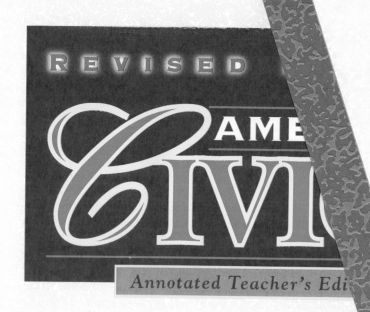

REVISED

AMERICAN
CIVICS

Annotated Teacher's Edition

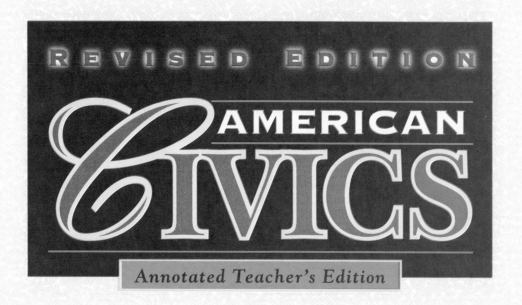

REVISED EDITION

AMERICAN CIVICS

Annotated Teacher's Edition

HOLT, RINEHART AND WINSTON

Harcourt Brace & Company

Austin • New York • Orlando • Atlanta • San Francisco • Boston • Dallas • Toronto • London

AUTHORS

WILLIAM H. HARTLEY, a former classroom teacher, is Professor of Education, Emeritus, at the Towson State University, Baltimore, Maryland. He is well known to teachers of the social studies as a past president of the National Council for the Social Studies. His monthly article "Sight and Sound" was for many years a highlight of *Social Education*. Dr. Hartley has written several textbooks, a number of motion picture and filmstrip scripts, and many articles in the field of education.

WILLIAM S. VINCENT, a former teacher of junior high school social studies, was Professor of Education, Emeritus, at Teacher's College, Columbia University, where he organized and directed the Citizen Education Project. Dr. Vincent wrote several books on citizenship and produced a number of educational films. He authored *Indicators of Quality*, a method of training teachers to measure the educational quality of schools and school systems.

CONSULTANTS AND REVIEWERS

John Benton
Richland Northeast High School
Columbia, South Carolina

Dr. F. Edward Blake, Jr.
Lancaster High School
Lancaster, Virginia

Margaret S. Branson
Associate Director
Center for Civic Education
Calabasas, California

Glenda Marilyn Cullum
Carver Middle School
Tulsa, Oklahoma

Martha Gould Daniel
Mann Magnet Junior High School
Little Rock, Arkansas

Steven E. Keefer
Bellmont High School
Decatur, Indiana

Julie E. Newton
Robert W. Groves High School
Garden City, Georgia

J. Garry Roberts
Central Junior High School
Springdale, Arkansas

Louis Roos
Cape Coral High School
Cape Coral, Florida

Alicia Sanderson
Canton High School
Canton, Oklahoma

Steven Schnell
Wilson Junior High School
Hamilton, Ohio

Georgianna B. Summerhill
Baptist Hill High School
Yonges Island, South Carolina

Senior Editor
Rachel Guichard Tandy

Project Editor
Holly Hammett Norman

Editorial Staff
Jim Eckel, *Managing Editor*; Daniel M. Quinn, *Editor*; Bob Fullilove, *Associate Editor*; Phyllis Salazar, *Department Secretary*

Editorial Permissions
Catherine J. Paré

Design
Design Five, New York; Diane Motz, *Art Director*; Lisa Walston, *Designer*; Greg Geisler, *Director, Image Services*; Elaine Tate, *Art Buyer Supervisor*; Linda Richey, *Art Buyer*

Photo Research
Peggy Cooper, *Photo Research Manager*; Tim Taylor, Victoria Smith, Kristin Hay, *Photo Research Team*

Production
Donna Lewis, *Senior Production Coordinator*; Amber Martin, *Production Assistant*; Jenine Street, *Manufacturing Coordinator*; Laura Cuellar, *Manufacturing Assistant*

For permission to reprint copyrighted material, grateful acknowledgment is made to the following sources:
Shirley Chisholm: From *Unbought and Unbossed* by Shirley Chisholm. Copyright © 1970 by Shirley Chisholm. **The Christian Science Monitor:** From "The School a No-Nonsense Principal Built" by Elizabeth Levitan Spaid from *The Christian Science Monitor*, June 20, 1994. Copyright © 1994 by The Christian Science Publishing Society. **Henry G. Cisneros:** Quote by Henry G. Cisneros from "What to Do?" from *The Los Angeles Times*, May 15, 1992. Copyright © 1992 by Henry Cisneros. **Indiana University Press:** Quote by a Vietnamese man in Kailua, Oahu, Hawaii, from *The Vietnamese Experience in America* by Paul James Rutledge. Copyright © 1992 by Paul James Rutledge. **The New York Times Company:** Quote by Elizabeth M. Watson from "Woman Named Police Chief of Houston" by Lisa Belkin from *The New York Times*, January 20, 1990. Copyright © 1990 by The New York Times Company. **Random House, Inc.:** From "On the Pulse of Morning" by Maya Angelou. Copyright © 1993 by Maya Angelou. **Scovil Chichak Galen Literary Agency, Inc. and Margaret Truman:** From a quote by President Harry S. Truman on his first five days in the White House. **U.S. News & World Report, Inc.:** Quote by Milton Friedman from *U.S. News & World Report*, March 7, 1977. Copyright © 1977 by U.S. News & World Report, Inc.

REFERENCES

"As a pupil I was neither particularly good nor bad . . ." from *Albert Einstein: Creator and Rebel* by Banesh Hoffmann with Helen Dukas. Copyright © 1972 by Helen Dukas and Banesh Hoffmann. Published by The Viking Press, Inc.

"Christ furnished the spirit and motivation, while Gandhi furnished the method." from *Stride Toward*

Freedom: The Montgomery Story by Martin Luther King, Jr. Copyright © 1958 by Martin Luther King, Jr. Published by HarperCollins Publishers Inc.

"Twenty-five years ago, . . ." from "After the Dream Comes True" by Charles Kuralt from *CBS Reports*. Copyright © 1985 by Columbia Broadcasting System.

". . . most important power is to set the agenda, . . ." from *Man of the House: The Life and Political Memoirs of Speaker Tip O'Neill* by Thomas P. O'Neill, Jr., with William Novak. Copyright © 1987 by Thomas P. O'Neill, Jr. Published by Random House, Inc.

Printed in the United States of America
ISBN 0-03-050762-6

1 2 3 4 5 6 7 069 00 99 98 97 96

Contents

UNIT 1 A TRADITION OF DEMOCRACY   1

UNIT 3   STATE AND LOCAL GOVERNMENT   136

UNIT 4 THE CITIZEN IN GOVERNMENT   182

UNIT 5   THE CITIZEN IN SOCIETY   240

*U*NIT **7**   THE UNITED STATES AND THE WORLD   **422**

UNIT 8   MEETING FUTURE CHALLENGES   466

REFERENCE SECTION

CASE STUDIES

CITIZENSHIP IN ACTION

AMERICAN BIOGRAPHIES

GLOBAL CONNECTIONS

DEVELOPING CIVICS SKILLS

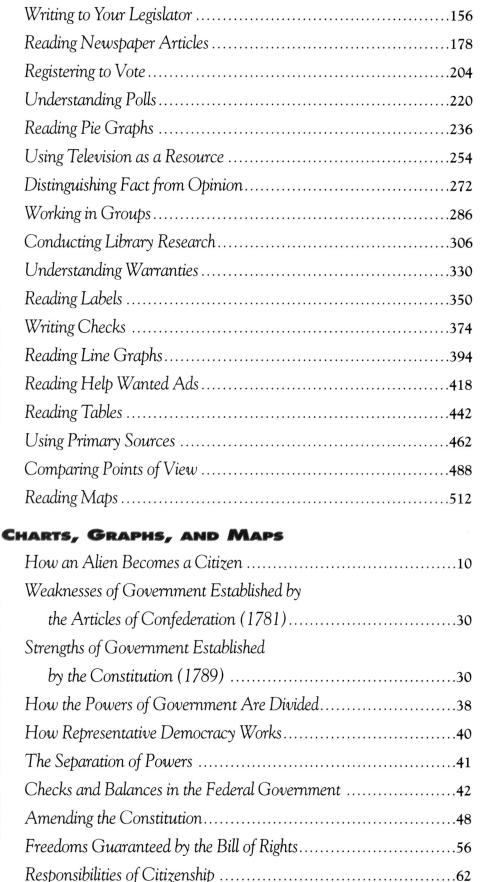

CHARTS, GRAPHS, AND MAPS

NATIONAL STANDARDS FOR CIVICS AND GOVERNMENT

It has been recognized since the founding of our nation that education has a civic mission: to prepare informed, rational, humane, and participating citizens committed to the values and principles of American constitutional democracy. That mission is reaffirmed in the National Education Goals included in the Goals 2000: Education America Act of 1994. Goal 3, Student Achievement and Citizenship, states:

> By the year 2000, all students will leave grades 4, 8, and 12 having demonstrated competency over challenging subject matter including . . . civics and government . . . so that they may be prepared for responsible citizenship, further learning, and productive employment. . . . All students will be involved in activities that promote and demonstrate . . . good citizenship, community service, and personal responsibility.

To help achieve these goals, the Center for Civic Education has developed voluntary *National Standards for Civics and Government* for students in kindergarten through grade twelve. More than a thousand teachers, scholars, parents, elected officials, and representatives of business and industry have contributed to their development.

The Need for Increased Attention to Civic Education

Although the National Education Goals, and the goals, curricular requirements, and policies of every state, express the need for and extol the value of civic education, this vital part of each student's education is seldom given sustained and systematic attention in the K–12 curriculum. Inattention to civic education stems in part from the assumption that the knowledge and skills citizens need emerge as by-products of the study of other disciplines or as an outcome of the process of schooling itself.

While it is true that history, economics, literature, and other subjects enhance students' understanding of government and politics, they cannot replace sustained, systematic attention to civic education. Civics should be seen as a central concern from kindergarten through twelfth grade, whether it is taught as a part of other curricula or in separate units or courses.

Effective and responsible participation in a constitutional democracy requires the acquisition of a body of knowledge and of intellectual and participatory skills. Effective and responsible participation also is furthered by development of certain dispositions or traits of character that enhance the individual's capacity to participate in civic life and contribute to the healthy functioning of the political system and improvement of society.

The Special Responsibility of Schools

Schools bear a special and historic responsibility for the development of civic competence and civic responsibility. Schools fulfill that responsibility through both formal and informal curricula beginning in the earliest grades and continuing through the entire educational process.

Formal instruction in civics and government should provide students with a basic understanding of civic life, politics, and government. It should help them understand the workings of their own and other political systems as well as the relationship of American politics and government to world affairs. Formal instruction provides a basis for understanding the rights and responsibilities of citizens in American constitutional democracy and a framework for competent and responsible participation. The formal curriculum should be augmented by related learning experiences in both school and community that enable students to learn how to participate in their own governance.

In addition to the formal curriculum, the importance of the informal curriculum should be recognized. The informal curriculum refers to the governance of the school community and relationships among those within it. These relationships should embody the fundamental values and principles of American constitutional democracy. Classrooms and schools should be managed by adults who govern in accordance with constitutional values and principles and who display traits of character worth emulating. Students should be held accountable for behaving in accordance with fair and reasonable standards and for respecting the rights and dignity of others.

The Importance of Knowledgeable, Skilled, and Dedicated Teachers

Ultimately, the value of the National Standards for Civics and Government will be determined in the classroom by knowledgeable, skilled, and dedicated teachers who have the capacity to make the study of civics and government the relevant, vital, and inspiring experience it should be. Teachers who foster students' natural, youthful idealism, and commitment to working together enhance the realization of the goals of American constitutional democracy.

The Center for Civic Education

CIVICS THEMES

American Civics focuses on several important civics themes that are closely tied to the national standards. Each chapter interleaf correlates that chapter's content to these fundamental themes.

★ The **Civics Skills** theme encompasses vocabulary development. Key civics terms are listed in the Civics Dictionary at the beginning of each chapter. Vocabulary instruction and development is then reinforced at the section level and in section and chapter reviews. Students also learn vital skills in the Developing Civics Skills feature at the end of each chapter. These skills are reinforced in unit reviews and in activities throughout the program.

★ The **Citizenship Values** theme focuses on the role of citizens in a democratic society. Students are encouraged to develop attitudes that foster good citizenship. These values are reinforced in the chapter and unit reviews and in Citizenship in Action features.

★ The **Principles of Democracy** theme focuses on the concept and purposes of democratic government. Students are introduced to various forms of government and are taught the basic values, principles, and ideals of American democracy.

★ The **American Government** theme focuses on the structure and purpose of the federal, state, and local governments. Students also learn how these governments operate within the federal system.

★ The **American Economic System** theme focuses on the U.S. economic system of free enterprise. Students learn how the U.S. system of government protects the economic rights of citizens and how citizens are encouraged to take risks and compete in the U.S. economic system.

★ The **Challenges in Today's World** theme focuses on the global, environmental, and social challenges facing U.S. citizens. Students learn about the U.S. role in world affairs, the challenge of improving life for all Americans, and the importance of protecting the environment.

GOALS

The American Civics program is designed to meet four goals of civic education:

• to provide students with a thorough understanding of our nation's system of government

• to instill in students the qualities of good citizenship that will enable them to put their knowledge into action

• to provide students with the skills they need to participate fully in a democratic society

• to familiarize students with the contemporary issues that face the United States, so that they will make the wise decisions on which the nation's future depends

These goals are supported throughout the entire American Civics program—the Pupil's Edition, the Annotated Teacher's Edition, the Skills Worksheets, Challenge/Enrichment Worksheets, Reteaching Worksheets, Chapter Tests, Portfolio Assessment Worksheets, Teaching Transparencies with Teacher's Notes, and Simulations and Case Studies with Block Scheduling Options.

PROGRAM COMPONENTS

PUPIL'S EDITION

American Civics is organized into 25 chapters divided into eight units. The program contains sufficient instructional material for a full-year, two-semester course. However, American Civics is designed so that teachers can easily focus on specific units and chapters of importance in a one-semester format.

The text's clear and engaging narrative takes a student-centered approach to the study of civics. Features throughout the textbook reinforce this emphasis and help tie civic concepts to real-world situations.

• **Citizenship in Action** features reveal how teenagers have taken action in their communities.

• **Case Study** features tie what students learn in a chapter to real-world situations and landmark court cases.

• **American Biography** features provide models of independent thinking by profiling Americans who have taken a stand and made a difference.

• **Did You Know That...** features provide interesting sidelights related to the textbook discussion.

• **Global Connections** features help students understand how civic values are expressed throughout the world.

• **Developing Civics Skills** features are located at the end of each chapter and help students develop and sharpen important citizenship, social studies, and life skills.

• **Learning from Technology** features in each Unit Review ask students to evaluate different media, such as virtual reality, telemetry, facsimile machines, and on-line computer services, as sources of information.

• **Citizenship in Your Community** features encourage students to explore and take action in their communities.

In the back of the textbook, students will find a **Reference Section** with maps, documents, biographical information about presidents, and statistical information about the 50 states. The **Glossary** provides definitions of all the boldface vocabulary terms in the text and includes their page references in the Pupil's Edition. The textbook also includes an **Index**, complete with cross-references.

THE ANNOTATED TEACHER'S EDITION

The Annotated Teacher's Edition of *American Civics* includes all the Pupil's Edition pages, slightly reduced in size to create top and side margins. This allows for convenient point-of-use teaching strategies and annotations designed to offer full instructional support.

At the beginning of each unit, teachers will find several features that provide background information and preparation to aid teaching.

Unit Overview provides summary statements that describe the focus of each unit.

Unit Objectives focus on broad concepts in each unit.

Using the Quotation links the introductory quotation at the beginning of each unit with civics concepts and materials discussed in the unit.

About the Author provides background information about the person quoted in the unit opener.

Chapter Interleaves provide several important teaching resources, including
- a planning guide box correlating all the components of the *American Civics* program to the text
- suggested print, multimedia, and Internet resources for teachers and students
- alternative teaching strategies to meet the individual learning styles found in many classrooms
- a themes section that correlates the chapter's content to the program's fundamental civics themes

Lesson Cycle

The lesson for each section is based on the following instructional model:

Objectives state the main concepts in each chapter and section and are tied to Section and Chapter Reviews.

Motivator introduces the lesson with a high-interest activity.

Building a Vocabulary refines and extends the definitions of key terms from the chapter Civics Dictionary.

Teaching strategies employ varied techniques to help students comprehend concepts in each section.

Guided Practice activities are suitable for the entire class.

Independent Practice activities build on Guided Practice activities and allow students of all ability levels to work independently or with partners.

Closure synthesizes the main concepts of each section.

Reviewing and Reteaching suggestions employ the Section Review and varied Reteaching activities in Reteaching Worksheets to help students master the content.

Extension activities extend the content of each section and enable students to develop research skills and make classroom presentations.

Side Margin Annotations

The side columns include **Global Perspectives**, **Multicultural Perspectives**, and **Civics Sidelight** annotations that support important civic concepts. Side margins also include suggested responses to Chapter Review and Section Review questions and to photo caption questions.

THE TEACHING RESOURCES

A rich collection of teaching resources accompanies *American Civics*. These materials include
- Professional Organizer
- Chapter Skills Worksheets
- Chapter Challenge/Enrichment Worksheets
- Chapter Reteaching Worksheets
- Chapter Tests, Forms A and B
- Chapter and Unit Portfolio Assessment Worksheets

ADDITIONAL RESOURCES

A variety of other resources are available for you to use with *American Civics:*

Teaching Transparencies with Teacher's Notes includes full-color transparencies of graphic illustrations found in *American Civics*, as well as teaching strategies.

Alternative Assessment Forms provide other means for assessing the progress of students who have difficulty on tests and in expressing themselves in standard formats.

Simulations and Case Studies with Block Scheduling Options offer expanded and dynamic teaching strategies and activities using case studies, simulations, and games.

Citizenship Skills Videodisc and Teacher's Guide is fully integrated with the Pupil's Edition. The 60-minute videodisc and the accompanying *Teacher's Guide* reinforce the teaching of citizenship and life skills in the Pupil's Edition and the Teacher's Edition. **This program is also available on videocassette.**

American Civics Test Generator provides a system for creating custom-designed tests on Macintosh® or Windows® computer systems.

Global Skill Builder CD-ROM is an interactive teaching software tool covering basic social studies skills in 13 skills segments.

The Constitution: Past, Present, and Future provides an annotated Constitution that takes your students through each article and amendment. Also included are built-in worksheets, selections from the Federalist Papers, and landmark Supreme Court cases.

MEETING INDIVIDUAL NEEDS

American Civics recognizes that most classrooms include students from a variety of backgrounds and with a variety of learning styles. Many of the activities in both the Pupil's Edition and the Annotated Teacher's Edition are suited to students with varying needs. In addition, activities in the chapter interleafs, located at the beginning of each chapter of the Annotated Teacher's Edition, focus explicitly on meeting the individual needs of the following categories of students.

Limited English Proficiency (LEP)

Instructional strategies in American Civics are designed to limit stress and anxiety for students who face difficulty in communicating in the classroom or in understanding instructions. Students who do not speak English as their first language may display conversational ability in English and understand a major part of a lesson. However, such students may not yet be able to express themselves in writing or orally well enough to indicate their level of understanding. LEP students also are students whose first language is English but who display insufficient language skills.

It is important to remember that all students for whom English is a second language do not fall within the same ability range, and that many of these students might otherwise be considered gifted or might have attained high academic skills if instructed in their own language.

Because of these diverse characteristics, LEP students benefit from a variety of instructional techniques. These include oral introduction to assignments and modeling by the teacher, vocabulary activities that emphasize context, opportunities to engage in role-playing and reader's theater, working in small groups or with partners, and responding to visuals. You might consider the following guidelines for effective interaction with LEP students:

Simplify Content
    Speak slowly.
    Pronounce words clearly.
    Use a controlled vocabulary.
    Minimize use of idioms.

Context Aids
    Use gestures.
    Use animated facial expressions.
    Act out meaning of words or concepts.
    Use varied visual materials.

Checking Understanding
    Make frequent checks for comprehension.
    Repeat important concepts.
    Expand meaning whenever possible.
    Use varied questions and techniques.

Last, remember that LEP students may be new immigrants to the United States—possibly from war-torn countries that are in economic and political turmoil. Students' difficulties in adapting to a new culture could prevent them from taking part in class discussions. Avoid questioning them about life in their former countries unless they are willing to share their experiences. When developing cooperative projects, try to use LEP students' knowledge, experiences, and cultural traditions in ways that will promote their self-esteem.

Learners Having Difficulty

To assist students who need repetition, have a short attention span, lack self-esteem, and/or learn at a slower rate than other classmates, American Civics activities provide the opportunity for review and reteaching of basic information in the chapter. Some activities also focus students on their own interests and experiences to motivate them and to encourage them to make connections. Specific methods include the use of audio and visual materials, teacher demonstrations, interactive activities, extended explanations, and summarizing and outlining exercises.

Auditory Learners

Strategies targeting students who respond particularly well to auditory stimuli include lectures (both by teachers and guest speakers), audiotapes (either listened to or created by students), class discussion, role playing, debate, reading aloud, and oral presentation.

Visual Learners

For students who are oriented toward visual learning, American Civics strategies suggest the examination, analysis, and interpretation of materials such as photographs, maps, graphs, and charts. Activities that make use of chalkboards, bulletin boards, and maps also are recommended. Students might be asked to create graphic organizers, posters, maps, or other visual displays.

Tactile/Kinesthetic Learners

Tactile/kinesthetic learners benefit from interactive activities and activities that utilize movement and action. Simulations, field trips, role playing, conducting interviews, using newspaper and magazine articles, constructing models, and creating maps, posters, time lines, and illustrations are all effective strategies used in American Civics.

Gifted Students

Activities requiring research beyond the textbook help meet the needs of gifted learners. Often such activities focus on real-world issues and problem solving through the use of investigation, debate, panel discussions, and other forums for the exchange of ideas. As almost every student is gifted in one way or another, teachers are encouraged to use these types of activities with as many students as possible.

PORTFOLIO ASSESSMENT

American Civics includes a variety of creative Building Your Portfolio projects that help students, teachers, and parents assess the learning and performance progress of an individual student. These projects offer teachers and students more than the traditional instructional pattern of lecture, reading, discussion, and test. Rather than relying simply on rote learning, the portfolio projects call on the creativity and enthusiasm of students to help them apply what they have learned in the text.

A student's portfolio—a collection of a student's work in a folder, envelope, box, or other container—serves as a tangible record of his or her progress and performance over a period of time. The portfolio activities are found at the end of each chapter in the Pupil's Edition. A unit portfolio project ties together the activities from these chapter projects throughout each unit. The variety of portfolio projects and materials provide a multidimensional view of a student's mastery of skills, understanding of information, and ability to apply those skills and knowledge. For example, students will write a Declaration of Education, outline a government for a new society, design and market a product, and plan a campaign for a student government office.

Flexibility and creativeness help make Portfolio Assessment an important part of the American Civics program. Activities throughout both the Pupil's Edition and the Annotated Teacher's Edition provide students with the opportunity to create a wide range of materials for their portfolios. Students should feel free to include any materials they consider representative of their progress.

Authentic Assessment

The Building Your Portfolio activities include real-world projects. The projects are designed to be authentic in both content and structure. Students might be asked, for example, to make presentations on education in a democracy or to develop proposals for creating an effective government. Students work toward completion of these projects by working on portfolio activities at the end of each chapter.

At the heart of authentic assessment lies the concept that students' most important learning takes place when students create the learning themselves. Rather than asking students to simply memorize information that may be forgotten at the end of the course, the unit portfolio projects involve students as the main participants in the learning process. The activities help students acquire skills they will need to know and use in their lives again and again—for jobs, for volunteer organizations, and for informed and active citizenship.

As they work on the projects, students will sharpen their research skills, learning what types of information to look for and where to find the information they need.

Students will also learn how to present information in a variety of forms, including writing; visual displays such as maps, charts, graphs, and illustrations; and oral presentations. Students' organizational skills also will improve as they complete their research and present their findings.

Alternative Assessment

The Building Your Portfolio projects provide a particularly valuable opportunity for students who are less comfortable with traditional assessment, such as in-class exams. Often such tests are not reliable indicators of progress for students who have difficulty expressing themselves in traditional formats. The unit projects allow students to work with a degree of flexibility in terms of content and structure.

The materials in the Portfolio Assessment Worksheets booklet support the portfolio projects. These chapter and unit worksheets provide checklists that students should follow as they work on their portfolio activities. These worksheets help students and teachers assess students' progress as they work through the projects.

The worksheets also assist students in planning their time by helping them pace their work over the entire unit, chapter by chapter. In addition, they help students by guiding them to sources of needed information and by teaching them how to manage large projects that require progress on various activities.

Also in Teaching Resources, teachers will find Alternative Assessment Forms that can be used to evaluate a student's progress on various kinds of assignments, such as writing projects, presentations, and group projects.

Cooperative Learning

The Building Your Portfolio projects provide an excellent opportunity for cooperative learning. Although students may work alone on a project, they might also accomplish the projects in a variety of ways. At the teacher's discretion, students might work cooperatively, rather than individually, on projects. Each project is divided into several specific steps, allowing group members each to take responsibility for one of the steps. Conversely, members might all work on each step together, dividing the tasks of research, writing, illustrating, and oral presentation.

BLOCK SCHEDULING

In recent years, many schools have changed to a system of block scheduling—combining standard 45- or 50-minute class periods into longer blocks of time, usually about 90 minutes. For those civics classrooms operating on a block schedule, the American Civics program includes alternative approaches to scheduling for the Simulations and Case Studies lessons, as well as the lessons that accompany the Citizenship Skills Videodisc or Videocassette segments.

MULTICULTURAL AWARENESS

The *American Civics* program helps students realize that U.S. society is increasingly influenced by the multicultural nature of our population. The cultural diversity that characterizes and enhances life in our society is also evident in most classrooms today. Multicultural issues are addressed throughout the narrative of the Pupil's Edition and are highlighted in discussions of civil rights and minority issues.

In the Annotated Teacher's Edition, teachers will find Multicultural Perspectives side annotations that highlight the contributions and viewpoints of various ethnic and cultural groups. Some of these side annotations also describe how cultures throughout history have addressed various subjects related to the study of civics.

GLOBAL AWARENESS

American Civics provides students a window through which they can see how people in other countries of the world approach various civic issues. The narrative of the Pupil's Edition discusses U.S. foreign policy and foreign relations in depth in both content and structure. Whenever appropriate, the text discusses links between the United States and the rest of the world. The Pupil's Edition also includes Global Connections features about such subjects as the new spirit of volunteerism in Russia and programs in Indonesia in which farmers effectively control the proliferation of harmful insects. The Annotated Teacher's Edition also addresses global issues in Global Perspectives side annotations.

COOPERATIVE LEARNING

Students have numerous opportunities in *American Civics* to practice cooperative learning skills. Citizenship in Your Community activities and Building Your Portfolio projects in the Pupil's Edition, as well as teaching strategies in the Annotated Teacher's Edition, help students master skills necessary to work in a group. The cooperative learning activities are designed for small groups of students. Each group member is assigned a task in helping complete a final, cooperative project.

LIFE SKILLS

The *American Civics* program helps students develop and sharpen important life skills, such as making decisions, reading labels and warranties, and working in groups. Developing Civics Skills features, cooperative learning activities, and various teaching strategies also focus student learning on the skills needed in today's complicated world.

MULTIMEDIA RESOURCES

AIMS: AIMS Media, 9710 DeSoto Avenue, Chatsworth, CA 91311, Tel. (800) 367-2467.

BARR: Barr Films, 12801 Schabarum Avenue, P.O. Box 7878, Irwindale, CA 91706, Tel. (800) 234-7878.

BEA: Beacon Films, 1560 Sherman Avenue, Suite 100, Evanston, IL 60201, Tel. (800) 323-9084.

BFA: BFA Educational Media, 468 Park Avenue South, New York, NY 10016, Tel. (800) 221-1274.

CF: Carousel Film & Video, 260 Fifth Avenue, Suite 405, New York, NY 10001, Tel. (212) 683-1660.

CINGLD: The Cinema Guild, Inc., 1697 Broadway, Suite 506, New York, NY 10019, Tel. (800) 723-5522.

COR/MTI: Coronet/MTI Film & Video, 108 Wilmot Road, Deerfield, IL 60015, Tel. (800) 777-8100.

CSS: Cambridge Social Studies, P.O. Box 2153, Dept. SS6, Charleston, WV 25328, Tel. (800) 468-4227.

CU: Close Up Publishing, Dept. K94, 44 Canal Center Plaza, Alexandria, VA 22314, Tel. (800) 765-3131.

EBEC: Encyclopaedia Britannica Educational Corporation, 310 South Michigan Avenue, Chicago, IL 60604, Tel. (800) 554-9862.

FH: Films for the Humanities & Sciences, P.O. Box 2053, Princeton, NJ 08543, Tel. (800) 257-5126.

FM: Focus Media, Inc., 485 South Broadway, Suite 12, Hicksville, NY 11801, Tel. (800) 645-8989.

GA: Guidance Associates, P.O. Box 1000, Mount Kisco, NY 10549, Tel. (800) 431-1242.

GL: Glencoe, P.O. Box 543, Blacklick, OH 43004, Tel. (800) 334-7344.

IU: Indiana University Center for Media and Teaching Resources, Bloomington, IN 47405, Tel. (800) 552-8620.

JF: Journal Films, 1560 Sherman Avenue, Suite 100, Evanston, IL 60201, Tel. (800) 323-9084.

MOD: Modern, 5000 Park Street North, St. Petersburg, FL 33709, Tel. (800) 243-6877.

NDF: New Day Films, Inc., 22-D Hollywood Avenue, Hohokus, NJ 07423, Tel. (201) 652-6590.

NGS: National Geographic Society, Educational Services, P.O. Box 98019, Washington, DC 20090, Tel. (800) 386-2728.

NPR: National Public Radio, Outreach, 635 Massachusetts Avenue, NW, Washington, DC, 20001, Tel. (202) 414-2843.

PBS: Public Broadcasting Service, PBS Video, 1320 Braddock Place, Alexandria, VA 22314, Tel. (800) 344-3337.

PHX: Phoenix Films, Inc., 468 Park Avenue South, New York, NY 10016, Tel. (800) 221-1274.

PSU: Pennsylvania State University Audio-Visual Services, Special Services Building, University Park, PA 16802, Tel. (800) 826-0132.

SRA: SRA, P.O. Box 543, Blacklick, OH 43004, Tel. (800) 843-8855.

SSSS: Social Studies School Service, 10200 Jefferson Boulevard, Room 1121, P.O. Box 802, Culver City, CA 90232, Tel. (800) 421-4246.

WHAT'S IN A NAME? EVERYTHING!

AMERICAN CIVICS

from Holt, Rinehart and Winston

What does it take to be an active, informed citizen? *American Civics* holds the answer for today's students, no matter what their interests, abilities, or learning styles. It thoroughly integrates the national civics standards to teach valuable lessons— registering to vote, working in groups, and respecting and protecting the rights of others— and to develop students' critical-thinking and decision-making skills. Your students must also be prepared to participate in our country's democratic processes. That participation requires the acquisition of skills that allow them to contribute to the political system and improvement of society. *American Civics* accomplishes all of this and more by building students' understanding of what it means to be productive, thoughtful, and responsible citizens.

> "*A* nation is formed by the willingness of each of us to share in the responsibility for upholding the common good. A government is invigorated when each of us is willing to participate in shaping the future of this nation."
>
> *Barbara Jordan*
> *Former U.S. Congresswoman*

Developing Civics Skills

shown 50% of actual size

CITIZENSHIP SKILL

Registering to Vote

Voting for candidates is a right we enjoy as citizens. Under the U.S. Constitution you must be at least 18 years old to vote. In addition, some states require you to live in the state for a certain period of time before you can register to vote. Many states require you to register in person; other states allow you to register by mail. Whatever the requirements in your state, it is important that you fulfill them so that you, too, can exercise your right to vote.

How to Register to Vote

1. Learn the registration procedure. The registration process varies from state to state. To find out how to register, contact your state or local election office. You should request a registration form and ask what deadlines you must meet.

2. Follow the procedure. Usually, registering to vote is as simple as filling out a form. The forms in most states ask for basic information: your name, your age, your residence, and whether you are a citizen. You must also sign the form, swearing that the information you have given is correct.

Applying the Skill

Study the registration form below. Then answer the following questions.

1. Which section should not be filled in? Why?
2. What do you think is the main purpose of the "Place of Birth" section?
3. Why must you sign a voter registration form?
4. Why do you think the form shown on this page is printed in Spanish as well as in English?

204 UNIT 4 THE CITIZEN IN GOVERNMENT

" *This country, with its institutions, belongs to the people who inhabit it.*"

Abraham Lincoln
Sixteenth President of the United States

Citizenship in Your Community

Individual Project

Investigate the beginnings of your community. Who first settled the community? From what countries or areas of the world did these immigrants come? What cultural influences brought by these immigrants are evident in your community? What are the ethnic and cultural backgrounds of the people who live in your community today? What languages do they speak? What foods do they enjoy? Create a poster showing how the ethnic and cultural mix of your community has changed over time.

BUILDS CIVIC COMPETENCY

With *American Civics,* your students learn about their individual rights and responsibilities in our society. To help students grasp these building blocks of civic competency, *American Civics* focuses on six central themes:

• **Principles of Democracy** examines the purpose of government and the basic values, principles, and ideals of American democracy.

• **Civics Skills** encourages students to learn and apply vocabulary terms and skills taught in the chapter, including the ones in the Civics Dictionary and in the Developing Civics Skills features.

• **American Government** covers the structure, purpose, and branches of federal, state, and local governments so your students learn how each functions.

• **American Economic System** describes the American economic system and free enterprise, enabling students to see how they—as consumers—impact the nation's financial health.

• **Citizenship Values** teaches students the rights and responsibilities of citizenship.

• **Challenges in Today's World** covers global challenges to U.S. foreign policy and other important issues facing all Americans.

Citizenship IN ACTION

FEEDING THE HUNGRY

Although most older people in the United States are active and vital citizens, some suffer from ill health, loneliness, and hunger. Thanks to the unselfish efforts of a teenage girl, some older citizens in Miami, Florida, have found unexpected help.

Alison Stieglitz started helping people in her community by filling Thanksgiving baskets for older citizens.

Sharing Good Fortune

When Alison Stieglitz was 12 years old, she celebrated her bat mitzvah, a Jewish ceremony marking a girl's acceptance of religious duty and responsibility. To honor Alison's hard work in preparation for the ceremony and her commitment to her faith, Alison's family members, relatives, and friends gave her gifts and money. Rather than spending the money on herself, however, Alison resolved to take her new responsibilities seriously and share her good fortune with people in need.

She decided to focus her efforts on providing Thanksgiving dinners for older people who were unable to leave their homes due to illness. With the money she received, Alison was able to assemble and distribute 15 baskets of food, which included turkeys. With each basket feeding four people, 60 older Miami citizens were able to enjoy a happy Thanksgiving. But Alison did not stop there.

The Sharing Grows

Each year from the date of that first act of good will, Alison expanded her efforts. By the time she was 17, she was able to provide more than 120 Thanksgiving baskets, feeding 480 housebound older citizens.

12 UNIT 1 A TRADITION OF DEMOCRACY

With the help of friends, relatives, and other volunteers, Alison (right) and her sister Leigh have given hundreds of people a helping hand.

By now Alison was not alone in her efforts. In response to the teenager's countless telephone calls and letters, community members, social workers, friends, and relatives pitched in to help. In addition to donating funds, these people volunteered to assemble the Thanksgiving food baskets and coordinate their delivery. With all the additional help, Alison was able to expand her work further by providing baskets of food to hurricane victims, Soviet Jewish immigrants, people with disabilities, and hospital patients, among others.

With the success of the Thanksgiving basket project as an inspiration, Alison then helped to organize the Hungry and Homeless Committee in her community synagogue. Because "soup kitchens" designed to feed the homeless in her area were closed on Sundays, Alison's committee worked with another Miami synagogue to provide food for the homeless on that day. Their combined efforts enabled them to serve breakfast and lunch to several hundred homeless people each Sunday.

In recognition of Alison's tireless work to feed the hungry, she was invited to the White House to receive the President's Volunteer Action Award. She also was the recipient of the Kimberly-Clark Corporation "Bless You" Award. Alison donated this cash award to a shelter for abused and neglected teenagers in her community.

Although she has received a great deal of recognition for her efforts, the down-to-earth Miami girl realizes that it is the caring rather than the recognition that is important. As Alison herself says, "Giving is not a one-time experience. It's something you do throughout your life."

YOU DECIDE

1. Why did Alison Stieglitz first become involved in helping the hungry?
2. Find out what efforts are being made in your community to feed the homeless and the hungry. What can you and other teenagers in your community do to become involved in this effort?

ENCOURAGES STUDENT INVOLVEMENT

American Civics stresses the importance of civic duty for all citizens and shows students how their involvement in community issues affects their lives. Activities in the *Pupil's Edition* and *Annotated Teacher's Edition* promote cooperative learning, decision making, and student involvement in the community, in society, and in government.

- **Citizenship in Your Community** activities—such as students working together to organize a mini–Earth Day in your class or school—in each chapter and unit review encourage students' involvement.

- **Citizenship in Action** features highlight students nationwide—like the high school students in Iowa tutoring elementary schoolchildren—who are taking an active role in their communities.

- **Developing Civics Skills** lessons in the *Pupil's Edition*—organized around citizenship, life, and social studies skills—develop students' ability to act as knowledgeable, contributing citizens.

PIQUES STUDENTS' INTEREST

"What's civics?" "Why do I have to take this class?" If this is what you hear from some of your civics students, it's probably because they have no idea how civics relates to them. *American Civics* solves this problem!

With inviting activities and a narrative style that piques students' interest, *American Civics* engages students in their individual civic development by providing them with the knowledge and understanding they need and by challenging them to develop their own ideas and draw their own conclusions about issues that affect them.

- **Case Studies** examine important topics and stimulate student discussion, debate, and decision making.

- **American Biography** features highlight individuals—such as James Madison, Thurgood Marshall, Rachel Carson, and Colin Powell—who took a stand on important issues and made a difference, demonstrating how individuals help shape society.

- **Global Connections** compares institutions and processes in other countries with those in the United States.

- **Did You Know That...** offers interesting facts about the nation's history and government, increasing your students' enjoyment of and interest in civics.

- **You Decide** questions encourage students to draw their own conclusions and develop their own ideas about topics such as landmark court cases.

- **Learning from Technology** features ask students to evaluate different media—such as virtual reality, telemetry, facsimile machines, and on-line computer services—expanding their use of a variety of sources to help them make informed decisions.

- **Global Skill Builder CD-ROM** helps students master social studies skills with 13 interactive lessons about topics such as reading charts and graphs, and navigating the Internet.

- **Internet Resources** in every chapter provide search words to help students find information on the Internet about topics such as Supreme Court cases, local city council meetings, and e-mailing their congressperson.

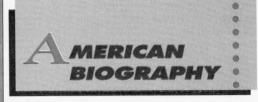

AMERICAN BIOGRAPHY

Colin Powell

Colin Powell was born in 1937 in the Harlem section of New York City. Powell's parents taught their children that education is the key to opportunity. Powell realized this while he was a student at City College of New York.

On his way to class one day, Powell stopped to watch the Reserve Officers Training Corps (ROTC). Impressed by what he saw, he joined the ROTC. He graduated from college with the highest grades in his ROTC class and the highest rank in the Corps—cadet colonel.

Powell swiftly moved up the military ranks. After serving in Vietnam, where he [won] numerous medals, he was selected to [help develop defense] policies.

[... Afri]can [... secu]rity [... Po]well [... post—] [... st]aff. [... was] [... ag]ainst Iraq in [... Powe]ll retired [... years of] [... con]tinued to [... Ho]wever, such [... H]aiti in 1994.

Learning from Technology

Virtual Reality

Virtual reality is a new technology that simulates the sights, sounds, and feel of real or imaginary events. Special goggles and gloves allow users to witness reenactments of events and interact with characters.

Imagine that you are using a virtual reality program that places you at the Constitutional Convention. You can talk to the delegates and view events as they unfold. What might be the advantages of using this form of technology to learn about the Convention? What might be the disadvantages? For example, would you consider answers from the "delegates" to be necessarily accurate? Would you rely on this technology as your sole source of information?

shown 50% of actual size

The First Amendment right to free speech helped the Gallaudet students change a long-standing practice.

Case STUDY — GALLAUDET UNIVERSITY

The freedom of Americans to express ideas and opinions is a priceless right guaranteed by the First Amendment. This right allows us not only to express our thoughts freely, but also to question actions we believe to be wrong or unfair. It lets us propose new actions we consider to be right and fair. Students at Gallaudet (gal-uh-DEHT) University in Washington, D.C., exercised their constitutional right to free speech and, in so doing, changed one of the school's long-standing traditions.

A Surprising Decision

Gallaudet University, founded in 1864, is the only liberal arts university for deaf people in the world. Known for its excellent teaching, Gallaudet has trained approximately 95 percent of the nation's hearing-impaired professionals. Until 1988, however, Gallaudet, whose 2,100 students are all hearing impaired, had never had a deaf president.

The long-standing practice of appointing only hearing presidents came under fire when the university's board of trustees had to choose a new president in 1988. Since two of the candidates for the position were hearing impaired, the students eagerly anticipated the historic moment when a deaf person would be chosen to lead the university.

This moment was not to be, however. Students and faculty were shocked to learn that the trustees had chosen a hearing person for the university's highest position. Their shock turned to outrage when it became clear that the new president had no experience in educating the deaf. Moreover, the new president did not know sign language—the only language used by most of the students at the university.

The Protests Begin

Protests over the decision erupted within minutes of the announcement. The students argued that, by choosing a hearing person to lead a university for the deaf, the trustees had sent the message that people with disabilities need able-bodied people to take care of them.

The students wanted a president who would serve as a role model. They wanted a president who would show the rest of the nation that people with disabilities are entitled

The slogan "Deaf President Now" expressed the goal of the Gallaudet students to have a president who would serve as their role model.

to the same freedom of opportunity granted to all Americans. They wanted a president who, like themselves, was hearing impaired.

"Deaf President Now"

For the next several days the students waged their fight through active protests. They blocked the entrances to the university and marched on the U.S. Capitol, located only one mile (1.6 km) from the school. Many chanted slogans that they themselves could not hear. Most used sign language to communicate their outrage. Other banners and posters expressed the students' demand, summed up by the simple slogan "Deaf President Now."

Faced with this outcry, the new president resigned on the fourth day of the protests. Soon after, the board of trustees appointed a hearing-impaired person as president. The students had won their fight, and they had struck a blow for the rights of people with disabilities everywhere. Most important, they had proved the value—and power—of free speech.

Protecting the Freedom of Speech

Freedom of speech is essential to a democracy. Only when citizens are free to express themselves can a government truly reflect the wants and needs of the people. Benjamin Franklin knew this. He said, "Whoever would overthrow the liberty of a nation must begin by subduing the freeness of speech. . . ." The students of Gallaudet also recognized the importance of this priceless right. To protect democracy, we must all guard our First Amendment right to free speech.

YOU DECIDE

1 What was the decision made by the university's board of trustees? Why did the Gallaudet students protest this decision?

2 How did the students make their concerns known?

3 What was the result of the students' actions?

4 Conduct library research to find another case in which students used their freedom of speech to bring about change. Summarize the case to share with the rest of the class.

" **The genius of the United States is not best or most in its executives or legislatures...but in the common people.** "

Walt Whitman
American Poet and Writer

GLOBAL CONNECTIONS

Voting in Australia

Even though voting is a right and responsibility of U.S. citizenship, some Americans choose not to vote. Not all nations give their citizens this choice. In Australia, for example, voting is compulsory.

All Australian citizens age 18 and over are required by law to register as voters. Citizens must vote in all national and state elections and in most local elections. People too ill to go to the polls on election day are allowed to mail in their ballots. Australians who fail to vote may have to pay heavy fines. Not surprisingly, Australia has one of the highest voter turnout rates of any indu...

SUPPLIES COMPLETE TEACHER SUPPORT

*W*ith an easy-to-use, wraparound format, our Annotated Teacher's Edition contains everything you need to teach civics. It gives you comprehensive instructional strategies, including strategies for students with individual needs. Complete on-page lesson plans provide convenient point-of-use teaching strategies and suggestions, offering background information and full instructional support for all elements in the Pupil's Edition.

TEACHING RESOURCES

- Skills Worksheets
- Challenge/Enrichment Worksheets
- Reteaching Worksheets
- Chapter Tests
- Portfolio Assessment Worksheets
- Simulations and Case Studies with Block Scheduling Options
- Teaching Transparencies with Teacher's Notes
- Alternative Assessment Forms
- The Constitution: Past, Present, and Future
- The Constitution: Past, Present, and Future Answer Key
- Test Generator: Test Item Listing
- Test Generator for both IBM® PCs and compatibles and Macintosh® computers
- Global Skill Builder CD-ROM
- Citizenship Skills Videocassette
- Citizenship Skills Videodisc

Citizenship Skills is available in two different formats—videocassette or videodisc—to best meet your needs. This program is designed to enhance the teaching of citizenship skills with interactive video segments tied to each unit in the text. Students are asked to solve problems, engage in citizenship activities such as voting or taking a poll, and use critical-thinking and other life skills to acquire, evaluate, and apply civics-related information. Both the videocassette and the videodisc are fully integrated with the text. The Annotated Teacher's Edition contains point-of-use references for both the videocassette and the videodisc to ease use and reduce planning time. Each program is accompanied by a Teacher's Guide with teaching suggestions and activities, including block scheduling strategies.

CHAPTER OVERVIEW

Chapter 1 examines the role of civics in our lives. It also explains how people become U.S. citizens and how American society has changed over the years, through immigration and shifts in population. The underlying theme of the chapter is that we must accept our responsibilities as citizens and work together to protect the American Dream of freedom and equality for all.

Motivator

Conduct a brainstorming session in which students identify the rights they enjoy as Americans. Examples might include the right to an education or to express opinions openly. Ask students if, in return, they have any obligations. Encourage them to see that if people do not take part in government, they may allow their rights to be reduced or perhaps even taken away.

CHAPTER OBJECTIVES

After studying Chapter 1, students should be able to do the following.

1. Describe what it means to be a U.S. citizen.
2. List the ideals that guide the American way of life.
3. Describe the early immigrants to the United States.
4. Explain how people become U.S. citizens.
5. Describe what the census tells us and how the U.S. population is changing.

SIMULATIONS AND CASE STUDIES

Lesson 1: Founding Documents Treasure Hunt

Block Scheduling Option

CHAPTER 1

We the People

CIVICS DICTIONARY

citizen	naturalization
civics	census
government	birthrate
ideal	death rate
immigrant	rural area
quota	urban area
refugee	suburb
native-born citizen	metropolitan area
alien	migration
deport	Sunbelt

2

UNMATCHED TEACHING RESOURCES

Each chapter in *American Civics* begins with a two-page chapter interleaf that provides several important teaching resources, including:

- A Planning Guide box, correlating all components of the *American Civics* instructional program to the text
- Suggested print, multimedia, and Internet resources for you and your students
- Alternative teaching strategies that meet the individual learning styles found in your classroom
- A Themes section that correlates each chapter's content to the fundamental civics themes found throughout *American Civics*

Building a Vocabulary refines and extends the definitions of key terms from each chapter's Civics Dictionary.

SECTION OBJECTIVES

After studying Section 1, students should be able to do the following.

1. Explain the obligations of a U.S. citizen.
2. Name the ideals that form the basis of U.S. government and the American way of life.
3. Identify at least three ways that citizens can become involved in government.
4. Identify qualities of a good citizen.

Teaching Section 1

Building a Vocabulary

Have students explain what a **citizen** is. *(a member of a political entity, such as a city, state, or nation)* Have students name specific political entities of which they are citizens. *(Students should name their hometown, county, state, and the United States.)* Explain that *civics* comes from the Latin word *civis*, meaning "citizen," and is the study of the rights and duties of citizens. Tell students that they will also learn about the institution that rules on behalf of citizens. Ask students what that institution is called. *(government)*

Side-Margin notes—Global Perspectives, Multicultural Perspectives, Civics Sidelights—support important civic concepts and provide interesting facts that make the study of civics applicable to your students' daily lives. These notes also provide handy point-of-use references to the Teaching Transparencies with Teacher's Notes, Simulations and Case Studies, and Citizenship Skills videocassette and videodisc, making your preparation fast and efficient.

CHAPTER FOCUS

Have you ever heard the term *American Dream?* The United States is built on this dream—the hope of a better life for everyone. This dream has been shared by millions of people who have believed that in this nation all men and women could truly be free.

It is a dream that began in colonial times and continues to draw thousands of people to the United States each year. For many people the American Dream has meant freedom from religious persecution. For others it has meant freedom from political upheavals and wars. For still others it has meant freedom to achieve economic success.

As an American, you have the freedom to pursue your own American Dream, whatever it may be. But the American Dream will remain a reality only as long as you, and all Americans, work to protect our precious heritage of freedom. This is your responsibility as an American **citizen**—a member of our nation.

GLOBAL PERSPECTIVES

While almost everyone today is a citizen of a nation, throughout history governments have limited the rights of some of their citizens (such as the right to vote), in effect conferring upon them a sort of second-class citizenship. At various times in history, governments have come to see citizenship in more egalitarian terms. One result of the French Revolution in 1789, for example, was the elimination of privileged classes in France. After the Revolution, people began to address everyone simply as "citizen." This equalizing title reflected their belief in the freedom and equality of all people.

STUDY GUIDE

• What does it mean to be a U.S. citizen, and what ideals guide the American way of life?
• Who were the early immigrants to America, and how do people become U.S. citizens today?
• What is the purpose of the census, and how is the American population changing?

The Meaning of Civics

Civics is the study of what it means to be an American citizen. The word *civics* comes from the Latin *civis*, meaning "citizen." The meaning of this word has changed since the ancient Romans first used it many hundreds of years ago. At that time, only a small group of wealthy people who owned property could be Roman citizens. Today almost everyone is a citizen of a nation.

The rights and responsibilities of being a citizen also have changed over time. Moreover, they differ from nation to nation. They depend on a nation's type of government. **Government** is the authority, or power, that rules on behalf of a group of people. Under the American system of government, citizens have many rights and responsibilities. Your civics course will help you discover the most important ones.

You will discover that American citizenship means more than being a productive and sharing member of the nation. It includes being a productive and sharing member of... most all Americans belong to a... school for several years, and w... people. Americans also are me... communities—villages, towns... and of states. Being an effective... United States are fulfilling y...

1	Civics in Our Lives

What is civics? Why do we study this subject in school? What does civics have to do with my life? These are some of the questions you may be asking as you begin your civics course.

Many of the subjects you study in school teach you about the American way of life and the priceless rights you enjoy as an American. The civics course you are about to begin will explain how you, as a citizen of the United States, can help to keep this heritage alive.

◄ *The Statue of Liberty* **CHAPTER 1** WE T...

Name _____ Date _____ Class _____

| **UNIT 1** | A TRADITION OF DEMOCRACY | PORTFOLIO ASSESSMENT WORKSHEET |

The Unit 1 portfolio project is described below. You will also find the project outlined on page 67 of your textbook. A checklist following the project's description will help you track your work and put the project together. Whether you work individually or in a group, be sure to show your teacher each step of your project as you complete it.

Name _____ Date _____ Class _____

| **CHAPTER 1** | WE THE PEOPLE | PORTFOLIO ASSESSMENT WORKSHEET |

WE THE STUDENTS

e Unit Project

...outlined on page 67 of your textbook. Your teacher will tell you if ...individually or in a group. By the end of the unit, you should be ...ver your information in a 10- to 15-minute presentation to the rest

...research to learn about the history of your school. You might ...administrators and teachers to find out how the number of stu-...in your school has changed over time. Also use these interviews ...e ethnic makeup of the school has changed over the course of your ...Make sure that you take careful notes during the interviews.

...use school yearbooks and old issues of your school newspaper to ...riculum changes and the ways in which students have shown their ...nsult your school librarian for additional sources of information ...y of your school.

...tion you gather to draw an illustrated time line showing how your ...nged over time. First make a rough draft of your time line. Make ...ur time line appropriately, such as "Our School: Then and Now." ... will illustrate the time line and what form the illustrations will ...ches of the illustrations you will use. Show your teacher the rough ...e line and sketches. Use the following checklist:

...s with administrators and teachers
...ion of notes from interviews
...school yearbooks
...school newspapers
...ion with school librarian
...ft of time line
...titled appropriately
...of illustrations
...initials

(continued)

CHAPTER 1 • PORTFOLIO ASSESSMENT WORKSHEET **1**

Name _____ Date _____ Class _____

| **CHAPTER 1** | WE THE PEOPLE | CHALLENGE/ENRICHMENT WORKSHEET |

Completing a Census Form

In the future, you will be asked to participate in the nation's census by filling out a census form. What does this form look like? What kinds of information will you be asked to provide?

The form on this page is based on part of the 1990 census form. Imagine, however, that it is the year 2010. You have just received the form in the mail. Complete the form.

CHAPTER 1 • CHALLENGE/ENRICHMENT WORKSHEET **1**

For permission to reprint copyrighted material, grateful acknowledgment is made to the following source: BARBARA JORDAN: From a statement of the Honorable Barbara Jordan, a United States Representative from The State of Texas, at the 1976 Democratic National Convention. Copyright © 1976 by Barbara Jordan.

Using the Quotation

Ask students to read the quotation by James Truslow Adams, an American historian and essayist of the early 1900s. Have them identify what, in Adams's view, the American Dream is. Help students see that the American Dream is an ideal—a goal of perfection—that we may never achieve, yet moving toward that goal is basic to our democracy.

About the Author

James Truslow Adams (1878–1949) was an American historian and Pulitzer Prize-winning author of many scholarly and popular books. Born in Brooklyn, New York, Truslow worked for a time as a successful stockbroker before embarking on his writing career. His long list of books includes *The Founding of New England* (1921), for which he won a Pulitzer Prize, and *The Epic of America* (1931).

xviii

"The American dream that has lured tens of millions of all nations to our shores in the past century has not been a dream of merely material plenty, though that has doubtless counted heavily. It has been much more than that. It has been a dream of being able to grow to fullest development as man and woman, unhampered [unrestricted] by the barriers which had slowly been erected [built] in older civilizations, unrepressed by [free from] social orders which had developed for the benefit of classes rather than for the simple human being of any and every class. And that dream has been realized more fully in actual life here than anywhere else."

— *James Truslow Adams*
SOCIAL HISTORIAN

The first unit in *American Civics* sets the stage for an understanding of the rights and duties of U.S. citizenship. Beginning with the introduction to the first chapter, students learn about the American Dream of freedom and equal opportunity for all. Unit 1 goes on to provide specific information concerning the American people, their basic freedoms, and the nature of the government established to protect, promote, and defend those freedoms.

After studying Unit 1, students should be able to accomplish the following.

1. Explain the importance of the study of civics.
2. Identify how people become U.S. citizens.
3. Describe the basic purposes and the development of U.S. government.
4. Explain the basic principles of the U.S. Constitution.
5. Discuss the organization of U.S. government.
6. Outline U.S. citizens' rights and responsibilities.

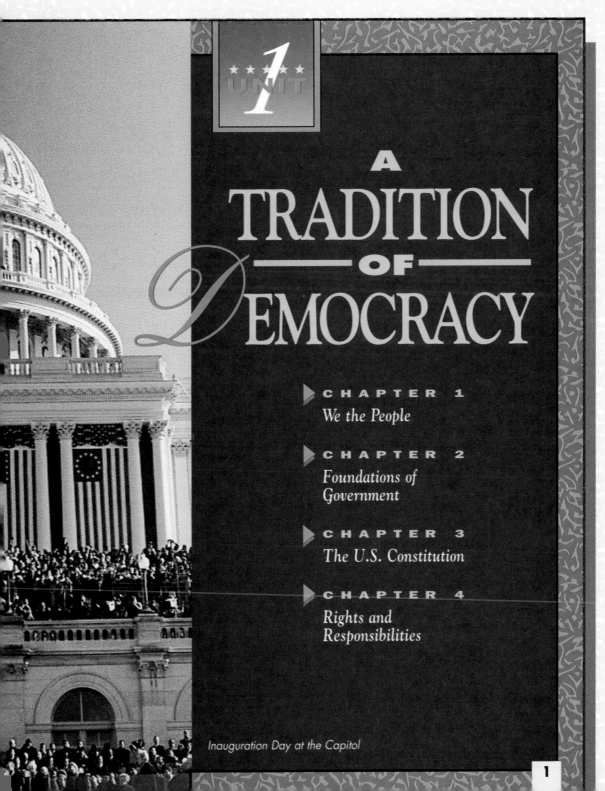

UNIT 1

A TRADITION —OF— DEMOCRACY

▶ **CHAPTER 1**
We the People

▶ **CHAPTER 2**
Foundations of Government

▶ **CHAPTER 3**
The U.S. Constitution

▶ **CHAPTER 4**
Rights and Responsibilities

Inauguration Day at the Capitol

Block Scheduling Option

CIVICS VIDEOCASSETTE

Segment 1: The Roles of a Citizen

CIVICS VIDEODISC

Segment 1: The Roles of a Citizen

Segment 1, Side A

Search Chapter 1

Play   Pause

BUILDING YOUR PORTFOLIO

"Building Your Portfolio" on page 67 outlines a unit project for students to work on as they study Unit 1. The unit project is supported by materials in the *Portfolio Assessment Worksheets* booklet.

We the People

TEXTBOOK	TEACHING RESOURCES	OTHER AVAILABLE RESOURCES
Chapter	• Skills Worksheet 1 • Challenge/Enrichment Worksheet 1	• Simulations and Case Studies Lesson 1
Section **1** Civics in Our Lives Page 3	• Reteaching Worksheet 1.1	
2 Who Are U.S. Citizens? Page 7	• Reteaching Worksheet 1.2	
3 The American People Today Page 11	• Reteaching Worksheet 1.3	
Review and Assessment Chapter 1 Review, Page 19	• Test, Form A • Test, Form B • Portfolio Assessment Worksheet 1	• *Test Generator,* Chapter 1

Block Scheduling Option

ADDITIONAL RESOURCES

BOOKS FOR TEACHERS

Briggs, Vernon M., *Immigration Policy and the American Labor Force,* Johns Hopkins.

Franzosa, Susan D., ed., *Civic Education: Its Limits and Conditions,* Prakken.

Loescher, Gil, and John Scanlan, *Calculated Kindness: Refugees and America's Half-Open Door, 1945 to the Present,* Free Press.

Praetorius, Henry, *An Immigrant Settler,* Binford & Mort.

BOOKS FOR STUDENTS

Bode, Janet, *New Kids on the Block,* Watts. Immigrant teenagers from developing countries tell their stories of living in a new culture in the United States.

Golding, William, *Lord of the Flies,* Putnam. Novel in which boys stranded on an island create their own power structure.

Graff, Nancy Price, *Where the River Runs: A Portrait of a Refugee Family,* Little, Brown. The story of a Cambodian refugee family who came to the United States.

Reimers, David, *The Immigrant Experience,* Chelsea House. Explores the experiences of immigrants in the United States.

Robbins, Albert, *Coming to America: Immigrants from Northern Europe,* Delacorte. Immigrants tell of coming to America, what they left behind, and what they did here and how.

MULTIMEDIA RESOURCES

America—It's All the Difference (f, c, 26 min.), MOD. Explores the range of backgrounds that have contributed to the exchange of ideas in the United States.

The American Experience: Our Living Traditions (f, c, 19 min.), BFA. How immigrants enrich American life and culture.

The Black West (f, VHS, 30 min.) BEA. Illustrates the role of African Americans in settling the American West.

Indians of Early America (VHS, c, 22 min.), EBEC. Explores the lives of a number of early Indian tribes by re-creating their daily activities.

A Nation of Immigrants (VHS, c, 16 min.), GA. Traces the history of immigration from the Pilgrims' landing to the Immigration Act of 1965.

The Way of the Willow (f, VHS, c, 30 min.), BEA. Focuses on a family of Vietnamese boat people to illustrate some of the problems faced by new immigrants to the United States.

THE INTERNET

Have students use these search words to locate more information about chapter topics on the Internet: *civics, citizenship, naturalization, immigration, census.*

 GLOBAL SKILL BUILDER

You might wish to use **Navigating the Internet** from the interactive *Global Skill Builder* CD-ROM to aid students' understanding of the Internet as a resource.

Abbreviations: b&w=black and white; c=color; f=film; fs=filmstrip; sd=sound; tr=transparency; VHS=videotape

PRINCIPLES OF DEMOCRACY

* **Living in a Democracy** Students will learn about the basic freedoms traditionally enjoyed by American citizens and about the qualities of a good citizen.

* **Living in a Diverse Society** Students will learn how the immigration policy of the United States has changed over time, how a person becomes a U.S. citizen, the ways in which a country's population grows, and trends in U.S. life today.

CIVICS SKILLS

Students will learn how to use the various parts of the *American Civics* textbook. They will also learn terms related to citizenship and the role of civics in their lives.

CITIZENSHIP VALUES

Students will be encouraged to take pride in their nation and its ideals and to understand that many people view the United States as a refuge for the oppressed peoples of the world.

MEETING INDIVIDUAL NEEDS

LIMITED ENGLISH PROFICIENCY (LEP)

Have pairs of students choose from the chapter a picture that interests them. Ask them to describe what is happening in the picture, using as many words from the Chapter 1 Civics Dictionary as they can. One member of each pair should write down a description. The other member should read the description to the class.

LEARNERS HAVING DIFFICULTY

Have students read the Chapter 1 Summary. Ask them to choose one sentence from each of the paragraphs in the summary and write it on a sheet of paper. Then have them find two or three details from the chapter to support each idea. Call on volunteers to share their findings.

AUDITORY LEARNERS

Have students work together to create a profile of a U.S. citizen. The first student might say, "The citizen is a woman." The second might give the person a name or an address. Others might add age, ethnic group, and so forth. Students should use as many ideas from the chapter as possible, including whether the character is a good citizen; whether he or she immigrated or migrated; and where the citizen lives—in the city, in the suburbs, or in the country.

VISUAL LEARNERS

Have students create a collage of rural, urban, and suburban scenes, using their own illustrations and/or images from periodicals. They should arrange their collages so that each tells the story of the movement of Americans from farm to city to suburb. Invite volunteers to present their collages to the class.

TACTILE/KINESTHETIC LEARNERS

Organize students into small groups. Have the groups form a "national citizenship committee." Have them design and write poster-sized advertisements seeking U.S. citizens. Advertisements might include several requirements of a good citizen, or students might use other appropriate ideas or statements from the chapter. Encourage creativity.

GIFTED LEARNERS

Set up a panel of students to discuss the following problem: The percentage of young adults who vote is consistently the lowest of all age groups. What can be done to encourage higher levels of participation in government? Students might wish to work together to break down the issue into several categories, such as educating people about the process of voting, keeping people informed about the issues, and raising people's interest levels. The panel should accept questions from the rest of the class.

CHAPTER OVERVIEW

Chapter 1 examines the role of civics in our lives. It also explains how people become U.S. citizens and how American society has changed over the years, through immigration and shifts in population. The underlying theme of the chapter is that we must accept our responsibilities as citizens and work together to protect the American Dream of freedom and equality for all.

Motivator

Conduct a brainstorming session in which students identify the rights they enjoy as Americans. Examples might include the right to an education or to express opinions openly. Ask students if, in return, they have any obligations. Encourage them to see that if people do not take part in government, they may allow their rights to be reduced or perhaps even taken away.

CHAPTER OBJECTIVES

After studying Chapter 1, students should be able to do the following.

1. Describe what it means to be a U.S. citizen.
2. List the ideals that guide the American way of life.
3. Describe the early immigrants to the United States.
4. Explain how people become U.S. citizens.
5. Describe what the census tells us and how the U.S. population is changing.

SIMULATIONS AND CASE STUDIES

Lesson 1: Founding Documents Treasure Hunt

Block Scheduling Option

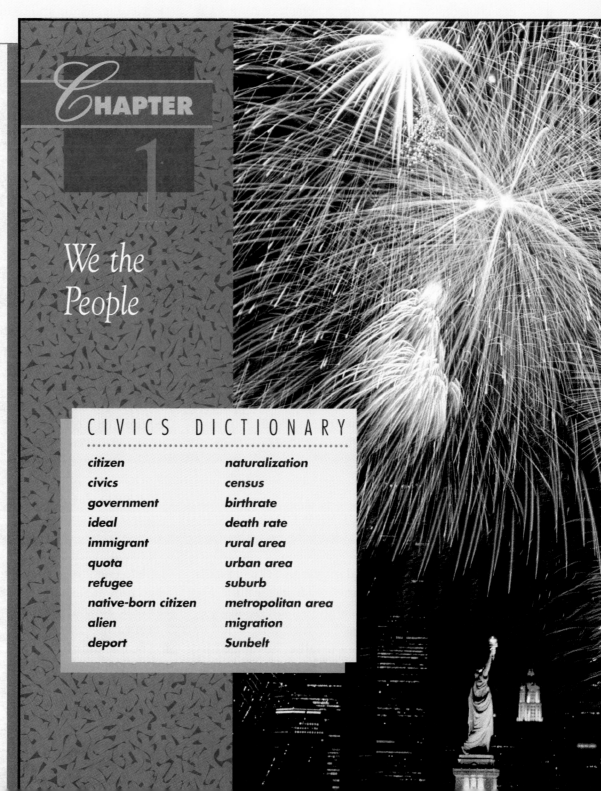

CHAPTER 1

We the People

CIVICS DICTIONARY

citizen	naturalization
civics	census
government	birthrate
ideal	death rate
immigrant	rural area
quota	urban area
refugee	suburb
native-born citizen	metropolitan area
alien	migration
deport	Sunbelt

SECTION OBJECTIVES

After studying Section 1, students should be able to do the following.

1. Explain the obligations of a U.S. citizen.

2. Name the ideals that form the basis of U.S. government and the American way of life.

3. Identify at least three ways that citizens can become involved in government.

4. Identify qualities of a good citizen.

Teaching Section 1
Building a Vocabulary

Have students explain what a **citizen** is. *(a member of a political entity, such as a city, state, or nation)* Have students name specific political entities of which they are citizens. *(Students should name their hometown, county, state, and the United States.)* Explain that **civics** comes from the Latin word *civis*, meaning "citizen" and is the study of the rights and duties of citizens. Tell students that they will also learn about the institution that rules on behalf of citizens. Ask students what that institution is called. **(government)**

CHAPTER FOCUS

Have you ever heard the term *American Dream*? The United States is built on this dream—the hope of a better life for everyone. This dream has been shared by millions of people who have believed that in this nation all men and women could truly be free.

It is a dream that began in colonial times and continues to draw thousands of people to the United States each year. For many people the American Dream has meant freedom from religious persecution. For others it has meant freedom from political upheavals and wars. For still others it has meant freedom to achieve economic success.

As an American, you have the freedom to pursue your own American Dream, whatever it may be. But the American Dream will remain a reality only as long as you, and all Americans, work to protect our precious heritage of freedom. This is your responsibility as an American **citizen**—a member of our nation.

GLOBAL PERSPECTIVES

While almost everyone today is a citizen of a nation, throughout history governments have limited the rights of some of their citizens (such as the right to vote), in effect conferring upon them a sort of second-class citizenship. At various times in history, governments have come to see citizenship in more egalitarian terms. One result of the French Revolution in 1789, for example, was the elimination of privileged classes in France. After the Revolution, people began to address everyone simply as "citizen." This equalizing title reflected their belief in the freedom and equality of all people.

STUDY GUIDE

● What does it mean to be a U.S. citizen, and what ideals guide the American way of life?

● Who were the early immigrants to America, and how do people become U.S. citizens today?

● What is the purpose of the census, and how is the American population changing?

1 Civics in Our Lives

What is civics? Why do we study this subject in school? What does civics have to do with my life? These are some of the questions you may be asking as you begin your civics course.

Many of the subjects you study in school teach you about the American way of life and the priceless rights you enjoy as an American. The civics course you are about to begin will explain how you, as a citizen of the United States, can help to keep this heritage alive.

The Meaning of Civics

Civics is the study of what it means to be an American citizen. The word *civics* comes from the Latin *civis*, meaning "citizen." The meaning of this word has changed since the ancient Romans first used it many hundreds of years ago. At that time, only a small group of wealthy people who owned property could be Roman citizens. Today almost everyone is a citizen of a nation.

The rights and responsibilities of being a citizen also have changed over time. Moreover, they differ from nation to nation. They depend on a nation's type of government. **Government** is the authority, or power, that rules on behalf of a group of people. Under the American system of government, citizens have many rights and responsibilities. Your civics course will help you discover the most important ones.

You will discover that American citizenship means more than being a responsible member of the nation. It includes being a productive and sharing member of society. Almost all Americans belong to a family, go to school for several years, and work with other people. Americans also are members of their communities—villages, towns, and cities—and of states. Being an effective citizen of the United States means fulfilling your duties and

Evaluating Ideas

Write the phrases *government by the people* and *rule through elected officials* on the chalkboard. Remind students that Americans believe in government by the people, yet in the United States the people rule through elected officials. Have students hold a panel discussion to debate how these two ideals, which seem opposed, can logically exist together. Call on volunteers to suggest how these two ideals are exemplified in U.S. society. *(Periodic elections allow the people to decide who will be responsible for governing, or ruling, the nation.)*

COOPERATIVE LEARNING

Refer students to the 10 qualities of a good citizen listed on pages 5–6. Divide the class into small groups. Within each group, assign each member one or more of these qualities. Have group members decide why their assigned qualities represent characteristics of a good citizen. Then have group members offer examples of how these qualities might show up in their daily lives. Have each group choose a member to write the group's examples on the board and explain them to the rest of the class.

CIVICS SIDELIGHT

"Government by the people" requires people capable of governing. Thomas Jefferson believed that the new American nation could succeed only if it had a well-informed electorate. Enlightened citizens, he thought, must be educated citizens. To that end, he introduced several education bills in Virginia. In 1814 he wrote: "It is highly interesting to our country, and it is the duty of its functionaries, to provide that every citizen in it should receive an education."

The success of the United States depends on well-educated citizens. These students know that studying is the key to a good education.

responsibilities as a member of each of these groups and communities.

American Ideals

The importance of being a responsible citizen cannot be stressed too much. As a citizen of the United States, there are many different reasons to take pride in your nation. It is a land of great natural beauty and of hardworking, creative people. Even more important are the **ideals**, or beliefs, that form the basis of this great nation.

The American government and way of life are based on the ideals of freedom and equality. As a citizen of this nation, each one of us is guaranteed the same rights and freedoms. These rights and freedoms are protected by laws and cannot be taken from any citizen. As a U.S. citizen, you must be willing to do your share to protect this great heritage of freedom, or liberty. It has been handed down from one generation of Americans to the next for more than 200 years.

A Heritage of Freedom

One important American freedom concerns you directly as you read this. It is the freedom to learn. Americans believe that every young citizen should have the opportunity to learn about our nation and the world by receiving a well-rounded education. To that end, our states and communities spend billions of dollars each year to provide free public schools for all young citizens. Each state also has public and private colleges and universities for those who wish to continue their education.

Another important freedom is the freedom to choose a job or career. Americans believe that all persons qualified for a job should have an equal opportunity to secure it.

Americans are fortunate to have many other freedoms as well. We may live as we wish as long as we respect the rights of others. We are free to own a house, marry the person of our choice, and raise a family. We may start our own business, travel, and live anywhere in the nation. We are free to speak and write what

4

Help students create a profile of a "good citizen." Start by writing on the board a phrase that describes one aspect of "Good Citizen X," such as "well informed." Then have students suggest other terms or phrases and explain why it is important that good citizens have each of these characteristics. Students should provide examples showing how "Good Citizen X" can meet these standards. For example, staying informed requires identifying and using sources of information, such as newspapers, on a regular basis.

Have students write several scenarios dealing with the following statement: *If you obey all the laws, you have fulfilled your responsibilities as an American citizen.* Students' scenarios should describe situations in everyday life supporting or refuting the statement. In particular, students should address the question of whether or not being a good citizen means more than just obeying laws. Call on volunteers to read one of their scenarios aloud for the class to discuss.

we wish as long as our words do not harm another person. We may not be arrested or imprisoned without just cause.

Government by the People

The leaders who planned our government created a system that would guarantee freedom. The form of government that they established remains strong today. Under the American form of government, the people rule through the officials they elect.

These elected officials are responsible to the people. Citizens are free to vote for new officials at election time if those in office do not do their jobs properly. Officials also can be removed from office before the end of their terms if necessary. By making officials answerable to the people they represent, the founders of this country made sure that our system of government would continue to serve the American people.

The Role of the Citizen

As a U.S. citizen, you have many freedoms. Being a citizen involves many responsibilities as well. Voting in elections is one of the most important of these responsibilities.

You can also help in other ways to choose the men and women who will govern. You can work for a political party, for example. Anyone who answers telephones, stuffs envelopes, or helps prepare for meetings of a political party is playing a part in the American system of government.

It is also your responsibility as a thoughtful citizen to inform officials of your needs or disagreements with government actions. You can do this by taking direct action. For example, you can write or call public officials or write to newspapers. Knowing how your government works will help you carry out your duties and responsibilities as a citizen.

Studying civics is one key to understanding these workings of government—at the national, state, and local levels. As you study the structure and purposes of these governments, you will learn what an important part each of them plays in your life. You will also learn your role in government.

Qualities of a Good Citizen

As a U.S. citizen and a future voter, you will play a vital role in determining the future of the nation. Your participation in government is necessary for the American form of government to work.

How can you become an effective citizen? What qualities will you need? Here is a list of 10 characteristics of a good citizen. You probably can think of several more. Good citizens

- are responsible family members,
- respect and obey the laws of the land,

Like these baseball players, citizens in a free nation must act as members of a team. For government to work, everyone must obey the rules and cooperate.

MULTICULTURAL PERSPECTIVES

Various cultures and societies emphasize different aspects of good citizenship. Among the Old Order Amish, for example, devotion to family, the land, and "plain living" are marks of good citizenship. The Amish, the majority of whom live today in Pennsylvania, Ohio, and Indiana, are a strict religious group whose members avoid anything of a worldly nature. They do not use automobiles, electricity, telephones, indoor plumbing, modern technology, or anything else from the "English" (non-Amish) world.

All aspects of the Amish culture revolve around the home and family life. Amish families are self-sufficient units. They produce their own food, clothing, soap, quilts, and furniture. Amish communities focus on intensive farming. Because modern farm equipment is forbidden, the work is difficult and demanding. The Amish rarely complain, however—hard work is expected of good citizens.

Closure

Ask students to list the rights of U.S. citizens. Write their responses on the chalkboard. Then ask what the responsibilities of a citizen are. Write the responses in a second list. Lead a discussion in which students compare the lists, emphasizing the give-and-take of citizenship.

Reviewing

Have students complete the Section 1 Review.

Reteaching

Assign Section 1 of the Chapter 1 Reteaching Worksheet.

SECTION 1 REVIEW
A N S W E R S

1. See the following pages: citizen, civics, government (p. 3); ideal (p. 4).

2. to fulfill the duties and responsibilities of citizenship

3. freedom and equality

4. vote in elections, work for political parties, contact public officials

5. Good citizens are responsible family members, respect and obey laws, respect rights and property, are loyal to nation, participate in community life, take an active part in government, use natural resources wisely, become well informed on issues, believe in equality of opportunity, and respect individual differences.

6. Goals might include increasing voter registration, encouraging community clean-ups, circulating petitions, encouraging volunteerism, and starting community watch programs.

6

- respect the rights and property of others,
- are loyal to their nation and proud of its accomplishments,
- take part in and improve life in their communities,
- take an active part in their government,
- use natural resources wisely,
- are well informed on important issues,
- believe in equality of opportunity for all people, and
- respect individual differences and ways of life that are different from their own.

The Importance of Civics

It is important for every American to understand how our system of government operates and why citizens must take part in it. Participation in government has always been a basic principle of the American form of government.

In your study of civics you will learn a great deal about American government. Your study also will include many other topics that

Our training as members of a family is our first lesson in civics. With other members of our families, we learn to work together toward shared goals.

concern all U.S. citizens. You will study how communities serve their people and some of the challenges these communities face.

You will also read about the nation's free-economic system and how it provides opportunities for all people. You will learn why citizens must pay taxes. You will study jobs and careers and learn what training and abilities they require. You will discover how the education system works and how you can get the most from your school years. You will read about America's relations with other nations and learn how over the years the United States has taken a position as a world leader.

Being a U.S. citizen is something we often take for granted. To become a responsible and effective citizen, however, requires effort and training, just as becoming a good athlete or a good musician does. The nation needs citizens who are well informed and who are willing to take part in determining how the nation acts. Meeting the obligations of citizenship is an important challenge. This textbook was written to help you meet that challenge.

SECTION 1 REVIEW

1. Define or identify the following terms: citizen, civics, government, ideal.

2. What obligations do you have as a U.S. citizen?

3. What ideals form the basis of U.S. government and the American way of life?

4. Identify three ways that citizens can become involved in government.

5. Identify 10 qualities of a good citizen.

6. **THINKING CRITICALLY** You head a committee to encourage good citizenship in your community. Create a chart showing five goals you want your committee to achieve and suggestions for achieving each goal.

SECTION OBJECTIVES

After studying Section 2, students should be able to do the following.

1. Describe America's earliest immigrants.

2. Explain changes in U.S. immigration policy since the early 1800s.

3. Name the two ways that a person can be a U.S. citizen by birth.

4. Compare the rights of U.S. citizens and legal aliens, and identify the problems of illegal aliens.

Teaching Section 2
Building a Vocabulary

Have a volunteer define **immigrants**. *(people who came here from other lands)* Then ask them why some immigrants are called **refugees**. *(They come to a country for refuge; they are fleeing persecution in their homeland.)* Ask whether anyone can name the process by which immigrants become citizens. *(naturalization)* Then ask them what they think **native-born citizens** are. *(Native-born citizens are those citizens born in this country.)*

2 | Who Are U.S. Citizens?

America's heritage of freedom and equality was formed bit by bit as groups from various parts of the world settled here. Today all Americans can be proud of the background we share. For we are all **immigrants**—people who came here from other lands—or descendants of immigrants.

From their countries of origin, immigrants brought different languages, ideas, beliefs, customs, hopes, and dreams. These different ways of life mixed with the ideas and ways of life of those already present in America. This multicultural heritage has given a special energy and richness to American society that would not be possible otherwise.

Early Americans

As you know from your study of American history, the first people to settle in America were Native Americans. Archaeologists—scientists who study the remains of past cultures—estimate that the ancestors of modern-day Native Americans came here from Siberia in Asia between 12,000 and 60,000 years ago. Gradually, over thousands of years, they moved into many parts of North, Central, and South America.

The Vikings came next but did not stay long. The Spaniards were the first Europeans to build lasting settlements in the Americas. They settled in Mexico, Central and South America, and what are now Florida, California, Texas, and the southwestern United States.

The original 13 colonies were settled mostly by people from England. Colonists from other countries included German settlers in Pennsylvania, the Dutch along the Hudson River, and the Swedes in New Jersey and Delaware. Many black people also came to America from Africa. Unlike other immigrants, most of them were brought to America as slaves. They and their children were forced to live in bondage for many years.

GLOBAL CONNECTIONS

The Americas

As you know, citizens of the United States are called Americans. What you may not know is that our neighbors to the north and south could be called Americans, too. After all, the two continents that make up the Western Hemisphere are North *America* and South *America*. Why, then, do the people of Canada, or Mexico, or Brazil not call themselves Americans?

The reason is that the United States was the first independent nation in the hemisphere. By the time Mexico and the other nations achieved independence in the 1800s, the "American" label already had a specific meaning. It meant a citizen of the United States.

U.S. Immigration Policy

Over the years, the United States has been settled and populated by people from all over the world. During its early history, the new American nation struggled to survive. As a result, most immigrants were welcomed to the United States. Agricultural workers and factory laborers, for example, were needed as the nation expanded from the Atlantic Ocean to the Pacific Ocean. As a result, during the first half of the 1800s, the U.S. government adopted an "open-shore" policy. This policy allowed unlimited immigration to the United States. The only persons who were not admitted to the country were criminals and those who had certain diseases.

MULTICULTURAL PERSPECTIVES

European newcomers to the American colonies included groups other than Christians. Several sizable Jewish settlements also existed in colonial America. The first such settlement was in the Dutch colony of New Amsterdam (now New York) in 1654. Groups of Jews also settled in Newport, Rhode Island (by 1678), and Savannah, Georgia (1733), among other locations. In 1800 the 600 Jews of Charleston, South Carolina, comprised the largest Jewish population of any U.S. city.

Dramatizing Government

Pair up students who take turns playing the roles of an alien applying for citizenship and an immigration official. Ask students to write questions the immigration official might ask, as well as possible answers. Have one volunteer pair present a dramatization to the class. (You might set up a mock immigration office.) Have the class discuss each character's goals and concerns in the exchange.

COOPERATIVE LEARNING

Organize the class into small groups. Have some group members make up characteristics of hypothetical immigrants (such as age, education, health, criminal record [if any], and years of U.S. residency). Other group members should ask questions to determine whether or not the immigrant may become a naturalized citizen. Have members record which immigrants are approved for citizenship, which are not, and why. Have a volunteer from each group present one "immigrant case" for the class to discuss.

GLOBAL PERSPECTIVES

Point out that many immigrants to the United States throughout the country's history have been refugees trying to escape from world trouble spots. Refugees are a major part of the massive movement of people throughout the world. In fact, some officials put the total number of refugees in the world in 1994 at 16 million. Some reports indicate that five million were displaced during the 1990–1991 Persian Gulf conflict alone. The massive number of refugees throughout the world is a major financial and logistical burden for the world community.

The faces of America show the many lands from which our citizens have come. Though our backgrounds may be different, we are all Americans.

As America began to fill and land and jobs became less available, however, some Americans wanted to change the immigration policy. Slowly the United States began to limit the number of people who were allowed to immigrate to this country. During the 1880s the government placed some restrictions on immigration. It was not until the 1920s, however, that a **quota**, or limit, was established on the number of immigrants who could be admitted to the nation each year.

U.S. immigration policy today is guided by the Immigration Act of 1990. Under this act the cap on immigration for 1995 and beyond was set at 675,000 immigrants a year—up considerably from the annual limit of 270,000 that existed until 1992. Preference is given to immediate relatives of U.S. citizens and to persons who have valuable employment skills. **Refugees**, or persons fleeing persecution in their home countries, are not subject to this annual quota.

In recent years the majority of immigrants to the United States have come from Asia, Latin America, and Europe. Many of these people immigrated to the United States to escape wars, political conflicts, and other crises in their home countries.

Citizenship by Birth

Millions of immigrants have become U.S. citizens. Some citizens belong to families that have lived here for many generations. Other Americans were born in foreign countries. All citizens, regardless of their heritage, have the same legal rights and responsibilities.

Americans gain their citizenship either by birth or by a special legal process. Most of us became citizens of the United States by birth. If you were born in any one of the 50 states or in any U.S. territory, you automatically became a **native-born citizen**. If one or both of your parents were U.S. citizens, you were a

Refer students to the map on pages 520–521. Have students use what they know from the news to list those countries near the United States from which many legal and illegal immigrants have come. Explain that difficult economic and/or political conditions in certain nearby countries are some of the reasons for this immigration. Have students debate what they believe U.S. immigration policy should be regarding these countries.

Have students find out when their ancestors (or those of a friend or a famous American) entered this country and from where they came. Students should use classroom and library resources to research conditions in the country of origin of their ancestors when the ancestors emigrated. Then have each student take the role of one of the immigrants and write personal journal entries describing the feelings he or she has about immigrating to the United States.

citizen by birth even if they were living in a foreign land when you were born. Citizenship, then, can be acquired by the place of birth or through one's parents.

What about children born in this country whose parents are citizens of a foreign country? Are they citizens of the United States? In most cases they are, if their parents were under the authority of the United States at the time the children were born.

What about children born here whose parents are officials representing a foreign country? They are not U.S. citizens because their parents are under the authority of another country. All cases involving claims of U.S. citizenship are handled by the U.S. Department of Justice.

Aliens in the United States

More than 21 million people living in the United States are citizens of other countries. These people are called **aliens**. Some of these people are here on a visit. Others live and work here or attend school but expect someday to return to their homelands. Many other aliens in the United States expect to live in the country permanently.

While in the United States, all aliens must obey the laws of this country. They are also entitled to be protected by its laws. Aliens enjoy most of the benefits of U.S. citizenship. They cannot, however, vote or hold public office. In addition, various state laws prohibit aliens from working at certain jobs, such as teaching in public schools.

All aliens living in the United States must register with the U.S. Immigration and Naturalization Service, an agency of the Department of Justice. They also must keep the agency informed of their current address.

Illegal Aliens

No one knows exactly how many aliens live in the United States illegally, but estimates range from 3.5 million to 4 million. In 1986 the Immigration Reform and Control Act was passed

to legalize the status of illegal aliens who meet certain requirements, but the flow of illegal immigration remains high.

Nearly half of all illegal aliens come from Mexico. Most come to the United States to find work and a better life. Life is often difficult for illegal aliens, however. Many become migrant workers, moving from farm to farm picking crops. Illegal aliens often have to work for very low wages under harsh working conditions. Some citizens resent these aliens, who they believe are taking jobs away from U.S. citizens. Illegal aliens also face the danger of being caught and **deported**, or forced to leave, the United States.

By learning English, these aliens are taking an important step toward becoming U.S. citizens. What other steps must aliens take to become citizens of the United States?

CIVICS SIDELIGHT

Many aliens who immigrate to the United States hope to obtain a permanent residence visa, or "green card," which allows them to live in the country indefinitely. Despite its name, the prized green card is no longer green. It is a white card about the size of a credit card.

Photo Caption Answer

declare intent (optional), file a petition, pass an examination, appear at a hearing to take oath of allegiance

Closure

Draw a chart on the chalkboard, with the following column headings: *Native-Born Citizen, Legal Alien, Illegal Alien, Naturalized Citizen.* Ask students for characteristics of each category. Write their answers in the appropriate columns. When the chart is complete, discuss the similarities and differences among the categories. Students may copy the chart into their notebooks as a study guide.

Reviewing

Have students complete the Section 2 Review.

Reteaching

Assign Section 2 of the Chapter 1 Reteaching Worksheet.

Citizenship by Naturalization

Under certain circumstances, citizens of other countries may become U.S. citizens. The legal process by which an alien may become a citizen is called **naturalization**. The first part of the naturalization process is entering the United States legally.

To be eligible to enter the country, foreigners must prove that they can support themselves and that they can read and write. They must prove they do not have certain diseases or a mental illness and are not drug addicts or criminals. There are several other restrictions that bar people from entering the United States. One restriction bars persons who favor violent revolution, that is, the overthrow of the government by force.

Only immigrants or aliens admitted as permanent residents may become American citizens. This rule excludes foreign visitors and students and others who do not plan to stay in the United States. Although not required, immigrants may file a "declaration of intention," stating that they plan to become citizens. Some employers ask for this document as evidence that the employee plans to stay in the country.

Aliens may apply for citizenship after they have lived in this country for five years. This period is reduced to three years for an alien married to an American citizen. Aliens must be at least 18 years old to apply for citizenship in the United States.

The first step is to fill out an application called a "petition for naturalization." When immigration authorities receive this application, they set a date for the person to appear before a naturalization official for a hearing.

During the hearing the applicant must show that he or she is a person of good moral character who believes in the principles of the U.S. Constitution. The applicant also must prove that he or she can read, write, and speak English acceptably and is familiar with U.S. history and government. After the examination the applicant files the petition for naturalization in a naturalization court.

Before they become citizens, applicants may be investigated to check their qualifications. If they prove to have the background needed to become citizens, they are called to court for a final hearing. There they take an oath of allegiance to the United States and are granted a certificate of naturalization. Children automatically become citizens when their parents' naturalization is officially completed.

Naturalized citizens have the same rights and duties as native-born Americans. There is only one exception. Naturalized citizens are

How an Alien Becomes a Citizen

Declaration of Intention (Optional)

An alien may file this declaration in any naturalization court. This written statement declares that the alien intends to seek U.S. citizenship.

Petition for Naturalization

After an alien has lived in the United States at least five years (or three years if married to a U.S. citizen), he or she files an application called a petition for naturalization.

Examination

A naturalization examiner conducts an examination in which the applicant must show that he or she is a person of good moral character who believes in the principles of the Constitution. The applicant also must prove that he or she can read, write, and speak English and knows about the history and government of the United States.

Final Hearing

If the applicant meets all of the qualifications, he or she is granted citizenship at a final hearing. There, the alien swears an oath of allegiance and is given a certificate of naturalization.

After studying Section 3, students should be able to do the following.

1. Explain the value of census information.

2. Cite ways in which a population can grow.

3. Describe migration patterns of Americans from early times to the present.

4. Understand the diversity of America's population.

Teaching Section 3
Building a Vocabulary

Have students describe their image of a typical **rural area** and a typical **urban area**. Explain that *rural* comes from a Latin word meaning "open land." Have students use dictionaries to determine the word origin of *urban*. *(comes from a Latin word meaning "city")* Then ask students whether a **suburb** is a mix of rural and urban or something completely different. Break *suburb* into its Latin parts: *sub-*, meaning "near," and *-urbs*, meaning "city."

not eligible to become president or vice president of the United States.

SECTION 2 REVIEW

1. Define or identify the following terms: immigrant, quota, refugee, native-born citizen, alien, deport, naturalization.

2. Who were the first immigrants to America and when did they come here?

3. How does U.S. immigration policy today differ from that of the early 1800s?

4. What are the two ways that a person becomes a citizen of the United States by birth?

5. What rights do U.S. citizens have that legal aliens do not?

6. What problems do illegal aliens face?

7. **THINKING CRITICALLY** You have just become a naturalized citizen of the United States. Write a letter to a friend in the country in which you were born explaining why and how you became a U.S. citizen.

3 The American People Today

The leaders who planned the American government realized that they would need to know how many people—citizens as well as noncitizens—lived in the nation. They decided that every 10 years the national government would make an official count of the number of people living in the United States. This count is called a **census**. The most recent census was taken in 1990.

What the Census Tells Us

The main purpose of the census is to find out the size of each state's population. This information is used for many purposes, including to determine how many people from each state will be elected to Congress.

The census also tells us a great deal about the United States and the people who live here. For example, it tells us how many children there are in each family and how many people have moved and where. In addition, the census indicates the rate of population growth in the United States. This and other information gathered by census takers helps the government, businesses, and individuals plan for the future. It also helps us learn something about ourselves and our nation.

Population Growth

When the first census takers counted the nation's population in 1790, they reported fewer than four million people living in the original 13 states. Since that time, the nation has grown in both size and population. Instead of 13 states, there are now 50. And, according to current projections, the nation's population will exceed 275 million by the year 2000. How did the United States grow to its present size and population?

All nations grow in three ways. One way is by natural increase in population. A natural population increase occurs when the birthrate is greater than the death rate. The **birthrate** refers to the annual number of live births per 1,000 members of a population. The **death rate** refers to the annual number of deaths per 1,000 members of a country's population.

The second way a nation grows is by adding new territory. The United States has gained new areas of land through war, purchase, and annexation. The people living in these new lands have added to the size of the country's population.

The third source of population growth is immigration, or the arrival of people from

(continued on page 14)

CIVICS SIDELIGHT

Today the census contains very detailed information about the population of a given country or region. Until about the seventeenth century, however, many governments used censuses for more limited purposes. Many census officials in earlier societies were selective in determining who should be counted and why. For example, governments primarily wanted to know who should be taxed, or who was available for work and military training. Consequently, certain societal groups, such as property owners and males, were more important than others to the census takers.

Linking Civics and History

Have students research the history of homelessness in the United States and other countries. Students should try to answer the following questions: How severe is the problem in the United States compared to other industrialized countries? Why is homelessness a difficult problem in many industrializing countries? How have some governments and private organizations tried to solve the problem? Ask students to write editorials advocating possible remedies for the problem in the United States.

CIVICS SIDELIGHT

Point out that various organizations provide food to needy people. The National Meals on Wheels Foundation, for example, provides nutritious meals to homebound people in the United States. This nonprofit organization delivers more than a million meals each day right to the door of those in need. The 1972 Older Americans Act provided the funds to help expand a model for home-delivered meals throughout the country. Today there are nearly 20,000 federally funded and privately sponsored Meals on Wheels programs across the United States. Volunteers from charitable organizations and church groups are among those who help deliver the meals. The National Meals on Wheels Foundation also sponsors "Miles for Meals," walkathons that raise money to help support the program.

Citizenship IN ACTION

FEEDING THE HUNGRY

Although most older people in the United States are active and vital citizens, some suffer from ill health, loneliness, and hunger. Thanks to the unselfish efforts of a teenage girl, some older citizens in Miami, Florida, have found unexpected help.

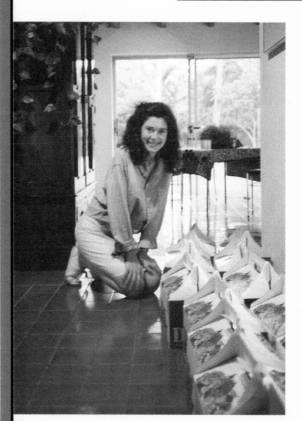

Alison Stieglitz started helping people in her community by filling Thanksgiving baskets for older citizens.

Sharing Good Fortune

When Alison Stieglitz was 12 years old, she celebrated her bat mitzvah, a Jewish ceremony marking a girl's acceptance of religious duty and responsibility. To honor Alison's hard work in preparation for the ceremony and her commitment to her faith, Alison's family members, relatives, and friends gave her gifts and money. Rather than spending the money on herself, however, Alison resolved to take her new responsibilities seriously and share her good fortune with people in need.

She decided to focus her efforts on providing Thanksgiving dinners for older people who were unable to leave their homes due to illness. With the money she received, Alison was able to assemble and distribute 15 baskets of food, which included turkeys. With each basket feeding four people, 60 older Miami citizens were able to enjoy a happy Thanksgiving. But Alison did not stop there.

The Sharing Grows

Each year from the date of that first act of good will, Alison expanded her efforts. By the time she was 17, she was able to provide more than 120 Thanksgiving baskets, feeding 480 housebound older citizens.

Summarizing

Have students reread this feature to find answers to the standard reporter's questions: *Who? What? When? Where?* and *How?* Students should then write newspaper articles reporting on efforts to help hungry and homeless people in Miami. Students may wish to gather their articles into a class newsletter.

With the help of friends, relatives, and other volunteers, Alison (right) and her sister Leigh have given hundreds of people a helping hand.

By now Alison was not alone in her efforts. In response to the teenager's countless telephone calls and letters, community members, social workers, friends, and relatives pitched in to help. In addition to donating funds, these people volunteered to assemble the Thanksgiving food baskets and coordinate their delivery. With all the additional help, Alison was able to expand her work further by providing baskets of food to hurricane victims, Soviet Jewish immigrants, people with disabilities, and hospital patients, among others.

With the success of the Thanksgiving basket project as an inspiration, Alison then helped to organize the Hungry and Homeless committee in her community synagogue. Because "soup kitchens" designed to feed the homeless in her area were closed on Sundays, Alison's committee worked with another Miami synagogue to provide food for the homeless on that day. Their combined efforts enabled them to serve breakfast and lunch to several hundred homeless people each Sunday.

In recognition of Alison's tireless work to feed the hungry, she was invited to the White House to receive the President's Volunteer Action Award. She also was the recipient of the Kimberly-Clark Corporation "Bless You" Award. Alison donated this cash award to a shelter for abused and neglected teenagers in her community.

Although she has received a great deal of recognition for her efforts, the down-to-earth Miami girl realizes that it is the caring rather than the recognition that is important. As Alison herself says, "Giving is not a one-time experience. It's something you do throughout your life."

YOU DECIDE

1 Why did Alison Stieglitz first become involved in helping the hungry?

2 Find out what efforts are being made in your community to feed the homeless and the hungry. What can you and other teenagers in your community do to become involved in this effort?

ANSWERS TO
YOU DECIDE

1. She used her bat mitzvah money to show her acceptance of responsibility to help others.

2. Community efforts might include soup kitchens, Meals on Wheels, and food vouchers. Possible ways to become involved include donating money, collecting and distributing food, and forming organizations to help the homeless and the hungry.

Illustrating Ideas

Have students use newspapers and other periodicals to create collages illustrating the reasons for population growth. For example, students might use articles about birthrates or pictures of maternity wards to illustrate natural increases in population. Use the collages to prompt a discussion on the importance of accurate censuses. For example, students might say rapidly increasing birthrates mean increasing numbers of children and subsequent needs to improve and enlarge educational facilities.

Have small groups of students create sketch maps showing how the U.S. population has gradually shifted westward over time. Some groups may want to show the location of large cities at different points in U.S. history, for example, while other groups might want to create maps showing the most populous states at various points in time. Each group member should use classroom and library resources (such as almanacs and encyclopedias) to find population information for specific states and cities or for specific years.

CIVICS SIDELIGHT

To help students visualize how the population of the United States has shifted over time, explain how the country's center of population has moved. The center of population is the point at which a flat, weightless map of the country would balance if weights of identical value were placed on it so that each weight represented the location of one person. In 1790 the U.S. center of population was 23 miles east of Baltimore, Maryland. As Americans moved westward, so did the center of the population. By 1900 the center of population was six miles southeast of Columbus, Indiana. In 1990 the country's center of population was 10 miles southeast of Steelville, Missouri.

other lands. Since 1820 more than 60 million immigrants from all over the world have come to the United States. As you know, the United States has been called a nation of immigrants.

How America's Population Grew

As the United States expanded from the Atlantic coast to the Pacific coast, it needed a rapidly growing population to settle the land. In the early years of the nation, however, the population grew relatively slowly.

Life was very difficult in those early pioneer days, and the death rate of Americans was high. Many infants and children died, disease was common, and there were few doctors. Little was known about diseases and how to cure them. Although some Americans lived to an old age, disease, poor diet, and the hazards of pioneer living made the average life expectancy short.

Between 1790 and 1830 the population of the nation more than tripled, reaching nearly 13 million. Almost all of this growth was the result of births in the United States. It was common for families to have large numbers of children. Large families were a necessity at this time. Most people lived on farms, and large families were needed to help work the farms. Thus even though many children died young and the death rate was high, the population grew significantly.

Beginning in the 1830s large numbers of immigrants started to arrive in the United States. Between 1831 and 1840 almost 600,000 immigrants came, many from Ireland. Over the next 10 years more than a million and a half new immigrants arrived. The population had exceeded 23 million by 1850.

By 1920 the nation's population had risen to nearly 106 million. Immigrants from many lands, particularly the countries of southern and eastern Europe, accounted for a large part of this increase in total population. As you have read, however, after 1920 the United States began to limit the number of immigrants admitted into the country each year.

Most of the population growth after this time was due to natural increase.

Today's Population Growth

Today the population of the United States continues to grow, although not as rapidly as in the past. In 1970, for example, 203 million people lived in the nation—nearly 24 million more than in 1960. By 1980, however, a new trend had appeared. Although the population increased by 23 million, this represented a change of only 11 percent since 1970. This was the second-smallest increase in any 10-year period since 1790.

Population projections indicate that the rate of increase will continue to drop, falling to 9 percent by the year 2000. One reason the U.S. population is growing at a slower rate is that many people are having smaller families.

A People on the Move

Where do the people of the United States live? The first census found most Americans living on farms, with a smaller number living in villages and in a few medium-sized cities. Over the years this changed. The farm population has become smaller every year. In 1993 fewer than 5 million Americans lived in households associated with farming operations.

Beginning in the 1800s many Americans began to move away from **rural areas**, or regions of farms and small towns. Most of them went to live in **urban areas**, or cities, where they worked in factories and offices. By 1830 the census showed that urban areas were growing faster than rural areas. With each census, the proportion of Americans living in or near cities continued to grow. By 1920 the census showed that more Americans lived in urban areas than in rural areas.

As the population continued to grow rapidly and people moved to the cities, urban areas became crowded. Many Americans could afford to buy automobiles, which made it possible to travel longer distances to work. As a result, beginning in the mid-1900s, people liv-

Ask volunteers to gauge the potential for population growth in their neighborhoods by describing the population that already lives there (such as the estimated number of people by age group). Then have students discuss what these characteristics mean for potential population growth in the neighborhood. For example, if the neighborhood is populated mainly by older people, the most likely avenue for population growth might be new families moving into the neighborhood (immigration, rather than births).

Have each student create a class bulletin-board display entitled "How the American people have changed in the past 20 years." Each student should draw or find images, write extended captions, create maps or charts, and design the display. Some students might illustrate changes in their own neighborhoods over time. Call on volunteers to present their displays to the class.

ing in cities started to move to surrounding areas—the **suburbs**.

They moved to the suburbs in search of better homes, schools, and communities. Sixteen of the 25 largest cities in the United States lost population between 1960 and 1970. Only nine showed a gain. Today the people who live in the suburbs outnumber those who live in the cities.

Taken together cities and their suburbs account for a vast majority of the nation's population. Today more than three fourths of the U.S. population live in **metropolitan areas**, or areas made up of cities and their suburbs. More than half live in areas with populations of 1 million or more.

Another Population Shift

Throughout the nation's history, Americans have been on the move. This movement continues today, with many Americans moving to different parts of the nation. Such large movements of people from region to region is called **migration**. The migration pattern in the United States in recent years shows people moving from the Midwest and the Northeast to the South and West.

States in the Midwest and older industrial areas in the Northeast are losing population. Americans from these areas are moving to states in the South and West. These states are known as the **Sunbelt**. People are moving to the Sunbelt because of the region's warmer climate. Also, they are looking for better jobs and better opportunities.

California now has the largest population. Nevada, Arizona, Florida, and Alaska are among the fastest growing states, showing enormous increases in population since 1980. States such as Iowa, West Virginia, Rhode Island, and North Dakota, however, have shown losses in population in the past several years.

Because of the population shift to the Sunbelt, cities in the South and West are growing. Los Angeles, California, and Phoenix, Arizona, are now among the nation's 10 largest cities. Mesa, Arizona, is one of the fastest growing

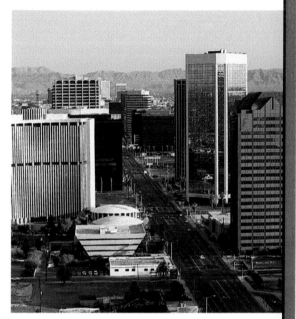

People are attracted to Phoenix, Arizona, because of its warm climate and many job opportunities.

cities. At the same time, cities in the North and East such as Newark, New Jersey; Detroit, Michigan; and Pittsburgh, Pennsylvania, are losing population. Despite this population trend, New York City remains the nation's most populous city.

A Diverse Population

The United States has been shaped by people from all over the world. Today's Americans come from many different cultural backgrounds and represent a wide variety of ethnic groups. Despite this diversity, however, the people are united by a common bond—they are all Americans.

The 33 million African Americans living in the United States today make up 13 percent of the population, forming the largest minority group. Hispanic Americans are the country's second-largest minority group—a group that has seen tremendous growth since

MULTICULTURAL PERSPECTIVES

Explain that Miami, Florida, is a good example of the diverse nature of the U.S. population. The city's mild climate has attracted many migrants from the North, especially Jews from the New York–New Jersey area. The city's location near the Caribbean Sea, on the other hand, has attracted many immigrants from that region, including Haitians, Cubans, Puerto Ricans, Mexicans, and other Hispanic immigrants. Cuban Americans, in particular, are important political, economic, and social leaders in Miami.

Closure

Begin an outline on the chalkboard by writing the main headings throughout the section. Then have students complete the outlines at their desk, with each student listing the major points discussed under each heading. Students should save the outlines for use as study guides.

Reviewing

Have students complete the Section 3 Review.

Reteaching

Assign Section 3 of the Chapter 1 Reteaching Worksheet.

CIVICS SIDELIGHT

You might point out that studying population demographics helps the government provide for current needs and plan for the future. The "baby boom," for example, is an aging wave of people moving toward "retired" status. After World War II, the return of millions of U.S. soldiers and general prosperity brought about greatly increased birthrates between 1946 and 1964. Since baby boomers will reach retirement age in the first part of the twenty-first century, government officials must find ways to make sure that the large number of baby boomers do not swamp programs such as Social Security and Medicare.

1980. Hispanic Americans today account for nearly 27 million Americans. The fastest growing minority group, however, is the third-largest group—Asian Americans. Since 1980, the Asian American population has increased an extraordinary 147 percent—to more than nine million. Much of this growth took place as a result of immigration.

Smaller Families

Recent statistics also show that other changes are taking place in the United States. The size of U.S. households has decreased since 1970. Many couples are having fewer children. Many people, too, now live alone. As a result, today there are more households with fewer people living in them. Since 1970 the total

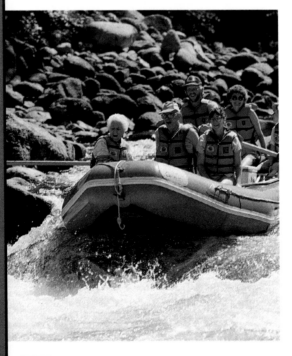
Older citizens stay active for many years past retirement. Here, some older Americans experience the excitement of white-water rafting.

number of households increased from about 63 million to more than 97 million. The average number of persons living in a household, however, declined from more than three people to fewer than three people.

Another change taking place is the increase in the number of one-parent households. Since 1970 the number of one-parent families in the United States has more than doubled. As more couples divorce, a larger number of women are becoming heads of households. In general, women remain responsible for child care. Today less than 30 percent of the nation's households include the traditional family of mother, father, and one or more children.

Changing Roles

Along with changes in the family have come changes in the roles of men and women. Perhaps one of the most significant changes has come about as more women have expanded their role from the traditional one of homemaker. In recent years more women than men have been entering and graduating from college. And, after receiving their education, more women than ever before have been entering the workforce.

In 1970 about 31 million women worked outside the home. Today more than 60 million women work outside the home. Estimates show that this number will reach nearly 72 million by the year 2005. Most women work for the same reason that most men do—economic necessity. Women who head households depend on their jobs as a source of income. So do many married women. Today more than 60 percent of the married women in the United States work outside the home. One result of the increased number of women in the workforce is that more women are entering professions that once were open only to men.

An Older Population

Statistics also show that the nation is "growing older" every year. In the early years of the

Have students research population trends in other countries of the world. Students should identify countries experiencing slow increases in their populations (such as in some countries of Europe) and countries experiencing rapid rates of population growth (such as in some countries of Africa and Asia). Students should write short paragraphs about selected countries and their growth rates and should include reasons for those rates. Call on volunteers to report their findings to the class.

---

nation, when both birthrates and death rates were high, the country had a young population. In 1850, for example, half the population of the United States was under the age of 19. Until the 1980s half the population was under the age of 30.

Today people between the ages of 25 and 64 make up the largest group in the population. In this group of almost 134 million people are most of the nation's wage earners and heads of families. They control much of business and government, and greatly influence the nation's values and actions.

An increasing part of the population consists of people who are 65 or older. This trend has resulted from a drop in both birthrates and death rates. The birthrate dropped steadily beginning in the 1960s before leveling off in the 1980s. Also, Americans are living longer. In 1920 the average American lived 54 years. Currently, the average life expectancy is around 76 years.

Today about 33 million Americans are 65 or older. This means that a large number of Americans are retired. Many older people, however, are eager to remain in the workforce. Some work part-time, and others have started new careers or returned to school.

Although most older citizens continue to be active and productive, many are troubled by the problems of low income and poor health. Using the experience and talents of older citizens offers both a challenge and an opportunity for the nation.

SECTION 3 REVIEW

1. Define or identify the following terms: census, birthrate, death rate, rural area, urban area, suburb, metropolitan area, migration, Sunbelt.

2. Why is the information gathered by census takers important?

3. In what three ways can a population grow?

4. Describe the movement of the American people from the early years of the nation to the present.

5. What has been the migration pattern in the United States in recent years?

6. Why is it correct to say that the United States has a diverse population?

7. **THINKING CRITICALLY** It is the year 2020 and you are a history textbook author. Describe for your readers the U.S. population in the mid-1990s. Focus your description on population diversity, household and family size, changing roles, and the aging of the population.

CHAPTER 1 SUMMARY

Civics is the study of what it means to be a U.S. citizen. It teaches us our responsibilities and rights as members of our nation. As citizens, we must protect the ideals of freedom on which the nation was built. We also have important citizenship responsibilities as members of our local community and state.

U.S. citizenship is gained by birth or by naturalization. Naturalized citizens enjoy the same rights as native-born citizens except that naturalized citizens are not eligible to become president or vice president.

The national government has taken a census every 10 years since 1790 to determine how many people live in the United States. The information gathered by census takers tells us how the nation has grown and changed over the years. A nation of farms has become a nation of cities and suburbs.

Recent statistics reveal that Americans are living longer, having smaller families, and moving to the Sunbelt. The number of African Americans, Hispanic Americans, and Asian Americans is increasing, as is the number of women in the workforce.

SECTION 3 REVIEW
A N S W E R S

1. See the following pages: census, birthrate, death rate (p. 11); rural area, urban area (p. 14); suburb, metropolitan area, migration, Sunbelt (p. 15).

2. It helps government, business, and individuals plan for the future.

3. natural increase, addition of new territory, immigration

4. Most Americans once lived on farms and in rural areas. Now most live in cities and metropolitan areas (including suburbs).

5. to the Sunbelt of the South and West from the older industrial areas of the Midwest and Northeast

6. Americans come from many different cultural backgrounds and represent a wide variety of ethnic groups.

7. Answers should address minority groups, smaller households and families, increased numbers of women in the workforce, and the aging population.

Point out to students that the study of civics has received a lot of attention in recent years. From the president of the United States to the local registrar of voters, from the secretary of education to the local school board, officials are concerned about young people's participation in government.

This textbook reflects that concern. Tell students that their textbook contains not only facts but also ideas—ideas that will help them discover what it means to be a citizen of the United States. Still, a textbook is merely a starting point. Encourage students to look around them as they explore the world outside of school and think about how government and society as a whole affect the daily lives of their families and them.

Developing Civics Skills

SOCIAL STUDIES SKILL
Using Your Textbook

Have you ever heard the phrase "tools of the trade"? These are the tools that help people do their jobs. Right now, your job is studying civics. Your basic learning tool is your textbook.

Even though you have already had a great deal of practice using textbooks, remember that each textbook is a specialized tool. You have to treat this book as you would any new tool. You need to explore all its features to discover how it works and how it can best serve you.

How to Use Your Textbook

1. **Use the Table of Contents.** Look first at the Table of Contents, which begins on page v. The Table of Contents will give you an overview of the topics in the textbook and show you how the book is organized.
2. **Study each unit's opening pages.** Begin each unit by looking at the unit's opening pages. For example, review the opening pages of Unit 1 (page 1). Read the title of the unit and the titles of the chapters found in the unit. Study the photographs and read the quotation.
3. **Study each chapter's opening pages.** Turn to pages 2–3 for the opening of Chapter 1. Read the chapter title and look at the photograph. Note what these items say about the theme of the chapter. Next, read the Civics Dictionary, the Chapter Focus, and the Study Guide. These features will guide you in studying the chapter material.
4. **Read the chapter.** Use the headings and subheadings as clues to main ideas and supporting details. Also note the words printed in bold type. These terms are highlighted to show their importance to

the study of civics. The meaning of a boldfaced term can be learned from the sentences surrounding it. Use the Section Review at the end of each section to check your progress. Read the Chapter Summary (page 17).

5. **Study the visuals.** Note the photographs and other visuals in each section.
6. **Study the special features.** Each unit of the textbook contains a number of special features that will add to your knowledge and enjoyment of civics. Be sure to read each feature carefully.
7. **Review your learning.** The textbook contains Chapter Reviews (page 19) and Unit Reviews (pages 66–67). Each of these reviews will help you to check your understanding of the material.
8. **Use the end-of-book material.** The textbook contains a large Reference Section, including an extensive selection of historical documents, a Glossary, and an Index (pages 517–605). Familiarize yourself with this material now so that you may use it as needed.

Applying the Skill

Complete the following activities.

1. Turn to the Table of Contents. How many units and chapters does the textbook have? What is the title of Unit 6?
2. Turn to the unit opening pages of Unit 2 (pages 68–69). Who is the author of the quotation? What are the titles of the chapters in this unit?
3. Turn to the Glossary beginning on page 579. What does the term *currency* mean? What is the second entry under "G"?

---

1. 8 units, 25 chapters; The American Economy

2. Abraham Lincoln; The Legislative Branch, The Executive Branch, The Judicial Branch

3. coins and paper money; general trial court

CHAPTER 1 REVIEW
A N S W E R S

Vocabulary Workshop
1. naturalization
2. government
3. count population every 10 years
4. rural—regions of farms and small towns; urban—cities
5. beliefs; freedom and equality

6. native-born citizen
7. persons fleeing persecution in their home countries

Reviewing Main Ideas
1. early 1800s—"open-shore" policy, late 1800s—government began to restrict immigration
2. birth or naturalization
3. enter country legally, file "petition for naturalization," pass examination, appear at a hearing to take oath

4. African Americans, Hispanic Americans, Asian Americans
5. fewer children, more people living alone, more one-parent families, more women becoming heads of households
6. more graduating from college, more entering workforce
7. Drop in birthrate and death rate and longer life expectancy have produced higher proportion of older citizens.

Thinking Critically
1. Students should use sound reasoning in their answers.
2. Immigrants with U.S. relatives have a support system already in place. Skilled immigrants can contribute their knowledge and expertise to the labor force.
3. Posters should reflect the multicultural nature of the nation.
4. Answers should focus on the benefits of diversity.

CHAPTER 1

R·e·v·i·e·w

Vocabulary Workshop

1. Identify the legal process by which an alien becomes a citizen.
2. What term refers to the authority that rules on behalf of a group of people?
3. What is the purpose of a census?
4. What is the difference between rural areas and urban areas?
5. What are ideals? Identify two ideals that form the basis of the American way of life.
6. What is the term for a person born in the United States or in any U.S. territory?
7. Define the term *refugees*.

Reviewing Main Ideas

1. How did U.S. immigration policy change from the early 1800s to the late 1800s?
2. By what two ways can a person become a citizen of the United States?
3. What are the main steps by which an alien becomes a U.S. citizen?
4. What are the three largest minority groups in the United States?
5. How has the American family been changing in recent years?
6. What changes have taken place in women's roles over the past few decades?
7. Why is it correct to say that the U.S. population is "growing older"?

Thinking Critically

1. The founders of the American government made elected officials answerable to the people so that government would continue to serve the people. Do you think the people of the United States today are being adequately served by government? Explain your answer.
2. Why do you think current immigration law gives preference to immigrants who

are immediate relatives of U.S. citizens or who have certain employment skills?
3. Using photographs from magazines and newspapers, create a poster that illustrates the multicultural nature of life in the United States.
4. In what ways has the United States benefited from the diversity of its people?

Citizenship in Your Community

Individual Project

Investigate the beginnings of your community. Who first settled the community? From what countries or areas of the world did these immigrants come? What cultural influences brought by these immigrants are evident in your community? What are the ethnic and cultural backgrounds of the people who live in your community today? What languages do they speak? What foods do they enjoy? Create a poster showing how the ethnic and cultural mix of your community has changed over time.

Building Your Portfolio

The first step of your unit portfolio project (see page 67) is to conduct research to learn about the history of your school. Use this information to draw an illustrated time line showing how your school has changed over time, including changes in the number of students and teachers, changes in the ethnic makeup of the school population, curriculum changes, and how students have shown their school spirit. Title your time line "Our School: Then and Now." Place your time line in your individual portfolio for later use.

Citizenship in Your Community

Posters should show how the cultural and ethnic mix of the community has changed over time.

Building Your Portfolio

Assign Portfolio Assessment Worksheet 1 in the *Portfolio Assessment Worksheets* booklet.

Assessment

- **Chapter 1 Tests**, *Chapter Tests* booklet
- **Test Generator**, Chapter 1
- **Portfolio**, Portfolio Assessment Worksheet 1, *Portfolio Assessment Worksheets* booklet

CHAPTER 2

Foundations of Government

TEXTBOOK	TEACHING RESOURCES	OTHER AVAILABLE RESOURCES
Chapter	• Skills Worksheet 2 • Challenge/Enrichment Worksheet 2	• Simulations and Case Studies Lesson 1
Section **1** Why Americans Have Governments Page 21	• Reteaching Worksheet 2.1	
2 The First American Government Page 24	• Reteaching Worksheet 2.2	
3 A New Constitution Page 28	• Reteaching Worksheet 2.3	
Review and Assessment Chapter 2 Review, Page 35	• Test, Form A • Test, Form B • Portfolio Assessment Worksheet 2	• *Test Generator,* *Chapter 2*

Block Scheduling Option

ADDITIONAL RESOURCES

BOOKS FOR TEACHERS

Beer, Samuel H., *To Make a Nation: The Rediscovery of American Federalism*, Belknap.

Boorstin, Daniel J., *The Americans: The Democratic Experience*, Random House.

Bowen, Catherine D., *Miracle at Philadelphia: The Story of the Constitutional Convention, May to September 1787*, Little, Brown.

Gabriel, Ralph, and Robert Walker, *The Course of American Democratic Thought*, Greenwood.

Tuchman, Barbara, *The First Salute: A View of the American Revolution*, Knopf.

BOOKS FOR STUDENTS

Commager, Henry Steele, *The Great Constitution: A Book for Young Americans*, Bobbs. Describes the work of those who created the Constitution and discusses the states' reactions to this new plan of government.

McPhillips, Martin, *The Constitutional Convention*, Silver Burdett. Describes the events surrounding this historic meeting in Philadelphia.

Morris, Richard B., *The Forging of the Union: 1781–1789*, HarperCollins. Examines the founding of our government and the writing of the Constitution.

Vaughan, Harold C., *The Constitutional Convention*, Franklin Watts. Explains the challenges faced in ratifying the Constitution.

MULTIMEDIA RESOURCES

The Constitution of the United States (VHS, c, 19 min.), EBEC. Studies events leading up to the framing of the Constitution, the Constitutional Convention, ratification difficulties, and the basic principles of the document itself.

Declaration of Independence (VHS, c, 9 min.), BFA. A reenactment of the delegates' debate over independence.

A Design for Liberty: The American Constitution (VHS, c, 30 min.), MOD. Discusses the idea of liberty as it was understood by the revolutionary generation and how concern for its preservation led to the writing of the Constitution.

THE INTERNET

Have students use these search words to locate more information about chapter topics on the Internet: *federal government, Constitution, civics, Articles of Confederation.*

 GLOBAL SKILL BUILDER

You might wish to use **Navigating the Internet** from the interactive *Global Skill Builder* CD-ROM to further students' understanding of the Internet as a resource.

Abbreviations: b&w=black and white; c=color; f=film; fs=filmstrip; sd=sound; tr=transparency; VHS=videotape

PRINCIPLES OF DEMOCRACY

✶ **Resolving Differences** Students will learn about the ideals expressed in the Declaration of Independence, how compromise made it possible to ratify the Constitution, and how and why the new Constitution was ratified by the states.

CIVICS SKILLS

Students will learn how to interpret paintings and photographs. They also will learn terms important to understanding government and the foundations of American government.

CITIZENSHIP VALUES

✶ **Resolving Differences** Students will be encouraged to appreciate the need to cooperate, to value important ideals underlying the Declaration of Independence, and to recognize the skill and foresight of the people who planned and wrote the Constitution.

MEETING INDIVIDUAL NEEDS

LIMITED ENGLISH PROFICIENCY (LEP)

Have students work in pairs to illustrate the following terms: *democracy, direct democracy, representative democracy, constitution, federalism, legislature.* Have them sketch drawings or create graphic organizers that show each term's meaning. For example, for *federalism* students might draw a large circle for the national government; smaller circles for the states; and lines connecting them to suggest the sharing of power and resources.

LEARNERS HAVING DIFFICULTY

Encourage students to summarize Sections 2 and 3 of the chapter by presenting mock radio news reports. For each section, students might begin by announcing the main result. Then they could review the events leading up to that result.

AUDITORY LEARNERS

Invite students to read aloud Thomas Paine's *Common Sense* (Penguin Classic series), Patrick Henry's speech to the Virginia Convention (textbook page 524), or Nathan Hale's brief speech before his execution (textbook page 528). Discuss how the ideals expressed in these passages have influenced American government and society.

VISUAL LEARNERS

Compare government under the Articles of Confederation with that under the Constitution by drawing two "ships of state" on the board. Start with the Articles of Confederation. Ask: Did the government have the power to (1) make laws? (2) control trade? (3) collect taxes? (4) raise an army? (5) Did the government have a president to lead it? Then ask the same questions about the Constitution. For each yes answer, draw (1) a hull, (2) masts, (3) sails, (4) cannons, and (5) the captain at the helm. (Articles of Confederation has only a hull; Constitution is complete.)

TACTILE/KINESTHETIC LEARNERS

Have students examine the Great Compromise by cutting out two sets of 13 squares. Squares in the first set (representing the Senate) should all be the same size. The second set (House) should be of different-sized squares, with squares sized in proportion to the populations of each of the 13 states in 1790. (Refer to *Historical Statistics of the United States* for state populations in 1790.) Elicit how the first set shows each state with equal representation (all squares are the same size) and how the second set shows states represented according to population.

GIFTED LEARNERS

Have students research and report on similarities between the U.S. government under the Constitution and other governments in the world's history, such as those of the Iroquois League, England, the Roman Empire and Republic, and ancient Greece.

Chapter 2 begins by defining the term *government* and presenting various historical forms that government has taken. Then it describes the development of the government of the United States, including discussions of the Articles of Confederation and the Constitution. The underlying theme of the chapter is that a sound government rests on cooperation and concern for the needs and ideals of the people.

Motivator

Tell students that you are going to say a word and that you want to know what images the word brings to mind. Then say the word *government.* Ask volunteers to describe their mental images and explain them. Or, instead, you might wish to have students quickly sketch a picture that, for them, represents "government." (*Students might visualize, among other things, concrete manifestations of government, such as the White House, the president, the Capitol, schools, or prisons.*)

CHAPTER OBJECTIVES

After studying Chapter 2, students should be able to do the following.

1. Explain why government is necessary.
2. List the types of government that exist around the world.
3. Identify the weaknesses of the nation's first government.
4. Explain how the Constitution created a strong nation.

SIMULATIONS AND CASE STUDIES

Lesson 1: Founding Documents Treasure Hunt

Block Scheduling Option

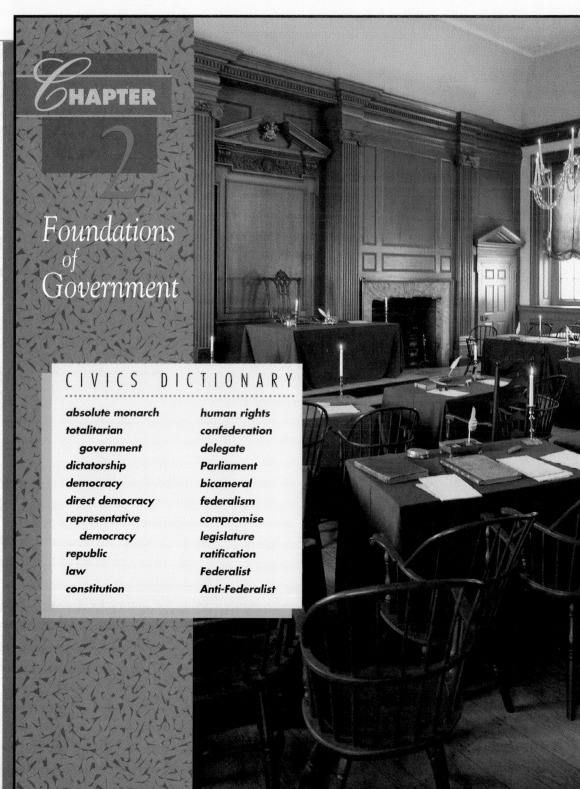

CHAPTER 2

Foundations
of
Government

CIVICS DICTIONARY

absolute monarch	human rights
totalitarian	confederation
government	delegate
dictatorship	Parliament
democracy	bicameral
direct democracy	federalism
representative	compromise
democracy	legislature
republic	ratification
law	Federalist
constitution	Anti-Federalist

After studying Section 1, students should be able to do the following.

1. Identify the factors that shape a nation's government.
2. Describe the basic forms of government and who holds power in each.
3. Compare and contrast direct democracy and representative democracy.
4. List the basic purposes of government.

Teaching Section 1
Building a Vocabulary

Ask students what system of government we have in the United States. Is it a **representative democracy** or a **republic**? Tell them that both answers are correct—they mean the same thing. Then ask students how they think representative democracy differs from **direct democracy**. *(In a direct democracy, the people rule directly, not through representatives.)*

CHAPTER FOCUS

What do you think of when you hear the term *government*? Perhaps you think of the Capitol in Washington, D.C., or your state capital, or your city hall. Perhaps you think of the president, your state governor, or your town mayor. Or maybe you think of laws you must obey or the rules of your school's student council. If any of these things come to mind, you are on the right track.

Government, though, is not only buildings, leaders, and laws. Government is the entire system of authority, or power, that acts on behalf of a group of people.

The American government is a government "of the people, by the people, and for the people." It has been established to serve the people. It protects our rights and safeguards our freedom. The American government is you—it is all of us.

STUDY GUIDE

● What types of government exist around the world, and why is government necessary?

● What was the nation's first plan of government, and why was it a weak plan?

● How did the Constitutional Convention create a strong new nation?

1 Why Americans Have Governments

To govern means to rule. A government is any organization set up to make and enforce rules. You actually live under three different levels of governments.

The city or town in which you live has a government. It makes and enforces rules for the people in your community. At the next level, your state government makes and enforces rules for you and the other people in your state. At the national level, the U.S. government makes and enforces rules for all the people in the United States.

Types of Governments

Every nation in the world has a government. These governments, however, are not all alike. There are many important differences in the way they govern. They differ in the way their leaders are chosen and in the amount of power held by their people. Each nation's government has been shaped by the beliefs of the people and by their history.

In times past, the governments of many nations were controlled by kings or queens. They often held all the power in their nation's governments, and they were able to rule by force. Because they held absolute, or total, power, they were called **absolute monarchs**. Today there are few absolute monarchs left. Most nations that have monarchs greatly limit the monarchs' power.

In some nations one person or a small group of people holds all the power. The government has total control over the lives of the people. It rules the nation by force. This type of government is a **totalitarian government** or a **dictatorship**.

Other nations have a democratic form of government. In a **democracy** the people of a nation either rule directly or they elect officials who act on their behalf. The word *democracy* comes from an ancient Greek term meaning "rule of the people."

There are two forms of democracy. In a **direct democracy** all voters in a community

CIVICS SIDELIGHT

You might point out that leaders in all governments seek to justify their power. In democracies elections are the main justification. Governments not chosen by popular vote, however, must find other justifications. Communist dictatorships, for example, have often tried to justify their power by claiming to represent the working classes against what they believed was a tyrannous wealthy class. Louis XIV of France, who ruled from 1643 to 1715, is a prime example of an absolute monarch. Like other European rulers of the time, Louis XIV believed his power came directly from God—that he ruled his country by divine right.

Reasoning from Personal Experience

Have students write down all the rules they follow, from the time they leave school to the time they go to bed. These could include rules about riding a bus, crossing a street, playing a game, or doing homework. They might make a chart showing the time, activity, and rule. For each rule they list, have them answer the question "Who made that rule?" Ask what they believe are the purposes of these rules.

COOPERATIVE LEARNING

Organize the class into small groups. Have each group member locate a newspaper or magazine article about a foreign country and then find as much information as he or she can about that nation's system of government. Have group members discuss among themselves similarities and differences between each government and our representative democracy. Each group should develop a list that provides at least one country as an example for each kind of government the group has studied.

meet in one place to make laws and decide what actions to take. This form works only in small communities.

In a **representative democracy** the people elect representatives to carry on the work of government for them. This system of government is also called a **republic**. It is the form of government found in the United States.

Americans are fortunate to live in a republic. We believe that the people should rule themselves. We have a form of government in which leaders are responsible to the people.

Do We Need Government?

Would it be possible for all of us to live as we choose? Could we manage our own affairs without a government? Do we need rules for getting along with one another? To answer these questions, it is important to understand the basic purposes of government.

Helping People Cooperate

One of the earliest lessons people learned was that cooperation was useful. It was easier to hunt and kill a large animal for food if the members of the group worked together. The people could also better protect themselves against enemies when they were united. Thus whenever large groups of people have lived together, they have found it necessary and useful to have a government.

Under early forms of government, the strongest person was often made the leader of the people. This person could best help the people defend themselves against their enemies. When food was scarce, the best hunter might be the leader. In other matters, such as whether the people should move to better land, a group of the oldest and wisest leaders might decide. Even the simplest form of government helped to make life safer and easier.

Providing Services

Over the years government has grown more and more complex. Yet its basic purposes have

remained the same. It not only provides ways for people to live and work together, it also enables a large group of people to get things done. It might be possible for each person in the group to do some of these things alone. It usually would be more difficult and expensive, however, for each person to do so.

For example, what would happen if each family in your community had to educate its own children? Even if parents had time to teach, would they be able to teach all subjects well? By establishing schools, the government makes it possible for all children to receive a good education.

Government also performs other services that would be difficult or impossible for individual citizens to provide for themselves. Government protects the people from enemy nations. It provides police to protect lives and property. Fire departments protect our homes.

Because of government, you can travel over highways that stretch from border to border. A system of money makes it easy for you to buy and sell things and to know the value of these things. Your trash is collected, and health laws are enforced to protect you. You can go to public libraries. The government provides these and many more services.

Providing Rules

Large groups of people need rules to help them live together in peace. When there are rules, all people know what they may and may not do. Without rules, any disagreement would probably end with the strongest members of the group settling things their way.

Providing rules of conduct for a group is therefore one of the most important reasons for establishing governments. These rules are known as **laws**. They are written down so that people can know them and obey them. Laws are written by the government to guide, as well as to protect, all of us.

For example, if you own a house on a city or village street, a law may require you to keep your sidewalk in good repair. If you fail to repair cracks, someone may fall and be injured.

Closure

Have a volunteer look up the meaning of the word *anarchy*. *(comes from a Greek word meaning "having no ruler;" a condition or situation characterized by disorder, an absence of authority)* Then ask the class what life might be like if there were no laws governing society. Have students identify specific rules in your school or laws in your community that help keep order. Conclude by discussing the advantages of living in a democracy.

Reviewing

Have students complete the Section 1 Review.

Reteaching

Assign Section 1 of the Chapter 2 Reteaching Worksheet.

Government provides its citizens with hundreds of services, such as free public libraries and the maintenance of community-owned trees.

This law also protects you and your family, because you depend on your neighbors to keep their sidewalks in good condition.

Many of the laws under which we live are contained in **constitutions**, or written plans of government. Americans have used constitutions to establish national and state governments. A constitution states the purposes of the government. It describes how the government is to be organized. It also contains important laws the government is to uphold.

Putting Ideals into Practice

A nation's government helps put into practice the ideals of the people, the things in which they believe. Americans believe that the people should rule themselves. We also believe that each person is important and that no one should be denied his or her rights.

What are these rights? In the Declaration of Independence (discussed later in this chapter), they are described as "life, liberty, and the pursuit of happiness." This means that all Americans have the right to live their lives in liberty, or freedom, and to seek happiness.

To safeguard each citizen's liberty, the government guarantees certain freedoms, such as freedom of speech, freedom of the press, and freedom of religion. These freedoms can never be taken away from any U.S. citizen by the government. Nor can they ever be restricted,

except to keep people from using these freedoms to violate the rights of others.

For example, free speech and a free press do not mean freedom to tell lies or write false statements about another person. Each citizen has the right to have his or her reputation protected from efforts to hurt it with untruths.

Americans believe that if any citizen is denied his or her rights, the liberty of all is endangered. The U.S. government has helped its people put these ideals into practice by passing and enforcing laws that guarantee equal rights for all citizens. For example, there are laws requiring that all Americans be given equal opportunities to receive an education, to vote, and to seek jobs.

SECTION 1 REVIEW

1. Define or identify the following terms: absolute monarch, totalitarian government, dictatorship, democracy, direct democracy, representative democracy, republic, law, constitution.

2. What factors shape a nation's form of government?

3. What are the basic forms of government found around the world? Who holds the power in these forms of government?

SECTION 1 REVIEW
A N S W E R S

1. See the following pages: absolute monarch, totalitarian government, dictatorship, democracy, direct democracy (p. 21); representative democracy, republic, law (p. 22); constitution (p. 23).

2. beliefs of the people and their history

3. absolute monarchy (king or queen), totalitarian government (one person or small group of people), democracy (the people)

4. direct democracy—all voters meet together to make laws and take actions; representative democracy—the people elect representatives to do the work of government

5. enable people to live together in cooperation, perform services that are difficult for people to perform themselves, provide rules for living, put ideals into practice

6. Speeches will vary but should address the purposes of government (pages 22–23).

After studying Section 2, students should be able to do the following.

1. Assess the importance of the outcome of the Second Continental Congress.
2. Identify the weaknesses of the Articles of Confederation.
3. Relate how a lack of strong national government created problems for the United States.

Ask students whether they think all people, as human beings, have rights. Have volunteers name a few of those rights. Tell students that those rights are **human rights**. Americans broke away from Great Britain partly because it violated their human rights. Americans made sure that their first government, a **confederation**, would not have the power to deny people's rights.

GLOBAL PERSPECTIVES

Ironically, Jefferson and others were strongly influenced by the writings of a renowned British thinker, John Locke. After Britain's own Glorious Revolution in 1688 (in which Parliament won new authority over the monarchy), Locke had published his *Two Treatises on Government* (1690). In this work he declared that people have an absolute right to overthrow any government that denies or interferes with their natural, or human, rights.

4. How does a direct democracy differ from a representative democracy?

5. What are the basic purposes of government?

6. **THINKING CRITICALLY** You are the new leader of the nation Civicus. Write a speech to the people of Civicus in which you explain how the new government will serve the people. Include examples of how you will work to fulfill the four basic purposes of government.

2 The First American Government

As you know from your study of U.S. history, America was once ruled by Great Britain. Great Britain, however, was far away on the other side of the Atlantic Ocean. This great distance allowed American colonists to make many of their own rules and regulations without interference from British leaders.

When the British government under King George III began to enforce its rules and regulations in the colonies, the Americans were angry. They had become used to doing things their own way, and they resented being forced to obey laws they considered unjust. Americans wanted to be free to govern themselves. They fought the Revolutionary War to gain their independence as a nation and to be free.

The Declaration of Independence

When fighting broke out between the American colonies and Great Britain in 1775, the Americans were not yet officially seeking independence. The next year, however, leaders from the 13 colonies met in Philadelphia. At this meeting, called the Second Continental Congress, they named a committee to draw up a Declaration of Independence. Most of the

The artist John Trumbull painted this version of the signing of the Declaration of Independence. The tallest figure in the center is the Declaration's author, Thomas Jefferson.

Have students read the Declaration of Independence (pages 525–527), paying special attention to mentions of human rights. Have students list the king's human rights abuses alleged by the Second Continental Congress in the Declaration of Independence. Then have students take the role of colonists and write journal entries explaining why declaring independence was justified by these abuses.

COOPERATIVE LEARNING

Divide the class into small groups, and explain that each is a committee of citizens appointed to critique the Articles of Confederation. Assign each group member an identity, such as farmer, merchant, banker, ex-Revolutionary War soldier, or member of Congress. Each member should argue for or against the Articles. Caution students to stay within the assigned identity. The group should draft a consensus report for or against the Articles to present to the class.

Declaration was written by Thomas Jefferson. It was approved by members of the Continental Congress on July 4, 1776.

The Declaration explains the reasons the 13 colonies decided to separate from Great Britain and form a free nation. By doing so it upholds the philosophy that the power of government comes from the consent of the governed—the people. If a government ignores the will of the people, the people have a legitimate right to change the government.

Yet the Declaration of Independence is much more than a document to justify independence. It also is a statement of American ideals. It explains to the world, in clear and inspiring language, that the purpose of government is to protect **human rights**—the basic rights to which all people are entitled as human beings.

Ideals of American Government

These basic human rights are clearly stated in the Declaration of Independence:

> We hold these truths to be self-evident: That all men are created equal; that they are endowed by their Creator with certain unalienable rights; that among these are life, liberty, and the pursuit of happiness.

This passage is one of the most famous in American writing. Over the years it has come to mean that all Americans—members of all groups and including both men and women—are equal under the law.

For example, the right of each individual to life, liberty, and happiness must be equal to that of every other individual. No person has the right to consider his or her own life and liberties more important than those of others.

The leaders who signed the Declaration of Independence realized that these ideals would be difficult to achieve. Yet they believed these ideals were worth "our lives, our fortunes, and our sacred honor."

The Declaration of Independence is one of the greatest documents in the history of the

DID YOU KNOW THAT...

There was no official ceremony for the signing of the Declaration of Independence. Although paintings show delegates to the Second Continental Congress signing the document as a group, such a ceremony did not actually take place.

The Congress did adopt the Declaration on July 4, 1776—the occasion we celebrate as Independence Day. But only John Hancock, president of the Congress, signed the Declaration on that day. Other signers added their names between then and November 4. The last signature on the Declaration was not added until 1781.

Maybe you have seen a copy of Hancock's signature on the Declaration. He wrote it with such a flourish that we still use the expression "John Hancock" to mean a person's signature.

nation. Although it was written more than 200 years ago, it remains a lasting symbol of American freedom. (See pages 525–527.)

The Articles of Confederation

The Declaration of Independence did not provide a government for the new nation. Therefore in 1777, while the Revolutionary War was still being fought, the Continental Congress drew up a plan of government—the Articles of Confederation. It was approved by the 13 states and began to operate in 1781.

A **confederation** is a loose association, rather than a firm union, of states. The Articles of Confederation set up a "firm league of

CIVICS SIDELIGHT

The "pursuit of happiness" may seem a trivial concept alongside "life" and "liberty." But in the 1700s happiness was at the center of philosophical debate about good government. Enlightenment thinkers, such as Thomas Jefferson, were not so concerned with private happiness—the amusements of daily life. They were interested in public happiness. Public happiness had to do with such things as having enough to eat, a roof over one's head, and clothes on one's back. And good government, they believed, exists to help its people pursue such "happiness."

Guided Practice

Draw a chart with two columns on the chalkboard. Ask students to fill in the first column with the basic ideals and structures of the Articles of Confederation. *(loose association of states, limited central government powers, one vote per state in Congress, no taxation powers for Congress, no national executive or judicial branches)* For the second column, students should suggest how each of the items in the first column weakened the new government.

Independent Practice

Ask students to imagine the United States today under the Articles of Confederation. Have each student write a paragraph explaining how one aspect of the Articles of Confederation might affect government and life in the country today. (For example, one student might choose to write how having no executive branch would affect U.S. foreign policy.) Ask volunteers to share their opinions with the class.

CIVICS SIDELIGHT

Shays's Rebellion, in 1786, began because farmers could not pay their debts and were losing their farms. This uprising of Massachusetts farmers, many armed with pitchforks and posts, alarmed Americans and made clear the weakness of the Articles. Massachusetts called on the national government for help, but Congress had no power to act. (After the uprising, Thomas Jefferson remarked, "A little rebellion now and then is a good thing. . . . The tree of liberty must be refreshed from time to time with the blood of patriots and tyrants.")

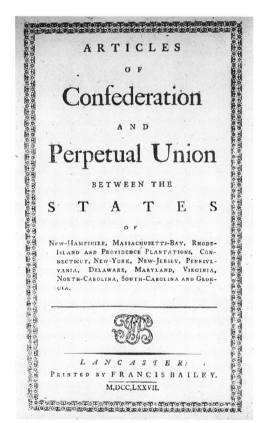

ARTICLES
OF
Confederation
AND
Perpetual Union
BETWEEN THE
STATES
OF
NEW-HAMPSHIRE, MASSACHUSETTS-BAY, RHODE-ISLAND AND PROVIDENCE PLANTATIONS, CONNECTICUT, NEW-YORK, NEW-JERSEY, PENNSYLVANIA, DELAWARE, MARYLAND, VIRGINIA, NORTH-CAROLINA, SOUTH-CAROLINA AND GEORGIA.

LANCASTER:
PRINTED BY FRANCIS BAILEY.
M,DCC,LXXVII.

The Articles of Confederation created a new plan of government for the young nation.

friendship" among the 13 states. Each state in the nation was to have equal powers and in most ways was independent of the other states. The central, or national, government had very limited powers. The people of the 13 states did not want a strong central government. They feared that such a government might use its power to limit the freedom of the separate states.

Under the Articles of Confederation, the national government consisted of a lawmaking body of one house, called Congress. The states sent representatives to Congress. Each state had one vote in Congress, regardless of the number of people living in the state.

There was no provision in the Articles for a president or an executive branch to carry out the nation's laws. Instead, the Articles gave the states the power to enforce the laws passed by Congress. In part, this arrangement stemmed from the people's suspicion of strong leaders after their experience with King George III of Great Britain. The Articles also did not establish a national court system to interpret the laws and punish lawbreakers.

During the Revolutionary War, the 13 states were willing to work together and make sacrifices to achieve victory. Things were different in the years following the Revolution, however. Many Americans suffered difficult times after the war. Property had been destroyed. Trade with other nations had slowed. American businesses had suffered. Moreover, the war left the nation deeply in debt. The new government tried to handle these problems, but it was too weak to solve them.

Weaknesses of the Confederation

There were many reasons for the weakness of the nation's government under the Articles of Confederation. Congress had trouble passing laws because a vote of 9 of the 13 states was needed to pass important measures. Without a president or an executive branch, there were no officials to ensure that the laws passed by Congress were carried out. Nor were there national courts to interpret the laws or to judge those who broke them.

In addition, changing the Articles of Confederation to make the national government stronger was difficult. Changes in the Articles required the unanimous vote of all 13 states.

Another weakness of the new government was that Congress lacked the power to collect taxes. Congress could ask the states to contribute money to pay the national government's expenses, but Congress had no power to force states to make these contributions.

Without money, Congress could not pay the nation's debts or carry on any government programs that might be needed. Congress also

Closure

Return to the list of weaknesses on the chalkboard (from the Guided Practice activity on page 26). Have students suggest how the problems related to government under the Articles of Confederation might be solved. Write their responses on the chalkboard. Review the results, focusing on the lack of a strong central authority. Point out that the next section discusses how the young nation tried to solve these problems.

Reviewing

Have students complete the Section 2 Review.

Reteaching

Assign Section 2 of the Chapter 2 Reteaching Worksheet.

could not pay the soldiers who had fought in the Revolutionary War.

Under the Articles of Confederation, the national government also lacked other important powers. It could not regulate, or control, trade between the states or with foreign nations. Each state regulated its own trade, causing many disputes among the states and with other nations. In addition, most of the states issued their own money.

The states acted more like small, separate nations than states that were members of a confederation. The states often refused to obey the laws of Congress. As a result, relations between the states and Congress worsened.

The Confederation Fails

The Articles of Confederation succeeded in establishing a new nation—a major achievement. Yet the national government set up by the Articles failed in a number of important ways.

The main trouble with the government set up by the Articles was that the states refused to give the national government enough power to operate effectively. The states feared a strong central government and thus kept most of the real power in their own hands.

The people of each state continued to think of themselves as belonging to their particular state rather than to the nation as a whole. This was natural because the states were separated by great distances and transportation was poor. Also, there was little contact between many of the states. It took years before the states began to think of themselves as parts of a single nation.

The weaknesses of the national government became clear as the young nation began to face new problems. The states quarreled over the location of boundary lines. They became involved in disputes over trade. The national government was powerless to end these disagreements. It seemed to many that the new nation was about to break up into several small nations.

Many leaders began to favor strengthening the national government. As a result, in 1787

Under the Articles of Confederation each state issued its own money. The currency shown here is a Massachusetts-Bay dollar.

Congress asked the states to send representatives to a meeting to consider what could be done to improve the national government.

SECTION 2 REVIEW

1. Define or identify the following terms: human rights, confederation.

2. What was the outcome of the Second Continental Congress?

3. What were the weaknesses of the Articles of Confederation?

4. How did the lack of a strong national government create problems?

5. **THINKING CRITICALLY** You are a farmer living in Virginia in the 1780s. Write a letter to the editor of your local newspaper describing the problems you have encountered as a result of government under the Articles of Confederation. Suggest what needs to be done to improve your situation.

SECTION 2 REVIEW
A N S W E R S

1. See the following page: human rights, confederation (p. 25).

2. The Declaration of Independence was signed.

3. no national executive to enforce laws; no national courts to interpret laws or to judge those who broke them; change required unanimous vote of states; Congress could not collect taxes to pay the nation's debts or for necessary programs, could not regulate trade, and could not issue an official currency.

4. The national government did not have the power to operate effectively or to help engender a feeling that all citizens were part of one nation. States quarreled over such things as boundary lines and trade. The government had no power to end these disputes.

5. Letters will vary but might mention difficulties obtaining government services, regarding trade, and exchanging money across state lines.

After studying Section 3, students should be able to do the following.

1. Identify the ideas about government that delegates to the Constitutional Convention borrowed from Great Britain.

2. Explain how the Constitution strengthened the American government.

3. Describe how Federalists and Anti-Federalists resolved their differences.

Ask students what it means to delegate. *(to assign responsibility or authority)* A **delegate** is someone who is assigned authority. Tell students that the delegates to the Constitutional Convention created a government based on the concept of **federalism**. In a federal system (from the Latin word *foedus*, meaning "compact" or "league"), the states share power with the national government. A **con*fed*eration** is a loose association or league of people or governments (such as states).

MULTICULTURAL PERSPECTIVES

You might point out that custom and law limited political authority almost exclusively to white, male, property owners for many years of the young American republic. Also, many early Americans were Protestants. Not surprisingly, then, the delegates to the Constitutional Convention in 1787 were all males, all white Anglo–Saxon Protestants, and all fairly well-off financially. While drafting a Constitution that reflected their particular interests, however, they also succeeded in creating a flexible system that has served (over time) to guarantee the rights of women and members of other races, religions, ethnic groups, and economic classes.

3 A New Constitution

In May 1787 a group of the nation's most respected leaders met in Independence Hall in Philadelphia. They had been sent as **delegates**, or representatives, of their states to find ways to improve the national government. The delegates soon became convinced that changing the Articles of Confederation was not enough. They decided instead to create a completely new plan of government—a new constitution.

The meeting became known as the Constitutional Convention. The leaders who attended the Convention wrote a constitution that established a government for the United States that has endured for more than 200 years. The new plan of government drafted by the delegates is the Constitution of the United States. It is the world's oldest written constitution still in effect.

The Delegates

The 55 delegates who attended the Constitutional Convention included many of those who had been involved in the nation's struggle for independence. George Washington had led the American army to victory over the British in the Revolutionary War. Respected by all, he was chosen to preside over the Convention. He called on speakers and kept the meetings running smoothly.

At 81 years of age, Benjamin Franklin—diplomat, inventor, writer—was the oldest delegate to the Constitutional Convention. Among the other delegates were James Madison, Alexander Hamilton, James Wilson, Roger Sherman, William Paterson, and Edmund Randolph.

An English Heritage

These leaders knew history well, and they had learned many important lessons from the past.

The Constitutional Convention owed much of its success to the wisdom and work of these two delegates—Benjamin Franklin (left) and George Washington (right).

Dramatizing Government

Assign students roles as delegates to a Constitutional Convention. Each "delegate" should be given a profile, such as home state and profession. You might have some students portray important figures, such as Madison, Randolph, Franklin, and Washington. Arrange the classroom into a meeting hall, and ask each "delegate" to sit with others from his or her "home state."

Among the issues to be decided are the structure of the central government, the extent of power granted to the government, and how the states should be represented in the government. Have the "delegates" prepare speeches and position papers to defend their ideas. Speeches and papers might include references to aspects of English political ideas that might be important to the new U.S. government.

The delegates wanted the American people to enjoy the rights the English had fought for and won during past centuries.

This heritage from England included the rights mentioned in the Magna Carta (the "Great Charter"), which the English people had won from King John in 1215. This important document guaranteed that free people could not be arrested, put in prison, or forced to leave their nation unless they were given a trial by other free people who were their equals. It also guaranteed that the citizens of England were to be judged only according to English law.

The members of the Constitutional Convention also wished the new American nation to have the rights contained in the English Bill of Rights of 1689. One of these rights was the right to petition, or request, the government to improve or to change laws. Another was the right to a fair punishment if a citizen were found guilty of a crime.

The Convention delegates in Philadelphia also studied carefully the example of parliamentary government in England. **Parliament** is the lawmaking body of the British government. It is **bicameral**. That is, it consists of two parts, or houses. It is made up of the House of Lords, appointed by the monarch, and the House of Commons, elected by the people. This system enables each house to check and improve the work of the other house.

Secret Meetings

The delegates to the Constitutional Convention held their meetings in secret. They were forbidden to discuss any of the business of the Convention with outsiders. This rule was put into effect so that the delegates could speak freely at the Convention.

The Convention had drawn a great deal of public attention. Many delegates feared that if they spoke publicly on a particular issue, they might be subjected to pressure from outsiders. Taking a public stand would also make it more difficult for delegates to change their minds after debate and discussion.

AMERICAN BIOGRAPHY

James Madison

James Madison was born in 1751 to a prosperous Virginia family. Frail and ill throughout his childhood, Madison relied on private tutors for his early education. He did not let poor health, however, keep him from developing his mind. At the age of 20, Madison graduated from the College of New Jersey (now Princeton University) and began what would prove to be a distinguished political career.

In 1776 Madison helped draft Virginia's state constitution. He also served in the Continental Congress from 1780 to 1783. As a delegate to the Constitutional Convention, Madison helped the often-angry debaters to find common ground. Even though he disliked public speaking, his skillful conduct in the debates and his leadership qualities earned Madison the name "Father of the Constitution."

As a member of the first U.S. Congress, Madison was the primary author of the Bill of Rights. In 1809 he became the fourth president of the United States, after serving as secretary of state under Thomas Jefferson. Madison died in 1836, the last remaining framer of the U.S. Constitution.

GLOBAL PERSPECTIVES

Point out that today the House of Lords has little real power in Parliament. The House of Commons is, in practice, the only real lawmaking body in Britain. It has complete control of all money bills and most other public legislation. What power the House of Lords has is limited primarily to being able to delay the passage of legislation.

Some delegates favored open public debate and criticized the secrecy rule. Without it, however, agreement on difficult issues might not have been possible.

If the meetings were held in secret, how do we know today what took place during the

Divide the class into groups of five. Each group should create a constitution for the school's student government. The constitution should include at least three branches: executive, legislative, and judicial. A different group member should perform each of the following tasks: develop proposals for each branch, act as recording secretary, and preside over the "Constitutional Convention." The group should present its proposed constitution to the class for approval.

Guided Practice

On the chalkboard draw a triangle with the name of one of the three branches of government at each point. *(legislative, executive, judicial)* Ask students which governmental powers were created for each branch under the new Constitution. Facilitate a debate between students about which new powers were most important to creating a strong national government.

CIVICS SIDELIGHT

Amazingly, the delegates to the Constitutional Convention managed to create the foundation of the nation in just five months—May to September. More amazing still, they did it in spite of the heat, humidity, and bugs of a season some Philadelphians called the "worst summer since 1750." Commenting on the stifling heat, a French visitor wrote home, "At each inhaling of air, one worries about the next one. The slightest movement is painful."

Weaknesses of Government Established by the Articles of Confederation (1781)			Strengths of Government Established by the Constitution (1789)
States given most powers; few powers given to the national government.			States keep many powers; important powers given to the national government.
• Congress elected by the state legislatures			• Congress elected by the people (after the 17th Amendment)
• Laws difficult to pass (approval of 9 out of 13 states required)	One-House Congress	Two-House Congress	• Laws easier to pass (majority vote required)
• Congress given no power to collect taxes			• Congress given power to collect taxes
• Congress given no power to regulate trade			• Congress given power to regulate interstate and foreign trade
• Congress given no power to coin money	No President	A President	• Congress given power to coin money
• Congress given no power to establish armed forces—each state had its own troops			• Congress given power to establish an army and a navy to defend the nation
• No president or executive branch			• President given power to enforce the laws
• No system of national courts	No Court System	A Court System	• National court system, including a Supreme Court, given power to interpret the laws

Convention? We know because of James Madison of Virginia. Madison kept a journal, or record, of the proceedings of each meeting. His journal, which was kept secret until after his death, is the chief source of information about the Convention.

Writing the Constitution

The framers of the Constitution agreed that the national government had to be given greater power. At the same time, most of the framers agreed that the states should keep the powers needed to govern their own affairs. To achieve this balance, the framers established a system of government known as **federalism**, or a federal system. In a federal system the many powers of government are divided between the national government, which governs the whole nation, and state governments, which govern the people of each state.

The framers worked out the new plan of a federal system at their meetings during the hot summer months of 1787. They discussed many ideas and proposals and settled many differences of opinion by a series of compromises. A **compromise** is an agreement in which each side gives up part of its demands.

The most serious disagreement arose over the question of representation in the new national **legislature**, or lawmaking body. The larger states favored a legislature in which representation would be based on the size of a state's population. The smaller states wanted

Randomly assign students to be either Federalists or Anti-Federalists. Have each student create a pamphlet (using folded sheets of paper) in support of his or her side of the ratification issue. Using such things as slogans, headlines, articles, editorials, and political cartoons, the finished pamphlets should make an argument for or against the proposed strong national government. Have students vote on the most persuasive pamphlets.

Have students review the section by outlining the material. Suggest that students write each of the headings from the section on a sheet of paper, followed by one or two sentences summarizing the material under each heading. Students should save their outlines for use as study guides.

each state to have an equal number of representatives in the legislature.

For weeks the framers argued over this issue. Finally, both sides agreed to a compromise. Their agreement provided for a law-making body of two houses, called Congress. In one house, the Senate, the states were to have equal representation. In the other house, the House of Representatives, each state was to be represented according to the size of its population. This agreement is known as the Great Compromise.

A Strong New Nation

Many other compromises were reached as the Convention delegates worked on the Constitution. The framers agreed to take away some of the powers of the states and to increase the powers of the new national government. The national government was given the power to tax, to regulate trade among the states and with foreign nations, to raise armed forces, and to coin and print money.

Provision was made for a president to carry out the nation's laws. A Supreme Court and other national courts would interpret these laws. The charts on page 30 show the major differences between the Articles of Confederation and the Constitution.

By September 1787 the delegates had completed their work. Probably no delegate was satisfied with every part of the document. Benjamin Franklin, for example, did not approve of parts of the Constitution. Yet he believed that the framers had written the best Constitution possible. For this reason, he urged the delegates to sign the document.

Most of the delegates shared Franklin's belief. Of the 42 framers present that day, 39

CIVICS SIDELIGHT

James Madison echoed the thoughts of most delegates when he said he hoped the Constitution would "last for ages." Benjamin Franklin stated this idea in another way. "Our new Constitution is now established, and has an appearance that promises permanency," he declared, "but in this world nothing can be said to be certain, except death and taxes."

As this political cartoon shows, the states formed the base, or pillars, of a strong new nation under the Constitution. North Carolina and Rhode Island were the last two states to ratify the Constitution.

Reviewing

Have students complete the Section 3 Review.

Reteaching

Assign Section 3 of the Chapter 2 Reteaching Worksheet.

Extension

Ask students to list some ideas about government that the convention delegates borrowed from Great Britain. Then assign students to find and research countries that have modeled their constitutions on the U.S. Constitution. Have students present reports about the constitutions of specific countries to the class.

CIVICS SIDELIGHT

Three of the most influential Federalists were Alexander Hamilton, James Madison, and John Jay. They wrote the 85 essays known today as *The Federalist*. In the essays, two thirds of which Hamilton wrote, they defended the Constitution and republican government against attacks by opponents. The essays not only influenced states toward ratification but also served to explain and give form to the emerging institutions of U.S. government.

signed the Constitution. After a farewell dinner, the delegates left for home.

Approving the Constitution

The work of the members of the Constitutional Convention was not over after they left Philadelphia. The Constitution now had to be sent to the states for their **ratification**, or approval. Before the Constitution could go into effect, it had to be ratified by 9 of the 13 states. Each state set up a special convention of delegates to vote on the Constitution.

People quickly divided into two groups over the issue of adopting the Constitution. Some people strongly supported the new plan of government. Others were opposed to it. The public was swamped with pamphlets, letters to newspapers, and speeches representing both sides of the debate.

Federalists and Anti-Federalists

Supporters of the Constitution were called **Federalists**. They favored a strong national government. The Federalists argued that the government under the Articles of Confederation was too weak to keep the country united. They feared that unless the Constitution was adopted, the United States would break up into 13 separate nations.

George Washington was inaugurated as the first president of the United States in New York City on April 30, 1789.

Extension

Remind students how important compromise was to the success of the Constitutional Convention. Have students think of a factual or fictional issue in their own lives that has been (or might be) resolved through compromise. Have them write a detailed description of how that compromise was (or might be) carried out.

People who opposed the new Constitution were called **Anti-Federalists**. They feared that a constitution that established a strong national government defeated the purpose of the recent war against Great Britain. The Anti-Federalists did not believe that the proposed Constitution would protect the power of the states and the freedom of the people.

The Constitution Is Ratified

Gradually, those who favored the Constitution gained support. Many citizens, however, were upset that the Constitution did not contain a list of the rights of the people. Finally, it was agreed that such a list, or bill, of rights for the people would be added if the new Constitution were ratified.

Most of the states ratified the Constitution in 1787 and 1788. The new government of the United States began to operate in March 1789. Two states, North Carolina and Rhode Island, did not approve the Constitution until after it went into effect.

New York City was chosen as the nation's temporary capital. There, on April 30, 1789, George Washington was sworn in as the first president of the United States. Members of the new Senate and House of Representatives arrived to begin their work. The nation's new government was underway.

The U.S. Constitution is a remarkable and important document. Every American should read and study it carefully. (See pages 529–549.) You will learn more about the government established by the Constitution in Chapter 3.

SECTION 3 REVIEW

1. Define or identify the following terms: delegate, Parliament, bicameral, federalism, compromise, legislature, ratification, Federalist, Anti-Federalist.

2. What ideas of government did the Constitutional Convention delegates borrow from Great Britain?

3. How did the U.S. Constitution strengthen the American government?

4. What did the Federalists and the Anti-Federalists disagree about and how did they settle their differences?

5. **THINKING CRITICALLY** Draw a "family tree" chart of the United States Constitution that traces the origins its main ideas, institutions, organization, and compromises. Use lines and arrows to connect the sources (countries, people, events, experiences) to the Constitution's main ideas.

CHAPTER 2 SUMMARY

Government serves many important purposes. Above all, government makes it possible for people to live and work together. Government also provides many services that citizens acting alone could not perform.

Americans believe that the people should rule themselves. Americans also believe that no person should be denied his or her rights. These ideals of the American people are clearly set forth in the Declaration of Independence, one of the greatest documents in the history of the nation.

The Articles of Confederation established the first government of the 13 states. Under this plan, the weak national government could not operate effectively.

In 1787 delegates to the Constitutional Convention wrote a new plan of government for the nation. This plan, the Constitution of the United States, has lasted for more than 200 years. It created a stronger national government and established a lawmaking body of two houses, called Congress. It also provided for a president to carry out the laws and for national courts to interpret the laws. Government under the Constitution began operating in 1789.

Have students look at the painting on page 24 and apply the guidelines for effectively gathering information from pictures. Ask: What is the subject of the picture? How does the artist draw your eye to Thomas Jefferson? Remind students that photography did not exist at this time, but suggest that this artist was attempting to document an important event as a photographer might today. Ask: Do you think a photograph of the signing of the Declaration of Independence would have looked different from this painting? Why? Point out, first, that the artist was not actually in attendance at the signing of the Declaration of Independence. Then have students scan the faces of the signers. They should note that every face is clearly visible, something that would rarely happen in real life.

SOCIAL STUDIES SKILL
Learning from Pictures

According to an old saying, "One picture is worth a thousand words." A painting or a photograph, however, does not speak for itself. You have to know how to read and interpret a picture before you can fully grasp its meaning.

There are easy guidelines you can follow that will help you learn to get the most information from the paintings and photographs in your textbook.

How to Learn from Pictures

1. **Determine the subject.** Look at the people who are portrayed in the picture and take note of any objects around these people. Determine what the people portrayed in the picture are doing. Read the title and caption of the picture for clues to its subject matter.
2. **Examine the details.** Study the details of the picture, including the picture's background. All of the visual evidence in a picture is important to understanding a historical event or time period. The picture's details are clues to its content, importance, and relevance.
3. **Determine the artist's point of view.** Most people think that a picture presents only facts. Any photograph or painting, however, also expresses the artist's ideas and feelings about a subject. Certain details are emphasized over the rest. Other details are left out. Determine whether the artist is portraying the events in the picture favorably or unfavorably.
4. **Put the data to use.** Determine whether the information presented in the picture is an accurate description of the actual events. Remember that a picture is an artist's interpretation of an event. Therefore, consider what you already know about the event or time period. Knowing whether the picture is accurate will give you clues about how to interpret and use the information.

Applying the Skill

Examine the painting below, which shows George Washington addressing the delegates to the Constitutional Convention. Then answer the following questions.

1. Which details in the painting is the artist trying to emphasize?
2. How does the artist want you to feel about George Washington? Which details in the painting support your answer?
3. Using what you have learned about the Constitutional Convention, why do you think the artist made George Washington the center of attention?

ANSWERS TO
Applying
the Skill

1. Answers will vary. Students might mention the document held by Washington and the identities of the people.

2. respect and admiration; all attention focused on Washington; Washington standing on a platform above everyone else; Washington rather than another delegate is holding the Constitution.

3. Washington was seen as a central authority figure and a trusted hero of the Revolution.

Vocabulary Workshop

1. direct democracy—All voters meet together to make laws and take actions. representative democracy—Elected representatives govern.

2. constitution

3. federalism

4. confederation

5. Great Compromise; some power of states taken away, powers of national government increased

6. Federalists and Anti-Federalists

Reviewing Main Ideas

1. beliefs of the people and their history

2. foster cooperation, perform services, provide rules for living, put ideals into practice

3. to explain why colonists wanted to break from Great Britain, to put American ideals in writing

4. no president or national court system; could not collect taxes, regulate trade, or issue official currency; no strong central government to foster national unity

5. strong central government had power to tax, regulate trade, raise armed forces, coin money; provided for president and national courts

6. for free discussion

7. Federalists—Articles too weak to keep country united; Anti-Federalists—Constitution would not protect states or the people

Thinking Critically

1. Students should offer specific examples.

2. Students should make reasoned arguments.

3. A free press and the demands of citizens for information might make secrecy difficult.

4. Compromise permits people with opposing views to agree on a final product.

Vocabulary Workshop

1. Distinguish between a direct democracy and a representative democracy.

2. What is another term for a written plan of government?

3. In what kind of a system are powers divided between the national government and the state governments?

4. What is the term for a league of states loosely bound together?

5. What important compromises were made at the Constitutional Convention?

6. What two groups clashed over support for the new Constitution?

Reviewing Main Ideas

1. What two factors shape the government of a nation?

2. What are four reasons why people form governments?

3. What were the main purposes of the Declaration of Independence?

4. What were the weaknesses of government under the Articles of Confederation?

5. How did the U.S. Constitution correct the weaknesses of government under the Articles of Confederation?

6. Why did the Constitutional Convention delegates hold their meetings in secret?

7. What were the arguments of the supporters and opponents of the Constitution?

Thinking Critically

1. Describe what life might be like for U.S. citizens today if government did not provide services.

2. Do you think that the United States would have grown from its original 13 colonies if the nation were still governed by the Articles of Confederation? Explain your answer.

3. If the Constitutional Convention were held today, how difficult would it be for the delegates to conduct their meetings in secret? Explain your answer.

4. Explain the role of compromise in the Constitutional Convention. How have you used compromise to settle a disagreement about an issue?

Citizenship in Your Community

Cooperative Project

With your group, ask several members of your community to define the term *human rights*. Use this information to create a visual display entitled "How the United States Protects Human Rights." Your display may include pictures from magazines, photographs you take in your community, newspaper articles, and poems.

Building Your Portfolio

The second step of your unit portfolio project (see page 67) is to write a "Declaration of Education" statement. In your Declaration express what you believe are the ideals of American education. Begin your Declaration of Education with the following phrase: "We, the American students, hold these truths to be self-evident. . . ." Your Declaration should then explain how your school upholds each of the educational ideals listed. Place your statement in your individual portfolio for later use.

Citizenship in Your Community

Make sure visual materials are based on survey results.

BUILDING YOUR PORTFOLIO

Assign Portfolio Assessment Worksheet 2 in the *Portfolio Assessment Worksheets* booklet.

Assessment

- **Chapter 2 Tests**, *Chapter Tests* booklet
- **Test Generator**, Chapter 2
- **Portfolio**, Portfolio Assessment Worksheet 2, *Portfolio Assessment Worksheets* booklet

PLANNING GUIDE

TEXTBOOK	TEACHING RESOURCES	OTHER AVAILABLE RESOURCES
Chapter	• Skills Worksheet 3 • Challenge/Enrichment Worksheet 3	• Simulations and Case Studies Lesson 2
Section **1** Ideals of the Constitution Page 37	• Reteaching Worksheet 3.1	• Transparency 1: How Representative Democracy Works
2 The Three Branches of Government Page 41	• Reteaching Worksheet 3.2	
3 A Flexible Document Page 43	• Reteaching Worksheet 3.3	
Review and Assessment Chapter 3 Review, Page 49	• Test, Form A • Test, Form B • Portfolio Assessment Worksheet 3	• *Test Generator,* Chapter 3

Block Scheduling Option

ADDITIONAL RESOURCES

BOOKS FOR TEACHERS

Belz, Herman, et al., eds., *To Form a More Perfect Union: The Critical Ideas of the Constitution,* University Press of Virginia.

Bryner, Gary C., and Dennis L. Thompson, eds., *The Constitution and the Regulation of Society,* State University of New York Press.

Lieberman, Jethro K., *The Enduring Constitution,* West Publishing Co.

BOOKS FOR STUDENTS

Bye, Thomas, *Our Constitution: A Working Plan for Democracy,* Janus Books. Short, easy-to-read study of the ways in which the Constitution of the United States upholds American ideals.

Kammen, Michael, *A Machine That Would Go of Itself,* Knopf. Describes how the Constitution is a part of our everyday lives.

Mee, Charles L., *The Genius of the People,* Harper & Row. Takes an in-depth look at the Constitutional Convention of 1787.

Padover, Saul K., *The Living U.S. Constitution,* New American Library/Dutton. A guide to the Constitution of the United States, including important Supreme Court cases and their meanings.

Ratcliffe, Robert, ed., *Vital Issues of the Constitution,* Houghton Mifflin. A discussion of the freedoms and rights granted by the U.S. Constitution.

MULTIMEDIA RESOURCES

American Civics (tr) GA. An overview of American citizenship, including maps and diagrams of the electoral system, branches of government, and laws.

The Constitution at 200: Why Does It Still Work? (VHS, c, 48 min.), SSSS. Describes how the basic principles of the Constitution still guide the nation today.

The Faces of Freedom (VHS, c, 27 min.), EBEC. A look at some of the people who have helped make the United States a great nation.

Federalism (f, VHS, c, 19 min.), COR/MTI. Examines the concurrent and conflicting powers of the federal and state governments.

THE INTERNET

Have students use these search words to locate more information about chapter topics on the Internet: *Constitution, legislative branch, executive branch, judicial branch.*

 GLOBAL SKILL BUILDER

You might wish to use **Navigating the Internet** from the interactive *Global Skill Builder* CD-ROM to aid students' understanding of the Internet as a resource.

Abbreviations: b&w=black and white; c=color; f=film; fs=filmstrip; sd=sound; tr=transparency; VHS=videotape

CIVICS SKILLS

Students will learn how to read and construct a flow-chart. They will also learn terms important to understanding the Constitution of the United States and its development.

CITIZENSHIP VALUES

☆ **Living in a Democracy** Students will be encouraged to appreciate the Constitution as a groundbreaking model for republican government, to value the ways in which the Constitution has put its ideals into effect, and to recognize the great flexibility of the Constitution and its ability to meet the test of time.

AMERICAN GOVERNMENT

☆ **Structures and Functions** Students will learn the major goals of the Constitution, how power is shared by national and state governments in a federal system, and how the system of checks and balances works.
☆ **Resolving Differences** Students will learn the various steps in the amendment process and the other ways in which the Constitution may be changed.

MEETING INDIVIDUAL NEEDS

LIMITED ENGLISH PROFICIENCY (LEP)

Have pairs of students use dictionaries to identify the roots for the terms *executive, legislative,* and *judicial.* Ask the students to write and illustrate the definitions of these roots (*execute, legislate, judge*). Then ask the students to use those definitions to explain the duties of each branch of government.

LEARNERS HAVING DIFFICULTY

Begin a word web by drawing a circle on the board and labeling it "Constitution." On lines radiating from the circle, have volunteers write adjectives that describe the U.S. Constitution. You might start off by adding the label "flexible."

AUDITORY LEARNERS

Call on a volunteer to read aloud the Preamble to the Constitution. Tell students that the Preamble states the purposes of the Constitution. Ask students to illustrate each of the American ideals incorporated in the Preamble.

VISUAL LEARNERS

Have students draw their own diagrammatic sketch of the "tree of government." You might suggest that a tree has roots, a trunk, and branches, which all could be labeled with parts of government. Some students might label the roots as the people, others as the states. Some might add leaves or fruit to represent laws or new programs. Or they might wish to use a completely different diagram.

TACTILE/KINESTHETIC LEARNERS

Illustrate checks and balances with a simple two-pan balance scale borrowed from science class. Make labels for the three branches of government. Compare two branches at a time by attaching a label to each pan. Use different-sized batteries—sources of "power"—as weights. First, have a student place equal-sized batteries on each pan, and note that the power of the branches is balanced. Have another student add another battery to one side. Ask the class which branch has more power. Explain that the lighter (weaker) branch must add weight (power) to balance the scales. Explain that each branch of government has specific powers that balance, or check, the powers of the other branches.

GIFTED LEARNERS

Have students research the status (or lack of status) of women in the Constitution. They should examine amendments that pertain to women. Other possible approaches include showing how the interpretation of the Constitution has changed over the years and examining the appointments of women to government positions. Have students report their findings to the rest of the class.

CHAPTER OVERVIEW

Chapter 3 shows how the ideals underlying the American Revolution formed the foundation of the Constitution. The chapter discusses the three branches of government and why they are separated. It also focuses on the provisions in the Constitution that have allowed the government to adapt to the changing needs of the nation. The underlying theme of the chapter is that the U.S. Constitution truly is a "living document."

Motivator

Ask students what technological inventions did not exist at the time the U.S. Constitution was written. *(television, telephone, CD player, airplane, electric lightbulb)* Point out that these innovations and hundreds of other changes have taken place in the more than 200 years since the Constitution was written. Ask students why they think the Constitution has been able to govern the country successfully through such profound changes and development.

CHAPTER OBJECTIVES

After studying Chapter 3, students should be able to do the following.

1. Name the ideals expressed in the Constitution.
2. Identify the branches of government and their powers.
3. Describe how the Constitution provides for changing needs and conditions.

SIMULATIONS AND CASE STUDIES

Lesson 2: Decoding the Document

Block Scheduling Option

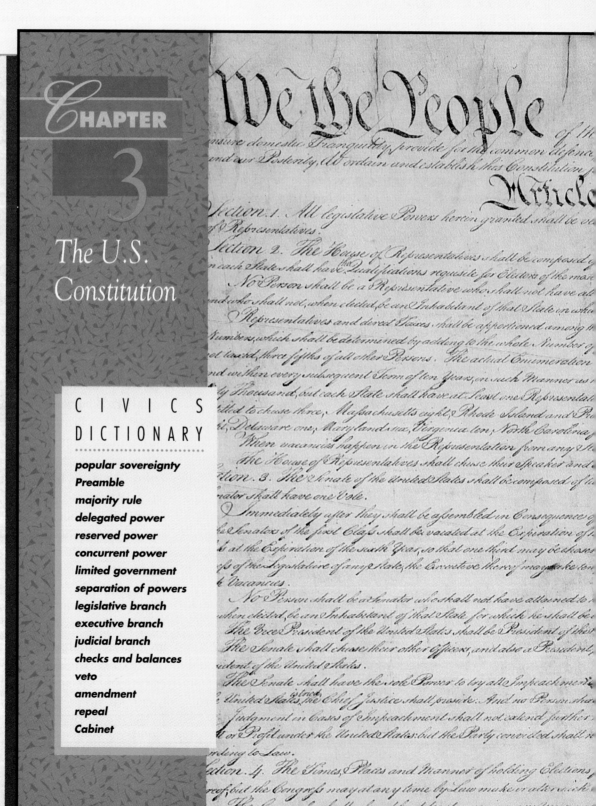

CHAPTER 3

The U.S. Constitution

CIVICS DICTIONARY

- **popular sovereignty**
- **Preamble**
- **majority rule**
- **delegated power**
- **reserved power**
- **concurrent power**
- **limited government**
- **separation of powers**
- **legislative branch**
- **executive branch**
- **judicial branch**
- **checks and balances**
- **veto**
- **amendment**
- **repeal**
- **Cabinet**

SECTION OBJECTIVES

After studying Section 1, students should be able to do the following.

1. Describe how the Pilgrims influenced the nation's founders.

2. List the goals of the U.S. government.

3. Explain the principle of majority rule.

4. Explain why the Constitution limits the powers of the federal government.

Teaching Section1
Building a Vocabulary

Explain that the word *reign*, part of *sovereign*, means "to rule." *Popular* indicates "the will of the general public." Thus, **popular sovereignty** means "rule by the will of the people." Also, break the word *concur* into the French *con* (together) and *currere* (to run). **Concurrent powers**, then, would be powers that run together, or that are shared. Explain that both terms are important to American government under the Constitution.

CHAPTER FOCUS

The framers of the U.S. Constitution lived in an age without telephones, automobiles, televisions, and satellites. How could the nation's founders have planned for governing your life in the modern age?

The answer is that the framers created a plan of government that could stand the test of time—more than 200 years so far. They wrote a Constitution based on fundamental ideals of democratic government. This Constitution created a government flexible enough to change with the changing times while still being true to its basic ideals. As a result, the Constitution is as relevant to your life today as it was to Americans living more than 200 years ago. The Constitution is the bond that unites all Americans—past, present, and future.

● ●

STUDY GUIDE

● What ideals are expressed in the Constitution?

● What are the branches of government, and how does the Constitution control their power?

● How does the Constitution provide for changing needs and changing conditions?

1 Ideals of the Constitution

The Declaration of Independence states that governments should receive their powers from "the consent [approval] of the governed [people]." This is one of the basic ideals on which the nation was founded.

This ideal, treasured by the framers of the Constitution, can be traced in part to the Mayflower Compact. (See page 523.) The Compact was drawn up on November 21, 1620, when the Pilgrims on the *Mayflower* reached North America. They were far off course and had no charter from the king to settle in New England or to form a government.

The Pilgrims wrote the Compact to create a new government based on cooperation and the consent of the people.

Consent of the Governed

Government by **popular sovereignty**, or consent of the governed, is one of our most cherished ideals. It is stated in the opening sentence of the Constitution, which is known as the Preamble. The **Preamble** is an introduction that explains why the U.S. Constitution was written.

The Preamble begins with the words "We the people." The framers of the Constitution wanted to emphasize the importance of the people. These words stress that our government was established by the people. As the Preamble clearly states, "We the people of the United States, . . . do ordain [order] and establish this Constitution. . . ."

Goals of the Constitution

The Preamble itself is not law. Rather, it is a statement of goals. The Preamble lists six goals for the government of the United States:

1. "To form a more perfect union." The new government should be a better union of states than that under the Articles of Confederation.

2. "To establish justice." The government

The Constitution protects religious worship and diversity in the United States. This ideal of religious toleration reaches back to some of the earliest English settlements in what Europeans called the New World. Religious toleration, however, was not the objective of the Pilgrims and their Plymouth colony in Massachusetts. In England the Pilgrims, or Separatists, had struggled to maintain their unity and their self-sufficiency in the face of government attempts to impose the state religion on them, and they had finally been forced to flee. The Plymouth Pilgrims wanted nothing to do with people outside their faith.

Gathering Information

Have students find newspaper articles that illustrate examples of state powers, national powers, and powers that are shared between the two levels of government. Have students make a three-column list classifying the powers that they were able to find. Call on volunteers to write items from their lists on the chalkboard. Resolve any disagreements about classifying powers in a class discussion about delegated, reserved, and concurrent powers.

Have students work in small groups to develop a list of goals for the school's student government. Each student should offer a proposed goal. They might wish to use the "Goals of the Constitution" as a model. Have each group write its finished list on the board and present it to the class. Discuss similarities and differences in the lists, and vote on a final list of goals. Compare it with any existing list of student government goals, and discuss variations.

GLOBAL PERSPECTIVES

Point out to students that the chart on this page indicates how the powers of government are divided in the U.S. federal system. In some other governments, under what are called unitary, rather than federal, systems, power divisions are less distinct. In Nazi Germany between 1933 and 1945, for example, the national government appointed officials who were responsible for running the affairs of territorial subdivisions. Locally elected officials had little real power. In France up to 1982, the national government appointed important officials to supervise the actions of locally elected officials. In 1982, however, some locally elected governments in France were given more power. In Great Britain the national government officially has power over local governments. In practice, however, local governments have considerable autonomy to act on their own. Other countries with unitary governments of one form or another include Japan and countries in Middle and South America and in Africa.

should make laws and establish a system of courts that are fair to all.

3. "To insure domestic tranquillity." The government should preserve peace within the nation.

4. "To provide for the common defense." The government should protect the nation from its enemies.

5. "To promote the general welfare." The government should help ensure the well-being of all the people.

6. "To secure the blessings of liberty." The government should safeguard the freedom of the people.

These goals reflect the belief that government should serve its citizens. They remain the goals of the nation today.

A Representative Democracy

The representative democracy, or republic, set up by the Constitution is based on the consent of the people who are governed. What happens, though, if the people become dissatisfied with the way their representatives are governing? In this case, the people can let their representatives know what they believe should be done. If people do not approve of their representatives' actions, in the next election they can elect new representatives who they believe will do a better job.

Our republic works successfully because Americans believe in **majority rule**. The majority is more than half of the people. When disagreements occur between people, the

How the Powers of Government Are Divided

Federal Government Powers (Delegated Powers)	Powers Shared by Federal and State Governments (Concurrent Powers)	State Government Powers (Reserved Powers)
• To regulate interstate and foreign trade	• To collect taxes	• To regulate trade within the state
• To coin and print money	• To borrow money	• To establish local governments
• To conduct foreign relations	• To establish courts	• To conduct elections
• To establish post offices and roads	• To charter banks	• To determine qualifications of voters
• To raise and support armed forces	• To enforce laws and punish lawbreakers	• To establish and support public schools
• To declare war and make peace	• To provide for the health and welfare of the people	• To incorporate business firms
• To govern American territories and admit new states		• To make marriage laws
• To pass naturalization laws and regulate immigration		• To license professional workers
• To make all laws "necessary and proper" to carry out its powers		• To keep all powers not granted to the federal government nor prohibited to the states

Divide the class into two groups: those who would like each school day to start and end later than it currently does and those who would like school to start and end earlier. Have volunteers from each group argue for their positions, and allow students to change sides if they are persuaded by opposing arguments. Then ask the class to vote on the issue. Ask: How did this process illustrate the ideal "majority rule with minority rights"? *(minority is allowed to voice its opinion)* Ask for other situations that illustrate this ideal.

Have students discuss how the Constitution limits government. *(by specifying certain powers that are forbidden to both the federal government and the states)* Then have students write newspaper editorials explaining how limited government works in a system of majority rule. (Students might point out that the majority of the people decide, through the Constitution and laws, how much power the government has.) Invite volunteers to share their editorials with the class.

decision of the majority is accepted by all. Under our system of government, however, the majority must always respect the rights of the minority—the smaller group of people. Moreover, the minority must be free to express its views on issues and to try to convince the majority to accept its ideas.

A Federal System

As you learned in Chapter 2, the delegates at the Constitutional Convention agreed to establish a federal system of government. Under federalism the powers of government are divided between the national government, which governs the whole nation, and the state governments, which govern the people living in each state.

The national government, which is usually referred to as the *federal government*, is centered in Washington, D.C. The term *federal system* refers to the country's entire system of government. This system includes both the federal government and each of the 50 state governments.

Under a federal system, the federal government has certain important powers. All powers that are not given to the federal government remain with the state governments.

Federal Government Powers The powers given to the federal government by the Constitution, called **delegated powers**, apply to matters concerning all the people. For example, only the federal government can coin money. Only the federal government has the power to control trade with foreign nations. The federal government alone has the power to provide for the common defense, because an attack on the United States would threaten all Americans.

You recall that under the Articles of Confederation, the federal government did not have these important powers. The Constitution gave these powers to the federal government to strengthen it.

State Government Powers The U.S. Constitution leaves to the states several

Responsibility for running the nation's postal service is one of the powers given to the federal government.

important powers to manage their own affairs. The states or the people have all the powers not specifically given to the federal government by the Constitution. These are known as **reserved powers** because they are reserved, or set aside, for the states or the people. The state governments, for example, conduct elections, regulate trade within the states, and establish local governments.

Shared Powers The federal and state governments also share many powers. These are known as **concurrent powers**. Both the federal and state governments, for example, can raise funds through taxation. Both also have the power to borrow money. Moreover, they share the power to establish courts, to charter

CIVICS SIDELIGHT

Point out that some people today believe that the power of the federal government often surpasses what the founders might have envisioned. If, for example, individual states are reluctant to implement its legislation, the federal government may choose to withhold vitally needed funding, such as that for constructing and maintaining interstate highways.

Closure

Have students read the Mayflower Compact on textbook page 523. Lead a class discussion of the Compact's relationship to government by the consent of the governed. Have students write their own compacts (perhaps named after their school) regarding student government and the consent of students. Invite volunteers to read their compacts to the rest of the class.

Reviewing

Have students complete the Section 1 Review.

Reteaching

Assign Section 1 of the Chapter 3 Reteaching Worksheet.

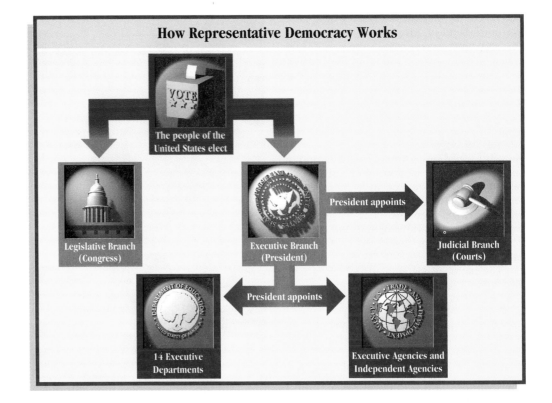

banks, to enforce laws and punish lawbreakers, and to provide for the health and welfare of the American people.

Whenever a state law disagrees with the Constitution or with a federal law, the state must give way to the federal government. The framers of the Constitution made this clear by writing that the Constitution and the laws of the federal government shall be "the supreme law of the land."

Limited Powers

By establishing the federal system, the framers of the Constitution set up the stronger national government that the new nation needed. The framers were determined, however, to keep the new federal government from becoming too powerful. This ideal of **limited government** led the founders to spell out the powers of the federal government. As a result, citizens know exactly what the powers of the federal government are.

The Constitution also provides that all powers not mentioned are reserved for the states or the people. Furthermore, the Bill of Rights (discussed in the next chapter) specifies certain powers that are forbidden to both the federal government and the states. It describes the many freedoms that belong to every citizen of the United States.

As you have read, the framers of the Constitution believed that all governments should have the consent of the people. They made sure that the new government could have only as much power as the people wanted to give it. The American people wanted to limit, or to check, the powers of the federal government so that the government would be responsible to the American people.

After studying Section 2, students should be able to do the following.

1. Explain why the Constitution provides for the separation of powers.
2. Identify the main responsibility of each of the three branches of government.
3. Describe how the system of checks and balances works.

Write **executive branch**, **judicial branch**, and **legislative branch** in a row on the chalkboard. Ask students to tell you in which branch the Congress, the president, and the courts belong. Position the answers beneath the terms. Then draw two "walls" with chalk to separate the terms, and ask what this shows (the **separation of powers**).

SECTION 1 REVIEW

1. Define or identify the following terms: popular sovereignty, Preamble, majority rule, delegated power, reserved power, concurrent power, limited government.

2. How did the Pilgrims influence the nation's founders? How is the ideal of popular sovereignty expressed in the Preamble?

3. What are the goals of the government of the United States?

4. Explain the principle of majority rule.

5. Why does the Constitution limit the powers granted to the federal government?

6. **THINKING CRITICALLY** Write a poem or a rap song that describes how the ideals in the Constitution affect your life today.

2 The Three Branches of Government

The Constitution contains provisions designed to prevent any person or group of people, or any part of the government, from taking too much power. As you have learned, the Constitution set up a federal system that divides powers between the federal and state governments. The Constitution also divides power among three separate branches of the federal government.

This three-way division of power is called the **separation of powers**. It ensures that no branch of the federal government becomes too powerful. The three branches are the legislative branch, the executive branch, and the judicial branch. They were created by the first three articles of the Constitution.

Legislative Branch

Article 1 of the Constitution established Congress as the **legislative branch**, or lawmaking branch, of the government. Congress is made up of two houses—the Senate and the House of Representatives.

The Constitution places great emphasis on Congress. It is the first branch of government discussed in the Constitution. The workings of Congress are described in greater detail than either of the other two branches. Moreover, the other branches depend on Congress for the money they need to carry out their duties.

Executive Branch

The **executive branch**, created in Article 2 of the Constitution, is responsible for executing, or carrying out, the nation's laws. It is headed

SECTION 1 REVIEW
A N S W E R S

1. See the following pages: popular sovereignty, Preamble (p. 37); majority rule (p. 38); delegated power, reserved power, concurrent power (p. 39); limited government (p. 40).

2. The Constitution's ideal of popular sovereignty can in part be traced to the Pilgrims' Mayflower Compact. The Preamble's goals reflect the beliefs that government should serve its citizens.

3. form a more perfect union, establish justice, insure domestic tranquillity, provide for the common defense, promote the general welfare, secure the blessings of liberty

4. When disagreements occur, the majority prevails. The rights of the minority must be respected, and the minority must be allowed to have its views heard.

5. so that the federal government will not become too powerful

6. Poems and rap songs will vary. Students should refer to at least four ideals in their works.

The Separation of Powers

Legislative Branch (Congress)	Executive Branch (President)	Judicial Branch (Courts)
makes the laws.	carries out and enforces the laws.	interprets laws and punishes lawbreakers.

Guided Practice

Divide the class into three groups, each representing one branch of government. Have students from each branch suggest real-life actions their branch might take. Then have students from each branch suggest actions they could take in response to actions taken by other branches. For example, students in the legislative branch should say that they have the right to approve court appointments of the executive branch. You might ask for volunteers to act as spokespersons for each branch.

Closure

Point out to students that the Constitution allows for many leaders in both the legislative and the judicial branches of government. Then ask: Why do you think the Constitution allows for just one leader of the executive branch—the president? What might be some consequences if several leaders headed the executive branch?

Checks and Balances in the Federal Government

Powers	Checks on Powers
The Congress • Passes bills into laws • Can pass laws over the president's veto if two thirds of the Congress approve the law • Approves appointments of federal court judges	• President can veto bills. • The Supreme Court can rule that a law is unconstitutional.
The President • Can approve or veto laws • Carries out the laws • Appoints federal court judges	• Congress can pass laws over the president's veto by a two-thirds vote. • Congress can impeach and remove the president for high crimes or for misdemeanors. • Senate approves the president's appointments to the federal courts.
The Supreme Court • Interprets the meaning of laws • Can rule that laws passed by Congress and actions taken by the executive branch are unconstitutional	• Congress (or the states) can propose an amendment to the Constitution if the Supreme Court rules that a law is unconstitutional. • Senate can refuse to approve the appointments to the federal courts. • Congress can impeach and remove a federal judge from office.

by the president. This branch also includes the vice president and many other people who help the president enforce the nation's laws.

Judicial Branch

Article 3 established the **judicial branch**, or federal court system, to interpret laws and punish lawbreakers. The Constitution makes the Supreme Court the head of the judicial branch. As such, the Court can declare a law invalid if it is in conflict with the Constitution. The Constitution also gives Congress the power to establish lower courts to help carry out the work of the judicial branch.

Checks and Balances

To ensure that no branch of the federal government becomes too powerful, the Constitution provides for a system of **checks and balances**. Each branch has powers that check, or limit, the powers of the other two branches. Moreover, each branch has its own powers, which no other branch can assume. In this way the powers of government are balanced by being divided three ways.

How does the system of checks and balances work? Consider lawmaking, for example. Congress has the power to make laws. The president, however, has the power to **veto**, or turn down, proposed laws. With the veto

SECTION OBJECTIVES

After studying Section 3, students should be able to do the following.

1. Explain why the Constitution often is called a "living document."

2. Describe the amendment processes, including proposal, ratification, and repeal.

3. Explain how interpretation and custom add flexibility to the Constitution.

power, the president can check the lawmaking power of Congress.

Does this mean that the president can stop any law passed by Congress from taking effect? That would give the president too much power. The Constitution, therefore, balances the president's power by giving Congress the power to pass laws over the president's veto. Overriding a presidential veto requires a two-thirds vote of both houses of Congress. In this way Congress can check the lawmaking power of the president.

The Supreme Court also can become involved in lawmaking because it has the power to interpret the meaning of laws in its decisions. In addition, the Court can declare that certain laws are in conflict with the Constitution and cannot be enforced.

There are many other checks and balances in the federal government. You will learn more about how the three branches of the federal government check and balance each other in Chapters 5, 6, and 7.

SECTION 2 REVIEW

1. Define or identify the following terms: separation of powers, legislative branch, executive branch, judicial branch, checks and balances, veto.

2. Why does the U.S. Constitution provide for separation of powers?

3. What is the primary responsibility of each of the three branches of the federal government?

4. How does the federal government's system of checks and balances work?

5. **THINKING CRITICALLY** Imagine that there is a national debate underway concerning the federal government's system of checks and balances. Some people would like to eliminate the system, while others would like to

keep it in place. Write a newspaper editorial explaining what might happen if the system were eliminated and why this would prove harmful to the U.S. government and the American way of life. Be as persuasive as possible in your arguments.

3 A Flexible Document

Changing times may call for changes in the government. In 1787, when the Constitution was written, the United States was a nation of 13 states with fewer than 4 million people. Today the states are home to more than 260 million people. The nation has changed in other ways as well.

How can the U.S. Constitution, which was written during the age of sailing ships, meet the needs of a nation in the age of space exploration? The answer is that the framers of the Constitution planned a system of government that could change to meet changing conditions and changing needs. The U.S. Constitution truly is a "living document."

Providing for Change

One of the most important features of the Constitution of the United States is that it is a flexible document. The framers of the Constitution knew that the plan of government they were creating would have to meet the needs of a growing nation.

They could not possibly foresee all the changes the United States would undergo. Yet the government established by the Constitution has been able to change and adapt to new circumstances and challenges. There are three ways in which the Constitution and the government can adapt to the changing needs and conditions of the nation: amendment, interpretation, and custom.

(continued on page 46)

SECTION 2 REVIEW
A N S W E R S

1. See the following pages: separation of powers, legislative branch, executive branch (p. 41); judicial branch, checks and balances, veto (p. 42).

2. to ensure that no branch of government becomes too powerful

3. legislative branch—make laws; executive branch—carry out laws; judicial branch—interpret laws and punish lawbreakers

4. Each branch has a specific job. At the same time, each branch can limit the actions of the other branches. Thus, the powers of government are balanced among the branches.

5. Editorials will vary. Students should refer to the possibility of one branch of government becoming too powerful and infringing on the rights of the people.

Illustrating Ideas

Help students summarize the events of Watergate by making a time line. Draw a long horizontal line on the chalkboard. At the left, write *1972*. Have students identify the main events of this constitutional drama. On the time line, you may wish to note only events that are dated in the feature, or you may wish to insert undated events as well, to make the story more complete.

Linking Civics and History

Have students work in small groups to research other government scandals in the nation's past. Have each group prepare and present a report to the class. Encourage groups to illustrate their reports with graphics and visual aids. The class might discuss how each scandal's effects on government and the nation compare with the effects of Watergate.

CIVICS SIDELIGHT

What are the key players in the Watergate scandal doing today? A number have died, including Richard M. Nixon in 1994. John Dean served 127 days in prison and is the author of the best-selling book *Blind Ambition*. Archibald Cox became chairman of Common Cause and a professor at Boston University. Leon Jaworski died in 1982. Sam Ervin died in 1985, the year Howard Baker retired from the Senate. Baker later served as President Ronald Reagan's chief of staff for two years.

Among the top Nixon aides implicated in Watergate, White House Chief of Staff H.R. Haldeman served 18 months in prison and died in November 1993. John Ehrlichman, Nixon's domestic counselor, also served 18 months in prison. A published author, Ehrlichman was working in 1994 for an international consulting company. John Mitchell, Nixon's attorney general, served 19 months in prison for his part in the Watergate cover-up and died in 1988.

Case STUDY — WATERGATE

In 1972 the Watergate building in Washington, D.C., housed the headquarters of the Democratic National Committee. Before dawn on June 16, 1972, five burglars broke into these offices, setting off a chain of events that eventually led to a test of the Constitution and the resignation of a president.

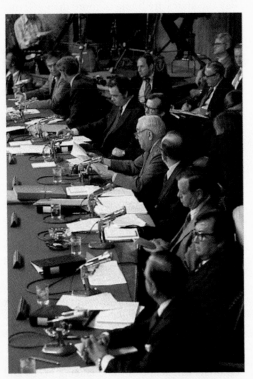

The Senate Watergate Committee was created in 1973 to investigate charges stemming from the Watergate break-in.

The White House Is Involved

When the burglars were arrested, the police found that they were carrying electronic spy equipment that made it clear that this was not just a routine burglary. Reporters immediately began asking questions about the incident. Why would anyone want to break into Democratic party headquarters?

The year 1972 was a presidential election year. Some people wondered if the burglars had been looking for material to help defeat Democratic candidates and reelect Republican President Richard M. Nixon. Most Americans, however, dismissed the possibility of White House involvement, and Nixon was reelected by a wide margin. Still, reporters and others had suspicions. Early in 1973 the Watergate burglars were tried and found guilty. Threatened with a long imprisonment, one of the burglars broke his silence and described conversations with top White House aides.

Executive Privilege

The Senate formed a special committee to investigate the charges against Nixon's aides. At first Nixon refused to allow the committee to question the aides. He claimed executive privilege—the right and need of the president and his aides to keep silent about official conversations. But as Congress grew increasingly angry, Nixon announced that his aides would testify. Before the hearings began, news reports made it clear that some White House people had been involved. Moreover, they had tried to cover up their actions. In April 1973 Nixon's top aides resigned.

The Senate Watergate Committee began public hearings in May. One top aide, John

Summarizing

Have students write, in their own words, a paragraph summarizing the Watergate scandal and its significance. Then have them write a second paragraph stating how they might have reacted to the incident at the time it occurred. Would it have changed their attitude toward the government? Are any attitudes they hold today a result of what they know about Watergate and the issues it involved?

Dean, testified that Nixon knew about the cover-up. The president denied the charge. But many wondered if Nixon was telling the truth. Then it appeared there was a way to find out. The public learned that every conversation between Nixon and his aides had been recorded on tape-recording machines placed in the White House by order of Nixon himself.

Conflict over the Tapes

The Senate Committee and Archibald Cox, Watergate special prosecutor, immediately requested a number of the tapes. Nixon refused, again claiming executive privilege. In October 1973 a federal court of appeals denied the claim of executive privilege, ruling that Nixon must turn over the tapes.

Instead, Nixon offered to release a written summary of the tapes and ordered Cox not to request any more tapes. When Cox refused, he was fired. After great protest from Congress and the public, Nixon agreed to release the tapes and named a new special prosecutor.

Then came another shock. Some of the requested tapes were missing. Criticism of Nixon grew, and the House Judiciary Committee began to investigate the possible impeachment of the president. The House Committee and the special prosecutor also demanded the missing tapes. Finally, the question was put before the Supreme Court. On July 24, 1974, the Court ruled that President Nixon had to release the tapes.

Nixon Leaves Office

Meanwhile, the House Judiciary Committee voted to recommend Nixon's impeachment on three counts: obstruction of justice, abuse of power, and contempt of Congress and the courts. It was now up to the full House to vote.

Before the House could act, however, the newly released tapes proved that Nixon had been involved in the cover-up of the Watergate break-in. It quickly became certain that the president would be impeached by the House. Thus, on August 9, 1974, Richard M. Nixon

left the nation's capital—the only person ever to resign the presidency.

The Watergate case proved that the system of checks and balances set up by the Constitution works. Together the courts and Congress had restrained a president engaged in wrongdoing. Moreover, they reminded the world that even a president is not above the law.

Richard M. Nixon waved good-bye as he left the capital and the presidency on August 9, 1974.

YOU DECIDE

1 Do you think Nixon should have faced criminal charges for his involvement in Watergate?

2 How did the Watergate case prove that the system of checks and balances set up by the Constitution works?

45

ANSWERS TO YOU DECIDE

1. Answers will vary. Some students might say that everyone, including the president of the United States, should have to face legal action for possible wrongdoing. Other students might say that having to resign the presidency was punishment enough for Nixon's involvement in the cover-up.

2. It showed that the Constitution's system of checks and balances works because Congress and the courts were able to use their constitutional powers to restrain the power and actions of the president.

Teaching Section 3
Building a Vocabulary

Ask students what it means to amend something. *(to make a change)* Ask if they can name any **amendments** to the Constitution. Then ask what it would mean if an amendment were **repealed.** *(It would be canceled—no longer in effect.)* The French used the word *cabinet* to describe a small, private apartment in which the king met with his advisers. Ask students what officials they think are part of the U.S. president's Cabinet.

Summarizing Information

After reviewing the amendment process, have students write short summaries of the process. Then assign one Constitutional amendment to each student. Have each student neatly write a short paragraph explaining when his or her amendment was ratified and how it changed the Constitution. Collect the papers to make a "Constitutional Amendments Handbook" that students can use as a study guide.

Civics Sidelight

The Eighteenth Amendment, ratified in 1919 and known as the Prohibition Amendment, made the manufacture, sale, or transportation of alcoholic beverages illegal. Prohibition did not work. Gangsters thrived on the illegitimate business of bootlegging; millions of people continued to drink liquor; and with such widespread flouting of the law, the police could not enforce it. The Twenty-first Amendment, ratified in 1933, repealed prohibition.

Did You Know That...

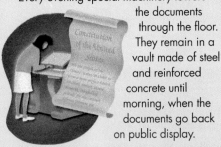

The Declaration of Independence, the Constitution, and the Bill of Rights are on display at the National Archives Building in Washington, D.C. These valued safeguards of American liberties are displayed in a special glass case that prevents air and moisture from seeping in.

Every evening special machinery lowers the documents through the floor. They remain in a vault made of steel and reinforced concrete until morning, when the documents go back on public display.

The Amendment Process

An **amendment** is a written change made to the Constitution. The process for amending, or changing, the Constitution is set forth in Article 5 of the Constitution.

It is not easy to amend the Constitution. All proposed amendments require the approval of three fourths of the states. Securing this approval for an amendment may take a long time. As a result, it is likely that long, careful thought will be given to a proposed amendment before it is passed. Since the Constitution went into effect in 1789, only 27 amendments have been added to it.

Proposing an Amendment An amendment may be proposed in two ways. In either way, both the U.S. Congress and the states must be involved in the process. The first way is to have Congress propose an amendment by a two-thirds vote in both houses. Because a two-thirds vote in Congress

is difficult to obtain, members must be certain the amendment is needed.

The second way of proposing an amendment to the Constitution begins with the states. Under this method, the legislatures of two thirds of the states—34 out of 50—can ask Congress to call a national convention to propose an amendment. This method has never been used successfully. It could be used, however, if Congress should refuse to propose an amendment that the American people believe is necessary.

Ratifying an Amendment After an amendment has been proposed, it then must be ratified, or approved, by three fourths, or 38, of the states. There are two ways an amendment may be ratified. The method of ratification must be described in each proposed amendment.

One method involves sending the proposed amendment to the state legislatures for approval. All but one of the amendments to the Constitution were approved this way. The second method involves sending the proposed amendment to state conventions elected by the people of each state to consider the amendment. This method has been used only once.

After an amendment has been ratified by the required number of states, it becomes part of the written Constitution. What happens if the people decide they do not like the way an amendment is working? In that case, the amendment in question can be **repealed**, or canceled, by another amendment. Only one of the amendments to the Constitution, the Eighteenth Amendment, has been repealed.

Interpreting the Constitution

The government also changes when some part of the Constitution is interpreted in a new way. Congress may interpret a certain clause in the Constitution as giving it the right to pass a particular law.

For example, Congress has passed laws setting the minimum wage that workers in the

Closure

Divide the class into three groups. Assign each group one of the three ways in which the Constitution can be changed: by amendment, by interpretation, and by custom. Have each group argue that its method of amendment is the best way to change the Constitution. When all arguments and discussion are finished, have the class vote on the most effective way to change the Constitution.

Reviewing

Have students complete the Section 3 Review.

Reteaching

Assign Section 3 of the Chapter 3 Reteaching Worksheet.

United States must be paid. A minimum wage is not mentioned anywhere in the Constitution. The Constitution does, however, give Congress the power to control trade among the states. The goods made by workers usually travel from one state to another. Therefore, Congress has interpreted the Constitution to mean that Congress has the power to pass laws affecting working conditions. These conditions include wage rates.

The Supreme Court has the power to decide if Congress has interpreted the Constitution correctly. The Court's rulings are final.

Custom and Tradition

A number of changes in the federal government also have come about through custom and tradition. For example, the Constitution does not provide for regular meetings of the leaders in the executive branch of the federal government. President George Washington, however, brought these leaders together regularly to serve as his advisers, or **Cabinet**. Since that time, regular meetings between a president and the Cabinet have become an accepted part of the government.

Many other important traditions and customs have developed in the nation's government. These traditions are seldom written down or passed into law. For this reason, they are sometimes referred to as part of the "unwritten Constitution."

SECTION 3 REVIEW

1. Define or identify the following terms: amendment, repeal, Cabinet.

2. Why can it be said that the U.S. Constitution is a "living document"? What are the advantages of this flexibility?

3. What are the two ways that an amendment can be proposed and the two ways that a proposed amendment can be ratified?

4. How can an amendment to the U.S. Constitution be repealed?

5. Explain how interpretation of the Constitution and custom and tradition help the government change to meet changing times.

6. **THINKING CRITICALLY** You are a delegate to the Constitutional Convention in Philadelphia. Write a short speech that will convince the other delegates at the Convention how important it is to make the United States Constitution a flexible document.

CHAPTER 3 SUMMARY

The nation's government is based on the U.S. Constitution. This Constitution provides a workable plan of government.

The U.S. government is based on the ideal of popular sovereignty, or the consent of the people who are governed. It is a federal system in which certain powers are given to the federal government and other powers are left to the state governments and the people. Certain other powers are shared by both the federal and state governments.

The Constitution provides for three separate branches of government—the legislative branch, the executive branch, and the judicial branch. This separation of powers is designed to prevent any person or group of people from taking too much power. Each branch of government has powers that check, or limit, the powers of the other two branches.

The Constitution and the federal government have been able to meet the needs of a growing and changing nation. The Constitution can be amended, and it can be interpreted in new ways. Changes can also come about through custom and tradition. The Constitution truly is a "living document."

SECTION 3 REVIEW
ANSWERS

1. See the following pages: amendment, repeal (p. 46); Cabinet (p. 47).

2. Its provisions enable government to change to meet changing conditions. The founders could not foresee all the changes the United States would undergo.

3. proposed—either by a two-thirds vote in both houses of Congress, or the legislatures of two thirds of the states can ask Congress to call a convention; ratified—either by legislatures in three fourths of the states or by conventions held in three fourths of the states

4. by another amendment

5. Interpretation enables Congress to pass new laws. Custom helps change become an accepted part of government.

6. Speeches will vary. Students should argue that making the Constitution flexible will enable it to serve the nation's changing needs in the future.

Developing Civics Skills

The flowchart on this page shows a process. Point out to students that in their study of civics, they will discover that many aspects of government are processes. Amending the Constitution is just one example. Rules usually govern how a process is started and how it is continued through various stages until it is completed. For this reason, government processes lend themselves to graphic representation, such as flowcharts.

Students should be able not only to read a flowchart but also to construct one. You might have students practice this skill by creating a flowchart of the steps involved in making a sandwich or in completing a research project. Invite volunteers to share their flowcharts with the class.

ANSWERS TO Applying the Skill

1. Congress calls a national convention, which then may propose a constitutional amendment.

2. Most students will probably point to the two-thirds and three-fourths votes required for proposal and ratification. Students also might note that elected officials—the chosen representatives of the people—play an important role in the amendment process.

Developing Civics Skills

SOCIAL STUDIES SKILL
Reading Flowcharts

A flowchart is a diagram that presents information in a visual, easy-to-understand way. Its main purpose is to show the various steps that a process follows. Once you learn how to read a flowchart, you will be able to trace the movement of a process through time.

How to Read Flowcharts

1. Determine the subject. Read the title of the chart to determine its subject matter. Look at any major headings for an overview of the process shown in the flowchart.

2. Identify the beginning and the end points. Study the arrows in the chart, noting their direction. They will tell you how the process begins and how it ends. A process may have more than one beginning and more than one end.

3. Study the middle stages. The middle stages show you movement through time by connecting all the stages in the order they take place. They also show you where the process may become stalled.

Applying the Skill

Examine the flowchart below. Then answer the following questions.

1. What happens if two thirds of the state legislatures request that a constitutional convention be held?

2. What evidence in the flowchart supports the following statement: "A majority of the people must favor an amendment before it can be added to the Constitution."

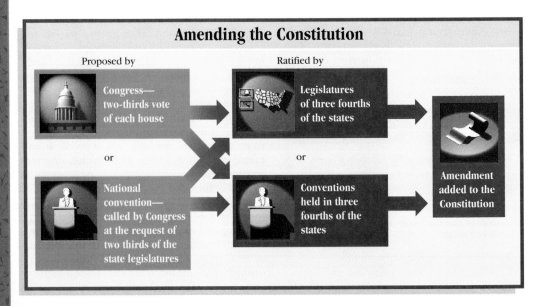

Amending the Constitution

Proposed by

Congress—two-thirds vote of each house

or

National convention—called by Congress at the request of two thirds of the state legislatures

Ratified by

Legislatures of three fourths of the states

or

Conventions held in three fourths of the states

Amendment added to the Constitution

CHAPTER 3 REVIEW
A N S W E R S

Vocabulary Workshop
1. amendment
2. a power given to the federal government by the Constitution
3. veto
4. Preamble

5. concurrent powers
6. to advise the president

Reviewing Main Ideas
1. form a more perfect union, establish justice, insure domestic tranquillity, provide for common defense, promote general welfare, secure blessings of liberty
2. When disagreements occur, the majority decision prevails; majority rule reduces tensions and allows actions to be taken while taking into account the views of the minority.
3. legislative branch—make laws; executive branch—carry out laws; judicial branch—interpret laws and punish lawbreakers
4. Powers are separated and limited by a system of checks and balances.
5. amendment, interpretation, custom
6. proposal by Congress or by a convention called by the states; ratification by state legislatures or state conventions

Thinking Critically
1. Answers will vary. Students should support their choices.
2. Answers should address the balance between majority rule and the rights of the minority to be heard.
3. Their experiences under British control made them wary of government.
4. Students might point to the Constitution's flexibility.

Citizenship in Your Community
Students' summaries should focus on concurrent powers.

BUILDING YOUR PORTFOLIO
Assign Portfolio Assessment Worksheet 3 in the *Portfolio Assessment Worksheets* booklet.

Assessment
- **Chapter 3 Tests**, *Chapter Tests* booklet
- **Test Generator**, Chapter 3
- **Portfolio**, Portfolio Assessment Worksheet 3, *Portfolio Assessment Worksheets* booklet

CHAPTER 3 R·e·v·i·e·w

Vocabulary Workshop
1. What is the term for a written change in the U.S. Constitution?
2. Define the term *delegated power*.
3. What is the term for the president's power to turn down a law passed by Congress?
4. What is the term for the introduction to the Constitution that explains why the Constitution was written?
5. What type of powers do the federal and the state governments share?
6. What is the purpose of the president's Cabinet?

Reviewing Main Ideas
1. What are the six purposes of government as stated in the Preamble?
2. What is the principle of majority rule, and why is this principle important?
3. What are the three branches of the federal government, and what are their primary responsibilities?
4. How does the U.S. Constitution ensure that no branch of the federal government becomes too powerful?
5. What are the three ways that the Constitution can be changed?
6. What are the steps in the amendment process?

Thinking Critically
1. The Constitution is based on many great ideals of government. Which of these ideals do you consider the most important to the American way of life, and why?
2. The principle of majority rule means that sometimes the wishes of the minority go unfulfilled. Do you think this is fair?
3. What experiences do you think led the framers of the Constitution to ensure that no one person or group in the government could gain too much power?
4. The U.S. Constitution is the world's oldest plan of government still working successfully. What do you think is responsible for this lasting success?

Citizenship in Your Community

Individual Project
One of the ideals on which the U.S. Constitution is based is federalism, the sharing of powers between the federal government and the state governments. Collect newspaper articles that show examples of powers shared by your state and the federal government. Summarize each article and explain how these shared powers allow both the federal government and your state government to operate effectively.

Building Your Portfolio

The third step of your unit portfolio project (see page 67) is to create a chart entitled "The Three Branches of Education." Write the following headings across the top of your chart: Administration, Teachers, Students. Under each heading, answer the following questions. What are the primary duties of this branch? What responsibilities does this branch share with the other branches? How does this branch work with the other branches? Then write a caption explaining why cooperation among the branches of education is a vital part of the U.S. educational system. Place your chart in your individual portfolio for later use.

CHAPTER 4

Rights and Responsibilities

TEXTBOOK	TEACHING RESOURCES	OTHER AVAILABLE RESOURCES
Chapter	• Skills Worksheet 4 • Challenge/Enrichment Worksheet 4	• Simulations and Case Studies Lesson 3
Section **1** The Bill of Rights Page 51	• Reteaching Worksheet 4.1	• Transparency 2: Freedoms Guaranteed by the Bill of Rights
2 Guaranteeing Other Rights Page 58	• Reteaching Worksheet 4.2	
3 Citizen Duties and Responsibilities Page 61	• Reteaching Worksheet 4.3	
Review and Assessment Chapter 4 Review, Page 65 Unit 1 Review, Page 66	• Test, Form A • Test, Form B • Portfolio Assessment Worksheet 4 • Unit 1 Portfolio Assessment Worksheet	• *Test Generator,* Chapter 4 • *Test Generator,* Unit 1

Block Scheduling Option

ADDITIONAL RESOURCES

BOOKS FOR TEACHERS

The Bill of Rights: Opposing Viewpoints, Greenhaven Press.

Burns, James MacGregor, and Stewart Burns, *A People's Charter: The Pursuit of Rights in America,* Knopf.

Lacey, Michael J., and Knud Haakonssen, eds., *A Culture of Rights: The Bill of Rights in Philosophy, Politics, and Law 1791 and 1991,* Cambridge University Press.

Mellon, James, ed., *Bullwhip Days: The Slaves Remember,* Grove-Atlantic.

BOOKS FOR STUDENTS

Archer, Jules, *You Can't Do That to Me: Famous Fights for Human Rights,* Macmillan. Americans who fought for rights.

Colman, Warren, *The Bill of Rights,* Children's Press. Short, easy-to-read overview of the first ten amendments to the U.S. Constitution.

Gordon, Dorothy, *You and Democracy,* Dutton. Discusses the advantages of living in a nation in which people are free.

Lawson, Don, *The Changing Face of the Constitution,* Franklin Watts. Explains how the Constitution has been amended and interpreted to extend civil rights.

MULTIMEDIA RESOURCES

The Amendments (f, VHS, c, 19 min.), COR/MTI. Examines how constitutional amendments became law and the impact they have had.

The Bill of Rights in Action: Due Process of Law (f, c, 23 min.), IU. Presents opposing interpretations of the due process clause of the Fifth Amendment.

The Bill of Rights in Action: Freedom of Speech (f, c, 20 min.), IU. Discusses whether free speech is an absolute or should be controlled when it threatens law and order.

The Bill of Rights Today: The 4th Amendment (VHS, c, 18 min.), BARR. Cases related to an antidrug campaign reveal issues related to the Fourth Amendment.

Susan B. Anthony (f, b&w, 19 min.), IU. Depicts the story of Susan B. Anthony's efforts in establishing the vote for women.

THE INTERNET

Have students use these search words to locate more information about chapter topics on the Internet: *Bill of Rights, Constitution, voter participation.*

 GLOBAL SKILL BUILDER

You might wish to use **Navigating the Internet** from the interactive *Global Skill Builder* CD-ROM to aid students' understanding of the Internet as a resource.

Abbreviations: b&w=black and white; c=color; f=film; fs=filmstrip; sd=sound; tr=transparency; VHS=videotape

AMERICAN GOVERNMENT

☆ **Living in a Diverse Society** Students will learn the ways in which amendments to the Constitution have extended civil and voting rights to various groups of Americans.

CIVICS SKILLS

Students will learn how to interpret information in a bar graph. They will also learn terms important to understanding their constitutional and civil rights.

CITIZENSHIP VALUES

☆ **Rights and Responsibilities** Students will learn the important duties and responsibilities of citizenship. Students will be encouraged to value the Bill of Rights and the many freedoms it protects, and to appreciate that the United States has over time brought more groups into active citizenship through the extension of civil and voting rights.

MEETING INDIVIDUAL NEEDS

LIMITED ENGLISH PROFICIENCY (LEP)

Pair each LEP student with an English-proficient student. Have them examine and interpret each photograph in the chapter. They should read any signs or other written matter in each photograph and verbalize the action or content. For each photograph, the pair should produce a written description of what they see—a listing of the elements of the photograph and a statement of what seems to be going on, in the context of a chapter on citizenship.

LEARNERS HAVING DIFFICULTY

Review Chapter 4 by writing on the chalkboard the open-ended question "Why is it important that . . . ?" For each amendment or duty of citizenship that you wish to review, ask students to complete that question. For example, for the First Amendment, students might ask: Why is it important that Americans have the right to free speech? Students should complete the activity by answering each question.

AUDITORY LEARNERS

Ask an attorney to visit your class to discuss how the amendments introduced in Section 2 have influenced Americans' civil rights. Before the speaker arrives, students should prepare a list of appropriate questions. You might also wish to have copies of the amendments available for reference.

VISUAL LEARNERS

Have students bring old newspapers and newsmagazines to class. Have them find one or more articles dealing with the rights of citizens. Display the articles on a bulletin board. Students should label their articles with the constitutional amendment(s) relevant to the issues involved. Have students discuss how the rights found in the stories are protected.

TACTILE/KINESTHETIC LEARNERS

Have students role-play an important aspect of citizenship. They might choose one of the duties or responsibilities of citizenship described in the text, or think of other aspects from their daily lives. They might present their role-play with a written script or with no dialogue at all. Students might role-play taking part in a civic or political activity such as a rally or speech. The rest of the class should be prepared to discuss the presentation.

GIFTED LEARNERS

Have students conduct research on the history of free public education in the United States and write a paper on the reasons that attending school is a duty of citizenship. Encourage students to take a creative approach to the presentation of this information. They might focus on biographical material, for example, or case studies. Invite volunteers to present their research to the class for discussion.

Chapter 4 takes a close look at the Bill of Rights and at later amendments that extended the civil rights of Americans. The chapter also examines the duties and responsibilities required to maintain citizens' rights and freedoms. The underlying theme of the chapter is that citizens must accept the responsibilities as well as the privileges of freedom.

Motivator

Divide the class into three or four groups. Remind them that the states ratified the Constitution only when assured that a list of the rights of the people would be added. Ask each group to create a list of 10 rights they believe are important. Compare lists to find the 10 rights mentioned most often. Write that final list on the chalkboard for later reference. Conduct a class vote to see whether or not a three-fourths majority of students would support all of the rights listed on the board.

CHAPTER OBJECTIVES

After studying Chapter 4, students should be able to do the following.

1. Describe the Bill of Rights and explain its significance.
2. Understand how the Constitution has changed over time to better guarantee citizens' rights.
3. Identify the duties and responsibilities of U.S. citizens.

SIMULATIONS AND CASE STUDIES

Lesson 3: Illustrating the Amendments

Block Scheduling Option

CHAPTER 4

Rights and Responsibilities

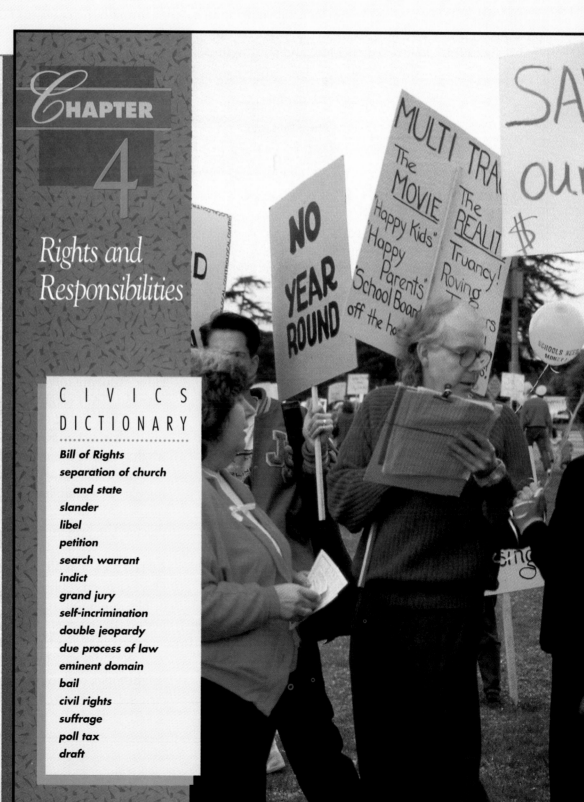

CIVICS DICTIONARY

Bill of Rights
separation of church and state
slander
libel
petition
search warrant
indict
grand jury
self-incrimination
double jeopardy
due process of law
eminent domain
bail
civil rights
suffrage
poll tax
draft

After studying Section 1, students should be able to do the following.

1. Describe the Bill of Rights.

2. Explain the reasons why the Bill of Rights was added to the Constitution.

3. Name the rights guaranteed by the first 10 amendments to the Constitution.

Teaching Section 1

Building a Vocabulary

To help students remember the difference between **libel** and **slander**, explain that there are many words that have the same root as or are similar to *libel*. *Liber* (in Latin) and *libro* (in Spanish) mean "book." We find written material in a *lib*rary. Tell students that these word associations will help them remember that libel is written, while slander is spoken. Ask students to suggest similar word associations and roots for other vocabulary words in this section.

CHAPTER FOCUS

Do you know how many years, months, and days are left until your 18th birthday? That time represents the countdown to the day you will receive the right to vote. Why is this day so important? From that day on, you can participate fully in your government. You can vote on important issues and help elect the nation's leaders.

Voting is only one of the many rights guaranteed to U.S. citizens. We have the right to express our ideas both in speech and in writing. We have the right to live in any city or state in the nation. We have the right to own property. Each of these rights, along with many others, is protected by the Constitution.

As a U.S. citizen, you share these rights with all other Americans. You must realize, however, that in exchange for your rights, you have certain responsibilities. For example, in exchange for the right to a free education, you have the responsibility to learn all that you can. Appreciating your rights and fulfilling your responsibilities will help you become a good citizen.

. . . .

STUDY GUIDE

● What is the Bill of Rights, and why is it important?

● How has the Constitution changed over time to better guarantee our rights?

● What are my duties and responsibilities as a U.S. citizen?

1 The Bill of Rights

Most of the framers of the Constitution believed that the safeguards written into that document would protect the rights of Americans. When the Constitution was sent to the states in 1787 for ratification, however, many Americans wanted a bill, or list, of rights added to the Constitution. A number of states ratified the Constitution only on the condition that a bill of rights would be added.

Two years after the new American government went into effect, the **Bill of Rights** was added as the first 10 amendments to the Constitution. Congress discussed nearly 200 proposals for amendments before it presented these 10 to the states for approval. The states ratified these amendments, and they became part of the U.S. Constitution in 1791. (See pages 541–542.)

The First Amendment

The rights described in the First Amendment of the Constitution are probably the most familiar to us because they are so close to our daily lives. First Amendment rights are basic rights that are essential to a free people.

Freedom of Religion The first right, or freedom, guaranteed in the Bill of Rights is freedom of religion. This freedom guarantees Americans the right to practice any religion, or to practice no religion at all.

The First Amendment forbids Congress from establishing an official national religion, or from favoring one religion in any way. This division between religion and government is known as the **separation of church and state**.

Like all rights in the Bill of Rights, freedom of religion had its origins in colonial times. As you know, several colonies were established mainly by settlers seeking the freedom to practice their religion. This right eventually was guaranteed to all Americans by the First Amendment.

GLOBAL PERSPECTIVES

The United States is not the only nation with a "Bill of Rights" that guarantees the basic rights of its citizens. As students read earlier, delegates at the Constitutional Convention were influenced by the English Bill of Rights. The French government, its society convulsed by revolution, passed the Rights of Man and of the Citizen in 1789. The Canadian Charter of Rights and Freedoms also guarantees basic rights. In 1948 the United Nations General Assembly adopted the Universal Declaration of Human Rights, which proclaims itself "as a common standard of achievement for all peoples and all nations."

Circulating a Petition

Create a petition, with the text of the First Amendment at the top and lines underneath for signatures. Organize the class into small groups, and give each group a copy of the petition. Petitions in hand, the groups should seek signatures of other students and faculty during their lunch period or after school, not identifying the text as the First Amendment. They should keep track of how many people support the petition and how many oppose it. Have students ask petition signers why they think these rights are important. Discuss the results with the class.

COOPERATIVE LEARNING

Organize the class into small groups. Have the members of each group choose which amendment they believe is the most important of the first 10 amendments. Then have one member of each group briefly research the amendment's history and another member provide real-life examples involving the amendment's guaranteed rights. One member should serve as a secretary to record the group's arguments that this amendment is the most important one in the Bill of Rights. Other members should present the group's arguments to the class for discussion and debate.

CIVICS SIDELIGHT

In 1977 the National Socialist Party of America, a neo-Nazi group, wanted to hold a "white supremacy" rally in Skokie, Illinois. Skokie, a suburb of Chicago, is home to some 7,000 Jewish survivors of Nazi concentration camps. Town officials tried to block the rally, and the state courts backed their decision. The U.S. Supreme Court disagreed. In a 5–4 ruling, the Court said the ban was unconstitutional on grounds of the First Amendment, which guarantees the freedom of speech. As former Justice Oliver Wendell Holmes once wrote, the Constitution protects not only "free thought for those who agree with us but freedom for the thought that we hate."

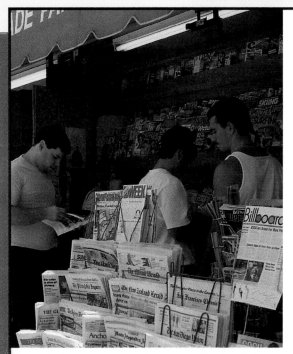

A trip to any newsstand in your neighborhood gives evidence of the freedom of the press guaranteed by the First Amendment.

Freedom of Speech The right to express ideas and opinions through speech is called freedom of speech. Freedom of speech also means the right to listen to the ideas and opinions of others. This freedom guarantees that Americans are free to express their thoughts and ideas. We may talk freely to friends and neighbors or deliver a speech in public to a group of people.

The First Amendment guarantees Americans the right to express opinions about the government and to criticize the actions of government officials. In contrast, people living under a totalitarian government have no right to speak freely. If they criticize the actions of the government, they may be punished.

Of course, people cannot use their right to freedom of speech to injure others. People do not have the right to tell lies or to spread false rumors about others. If they do, they may be sued in court for **slander**, or knowingly making false statements that hurt another person's reputation.

Furthermore, the right of free speech cannot be exercised in a way that might cause physical harm to others. A person does not have the right to call out "Fire!" in a crowded room just to see what might happen. Such an action could cause panic, and many people could be injured in the rush to escape.

In other words, like all freedoms, the right of free speech is not an absolute freedom. There are limits based on the rights of others and on what is good for all.

Freedom of the Press The freedom to express ideas in writing is freedom of the press. This freedom is closely related to freedom of speech and is also guaranteed by the First Amendment.

Americans struggled in colonial times for this important right. At that time newspapers were forbidden to criticize the government or public officials. An important court case, however, increased the freedom of the press.

A printer named John Peter Zenger was arrested and jailed in 1734 for publishing newspaper articles that criticized the royal governor of New York. According to the law, Zenger was guilty even if what he had written were true. The jury, however, found Zenger not guilty. The jury agreed that writing the truth was not a crime.

Freedom of the press gives all Americans the right to express their thoughts freely in writing, provided they do not state falsehoods that damage a person's reputation. If they do, they may be sued for **libel**.

The courts have decided that freedom of the press applies to electronic media as well as to written works such as books. Thus, television and radio broadcasts also are protected under the First Amendment.

Freedom of Assembly Another of the priceless freedoms guaranteed by the First Amendment is freedom of assembly, or freedom to hold meetings. Americans are free to meet to discuss problems and plan actions.

Guided Practice

Lead a class discussion about real-life situations in which various freedoms guaranteed in the Bill of Rights affect teenagers specifically. On the chalkboard, write such situations for each of the first 10 amendments. For example, students might discuss how freedom of the press affects their activities in working on the school newspaper. Students might also discuss how the freedoms of speech and of petition protect their right to have their concerns heard by their student government.

Independent Practice

Have students exercise their freedom of petition by writing letters to school officials about issues important to them (such as cafeteria hours, school dances, or dress codes). You might have volunteers read their letters to the class. Then have students vote on the issue most important to them and have them circulate a petition about it.

They can gather to express their views about government decisions. Of course, such meetings must be peaceful.

Freedom of Petition The right to ask the government to do something or stop doing something is freedom of petition. A **petition** is a formal request. The First Amendment contains this guarantee. Freedom of petition gives you the right to contact your representatives in Congress and ask them to pass laws you favor. You are similarly free to ask your representatives to change laws you do not like. The right of petition helps government officials learn what citizens want done.

The Second Amendment

During the colonial period, Americans organized militias, or volunteer armies, to defend their communities. These militias played an important part in the American Revolution.

Later, in the early years of the nation, Americans needed weapons to serve in the militias that were established to defend the states. The militias also provided protection during emergencies. Many Americans believed that, without weapons, they would be powerless if the government tried to overstep its powers and rule by force. For these reasons, the Second Amendment to the Constitution gives Americans the right to bear arms.

Today, because of the increase of crime in the United States, gun control is widely debated. Some people demand that guns be regulated. They say that gun control laws would lower the crime rate. Other people argue that the Second Amendment prevents the government from passing laws that limit the right to bear arms. (See "Case Study: Gun Control" on pages 104–105.)

The Third Amendment

The Third Amendment states that the government cannot force Americans to quarter, or give housing to, soldiers in peacetime. Under British rule, the colonists were sometimes forced to house and feed British soldiers. As a result, Americans wanted a "no quartering" right in the Bill of Rights.

The Fourth Amendment

The Fourth Amendment protects people from unreasonable searches and seizures. This means that in most cases our persons or property cannot be searched and our property cannot be taken from us by the government.

A search is considered reasonable, however, if a judge has issued a **search warrant**—a legal document that describes the place to be searched and the persons or things to be seized. A search warrant can be issued only if there is good reason to believe that evidence about a crime will be found.

The Fifth Amendment

The Fifth Amendment contains several provisions protecting the rights of a person accused of a crime. Before a person can be brought to

(continued on page 56)

These citizens are attending a town meeting in Gloucester, Massachusetts, to give their views and to listen to the views of other citizens.

CIVICS SIDELIGHT

The right to privacy inherent in the Fourth Amendment does not prevent school principals or teachers from searching a student's locker if they have reasonable grounds to suspect a violation of law or school regulations. The key word, according to the Supreme Court, is *reasonable*. School authorities do not need a search warrant or have to show probable cause, but they cannot act unreasonably.

Illustrating Ideas

Draw a flowchart on the chalkboard to show the sequence of events at Gallaudet University in 1988. Have students recount the action that launched the protests, the form protest took, and its results. Isolate each event in a box, and draw an arrow connecting one box to the next in the sequence. Have a volunteer use the graphic organizer to tell the story in his or her own words.

MULTICULTURAL PERSPECTIVES

The actions of the students at Gallaudet University fueled the fires of an ongoing debate among the nation's deaf and hearing-impaired citizens. Some of these citizens believe that deaf and hearing-impaired people should make efforts to use speech and lip-reading for communication. They are also in favor of cochlear implants, devices surgically set into the ear that may enhance hearing. Other people, however, believe that deaf people have their own culture, much like some other minority groups. As such, these people are opposed to any devices or styles of communication that attempt to "fix" deaf people and make them more like hearing people. They further assert that sign language and finger spelling allow them to communicate among themselves without difficulty and that hearing people should make efforts to learn their language.

Case STUDY

GALLAUDET UNIVERSITY

The freedom of Americans to express ideas and opinions is a priceless right guaranteed by the First Amendment. This right allows us not only to express our thoughts freely, but also to question actions we believe to be wrong or unfair. It lets us propose new actions we consider to be right and fair. Students at Gallaudet (gal-uh-DEHT) University in Washington, D.C., exercised their constitutional right to free speech and, in so doing, changed one of the school's long-standing traditions.

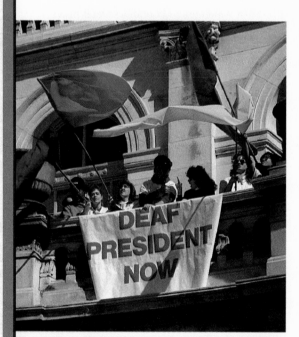

The slogan "Deaf President Now" expressed the goal of the Gallaudet students to have a president who would serve as their role model.

A Surprising Decision

Gallaudet University, founded in 1864, is the only liberal arts university for deaf people in the world. Known for its excellent teaching, Gallaudet has trained approximately 95 percent of the nation's hearing-impaired professionals. Until 1988, however, Gallaudet, whose 2,100 students are all hearing impaired, had never had a deaf president.

The long-standing practice of appointing only hearing presidents came under fire when the university's board of trustees had to choose a new president in 1988. Since two of the candidates for the position were hearing impaired, the students eagerly anticipated the historic moment when a deaf person would be chosen to lead the university.

This moment was not to be, however. Students and faculty were shocked to learn that the trustees had chosen a hearing person for the university's highest position. Their shock turned to outrage when it became clear that the new president had no experience in educating the deaf. Moreover, the new president did not know sign language—the only language used by most of the students at the university.

The Protests Begin

Protests over the decision erupted within minutes of the announcement. The students argued that, by choosing a hearing person to lead a university for the deaf, the trustees had sent the message that people with disabilities need able-bodied people to take care of them.

The students wanted a president who would serve as a role model. They wanted a president who would show the rest of the nation that people with disabilities are entitled

The First Amendment right to free speech helped the Gallaudet students change a long-standing practice.

to the same freedom of opportunity granted to all Americans. They wanted a president who, like themselves, was hearing impaired.

"Deaf President Now"

For four long days the students waged their peaceful but active protests. They blocked the gates of the university and marched on the White House, located only one mile (1.6 km) from the school. Many chanted slogans that they themselves could not hear. Most used sign language to communicate their outrage. Colorful banners and posters expressed the students' demand, summed up by the simple phrase "Deaf President Now."

Faced with this outcry, the new president resigned on the fourth day of the protests. Soon after, the board of trustees appointed a hearing-impaired person as president. The students had won their fight, and they had struck a blow for the rights of people with disabilities everywhere. Most important, they had proved the value—and power—of free speech.

Protecting the Freedom of Speech

Freedom of speech is essential to a democracy. Only when citizens are free to express them-selves can a government truly reflect the wants and needs of the people. Benjamin Franklin knew this. He said, "Whoever would overthrow the liberty of a nation must begin by subduing the freeness of speech. . . ." The students of Gallaudet also recognized the importance of this priceless right. To protect democracy, we must all guard our First Amendment right to free speech.

YOU DECIDE

1. What was the decision made by the university's board of trustees? Why did the Gallaudet students protest this decision?
2. How did the students make their concerns known?
3. What was the result of the students' actions?
4. Conduct library research to find another case in which students used their freedom of speech to bring about change. Summarize the case to share with the rest of the class.

Closure

Have students compare the Bill of Rights with the list of 10 rights that the class created in the "Motivator" activity on page 50. Discuss the differences, and have volunteers come to the board to create a chart with the 10 amendments of the Bill of Rights listed in one column and the class's 10 rights listed in a second column. Have students discuss which list best covers the most important rights of citizens.

Reviewing

Have students complete the Section 1 Review.

Reteaching

Assign Section 1 of the Chapter 4 Reteaching Worksheet.

An overhead transparency of "Freedoms Guaranteed by the Bill of Rights" is available in *Teaching Transparencies with Teacher's Notes.*

CIVICS SIDELIGHT

The Fifth Amendment protection against self-incrimination is associated with the words "I take the Fifth." Usually, the defendant in a criminal investigation "pleads the Fifth" in order to avoid revealing potentially damaging information. This plea is not an admission of guilt. But outside of the courtroom, in popular jargon, the phrase has come to mean, to some people, "I'm guilty, but I'm not going to admit it." You might discuss with students the importance of not necessarily associating silence with evidence of guilt.

Freedoms Guaranteed by the Bill of Rights

Freedom of Religion
- Freedom of worship
- Freedom to belong to any religion, or to none
- No official religion may be established.

Right to Equal Justice
- All persons accused of a crime must receive fair and equal treatment in a court of law.

Freedom of Assembly
- Freedom to hold meetings
- Meetings must be peaceful and obey local laws.

Freedom of the Press
- Freedom to print books, newspapers, and magazines
- No one may print falsehoods or writings that harm citizens.

Right to Freedom and Security
- No unlawful search may be made of homes or persons.
- Right to bear arms
- No troops may be stationed in citizens' homes.

Freedom of Petition
- Freedom to urge the government to pass laws
- Freedom to ask the government to take certain actions

Freedom of Speech
- Freedom to express ideas and opinions
- No one may use this freedom to speak falsely in order to harm or injure other citizens.

trial, he or she must be **indicted**, or formally accused of a crime, by a **grand jury**. The grand jury decides if there is enough evidence to go to trial. This system protects an accused person from hasty government action.

The Fifth Amendment also protects an accused person against **self-incrimination**, or having to testify against oneself. Furthermore, it protects people from **double jeopardy**. This means that a person cannot be tried a second time for the same crime.

Another Fifth Amendment protection states that no person can be denied life, liberty, or property without **due process of law**. This means that a person can be punished for a crime only after receiving a fair trial.

The last clause of the Fifth Amendment guarantees all Americans the right to own private property. It states that the government cannot take private property for public use without paying a fair price for it. For example, if the government needs to build a road or a school, property owners may have to give up their property to make way for a public need. The government, however, must pay a fair price for the property.

The government's power to take citizens' private property for public use is known as

Have students read the Ninth Amendment and write essays discussing how this amendment further establishes the flexibility of the Constitution. Students might name other basic rights and freedoms that are not specified in the Bill of Rights or the rest of the Constitution. Invite volunteers to discuss their essays with the class.

eminent domain. Property may be taken only for the public good and with just compensation to the property owner.

The right to own private property is one of the nation's basic freedoms. The U.S. economic system is based on this right.

The Sixth and Seventh Amendments

The Sixth Amendment guarantees a person accused of a crime the right to a prompt, public trial by a jury. Accused people must be informed of the crimes they are charged with committing. They also have the right to hear and question all witnesses against them and to call witnesses to appear in court.

The Sixth Amendment also guarantees a person accused of a crime the right to have the help of a lawyer. The Supreme Court has ruled that if an accused person cannot afford to hire a lawyer, one will be provided by the courts. The government pays the lawyer's fee.

The Seventh Amendment provides for a trial by jury in certain kinds of cases that involve conflicts over money or property.

The Eighth Amendment

The Eighth Amendment states that the court cannot set bail that is excessive, or too high. **Bail** is the money or property an accused person gives a court to hold as a guarantee that he or she will appear for trial. After the bail is paid, the accused person can leave jail. The bail is returned to the accused after the trial.

The Eighth Amendment also forbids "cruel and unusual" punishment. The exact meaning of what is "cruel and unusual" has been debated for a long time.

The Ninth Amendment

The writers of the Bill of Rights did not want to imply that the people had only those rights that are specifically mentioned in the Constitution and in the first eight amendments. To ensure that Americans would enjoy every right and freedom possible, they added the Ninth Amendment. This amendment states that the people of the United States enjoy many other basic rights that are not listed in the Constitution. These rights are as important as those that are mentioned in the Constitution. Among these rights are the freedoms to

- live or travel anywhere in the nation,
- work at any job for which we qualify,
- marry and raise a family,
- receive a free education in public schools, and
- join a political party, a union, and other legal groups.

The Tenth Amendment

As a final guarantee of citizen rights, the Tenth Amendment sets aside, or reserves, many powers of government for the states or for the people. This amendment states that all powers not expressly given to the federal government or forbidden to the states by the Constitution are reserved for the states or for the people. This provision gives the states the power to act to guarantee the rights of citizens.

SECTION 1 REVIEW

1. Define or identify the following terms: Bill of Rights, separation of church and state, slander, libel, petition, search warrant, indict, grand jury, self-incrimination, double jeopardy, due process of law, eminent domain, bail.

2. What is the Bill of Rights, and why was it added to the Constitution?

3. What rights are guaranteed by the First Amendment?

4. What rights are guaranteed to a person accused of a crime?

5. What is the purpose of the Ninth Amendment?

SECTION 1 REVIEW ANSWERS

1. See the following pages: Bill of Rights, separation of church and state (p. 51); slander, libel (p. 52); petition, search warrant (p. 53); indict, grand jury, self-incrimination, double jeopardy, due process of law (p. 56); eminent domain, bail (p. 57).

2. first 10 amendments; many states ratified Constitution on the condition that a bill of rights be added

3. freedoms of religion, speech, press, assembly, and petition

4. cannot go to trial unless indicted by grand jury; right to due process of law; protections against self-incrimination and double jeopardy; rights to silence, to speedy trial, to hear charges, to question witnesses, to have lawyer, to trial by jury; freedom from excessive bail and from cruel and unusual punishment

5. ensure Americans enjoy every possible right and freedom

6. Answers might include writing letters to the editor, petitioning government, organizing protesters, and carrying signs.

After studying Section 2, students should be able to do the following.

1. Explain why the Thirteenth and Fourteenth Amendments are called the "Civil War Amendments," and describe how these amendments extended civil rights.

2. Identify the amendments that extended the voting rights of Americans.

Civil is related to *civics* or *citizen*. All Americans have **civil rights**, the rights and privileges of a citizen. Tell them that one of the most important civil rights is **suffrage**, which comes from a Latin word that means "political support." Ask students what they think the civil right of suffrage is. *(the right to vote)* Then tell them that poor people, especially African Americans, were once deprived of their right to vote because of the **poll tax**. Have students analyze this term to determine its meaning. *(a tax on voting)*

MULTICULTURAL PERSPECTIVES

Shortly after the Civil War, former slaves from North Carolina petitioned President Andrew Johnson for measures that would guarantee African Americans the right to vote. "Some of us are soldiers and have had the privilege of fighting for our country in this war. Since we have become Freemen, we begin to feel that we are men, and are anxious to show our countrymen that we can and will fit ourselves for the creditable discharge of the duties of citizenship. We want the privilege of voting." The Fifteenth Amendment, ratified in 1870, guaranteed African Americans the right to vote.

6. **THINKING CRITICALLY** Members of a "hate group" have used their First Amendment rights to gain permission for a parade in your community. Although you believe in the group's First Amendment rights, you strongly disagree with the group's views. Describe the various legal ways you can use *your* First Amendment rights to make your disagreement known.

2 Guaranteeing Other Rights

Since the passage of the Bill of Rights, other amendments have been added to the Constitution. These amendments were passed as changing conditions and changing beliefs in the country required changes in the government. Today the Constitution has a total of 27 amendments. Some of these amendments expanded the rights of U.S. citizens.

Extending Civil Rights

Rights guaranteed to all U.S. citizens are called **civil rights**. The Constitution, especially the Bill of Rights, is the foundation for civil rights in this nation. The protection of civil rights, however, was left largely to the individual states until after the Civil War. The Thirteenth and Fourteenth Amendments were added after the war to protect the rights of newly freed African Americans.

The Thirteenth Amendment The Thirteenth Amendment, ratified in 1865, outlawed slavery in the United States. President Abraham Lincoln had ordered an end to slavery in the Confederate states during the Civil War. But his order, the Emancipation

Women held marches and demonstrations for years before finally gaining the right to vote with the ratification of the Nineteenth Amendment in 1920.

Writing a Letter

Invite students to imagine that they lived during the period just after the Civil War. Have each student write a letter to a friend overseas explaining the necessity of passing the Thirteenth, Fourteenth, and Fifteenth Amendments. Each letter should explain what rights and principles are behind the amendments, why the amendments are necessary, and what effects the amendments will have on *all* Americans, including African Americans. Ask for volunteers to share their letters with the class.

COOPERATIVE LEARNING

Divide the class into small groups, and assign each group one of the amendments discussed in this section. Have them research the amendment's passage and prepare a dramatization of its adoption process. Each group member should portray one of the people in the process. Have each group present its dramatization to the class.

Proclamation, led to the freedom of very few slaves. (See page 553.) The Thirteenth Amendment officially ended slavery in all the states and in all lands governed by the United States.

The Fourteenth Amendment The Fourteenth Amendment, ratified in 1868, was intended mainly to protect the rights of African Americans. It contains important rights, however, for all the American people.

The first part of the amendment grants full citizenship to African Americans. Next the amendment says that no state can take away a citizen's "life, liberty, or property, without due process of law." Also, no state can deny citizens equal protection of laws. Thus the Fourteenth Amendment protects citizens against unfair actions by state governments, just as the Fifth Amendment protects citizens against unfair actions by the federal government.

Extending Voting Rights

One of the most important civil rights is **suffrage**, or the right to vote. The struggle to gain the right to vote for all Americans was not won easily. Voting rights are the subject of six amendments to the Constitution.

The Constitution at first made no mention of voting rights. It was left to the states to decide who could vote. Most states limited the vote to white males over the age of 21 who owned a certain amount of property. Some states allowed only those people who held certain religious beliefs to vote.

Gradually the states eliminated property and religious qualifications for voting. Between the late 1800s and the 1970s, amendments to the Constitution extended the right to vote to all U.S. citizens.

The Fifteenth Amendment African Americans were guaranteed the right to vote by the Fifteenth Amendment, ratified in 1870. It states that no person can be denied the right to vote because of race or color. In the late 1800s and early 1900s, however, many states, especially in the South, passed laws

GLOBAL CONNECTIONS

Women's Suffrage

American women were not the only women who struggled for the right to vote. Nor were they the first to achieve it. This distinction belongs to the women of New Zealand, who fought a years-long campaign for suffrage.

When a petition of signatures requesting women's suffrage was first sent to the New Zealand Parliament, the members laughed. It was not until suffragist Kate Sheppard presented the legislature with a 300-yard-long (274 m) petition, signed by almost one fourth of all New Zealand women, that the women were taken seriously.

In 1893 New Zealand became the first self-governing country to grant women suffrage. U.S. women struggling for this right used the New Zealand victory as proof against the widespread notion that "women didn't really want the vote." It would be years, however, before U.S. women, too, could vote.

that kept African Americans from voting. Finally, in the 1960s, Congress passed civil rights laws that truly established equal voting rights for African Americans.

The Seventeenth Amendment The right of eligible voters in a state to elect the state's U.S. senators was granted by the Seventeenth Amendment. Before this amendment was ratified in 1913, U.S. senators were chosen by members of the state legislatures.

CIVICS SIDELIGHT

New Jersey's first constitution said that "any person" with property worth a certain amount of money could vote. At first, not many women voted. Soon, however, their votes began to decide some close elections. As a result, the state's all-male legislature in 1807 took away women's right to vote. New Jersey women would not vote again until the Nineteenth Amendment was ratified—more than a century later.

Closure

Have students read the Seneca Falls Declaration (textbook page 552), noting the date and briefly discussing the points it makes. Ask: Do these points seem valid to you? Have a volunteer find the date of the Nineteenth Amendment, and then ask students why, in their opinion, it took so long for women to receive this particular civil right.

Reviewing

Have students complete the Section 2 Review.

Reteaching

Assign Section 2 of the Chapter 4 Reteaching Worksheet.

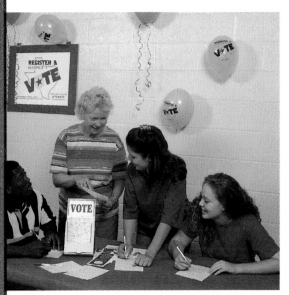

The young people here show their eagerness to take advantage of the Twenty-sixth Amendment. They are registering to cast their first votes in an election.

The Nineteenth Amendment American women were granted the right to vote with the Nineteenth Amendment. They won this right only after a long, hard struggle. It was led by such courageous women as Lucretia Mott, Elizabeth Cady Stanton, Susan B. Anthony, and Carrie Catt. They argued that women should not be treated as second-class citizens.

In 1869 Wyoming became the first state in the nation to give women the right to vote. Gradually other states began to grant the vote to women. The suffragists, those who fought for the right of women to vote, finally won their national struggle in 1920 when the Nineteenth Amendment was ratified.

The Twenty-third Amendment The Twenty-third Amendment, ratified in 1961, further extended citizen voting rights. It gave people living in the District of Columbia (Washington, D.C.) the right to vote for president and vice president. Before this amendment, residents of the District of Columbia could not vote in national elections.

The Twenty-fourth Amendment Beginning in the 1890s some states required all persons to pay a special tax, called a **poll tax**, to vote. Many Americans believed this tax was aimed at the poor, and especially at African Americans, to discourage them from voting. In 1964 the Twenty-fourth Amendment forbade the use of a poll tax as a qualification for voting in national elections. In 1966 the Supreme Court ruled that the poll tax is also unlawful in state elections.

The Twenty-sixth Amendment The right to vote was extended to another large group of Americans in 1971. In that year the Twenty-sixth Amendment lowered the voting age in national, state, and local elections to 18. Previously, most states had set 21 as the age at which people could vote for the first time. This amendment gave young Americans a greater voice in government.

SECTION 2 REVIEW

1. Define or identify the following terms: civil rights, suffrage, poll tax.

2. Why are the Thirteenth and Fourteenth Amendments called "Civil War Amendments"? How did these amendments extend civil rights?

3. Which amendments extended the voting rights of Americans?

4. **THINKING CRITICALLY** Create a chart entitled "Voting Rights for Americans." For each constitutional amendment that extended voting rights, indicate in the chart the year it was ratified and the group(s) that benefited from its ratification. Write a caption explaining how the extension of voting rights helped make the nation more democratic.

After studying Section 3, students should be able to do the following.

1. Explain the difference between a citizen's duties and a citizen's responsibilities.

2. Identify and explain five duties and five responsibilities of citizenship.

Teaching Section 3

Building a Vocabulary

Write the word **draft** on the chalkboard. Tell students that one meaning of *draft* is "to draw along or to pull [something] along." Explain that one can be drafted to perform a particular service, such as to run for political office or to serve in the armed forces.

3   *Citizen Duties and Responsibilities*

You have been learning about the rights that are guaranteed to all U.S. citizens. Along with these rights, citizens also have important duties and responsibilities.

Duties of Citizenship

Certain actions are the duty of all citizens. These duties are the *musts* of citizenship. That is, all U.S. citizens are required by law to perform these actions. The duties required of all citizens are described in the Constitution and in the laws of the nation and the states.

Most Americans are familiar with these duties of citizenship, but sometimes we forget how important they are. The success of our system of government depends on all citizens fulfilling these duties.

Obeying the Law One of the most important duties of citizenship is to obey the law. The U.S. system of government can work only if citizens respect and obey the laws. Of course, it is important to know what the laws are. For example, when you learn to drive a car, you must also learn the traffic laws. Ignorance of the law excuses no one.

Attending School One of the first duties of all Americans is to attend school. The nation places a high value on education. Free public schools guarantee all young Americans the opportunity to study and learn in order to develop their talents and abilities. Education also teaches the skills and knowledge needed to fulfill the duties and responsibilities of citizenship. To ensure freedom and the future of the nation, citizens must be educated.

Paying Taxes Another important duty of citizenship is to pay taxes. Taxes pay for the many different services provided by government. In paying taxes, citizens pay for police and fire protection, paved streets, schools, electricity, water, and countless other services. Tax money also pays for the costs of maintaining the nation's military defenses. The United States must be able to defend itself in order to protect the rights and freedoms of its citizens.

Serving in the Armed Forces As a citizen, you have a duty to help the nation if it is threatened. You may be called to help defend the nation by serving in the armed forces.

During several periods in its history, the United States has used a **draft**. That is, men were required to serve in the military. Since 1975 the United States has used only volunteers in the armed forces. Since 1980, however, 18-year-old men have had to register, or sign up, for military service. This process lets the government know the names and addresses of

These young Americans are aware that recreational areas are more enjoyable for all people when everyone respects and obeys the rules.

G LOBAL PERSPECTIVES

In most nations that draft their citizens into the armed forces, only men are called. But Israel, a small country surrounded by real and potential enemies, has required service by both men and women since its founding in 1948. China did the same, starting in 1949, but with so many young people available each year, the Chinese draft has since become highly selective.

Expressing a Point of View

Some citizens object to some of the *musts* or *shoulds* presented in the textbook, which is their right as citizens. Students can learn a lot by taking a contrary position. Have them write a position statement arguing *against* one of the duties or responsibilities discussed in the section. Students should be sure to explain their reasoning. Call on volunteers to present their statements to the class and answer any challenges to their arguments.

Guided Practice

Make a chart titled "Citizenship" on the chalkboard, with two column headings: *Duties* and *Responsibilities*. Have students provide a word or phrase to name each of the duties and responsibilities mentioned in the section. They might wish to add others. Then ask volunteers to tell why each one is important.

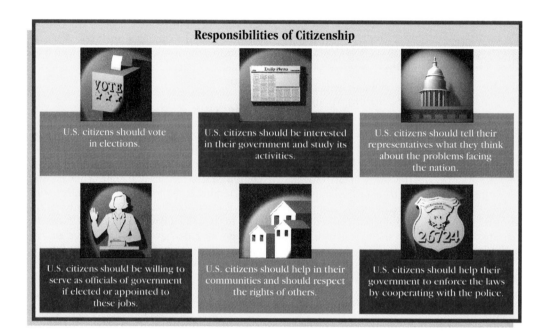

Responsibilities of Citizenship

U.S. citizens should vote in elections.

U.S. citizens should be interested in their government and study its activities.

U.S. citizens should tell their representatives what they think about the problems facing the nation.

U.S. citizens should be willing to serve as officials of government if elected or appointed to these jobs.

U.S. citizens should help in their communities and should respect the rights of others.

U.S. citizens should help their government to enforce the laws by cooperating with the police.

all men of draft age. Registration ensures that if a war or other crisis requires that the nation quickly expand its armed forces, the draft could be used again.

Appearing in Court Citizens must, if called, serve as members of a jury. Citizens must also testify in court if called as witnesses. Appearing in court can be inconvenient. Often we must take time off work to attend court. The right to a trial by jury, however, depends on citizens fulfilling their duty to serve on juries and appear as witnesses.

Responsibilities of Citizenship

In addition to the duties of citizenship, Americans have many responsibilities of citizenship. These responsibilities are the *shoulds* of citizenship. That is, although citizens are not required by law to carry out these actions, most Americans accept these responsibilities. They are important to the success of the nation and the well-being of the people.

Voting As you know, voting is one of the most important rights of U.S. citizens. Voting is also one of our most important responsibilities. By voting, each citizen plays a part in deciding who will be the leaders of government. Each voter also helps determine what actions the government will take because the people we elect plan the government's activities.

The vote of every citizen counts. Only by exercising the right to vote can citizens carry out the constitutional ideal of government by consent of the governed. Voting is one of the great privileges citizens of the nation have.

Being Informed To cast their votes wisely, citizens have a responsibility to be well informed. Education helps prepare citizens for this important responsibility.

Americans should take an active interest in the programs and activities of the government. They also should learn what policies are favored by each candidate running for office. Furthermore, Americans have a responsibility to tell their representatives what they think about public issues.

Closure

Have students compose a slogan or a rap that encourages Americans to accept the duties and responsibilities of citizenship. Have students present their creations to the class. The students should explain how their slogans or rap songs accomplish the assigned task.

Reviewing

Have students complete the Section 3 Review.

Reteaching

Assign Section 3 of the Chapter 4 Reteaching Worksheet.

Taking Part in Government Citizens should be involved in their government either as members of a political party or as independent voters. In addition, citizens should be willing to serve as officials of government if they are asked to serve by election or appointment to public office. The quality of any government depends on the quality of the people who serve in that government.

Helping Your Community One of the most important ways to be a responsible citizen is to take pride in your community and make sure that your community can take pride in you. For example, it is essential that all members of the community respect the property of others. Being careful not to litter, and even picking up after those who do, is an important part of citizenship.

It is also important to take an active part in the affairs of your community. Citizens should be willing to give their time to help improve their neighborhood, town, or city. People can volunteer their services and time at the library, for example. Cooperating with the police is another important way to help the community.

Respecting and Protecting Others' Rights The nation's success depends on the rights of citizens. You can play an important role in protecting these priceless rights. By knowing what rights all people share, you can be sure to respect those rights. You will also know when people's rights are being violated and can help protect those rights. All Americans must take part in defending human rights for the nation to truly have a "government of the people, by the people, for the people."

SECTION 3 REVIEW

1. Define the following term: draft.

2. What is the difference between a citizen's duties and a citizen's responsibilities?

3. Identify five duties and five responsibilities of citizenship.

4. THINKING CRITICALLY Create a Community Service Action Plan. First, identify a problem or issue in your community that needs to be addressed. Next, list the ways that citizens in the community can help to solve the problem. Then, describe how you will alert the community to the problem or issue and involve citizens, businesses, and local officials in solving it.

CHAPTER 4 SUMMARY

The Constitution has 27 amendments. The first 10 amendments, known as the Bill of Rights, clearly define the rights of all Americans. These amendments guarantee such priceless rights as freedom of speech, freedom of the press, freedom of assembly, freedom of religion, and the right to a speedy and fair trial by a jury.

The Ninth Amendment states that the rights listed in the Constitution are not the only rights held by the American people. The Tenth Amendment reserves to the state governments and to the people all powers not specifically given to the federal government by the Constitution.

Later amendments to the Constitution further expanded the rights of all Americans. The Thirteenth and Fourteenth Amendments protected the rights of the newly freed African Americans after the Civil War. Six other amendments to the Constitution expanded the voting rights of the American people.

Along with the rights and freedoms of U.S. citizenship come important duties and responsibilities. The nation can remain free and strong only if citizens respect and obey laws and carry out the other duties and responsibilities of citizenship.

SECTION 3 REVIEW ANSWERS

1. See the following page: draft (p. 61).

2. duties—required by law; responsibilities—necessary, but not required by law

3. duties—obeying the law, attending school, paying taxes, serving in the armed forces, appearing in court; responsibilities—voting, being informed, taking part in government, helping one's community, respecting and protecting others' rights

4. Plans will vary but should be realistic in scope and logically developed.

Point out to students that a bar graph compares two or more things at the same point in time. The bar graph on this page shows the participation of voters of different age groups in the November 3, 1992, election. You might ask students to locate the same data for the 1996 presidential election and for earlier presidential elections. Have them make bar graphs for each election to see whether there is a trend in voter participation by age. Ask students which age groups have historically been more or less likely to vote.

🌐 **GLOBAL SKILL BUILDER**

You might wish to use **Reading Graphs** and **Presenting Data Graphically** from the interactive *Global Skill Builder* CD-ROM to reinforce students' understanding of bar graphs and other types of graphs.

ANSWERS TO
Applying
the Skill

1. Voter participation rates increase with age. Some students might suggest that a candidate could slant his or her campaign to appeal to groups that have high voter participation rates.

2. Students' paragraphs should address the differences in voter participation rates between the various age groups. Students should note that the graph condenses data and facilitates comparisons.

64

Developing
Civics
Skills

SOCIAL STUDIES SKILL
Reading Bar Graphs

On November 3, 1992, more than 104 million Americans cast their votes for president. Although this sounds like an impressive figure, it represents only about 55 percent of the voting-age population.

How often have you heard statements such as the one above? If you are like most Americans, you probably encounter figures like these nearly every day. One effective way to make sense of this information is to use graphs.

Graphs are important tools for understanding data. A single graph can condense large amounts of written information into one easy-to-read diagram.

How to Read Bar Graphs

1. **Identify the type of graph.** The graph on this page is called a bar graph, because it uses bars to show amounts. Other graphs use different symbols, such as lines, pictures, or parts of circles to display data.
2. **Determine the subject.** Read the title of the graph to determine the subject and purpose of the graph.
3. **Study the labels.** Bar graphs usually have two labels. One label reads across the bottom of the graph. This label identifies the data on the line called the horizontal axis. Now look at the label that appears on top of the line running up and down. This line is called the vertical axis. What information is indicated by the label for the vertical axis? Studying the labels will help you understand the information presented in the graph.
4. **Analyze the data.** Compare the height of the bars in the graph. Use these bars to determine how the items or groups being compared on the horizontal axis differ.

5. **Put the data to use.** Use the data to draw conclusions about the subject of the graph.

Applying the Skill

Examine the bar graph below. Then answer the following questions.

1. What conclusions can you draw about the relationship between age and voter participation? How might a presidential candidate use the graph on this page?
2. Write a paragraph that summarizes the data presented in the bar graph. Which is more effective in describing the data—the bar graph or your paragraph? Explain your answer.

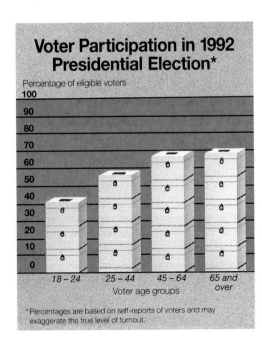

Voter Participation in 1992 Presidential Election*

Percentage of eligible voters

18 – 24 | 25 – 44 | 45 – 64 | 65 and over
Voter age groups

*Percentages are based on self-reports of voters and may exaggerate the true level of turnout.

Vocabulary Workshop
1. suffrage
2. libel—written false statements; slander—spoken false statements
3. bail
4. rights guaranteed to all citizens
5. search warrant

Reviewing Main Ideas
1. to win ratification
2. Some people believe gun regulation would reduce crime. Others believe gun regulation is unconstitutional.
3. 4th—no unreasonable searches and seizures; 5th—cannot go to trial unless indicted by grand jury, right to due process of law, right to silence, protection against self-incrimination, no double jeopardy; 6th—speedy trial, trial by jury, hear charges, question witnesses, have lawyer; 8th—no excessive bail or cruel and unusual punishment
4. to give Americans every right and freedom possible
5. 13th—outlawed slavery; 14th—citizenship for African Americans, due process rights, ensured equal protection under the law
6. 15th, 17th, 19th, 23rd, 24th, 26th
7. duties—obey laws, attend school, pay taxes, serve in military, appear in court; responsibilities—vote, be informed, take part in government, help community, respect and protect others' rights

Thinking Critically
1. Some students might point out that quartering of soldiers is still possible.
2. Students should use sound reasoning in their responses.
3. Students should support their responses.
4. A minority of people would make all decisions.

Citizenship in Your Community
Students should focus on voter participation.

BUILDING YOUR PORTFOLIO
Assign Portfolio Assessment Worksheet 4 in the *Portfolio Assessment Worksheets* booklet.

Assessment
- **Chapter 4 Tests**, *Chapter Tests* booklet
- **Test Generator**, Chapter 4
- **Portfolio**, Portfolio Assessment Worksheet 4, *Portfolio Assessment Worksheets* booklet

---

CHAPTER 4
R · e · v · i · e · w

Vocabulary Workshop
1. What is the term for the right to vote?
2. Distinguish between libel and slander.
3. What might an accused person have to give the court to hold as a guarantee that he or she will appear for trial?
4. Define the term *civil rights*.
5. What legal document describes a place to be searched and a person or things to be seized?

Reviewing Main Ideas
1. Why was the Bill of Rights added to the U.S. Constitution?
2. Why is the Second Amendment to the Constitution controversial?
3. Which amendments focus on the rights of people accused of crimes? What rights do these amendments guarantee?
4. Why was the Ninth Amendment included in the Bill of Rights?
5. How did the Thirteenth Amendment and the Fourteenth Amendment extend the civil rights of Americans?
6. Which amendments to the Constitution focus on voting rights?
7. What are the duties of citizenship? What are the responsibilities of citizenship?

Thinking Critically
1. Unlike most of the amendments contained in the Bill of Rights, the Third Amendment's "no quartering" rule has never been tested in a court of law. Because this amendment seems to be far removed from Americans' modern-day lives, should it be repealed? Why or why not?
2. There are some people who believe that capital punishment, or the death penalty, is "cruel and unusual." Do you agree or disagree? Explain your answer.
3. Which freedom in the Bill of Rights do you consider to be the most important, and why?
4. Voting is not required by law, but it is a responsibility of citizenship. Why might it be harmful for the nation if citizens did not fulfill this responsibility?

Citizenship in Your Community

Cooperative Project
With your group, research voter participation in your community. What percentage of the eligible voters in your community are registered to vote? Is voter participation highest in local, state, or national elections? Is participation increasing or decreasing? What is being done to encourage people to register and to vote? How can you and other teenagers become involved in this process? You might want to create charts and graphs to present the information you collect.

Building Your Portfolio

The fourth step of your unit portfolio project (see page 67) is to create a chart entitled "Student Rights and Responsibilities." In one column of the chart, list the rights to which you are entitled as a student in the U.S. educational system. In the second column list the responsibilities that accompany each of your rights. Then write a caption explaining why appreciating your rights and fulfilling your responsibilities help your school operate more effectively. Place your chart in your individual portfolio for later use.

UNIT 1 REVIEW
A N S W E R S

Reviewing Main Ideas

1. All Americans either came here from other lands or are descended from immigrants.
2. natural increase, addition of new territory, immigration
3. ideal of popular sovereignty from Mayflower Compact and ideals of freedoms from Magna Carta and English Bill of Rights
4. Great Compromise, under which states were given equal representation in the Senate and representation in the House according to population size
5. keep one person or group from becoming too powerful
6. form a more perfect union, establish justice, insure domestic tranquillity, provide for common defense, promote general welfare, secure blessings of liberty
7. duties—required by law; responsibilities—necessary, but not required by law

Thinking Critically

1. Citizens would not have rights and freedoms they now have.
2. It contains many provisions that protect the rights of the accused.
3. Thirteenth—outlawed slavery; Fourteenth—guaranteed equal protection under the law; Nineteenth—gave suffrage to women

Practicing Civics Skills

1. Flowcharts should show steps of naturalization procedure.
2. Washington's inauguration; Washington's hand on his heart, book he is touching, attention on Washington; Washington was respected and admired as a leader
3. Students should demonstrate an understanding of bar graphs and accurately graph the collected data.

Citizenship in Your Community

Reports should focus on volunteer groups.

Learning from Technology

Answers should include the advantages and disadvantages of learning about the Constitution in this way.

R·e·v·i·e·w

Reviewing Main Ideas

1. Why can it be said that the United States is a nation of immigrants?
2. What are the three ways in which a nation's population may grow?
3. How were the nation's founders influenced by the Mayflower Compact, the Magna Carta, and the English Bill of Rights?
4. How did the nation's founders settle the argument over representation in the U.S. legislature?
5. What is the purpose of the separation of government powers?
6. What are the six goals of government contained in the Preamble?
7. How do the duties of citizenship differ from the responsibilities of citizenship?

Thinking Critically

1. How do you think your life would be different from what it is today if you lived under a totalitarian government?
2. How does the Bill of Rights help ensure that people accused of crimes are "innocent until proven guilty"?
3. How did the Thirteenth Amendment and the Fourteenth Amendment affect the lives of African Americans? How did the Nineteenth Amendment affect the lives of American women?

Practicing Civics Skills

1. Draw a flowchart showing the steps involved in becoming a naturalized citizen.
2. Examine the painting on page 32 of your textbook. What event does the painting show? What details does the artist emphasize? What do you think the artist is trying to convey in the painting?

3. Conduct research to find the percentage of eligible voters that voted in presidential elections from 1972 to 1996. Use this information to create a bar graph showing trends in voter participation.

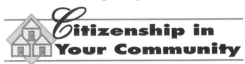

Citizenship in Your Community

Cooperative Project

With your group, contact your local Chamber of Commerce and City Hall to learn about volunteer groups in your community. Interview the representatives of one of the volunteer groups. What is the purpose of the group? How many members does the group have? How long has the group been in existence? What problems has the group encountered in trying to fulfill its goals? Present your findings to the class.

Learning from Technology

Virtual Reality

Virtual reality is a new technology that simulates the sights, sounds, and feel of real or imaginary events. Special goggles and gloves allow users to witness reenactments of events and interact with characters.

Imagine that you are using a virtual reality program that places you at the Constitutional Convention. You can talk to the delegates and view events as they unfold. What might be the advantages of using this form of technology to learn about the Convention? What might be the disadvantages? For example, would you consider answers from the "delegates" to be necessarily accurate? Would you rely on this technology as your sole source of information?

Individually or in a group, complete the following project to show your understanding of the civics concepts involved.

We the Students

In Unit 1 you have read about the nation's long tradition of democracy under a government established to serve the people. Imagine that you are the U.S. representative at an international conference on education. The other delegates at the conference represent nations that have governments other than a democracy.

Your job is to explain to the other delegates that education under a democratic system of government serves the needs of students and the nation. Your presentation to the delegates will consist of a report accompanied by visual materials. To prepare these materials, you will need to do the following.

1. Conduct research to learn about the history of your school. Use this information to draw a large illustrated time line showing how your school has changed over time, including changes in the number of students and teachers, changes in the ethnic makeup of the school population, curriculum changes, and how students have shown their school spirit. Title your time line "Our School: Then and Now."

2. Write a "Declaration of Education" statement. In your Declaration, express what you believe are the ideals of American education. Begin your Declaration of Education with the following phrase: "We, the American students, hold these truths to be self-evident. . . ." Your Declaration should then explain how your school upholds each of the educational ideals listed.

3. Create a chart entitled "The Three Branches of Education." Write the following headings across the top of your chart: Administration, Teachers, Students. Under each heading, answer the following questions. What are the primary duties of this branch? What responsibilities does this branch share with the other branches? How does this branch work with the other branches? Then write a caption explaining why cooperation among the branches of education is a vital part of the U.S. educational system.

4. Create a chart entitled "Student Rights and Responsibilities." In one column of the chart, list the rights to which you are entitled as a student in the U.S. educational system. In the second column list the responsibilities that accompany each of your rights. Then write a caption explaining why appreciating your rights and fulfilling your responsibilities help your school to operate more effectively.

Organize your materials, and make your presentation to the other conference delegates (the rest of the class).

THE FEDERAL GOVERNMENT

Using the Quotation

Tell students that each of the three branches of government has offices in a number of buildings in Washington, D.C. These buildings, as well as the memorials to former presidents, represent the federal government and the officials who have been a part of that government. Have students discuss the quotation, which speaks of the rights of the people to control their government and its institutions.

About the Author

Although Abraham Lincoln (1809–1865) championed the right of the people to choose their government, he insisted on the preservation of the Union formed by the people and their government. Lincoln was assassinated just days after the Confederate surrender at Appomattox Court House ensured the preservation of the Union.

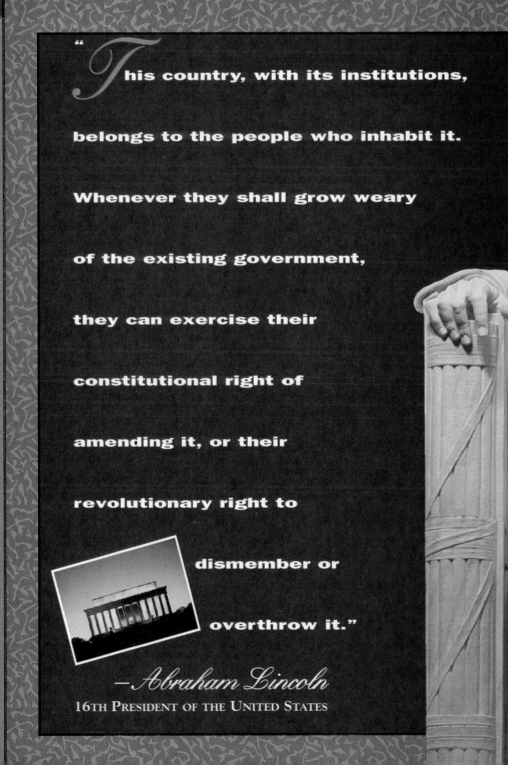

"This country, with its institutions, belongs to the people who inhabit it. Whenever they shall grow weary of the existing government, they can exercise their constitutional right of amending it, or their revolutionary right to dismember or overthrow it."

—*Abraham Lincoln*
16TH PRESIDENT OF THE UNITED STATES

Unit 2 provides a detailed study of our federal system of government and the machinery under which it operates. It also explains the functions and activities of each of the three branches of government: the legislative branch, the executive branch, and the judicial branch.

After studying Unit 2, students should be able to accomplish the following.

1. Explain the organization and powers of Congress.

2. Trace the process of how a bill becomes a law.

3. List the main powers and responsibilities of the president of the United States.

4. Discuss the roles played by the executive departments, the Cabinet, and independent agencies.

5. Identify the types of law found in the United States.

6. Describe the organization of the federal court system.

Block Scheduling Option

CIVICS VIDEOCASSETTE

Segment 2: Who Has the Power?

CIVICS VIDEODISC

Segment 2: Who Has the Power?

Segment 2, Side A

Search Chapter 2

Play   Pause

BUILDING YOUR PORTFOLIO

"Building Your Portfolio" on page 135 outlines a unit project for students to work on as they study Unit 2. The unit project is supported by materials in the *Portfolio Assessment Worksheets* booklet.

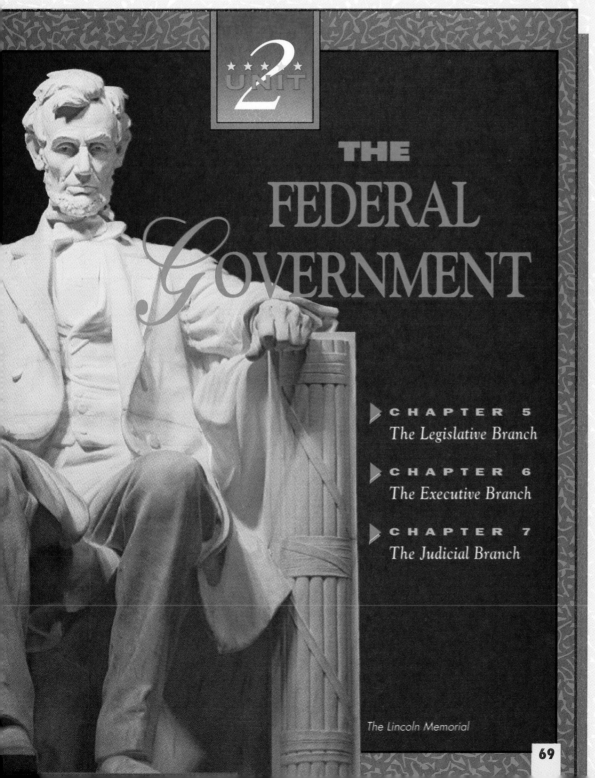

UNIT 2

THE FEDERAL GOVERNMENT

The Lincoln Memorial

CHAPTER 5

The Legislative Branch

TEXTBOOK	TEACHING RESOURCES	OTHER AVAILABLE RESOURCES
Chapter	• Skills Worksheet 5 • Challenge/Enrichment Worksheet 5	• Simulations and Case Studies Lesson 4
Section **1** Senate and House of Representatives Page 71	• Reteaching Worksheet 5.1	• Transparency 3: Congressional Representation After the 1990 Census Transparency 4: The Congress of the United States
2 How Congress Is Organized Page 75	• Reteaching Worksheet 5.2	
3 The Powers of Congress Page 79	• Reteaching Worksheet 5.3	
4 How a Bill Becomes a Law Page 84	• Reteaching Worksheet 5.4	• Transparency 5: How Ideas for Bills Begin
Review and Assessment Chapter 5 Review, Page 91	• Test, Form A • Test, Form B • Portfolio Assessment Worksheet 5	• *Test Generator*, Chapter 5

Block Scheduling Option

ADDITIONAL RESOURCES

BOOKS FOR TEACHERS

Barone, Michael, *The Almanac of American Politics* (biennial), National Journal.

Ferguson, John H., and Dean E. McHenry, *The American Federal Government*, McGraw-Hill.

Polsby, Nelson W., *Congress and the Presidency*, Prentice-Hall.

Price, David E., *The Congressional Experience: A View from the Hill*, Westview.

BOOKS FOR STUDENTS

How Congress Works, Congressional Quarterly. Studies the structure and operation of the legislative branch.

Kennedy, John F., *Profiles in Courage*, Harper & Row. This prize-winning book by President Kennedy includes the story of the senator who voted his conscience in the acquittal of Andrew Johnson.

MULTIMEDIA RESOURCES

A Day in the Life of Congress (VHS, c, 23 min.), SRA. Follows a member of Congress through a typical hectic day.

Focus on Government: Congress (VHS, c, 15 min.), CU. Students discuss Congress's roles and responsibilities.

Powers of the Congress (videodisc), COR/MTI. Studies Congress and the legislative process. (English/Spanish)

THE INTERNET

Have students use these search words to locate more information about chapter topics on the Internet: *United States Congress, House of Representatives, United States Senate, legislative branch.*

 GLOBAL SKILL BUILDER

You might wish to use **Navigating the Internet** from the interactive *Global Skill Builder* CD-ROM to aid students' understanding of the Internet as a resource.

Abbreviations: b&w=black and white; c=color; f=film; fs=filmstrip; sd=sound; tr=transparency; VHS=videotape

CIVICS SKILLS

Students will learn how to interpret political cartoons. They will also learn terms important to understanding the role of Congress in U.S. government and the process of making laws.

CITIZENSHIP VALUES

✷ **Rights and Responsibilities** Students will be encouraged to develop an interest in government, to appreciate the responsibilities of members of Congress, and to realize their own civic responsibility to communicate with their elected officials.

AMERICAN GOVERNMENT

✷ **Structures and Functions** Students will learn why the framers of the Constitution created a bicameral legislature, the basic organization of Congress, and the membership qualifications for both the House of Representatives and the Senate. They also will learn how the committee system in Congress works, the delegated and implied powers of Congress, the ways in which the powers of Congress are limited, and steps by which a bill becomes law.

MEETING INDIVIDUAL NEEDS

LIMITED ENGLISH PROFICIENCY (LEP)

Have pairs of students write lists of the constitutional powers of Congress. Then have the students find newspaper and magazine articles that illustrate each of the powers of Congress. Have the students present their examples to the class.

LEARNERS HAVING DIFFICULTY

Review the principle of checks and balances. Have students discuss how this principle applies to Congress. Ask: How does each house serve as a check on the other's power? Have students draw illustrations of checks and balances to support their responses.

AUDITORY LEARNERS

Have students listen to local news-radio programs or to a National Public Radio broadcast and take notes on national issues dominating the current session of Congress. Students should write newspaper headlines about these issues and their progress through Congress (such as, "Senator filibusters on gun bill"). Students should present and explain their headlines to the class.

VISUAL LEARNERS

Have students assign visual symbols to as many vocabulary terms for this chapter as they can. They should find terms that lend themselves to graphic representation. For example, *bicameral* might be symbolized by two houses within a diagram of the Capitol; *Speaker* might be symbolized by a politician in the shape of a loudspeaker. For each vocabulary term, students should draw the symbol, write the term, and define the term.

TACTILE/KINESTHETIC LEARNERS

Organize the class into five groups. Assign each group one of the five delegated powers of Congress. Have each group prepare a scene that deals with its assigned power. The power itself must not be mentioned. Have the groups perform their scenes in front of the class. Ask the students in the rest of the class to guess which power is being illustrated.

GIFTED LEARNERS

Have a group of students draw up an imaginary bill to provide trips to Washington, D.C., for civics students (or a bill that would accomplish some other worthy goal). Then divide the rest of the class into a number of groups representing various interests in Congress. Have the first group present its bill to each group for consideration. Each group must decide whether it will support the bill and then should explain its decision to the class.

CHAPTER OVERVIEW

Chapter 5 focuses on Congress. It examines the division of Congress into the Senate and the House of Representatives. Then it looks at how the two houses are organized and what powers they hold. The chapter concludes with an in-depth study of how a bill becomes a law. The underlying theme of the chapter is that Congress is the central institution of our representative democracy.

Motivator

Have students imagine that they have one of the most important jobs in government. They work long hours to help people, and they are paid well for their efforts. Ask students how they feel about this job. Now tell them that every two years they have to battle to keep their job for another two years. How do they feel now? *(like a member of the House of Representatives must feel)*

CHAPTER OBJECTIVES

After studying Chapter 5, students should be able to do the following.

1. Identify how many people serve in Congress.
2. List the qualifications one must have to become a member of Congress.
3. Tell how both houses of Congress are organized.
4. Identify the powers and limitations of Congress.
5. Explain the process by which a bill becomes a law.

SIMULATIONS AND CASE STUDIES

Lesson 4: Senate Subcommittee Hearing on Limiting Congressional Terms

Block Scheduling Option

CHAPTER 5

The Legislative Branch

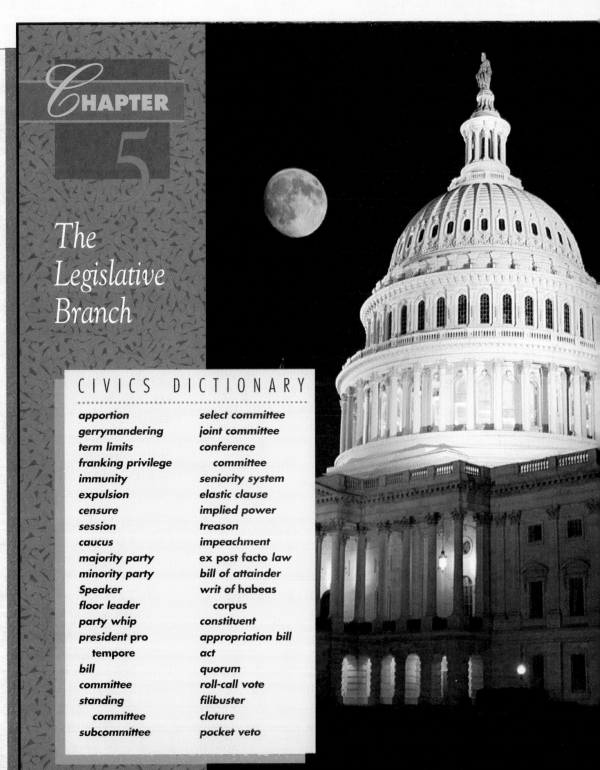

CIVICS DICTIONARY

apportion
gerrymandering
term limits
franking privilege
immunity
expulsion
censure
session
caucus
majority party
minority party
Speaker
floor leader
party whip
president pro tempore
bill
committee
standing committee
subcommittee

select committee
joint committee
conference committee
seniority system
elastic clause
implied power
treason
impeachment
ex post facto law
bill of attainder
writ of habeas corpus
constituent
appropriation bill
act
quorum
roll-call vote
filibuster
cloture
pocket veto

SECTION OBJECTIVES

After studying Section 1, students should be able to do the following.

1. Identify the number of members in the House and Senate and the length of term for members of each house.

2. Compare the qualifications and salaries of members of the House and Senate.

3. Explain the ways Congress deals with misconduct by its members.

Teaching Section 1
Building a Vocabulary

Have pairs of students create sets of flash cards, with a vocabulary term on the front of each card and a definition or descriptive illustration of the term on the back of the same card. Then have the students take turns quizzing each other with the flash cards until both students know the definition of each vocabulary term.

CHAPTER FOCUS

Do you remember where you were on January 3 of this year? Every year on that day in Washington, D.C., representatives, senators, clerks, and congressional staffs take their places in the Capitol Building for the start of a new session of Congress.

What is the role of the members of Congress during each session? Under the Constitution, it is the responsibility of the legislative branch to make the nation's laws. Thus Congress decides issues such as how large the U.S. armed forces will be and whether federal taxes will rise. Each session lawmakers make decisions that affect your life, your school, and your community.

● ●

STUDY GUIDE

● How many people serve in Congress, and what are their qualifications?

● How is Congress organized, and what are its powers and limitations?

● How does a bill become a law?

1 Senate and House of Representatives

As you know, the work of the federal government is divided among three separate branches—the legislative branch, the executive branch, and the judicial branch. The framers of the Constitution believed the legislative branch was so important that they discussed it first, in Article 1 of the Constitution.

Two Houses of Congress

The work of the legislative branch is carried out by the Congress of the United States. Congress is the lawmaking body of the federal government. The Constitution provides that the Congress shall be composed of two houses— the Senate and the House of Representatives.

The leaders who drew up the U.S. Constitution in 1787 had two main reasons for creating a lawmaking body of two houses, or a bicameral legislature. First, a lawmaking body of two houses would help to check and balance the work of this branch of the government. Having two houses to share the responsibility of making the nation's laws allows each house to check the actions of the other. As a result, there is less danger that Congress will pass laws in haste or pass laws that are not needed or wanted by the people.

Second, the framers established a bicameral legislature to settle a dispute between the large and the small states. As you have learned, the smaller states feared they would be dominated by the larger ones. The dispute was settled by the Great Compromise. It provided that the states be represented equally in the Senate and according to the size of their populations in the House of Representatives.

House of Representatives

The House of Representatives, or the House as it is often called, has 435 members. It is the larger of the two houses of Congress. Members of the House are called representatives. According to the Constitution, the number of representatives each state can elect to the House is based on the size of the state's population. Each state, regardless of its population size, is entitled to at least one representative.

Originally, each state elected one representative for every 30,000 people living in the state. In the first Congress, which met in 1789, there were 65 representatives in the House. Then, as new states joined the union and the

GLOBAL PERSPECTIVES

Bicameral legislatures are found in many countries with federal systems, such as Australia, Brazil, and Canada. In these federal systems, one house in the legislature often represents the interests of states or provinces in relation to the central government. In some countries with bicameral legislatures (but not necessarily federal systems of government), such as Japan, Canada, the United Kingdom, and France, one chamber of the legislature has considerably less authority than the other.

Illustrating Ideas

Have students cut construction paper into squares, assigning one square for each U.S. state. The size of each square should be in proportion to its state's congressional representation. The largest square represents California, for example. Then have students use the squares to construct a U.S. "map." Ask: Which states have the largest physical size? the largest representation in Congress?

Comparing Qualifications

Have pairs of students draw a two-column chart, each student taking one column. One student should list the qualifications of a member of the House of Representatives, the other, those of a Senator. Then have each pair use the chart to develop qualifications for student government representatives. Pairs should be able to explain the rationale behind their lists of qualifications. Call on volunteers to present their lists to the class.

CIVICS SIDELIGHT

State legislatures responsible for drawing the boundaries of congressional districts have often been accused of gerrymandering. The term is a cross between *Gerry* and *salamander*. In 1812 political opponents criticized (perhaps unfairly) Governor Elbridge Gerry of Massachusetts for the creative drawing of congressional district boundaries in a way that benefited his party. The bizarre shape of one congressional district reminded some observers of a salamander, called by some people a "Gerrymander."

CIVICS TRANSPARENCIES

An overhead transparency of "Congressional Representation After the 1990 Census" is available in *Teaching Transparencies with Teacher's Notes.*

nation's population increased, membership in the House grew. To prevent the membership from growing too large, in 1929 Congress limited the size of the House to 435 members. Today each member of the House represents on average more than 500,000 people.

How Membership Is Divided Every 10 years, after the census is taken, Congress determines how the 435 seats in the House are to be **apportioned**, or distributed. Congress itself divides these seats among the states according to population.

If a state's population decreases from one census to the next, the number of its representatives may be reduced. Likewise, states whose populations grow may be entitled to more representatives. The total size of the House, however, cannot be more than 435 members. The map on this page shows the number of representatives each state sends to the House as a result of the 1990 census.

Congressional Districts Each representative is elected from a congressional district. Each state legislature is responsible for dividing the state into as many congressional districts as it has members in the House. The boundaries must be drawn so that each district is nearly equal in population.

State legislators sometimes draw district lines that favor a particular party. This practice is called **gerrymandering**. For example, a state legislature made up mostly of Democrats might draw district lines that place Democratic voters in a majority in as many districts as possible. Gerrymandering often results in oddly shaped districts.

Electing Representatives Elections for members of the House of Representatives are held in November of each even-numbered year. All representatives are elected for two-year terms. If a representative dies or resigns before the end of a term, the governor of the representative's home state must call a special election to fill the vacancy.

Senate

The Senate is the smaller of the two houses of Congress. The Constitution provides that each

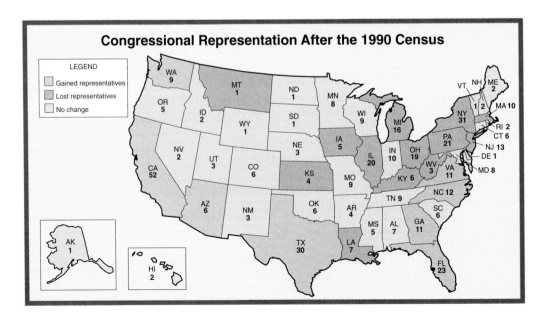

Congressional Representation After the 1990 Census

LEGEND
- Gained representatives
- Lost representatives
- No change

Help students complete a web diagram about good conduct. Write "Reasons for Good Conduct" in a circle on the board. Then call on volunteers to suggest reasons why society and its organizations require good conduct from their members. You might start by writing "fosters respect for other people" on one line radiating from the circle.

Have each student create a code of conduct for students, detailing duties and responsibilities, as well as punishments for violations. A preamble should explain the importance of the code. The codes can be in a variety of forms, including a brochure (from folded paper) or a booklet. Call on volunteers to share their codes with the class. You might have volunteers compare their codes with a conduct code developed by school officials.

state, regardless of size, be represented in the Senate by two members, or senators.

The first Senate consisted of 26 senators, representing the 13 original states. As the number of states in the United States increased, membership in the Senate grew. Today the Senate has 100 members—two senators elected from each of the 50 states. Each senator represents his or her entire state.

Senators are elected to Congress for six-year terms. Elections for senators, like those for representatives, are held in November of each even-numbered year. Only one third of the Senate's membership comes up for election every two years. Therefore, a new Senate begins its work with at least two thirds of the members having experience in the Senate.

The senator from each state who has served the longer period of time is the state's senior senator. If a senator dies or resigns before the end of a term of office, the governor of the state may appoint someone to fill the vacancy until the next regular election or until a special state election is held.

Recently, there has been a drive to limit the number of terms members of Congress can serve. In 1995, however, the Supreme Court ruled that such **term limits** are unconstitutional, because the Constitution reserves to the people the right to choose federal lawmakers.

Qualifications of Members

The Constitution lists the qualifications that members of Congress must meet. The following are qualifications for members of the House. A representative must

- be at least 25 years old,
- have been a U.S. citizen for at least seven years, and
- be a legal resident of the state he or she represents. (Usually a representative lives in the district from which he or she is elected. The Constitution does not, however, make this a requirement for office.)

The qualifications for members of the Senate differ slightly from those for members of the House. The Constitution lists the following qualifications for senators. A senator must

- be at least 30 years old,
- have been a U.S. citizen for at least nine years, and
- be a legal resident of the state he or she represents.

In addition to these qualifications, members of Congress traditionally have shared other characteristics. For example, they usually have had previous political experience, often in their state legislatures. Most members of Congress also have been active members of community and volunteer organizations.

Many members of Congress are lawyers, businesspeople, bankers, or educators. Senators tend to be older than representatives. In 1995, nearly half of the representatives were under the age of 50. In contrast, only 15 senators were under the age of 50.

Traditionally, most members of Congress have been white men. In recent years the number of women, African Americans, Hispanic Americans, Asian Americans, and Native Americans in Congress has increased. In 1995, for example, there were 47 women in the House and 8 women in the Senate. Forty African Americans served as representatives. However, the numbers of women and ethnic minorities in Congress remain far below their percentages in the population.

Salary and Benefits

Each member of Congress receives a yearly salary of $133,600. For years the power of Congress to set its own salary has been a matter of heated debate. In response to this debate, the Twenty-seventh Amendment to the Constitution was ratified in 1992. The amendment states that no increase in congressional pay can take effect until after the next congressional election. This condition allows voters to respond to the proposed increase.

All members of Congress have offices in the Capitol Building and receive an allowance to pay staff members. Members receive free

CIVICS SIDELIGHT

In January 1993 Congress changed its rules to allow delegates from the District of Columbia, Puerto Rico, Guam, American Samoa, and the U.S. Virgin Islands to have voting privileges in the House of Representatives, except for final votes on legislation. Previously, those delegates could participate only in committee work because they did not meet the constitutional requirement that legislators represent states. Proponents of the new rules argued that initial votes on legislation and amendments from the floor actually take place in the "committee of the whole"—the entire House.

Closure

Have students write help-wanted ads for the position of representative or senator. The ads should include job requirements and qualifications for the positions. Encourage students to be creative in their attempts to attract people to work in the Congress of the United States.

Reviewing

Have students complete the Section 1 Review.

Reteaching

Assign Section 1 of the Chapter 5 Reteaching Worksheet.

CIVICS TRANSPARENCIES

An overhead transparency of "The Congress of the United States" is available in *Teaching Transparencies with Teacher's Notes*.

SECTION 1 REVIEW
ANSWERS

1. See the following pages: apportion, gerrymandering (p. 72); term limits (p. 73); franking privilege, immunity, expulsion (p. 74); censure (p. 75).

2. 435; November of even-numbered years; 100; six years

3. House—at least 25 years old, citizen at least seven years, legal resident of the represented state; Senate—at least 30 years old, citizen at least nine years, legal resident of the represented state

4. $133,600; pay increase cannot go into effect until after intervening election

5. serious misconduct—expulsion from office; less serious misconduct—censure

6. Answers should include specific advantages or disadvantages of term limits.

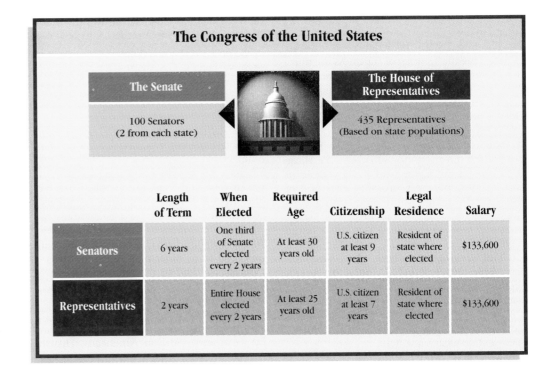

The Congress of the United States

The Senate		The House of Representatives
100 Senators (2 from each state)		435 Representatives (Based on state populations)

	Length of Term	When Elected	Required Age	Citizenship	Legal Residence	Salary
Senators	6 years	One third of Senate elected every 2 years	At least 30 years old	U.S. citizen at least 9 years	Resident of state where elected	$133,600
Representatives	2 years	Entire House elected every 2 years	At least 25 years old	U.S. citizen at least 7 years	Resident of state where elected	$133,600

trips to their home states, an allowance for local district offices, and a stationery allowance. In addition, they have the **franking privilege**—the right to mail official letters free of charge.

Members of Congress cannot be arrested when they are in Congress or are on their way to or from a meeting of Congress, unless they have committed a serious crime. This congressional **immunity**, or legal protection, ensures that no one can interfere needlessly with federal lawmakers as they perform their duties.

Members of Congress cannot be sued for anything they say while they are speaking in Congress. This provision in the Constitution is intended to protect their freedom to debate.

Rules of Conduct

Both houses of Congress have the right to decide who shall be seated as members. That is, if the Senate or the House of Representatives questions the constitutional qualifications of a newly elected member, the member may not be seated in Congress until an investigation of the charges is made. The Supreme Court must review the actions of Congress in this regard. Congress seldom has to refuse to seat one of its members.

The House and Senate have passed strict codes of conduct for their members. For example, members of Congress may not use campaign funds for personal expenses. Also, there is a limit on the amount of outside income they may earn. In addition, members of Congress are required to make a full disclosure of their financial holdings.

Serious misconduct by a member of the Senate or House may result in **expulsion** from office by a vote of two thirds of the senators or representatives. Expulsion of a member means that the person must give up his or her seat in Congress. Grounds for expulsion are limited to serious offenses, such as treason or other conduct unbecoming a member of Congress.

After studying Section 2, students should be able to do the following.

1. Describe a regular session of Congress.

2. Identify the congressional officers provided for in the Constitution.

3. Explain how the leaders of each house of Congress are chosen.

4. Describe congressional committees, including their power to affect bills.

A **party whip** is an important member of a political party's leadership in Congress. In fox hunting the job of a whipper-in is to keep fox-sniffing dogs from straying during a hunt. To do so, the whipper-in literally whips the dogs back into the pack. The British Parliament first used the term for political purposes, applying the name *whip* to officials whose job it is to keep party members in line with the party's leadership. Have students draw political cartoons illustrating the job of a congressional whip.

Less serious offenses may bring a vote of **censure**, or formal disapproval of a member's actions. A censured member must stand alone at the front of the House or Senate and listen as the charges are read.

SECTION 1 REVIEW

1. Define or identify the following terms: apportion, gerrymandering, term limits, franking privilege, immunity, expulsion, censure.

2. How many members sit in the House of Representatives, and when are elections for the House held? How many members sit in the Senate, and how long do senators serve?

3. Compare the qualifications for members of the House and Senate.

4. What salary do representatives and senators receive? How does the Twenty-seventh Amendment affect the power of Congress to set its own salary?

5. How does Congress deal with misconduct by members?

6. **THINKING CRITICALLY** How might term limits help Congress better serve the needs of the American people? How might such limits hurt the ability of Congress to serve the people? Write a position statement agreeing or disagreeing with the Supreme Court's decision on the issue of congressional term limits.

2 How Congress Is Organized

Beginning with the first Congress in 1789, each Congress has been identified by number. Thus

the Congress that began its term in 1789 was known as the First Congress. The Congress that began its term in 1997 is called the 105th Congress.

Terms and Sessions

In each term of Congress, there are two regular **sessions**, or meetings. The first session begins on January 3 in the odd-numbered year following the congressional election in November. The second session begins on January 3 of the next year.

Each session may last as long as Congress wishes. In the past, sessions usually lasted from January 3 until August or September. In recent years, the growing workload has led to longer sessions. Both houses of Congress agree on the date to adjourn, or end, the session.

Occasionally, serious problems arise after Congress has adjourned its regular session. In such cases, the president of the United States can recall Congress to meet in a special session. Usually, the president calls both houses into special session. The president may decide, however, to call only one of the two houses.

Under certain circumstances, the House of Representatives and the Senate will meet together. This is known as a joint session of Congress. For example, a joint session will be called if the president wants to address Congress. Such sessions are often televised.

Organization

The Constitution provides for only three congressional officers. First, it directs the House of Representatives to select a presiding officer. Second, it names the vice president of the United States as president of the Senate. Third, it calls for the selection of a senator to preside in the vice president's absence. These are the only directions given by the Constitution about the organization of Congress.

Over the years, Congress has developed procedures to organize itself. Shortly after the opening day of each term, the Republican and Democratic members in each house gather

CIVICS SIDELIGHT

One of the most famous special sessions of Congress was called by Franklin D. Roosevelt in 1933. During the so-called Hundred Days that began his presidency, he pushed Congress to pass many bills aimed at combating the Great Depression. This special session produced many fiscal and social reform measures that became the foundation of the New Deal.

Seeing Relationships

To show how congressional terms and sessions are related, display two calendars, one for 1996 and one for 1997. Ask students when the congressional election was held *(November 1996)* and when the new term of Congress began *(January 1997)*. You might then point to a month and ask volunteers which session of Congress it falls in *(105th beginning in January 1997)* or how many more months till the next election.

Have small groups of students hold majority or minority party caucuses. With Congress as a model, each group should draw up a list of school government leadership positions and elect members to the positions. Each "leader" should develop a list of qualifications and responsibilities for his or her office. Have the group present its leaders, each of whom should explain the qualifications and responsibilities of his or her office.

MULTICULTURAL PERSPECTIVES

Besides party caucuses, the Congress is also home to several unofficial caucuses. Among the most powerful has been the Congressional Black Caucus, formed in 1969 to further the interests of African Americans. Other caucuses include the Congressional Hispanic Caucus and the Older Americans Caucus. These caucuses combine the clout of individual members of Congress, often providing political pressure to pursue the interests of their members. The Congressional Black Caucus, for example, often provides support for African American nominees to government posts and to policies that directly affect African Americans.

CIVICS SIDELIGHT

Former Speaker Thomas P. "Tip" O'Neill (1912–1994) knew just how much influence he had in deciding the order of business in the House. In his autobiography, he put it bluntly: "[The Speaker's] most important power is to set the agenda, and if he doesn't want a certain bill to come up, it usually doesn't."

separately in private meetings. These private meetings are called party **caucuses**. At these caucuses, the Republican members of each house choose their own leaders, and the Democratic members choose theirs.

The political party that has more members in each house is known as the **majority party**. The political party that has fewer members is called the **minority party**.

Leaders of the House

According to the Constitution, the presiding officer of the House of Representatives is the **Speaker** of the House. The Speaker is the most powerful officer in the House. No representative may speak until called on, or recognized, by the Speaker. The Speaker also greatly influences the order of business in the House.

The Speaker, because of these important responsibilities, is paid $171,500 a year. The Speaker is always a member of the majority party. Like other leaders in the House and Senate, the Speaker is usually a longtime member of Congress.

House members also choose a number of other leaders. At their private caucuses, House Democrats and Republicans each choose a floor leader and a party whip. The **floor leader** of each party guides the party's proposed laws through Congress. The floor leader of the majority party is called the majority leader. The floor leader of the minority party is the minority leader. Each floor leader is assisted by a **party whip**, who tries to persuade members to vote for party-sponsored legislation.

Leaders of the Senate

The Constitution provides for the vice president of the United States to serve as the presiding officer of the Senate. The vice president, however, is not a senator and therefore cannot take part in Senate debates. The vice president may vote only in the case of a tie.

In recent years, the vice president has had many other responsibilities and has spent little time in the Senate. During the vice president's absence, the Senate is presided over by the **president *pro tempore***, a president "for the time being." This leader is elected by the members of the Senate. The president *pro tempore* is by custom the longest-serving member of the majority party.

The most powerful officers of the Senate are the majority leader and the minority

The Senate and the House of Representatives meet together in a joint session when the president wishes to address Congress.

Write the following goal on the board: Develop a health-care system that benefits everyone. Then have students suggest which congressional committees might be involved in a process that tackles this issue. For example, the Senate Labor and Human Resources Committee might want to study bills that affect the health benefits of workers. Write students' suggestions on the board, and have the class discuss which kinds of issues affecting health-care reform each committee would be most concerned with.

Assign one congressional committee to each student. Have each student find newspaper and magazine articles about the assigned committee and its work. Each student should list specific bills the committee considers. Then have each student identify the committee's counterpart in the other chamber. Call on volunteers to report their findings to the class as part of a discussion on the work of committees.

leader. Like the floor leaders of the House, the majority leader and the minority leader are elected in party caucuses. They, too, are assisted by party whips.

Committees

Every year Congress has to consider thousands of **bills**, or proposed laws. Members of the First Congress could have read each of the 268 bills they considered. Today Congress handles around 8,000 bills in a two-year term. It would be impossible for all members of each house to consider every bill that is proposed. Therefore, the members divide their work among many smaller groups, or **committees**.

Most of the work of Congress is done in committees. The congressional committees study all bills before they are considered by Congress. To obtain information needed to do their work, committees hold meetings and conduct investigations.

Standing Committees Each house of Congress has a number of permanent committees, or **standing committees**. As you can see in the chart on page 78, the Senate has 17 standing committees and the House has 19. Each committee is responsible for a special area. In the House, for example, the Ways and Means Committee handles all matters concerning taxes. In the Senate, bills related to taxes go to the Finance Committee.

Before any bill is considered by Congress, it is carefully studied by a standing committee. The committee holds special meetings, or hearings, to gain information on the positive and negative aspects of a bill. Committee members may revise a bill. It is then sent to the entire membership for consideration, with the committee's recommendation for or against it. This recommendation usually determines whether the members will or will not approve the bill.

Subcommittees Each standing committee is divided into **subcommittees**. These subcommittees deal with specific issues in the area handled by the committee as a whole. For example, the subcommittees of the Senate Foreign Relations Committee include those on Africa, Asia, and Europe.

Daniel Inouye

Daniel Inouye, the first Japanese American to serve in Congress, was born in 1924 in what was then the territory of Hawaii. A second-generation American, Inouye grew up in a home where both Japanese and American customs were practiced. Inouye studied and worked hard as a teenager and planned to become a surgeon.

Inouye's dream of a medical career ended, however, when a World War II injury led to the loss of his right arm. Inouye's bravery in defense of his nation earned him the Distinguished Service Cross, the Bronze Star, and the Purple Heart.

Inouye then turned his sights on law school and a career in politics. While studying law in Washington, D.C., he often went to watch Congress at work. In 1954 Inouye was elected to Hawaii's territorial House of Representatives. Four years later, he joined Hawaii's Senate.

In 1959 Congress granted statehood to Hawaii, making it the nation's 50th state. Daniel Inouye became the first member of Congress from the new state of Hawaii, joining the U.S. House of Representatives. In 1962 Inouye was elected to the Senate, where he continues to serve his state and the nation as a respected and dedicated member of Congress.

MULTICULTURAL PERSPECTIVES

Some Native American peoples had complex systems of government that included councils and specific leadership positions. For example, the Cheyenne were governed by a civil council comprised of 44 chiefs. Within that council, certain chiefs had designated leadership and spiritual duties. The highest ranking of these 44 chiefs were the five priestly chiefs, one of whom (called the Prophet) presided over the council meetings. Two council members were designated as "doormen," whose duties included moving the council toward decisions on issues before it. A separate council of 24 war chiefs was responsible for the Cheyenne's military affairs. The war chiefs appointed the war leader for a single military operation.

Closure

Invite a member of the student government in your school to speak to your class about the responsibilities and procedures of the school government. Have students prepare a list of questions to ask the speaker. Conclude by having the class discuss the similarities and differences between Congress and the student government.

Reviewing

Have students complete the Section 2 Review.

Reteaching

Assign Section 2 of the Chapter 5 Reteaching Worksheet.

Shirley Chisholm, who in 1969 became the first African American woman to serve in the House of Representatives, believed that the seniority system stood in the way of progress. In the forthright style that marked her years in the House, she wrote: "The seniority system keeps a handful of old men . . . in control of the Congress. These old men stand implacably across the paths that could lead us toward a better future. But worse than they, I think, are the majority of members of both Houses who continue to submit to the senility system."

Select Committees From time to time, each house of Congress will appoint **select committees** to deal with issues that are not handled by the standing committees. Select committees have investigated government scandals, for example. After holding hearings on a problem area, a select committee recommends solutions that may lead to new laws. Select committees are disbanded when they have finished their work.

Joint Committees Congress also has committees made up of an equal number of representatives and senators. These **joint committees** are set up when the two houses of Congress decide they can take care of certain matters better by working together.

Conference Committees Another kind of House-Senate committee is known as a **conference committee**. This is formed to work out a compromise when the House and Senate pass different versions of the same bill. Each conference committee is temporary and considers only one bill.

Committee Membership

Each member of the House usually serves on only one of the major standing committees. This enables each representative to specialize in one subject area. In the Senate, each senator serves on at least two major standing committees. Members of Congress seek assignment to these major standing committees.

The membership of the standing committees is divided in proportion to the number of members each party has in each house. If the Senate contains 60 Republicans and 40 Democrats, a ten-member committee would include six Republicans and four Democrats. Thus the majority party has a great advantage over the minority party. It is able to control much of a committee's work.

Each party in each house of Congress has its own committee on committees. This group nominates, or names, members of the party to serve on the various standing committees. A party caucus then reviews the nominations. Loyal party members and longtime members of Congress usually are rewarded with important committee assignments.

Committee Chairpersons

Because congressional committees are so important, their chairpersons are very powerful.

Standing Committees of Congress

House Committees	Senate Committees
Agriculture	Agriculture, Nutrition, and Forestry
Appropriations	Appropriations
Banking and Financial Services	Armed Services
Budget	Banking, Housing, and Urban Affairs
Commerce	Budget
Economic and Educational Opportunities	Commerce, Science, and Transportation
Government Reform and Oversight	Energy and Natural Resources
House Oversight	Environment and Public Works
International Relations	Finance
Judiciary	Foreign Relations
National Security	Governmental Affairs
Resources	Indian Affairs
Rules	Judiciary
Science	Labor and Human Resources
Small Business	Rules and Administration
Standards of Official Conduct	Small Business
Transportation and Infrastructure	Veterans' Affairs
Veterans' Affairs	
Ways and Means	

Extension

Lead students in a discussion of the process of cooperative learning—group projects—including compromise and the resolution of disagreements. (For a discussion of cooperative learning, see page T23 in the front of this Teacher's Edition.) Have them extend this discussion to congressional committees. Encourage students to speculate about the workings of those committees and to show how cooperative learning relates to the work of committees.

After studying Section 3, students should be able to do the following.

1. Name the five major areas in which Congress has the power to make laws.

2. Describe the impeachment process.

3. Identify the special powers of the House and the Senate.

4. Explain the ways in which the Constitution limits the power of Congress.

Chairpersons decide when a committee will meet and when it will hold hearings. They create subcommittees and hire and fire committee staff. Their importance gives them great influence in Congress.

How does someone reach this position? For many years, the post of committee chairperson automatically went to the member of the majority party who had the most years of service on the committee. This **seniority system** was a long-established custom.

Some people believe the seniority system works well. They say it assures experienced leadership. In recent years, however, some people have questioned the use of seniority in choosing committee chairpersons. Critics believe that younger members with fewer years of service might provide new ideas and more active leadership.

As a result of such criticism, Congress has changed its method of selecting chairpersons. The majority party in each house now chooses the heads of committees by secret vote in a party caucus. The person with the longest service, however, is almost always chosen.

Congressional Staffs

Congressional staffs include special assistants, clerks, and secretaries. Members of Congress need large staffs to run their offices in Washington and in their home districts or states. Their staffs also provide information on bills being considered by Congress and help keep senators and representatives informed on important issues. Furthermore, congressional staffs keep members of Congress informed on what the people they represent think about issues under consideration.

SECTION 2 REVIEW

1. Define or identify the following terms: session, caucus, majority party, minority party, Speaker, floor leader, party whip, president *pro tempore*, bill, committee, standing committee, subcommittee, select committee, joint committee, conference committee, seniority system.

2. When does each session of Congress begin? How long does each regular session of Congress last, and how is a date of adjournment chosen?

3. For what three congressional positions does the U.S. Constitution provide? How are the leaders in each house of Congress chosen?

4. Why does Congress work through committees? What usually determines whether Congress will approve a bill?

5. How are committee assignments made? Who usually receives the most important congressional committee assignments?

6. THINKING CRITICALLY How should committee chairpersons be chosen? Write a statement that outlines what you believe is the best method for choosing chairpersons. Include the reasons why you believe your system will be both efficient and democratic.

---

3 The Powers of Congress

The U.S. Congress is very powerful. Under the Constitution, Congress's most important responsibility is to make laws. These laws do not simply tell us what we can and cannot do. They affect us in other ways as well. For example, laws passed by Congress determine how high taxes will be. They provide for the building of highways and dams. They decide what military equipment to sell to other nations. Congress's actions affect the lives of millions of people in the United States and throughout the world.

SECTION 2 REVIEW
ANSWERS

1. See the following pages: session (p. 75); caucus, majority party, minority party, Speaker, floor leader, party whip, president *pro tempore* (p. 76); bill, committee, standing committee, subcommittee (p. 77); select committee, joint committee, conference committee (p. 78); seniority system (p. 79).

2. first session—Jan. 3 in odd-numbered year; second session—Jan. 3 of next year; lasts as long as Congress wishes; adjournment date agreed on by both houses

3. Speaker, vice president as president of Senate, president *pro tempore* of Senate; chosen by party caucuses

4. to divide large workload; standing committee's recommendation

5. committee on committees nominates, decisions reviewed by caucuses; loyal, longtime members

6. Students should provide specific reasons for their positions.

Tell students that the **elastic clause** shows the Constitution's flexibility. Ask: What does this clause do to Congress's power? *(stretches it)* Still, the Constitution denies Congress certain powers, including the passage of an ***ex post facto*** law. Ask: If *ex post facto* is Latin for "after the fact," what is an *ex post facto* law? *(a law enacted after something has happened—a retroactive law)*

Have students name the powers of Congress, including its special powers. Invite volunteers to write their responses in a column on the chalkboard. Briefly discuss the elastic clause. Then have students write a short editorial on the following question: Does Congress have too much power? (Leave the list on the chalkboard for later reference.)

CIVICS SIDELIGHT

Chief Justice John Marshall expressed the Supreme Court's interpretation of the elastic clause in the case of *McCulloch v. Maryland* (1819). "Let the end be legitimate, let it be within the scope of the Constitution," he wrote in the Court's opinion, "and all means which are appropriate, which are plainly adapted to that end, which are not prohibited, but [are consistent] with the letter and spirit of the constitution, are constitutional."

DID YOU KNOW THAT...

Every member of Congress has the franking privilege—the right to send official mail without paying postage. Instead of a stamp, a copy of the congressperson's signature appears on the envelope. In the past, the franking privilege was sometimes abused. The most extreme example of this abuse involved a senator in the 1800s. He declared his horse to be a "public document," put his signature on the horse's bridle, and had his horse shipped home for free.

Powers Granted to Congress

Article 1, Section 8, of the Constitution lists the powers granted to Congress. As you know, these powers are called delegated powers because they are granted, or delegated, to Congress by the Constitution. Delegated powers give Congress the right to make laws in five important areas.

Financing Government Congress can raise and collect taxes, borrow money, and print and coin money. It can use the funds it collects to pay the debts of the United States and to provide for the nation's defense and for the general welfare.

Regulating and Encouraging U.S. Trade and Industry Congress can regulate trade with foreign nations and among the states. It can also help U.S. businesses by setting a uniform standard of weights and measures and by passing laws that protect the rights of inventors. Congress also establishes post offices and builds roads that help business and industry in the nation. Congress can set

punishments for piracy and other major crimes committed against U.S. ships on the high seas.

Defending the Nation Congress has the power to declare war and to maintain an army and a navy. It also can provide for a citizen army that can be called to duty during wartime or national emergencies.

Enforcing Laws Congress can pass laws concerning such crimes as counterfeiting and treason. To ensure that these and other federal laws are upheld, Congress can establish a system of national courts.

Providing for Growth Congress has the power to govern the nation's territories and to provide for the admission of new states. Congress also has the power to regulate immigration and to pass naturalization laws. Naturalization laws make it possible for aliens to become U.S. citizens.

The Elastic Clause

The last power listed in Section 8 of Article 1 is among the most important and far-reaching. It states that Congress has the power "to make all laws which shall be necessary and proper for carrying into execution [carrying out] the foregoing powers."

This statement is the necessary and proper clause, also called the **elastic clause**. It is called the elastic clause because it allows Congress to stretch the delegated powers listed in the Constitution to cover many other subjects. The clause has permitted Congress to pass laws on situations that developed long after the Constitution was written.

For example, Congress has set up national military academies to train army, navy, and air force officers. The Constitution does not specifically give Congress this power. Congress, however, argues that the academies are "necessary and proper" for it to carry out its constitutional right to establish an army and a navy. Congress claims that this clause of the U.S. Constitution implies, or suggests, that

Have small groups review the impeachment process and prepare answers to the following questions: Does the process of impeachment treat the person being impeached fairly? Are the people of the United States well served by this process? Each group member should find specific historical examples of the impeachment process to support the group's answers. Call on volunteers to present their groups' opinions and examples to the class.

Have volunteers name the limits on the powers of Congress and write their responses in a column on the chalkboard, beside the earlier-compiled list of powers. (See "Expressing a Point of View" on page 80.) Then have students discuss the following question: Do these limits "tie the hands" of Congress? In light of these limits, review students' earlier opinions on the question of whether Congress has too much or too little power.

Congress has the right to establish military academies to train military officers. For this reason, the powers that Congress claims under the elastic clause are called **implied powers**.

Power to Impeach

The Constitution gives Congress other powers in addition to lawmaking. One of Congress's most important powers is its power to accuse high federal officials of serious crimes against the nation and to bring them to trial. The highest officials in the government—including the president, vice president, and federal judges— may be removed from office if they are found guilty of serious crimes such as **treason**, an act that betrays or endangers one's country.

The charges against the accused official must be drawn up in the House of Representatives. The list of charges is read before the entire House. Then the representatives vote. If a majority of them vote in favor of the list of charges, the official is formally accused, or impeached, and will be put on trial. The procedure of drawing up and passing the list of charges in the House is called **impeachment**.

The trial on the impeachment charges is held in the Senate. During this trial, the Senate becomes a court. The vice president usually acts as the judge. If the president is impeached, however, the chief justice of the Supreme Court presides instead. In this case the vice president cannot preside because he or she would become president if the president were found guilty.

The members of the Senate act as the jury. They hear the evidence and examine all witnesses. They then vote on the guilt or innocence of the official. Two thirds of the Senate must find the official guilty before he or she can be dismissed from office.

The impeachment process has been used rarely. Altogether, 15 federal officials have been impeached. Only seven of them, all judges, were found guilty and dismissed from office. Only one president, Andrew Johnson, has ever been impeached. At his impeachment trial in the Senate in 1868, President Johnson was found not guilty by only one vote. In 1974 the threat of impeachment caused President Richard M. Nixon to resign from office. (See "Case Study: Watergate" on pages 44–45.)

Special Powers

The Constitution gives each house of Congress a number of special powers. The House of Representatives has three special powers:

- The House alone can start impeachment proceedings.
- All bills for raising money must start in the House.

Powers of Congress

| The Senate | The House of Representatives |

Delegated Powers

- Collect taxes to pay for the cost of the federal government
- Regulate foreign and interstate trade
- Set a uniform standard of weights and measures and grant patents and copyrights
- Declare war and make peace
- Raise armed forces to defend the nation
- Establish post offices and roads
- Print and coin money
- Make rules about naturalization and immigration
- Govern the District of Columbia and the nation's territories
- Admit new states to the Union
- Borrow money
- Establish a system of national courts

Implied Powers

- Make all laws necessary and proper to carry out the delegated powers
- Provide for the general welfare of the United States

Removal of the president by impeachment is a long and difficult process in the United States. In countries with a parliamentary system, the leader of the country can be removed much more easily. In nations such as Great Britain and Germany, the parliament plays an important role in selecting the head of government. In those countries the head of government can be dismissed simply by a vote that shows a lack of confidence in the leader.

Independent Practice

Ask students to review the list of limits on the powers of Congress and choose the limit they believe most protects the rights of U.S. citizens. Have students write a paragraph explaining which limit they chose and why. Volunteers may read their paragraphs aloud.

Closure

Have students use newspapers and other periodicals to create collages illustrating the powers of Congress. Students should be prepared to discuss how each part of their collages represents these powers. Call on volunteers to present their collages to the class. Have the class suggest ways in which powers illustrated in the collages are limited.

CIVICS SIDELIGHT

The Latin words *habeas corpus* literally mean "you should have the body." In practice, the court is saying to law-enforcement officials, "bring us the accused person" (so that the person can be charged with a specific crime). The right of *habeas corpus* helps prevent unlawful imprisonment and thus protects the rights of all individuals.

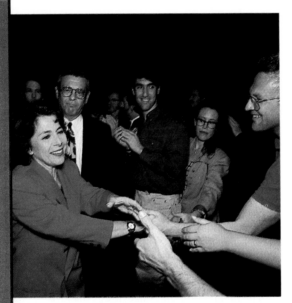

Members of Congress, such as Senator Barbara Boxer, meet often with their constituents.

- If no candidate for president receives the number of votes needed to be elected, the members of the House of Representatives choose the president.

The Senate has four special powers:

- All impeachment trials must be held in the Senate.
- If no candidate for vice president receives the number of votes needed to be elected, the members of the Senate choose the vice president.
- All treaties, or written agreements, with foreign nations must be approved in the Senate by a two-thirds vote.
- Certain high officials appointed by the president must be approved in the Senate by a majority vote.

Limits on Powers

The powers of Congress are limited in several important ways. The Supreme Court has the power to decide when Congress has reached beyond the powers granted to it by the Constitution. (You will read more about this in Chapter 7.) When the Court rules that Congress has passed a law that exceeds Congress's constitutional powers, this law has no force.

Another limit on Congress's powers is the Tenth Amendment to the Constitution. It declares that the states shall keep all the powers not specifically granted to the national government. These powers, as you recall, are the reserved powers. They include the states' authority with regard to elections, education, and marriage.

In addition, Article 1, Section 9, of the Constitution denies certain powers to Congress. The Constitution specifically forbids Congress from the following.

Passing *Ex Post Facto* Laws A law that applies to an action that took place before the law was passed is called an ***ex post facto* law**. For example, it is not against the law today to buy and sell foreign automobiles. If tomorrow Congress forbids the buying and selling of foreign cars, a person cannot be arrested for having bought or sold one of these cars in the past.

Passing Bills of Attainder A law that sentences a person to jail without a trial is called a **bill of attainder**. The Constitution provides that anyone accused of a crime must be given a trial in a court of law.

Suspending the Writ of *Habeas Corpus* A person accused of a crime has the right to a **writ of *habeas corpus***. This writ is a court order requiring that the accused person be brought to court to determine if there is enough evidence to hold the person for trial. If Congress had the right to suspend, or set aside, the writ of *habeas corpus*, a person might be kept in jail indefinitely with no formal charges being brought. The only exception to this rule is in times of rebellion or invasion.

Taxing Exports Goods that are sent to other countries are called exports. A tax on

Extension

Have students write an essay comparing and contrasting the powers (and limits on those powers) of legislative bodies in other countries with those of the U.S. Congress. You might assign countries to students to ensure that the class researches various forms of government. Call on volunteers to report their findings to the class.

Reviewing

Have students complete the Section 3 Review.

Reteaching

Assign Section 3 of the Chapter 5 Reteaching Worksheet.

exports would harm the nation's foreign and domestic trade. Congress can, however, tax imports—goods that are brought into the country from abroad.

Passing Laws Violating the Bill of Rights As you recall, the Bill of Rights, the first 10 amendments to the Constitution, spells out the rights and freedoms of all U.S. citizens. Congress may not pass any law that violates these rights.

Favoring Trade of a State Congress cannot pass laws giving a state or group of states an unfair trade advantage. Of course, Congress can pass laws regulating trade, but these laws must apply equally to all states.

Granting Titles of Nobility Americans believe that all people are created equal. Therefore, they are opposed to establishing a noble class, or small group of persons with rights superior to those of other citizens.

Withdrawing Money Without a Law Congress must pass a law telling how money shall be spent and the exact amount to be spent before public funds are made available. This limitation means that Congress must pass additional laws to provide the money for carrying out the other laws it passes.

Other Roles of Congress

Over the years, the job of members of Congress has expanded greatly. Their responsibilities have grown to include roles that were not anticipated in the Constitution.

Helping Constituents One of the most important jobs of members of Congress is to serve the interests of the people who live in their home districts or states. These people are called **constituents**.

Members of Congress receive thousands of letters from their constituents every week. Some of this mail gives opinions on issues. Other letters ask a representative or senator to vote for or against a certain bill.

Most mail is from people asking for help. For example, a veteran with a disability may complain that the government has misplaced his claim. The owner of a small company may ask how to apply for a government contract.

Conducting Investigations Another important responsibility of Congress is its power to conduct investigations. Either house of Congress may investigate national issues. The purpose of these investigations usually is to determine whether a new law is needed or if an existing law is being carried out as Congress intended.

SECTION 3 REVIEW

1. Define or identify the following terms: elastic clause, implied power, treason, impeachment, *ex post facto* law, bill of attainder, writ of *habeas corpus*, constituent.

2. In what five major areas does Congress have the power to make laws?

3. What are the steps in the impeachment process?

4. What special powers does the House of Representatives have? What special powers does the Senate have?

5. Identify the ways that the Constitution limits the power of Congress.

6. **THINKING CRITICALLY** As the nation's lawmakers, members of Congress consider proposals for new laws on a variety of issues. Although they have been elected as representatives of the people, members of Congress bring their own experiences, talents, and beliefs to the job. How should members of Congress vote on proposals —according to their own beliefs or according to the wishes of their constituents? Explain your answer.

SECTION 3 REVIEW
A N S W E R S

1. See the following pages: elastic clause (p. 80); implied power, treason, impeachment (p. 81); *ex post facto* law, bill of attainder, writ of *habeas corpus* (p. 82); constituent (p. 83).

2. finance, trade and industry, defense, enforcing laws, providing for nation's growth

3. charges by House; majority vote required; tried in Senate; two-thirds vote to convict

4. House—starts impeachment cases, initiates money bills, chooses president if no Electoral College majority; Senate—tries impeachment cases, chooses vice president if no Electoral College majority, approves treaties and appointments

5. Court review of laws; reserved powers; rarely may suspend *habeas corpus*; cannot pass *ex post facto* laws or bills of attainder, tax exports, violate Bill of Rights, favor trade of one state, grant titles, or withdraw money from Treasury without law

6. Answers will vary but should include sound reasoning.

SECTION OBJECTIVES

After studying Section 4, students should be able to do the following.

1. Identify where ideas for bills originate.

2. Describe what happens after a bill is introduced in the House of Representatives.

3. Explain what happens if each house passes a different version of a bill.

4. Identify the actions a president might take on a bill passed by both houses.

Teaching Section 4
Building a Vocabulary

Ask: If to *appropriate* means to set aside something (such as money) for a specific purpose, what is an **appropriation bill**? Remind students that such money bills start in the House. Tell them that 218 members—a **quorum**—must be present to consider a bill. Ask students to define *quorum*. (*majority*) Remind students that you "take roll" each morning. Then ask what they believe a **roll-call vote** is.

CIVICS SIDELIGHT

The complex process of passing a bill would be even more difficult if politicians were unwilling to compromise—to accept what *can* be accomplished instead of holding out for the impossible. Otto von Bismarck, Chancellor of Germany in the late 1800s, recognized this fact. He is credited with saying: "Politics is the art of the possible."

4 How a Bill Becomes a Law

Each day that Congress is in session, an interesting scene takes place. As the members of the House enter their legislative hall, some of them approach the front of the chamber. They drop papers into a box on the clerk's desk. This box is called the hopper. The papers dropped into it by the members are bills, or written proposals for laws.

Of course, not all these proposals become laws. The process of getting a law passed is long and difficult. This sometimes makes us think that government is not responsive enough. In the long run, however, the careful process helps ensure that the nation's laws will be good laws.

The Idea for a Bill Begins

Each year the Senate and the House of Representatives consider thousands of bills. These bills may be introduced in either house. The only exception to this rule is an **appropriation bill**, or bill approving the spending of money. An appropriation bill must originate in the House of Representatives. Every bill must be passed by both houses of Congress before it can be signed by the president and become a law. A law is also known as an **act**.

Where do the ideas for these bills begin? Ideas can come from the following sources.

From U.S. Citizens The people are a powerful force in influencing laws. When a large number of constituents requests a law, a representative or senator usually introduces a bill containing the constituents' ideas.

From Organized Groups Members of Congress sometimes introduce bills because they are requested to do so by certain groups. For example, businesspeople may want to limit competition from industries in other countries. Labor groups may call for laws establishing improved working conditions or higher hourly wages.

From Committees of Congress Many bills begin in Congress itself. Suppose that a congressional investigating committee conducts a study of certain kinds of crime. Its findings convince the committee that the federal government needs a new law for crime control. The committee can then draw up a bill and introduce it in Congress.

From Members of Congress Members of Congress often become experts in certain fields. A member who has experience with farming issues, for example, may introduce a bill to fund an agriculture program.

From the President The president has great influence on bills introduced in Congress. Early in each session of Congress, the president appears before a joint session of the two houses to deliver a speech on the state of the nation. In this speech the president recommends laws that the president believes are needed to improve the nation's well-being. Many of these ideas are soon introduced as bills by members of Congress.

An Idea Becomes a Bill

Although anyone can suggest an idea for a bill, only members of Congress can introduce the bill itself. Suppose, for example, that a group of citizens favors the creation of a new national park. The citizens write to their senators and representatives to explain their idea. The leader of the group arranges for a meeting with one of the senators or representatives to discuss the group's idea in more depth.

At this meeting the leader of the group provides facts and figures on the subject and urges that a bill be introduced. If the senator or representative is convinced that the group's idea is a good one, he or she may agree to introduce the bill in Congress.

To learn how a bill becomes a law, follow the progress of the national park bill as it is considered first by the House of Representatives and then by the Senate.

Practicing Interviewing Skills

Invite a staff member of a senator or representative to speak to your class about the day-to-day business of getting a bill through Congress, including the sources of ideas for bills. Have students prepare a list of appropriate questions to ask the speaker. Ask the staff member to explain the process of researching and preparing the bill to be introduced. Who does the research, staff or outside groups?

Writing to Persuade

Have students write a letter to the editor supporting or opposing a bill before Congress. Each student will need to review newspapers and other periodicals. The letter should follow standard business form. Call on volunteers to read their letters to the class. Ask: What role in the process of passing a bill does each citizen play?

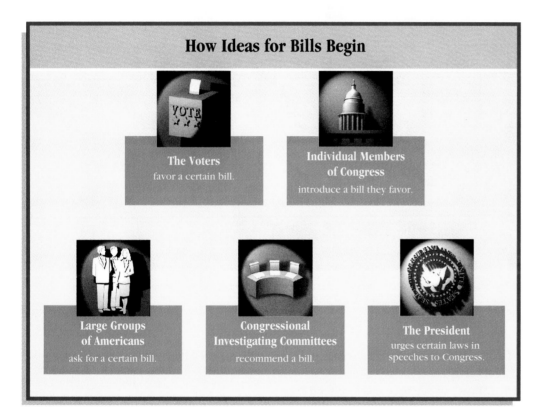

How Ideas for Bills Begin

The Voters favor a certain bill.

Individual Members of Congress introduce a bill they favor.

Large Groups of Americans ask for a certain bill.

Congressional Investigating Committees recommend a bill.

The President urges certain laws in speeches to Congress.

The Bill Is Introduced in the House

How does the representative introduce this bill in the House? First the proposed bill is carefully written out. Bills are not always written by representatives. In fact, many bills are written by a committee, by the group that suggested the bill, or by an assistant on the representative's staff.

After the bill is dropped into the hopper, it is given letters and a number. Suppose that the bill to create a new national park is marked HR 1215. The letters *HR* indicate that the bill is being considered by the House of Representatives. The number *1215* indicates the bill's place among all the bills introduced in this session of Congress.

What happens to the bill after it is introduced? It is sent to a standing committee for study. Usually the subject of the bill determines which committee will study it. In some cases, two committees may want to study the bill. The Speaker of the House decides to which committee the bill will be sent.

The Bill Is Sent to Committee

In the case of HR 1215, the Speaker sends the bill to the House Resources Committee. This committee deals with all bills concerning the national park system.

Each bill is given careful attention by the committee to which it is sent. Many bills are found to be unnecessary. These are set aside and are never returned to the House for action. In this way the committees reduce the amount of legislation Congress must consider.

Assign each of five groups one of the sources of ideas for bills listed in the textbook. Have each group assume the identity of one source and submit an idea for a bill. The "U.S. citizen" and the "organized group" should write letters to their congressional representatives. The "committee" and "member of Congress" might write memos. The "president" might prepare a speech with each member acting as adviser to the president. Have groups present their ideas to the class for discussion.

Writing Creatively

Have students write a story from the point of view of a bill submitted to Congress. Students should use the first person. For example, they might begin, "I am a bill to raise the minimum wage. My sponsor dropped me into the hopper of the House of Representatives on June 3. . . ." The bill should also address what happens to it after it has been passed and reaches the president's desk.

CIVICS SIDELIGHT

Members of Congress use many creative terms to describe certain parts of the legislative process. For example, a "Christmas-tree bill" is a piece of legislation to which many amendments have been added. Typically, these amendments confer various benefits to specific groups. A critic might say such a bill was loaded with "pork" or represented "pork-barrel spending," meaning the amendments amounted to wasteful public spending favoring a congressperson's district or state. The targets of such criticism might call the critic's words "buncombe," "bunkum," or just "bunk." These words come from an obviously insincere speech given by a nineteenth-century congressman from Buncombe County, North Carolina. Buncombe County's name came to be used to describe irrelevant or insincere political speeches.

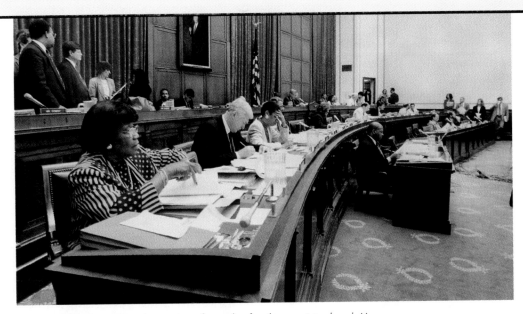

Bills are sent to congressional committees for study after they are introduced. Here, a House committee makes changes to a bill under consideration.

The Committee Holds Hearings

HR 1215 is not set aside. Instead, the House Resources Committee holds hearings on the bill. Most committee hearings are open to the public. Some important hearings are shown on television.

At the hearings the committee calls witnesses to testify for and against the bill. These witnesses give committee members the information they need to recommend that the bill be accepted, rejected, or changed. Testimony from witnesses, letters from citizens, and evidence that committee members gather from many other sources all help the committee reach a decision on the bill.

The Committee Studies the Bill

In the case of HR 1215, the Resources Committee decides to change parts of the bill in certain ways. Members rewrite paragraphs and add new sections. When they are finished, the bill is very different from the one they originally received. The majority of committee members decide to recommend that the House pass the bill as amended, or changed, by the standing committee.

The House Considers the Bill

When HR 1215 is reported out of committee and sent back to the House of Representatives, it is placed on the House calendar. The calendar is the schedule that lists the order in which bills are to be considered. In an emergency a bill can be moved up on the calendar so that action may be taken quickly.

HR 1215 must be given three readings in the House of Representatives. By the time its turn comes on the calendar, the first reading has already occurred. It took place when the Speaker first read the title of the bill to the House before sending it to the appropriate standing committee. The second reading will occur while the bill is debated.

Guided Practice

Have students offer details to support this statement: The process of getting a law passed is long and difficult. Then ask: Is it worth all this trouble to transform a bill into a law? Lead the class in a panel discussion on whether the process should be simplified and how that could be accomplished. Ask what value there is in such a lengthy process.

Independent Practice

Have each student create an alternative process for passing a bill. Students may simplify the process or add steps, if they desire. The students should illustrate their processes in some way, using diagrams or flowcharts on posterboard, for example. Make sure students include the role of presidential vetoes in their processes. Call on volunteers to explain how their ideas would improve the process.

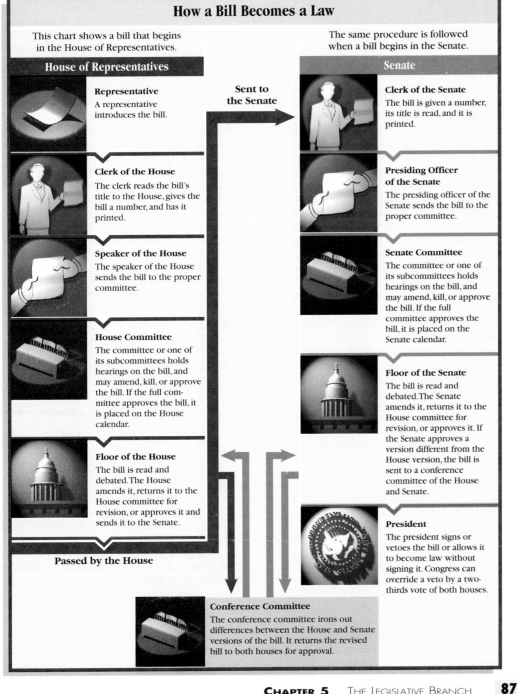

How a Bill Becomes a Law

This chart shows a bill that begins in the House of Representatives.

The same procedure is followed when a bill begins in the Senate.

House of Representatives

Representative
A representative introduces the bill.

Clerk of the House
The clerk reads the bill's title to the House, gives the bill a number, and has it printed.

Speaker of the House
The speaker of the House sends the bill to the proper committee.

House Committee
The committee or one of its subcommittees holds hearings on the bill, and may amend, kill, or approve the bill. If the full committee approves the bill, it is placed on the House calendar.

Floor of the House
The bill is read and debated. The House amends it, returns it to the House committee for revision, or approves it and sends it to the Senate.

Passed by the House

Sent to the Senate

Senate

Clerk of the Senate
The bill is given a number, its title is read, and it is printed.

Presiding Officer of the Senate
The presiding officer of the Senate sends the bill to the proper committee.

Senate Committee
The committee or one of its subcommittees holds hearings on the bill, and may amend, kill, or approve the bill. If the full committee approves the bill, it is placed on the Senate calendar.

Floor of the Senate
The bill is read and debated. The Senate amends it, returns it to the House committee for revision, or approves it. If the Senate approves a version different from the House version, the bill is sent to a conference committee of the House and Senate.

President
The president signs or vetoes the bill or allows it to become law without signing it. Congress can override a veto by a two-thirds vote of both houses.

Conference Committee
The conference committee irons out differences between the House and Senate versions of the bill. It returns the revised bill to both houses for approval.

Civics Sidelight

The Speaker of the House wields great power in the lawmaking process. Sometimes it is unclear which committee should deal with a particular bill. If the Speaker (who belongs to the majority party) wants a bill to pass, he or she can choose to send it to the committee that is most likely to report it out favorably. Likewise, a bill opposed by the Speaker might end up in a committee hostile to the proposed legislation.

Closure

Refer students to the chart on how a bill becomes a law on page 87. Ask your local congressperson for a copy of a bill he or she has filed and a summary of its process to passage. Organize the class into a mock Congress and have the class re-enact the passage of the bill. Include a volunteer who acts as president.

CIVICS SIDELIGHT

Some senators have read telephone books, almanacs, and baseball statistics in their filibuster attempts. These efforts to prolong debate have galled many senators, especially those in the majority, who want to pass the bill. Yet others, such as the late Illinois Senator Everett Dirksen, have taken a different view. He once called the filibuster "the only weapon which the minority has to protect itself."

The Rules Committee decides how much time will be given to debate this bill. The time to be spent in debate, or discussion, is divided evenly between those members who are in favor of the bill and those members who are against the bill.

For the debate, the House usually acts as a Committee of the Whole. As one large committee, the House can act less formally and turn the meeting into a work session. The bill now is given its second reading. A clerk reads a paragraph, and then amendments may be offered. Debate on each amendment is usually limited to five minutes for each member who speaks. A vote is then taken on the amendment. It is usually a voice vote with all members in favor saying "yea" and all those opposed saying "nay."

Each paragraph of the bill is read and amended in similar fashion until the entire bill has been considered. When the House meets again in formal session, a member may demand a "quorum call." A **quorum**, or majority of the members, must be present in Congress to do business.

The House Votes on the Bill

When a quorum is present, the House is ready for the third reading. This reading is usually by title only. Any member may demand, however, that the bill be read in its entirety. The vote is then taken. A majority of the members present is needed to pass a bill.

On important bills a **roll-call vote** is usually taken. Each member's name is called and a record is made of his or her vote. The bill to create a new national park, as amended, passes the House. But it is not yet a law. Like all bills, it must now be considered by the other house of Congress, the Senate.

The Senate Acts on the Bill

In the Senate, the bill is called S 2019. The way in which a bill is handled in the Senate is similar to the process followed in the House. Bill S 2019 is read by title, for its first reading. It is then sent to the Senate Energy and Natural Resources Committee.

After holding hearings, the committee revises S 2019. The committee then recommends that the bill be passed by the Senate.

The senators usually are not limited in their debate, as are members of the House of Representatives. In the Senate, speeches may last a long time. To prevent the Senate from taking a vote on a bill, some senators have talked for many hours, thereby "talking the bill to death." This method of delay by making lengthy speeches is called a **filibuster**. Debate in the Senate can be limited only if three fifths of the full Senate vote to limit it. Limit on debate in the Senate is called **cloture**.

After the members of the Senate finish their debate on S 2019, a roll call is taken. Bill S 2019 passes. What happens next?

The House and the Senate Agree on the Final Bill

When a bill passes the House and Senate in identical form, it is ready to be sent to the president. Usually, however, the two houses pass different versions of the same bill. If a bill is changed in any way, it must be sent back to the house in which it originated for another vote. In the example of the national park bill, the House of Representatives does not agree to the Senate changes. When this happens, a conference committee must be called.

A conference committee meets to reach an agreement on the bill. The committee is made up of an equal number of senators and representatives. The committee members from each house may have to give up something to reach a compromise.

Finally, a compromise bill is sent back to both houses. Usually both houses approve the work of the conference committee.

The President Approves the Bill

The bill as passed by both houses is sent to the president of the United States. The president

Extension

Have students interview a member of the town or city council or other local governing body to see how ideas are turned into local laws. Students should then illustrate the similarities between the processes at the local and congressional levels. Call on volunteers to present their illustrations to the class. Ask: Who would you suppose receives the most pressure from interest groups, local or congressional officials? Why do you think this might be true?

may take one of three possible actions on a bill from Congress:

1. The president may sign the bill and declare it to be a law.

2. The president may refuse to sign the bill and send it back to Congress with a message giving the reasons for rejecting it. This action, as you know, is called a veto.

3. The president may keep the bill for 10 days without signing it. If Congress is in session during this 10-day period, the bill becomes a law without the president's signature. If Congress is not in session, however, and the president does not sign the bill within 10 days, the bill does not become a law. Instead, the bill has been killed by a **pocket veto**.

The president does not use the veto often. Although Congress can pass a bill over a presidential veto by a two-thirds vote of both houses, it is very difficult to obtain the necessary votes. In the case of the national park bill, it becomes a law and goes into effect after the president signs it.

The long and involved process of making laws may be slow, but it prevents hasty legislation while providing a way for the federal government to pass needed laws.

SECTION **4** REVIEW

1. Define or identify the following terms: appropriation bill, act, quorum, roll-call vote, filibuster, cloture, pocket veto.

2. From what sources do the ideas for bills introduced into Congress originate?

3. What happens after a bill is introduced in the House?

4. What happens if the two houses pass different versions of the same bill?

5. What three possible actions can the president take on a bill that has been passed by both houses of Congress?

6. THINKING CRITICALLY Imagine that you head a citizens' group that has submitted a proposal to Congress to reduce the amount of violence shown on television. Your representative has introduced a bill on your group's behalf, and the bill has just had its first reading in the House. Write a letter to the members of your group updating them on the bill's status. Describe the stages through which the bill must now pass before it becomes a law. Be sure to tell the group how it can become further involved in the lawmaking process.

CHAPTER 5 SUMMARY

The legislative, or lawmaking, branch of the federal government is called Congress. It consists of two houses, the House of Representatives and the Senate. Each state is represented in the Senate by two senators. The number of representatives each state elects to the House of Representatives is based on the size of the state's population.

Congress meets for two regular sessions in each of its terms. The two houses organize their work and operate in similar ways. Much of the work of Congress is done by various types of committees.

Congress has been given many important powers by the Constitution. The delegated powers set forth specific functions of Congress. The elastic clause, meanwhile, allows Congress to exercise powers suggested but not specifically granted to it. These are called implied powers. The Constitution also limits the powers of Congress. It reserves certain powers for the states and specifically forbids some powers to Congress.

Congress considers thousands of bills each year. To become a law, each bill must be passed by both houses of Congress before being signed by the president.

Point out to students that several symbols used in political cartoons have been around for many years. In the 1870s American political cartoonist Thomas Nast used the donkey as a symbol of the Democratic party and the elephant as a symbol of the Republican party. (See page 578.) Cartoons such as Nast's appeared on editorial pages of newspapers throughout the country.

Today political cartoons occasionally move off the editorial pages and into the entertainment, or comics, section of the newspaper. One example is the daily cartoon strip *Doonesbury*, drawn by Garry Trudeau, which often follows controversial political issues. As an extension exercise, have students draw a political cartoon expressing an opinion on a current local, state, or national issue.

Developing Civics Skills

CITIZENSHIP SKILL
Interpreting Political Cartoons

ANSWERS TO Applying the Skill

1. seniority system

2. Answers will vary. Students should recognize the relationship between the cartoonist's use of age and the basis for choosing committee heads under the seniority system. If students have difficulty understanding why the artist equates the seniority system with a king, point out that kings usually hold their positions for life.

3. The cartoonist believes the seniority system is incompatible with representative government. This point is made by showing representative government (the people) throwing the seniority system out of Congress.

Most Americans recognize him at a glance. He has been wearing the same outfit for more than 100 years: striped pants, a cutaway coat, and a hat decorated with stars and stripes. His name is Uncle Sam—the figure that has come to represent the United States. (See page 578.)

Uncle Sam and many other famous characters appear regularly in political cartoons. Political cartoons typically are found in the editorial sections of newspapers. These cartoons use pictures to express a point of view. Because the pictures often are humorous, your first reaction might be to laugh. It is important, however, to look beyond the humor. Every political cartoon has an underlying message.

How to Interpret Political Cartoons

1. **Identify the symbols.** As you look at the cartoon, keep in mind that the artist often uses symbols, or drawings with special meanings. Some symbols, such as Uncle Sam, represent countries, groups of people, or places. Other symbols represent ideas. Justice, for example, often is shown as a blindfolded, robed woman holding a set of scales.
2. **Identify the caricatures.** Caricatures are sketches that exaggerate, or distort, a person's features. Caricatures can be positive or negative, depending on the cartoonist's point of view. Determine whether the cartoonist is portraying the subject in a favorable or unfavorable manner.
3. **Read the labels.** Editorial cartoons often use labels to identify people, objects, events, or ideas. How do the labels help express the cartoonist's point of view?
4. **Read the caption.** Many cartoons have a caption. If the cartoon has a caption, note

how it relates to the cartoon. Identify whose point of view is being expressed in the caption—that of the cartoonist, the cartoon figure, or some other person.

Applying the Skill
Examine the political cartoon below. Then answer the following questions.
1. What is the subject of the cartoon?
2. Why do you think the cartoonist chose to portray the seniority system of Congress as an old king?
3. What is the cartoonist's opinion of the seniority system? Do you agree with this opinion? Why or why not?

American Revolution Bicentennial

Copyright 1975 by Herblock in The Washington Post

SECTION OBJECTIVES

After studying Section 1, students should be able to do the following.

1. Identify the qualifications for the presidency and rules regarding the term of office.
2. Cite the salaries of the president and vice president.
3. Identify the order of presidential succession.
4. Explain what happens if a president becomes too ill to fulfill the duties of office.

Teaching Section 1
Building a Vocabulary

Tell students that if one person succeeds another, he or she takes the other person's place. Such an event is known as a succession. Have students deduce what **presidential succession** refers to. *(the order of people who would succeed to the office of president should it become vacant)* Explain that the prefix *vice* has Latin origins and refers to one who takes the place of another. Ask: In addition to the vice president, what other such titles can you name with the prefix *vice? (vice principal, vice chairman)*

CHAPTER FOCUS

Every four years Inauguration Day draws thousands of visitors to the nation's capital. These visitors and millions more watching on television will witness the swearing in of a new president. Perhaps you were one of the people watching the most recent inaugural ceremony on television. If so, you know that the ceremony is held on a large, flag-draped platform set up at the Capitol. There, the president-elect takes the oath of office, repeating these words from the Constitution:

> I do solemnly swear (or affirm) that I will faithfully execute the office of the President of the United States, and will, to the best of my ability, preserve, protect, and defend the Constitution of the United States.

The president then delivers an Inaugural Address, a speech listened to by people throughout the world. They know, as you know, that one of the most powerful people in the world is speaking—the person who will lead the United States for the next four years.

• •

STUDY GUIDE

- What are the qualifications for president?
- What are the president's powers and roles?
- How is the executive branch organized?
- What are the executive departments and the independent agencies?

1 | The Presidency

The executive branch of the federal government, described in Article 2 of the Constitution, is responsible for executing, or carrying out, the nation's laws. The executive branch is headed by the president of the United States.

In 1789 George Washington became the nation's first president. Since then only 41 others have served as president. Hundreds of people, however, have sought the office. The president is the nation's most powerful elected official.

Qualifications

The Constitution sets forth certain qualifications that the president of the United States must meet. The president must

- be a native-born U.S. citizen,
- be at least 35 years of age, and
- have been a resident of the United States for at least 14 years.

These are the only qualifications for president mentioned in the Constitution. There also have been a number of "unwritten rules," however, about who could be elected president. For example, all U.S. presidents have been men. All have been white. All have been Christian. Most presidents have attended college. Many have been lawyers. Most have held other political offices at the state or national level for several years before becoming president.

These unwritten rules, however, can change. For example, for most of the nation's history, only Protestants were elected president. John F. Kennedy, who was a Roman Catholic, broke that unwritten rule when he was elected president in 1960.

Recently, more women and other minority group members have become involved in

MULTICULTURAL PERSPECTIVES

On January 20, 1993, Maya Angelou, an African American writer, read her poem "On the Pulse of Morning" at the presidential inauguration of Bill Clinton. She stirred the crowd with her call for peace and harmony among all ethnic groups and cultures. Her poem ends with a hopeful appeal: "Here, on the pulse of this new day / You may have the grace to look up and out / And into your sister's eyes, and into / Your brother's face, your country / And say simply / Very simply / With hope— / Good morning."

CIVICS SIDELIGHT

The ages of presidents upon taking office have varied widely. John F. Kennedy, at 43, was the youngest person ever elected president. Theodore Roosevelt, however, who succeeded to the presidency at age 42 upon William McKinley's assassination in 1901, was actually the youngest president. Ronald Reagan, at 69, was the oldest person elected president.

Evaluating Ideas

Have students review the qualifications for president. Ask: Would you be in favor of eliminating or replacing one of the three constitutional qualifications for the presidency, or do you think they are sufficient as is? Lead students in a panel discussion of the effects of replacing one or more of these qualifications.

Testing Presidential History

Allow students a few minutes to study pages 562–565. Then divide the class into two groups, each lined up single file (similar to a spelling bee). Begin the game by naming a president. Alternating between groups, ask the student at the head of each line to state when the president served in office and the number of years and terms in office. Award one point for each correct answer. The side accumulating the most points wins.

CIVICS SIDELIGHT

No matter how many terms a president serves, the end of the last term can be frustrating. The presidents become "lame ducks," lacking political clout because they are about to leave office. Before 1933 and the passage of the Twentieth Amendment, presidents were lame ducks from the election in November to the inauguration of the new president in March of the next year. The reason for the four-month interval between the election and the inauguration was that newly elected officials needed time to travel the often great distances from their homes to the capital. The Twentieth (or "Lame Duck") Amendment, passed in the era of the automobile, moved up the inauguration to January, thus cutting the lame-duck period in half.

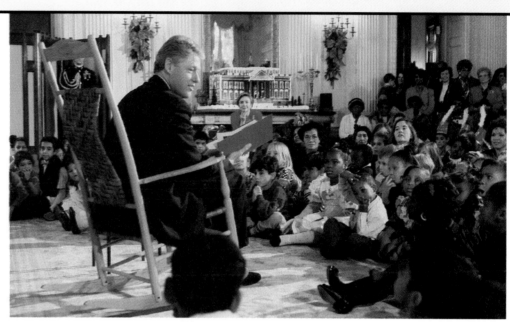

The president of the United States lives in the White House. Here, President Clinton reads a story to young guests visiting the White House.

presidential politics. In 1984, for example, Geraldine Ferraro was the Democratic nominee for vice president. Jesse Jackson, an African American, made a strong bid for the presidency in 1984 and again in 1988.

Term of Office

The president is elected to a four-year term and may be reelected for a second term of office. The original U.S. Constitution, however, did not state how many terms the president could serve.

George Washington set the tradition of a limit of two terms. He refused to run for the presidency a third time when he was urged to do so. This two-term tradition was not broken until Franklin D. Roosevelt was elected to a third term as president in 1940. In 1944 he won a fourth term.

In 1951 the number of terms a president can serve was limited by passage of the Twenty-second Amendment. This amendment set a two-term limit to the presidency.

Salary and Benefits

The salary the president receives is set by Congress. Congress cannot, however, change the salary during a president's term of office. This restriction was included in the Constitution to prevent Congress from punishing or rewarding a president.

Today the president is paid a salary of $200,000 a year plus $50,000 for official expenses. Since the president must travel frequently, there is also an annual allowance for travel costs.

The president is provided with many additional benefits. The president's family lives in the White House. This beautiful building has been the home of all U.S. presidents since John Adams. The White House is also the site of the president's office and the offices of the president's closest assistants. Parts of the White House are open to the public.

For special meetings and for relaxation on weekends or holidays, the president can use Camp David, located in the mountains of Maryland. A large fleet of cars, helicopters, and

Have students write help-wanted ads for the position of president or vice president of the United States. Each student should choose one or the other. Have volunteers present their ads in class, noting similarities and crucial differences between the two jobs, as well as salaries. Display ads on a bulletin board.

Call on a group of volunteers to develop various situations in which the rules of presidential succession and the Twenty-fifth Amendment would be important. These situations should be fully developed, including the condition and location of important government officials. List these situations on the board and work with the class to provide the correct procedures for succession in each case.

planes—including the special jet *Air Force One*—is also available to the president.

The Vice President

The Constitution provides that if the president dies, resigns, or is removed from office, the vice president becomes president. The Constitution gives the vice president only one other job—to preside over the Senate. Because the power of the vice president is so limited, John Adams, the first vice president of the United States, called the office "the most insignificant" ever invented.

In recent years, however, presidents have given their vice presidents more responsibilities. Vice presidents must be fully informed and prepared to take over the important job that could become theirs. In fact, nine vice presidents have taken over the office of president. The first was John Tyler, who became president in 1841 when President William Harrison died. In the twentieth century, five vice presidents have assumed the presidency.

The vice president must meet the same constitutional qualifications as the president. The vice president also serves a four-year term, and receives a salary of $171,500 a year plus a sum for official expenses.

Vice presidential candidates often are chosen for their ability to help the presidential candidates win election. Increasingly, political parties have also chosen vice presidential nominees who are fully qualified in experience to succeed to the presidency.

Presidential Succession

Eight U.S. presidents died while in office. One president resigned. In each case, the vice president took the oath of office and became president as provided by the Constitution.

What would happen if both the president and the vice president should die while in office? The Constitution gave Congress the right to decide who should then fill the office of the presidency. This is known as the order of **presidential succession**.

According to a law passed by Congress in 1947, the Speaker of the House of Representatives becomes president if both the regularly elected president and vice president die or are removed from office. If the Speaker dies or is removed from office, then the president *pro tempore* of the Senate succeeds to the presidency. Following them in succession to the presidency are the members of the president's Cabinet, in the order in which their departments were created.

The Twenty-fifth Amendment

If the president dies or resigns and is succeeded by the vice president, who then becomes vice president? Until 1967 the answer to this question was no one. The office of the vice president remained empty when the vice president assumed the presidency.

Chief Justice Warren Burger swore in Gerald R. Ford as the 38th president of the United States on August 9, 1974, the day that President Richard M. Nixon resigned from office.

CIVICS SIDELIGHT

Following are the nine vice presidents who have succeeded to the presidency following the death or resignation of the president. The presidents they succeeded are in parentheses: Gerald Ford (after Richard Nixon's resignation in 1974); Lyndon Johnson (after John Kennedy's assassination in 1963); Harry Truman (after Franklin Roosevelt's death in 1945); Calvin Coolidge (after Warren Harding's death in 1923); Theodore Roosevelt (after William McKinley's assassination in 1901); Chester Arthur (after James Garfield's assassination in 1881); Andrew Johnson (after Abraham Lincoln's assassination in 1865); Millard Fillmore (after Zachary Taylor's death in 1850); John Tyler (after William Henry Harrison's death in 1841).

Closure

Point out that the Cabinet members in line to succeed the president are appointed, not elected, officials. Also point out that, as students have read, events in 1973 produced a situation in which neither the president nor the vice president had been elected. Remind students that ours is a "government by the people." Have students write a position statement and a list of supporting facts and opinions to answer the following question: Should the nation ever be run by appointed officials? Call on volunteers to present their reasoned positions to the class.

Reviewing

Have students complete the Section 1 Review.

Reteaching

Assign Section 1 of the Chapter 6 Reteaching Worksheet.

SECTION 1 REVIEW
A N S W E R S

1. See the following page: presidential succession (p. 95).

2. native-born citizen, at least 35 years old, U.S. resident for at least 14 years

3. two terms; president—$200,000; vice president—$171,500

4. vice president, Speaker, president *pro tempore* of Senate, Cabinet members in the order in which their departments were created

5. vice president serves as acting president until president is well again

6. Answers will vary. Students might say limits ensure that presidents do not become too powerful or unresponsive. Disadvantages might include insufficient time to tackle complex objectives and a president weakened by the inability to use possible reelection as a political tool.

96

Adopted in 1967, the Twenty-fifth Amendment to the U.S. Constitution provides for the new president nominating a new vice president. The nomination of the vice president must then be approved by a majority vote of both houses of Congress.

The first use of the Twenty-fifth Amendment occurred in 1973. Vice President Spiro Agnew resigned after he was charged with income tax evasion. President Richard M. Nixon nominated Gerald R. Ford as the new vice president. Ford's nomination was confirmed by Congress.

The amendment was used again in 1974. When President Nixon resigned because of the Watergate scandal, Vice President Ford became president. Ford then nominated Nelson A. Rockefeller as vice president, and Congress approved the nomination. For the only time in its history, the nation had a president and a vice president who had not been elected to office by the people.

The Twenty-fifth Amendment also provides that if the president is too ill to serve, the vice president will serve as acting president until the president is well again. Suppose, however, that the president wants to resume the duties of office, but the vice president and the Cabinet do not think the president is fit to do so. Then Congress must decide by a two-thirds vote whether the president will return to office or whether the vice president will continue as acting president.

SECTION 1 REVIEW

1. Define the following term: presidential succession.

2. What are the constitutional qualifications for the presidency and the vice presidency?

3. How many terms can a president serve, and what salaries do the president and vice president receive?

4. Identify the order of presidential succession.

5. What happens if a president becomes too ill to serve?

6. **THINKING CRITICALLY** As you have learned, the Twenty-second Amendment places a limit on the number of terms that a president can serve in office. What advantages might there be to limiting a president's length of time in office? What disadvantages might there be to this limit? Write a position statement for or against repealing the Twenty-second Amendment.

---

2 | Powers and Roles of the President

Article 2, Section 1, of the Constitution provides that "the executive power shall be vested in [given to] a President of the United States of America." This clause means that the president, as head of the executive branch, is responsible for executing, or carrying out, the laws passed by Congress.

Because the president has the job of executing the nation's laws, the president is often called the nation's chief executive. As chief executive, the president must take an active role in all phases of government.

Legislative Leader

The president plays a large role in shaping the laws of the United States. As you know, the president recommends, or suggests, needed laws to Congress. In fact, the Constitution requires that the president "shall from time to time give to the Congress information of [about] the state of the Union, and recommend to their [Congress's] consideration such measures as he shall judge necessary. . . ."

After studying Section 2, students should be able to do the following.

1. Identify and describe the president's legislative influence and judicial powers.

2. Explain the ways in which Congress limits the president's military powers.

3. Identify the president's duties both as foreign policy leader and as chief of state.

Ask students what piece of paper they will receive when they graduate. *(a diploma)* Diploma comes from a Greek word meaning "folded paper." **Diplomatic notes** and **diplomacy** have the same root as *diploma*. In the world of **foreign policy**, officials sometimes exchange diplomatic notes—official communications in document ("folded paper") form—between governments. The dealing between governments is known as diplomacy because such dealings in the past relied so much on the trafficking of these notes.

To carry out this constitutional provision, the president delivers several messages to Congress each year. These messages may be delivered as speeches before Congress or be sent in writing.

Every year, usually in late January, the president delivers to Congress a **State of the Union Address**. This speech, which is televised to the public, sets forth the programs and policies that the president wants Congress to put into effect as laws. These programs and policies usually address the nation's most pressing concerns.

The president also sends Congress a budget message, recommending how the federal government should raise and spend its money. In an economic message to Congress, the president reviews the nation's economic condition and recommends various laws and programs to help the economy.

The president also influences legislation by the power to veto, or reject, laws. Sometimes the threat of a presidential veto discourages Congress from passing a bill. Congress knows how difficult it is to pass a bill after it has been vetoed by the president. For this reason, Congress considers the issues carefully before passing a bill it knows the president does not favor.

Commander in Chief

As head of the U.S. armed forces, or commander in chief, the president has important powers. All military officers, in time of war or in peacetime, take their orders from the president. The president does not actually lead U.S. forces into battle. The president is, however, in constant contact with the nation's military leaders. The president also has the final word in planning how a war is to be fought.

Under the Constitution, only Congress can declare war. As commander in chief of the armed forces, however, the president may send U.S. forces into any part of the world where danger threatens. Presidents have sent troops into action in foreign lands many times in the nation's history.

In his role as U.S. foreign policy leader, President Bill Clinton helped Yitzhak Rabin (left) of Israel and Palestinian Yasser Arafat (right) work out a peace agreement between their two peoples.

Sending U.S. troops into certain situations sometimes involves the risk of war. Therefore, Congress passed the War Powers Act in 1973 to limit the president's military power. This act requires that troops sent abroad by the president be recalled within 60 days unless Congress approves the action. The 60 days may be extended to 90 days if needed to ensure the safe removal of U.S. troops.

Foreign Policy Leader

The president, as chief executive of one of the most powerful nations of the world, must give constant attention to U.S. **foreign policy**—the nation's plan for dealing with the other nations of the world. As the person in charge of conducting U.S. foreign policy, the president seeks to secure friendly relations with foreign governments while preserving the security of the United States.

To conduct relations with other governments, the president appoints officials to represent the United States government in foreign nations. The president also meets with leaders of other nations and with their representatives in the United States. In addition, the president

GLOBAL PERSPECTIVES

The United States is not the only country in the world whose civilian chief executive also is the commander in chief of the country's armed forces. The presidents of France and Argentina, for example, are the supreme commanders of their respective country's armed forces. In some cases military commanders have overthrown elected civilian governments and taken control of the government. In 1976, for example, military commanders overthrew the civilian president of Argentina. The Argentine military turned the government back over to an elected civilian president in 1983.

As an extension exercise, you might have some students research who serves as commander in chief of armed forces in other countries.

Writing to Persuade

Review the function of the president in the system of checks and balances. Ask students to consider how the president helps shape U.S. laws and interacts with the judicial branch. Have students write a speech outlining what they believe is the president's most important power in "checking" or "balancing" either the legislative branch or the judicial branch.

GLOBAL PERSPECTIVES

The nation's chief diplomat occasionally makes a cultural mistake. President Kennedy, delivering a speech to a supportive crowd in Berlin, Germany, in 1963, spoke the heartfelt words *"Ich bin ein Berliner."* Most people knew he meant to say "I am a Berliner," but *ein Berliner* in German actually means a popular Berlin pastry similar to a jelly-filled doughnut. Popular history, however, records Kennedy's line as he meant it.

CIVICS TRANSPARENCIES

An overhead transparency of "Powers of the President" is available in *Teaching Transparencies with Teacher's Notes.*

often travels abroad to other countries to meet with foreign leaders.

In pursuing its foreign policy, the U.S. government makes written agreements, called **treaties**, with other nations. The president is responsible for making these treaties with foreign governments. Many officials work to reach agreements with other nations. The president, however, assumes the final responsibility for all treaties.

All treaties must be made with the advice and consent of the Senate. The Senate must approve a treaty by a two-thirds vote before it becomes effective. If the treaty is approved, the president has the responsibility of seeing that its provisions are carried out.

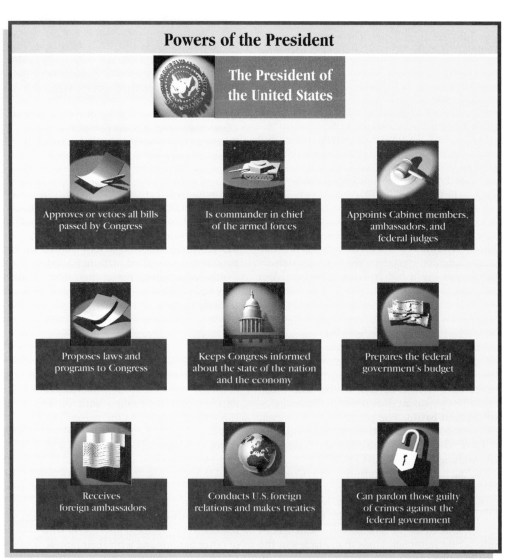

Powers of the President

The President of the United States

Approves or vetoes all bills passed by Congress

Is commander in chief of the armed forces

Appoints Cabinet members, ambassadors, and federal judges

Proposes laws and programs to Congress

Keeps Congress informed about the state of the nation and the economy

Prepares the federal government's budget

Receives foreign ambassadors

Conducts U.S. foreign relations and makes treaties

Can pardon those guilty of crimes against the federal government

Tell students that the president must wear many "hats" as chief executive. Call on volunteers to use the board to draw hats (or other articles of clothing) that represent the roles the president has. For example, students might draw a general's hat to represent the president's role as commander in chief or a judge's robe to represent the judicial powers of the presidency. When the president's roles have been illustrated, ask: Are the skills needed to be chief diplomat different from the skills needed to be chief of state?

Have students pick three of the president's roles and suggest specific activities that might fit into each category. Have them write each activity in the form of a newspaper headline. For example, a headline for the president in the role of chief of state might read: "President tosses first pitch to open baseball season."

Chief Diplomat

Great skill and tact are required in dealing with friendly and unfriendly nations. The art of dealing with foreign governments is called **diplomacy**. The president is the nation's chief diplomat. Presidential visits to foreign nations build international friendship and security and promote U.S. interests.

As the nation's chief diplomat, the president often corresponds with the leaders of foreign governments. These written communications are called **diplomatic notes**. Also, the president has access to a computerized communications system. This system enables the president to make a direct connection with other governments quickly in an emergency. Such a method of communication between world leaders is important. It can prevent governments from taking hasty actions that might have dangerous consequences for the United States and the world.

Judicial Powers

The Constitution gives the president the power to appoint Supreme Court justices and other federal judges. These judicial appointments must be approved by a majority vote of the members of the Senate.

The president also has the power to grant reprieves and pardons to those who have committed certain federal crimes. A **reprieve** postpones the carrying out of a person's sentence. It gives a convicted person the opportunity to gather more evidence to support his or her case or to appeal for a new trial. A **pardon** forgives a person convicted of a crime and frees him or her from serving out the sentence. The president also has the judicial power known as **commutation**, or making a convicted person's sentence less severe.

Other Presidential Roles

Over the years the president has assumed other roles that are not mentioned in the Constitution. These roles include chief of state and political party leader.

Presidents, such as Bill Clinton, enjoy meeting with younger generations of Americans who will someday lead the country.

As chief of state, the president is the symbol of the United States and its people. It is the president who greets visiting foreign leaders and travels to other countries to strengthen ties and improve relations. The president performs many ceremonial duties as well. These include awarding medals to honor worthy citizens, lighting the nation's Christmas tree, and throwing out the first baseball to open the baseball season.

The president is also the leader of a political party. Members of the president's political party worked hard to help elect the president. In return, the president makes speeches to help other party members who are running for public office. The president also helps the party raise money for its political campaigns, candidates, and programs.

Civics Sidelight

The Senate checks the judicial power of the president by confirming or rejecting the president's appointments to the bench. At times confirmation battles have been fierce. Battles over the Supreme Court nominations of Robert Bork in 1987 and Clarence Thomas in 1991, for example, were particularly bitter. The Senate rejected Bork but approved Thomas. Up to 1995, 16 presidents had at least one of their Supreme Court nominees rejected by the Senate. Only 6 of 28 total court rejections (up to 1995) had come in this century.

Closure

Have students locate the salary figures for the president and vice president, from Section 1. Ask whether the salaries are too much or too little money for the job each performs. Have students write job profiles for the two offices, including the salary level for each and an explanation of the requirements that go with the salaries. Students might consider the president's power and responsibilities as well as the salaries of comparable executives in business.

Reviewing

Have students complete the Section 2 Review.

Reteaching

Assign Section 2 of the Chapter 6 Reteaching Worksheet.

SECTION 2 REVIEW
A N S W E R S

1. See the following pages: State of the Union Address, foreign policy (p. 97); treaty (p. 98); diplomacy, diplomatic note, reprieve, pardon, commutation (p. 99).

2. recommends legislation, gives annual State of the Union Address, sends economic and budget messages to Congress, may veto bills; appoints Supreme Court and other federal judges, may grant pardons, reprieves, and commutations

3. with War Powers Act, which requires that troops sent abroad by the president be recalled within 60 days unless Congress approves the action

4. appoints representatives to foreign countries, meets with foreign representatives and dignitaries, makes treaties, serves as chief diplomat of the United States

5. greets foreign leaders and serves as nation's representative abroad, performs ceremonial duties

6. Speeches should address suggested solutions to problems.

100

Presidential Daily Life

The president must find time to carry on a wide range of activities from day to day. At all times the president's office must be in touch with other key officials of the nation's government. Thus the president can never be far away from the telephone.

The activities that occupy the president's time are varied. Many hours of the day are spent in meetings with presidential advisers. When Congress is in session, the president may have a breakfast or luncheon meeting with congressional leaders. Meetings are also held with members of the president's political party to discuss the bills before Congress, appointments of officials, or political plans and strategies important to the party. In addition, the president meets regularly with members of the Cabinet.

The president delivers a great number of speeches. President Franklin D. Roosevelt established the custom of reporting directly to the American people. He did so by radio talks, which he called "fireside chats."

Today the president still delivers radio talks to the public, usually every week. More and more, however, presidents rely on television broadcasts. The president appears on television to speak directly to the American people, to inform them of proposed new programs, and to ask for their support. The president also holds press conferences to explain government decisions and answer questions from reporters.

The president must find time to attend to many other important duties. The president must sign (or veto) bills submitted by Congress, write speeches, appoint officials, and examine budget figures. The president must deal with matters of foreign policy and reach decisions on national defense issues. The president must find time to read newspapers and magazines and to study reports received from government officials at home and abroad. This enables the president to stay informed about events taking place in the nation and throughout the world.

SECTION 2 REVIEW

1. Define or identify the following terms: State of the Union Address, foreign policy, treaty, diplomacy, diplomatic note, reprieve, pardon, commutation.

2. How does the president influence legislation? What are the judicial powers of the president?

3. How does Congress limit the military powers of the president?

4. What are the president's duties as foreign policy leader?

5. What duties does the president have as chief of state?

6. **THINKING CRITICALLY** Using the president's State of the Union Address as a model, write a "State of the School Address." In your speech identify some of the challenges facing your school. For each issue, propose a possible solution. Conclude by telling the school's citizens (your class) what you will do to help the school prosper.

---

3 | Executive Departments and the Cabinet

The duties of the executive branch of the federal government have grown significantly since George Washington served as the nation's first chief executive. During the early years of the nation, presidents carried out their executive duties with the help of a few assistants. Today there are thousands of people who assist the president.

Executive Office of the President

The president's closest advisers and aides are part of the Executive Office of the President.

SECTION OBJECTIVES

After studying Section 3, students should be able to do the following.

1. Identify and explain the purpose of the Executive Office of the President.

2. Describe the relationship between the Cabinet and the executive departments.

3. Name the 14 executive departments.

Teaching Section 3
Building a Vocabulary

Point out that **ambassador** and **embassy** come from the same root word meaning "service." Explain that the residence of an *ambassador* to a country is the *embassy*. Ask students where they would go if they lost their **passport** in a foreign country. *(to an embassy or a **consulate**)*

The Executive Office was established in 1939. It has been reorganized by every president since then. The agencies and offices that make up the Executive Office advise the president on current issues, including important domestic and international matters.

The Council of Economic Advisers, for example, furnishes the president with facts and figures about the nation's economy. It recommends programs to promote economic growth and stability.

Another agency of the Executive Office is the Office of Management and Budget. This agency assists in the preparation of the federal budget, which the president must present to Congress. A **budget** is a plan of income and spending.

The National Security Council (NSC) is the president's top-ranking group of advisers on all matters concerning the nation's defense and security. The Office of National Drug Control Policy coordinates federal, state, and local activities designed to stop the use of illegal drugs. The Council on Environmental Quality monitors the environment and makes recommendations to the president.

The White House Office includes the president's closest personal and political advisers. Also part of this office are researchers, clerical staff, social secretaries, and the president's doctor. Members of the White House staff perform many important jobs for the president. They schedule the president's appointments and write speeches. They help maintain good relations with Congress and with other departments and agencies of the government. A press secretary represents the president to the news media and the public.

Executive Departments

The leaders who wrote the U.S. Constitution drew up a plan of government with plenty of room for growth. They did not try to work out every detail of government. For example, they did not try to plan for each person who would help the president carry out the nation's laws. Thus the Constitution makes no mention of

DID YOU KNOW THAT...

When George Washington became the nation's first president, no one knew what to call him. Vice President John Adams wanted to call him "His Highness, The President of the United States and Protector of the Rights of the Same." The Senate called him "His Highness." This was the title used for the British king.

It was the House of Representatives that began to refer to the nation's chief executive as "the President of the United States." This simple title soon won everyone's approval.

His Highness?

Mr. President?

the president's assistants other than to state that "he may require the opinion, in writing, of the principal officer in each of the executive departments. . . ."

Today there are 14 **executive departments** in the federal government. Each department has specific areas of responsibility. The chart on page 107 shows the principal duties of each executive department.

Congress has the power to establish executive departments, reorganize and combine different departments, or even eliminate a department. The power to change the executive departments helps the presidency and the nation adapt to changing times.

Of course, the president, as chief executive, has a great deal of influence in these changes. Congress listens carefully to the president's wishes and requests regarding the executive departments. The president also has the power to direct the executive departments, working within the structure established by Congress.

CIVICS SIDELIGHT

The genesis of the Executive Office of the President was the *Report of the President's Committee on Administrative Management* in 1937. "The president needs help," concluded the committee upon its review of the administrative needs of an executive branch whose policy authority had been greatly expanded. Indeed, the Great Depression and the New Deal programs that were instituted to battle that economic catastrophe were important factors in the growth of the executive branch. Congressional action also lent a hand in the expansion of the executive branch. For example, Congress created the Bureau of the Budget as part of the Treasury Department in 1921. The Bureau of the Budget (later changed to the Office of Management and Budget) moved to the Executive Office of the President in 1939. Congress also expanded the president's role in areas such as labor, national security, and atomic energy policy.

Making Comparisons

Invite a member of the school board (preferably the president or chairperson) to your class to discuss how the budget for schools in your community is prepared. Have students prepare and ask questions about the budget process and about key players in that process. Then have students create charts that compare the budget process for the Executive Office of the President with that for the local school board.

CIVICS SIDELIGHT

The first female Cabinet member, Frances Perkins, served as secretary of labor in 1933. During her 12-year tenure, Perkins was a proponent of legislation setting a minimum wage, establishing a maximum work week, limiting child employment, and providing unemployment compensation. She also helped forge the Social Security Act and the Fair Labor Standards Act. The latter provided workers with a minimum wage and a maximum 40-hour week.

GLOBAL PERSPECTIVES

Point out that ambassadors and other diplomats to and for the United States may not be arrested in a foreign land. Among the reasons for the policy of diplomatic immunity is the desire for officially accredited diplomats to be able to perform their duties with complete independence. Also, diplomats are direct representatives of foreign countries and, as such, remain under the authority of their own governments.

The Cabinet

George Washington had the help of only three executive departments: the Departments of State, Treasury, and War. He met frequently with the heads of these departments to discuss policy and to seek their advice on important matters. The heads of these executive departments, as you recall, became known as the president's Cabinet. Every president since Washington has followed the custom of holding Cabinet meetings.

The Cabinet consists of the heads of the 14 executive departments and any other officials the president chooses. The president often invites other key government officials, such as the vice president, to attend Cabinet meetings. Cabinet meetings are led by the president.

Members of the Cabinet are appointed by the president. These appointments, however, must be approved by a majority vote of the Senate. The title of most Cabinet members is **secretary**. For example, the head of the Department of State is called the secretary of state. The head of the Department of the Treasury is called the secretary of the treasury. The head of the Department of Justice, however, is known as the **attorney general**.

On the next few pages, you will read about each of the 14 executive departments. All of these departments work to improve the lives of all Americans.

Department of State

The conduct of the nation's relations with other countries is the special responsibility of the Department of State. The secretary of state heads a large staff of officials in Washington, D.C., who direct the worldwide work of the department. U.S. officials sent to other countries to represent the nation also report to the Department of State.

Ambassadors are the highest-ranking U.S. representatives in foreign countries. The official residence of an ambassador in a foreign country is called an **embassy**. In a few smaller countries, the United States is represented by officials called **ministers**.

There is another kind of representative, called a **consul**. An American consul's office,

These pictures show the steady growth of the size of the Cabinet from President Washington's time (left) to President Clinton's time (right).

Consult the telephone directory under "United States Government" for executive departments or agencies with offices in or near your community. Arrange for a speaker from one of these offices to talk to the class about his or her work. Have students prepare a list of pertinent questions to ask the speaker.

Have students use newspapers and other periodicals to create a collage illustrating the major responsibilities of each of the executive departments. Students should include short, explanatory captions under each illustration in their collages. Display some of the collages to the class.

or **consulate**, can be found in most large foreign cities. The consuls and the members of their staffs work hard to improve trade between the United States and other nations. They also help protect American citizens who conduct business and own property in foreign countries. American citizens traveling in foreign lands may go to U.S. consulates if they need help.

At home the Department of State is the keeper of the Great Seal of the United States. The Great Seal is put on all laws and treaties. (See page 577.) The Department of State also issues documents known as passports and visas. **Passports** allow U.S. citizens to travel abroad. **Visas** allow people from other nations to come to the United States.

Department of the Treasury

The Department of the Treasury manages the nation's money. It collects taxes from citizens and businesses and pays out the money owed by the federal government. When necessary, the Department of the Treasury borrows money for the government. It also supervises the coining and printing of money, and it keeps the president informed about the financial condition of the country.

There are several divisions within the Department of the Treasury. The Internal Revenue Service (IRS) collects individual and corporate income taxes. The Customs Service collects taxes on goods brought into the country. The Secret Service protects the president and helps prevent **counterfeiting**—the making or distributing of fake money.

Department of Defense

Until 1947 the nation's armed forces were directed by two separate departments—the Department of War and the Department of the Navy. In 1947 Congress placed all the armed forces—the Army, Navy, and Air Force—under one department, the Department of Defense. Its head, the secretary of defense, is always a **civilian**, or nonmilitary person. The

GLOBAL CONNECTIONS

Women in the Military

In the history of the United States, nearly two million American women have served in the defense of the nation. Military service has never been compulsory for women—they have always served as volunteers. Recently, some of the restrictions preventing American women from serving in combat positions in the armed forces have been lifted.

Military life for women in Israel is much different. There, women as well as men are required to serve in the Israeli Defense Forces. Young Israelis begin their military service at the age of 18. Men serve for three years, while women serve for two years.

Although there are many sections of the army to which Israeli soldiers may be assigned, women usually are assigned to noncombat roles. Even so, Israeli women undergo a three-month course that teaches them combat and weapons skills. In addition, many combat instructors are women.

Most young Israeli women are eager to perform their military duty. They consider it a natural stage on the way to adulthood.

CIVICS SIDELIGHT

The oldest U.S. officer-training school is the Military Academy at West Point, founded by an act of Congress and opened in 1802. Entrance into West Point is by invitation only. Sources of appointment include the president, the vice president, each senator, each representative, and the armed forces. Women cadets were first admitted to West Point in 1976. Congress may permit foreign nationals from U.S. allies to attend U.S. military academies. The other major service academies are the Naval Academy at Annapolis, Maryland, and the Air Force Academy at Colorado Springs, Colorado.

secretary has, however, many military officers as assistants. These officers help the secretary plan military defense and provide for the training and equipping of the armed forces.

There are three major divisions within the Department of Defense. The Department of
(continued on page 106)

Linking Civics and History

Have small groups of students work to research past efforts at passing gun control legislation in your community, in your state, in other states, and in the nation. The groups may employ the use of time lines, diagrams, or other methods to illustrate their findings. Have each group share its findings with the class.

CIVICS SIDELIGHT

According to the U.S. Department of Justice, the number of violent crimes committed by people armed with handguns is increasing. In 1992, for example, nearly 931,000 violent crimes in the nation involved the use of handguns. This figure represents approximately 13 percent of all the violent crimes committed in 1992. Moreover, each year over a five-year period, an average of 62,000 victims of violent crime defended themselves against their attackers by using firearms.

Not all groups in the United States are equally likely to be the victims of handgun crime. According to the Justice Department, African American males between the ages of 16 and 19 are four times as likely as white males in this age group to be the victims of handgun crime. Similarly, African American males aged 20 to 24 are three times as likely to be victims as white males their age.

Case STUDY

GUN CONTROL

Guns have played an important role in American history. Colonists used muskets to hunt food for their families and to win the American Revolution. As the country expanded westward, rifles and pistols were used for hunting game, settling disputes, and defending against cattle rustlers.

Guns are still an important part of American life. Some 42 percent of Americans own firearms. Americans use their guns primarily for recreation—hunting, target shooting, and collecting. Many people keep guns in their homes for protection.

Unfortunately, firearms have a darker side. About 38,000 Americans are killed by firearms each year. Most of these deaths involve crimes. Gun accidents, however, kill about 1,400 Americans annually. And firearms kept for self-protection often end up injuring or killing friends or family members instead of scaring off intruders.

Because so many Americans are hurt and killed by firearms, many citizens want the government to restrict gun ownership. Other people argue that gun ownership is a basic right guaranteed to all Americans. At the center of this debate is the Second Amendment to the Constitution.

Both the supporters and the opponents of handgun control believe strongly in their positions.

"A Well Regulated Militia"

The Second Amendment states that "A well regulated militia being necessary to the security of a free state, the right of the people to keep and bear arms shall not be infringed."

This amendment allows each state to form and arm its own "well regulated militia," what we know today as the National Guard. National Guard units maintain the internal security of each state during emergencies. The amendment also gives local, state, and federal governments the right to establish and arm security forces, such as police departments.

Few people would argue against giving police and military forces the right to use weapons to maintain the peace and security of the nation. But what about average citizens? Does the Second Amendment give everyone the right to own and use guns?

Summarizing

Pose the following debate proposition: Handguns should be banned completely. Have half the class support the proposition and half oppose it. Tell them to use the case study to find points they would make in a debate on this issue. List points for and against the proposition on the chalkboard. You may wish to have selected students do further research and then conduct a panel discussion on this issue.

Interpreting the Constitution

In 1981 the town of Morton Grove, Illinois, became the first town to completely ban handguns. The U.S. Court of Appeals ruled that the Morton Grove law did not violate the Second Amendment, and the Supreme Court refused to hear the case, allowing the lower court's ruling to stand.

The Morton Grove decision is in keeping with the judiciary's view of the Second Amendment. In fact, every Supreme Court and federal court decision involving the Second Amendment has held that the amendment does not guarantee the right of individuals to own or to carry arms. Gun control laws, therefore, are constitutional.

The federal government, most states, and many communities have some level of restrictions on gun ownership. The Brady Handgun Violence Prevention Act, which went into effect in 1994, makes it more difficult for people to buy handguns. The "Brady law" sets a national five-day waiting period on handgun purchases. The law also requires that local law-enforcement agencies check the backgrounds of people who want to buy handguns. Convicted criminals, minors, drug abusers, and illegal immigrants are not eligible to buy handguns in the United States.

Battling over Gun Control

Despite court rulings and new laws, gun control continues to be hotly debated. The National Rifle Association (NRA), a highly vocal supporter of gun ownership, argues that the Second Amendment guarantees Americans "the right to keep and bear arms."

Among the most prominent of the groups opposing this view is Handgun Control. Handgun Control argues that stronger gun control laws, by keeping guns out of the hands of criminals, will reduce the number of Americans killed and injured by guns each year. The battle over gun control continues.

Jim Brady, former presidential press secretary, was shot in an assassination attempt on President Ronald Reagan in 1981. His efforts to restrict handgun ownership were rewarded in 1994 when the Brady Handgun Violence Prevention Act went into effect.

YOU DECIDE

1 What role have guns played in American life?

2 Why do some people support gun control laws? Why do others oppose these laws?

3 Find out what, if any, gun control laws exist in your community or state. Are they effective? How restrictive are they?

CIVICS SIDELIGHT

Jim Brady suffered a head wound in the 1981 attempt to assassinate President Reagan. Brady's recovery from the handgun shooting has been a long and painful process, and he now must use a wheelchair. Since the shooting, Brady and his wife, Sarah, have been among the nation's most vocal advocates for gun control.

ANSWERS TO YOU DECIDE

1. Colonists used guns to hunt and to fight the British. Settlers used guns to hunt, settle disputes, and defend against rustlers. Today guns are used for hunting, target shooting, collecting, and protection.

2. People support such laws because they believe they will reduce the number of people killed by guns. Opponents believe such laws violate their Second Amendment rights.

3. Students' opinions on effectiveness and restrictiveness of laws may vary according to point of view.

Refer students to the chart of executive departments on page 107. Suggest various issues or policies and ask the class to supply the name of the executive department(s) that would have jurisdiction over each issue or policy. Have students record these issues and policies for use in the following "Independent Practice" activity.

Ask each student to pick one executive department and create a brochure about it. The brochure should include information about the department's history, duties, and structure, as well as information about issues affecting the department. Students might need to refer to newspapers and other periodicals and to classroom resources, such as encyclopedias. Collect the brochures to create a "Guide to the Executive Departments."

CIVICS SIDELIGHT

At first glance, the Department of Commerce may seem an odd place to find the Bureau of the Census and the National Oceanic and Atmospheric Administration. But the department is required by law to provide statistics and analyses for business and government planners and to seek to improve knowledge of the earth's physical environment and oceanic resources.

the Army commands land forces. The Department of the Navy has charge of seagoing forces and includes the Marine Corps. The Department of the Air Force is responsible for air defenses. Each of these divisions is headed by a civilian secretary.

The highest-ranking military officers of the Army, Navy, and Air Force are members of the **Joint Chiefs of Staff**. The head of the Marine Corps attends all meetings of the Joint Chiefs and takes part as an equal member when matters concerning the Marines are discussed. Members of the Joint Chiefs of Staff have the duty of advising the president on military matters.

The Department of Defense is also responsible for four officer-training schools. These are the U.S. Military Academy at West Point, New York; the U.S. Naval Academy at Annapolis, Maryland; the U.S. Air Force Academy at Colorado Springs, Colorado; and the U.S. Coast Guard Academy at New London, Connecticut.

Academy candidates are nominated by their district representatives or by their state senators. Usually, four candidates are named for each opening. All candidates must have good high school academic records and must pass scholastic and physical tests.

The successful candidate receives a free four-year college education and upon graduation becomes an officer in one of the military services. Since 1976 women have been admitted into all the service academies on an equal basis with men.

Department of Justice

The Department of Justice, under the attorney general, enforces federal laws. This department also defends the United States in court when a lawsuit is brought against the federal government for any reason.

The Federal Bureau of Investigation (FBI) is an important agency of the Department of Justice. The FBI investigates crimes that break federal government laws and arrests those accused of crimes against the United States.

The Immigration and Naturalization Service (INS) and the Bureau of Prisons are also part of the Department of Justice.

Department of the Interior

The Department of the Interior manages the nation's natural resources. Its duties are to encourage the wise use of U.S. land, minerals, water, fish, and wildlife. The department also manages national parks and federal dams.

There are several important divisions within the Department of the Interior. The Bureau of Indian Affairs deals with matters involving Native Americans. The Bureau of Reclamation sponsors irrigation, flood control, and hydroelectric power projects. Other divisions include the National Park Service, the Bureau of Mines, and the U.S. Fish and Wildlife Service.

Department of Agriculture

The Department of Agriculture helps farmers in the important task of raising and marketing crops. Special agencies in the department, such as the Agricultural Research Service and the Natural Resources Conservation Service, encourage better methods of farming. The department also prepares reports on market conditions for crops and livestock that assist farmers in their planning and planting.

Other divisions within the Department of Agriculture include the Farmers Home Administration (FmHA), which provides loans for buying and operating farms, and the U.S. Forest Service, which helps protect the nation's woodlands. The Food and Consumer Service manages the Food Stamp and National School Lunch programs.

Department of Commerce

The Department of Commerce encourages U.S. trade and business. There are many important agencies within this department. For example, the Bureau of Economic Analysis studies business conditions in the United

Closure

Have each student write the name of one of the 14 executive departments on a slip of paper, along with three adjectives or responsibilities that correspond to that department. Collect the lists by department. Without revealing the name, read the description of each department in turn, asking students to guess the department.

Reviewing

Have students complete the Section 3 Review.

Reteaching

Assign Section 3 of the Chapter 6 Reteaching Worksheet.

Principal Duties of the Executive Departments

 Department of State (1789) [1]

Conducts foreign relations

Protects U.S. citizens abroad

Issues passports and visas

 Department of the Treasury (1789)

Prints, coins, and issues money

Collects taxes and pays bills

Manages government funds

 Department of Justice (1789) [2]

Investigates violations of federal laws

Prosecutes cases before courts

Administers naturalization laws

Enforces immigration laws

 Department of the Interior (1849)

Controls public lands

Maintains public parks

Supervises Native American reservations

Controls water resources

 Department of Agriculture (1862)

Conducts studies to help farmers

Manages Food Stamp and School Lunch programs

Helps farmers raise and market crops

Directs soil conservation programs

Department of Commerce (1903)

Sets standards for weights and measures

Encourages and regulates foreign trade

Publishes reports on business and trade

 Department of Labor (1913)

Determines standards of labor

Publishes employment information

Directs public employment services

 Department of Defense (1949)

Maintains U.S. armed forces

Conducts military studies

Operates military bases

 Department of Health and Human Services (1953) [3]

Directs public health services

Sees that foods and medicines are safe

 Department of Housing and Urban Development (1965)

Helps urban housing programs

Helps cities plan traffic control

Helps cities plan mass transportation

Cooperates with metropolitan area planners

 Department of Transportation (1966)

Helps develop the nation's transportation policy

Supervises federal-aid highway program

Promotes transportation safety

Department of Energy (1977)

Helps develop the nation's energy policy

Promotes conservation of energy

Regulates energy resources

 Department of Education (1979)

Sets guidelines for granting financial aid to schools

Conducts research on educational subjects

Administers federally sponsored education programs

 Department of Veterans Affairs (1949)

Administers medical and disability benefits to veterans and their families

Provides pensions and death benefits for veterans

Guarantees home loans to veterans

1. Year in parentheses indicates the year the department was established.
2. Attorney General position established in 1789; department set up in 1870.
3. Department of Health, Education, and Welfare established in 1953; split into Department of Education and Department of Health and Human Services in 1980.

MULTICULTURAL PERSPECTIVES

President Clinton's Cabinet appointments in 1993 represented a mix of racial and ethnic groups, including more African Americans (Mike Espy, Department of Agriculture; Ronald H. Brown, Department of Commerce; Hazel R. O'Leary, Department of Energy) and Hispanic Americans (Federico F. Pena, Department of Transportation; Henry G. Cisneros, Department of Housing and Urban Development) than ever before.

Extension

Have students write a paragraph explaining which of the 14 executive departments has the most impact on their daily lives. They should provide concrete examples of this impact. Ask: Do you think the actions of other departments will affect you more or less the older you become? Which ones? Why?

SECTION 3 REVIEW
A N S W E R S

1. See the following pages: budget, executive department (p. 101); secretary, attorney general, ambassador, embassy, minister, consul (p. 102); consulate, passport, visa, counterfeiting, civilian (p. 103); Joint Chiefs of Staff (p. 106).

2. advise president on domestic and foreign matters

3. Heads of executive departments are all members of the Cabinet.

4. State, Treasury, Defense, Justice, Interior, Agriculture, Commerce, Labor, Health and Human Services, Housing and Urban Development, Transportation, Energy, Education, Veterans Affairs

5. Memos will vary. Students should demonstrate an understanding of their department's purpose.

108

States. The Minority Business Development Agency assists in creating and strengthening minority-owned businesses. The Patent and Trademark Office protects the rights of inventors. The International Trade Administration promotes world trade and seeks to strengthen the U.S. position in such trade.

Also within this department is the Bureau of the Census, which counts the U.S. population every 10 years. The National Oceanic and Atmospheric Administration, which monitors and forecasts the nation's weather, is also part of the Department of Commerce.

Department of Labor

American workers receive important services from the Department of Labor. This department gathers information on working conditions in various businesses and industries. The Employment Standards Administration is responsible for carrying out federal laws that regulate the wages and hours of workers and seeks to improve working conditions.

Another division of the Department of Labor is the Bureau of Labor Statistics, which collects information about employment and labor-management relations. The Women's Bureau is responsible for promoting the employment opportunities and personal well-being of working women.

Department of Health and Human Services

The Department of Health and Human Services gathers information, conducts research, and runs programs to promote the health and well-being of all citizens. It was created from the Department of Health, Education, and Welfare (HEW) in 1980. Its largest division, the Social Security Administration, became an independent agency early in 1995.

Department of Housing and Urban Development

The Department of Housing and Urban Development (HUD) seeks to improve the housing conditions in U.S. cities. It runs programs to help people buy homes, and it helps city and state governments provide public housing and improve neighborhoods.

Department of Transportation

The Department of Transportation helps coordinate and develop the nation's ground, water, and air transportation systems. It also promotes public safety and deals with mass transportation issues. The Coast Guard is part of the Department of Transportation in peacetime. In wartime it becomes part of the Navy and the Department of Defense.

Department of Energy

The Department of Energy helps plan and manage the nation's energy policy. One of the department's main goals is to lessen the amount of energy that is wasted in the nation. In addition, this department is responsible for enforcing energy laws. It also regulates the development and use of nuclear and hydroelectric power, gas and oil pipelines, and other energy resources.

Department of Education

The Department of Education provides advice and information to the nation's school systems. It is also responsible for distributing federal funds and administering federal programs in schools throughout the United States.

Department of Veterans Affairs

The Department of Veterans Affairs replaced the Veterans Administration (VA), a government agency, in 1989. This department is responsible for administering government benefits to U. S. veterans and their families. These benefits include health care, pensions, and education loans.

SECTION OBJECTIVES

After studying Section 4, students should be able to do the following.

1. Explain why the independent agencies are separate from the executive departments.

2. Compare and contrast independent agencies and regulatory commissions.

Teaching Section 4
Building a Vocabulary

Point out that **independent agencies** and **regulatory commissions** are part of the federal **bureaucracy**. *Bureaucracy* comes from the French word *bureau* (desk or office). *Cracy* is derived from a Greek word meaning "strength or power." *Bureaucracy*, then, literally means "power of office." Ask students if they can identify government offices that are part of the federal bureaucracy. *(For example, students might say the Social Security Administration and the Federal Communications Commission.)*

SECTION 3 REVIEW

1. Define or identify the following terms: budget, executive department, secretary, attorney general, ambassador, embassy, minister, consul, consulate, passport, visa, counterfeiting, civilian, Joint Chiefs of Staff.

2. What is the purpose of the Executive Office of the President?

3. What is the relationship between the Cabinet and the executive departments?

4. Identify the 14 executive departments.

5. **THINKING CRITICALLY** Imagine that your recent appointment to head an executive department (of your choice) has been approved by the Senate. As a new secretary, your first task is to write a memo to the president. In the memo describe what you believe is the most pressing national issue facing your department, and explain how your department will address it.

4 Independent Agencies and Regulatory Commissions

In addition to the executive departments, Congress has set up a number of **independent agencies**. These agencies help the president carry out the duties of office.

The independent agencies are separate from the executive departments because they perform specialized duties that often do not fit into any regular department. In addition, some of these agencies serve all the departments. Therefore, they function best as separate and independent organizations.

Independent Agencies

There are more than 60 independent agencies. Each was created by Congress to perform a

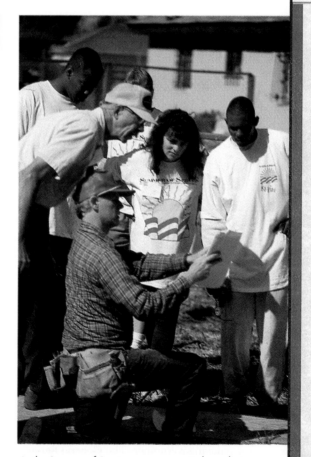

In the Summer of Service program, an independent agency project, young people spent their summers helping communities in need.

specific job. For example, the Commission on Civil Rights collects information about discrimination. The Farm Credit Administration helps farmers obtain loans. The Small Business Administration makes loans to small businesses. The National Aeronautics and Space Administration (NASA) runs the nation's space program.

Several independent agencies assist the work of the entire government. For example, the Office of Personnel Management gives tests to people who want to apply for jobs with

CIVICS SIDELIGHT

Explain that "independent" agencies are often heavily influenced by various interest groups. For example, the Nuclear Regulatory Commission (NRC)—an independent regulatory agency—licenses nuclear reactors through a long and formal process. Despite the lengthy approval process for big utilities seeking to build nuclear power plants, since 1967 the NRC has rarely denied approval for construction permits or operating licenses. Some people have been critical of what they believe is lax regulation of the nuclear energy industry. In 1979 a number of mechanical problems and human errors caused a serious accident at the Three Mile Island nuclear power plant in Pennsylvania. The accident highlighted a number of problems in the nuclear energy industry, including problems with regulation. Industry and government have worked to improve safety since that accident.

Guided Practice

Write *Independent Agencies* in a large circle on the chalk-board. Draw a smaller circle inside the other one, and write *Regulatory Commissions*. Help students see that all regulatory commissions are independent, but not all independent agencies are regulatory. Call on volunteers to write the names of regulatory agencies in the smaller circle and the names of other independent agencies in the larger circle.

Independent Practice

Have students choose one of the agencies discussed in the section and draw a picture that illustrates one of that agency's responsibilities. The identity of the agency should be put on the back of the picture. Have each student display his or her work and ask the class to guess which agency he or she has chosen to represent.

CIVICS SIDELIGHT

Presidential appointments to head independent agencies and other parts of the federal bureaucracy are considered "plums"— very desirable jobs. Every four years a House Committee on Post Office and Civil Service prepares a book called *Policy and Supporting Positions*, which is also known as the "plum book." The book, printed by the Government Printing Office, lists all the available political positions to be filled by the new presidential administration.

THE SPIDER'S PARLOR

This cartoon is more than 40 years old, yet it illustrates a complaint still common today. What point is the cartoonist trying to make?

the federal government. The General Services Administration buys supplies for the federal government. It also builds and maintains federal buildings.

Regulatory Commissions

Some independent agencies have the power to make rules and bring violators to court. These are called **regulatory commissions**. Their decisions often have the force of law.

The Interstate Commerce Commission (ICC), for example, regulates railroad, bus, truck, and water transportation that crosses state lines. The commission has the power to regulate rates and services. Established by Congress in 1887, it is the nation's oldest independent regulatory commission.

The Consumer Product Safety Commission (CPSC) sets and enforces safety standards for consumer products. It also conducts safety research and provides education programs.

The Securities and Exchange Commission (SEC) helps enforce laws regulating the buying and selling of stocks and bonds. This helps protect Americans' investments.

The National Labor Relations Board (NLRB) helps enforce federal labor laws. It also works to prevent and remedy unfair labor practices among businesses.

Who Runs the Regulatory Commissions?

The regulatory commissions were made independent so that they could have the freedom

Closure

Have students draw a political cartoon about a single independent agency or regulatory commission and a particular relevant issue. Students may need to refer to newspapers and other periodicals, as well as to classroom resources. Each cartoon should somehow illustrate the purpose of the agency and its effect on the issue the student has chosen. Display these cartoons for the class.

Reviewing

Have students complete the Section 4 Review.

Reteaching

Assign Section 4 of the Chapter 6 Reteaching Worksheet.

---

they need to do their jobs. The heads of these commissions are appointed by the president, with the approval of the Senate. These officials serve long terms, however—as long as 14 years. Because of these long terms, a single president cannot appoint more than a few commission leaders.

The independence of the regulatory commissions often has been criticized on the grounds that it makes them too powerful. Some people say that these commissions regulate too much and interfere too much in our lives. Other people defend these commissions. They say that their regulations are needed to protect the public.

The Federal Bureaucracy

The many departments and agencies in the executive branch of the government form the federal **bureaucracy**. Roughly three million people work in the bureaucracy. They include administrators, lawyers, scientists, doctors, engineers, secretaries, and clerks. People in the bureaucracy perform the day-to-day work of the executive branch. They work in Washington, D.C., in other cities throughout the United States, and in other nations.

The bureaucracy has many rules and regulations for carrying out a wide range of activities. Often these rules and regulations lead to bureaucratic delay, or "red tape." People dealing with a government agency often must spend a lot of time filling out forms. They must stand in seemingly endless lines. Sometimes they must go from department to department before getting the help they need. Despite these problems, the people in the bureaucracy keep the executive branch functioning under every president.

SECTION 4 REVIEW

1. Define or identify the following terms: independent agency, regulatory commission, bureaucracy.

2. Why are the independent agencies separate from the executive departments?

3. In what ways are independent agencies and regulatory commissions similar? In what ways are they different?

4. THINKING CRITICALLY Examine the political cartoon on page 110 of your textbook. Then think of a personal experience you have had with bureaucratic red tape in the government or another large organization. Illustrate this experience in a political cartoon. Be sure to include symbols and labels or a caption for your cartoon.

CHAPTER 6 SUMMARY

As the head of the executive branch, the president is responsible for seeing that the nation's laws are carried out. The president is elected for a four-year term. Presidents may be elected to no more than two terms.

The president has a difficult and demanding job. The president must provide leadership in such vital areas as setting foreign policy, dealing with foreign governments, planning national defense needs, and promoting the nation's prosperity. As chief executive of one of the world's most powerful nations, the president plays a large part in shaping the history of the nation and the world.

For help in these tasks, the president turns to the members of the Cabinet—the heads of the executive departments. These departments carry on much of the work of the executive branch of the federal government. A number of independent agencies also assist in the day-to-day work of the executive branch. These agencies deal with matters such as interstate commerce, protection of the environment, national defense, and many other important activities of government.

SECTION 4 REVIEW
A N S W E R S

1. See the following pages: independent agency (p. 109); regulatory commission (p. 110); bureaucracy (p. 111).

2. because they perform specialized duties that often are not the job of any regular department and because some of them serve all the executive departments

3. Both are independent of the executive departments, and both carry out specialized functions. Regulatory commissions have the power to make rules and bring violators to court; independent agencies do not have such powers.

4. Cartoons will vary. Students should demonstrate an understanding of bureaucratic red tape.

Tell students that a chart is an effective way to visualize any organization, from a complex government bureaucracy to a small school group. Businesses, for example, often follow a pattern similar to the one shown below. They have a leader (president) and other executive officers.

Have students draw a chart to represent the organization of the business where a family member or friend works. Point out the similarities with the chart of the Department of Defense. Suggest to students that organizational charts are most useful for sorting out complex organizations. They reveal not only levels of authority but also the "chain of command"—how decisions from above flow through the organization.

ANSWERS TO Applying the Skill

1. secretary of the Air Force

2. secretaries of the Army, Air Force, and Navy and the Joint Chiefs of Staff (advisory role); secretary of defense

3. Civilians hold all the top positions to ensure that the military remains accountable to the people.

Developing Civics Skills

SOCIAL STUDIES SKILL
Reading Organizational Charts

An effective way to visualize the executive branch is to use an organizational chart. An organizational chart is a diagram that helps you see how the various parts of an organization are related to each other.

Organizational charts have two basic parts: boxes and lines. The boxes represent certain offices or people. The lines that connect the boxes represent lines of communication and authority. Generally, the offices or people with the most authority are at the top of the chart and those with the least authority are at the bottom.

How to Read Organizational Charts

1. **Determine the subject.** Read the title of the chart to learn which organization is being diagrammed.
2. **Identify the symbols and colors.** Most organizational charts include a key. The key identifies what the symbols and colors in the chart represent.
3. **Analyze the chart.** Read the labels of the various boxes, and notice how the lines of authority and communication connect the boxes.
4. **Put the data to use.** Draw conclusions about the organization from the chart.

Applying the Skill

Examine the organizational chart below. Then answer the following questions.

1. To whom does the chief of staff of the Air Force report?
2. Who reports to the secretary of defense? Who reports directly to the commander in chief?
3. What role is played by civilians in the Department of Defense? Why do you think this is so?

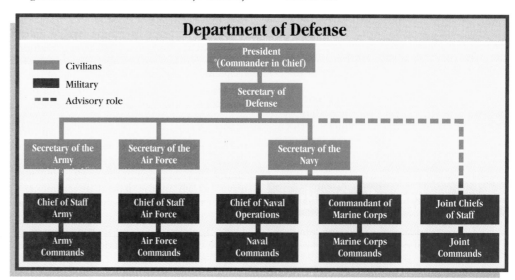

Department of Defense

Key:
- Civilians
- Military
- - - Advisory role

- President (Commander in Chief)
- Secretary of Defense
- Secretary of the Army
- Secretary of the Air Force
- Secretary of the Navy
- Chief of Staff Army
- Chief of Staff Air Force
- Chief of Naval Operations
- Commandant of Marine Corps
- Joint Chiefs of Staff
- Army Commands
- Air Force Commands
- Naval Commands
- Marine Corps Commands
- Joint Commands

CHAPTER 6 REVIEW
A N S W E R S

Vocabulary Workshop
1. order in which office of president is filled if it becomes vacant
2. sets forth the programs and policies the president wants Congress to pass
3. Joint Chiefs of Staff
4. treaties
5. attorney general; secretary
6. pardon, reprieve, commutation
7. ambassador

Reviewing Main Ideas
1. native-born citizen, at least 35 years old, U.S. resident for at least 14 years
2. recommends legislation, gives annual State of the Union Address, sends economic and budget messages to Congress, may veto bills; appoints Supreme Court and federal judges and grants pardons, reprieves, and commutations
3. foreign policy—appoints representatives to foreign lands, makes treaties, meets with foreign representatives and dignitaries, serves as nation's chief diplomat; chief of state—greets foreign visitors, travels to foreign lands, performs ceremonial functions
4. independent of executive departments, carry out specialized functions; only regulatory commissions have power to make rules and bring violators into court

Thinking Critically
1. Students should use sound reasoning in their responses.
2. Students should address advantages and disadvantages.
3. people and Constitution

Citizenship in Your Community
Collages should reflect the activities of the president.

Building Your Portfolio
Assign Portfolio Assessment Worksheet 6 in the *Portfolio Assessment Worksheets* booklet.

Assessment
- **Chapter 6 Tests**, *Chapter Tests* booklet
- **Test Generator**, Chapter 6
- **Portfolio**, Portfolio Assessment Worksheet 6, *Portfolio Assessment Worksheets* booklet

---

CHAPTER 6
R·e·v·i·e·w

Vocabulary Workshop
1. Define the term *presidential succession*.
2. What are the purposes of the president's State of the Union Address?
3. What group of military officers advises the president on military matters?
4. What is the term for written agreements made between nations?
5. What is the head of the Department of Justice called? What title is used for the heads of the other executive departments?
6. What three actions may the president take regarding persons who have committed certain federal crimes?
7. What is the term for the highest-ranking U.S. representatives in foreign countries?

Reviewing Main Ideas
1. What qualifications must a president meet? a vice president?
2. What are three ways that the president can influence legislation? How can the president influence the judicial branch?
3. What is the president's role in foreign policy? as chief of state?
4. How are independent agencies and regulatory commissions similar? How do they differ?

Thinking Critically
1. As you have learned, John Adams, the first U.S. vice president, called the office of the vice president "the most insignificant" ever invented. Do you think this statement holds true today? Why?
2. Officials in Washington have considered creating an executive department whose responsibilities would focus on the environment. What advantages would a Department of the Environment bring? Why might such a department be controversial?
3. The president is the most powerful member of the executive branch. Who or what has authority over the president?

Citizenship in Your Community

Cooperative Project
With your group, collect newspaper and magazine articles and photographs that illustrate the president's daily activities. Determine how each of the president's activities affects your community. What policies or laws has the president carried out that affect your daily life and that of the other members of your community? Create a collage with the materials you have collected, and present it to the class. Each member of your group should explain how one of the president's activities shown affects your community.

Building Your Portfolio

The second step of your unit portfolio project (see page 135) is to create a list of the responsibilities of the executive branch. Next to each item, indicate which part of the executive branch handles that responsibility—the president and the Executive Office, an executive department, or an independent agency. Analyze your list. Do responsibilities overlap, causing conflict and inefficiency? Are there too many departments and agencies? Too few? Write a paragraph explaining any changes you would make to the executive branch. If no changes are needed, explain why. Place your list and your paragraph in your individual portfolio for later use.

CHAPTER 7

The Judicial Branch

TEXTBOOK	TEACHING RESOURCES	OTHER AVAILABLE RESOURCES
Chapter	• Skills Worksheet 7 • Challenge/Enrichment Worksheet 7	• Simulations and Case Studies Lessons 6 and 7
Section **1** Equal Justice Under the Law Page 115	• Reteaching Worksheet 7.1	
2 The Federal Court System Page 119	• Reteaching Worksheet 7.2	• Transparency 7: The United States Court System
3 The Supreme Court Page 123	• Reteaching Worksheet 7.3	
Review and Assessment Chapter 7 Review, Page 133 Unit 2 Review, Page 134	• Test, Form A • Test, Form B • Portfolio Assessment Worksheet 7 • Unit 2 Portfolio Assessment Worksheet	• *Test Generator,* Chapter 7 • *Test Generator,* Unit 2

Block Scheduling Option

ADDITIONAL RESOURCES

BOOKS FOR TEACHERS

Cox, Archibald, *The Court and the Constitution*, Houghton Mifflin.

Cox, Archibald, *The Role of the Supreme Court in American Government*, Oxford University Press.

Elliot, Stephen P., ed., *A Reference Guide to the United States Supreme Court*, Facts on File.

Lieberman, Jethro K., *The Evolving Constitution: How the Supreme Court Has Ruled on Issues from Abortion to Zoning*, Random House.

BOOKS FOR STUDENTS

Aaseng, Nathan, *Great Justices of the Supreme Court*, Oliver. The Court's history told through biographical sketches.

Congressional Quarterly and Elder Witt, *The Supreme Court and Individual Rights*, Congressional Quarterly. Examines the relationship between judicial decision making and the rights of the individual.

Rappaport, Doreen, *Tinker vs. Des Moines: Student Rights on Trial*, HarperCollins. An interactive book about the Supreme Court decision that protected students' rights to free speech.

MULTIMEDIA RESOURCES

Focus on Government: The Supreme Court and the Constitution (VHS, c, 15 min.), CU. Students debate the Court's interpretation of controversial issues.

The Research Companion: Supreme Court Decisions (Apple 5.25" disk), FM. Role-playing simulations dealing with landmark Court cases.

THE INTERNET

Have students use these search words to locate more information about chapter topics on the Internet: *judicial branch, federal courts, United States Supreme Court.*

 GLOBAL SKILL BUILDER

You might wish to use **Navigating the Internet** from the interactive *Global Skill Builder* CD-ROM to aid students' understanding of the Internet as a resource.

Abbreviations: b&w=black and white; c=color; f=film; fs=filmstrip; sd=sound; tr=transparency; VHS=videotape

CIVICS THEMES

AMERICAN GOVERNMENT

★ **Structures and Functions** Students will learn about the role of the judicial branch in our republican form of government, the four kinds of law in the United States, the procedures that ensure the right to a fair trial, and the significance of the Supreme Court's power of judicial review. Students also will learn how the Supreme Court has acted to protect our basic rights and freedoms, and the Supreme Court's role in keeping the Constitution a document for all generations.

CIVICS SKILLS

Students will learn how to evaluate alternatives in the decision-making process. They also will learn terms important to understanding the role and responsibilities of the judicial branch.

CITIZENSHIP VALUES

★ **Rights and Responsibilities** Students will be taught that the federal courts provide for equality under the law, and they will be led to appreciate the importance of the right to a fair trial.

MEETING INDIVIDUAL NEEDS

LIMITED ENGLISH PROFICIENCY (LEP)

Have students organize the information about the federal court system by creating web diagrams. Students might focus on the three main levels of courts: district courts, courts of appeals, and the Supreme Court. Each of these names would appear in a central circle. Lines branching from that circle would lead to other circles in which related information appears. Encourage students to include as many important details about each level of courts as they can.

LEARNERS HAVING DIFFICULTY

Have students read Section Review questions from the chapter (except for the vocabulary activity and "Thinking Critically"). Clarify any terms or concepts that may be confusing. Then have pairs of students locate the answers in the textbook. Students should alternate quizzing each other.

AUDITORY LEARNERS

After students complete the chapter, have them take turns reading aloud the first two sections of Article III of the Constitution. (See pages 538–539.) They should make connections between the material they have just learned and the more formal presentation of it in the Constitution. Have students volunteer to paraphrase individual paragraphs in this article.

VISUAL LEARNERS

Have students use newspapers and other periodicals to illustrate the U.S. court system. Some students might choose to create collages with pictures of individuals or actions involved in trial cases. Students should illustrate individuals and actions from all levels of the federal courts. Illustrations should include descriptive captions. Invite volunteers to explain their work to the class.

TACTILE/KINESTHETIC LEARNERS

If possible, lead students on a field trip to a federal courthouse or to a county or state district courtroom. You might wish to arrange in advance to sit in on a trial or hearing. Have students create court illustrations similar to those used by the news media when covering trials where photographic equipment is prohibited. If possible, have a judge speak with students about his or her role in the court system.

GIFTED LEARNERS

Have students conduct further research on cases presented in the chapter or on other famous cases that they find interesting. Have them focus on the historical context of each case, including contemporary events and public opinion. Invite students to report their findings to the class.

CHAPTER OVERVIEW

Chapter 7 examines how the federal court system has evolved since the Constitution was written. It focuses on the constitutional guarantees at the heart of the justice system and the ways in which the federal courts defend those guarantees. The underlying theme of the chapter is that the federal courts are dedicated to the principle of equal justice under the law.

Motivator

Ask students to quote the last six words of the Pledge of Allegiance. *(with liberty and justice for all)* Tell students that the word *liberty* comes from the Latin word for "free." Ask: What does justice have to do with freedom? *(Justice guarantees freedom.)* Ask students to interpret and discuss this statement.

CHAPTER OBJECTIVES

After studying Chapter 7, students should be able to do the following.

1. Explain how laws guarantee equal justice for all citizens.
2. Describe how the federal court system is organized.
3. Identify the role of the Supreme Court in the federal court system.
4. Determine how cases reach the Supreme Court.

SIMULATIONS AND CASE STUDIES

Lesson 6: *Bethel School District v. Matthew Fraser*
Lesson 7: Moot Court: *Jones v. Clear Creek ISD*

Block Scheduling Option

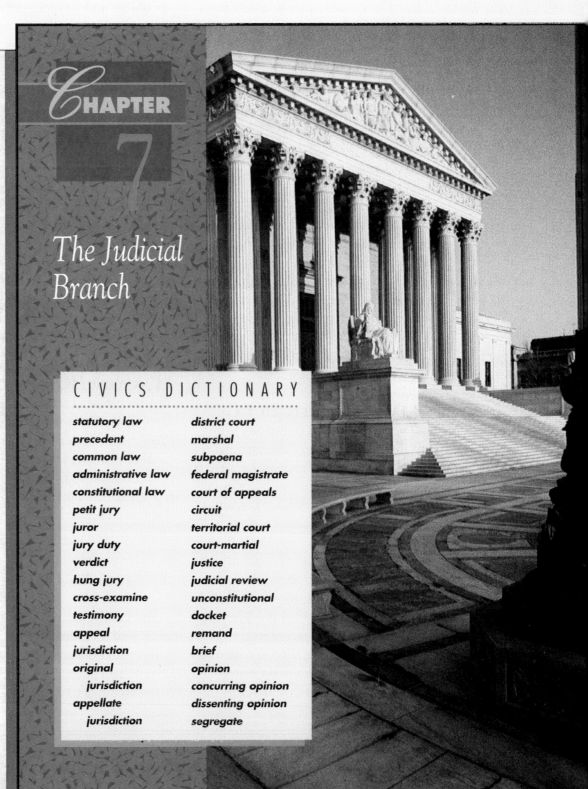

CHAPTER 7

The Judicial Branch

CIVICS DICTIONARY

statutory law	district court
precedent	marshal
common law	subpoena
administrative law	federal magistrate
constitutional law	court of appeals
petit jury	circuit
juror	territorial court
jury duty	court-martial
verdict	justice
hung jury	judicial review
cross-examine	unconstitutional
testimony	docket
appeal	remand
jurisdiction	brief
original	opinion
jurisdiction	concurring opinion
appellate	dissenting opinion
jurisdiction	segregate

After studying Section 1, students should be able to do the following.

1. Explain how majority rule affects the making of laws and why obeying laws is important.

2. Identify the four types of U.S. law.

3. Describe the role of the courts.

4. Define the phrase "beyond a reasonable doubt."

5. Explain the right of appeal.

Teaching Section 1
Building a Vocabulary

The Latin root *jur* means "law." Americans are subject to serving **jury duty**, which means they may be required to sit as a **juror** to decide guilt or innocence in a trial. A **trial jury** is also called a **petit jury**. Point out that the word *petit* in the term *petit jury* comes from the French (meaning "small"), but it has lost its French pronunciation. As a legal term, *petit* is pronounced "PEH-tee".

CHAPTER FOCUS

If you have ever played a sport, you know that the sport is governed by a set of rules. When a player breaks those rules, the player is penalized. What happens when players disagree about the meaning of a certain rule? In that instance, an official makes a final decision about the rule.

The U.S. government also needs officials to interpret its rules, or laws, and to punish law-breakers. These functions are the responsibility of the judicial branch of the federal government. In interpreting the laws, the judicial branch is guided by the ideal of equal justice for all. This ideal, essential to a free nation, protects your rights and the rights of all Americans.

• •

STUDY GUIDE

● How do the laws guarantee equal justice for all citizens?

● How is the federal court system organized?

● What role does the Supreme Court play in the court system, and how do cases reach the Supreme Court?

1 — Equal Justice Under the Law

Carved in marble over the entrance of the Supreme Court Building in Washington, D.C., is the motto "Equal Justice Under Law." This motto means that in the United States all citizens are considered equal and are guaranteed equal protection by the law.

Laws for the Good of All

American citizens enjoy freedom because the United States has laws to protect their rights. Of course, some laws limit freedom. A law against robbery, for example, denies the robber's freedom to steal. This law gives other citizens, however, freedom to use and enjoy their personal property.

Laws usually represent majority rule, or what the majority of citizens believe to be right and wrong. When most of the people believe strongly that something should or should not be done, a law is passed on this issue. If the American people later change their position on the issue, the law can be changed. In this way laws grow and change with the times.

Every U.S. citizen has the duty to know and obey the laws, especially those that concern an activity we undertake. If you ride a bicycle, for example, you must learn about road signs and traffic regulations. Law-abiding citizens realize that laws are passed for the good of all. By learning and obeying the nation's laws, you are practicing good citizenship.

Kinds of Law

There are four kinds of law in the United States. All these laws must follow the principles set forth in the Constitution, which is the supreme law of the land.

Statutory Law Laws that are passed by lawmaking bodies are known as **statutory laws**. They are passed by Congress and by state and local governments. For example, a state law that requires fire exits in all public buildings is a statutory law.

Common Law What happens if there is no statutory law covering a specific situation? Then we follow certain rules that have been accepted by Americans as the proper

MULTICULTURAL PERSPECTIVES

Common law has roots in England in the Middle Ages after the Norman Conquest in 1066. Before that time, local custom, strongly influenced by the church, formed the basis for law in England. The Normans, descendants of Vikings who settled in France, established a central judiciary in England. Judges' decisions began to be recorded so that other judges could read and profit by them. This led to the development of the common law legal tradition that later spread throughout the British Empire, including the British colonies in North America.

Applying Ideas

Review with students the idea that a law against robbery limits the robber's freedom but safeguards the freedom of other citizens. Ask students to suggest "laws" based on this concept for their school. For example: "Students should maintain quiet during testing periods." Lead a debate on each proposed law, and then conduct a vote on each law. Ask why it is important that everyone, including those who voted against establishing a particular law, obey these new school laws.

COOPERATIVE LEARNING

Organize the class into small groups. Assign each group one of the four types of law. Have students become "experts" on each type of law so that they can explain it to the rest of the class. Each group member should find at least one example of the assigned type of law. Members should then work together to illustrate the group's examples and present their group's findings to the class.

CIVICS SIDELIGHT

The historical basis for many of the rights U.S. citizens hold dear, including the right to a fair trial, is the Magna Carta (Latin words for "Great Charter"). For example, one part of the Magna Carta reads: "No freeman shall be captured or imprisoned . . . except by the lawful judgment of his peers [and] by the law of the land."

English nobles forced King John to approve the charter in 1215. Although the charter specifically granted rights only to the aristocracy, not the common people of England, the Magna Carta provided a foundation for later strides in guaranteeing rights and liberties to all people.

ways in which to act. Some of these rules are based on common sense. Some are based on common practice.

For example, before automobiles became a major form of transportation, there were no laws about driving them. Suppose that someone was driving an automobile at its top speed and ran into a horse-drawn wagon, crushing the wagon. The driver of the automobile might argue that the case should be dismissed because there is no existing law regulating the speed of automobiles.

The judge might reply that there is an established principle that people cannot use their property to injure others. Thus the judge would apply the rule of common sense and common practice in such a case.

The judge's decision might be remembered by another judge hearing a similar case. Eventually, most judges might follow the same **precedent**, or earlier decision, in such cases. In time, those guilty of driving their automobiles recklessly would be punished according to this customary rule. This rule would become a part of the nation's customary, or common, law. Thus **common law** is law that comes from judges' decisions.

In time, most common law is passed as statutory law by the nation's lawmaking bodies. In this way, it is written down so that all of the nation's citizens may know it.

Administrative Law Many of the laws that affect our daily lives are made by government agencies. These laws are known as **administrative laws**. For example, the Consumer Product Safety Commission (CPSC) makes an administrative law when it rules that a particular toy is unsafe and must be taken off the market immediately.

Constitutional Law The U.S. Constitution, as you know, is supreme above all other types of law. Therefore, if any law comes into conflict with the Constitution, the Constitution prevails. **Constitutional law** is law based on the Constitution of the United States and on Supreme Court decisions interpreting the Constitution.

Role of the Courts

Courts use the different kinds of law to settle disputes. Disputes between people, disputes between people and the government, and disputes between governments are brought before a court. The court applies the law and reaches a decision in favor of one side or the other.

To be just, a law must be enforced fairly. For example, it is against the law for workers in a nuclear power plant to give or sell secrets about their work to a foreign government. What might happen if an FBI agent found an engineer who worked in a nuclear power plant talking to a foreign spy? Could the federal government arrest the engineer on suspicion of treason and put the engineer in prison for years? The answer is no. Even though the crime is serious, under the U.S. system of justice the engineer, like any accused person, must be given a fair public trial.

To guarantee justice, U.S. law assumes that a person is innocent until proven guilty. The proper way to determine whether or not a person is guilty is to hold a trial in a court of law. The courts are made up of persons who have been given the authority to administer justice. Americans believe that only a system of courts can assure equal justice to all people.

Right to a Fair Trial

The Constitution guarantees every American the right to a fair public trial. It is important to understand this guarantee as you study the federal court system and the principle of equal justice under the law. What does the right to a fair trial mean? Consider the example of the engineer who is accused of giving secret information to a foreign government.

Right to Have a Lawyer All persons accused of crimes are entitled to the services of a lawyer. The lawyer will represent them in court and help protect their rights. If the engineer cannot afford a lawyer, the court will appoint one and pay the lawyer's fees out of public funds.

Use the board to help students make a flowchart showing the rights of accused persons as they move through the court process. Each item in the chart might be boxed, with an arrow leading to the next item. To help students begin the chart, ask: If you were accused of a serious crime, what is the first thing you would do? *(hire a lawyer)* Continue prompting students through the process.

Part of the court process is the actual trial at which the accused person is to be found innocent or proved guilty *beyond a reasonable doubt.* Have students write a position statement about how the court process helps ensure that the accused person will be found innocent or proved guilty beyond a reasonable doubt.

Right to Be Released on Bail A person accused of a crime does not usually spend months in prison waiting for a trial. Usually the accused person may be released if he or she can put up bail.

Bail, as you have learned, is a sum of money deposited with the court as a pledge that the accused will appear in court at the time of the trial. The amount of bail is set by a judge. A person accused of a serious crime, such as murder or treason, however, may be denied bail by the court and have to remain in jail until the trial is held.

Indictment by a Grand Jury Because a person is arrested on suspicion of a crime does not mean that this person will go to trial. There must be enough evidence against someone to justify bringing that person into court for trial. As you know, the group that decides whether there is enough evidence to bring the accused person to trial is the grand jury. In federal courts, the grand jury is made up of 12 to 23 citizens who live in the court district in which the trial is to be held.

The grand jury examines the evidence against the accused person. It questions witnesses and investigates the facts. If a majority of grand jury members decides that the evidence against the accused is strong enough, the person is indicted, or formally accused of a crime. In the case of the engineer, the grand jury finds the evidence strong enough. The engineer is indicted and held for trial.

Right to a Jury Trial Individuals who go on trial must be judged on the basis of the evidence for and against them. But who shall judge the evidence? The Sixth Amendment to the Constitution guarantees an accused person the right to be tried before a trial jury. A trial jury is also called a **petit jury**. It is usually made up of 6 to 12 persons who live in the community. The men and women of the trial jury are called **jurors**.

Jurors on trial juries and grand juries are selected from a list of people who live in the community. A court official selects the names at random and sends notices ordering the people to report for **jury duty**. From this group, or

The right to a jury trial is a cornerstone of the U.S. justice system. This system relies on the willingness of all citizens to serve on juries.

Closure

Invite a parent or a teacher from your school who has served on a jury to visit your class to discuss courtroom procedure. Have students prepare a list of appropriate questions to ask the speaker. Then have the class work with the guest to diagram the sequence of events in a typical trial (impaneling jurors, making opening arguments, calling and questioning witnesses, and so on).

Reviewing

Have students complete the Section 1 Review.

Reteaching

Assign Section 1 of the Chapter 7 Reteaching Worksheet.

SECTION 1 REVIEW
A N S W E R S

1. See the following pages: statutory law (p. 115); precedent, common law, administrative law, constitutional law (p. 116); petit jury, juror, jury duty (p. 117); verdict, hung jury, cross-examine, testimony, appeal (p. 118).

2. Laws usually reflect the beliefs of the majority. Laws are for the good of all.

3. statutory, common, administrative, constitutional; constitutional law

4. provide fair public trials and ensure equal justice for all

5. case brought against the accused must be so convincing that there is no reasonable doubt in jurors' minds

6. to ensure that cases are decided fairly

7. Charts will vary but should reflect the importance of protecting the rights of all.

The Right to a Fair Trial

- The right to have a lawyer
- The right to be released on reasonable bail before the trial is held
- The right to be considered innocent until proven guilty
- The right to expect the grand jury to find enough evidence before an indictment is made

- The right to a jury trial
- The right to not testify against oneself
- The right to hear and question all witnesses
- The right to appeal the verdict if there is reason to believe that the person did not receive a fair trial

panel of jurors, the required number of jurors is chosen for the trial.

The trial jury must try to reach a decision, or **verdict**, in the case. Usually the jury's verdict must be a unanimous vote. This means that all the members of the jury must agree on whether the accused person is guilty or innocent of the charges. If a jury cannot reach a verdict, it is called a **hung jury**. Usually a new trial with a new jury is held.

Innocent Until Proven Guilty The burden of proof in a jury trial rests with those people who bring charges against the person on trial. They must prove their case "beyond a reasonable doubt." Accused persons cannot be forced to testify against themselves. Their lawyers have the right to **cross-examine**, or question, witnesses to ensure that their **testimony**, or evidence given in court, is accurate. Accused persons have the right to call their own witnesses to defend themselves.

Suppose the engineer accused of selling secrets is found guilty by a trial jury. This means the jury believes that the lawyers for the government have proved the engineer's guilt beyond a reasonable doubt.

Right of Appeal Because courts are made up of human beings, they sometimes make mistakes. To ensure that cases are decided fairly, the U.S. court system provides the right to **appeal**, or to ask for a review of the

case. If there is reason to doubt that the engineer received a fair trial, the engineer can appeal to a higher court.

SECTION 1 REVIEW

1. Define or identify the following terms: statutory law, precedent, common law, administrative law, constitutional law, petit jury, juror, jury duty, verdict, hung jury, cross-examine, testimony, appeal.

2. How does majority rule affect the making of laws? Why is it the duty of citizens to obey laws?

3. What are the four types of law found in the United States? Which type prevails?

4. What is the role of the courts?

5. What must people who bring charges prove in court?

6. Why do people found guilty of crimes have the right to appeal?

7. **THINKING CRITICALLY** Create a chart with two columns. In one column list the eight rights to a fair trial given to persons accused of crimes. For each right you have listed, explain in the other column what might happen if accused persons did not have this right.

After studying Section 2, students should be able to do the following.

1. Determine the types of cases tried in federal courts.
2. Identify which type of federal court holds jury trials.
3. Explain the purpose of courts of appeals and the various special courts.
4. Identify the Supreme Court's role in the judicial system.

Teaching Section 2
Building a Vocabulary

Remind students that the Latin *jur* means "law." The Latin word *diction* means "to say." Courts with the authority to talk about (say), or interpret, the law are said to have **jurisdiction**. Have students try to deduce the meaning of **original jurisdiction** *(the right to hear a case first)* and the meaning of **appellate jurisdiction** *(the right to deal with court appeals).*

2 The Federal Court System

Under the federal system of government, the United States has two court systems. One is the federal court system. The other is the system of state courts. (You will read about the state court system in Chapter 8.)

Article 3 of the U.S. Constitution provides that "the judicial power of the United States shall be vested in one Supreme Court, and in such inferior [lower] courts as the Congress may from time to time . . . establish." The First Congress used this constitutional power to set up a system of federal courts.

In 1789 Congress passed the Judiciary Act, which established what has grown into one of the great court systems of the world. This system of federal courts makes up the judicial branch of the federal government.

Cases Tried in Federal Courts

The Constitution grants the federal courts jurisdiction in several different kinds of cases. **Jurisdiction** means the authority to interpret and administer the law. Listed below are the kinds of cases that are brought to trial in federal courts:

- any person accused of disobeying any part of the U.S. Constitution, including its amendments
- anyone accused of violating a U.S. treaty
- anyone accused of breaking laws passed by Congress
- charges brought by a foreign nation against the U.S. government or a U.S. citizen
- crimes committed on U.S. ships at sea
- U.S. ambassadors and consuls accused of breaking the laws of the nation in which they are stationed
- crimes committed on certain types of federal property
- disagreements between the states (The Eleventh Amendment, however, provides

that any lawsuit against a state brought by a citizen of another state or of a foreign country shall be tried in a state court.)
- lawsuits between citizens of different states (Most federal court cases are of this type.)

Organization of the Federal Courts

The federal courts are organized into several levels. They are also classified according to their jurisdiction. The lowest courts are trial courts, which have **original jurisdiction**. That is, they have the authority to be the first courts in which most federal cases are heard.

Above these trial courts are courts that have **appellate jurisdiction**. That is, they review decisions made by lower courts. The word *appellate* means "dealing with appeals." Every convicted person has the right to appeal to an appellate court. An appeal is usually made when lawyers believe the law was not applied correctly in the lower court. A case can also be appealed if new evidence is found.

U.S. District Courts

There are three main levels of federal courts. The chart on page 120 is an organizational chart of the courts in the federal system.

At the base of the federal court system are the **district courts**. There is at least one district court in each of the 50 states and in the District of Columbia. Some of the larger states are divided into as many as four federal court districts, each with its own district court. Today there are 91 federal district courts in the United States and its territories.

The district court is the only federal court in which jury trials are held. District courts have original jurisdiction in most federal cases. They cannot hear appeals from other courts.

The Constitution is definite about where federal cases shall be tried. Article 3, Section 2, states in part that "such trial shall be held in the State where the said crimes shall have been committed. . . ."

CIVICS SIDELIGHT

Federal courts help clear up conflicts of authority between federal and state law. One of the most famous cases in federal courts was a dispute between two steamboat operators—Thomas Gibbons and Aaron Ogden—that went all the way to the Supreme Court. Gibbons sued Ogden to keep him from carrying passengers between ports in New York and New Jersey. Was interstate commerce to be controlled by states or by the federal government? In *Gibbons v. Ogden* (1824), the Supreme Court decided that the commerce clause of the Constitution (Article I, Section 8) gave control over interstate commerce to the United States Congress.

Applying Ideas

Pose the following question: What if federal cases all had to be tried in Washington, D.C., and not in the state where the crime was committed? Invite students to suggest scenarios that reveal the problems involved in moving a case from its origin to a distant site.

The reason for this provision is to ensure that the accused person receives a fair and convenient trial. The witnesses who will testify are usually close at hand. No one has to travel long distances to be heard. Furthermore, the jury will be familiar with the location of the crime, and it can judge the truth of the evidence more fairly.

District Court Officials

Each district court has from 2 to 28 judges, depending on the caseload of the individual court. All district court judges, except those in U.S. territories, are appointed for life. District court judges decide matters of court procedure and explain the law involved in the case to the jury. They decide the punishment if the accused person is found guilty.

A number of other officials help the district courts work smoothly. Each district court has a U.S. **marshal**. Marshals arrest persons accused of breaking federal laws. They also deliver official court orders, called **subpoenas**, that require persons to appear in court. In addition, U.S. marshals keep order in the district courtrooms and see that the courts' verdicts are carried out.

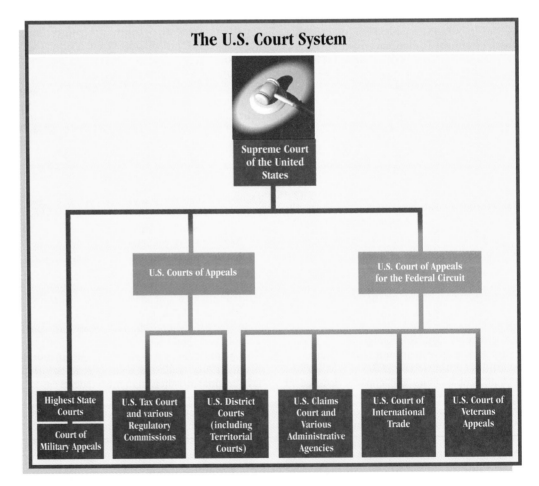

The U.S. Court System

Supreme Court of the United States

U.S. Courts of Appeals

U.S. Court of Appeals for the Federal Circuit

Highest State Courts / Court of Military Appeals

U.S. Tax Court and various Regulatory Commissions

U.S. District Courts (including Territorial Courts)

U.S. Claims Court and Various Administrative Agencies

U.S. Court of International Trade

U.S. Court of Veterans Appeals

Help students examine the organizational chart on page 120. Have students identify the subject of the chart. *(the U.S. court system)* Ask them to describe the lines of authority. Then have them draw conclusions. For example, they might determine which court would hear an appeal from a district court. *(a U.S. Court of Appeals or the U.S. Court of Appeals for the Federal Circuit)*

Review with students the three types of cases in which the Supreme Court has original jurisdiction. *(cases involving foreign diplomats, disputes between states, cases involving a state and the federal government)* Have students apply map and chart skills to show an example of each type of case. For example, for cases involving disputes between states, they might draw the two states as if they were boxers. Have students title and describe each illustration.

District court officials also include **federal magistrates**. These officials hear the evidence against accused persons and decide whether the cases should be brought before a grand jury. Magistrates also hear some minor cases.

Another district court official is the U.S. attorney. This official is a lawyer for the federal government. It is the job of the U.S. attorney to prove to a jury that the accused person is guilty of the federal crime he or she is charged with committing.

U.S. Courts of Appeals

The next level of the federal court system consists of **courts of appeals**. These courts review cases that are appealed from the district courts. Courts of appeals also hear appeals from decisions of federal regulatory commissions. For instance, a railroad company might believe that the rates for fares set by the Interstate Commerce Commission are unfair. If so, the railroad company can ask a court of appeals to review the commission's decision.

There are 12 U.S. courts of appeals. Each court of appeals covers a large judicial district known as a **circuit**. The 50 states are divided into 11 circuits. The twelfth circuit is the District of Columbia. There is also a court of appeals for the federal circuit. This court of appeals has national jurisdiction.

Each court of appeals has 6 to 28 judges. The senior judge of each circuit serves as the chief judge. The judges of the courts of appeals are appointed for life.

Jury trials do not take place in the courts of appeals. Instead, a panel of at least three judges reviews the evidence and makes the decision. The judges examine the records of the district court trial and hear arguments by the lawyers for both sides. The judges do not determine whether the accused person is guilty or innocent. They are not holding another trial of the case. Instead, their job is to determine if the person who appealed the case was granted full legal rights during the trial.

The judges reach their decision by majority vote. If the court of appeals finds that

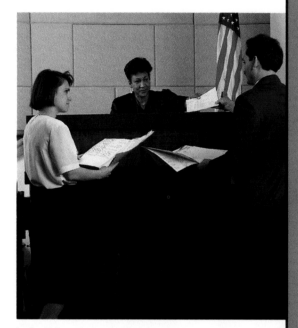

In the U.S. court system, justices are sworn to act "without fear or favor" in making their decisions.

justice was not done, it sends the case back to the district court for a new trial. If the court of appeals finds that justice was done, it upholds, or accepts, the district court's decision. In most cases the decision of the court of appeals is final. Sometimes, however, yet another appeal is made to the U.S. Supreme Court.

The U.S. Supreme Court

The highest court in the land is the U.S. Supreme Court, which meets in Washington, D.C. The Supreme Court works chiefly as an appeals court, reviewing cases that have been tried in lower federal courts and in state courts.

In addition, the Constitution gives the Supreme Court original jurisdiction in the following three types of cases:

• cases involving diplomatic representatives of other nations

CIVICS SIDELIGHT

Today a circuit refers simply to a judicial district. But in the early decades of U.S. history, the circuit was an actual route; and even justices of the Supreme Court were required by law to "ride the circuit." Supreme Court justices complained about the rough roads and other hardships of this duty, and they even promised to take a pay cut if Congress would hire separate circuit judges. Congress refused. The legislators thought the high-court circuit riders helped link the people in a personal way with the distant national government. Circuit riding did not completely disappear until 1891.

Closure

Have students create a flowchart showing a case moving through the U.S. court system. Students should identify or be assigned a hypothetical case and determine which court would hear the case, then carry the case through the appeals process all the way to the Supreme Court. Students should save their flowcharts for use as study guides.

Reviewing

Have students complete the Section 2 Review.

Reteaching

Assign Section 2 of the Chapter 7 Reteaching Worksheet.

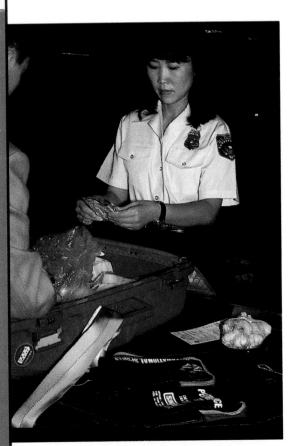

This customs agent is examining the luggage of people entering the United States. Travelers can appeal to the Court of International Trade if they believe they are being taxed unfairly by the U.S. government.

- cases involving disputes between states (For example, the Supreme Court once settled a dispute between Arizona and California over the use of water from the Colorado River basin.)
- cases involving a state and the federal government (For example, the ownership of public lands has often been a source of conflict between the states and the federal government.)

Decisions of the Supreme Court are final. The Court's decisions cannot be appealed.

Other Federal Courts

Congress also set up a number of special courts to handle specific types of cases. These courts are identified in the chart of the federal court system on page 120.

U.S. Claims Court This court hears cases involving money claims against the federal government. If the court rules against the government, the person bringing the suit is usually granted a sum of money. Congress must then authorize the payment of the claim.

U.S. Court of International Trade This court hears cases involving taxes on imports. Individuals or businesses importing certain goods into the United States from other countries must pay taxes on those goods. People who think that the tax is too high, for example, may take their cases to the Court of International Trade. This court is in New York City, but it also hears cases in other port cities.

Territorial Courts Territorial courts were established by Congress to administer justice to the people living in U.S. territorial possessions. There is one territorial court each in the Northern Mariana Islands, Guam, the Virgin Islands, and Puerto Rico. These courts handle the same kinds of cases as district courts. They also hear the types of cases that would go to a state court.

U.S. Tax Court This court hears appeals from taxpayers who disagree with rulings of the Internal Revenue Service (IRS) concerning their payment of federal taxes. The Tax Court is actually an independent agency, but it has powers like those of a court.

Court of Military Appeals This court is the appeals court for the nation's armed services. People in the armed services who are accused of breaking a military law are tried at a **court-martial**. This is a trial conducted by military officers. The Court of Military Appeals consists of three civilian judges. Appeals of this court's decisions can be, but rarely are, heard by the Supreme Court.

Extension

Have students list the qualifications they think the ideal federal court judge should have. Then ask students to research the qualifications of current or prominent former Supreme Court justices to see how they compare with the students' lists. Have the class debate the issue and list consensus qualifications on the board.

After studying Section 3, students should be able to do the following.

1. Identify and explain how appointments to the Supreme Court are made.
2. Explain how the power of judicial review strengthened the Court and how Congress limits the Court's power.
3. Explain how the Supreme Court decides to hear a case and what happens if it refuses.
4. Explain why the Court should be able to change its opinion over time.

U.S. Court of Veterans Appeals

Another special court is the recently created Court of Veterans Appeals. This court hears appeals brought by military veterans against the Department of Veterans Affairs. Cases brought before this court always involve claims for veterans benefits.

Federal Court Judges

All the federal courts are presided over by judges who are appointed by the president. These appointments must be approved by the Senate by a majority vote.

Federal judges are appointed for life. That is, the job is theirs for as long as they want it. Federal court judges can be removed from office only by impeachment by Congress. Congress may not lower a judge's salary during her or his time in office. These guarantees were written into the U.S. Constitution to ensure that judges are not punished or rewarded for their decisions in cases. Judges are assisted in their work by many other people, including clerks and court reporters.

SECTION 2 REVIEW

1. Define or identify the following terms: jurisdiction, original jurisdiction, appellate jurisdiction, district court, marshal, subpoena, federal magistrate, court of appeals, circuit, territorial court, court-martial.

2. Why are federal cases tried in the same states in which the crimes are committed?

3. In which type of federal court are jury trials held? What is the purpose of the courts of appeals?

4. In what types of cases does the Supreme Court have original jurisdiction? Why has Congress set up special courts?

5. THINKING CRITICALLY How might lifetime appointments for judges benefit the U.S. system of justice? How might such appointments be harmful to the system? Write a position statement supporting or opposing a constitutional amendment to end the system of lifetime appointments for federal judges.

3 The Supreme Court

The Supreme Court is the head of the judicial branch of the federal government. It is the only court specifically established by the Constitution. Decisions of the Supreme Court affect the lives of all Americans.

Supreme Court Justices

The size of the Supreme Court is determined by Congress. The number of **justices**, or judges, of the Supreme Court has been set at nine since 1869. The Court has a chief justice and eight associate justices.

Supreme Court justices, like other federal judges, are appointed by the president. Their appointments must be approved by a majority vote of the Senate. Justices are appointed for life and can be forcibly removed from office only by the impeachment process. The annual salary of the chief justice is $171,500. Associate justices are paid $164,100 per year.

The Constitution does not set any requirements for Supreme Court justices. All have been lawyers, however, and many have served as judges on lower courts. Others have taught law or held public office. Until recently, all justices were men. In 1981 Sandra Day O'Connor became the first woman to serve on the Supreme Court. A second woman, Ruth Bader Ginsburg, joined the Court in 1993.

Presidents generally try to appoint justices who share their political beliefs. Once appointed, however, a justice of the Supreme

(continued on page 126)

SECTION 2 REVIEW ANSWERS

1. See the following pages: jurisdiction, original jurisdiction, appellate jurisdiction, district court (p. 119); marshal, subpoena (p. 120); federal magistrate, court of appeal, circuit (p. 121); territorial court, court-martial (p. 122).

2. Defendant and witnesses are nearby and jury is familiar with crime location and can judge truth of evidence more fairly; helps to ensure the accused receives a fair trial.

3. district courts; determines whether accused was granted full legal rights during trial

4. cases involving diplomats of other nations, disputes between states, or disputes between a state and the federal government; to hear specific types of cases

5. Answers will vary. Students should use sound reasoning in stating their positions.

Illustrating Ideas

Have students illustrate the Tinkers' probable course through the court system in a flowchart titled "The Tinkers' Route to the Supreme Court." Be sure students understand why the case was tried in federal courts. *(The dispute was a constitutional issue.)* They might turn to the chart on page 120 for assistance.

MULTICULTURAL PERSPECTIVES

The Quaker religion heavily influenced the antiwar sentiments of Mary Beth and John Tinker, whose parents were Quakers who strongly opposed war. Quakers, or Friends, as they are called, devote themselves to the causes of peace and benevolence. The Quaker religion was founded in England in the 17th century by religious leader George Fox. Facing persecution in England for refusing to take oaths or to fight in wars, many Quakers moved to America and settled in Pennsylvania. The United States today is home to more than 100,000 people of the Quaker faith. They avoid formal church structures, preferring to worship together in "meeting houses." Many Quaker groups have no formal clergy. Best known for their humanitarian and pacifist beliefs, Quakers have established relief organizations and peace organizations that serve throughout the world.

Citizenship **IN ACTION**

THE TINKERS TAKE A STAND

Mary Beth Tinker, her brother John, and Christopher Eckhart did not set out to put their names in U.S. law books. All they wanted was to take a stand on an important national issue. That is why they wore black armbands to school in December 1965. Little did they realize that their actions would lead all the way to the Supreme Court.

Mary Beth Tinker and John Tinker went all the way to the Supreme Court in their fight to wear the black armbands they are holding.

Protesting the War

In 1965 the United States was deeply involved in a war between communist North Vietnam and noncommunist South Vietnam in Southeast Asia. Many Americans were in favor of supporting South Vietnam in the war. Others, however, believed that the United States should stay out of the conflict.

A group of students in Des Moines, Iowa, where the Tinkers and Chris Eckhart lived, decided to wear black armbands to school to protest the war. The armbands were meant to be a symbol of mourning for the U.S. soldiers who were dying in Vietnam.

Members of the Des Moines school board heard about the armbands and became worried. They thought the armbands might cause trouble and banned them from the schools. When several students wore the armbands to school anyway, the students were suspended from school.

The Supreme Court Hears the Case

The Tinker family took the school board to court on behalf of Mary Beth, John, and Chris Eckhart. Their lawyers argued that the school

Linking Civics and History

Have pairs of students research the Vietnam War era in the United States to find other examples of student protest. Each pair of students should focus on one incident and report to the class in detail on their findings. Some students might research protests against other wars to determine the extent of student activism during those periods.

board had denied them their constitutional right of free speech.

The case went all the way to the U.S. Supreme Court. The justices agreed to hear the case because they believed it raised two important constitutional questions. First, should wearing an armband be considered a form of free speech? Second, how far did the right of free speech apply to students? Schools must keep discipline in the classrooms and hallways to allow all students to learn.

A Decision for Free Speech

The Supreme Court announced its decision in the case of *Tinker v. Des Moines Independent Community School District* in 1969. The Court ruled that wearing a symbol, such as an armband, is a form of speech. It is therefore protected by the U.S. Constitution.

The second question was more difficult to decide. All the justices stressed that schools must be protected against disturbances. What the justices could not agree on was whether the students wearing armbands had caused trouble in school.

Two justices sided with the Des Moines school board. They maintained that wearing armbands had taken the students' minds off their studies. Therefore, the schools had acted properly in banning the armbands.

The majority of the justices, though, supported the students. They believed there was no evidence that the armbands had caused any disturbances. The Court ruled that the ban on armbands was unfair. The justices also pointed out that schools allowed students to wear campaign buttons for political candidates. Wearing buttons is also a form of "speech."

The Supreme Court justices did not say that schools could never limit the expression of opinions by students. What they said was that in this case the students had acted within their rights.

The Court's ruling is now part of U.S. law. As a result, students and school officials have a clearer idea of the rights of free speech for students and teachers.

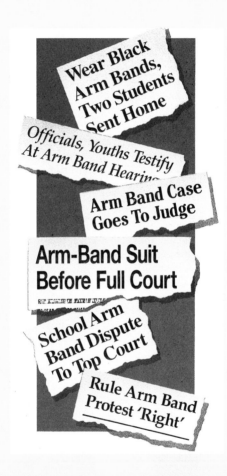

Wear Black Arm Bands, Two Students Sent Home

Officials, Youths Testify At Arm Band Hearing

Arm Band Case Goes To Judge

Arm-Band Suit Before Full Court

School Arm Band Dispute To Top Court

Rule Arm Band Protest 'Right'

YOU DECIDE

1 What were the two main questions in the *Tinker* case?

2 Conduct research to learn if former students in your school or in schools in your area engaged in similar protests in the 1960s. What was the reaction of school officials?

3 Have you ever expressed your political opinions in school? What forms of expression did you use?

MULTICULTURAL PERSPECTIVES

In another case involving students, the Supreme Court ruled in 1943 that government could not force citizens to recite the Pledge of Allegiance to the U.S. flag. Two students had been sent home from their West Virginia grade school after refusing to recite the pledge. They argued that their religious faith as Jehovah's Witnesses prohibited them from pledging allegiance to anyone or anything but God. The Court ruled that officials could not "prescribe what shall be orthodox in politics, nationalism, religion, or other matters of opinion."

ANSWERS TO YOU DECIDE

1. Is wearing armbands a form of speech? How does the right of free speech apply to students?

2. Students might want to examine yearbooks and interview former students, teachers, and officials in researching this question.

3. Answers will vary. Help students see the variety of ways people express opinions.

Teaching Section 3
Building a Vocabulary

Point out that *concur* is derived from the Latin roots *con- (com-)*, meaning "with" or "together," and *cur (currere)*, meaning "to run." Thus, **concurring opinions** are those in which the views of individuals come (run) together, or agree. *Dissent* is derived from Latin roots meaning "apart" *(dis-)* and "to perceive" *(sentire)*. Have students deduce the meaning of **dissenting opinions**. *(opposing opinions)*

Creating a Court

Have students set up a "Supreme Court" for your school's student government by using the U.S. Supreme Court as a model. Divide the class into three groups. One group should decide what kind of cases the court can hear. The other groups should decide the size of the court and how justices to the court are to be appointed. Have volunteers from each group present their proposals to the class.

CIVICS SIDELIGHT

The head of the Supreme Court is officially known as the "Chief Justice of the United States." The president's nominee for this position must undergo Senate confirmation even if he or she is already an associate justice on the Court. President Ronald Reagan, with Senate approval, elevated Associate Justice William Rehnquist to chief justice in 1986, for example. The appointment is for life.

CIVICS SIDELIGHT

You might want to point out what eventually happened to Marbury. In spite of its declaration that the Judiciary Act was unconstitutional, the Supreme Court said that Marbury deserved the job on other grounds. The Court, however, did not have the power to force Madison to act. Marbury did not receive the appointment.

Court is free to make decisions with which the president disagrees.

Power of Judicial Review

A unique feature of the Supreme Court is its power of **judicial review**. That is, the Court has the power to determine whether a law passed by Congress or a presidential action is in accord with the Constitution. If the Supreme Court decides that a law conflicts with the Constitution, that law is declared **unconstitutional**, and it is no longer in force. Before a law is declared unconstitutional, however, someone must challenge the law and bring a case to court.

The Constitution does not say that the Supreme Court has the power of judicial review. This power was established for the Court by John Marshall. As chief justice from 1801 to 1835, Marshall laid the foundations for the Supreme Court's great power.

John Marshall was one of the nation's most influential chief justices. Under his leadership the Supreme Court made some of its most far-reaching decisions.

Influence of John Marshall

During his 34 years as chief justice, John Marshall established three basic principles of U.S. law. Marshall stated the idea of judicial review for the first time in 1803 in the case of *Marbury v. Madison*. The case involved William Marbury, who had been promised appointment as a justice of the peace, and Secretary of State James Madison.

Marbury claimed that the Judiciary Act of 1789 gave the Supreme Court the power to order Secretary of State Madison to give him the promised appointment. In his now-famous opinion, Chief Justice Marshall found that the Judiciary Act was in conflict with the Constitution. The act gave the Supreme Court powers not granted by the Constitution. Because the Constitution is the supreme law of the land, the Judiciary Act passed by Congress was declared unconstitutional.

Under Chief Justice Marshall, the Supreme Court also established the principle that laws passed by state legislatures can be set aside if they conflict with the Constitution. The third principle established by Marshall is that the Supreme Court has the power to reverse the decisions of state courts. Over the years the Supreme Court has come to have the final power to interpret the Constitution.

Hearing Cases

As you know, the Supreme Court cannot begin a case itself. It serves mainly as an appeals court. All cases heard by the Court involve real legal disputes. A person cannot simply ask the Supreme Court for an opinion about whether or not a law is constitutional.

The Supreme Court decides what cases it will hear. Thousands of cases are appealed to the Court each year. The Court, however, chooses only about 100 to 200 cases each year to place on its **docket**, or calendar, for review. If the Supreme Court had to review all cases that were appealed to it, it would still be deciding cases that originated decades ago.

Summarizing Ideas

Have students write the names of several fictional cases that might be appealed to the Supreme Court. Make sure that some cases involve the court's review of a legislative act. With each name, students should supply a brief description of the case. They then should decide whether the Supreme Court would choose to hear the case and explain their reasoning. Call on volunteers to present some of their cases to the class for discussion.

The Supreme Court serves as the final court of appeals. Shown here are (standing, left to right) Justices Ginsburg, Souter, Thomas, Breyer; (seated, left to right) Scalia, Stevens, Rehnquist, O'Connor, and Kennedy.

How, then, does the Supreme Court decide what cases to hear? The justices accept only those cases that involve issues of significant public interest. Cases heard by the Court generally deal with important constitutional or national questions. At least four of the nine justices must vote to hear a case. If the Supreme Court refuses to review a case, the decision of the lower court remains in effect. The Court may also **remand**, or return, a case to a lower court for a new trial.

The Court in Action

The Supreme Court begins its session each year on the first Monday in October. The Court usually adjourns in late June. The justices spend much of their time reading written arguments, hearing oral arguments, and holding private meetings.

After the Supreme Court has agreed to hear a case, the lawyers for each side prepare a **brief**. This is a written statement explaining the main points of one side's arguments about the case. Each justice studies the briefs.

The next step takes place in a public session. The lawyers for each side appear before the Court to present an oral argument. Each presentation is limited to 30 minutes, and the time limit is strictly enforced. The justices often question the lawyers about the case. The entire procedure is designed to bring out the facts in each case as quickly as possible.

On most Fridays, the justices meet privately to discuss and vote on the cases they have heard. Each justice has one vote, but all justices do not have to vote. Decision is by majority vote. If there is a tie vote, the decision of the lower court remains in effect.

Supreme Court Opinions

One of the justices who supported the majority decision is assigned to write the opinion of the Court. An **opinion** explains the reasoning that led to the decision. The Court's opinion is binding on all lower courts.

Ask: Did *Marbury v. Madison* give the Supreme Court too much power? Draw a large balance scale on the chalkboard and label one side *Supreme Court* and the other side *Congress*. Have students take turns writing the three principles established by the Marshall Court on one side and the Congress's actions to check the Court on the other. Discuss this example of checks and balances.

Have students draw political cartoons that deal with judicial review or with one of Congress's historical actions to check the power of the Supreme Court. Students might choose a particular case to lampoon. Call on volunteers to share their cartoons with the class.

CIVICS SIDELIGHT

In the first century of the nation's history, the Supreme Court declared 23 federal laws unconstitutional. Since then the Court has become much more active in this area, negating more than 100 federal laws. (For example, in 1989 the Court ruled unconstitutional a law criminalizing flag burning.) In the same 200-year period, the Court declared more than a thousand state and local laws to be unconstitutional.

DID YOU KNOW THAT...

The words "Oyez, oyez, oyez!" are called out as the Supreme Court justices file into the courtroom. *Oyez* sounds like "Oh, yes." An odd way to open a court? Actually, the word means "Hear ye," and it comes from the French language. In fact, several French words are used in conducting U.S. government business. Many of our nation's founders were heavily influenced by the great French philosophers' ideas about government.

Oyez, Oyez!

Sometimes a justice agrees with the decision of the majority, but for different reasons. In that case the justice may decide to write a **concurring opinion**.

Justices who disagree with the decision of the Court may explain their reasoning in a **dissenting opinion**. Although dissenting opinions have no effect on the law, they are still important. Many dissenting opinions have eventually become the law of the land when the beliefs of society and the opinions of the justices changed.

Checking the Court's Power

The Supreme Court has gained great power over the years. How do the other branches of government check the powers of the Court?

Consider what happens when the Supreme Court rules that a law passed by Congress is unconstitutional. As you know, this means that the law has no force. Congress, however, may pass a new law that follows the Constitution and that the Supreme Court may uphold.

In this way laws can be improved while the rights of U.S. citizens under the Constitution remain protected.

Another way to make a desired law constitutional is to amend the Constitution. For example, in 1895 the Supreme Court declared that an income tax law passed by Congress was unconstitutional. The Court pointed out that the Constitution (Article 1, Section 9, Clause 4) states that direct taxes must be apportioned according to the population of each state. In other words, such taxes must fall evenly on all people.

The income tax law did not meet this constitutional requirement, and thus was declared unconstitutional by the Court. In 1913, however, the states ratified the Sixteenth Amendment, which gave Congress the power to tax incomes. The income tax became legal and constitutional.

Changing Court Opinions

The Supreme Court has helped make the Constitution a long-lived document by interpreting it differently at different times. In this way the Court helps the Constitution meet the demands of changing times. Supreme Court justices are aware of changing social, political, and economic conditions. In reaching decisions, they consider the beliefs of the people and the advancing ideas of justice for all.

The following example illustrates how the Court can change its opinion to meet changing times. In the late 1800s many of the states passed segregation laws. These laws **segregated**, or separated, African Americans in society. Black people and white people could not share the use of public services such as trains, schools, hotels, and hospitals.

A Decision for Segregation In 1896 an important case about segregation was brought before the Supreme Court. The case, *Plessy v. Ferguson,* challenged a Louisiana law that required blacks and whites to ride in separate railroad cars. Homer Plessy, who was part African American, had taken a seat in a

Write *Plessy* and *Brown* in two headings on the chalkboard. Then call on volunteers to explain the history of the *Plessy v. Ferguson* and *Brown v. Board of Education of Topeka* cases and the Supreme Court's reasoning in both decisions. Write their answers under the appropriate headings on the chalkboard. Then ask: What principle did the Supreme Court repudiate in *Brown*? *(separate but equal)* Why is it important that the Supreme Court be able to change its opinion? *(important to meet changing times and attitudes)*

Ask: How did the *Brown* decision strengthen constitutional rights? *(suggested that all segregation laws were unconstitutional)* Have students write newspaper editorials about Supreme Court decisions that strengthened constitutional rights (including the *Brown* decision). Students should focus on why these decisions were important and why the decisions have been obeyed despite strong opposition from some parts of society. *(The Court's appearance of being above politics has enhanced its power and prestige.)*

passenger car that had a sign reading "For Whites Only." When Plessy refused to move to a car for blacks, he was arrested.

Plessy was found guilty of breaking the Louisiana law and appealed the decision to the Supreme Court. He argued that Louisiana's segregation laws denied him the "equal protection of the law" guaranteed by the Fourteenth Amendment to the Constitution.

The Supreme Court did not accept Plessy's argument. The Court ruled that segregation laws did not violate the Fourteenth Amendment if the separate facilities provided for blacks were equal to those for whites. This decision established the "separate but equal" principle. That is, the decision legalized separate but equal facilities for blacks and whites in all areas of life.

A Decision Against Segregation In most places, however, facilities for blacks clearly were not equal to those for whites. For example, schools for black students often were overcrowded and lacked much of the equipment provided for white students.

After World War II, conditions in the nation began to change. Many people began to realize that the nation's African American citizens were not being treated fairly under the system of segregation.

In 1954 the Court decided another important segregation case. The case of *Brown v. Board of Education of Topeka* concerned eight-year-old Linda Brown, an African American girl living in Topeka, Kansas. The school located only five blocks from Linda's home was for whites only. Linda traveled 21 blocks to a school for blacks. Her father sued the school district, claiming segregated schools were unconstitutional.

In a unanimous decision, the Supreme Court agreed. It ruled that segregated schools were not equal and therefore violated the Fourteenth Amendment. Segregated schools, argued the Court, denied students equal protection under the law. Therefore, the Court ruled that public schools in the United States should be desegregated "with all deliberate

speed." The Supreme Court had reversed its earlier decision. (See page 557.)

Strengthening Constitutional Rights

In recent years Supreme Court decisions have made far-reaching changes in three areas of American life—the rights of accused persons, voting, and civil rights.

Rights of Accused Persons A number of Supreme Court decisions in the 1960s greatly strengthened the rights of accused persons. For the most part, these decisions apply to the period of time immediately following a person's arrest.

In the 1966 case of *Miranda v. Arizona,* the Supreme Court declared that the police must inform arrested suspects of their rights before police may question them. Suspects must be told that they have the right to remain silent, that anything they say may be used

Thurgood Marshall (center) argued for Linda Brown (inset) in Brown v. Board of Education of Topeka. *The case led to desegregation of U.S. schools.*

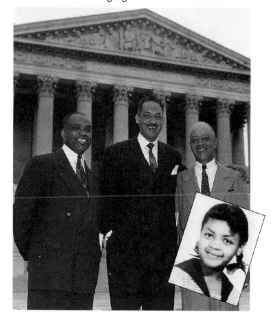

MULTICULTURAL PERSPECTIVES

Has desegregation, as ordered by the Court in the *Brown* case, worked? Statistics on the integration of public schools show that one third of the African American public school students in the nation attend schools where minority students make up 90 to 100 percent of the enrollment.

Opposition to specific integration plans and the movement of white students to private and suburban schools have often slowed or negated desegregation efforts. A significant blow to desegregation came in 1995, when the Supreme Court reversed a federal district court's order to the state of Missouri to make expenditures on its school system specifically designed to attract suburban white students.

Since the Court's ruling, cities across the nation have been working toward eliminating mandatory desegregation. As a result, the separation of African American children and white children in public schools is on the rise. Those seeking to undo mandatory desegregation point to the enormous expense and difficulty involved in trying to achieve a racial balance in the schools.

Closure

Ask students to brainstorm adjectives to describe Supreme Court justices. Have a volunteer list the words on the chalkboard. (There will likely be more positive adjectives than negative.) Ask: Why do we have positive feelings about the Supreme Court? Do we feel the same about the legislative branch? the executive branch? Discuss the differences in image among the branches of government.

Reviewing

Have students complete the Section 3 Review.

Reteaching

Assign Section 3 of the Chapter 7 Reteaching Worksheet.

CIVICS SIDELIGHT

In 1987 the Sumner Elementary School, which denied Linda Brown admission, was made a National Historic Landmark. Four years later Linda Brown's all-black school, Monroe Elementary, received the same designation. In 1992 Congress designated both schools to be part of the *Brown v. Board of Education* National Historic Site in Topeka.

AMERICAN BIOGRAPHY

Thurgood Marshall

Thurgood Marshall, the first African American to serve on the Supreme Court, dedicated his life to providing all Americans with equal justice under the law.

Encouraged by his father to pursue a career in law, Marshall graduated first in his class from Howard Law School in 1933. He opened a law office in Baltimore and soon caught the attention of the National Association for the Advancement of Colored People (NAACP). In 1934 he joined the local NAACP as its lawyer.

Marshall's greatest courtroom victory came in 1954 when he argued and won *Brown v. Board of Education of Topeka*, the Supreme Court case that outlawed segregation in public schools in the United States. Marshall continued his battle for civil rights both as a Court of Appeals judge and later as U.S. solicitor general, the nation's top-ranking courtroom attorney.

In 1967 Marshall was appointed to the Supreme Court, where he defended individual rights and equal justice under the law for more than two decades. Marshall died in 1993, two years after he retired from the nation's highest court.

against them, and that they have the right to have a lawyer present during questioning. If a suspect cannot afford a lawyer, a lawyer will be appointed for the suspect. (See "Case Study: Miranda Rights" on pages 152–153.)

There have been differences of opinion over the Supreme Court decisions involving the rights of accused persons. Some Americans have argued that the Court's decisions protect criminals. Others have said that they guarantee justice to all Americans. What is the proper balance between the rights of the individual and the rights of society as a whole? This is a difficult question of ongoing debate.

"One Person, One Vote" The Supreme Court also made several important decisions in the 1960s concerning voting and representation in state legislatures and the House of Representatives. The "one person, one vote" decision was the most far-reaching of these rulings.

According to this decision, election districts for choosing representatives to Congress and the state legislatures must be divided by population as equally as possible. This means that every citizen's vote in an election must be equal in value. Only in this way will there be genuinely representative government at both the state and federal levels.

Civil Rights and Civil Liberties The third area in which the Supreme Court's rulings have had important results is in civil rights and civil liberties. The 1954 *Brown* decision against segregated schools did not completely eliminate segregation in U.S. schools or in American life. The Court's decision, however, struck a blow against segregation in the nation by suggesting that all segregation laws were unconstitutional.

The civil rights movement and civil rights legislation followed. Segregation laws were removed, while laws guaranteeing African Americans the right to vote were passed. In its decisions, the Court has provided leadership by showing that the rights guaranteed in the Constitution apply to all Americans.

The Court's Prestige

Throughout the nation's history, the prestige and dignity of the Supreme Court have grown. The Supreme Court justices, for the most part, remain uninvolved in politics and have not

Have groups of students research the history of famous Supreme Court cases, such as *Brown v. Board of Education of Topeka*. Then have these groups re-enact the cases as they were presented before the Supreme Court, with some students acting as the plaintiff's attorneys (such as Thurgood Marshall in *Brown*) and others taking the roles of Supreme Court justices.

Invite students to consider a lawyer arguing his or her case before the Supreme Court. How would he or she prepare? Have students write brief journal entries as if they are lawyers at the end of their first day arguing a case in front of the highest court in the land.

been influenced by favors or bribes. Most Americans believe the Court is an important part of our democratic system.

The decisions of the Supreme Court have not, however, been free of controversy. Some have criticized the Court for being too liberal or too conservative.

In the late 1930s President Franklin D. Roosevelt attempted to change the nature of the Supreme Court by adding more justices to the Court. Public outcry, however, caused Roosevelt's plan to be dropped. Americans did not want to change the balance of power among the executive, legislative, and judicial branches in the federal government. They wanted the Court to remain free of political influence.

The debate over the Supreme Court's power continues today. Limits on the Court's power do exist. Although the Court makes important decisions that affect U.S. policies and American life, it cannot enforce these decisions. The Court must depend on the executive branch to carry out its decisions. The cooperation of the public also is necessary if Supreme Court decisions are to be effective.

SECTION 3 REVIEW

1. Define or identify the following terms: justice, judicial review, unconstitutional, docket, remand, brief, opinion, concurring opinion, dissenting opinion, segregate.

2. How many justices sit on the Supreme Court? How are appointments to the Supreme Court made?

3. How did the power of judicial review strengthen the Supreme Court? How is the power of the Supreme Court limited by Congress?

4. How does the Supreme Court decide which cases to hear? What happens if the Court refuses to hear a case?

5. Why is it important that the Court be able to change its opinion?

6. **THINKING CRITICALLY** Imagine that you are a justice of the Supreme Court in 1954. The Court has just made a ruling in the case of *Brown v. Board of Education of Topeka*, and you have been assigned to write the Court's opinion on the case. In your opinion explain why the Court has decided to overturn *Plessy v. Ferguson* and why segregated schools are unconstitutional.

CHAPTER 7 SUMMARY

The federal courts make up the judicial branch of the federal government. The job of these courts is to interpret laws and to bring to trial those people accused of breaking laws. In the United States we believe in the idea of government by law. These laws, however, must be enforced fairly. Thus the federal courts also ensure that every accused person enjoys the Constitution's guarantee of a fair trial.

There are four different kinds of law in the United States. These are statutory law, common law, administrative law, and constitutional law.

The Constitution gives the federal courts jurisdiction, or authority, to hold trials in a wide variety of cases and to judge these cases. District courts are the only federal courts in which juries are used. Under certain conditions, convicted persons may take their cases to a court of appeals and then perhaps even to the Supreme Court.

The U.S. Supreme Court is the highest court in the land. It hears appeals from lower federal courts and from state courts. Its decisions are final. Through its power of judicial review, the Supreme Court can decide if laws and presidential actions are constitutional. Decisions of the Supreme Court affect the daily lives of all Americans.

SECTION 3 REVIEW ANSWERS

1. See the following pages: justice (p. 123); judicial review, unconstitutional, docket (p. 126); remand, brief, opinion (p. 127); concurring opinion, dissenting opinion, segregate (p. 128).

2. nine; by president with Senate approval

3. asserted Court's power to declare congressional laws and presidential acts unconstitutional; if Court declares a law unconstitutional, Congress may pass similar law that will be accepted by Court, or Constitution may be amended

4. accepts (by vote of at least four justices) cases involving issues of significant public interest; decision of lower court stands or case is remanded to lower court

5. helps Constitution meet demands of changing times

6. Students should demonstrate an understanding that the 1954 Court believed segregated schools denied students equal protection under the law.

Suggest to students that justices of the Supreme Court follow guidelines for decision-making that are similar to the ones listed here. Concurring and dissenting opinions often include a definition of the problem, an evaluation of its importance, a list of options, and a final determination. As an extending exercise, have students list three decisions that they made in the past week or month and explain how they came to those decisions. Then have them compare their methods of making decisions with the list of guidelines on this page. Ask students to illustrate their decision-making process and compare it to the guidelines on this page.

ANSWERS TO Applying the Skill

1. She can accept or decline the job, or she can find another way to pay for college.

2. If she accepts the job, she will have to give up basketball and her grades might drop, perhaps jeopardizing her chances to be accepted into college. However, she will be able to save money. If she declines the job, she can continue to play basketball and have time to study. However, she will have to find another way to pay for college.

3. Students should think in terms of Rosa's ultimate goal: a college education. If accepting or declining the job seems an impossible choice for students, encourage them to come up with creative solutions to Rosa's problem.

132

Developing Civics Skills

LIFE SKILL
Making Decisions

Federal court judges and Supreme Court justices are in powerful positions. The decisions they make directly affect your life and the lives of all Americans.

You, too, must make important decisions. You must decide, for example, how best to study for your tests. You must decide what extracurricular clubs to join. Many of the decisions you make have important effects not only on you but also on the people around you. It is important that you—like the nation's judges—make the right decisions.

How to Make Decisions

1. Define the problem. It often helps to write down the decision facing you in the form of a question, such as "Should I take an after-school job?" Writing the question down helps clarify the problem. It also helps you see if you are asking the right question. For example, instead of deciding if you need an after-school job, you might first decide if you need more money.

2. Determine the importance of the decision. Many decisions are simple. For example, you decide what you will eat for lunch and what you will wear each day. Other decisions are much more complex and important, such as deciding where you will go to college. Take more time and care when making important decisions.

3. Identify your options. For some decisions, your options are limited. For example, if the question before you is "Should I write a research paper on the Supreme Court?" your only options are yes or no. But if the question is "What should be the topic of my research paper?" then you are faced with a great many more options. Make a list of all your options. Then write down the advantages and the disadvantages each option offers.

4. Choose an option. Once you have identified the advantages and disadvantages of each option, you can weigh the options and reach a decision. Take your time studying the lists you have made. Narrow your choices by ruling out less desirable options until you are left with the one best option for you.

5. Carry out your decision. Once you have made your decision, follow through with it fully.

6. Evaluate your decision. After you have carried out your decision, decide if you made the correct one. Judging whether you made a mistake will help you make wise decisions in the future.

Applying the Skill

Read the following situation. Then answer the questions.

Should Rosa take a part-time job at the ice cream shop? She needs to save at least $500 a year for college, and she might not find work this summer. The hours could be a problem—three hours every day after school and all day every Saturday. She would have to miss basketball practice. And she would have less time to study. Her grades might drop, and she might not be accepted into college. What should she do?

1. What are Rosa's options in this situation?
2. What are the advantages and disadvantages of each of her options?
3. If you were in Rosa's position, which choice would you make? Explain the reasoning behind your choice.

Vocabulary Workshop

1. statutory, common, administrative, constitutional; constitutional law

2. petit jury

3. original—hear cases first; appellate—review lower court rulings

4. court-martial

5. Court may determine constitutionality of laws or presidential actions.

6. subpoenas

Reviewing Main Ideas

1. statutory—laws passed by Congress and by other lawmaking bodies; common—law developed from judges' decisions, precedents, earlier court decisions

2. to a lawyer, to fair bail, to indictment by grand jury, to jury trial, to be considered innocent until proven guilty, to not testify against oneself, to question witnesses, to appeal

3. decides if enough evidence to try

4. to ensure impartiality of judges

5. established "separate but equal" principle; banned segregation as unequal

6. can declare congressional actions unconstitutional

7. judicial review, right of Court to set aside state laws violating U.S. Constitution and to reverse decisions of state courts

8. established principle of judicial review; established that police must tell suspects their rights before questioning them

Thinking Critically

1. Students should consider the Court's workload.

2. Students might say equality under the law requires protecting the rights of all.

3. Students should use sound reasoning in their responses.

Citizenship in Your Community

Paragraphs should compare the views of the sources.

BUILDING YOUR PORTFOLIO

Assign Portfolio Assessment Worksheet 7 in the *Portfolio Assessment Worksheets* booklet.

Assessment

• **Chapter 7 Tests**, *Chapter Tests* booklet

• **Test Generator**, Chapter 7

• **Portfolio**, Portfolio Assessment Worksheet 7, *Portfolio Assessment Worksheets* booklet

---

CHAPTER 7 — R·e·v·i·e·w

Vocabulary Workshop

1. What are the four types of law? Which type is supreme above all others?

2. What is another term for a trial jury?

3. What is the difference between original jurisdiction and appellate jurisdiction?

4. What is another term for a military trial?

5. Define the term *judicial review*.

6. What are the official court orders delivered by U.S. marshals called?

Reviewing Main Ideas

1. What is the difference between statutory law and common law?

2. Identify the eight rights that guarantee an accused person a fair trial.

3. What is the role of a grand jury?

4. Why are federal judges appointed for life?

5. What was the significance of *Plessy v. Ferguson*? of *Brown v. Board of Education of Topeka*?

6. How does the Supreme Court limit Congress's power?

7. What principles of U.S. law were established by John Marshall?

8. What was the significance of *Marbury v. Madison*? of *Miranda v. Arizona*?

Thinking Critically

1. When the Supreme Court hears a case, it limits the lawyers for each side to a 30-minute presentation. In your opinion, is this enough time to present all the facts of a case? Why do you think such a time limit exists?

2. Some people believe that the rights guaranteed to criminal suspects offer too much protection to criminals. Other people believe that these rights are needed to protect those who are unjustly accused.

What is your position on this issue? Explain your answer.

3. Justices of the Supreme Court vote to decide which cases they will review. Is this a fair system, or should an impartial panel of judges decide which cases the justices should hear? Explain your answer.

Citizenship in Your Community

Individual Project

Interview a member of your local police force. Ask the police officer how your police force protects the rights of the accused. Does the officer believe that these rules help or hinder the work of the police? Next, arrange to interview a local, state, or federal judge in your community concerning the ways in which the courts protect the rights of the accused. Finally, write a paragraph comparing the views of these two sources.

Building Your Portfolio

The third step of your unit portfolio project (see page 135) is to draw an organizational chart of the federal court system. Then draw a second organizational chart showing any changes you would make to the system. Consider how judges are chosen, the terms judges serve, the number of judges in each court, the types of cases each court handles, and each court's power to review other courts' and other federal branches' decisions. In a caption explain the reasoning behind each change or the lack of changes. Place your charts in your individual portfolio for later use.

UNIT 2 REVIEW
A N S W E R S

Reviewing Main Ideas

1. to check and balance the work of both houses and to settle disputes between states regarding representation
2. also called necessary and proper clause in Constitution; enables Congress to stretch its delegated powers to cover many other subjects
3. helps ensure that the nation's laws will be good laws
4. executive department heads; advise president
5. Supreme Court; power of Court to declare congressional laws and presidential acts unconstitutional
6. permanent committees of Congress with each responsible for a special area
7. recommends legislation, gives annual State of the Union Address, sends economic and budget messages to Congress, may veto bills; appoints judges, grants pardons, reprieves, and commutations
8. *Brown* case overturned *Plessy* decision by ruling school segregation unconstitutional

Thinking Critically

1. Answers will vary but should address the principle of not allowing any one group or branch of government to become too powerful or dominant.
2. Students should mention qualities that would be needed by a person who might have to assume the presidency.

3. Answers will vary. Students should use sound reasoning.

Practicing Civics Skills

1. Projects should include all elements of a political cartoon.
2. Charts should show the organization of your local government.
3. Encourage students to explain why they choose certain options over others.

Citizenship in Your Community

Students should compare the systems of government.

Learning from Technology

Answers will vary but should address the advantages and disadvantages of such a system.

UNIT 2 R·e·v·i·e·w

Reviewing Main Ideas

1. Why is Congress a bicameral legislature?
2. What is the elastic clause?
3. Why is lawmaking such a complex process?
4. What is the president's Cabinet?
5. Which court serves as the head of the judicial branch? What is judicial review?
6. What are standing committees?
7. How does the president influence the legislative branch of government? the judicial branch?
8. What is the relationship between *Plessy v. Ferguson* and *Brown v. Board of Education of Topeka*?

Thinking Critically

1. Explain to a visitor from a totalitarian nation why the separation of powers in the U.S. government helps ensure the freedom of Americans.
2. Imagine that you are a candidate for president. What qualities will you look for in a vice presidential candidate?
3. Over the past several years, the number of decisions made by the Supreme Court has decreased even though the caseload of the Court has increased. Do you think a quota should be set on the number of cases the Court must decide each year?

Practicing Civics Skills

1. Select an issue at the local, state, or federal level that interests you and portray it in a political cartoon. Be sure to use symbols, caricatures, labels, and a caption.
2. Create an organizational chart of your local government. For information about how your community government is organized, contact city officials or the local chapter of the League of Women Voters.
3. Keep a decision-making journal for a period of one week. Note when you make decisions, what your options are, and your reasons for choosing options. How can you improve your decision-making skills?

Citizenship in Your Community

Cooperative Project

With your group, conduct research to find out how you can become pen pals with teenagers living around the world. In your letters to pen pals, describe the U.S. system of government. Then ask these teenagers to describe the system of government in their countries. Present your letters to the class and discuss the similarities and differences in government.

Learning from Technology

Communications Satellites

Recently, two of the nation's leading technology companies announced plans to create a $9 billion global communications network. This network will put into orbit around the earth some 840 communications satellites, linking computer users in 95 percent of the world's governments, universities, and hospitals. What positive or negative effects might such a communications system have on U.S. foreign relations? How might such a system affect the federal government's ability to keep national secrets? How might Americans' right to privacy be affected?

Building Your Portfolio

Students have been working on a Building Your Portfolio project throughout Unit 2. You might ask volunteers to present their work to the class. Have all of the students add their work to their individual portfolios. Assign the Unit 2 Portfolio Assessment Worksheet in the *Portfolio Assessment Worksheets* booklet.

Building Your Portfolio

Individually or in a group, complete the following project to show your understanding of the civics concepts involved.

Reinventing Government

Many Americans believe that government has grown too large. These citizens believe the size and complexity of the federal government are interfering with its effectiveness. In response to such concerns, many citizens and elected officials are working to "reinvent" government—to make it more efficient and responsive to the people.

Prepare a proposal entitled "Reinventing Government." In your proposal explain what changes you wish to make to each branch of the federal government. Be sure to explain why these changes are needed and how they can be made within a democratic system. Any changes you propose must uphold the Constitution's principles and ideals, such as checks and balances, the separation of powers, and the accountability of government to the people. To prepare your proposal, you will need to do the following.

1. Write a bill outlining the changes you propose to make Congress more efficient and responsive. It might be helpful to show your proposed changes in a two-column chart. In one column list current membership requirements, procedures, and organizational structures for Congress. In the second column describe how you would change (or keep) each item in the first column. Your bill should summarize the chart's information and explain the purpose and reasoning behind each change.

2. Create a list of the responsibilities of the executive branch. Next to each item, indicate which part of the executive branch handles that responsibility—the president and the Executive Office, an executive department, or an independent agency. Analyze your list. Do responsibilities overlap, causing conflict and inefficiency? Are there too many departments and agencies? Too few? Write a paragraph explaining any changes you would make to the executive branch. If no changes are needed, explain why.

3. Draw an organizational chart of the federal court system. Then draw a second organizational chart showing any changes you would make to the system. Consider how judges are chosen, the terms judges serve, the number of judges in each court, the types of cases each court handles, and each court's power to review other courts' and other federal branches' decisions. In a caption, explain the reasoning behind each change or the lack of changes.

Organize your materials, and present your proposal to a local citizens' group (the rest of the class).

STATE AND LOCAL GOVERNMENT

▶**CHAPTER 8**
State Government
▶**CHAPTER 9**
Local Government

Using the Quotation

Have students read the quotation by Walt Whitman. Ask them to think about Whitman's words and then to give a short answer to the following question: Of all the components that make up the U.S. system of government, which one is the most important? *(the people)*

About the Author

Walt Whitman (1819–1892) was born on Long Island in New York. Whitman's varied career included work as a journalist, teacher, house builder, and poet. He cared for wounded soldiers during the U.S. Civil War and produced a number of well-known poems about the war and President Abraham Lincoln's death. He first published *Leaves of Grass*, a widely read book of his poems, in 1855. Revised and enlarged editions of the book were published up to Whitman's death in 1892.

136

" . . . The genius of the United States is not best or most in its executives or legislatures, nor in its ambassadors or authors, or colleges or churches or parlors, nor even in its newspapers or inventors—but almost most in the common people, south, north, west, east, in all its states, through all its mighty amplitude [range]."

—*Walt Whitman*
AMERICAN POET AND WRITER

Unit 3 describes how state and local governments function in the United States. By examining the powers, duties, and organization of each of these levels of government, students receive a clearer understanding of how the federal system works. They also gain insight into the importance of state and local governments in meeting the special needs of all their citizens.

UNIT OBJECTIVES

After studying Unit 3, students should be able to accomplish the following.

1. Describe the ways in which state governments serve their citizens.

2. Explain the organization of state governments.

3. Define various units of local government.

4. Identify kinds of city government.

5. Explain how all levels of government work together to serve U.S. citizens.

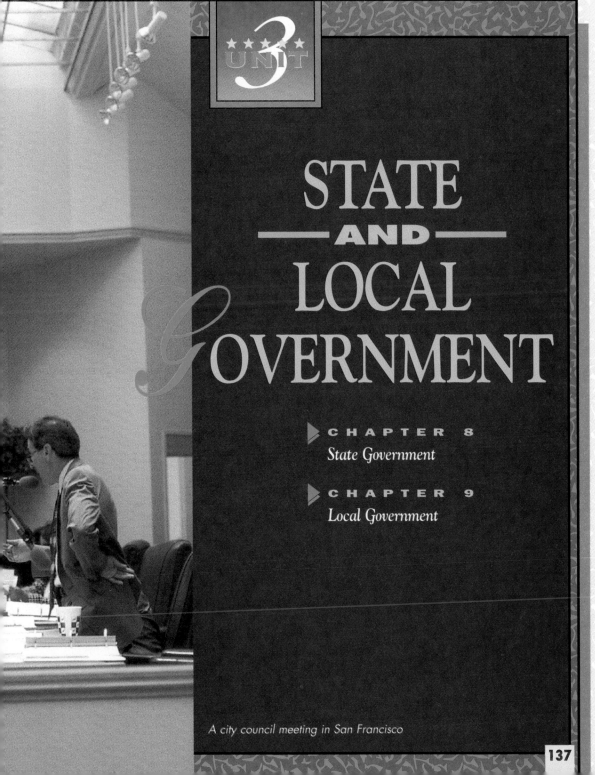

UNIT 3

STATE —AND— LOCAL GOVERNMENT

▶ **CHAPTER 8**
State Government

▶ **CHAPTER 9**
Local Government

A city council meeting in San Francisco

Block Scheduling Option

CIVICS VIDEOCASSETTE

Segment 3: The Citizen and Local Media

CIVICS VIDEODISC

Segment 3: The Citizen and Local Media

Segment 3, Side A

Search Chapter 3

Play   Pause

BUILDING YOUR PORTFOLIO

"Building Your Portfolio" on page 181 outlines a unit project for students to work on as they study Unit 3. The unit project is supported by materials in the *Portfolio Assessment Worksheets* booklet.

CHAPTER 8

State Government

TEXTBOOK	TEACHING RESOURCES	OTHER AVAILABLE RESOURCES
Chapter	• Skills Worksheet 8 • Challenge/Enrichment Worksheet 8	• Simulations and Case Studies Lessons 8 and 9
Section **1** The States Page 139	• Reteaching Worksheet 8.1	
2 State Legislatures Page 143	• Reteaching Worksheet 8.2	• Transparency 8: State Government
3 The State Executive Branch Page 147	• Reteaching Worksheet 8.3	• Transparency 9: The Powers and Duties of the Governor
4 State Courts Page 150	• Reteaching Worksheet 8.4	
Review and Assessment Chapter 8 Review, Page 157	• Test, Form A • Test, Form B • Portfolio Assessment Worksheet 8	• *Test Generator, Chapter 8*

Block Scheduling Option

ADDITIONAL RESOURCES

BOOKS FOR TEACHERS

Book of the States (biennial), Council of State Governments.

Burns, James MacGregor, et al., *State and Local Politics: Government by the People,* Prentice-Hall.

Ferguson, John H., and Dean E. McHenry, *The American System of Government,* McGraw-Hill.

Levine, Erwin, and Elmer E. Cornwell, *An Introduction to American Government,* Macmillan.

Van Horn, Carl E., *The State of the States,* Congressional Quarterly.

BOOKS FOR STUDENTS

Beyle, Thad L., ed., *State Government: CQ's Guide to Current Issues and Activities,*

Congressional Quarterly. Examines the influence of the states, and addresses issues of concern to state governments.

Feinberg, Barbara S., *State Governments,* Watts. Explains various jobs of state government officials, the effects of state government agencies on people's lives, and the division of power between federal and state governments.

MULTIMEDIA RESOURCES

Federalism (f, VHS, c, 19 min.), COR/MTI. Examines the powers of the federal government and state governments.

State and Local Government in Action (fs, c), SRA. Six filmstrips provide a comprehensive introduction to state and local governments.

State Government: Resurgence of Power (VHS, c, 21 min.), EBEC. Examines legislative sessions in two key states.

THE INTERNET

Have students use these search words to locate more information about chapter topics on the Internet: *federal government, state governments, state legislatures.*

 GLOBAL SKILL BUILDER

You might wish to use **Navigating the Internet** from the interactive *Global Skill Builder* CD-ROM to aid students' understanding of the Internet as a resource.

Abbreviations: b&w=black and white; c=color; f=film; fs=filmstrip; sd=sound; tr=transparency; VHS=videotape

AMERICAN GOVERNMENT

* **Levels of Government** Students will learn how powers are divided between federal and state governments, what powers are reserved to the states, and how the federal and state governments cooperate with each other. Students also will learn the procedure by which the majority of the states were admitted to the Union.

* **Structures and Functions** Students will trace the process by which state laws are passed and will learn the kinds of work done by each branch of state government. Students also will learn the qualifications and duties of key state officials.

CIVICS SKILLS

Students will learn how to write effective letters to public officials. They also will learn terms important to understanding the structures and functions of state governments.

CITIZENSHIP VALUES

* **Levels of Government** Students will be encouraged to appreciate the importance of the nation's state governments, the need for cooperation among the various levels of government, and the role of state courts in working to preserve "domestic tranquillity."

MEETING INDIVIDUAL NEEDS

LIMITED ENGLISH PROFICIENCY (LEP)

Pair LEP students with English-proficient students. Have the students list and illustrate the major powers of state government. (See the chart on page 140.) For example, the students might draw a ballot and a ballot box to illustrate the state's power to hold and regulate elections.

LEARNERS HAVING DIFFICULTY

Have students outline part or all of the chapter to review the main points of each lesson. Encourage them to use the proper format of Roman numerals, capital letters, Arabic numerals, and lowercase letters in order to show section titles, headings, main ideas, and supporting details.

AUDITORY LEARNERS

Invite students to follow the activities of the governor of your state for a week by watching television news reports and listening to radio news. They should take notes on everything the governor does for a full week and then report back to the class. Students might try categorizing the governor's activities into the roles given in the textbook: chief legislator, chief executive, political party leader, and so on.

VISUAL LEARNERS

Have students collect news stories showing the activities of or the services provided by their state government. Encourage students to summarize each article by identifying the state agency covered and by describing its involvement in current events. Students should refer to their textbooks as needed to categorize the agency as part of an executive department or another arm of the government. Call on volunteers to present their summaries to the class for discussion.

TACTILE/KINESTHETIC LEARNERS

Have students draw four pictures or diagrams to represent the four types of courts found in most states. Students should be sure their pictures clearly show the differences among the types of courts. They should label each type and add any other descriptive notes and a caption as needed. Display students' finished illustrations for the class to discuss.

GIFTED LEARNERS

Have pairs of students debate whether governors should be limited to two terms in office, as the U.S. president is. Students may be able to find arguments both for and against term limits in newspapers or other periodicals.

CHAPTER OVERVIEW

Chapter 8 introduces the powers of states as an integral part of the federal system of shared powers. It examines the organization of state government and investigates some of the many ways in which state and federal governments work together. The underlying theme of the chapter is that state governments serve the needs of their citizens.

Motivator

Have students consider these questions: What features set our state apart from other states? Is it a densely populated state, with large cities, or mainly a rural state? What is the basis of our state's economy? After a brief discussion, ask: Why might state governments sometimes be better able to meet people's needs than the federal government might be able to? *(People's needs vary from state to state.)*

CHAPTER OBJECTIVES

After studying Chapter 8, students should be able to do the following.

1. Identify the constitutional powers held by states.
2. Identify the contents of state constitutions.
3. Explain how state legislatures are organized and how a bill becomes a state law.
4. Explain how the state executive branch is organized.
5. Explain how state courts carry out their work.

SIMULATIONS AND CASE STUDIES

Lesson 8: The State Executive Branch in the News
Lesson 9: Television Talk Show: *Herrera v. Collins*

Block Scheduling Option

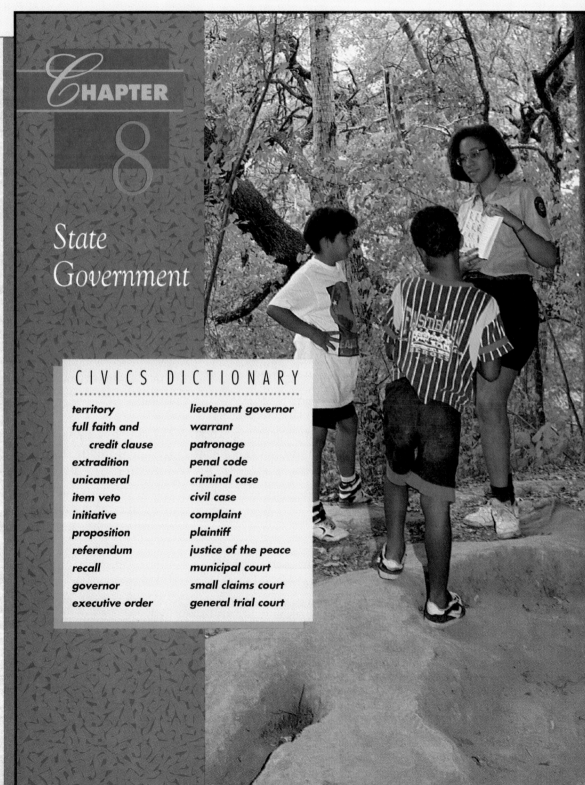

CHAPTER 8

State Government

CIVICS DICTIONARY

territory	*lieutenant governor*
full faith and credit clause	*warrant*
	patronage
extradition	*penal code*
unicameral	*criminal case*
item veto	*civil case*
initiative	*complaint*
proposition	*plaintiff*
referendum	*justice of the peace*
recall	*municipal court*
governor	*small claims court*
executive order	*general trial court*

After studying Section 1, students should be able to do the following.

1. Identify the states' reserved powers.
2. Explain how new states were added under the Articles of Confederation.
3. Identify the six parts of most state constitutions.
4. Explain how states cooperate with each other and with the federal government.

Teaching Section 1
Building a Vocabulary

Introduce the term **extradition** by explaining that the prefix *ex-* means "out" and the Latin *traditio* means "the act of handing over." *Extradition* thus means to hand over someone or something out of one area to another. Reinforce the term **territory** by having students consider these places: Puerto Rico, Guam, American Samoa. Ask: What is their relationship to the United States? *(They are U.S. territories.)*

CHAPTER FOCUS

Have you ever wondered who decides how many days you must attend school each year? This decision is made by your state government. Some state governments even decide what will be taught in school and what textbooks students will use. State governments make many decisions that affect your life on a daily basis.

Your state government makes laws that govern and protect you and the other people who live in your state. It helps pay for public education and provides hospitals to care for the ill. It builds and maintains the highways and bridges you use. Your state government does all these things and more because, like the federal government, it has been established to serve the people.

STUDY GUIDE

● What powers do the states have, and what is included in state constitutions?

● How are state legislatures organized, and how does a bill become a state law?

● What is the state executive branch, and how is it organized?

● How do state courts carry out their work?

1 The States

When the American colonies won their independence, the original 13 states acted like small, separate nations. As you know, under the Articles of Confederation each state issued its own money. Each state regulated trade crossing its borders and often treated neighboring states as though they were foreign nations. There was no provision for a president or a system of national courts, and the Congress had little power. For a while it seemed as though the United States would break up into 13 small, weak nations.

In 1787 the delegates to the Constitutional Convention worked long hours to establish a better form of government with a stronger national government. The delegates agreed to take away some of the powers of the states in order to form "a more perfect union." The states, however, were allowed to keep certain powers for themselves. The resulting form of government, as you read earlier, is known as federalism, or a federal system.

Division of Powers

In the U.S. federal system, the powers of government are divided between the 50 states and the federal government. How were these powers divided?

The states gave to the federal government those powers that affected all the people of the nation. For example, only the federal government can regulate trade between the states, coin money, and conduct foreign affairs. The federal government alone can set up a postal service and maintain an army and a navy.

The states, meanwhile, have considerable power to govern the people who live within their borders. State governments are close to the people and can better provide them with many needed services.

Reserved State Powers

When the states approved the Constitution, they wanted to make certain that the rights of the state governments would always be protected. Therefore, the Tenth Amendment was added to the Constitution. As you have read,

CIVICS SIDELIGHT

You might point out to students that the problem of all 13 states distributing their own currencies had its beginnings in the 17th century. In fact, early American colonists often used various goods or foreign coins (if they could get them) for money. They did this because the British government (which was trying to prevent colonists from trading with foreign powers) would not provide coins or allow the colonies to mint coins. The Massachusetts Bay Colony began producing coins in 1652. Eventually other colonies began to produce their own money. An attempt to create a common currency (and cover the costs of war) brought Americans the *continental*, authorized by the Continental Congress during the American Revolution. However, the *continental* became virtually worthless, and the Congress stopped issuing it. The U.S. Constitution in 1787 finally gave the national government, rather than the states, the power to produce a currency.

Summarizing

Have students read the Tenth Amendment to the U.S. Constitution (page 542) and also Article I, Sections 8–10 (pages 533–535) to review the constitutional basis of the states' reserved and concurrent powers. Then have students write paragraphs summarizing what they know about these two types of powers. Call students to the board to list examples of each of the types of powers.

Illustrating Ideas

On the board begin a flowchart of the process by which new states were admitted under the Articles of Confederation. Begin the flowchart by writing "territory of the United States." Call on volunteers to fill in other steps in the process. Then ask volunteers to debate whether Congress should be required to grant statehood to any territory that meets the requirements for statehood listed in the flowchart on the chalkboard.

CIVICS SIDELIGHT

Point out that all states have the power to tax and that each government approaches the issue with an eye toward its own domestic realities. So-called "sin taxes" serve as an example. The taxes on cigarettes and alcohol are known as "sin taxes," which implies that some people believe that those who smoke and consume alcohol should suffer economically for their bad habits. Raising sin taxes is much more acceptable to some Americans than raising taxes on income or property. Also, in an era of health consciousness, asking Americans to pay more for products that can lead to health problems makes sense to many politicians. On the other hand, some politicians and other Americans, especially in states where the liquor and tobacco industries are important to local economies, oppose sin taxes. They argue that such taxes endanger jobs in those industries.

the amendment provided that "the powers not delegated [given] to the United States by the Constitution, nor prohibited by it to the states, are reserved to [set aside for] the states respectively, or to the people." These reserved powers make it possible for states to govern their residents effectively.

State governments are responsible for conducting elections. They decide most of the qualifications for voting, although they must respect the U.S. Constitution's provisions about voting. States also establish procedures for holding all local, state, and national elections. The federal system of government depends on the states to ensure that Americans are given the opportunity to elect their own representatives.

Another important function of state governments concerns education. The power to establish and maintain schools belongs to the state governments. The states have the power to decide what kinds of schools they will provide. Again, however, state school regulations cannot conflict with the U.S. Constitution or with the rulings of the Supreme Court.

The states make laws concerning marriage and divorce, and they regulate traffic on the highways. State laws deal with health, safety, welfare, and the regulation of business within state borders. In addition, state governments have control over all local governments within their boundaries—cities, towns, townships, and counties. Local governments receive their powers from the states.

Concurrent Powers

The states also share many powers with the federal government. These shared powers, as you recall, are called concurrent powers. Even

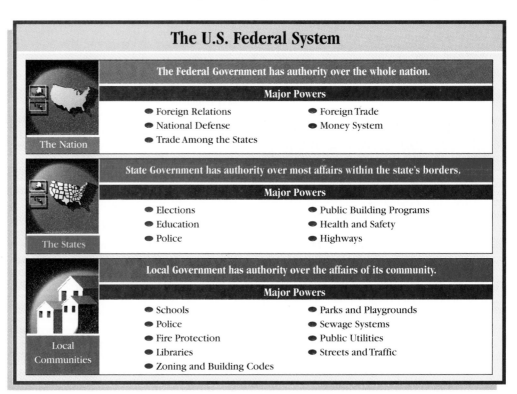

The U.S. Federal System

The Federal Government has authority over the whole nation.	
Major Powers	
● Foreign Relations	● Foreign Trade
● National Defense	● Money System
● Trade Among the States	

The Nation

State Government has authority over most affairs within the state's borders.	
Major Powers	
● Elections	● Public Building Programs
● Education	● Health and Safety
● Police	● Highways

The States

Local Government has authority over the affairs of its community.	
Major Powers	
● Schools	● Parks and Playgrounds
● Police	● Sewage Systems
● Fire Protection	● Public Utilities
● Libraries	● Streets and Traffic
● Zoning and Building Codes	

Local Communities

Help students create a two-column chart that compares the typical state constitution with the federal Constitution. The title might be *Constitutions,* and the column headings might be *Most States* and *Federal.* Have students list the six parts of most state constitutions in the chart's first column. Then have them find parallel elements in the federal Constitution and list those elements in the second column. Ask volunteers to note any similarities and differences between the two columns.

Have students write an advertisement for selling a "new and improved" state constitution. The advertisement might boast about the constitution's provisions and elements as listed in the textbook. Advertisements might also describe the document's value as an instrument of government. Some students might wish to turn their work into posters. Display students' work and ask them which state constitutions they would "buy" and why.

if certain powers are granted to the federal government in the Constitution, state governments may also have these powers. Unless a power is forbidden to the states by the U.S. Constitution, state governments may exercise that power.

A good example of a shared, or concurrent, power is the power of taxation. Both the federal government and the state governments have the power to tax the American people. Federal and state governments must collect various kinds of taxes to carry on their activities. State governments may raise money by taxing items such as gasoline, liquor, cigarettes, real estate, income, and personal property. The money raised through state taxes is used to pay for education, highways, health and safety programs, and other state activities.

From 13 States to 50 States

The 13 original states became part of the United States when they approved the Constitution. The states that joined the country later had to apply for admission. Most of these states were once U.S. territories. A **territory** is an area, governed by the United States, that is eligible to become a state.

In 1787, under the Articles of Confederation, Congress passed an important law called the Northwest Ordinance. This law provided a way for territories to join the nation as new and equal states.

Under the Northwest Ordinance a territory was eligible to become a state once it had a population of 60,000. If it wished to join the United States, the territory lawmakers sent a petition to Congress asking to be organized as a state.

If Congress agreed to the request, it asked the territory lawmakers to write a state constitution. This constitution had to be approved by the people of the territory and by the U.S. Congress. After these steps were completed, Congress voted whether to admit the territory as a new state.

The United States has admitted 37 states since it became an independent nation. In

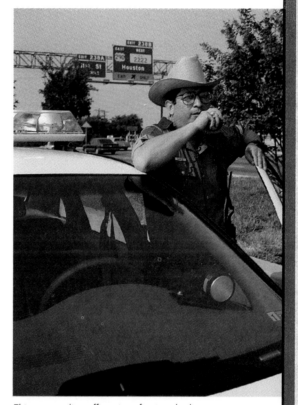

This state police officer is enforcing the law in an area over which each state has control—safety along the state's highways.

1959 Hawaii became the 50th state. The United States could grow larger still. U.S territorial possessions include Puerto Rico, Guam, American Samoa, the U.S. Virgin Islands, and parts of the Pacific islands. In a 1993 election Puerto Rican voters rejected the opportunity to petition the U.S. Congress for statehood. Puerto Ricans chose instead to keep a territorial status.

State Constitutions

Each of the 50 states has its own constitution, which contains the rules that direct how the state government will be organized and carry

MULTICULTURAL PERSPECTIVES

Students might wonder where Native American reservations fit into the federal-state-local framework. Even scholars are confused about this issue. The courts have defined Native American lands as "domestic, dependent nations." This allows Native Americans a certain amount of self-rule and a special relationship with the federal government. Recently, Native Americans have begun to exercise more of that self-rule. This development has led to conflicts with states over who should have governmental authority over non-Native Americans living on reservations, because non-Native Americans sometimes make up a large percentage of the reservation population. The answers to this and related questions are still evolving in the nation's courts.

Closure

Instruct students to examine the chart on textbook page 140. Ask: Why do you suppose the federal government regulates trade among the states? Why don't state governments have the power to set local traffic laws? Responses should center around the reasons for having different levels of government in the federal system.

Reviewing

Have students complete the Section 1 Review.

Reteaching

Assign Section 1 of the Chapter 8 Reteaching Worksheet.

GLOBAL PERSPECTIVES

Point out that extradition is also an international practice, an important part of any two countries' diplomatic relationship. The nations usually sign an extradition treaty declaring what crimes can lead to extradition.

The United States allows a U.S. citizen to be extradited only if authorized in such a treaty. The governments of Argentina and the United Kingdom follow the same policy. Most countries, however, prefer not to release their citizens into the custody of another country for any reason. Germany, France, Switzerland, the Netherlands, and Belgium prohibit extradition altogether.

The other side of the extradition coin is political asylum. Most nations recognize the need to provide a haven for people wanted in their home countries for political reasons alone. Many nations will not allow foreign nations to extradite such political refugees.

on its work. Most state constitutions contain the following:

- a preamble, or beginning, that states the basic ideas and ideals on which the state government is founded
- a bill of rights, sometimes called a declaration of rights, that lists the rights and freedoms guaranteed to all citizens who live in the state
- an outline of the organization of the state's government, with the duties of the legislative, executive, and judicial branches carefully spelled out
- provisions for elections, including qualifications for voting that must be met by the citizens of the state, as well as rules for conducting elections
- provisions for managing state affairs, including education, keeping law and order, building highways, regulating business, and raising money by means of taxes
- methods of amending, or changing, the state constitution, and a list of the amendments passed

Most state constitutions have gone through the amendment process many times. Amendments have been necessary because the powers and duties of state governments have changed greatly since their constitutions were first written. The Texas state constitution, for instance, has been amended more than 300 times. In recent decades a number of states have drawn up new constitutions. A new constitution usually is written and proposed at a state constitutional convention by delegates who are elected by the people.

States Working Together

In joining the Union, the states agreed to work together in harmony. One way they promised to cooperate is stated in Article 4, Section 1, of the U.S. Constitution. It states that "Full faith [belief] and credit [acceptance] shall be given in each State to the public acts, records, and judicial proceedings [court decisions] of every other State."

The **full faith and credit clause** ensures that each state will accept the decisions of courts in other states. If a court in California, for instance, decides that one of its citizens owns a certain piece of land, the other states will accept this legal decision. Another example of the full faith and credit clause is the acceptance of the official records of other states. A marriage certificate, birth certificate, will, contract, or deed issued by any state is accepted by all other states.

States work together in other ways, too. For example, a person accused of a crime cannot escape justice by fleeing to another state. If a person commits a crime in Utah and flees to Arizona, the governor of Utah can ask the governor of Arizona to return the person to Utah. This method of returning fugitives from justice is called **extradition**.

States cooperate on many projects. A bridge that crosses a river bordering two states is built and maintained by the governments of both states. States also work together to reduce water and air pollution.

The States and the Federal Government

For the federal system to work well, it is important that the 50 states and the federal government cooperate. What are some of the ways in which the federal and state governments join to provide services for Americans?

The U.S. Constitution, in Article 4, Section 4, promises that "The United States shall guarantee to every State in this Union a republican form of government. . . ." As you have read, in a republican form of government the people elect representatives to carry out the work of government. Every state, as it joined the Union, has been required to provide for a republican form of government in its state constitution.

The Constitution also promises that the federal government will "protect each of them [the states] against invasion." It is the responsibility of the federal government to provide

Extension

Have students research examples of disputes (such as disagreements about borders or mineral rights) between states. Students should write a paragraph explaining each dispute, presenting both sides of the issue and detailing how the dispute was settled. Students should create maps or other visuals to illustrate their examples. Ask volunteers to present their examples to the class.

SECTION OBJECTIVES

After studying Section 2, students should be able to do the following.

1. Explain why state election districts must have nearly equal populations.

2. Identify and explain the qualifications and terms of office of state legislators.

3. Describe how presiding officers are chosen and how the work of state legislatures is done.

4. Describe how a state bill becomes a law.

strong military forces to defend the states and the nation against attack.

In addition, the Constitution states that the federal government must stand ready to help any state put down "domestic violence" within its borders. An example of domestic violence might be rioting in a town. The governor may call on the National Guard of the state if local police cannot control the disorder. In extreme cases, the governor may ask the federal government for assistance.

The federal and state governments share the costs of furnishing a number of services to the American people. Federal and state governments work together to build highways, assist jobless workers, help the needy, and conserve natural resources. Together the federal and state governments provide low-cost lunches for schoolchildren and offer job training to people with disabilities.

SECTION 1 REVIEW

1. Define or identify the following terms: territory, full faith and credit clause, extradition.

2. What powers are reserved to the states by the Constitution?

3. How did the Articles of Confederation provide for the addition of new states?

4. What are the six parts that make up most state constitutions?

5. What are two ways that the states cooperate with each other? Identify three ways that the states and the federal government cooperate.

6. **THINKING CRITICALLY** Imagine that the Constitution does not contain the full faith and credit clause and that your family is planning a move to another state. Explain how the lack of a full faith and credit clause will affect your family after the move.

2 State Legislatures

Each state has a lawmaking body elected by the people of the state. In 26 states this lawmaking body is called the legislature. The term *general assembly* is used in 19 states. In Montana, North Dakota, and Oregon, the lawmaking body is the legislative assembly. In Massachusetts and New Hampshire, it is the general court. In this chapter we shall use the general term *state legislature.*

Organization

All but one of the states have a bicameral legislature. The larger of the two houses usually is called the House of Representatives. The smaller house is known as the Senate. Only Nebraska has a one-house, or **unicameral**, legislature called the Senate.

State legislatures vary greatly in size. Alaska has the smallest legislature, with 40 representatives and 20 senators. The largest legislature is in New Hampshire, which has 400 representatives and 24 senators.

The members of each state legislature are elected by the people of the state. Each member represents the people who live in a particular district of that state. The state legislature divides the state into districts.

Originally, the upper house (Senate) of the state legislature usually had one senator from each county or from each election district into which the state was divided. The counties or districts, however, often were unequal in population. Therefore, sparsely populated areas of the state often had as many senators as heavily populated areas.

In 1964 the U.S. Supreme Court ruled that all state election districts must be equal in population—or as nearly equal as possible. As you read in Chapter 7, this is the famous "one person, one vote" ruling. The states now are required to establish election districts nearly equal in population.

SECTION 1 REVIEW ANSWERS

1. See the following pages: territory (p. 141); full faith and credit clause, extradition (p. 142).

2. elections and rules on voting; laws on education, marriage, divorce, highway traffic, and public health, safety, and welfare; regulate business; grant powers to local government

3. Northwest Ordinance—territory eligible when it has 60,000 people; petition Congress; write constitution to be approved by residents and Congress; Congress votes

4. preamble; bill of rights; state's organization; elections; managing state affairs; amending the constitution and a list of amendments

5. full faith and credit clause, extradition, interstate projects; share services, such as highway building, job training, aid to needy, conservation

6. Students should demonstrate an understanding of the full faith and credit clause.

Teaching Section 2
Building a Vocabulary

Ask students what it means to *initiate* an action. *(to start it)* Tell them that people have the right to start new state legislation. Have them deduce what that process might be called. *(initiative)* The people or government also can initiate a vote on an issue—that is, *refer* the matter to voters. Ask students if they can name any recent **refer**endum decided by voters in their state.

Drawing a Map

Have each student sketch a map of a fictional state. Have students divide their maps into nine election districts equal in area, but with populations that vary significantly in size. Students should explain in their map captions how districts with a minority of the state's population can disproportionately influence the state's legislature. Then have each student draw a second map that redivides the state into districts roughly equal in population. The second map's caption should explain the advantages of this system.

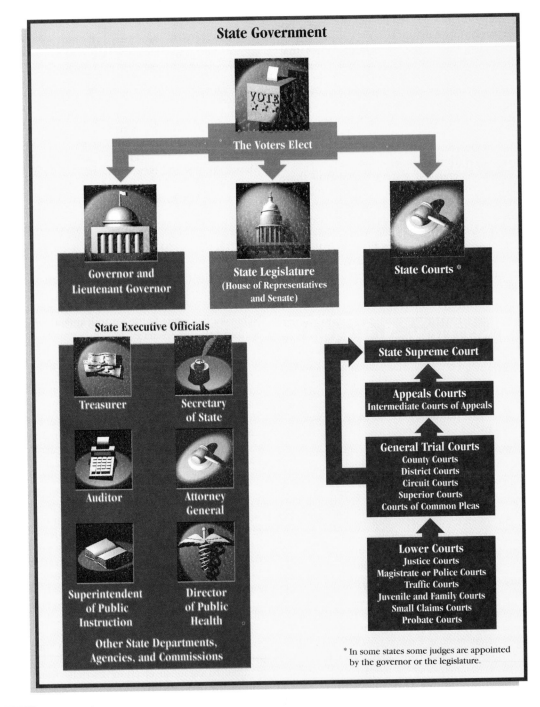

State Government

The Voters Elect

Governor and Lieutenant Governor

State Legislature (House of Representatives and Senate)

State Courts *

State Executive Officials

Treasurer

Secretary of State

Auditor

Attorney General

Superintendent of Public Instruction

Director of Public Health

Other State Departments, Agencies, and Commissions

State Supreme Court

Appeals Courts Intermediate Courts of Appeals

General Trial Courts County Courts District Courts Circuit Courts Superior Courts Courts of Common Pleas

Lower Courts Justice Courts Magistrate or Police Courts Traffic Courts Juvenile and Family Courts Small Claims Courts Probate Courts

* In some states some judges are appointed by the governor or the legislature.

Ask: How old must a person be to serve in most state legislatures? Use the board to create a profile of "State Legislature Candidate X" by discussing with students other requirements a person must meet to run for a seat in the legislature. *(The person must be a citizen who lives in the state and district he or she wants to represent; also, the person cannot have already served the maximum number of years in a state with term limits.)*

Invite students to imagine they want to run for the legislature in their state. Have them write a fictional résumé—a summary of their experience and skills—with which they can sell themselves to the voting public. "Candidates" should show that they meet the basic legal qualifications for the position and have other skills needed to serve the people of their state.

Qualifications and Terms

Members of a state legislature must be U.S. citizens. They must live in the state and district that they represent. In most states a state senator must be at least 25 years of age. Most states require state representatives to be at least 21 years old. Some states, however, have lowered the age requirement to 21 for senators and 18 for representatives.

In most states senators are elected for four years and representatives for two years. In a few states, however, both senators and representatives are elected for four-year terms. In some states senators and representatives both serve two years. The senators who serve in Nebraska's one-house legislature are elected for four-year terms.

The 1995 Supreme Court ruling that declared term limits for federal lawmakers unconstitutional (see page 73) does not apply to state legislators. Currently, 20 states limit the number of terms their legislators can serve. These term limits, however, are also being challenged.

Salaries and Benefits

The salaries and benefits received by state legislators vary widely from state to state. Even so, the salaries of all state legislators are surprisingly low, considering the important work that they do. In Rhode Island, for example, state legislators each receive only $10,000 a year. New York's legislators are among the highest paid, each receiving an annual salary of $57,500, plus $89 a day for expenses.

State Legislatures at Work

The legislatures in the majority of the states meet in regular sessions every year. Other state legislatures meet once every two years. California has a two-year session that meets for that entire period. In other states a session can last from thirty days to six months or more. The governor, or sometimes the state legislature, may call special sessions.

At the beginning of the session, the presiding officer and other leaders are chosen. Committees are appointed. In most states there is a lieutenant governor who presides over the Senate. In other states the Senate chooses its own presiding officer. Members of the lower house in all states choose their own presiding officer, usually called the Speaker.

As in the U.S. Congress, most of the work of the state legislatures is done in committees. In the upper house, committee members are chosen by the presiding officer or by all the upper house members. In the lower house the Speaker usually has the responsibility of appointing committee members.

Passing State Laws

The lawmaking process in state legislatures is similar to the procedure followed in Congress. (See Chapter 5.) The following summarizes the way in which a bill becomes a state law.

A Bill Is Introduced Any member of either house may introduce a bill. It is first handed to the clerk and given a number. The presiding officer reads aloud the title of the bill and sends it to the appropriate committee.

The Bill Is Sent to Committee The committee listens to various witnesses for and against the bill and then questions them to obtain necessary information. The members may discuss the bill for many hours. The committee may vote to pass the bill, to change it, or to kill it.

The Bill Reaches the Floor If the committee approves the bill, it is returned to a full meeting of the house. The bill is read aloud, line by line. The members of the house discuss each part of the bill. Amendments may be offered, and if passed they become part of the bill. The members then vote on the bill. Bills that are passed are signed by the presiding officer and sent to the other house.

The Bill Is Sent to the Second House When the bill is introduced in the

CIVICS SIDELIGHT

Point out that states differ in required qualifications for their legislators and in how many terms they may serve. In September 1990, Oklahoma became the first state in the nation to limit the terms of its state legislators. Two months later California and Colorado followed suit. Term-limit fever spread to 11 other states in 1992. By 1995, 20 states had imposed term limits on their state legislators. Representatives in these states are limited to serving 6 to 12 years, depending on the state, and senators are limited to serving 8 to 12 years, also depending on the state.

Closure

Have students line up to enact the process of passing a state law. Have individual students represent each step of the process by identifying themselves and describing the action that takes place. For example, the first student in line might say, "I am a representative, and I am introducing a bill." The second student would play the role of presiding officer, the third the committee, and so forth.

Reviewing

Have students complete the Section 2 Review.

Reteaching

Assign Section 2 of the Chapter 8 Reteaching Worksheet.

146

The state legislature is the lawmaking branch of state government. Here, members of the Texas House of Representatives debate a bill under consideration.

second house of the state legislature, it is sent to a committee. If the bill survives the hearings, debates, and changes in this committee, it is sent back to the floor of the second house. Here it is debated, perhaps changed again, and then put to a vote.

Bills that pass one house and fail in the second house are dead. If both houses of the legislature pass a bill in the same form, it is then sent to the governor to be signed. Frequently, however, both houses pass the bill, but in different forms. In this case, it is sent to a joint conference committee.

The Bill Is Sent to a Joint Conference Committee Joint conference committees are made up of members selected from both houses. Committee members must try to reach a compromise that will be acceptable to both houses. The compromise bill of the joint conference committee is then voted on by the two houses. Each house usually accepts this final version of the bill.

The Bill Is Sent to the Governor The final step in making a state law is to send the bill to the governor. If the governor signs the bill, it becomes a law. In all states except North Carolina, the governor may veto a bill he or she does not support. In most states the

governor also has the power to veto only one part, or item, of an appropriation bill. This is called an **item veto**. The legislature can pass a bill over the governor's veto by a two-thirds vote in each house.

Citizen Action

Some state constitutions allow the people to take a direct part in making laws. Citizens are able to initiate, or start, new legislation through a process called the **initiative**.

Citizens must draw up a petition describing the proposal. If a required number of voters sign the petition, the **proposition**, or proposed law, appears on the ballot at the next general election. If enough people vote for the bill, it becomes law.

In many states certain bills passed by the legislature must be approved by the voters before the bills become laws. This method of referring questions directly to the people is called a **referendum**.

Some states also provide voters with the means to remove elected officials from office. This process, known as a **recall**, begins when a required number of voters sign a petition. A special election on the petition is then held. If a majority of voters favors the recall, the official is removed.

SECTION OBJECTIVES

After studying Section 3, students should be able to do the following.

1. Identify the qualifications, term of office, duties, and powers of most governors.

2. Identify the other officials of state executive branches.

3. Describe how most state government employees get their jobs.

Teaching Section 3

Building a Vocabulary

Ask students what a **governor** is. Elicit that a governor is the chief executive of a state. Then ask: What do you think an **executive order** is? *(the governor's formal command to carry out a law)* Given that a lieutenant is a subordinate officer in the military, have students speculate on the duties of a **lieutenant governor**. *(to assist the governor or succeed the governor if necessary; often presides over a state's Senate)* Point out to students the similarity of the lieutenant governor to the U.S. vice president.

SECTION 2 REVIEW

1. Define or identify the following terms: unicameral, item veto, initiative, proposition, referendum, recall.

2. Why must state election districts be nearly equal in population?

3. What are the qualifications for members of state legislatures? How long do members of state legislatures serve?

4. How are presiding officers chosen, and how is the work of state legislatures carried out?

5. How does a state bill become a state law?

6. **THINKING CRITICALLY** Create a chart that compares the U.S. Congress with a typical state legislature in terms of qualifications, organization, structure, and duties. In what ways are they similar? How do they differ?

The State Executive Branch

The state's legislative branch makes the laws for the state. These laws are carried out by the state's executive branch. The executive branch is headed by the **governor**. It also includes other officials, as well as numerous agencies, who assist the governor.

Qualifications and Terms of Governors

The governor is the chief executive in each state. He or she is elected by the people of the state in a statewide election. The qualifications for governor are listed in each state constitution. In general, a candidate for governor must be a U.S. citizen and must have lived in the state for a certain number of years. Most states require a governor to be at least 30 years old. A few, however, allow persons at least 25 years of age to run for governor.

Most governors serve four-year terms. In some states they are elected for two years. About one third of the states limit their governors to one or two terms in office.

The salaries of governors vary greatly from state to state. For example, the governor of New York receives $130,000 a year, while the governor of Montana receives $59,310. In addition to a salary, governors usually receive an allowance for expenses. In most states governors and their families live in an official residence in the state capital.

Powers and Duties of Governors

The main job of a governor, as chief executive of the state, is to carry out the laws. Like the president of the United States, however, many governors also have legislative and judicial responsibilities.

Chief Legislator Only the state legislature can pass laws. The governor, though, plays an important part in proposing new laws. The governor usually appears before the state legislature at one of its early meetings. At this meeting, the governor outlines laws he or she thinks should be passed. The governor talks to leaders of the legislature, urging them to pass specific bills and oppose others. State legislators know that if they pass a bill the governor opposes, it may be vetoed.

After the legislature has passed a law, it is the responsibility of the governor to put it into force. If the legislature passes a new tax law, for example, it is the duty of the governor to issue orders that will determine how the taxes are to be collected. The orders that set up methods of enforcing laws are called **executive orders**. Almost every new law requires an executive order.

GLOBAL PERSPECTIVES

Students might be familiar with the term *governor general*. Help students distinguish between governors general and state governors in the United States. A governor general is the chief executive of an overseas possession of a foreign power. He or she is the representative of the foreign power's head of government. For example, European colonial powers, such as the United Kingdom, Portugal, the Netherlands, and Spain are represented in their possessions by governors general. Members of the British Commonwealth of Nations have governors general that represent the British monarch. The powers of governors general vary, depending on the laws of the country. Canada's governor general, who represents the British monarch, has little real power; however, some governors general have almost absolute authority in their particular countries.

Learning Through History

Have pairs of students use classroom resources (such as encyclopedias) to research a powerful governor from U.S. history. Ask the students to determine how each governor acquired power and then to distill their findings into one or more generalizations, such as, "A governor acquires power through hard work." Use some of these generalizations to prompt a discussion of unofficial qualifications for being a state governor.

Invite small groups of students to imagine they are producing a popular talk show with a fictional governor as today's featured guest. Have them introduce the governor, giving as many details as possible. Groups should supply—in some creative way—the governor's name, age, salary, roles, and other powers. Students can be assigned to play the various roles of host(s), featured guests, and so on. Invite volunteers to present their talk shows to the class.

CIVICS SIDELIGHT

The state legislature is a common breeding ground for gubernatorial hopefuls. There, governors-to-be can learn the ins and outs of state government. In the same way, the position of governor can be a stepping-stone to the presidency. Up to 1995, nine presidents had moved directly from a governorship to the White House. Twelve presidents began their political careers as state legislators.

CIVICS TRANSPARENCIES

An overhead transparency of "The Powers and Duties of the Governor" is available in *Teaching Transparencies with Teacher's Notes.*

Chief Executive   In most states one of the governor's most important responsibilities is to draw up a budget for the state. A budget director or a budget bureau usually assists the governor in this task. Long hours are spent determining how much money the state will need during the next one- or two-year period, and what taxes will be required to meet this need. The completed budget is sent to the legislature for approval.

As chief executive of the state, the governor also may appoint a number of state officials with the approval of the state Senate. The governor works with these officials to carry out state laws.

Political Party Leader   The governor is the head of his or her political party in the state. State senators and representatives pay close attention to what the governor says. They know the governor can help them during their next election campaigns.

Other Powers   The governor has many other powers. The heads of the state police force and state militia report to the governor. In times of emergency, such as floods or

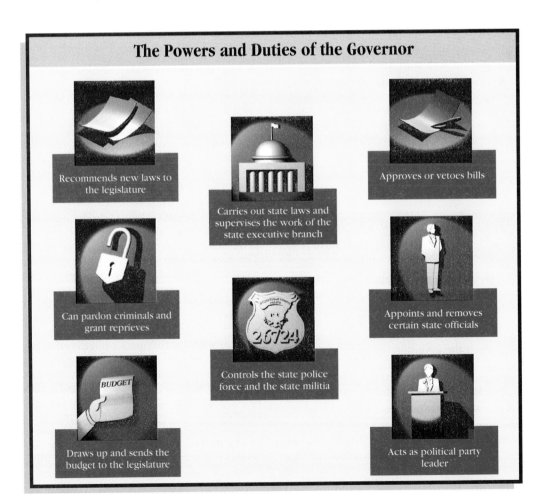

The Powers and Duties of the Governor

- Recommends new laws to the legislature
- Carries out state laws and supervises the work of the state executive branch
- Approves or vetoes bills
- Can pardon criminals and grant reprieves
- Appoints and removes certain state officials
- Draws up and sends the budget to the legislature
- Controls the state police force and the state militia
- Acts as political party leader

BUDGET

26724

Conduct a "civics bee" by organizing the class into two groups and lining up students single file. Alternating between students at the front of each line, ask a student to identify the state official responsible for a specific function that you read aloud. After each student answers a question, have him or her move to the back of the line. Each side is awarded one point for each correct response. Continue until all the students have had at least one opportunity to participate.

Ask students how most state employees get their positions. *(apply through a government office)* Then ask: How are the rest of the jobs filled? *(recommendations of party leaders)* Invite students to imagine each is the head of one of the state executive offices or agencies. Have each student create a job description for an assistant to be hired soon. The description should include skills as well as political qualifications necessary for the job.

---

hurricanes, the governor may call out the National Guard to help keep order. The governor also has the judicial power to pardon, or free, certain prisoners. A reprieve issued by a governor will postpone a prisoner's sentence.

Other State Executive Officials

The voters of each state elect a number of officials in addition to the governor to help run the state government and enforce state laws. The following officials are the most important members of each state's executive branch. In most states these officials are elected by the voters. In some states, however, they are appointed by the governor.

Lieutenant Governor All but seven states have a **lieutenant governor**. The lieutenant governor becomes head of the state executive branch if the governor dies, resigns, or is removed from office. In some states it is possible for the lieutenant governor and the governor to belong to different political parties. The lieutenant governor often serves as presiding officer of the state senate.

Secretary of State The secretary of state keeps state records and carries out election laws. This official is sometimes called the secretary of the commonwealth. Only Alaska, Hawaii, and Utah do not have this official. In states that do not have a lieutenant governor, the secretary of state takes over as governor if the office of governor becomes vacant.

Attorney General The attorney general takes care of the state's legal business, or matters concerning the law. If a state official wants advice about the meaning of a law, the attorney general provides it. The attorney general or an assistant represents the state in court when the state is involved in a lawsuit. The attorney general may also assist local officials in the prosecution of criminals.

State Treasurer The state treasurer is in charge of handling all state funds. This official supervises the collection of taxes and pays the state's bills.

State Auditor The state auditor ensures that no public funds are paid out of the state treasury unless payment is authorized by law. Usually the treasurer cannot pay any bills without a written order that is signed by the auditor. This order to pay out money is called a **warrant**. The auditor also examines the state's financial records regularly to make sure they are correct. The auditor is sometimes called the comptroller.

Superintendent of Public Instruction The most important duty of the superintendent of public instruction is to carry out the policies of the state board of education (known in some states by other titles). The state board makes regulations, under state law, that govern the various local school districts. The superintendent is in charge of the distribution of state funds to local school systems according to state and federal laws. In some states this official is called the superintendent of public schools or the state commissioner of education.

The Cabinet

In some states the officials you have just read about are a part of the governor's Cabinet. In other states they are not considered members of the Cabinet unless they are appointed by the governor. Like the president's Cabinet, the governor's official advisers head the executive departments of the state government.

Most states have a Department of Justice (headed by the attorney general), a Department of Labor, a Department of Agriculture, a Department of Transportation, and a Department of Public Safety, which includes the state police. The Department of Public Works is responsible for all public construction projects in the state except work done on highways.

State Executive Agencies

A number of state agencies help the governor carry out the laws. These agencies are part of

MULTICULTURAL PERSPECTIVES

The number of African Americans in state government and other offices is on the rise. In 1970 there were just 1,500 black elected officials. By 1993 that number had risen to more than 8,000.

African Americans held a number of state and local offices in southern states during Reconstruction after the U.S. Civil War. In fact, six African Americans were lieutenant governors in the South during that period, and one served briefly as governor of Louisiana after the removal of the white governor in 1873. African Americans also served in the U.S. House of Representatives and the U.S. Senate.

Even before the end of Reconstruction, however, African Americans began to lose political power in the South as whites reasserted their control in the region. Finally, in 1989 Douglas Wilder of Virginia became the first elected African American governor in the United States.

Closure

Have students discuss the following questions: Why would service as a governor be good experience if one wanted to become president? *(similar executive duties and responsibilities)* What experience might a governor lack? *(foreign policy experience; knowledge of the Washington scene)* Conduct a panel discussion on whether lack of foreign policy or Washington experience should preclude a governor from being president.

Reviewing

Have students complete the Section 3 Review.

Reteaching

Assign Section 3 of the Chapter 8 Reteaching Worksheet.

SECTION 3 REVIEW
A N S W E R S

1. See the following pages: governor, executive order (p. 147); lieutenant governor, warrant (p. 149); patronage (p. 150).

2. U.S. citizen, resident of state for a certain number of years, certain minimum age; most serve four-year terms, some two-year terms; terms limited to one or two in about one third of the states

3. proposes and may veto legislation, issues executive orders, prepares state budget; appoints certain officials, heads state political party, oversees state police and National Guard; grants pardons and reprieves

4. lieutenant governor, secretary of state, attorney general, state treasurer, state auditor, superintendent of public instruction

5. most jobs open to those who pass state examination; other state jobs filled by political appointments

6. Students should be able to explain their rankings.

150

the state executive branch and are sometimes called boards, commissions, or departments.

Most state agencies are headed by officials appointed by and responsible to the governor. In some states the heads of the agencies are appointed by the state legislature and are responsible directly to the legislature.

Each state agency has a specific area of responsibility. For example, the state Board of Health enforces health laws and recommends measures to improve the health of state citizens. The Department of Human Services supervises programs that help people who are poor, unemployed, or disabled. The state Civil Service Commission is in charge of hiring most of the people who work for the state. Other state agencies administer state laws on agriculture, highways, and conservation or regulate banks and public utilities.

State Government Employees

The 50 state governments employ more than four million people. Most state government jobs are open to any qualified citizen who passes a state examination. Some state jobs, however, are filled through **patronage**. That is, the jobs are given to people recommended by political party leaders and officeholders. Such jobs often go to those people in the party who have helped in some important way during the election campaign.

SECTION 3 REVIEW

1. Define or identify the following terms: governor, executive order, lieutenant governor, warrant, patronage.

2. What are the qualifications for governor in most states? How long do most governors serve?

3. What are the main duties and powers of a state governor?

4. What state officials help the governor carry out the duties of the executive branch?

5. How do most state government employees get their jobs?

6. **THINKING CRITICALLY** Examine the chart on page 148, which shows the powers and duties of state governors. Then create a two-column chart. In the first column rank the governor's powers and duties in order of importance, from most important to least important. In the second column explain why you ranked each item in this way. Might the governor rank these powers and duties differently than you, a member of the general public? Explain your answer.

State Courts

Each state government has the power to maintain peace and order within its boundaries and to establish its own **penal code**, or set of criminal laws. This power is shared by all three branches of state government. The legislature passes laws to provide for the welfare and safety of the people of the state. The executive branch ensures that these laws are enforced. The judicial branch—the state court system—is responsible for interpreting state laws and punishing those people who break them.

Work of the State Courts

Federal and state courts handle both criminal and civil cases. **Criminal cases** deal with violations of the law. Such cases involve acts that harm individuals or the community as a whole. A criminal act is considered an offense against society. In such a case, an attorney for the state presents the evidence against the

SECTION OBJECTIVES

After studying Section 4, students should be able to do the following.

1. Describe the area of responsibility of each of the four types of state courts.

2. Explain how small-claims courts differ from other courts.

3. Identify what citizens can do if they are not satisfied with an appeals court decision.

Teaching Section 4
Building a Vocabulary

Help students remember the difference between **criminal cases** and **civil cases** in federal and state courts. *Criminal* is derived from a Latin word meaning "accusation" or "reproach." Criminal cases cover those accused of committing an offense against society. *Civil* is derived from a Latin word meaning "citizen." Civil cases involve disputes between individuals (citizens), between individuals and the government, or between businesses and individuals or the government.

accused. The state's attorney represents the people of the state, because breaking a state law is a crime committed against the people of the state.

Civil cases deal with disputes between individuals or businesses. They may also involve disputes between a business and the government or between an individual and the government. These disputes usually focus on property or money. For example, if one person claims that another person owes him or her money and asks a state court for help in collecting the money, the case would be a civil case. Another example is a lawsuit brought by one company against another company for not carrying out its part of a business contract.

In a civil case the person or company filing the **complaint**, or lawsuit, is referred to as the **plaintiff**. The state court must decide who is right according to the law and must award damages in civil cases.

Organization

Each state has its own system of courts to interpret the law and punish lawbreakers. The organization of state courts varies from state to state. Four types of courts are found in most states: lower courts, general trial courts, appeals courts, and a state supreme court. The chart on page 144 shows the organization of most state court systems.

Lower Courts The lower courts generally hear minor cases, including misdemeanors and civil cases involving small amounts of money. In most rural areas and small towns these cases are heard by a **justice of the peace**. This elected official presides over a justice court and tries misdemeanors and civil cases involving small sums. For misdemeanors the justice of the peace can hand down fines or short jail sentences.

In larger towns and small cities such cases are handled by a magistrate's court or police court. These courts usually are presided over by an elected judge. All cases are heard by the judge and not by a trial jury.

Many large cities have **municipal courts**. These courts are often divided into smaller courts that handle specific types of cases. Traffic courts, for example, hear cases involving traffic violations. Family relations courts hear cases involving family disputes. Juvenile courts hear cases involving young persons.

Judges with special legal training usually preside over the lower courts. These judges conduct hearings without a jury. They are interested in discovering the cause of the trouble and preventing further difficulty. Judges in juvenile and family relations courts work closely with social workers to help families who are in trouble. In serious cases the decisions of the judges may be appealed to a trial court.

Most states have also established special courts that hear civil cases involving small amounts of money. These **small claims courts** usually handle cases involving less than $5,000. No lawyers are needed. The people in the dispute explain their side of the argument to the judge. After questioning each side to discover all the facts, the judge makes a decision in the case.

(continued on page 154)

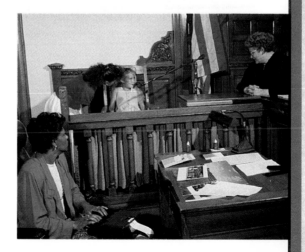

Many cities have established various special lower courts. In this family relations court, the judge must consider the best interests of the child.

CIVICS SIDELIGHT

Justices of the peace have been criticized because, although many are not lawyers, they handle legal cases. In fact, a presidential Task Force on the Courts in 1967 recommended completely dismantling the justice-of-the-peace system. Nevertheless, many people believe justices of the peace have important functions, including handling many minor civil responsibilities (such as conducting weddings, issuing arrest warrants, and dealing with traffic offenses). Having justices of the peace be responsible for such duties leaves more important cases to already overcrowded higher courts.

Illustrating Ideas

Have students use a flowchart to track *Miranda v. Arizona* through the courts. Each event should be boxed, with an arrow leading to the next event in sequence. The first event might be "Miranda arrested on kidnapping charges." The last event in the sequence might be "Miranda reconvicted at a new trial."

CASE STUDY

MIRANDA RIGHTS

If you have ever watched a movie or television show dealing with crime, you are familiar with the following scene: A robbery is committed late at night, and the police jump into action. After an exciting chase by car and on foot, the officers corner the fleeing suspect. As one officer handcuffs the suspect, the other officer pulls out a small card and reads the suspect a brief statement similar to the following: You have the right to remain

Police officers must inform suspects of their legal rights before they can arrest them. They do this by reading the Miranda Warning.

silent. If you give up the right to remain silent, anything you say can and will be used against you in a court of law. You have the right to be represented by an attorney and to have an attorney present during questioning. If you cannot afford an attorney, one will be provided for you.

This scene does not happen just in the movies and on television. Real-life police officers are required to read this brief statement, known as the "Miranda Warning," to all arrested suspects before questioning them. This requirement comes from a landmark 1966 U.S. Supreme Court decision, *Miranda v. Arizona*. At the heart of the decision are important freedoms guaranteed to all Americans in the Fifth and Sixth Amendments to the U.S. Constitution.

Ernesto Miranda Is Arrested

In 1963 a young woman was kidnapped near Phoenix, Arizona. A few days after the kidnapping, the police arrested Ernesto Miranda, a warehouse worker, and took him to the police station. After he was questioned by the police for several hours, Miranda confessed to the crime.

At Miranda's trial, the arresting officers testified that they had warned Miranda that anything he said could be used against him in court. They also testified that no threats or force had been used to make Miranda confess to the crime. The officers admitted, however, that they had not told Miranda about his right to remain silent or to have an attorney present. Nevertheless, Miranda was found guilty of kidnapping and given a prison sentence of 20 to 30 years.

Organize the class into small groups. Invite students to write a dramatic scene from a movie about the *Miranda v. Arizona* case. Students might choose to focus on the questioning of the suspect, the first trial, or the Supreme Court argument. Tell students that their scenes can be dramatized, so they should use their imaginations. Each group member should assume a role in the enactment. Have groups present their scenes to the class for discussion.

The Supreme Court Decides

Miranda's lawyers appealed the decision to the Arizona Supreme Court, arguing that Miranda had not been informed of his rights and that he had been denied consultation with a lawyer. The Arizona Supreme Court justices were unconvinced, however, that Miranda's rights had been violated. The Arizona justices upheld the conviction. Miranda's lawyers then appealed the case to the U.S. Supreme Court.

In Court, Miranda's lawyers argued that the Fifth Amendment to the Constitution guarantees citizens the right to refuse to give information about themselves. In other words, people have the right to remain silent. Furthermore, under the Sixth Amendment to the Constitution, the lawyers argued, persons accused of crimes are guaranteed the right to an attorney.

The Supreme Court agreed. It ruled that, by taking Miranda's confession without informing him of his right to silence and his right to an attorney, the police officers had deprived Miranda of these rights. Although Miranda was later reconvicted at a new trial, his case forever changed the way that the police must treat criminal suspects.

Innocent Until Proven Guilty

If the police or the courts fail to follow the guidelines established by the Fifth and Sixth Amendments, charges against a suspected criminal—even a guilty one—may have to be dropped. The criminal may even go free. Because the *Miranda* ruling has allowed some criminals to escape justice, some people argue that the laws go too far in protecting the rights of suspects. They believe the public's right to safety is more important.

As free citizens, however, we must remember that the entire U.S. judicial system is based on the belief that people are innocent until proven guilty. To protect the innocent, we must guard the rights of all who are accused of crimes.

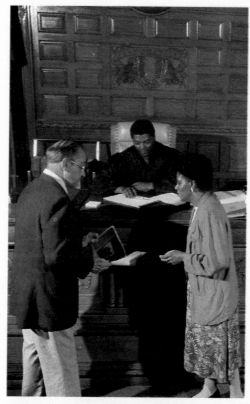

The right to be represented by a lawyer is guaranteed by the Sixth Amendment to the Constitution.

YOU DECIDE

1 What is the Miranda Warning? What is its purpose?

2 According to the Supreme Court, which of Miranda's constitutional rights were violated?

3 Some people argue that it is better to let 10 guilty people go free than to imprison one innocent person. Do you agree or disagree with this statement? Why?

ANSWERS TO YOU DECIDE

1. statement that police officers must read to suspects they are arresting; informs suspects of the legal rights to which they are entitled

2. Fifth Amendment right to silence and Sixth Amendment right to consult with attorney

3. Answers will vary. Some students might say it is important to make sure no innocent people are punished for crimes they did not commit.

Discuss with students how the four types of courts differ and how each level has its own purpose. Then set up a small claims court ("The Students' Court") in class. Have small groups of students invent disputes—with rational stories from both the plaintiffs and the defendants. With individual group members playing the roles of judge, plaintiff(s), defendant(s), witness(es), and so on, groups should present their cases. The class should render decisions on the cases.

Guided Practice

Divide the class into three groups, assigning each group to represent a general trials court, an appeals court, or a state supreme court. Call on volunteers from each group to discuss the role of their type of court in accepting and hearing court cases. Then suggest a hypothetical court case and move it through the courts. Call on volunteers to explain what will happen to the case as it reaches their court.

Photo Caption Answer

Making sure these rights are protected often leads to lengthy court cases and contributes to an overcrowded court system.

CIVICS SIDELIGHT

"The People's Court," a popular television show that first aired in 1981, showed millions of viewers how a small claims court operates. The litigants and their cases were real, and the judge—Joseph A. Wapner—was a veteran of the California court system. Judge Wapner, in his no-nonsense way, persuaded viewers that the best means of winning in small claims court is to be prepared. He commended litigants who could back up their claims with receipts, photographs, and other necessary documentation.

The right to bring lawsuits and the right to appeal a court's decision are protected in the United States. These rights, however, have a price. What is it?

General Trial Courts Major criminal and civil cases are handled in **general trial courts**. Most cases are heard by a jury, and a judge presides. In many of the states, the judges are elected by the people of the county or district in which they serve.

Larger cities usually have several general trial courts. Sometimes one of these courts hears only civil cases and another hears only criminal cases.

Some of the states have trial courts called county courts. The county court is located in the county seat, which is the center of county government in most states. In other states trial courts are called district courts. In some states there are also circuit courts. In the circuit court the trial judge travels a circuit (complete route) from one county to another to hold court trials. Other names for trial courts in some states are superior courts and courts of common pleas.

Appeals Courts Sometimes a person believes his or her case was not handled fairly in a trial court. That person may appeal the decision to an appeals court. These courts are often called intermediate courts of appeals. The usual basis for appeal is that the rights to a fair trial guaranteed to all citizens were somehow violated during a person's trial.

Appeals courts do not use juries. Instead, a group of judges examines the trial record of the lower court and hears arguments from the lawyers on both sides.

The group of judges decides the case by majority vote. The judges must decide whether the trial in the lower court gave the person on trial all the rights guaranteed under the Constitution. If the person is still not satisfied with the appeals court's decision, he or she can appeal to the state supreme court.

State Supreme Court The state supreme court is the highest court in most states. The judges who sit on the state supreme court hear cases on appeal in much the same way as the U.S. Supreme Court. In some states the supreme court is called the court of appeals or the supreme judicial court.

State supreme court judges are elected in most states. In other states they are appointed by the governor with the consent of the state Senate. The decision of the state supreme court is final unless a federal law or a question about the U.S. Constitution is involved. Then the case may be appealed to the U.S. Supreme Court for review.

Overcrowded Courts

There have been many proposals in recent years for the reform of the state court systems. The state courts are overburdened with work. So many cases come before them that the court calendar is often a year or more behind schedule. It is not unusual to find automobile accident cases that have waited two or three years for a court settlement.

In many large cities the jails are crowded with accused persons who are awaiting trial.

After reviewing the overcrowding problem in state courts, remind students that Amendment 6 of the Constitution states that "the accused shall enjoy the right to a speedy . . . trial." Then lead a discussion in which students try to determine what speedy should mean.

Have students complete the Section 4 Review.

Assign Section 4 of the Chapter 8 Reteaching Worksheet.

Some have waited for more than a year. They may or may not be guilty. They have remained in jail because they do not have the money to post bail. They have not been brought to trial because there are so many other cases ahead of theirs.

This backlog of cases makes it impossible to fulfill every American's constitutional guarantee of a speedy public trial. Critics point to three reasons for this situation. First, there are more cases than ever before and not enough judges to handle the increasing caseload. Second, trials are long and slow. The very guarantees that protect American citizens often cause trials to take a long time. Third, some courts are not conducted in an efficient manner. Judges call frequent recesses, or breaks, in a trial. Lawyers sometimes use delaying tactics to help their clients.

Some people believe that the courts are behind the times. They suggest that all courts should use modern technological tools, such as computers, as much as possible to make the courts work more efficiently.

The conditions in the courts are serious. Their improvement is a pressing concern to all citizens in our democratic society.

SECTION 4 REVIEW

1. Define or identify the following terms: penal code, criminal case, civil case, complaint, plaintiff, justice of the peace, municipal court, small claims court, general trial court.

2. What are the roles of the four types of state courts?

3. How do small claims courts differ from other courts?

4. What can citizens do if they are not satisfied with an appeals court decision?

5. **THINKING CRITICALLY** You have just been appointed to your state's

Judicial Council, an advisory group made up of judges, lawyers, and citizens. The purpose of this council is to make recommendations for the efficient operation of the state courts. Write a statement to the council outlining the problems you see in your state court system and what might be done to make the courts more efficient. Be sure to explain who you are, how the state court system affects you, and why you are concerned.

CHAPTER 8 SUMMARY

Each of the 50 states has its own state government. The state government manages the internal affairs of the state. Like the federal government, every state government is based on a written constitution.

The U.S. Constitution leaves many powers to the states. The states have power over areas such as public education, elections, highways, and the establishment of local governments. The states share with the federal government powers such as taxation, law enforcement, and the protection of the health, safety, and welfare of the people.

Each state government has a legislative branch, executive branch, and judicial branch. Most states have a two-house legislative body similar to Congress. The process of passing state laws is similar to that of putting federal laws through Congress.

The governors of the states are the chief executive officers of the state governments. They ensure that state laws are enforced. Other executive officials and state executive agencies assist governors in their work.

State courts interpret state laws and bring to trial those people accused of breaking state laws. The court system in the states includes lower courts, general trial courts, appeals courts, and state supreme courts.

SECTION 4 REVIEW
A N S W E R S

1. See the following pages: penal code, criminal case (p. 150); civil case, complaint, plaintiff, justice of the peace, municipal court, small claims court (p. 151); general trial court (p. 154).

2. lower courts—misdemeanor cases and minor civil cases; general trial courts—major criminal and civil cases; appeals courts—cases from people dissatisfied with fairness of lower court trials; state supreme court—court of final appeal (unless federal law or question about U.S. Constitution is involved)

3. no lawyers needed; people in the dispute speak directly to judge

4. appeal to state supreme court

5. Answers will vary. Students might suggest using computers, hiring more staff and judges, and setting new rules that cut down on delaying tactics used by lawyers.

Ask students to consider what a legislator's job might be like. Even local legislators are very busy people, with dozens of issues needing their attention. They receive mounds of mail every day about a variety of important and not-so-important matters. Still, legislators cannot ignore their constituents. Help students understand that their concerns are just as important as anyone else's. Most legislators have a staff of assistants to find answers to constituents' questions and to deal with their problems.

Have students use the guidelines on this page to put together a class letter to one of your legislators about a local or national issue. If a student feels strongly about the issue, encourage her or him to send the letter to the legislator.

Developing

Civics

Skills

CITIZENSHIP SKILL
Writing to Your Legislator

One of the best ways to let your legislator know what you are thinking is to write a letter. Well-written letters receive more attention than poorly written ones. Fortunately, there are some basic rules to follow to make sure that yours is the kind of letter that receives an answer.

How to Write to Your Legislator

1. **Include your return address.** Make sure that your return address is on the letter. This will allow your legislator to respond to you.
2. **Use the proper term of address.** Always address a legislator as "The Honorable (name)." This applies to both the inside address and the address on the envelope.
3. **Use the correct opening and closing.** In the salutation, or greeting, use the person's correct title. For members of the U.S. House of Representatives, "Dear Representative (name)," "Dear Congresswoman (name)," or "Dear Congressman (name)" are all acceptable. For members of the Senate, "Dear Senator (name)" is the usual style. Titles of state officials vary. Find out the exact title of a state official before you write. End your letter with the proper closing, such as "Respectfully yours," or "Sincerely yours." Then add your signature.
4. **Use your writing skills.** Keep the body, or main part, of the letter as brief as possible. Clearly state your position or request in the first paragraph. Point out the relevant facts that will help your legislator understand your concerns.
5. **Be considerate of your reader.** Put yourself in the legislator's place. Be polite—even if you are angry. Also, your letter will receive more attention if it is neatly typed or handwritten.

Applying the Skill
Read the letter below. Then answer the following questions.

1. To whom is the letter addressed? What closing does the writer use?
2. What issue is Peter Gill concerned about in his letter?
3. Why might a letter be more convincing than a telephone call?

> 32 Wadel Avenue
> Elkhart, IN 46516
> January 15, 1995
>
> The Honorable Ann Downing
> The State House
> Indianapolis, IN 46204
>
> Dear Representative Downing:
>
> As you know, there is a bill currently before the legislature that would create 3,000 summer jobs for teenagers in our state. I strongly urge you to support this bill.
>   Passage of Bill HR 1026 will give many teenagers the chance to earn money for school. It will also provide them with experience for future jobs. Finally, the state stands to benefit from all the work these teenagers will be doing in our parks, hospitals, and civic centers.
>   I would appreciate knowing your position on this very important issue.
>
>   Sincerely yours,
>
>   *Peter Gill*
>   Peter Gill

---

1. The Honorable Ann Downing; Sincerely yours

2. summer jobs for teenagers

3. Answers will vary. Some students might say that an official might be more persuaded by a constituent who has taken the time to write a letter, rather than just calling, about an issue important to him or her.

After studying Section 2, students should be able to do the following.

1. Explain how town government began.

2. Describe how the concepts of direct democracy and representative democracy relate to some town governments.

3. Explain the origins and status of townships.

4. Identify the purpose and forms of special districts.

5. Describe the advantages to a rural community of becoming a village.

Teaching Section 2
Building a Vocabulary

Have students suggest what goes on at a **town meeting**. Ask: Does the whole town meet? *(This is possible.)* Then help students distinguish among a **town**, a **township**, and a **village** by pointing out that these forms of local government are closely related, but that each form may be slightly different in various parts of the country. Tell students that they will learn about the differences in this section.

grant of land from the British king. The colonists established small towns, where they built their homes and churches.

At the edges of the towns, the settlers established their farms. Each day they left their homes and worked on the farms. The colonists considered these outlying farms to be part of their towns. Later some of the settlers moved to the farms. As long as these farms were located within the town limits, the people who lived on them were counted as members of that town. New England towns stretched out into the countryside.

In the New Amsterdam colony (now called New York), the settlers set up a **village** form of government. Only the village itself, which included the homes of the settlers as well as other buildings, were overseen by the village government. The outlying parts of the settlement were not considered part of the village, and they later came under the rule of the county government.

As other people pushed farther west, they established new settlements. Some of them called their settlements towns. In Pennsylvania, settlements were often called boroughs. Thus many different names were used for these small settlements.

Early Town Government

The people of the early New England towns worked out a simple yet effective form of local government—the **town meeting**. All the people who lived in a town, as well as those from the surrounding farms, met regularly in the town hall. At these public meetings, citizens discussed issues and problems and decided how they should be handled.

Every citizen had a chance to speak on any issue. After all opinions were heard, the people at the meeting voted on the issue. In this way each citizen had a direct vote in the government. A New England town meeting was direct democracy in action. Some small New England towns still carry on their business in this manner. Town meetings are also held in several states in the Midwest.

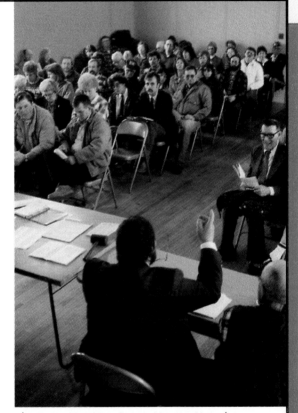

This town meeting is in Panton, Vermont. Here, the tradition of town meeting government, begun in colonial times, continues today.

Town Meetings Today

The town meetings held in New England today are usually in the spring. A notice of the town meeting is posted in various parts of town well before the meeting. This notice gives the time of the meeting and lists the business to be discussed by the voters.

On meeting day the voters gather in the town hall. Before the meeting begins, the town elections are held. Some towns, however, wait until after the meeting to hold their elections. The voters elect several (usually three to five) officials, called selectmen and selectwomen. These people are responsible for managing the town's affairs during the period between regular town meetings. The voters also elect the

---

CIVICS SIDELIGHT

The direct democracy of the town meeting has its roots in ancient Greece. In the fifth century B.C., the city-state of Athens developed a true democracy. Athens's citizens—free adult males—ruled themselves. In the Athenian Assembly, which met 40 times a year, citizens could speak their minds on any subject, not unlike citizens at a present-day town meeting. To maintain order and keep meetings moving along, however, a council of 500 men set an agenda for each meeting.

Advertising a Meeting

Ask: What is unique about the town meeting form of government? (*all citizens debate and vote directly on local issues*) Discuss direct democracy and why people might favor it over representative democracy. Then have students create fliers advertising a school meeting. The flier should include information about what will be decided at the meeting, the time and location of the meeting, and why students should attend the meeting.

COOPERATIVE LEARNING

Have small groups of students create township governments. Members should assign each other different roles, such as township supervisor, treasurer, and board commissioner. Have each member use classroom or library resources to write a brief description of his or her job responsibilities. Then have the group create a special "Township Government Handbook" that lists the members, their official titles, and their duties.

GLOBAL PERSPECTIVES

Township government is decreasing in importance in the United States. That is not so in China, which just began forming township governments in rural areas in the 1980s. The Chinese did so as part of a nationwide move toward economic reforms. China's leadership believed that township governments could relieve other local governments of their political and administrative duties, leaving them free to concentrate on increasing economic production. Responsibilities of the new township governments include economic planning, education, and public health. China's economic boom in the 1990s suggests that township government there might have a bright future.

other town officials. These officials include a town clerk, members of the school board, a tax collector, a tax assessor, and fish and game wardens. Some towns elect these officials on a separate election day rather than at the town meeting itself.

During the town meeting, the voters discuss the town's business. They elect a moderator to preside over this part of the meeting. The selectmen and selectwomen report on their activities over the past year. The treasurer gives the financial report, explains the town's debts, and asks the citizens to vote to pay these debts.

Next, the officials discuss town business for the coming year. The voters may be asked to give their opinions on such matters as street lighting, the building of a new school or fire station, and the purchase of more snow removal equipment. After the discussion ends, a vote is taken on each item. Voting is usually by voice vote.

Representative Town Meetings

The town meeting form of government works well in areas that have small populations. Direct democracy is practical in such towns because it is easy for all the voters to gather in one central location. For many other towns, however, increases in population and the need for more local services have led to changes.

Some towns no longer hold town meetings. They have hired town managers to take their place. Other towns have turned to representative town meetings. In this type of town government, the voters elect representatives to attend the town meetings and make decisions for them.

Early Township Governments

In some of the Middle Atlantic states (New York, Pennsylvania, and New Jersey), counties were divided into smaller units of local government called **townships**. These served many

of the same purposes as the towns in New England. Townships were responsible for maintaining local roads and rural schools and for looking after the poor.

As county governments grew in the Middle Atlantic states, township governments became less important. In time these states developed a form of local government called county-township government. In this mixed form of local government, county and township officials worked side by side.

A stronger type of township developed in those midwestern states that were carved out of the old Northwest Territory between the Ohio and Mississippi rivers. In 1785 Congress worked out a system of surveying, or measuring, this vast area. According to the system, the Northwest Territory was divided into areas six miles square (15.5 sq. km) called congressional townships.

Early congressional townships were not units of government. They were only divisions of land. As settlers from New England moved into this territory, they set up governments similar to the town governments in the states from which they came. The new units of government were called civil townships. Sometimes a civil township occupied the same area as a congressional township, but usually it included more territory.

Township Government Today

Township government generally has decreased in importance. In many areas municipal and county governments have taken over the services once provided by townships. Found today in 20 states—mostly Middle Atlantic states and states in the Midwest—townships serve mainly rural areas.

Township governments vary from state to state. Usually the township is headed by a chairperson, or township supervisor. This official is elected by the voters. The voters also elect a township board of commissioners, or board of trustees, who make the laws or regulations for the township. **Constables** enforce

Summarizing

Have students list the steps taken by the Scio Bridge Brigade to save the covered bridges in their county. Help students see that in our free society, anyone may take similar steps to try to achieve what he or she wants. Students should save their lists for use as study guides.

students, though, who acted. Many of them passed through a covered bridge every day on their way to and from school. They had fond thoughts about the bridges. One student remembered catching his first fish from a covered bridge. Another thought of the many times she had stopped her bicycle to rest under the roof of a covered bridge. Still others knew what the bridges meant to their parents and grandparents and what they would mean to people in the future. According to one student, "We need touches of the past for our future."

At the urging of a social studies teacher, the students organized themselves into the Scio Bridge Brigade. They wrote down their thoughts about the bridges and sent them to county officials. They went door to door trying to win support for their cause. They spoke about the bridges at public hearings. They wrote letters to newspapers. They invited the Covered Bridge Society of Oregon to meet in Scio. With money they earned from a jog-a-thon, brigade members published a pamphlet of their poems and drawings about the bridges.

The members of the Scio Bridge Brigade were successful. As a result of their efforts, five of the county's ten covered bridges were listed on the *National Register of Historic Places.* For its work the Scio Bridge Brigade won an award from the National Trust for Historic Preservation. The students succeeded in preserving part of the nation's heritage because they cared enough to take action.

Members of the Scio Bridge Brigade worked to protect covered bridges like this one.

The Scio Bridge Brigade logo

YOU DECIDE

1 What were the arguments for and against placing the covered bridges on the *National Register of Historic Places?*

2 Why do you think the students were able to convince public officials to preserve some of the bridges?

3 Do you think a special effort should be made to preserve links to the nation's past, such as covered bridges? Why? What other links with the nation's past can you think of?

CIVICS SIDELIGHT

Some of the nation's covered bridges are being lost to arson. In New Hampshire, for example, seven wooden bridges were burned between 1965 and 1981. The state lost three more bridges to arson during a three-month period in 1993. Many covered bridges are located in small towns that cannot afford the high rebuilding costs. The Slate Bridge in Swanzey, New Hampshire, for example, cost about $1,850 to build in 1862. Officials estimated a cost of up to $2 million to replace the covered bridge after it was burned in 1993.

ANSWERS TO YOU DECIDE

1. for—bridges could not be torn down, possible federal funding to preserve bridges; against—federal government would become too involved in local affairs

2. Students should note that Scio students took direct action to persuade officials.

3. Students should make reasoned arguments.

Understanding Ideas

Have students make a list of all the people who use roads. *(examples: pedestrians, bicyclists, commuters, vacationers, truckers)* Ask whether there are many people in the United States who do not need roads. *(very few)* Then ask: Why is the government interested in building and maintaining roads? *(Government serves the needs of the people.)* Save the lists for use in the "Cooperative Learning" activity on this page.

CIVICS SIDELIGHT

Today the federal government funds most of highway construction and repair costs. Expense was one factor that forced the federal government into highway construction in the first place. The National Pike cost $6,825,000 to build, a monumental sum when it was completed in the 1830s. This was no mud road; it was a highly engineered highway, 20 feet (6.1 m) wide, with a thick surface of broken stone. Today the cost of building a new highway can be astronomical, depending on where it is. A new rural interstate might cost $2 million per mile, not counting interchanges. A complex highway through a major city, meanwhile, can cost hundreds of millions of dollars per mile of roadway.

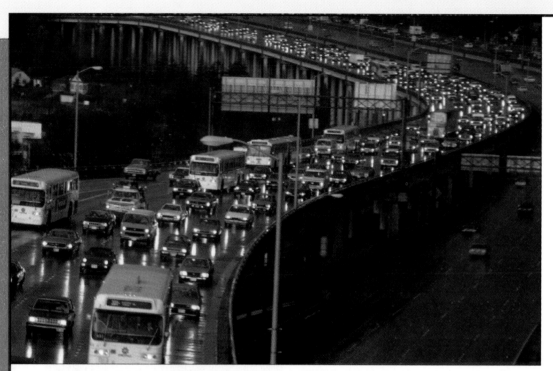

This well-traveled highway in Washington is part of a vast coast-to-coast highway system. It is just one example of cooperation between federal and state governments.

county assumed the responsibility of building connecting roads. The counties called on local farmers and townspeople to supply the labor to build the roads. Local residents also provided money to hire workers.

These early roads were often twisting and rutted, dusty in dry weather, and muddy after rain. They were, however, cheap to build and repair. Local governments could easily plan and pay for such roads.

As the nation grew, highways were needed to connect the East with the growing West. In response, Congress voted to have the federal government build main roads to the West. The most important of these early roads was the National Road, also known as the Cumberland Road. It started at Cumberland, Maryland, and made its way as far west as Vandalia, Illinois.

Still, for a long time local governments and private companies built most roads in the United States. These roads were paid for by collecting tolls, or fees, from the people who used them. When the automobile was invented, however, it became clear that road building was no longer a local matter. Motorists needed dependable, well-maintained highways that would stretch across their home states and connect with roads in other states.

Cooperation in Road Building

Late in the 1800s New Jersey became the first state to use state funds to help its counties improve their local roads. Massachusetts went a step further in 1894, when it began to build a statewide highway system. Other states soon followed the lead of New Jersey and Massachusetts and set up state highway departments to build main roads.

Guided Practice

Help students draw a chart to show how governments cooperate. Ask for suggestions about how to design this chart. Column headings should be *Federal, State,* and *Local.* Categories of cooperation might include *Road Building, Education, Law Enforcement,* and *Funding.* For each category, have students fill in the details of how each level of government contributes in each category.

Independent Practice

Have students find a newspaper article that describes cooperation or competition among levels of government. Ask them to summarize the article, paying particular attention to the agencies that are involved at each level. For example, the local public works department might be working with the state transportation department to upgrade local bridges. Have students discuss why intergovernmental cooperation is (or is not) necessary for the project.

Today most well-traveled roads are built and maintained by the states. Each year state governments spend billions of dollars to build and improve roads.

The federal government also plays an important role in the states' many road-building programs. It pays a large part of the cost of new state highways. It does so because good roads contribute to the safety and well-being of all U.S. citizens. Good roads make the movement of people and goods easier.

The interstate highway system, planned by the federal government, now connects all parts of the nation. It is a joint project of the federal and state governments. The state governments plan the routes and supervise construction of the roads. The roads must meet federal requirements.

The federal government pays 80 cents of every dollar of the cost of building and maintaining the nation's highways. This money comes from a highway trust fund to which motorists contribute every time they pay taxes on gasoline purchases. The federal government also assists state and local governments in building and maintaining other highways, bridges, and tunnels.

Cooperation in Education

Public education is one of the most important areas in which governments cooperate to serve the public. State governments grant funds to local communities to help them operate their schools. State boards of education provide services for local school districts and see that they obey state laws. Actual control of the schools, however, is left to local boards of education. These local boards know the needs of the students in their schools.

The federal government cooperates by helping with special funds for schools. Schools with a large number of disadvantaged students receive special federal aid to enrich their educational programs. The federal government also provides school lunch programs for needy students. In addition, the federal government supports research in education.

Other Forms of Cooperation

Local, state, and federal governments work together in many other ways as well. For example, local and state police cooperate with the Federal Bureau of Investigation (FBI) to capture suspects. Most states have crime laboratories, whose services also are used by local police officials. State and local police may obtain helpful information, such as fingerprints, from FBI files. Suspects arrested and convicted by local governments often are sent to prisons maintained by state governments.

Stores and businesses must obey many state laws that promote good business practices. Workers in local factories and mines are protected by state inspectors who see that safety regulations are obeyed. State bank inspectors help keep savings safe.

State governments also set up state licensing boards. These boards give examinations and issue licenses to doctors, dentists, lawyers, engineers, nurses, teachers, and accountants. This service helps ensure that communities have qualified professional workers.

The federal government provides state and local governments with funds to help them

Through the FBI, the federal government keeps millions of sets of fingerprints on file. Local and state criminal investigators often make use of these files.

CIVICS SIDELIGHT

When the U.S. Conference of Mayors met in 1994 to discuss issues of concern, one common problem stood out. Mayors across the nation complained of having to pay the costs of enforcing federal legislation. These so-called unfunded mandates include laws passed by Congress requiring water and air pollution controls and public access for individuals with disabilities. Mayors estimated that cities set aside an average 11 percent of their budgets just to cover the costs of federal regulations that are passed without funding. Local officials often complain about unfunded state mandates, also. Such issues often make their way into political debate during campaigns.

Closure

Have students examine the flowchart on page 171. Discuss how the three levels of government are separate and distinct but also connected. Then have students list examples of intergovernmental cooperation that directly affects their lives and those of other citizens.

Reviewing

Have students complete the Section 4 Review.

Reteaching

Assign Section 4 of the Chapter 9 Reteaching Worksheet.

CIVICS SIDELIGHT

Point out that the competition between governments sometimes involves the courts. School funding is one example. Although the federal government provides some funding, public education is primarily a responsibility of state and local government. Courts in a number of states have declared that inequalities in funding between rich and poor school districts violated state constitutions. The Texas Supreme Court, for example, ruled just that in 1989. Some recommended remedies for the Texas dilemma have included forcing wealthy school districts to share some of their funds with poorer school districts. Inevitably, such proposals have pitted wealthy and poor school districts and their supporters against one another in the state legislature and in the courts. A number of states continue to grapple with the problem of equitable education funding.

Because communities face the risk of fires, local governments must have the funds to keep fire departments ready for action.

carry out important programs. **Grants-in-aid** are federal funds given to state and local governments for specific projects, such as airport construction or pollution control. The receiving government must meet certain standards and conditions, and often must provide some money of its own for the project. Grant-in-aid projects are subject to supervision by the federal government.

Block grants are funds given by the federal government for broad purposes. State and local governments develop and carry out the programs and decide how the funds will be spent. They must, however, develop a spending plan and report how the funds were spent.

City Governments Work Together

Cities face many common challenges. For example, city governments are concerned about increasing funds for police, fire departments,

and education. They look for ways to lessen air pollution and to dispose of trash safely. The U.S. Conference of Mayors meets regularly so that the nation's mayors may compare problems and discuss possible solutions.

As neighboring cities grow closer together, they often share problems. For example, many villages and townships lie in Nassau County on Long Island, New York. The population of this area grew from 300,000 in 1947 to nearly a million and a half in 1970. Soon one community had merged into the next in an almost continuous line. The officials of the various local units realized that cooperation among Nassau County communities was needed.

For greater efficiency and better service, the officials of the various localities agreed that their communities should combine and share some services. Fire alarms now may be answered by the fire departments of several neighboring communities. The costs of trash collection, water, and other services may be

Extension

Have students create a board game in which participants buy and improve properties as they move around the playing board. Along the way students might collect "Funding Cards" and "Regulation Cards" that help (or limit) them in building such things as bridges, roads, civic centers, and parks on their properties. Students might refer to popular board games to help them develop specific rules. The purpose of the game is to illustrate how governments influence commerce and the lives of citizens.

---

shared. Although police departments are maintained separately by the various communities, Nassau County communities cooperate closely in law enforcement.

Government Competition

Although cooperation among governments is growing, governments also compete with one another. For example, governments compete for citizens' tax dollars. A person may have to pay income taxes to both state and federal governments. There may be a city income tax as well. Residents may also have to pay property taxes to their local governments. State and local governments may collect sales taxes.

States compete with each other to attract industry. They offer businesses lower taxes, a good supply of labor, good highways, and favorable laws to encourage industry to move to their state. Cities compete for trade and industry in similar fashion.

The federal government and federal laws sometimes seem to interfere or compete with local laws and customs. For example, the federal government may challenge the election procedures in a state or locality if such procedures conflict with federal law.

The combined system of federal, state, and local governments is complex. It would be surprising if there were not instances of conflict. Only by working together, though, can the nation's three levels of government fulfill their duty to serve the American people.

SECTION 4 REVIEW

1. Define or identify the following terms: grant-in-aid, block grant.

2. Why did the federal government become involved in road building?

3. Name three ways in which governments cooperate and three ways in which they compete.

4. **THINKING CRITICALLY** You have been invited by your local government to give a short speech entitled "How Governmental Cooperation Serves Our Community." In your speech explain how the three levels of government work together to improve life in your community.

CHAPTER 9 SUMMARY

Each of us is directly affected by local government. The governments of the nation's cities, towns, townships, and counties take care of many of the practical needs of our lives. They provide fire and police protection, a water supply, a sewage system, trash removal, and other necessary services.

County governments serve the common needs of people over a fairly large area. In some states more and more power has been given to the towns and cities, and the counties serve mainly as election districts.

Town meetings still serve areas of New England and some parts of the Midwest. Population growth in these regions, however, has caused some larger New England towns to hire town managers or to hold representative town meetings.

Town and township governments in many areas work with the county in governing and in providing services to their communities. Special districts, especially in rural areas, provide services such as sewage systems, a water supply, and local schools.

City government faces many challenges. Some cities have the mayor-council plan of government. Others have turned to the commission plan or are using the council-manager plan of government.

Federal, state, and local governments cooperate in many ways. Sometimes, though, the various governments compete for taxes, trade, and industry.

SECTION 4 REVIEW
ANSWERS

1. See the following page: grant-in-aid, block grant (p. 176).

2. As the nation expanded, highways were needed to connect the East with the growing West. The invention of automobiles created a need for highways that connected distant points. Good roads contribute to the safety and well-being of all citizens and facilitate the movement of people and goods.

3. cooperate—road building, public education, law enforcement, occupational safety, attracting business, regulation and licensing, public works and services; compete—taxes, attracting business, local laws and customs

4. Speeches will vary but should address ways governments work together.

Point out to students that the same newspaper may carry both a news story about an important national or international event and an editorial concerning that event. Students can develop a fuller picture of the event by reading both pieces. They should be aware, however, that the editorial may give only one side of the story. As an extending exercise, have students find a newspaper article that illustrates cooperation among different levels of government and write an editorial responding to the article.

Developing Civics Skills

LIFE SKILL
Reading Newspaper Articles

We live in a rapidly changing world in which the events happening in faraway nations can have an impact on our everyday lives. In fact, the world is fast becoming a global community. This means that there is a growing interdependence and cooperation among the nations of the world.

It is therefore important for all citizens to stay informed about what is happening in the nation and around the world. One source of information on current events is the newspaper. Newspaper articles generally are written according to a standard format. Learning to recognize that format is one key to becoming an informed and responsible citizen.

How to Read Newspaper Articles

1. **Read the headline.** A headline is a short statement printed in large, bold type above the article. It contains key words designed to capture your attention and present the main point of the article.
2. **Notice the dateline and the byline.** The dateline and the byline are located just below the headline. If a news story happens outside the area in which you live, it will probably contain a dateline. The dateline tells you where the article was written and may include the date it was written. The byline tells you who wrote the article—either a reporter or a news service. Two of the largest news services are Associated Press (AP) and Reuters.
3. **Read the lead.** The lead, or first sentence, of a news article is designed to tell you who did what, where, when, and how.
4. **Read the body.** The paragraphs following the lead make up the body of the article. The body usually contains the "why" of the story, including quotations and details.

Reading the body of the article will give you a well-rounded picture of the event or situation.
5. **Distinguish between news and editorials.** What you should *not* find in a news article is the writer's opinion or point of view. Writers present their points of view in editorials, found on the editorial pages of the newspaper. Citizens who disagree with editorials or who want to express their own opinions may write letters to the editor.

Applying the Skill

Read the article below. Then answer the following questions.

1. What is the headline of the article?
2. What does the byline tell you?
3. What questions are answered by the facts given in the lead? Does the article present an opinion?
4. What details does the body of the article provide?

Lakeville Cleans Up

by María López

LAKEVILLE, Mich. — The city's annual July Fourth cleanup was a great success, city officials said Tuesday.

"It was the most successful celebration we've ever seen," said Mayor Tamara Patterson.

In what has become a tradition, Lakeville residents once again did more than watch parades on Independence Day. Residents also swept sidewalks, planted flowers, and picked up litter.

The tradition began in 1976 when Lakeville residents decided to do something different for the nation's 200th birthday, Patterson said. Response to a citywide cleanup was so enthusiastic, the city council decided to make it a regular event, she said.

ANSWERS TO
Applying the Skill

1. Lakeville Cleans Up
2. The story was written by María López.
3. The lead answers three questions: *who* (Lakeville officials), *what* (the city's annual cleanup was a success), and *when* (July Fourth). The article reports the opinions of its sources.
4. most successful cleanup ever; residents swept sidewalks, planted flowers, picked up litter; tradition since 1976 when done to celebrate the nation's bicentennial; city officials made it an annual event after enthusiastic response to first cleanup

Vocabulary Workshop

1. parishes; boroughs
2. city
3. ordinances
4. home rule
5. mayor

Reviewing Main Ideas

1. established by and receive power from state government
2. help state collect taxes, supervise elections, enforce state laws; provide people such things as roads, schools, libraries, health and welfare services, law enforcement
3. all citizens may debate and vote directly on issues; population growth and need for more services
4. Congressional townships formed in midwestern states out of division of the Northwest Territory. These were divisions of land, not units of government. Settlers who moved into this territory created civil townships.
5. to handle special needs of some residents; school districts
6. give cities power to manage own affairs and local problems; tend to have large populations crowded into relatively small areas
7. cooperate—road building, education, law enforcement, business regulations and licensing, public works and services; compete—for tax dollars, to attract business, local laws and customs

---

CHAPTER 9 R·e·v·i·e·w

Vocabulary Workshop

1. What does Louisiana call its counties? What does Alaska call its counties?
2. What is the largest type of municipality?
3. What is the term for the regulations that govern a community?
4. What term describes the power of a city to write its own plan of government?
5. Who is the chief executive of a city government?

Reviewing Main Ideas

1. How are local governments established?
2. How does a county serve both the state and the people in that state?
3. How are town meetings "direct democracy in action"? Why do some towns use representative town meetings?
4. How were congressional townships formed, and how did they become civil townships?
5. Why are special districts formed? What is the most common type of special district?
6. What is the purpose of home rule? Why do cities sometimes have more difficult problems than other units of local government?
7. How do the three levels of government—local, state, and federal—cooperate and compete?

Thinking Critically

1. Recently, some communities in the nation have instituted teenage curfew laws. These laws regulate the time of night that teenagers must be off the streets. Why do you think communities have passed such laws? How might such laws protect the safety and well-being of teenagers? Are such laws constitutional?

2. Which of the three forms of city government do you think offers the most effective system of checks and balances in local government? Which offers the least effective system?

Citizenship in Your Community

Cooperative Project
With your group, research the history and current operations of your local government. Some group members should conduct library research. Other group members should interview local government officials and members of the local historical society, if one exists. In your report, discuss when and how your community was founded, the type of government established when the community was founded, how that government has changed over the years, and the number and type of local officials serving today.

Building Your Portfolio

The second step of your unit portfolio project (see page 181) is to create a poster that contains an organizational chart for each of the types of local government found on Earth. As you compare these organizational charts, consider the following issues: how leaders are chosen, what types of areas are governed, and the governments' purposes. Below the charts write a caption that explains which form of local government would best serve the people of Governus. Place your poster in your individual portfolio for later use.

Thinking Critically

1. Opinions may vary. Point out that communities have passed such laws to cut down on teenage crime and to protect young people.
2. Answers will vary. Students should demonstrate knowledge of city government.

Citizenship in Your Community

Student reports should focus on the development of your local government.

BUILDING YOUR PORTFOLIO

Assign Portfolio Assessment Worksheet 9 in the *Portfolio Assessment Worksheets* booklet.

Assessment

- **Chapter 9 Tests**, *Chapter Tests* booklet
- **Test Generator**, Chapter 9
- **Portfolio**, Portfolio Assessment Worksheet 9, *Portfolio Assessment Worksheets* booklet

Reviewing Main Ideas

1. provided way for territories to join nation as states

2. Citizens directly take part in government by proposing legislation, approving legislation, and removing elected officials from office.

3. Civil cases deal with disputes between individuals, businesses, and government. Criminal cases deal with violations of the law.

4. person accused of a crime cannot escape justice by fleeing to another state

5. States plan the routes and supervise construction. The roads must meet federal requirements. The federal government pays 80 percent of the costs of building and maintaining the nation's highways. The three levels of government compete for taxes. States and cities compete for business. Federal laws sometimes interfere or compete with local laws and customs.

6. bill is introduced, sent to committee, returned to house of origin; debated, voted on, and, if passed, sent to second house for similar process; conference committee to resolve differences; if passed, goes to governor for signing; powers and duties of governor— proposes laws, issues executive orders, prepares budget, appoints certain officials, heads state political party, oversees state police and National Guard

7. to make county government

more efficient; Colonial experiences with British governors who did not listen to the people's wishes made citizens wary of officials with too much power.

Thinking Critically

1. Students should note that police agencies exist at all government levels. Each has crime facilities that the others can call on for help.

2. Answers will vary. Students should use sound reasoning in their responses.

Practicing Civics Skills

1. Students should use the proper elements for a letter to state legislators.

2. Students should demonstrate an understanding of the elements of a newspaper article.

R·e·v·i·e·w

Reviewing Main Ideas

1. How did the Northwest Ordinance help the nation grow?

2. How do the initiative, referendum, and recall encourage direct democracy?

3. Distinguish between civil cases and criminal cases.

4. How does extradition uphold the full faith and credit clause?

5. How is the interstate highway system a joint project of the federal and state governments? In what ways do the three levels of government compete?

6. How does a state bill become a law? What are the powers and duties of a governor?

7. Why have some counties established the position of county manager? Why did some cities develop the weak-mayor plan of government?

Thinking Critically

1. Imagine that a criminal suspect is believed to be hiding in your community. How might local, state, and federal governments work together to find the suspect?

2. Are communities better served when one person holds executive power, or when a group of people shares such power?

Practicing Civics Skills

1. Write a letter to one of your state legislators. Request information about an aspect of state government or express your thoughts on a current issue that affects teenagers.

2. Select a recent newspaper story about your local government and another one

about a government in a foreign country. What information is given in the headlines? What do you learn from their bylines? What facts are given in their leads? What similarities and differences can you find in these two governments?

Citizenship in Your Community

Cooperative Project

With your group, conduct a town meeting in your classroom. Post a notice giving the date and time of the meeting and listing the town (class) business to be discussed. Elect a moderator from your group to preside over the meeting. Have other members of your group act as town citizens to discuss the issues and problems that concern your class. How effective is this type of meeting? What issues concern the members of your group? What democratic ideals guided the meeting?

Learning from Technology

Facsimile Machines

Facsimile machines, or fax machines as they most often are called, are becoming as commonplace as telephones. Fax machines are a form of technology that allows people to transmit printed material and pictures by means of electronic signals sent over telephone lines. In what ways can such a form of communication encourage the participation of citizens in state and local government? When dealing with government, is this means of communication more or less effective than other means of communication? Explain your answer.

Citizenship in Your Community

Before the meeting begins, have students suggest issues they would like to discuss. Decide which issues are appropriate and list them on the chalkboard. Make sure students stay on task during the meeting.

Learning from Technology

Students might mention that fax machines allow people to send written communications to officials. Fax messages are less time-consuming than sending letters through the mail, and faxes can be sent directly to specific officials.

Building Your Portfolio

Students have been working on a Building Your Portfolio project throughout Unit 3. You might ask volunteers to present their work to the class. Have all of the students add their work to their individual portfolios. Assign the Unit 3 Portfolio Assessment Worksheet in the *Portfolio Assessment Worksheets* booklet.

Building Your Portfolio

Individually or in a group, complete the following project to show your understanding of the civics concepts involved.

A Government for Governus

You are the leading government expert on the planet Governus, a small planet in a faraway galaxy. The people of Governus live on the planet's only landmass—Governus Island. Their society has been in chaos for centuries because the people cannot agree on what type of government would best serve them.

They have sent you on an exploration mission to the planet Earth to observe government in action. Your job is to develop a two-tiered plan of government for Governus based on the most effective aspects of Earth's state and local governments.

The Governus plan should include legislative, executive, and judicial aspects of government. The Governusians have agreed to accept your plan of government, but they insist on knowing the reasoning behind your recommendations. To prepare your plan, you will need to do the following.

1. Write the section of the Governus Constitution that deals with organization. First, write a summary of the typical form of state government. Next, write a second summary that describes how some state governments differ from this typical form of state government. Use these two summaries to write the Governus Constitution's section on organization. Be sure to explain why you have organized the government in this way.
2. Create a poster that contains an organizational chart for each of the types of local government found on Earth. As you compare these organizational charts, consider the following issues: how leaders are chosen, what types of areas are governed, and the governments' purposes. Below the charts write a caption that explains which form of local government would best serve the people of Governus.

Organize your materials, and present your plan to the Governusians (the rest of the class).

THE CITIZEN IN GOVERNMENT

Using the Quotation

Have students read the quotation by Barbara Jordan, who was the first African American congresswoman from the South. Ask them to summarize the quotation in their own words. Then have students read the titles of the chapters in this unit. Encourage students to suggest connections between Jordan's ideas and the subjects of this unit.

About the Author

Barbara Jordan (1936–1996) served in the Texas Senate for six years before her election to the U.S. House of Representatives in 1972. She served in Congress until 1979, when she became a professor at the Lyndon B. Johnson School of Public Affairs at the University of Texas at Austin.

"A nation is formed by the willingness of each of us to share in the responsibility for upholding the common good. A government is invigorated when each one of us is willing to participate in shaping the future of this nation. . . . We must . . . begin again to shape a common future. Let each person do his or her part. If one citizen is unwilling to participate, all of us are going to suffer. For the American idea, though it is shared by all of us, is realized in each one of us."

—*Barbara Jordan*
U.S. CONGRESSWOMAN (1973–1979)

SECTION OBJECTIVES

After studying Section 1, students should be able to do the following.

1. Identify the purposes of political parties.
2. Describe the founding of the Democratic and Republican parties and explain the advantages of a two-party system.
3. Explain why coalition governments can be unstable.
4. Describe how third parties have influenced U.S. politics.
5. Explain why the United States generally opposes one-party systems.

Teaching Section 1
Building a Vocabulary

Candidate is derived from the Latin *candidus* (white). People seeking office in ancient Rome often wore white togas. **Nominate** comes from *nomen*, the Latin word for "name." A candidate is nominated for office by a **political party**. Have students identify the two parties that dominate U.S. politics. *(Democratic and Republican)*

CHAPTER FOCUS

Are you ready to vote? The Twenty-sixth Amendment to the U.S. Constitution gives you the right to vote when you are 18. At that time you will be faced with the challenge of casting your vote wisely for national, state, and local officials. Your vote will help choose the nation's leaders and determine how billions of dollars will be spent on federal programs and policies.

Voting is a privilege that all citizens should take seriously. Learning all you can about the U.S. political process and becoming involved in that process now will help you become a careful and intelligent voter.

STUDY GUIDE

● What are political parties, and what purposes do they serve?

● How are political parties organized?

● How do people register to vote, and how does voting today differ from voting in the past?

● What is the Electoral College, and what part does it play in U.S. presidential elections?

1 A Two-Party System

Nowhere in the Constitution is there a provision for political parties. They are not an official part of the U.S. government's organization. Anyone who has lived in the United States at election time, however, knows that political parties are an important part of the American democratic process.

What Is a Political Party?

A **political party** is an organization made up of citizens who have similar ideas on public issues and who work together to put their ideas

into effect through government action. To achieve their purposes, political parties encourage voters to elect to public office those people favored by the party. Parties also work to have laws that they favor passed.

In the United States political parties are voluntary. Citizens are free to join the party of their choice. They also may decide not to join any party. Americans who join a political party usually do so because they agree with most of that party's ideas. Of course, not all members of a political party agree on every issue. If members are in serious disagreement with a party on important issues, they are free to leave the party.

As members of a political party, Americans join with other citizens in trying to put their ideas of government to work at the local, state, and federal levels. Political parties play a large role in helping the American people govern themselves.

Role of Political Parties

What is the role of political parties in the United States? Political parties offer a practical way for large numbers of people with similar ideas to get things done. Political parties are concerned with practical politics. In other words, parties are concerned with the actions that government should take.

Everyone's life is affected by practical politics. When you complain about the high cost of living, you are taking a practical interest in politics. If you complain as a single voice,

MULTICULTURAL PERSPECTIVES

Political parties must try to attract members of expanding groups of voters. These groups, in return, seek to influence the policies of the party with which they are primarily associated. For example, African Americans have been an important constituency in the Democratic party since Franklin Roosevelt's administration. They have supported the party's candidates often by huge margins. There are several reasons for this tendency, including the various economic and social policies pursued by Democratic leaders and perceived as beneficial to African Americans.

The importance of the African American constituency to the Democratic party has led party leaders to champion such causes as civil rights and urban aid. And in 1989 Ronald H. Brown became the first African American chairperson of the Democratic National Committee.

Ask students what purposes political parties serve in the United States. Students should list the purposes on the chalkboard. Have students suggest why each purpose is important. Then have the class vote on which they think is the most important purpose. A volunteer might tally the results for the class.

Ask members of the local Democratic and Republican parties (and others if appropriate) to speak to the class. Have students prepare pertinent questions for each speaker, covering such subjects as the founding of his or her party, the party's philosophy, and any similarities between the party and the Federalists and/or the Anti-Federalists. Have students write short news articles about the interviews.

CIVICS SIDELIGHT

In his Farewell Address, George Washington warned against the "baneful effects of the spirit of party." This spirit, he said, "serves always to distract the public councils, and enfeeble the public administration. It agitates the community with ill-founded jealousies and false alarms; kindles the animosity of one part against another, foments occasionally riot and insurrection. It opens the doors to foreign influence and corruption, which find a facilitated access to the government itself through the channels of party passions." You might ask students whether they think Washington's arguments are valid.

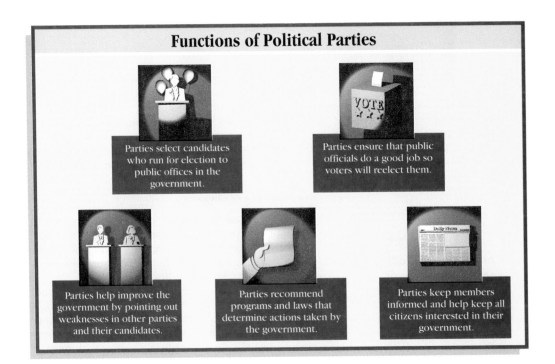

Functions of Political Parties

Parties select candidates who run for election to public offices in the government.

Parties ensure that public officials do a good job so voters will reelect them.

Parties help improve the government by pointing out weaknesses in other parties and their candidates.

Parties recommend programs and laws that determine actions taken by the government.

Parties keep members informed and help keep all citizens interested in their government.

though, you are not very effective. If instead you join with other citizens who agree with your complaint, you can make your voice heard in a way that gets results. Political parties serve this purpose.

Political parties also **nominate**, or select, candidates to run for public office. **Candidates** are the men and women who run for election to offices at various levels of the government. Most Americans who serve in public office have been elected to their offices as candidates of political parties. Although not impossible, it is difficult for a person to run for office without the support of a political party.

Political parties also take positions on public issues and work to have laws passed. During election campaigns, each political party tries to convince the voters that it offers the best program.

After an election, the winning candidates become the leaders of the government. The political party to which these leaders belong tries

to ensure that the leaders do a good job. In this way the party hopes to ensure that its candidates will win again in the next election.

The party whose candidates lost the election will be watching for weaknesses in the winning party's new leaders and any mistakes or missteps they may make while in office. This party will be quick to point out to the public any campaign promises not kept by the new leaders.

Beginnings of the Two-Party System

The first political parties began during President George Washington's administration. As you read in Chapter 2, those people who favored a strong federal government were called Federalists. Those people who favored limiting the power of the central government were called Anti-Federalists. Anti-Federalists later were known as Democratic-Republicans.

Assemble five dominoes, two large coffee mugs, and a textbook. Explain that the five dominoes represent political parties in a multiparty system. Call on volunteers to balance the textbook ("table top") on as few dominoes ("table legs"), standing on end, as possible. Ask: When is the textbook (table top) most stable? *(when there are more dominoes and when they are evenly distributed under the textbook)* Is it easy to upset that stability? *(Instability increases as the number of dominoes decreases.)*

Then balance the textbook first on the two coffee mugs and then on just one mug in the center. Ask students how this demonstrates the stability of two-party systems. *(In two-party systems, such as in the United States, either party may be strong enough to stabilize the government, much like one large coffee mug may hold up a book.)* Then ask: How do third parties affect the stability of the U.S. two-party system? *(Often they focus debate on specific issues and influence the main parties.)*

Alexander Hamilton became the leader of the Federalists. He proposed policies that would make the federal government strong. Thomas Jefferson, leader of the Democratic-Republicans, opposed Hamilton and the Federalist party. Jefferson and the Democratic-Republicans tried to limit the power of the federal government.

As President Washington watched these two different points of view lead to the establishment of political parties, he became worried. He feared that the growth of parties would weaken the new nation. In his Farewell Address as president, Washington warned Americans that political parties were dangerous because they could divide the nation.

Washington's warnings, however, were soon forgotten. Political parties became a lasting part of the American form of government.

Throughout most of its history, the United States has had two strong political parties, or a **two-party system**.

The Democratic and Republican Parties

For more than 140 years, the Democratic party and the Republican party have been the nation's two major political parties. The present Democratic party traces its roots to Jefferson's Democratic-Republican party. In the 1820s that party split into several groups.

One group, led by Andrew Jackson, became the Democratic party. Jackson believed that the federal government was acting to benefit the wealthy. He was determined that the federal government should represent frontier

Thomas Jefferson (left) and Alexander Hamilton (right) disagreed about how government should operate. They were the leaders of the first U.S. political parties.

CIVICS SIDELIGHT

Andrew Jackson's appeal to the common people was never more apparent than in the celebration following his inauguration on March 4, 1829. Crowds of people—farmers and country folk, men and women, black and white, young and old—celebrated in the streets and in the White House itself. The traditional post-inaugural gala for the new president turned into a free-for-all as Jackson's hungry and thirsty supporters mobbed the reception hall. The sound of shattering crystal and ripping silk accompanied the laughs and cheers of the frontier folk who came from miles around to congratulate their hero. Jackson, evading his admirers, fled the building, but the rowdy crowds left only when lured out onto the White House lawn by additional quantities of food and drink.

Closure

Draw a three-column chart on the board. Then have students summarize what they have learned about one-party, two-party, and multiparty systems. Call on volunteers to provide characteristics of each party system and compare it to the others. Start the chart by writing "governments often by coalition" beneath the column labeled "multiparty."

Reviewing

Have students complete the Section 1 Review.

Reteaching

Assign Section 1 of the Chapter 10 Reteaching Worksheet.

Presidential candidate Ross Perot ran in both the 1992 and 1996 campaigns. His candidacy challenged the two major parties.

settlers, farmers, and city laborers—the common people. Andrew Jackson was elected president of the United States in 1828, and the Democratic party that he helped establish began its long history.

The present Republican party was formed in 1854 when several small groups that opposed the policies of the Democratic party joined together. The Republican party was started by people who were against slavery and its spread into U.S. territories. In 1860 Abraham Lincoln became the first candidate nominated by the Republican party to be elected president of the United States.

Advantages of Two-Party Systems

Since the mid-1800s the Democratic and Republican parties have had almost equal strength, making the two-party system work remarkably well. When one party fails to please a majority of voters, there is another strong party ready to take over. The newly elected party often tries different programs and policies in dealing with the nation's problems.

If there were more than two strong political parties, all of about equal strength, no one party could win a majority of votes. To run the government, two or more of the political parties would have to agree to compromises and work together. This agreement between two or more political parties to work together to run the government is called a **coalition**.

In the Netherlands and other nations, coalition governments have worked well. This system, however, has certain disadvantages. Often the political parties disagree and the coalition breaks apart, weakening the government and the nation. Several European nations have this **multiparty system**. Some nations, such as Italy, have had great difficulty in forming a stable government because of the many small political parties.

Third Parties

There are a number of minor political parties, or **third parties**, in the United States. At certain times in the nation's history, third parties have had great influence.

In 1912 Theodore Roosevelt was denied the presidential nomination of the Republican party and organized a third party called the Progressive party. Roosevelt ran for president as the nominee of this party. He was not elected, but he took away enough votes from the Republican candidate, William Taft, to permit the Democratic candidate, Woodrow Wilson, to win.

The strongest showing of any third-party or independent presidential candidate since Theodore Roosevelt occurred in 1992 when independent Ross Perot ran against Democrat Bill Clinton and Republican George Bush. Although election results gave the nation's highest office to Clinton, Perot won an impressive 19 percent of the vote.

Third-party candidates have run for office throughout most of the nation's history, but few have done as well as Roosevelt and Perot.

Extension

Explain that some U.S. states, especially in the South, have had histories of one-party dominance. Have students research the effect of one-party government in these states, such as Alabama, Louisiana, and Texas. Have students write short paragraphs identifying which party was dominant in each state, when, and why. Are these states still dominated by one party?

Among the most notable third-party candidates are George Wallace and John Anderson. Wallace, former governor of Alabama, ran for president in 1968 as the candidate of the American Independent party. He received 9.9 million votes, or 13.5 percent of the vote. Representative John Anderson of Illinois, an independent presidential candidate, won almost 7 percent of the vote in 1980.

At various times in U.S. history, third parties have proposed new ideas that were opposed at first by the major political parties but were later adopted. For example, in the late 1800s the Populist party was formed by a group of Americans that favored several new ideas. One of these ideas was the election of U.S. senators directly by the voters. The leaders of the two major parties favored the election of senators by the state legislatures as provided in the Constitution.

When Populist ideas began to find favor with Americans, some of these ideas, including the direct election of senators, were adopted and put into effect by the major parties. The method of electing U.S. senators was changed by the Seventeenth Amendment to the Constitution.

One-Party Governments

In nations with more than one political party, the voters have a choice. They can decide which party to join and for which party to vote. They may change parties or choose not to join any party.

In some nations, however, governments are based on a **one-party system**. That is, there is only one political party in the nation. All other political parties are forbidden by law. As you know, such nations are sometimes called dictatorships or totalitarian governments.

In this type of government all power is in the hands of one person or a group of people. In a one-party government, a single party controls the government. It dictates, or commands, and the people must obey.

Italy under Benito Mussolini and Germany under Adolf Hitler had such a form of government. Today several nations, such as Cuba, the People's Republic of China, and other communist nations, have one-party governments. Some noncommunist nations, such as Libya, Syria, and Monaco, also have only one official political party.

The United States and other democratic countries have traditionally opposed dictatorships and totalitarian governments because such systems do not allow their citizens freedom of speech and action. Americans and citizens of other democratic nations consider these freedoms essential because they believe a government should serve and be responsible to its people.

SECTION 1 REVIEW

1. Define or identify the following terms: political party, nominate, candidate, two-party system, coalition, multiparty system, third party, one-party system.

2. What purposes do political parties serve?

3. When and by whom were the Democratic and Republican parties formed? What are the advantages of two-party systems?

4. Why do coalition governments often last only a short period of time?

5. How have third parties influenced American politics?

6. Why does the United States generally oppose one-party governments?

7. **THINKING CRITICALLY** Imagine that you have recently moved to the United States from a country that has a one-party system of government. Write a letter to a friend back home explaining how your life under a two-party system of government differs from the life you left behind.

Ask students to describe what happens at a **polling place**. Explain that the word *poll* in Middle English meant "head." To take a poll meant to count heads. A polling place is a place to count people's heads or, in an election, people's votes. Tell students that each polling place is in a voting district called a **precinct**.

COOPERATIVE LEARNING

Assign small groups one of the three basic levels of party committees: national, state central, or local. Assign students committee roles, such as chairperson, recording secretary, and committee members. Have each group create a planning document of the committee's responsibilities and goals during an imaginary election campaign. Each group should base its list on a set of fictional candidates, issues, and funding needs.

GLOBAL PERSPECTIVES

Political parties in many other democracies also have local and national structures. In the United Kingdom, for example, district organizations (constituency committees) nominate their own candidates for Parliament. Delegates from these constituency committees meet annually in national party conferences (attended also by affiliated organizations, such as unions for the Labor party).

In India, the world's most populous democracy, the main parties have national and state organizations. Power is divided between these national and state organizations in varying degrees. State and local party units generally are responsible for local elections.

Political parties in Costa Rica, one of the most stable democracies in Middle and South America, are organized in pyramidal structures. At the base are district assemblies. Above these district assemblies are, in hierarchical order, cantonal assemblies, provincial assemblies, and each party's National Assembly. The National Assembly chooses party officials and candidates for elections.

2 Political Party Organization

To work effectively a political party must be well organized. It must have leaders, committees, and workers able to carry out the party's program. It must be organized at the local, state, and national levels. The party must also be able to raise money to pay its expenses. The party must nominate its candidates for office and plan its campaign strategies to get these candidates elected.

Over the years party members have established procedures for carrying out all of the above activities. Both major parties are organized in much the same way.

Party Committees

The planning for each political party is done through a series of committees. Each political party has a national committee and state central committees in each state. Each party also has local committees at the county, city, and sometimes township levels.

Each of these party committees is headed by a chairperson. The committee members are usually elected by the party voters at election time. Sometimes, however, the members are chosen at meetings of party leaders. As you know, these meetings of political party leaders are called caucuses.

The National Committee The largest party committee is the national committee. Membership on this committee carries great distinction. For many years it consisted of one committeeman and one committeewoman from each state, each territory, and the District of Columbia. In the 1970s, though, each party enlarged the membership of its national committee.

Members of the national committee may be chosen in three ways. They may be elected by a state convention, elected by voters in a statewide election, or chosen by the state central committee. The national committee

chairperson is often chosen by the party's presidential candidate.

The national committee selects the city in which the national nominating convention will be held. At this official party meeting, the party's presidential and vice presidential candidates are chosen. The national committee is responsible for setting the date and drawing up rules for the convention.

During an election year, the national committee publishes and distributes party literature and arranges for campaign speakers. The committee also helps the presidential candidate to plan, conduct, and raise money for the election campaign.

State Central Committees Each political party has a state central committee to supervise the party's operation within each of the 50 states. The chairperson of the state central committee is one of the party's most prominent members in the state. He or she is often a member of the national committee.

The state central committee represents the party organization in each state. Like the national committee, it is busiest at election time. The state chairperson works with the members of the state central committee to maintain a strong state organization and party harmony. The committee works to raise money for campaigns and to help candidates win elections.

Local Committees At the local level are county committees and city committees. Township committees are sometimes found in rural areas. Members of local committees are elected by party members. Committee chairpersons are elected by committee members and serve as local party leaders.

The party's successes or failures often depends on the local committees and their leaders. The county or city committee is responsible for conducting all campaigns on the local level. It raises money for the party and party candidates. Through the local chairperson, the committee makes recommendations for political appointments and for candidates for office. A strong chairperson may stay in

Draw a circle on the board and label it "political party." On lines radiating from the circle, have volunteers write the sources of party finances. Then have a panel discussion on whether a citizen's constitutional freedoms of speech and association are infringed upon by government regulation of party financing. Students might discuss advantages and disadvantages of such regulations.

Have students write newspaper editorials supporting or opposing political financing regulations. Students might focus their editorials on existing regulations, or they might propose, or oppose, new regulations. Students might want to review newspaper and magazine articles on political financing reforms. Call on volunteers to read their editorials to the class for discussion.

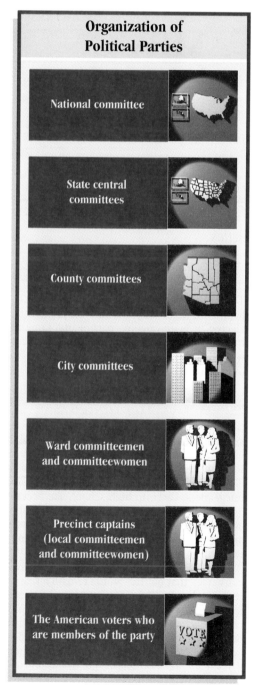

Organization of Political Parties

- National committee
- State central committees
- County committees
- City committees
- Ward committeemen and committeewomen
- Precinct captains (local committeemen and committeewomen)
- The American voters who are members of the party

office for many years and become powerful in the party.

Local Party Organization

To make voting easier for citizens, all counties, cities, and wards are divided into voting districts called **precincts**. The voters in each precinct vote at the same **polling place**. A rural precinct may cover large areas of countryside. A precinct in a crowded city may cover just a few blocks. The party leader in the precinct is called the precinct captain. The precinct captain encourages all voters to cast their ballots for the party's candidates.

Precinct captains are busy at election time. They organize volunteers to distribute campaign literature. They see that pictures of the party's candidates are displayed in local shops. Precinct captains may arrange to have voters with disabilities driven to the polling place. They may have party workers telephone voters and urge them to vote for party candidates. Between elections precinct captains get to know the people in the neighborhood.

Political Party Finances

Running for political office is expensive. Candidates for president, for example, need millions of dollars to run their campaigns. Their costs include office rent, assistants, campaign literature, radio and television broadcasts, and traveling expenses. From where does all this money come?

Until recently all political campaigns were paid for entirely with private contributions. Many campaigns are still paid for this way. Voters are urged to contribute to the political party of their choice. Business groups, labor unions, and many other groups also contribute to the political party that they believe best represents their interests.

Political parties work hard to raise money. Several times a year, they hold large fundraising events. The money raised at these events goes into the party's treasury. It will be used to pay election campaign expenses.

(continued on page 194)

CIVICS SIDELIGHT

What do candidates for Congress buy with their campaign funds? The following expenditures are typical: overhead (office equipment and supplies, rent, salaries, travel), fundraising efforts (events, direct mail, telemarketing), advertising, and other campaign activity (mailings, polling, stumping).

The amount of money members of Congress spend on campaigns can be staggering. The Democratic and Republican nominees together spent $42 million in the 1994 U.S. Senate race in California. During the 1986–1992 election cycle, at least 10 senators spent more than $4 million each on their campaigns. The top spender shelled out more than $11.5 million. The top spender during the 1990–1992 U.S. House election cycle spent nearly $5.5 million.

CIVICS TRANSPARENCIES

An overhead transparency of "Organization of Political Parties" is available in *Teaching Transparencies with Teacher's Notes.*

Linking Civics and History

Have students work together in small groups to research a campaign or a political issue from history that drew young people into the political process. Issues might include the Twenty-sixth Amendment, the civil rights movement, or the Vietnam War. Have each group explore which candidates most seemed to attract young people to the political process and why.

CIVICS SIDELIGHT

During the 1992 presidential campaign, a group of young people had the opportunity to meet with the candidates and explain their positions on the major issues of the day. These young people were the 12 winners of the Kids Caucus essay contest, sponsored by *Scholastic* magazine. One week before the Democratic National Convention was held, the 12 essay winners met together in New York to write "Hear Our Voice," a platform stating their positions on issues such as education, the economy, and the environment. Caucus members presented their platform at both the Democratic and Republican national conventions. One caucus member, 15-year-old Kelly Aldrich, was seen live on national television during the Democratic National Convention. At the Republican National Convention, the young people had a private meeting with then-President George Bush to explain their platform.

Citizenship IN ACTION

ON THE CAMPAIGN TRAIL

Janet Benson and Bill Chan live far apart and have never met. Janet is from Minot, North Dakota, and is a Republican. Bill is from Phoenix, Arizona, and is a Democrat. Yet the two teenagers have something in common. They both are active in party politics and have great respect for the work carried out by their political parties.

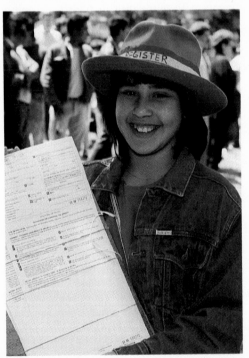

Even though this teenager is too young to cast her vote, she understands the importance of becoming involved in the political system.

To Janet and Bill, politics is not something that happens every four years when a president is elected. It is an ongoing part of life. Long before they entered high school, the two students were rounding up votes for the political party of their choice.

An Active Republican

Janet's interest in politics began when she was six years old. Her parents are active Republicans, who for a time advised a club of teenage Republicans. Janet began helping Republican candidates by putting up posters and passing out leaflets. Later, in high school, she became an officer of her local TAR (Teen-Age Republican) Club. With other TAR officers from around the country, Janet traveled to Washington, D.C., for a national TAR conference.

While still in high school, Janet became convinced that politics would remain a key interest in her life. "Some people want a career in science or sports," she says. "For me, it's politics. I love it." She believes that "politics doesn't end when an election is over." Members can help their political party at any time. They can, for example, hold discussions of bills being considered by the state legislature

◆ ***C*OOPERATIVE LEARNING**

Have small groups create television commercials encouraging teenagers to get involved in the political process. The commercials should include suggestions of ways to get involved. Roles for group members include narrator, script writer, and on-air personalities. Have groups present their commercials to the class.

 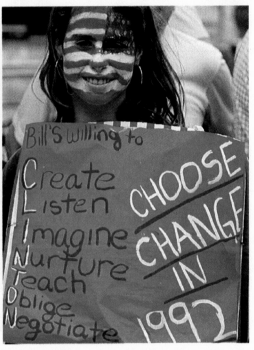

Campaigning for political candidates in whom you believe is an important way to make your voice heard in government.

or by Congress. They also can find out what programs are needed in their communities and work to address these issues.

An Active Democrat

Like Janet, Bill had an early introduction to politics. His mother held elective office and served on the Democratic national committee. To help her, Bill began distributing campaign leaflets when he was nine years old.

As a high school junior, Bill went with his mother to a Democratic committee meeting in Washington, D.C. The purpose of the meeting was to help draw up the party platform for the national Democratic convention. Bill read over the proposals with his mother and discussed them with other Democrats. Later he went to the White House and shook hands with the president.

In high school Bill joined the Young Democrats. He enjoys "working the polls" on election day. This means talking to voters and passing out leaflets near polling places.

Janet and Bill support different political parties. Yet both learned at an early age how important it is to take an active part in the nation's political life.

YOU DECIDE

1 What might be some of the advantages and disadvantages of joining a political party at a young age?

2 Do you think joining a party organization is a good way to have a say in government? Why or why not?

 ***C*IVICS SIDELIGHT**

Young people who want to work for their political parties may decide to join the Young Democrats of America or the Young Republican National Federation. With national headquarters in Washington, D.C., both of these organizations oversee community and campus chapters throughout the nation. Local chapters of both political organizations participate in such activities as voter registration drives, voter education, political campaigning, and fundraising.

ANSWERS TO YOU DECIDE

1. Some students might think involvement in a political party is one way for teenagers to make their voices heard before they are old enough to vote. Other students might believe teenagers should investigate the major and minor parties before deciding to join a party.

2. Answers will vary. Students should recognize the effects of collective action on government decision making.

Closure

On the chalkboard draw a triangle divided into three levels. As students name the three kinds of party committees, label the levels of the triangle (with "National Committee" at the top, "Local Committees" at the base). Ask: What might the placement of "Local Committees" at the base represent? *(The importance of citizens becoming involved locally to provide a foundation for parties.)*

Reviewing

Have students complete the Section 2 Review.

Reteaching

Assign Section 2 of the Chapter 10 Reteaching Worksheet.

194

Candidates hold fund-raising dinners and other events in communities throughout the country. The events raise money for the candidates' campaigns.

Whenever large campaign contributions are made, however, people worry about corruption. Will a big contributor receive special favors in return for helping the winning candidate? To lessen the possibility of political corruption, the U.S. Congress passed the Federal Election Campaign Act.

The Federal Election Campaign Act requires every political candidate to report the name of every person who contributes $200 or more in a year. The law also limits individual contributions to candidates to $1,000 for primary elections and another $1,000 for general elections. These provisions are enforced by the Federal Election Commission.

Public Financing

The act also introduced public financing of presidential elections. How does public financing work? Money is made available to candidates from the Presidential Election Campaign Fund in the U.S. Treasury. By checking a box on their federal income tax forms, Americans can contribute $3 of their taxes to the election fund. This neither raises nor lowers the amount of tax a person pays.

The U.S. Treasury distributes the fund's money to the candidates. To be eligible to receive this money, a candidate trying to win a party's nomination for president must first raise at least $100,000 from private contributions. The candidate then can receive up to a certain amount in matching public funds. The more money a candidate raises, the more he or she can receive. To receive matching funds, however, candidates must agree to limit their spending in nomination campaigns and to use public funds only for campaign expenses.

After winning nomination, presidential candidates of the major parties who accept public financing cannot accept private contributions. Their campaigns must be paid for only with the public funds they receive.

After studying Section 3, students should be able to do the following.

1. Explain how the Voting Rights Act protects voters, and identify who is disqualified from voting.

2. Explain why and how citizens register to vote.

3. Describe primary and general elections.

4. Explain how an independent candidate can become listed on a ballot.

5. Compare voting today with voting in the past.

Teaching Section 3
Building a Vocabulary

Ask students: Which comes first, the **general election** or the **primary election**? Tell students that *primary* comes from the Latin *primus*, meaning "first," and that a primary election is a preliminary, or first, race in which candidates of the same party run against each other. Each party's primary election winner faces the other primary winner(s) in the general election.

Minor-party candidates may receive public funds *after* the election if they win at least 5 percent of the vote.

In the 1992 presidential campaign, Democrat Bill Clinton and Republican George Bush each received, and were limited to spending, $55.2 million in public funds. Independent Ross Perot spent his own money on the campaign and so was not subject to a spending limit. The 1996 presidential candidates who accepted public funding each were limited to spending $61.8 million.

SECTION 2 REVIEW

1. Define or identify the following terms: precinct, polling place.

2. What committees make up each of the two major political parties?

3. From what sources do political candidates and parties obtain most of their funds? Why does Congress regulate the amount of money that can be contributed to political parties?

4. What are the basic provisions of the Federal Election Campaign Act?

5. **THINKING CRITICALLY** Some people believe that federal financing of presidential candidates helps prevent corruption. Others believe that these federal funds could be better spent elsewhere and that campaigns should be financed solely through private contributions. What is your position on this issue, and why?

3 — The Right to Vote

At the age of 18, all U.S. citizens have the right to vote in national, state, and local elections. The right to vote is one of the most important rights held by American citizens. It is the means through which citizens can most directly affect the actions of government.

State Qualifications for Voting

Each state decides qualifications for voting in state elections. All states, however, must follow the provisions about voting contained in the U.S. Constitution. Specifically, the Constitution forbids any state to deny a citizen the right to vote on the basis of race, color, or sex. To ensure these voting rights of all citizens, Congress in 1965 passed the Voting Rights Act. (See page 561.) This law, expanded in 1970, 1975, and 1982, also prohibits any state from using literacy tests, or reading tests, as a requirement for voting.

Many states disqualify certain people from voting. In most states a person who is convicted of a serious crime loses his or her right to vote. Most states also deny the right to vote to mentally incompetent persons, election-law violators, and vagrants, or persons with no established residence.

Registering to Vote

When a person goes to a polling place to vote, how do the officials know that he or she is a qualified voter? Most states require voters to register ahead of time. Registering places a voter's name on the official roll of eligible voters. When people register, they give their names, addresses, dates of birth, and other information showing that they meet the voting qualifications. They may be given cards showing that they are registered voters.

Almost all states have permanent registration. This means that people must register only once as long as they do not change addresses. Some of these states, however, require voters who do not vote in a certain number of elections to register again. A few states have periodic registration in some or all areas. This means that voters must register before each election or at regular intervals to remain qualified voters.

G LOBAL PERSPECTIVES

The first requirement one must meet to register to vote is age. The minimum voting age in the United States, 18, is a fairly common requirement in many other countries. The minimum age requirements do vary, however. Iranians may vote at age 15, for example, but Malaysians must wait until they are 21. Japanese are eligible to vote when they are 20. The minimum voting age in most European countries is 18. Following is a selection of countries and their minimum voting ages as of 1994: Argentina, 21; Brazil 18; Chile, 18; Egypt, 18; India, 21; Israel, 18; Kenya, 18; Mexico, 18; Morocco, 20; Mozambique, 21; Philippines, 15; Sweden, 18; Thailand, 21.

Creating a Pamphlet

Have students create pamphlets that explain the Voting Rights Act of 1965. (See page 561.) The audience for the pamphlets should be elementary school students. The pamphlets should restate each important idea in simple terms. Encourage students to be creative in the design of their pamphlets, including any visuals that might help explain the Act. Arrange to deliver the pamphlets to an elementary class that is interested in learning more about voting.

COOPERATIVE LEARNING

Have small groups develop voter registration procedures for school elections. Each group should review the textbook discussion on voter registration to decide why and how students should register. Then the group should decide how to advertise the necessary information (such as through posters and announcements over the school's public address system.) Roles for students might include chairperson, recording secretary, writer, and illustrator.

CIVICS SIDELIGHT

Many terms used to describe elections were first used to describe horse races. Elections often are referred to as *races*. This is natural, since candidates *run* to see who will *win*. A nominee for high office, such as the presidency, has a *running mate*, who is running for vice president. In horse racing a stable owner might use another horse, a running mate, to set the pace for another of his or her horses in a race.

In politics and horse racing, a *dark horse* (or *long shot*) is a contender who seems to have little chance of winning. The candidate or horse who is ahead is called the *front runner*—but the *finish* may be *neck and neck* after all.

When people register to vote, they may be asked to register as a member of the political party of their choice. Party membership may be changed later by registering again. Voters may also register as **independent voters** and not become a member of a political party. If a person does not register as a member of a political party, however, that person may not be allowed to vote in primary elections.

Primary Elections

Two separate elections are held in most states. The **primary election** takes place first and is usually held in the spring. The primary election allows voters to choose the candidates from each party who will run for public office in the later **general election**.

There are two types of primary elections, the closed primary and the open primary. In the **closed primary** only those voters who are registered in the party can vote to choose the party's candidates. Most states use the closed

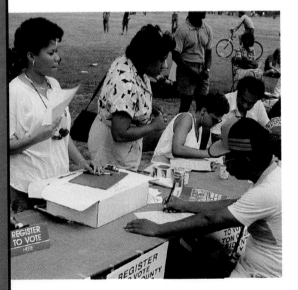

To encourage Americans to register to vote, registration tables may be set up on sidewalks to make the process as easy and convenient as possible.

primary. Thus in most states only registered Democrats can vote for Democratic candidates, and only registered Republicans can vote for Republican candidates. Those people who have registered as independent voters cannot vote in the closed primary. In the **open primary** voters may vote for the candidates of either major party, whether or not they belong to that party.

In most states the candidate who receives the highest number of votes is the winner of the primary election. The winning candidate does not have to receive a majority, or more than 50 percent, of the vote. In some states, however, the winner must receive a majority of the votes. If no candidate receives a majority, a **runoff primary** between the two leading candidates decides the winner. The winning candidate in the primary election then becomes the party's candidate in the general election.

Nomination by Convention

In some states political parties choose their candidates in a nominating convention. The people who attend and vote in the convention are elected as delegates by the various committees in the state's political organization. In a state convention the county and city committees select the delegates. In a national convention the state committees often select the delegates.

Independent Candidates

What about independent candidates who belong to no political party but wish to run for office? An independent candidate can have his or her name printed on the general election ballot if enough supporters sign a petition.

Independent candidates usually receive **grassroots** support—support from many individuals at the local level rather from national parties and other large organizations. Independent candidates are not elected as often as major-party candidates, but they do win some elections, mostly for local offices.

Guided Practice

Ask students how candidates have their names placed on general election ballots. *(by winning party primaries or by obtaining enough petition signatures to qualify as an independent candidate)* Lead a class discussion about whether independent candidates should be required to obtain signatures on petitions in order to be listed on a ballot. *(Some students might suggest that such rules prevent ballots from being encumbered with the names of many candidates who have little public support.)*

Independent Practice

Have students create a petition for themselves, as if they were independent candidates for your state's legislature. They might also wish to create a leaflet to accompany the petition. The leaflet would explain to prospective voters who they are and why people should vote for an independent candidate. Each student should then create a plan of action for obtaining the necessary petition signatures.

It is even possible for a person to be elected to an office when his or her name is not printed on the ballot. In some states space is included on the ballot to write in the name of a person the voter prefers. It is difficult to be elected by write-in votes, but it does occur.

General Elections

Congress has set the date for the general elections of the president and Congress as the first Tuesday following the first Monday in November. Presidential elections take place every four years. Congressional elections occur every two years. Most general elections for state officials are also held in November. The president and members of Congress are elected in even-numbered years. Some states elect their state officials in odd-numbered years. State elections, however, are held at different times in different states.

On election day, the American voter faces a great responsibility and privilege of citizenship. The voter must choose among the candidates of the various parties. The intelligent voter has studied hard to identify the candidate whose views most closely resemble his or her own. The voter has read newspapers and magazines, listened to the candidates on radio and television, and discussed the candidates with other people.

As voters enter the polling place, they may see several neighbors working. These people are acting as inspectors, or poll watchers. Each party has its own poll watchers to ensure that elections are conducted fairly.

Voting in the Past

During the first part of the 1800s, voting in the United States was usually by voice vote. Voters announced aloud to the election official the name of the candidate for whom they wanted to vote.

This system of voice voting made it possible to influence the way a person voted. Suppose a person's boss was standing nearby. The boss could hear how the employee voted and

Global Connections

Voting in Australia

Even though voting is a right and responsibility of U.S. citizenship, some Americans choose not to vote. Not all nations give their citizens this choice. In Australia, for example, voting is compulsory.

All Australian citizens age 18 and over are required by law to register as voters. Citizens must vote in all national and state elections and in most local elections. People too ill to go to the polls on election day are allowed to mail in their ballots. Australians who fail to vote may have to pay heavy fines. Not surprisingly, Australia has one of the highest voter turnout rates of any industrialized nation in the world.

might fire the employee who did not vote the way the boss wanted.

In 1888 a new system of voting using paper ballots was adopted. Paper ballots contain the names of the candidates and a place for the voter to mark a choice. This ballot is marked in secret, so that no one knows for whom a person votes. This method of voting is called the **secret ballot**. It helps make elections fair and honest.

Voting Today

Most states now use voting machines instead of paper ballots. Voting machines are large, curtained booths. The voter enters the booth and pulls a lever to close the curtains. On the

Global Perspectives

The secret ballot originated in Australia in the 1850s, and for that reason it is also called the Australian ballot. Prior to the adoption of the Australian ballot, votes not cast by voice in U.S. elections were cast using ballots in varying colors and sizes printed by political parties. The Australian ballot not only protected the secrecy of a voter's choice but also made split-ticket voting much easier because all candidates were listed on one ballot printed by the government.

Civics Sidelight

Since 1956 the majority of voters in nearly a quarter of all congressional districts have supported a presidential candidate of one party and a congressional candidate of another. Some people believe such voting patterns can foster "gridlock," with the party controlling one branch of government thwarting the policy efforts of the party controlling the other branch. Some people believe such a result is not necessarily bad.

Closure

Ask students whether the right to vote is more secure now than it was in the past. Have each student write an answer to that question and pick one reason to support it. Invite students to give their responses aloud, and have a volunteer write each new response on the chalkboard. Then discuss the progress that has taken place in extending and securing voting rights.

Reviewing

Have students complete the Section 3 Review.

Reteaching

Assign Section 3 of the Chapter 10 Reteaching Worksheet.

SECTION 3 REVIEW
A N S W E R S

1. See the following pages: independent voter, primary election, general election, closed primary, open primary, runoff primary, grassroots (p. 196); secret ballot (p. 197); straight ticket, split ticket (p. 198).

2. no disqualification based on race, color, sex, literacy; disqualified—convicted of serious crimes, mentally incompetent, election-law violators, vagrants

3. establish eligibility; provide name, address, birthdate, other proof of qualifications

4. primary—choose party nominees; general—nominees vie; closed—only party members may vote; open—anyone may vote; runoff—if no majority winner in first primary, voters choose from among top two candidates

5. by petition

6. past—usually voice vote, then secret ballot; now—secret ballot, voting machines

7. Plans should be workable.

198

Some voters cast their ballots for candidates by pulling levers on a voting machine. The ballots are then quickly and accurately counted by computers.

front of the voting machine, the voter sees several rows of small metal bars or levers with the name of a candidate under or next to each lever. A party's candidates are sometimes all on one row.

Many voters choose to vote a **straight ticket**—that is, for all the candidates of one party. Other voters choose to vote a **split ticket**—that is, for the candidates of more than one political party.

When the voter has finished, he or she pulls back the lever that opens the curtains. This action automatically records the voter's choices in the machine. All the levers shift back into position, so they are ready to be pulled down by the next voter. Voting machines keep a running count of the votes cast for each candidate. When the final vote is cast, election officials open the voting machine and read the total vote for each candidate.

On election day polling places are usually open from early in the morning until evening. In many states election day is a public holiday so that there is no excuse for failing to vote. In other states the law provides that all employers must give time off during the day to any employee who needs time to vote.

SECTION 3 REVIEW

1. Define or identify the following terms: independent voter, primary election, general election, closed primary, open primary, runoff primary, grassroots, secret ballot, straight ticket, split ticket.

2. How does the Voting Rights Act protect voters? Who is disqualified from voting?

3. Why are voters required to register? How do people register to vote?

4. How do primary elections differ from general elections? How do open primaries differ from closed primaries? What is the purpose of a runoff primary?

5. How can an independent candidate become listed on a ballot?

6. How does voting today differ from voting in the past?

7. **THINKING CRITICALLY** Imagine that you head a committee to increase voter registration and participation in your community. Create a plan of action that will guide the work of your committee toward its goals. In your plan be sure to state the goals of your committee and to outline the steps the committee will take to achieve these goals. You might want to create a slogan the committee can use to emphasize the importance of voting.

4 | Nominating and Electing Our Leaders

Every four years the nation stirs with excitement as the presidential election draws near. Americans like a good, hard-fought battle, and the election of the president is one of the best. Most Americans follow every step of the

198

x

SECTION OBJECTIVES

After studying Section 4, students should be able to do the following.

1. Explain the purpose of national nominating conventions and how convention delegates are chosen.

2. Explain how voters learn the views of U.S. presidential candidates.

3. State the main purpose of the Electoral College and the number of electors.

4. Explain what happens when none of the presidential or the vice presidential nominees wins an electoral majority.

Teaching Section 4
Building a Vocabulary

Discuss the common meaning of *platform. (a flat, raised structure)* Tell students that the earliest meaning comes from the French words *plat* and *forme* (meaning "flat form" or "map"). Soon the word simply meant "plan" or "design." Ask what a **party platform** is. *(a political plan, but also something solid for a candidate to "stand" on)* Note how the early and everyday meanings have been combined.

presidential election campaign in newspaper, magazine, radio, and television reports.

Convention Delegates

In each state members of each political party choose delegates to go to their party's nominating convention. Convention delegates may either be elected in presidential primaries or selected by party leaders.

In recent years **presidential primaries** have grown in importance. Today most states and the District of Columbia hold presidential primaries. In these primaries voters indicate for which candidate they want the delegates to vote at the national nominating convention.

In some states the candidate who receives the most votes wins all the delegate votes from that state. In other states each candidate wins some of the delegate votes based on the proportion of primary votes received. In still other states the primaries indicate only the voters' preference. Delegates from these states may vote as they wish at the convention.

In states that do not hold primaries, the delegates are chosen by the states' party leaders in state or local party conventions. They may also be selected by state committees.

Larger states send more delegates to the national nominating convention than smaller states. The Democratic and Republican parties have different formulas for determining how many delegates a state sends to the convention. Because the formulas differ, the number of delegates at each party's convention differs.

Each state may send additional delegates if the party's candidate won in that state in the last presidential election. Both parties use complicated formulas to choose these extra delegates. States also send alternates who vote if regular delegates become ill.

National Nominating Conventions

Each party's national nominating convention is held during the summer of the presidential election year. On the convention's opening

The Reverend Jesse Jackson ran a strong campaign for the 1984 and 1988 Democratic party presidential nominations.

day, the delegates from each state are seated in the vast convention hall. Sometimes there are rival delegates who claim to represent the regular party organization of their state. When disputes between delegates occur, the convention's credentials committee must decide which delegation to seat.

The chairperson of the convention then calls for order. The chairperson has been selected by the national committee beforehand from among the party's prominent members. After a keynote speaker delivers an opening address, a special committee presents the **party platform**. This written statement outlines the party's views on important issues and sets forth a proposed program for the nation. Each part of the platform is called a "plank." For example, the party platform may include a plank calling for an increase in environmental protections. After strong and often heated debate, delegates vote on and adopt a platform.

CIVICS SIDELIGHT

The first primaries were legally established in 1905 by the Progressive party in Wisconsin. The number and importance of primaries fluctuated over the years. After 1968 the primaries became increasingly important to choosing delegates to the Democratic and the Republican party conventions.

The parties also have made efforts to diversify by ethnicity and gender their convention delegations. For example, a Democratic party commission formed in 1969 proposed reforms that required state delegations to include members from ethnic groups and both genders in proportion to their numbers in the general electorate. Although these requirements have been modified over the years, the result has been increasingly diverse delegations to national conventions. In 1992 the Republican party continued its efforts toward diversification by adopting rules that instructed state party organizations to "endeavor to have equal representation" of both genders among their national convention delegations.

Writing a Song

Explain that nominating conventions can be very colorful events in which various methods are employed to focus attention on particular candidates. Tell students that their task is to "drum up" support for a candidate at a fictional national convention by writing a song or a rap to introduce their candidate's views. Students might base their creations on a real or fictional political figure. Call on volunteers to present their song or rap to the class.

Dramatizing to Learn

Hold a mock national nominating convention in class. Assign students various roles, such as speakers, convention delegation members that nominate a favorite son or daughter, delegation members that nominate a major candidate, the acceptance-speech writers, and party nominees. Divide the class into "states" and conduct a roll-call vote for the nomination. Students might create political hats and signs that support various fictional or real candidates.

CIVICS SIDELIGHT

The presidential nomination process has expanded recently to include the voices of the people more directly, through primaries and caucuses. In times past the president might have been chosen in a proverbial "smoke-filled room"—where cigar-chomping party bosses haggled over the nominees. Changes in party rules have weakened the power of party bosses and made the selection of delegates more democratic. In addition, technological advances in media have helped shed light on the nominating process. In 1844 the telegraph spread the news of James K. Polk's nomination. Radio opened the proceedings to interested listeners in 1924. In 1948 television cameras for the first time gave Americans an insider's view of party politics. And in 1996, all of the candidates in the presidential race opened electronic campaign offices, giving people with computers and modems access to the candidates' views and positions on the issues.

Presidential Candidates

The convention now tackles its most important item of business—choosing the party's candidate for president.

Nominations First there is a roll call of the states. As each state is called, one of its delegates may give a speech nominating, or naming, a candidate. Each nominating speech is followed by one or more seconding speeches.

Not all state delegations, of course, nominate candidates. There may be only half a dozen or so candidates nominated. Many of these nominees will have run in presidential primaries. When the political party has a president in power who is eligible to run again, the convention almost always nominates this person for a second term.

Favorite Sons and Daughters Some of the candidates named are **favorite sons or daughters**. They are the party leaders who are popular in their home states. In most cases favorite sons and daughters have little chance of winning their party's presidential nomination.

Why, then, do states nominate them? Sometimes the name of a favorite son or daughter is presented to honor the state's party leader. In other cases a state names a favorite son or daughter to delay its decision on which of the well-known candidates it will support. These delegates vote for their favorite son or daughter on the first ballot. In later ballots they usually switch their votes to one of the leading candidates.

Balloting After all candidates are nominated, the balloting begins. To win the nomination a candidate must receive a majority of the votes of all the delegates at the convention. A roll call of the states is taken again. A delegate from each state announces how many votes the delegation is casting for each candidate. In recent decades one of the candidates has almost always been nominated on the first ballot. When no candidate is strong enough to win a majority, however, many ballots may be needed.

Vice Presidential Candidates

Next the delegates nominate the vice president. Vice presidential candidates often are chosen for their ability to win votes. Sometimes they are from a state whose support the

Months of personal appearances and rallies mark the campaign trail for candidates like (left to right) Al Gore, Bill Clinton, Bob Dole, and Jack Kemp.

On the board begin a flowchart of the process of electing a president, beginning with the nominating conventions. Students should supply each step in the process. After you reach election day, split the chart into two forks. Have students explain the two main scenarios that might follow. *(One nominee wins a majority of votes in the Electoral College, or the election of the president is decided by the House of Representatives.)*

Invite students to imagine that no one in a hypothetical presidential election has won a majority of electoral votes. The nominee who won the most electoral and popular votes is not a member of the party that controls the House of Representatives. Have students write newspaper editorials on whether the House of Representatives should elect the nominee with the most electoral votes or the nominee of the party that controls the House.

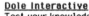

This photograph of 1996 Republican presidential candidate Bob Dole's campaign home page shows how computers have become an important tool for campaigning.

party needs. As you know, the vice presidential candidate must also have the qualifications to be president.

The nominee for president has the strongest voice in deciding who will be the vice presidential candidate. In 1984 Democratic presidential candidate Walter Mondale made a historic choice when he selected Geraldine Ferraro, a congresswoman from New York, as his running mate. This choice marked the first time a woman was nominated for the vice presidency by a major party.

The Election Campaign

The presidential election campaign gets underway soon after the convention ends. One of the most widely used methods of campaigning is the personal-appearance tour. Jet planes enable the candidates to crisscross the nation many times during an election campaign.

Television is another effective campaign device. Millions of Americans watch and listen as the candidates discuss their ideas and programs. Computers also have become a campaigning tool. The 1996 presidential campaign marked the first time Americans could use on-line computer services to learn about the candidates.

Election Day

Campaigning ends on the night before the election. Even so, election day itself is an active one for party workers. They are busy telephoning citizens and urging them to vote.

Closure

Have students create collages representing the presidential nomination and election process. Encourage students to use visuals that jog their memories about key points. For example, a student might use a campaign hat to represent the nominating convention, a speaker's platform to represent the party platform, and a ballot and graduation cap to represent the Electoral College.

Reviewing

Have students complete the Section 4 Review.

Reteaching

Assign Section 4 of the Chapter 10 Reteaching Worksheet.

An overhead transparency of "Electoral Map of the United States" is available in *Teaching Transparencies with Teacher's Notes.*

In the 1860 presidential election Abraham Lincoln received just 39.9 percent of the popular vote in a hotly contested, four-way race. However, he won the presidency with 59.4 percent of the votes in the Electoral College. Lincoln is one of 16 such "minority presidents," a list that also includes John F. Kennedy, Richard M. Nixon, and Bill Clinton. Clinton won the presidency in 1992 with a little more than 43 percent of the popular vote. However, he won 68.8 percent of the votes in the Electoral College.

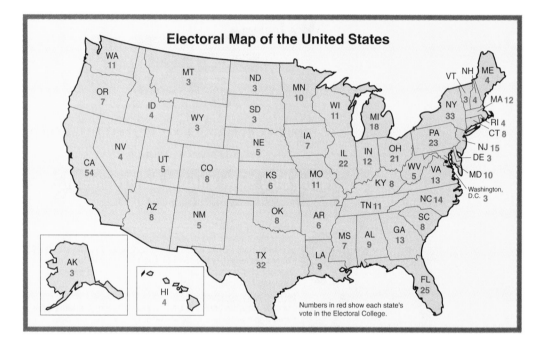

Electoral Map of the United States

Numbers in red show each state's vote in the Electoral College.

On election night many Americans watch the election returns on television. Because of the different time zones, the first election returns come from the eastern states. Gradually the election returns come in from the western states. The last reports usually come in from California, Hawaii, and Alaska. Sometimes the final results are not known until the next morning.

The Electoral College

In a presidential election Americans do not vote directly for the president. The votes they cast are known as the **popular vote**. This vote is actually for people called **electors**. Electors cast the official vote for president.

The names of the electors may or may not appear on the ballot. A vote for the Democratic candidate is a vote for the Democratic electors. A vote for the Republican candidate is a vote for the Republican electors. Each state has as many electors as it has senators and representatives in Congress. In addition, the

District of Columbia (Washington, D.C.) has three electoral votes. The nation's 538 electors are referred to as the **Electoral College**.

In each state the electors gather in the state capital on the first Monday after the second Wednesday in December. The electors of the party whose presidential candidate won a majority of the state's popular votes in the November election cast all the state's electoral votes at this December meeting.

For example, if the Democratic presidential candidate won a majority of the state's votes in November, it is the Democratic electors who cast the state's **electoral votes**. If the Republican candidate won, it is the Republican electors who gather at the state capital to cast the official votes. The electors are not required to vote for their party's candidate. Only rarely, however, do electors cast their votes for a candidate outside their party.

The votes cast by the electors are then sent to the president *pro tempore* of the Senate. On January 6, following the presidential election, the Senate and the House of Representatives

Extension

Have students research the election process for leaders of foreign countries. Among other issues, students should focus on how parties nominate contenders and whether a country has an Electoral College. Students can use graphs and diagrams to compare systems in other countries with that of the United States.

gather in a joint session of Congress. The votes of the electors are opened and officially counted. The candidate who receives a majority (270) of the electoral votes is officially declared the next president of the United States.

What happens if no presidential candidate receives a majority of the votes in the Electoral College? In that case the president is chosen by the House of Representatives from among the three leading candidates. If no candidate receives a majority of votes for vice president, that official is chosen by the Senate. The choice is made from among the two candidates with the highest number of electoral votes. Congress has had to choose the president or vice president only three times in U.S. history—in 1800, 1824, and 1836.

The Electoral College was originally set up in the Constitution because those who planned the government were uncertain how successful the people of the new republic would be in choosing wise leaders. You recall that they also provided for members of the Senate to be elected by state legislatures rather than directly by the people.

In recent years many plans have been proposed to replace the Electoral College with a system of direct election by popular vote. Many Americans favor the direct election of the president and vice president. Others favor keeping the present system.

SECTION 4 REVIEW

1. Define or identify the following terms: presidential primary, party platform, favorite son or daughter, popular vote, elector, Electoral College, electoral vote.

2. What is the purpose of the national nominating conventions? How are delegates to each party's national convention chosen?

3. How can voters learn about the views of presidential candidates?

4. How many electors are in the Electoral College? What is the main purpose of the Electoral College?

5. What happens if no candidate for president or vice president wins a majority of votes in the Electoral College?

6. **THINKING CRITICALLY** Which do you think should guide the presidential election process—the Electoral College or direct election by popular vote? Explain your answer.

CHAPTER 10 SUMMARY

Although political parties are not mentioned in the Constitution, they have become an important part of the U.S. system of government. Political parties choose the candidates who run for office and become the nation's leaders. Political parties offer a practical way for large numbers of people to work together to put their ideas and programs into effect.

The United States has a strong two-party system. The Republican and Democratic parties are organized at local, state, and national levels. Both parties work through a series of committees to have their candidates elected. Throughout U.S. history, there also have been many minor political parties.

American voters may belong to a political party, or they may choose not to join a party. In either case, voters are free to vote for any person or party they wish. The Constitution provides that the states set most of the qualifications for voting, subject to the restrictions established by the U.S. Constitution and by Congress.

The presidential election, held every four years, is a dramatic event. Americans closely follow the party nominating conventions, the election campaign, and the election results.

Various states impose their own voting requirements (within constitutional limits) and registration procedures. Have students research the history of voter registration in the United States. In particular, students should focus on arguments made by proponents and opponents of voter registration. Then have students write letters to the editor of a newspaper supporting or opposing voter registration requirements. Students should support their arguments, stating why they believe voter registration is wise or should be abolished.

Developing Civics Skills

CITIZENSHIP SKILL

Registering to Vote

Voting for candidates is a right we enjoy as citizens. Under the U.S. Constitution you must be at least 18 years old to vote. In addition, some states require you to live in the state for a certain period of time before you can register to vote. Many states require you to register in person; other states allow you to register by mail. Whatever the requirements in your state, it is important that you fulfill them so that you, too, can exercise your right to vote.

How to Register to Vote

1. Learn the registration procedure. The registration process varies from state to state. To find out how to register, contact your state or local election office. You should request a registration form and ask what deadlines you must meet.

2. Follow the procedure. Usually, registering to vote is as simple as filling out a form. The forms in most states ask for basic information: your name, your age, your residence, and whether you are a citizen. You must also sign the form, swearing that the information you have given is correct.

Applying the Skill

Study the registration form below. Then answer the following questions.

1. Which section should not be filled in? Why?
2. What do you think is the main purpose of the "Place of Birth" section?
3. Why must you sign a voter registration form?
4. Why do you think the form shown on this page is printed in Spanish as well as in English?

ANSWERS TO Applying the Skill

1. "For Official Use Only" space, because space is reserved for election officials

2. to determine citizenship status, residency, and eligibility

3. to attest to the truth of the information provided

4. It is the form used in Texas, a state with many Hispanic Americans, some of whom may have a limited English proficiency.

VOTER REGISTRATION APPLICATION (SOLICITUD PARA REGISTRO DE VOTANTE)

PLEASE COMPLETE ALL OF THE INFORMATION BELOW. PRINT IN INK OR TYPE.
(POR FAVOR COMPLETE LA SIGUIENTE INFORMACION. ESCRIBA EN LETRA DE MOLDE CON TINTA O ESCRIBA A MAQUINA.)

For Official Use Only
PCT   Cert. Num.   EDR

Last Name (Apellido)	First Name (NOT HUSBAND'S) (Nombre de Pila) (NO DEL ESPOSO)	Middle Name (If any) (Segundo Nombre) (si tiene)	Maiden Name (Apellido de Soltera)

Sex (Sexo) | Date of Birth: month, day, year (Fecha de Nacimiento): (el mes, el día, el año) | Place of Birth: city or county, state or foreign country (Lugar de Nacimiento): (ciudad o condado), (estado o país extranjero) | County and Address of Former Residence (Condado y dirección de su residencia previa)

Residence Address: Street Address and Apartment Number, City, State, and ZIP. If none, describe location of residence. (Do not include P.O. Box or Rural Rt.) (Dirección de Residencia: Calle y Número de Departamento, Ciudad, Estado, y Zona Postal; si no tiene, describa la localidad de su residencia.) (No incluya su caja postal o ruta rural.)

Mailing Address, City, State and ZIP: If mail cannot be delivered to your residence address. (Dirección Postal, Ciudad, Estado y Zona Postal) (Si es imposible entregar correspondencia a su dirección.)

Applicant is a United States citizen and a resident of the county and has not been finally convicted of a felony or if a felon eligible for registration under section 13.001, Election Code. I understand that giving false information to procure a voter registration is a misdemeanor. (Suplicante es ciudadano de los Estados Unidos y es residente del condado y no ha sido probado culpable finalmente de un crimen, o, si es criminal, está elegible para registrarse para votar bajo las condiciones de la sección 13.001 del Código de Elecciones. Yo entiendo que es un delito menor dar información falsa con motivo de conseguir un registro de votante.)

Social Security No. (Número de Seguro Social)*

Telephone No. (Optional) (Número de Teléfono) (Facultativo)

TX Driver's License No. or Personal I.D. No. (Issued by TX Dept. of Public Safety) (Optional) (Número de Licencia de Conductor de Tejas o Número de Identificación Personal) (Emitido por el Departamento de Seguridad Público de Tejas) (Facultativo)

X
Signature of Applicant or Agent or Printed Name of Applicant if Signed by Witness (Firma del Suplicante o Agente, o Nombre del Suplicante En Letra de Molde Si Fue Firmado Por Un Testigo)

FOR WITNESS (PARA TESTIGO):   Signature (Firma)   Printed name (Nombre en Letra de Molde)

Address (Dirección)

Court of Naturalization, If Applicable (Corte de Naturalización, Si Aplicable)

FOR AGENT (PARA AGENTE): Application may be made by agent, who must be a qualified voter of this county or have submitted a registration application and must otherwise be eligible to vote and must be the applicant's husband, wife, father, mother, son or daughter. (La solicitud podrá estar dirigida por un agente que deberá ser un votante capacitado de este condado o que habrá presentado una solicitud para registrarse para votar, y de otro modo deberá de estar elegible para votar. El agente deberá ser el esposo, esposa, padre, madre, hijo o hija del suplicante.)

Relationship (Parentesco)

☐ Check here if applicant is unable to make mark. (Marque aquí si el suplicante no puedehacer su marca.)

*The disclosure of social security number is voluntary. It is solicited by authority of sec. 13.122 and will be used only to maintain the accuracy of the registration records. (No es obligatorio dar su número de seguro social. Se solicita bajo la autoridad de la sec. 13.122 y se usará solamente para mantener la exactitud de los archivos.)

Vocabulary Workshop

1. secret ballot
2. popular votes—cast by all citizens; electoral votes—cast by Electoral College
3. candidates
4. independent

5. closed—only party members may vote; open—anyone may vote for candidates of either major party; select presidential nominees of party

Reviewing Main Ideas

1. way for people with similar ideas to accomplish things, help people make voices heard, nominate candidates, take stands on issues, ensure office-holders do good jobs, check conduct

of opposing parties; offers alternative for voters, one party has sufficient strength to run government

2. private contributions, public financing; Federal Election Campaign Act
3. to establish eligibility
4. governments formed by two or more parties; based on shaky compromises
5. encourages precinct voters to support party
6. believe in direct election of president by the people
7. candidates declare, national convention delegates selected, convention held, balloting until candidate wins majority of votes

Thinking Critically

1. Slogans should tout party membership.
2. to make sure only candidates with significant support get public funds
3. Students should make reasoned responses.

CHAPTER **R · e · v · i · e · w**

Vocabulary Workshop

1. What replaced the voice vote common in earlier times?
2. What is the difference between the popular vote and the electoral vote?
3. What is the term for people who run for election to public office?
4. What is the term for a voter who is not a member of a political party?
5. What is the difference between a closed primary and an open primary? What is the purpose of a presidential primary?

Reviewing Main Ideas

1. What purposes do political parties serve? What are the advantages of a two-party system?
2. How do political campaigns raise money? How does Congress regulate fund raising?
3. Why must voters be registered?
4. What are coalition governments, and why are they often unstable?
5. What is the role of a precinct captain in a campaign?
6. Why do some people want to replace the Electoral College?
7. How do the major political parties select their presidential candidates?

Thinking Critically

1. Imagine that you are living in the 1800s. Write a political slogan that reflects the views of either the Democratic party or the Republican party and that will encourage people to join that party.
2. As you have learned, minor-party presidential candidates are eligible to receive federal funds *after* the election has taken place. Why do you think such a waiting period is in place for minor-party candidates but not for major-party candidates?

3. The Constitution makes no provision for political parties. Why do you think this is so? If the framers of the U.S. Constitution were alive today, would they view the two-party political system as beneficial or harmful to the nation? Explain the reasoning behind your answer.

Citizenship in **Your Community**

Individual Project

Attend a political rally or other meeting of voters in your community. Observe the meeting, talk to the people in attendance, and record enough information so that you can answer the questions *who, what, when, where,* and *why.* Use this information and supporting details to write a newspaper article about the meeting. You may wish to submit the article to your school newspaper.

Building **Your Portfolio**

The first step of your unit portfolio project (see page 239) is to choose a U.S. president that you admire, and research that person's presidential campaign. What people were important to the campaign's success? How did volunteers help the campaign? How did the president raise campaign contributions? What kind of relationship did the president have with the media? Organize your findings in an illustrated time line entitled "The Election Campaign of President _____." Below your time line explain why this campaign was successful. Place your time line in your individual portfolio for later use.

Citizenship in **Your Community**

Articles should answer the five questions.

BUILDING **Y**OUR **PORTFOLIO**

Assign Portfolio Assessment Worksheet 10 in the *Portfolio Assessment Worksheets* booklet.

Assessment

- **Chapter 10 Tests**, *Chapter Tests* booklet
- **Test Generator**, Chapter 10
- **Portfolio**, Portfolio Assessment Worksheet 10, *Portfolio Assessment Worksheets* booklet

CHAPTER 11

The Political System

TEXTBOOK	TEACHING RESOURCES	OTHER AVAILABLE RESOURCES
Chapter	• Skills Worksheet 11 • Challenge/Enrichment Worksheet 11	• Simulations and Case Studies Lesson 13
Section **1** Shaping Public Opinion Page 207	• Reteaching Worksheet 11.1	• Transparency 15: Propaganda Techniques
2 Interest Groups Page 212	• Reteaching Worksheet 11.2	
3 Taking Part in Government Page 217	• Reteaching Worksheet 11.3	
Review and Assessment **Chapter 11 Review,** Page 221	• Test, Form A • Test, Form B • Portfolio Assessment Worksheet 11	• *Test Generator*, Chapter 11

Block Scheduling Option

ADDITIONAL RESOURCES

BOOKS FOR TEACHERS

Boyte, Harry C., et al., *Citizen Action and the New American Populism*, Temple University Press.

Kahn, Si, *Organizing: A Guide for Grassroots Leaders*, National Association of Social Workers.

Paletz, David L., and Robert Entman, *Media, Power, Politics*, Free Press.

Potholm, Christian, *Just Do It: Political Participation in the 1990s*, University Press of America.

Ranney, Austin, *Channels of Power: The Impact of Television on American Politics*, Basic Books.

BOOKS FOR STUDENTS

Harlan, Judith, *Hispanic Voters: A Voice in American Politics*, Watts. Introduction to Hispanic involvement in and impact on the U.S. political system.

Lewis, Barbara A., *The Kid's Guide to Social Action*, Free Spirit. A wealth of information on working for change at the local, state, and federal levels.

Remmes, Harold, *Lobbying for Your Cause*, Pilot Books. Explains how lobbying can influence legislation at the national level.

U.S. Government: Owner's Manual, Project Vote Smart/Center for National Independence in Politics. Lists members of Senate and House, with addresses, telephone numbers, performance evaluations, campaign finance history, sampler of key votes, and issue positions.

MULTIMEDIA RESOURCES

Lobbying: A Case History (VHS, c, 18 min.), EBEC. Viewers see lobbying in action as interest groups mobilize to influence Washington legislators.

Makers of Government (VHS, c, 16 min.), PHX. Shows how individuals can get involved in the political process at the local level by working for a candidate.

The Price of Power: Money in Politics (VHS, c, 30 min.), CSS. Documentary that shows how much influence money and the media have on modern political campaigns.

Why Bother Voting? (VHS, c, 60 min.), PBS. Uses humor, state-of-the-art graphics, and music to explain the mechanics of voting and the importance of the decision-making process.

THE INTERNET

Have students use these search words to locate more information about chapter topics on the Internet: *propaganda, polls, interest groups, voting.*

 GLOBAL SKILL BUILDER

You might wish to use **Navigating the Internet** from the interactive *Global Skill Builder* CD-ROM to aid students' understanding of the Internet as a resource.

Abbreviations: b&w=black and white; c=color; f=film; fs=filmstrip; sd=sound; tr=transparency; VHS=videotape

CIVICS SKILLS

Students will learn how to interpret information presented in a poll. Students also will learn terms important to understanding the political system.

CITIZENSHIP VALUES

★ **Living in a Democracy** Students will learn that public opinion makes government responsive to the needs of the people, that it is a citizen's duty to think critically about the information he or she receives through the media, and that the success of the republic depends on citizen participation.

AMERICAN GOVERNMENT

★ **Living in a Democracy** Students will learn how opinions are shaped and how propaganda techniques are used to influence public opinion. Students also will learn how public opinion is measured and why polls must be used carefully.

★ **Living in a Democracy** Students will learn how interest groups work and how citizens can directly participate in government.

MEETING INDIVIDUAL NEEDS

LIMITED ENGLISH PROFICIENCY (LEP)

Have pairs of students use newspapers and other periodicals to find references to vocabulary words (as many as possible) in this chapter. For example, one pair might find newspaper articles about lobbyists for or against particular piece of legislation in Congress. The students should write a summary of the article that explains information such as the legislation discussed, the lobbyists involved, and (if known) the fate of the legislation.

LEARNERS HAVING DIFFICULTY

Organize students into groups of three. Have each student summarize the main points in one section of the chapter. Each student also should identify and define vocabulary terms in his or her section. Then have the three students exchange their summaries. You might make copies to create a chapter study guide for all group members.

AUDITORY LEARNERS

Have pairs of students create radio commercials about a product, candidate, or desired activity. Then have each pair present its commercial to the class. Have students identify the propaganda technique used and the specific points made in each appeal.

VISUAL LEARNERS

Gather and display a collection of political cartoons from various newspapers and magazines. Ask students what point the cartoonist is trying to convey in each cartoon. After they have discussed the cartoons, have students debate whether political cartoons are effective tools in shaping public opinion.

TACTILE/KINESTHETIC LEARNERS

Arrange for students to attend a meeting of a local interest group, such as a union or a local Chamber of Commerce committee. Have students take notes to answer the following questions: How was the meeting run? What are the goals of the organization? How do the organization's members try to reach those goals? Have students share their observations about the meeting with the class.

GIFTED LEARNERS

Have students research laws the United States and other countries have regarding lobbying, including any restrictions on such practices. Some students should use charts and other visual guides to compare lobbying and lobbying regulations in the United States with similar practices and rules in other countries. Invite volunteers to report to the class.

CHAPTER OVERVIEW

Chapter 11 examines public opinion—what it is, how it is shaped, and how people in the United States can communicate opinions to their elected leaders. The underlying theme of the chapter is that the U.S. system of government rests on the active involvement of its citizens.

Motivator

Write the following quotation from Abraham Lincoln on the chalkboard: "Our government rests in public opinions. Whoever can change public opinion can change government. . . ." Ask: Do you agree with Lincoln that public opinion can change government? If so, how? Tell students that they will find out how in this chapter.

CHAPTER OBJECTIVES

After studying Chapter 11, students should be able to do the following.

1. Describe public opinion and explain how propaganda attempts to influence it.
2. Describe interest groups and how they work to influence government.
3. Explain why all Americans should take an active part in government.

SIMULATIONS AND CASE STUDIES

Lesson 13: Creating Campaign Commercials

Block Scheduling Option

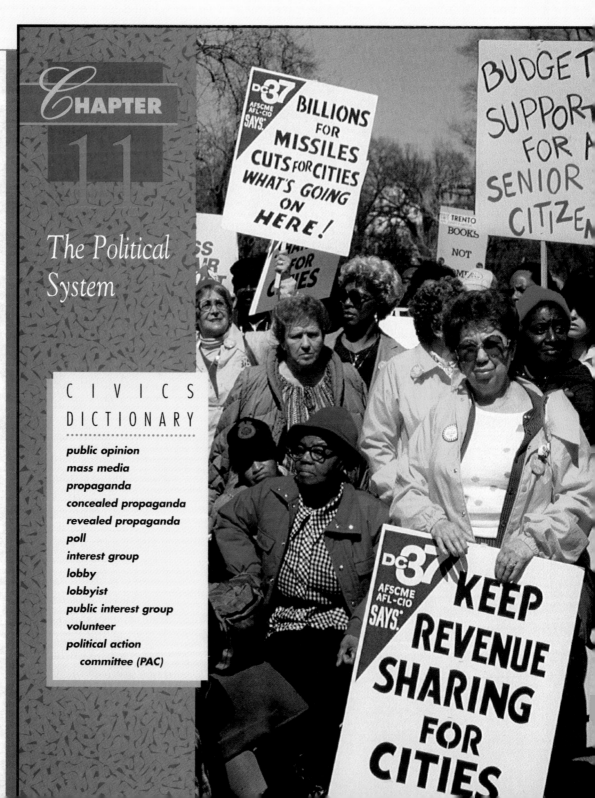

CHAPTER 11

The Political System

CIVICS DICTIONARY

public opinion
mass media
propaganda
concealed propaganda
revealed propaganda
poll
interest group
lobby
lobbyist
public interest group
volunteer
political action
   committee (PAC)

After studying Section 1, students should be able to do the following.

1. Identify the sources that influence opinions and explain why a person can have information but not be a well-informed citizen.

2. Contrast the use of propaganda in totalitarian societies with its use in democratic societies.

3. Explain the importance of using representative samples in polls.

4. Identify the possible disadvantages of polls.

Teaching Section 1

Building a Vocabulary

Tell students that the word **propaganda** is related to *propagate*. If you propagate an idea, you encourage public awareness of it. In 1622 Pope Gregory XV wanted to propagate the Roman Catholic faith, so he set up the Congregation of the Propaganda to spread Church ideas. The term *propaganda* came to mean any scheme for influencing public opinion. Have students deduce the meaning of **concealed propaganda** and **revealed propaganda**.

CHAPTER FOCUS

Will you run for public office in the future? Chances are that you, like most people, will not. There are many other ways, however, that you can participate in the political system. You can contact government officials and tell them what you think about public issues. You can work to elect political candidates who share your ideas. You can contribute your time and effort to help make your community a better place to live. When you are 18, you can vote in local, state, and national elections.

No matter how you choose to participate, your action is the key to democracy. A democratic nation such as the United States relies on citizens who are active participants in the political system. It is not enough to receive the benefits of living in a free society. You must also be willing to contribute to the preservation of this freedom.

CIVICS SIDELIGHT

Thomas Jefferson saw the value not only of public opinion but also of the newspapers that printed it. In 1787 he wrote: "The basis of our government being the opinion of the people, the very first object should be to keep that right; and were it left to me to decide whether we should have a government without newspapers, or newspapers without a government, I should not hesitate a moment to prefer the latter."

STUDY GUIDE

● What is public opinion, and how does propaganda attempt to influence it?

● What are interest groups, and how do they work to influence government?

● Why is it important for all Americans to take an active part in government?

1 Shaping Public Opinion

What is your opinion? You have probably been asked this question many times. Our opinions, those beliefs we hold to be true, are important to us. They can also influence what others believe or how they act.

In the United States the opinions of the people greatly influence government affairs. For example, an elected public official who ignores the opinions of the people is likely to lose the next election. But what are the opinions of the people? When do the opinions of individuals become public opinion?

What Is Public Opinion?

We have all heard such statements as "Public opinion demands that something be done." People sometimes think that public opinion is one opinion shared by all Americans. There are, however, very few issues on which all Americans agree.

On any particular issue, there are a number of opinions held by a number of separate groups. Each group is made up of people who share the same opinion. Each group, therefore, makes up a "public." Because each issue has many interested publics, **public opinion** is the total of the opinions held concerning a particular issue. Thus *public opinion* really refers to many opinions.

What Shapes Opinions?

Opinions are shaped by influences from many sources. The first influence on our opinions is our family. It is only natural for the ideas and beliefs of our family to become part of our own attitudes and values. Because we share so many of the same experiences with our family, we often have similar responses to many issues. As we grow older, other people and experiences also influence what we believe. Friends, teachers, and clubs play a major role in shaping our opinions.

Illustrating Ideas

Have students make a list of all the ways their opinions have been influenced in the last day or two, noting the source of each influence. Have students create collages (with explanatory captions) illustrating the sources of the influences they listed. A picture or sketch of a family, for example, could represent the influence of a student's family on his or her opinions.

Understanding Ideas

Use encyclopedias, history books, and other resources to show students examples of propaganda used by totalitarian governments, such as in Nazi Germany. Ask students to identify the purposes of each example. Have students write editorials encouraging audiences for propaganda to search for the truth. Each editorial should explain why it is important to stay informed of the truth.

GLOBAL PERSPECTIVES

Since the 1930s Chinese governments have used propaganda in the arts to help control the country's people. During the 1930s some 2,500 propaganda troupes began performing political dance-plays based on folk dances. Before they took power in the country, Chinese communists used one *yang-ko* folk dance, for example, to spread propaganda about their ideas on government and society. In 1942, Mao Zedong declared that art was a means of "uniting and educating the people." In China today the government strongly supports the performing arts, but freedom of expression is still restricted.

"You're wasting your time! . . My mind is totally controlled by what the mass media feeds into it!"

Try to identify what shapes your opinions on public issues. Are you like this man, or do other factors affect your thinking?

Information is also important in shaping opinions. Much of the information we need to make wise decisions about public issues comes from the mass media. The **mass media** include newspapers, television, radio, films, books, magazines, and other forms of communication that transmit information to large numbers of people.

Having information, however, does not always mean being well informed. Sometimes information is inaccurate or one-sided. A newspaper, for example, might give more favorable coverage to political candidates it supports and less favorable coverage to candidates it opposes. Magazine articles might express an opinion rather than simply report the facts.

Effective citizenship requires us to think critically about what we see, hear, and read. It is essential to be able to recognize the difference between fact and opinion and to gather information from reliable sources.

Propaganda and Public Opinion

Many of the ideas in the mass media have been directed at us for a purpose. Someone or some group is urging us to do something—to buy something, to believe something, or to act in a certain way. Ideas used to influence people are called **propaganda**.

It has been said that we live in the propaganda age. Propaganda is certainly nothing new, but it has become increasingly influential in recent years. One reason for this development is the tremendous growth of the mass media and advances in technology. Communications satellites, computer networks, and television broadcasts all help spread propaganda farther and faster than ever before.

There are always many people, groups, and advertisers using propaganda to influence public opinion. Advertisers use propaganda to urge consumers to buy their products. Political candidates use propaganda to convince voters to support them. When a political party tries to win public support, it is using propaganda.

People often think of propaganda as negative. Under dictatorships and totalitarian governments, this is true. In these societies the government uses propaganda techniques to control people's actions and limit their freedoms. In contrast, in democratic societies many groups, not just the government, use propaganda. These groups compete to influence the public. The propaganda they use is mostly neutral—neither good nor bad. It is simply a technique designed to sway people's attitudes, opinions, and behavior.

Kinds of Propaganda

Citizens must be alert to propaganda. They must be able to recognize it and be aware of the various methods used by propagandists. When propaganda is presented as being factual and its sources are kept secret, it is called **concealed propaganda**. Concealed propaganda is used to fool people without letting them know its purpose is to influence them.

Have small groups create a presidential campaign strategy using one of the six propaganda techniques. For example, one group might create a television commercial using testimonials. Roles for students for such a strategy might include scriptwriter, narrator, and individual citizens making testimonials. Ask the class to deduce which propaganda technique was used by each group.

Take two polls in your class on the following question: Should students sitting in the front row be exempted from homework? First poll (by secret ballot) half of the students in the front row. Then poll (by secret ballot) a sample of students from the whole class (the same number from each row). Reveal the results of both polls. Ask: Which poll is more representative of the class? Why? *(The poll of a sample of the whole class is more representative.)*

Sometimes concealed propaganda is relatively harmless. For example, press agents may make up interesting stories about television actors to give these actors publicity. At other times, concealed propaganda may be used to create a harmful impression. A photograph may be taken in a certain way or may be retouched to portray a political candidate in a negative light. False rumors may be spread to harm someone or to mislead people about a proposed program or policy.

Revealed propaganda is much more common in the United States and in other democracies. **Revealed propaganda** makes readers or listeners aware that someone is trying to influence them. Almost all advertising is revealed propaganda. You know when you see most advertisements that somebody wants you to buy something or to believe something.

Television and radio commercials are direct appeals to the public to buy products. In an election campaign, political parties often run commercials in an effort to get voters to support their candidates. These commercials must be clearly labeled as paid advertisements.

Your civics book also contains revealed propaganda. It is openly spreading the idea that all Americans should understand and take part in the nation's political system.

Propaganda Techniques

Some propaganda techniques are difficult to spot. Others can be easily recognized by people who carefully examine what they read and hear. What are some propaganda techniques?

Testimonials Political candidates and advertisers often seek endorsements from

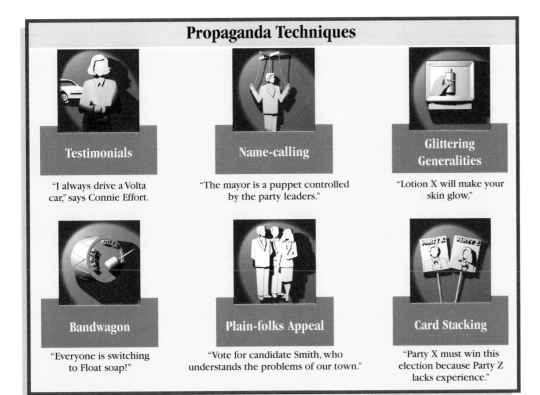

Propaganda Techniques

Testimonials
"I always drive a Volta car," says Connie Effort.

Name-calling
"The mayor is a puppet controlled by the party leaders."

Glittering Generalities
"Lotion X will make your skin glow."

Bandwagon
"Everyone is switching to Float soap!"

Plain-folks Appeal
"Vote for candidate Smith, who understands the problems of our town."

Card Stacking
"Party X must win this election because Party Z lacks experience."

Independent Practice

Have pairs of students develop a question and a poll for the entire school. Students should list the methods they would use to ensure that their polls include representative samples of the student body. Then have the students conduct two polls—one with a representative sample and one without—and write a short report on their results. Call on volunteers to report their results to the class.

Closure

Have students write a letter to the editor on an issue important to them. The letter should critique how the issue has been covered in the media. In particular, the letter should refer to any propaganda techniques and polls that have been used to influence or inform the public. Each student should decide whether the public has been well served by media coverage of the issue.

CIVICS SIDELIGHT

Candidates for high office today often hire professional organizations to conduct polls. In the 1990 congressional races, the five top pollsters each received more than a million dollars for their services. Critics charge that poll results (and statistics in general) can be manipulated to give a desired result. Consider this remark by President Harry Truman, who trailed his opponent in polls in the 1948 presidential campaign: "Polls are like sleeping pills designed to lull the voters into sleeping on election day. You might call them 'sleeping polls.' " Truman confounded the pollsters by winning the election against Thomas Dewey. One newspaper had been so confident that Truman would lose that its first edition the morning after the election incorrectly screamed "Dewey Wins."

famous people. Advertisers know, for instance, that people admire sports heroes. Therefore, they pay famous athletes to say they use and like their products.

Advertisers know that if a football hero says he drives a certain automobile, many people will believe the automobile must be good. Because these people admire the football hero, they trust his judgment. People who think for themselves, however, know that this testimonial by a famous athlete proves little. A football player may be a good quarterback, but this talent on the field does not make him an expert on automobiles.

Bandwagon People who write propaganda know that if you say something often enough and loud enough, many people will believe it. If you can win some people over to your ideas, eventually more and more people will come over to your side. This is known as the bandwagon technique. "Everybody's doing it! Jump on the bandwagon!" This method of propaganda appeals to people's desire to do what their friends and neighbors are doing. It takes advantage of the "peer pressure" factor.

Name-calling Another propaganda technique is name-calling, or using an unpleasant label or description to harm a person, group, or product. During an election campaign, both sides often use name-calling. For example, you may hear that some candidate favors "reckless spending" or that another is "opposed to progress." You must ask yourself, What proof is given? Are the charges supported by any facts?

Glittering Generalities Another technique used to influence people's thinking is the glittering generality. This technique uses words that sound good but have little real meaning. Many advertising slogans are glittering generalities. For example, statements such as "It contains a miracle ingredient!" or "It's new and improved to be better than ever!" tell nothing about the product or its ingredients.

Political candidates often use vague statements with which everyone can agree. These glittering generalities tell voters nothing about what a candidate really believes. This type of propaganda often uses words such as *home, country, freedom, patriotism,* and *American.* These words are chosen because they spark positive images with which most people in the nation identify.

Plain-folks Appeal During election campaigns, many candidates describe themselves as plain, hardworking citizens. They stress that they understand the problems of average Americans. This plain-folks appeal is designed to show people that, as one of them, the candidate can best represent the interests of the average citizen.

Card Stacking Another propaganda technique is card stacking. This technique uses facts in a way that favors a particular product, idea, or candidate. Newspapers, for example, may give front-page attention to the activities of the candidates they favor. The other political party and its candidates may be given smaller headlines or be reported only on the inside pages.

Measuring Public Opinion

Government officials are responsible for carrying out the wishes of the people. How do government officials find out what the public wants? The most obvious test of public opinion is an election. Another way to measure public opinion is to conduct a public opinion **poll**, or survey.

Polls are used to find out what people think about specific issues and about politicians and their policies. A poll attempts to measure public opinion by asking the opinions of a sample, or portion, of the public.

Choosing a Sample

Great care must be taken to choose a sample that is representative of the public that is

Reviewing

Have students complete the Section 1 Review.

Reteaching

Assign Section 1 of the Chapter 11 Reteaching Worksheet.

SECTION OBJECTIVES

After studying Section 2, students should be able to do the following.

1. Explain how interest groups differ from political parties.

2. Describe the different types of interest groups and determine why such groups have been criticized.

3. Explain how lobbyists try to influence government and public opinion.

being measured. An unrepresentative sample can cause serious errors in a poll's results. Suppose, for example, your school principal decides to conduct a poll to find out if people want the cafeteria to remain open during the entire school day. If only teachers and cafeteria workers are polled, the poll results will probably be different than if students are also included in the polling sample.

A well-known sampling error occurred in 1936. A popular magazine called *Literary Digest* conducted a public opinion poll to predict the outcome of the presidential election. President Franklin D. Roosevelt, the Democratic candidate, ran against Republican candidate Alfred M. Landon.

The *Digest* mailed more than 10 million ballots to people chosen at random from telephone directories and automobile registration lists. Approximately two million people filled out these ballots and mailed them back to the magazine. Based on the poll results, the *Digest* predicted that Landon would be elected. The election results were very different, however. Roosevelt won by a landslide, with 60 percent of the vote.

What went wrong with the poll? It failed because in 1936 only people with high incomes could afford to own telephones and automobiles. The sample did not represent the entire voting population.

Once a representative sample has been chosen, care must be taken in deciding what questions to ask. The way questions are phrased often affects the answers that will be given. For example, the neutral question "Should more firefighters be hired?" might receive one answer. The question "Should taxes be raised to hire more firefighters?" might receive a different answer.

Using Polls Carefully

Polls are a valuable tool for measuring public opinion. Some critics fear, however, that polls influence public opinion as well as measure it. For example, some people want to be on the winning side. Imagine that two days before the election, a poll predicts that Candidate Z will win by 15 percent. The possibility exists that some voters will decide in favor of Z in order to support a winner.

Polls can help us evaluate public opinion only if we look at more than just the percentages given in the results. Look also for the wording of the questions, the number of people responding, and the sample population surveyed in the poll.

Especially important is the number of people responding as "undecided." Often, the number of people who are undecided is so large that no prediction is possible. In election campaigns candidates usually try to address their strongest appeal to undecided voters.

SECTION 1 REVIEW

1. Define or identify the following terms: public opinion, mass media, propaganda, concealed propaganda, revealed propaganda, poll.

2. What sources influence opinions? Why is it possible to have information and yet not be well informed?

3. How does the use of propaganda in totalitarian societies differ from its use in democratic societies?

4. Why is it important that polls use representative samples? Why do some people criticize polls?

5. **THINKING CRITICALLY** Imagine that you are running for Student Council president. Write six different campaign slogans for yourself, each based on one of the propaganda techniques discussed in the section. Which of the slogans do you think would be most effective in winning votes, and why? Which of the slogans gives an honest assessment of your qualifications for the office? Explain your answers.

SECTION 1 REVIEW ANSWERS

1. See the following pages: public opinion (p. 207); mass media, propaganda, concealed propaganda (p. 208); revealed propaganda (p. 209); poll (p. 210).

2. family, friends, teachers, clubs, mass media; information may be inaccurate or one-sided

3. In totalitarian societies, government uses propaganda to control people and actions and to limit freedom. In democratic societies, competing groups, not just government, use neutral propaganda to influence public attitudes, opinions, and behavior.

4. It is important to avoid poll results that do not accurately represent the population. Critics say polls influence public opinion as well as measure it.

5. Students should recognize that none of the propaganda techniques gives an honest and complete assessment of the qualifications and character of a candidate.

Teaching Section 2
Building a Vocabulary

By the mid-1600s, members of the British House of Commons called the public room just outside the main chambers the *lobby* (derived from the Old High German word *lauba*, a shelter created by foliage). The British called people who gathered there in search of legislative aid members of the **lobby**, or "lobby-agents." Have students use the origin of this word to create pictures or cartoons that describe the functions of a **lobbyist**.

Have small groups represent different interest groups in your school. Have each group write up a list of goals and strategies for achieving them (such as advertising in the school newspaper, circulating flyers, or lobbying student government). Groups should assign tasks to each member, such as advertisement copywriting, illustrating, or lobbying. Have each group present its campaign to the class.

MULTICULTURAL PERSPECTIVES

The interest groups who opposed slavery included both whites and blacks. Their "interest" was not so much economic as it was moral. William Lloyd Garrison (1805–1879), who published an antislavery newspaper called *The Liberator*, saw himself as a radical crusader: "I do not wish to think, or speak, or write, with moderation. . . . I am in earnest—I will not equivocate—I will not excuse—I will not retreat a single inch—AND I WILL BE HEARD." Garrison's African American counterpart in the abolition movement was Frederick Douglass, an escaped slave. Douglass (1817–1895) believed in political action, and he used his own antislavery newspaper, the *North Star*, to that end. After the Civil War, Douglass's interest turned to civil rights for African Americans and for women.

AMERICAN BIOGRAPHY

Marian Wright Edelman

Marian Wright Edelman was born in 1939 in Bennettsville, South Carolina. The daughter of a Baptist minister, she was encouraged not only to pursue an education but also to use this education to help others. Her parents set the example. They opened the Wright Home for the Aged behind their church. In addition, over time 12 foster children shared the family's home.

Edelman soon set her own example of helping others. After graduating from Yale Law School, she joined the National Association for the Advancement of Colored People (NAACP) Legal Defense and Education Fund. While working for the Fund, she fought against segregation laws in the South. In 1965 she became the first African American woman to obtain the right to practice law in the state of Mississippi.

Edelman focused her efforts on safeguarding the rights of children as well. In 1973 she founded the Children's Defense Fund. This organization is aimed at helping children and at addressing children's issues in public policy. Edelman has testified before Congress several times on children's issues.

Today Edelman continues her lobbying efforts on behalf of children's health care, nutrition, education, and employment issues. The home where she was born in South Carolina is now a youth development center of the Children's Defense Fund. The Fund continues to help hundreds of children in need.

2 Interest Groups

Americans have many ways to express their opinions to government officials. As you know, they can write or call their government representatives. One of the most effective ways to express an opinion is by becoming part of an interest group.

What Is an Interest Group?

Many Americans are members of one or more **interest groups**. These are organizations of people with a common interest who try to influence government policies and decisions. An interest group is also known as a pressure group or **lobby**. A person who is paid by a lobby or interest group to represent that group's interests is called a **lobbyist**.

Interest groups differ from political parties. While both seek to influence government, interest groups are not primarily concerned with electing candidates to office. Although they often support particular candidates, their main interest lies in influencing public policies that affect their members.

Interest groups have existed throughout the nation's history. For example, people favoring the Constitution organized to work for its approval. Before the Civil War, people opposed to slavery organized to end it.

Kinds of Interest Groups

There are many different kinds of interest groups. They include business associations, labor unions, farm organizations, older citizens' groups, veterans' organizations, teachers' associations, and consumer groups. Each group works to promote the interests of its members.

Many interest groups represent the economic interests of their members. These interest groups include the National Association of Manufacturers, the United Mine Workers, and the American Farm Bureau Federation. Members of these and other economic interest

Present the following scenario to students: A member of the House introduces a bill to give a tax break to mining companies. Ask: What kinds of interest groups (including public interest groups) are likely to support or oppose this legislation? Have students take the roles of lobbyists for each group and give their responses "in character." *(Groups might include miners, jewelers, and environmentalists.)*

Have students choose a bill (fictional or real) recently passed by Congress and write a newspaper account of the bill's passage. (A local congressperson's office might be able to provide information about a particular bill.) The article should include information about the arguments of interested groups for and against the bill and how the bill was passed.

groups seek to influence government policies that affect them.

For example, the American Farm Bureau Federation is a nationwide organization of farmers. It works to have bills passed that help farmers recover losses from natural disasters and falling crop prices.

Some interest groups consist of people whose concerns are issue-oriented. That is, they focus on a specific issue or cause. For example, the National Association for the Advancement of Colored People (NAACP) works to promote racial equality. The National Organization for Women (NOW) seeks to protect the rights of women.

Other groups, referred to as **public interest groups**, seek to promote the interests of the general public rather than just one part of it. These include groups working to protect consumers, wildlife, and the environment.

How Interest Groups Work

Interest groups vary in size, goals, and budgets. Most, though, use similar methods to influence government decisions. They encourage members to write to the president or to their senators or representatives about specific bills. Many interest groups also hire lobbyists to speak for them and to represent their interests. Lobbyists work at all levels of government, although most are located in Washington, D.C.

Lobbyists get their name from the way they operated many years ago. In the past, they waited for lawmakers in the lobbies outside the legislatures' meeting rooms. There they talked to lawmakers and tried to influence their decisions on the issues of the day.

Most lobbyists today are highly skilled people with a staff of research assistants. Some lobbyists are former members of the legislatures or public agencies they now seek to influence. Other lobbyists are lawyers, public relations experts, journalists, or specialists in particular fields.

Influencing Government Many of the nation's laws are the result of a struggle

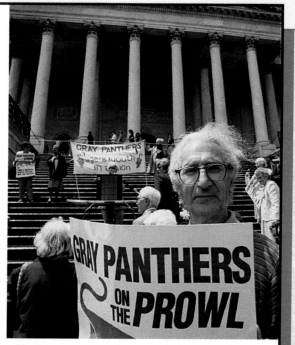

Older citizens are a steadily growing percentage of the population. As their numbers increase, so does their power as an interest group.

among various interest groups. One example is the minimum wage law. This law states that workers may not be paid less than a certain amount of money per hour. Labor groups often seek an increase in the minimum wage. Business groups generally oppose such an increase. Lobbyists for both interest groups present their arguments to Congress. After listening to both sides and considering all the facts, Congress makes its decision.

The minimum wage has increased over the years. The amount of each increase, however, has been a compromise between those people who want a higher increase and those who want a smaller one.

Lobbyists use a number of different methods to promote the action they seek. They argue in support of bills they favor and against bills they oppose. Sometimes lobbyists ask members of Congress to sponsor bills favored by members of the lobbyist's interest group.

(continued on page 216)

CIVICS SIDELIGHT

Sometimes the methods that lobbyists use to influence legislation are suspect, even unlawful. Some lobbyists have been known to offer money to members of Congress in return for favors on Capitol Hill. Occasionally, a member of Congress succumbs to this temptation. In the late 1970s the FBI ran an undercover operation, dubbed "Abscam," in which agents posing as wealthy foreign businesspeople offered bribes of up to $50,000 to various members of Congress. One U.S. senator and six representatives were convicted of accepting the bribes.

Illustrating Ideas

Have students create diagrams to organize the information in this article by cause and effect. Students might choose to create flowcharts or time lines, for example, to illustrate the article. The first piece of information might be the death of Cari Lightner by a drunk driver. Ask: What did Cari's mother do as a result of this accident? Have students complete the cause-and-effect diagram.

CIVICS SIDELIGHT

In its continuing campaign to stop drunk driving, Mothers Against Drunk Driving released a national report card in November 1993 that graded the 50 states according to their anti–drinking-and-driving efforts. Completed in conjunction with the National Highway Traffic Safety Administration, the survey on which each state's grade is based examined 12 separate factors. These factors included the governor's leadership, statistics and record-keeping, administrative and criminal sanctions, and state legislation concerning drunk driving. Illinois earned the highest grade in the report, an A-minus. The national average of all the states was a B-minus. According to the report, 45 percent of traffic deaths nationally in 1992 were related to alcohol.

Case STUDY

MOTHERS AGAINST DRUNK DRIVING

You may sometimes think that there is nothing you can do to change something you believe is wrong. It may seem that the odds are so against you that any action you take will go unnoticed. But under the First Amendment right of petition, you—like all Americans—are free to work toward any cause you believe to be worthy and right. One woman used her First Amendment right of petition to turn a personal tragedy into a triumph for people all across the nation.

A Child Is Killed

In May 1980, 13-year-old Cari Lightner was struck and killed by an automobile as she

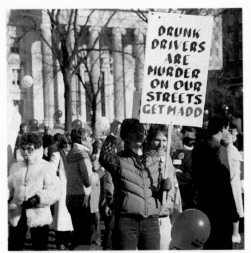

Mothers Against Drunk Driving (MADD) is an organization with branches throughout the nation. It began when one woman exercised her First Amendment right of petition.

walked near her home in California. The driver of the automobile was drunk. Candy Lightner, the young victim's mother, was horrified to learn that the driver had been arrested in the past for drunk driving. Moreover, the police told Lightner that the driver probably would not go to jail, even though Cari had died in the accident. Why would the driver not go to jail? Because according to California law, driving under the influence of alcohol was a misdemeanor, or minor crime.

Lightner knew that there was nothing she could do to bring back her daughter. But she also knew that something had to be done to protect other people from suffering her daughter's tragic fate.

A Mother Takes Action

Lightner decided that her first plan of action would be to work for stronger laws against drunk driving. To this end, she formed an organization called Mothers Against Drunk Driving, or MADD. She and the other concerned citizens of MADD then contacted dozens of elected officials in the state of California, including the governor. Lightner used her First Amendment right of petition to urge these officials to work for stiffer penalties for drunk drivers. California lawmakers soon saw the wisdom of MADD's arguments and strengthened the laws.

A Nation Responds

Acting as the voice of concerned citizens everywhere, MADD expanded its crusade throughout the nation. As a result, all 50 states have strengthened their drunk driving laws in recent years. Many states, for example, have

Creating a Campaign

Have pairs of students create campaigns supporting MADD's goals in your school. Each pair should develop graphics and other visual guides to provide information to the student body about the dangers of drinking and driving. To develop their campaigns, students may want to review how interest groups influence public opinion.

raised the drinking age from 18 or 19 to 21. Many states also take away the driver's license of drivers convicted of driving while intoxicated. More than half the states in the nation allow police officers to take the driver's licenses—on the spot—of drivers who fail or refuse to take a test to determine intoxication.

The work of MADD continues today. The organization now has more than three million members nationwide. Located in every state in the nation, MADD's members petition for stricter laws against drunk driving, provide assistance to victims of drunk drivers, serve on advisory boards, and sponsor workshops about the dangers of driving and drinking.

Students Become Involved

One of MADD's most important accomplishments was to inspire students across the nation to join the fight against drunk driving. Students Against Driving Drunk (SADD) was

formed in 1982 and now has millions of members in state and local chapters nationwide. The goal of SADD is to reduce the number of young people killed in alcohol-related traffic accidents. To this end, members of SADD work to educate young people about the dangers of underage drinking, driving drunk, and riding in automobiles with drunk drivers. SADD's strongest message is that young people should strive to live alcohol-free lives.

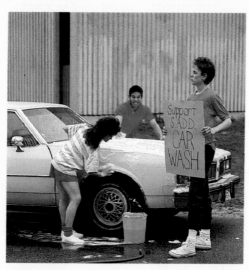

Students Against Driving Drunk (SADD), an offshoot of MADD, reflects the commitment of the nation's young people to keep drunk drivers off the road.

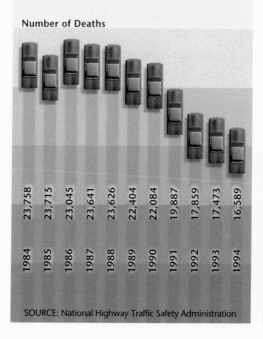

Alcohol-Related U.S. Traffic Deaths

Number of Deaths

Year	Number of Deaths
1984	23,758
1985	23,715
1986	23,045
1987	23,641
1988	23,626
1989	22,404
1990	22,084
1991	19,887
1992	17,859
1993	17,473
1994	16,589

SOURCE: National Highway Traffic Safety Administration

YOU DECIDE

1 Why did Candy Lightner form MADD?

2 What do the members of MADD do to combat drunk driving?

3 Contact the SADD chapter in your state or local community. What does this chapter do to educate young people about the dangers of drunk driving? How effective are its efforts? What more can be done?

ANSWERS TO YOU DECIDE

1. Her daughter was killed by a drunk driver, and she wanted to work for stricter laws against drunk driving.

2. petition for stricter laws, provide help for victims of drunk drivers, serve on advisory boards, sponsor workshops on the dangers of drinking and driving

3. Students might mention anti–drunk-driving campaigns, local conferences and workshops, and speeches.

Closure

Invite a member of a teacher's association (or another interest group) to meet with the class. Ask the speaker to bring along any pamphlets or other literature the group may have produced recently in an attempt to influence government or public opinion. Help students prepare to ask critical questions based on what they have learned in Section 2.

Reviewing

Have students complete the Section 2 Review.

Reteaching

Assign Section 2 of the Chapter 11 Reteaching Worksheet.

SECTION 2 REVIEW
ANSWERS

1. See the following pages: interest group, lobby, lobbyist (p. 212); public interest group (p. 213).

2. An interest group's main purpose is to influence public policies, not to elect candidates to office.

3. Some represent economic interests of members. Some (such as civil rights groups) focus on specific issues or causes. Some (such as consumer and environmental groups) promote interests of the general public. Critics say they play too great a role in the lawmaking process; interests of groups lacking in money and organization are overshadowed by those of better-funded and organized groups.

4. argue for or against legislation, ask Congress members to sponsor bills, supply information, help write bills, testify at hearings, advertise, provide workers and contributors for candidates, urge people to contact public officials

5. Students should address the freedom of all to be heard.

216

They supply facts for the bill and may help write the bill. Government officials often contact lobbyists to learn what interest groups think about issues affecting those groups.

Lobbyists testify at committee hearings as well. In fact, lobbyists from different interest groups often present evidence on opposite sides of the issue. Each lobbyist comes to the hearings prepared with facts and well-developed arguments.

Supplying information is one of a lobbyist's most important jobs. As you read in Chapter 5, members of Congress are faced with thousands of bills each year covering many different subjects. No lawmaker can be fully informed in all these areas. Lawmakers appreciate the help provided by lobbyists.

Influencing Public Opinion Interest groups attempt to influence not only the government but public opinion as well. For example, interest groups place advertisements in the mass media in support of their positions. They often promise to help government officials in their next election campaigns by supplying workers and contributions. Sometimes lobbyists urge local groups and individuals to send letters and telegrams to public officials. They hope that public support will influence the lawmakers' decisions.

Regulating Interest Groups

Interest groups may use any legal means to influence public officials and the public itself. To keep the activities of lobbyists in the open, federal and state governments require lobbyists to register. They must indicate for whom they are working and how much money they spend in lobbying. In recent years laws regulating lobbying have been strict. The Lobbying Disclosure Act of 1995 closed many loopholes, or ways of evading the laws.

Role of Interest Groups

Lobbyists once were viewed with suspicion because many of them worked in secret. Today they are usually welcomed as sources of information and help by overworked lawmakers and government officials.

Some people, however, are critical of interest groups and their lobbyists. They believe these groups play too great a role in the lawmaking process. Critics charge that too much attention is paid to the interest group that is best organized and has the most money. As a result, important interests—such as those of disadvantaged citizens—do not always have an equal hearing.

Despite this suggested imbalance, interest groups play an important role in the political process. You are probably a member of a number of interest groups even though you may not be aware of it. Interest groups are made up of people—in our roles as students, businesspeople, consumers, farmers, workers, and veterans. In a free society, citizens have the right to make their opinions known to government leaders. Interest groups are evidence of our political freedom.

SECTION 2 REVIEW

1. Define or identify the following terms: interest group, lobby, lobbyist, public interest group.

2. How do interest groups differ from political parties?

3. What kinds of interest groups exist? Why have interest groups been criticized?

4. How do lobbyists try to influence government and public opinion?

5. **THINKING CRITICALLY** The textbook states that interest groups "are evidence of political freedom." What does this statement mean? Do you agree or disagree with the statement? Why? What might be done to better serve the interests of groups lacking in money and representation?

SECTION OBJECTIVES

After studying Section 3, students should be able to do the following.

1. Identify four ways that all citizens can participate in government.

2. Explain the importance of voting, and determine why so few U.S. citizens vote.

3. Explain how volunteers and interest groups help political campaigns.

Teaching Section 3
Building a Vocabulary

Ask students to define **volunteer**. Tell them that the origin of the word comes from the Latin word meaning "will." A person who volunteers does so willingly. Ask: Does a volunteer get paid? *(no)* Ask students to name some organizations and activities for which teenagers might volunteer their time and their help.

3 Taking Part in Government

As you have learned, Americans can influence government decisions through public opinion and interest groups. Citizens also can make government more responsive by taking an active part in government.

Americans can participate in government in many ways. We can vote in elections—local, state, and national. We can work for political parties. We can speak out on public issues and help make our communities better places to live. All these activities are responsibilities of citizenship. They are vital to the preservation of a democratic government.

Voting: Democracy in Action

Voting is the most important opportunity for citizens to participate in government. Because only a small percentage of citizens can actually serve in the government, we elect officials to represent us. All citizens can take part in selecting the leaders who will represent and serve the people.

Elections offer every citizen the chance to be involved in governing the nation. Each voter helps determine what actions the government will take. We are making known our opinions on public issues when we vote. When we choose candidates, we are expressing our opinions on their leadership abilities as well as on their programs.

Voting is not only a right, it is an important responsibility. Yet millions of U.S. citizens do not vote. In fact, the United States has one of the lowest voter turnouts of any free nation in the world. In recent presidential elections little more than half the voting-age population has voted. In 1992 only about 55 percent of the voting-age public voted for the nation's president. In non-presidential elections the percentage of voters is even smaller. This low voter turnout leaves the selection of

What is the cartoonist saying about voter participation in the United States? What do you think could be done to encourage more Americans to vote? What can you do to prepare yourself to vote?

government officials to a small percentage of the nation's people.

Why do so few people vote? Some people do not register and thus are not eligible to vote. Some people do not like any of the available candidates. Some are ill and cannot reach the polling places on election day. Some are unexpectedly away from home and cannot reach the polling places at which they are registered to vote. Others move and do not meet residency requirements for voting.

Every Vote Counts

The most common reason for not voting, however, is a person's belief that his or her vote will not make a difference in the outcome of an election. Of course, this is not true. The vote of every individual helps determine who

Cartoon Caption Answer

Voter participation is lacking. Students should consider actions suggested in this section.

CIVICS SIDELIGHT

As the post-World War II baby-boom generation has aged, older Americans have made up an increasingly larger part of the electorate (people aged 18 and over). For example, people aged 45 to 64 made up 26.7 percent of the voting-age population in the November 1994 elections. That figure was up from 25.7 percent for the November 1990 elections. Over the same period, the percentage of eligible voters aged 18 to 24 fell from 13.6 percent in 1990 to 13.2 percent in 1994. Also, 43.6 percent of eligible voters in 1994 were aged 25 to 44. That percentage was down from 44.3 percent in the November 1990 elections.

There were 8.3 million more female eligible voters than male eligible voters in November 1994. Of all eligible voters, 52 percent were women.

Guided Practice

Help students create a profile of "Good Citizen A." On the board write "Citizen A participates in government by. . . ." Call on volunteers to supply the four ways one can participate in government (along with specific examples where appropriate). Then group students according to which method of participation they believe is most important. Facilitate a four-way debate among the groups.

Independent Practice

Have students draw cartoons featuring "Good Citizen A" and "Could-Be-Better Citizen B." The cartoons should illustrate why and in what ways Citizen B should participate in government and political campaigns. Display the cartoons for the class. Some students might want to submit their cartoons to the school newspaper for publication on the editorial page. Have the class discuss volunteers' cartoons.

CIVICS SIDELIGHT

Congressional incumbents have been major beneficiaries of PAC contributions. PAC contributions to all congressional candidates increased from $56.6 million in 1993 to $67.6 million in 1995. Much of that funding has gone to incumbents, contributing to a situation in which incumbents continue to raise and spend far more money for elections than do many of their challengers. By the early 1990s incumbents in the U.S. House of Representatives were outspending election challengers by nearly four to one. Some wealthy challengers have tried to close the gap by pumping considerable sums of their personal money into their campaigns.

wins or loses an election. Only by exercising the right to vote can we influence the laws and policies that greatly affect our lives. The importance of every person's vote can be seen by looking at the results of two presidential elections in the twentieth century.

In 1916 Charles Evans Hughes, the Republican candidate, went to bed believing he had been elected president. Hughes would have been right if 1,983 people in California had voted for him instead of for the Democratic candidate, Woodrow Wilson. Because Wilson received a majority of California's popular vote, however, he was awarded all of that state's electoral votes. California's electoral votes gave Wilson enough votes to win the election over Hughes.

In 1976 Jimmy Carter, the Democratic candidate, defeated Gerald R. Ford, the Republican candidate, by nearly 1,700,000 popular votes. The electoral vote was much closer, however. A shift of just 5,599 votes in Ohio and another 3,687 votes in Hawaii would have changed the electoral vote enough to give the election to Ford. Clearly, every American's vote is important in every election.

Signing petitions for causes in which you believe is one way you can influence government officials.

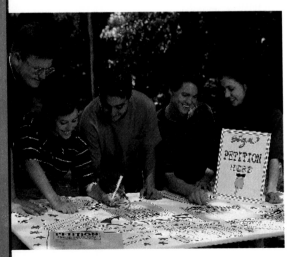

Taking Part in Political Campaigns

Another way to influence political decisions is to take part in election campaigns. Although you must be 18 years old to vote, people of any age can work as volunteers in political campaigns. **Volunteers** are people who work without pay to help others. Playing an active role as a volunteer in a political party is an effective way to have a say in who represents you in the government. You can also learn firsthand how the political system works.

There are many jobs for volunteers during an election campaign. You can ring doorbells or make phone calls to inform voters about your candidate and his or her ideas. You can encourage your friends and family members to vote. People are always needed to distribute campaign literature to passersby on the street. Envelopes must be addressed and stuffed with information about the candidate.

On election day, campaign workers urge people who support their candidate to vote. They may stay with young children to allow voters to go to the polling places. All these efforts can make the difference in the outcome of an election.

Interest Groups and Political Campaigns

Interest groups take part in political campaigns. They may provide volunteers to help candidates who are sympathetic to their causes. They also may make financial contributions to election campaigns.

Although interest groups are prohibited by law from contributing money directly to candidates, they may contribute through **political action committees (PACs)**. PACs collect voluntary contributions from members and use this money to fund candidates and issues the committees favor. The number of PACs has risen dramatically in recent years—from 608 in 1974 to about 4,200 today. In 1995 PACs contributed approximately $68 million to political candidates.

Closure

Have students reflect on the thoughts a volunteer might have at the end of a hard-fought political campaign. Ask them to write a journal entry that a political volunteer might write after the votes have been counted. Students might review what the volunteer did and how he or she feels about it. They might choose to imagine that the volunteer supported a local, state, or national candidate or issue.

Reviewing

Have students complete the Section 3 Review.

Reteaching

Assign Section 3 of the Chapter 11 Reteaching Worksheet.

Contacting Public Officials

Suppose the street corner near your home needs a traffic light. Or suppose you are against a proposed 15-cent increase in your city's bus fare. Or suppose the House of Representatives will vote soon on an issue important to you. How can you make your opinion on these issues known quickly?

Writing a letter to local officials or members of Congress is an excellent way to let them know what is on your mind. As you read in Chapter 5, members of Congress receive a lot of mail. They welcome these letters as a way of learning what the people they represent think about the issues.

You also can contact public officials by telephone, facsimile (fax) machine, or telegram. A visit to an official's office is another way to express your opinions. Many officials have regular office hours for meeting with their constituents. Of course, it is always best to call first to make an appointment.

Community Action

The activities of local government touch our lives most often and most directly. The quality of life in towns and cities depends to a large extent on how well local governments serve us. It is therefore important for all Americans to take part in their communities. Citizens can greatly influence their local governments.

Citizens often work together in community groups. For example, in many cities people working to improve their neighborhoods have formed block associations. Residents of an apartment house might form a tenants' group to improve the condition of their building. Citizens in a town might organize to raise money to buy new books for the library or repair the school's baseball field.

Community groups are active in large and small cities, in towns, and in villages. Working together makes it easier for citizens to bring about needed improvements and changes in their communities. Citizen involvement helps make democracy work.

SECTION 3 REVIEW

1. Define or identify the following terms: volunteer, political action committee (PAC).

2. Identify four ways that citizens can participate in government.

3. Why is it important for all eligible citizens to vote? Why do so few U.S. citizens vote?

4. How do volunteers help political campaigns? How do interest groups help political campaigns?

5. **THINKING CRITICALLY** The president of the United States has invited you to the White House to deliver a speech entitled "How to Encourage Citizen Participation in Politics." Write a draft of the speech.

CHAPTER 11 SUMMARY

In a democratic republic, government must be aware of the concerns and needs of all the people. One way to measure public opinion is by using public opinion polls. If used carefully, these polls can provide helpful information to candidates and government officials.

Opinion is shaped by many different sources, beginning with the family. Information provided by the mass media also plays a major role in shaping opinions. Propaganda is often used to try to influence people. Citizens must be able to recognize propaganda.

Interest groups play an important role in influencing government decisions and in shaping public opinion. Interest groups often hire lobbyists to promote the policies they favor.

Responsible citizens take an active part in public affairs. By voting in elections, citizens can help select the officials who will represent them. Citizens can also take part in political campaigns and work with community groups.

SECTION 3 REVIEW
A N S W E R S

1. See the following page: volunteer, political action committee (PAC) (p. 218).

2. vote in elections, work for political parties, speak out on public issues, help make their communities better places to live

3. Low turnout leaves selection of officials to a small percentage of the people. Some people believe their votes will not matter, do not register, do not like the candidates, are too ill to go to the polls, are not at home on election day, or move and do not meet residency requirements.

4. ring doorbells or make phone calls to talk about candidates, encourage others to vote, distribute campaign literature, address and stuff envelopes, baby-sit for voters; interest groups provide volunteers, give money through PACs

5. Speeches will vary but should include clear proposals for encouraging participation.

Point out that pollsters often ask the same question over and over to gauge shifts in public opinion. Since 1945 the Gallup Poll has asked Americans the following question: "Do you approve or disapprove of the way [name of the president] is handling his job as president?" The results of this polling are known as the presidential approval rating.

News organizations usually report the results because changes in the approval rating often signal the perceived success or failure of a president's policies. Have pairs of students conduct a student "approval rating" poll on the president over the next month. Have the pairs use graphics to illustrate their polls' results and report them to the class.

Developing Civics Skills

CITIZENSHIP SKILL

Understanding Polls

Each year millions of Americans participate in public opinion polls. In fact, chances are that someday you will be asked by a pollster to give your opinion on a topic. Poll results often are reported in the media. By learning to understand polls you can gain insight into what Americans think about important issues.

How to Understand Polls

1. **Examine the questions.** Questions must be worded in such a way that they mean the same thing to every person in the poll. Confusing questions often bring inaccurate answers. Questions also must be neutral. If they lead respondents toward any one answer, they do not truly measure public opinion.
2. **Examine the answers.** Pollsters rarely ask people to supply answers of their own. Rather, they provide a limited set of answers and let people choose the ones that apply to them. Pollsters use a limited set of answers because this makes it easy to put large numbers of people into a few answer categories. Otherwise, if pollsters questioned 1,000 people, they might receive 1,000 different responses.
3. **Examine the results.** When a poll is complete, the pollsters compute the percentage of people who selected each answer. These figures are the poll's facts. Pollsters use these facts to make generalizations, or broad statements that describe the patterns and relationships among the facts.

    Every generalization *must* be supported by the facts. If any of the facts do not fit, the generalization is not valid, or correct. For example, consider this statement: "I like spaghetti, lasagne, and ravioli." This

statement lists the facts. A generalization supported by these facts is "I like pasta."

Applying the Skill

Study the poll results below. Then answer the following questions.

1. Does the question posed by the poll meet the standards for a good question? Why or why not?
2. What are the facts of the poll?
3. "Only some people have a great deal of confidence in television news." Is this a valid generalization? Explain your answer.

"As far as people in charge of running television news are concerned, would you say you have a great deal of confidence, only some confidence, or hardly any confidence at all in them?"

	Great Deal	Only Some	Hardly Any	Not Sure
	29%	54%	16%	1%

SOURCE: Louis Harris Associates.

Vocabulary Workshop

1. public opinion
2. volunteer
3. mass media
4. lobby or pressure group
5. ideas used to influence; concealed—presented as fact, but source is secret; revealed—public aware that someone is trying to influence them
6. collect money from people to fund candidates and issues

Reviewing Main Ideas

1. totalitarian—government tries to control people, limit freedom; democratic—competing groups try to influence with neutral propaganda; interest groups not primarily concerned with electing candidates
2. argue for or against bills, ask Congress members to sponsor bills, supply information, help write bills, testify, meet with officials to discuss needs of clients; interest groups—hope public will pressure officials
3. testimonial, bandwagon, name-calling, glittering generalities, plain-folks appeal, card stacking
4. to find out opinions; to accurately show public opinion
5. People might change opinions to be on winning side.
6. to select who will lead, represent; believe votes do not matter, do not register, do not like candidates, too ill to vote, not home on election day, do not meet residency requirements
7. vote, volunteer work, speak out, encourage voting, distribute literature

Thinking Critically

1. Answers should be reasoned.
2. possible positive—wider audience; negative—elections based on who has best media presence
3. A democracy needs well-informed citizens.

Citizenship in Your Community

Posters should focus on actions of the interest group.

Building Your Portfolio

Assign Portfolio Assessment Worksheet 11 in the *Portfolio Assessment Worksheets* booklet.

Assessment

- **Chapter 11 Tests,** *Chapter Tests* booklet
- **Test Generator**, Chapter 11
- **Portfolio**, Portfolio Assessment Worksheet 11, *Portfolio Assessment Worksheets* booklet

---

R·e·v·i·e·w

Vocabulary Workshop

1. What is the term for the total of the opinions held concerning a particular issue?
2. What is the term for a person who donates his or her time?
3. What source of information includes newspapers, television, radio, films, books, and magazines?
4. What is another term for an interest group?
5. Define the term *propaganda*. What is the difference between concealed propaganda and revealed propaganda?
6. What is the purpose of a political action committee?

Reviewing Main Ideas

1. How does the use of propaganda differ in totalitarian societies and democratic societies? How do interest groups differ from political parties?
2. How do lobbyists help government officials? Why do interest groups try to influence public opinion?
3. What are the six different types of propaganda techniques?
4. What is the purpose of polls? Why must polls use representative samples?
5. What do critics mean when they say that polls can influence public opinion?
6. Why is voting important? Why do so few Americans vote?
7. How can citizens take part in the political system?

Thinking Critically

1. Public opinion polls are an ever-present part of the American political system. Should elected officials use their own best judgment when voting on the issues or should they follow the public opinion positions of the voters? Explain your answer.
2. It is common for presidential candidates to debate election issues on television. What positive and negative effects has television had on presidential politics?
3. Explain why citizens should be aware of the propaganda techniques used by advertisers and politicians.

Citizenship in Your Community

Individual Project

Research an interest group active in your community. What is the purpose of the group? How many members does the group have? How do people join the group? How long has the group been in existence? How does the group try to achieve its goals? What problems has the group encountered in its work toward these goals? Create a poster illustrating the goals and activities of the interest group.

Building Your Portfolio

The second step of your unit portfolio project (see page 239) is to conduct a poll in which you ask a representative sample of students in your school to identify the problems and issues facing students today. Show the results in a bar graph that indicates what percentage of poll respondents identified each issue or problem as a concern. Use your poll results to create a list of campaign goals that will address students' concerns. Place your graph and your list in your individual portfolio for later use.

PLANNING GUIDE

TEXTBOOK	TEACHING RESOURCES	OTHER AVAILABLE RESOURCES
Chapter	• Skills Worksheet 12 • Challenge/Enrichment Worksheet 12	
Section **1** Raising Money Page 223	• Reteaching Worksheet 12.1	• Transparency 16: Why the Costs of the Federal Government Have Increased
2 Types of Taxes Page 227	• Reteaching Worksheet 12.2	• Transparency 17: State Sales and Income Taxes
3 Managing the Nation's Money Page 232	• Reteaching Worksheet 12.3	• Transparency 18: The National Debt
Review and Assessment **Chapter 12 Review,** Page 237 **Unit 4 Review,** Page 238	• Test, Form A • Test, Form B • Portfolio Assessment Worksheet 12 • Unit 4 Portfolio Assessment Worksheet	• *Test Generator,* Chapter 12 • *Test Generator,* Unit 4

ADDITIONAL RESOURCES

BOOKS FOR TEACHERS

Congressional Quarterly Almanac, Congressional Quarterly.

Pechman, Joseph A., *The Rich, the Poor, and the Taxes They Pay,* Westview Press.

Schick, Allen, *Crisis in the Budget Process: Exercising Political Choice,* American Enterprise.

BOOKS FOR STUDENTS

Hall, Robert E., and Alvin Rabushka, *The Flat Tax,* Hoover Institution Press. Explains the concept of a uniform tax.

Lubov, Andrea, *Taxes and Government Spending,* Lerner. Explains the economics of government in a way that is accessible to students.

Walston, Mark, *The Department of the Treasury,* Chelsea House. Chronological study of the nation's attempts to raise revenue, establish credit, and develop policies to suit changing needs, from its early history to the present.

MULTIMEDIA RESOURCES

The Budget Crunch (VHS, c, 60 min.), PBS. Hypothetical case study of gridlock in the federal budget process.

Slicing the Pie: A Federal Budget Game (simulation), CU. Students role-play members of Congress, committee chairs, and lobbyists as they try to draft specific components of the federal budget.

Taxes Behind Closed Doors (VHS, c, 60 min.), IU. Provides a look at the behind-

the-scenes maneuvering involved in writing major tax-reform legislation.

THE INTERNET

Have students use these search words to find more information about chapter topics on the Internet: *taxes, government bonds, Social Security, Internal Revenue Service, federal budget, national debt.*

 GLOBAL SKILL BUILDER

You might wish to use **Navigating the Internet** from the interactive *Global Skill Builder* CD-ROM to aid students' understanding of the Internet as a resource.

Abbreviations: b&w=black and white; c=color; f=film; fs=filmstrip; sd=sound; tr=transparency; VHS=videotape

AMERICAN GOVERNMENT

★ **Funding Government** Students will learn reasons for the high cost of government. Students will be taught the purpose of taxes, the principles of fair taxation, and the basic kinds of taxes paid by U.S. citizens. Students also will learn the citizen's role in paying the costs of government and how the government manages the public revenue.

CIVICS SKILLS

Students will learn how to interpret information presented in a pie graph. Students also will learn terms important to understanding how the government collects, spends, and manages money.

CITIZENSHIP VALUES

★ **Funding Government** Students will be encouraged to consider the high costs of government and to appreciate the many services provided by citizens' taxes. Students also will be encouraged to recognize a citizen's responsibility to watch over government expenditures.

LIMITED ENGLISH PROFICIENCY (LEP)

Have pairs of students list the kinds of taxes discussed in Section 2 of this chapter. Have the students use dictionaries to look up the words of each tax name. For example, students should find the definitions of *individual* and *income* for the term *individual income tax*. Have the students create charts with dictionary definitions or sketches of the terms in one column and textbook descriptions of each tax in a second column.

LEARNERS HAVING DIFFICULTY

Have students play a vocabulary game using all the different kinds of taxes discussed in Section 2. Assign each type of tax to a pair of students. Have other students take turns asking each pair descriptive questions about their tax. They might ask, for example, "Is it a regressive tax?" A recorder might keep track of questions and answers on the chalkboard. When all the taxes have been guessed, use the material on the chalkboard to review them.

AUDITORY LEARNERS

Invite an accountant or other tax-preparation expert to speak to students about the federal income tax. The speaker might focus on aspects of paying taxes and filling out income tax forms that would be most helpful to young wage earners. Students would benefit from analyzing the form ahead of time so that they can ask the speaker pertinent questions.

VISUAL LEARNERS

Assign each student one or more of the charts and maps in Chapter 12. Have them study these visual guides and write a summary of the content of each one. Then call on volunteers to lead discussions of each of the charts and maps.

TACTILE/KINESTHETIC LEARNERS

Invite students to present short skits in which each student plays the role of a different taxpayer. One student might play the owner of a small business, another a farmer, another a corporation executive, another a miner, and so on. Have each student describe the taxes he or she pays and the concerns he or she has.

GIFTED LEARNERS

Have students research attempts to eliminate or shrink the federal budget since the 1970s. Then have each student create an outline that addresses the following questions: What methods were used to pare the deficit—tax hikes, spending cuts or freezes, or others? How successful have these efforts been? What were the general public reactions to methods employed to cut the deficit? Call on volunteers to present their findings to the class.

CHAPTER OVERVIEW

Chapter 12 examines how federal, state, and local governments raise and spend money for the services they provide. It also explores why the costs of government have risen dramatically in recent years. The underlying theme of the chapter is that U.S. citizens have a dual responsibility to pay their taxes and to oversee how the government spends these funds.

Motivator

Call on volunteers to suggest the names of almost any building, product, or service. Then have other students provide the source of funding for each item. For example, students might say a car is paid for by a consumer or a school is built and paid for by government. Then ask: How does each of these sources get the money to pay for these items? In particular, focus on the source of revenue for governments. *(taxes and fees)*

CHAPTER OBJECTIVES

After studying Chapter 12, students should be able to do the following.

1. Explain how the government raises money.
2. Identify the different kinds of taxes.
3. Describe how the government manages its money.
4. Explain the reasons for the national debt.

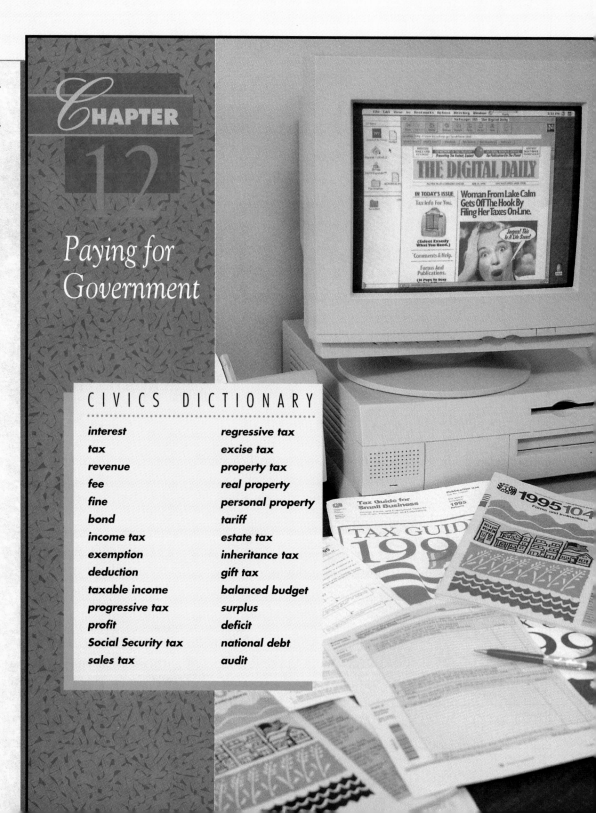

CHAPTER 12

Paying for Government

CIVICS DICTIONARY

interest	regressive tax
tax	excise tax
revenue	property tax
fee	real property
fine	personal property
bond	tariff
income tax	estate tax
exemption	inheritance tax
deduction	gift tax
taxable income	balanced budget
progressive tax	surplus
profit	deficit
Social Security tax	national debt
sales tax	audit

After studying Section 1, students should be able to do the following.

1. Identify reasons for the high cost of government.

2. Explain how government priorities affect government spending.

3. Identify the purposes and the principles of taxation.

4. Explain how governments raise money and why they borrow money.

Ask: What is the difference between a **tax** and a **fee**? *(tax: payment to support government; fee: a charge for a service)* Then ask what **revenue** refers to. *(income)* Have students try to identify the term's origin. *(Latin or French word meaning "come back" or "return")* Tell students that revenue is usually a return on an investment, but most government revenue comes in as taxes, fees, or **fines**.

CHAPTER FOCUS

Try to imagine a stack of $1,000 bills that reaches 100 miles (1,609 km) into the sky. This is the amount of money that the federal government spends each year—around $1.5 trillion. State and local governments spend many more billions of dollars. From where does all this money come? It comes from the American people. We must all pay for the costs of government.

Because the costs of government are paid with public funds, it is important to understand how the government raises and spends money. Making sure that the government manages money wisely is a serious responsibility that faces all citizens, including you.

● ●

STUDY GUIDE

● How does the government raise money?

● What are the different kinds of taxes?

● How does the government manage money, and why is there a national debt?

Raising Money

Each year the local, state, and federal governments spend huge amounts of money. Local governments, for example, provide the American people with police and firefighters. Public health programs and schools are paid for largely by local governments. They also provide paved streets, sewers, trash removal, parks, playgrounds, and many other services.

State governments provide highways and state police. They provide help to public schools and to people who have lost their jobs. State governments also provide funds to people who cannot afford food and housing.

The federal government provides for the nation's defense. It helps business, labor, and agriculture. It provides agencies to protect the public's health, helps in highway construction, and serves its citizens in hundreds of other ways. All these services cost money.

The High Cost of Government

It costs an enormous amount of money today to run the government. One reason why it costs so much is that the United States serves a larger population than ever before—about 261 million people. In addition, the government engages in many more programs and activities than in the past. Furthermore, the cost of living continues to rise. Today's dollar will not buy as much as in earlier years.

The largest cost to the federal government, however, is in benefit payments to individuals—people who are retired, elderly, disabled, or needy. The number of people who receive these benefit payments has been growing steadily over the years and will continue to rise as the population ages.

A large amount of money also is spent by the government on national defense. Although the amount of money spent in this area will gradually decrease over the next few years, defense will continue to account for a large portion of government spending.

Another reason for the high cost of government is the national debt (which you will read more about later in this chapter). Over the years the government has spent more money than it has raised. To make up the difference, the government has had to borrow money. Paying the interest on this national debt costs a great deal of money each year. **Interest** is the payment made for the use of the money. It is

CIVICS SIDELIGHT

Californians began a wave of "taxpayer revolts" in 1978 when they approved Proposition 13, which cut property taxes 57 percent. "Prop 13," an initiative amending the California Constitution, significantly reduced the funds available to public schools and local governments. By 1980, 38 states had followed California's lead and reduced or stabilized their tax rates.

Explaining Ideas

Discuss the reasons for the high cost of government: rising population, shrinking dollar, growth in services and benefits, national defense, and servicing the national debt. Then have students write short paragraphs explaining how each of these factors has contributed to higher government costs. Invite volunteers to share their paragraphs with the rest of the class.

COOPERATIVE LEARNING

Have small groups of students create collages prioritizing and illustrating various areas of government spending. Each group member should be responsible for illustrating at least one example. Groups should place their images on the collages in order from top to bottom according to their priorities. Groups should present their collages to the class and explain why they prioritized the spending areas as they did.

An overhead transparency of "Why the Costs of the Federal Government Have Increased" is available in *Teaching Transparencies with Teacher's Notes.*

Taxes have not always been paid in money. For example, some governments have taxed agricultural production by requiring farmers to turn over a portion of their grain to the government. Certain commodities were used to pay taxes in the Confederacy during the U.S. Civil War, for example. In early frontier communities in the United States, some citizens paid their taxes by working to construct roads, schools, and other community facilities. You might ask students if they can think of other ways, besides with money, people today could pay taxes. What purposes would be served by paying taxes in such ways?

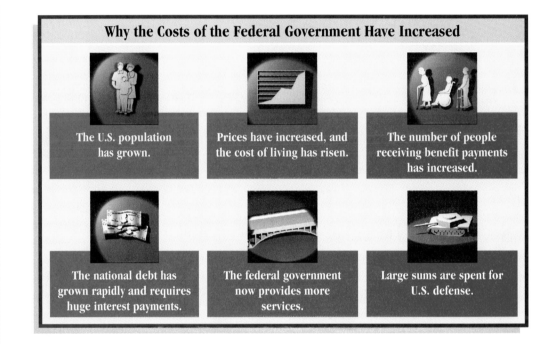

Why the Costs of the Federal Government Have Increased

The U.S. population has grown.

Prices have increased, and the cost of living has risen.

The number of people receiving benefit payments has increased.

The national debt has grown rapidly and requires huge interest payments.

The federal government now provides more services.

Large sums are spent for U.S. defense.

generally a certain percentage of the amount of money borrowed.

Establishing Priorities

All levels of government—federal, state, and local—raise most of the money to pay for services and programs by collecting taxes. A **tax** is a payment of money that citizens and businesses must make to help pay the costs of government. A tax is compulsory. That is, citizens must pay it whether they want to or not.

Many Americans complain about the high cost of government. It is understandable that they do so. All citizens have the right to expect that the government will spend their—the taxpayers'—money wisely.

In recent years taxpayers have questioned the need for many government programs and criticized wasteful spending practices. Taxpayer revolts across the nation have forced governments to reduce spending. In a number of states and local communities, taxpayers have voted to place limits on the amount they can be taxed.

Government officials, therefore, face difficult decisions. What government programs most need money? What programs will bring the greatest benefits to the most people?

Government officials first must list those activities that need money. These are listed in order of their urgency and need. This is called establishing priorities. Programs at the top of the list have high priority. Programs lower on the list have lower priority. Government officials spend funds for those programs high on the list. Programs of very low priority may not be funded. In recent years there has been much debate over the nation's priorities.

The Purpose of Taxes

The chief purpose of taxes is to raise money, or **revenue**. This revenue pays the costs of government. Another purpose of taxes is to regulate, or control, some activities.

Demonstrating Ideas

Have students say which principle of taxation is followed or broken in hypothetical situations that you suggest. For example, you might suggest that workers in Ohio and Iowa with the same level of income also pay the same federal income tax rate. Students should say this is correct because taxes must be applied equally to all persons regardless of where they live. Have students use these examples to create a poster showing the principles of the U.S. tax system.

Guided Practice

Help students create a fictional budget for their school government. First, list on the chalkboard the ways government raises money. Then call on volunteers to suggest how the student government might raise money and for what purposes. After a discussion of why and how the federal government borrows money, have a panel discussion on whether and how student government should be allowed to borrow money to cover its budget.

Taxes on imports, for example, are sometimes fixed at a high level. Their aim is not to raise large sums of money but to discourage imports and to encourage business activity in the United States. High taxes on cigarettes and alcoholic beverages, meanwhile, are partly intended to discourage their use.

Principles of Taxation

Governments try to follow certain rules, or principles, when they set up taxes. These rules aim to make taxes as fair as possible for all citizens. What are these principles of taxation?

Ability to Pay Taxes should not be so high that they are difficult for people to pay. To make it possible for all citizens to pay, taxes on the money people earn should be lower for those citizens with low incomes and higher for those with high incomes. Other taxes, such as taxes on items people buy, are at a fixed rate for all citizens within a given area. These taxes should be set at a reasonable level that all can pay.

Equal Application A local tax on property, for example, should be the same for all property worth the same amount of money. Taxes collected on the goods we buy should be the same for everyone purchasing these goods.

Easy Payment People want to pay their taxes quickly and easily. Therefore, a large part of some taxes is taken out of workers' paychecks before they receive their checks. These taxes are withheld by employers, who send the tax money directly to the government.

Convenient Collection Suppose that all taxes had to be paid at the time of the Christmas holidays when many people have extra bills to pay. Most Americans would find paying taxes then particularly difficult. Instead, governments collect taxes at a time when it is easier for citizens to pay them. The federal government also makes it easier for citizens to pay certain taxes by collecting part of

the total tax quarterly rather than requiring the entire tax all at once.

Other Methods of Raising Revenue

Governments also raise money through fees, fines, and payments for special services. **Fees**, or small payments, are charged for various licenses such as hunting licenses and marriage licenses. State governments raise large sums of money from fees paid for drivers' licenses and automobile license plates. The federal government recently was engaged in a controversial effort to raise the fees paid by western ranchers to graze their livestock on federal lands.

Money charged as a penalty for breaking certain laws is a **fine**. Local governments in particular raise revenue by charging fines for actions such as illegal parking, speeding, and other traffic violations.

Governments provide special services that are paid for directly by those who use these

"Only two things are certain," goes an old saying, "death and taxes." In recent years, though, Americans have been protesting that taxes are too high.

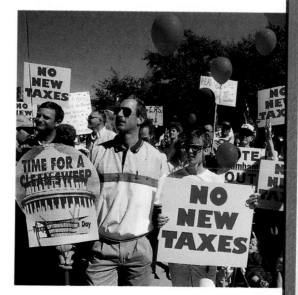

CIVICS SIDELIGHT

One controversial new source of government revenue is asset forfeiture. In 1984 law-enforcement agencies began seizing not just drug dealers but also their assets—boats, cars, planes, even houses. They can then resell the property to help pay for the tools, weapons, and personnel needed to fight the war on drugs. Between 1985 and 1994, the U.S. Justice Department's Assets Forfeiture Fund collected more than $3.5 billion worth of forfeited assets, $486 million of it in 1994 alone. In 1985 Congress allowed the proceeds from these asset seizures to be shared with state and local law enforcement agencies. In 1994 state and local law enforcement agencies received a combined figure of $220 million from the Assets Forfeiture Fund. Almost any property alleged to have a connection with a person's illegal drug-related activities might be seized, even if the person is not convicted of a crime. For this reason, some critics have condemned the practice as unconstitutional.

Closure

Have students draw a picture or a political cartoon characterizing how government obtains revenue or spends money. Students might want to illustrate one aspect of government funding or spending. Some students might want to portray government funding and spending in their cartoons. Encourage students to be creative. Students should be prepared to explain how their cartoons depict government funding, spending, or both. Display students' cartoons for the class.

Reviewing

Have students complete the Section 1 Review.

Reteaching

Assign Section 1 of the Chapter 12 Reteaching Worksheet.

Not many local governments have on hand the millions of dollars needed to build a school like this one. Instead, they must borrow the money, often by issuing school bonds.

services. For example, the federal government sells timber from national forest reserves and electricity from certain federal dam projects. Those who receive this timber or electric power must pay for this service. State governments collect payments from drivers who use certain toll roads and bridges. Local governments sometimes install parking meters to collect payments from those who park their cars on the street.

Government Borrowing

Although governments raise most of their funds through taxes and other forms of revenue, their needs are sometimes so great that they must borrow money. In recent years the federal government has tried to reduce the amount of money that it spends. It still spends much more money each year than it takes in, however. As a result, the federal government is in debt for more than $4.9 trillion.

On state and local levels, a large project, such as a school or a bridge, costs so much to build that it usually cannot be paid for fully out of the government's income in any single year. State and local governments, therefore, must borrow from citizens the additional money needed.

Governments borrow money by issuing bonds. A government **bond** is a certificate stating that the government has borrowed a certain sum of money from the owner of the bond. The government promises to repay the full amount of the loan on a certain date and to pay interest on the amount borrowed.

After studying Section 2, students should be able to do the following.

1. Explain what the individual income tax is based on and how citizens pay it.

2. Contrast sales and excise taxes and contrast estate and inheritance taxes.

3. Compare corporate and individual income taxes.

4. Describe how real property is taxed.

5. Explain how tariffs can protect U.S. industry.

Teaching Section 2
Building a Vocabulary

Ask students what the verb *progress* means. *(move forward)* Break the word into the Latin *pro (forward)* and *gradi (go)*. Do the same for *regress (go backward)*. Then tell students that a **progressive tax** rate rises or "goes forward" as income level rises. Have students deduce the meaning of the term *regressive tax*. You might have students sketch visual representations of the meanings of these terms.

SECTION 1 REVIEW

1. Define or identify the following terms: interest, tax, revenue, fee, fine, bond.

2. What are six reasons for the high cost of government?

3. How do government priorities affect government spending?

4. What are the purposes of taxes? What are the four principles of taxation?

5. How do governments raise money? Why do governments borrow money?

6. **THINKING CRITICALLY** You are a local government official who sets spending priorities. List the government services that should have the highest priority, and why. How will the government fund these services?

2 — Types of Taxes

As you have learned, taxes are the main source of revenue for the federal, state, and local governments. All levels of government depend on many types of taxes to raise the large sums of money they need.

Individual Income Taxes

The largest source of revenue for the federal government is **income taxes**, or taxes on the income that individuals and companies earn. An individual's income taxes are not based on that person's total income. Instead, they are based on the amount of income left over after certain amounts have been subtracted from that person's total income.

How Much Do We Pay? All taxpayers are allowed to deduct, or subtract, a certain amount of money for themselves and for each dependent, or each person they support in their family. These amounts are called **exemptions**. The amount of the exemption depends on the rate of inflation. If prices increase, the amount of the exemption also increases. In 1995 the exemption was $2,500.

Taxpayers also are allowed to deduct certain expenses. These amounts are **deductions**. For example, taxpayers can deduct charitable contributions, most business expenses, and the interest paid on home mortgages.

The amount of income left after all subtractions are made from the total income is

CIVICS SIDELIGHT

Income taxes were not always the largest source of revenue for the federal government. In fact, the first income taxes were not levied until the Civil War. The initial tax rate was 3 percent on incomes of more than $800 for U.S. residents. This income tax was repealed in 1872. Efforts in the 1890s by several progressive organizations, including the Populist party, the Greenback party, the Grange, the National Farmers' Alliance, and the Knights of Labor, led to a second federal income tax law in 1894, but the Supreme Court declared it unconstitutional a year after its enactment. Finally, in 1913 the Sixteenth Amendment permitted Congress to pass an income tax.

How the Federal Government Spends Its Money

Sources of Income	Expenditures
Individual income taxes	Benefit payments to individuals
Social Security taxes	National defense
Corporate income taxes	Interest on debt
Excise taxes	Veteran's benefits
Import taxes (tariffs)	Health and education
Borrowing (public debt)	Transportation and commerce
Estate taxes	Grants to states and local areas
Gift taxes	Foreign relations
	Science, space, and technology
	Energy and the environment

The Federal Government

Demonstrating Ideas

Make photocopies of a paycheck stub (with all identifiable personal information blotted out) and distribute the copies to students. Call on volunteers to identify the section on the pay stub that lists the amounts of money withheld for taxes, particularly income taxes. Have students discuss the advantages of having a small portion of one's salary withheld for taxes with each paycheck. *(keeps taxpayer from having to come up with all necessary taxes at one time)*

Gathering Information

Call on volunteers to create three charts on the chalkboard to contrast the following pairs of taxes: individual income tax and corporate income tax; sales tax and excise tax; estate tax and inheritance tax. Each tax's name should be a column heading. Comparative details and definitions for each tax should be listed underneath the appropriate headings. Students should copy the three charts in their notebooks for use in reviewing the section.

GLOBAL PERSPECTIVES

Compared with citizens of many other democracies, U.S. taxpayers pay less in taxes on a per capita basis. In 1992 U.S. tax revenues (national and local) amounted to $6,757 per person. In many other democratic countries, taxes per capita are higher. In Sweden, for example, tax revenues in 1992 were $14,234 per person. Other high averages were $13,498 in Denmark, $12,278 in Norway, and $11,175 in Switzerland. At $8,694, the per capita average for Japan was still higher than the U.S. average. Taxes per capita were slightly lower in the United Kingdom and even more so in Australia and New Zealand.

called **taxable income**. This is the amount on which individual income tax is paid.

The individual income tax is a progressive tax. A **progressive tax** is a type of tax that takes a larger percentage of income from higher-income groups than from low-income groups. Thus it is based on ability to pay. As a person's taxable income increases to a certain level, the tax rate that is applied to that income increases to a higher level as well.

The amount of income taxes that people pay changes. Congress changes tax rates when it wants to help the economy. It also does so to encourage saving, to encourage or discourage some kinds of spending, or to improve the system of taxation.

How Do We Pay? U.S. taxpayers must fill out and mail their tax forms on or before April 15 each year. Some taxpayers take advantage of electronic filing systems.

Most taxpayers do not pay all their income tax at the time they file tax returns. Income tax payments have already been taken out of each paycheck by their employers, who forward the tax money to the government. This system of making small tax payments each payday makes it easier for Americans to pay their individual income taxes.

Filling out the tax forms shows taxpayers how much they owe in taxes for the previous year. Sometimes people learn they will receive a refund, or get back some of the tax money withheld by their employers during the year. Sometimes people find they owe the government more money.

State and Local Taxes All but a few of the state governments and some city governments also collect an individual income tax. Each of these states and cities has its own income tax laws and sets its own tax rates.

Some states use the amount of federal income tax a person pays to determine the amount of state income tax he or she will pay. For example, a person might pay 5 percent of what he or she owes in federal income tax to the state government. Most states, however, create their own tax rates that are not based on federal income tax. Like state income tax rates, city income tax rates are much lower than those for the federal income tax.

This paycheck stub shows the deductions that employers take from workers' paychecks for taxes. Employers send this tax money to the government directly.

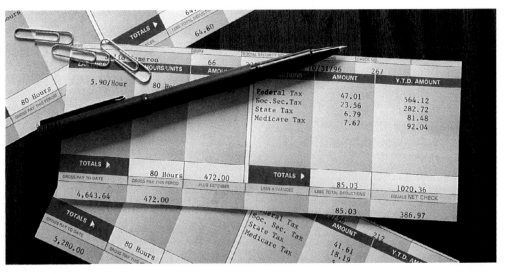

Drawing a Political Cartoon

Have students draw political cartoons to portray the collection of public money for one level of government. Because such activities are often portrayed negatively, you might ask some students to portray positive aspects of how each level of government accomplishes the task. Display the cartoons for the class.

settle disputes over the collection and spending of public money.

Preparing the Federal Budget

In the federal government the president recommends how public funds are to be raised and how they are to be spent. The job of planning the federal budget is so large and so complicated that the president needs the help of several government agencies.

One of the chief agencies involved in helping the president prepare the federal budget is the Office of Management and Budget (OMB). This important agency studies the nation's economy. It then forecasts the amount of tax income the government will receive in the coming year.

Each of the executive departments makes a careful estimate of how much money it plans to spend the following year. All these estimates are submitted to the president. The president and the director of the OMB study the many requests and establish priorities for the various items. Some requests may be cut to bring the total expenditures closer to estimated revenues.

After the budget is prepared each year, it is published in book form. This huge budget book contains hundreds of pages, listing thousands of separate items.

Congress and the Budget

The president sends the finished federal budget to Congress. Along with the budget, the president sends a message explaining the budget and urging that it be passed. Often the president addresses a joint session of Congress to seek support for the federal budget.

Congress makes its own study of the proposed budget. As you recall, only Congress has the power to raise and spend money. The House of Representatives and the Senate debate the various items in the budget and make changes. Both houses of Congress must approve the final version of the federal budget.

This scene is a common one each year as April 15 approaches. It is time to take out bills, receipts, and bank statements and fill out an income tax form.

The revised budget is then sent back to the president to be approved or vetoed.

The process of preparing the federal budget takes many months. There is much heated debate before the final budget is approved. When finally completed, the federal budget becomes the law under which public money will be spent during the coming year.

The National Debt

When a government has a **balanced budget**, its revenue equals its expenditures. That is, the amount of money it collects equals the amount of money it spends. Sometimes, however, a government budget is not balanced. When a government collects more money than it spends, it has a **surplus**, or an excess of money. When a government spends more money than it collects, it has a **deficit**, or a shortage of money.

Guided Practice

Call on volunteers to start a chart by listing on the chalkboard financial mismanagement safeguards for federal, state, and local governments. Then have students suggest similar safeguards against financial mismanagement for your school's student government. After you have finished the chart, have students debate whether they believe running budget deficits is mismanagement of money.

Independent Practice

Invite each student to imagine he or she is a member of Congress who has been invited to appear on a national news show to discuss a bill he or she has introduced. The bill will eliminate the national debt over a period of 10 years. Have students write the dialogue for the interview. They should cover the following topics: the amount of the national debt, how it got so large, why it is a problem, and why it is important to pass legislation eliminating it.

CIVICS TRANSPARENCIES

An overhead transparency of "The National Debt" is available in *Teaching Transparencies with Teacher's Notes.*

CIVICS SIDELIGHT

The national debt, it must be remembered, is really the *public* debt. All Americans are responsible for it. In fact, if every man, woman, and child in the United States in 1994 had been willing and able to pay $17,806 to the government, the national debt would have vanished. On the eve of the Civil War, the public debt on a per capita basis had been brought down to $2.06 since the beginning of the nineteenth century, when it was nearly $16 a head. Government spending during the Great Depression and World War II dramatically increased the public debt. In 1960 everyone owed $1,572. Deficit spending, in part to finance defense and increasingly expensive government social programs, greatly increased the national debt over the next decades.

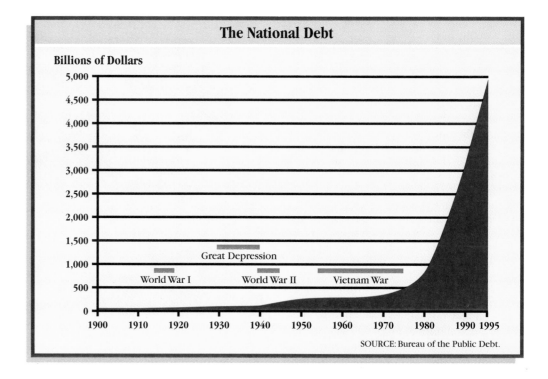

The National Debt

Billions of Dollars

SOURCE: Bureau of the Public Debt.

For decades, the government of the United States has operated at a deficit each year. That is, the federal government has spent more money than it has collected in revenue. To make up this difference, the federal government each year has had to borrow increasing amounts of money. The total amount of money owed by the U.S. government, plus the interest that must be paid on this borrowed money, makes up the **national debt**, which has soared to an astonishing $4.9 trillion.

The chart on this page shows how the national debt has grown over time. The enormous growth in this debt has been one of the most controversial public issues in recent years. Many people charge that the government's practice of operating under a budget deficit is harmful to the nation.

For example, part of the money collected in revenue each year must be used to pay the interest on the national debt. This portion cannot be used to fund programs and services for the people. Also, the interest on the debt is so high that future generations will be repaying the money that is borrowed now. The future taxes needed to pay interest on the debt may seriously strain the economy.

In addition, the government borrows much of the money it needs to make up for the deficit by issuing government bonds. Increasingly, these bonds are being bought by foreign investors. Thus increased amounts of public tax dollars are going overseas to pay interest on these debts.

There is no constitutional limit on the size of the national debt. Congress establishes a limit above which the debt cannot go, but it periodically raises this limit as the need for more money arises. To help control federal spending, Congress in 1996 voted to give the president the line-item veto. This power would allow the president to veto specific

Closure

Have students create pamphlets encouraging citizens to take seriously their responsibility to make sure public money is managed well and spent wisely. The pamphlets should include ways citizens can exert influence on the management of public money (such as through voting). Encourage students to be creative, using graphics, cartoons, or other visuals. Each student should title his or her pamphlet.

Reviewing

Have students complete the Section 3 Review.

Reteaching

Assign Section 3 of the Chapter 12 Reteaching Worksheet.

---

parts of a spending bill without vetoing the entire bill. The constitutionality of the presidential line-item veto, however, is expected to be challenged in the courts.

Public Money Is a Public Trust

To ensure that public funds are spent according to law, all levels of government provide for an **audit** of their accounts. An audit is a careful examination by trained accountants of every item of income and expenditure.

A department of the state government usually audits expenditures of local governments. Auditors from the state Department of Education or an independent auditing firm examine expenditures of local school districts. In state governments an independent agency of the state under the comptroller's direction usually conducts state audits. The General Accounting Office examines federal expenditures.

Citizen Responsibility

The well-being of the nation depends on how wisely our governments handle public funds. If wise policies of raising and spending money are to be followed, citizens must take an active part in understanding taxes, the use of public funds, and the national debt. They must make their voices heard on these issues.

SECTION 3 REVIEW

1. Define or identify the following terms: balanced budget, surplus, deficit, national debt, audit.

2. How do the three levels of government collect public money?

3. How is the federal budget prepared?

4. Identify safeguards used to prevent mismanagement of public funds.

5. Why does the federal government have such a large debt?

6. Why do many people believe that the large national debt is harmful to the nation?

7. **THINKING CRITICALLY** There are two ways that the federal government can reduce the budget deficit. One way is to increase revenue. The other way is to reduce spending. First, consider the advantages and disadvantages of each of these options. Then write a letter to the president with your recommendations for reducing the federal budget deficit. Be sure to tell the president why you think your recommendations will be effective.

CHAPTER 12 SUMMARY

Government costs a great deal of money. This money must be provided by citizens—each of us shares the costs of government. Over the years the costs of running the government have increased greatly.

Government raises revenue through taxes, fees, fines, special payments, and borrowing. There are many kinds of taxes. Americans pay taxes on individual incomes, property, purchases, imported goods, corporate profits, gasoline, and many other items. Federal, state, and local governments all collect a share of these taxes.

Various agencies collect this money and ensure that it is spent properly. The executive branches of the governments work closely with the legislative branches to plan revenue collection and spending.

Governments also borrow large sums to help pay their expenses. Federal borrowing has created a large national debt, a problem that concerns all Americans. As taxpayers, we must make sure our money is used wisely.

SECTION 3 REVIEW ANSWERS

1. See the following pages: balanced budget, surplus, deficit (p. 233); national debt (p. 234); audit (p. 235).

2. federal—IRS and Customs Service; state and local—own tax collection agencies

3. OMB studies economy, forecasts amount of revenue government will collect next year; executive departments estimate money needs, submit estimates to president; president and OMB set priorities, draw up budget; budget published; sent to Congress for approval

4. U.S. treasurer, comptroller, auditors

5. Government has borrowed huge amounts of money to make up for budget deficits.

6. Interest payments take money away from needed programs and services; debt will burden future generations and the economy; tax dollars sent overseas to service debt.

7. Students should consider the consequences of raising revenues and cutting spending.

Suggest to students that they can use a pie graph to represent nearly anything that is composed of various elements. For example, the contents of a refrigerator might be broken down by percentage into meats, vegetables, drinks, and so on. Tell students that, as with all graphs, it is the visual representation that makes the pie graph helpful. In complex areas such as budgeting, people can see at a glance where their money is going.

As an extending exercise, invite students to keep track of their spending for a week. Have them determine a category for each sum spent, and show the categories as different-sized sections of a pie graph.

GLOBAL SKILL BUILDER

You might wish to use **Reading Graphs** and **Presenting Data Graphically** from the interactive *Global Skill Builder* CD-ROM to reinforce students' understanding of pie graphs (circle graphs) and other types of graphs.

ANSWERS TO Applying the Skill

1. payments to individuals; other federal expenses

2. 16 percent

3. Students should conclude that the highest government priorities are payments to individuals, spending for defense, and paying interest on the national debt.

4. One advantage is that pie graphs condense large amounts of information into one easy-to-read diagram. They also enable a comparison of the whole and its parts. One disadvantage is that only one total can be shown at a time. Thus they cannot show changes over time.

Developing Civics Skills

SOCIAL STUDIES SKILL
Reading Pie Graphs

The federal government collects more than $1 trillion in revenue each year. It uses the money to pay for the hundreds of federal programs and services it provides for American citizens. Because the government handles so much money, it can be difficult to visualize how the huge government budget operates. Where does all of this money go each year?

One effective way to visualize this information is to use a pie graph. Like other graphs, pie graphs summarize large amounts of information in easy-to-read diagrams.

Every pie graph equals 100 percent of something. The pie graph on this page, for example, represents 100 percent of the federal government's expenses for one year. Each slice of the pie represents a part of those expenses. Because national defense accounts for 16 percent of the government's expenses, 16 percent of the pie, or circle—almost one sixth—is colored to represent this expenditure.

How to Read Pie Graphs

1. **Determine the subject.** Read the title of the graph to determine its subject and purpose.
2. **Study the labels.** The graph's labels indicate the main categories, or "slices," into which the circle has been divided.
3. **Analyze the data.** Compare the sizes of the various sections of the graph. The size of each section is determined by the percentage of the total it represents. The larger the section in the graph, the greater the percentage of the total that section represents.
4. **Put the data to use.** Use the data to draw conclusions about the subject of the graph.

Applying the Skill

Study the pie graph below. Then answer the following questions.

1. What is the federal government's largest expense? How much of the budget is spent on grants to states and localities?
2. What percentage of the federal budget is devoted to interest payments?
3. What conclusions can you draw about government spending priorities?
4. What are the advantages and disadvantages of using a pie graph?

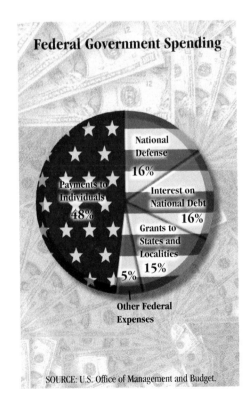

Federal Government Spending

National Defense 16%

Interest on National Debt 16%

Payments to Individuals 48%

Grants to States and Localities 15%

5%

Other Federal Expenses

SOURCE: U.S. Office of Management and Budget.

CHAPTER 12 REVIEW
A N S W E R S

Vocabulary Workshop
1. interest
2. revenue
3. corporate income tax
4. fine
5. progressive—takes higher percentage of income from high-income groups; regressive—takes higher percentage of income from low-income groups
6. revenues equal expenditures

Reviewing Main Ideas
1. high-priority programs funded before low-priority programs; population growth, more government services, rising cost of living, growth in benefit payments, higher defense spending, interest on national debt
2. president with OMB help; Congress
3. advantage—protects U.S. businesses by making imported goods as expensive as, or more expensive than, U.S. goods; disadvantage—makes goods more expensive in U.S.
4. U.S. treasurer, comptroller, auditors
5. to pay expenses not covered by other revenue; issue bonds
6. surplus—income greater than expenditures; deficit—expenditures greater; debt—interest payments take money from needed programs; burdens future generations; servicing debt requires sending tax dollars overseas

Thinking Critically
1. Some people believe actions to eliminate the deficit might hurt the economy.
2. Students might say releasing such information would violate one's privacy.
3. Citizens expect government to use their tax money wisely.

Citizenship in Your Community
Posters should illustrate local projects and services.

Building Your Portfolio
Assign Portfolio Assessment Worksheet 12 in the *Portfolio Assessment Worksheets* booklet.

Assessment
- **Chapter 12 Tests**, *Chapter Tests* booklet
- **Test Generator**, Chapter 12
- **Portfolio**, Portfolio Assessment Worksheet 12, *Portfolio Assessment Worksheets* booklet

CHAPTER 12

R·e·v·i·e·w

Vocabulary Workshop
1. What term refers to the payment made for the use of money?
2. What is government income called?
3. Which tax is based on the profits made by corporations?
4. What may a citizen have to pay as a penalty for breaking a law?
5. What is the difference between a progressive tax and a regressive tax?
6. Define the term *balanced budget*.

Reviewing Main Ideas
1. What is the relationship between government spending and government priorities? Identify six reasons for the high cost of government.
2. Who prepares the federal budget? Who must approve it?
3. What are the advantages and disadvantages of protective tariffs?
4. How is the public protected against the mismanagement of public funds?
5. Why must governments borrow money? How do they borrow money?
6. What is the difference between a surplus and a deficit? How might the national debt be harmful to the nation?

Thinking Critically
1. In recent years some federal officials and members of the public have sought a constitutional amendment to require a balanced federal budget each year. Congress and some economists, however, have strongly resisted such an action. Why do you think this is so?
2. The Internal Revenue Service (IRS) has more financial information on citizens than any other organization in the nation. How might this present the potential for abuse of citizens' rights?
3. What do you think the phrase "public money is a public trust" means?

Citizenship in Your Community

Cooperative Project
With your group, research taxing and spending in your community. Interview local officials about the taxes, fees, and fines paid by citizens. How does your local government set priorities and decide how to spend local revenue? Are citizens allowed to participate in this process? Create a poster showing the community projects and services that are paid for by public money. In a caption explain how they are funded.

Building Your Portfolio

The third step of your unit portfolio (see page 239) is to conduct research to learn what financial rules apply to Student Council elections in your school. Are there rules concerning the sources of campaign funds? How do Student Council candidates spend their campaign money? Then ask to see the Student Council budget for the past five years. How does the Student Council raise money? How are decisions made about how the money will be spent? Summarize your findings in a flowchart that shows how and where campaign funds flow in a campaign. Include captions that explain each step and any restrictions concerning the raising and use of the funds. Place your flowchart in your individual portfolio for later use.

Reviewing Main Ideas

1. to influence the ideas, opinions, and behavior of individuals; testimonial, bandwagon, name-calling, glittering generalities, plain-folks appeal, card stacking
2. provide practical way for large numbers of people with similar ideas to accomplish things, help people make their voices heard, nominate candidates for office, take positions on issues, try to ensure office-holders do good jobs, check conduct of opposing parties; primary—voters choose party's nominee(s) for office; general—all voters choose from among parties' nominees for office
3. to raise money and to regulate certain activities; progressive—takes higher percentage of income from high-income groups; regressive—takes higher percentage of income from low-income groups
4. provides alternative for voters; one party has sufficient strength to run government
5. means through which citizens can most directly affect actions of government; lets citizens select those who will lead and represent them
6. should be based on ability to pay, should be applied equally, should be easy to pay, should be collected at convenient times; make foreign goods as expensive as, or more expensive than, U.S. goods

Thinking Critically

1. Answers will vary. Students should use sound reasoning in their responses.
2. Students might say citizens might be hesitant to vote if others knew their preferences.
3. Students should recognize that everyone receives the benefits of democratic government, so everyone should help pay the costs.

Practicing Civics Skills

1. Answers should reflect the voter registration form used in your state.
2. Bar graphs should accurately reflect poll results.
3. Conclusions on taxing and spending should be based on the information presented in the graphs.

4 UNIT · R · e · v · i · e · w

Reviewing Main Ideas

1. Why do people use propaganda? Identify six propaganda techniques.
2. What are the functions of political parties in the United States? How do primary elections differ from general elections?
3. What are the purposes of taxes? What is the difference between a progressive tax and a regressive tax?
4. What are the advantages of a two-party political system?
5. Why is it important to vote?
6. What are the four rules of taxation? How do tariffs protect U.S. industry?

Thinking Critically

1. Candidates sometimes make campaign promises that they fail to keep. Do you think that these candidates mislead voters, or do the realities of political office sometimes make it difficult to keep promises? Explain your answer.
2. How would the election process in the United States be different today if there were no secret ballot?
3. Some Americans "cheat" on their taxes. Others refuse to pay their taxes at all. Why it is important that all Americans pay their fair share of taxes?

Practicing Civics Skills

1. Contact the election office in your community and request a copy of a voter registration form. Does the form include a space to enroll in a political party? Which information is optional? In what language(s) is the form printed?
2. Conduct a poll of students in your school about a school policy or a political event in your community. Be sure to survey a representative sample of students. Present your poll results in a bar graph.
3. Create pie graphs that illustrate the revenue and expenditures of your local government. One graph should show revenue. The other should show expenditures. What conclusions can you draw about taxing and spending in your community?

Individual Project

Contact voter organizations in your local community to learn about voter registration drives. When are these drives held? How effective are the drives? How can volunteers help? Create a poster advertising a community voter registration drive. Be sure your poster answers the questions *who, what, when, where,* and *why.*

Electronic Newspapers

Electronic newspapers are being developed to allow subscribers to receive news via their computers. Electronic newspaper subscribers will be able to choose whether to view advertisements at the bottom of the electronic page. To view the ads—complete with sound, music, and action—subscribers touch the ads' symbols. To encourage people to view the ads, advertisers may offer cents-off coupons, free tickets to events, and other incentives.

How might such a technology be used in political campaigns? Would you be more or less likely to vote for politicians who offer you an incentive to view their political commercials? Explain your answer.

Citizenship in Your Community

Posters should focus on the five questions: *who, what, when, where,* and *why.*

Learning from Technology

Some students might argue that a desire to be an informed voter should be sufficient incentive to view political commercials.

Building Your Portfolio

Students have been working on a Building Your Portfolio project throughout Unit 4. You might ask volunteers to present their work to the class. Have all of the students add their work to their individual portfolios. Assign the Unit 4 Portfolio Assessment Worksheet in the *Portfolio Assessment Worksheets* booklet.

Building Your Portfolio

Individually or in a group, complete the following project to show your understanding of the civics concepts involved.

Campaigning for Office

The superintendent of public schools has asked you to make a presentation to a group of students from schools in your state. The group is made up of students who are considering running for Student Council president in their schools. The title of your presentation will be "How to Run an Effective Election Campaign." Your presentation should consist of both written and visual materials. To prepare your presentation, you will need to do the following.

1. Choose a U.S. president that you admire, and research that person's presidential campaign. What people were important to the campaign's success? How did volunteers help the campaign? How did the president raise campaign contributions? What kind of relationship did the president have with the media? Organize your findings in an illustrated time line entitled, "The Election Campaign of President _____." Below your time line explain why this campaign was successful.

2. Conduct a poll in which you ask a representative sample of students in your school to identify the problems and issues facing students today. Show the results in a bar graph that indicates what percentage of poll respondents identified each issue or problem as a concern. Use your poll results to create a list of campaign goals that will address students' concerns.

3. Conduct research to learn what financial rules apply to Student Council elections in your school. Are there rules concerning the sources of campaign funds? How do Student Council candidates spend their campaign money? Then ask to see the Student Council budget for the past five years. How does the Student Council raise money? How are decisions made about how the money will be spent? Summarize your findings in a flowchart that shows how and where campaign funds flow in a campaign. Include captions that explain each step and any restrictions concerning the raising and use of the funds.

Organize your materials, and make your presentation to the prospective Student Council candidates (the rest of the class).

Using the Quotation

Have students read the quotation and find pictures in this unit that show people working together. Ask: What does volunteering have to do with the idea of citizenship? *(Students might review the qualities of a good citizen on pages 5–6.)* Invite students to share their own experiences with volunteering.

About the Author

Charlotte Lunsford–Berry (1931–   ) served as National Chairperson of Volunteers for the American Red Cross from 1986 to 1989. She was re-elected to a second three-year term on the Board of Governors of the National Red Cross in 1993. Lunsford–Berry, a graduate of Mary Baldwin College in Staunton, Virginia, and a resident of Columbia, South Carolina, has served in a wide variety of roles for the Red Cross since the early 1970s. She also has served on numerous boards, including the Mary Baldwin College Board of Trustees.

"Volunteerism still combines the best and most powerful values in our society—pride in the dignity of work, the opportunity to get involved in things that affect us, the freedom of choice and expression, the chance to put into practice an ethic of caring, and the realization that one person can make a difference."

Charlotte J. Lunsford

FORMER NATIONAL CHAIRPERSON OF VOLUNTEERS FOR THE AMERICAN RED CROSS

Expressing Ideas

Divide the class into two groups. Each student in one group should take the role of a parent in a one-parent family, and each student in the other group should take the role of a parent in a blended family. Students should write journal entries describing their fictional families, detailing the stresses and advantages family members have. Encourage volunteers to turn their journal entries into one-person skits or monologues. Have these volunteers present their dramas to the class.

Closure

Have students create diagrams (such as flowcharts or time lines) that trace the changing American family from colonial times to today. Students should write short descriptions of these changes under each entry in their diagrams. Have students save their diagrams for use as review and study guides.

---

scientists who study the family are interested in the ways in which the family continues to change. They have noted a number of trends in recent years. Among these trends are delayed marriage, two-earner marriages, one-parent families, and remarriage.

Delayed Marriage The average age at which people marry has risen steadily for several decades. In 1960, for example, the average age at first marriage for women was 20.3 years. The average age for men was 22.8. By 1994 the average age at first marriage had risen to 24.5 for women and 26.7 for men.

According to social scientists, there are several reasons for **delayed marriage**, or marrying at an older age. First, there is a growing acceptance of singlehood as a way of life. Second, young people are delaying marriage to finish their educations and start their careers. This is particularly true for women. Third, there is a large increase in the number of couples who live together without being married. Although most people who live with someone eventually get married, living together contributes to delayed marriage.

In addition to delaying marriage, couples are delaying having children. In the past, married women usually had their first baby when they were in their 20s. Today many women have their first child after the age of 30. Couples who delay childbearing usually wait until they are established in their careers.

Two-Earner Families In the past, husbands usually provided the sole income in the family. In recent years, however, the number of **two-earner families**, or families in which both partners work, has increased. This increase is due to the large number of married women who work outside the home. The percentage of women who work outside the home has risen steadily since about 1940. In 1940 about one in seven married women was in the workforce. Today more than 60 percent of married women work outside the home.

Married women work for the same reason that married men work—economic necessity.

GLOBAL CONNECTIONS

The One-Child Family in China

American families today are smaller than families of the past. For a number of reasons, Americans are choosing to have fewer children. In contrast, in China married couples have little choice about the size of their families. For more than a decade, the government in China has tried to limit family size to one child per family.

In 1981 China's population reached one billion. Knowing that this rapid population growth would interfere with plans for economic modernization, Chinese officials began a campaign to halt this growth.

In China today billboards proclaim the superiority of the one-child family. The government also uses educational programs and intense peer pressure to convince couples to have only one child. The strongest incentive, however, is economic. Couples who sign a pledge promising to have only one child receive payments for food, free health care and schooling for the child, and access to better jobs and housing. Couples who sign the pledge but then have a second child must repay all the benefits they have received.

Also, as more women pursue higher education, more of them want to put their skills to use in the workforce. Large numbers of women are finding success in fields once considered the domain of men—fields such as business, engineering, medicine, and law. It is also more

GLOBAL PERSPECTIVES

Statistics for 1994 showed that nearly 59 percent of all women in the United States over the age of 15 were in the workforce. This figure compares with 61 percent in Russia and 51 percent in Japan. Some cultures, however, still do not encourage women to work outside the home. In Argentina, for example, only 29 percent of women officially have entered the workforce. In the Islamic Republic of Iran, the figure is just 9 percent. Statistics, however, can be misleading. In Bangladesh, for example, an estimated 90 percent of women are involved in producing food. In Africa most of the agricultural work is done by women.

Reviewing

Have students complete the Section 1 Review.

Reteaching

Assign Section 1 of the Chapter 13 Reteaching Worksheet.

After studying Section 2, students should be able to do the following.

1. Explain why many states have a waiting period before issuing marriage licenses.

2. Explain the purpose of a blood test as a requirement for obtaining a marriage license.

3. Explain how state laws protect children.

4. Suggest reasons for the high divorce rate in the United States.

SECTION 1 REVIEW ANSWERS

1. See the following pages: delayed marriage, two-earner family (p. 245); one-parent family, remarriage, blended family (p. 246).

2. City families had to earn money to buy what they had once produced themselves on the farms.

3. a growing acceptance of singlehood, delay of marriage to finish education and start careers, large increase in number of people living together without being married; more married women working outside the home

4. more likely to be poor, single parents must handle responsibilities alone; blended—formed when one or both partners in a marriage bring children from previous marriage into the new marriage

5. Letters will vary but should mention economic and social changes a family likely would experience.

246

---

acceptable now than in the past for married women to work outside the home.

Along with the increase in the number of working women has been an increase in the amount of time that husbands devote to child care and household tasks. Although women still assume the major responsibility for these tasks, more men than ever before are sharing this responsibility with their wives. Social scientists find that men who share household tasks and child care with their wives tend to be younger and have more education than men who do not share such tasks.

One-Parent Families   Another trend noted in recent years is a large increase in the number of one-parent families. **One-parent families** are formed through divorce, widowhood, adoption by unmarried people, and births to unmarried women.

Most one-parent families in the United States are the result of divorce. About 26 percent of American families with children under the age of 18 are one-parent families.

Although every family has difficulties, the one-parent family is subject to added stresses. For example, one-parent families are more likely than two-parent families to be poor. In fact, more than half of all one-parent, female-headed families live in poverty. Also, parents in one-parent families must handle the responsibilities shared in two-parent families.

Remarriages   Although the United States has one of the highest divorce rates in the world, Americans continue to believe strongly in marriage and the family. More than 40 percent of the marriages taking place today are **remarriages**. This means that one or both of the partners have been married before.

In remarriage one or both of the partners often bring children from previous marriages into the new marriage. These new families are called **blended families**, or stepfamilies.

The people who become part of a stepfamily often must undergo a period of adjustment. For the marital partners this means taking on roles formerly occupied by biological parents.

For stepchildren this period of adjustment means learning to share a parent's attention with new stepbrothers and stepsisters.

Adjusting to life in a stepfamily sometimes brings conflict. It is important for all members of the new family to remember that they are undergoing a period of transition and to communicate openly and honestly with one another. To build a strong family unit, all members must have patience, understanding, and a willingness to cooperate.

SECTION 1 REVIEW

1. Define or identify the following terms: delayed marriage, two-earner family, one-parent family, remarriage, blended family.

2. How did the move to cities change the American family from a unit of producers to a unit of consumers?

3. Why has the average age at marriage risen in recent decades? What has led to the increase in two-earner families?

4. What special stresses face one-parent families? How are blended families formed?

5. **THINKING CRITICALLY**   Imagine that you are living in the early 1900s and that your family has just sold its farm and moved to the city. Write a letter to a friend back home explaining how life in the city differs from life on the farm.

2   Law and the Family

As you have learned, there are many different kinds of families in the United States today. Ways of life within these family units are affected by a number of factors.

Ask: How does state law legally protect children? *(State law protects children against improper care and against **child abuse**.)* Then ask: What if parents harm a child? *(Parents might be prosecuted; child might go to a **foster home**.)* A court might appoint a **guardian** for a child. Explain that *guardian* is related to an Old French word meaning "to guard" or "to defend." Ask students what it means to **adopt** someone. Explain that *adopt* comes from a Latin word meaning "to choose."

Have small groups of students design a marriage license. All students should contribute to the process of brainstorming what information will be called for on the license and how it will look. Assign one student to record why each item is included. You might wish to have students show, on the back of the license, the rights of the marriage partners as guaranteed by law. Obtain a copy of a real marriage license from your local government to compare with licenses created by the students.

For example, family life may differ depending on whether you live in a big city, a suburb, or a small town. Your family life may be affected by your ethnic, cultural, and religious background. Each ethnic, cultural, and religious group has its own rich heritage and traditions that it brings to family life. Family life also may be affected by factors such as income and age at marriage.

Although life within the family may vary, all families are subject to certain laws. These laws are designed to benefit everyone.

Marriage Laws

Because the family is so important, many laws have been passed to protect it. These laws have been passed by state legislatures because it is the state governments that have the power to regulate family law. **Family law** regulates marriage, divorce, and the duties of parents and children in the family.

The more than two million marriages that take place each year must meet the laws of the state in which they are performed. State laws, for example, have established the earliest age at which people may marry.

Most states require people to be at least 18 to marry without parental consent. In many states boys and girls may marry at age 16 with the consent of their parents. In a few states the couple also needs the consent of the court. Some states allow people to marry at even younger ages.

About half the states require a waiting period of one to five days from the time a couple applies for a marriage license until the license is issued. This waiting period is intended to discourage hasty marriages by allowing couples to "think it over."

Most states also require that a young man and woman applying for a marriage license take a blood test to show that they are in good health. This examination checks for diseases that can be passed on to another person.

All states require that marriages be performed by civil officials such as a justice of the peace, judge, or mayor, or by religious officials such as a minister, priest, or rabbi. Witnesses must be present at the ceremony to testify that a legal marriage was performed.

Protecting Family Members

When the marriage ceremony is completed, the newly married couple is considered a family unit. The husband and wife now have certain rights guaranteed by law. If the rights of the husband or wife are neglected, the courts may be asked to intervene, or take action.

Most cases of nonsupport, physical abuse, desertion, and other marital problems are tried in a family relations court. Before a case comes to trial, the court, lawyers, and social workers usually will recommend that the couple consult a marriage counselor to try to work out its problems.

Children, too, have certain legal rights as members of a family. If a child is not given proper care by the parents, the law can step in to protect the child. Every state requires doctors and other people to report instances of **child abuse**. Children who are mentally, physically, or sexually abused may be taken from their parents by the state.

These children may be placed in **foster homes**—homes of people who are unrelated to the children but who agree to act as their parents. The state pays the foster parents to care for the children. Parents who abuse their children may also have criminal charges filed against them. Sometimes parents who cannot take care of a child may ask the state to place the child in a foster home for a while.

If a child's parents die, a judge may appoint a relative or close family friend to act as a guardian for the child. A **guardian** is a person appointed by a state court to care for an individual who is not an adult or who is unable to care for himself or herself for some reason.

Sometimes the guardian will **adopt**, or legally establish, the child as his or her own. If no relative or family friend can be found to act as a guardian, the state may put the child up for adoption.

(continued on page 250)

Adoptive parents have always had to deal with the fact that their adopted child has another set of parents. Today that fact has become an issue at the center of the adoption process in the United States. Traditionally, the courts have severed all connections between the adopted child and the birth family. The adoption records were sealed. Now the trend is toward greater openness in the adoption process. Some state legislatures have given adult adoptees the right to look at their original birth records. Critics of the sealed-record system base their arguments on the importance of the biological link between child and birth parents. Supporters of the older system argue that the adoption system will fall apart unless the privacy of the birth parents—and of the new adoptive family—is secured.

Summarizing

Rewrite the freedom of religion clause of the First Amendment on the chalkboard as two separate headings: "Congress shall make no law respecting an establishment of religion" and "Congress shall make no law prohibiting the free exercise of religion." Have students place each Supreme Court case discussed here under the proper heading, write details of the case, and explain why it exemplifies a First Amendment right.

CIVICS SIDELIGHT

One year before the *Schempp* case was decided by the Supreme Court, the nation's highest court heard the case of *Engel v. Vitale.* This 1962 case was brought by a student and his parents in New Hyde Park, New York, against members of the local school board. Students in New Hyde Park were required to start each school day by reciting a prayer that had been written by the New York Board of Regents. The suit against the New Hyde Park school board argued that this requirement violated the separation of church and state. The Court agreed. Justice Hugo Black, speaking for the majority, said that "establishing governmentally composed prayers for religious services was one of the reasons which caused many of our early colonists to leave England and seek religious freedom in America."

Case Study

THE FREEDOM OF RELIGION

The United States has always been a haven of religious freedom. Many of the people who have settled in the United States came to this country to escape religious persecution in their own countries.

Even today, people come to the United States because it offers them the freedom to worship as they choose. This freedom to worship is guaranteed by the First Amendment to the U.S. Constitution.

The freedom to worship as we choose has always been one of the foundations on which our nation is based. This freedom is guaranteed to Americans under the First Amendment to the Constitution.

Religion in the United States

The First Amendment states that "Congress shall make no law respecting an establishment of religion, or prohibiting the free exercise thereof." Although these 16 words sound simple, they guarantee Americans many things. This amendment guarantees the separation of church and state. In other words, Congress may not establish a national religion and may not support one religion over another.

The First Amendment also gives Americans the freedom to belong to any religion they choose. There are now hundreds of religious groups in the United States, all free to worship as they wish. (The largest of these groups are shown in the chart on the next page.) Americans also may choose not to join a religious group or practice a religion.

Many cases concerning the interpretation of this First Amendment right have been brought before the U.S. Supreme Court. Two of the most interesting cases involve high school students taking action.

"A Position of Neutrality"

In 1962 Ellory Schempp was a senior at a public high school in Abington, Pennsylvania. Each day before school announcements were read over the loudspeaker, the principal of Schempp's school read aloud a passage directly from the Bible without comment. Schempp, however, was a member of a church that objects to reading the Bible without interpretation. He thought it was wrong for the principal to read religious material that violated his faith, so he complained about the Bible readings to school district officials.

Linking Civics and History

Have small groups of students research, write, and present a report about a historic case having to do with religious freedom. Cases might include the banishment of Roger Williams from Massachusetts in the 1600s or the Supreme Court cases of *Everson v. Board of Education, United States v. Seeger, Lynch v. Donnelly,* and *Wallace v. Jaffree.* Each group should illustrate its report with flowcharts or other diagrams that show the history of the case.

When the school district refused to halt the Bible readings, Schempp and his family sued. In 1963 the case went before the Supreme Court. The justices ruled that Bible readings in the public schools are a violation of the First Amendment. "In the relationship between man and religion," Justice Tom C. Clark wrote for the Court, "the State is firmly committed to a position of neutrality."

A Student's Request

Like Schempp, Bridget Mergens was a senior in a public high school when she started on a course that would lead all the way to the Supreme Court.

In 1985 Mergens asked the principal of her Omaha, Nebraska, school if she and her friends could meet after school to discuss the Bible. The principal refused her request, maintaining that to allow a Bible group to meet on school grounds would violate the separation of church and state.

Mergens argued that it was wrong to compare voluntary student clubs with enforced religious activities. The school board disagreed, however, and in 1990 the case reached the Supreme Court.

The Court ruled that religious clubs may meet on public school grounds as long as they are not sponsored by the school. According to the Supreme Court, schools that allow extracurricular activities cannot discriminate against student groups on religious, political, or philosophical grounds.

The Debate Continues

The place of religion in the public schools has been the subject of long and intense debate. Some people believe that schools should encourage religion and prayer. In fact some political candidates in recent elections have campaigned to place prayer or "moments of silence" back in school. Others maintain that the separation of church and state is a fundamental constitutional guarantee that prohibits prayer in school. The debate continues.

| Religious Groups in the United States* ||
Group	Total Members
Roman Catholic	59,858,042
Baptist	36,433,503
Methodist	13,563,129
Pentecostal	10,019,235
Lutheran	8,352,892
Islam	5,500,000
Latter-Day Saints	4,672,850
Jewish	4,300,000
Presbyterian	4,273,721
Eastern Orthodox	3,506,666
Episcopal	2,504,682
Reformed	2,079,634
Churches of Christ	1,651,103
Christian Churches and Churches of Christ	1,070,616
Christian Church (Disciples of Christ)	958,017
Jehovah's Witnesses	926,614
Hindu	910,000
Adventist	794,684
Church of the Nazarene	591,134
Community Churches	500,000
Salvation Army	446,403
Christian and Missionary Alliance	302,414
Churches of God	263,140
Mennonite	259,620
Buddhist Churches of America	230,000
Evangelical Free Church of America	226,391

*Groups of 200,000 or more.

SOURCE: *World Almanac and Book of Facts, 1996.*

YOU DECIDE

1 Why did Ellory Schempp sue his school district?

2 How did the Court rule in the Mergens case?

3 Should public school teachers lead students in prayer? Why or why not?

ANSWERS TO YOU DECIDE

1. He believed that the reading of the Bible over the school loudspeaker violated his religious beliefs.

2. Religious clubs may meet on school grounds as long as they are not sponsored by the school.

3. Answers will vary. Students who think teachers should lead students in prayer might say that religion is an integral part of American life. Students opposed might say that such practices violate the principle of separation of church and state.

Closure

Begin an outline on the chalkboard by writing the four main headings from this section on laws concerning marriage, protection of family members, separation, and divorce. Have volunteers help finish the outline on the board by describing the laws under each heading. Students should copy the outline in their notebooks for use as a review guide.

Reviewing

Have students complete the Section 2 Review.

Reteaching

Assign Section 2 of the Chapter 13 Reteaching Worksheet.

SECTION 2 REVIEW
A N S W E R S

1. See the following pages: family law, child abuse, foster home, guardian, adopt (p. 247); divorce, no-fault divorce (p. 250).

2. intended to discourage hasty marriages; to check for diseases that might be passed on to others

3. allow children to be placed in foster homes or with guardians when they have been abused or orphaned or when parents are unable to support them

4. division of property, child custody, visitation rights, spouse and child support payments

5. Divorce has become a less complicated and less expensive process. As more women work outside the home, they are less likely to stay in unhappy marriages for financial reasons. Society generally has become more tolerant of divorce.

6. Students should sufficiently explain why they believe their proposals would be effective.

As this photograph shows, most family relationships are loving and caring. When problems develop, though, state laws protect family members.

Divorce Laws

The final, legal ending of a marriage is called **divorce**. Each state makes its own laws concerning divorce. Some states make it difficult to obtain a divorce by limiting the causes for which divorces are granted. Some grounds for divorce in these states are desertion, mental or physical cruelty, felony conviction, drug addiction, and adultery.

Beginning in the 1970s with California, many states began offering **no-fault divorce**. Under this system, people seeking divorce do not have to charge their partners with grounds such as those mentioned above. Instead, couples simply must state that their marriages have problems that cannot be resolved.

All couples who divorce must make decisions, often through their lawyers, about the division of property, custody of children, visitation rights, and spouse support and child support payments. These decisions are reviewed by a judge. If the judge finds that the decisions are fair, the divorce agreement is approved. If the couple cannot agree on these issues, the judge will decide.

The United States has one of the highest divorce rates in the world. More than one million marriages in this country end in divorce each year, affecting more than one million children annually.

Social scientists who study the family note several reasons for the high divorce rate in the United States. First, the divorce process has become less complicated over the past few decades, and the cost of getting a divorce is much lower. Second, as more women work outside the home, they are less likely to stay in unhappy marriages for financial reasons. Third, society generally has become more tolerant and accepting of divorce.

Some Americans believe that the best way to reduce the number of divorces is to pass stricter marriage laws. Others believe that more preparation for marriage would result in better family life and fewer divorces. Many high schools and colleges now offer courses in marriage and the family to help young people understand the realities of marriage.

Laws designed to protect marriage partners and their children and to keep families together, however, sometimes do not succeed. The best way to achieve a happy and productive family life is to encourage family members to share and work together for the good of the family.

SECTION 2 REVIEW

1. Define or identify the following terms: family law, child abuse, foster home, guardian, adopt, divorce, no-fault divorce.

2. Why do many states have a waiting period before issuing marriage licenses? What is the purpose of a blood test?

3. How do state laws work to protect children?

250

After studying Section 3, students should be able to do the following.

1. Describe five important functions of the family.
2. Explain the importance of respecting the rights of other family members and the importance of compromising.
3. Explain how having a budget helps a family.

Teaching Section 3
Building a Vocabulary

Tell students to think about the items that might appear in a family budget. Ask: What kinds of items would appear month after month, with little or no change? *(items such as rent or mortgage, utilities, and insurance)* Have students suggest expenses they must regularly pay each month. *(Examples might include lunch money, club dues, and gas money.)* Tell students that these are examples of **fixed expenses**. Invite students to explain the use of the word *fixed* in this context. *(regular, relatively unchanging)*

---

4. What types of decisions must be made by couples who are planning to divorce?

5. What reasons do social scientists give for the high U.S. divorce rate?

6. **THINKING CRITICALLY** You head a national committee whose purpose is to suggest ways to reduce the high U.S. divorce rate. List three of your suggestions and explain why you believe they will be effective.

3 Your Family and You

The family continues to be the most important group in American society. It is the foundation on which the nation is built. Regardless of whether a family is large or small, rich or poor, it performs many important functions for its members and for the nation.

The Family Serves the Nation

There are more than 68 million families in the United States. We depend on these families to teach their children many of the responsibilities they will face as adults. What are some of the family's chief functions as it teaches these responsibilities?

Ensuring the Nation's Future A country is only as strong as its people. The family helps keep the nation strong when it provides a home in which children are raised as securely and happily as possible. In this way families shape the nation's future.

Educating its Members Children learn many things from their families. It is in the home that children learn to walk, talk, and dress themselves. The family also teaches children to get along with others and to share in household work.

Teaching Good Behavior The child's earliest ideas of right and wrong are taught in the home. Within the family, children learn how to behave.

Helping Manage Money The family earns and spends money to provide food, clothing, and a place to live for its members. The family should encourage children to learn to manage money, to save, and to share financial responsibilities.

Teaching Good Citizenship The family has the responsibility of helping children learn to respect the rights of others and to understand what their responsibilities are as good citizens.

Good Citizenship at Home

A home is more than just four walls, a roof, floors, windows, and doors. When most Americans think of home, they picture a special place where the family lives together in safety, comfort, and affection. The word *home* means the familiar place that members of the same family share.

The ideal home is loving and secure. Of course, no family can live up to the ideal all the time. Any group of people living together will disagree at times and need to find ways to solve their differences.

Using common sense and considering other people's points of view help prevent serious conflict. Remember that each member of the family is a person worthy of respect. Each person has rights. If people feel that their rights are respected, they are more likely to respect the rights of others.

Members of a family should take a sincere interest in one another's activities. They should take every opportunity to discuss the events of the day and to share their thoughts. Sharing problems and events of interest teaches family members to give and receive praise, advice, support, and criticism.

CIVICS SIDELIGHT

New parents living in extended families in the 1800s learned child-rearing skills from their parents and grandparents. Today many new parents rely on other sources of information, from advice columns in newspapers and magazines to books written by popular experts. Dr. Benjamin Spock's books on child care, for example, had a great influence on the upbringing of a whole generation of children—the post–World War II baby boomers.

Writing an Editorial

Assign each student one of the five chief functions of a family (page 251). Have students write editorials proclaiming the importance of the assigned functions. They might include comments about how some families are failing to meet those goals or illustrations of exemplary families. Invite at least one student to read aloud an editorial about each of the five functions.

COOPERATIVE LEARNING

Have small groups of students create fictional household budgets. Assign each group a monthly income for its household. Each group should illustrate on posters the different kinds of expenses its family has. Then each group member should suggest specific dollar amounts for at least one of the items in the budget. Students will need to use newspapers (classified ads for rental prices and store ads for grocery prices, for example) and other periodicals to determine realistic costs. Have a representative from each group present its household budget to the class.

CIVICS SIDELIGHT

The percentage of their income that Americans spend on housing has been rising steadily over the years. In 1993, for example, U.S. homeowners with mortgages spent a median of $799 per month, or 22 percent of their income, on housing costs. In 1975, Americans with mortgages spent only 18 percent of their income on housing costs. Among Americans who rented rather than owned their housing units, housing costs averaged 29 percent of income in 1993. In 1975, renters spent approximately 23 percent of their income on housing.

Although housing costs have been on the rise, Americans now are living better than ever before. For example, the percentage of U.S. houses that have central air conditioning increased from 17 percent in 1973 to 44 percent in 1993. Over the same period, the percentage of houses that have more than one bathroom increased from 31 percent to 53 percent, and three or more bedrooms, from 50 percent to 56 percent.

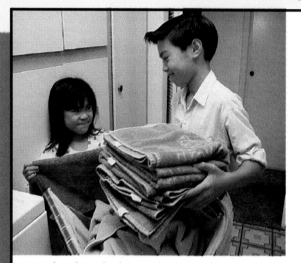

The relationship between brothers and sisters can be a rewarding experience. Both can learn patience, kindness, cooperation, and caring.

Solving Conflicts

Family members often can benefit from disagreements. Arguments, if kept in hand, can teach you how to present your ideas effectively and help you understand the other person's point of view.

Conflicts can occur between parents, between parents and children, or among the children in a family. These disagreements require members of the family to make compromises—to give a little and take a little. One of the signs of a well-adjusted family is that members of the family work together to find solutions to the minor problems of everyday living before they develop into crises.

By talking over ideas with members of your family, you learn to be understanding and patient. These traits are important in getting along with other people—friends, classmates, teachers, neighbors, and, later, coworkers.

Managing Family Funds

One issue all families face is how to spend the family's money. Adults try to earn enough money to pay for all the things the family needs and wants. They are concerned about feeding, clothing, and providing shelter for the family. The children in the family want money for school lunches, transportation, supplies for hobbies, movie and concert tickets, and many other things that seem important at the time.

When there are only so many dollars to divide among the various members of the family and each person cannot have everything that he or she wants, compromises must be worked out. Doing your share in handling family funds will help you learn about spending and saving money. Learning to manage money now will be a valuable skill to you as an adult.

Many families operate on some kind of a budget. The very thought of a budget discourages some people. When they think of a budget, they imagine a complicated bookkeeping system with column after column of figures. They also believe it usually means "pinching pennies" and having fewer good times.

In reality, though, a budget should not discourage anyone. It is simply a plan for spending the family's income. In fact, if a budget is carefully planned and faithfully followed, it can help reduce a family's worries about money matters.

Each family must decide how to budget its money. Financial advisers may make suggestions and explain ways to handle money. A family's own special interests and needs, however, require that the family make the final decisions about its spending plan.

The first step is to gather facts and make a plan based on these facts. The starting point in all budgets is the total amount of money available to spend. Most families have a fixed amount of income. They must keep their spending within this income.

First on a family's budget are certain **fixed expenses**. These are expenses that occur regularly and must be paid. There may be rent on an apartment or mortgage payments on a house. There is also the cost of food and regular payments such as insurance and telephone bills. The remaining money pays for clothing, medical expenses, entertainment, and other items. Families also try to set some money aside for savings.

Have students bring in articles from newspapers and other periodicals about issues facing families today. Call on volunteers to summarize these articles for the class. Students should look for articles about efforts to strengthen families in society and about specific financial and social problems families face. Organize a panel discussion on the most important issues facing families today.

Reviewing

Have students complete the Section 3 Review.

Reteaching

Assign Section 3 of the Chapter 13 Reteaching Worksheet.

Preparing for the Future

You can help your family follow its budget plan. One important way to do this is to help prevent waste in your home. In addition, try not to ask for things outside your family's budget. Talk to your parents or guardian before you agree to activities that cost money. Do not insist on doing things or buying things your family cannot afford.

If you receive an allowance or earn money on your own, draw up your own budget. Decide how much money you need for transportation, lunches, and other fixed expenses. Then, if you can, set aside some money for future expenses or emergencies.

Remember, too, that your home is the best place in which to learn about home management. Handling money is just one of the skills you will need for the future. By learning to get along with your family, you are preparing yourself for the day when you manage your own home.

Compare this picture to the one on page 244. It is still necessary and often fun for family members to work together to meet their needs.

SECTION 3 REVIEW

1. Define the following term: fixed expense.

2. What five important functions does the family serve?

3. Why is it important to respect the rights of other family members? Why is it important for family members to compromise?

4. How does having a budget help a family?

5. **THINKING CRITICALLY** Plan a personal budget. First list your weekly expenses. Then list your weekly sources of income. If you have a budget deficit, are you borrowing to pay your expenses? How can you improve your money managing skills? If you have a budget surplus, are you effectively saving this extra money?

CHAPTER 13 SUMMARY

The American family is the foundation on which the nation's future depends. It is the group in which young citizens learn lessons that stay with them for the rest of their lives.

As the nation has changed, so has family life. The United States has changed from a nation of farm families who provided for most of their own needs to a nation of city dwellers who must buy most of the products they need. People are marrying at older ages, and the number of two-earner families, one-parent families, and remarriages has increased. There no longer is a typical American family.

To protect the family, states pass laws regulating marriage, divorce, and the rights of parents and children. The practice of family law has grown as the stresses of modern life have caused family difficulties to increase. Among these problems are divorce and child abuse.

Many solutions have been offered for keeping the family together. There may be no one answer. All those who achieve a happy family life, however, work hard at it. You can help your family by cooperating, making compromises, and staying within the family budget.

SECTION 3 REVIEW
A N S W E R S

1. See the following page: fixed expense (p. 252).

2. ensuring the future of the nation, educating its members, teaching good behavior, helping manage money, teaching good citizenship

3. If people believe their rights are respected, they are more likely to respect the rights of others. Compromise helps people find solutions to their problems because everyone gives up or obtains something.

4. Staying within a budget helps families reduce their money worries.

5. Students should understand that saving is important to good money management.

Have students bring to class guides that list television and cablevision program schedules. Then have students use the guides to identify the many types of programs that provide information on one particular day. For example, students should list the number of programs that provide national news, local news, general interest and investigative features, and information on popular culture (about music and other entertainment, for example). Have students discuss the proportion of news and information programming to general interest programming such as movies, situation comedies, and other television entertainment. Ask: Is television a valuable source of information? How could it be better?

Developing
Civics
Skills

CITIZENSHIP SKILL
Using Television as a Resource

New York, 1929. Engineers focus a camera on a statue of cartoon hero Felix the Cat. In Kansas other engineers see a face flicker on a tiny screen called a viewer. It's Felix—America's first television star.

The Moon, 1969. A camera outside the lunar capsule sends pictures back to Earth. More than 500 million people all over the world hold their breath as astronaut Neil Armstrong steps onto the moon.

In the 40 years between these two events, television became the nation's main source of news and entertainment. Today more than 98 percent of U.S. households have televisions. Because so much of our news comes from television, it is important to watch it with a critical eye.

Most news programs follow definite formats. Once you become familiar with these formats, it will be easier for you to interpret what you see and hear.

How to Use Television as a Resource

1. **Listen for the important events of the day.** Regularly scheduled news programs shown each evening are set up like a newspaper. The opening stories are the headline news, or the most important events of the day.
2. **Distinguish between hard news and features.** Features are human-interest stories meant to amuse and entertain you. Features usually follow the hard news and often appeal more to the emotions than to the intellect.
3. **Watch the close of the program.** News programs usually close with sports and weather reports. Sometimes, though, the last report is a commentary. A commentary is a journalist's personal interpretation of an event.
4. **Recognize types of news programs.** In addition to the evening news, there are other types of news programs. The most popular are newsmagazines and documentaries. A newsmagazine usually studies several issues in one program. A documentary focuses on a single topic for the entire program.

Applying the Skill

Study the television schedule below. Then answer the following questions.

1. In which programs would you expect to find a report on the arrival of a foreign official in the United States?
2. Which program is a newsmagazine? Which programs are documentaries?

7:00 **2** **4** **7** NEWS

9 BEST OF NATIONAL GEOGRAPHIC: "Season of the Cheetah"

8:00 **2** 60 MINUTES: Includes segments about women in combat roles, health care reform and a cross-country bike trip

4 CHARLIE BROWN SPECIAL: "The Great Pumpkin"

7 COLLEGE BASEBALL: California Berkeley at Stanford

9 NATIONAL AUDUBON SOCIETY: "Greed and Wildlife: Poaching in America"

ANSWERS TO Applying the Skill

1. a regularly scheduled news program
2. 60 Minutes; Best of National Geographic and National Audubon Society

CHAPTER 13 REVIEW
A N S W E R S

Vocabulary Workshop
1. delayed marriage
2. person appointed by court to care for person who is not an adult or who is unable to care for self
3. family law
4. foster home
5. rent, mortgage payments, food costs, regular bills such as insurance
6. divorce

Reviewing Main Ideas
1. partner(s) brings children into new marriage
2. City families earn money to buy what they once produced themselves on the farms. City families had to share influence on children with schools and churches.
3. growing acceptance of singlehood, delay of marriage to finish education and start careers, more people living together outside marriage
4. no-fault—does not require people to charge partners with grounds
5. to discourage hasty marriages
6. divorce, widowhood, adoption by unmarried people, births to unmarried women; stresses—more likely to be poor, single parents handle responsibilities alone
7. reduces money worries by making sure family does not spend more than it earns
8. economic necessity, desire to put skills to use in workforce, new fields opened to women, greater acceptability of women working outside the home

Thinking Critically
1. Students should use sound reasoning.
2. Today's programs depict a variety of family forms.

Citizenship in Your Community
Students likely will find a variety of answers from various persons.

Building Your Portfolio
Assign Portfolio Assessment Worksheet 13 in the *Portfolio Assessment Worksheets* booklet.

Assessment
- **Chapter 13 Tests**, *Chapter Tests* booklet
- **Test Generator**, Chapter 13
- **Portfolio**, Portfolio Assessment Worksheet 13, *Portfolio Assessment Worksheets* booklet

---

CHAPTER 13

R · e · v · i · e · w

Vocabulary Workshop
1. What do social scientists call the tendency to marry at older ages?
2. Define the term *guardian*.
3. What regulates marriage, divorce, and the duties of parents and children?
4. What term is used for the home of people who are unrelated to a child but who agree to act as the child's parents?
5. Name four fixed expenses.
6. What term is used to describe the final, legal ending of a marriage?

Reviewing Main Ideas
1. How are blended families formed?
2. How has family life in the United States been affected by the move to the cities?
3. Why has the average age at marriage increased in recent years?
4. How does no-fault divorce differ from the traditional system of divorce?
5. Why do most states have a waiting period for couples applying for a marriage license?
6. How are one-parent families formed? What special stresses do these families face?
7. How can a budget help a family manage its income and spending?
8. What accounts for the increase in the number of married women who work outside the home?

Thinking Critically
1. There has been much discussion in recent years about the need to return to traditional family values. What are these values? Does everyone agree on them?
2. Watch an episode of a family-centered television program from the 1950s and 1960s, such as *Leave It to Beaver* and *Father Knows Best*. Do you think these programs accurately portrayed family life in the 1950s and 1960s? Compare these programs with current programs that focus on family life. Do today's television programs accurately reflect family life in the United States?

Citizenship in Your Community

Cooperative Project

With your group, conduct a poll in your community that asks the question "What do you think is the greatest problem facing families today?" Organize the group so that each member asks this question of a different group of people—police officers, religious leaders, judges, marriage counselors, older citizens, students. Tally the results. Which problems are mentioned most often? least often? How do the various groups differ in their opinions? Share your poll results with the rest of the class.

Building Your Portfolio

The first step of your unit portfolio project (see page 309) is to consider the factors that contribute to good citizenship in families. What obligations do young citizens have toward their families? What characteristics do all family members need to build a strong family? What challenges face the American family? How can young citizens work with their families to meet these challenges? Answer these questions in a speech entitled "Young Citizens Help Strengthen Their Families." Place your speech in your individual portfolio for later use.

CHAPTER 14

Citizenship in School

TEXTBOOK	TEACHING RESOURCES	OTHER AVAILABLE RESOURCES
Chapter	• Skills Worksheet 14 • Challenge/Enrichment Worksheet 14	• Simulations and Case Studies Lessons 14 and 15
Section **1** The U.S. School System Page 257	• Reteaching Worksheet 14.1	• Transparency 19: Local School Districts • Transparency 20: Education and Average Income
2 The Best Education for You Page 262	• Reteaching Worksheet 14.2	
3 Developing Your Life Skills Page 268	• Reteaching Worksheet 14.3	
Review and Assessment Chapter 14 Review, Page 273	• Test, Form A • Test, Form B • Portfolio Assessment Worksheet 14	• *Test Generator,* Chapter 14

Block Scheduling Option

ADDITIONAL RESOURCES

BOOKS FOR TEACHERS

Blumenfeld, Samuel L., *Is Public Education Necessary?* Paradigm (Idaho).

Bunzel, John H., ed., *Challenge to American Schools: The Case for Standards and Values,* Oxford University Press.

Flesch, Rudolph, *Why Johnny Can't Read: And What You Can Do About It,* Harper-Collins.

Gardner, Howard, *Multiple Intelligences,* Basic.

BOOKS FOR STUDENTS

Hentoff, Nat, *American Heroes: In and Out of School,* Delacorte. Examines civil rights issues in schools.

James, Elizabeth, and Carol Barkin, *How to Be School Smart: Secrets of Successful Schoolwork,* Lothrop. Offers informa-tion, and many practical hints, about ar-ranging study areas, managing time, studying, and taking tests.

Metos, Thomas H., *The Human Mind: How We Think and Learn,* Watts. A compre-hensive treatment of the brain and theo-ries of learning.

MULTIMEDIA RESOURCES

Career Direction: High School as Tryout (VHS, c, 47 min.), GA. Demonstrates how students can use their school experi-ences to identify potential careers.

Critical Thinking: How to Evaluate Infor-mation and Draw Conclusions (VHS, c, 42 min.), SSSS. Dramatizations show the everyday applications of thinking skills, from confronting drugs to buying a car.

How to Manage Your Time (VHS, c, 13 min.), GA. Shows students how to keep a record of time spent, decide on priorities, and design a basic weekly schedule.

THE INTERNET

Have students use these search words to lo-cate more information about chapter topics on the Internet: *United States school sys-tem, public school, education, higher education.*

 GLOBAL SKILL BUILDER

You might wish to use **Navigating the Inter-net** from the interactive *Global Skill Builder* CD-ROM to aid students' under-standing of the Internet as a resource.

Abbreviations: b&w=black and white; c=color; f=film; fs=filmstrip; sd=sound; tr=transparency; VHS=videotape

CIVICS SKILLS

Students will learn how to distinguish fact from opinion. Students also will learn terms important to understanding the role of citizenship in education.

CITIZENSHIP VALUES

★ **Structures and Functions** Students will learn the main purposes of education and how the education system developed. Students also will learn about the various levels of education in the United States and the goals of American schools.

★ **Learning Enrichment** Students will learn the traditional values of education in the United States, how people learn, and the importance of critical thinking skills.

★ **Developing Opportunities** Students will be encouraged to take advantage of the opportunities given to each individual by the U.S. system of education and to develop their talents and abilities to their full potential. Students also will be encouraged to give clear thought to all issues rather than to be ruled by prejudice.

MEETING INDIVIDUAL NEEDS

LIMITED ENGLISH PROFICIENCY (LEP)

Have students play "Vocabulary Wheel," a game in which players try to recognize vocabulary terms based on reading clues and guessing the letters in the term. *Materials:* (1) a spinner with an arrow that points to numbers; (2) vocabulary cards with a blank for each letter in the term and one clue to its meaning. *Play:* Have a student select a vocabulary card and copy its number of blank spaces and its clue on the board. Then have the first player spin and guess a letter. (Players "keep" the points represented by the number only if they correctly guess a letter in the term.) Write the correct letter(s) in position. After an incorrect guess, it is the next player's turn. Play continues until one player guesses the term.

LEARNERS HAVING DIFFICULTY

Direct groups of students to the Chapter 14 Summary (page 271). Assign each group one of the paragraphs in the summary. Ask students to copy that paragraph onto a sheet of paper. Then have them find at least three details from the chapter to support the ideas expressed in the paragraph. They should write the details below the paragraph. When students have completed this exercise, have them share their findings with each other.

AUDITORY LEARNERS

Have pairs of students take turns quizzing each other on their knowledge of chapter vocabulary terms. One student should read aloud the definition of each term (using the Glossary on pages 579–589) while the second student identifies the vocabulary term.

VISUAL LEARNERS

Have students design leaflets that summarize and illustrate the American Values in Education cited on pages 261–262 or "The Seven Cardinal Principles of Secondary Education" (pages 263 and 266). The leaflets might be handed out to all students in the school.

TACTILE/KINESTHETIC LEARNERS

Encourage students to find out what school systems in other countries are like by writing to foreign schools or establishing pen-pal relationships with foreign students. Pen-pal organizations often appear in the classified sections of magazines.

GIFTED LEARNERS

Have students research and report on the issue of bilingualism in schools. Specifically, students should address how bilingual education is related to American educational values.

CHAPTER OVERVIEW

Chapter 14 focuses on the U.S. system of education—its purpose, history, goals, and challenges, as well as the opportunities it offers everyone. The underlying theme of the chapter is that the future of the United States depends on having educated citizens who are willing to contribute their talents to the improvement of their community, their state, and their nation.

Motivator

Have students identify as many levels of education and school as they can. *(preschool, elementary school, middle and junior high school, high school, college, graduate school, trade school)* Ask students to discuss what they believe are the underlying purposes of education in general and the various levels of school in particular.

CHAPTER OBJECTIVES

After studying Chapter 14, students should be able to do the following.

1. Explain how the U.S. school system began and describe its form today.
2. Identify the challenges facing schools and what is being done to meet them.
3. Identify the goals that guide schools.
4. Describe how students can work to get the most from their educations.
5. Explain how people develop thinking skills.

SIMULATIONS AND CASE STUDIES

Lesson 14: Case Study Cartoon Strips: *Lamb's Chapel & John Steigerwald v. Center Moriches Union Free School District, et al.*

Lesson 15: The Case of the Coerced Confession: *Arizona v. Fulminante*

Block Scheduling Option

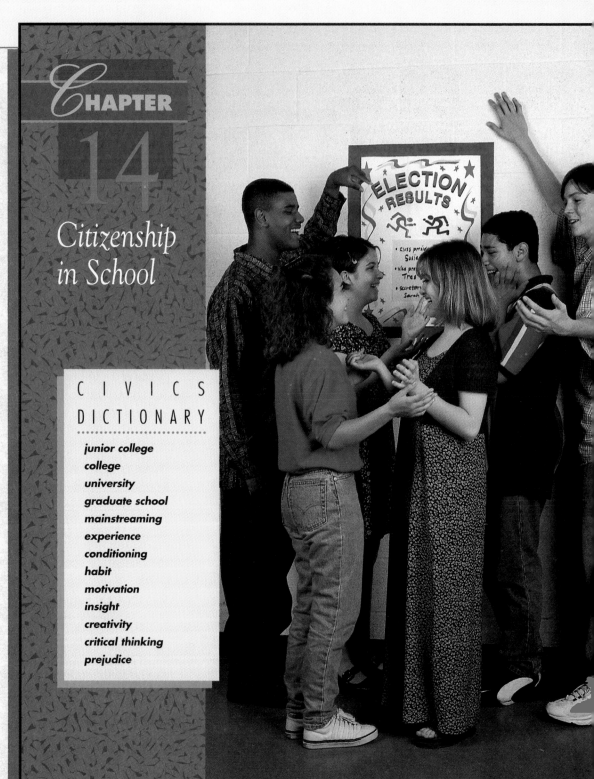

CHAPTER 14

Citizenship in School

CIVICS DICTIONARY

junior college
college
university
graduate school
mainstreaming
experience
conditioning
habit
motivation
insight
creativity
critical thinking
prejudice

SECTION OBJECTIVES

After studying Section 1, students should be able to do the following.

1. Identify the two main purposes of education.

2. Describe the debate in the 1800s over free public schools.

3. Identify the main levels on the educational ladder, and explain the advantages of higher education.

4. Identify challenges facing U.S. schools and how those challenges are being met.

Teaching Section 1
Building a Vocabulary

Ask students to name the various levels of education available after high school. Explain that a **university** may contain one or more **colleges** as well as a **graduate school**, which provides advanced degrees. *University* is derived from a Latin word meaning "entire" or "whole." Ask: What is the function of a **junior college**? (*training for specialized technical fields; often a stepping-stone to a four-year college or university*)

CHAPTER FOCUS

Have you thought about the kind of work you want to do when you become an adult? No matter what future you choose for yourself, you will profit from earning a good education. Not only will you benefit from developing your talents and abilities, the nation will benefit as well.

In this increasingly complex and technologically oriented world, the future of the United States depends on well-educated citizens who can make valuable contributions to the nation's progress. The future depends on you, your dedication, your training, and your hard work.

• •

STUDY GUIDE

● How did the American school system begin, and what is it like today?

● What challenges face American schools, and what is being done to meet these challenges?

● What goals guide schools, and how can you get the most from your education?

● How do we develop thinking skills?

1 The U.S. School System

There are about 63 million students enrolled in public and private schools and colleges in the United States. The cost of running these educational enterprises has risen to nearly $438 billion a year, or almost $7,000 per student. Around seven million teachers, administrators, and staff handle the day-to-day tasks of education in the nation. This vast education system affects every American citizen, young and old alike.

Purposes of Education

Americans place a high value on education for two main reasons.

Development of Individual Citizens From the earliest days of the nation, Americans have placed great value on the individual. One important purpose of education, therefore, is to serve the individual. Americans believe that all citizens should be given the opportunity to study and learn in order to develop their talents and abilities.

The Declaration of Independence sets forth the American belief "that all men are created equal; that they are endowed by their Creator with certain unalienable rights; that among these are life, liberty, and the pursuit of happiness." Over the years, Americans have come to believe that all citizens—men and women of all ethnic groups—should have equal opportunities to succeed through equal access to education.

Development of the Nation The well-being of all Americans depends on the willingness and ability of individuals to use their talents for the welfare of the entire nation. The aim of education is to teach young citizens how to contribute to society through good citizenship. Schools try to show how the well-being of each citizen and the future of the nation depend on all Americans learning to work together for the common good.

Beginnings of the American School System

The American system of education has been growing for more than 300 years. The first

GLOBAL PERSPECTIVES

Napoléon Bonaparte placed a high value on education. He established France's first secondary school system in 1802. In Paris six years later, he opened the world's first teachers' college. Paris had earlier been the site of the first school for the deaf (1760) and the first school for the blind (1784). Years before the French Revolution (1789), these two schools promoted equality of opportunity for individuals with disabilities.

MULTICULTURAL PERSPECTIVES

The United States has a long tradition of providing an education to immigrant children of many ethnic groups. The tradition continues today. In a single year, 1993, more than 65,000 children from 188 countries entered New York City's school system. Across the nation, the number of students whose first language was not English increased 20 percent during the 1990s. The large number of immigrant students and the variety of languages they speak offer a special challenge to the U.S. educational system.

Review with students the two main purposes of education. *(development of individual citizens, development of the nation)* Then ask: Why is individual development crucial to national development, and vice versa? Have students write their answers in the form of an imaginary biographical sketch in which an individual studies, develops an important skill, and contributes to national development, which opens doors to other individuals.

Assign pairs of students one side or the other of the debate over free public schools today. Have each pair expand on the points made in the textbook and conduct further research on the issue if they wish. Students may refer to relevant arguments made in the debates over free public schools in the 19th century. Then have the pairs debate the issue in class. Encourage each pair to use graphics and other visual guides to help them make their arguments.

MULTICULTURAL PERSPECTIVES

In the midst of the Civil War, before the Emancipation Proclamation, the first schools for escaped and freed slaves opened in the South, behind Union lines. Educated white and black men and women came from both the North and the South to teach in these schools. Charlotte Forten, a respected African American teacher in Port Royal, South Carolina, knew that education was an effective tool for ending prejudice and oppression. Forten's goals for her students were noble. She wrote: "I long to inspire them with courage and ambition (of a noble sort) and high purpose." Within a half dozen years after the Civil War, 11 colleges and universities and 61 normal schools (teachers' schools) had been founded for African Americans. Among those first traditionally African American schools are Howard University in Washington, D.C., and Fisk University in Nashville, Tennessee.

Artist Winslow Homer shows what an American country school looked like more than 100 years ago. Students of different ages all studied in the same room.

important step was taken in Massachusetts in 1647 when a law was passed requiring all but the smallest towns in the colony to set up public schools.

The purpose of this law was to make sure all children learned to read the Bible, so that they would not fall into evil ways. This law provided for every town of 50 families or more to hire a schoolteacher, who would be paid by the town. By doing so, Massachusetts shifted the responsibility for schooling from the home to the community.

In many of the other colonies, however, the education of some children was neglected. Although children of the wealthy were sent to private schools or were taught by tutors, children of poor parents often worked at an early age and had little or no schooling.

It was not until the first half of the 1800s that leaders such as Horace Mann began to demand free public schools for all children. The gradually developing public school system helped many children receive an education. The system did not, however, include African Americans. Many of them were slaves, and very few received an education.

Many Americans in those days were opposed to free public schools. Taxpayers did not want to pay to educate other people's children. Owners of private schools argued that free public schools would ruin their businesses. People who ran church-supported schools claimed that education should be under the control of the church and the home.

In contrast, the supporters of public education argued that a democratic society requires citizens who can read and write. By the time of the Civil War, the struggle for public, tax-supported schools was beginning to be won. Most northern states and some southern states had set up public school systems. These school systems, however, usually were limited to elementary education. There were few high schools in the United States in 1850. It was not until the period after the Civil War that a system of public secondary schools, or high schools, began to appear in the United States.

The Educational Ladder

Most Americans spend many years earning an education. There are several levels in the U.S.

Have small groups create ladders to represent the educational ladder. Each group may sketch its ladder or construct it from various materials, such as ice cream sticks. Each group should label the rungs of the ladder from the bottom to the top. Have each group member fill in the area above one rung with details or illustrations about that level of the educational system. Display the ladders for use as study and review guides.

Invite a local college student, a graduate student, and a professional with an advanced degree to the class to talk about the value of higher education. Have students develop pertinent questions for the guests. Make sure some students query the guests about their reasons for pursuing higher education, their goals, and what higher education has allowed them to accomplish. Have students use the interviews with your guests to write short newspaper articles about the value of higher education.

system of education. Schools range from nursery schools for young children to universities for adult higher education.

Nursery School Many children attend nursery school, or preschool. Nursery school usually accepts children three and four years old. In these schools children learn to play and get along with other children. Most nursery schools are private. Some communities, however, support nursery schools as part of their public school system. The federal government also grants funds for preschool programs in some communities.

Kindergarten Many public school systems start with kindergarten classes for five- and six-year-old children. The word *kindergarten* is German and means "garden for children." Kindergarten children spend a year learning how to get along with others and preparing for first grade. In many areas kindergartens teach the basics of reading and writing and number recognition.

Elementary School Most children enter the first grade of elementary school at the age of six. In elementary school students learn the building blocks of education—reading, writing, and arithmetic. The curriculum also includes subjects such as history, science, health, art, music, and physical education. Children attend elementary school for five to nine years, depending on how the school system is arranged.

Junior High School Grades 7, 8, and 9 usually make up junior high school. Many school systems have replaced junior high schools with middle, or intermediate, schools. Middle schools usually include grades 5 or 6 through 8. Some middle schools include only grades 7 and 8.

High School Students who have completed the first eight or nine grades enter high school. There are generally three kinds of high schools. Academic high schools prepare students for college. Technical and vocational

GLOBAL PERSPECTIVES

In the 1800s western powers dominated many poorer regions of the world. They influenced not only the economies and governments of their overseas possessions but also their educational systems. For example, the Philippines' educational system closely resembles that of the United States. In 1898, at the end of the Spanish-American War, the Philippines became a colony of the United States. Two years later, President William McKinley announced a policy of universal primary education for Filipino children. Filipinos soon established institutions of higher learning as well, including the University of the Philippines. As of 1994, 97 percent of elementary-school-age Filipinos were in school. The Philippines has a literacy rate of 93.5 percent.

Local School Districts*

The Voters of the school district or of the community elect

Board of Education hires

| Superintendent of Schools | Principals | Counselors | Coaches | Custodians Secretaries Cafeteria Workers | Teachers |

*School districts are separate units of local government. In some states, however, schools are governed by city, town, or county government. Local school boards are usually elected, but are appointed in some cities and counties.

CIVICS TRANSPARENCIES

An overhead transparency of "Local School Districts" is available in *Teaching Transparencies with Teacher's Notes.*

Call on volunteers to list across the top of the chalkboard American values in education. (See pages 261–262.) Then have students suggest why they think each of these values is important. List these reasons beneath the appropriate value heading on the board. Have students copy these reasons as a reference for the "Independent Practice" activity.

Ask students to use the chapter to identify issues currently challenging the educational system. *(violence in schools, need for education reform)* Then ask: How can the American values in education help solve these problems? Have students write short paragraphs answering this question. Students might want to refer to their lists (from the "Guided Practice" activity) of reasons why these values in education are important. Call on volunteers to read their paragraphs to the class for discussion.

An overhead transparency of "Education and Average Income" is available in *Teaching Transparencies with Teacher's Notes.*

An additional rung on the educational ladder is adult education, which is booming in the United States. In 1991, 32 percent of all adults took adult education courses to acquire new skills or knowledge. Of adults 55 or older, 15 percent enrolled in such courses. The percentages were 39 percent and 36 percent for adults aged 35–54 and 17–34, respectively.

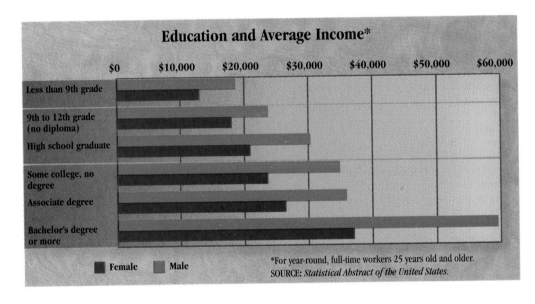

Education and Average Income*

*For year-round, full-time workers 25 years old and older.
SOURCE: *Statistical Abstract of the United States.*

high schools enable students to learn a trade or occupation. Comprehensive high schools offer college preparatory work as well as technical or vocational courses.

Higher Education

The need for higher education in the United States has grown with advances in knowledge and technology. Many jobs now require college and university training. Therefore, high school students are encouraged to earn as much education as they can.

Junior Colleges The growing demand for higher education is being met in part by two-year **junior colleges**. These schools are sometimes called community colleges. They are often supported by taxpayers and offer courses free or at low tuition to local high school graduates. Courses include training for specialized fields and preparation for more advanced study. Many junior college graduates transfer to four-year colleges or universities.

Colleges and Universities There are roughly 2,000 colleges and universities in

the United States. Most are coeducational. That is, they are open to both men and women students. They range in size from small **colleges** with only a few hundred students to large institutions with 10,000 students or more. The federal and state governments contribute around $65 billion to help support higher education institutions.

Some institutions of higher learning are organized as universities. A **university** includes one or more colleges as well as graduate programs in professional fields of learning, such as business, medicine, engineering, and law. A university also provides advanced studies in most of the subjects that are offered in colleges. After graduation from college, students may go on to **graduate school** to study for an advanced degree.

As you can see from the graph on this page, it pays to stay in school and earn as much education as you can. In addition to becoming a well-educated person, your income will likely increase with your level of education. This is true for both men and women. At every educational level, however, women traditionally have been paid less money than men for the same work.

Closure

Have students find articles in newspapers and other periodicals about issues in education today. The issues may concern any level of the educational ladder, higher education, or values in education. Students might want to focus on issues of particular importance locally. Students should summarize the articles in oral reports for the class.

Reviewing

Have students complete the Section 1 Review.

Reteaching

Assign Section 1 of the Chapter 14 Reteaching Worksheet.

Education for Students with Special Needs

U.S. citizens believe in equal opportunities through education for everyone. In the past, however, students with special needs were isolated in separate classrooms or separate schools. Today the law demands that students with special needs—gifted students and students with physical, mental, or learning disabilities—be taught in regular classrooms whenever possible. This practice is called **mainstreaming**.

Many students with disabilities attend regular classes for most of the day and then work with specially trained teachers for a few hours each day or each week. Others receive special instruction for much of the day and then join regular classes in subjects such as art and music. Gifted students may receive special enrichment instruction.

American Values in Education

Certain values have influenced the development of the nation's school system. The following are some of the traditional values that have developed over the years.

Free Public Education Citizens are entitled to a free public education. There should be no hidden charges to prevent any citizen from receiving a quality education at public expense. Public education in the United States costs taxpayers nearly $300 billion a year, including expenditures by the federal government of about $25 billion.

Equal Schooling Open to All No one should be discriminated against because of race, sex, religion, or financial status.

Freedom for any Creed or Religion U.S. schools are open to all Americans regardless of their religious beliefs. The Supreme Court has held that no special prayer or Bible reading shall be allowed during the school day. Private religious schools, however, are permitted to exist outside the public school system.

Local Control Local school boards operate the public schools under laws passed by the state legislature. State boards or departments of education assist local schools but do not give orders to district school boards. Actual control of the schools rests with the local school district, where the people best know the local needs.

CIVICS SIDELIGHT

Violence in school is a daily concern for many students. In 1992, 10 percent of students in tenth grade reported that they had carried a weapon into school at least once in the previous month. Fifty percent of tenth graders declared that they did not always feel safe at school. Since 1993, there have been 108 violence-related deaths in U.S. schools.

Violence can be stopped, however, as one school in New York City has proved. Violence, vandalism, and poor academic standards were some of the problems that led to the 1991 closing of an intermediate school in that city. Reopened as Frederick Douglass Academy the next fall, the school now faces a bright future. The new principal, Lorraine Monroe, and teachers enforce strict disciplinary and academic standards. Students wear uniforms. Chewing gum, eating candy, and listening to headphones are not allowed. Students are expected to do their work. "This school's about coming in here quietly and respecting your teachers," Monroe says. "We don't tolerate rudeness, unpreparedness. Kids respond to the kind of structure we're asking."

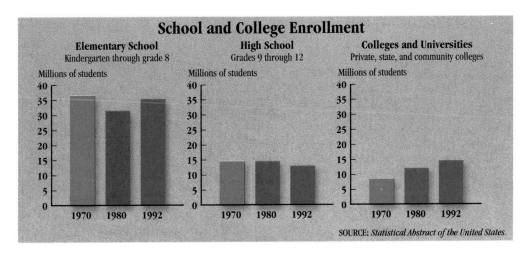

School and College Enrollment

Elementary School — Kindergarten through grade 8 — Millions of students

High School — Grades 9 through 12 — Millions of students

Colleges and Universities — Private, state, and community colleges — Millions of students

SOURCE: *Statistical Abstract of the United States.*

Extension

Arrange for a visit to a local college. Try to set up a talk with an admissions counselor and a tour of the campus, including a dormitory. You might wish to have students send off for brochures about the college before the trip, so they will be better prepared to absorb the experience. Encourage students to write to other colleges of interest and report to the class on the kinds of programs offered there.

SECTION OBJECTIVES

After studying Section 2, students should be able to do the following.

1. Identify the seven goals of education.

2. Explain the need to take notes in class and to go to class prepared.

3. Explain the best way to prepare for tests.

4. Describe what students can learn from extracurricular activities.

SECTION 1 REVIEW ANSWERS

1. See the following pages: junior college, college, university, graduate school (p. 260); mainstreaming (p. 261).

2. development of individual citizens, development of nation

3. opponents—said no to taxes to educate other people's children, would ruin business for private schools, education should be under control of church and home; supporters—argued that democratic society requires an educated citizenry

4. nursery, kindergarten, elementary, junior high and middle, high, junior college, college, university, graduate school; important—keep up with advances, many jobs require higher education, makes for a well-educated person, higher income

5. educational reform—Congress set goals for U.S. education; preventing school violence—security devices, violence prevention programs

6. Posters should encourage students to stay in school.

Compulsory Attendance Each state requires school attendance by young people, usually between the ages of 7 and 16. Some families, however, educate their children at home. Home schooling is legal, but the laws regulating this type of education vary from state to state. Current estimates of the number of children being educated at home range from 900,000 to 1.2 million.

Enriching Environment Schools should be places where young people can grow in mind, body, and spirit. Sports, clubs, social events, and creative arts are a part of each person's education. Schools should be lively places where individuals are encouraged to develop to their full potential.

Challenges in Today's School System

Americans have long believed that education is the backbone of democracy. Because education is so important to the nation and its citizens, all citizens must be aware of the challenges that face the U.S. educational system and work toward meeting them.

One issue that currently challenges the educational system is the need for educational reform. Test scores show that U.S. students are falling behind the students of other industrial nations in science, math, and reading. Many people fear that this situation will make it difficult for the nation to compete economically in the global community. In addition, technology is advancing so rapidly that the American economy increasingly needs highly skilled, well-educated workers.

To help young people meet the challenges of the future, Congress passed the Goals 2000: Educate America Act in 1994. This $370 million program sets goals for U.S. education and encourages the states to develop stricter educational standards. Included in the program are grants to states and local school agencies to help them institute educational reforms.

The U.S. educational system also faces an alarming increase in violence in schools. In some schools teachers must spend more time trying to maintain discipline than they do teaching. Some schools have installed metal detectors and other security devices to protect students and teachers against weapons that are brought to school. To help end such violence, many schools throughout the nation now offer violence-prevention programs that teach students how to settle disputes peacefully.

SECTION 1 REVIEW

1. Define or identify the following terms: junior college, college, university, graduate school, mainstreaming.

2. What are the two main purposes of education in the United States?

3. Describe the debate over free public schools that took place in the 1800s.

4. What are the main levels on the U.S. educational ladder? Why is it important to earn as much education as you can?

5. What two challenges currently face U.S. schools, and what is being done to meet these challenges?

6. **THINKING CRITICALLY** You head a panel in your community whose purpose is to encourage students to stay in school. Create a poster for a "Stay in School" campaign.

2 The Best Education for You

Luck has been defined as being in the right place at the right time. What we sometimes forget to add is that the lucky person is usually able to see opportunities and make good use of them. This is true in school and in studying, too. You must be aware of and take advantage

◈ COOPERATIVE LEARNING

Have small groups write creative stories about the ideal school—one that meets or exceeds "The Seven Cardinal Principles of Secondary Education." Groups should include examples of how the goals are achieved in the ideal school. Roles for members include writer, illustrators, and presenters. Have groups present their stories to the rest of the class for discussion.

Budgeting Time

Have students list the activities in which they participate. Then, using a chart or some other visual guide, students should assign days and times to each activity. All time spent doing anything (including eating and sleeping) should be accounted for. Have students indicate what schedule changes are possible should the need arise (such as the need to study for a test or to attend an unannounced club meeting). Call on volunteers to present their schedules to the class. Have students discuss whether the volunteers have budgeted their time wisely.

of the opportunities offered in school. What are these opportunities?

What Your School Has to Offer

Some years ago a group of teachers and school officials listed the goals of education that U.S. schools should try to achieve. The statement the group prepared is called "The Seven Cardinal Principles of Secondary Education." As you study these goals, or principles, think about how your school works to achieve them. Ask yourself if you are taking advantage of the opportunities offered by your school.

Using Basic Learning Skills One of the main goals of schools is to teach students the skills of reading, writing, and arithmetic. In addition, schools teach other skills that help students learn and study. These learning skills include public speaking, organizing and expressing ideas, using a dictionary, and conducting research. They also include the ability to read and interpret maps, graphs, charts, pictures, and cartoons.

You can use these skills to great advantage in many different courses in school. You also will discover that you will use these skills throughout your life.

Learning to Work with Others Many of your school activities require you to work with other students. This cooperation is good practice in helping you work with members of your family. It also will help you work with other people in your community and in the workplace now and in the future.

Health Education Most schools have a program in health education to teach students to develop good health habits. Health education usually also offers programs of physical activities and sports. You will benefit from the exercise these programs provide. Moreover, the practice in school will help you take care of your health and keep physically fit throughout your life.

Training for Your Life's Work Your school provides the educational foundation on which special job training can be based. Your school also helps you prepare for job opportunities after you graduate. Employers need well-educated, skilled workers. School makes it possible for you to become that kind of employee. By taking advantage of your education, you can prepare for a job in which you can contribute to the nation and find personal satisfaction.

Active Citizenship To help you become a good citizen your school seeks to develop your interest in community life. It teaches you about the history of the nation, its institutions, and the problems it faces today. Your classes and school activities help develop in you a sense of loyalty, love of country, good judgment, and willingness to do your fair share for the good of all.

Considerate Behavior Your school teaches students to adapt to accepted standards of behavior. It also tries to develop in all

(continued on page 266)

The students in this chemistry class know the value of a good education. The things they learn in school will help prepare them for the rest of their lives.

MULTICULTURAL PERSPECTIVES

Booker T. Washington (1856–1915), founder of the Tuskegee Institute in Alabama, believed education should include moral values and should train a person for his or her life's work. He favored teaching vocational skills and "the everyday practical things of life." W.E.B. Du Bois (1868–1963) thought this approach was too limited. He believed higher education should be the goal. Du Bois believed that African Americans with training in higher education would lead all African Americans to full equality. The arguments of these two famous African Americans reflect general questions that are still asked: What kind of education best promotes opportunity and equality? Is the role of schooling to produce skilled workers or to encourage scholarship, or both?

Extending Ideas

Have students suggest subjects they might be able to teach elementary students. Then have groups of students design brochures "advertising" their programs to an elementary school teacher or principal. The brochures should give such specific details as who will be taught, where, and how often. The brochures should also answer the following question: How does teaching others benefit both the teacher and the person who is taught? If possible, have students distribute the brochures to local elementary schools and encourage them to start their own tutoring programs.

CIVICS SIDELIGHT

Teenagers today are actively involved in a wide range of volunteer activities. According to a 1992 nationwide survey, six out of every ten adolescents between the ages of 12 and 17 participated in at least one volunteer activity each year. About 5 percent of the nation's adolescent volunteers provide tutoring services. Other young people volunteered their time to visit convalescent hospitals, provide baby-sitting services, help feed the hungry, and serve as youth-group leaders. On average, youthful volunteers donated 3.2 hours a week to volunteer work. In addition to donating their time to help others, young people also donate money. Fifty percent of the adolescents included in the survey donated an average of $56 to various causes.

Photo Caption Answer

Students might tutor in subjects in which they excel. Students might say they would learn important interpersonal skills and skills related to teaching and helping others.

Citizenship IN ACTION

KIDS TEACHING KIDS

Have you ever helped a classmate or a younger brother or sister with a homework assignment? If so, you probably realize that you have much to share with other students. There are many young people like yourself who value education so highly that they are helping other students take advantage of the opportunities offered by their schools. These kids are giving their time to teach other kids.

Both tutors and the schoolchildren they teach learn from a tutoring program. How might you help a younger student? What might you learn by doing so?

Starting Young

At Teller Elementary School in Denver, Colorado, several fifth-grade students are involved in a program to tutor first-, second-, and third-graders who need extra help with their learning. Three days a week, these young people meet together after school in the school library to complete homework assignments or to read together. The fifth-grade tutors give their young charges individualized help and attention with their schoolwork.

The students who come for tutoring sessions receive canvas bags that they are allowed to decorate themselves. Their teachers fill these bags with the day's homework assignments. The students then carry these bags to the library, where they and their tutors share donated cookies and complete the work. After each session, the children bring the bags back to the classroom and leave them there overnight. This way, the work cannot be lost or "eaten by the dog."

The tutors and the children they teach receive "credits" for the time they participate in the program. They can use these credits to purchase items from a school store set up es-

Have students write news features about tutoring at either Teller Elementary School or the schools of Waterloo, Iowa. Students should think of an interesting headline and include a byline (for the author) and dateline (for the location of the topic in the article). They might wish to make up some details to fill out their stories. Remind students to cover the *who, what, when, where,* and *how* questions.

pecially for this program. Among the items the students may purchase are school T-shirts, school supplies, and watches.

For most of the young students in the program, however, learning is its own reward. Administrators at Teller Elementary note how students who never completed their homework before are now finishing it every night. The tutoring program has made the difference.

The tutors in the program also are receiving the rewards of teaching. Many tutors are surprised at how eager the younger children are to participate. But as one tutor says, "I can remember when I was in the first grade—I would have liked help when I was in the first grade."

Another reward is better report cards. Both the tutors and the children they teach have improved their grades and test scores.

Attracting Future Teachers

In Waterloo, Iowa, another tutoring program is also finding success. In Waterloo more than 20 percent of the school district's students are African Americans. African Americans, however, make up only about 7 percent of Waterloo's teachers. In an effort to interest minority students in future careers as teachers, the Waterloo school system has undertaken a new program that links African American high school tutors with elementary schoolchildren who need extra help.

The tutors are chosen from lists of applicants compiled by school guidance counselors. The students to be tutored are chosen from lists submitted by teachers in Waterloo's seven elementary schools. The students who receive tutoring improve their learning skills by working with older students who serve as role models for achievement.

The high school student tutors, meanwhile, not only experience the satisfaction that comes from helping others, they also learn firsthand that teachers can make an enormous difference in the lives of young people. Most of the high school students in Waterloo's tutoring program have enrolled in college. Their goal? They want to be teachers.

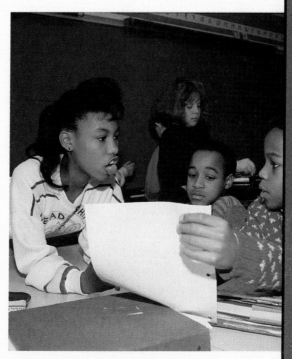

Tutoring gives you firsthand experience of a career in teaching. What skills might a tutor need?

YOU DECIDE

1 Why do you think the Denver tutors as well as the children they help were able to improve their grades?

2 How might the experience of tutoring encourage young people to choose careers as teachers?

3 Find out what kind of tutoring programs are available in your area. Do you think that young people who need tutoring might learn more from other young people than from adult tutors? Why or why not?

ANSWERS TO YOU DECIDE

1. Students might say tutors probably became more interested in their own studies while tutored children received individualized help and encouragement.

2. helps one discover satisfaction in helping others learn

3. Students should make reasoned responses.

Divide the class in half for an experiment. One half will take notes on the material you are about to read. The other half will just listen. Read a section aloud from an unfamiliar textbook. Tell students who took notes to study them briefly and then put them out of sight. Then, alternating between groups, ask questions about what you have just read. Keep score to determine which half correctly answers the most questions. Have students use this exercise to discuss the value of taking good notes.

Have students take notes on a television newscast. During the next class you might wish to have students compare notes through a current-events discussion of the events of the previous day. To gauge the accuracy of the notes, have the class determine how many versions of facts reported on the newscast were recorded by students.

CIVICS SIDELIGHT

A traditional study technique known as SQ3R (Survey, Question, Read, Recite, Review) was developed in the 1940s to help soldiers who were training for specialized positions. This technique is still a popular study method. In this method students survey the chapter headings and turn them into questions. Then they read the chapter to find answers to their questions, pausing after each section to recite the answer. When students finish the chapter, they review each of the major points.

students a feeling of consideration for their families, teachers, classmates, friends, and other members of the community. Your school stresses, too, the importance of respecting the privacy and property rights of other citizens.

Wise Use of Leisure Time Your school also tries to teach you to enjoy good books, art, and music so that they may enrich your life. Your teachers encourage you to develop interesting hobbies and to take part in school activities such as athletics and drama.

By encouraging you to undertake such activities, your school is trying to help you find a hobby or special interest to enjoy now and in the future. In this way your school helps make you a well-rounded person.

Getting the Most from School

To make the best use of the opportunities your school offers, you must remember the goals of your education. Your years in school are very important. The success you enjoy in school and the study and learning habits you develop will help determine the kind of person you will become. They also will influence the kind of job you will have. What kinds of study and learning habits should you try to develop?

One of the first and most important study habits all students must learn is the wise use of time. A well-organized student finds time in his or her daily schedule for study, school activities, exercise, relaxation, and the proper amount of sleep.

Just as your family budgets its money, it is wise to budget your time. Work out a daily schedule for your more important activities, and be sure to finish things on time.

How to Study

Study your schoolwork with care and concentration. If possible, select a regular place to study that is quiet and has good working space

School gives young people the opportunity to participate in a variety of activities. Taking part in the school band is one way for students to develop their talents.

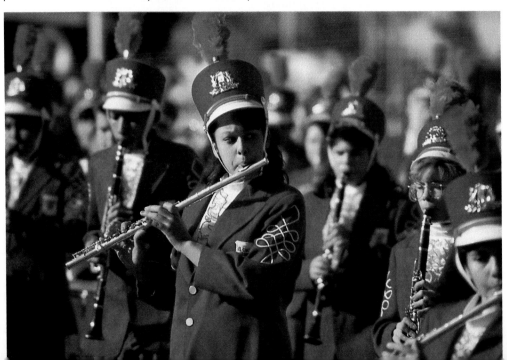

Closure

Review with students the importance of being prepared for taking part in class and for taking tests. Then have students make a list of other aspects of life in which they could benefit by being prepared—or be at a disadvantage if they are unprepared. Discuss the lists.

Reviewing

Have students complete the Section 2 Review.

Reteaching

Assign Section 2 of the Chapter 14 Reteaching Worksheet.

---

and proper light. Keep the materials you need close at hand.

Take notes while you read. You will soon find that writing down important ideas will help you understand and remember these ideas. Make sure you understand your assignment before you start. Then do the best job you can.

Your textbooks are written to help you learn quickly and efficiently. Here are some useful hints to help you get the most from your textbooks:

- Learn how to use the study helps in the book. Use the Table of Contents, Index, Glossary, maps, charts, appendices, and captions.
- Note the chapter title, the section headings, and other subheadings within the chapter. They give you clues to the chapter's most important ideas.
- Read through the assigned text carefully, noting topic sentences and summarizing paragraphs.
- Reread the assigned text. This time make written notes on the important ideas and facts included in the material.
- Answer the questions at the end of each section of the chapter. If you find a question you cannot answer, turn to the page in your textbook where the subject is discussed and find the correct answer.
- Some people find using a card file helpful. They create a file of cards containing definitions, formulas, important facts, and answers to key questions. These cards are helpful when reviewing for a test.

Taking Part in Classwork

Each day you go to class, bring the material you will need to take an active part in that day's lesson. Pay careful attention to what is being taught in class. Think about the lessons and do not be afraid to ask questions. Learn to form your own ideas and opinions. If you fall behind or fail to understand part of a lesson, ask for help.

If you come to class unprepared, you hurt yourself and your classmates, who will not benefit from what you might have contributed. A class is like any group that depends on each member to function at its best. The group performs well when everyone does his or her part. The failure of one person to carry out a responsibility deprives the others of information and the satisfaction of working together for a common purpose.

How to Do Well on Tests

When preparing to take a test, review your notes carefully. Some students find it helpful to have classmates ask them questions that might appear on the test. This review process helps them discover whether they really know the material.

When taking a test, it is a good idea to read each question carefully before trying to answer it. Before you begin, look over the entire test to see how many questions there are and how much time should be spent on each question. If there is time left at the end of the test period, reread your answers. Also check carefully that you have answered each question to the best of your ability.

Taking Part in Activities

School is more than classes, homework, tests, and class projects. School clubs, student government, sports teams, cheerleading, dances, and other social events are also part of your education. These extracurricular activities, in which you take part in addition to classes, can teach you a great deal.

Extracurricular activities add to your fun in school. At the same time, they help you develop your own special abilities and interests. You may learn new skills or new ways to express yourself. You may make new friends.

Students who take part in classwork and activities are not satisfied merely to "get by" in school. They realize that not taking part in school would cheat themselves of a rewarding education and perhaps of a richer future.

After studying Section 3, students should be able to do the following.

1. Identify how learning and experience are related.
2. Explain the role of insight in the thinking process.
3. Identify the steps involved in thinking critically.
4. Explain the difference between fact and opinion.
5. Explain why people should learn to think for themselves.

Teaching Section 3
Building a Vocabulary

Teach the term ***motivation*** by referring to its Latin root, *movere*, meaning "to move." Tell students that this is also the root of the words *motion* and *motor*. Teach the term ***prejudice*** by separating its parts: *pre-*, meaning "before," and *judice*, meaning "judgment." Ask students why prejudging often leads to incorrect and uninformed conclusions. Have students use the word parts to define the term ***insight***. (*"seeing within"*)

SECTION 2 REVIEW
A N S W E R S

1. teach students basic skills, teach students to work together, help students develop good health habits, prepare students for job training and opportunities, prepare students for active citizenship, teach considerate behavior, teach students to use leisure time wisely

2. Notes help students identify and remember main ideas and prepare for tests. Being prepared not only helps students learn, it also helps them contribute to the knowledge of others.

3. Review notes carefully and be quizzed on material by other students.

4. new skills and new ways of expression

5. Students might want to create charts listing strengths, weaknesses, and ways to improve skills.

SECTION 2 REVIEW

1. What are the seven goals of education?

2. Why should you take notes when you study? Why is it important to go to class prepared?

3. How can you best prepare for tests?

4. What can you learn from extracurricular activities?

5. **THINKING CRITICALLY** Analyze your personal study habits. What are your strengths? What are your weaknesses? Do your grades accurately reflect the amount of time you study? Do you study more effectively alone or with other people? What can you do to improve your study skills?

| 3 | *Developing Your Life Skills* |

One of the main purposes of education is to help people learn skills they will use all their lives, such as how to think. The dictionary tells us that to think is to form ideas in the mind. This sounds simple enough, but how do we form these ideas?

We think mainly with facts. When faced with a problem, thinking people consider all the facts. They then consider all possible solutions and decide which solution seems best. How do we obtain the facts with which we do our thinking? We learn them.

How We Learn

Almost everything we do—the way we act, think, pass along information, even the way we show emotion—is learned. People learn in many ways. All learning, however, is the result of some kind of **experience**, or the direct observation or participation in events.

The simplest kind of learning is the result of experience that involves the motor nerves—those nerves that control muscles. For example, a person who touches a hot stove pulls back his or her hand because of the pain. Next time, that person will avoid a hot stove.

Now suppose that while the person was reaching for the stove, someone said "Hot!" in a sharp tone. In the future, if near a hot stove, the person will draw back his or her hand whenever someone says "Hot!" This kind of learning is called **conditioning**.

Much of our behavior, or the way we act, is conditioned. People learn to do things because they expect to be rewarded or to gain satisfaction. Children will wash their hands before meals if they expect to receive praise or a hug. They will continue to behave in the desired way if they are rewarded occasionally. Behavior that is repeated often usually becomes a **habit**—an action that is performed automatically without thinking.

People also learn by copying, or imitating, others. Young children imitate their parents or guardians and other members of the family. They repeat their family's opinions and habits. As adults, people often imitate their friends and others they admire.

Learning in School

Much of what we know is also learned by looking and listening. Every day of our lives we learn through our senses and take in different kinds of information. In this complex society, however, there is so much information that it has to be organized, or arranged in groups, to be usable. A large part of the organized information we learn is taught in school and in books.

Schools teach students how to make the best use of information by comparing and analyzing facts, putting the facts together, and drawing conclusions. They also teach students where to find information.

The ability to learn depends on maturity, experience, and intelligence. It also depends on the degree of motivation. **Motivation** is the internal drive that stirs people and directs their behavior and attitudes.

How We Think

Thinking is a complex process. It involves awareness, understanding, and interpretation of what we see and know. We are thinking when we solve problems by considering all possible solutions. Every time we make a decision, we solve a problem.

Sometimes we cannot find an answer, no matter how hard we try. Then, suddenly, the answer will spring to mind. This is called **insight**. The answer seems to come out of nowhere. Actually, it comes to mind only after we have studied the problem and ruled out several possible answers. Without realizing it, people often take what they know about something else and apply it to the problem they are trying to solve.

Occasionally our solutions are original. The ability to find new ways of thinking and doing things is called **creativity**. Everyone can think creatively. We have other thinking abilities, too. The abilities to reason, question, and weigh information are ways of thinking.

Critical Thinking

There is no simple way to learn the truth about an issue or to solve a problem. The search for truth on many subjects is long and hard. How can we learn to think clearly in order to find solutions and make decisions? The kind of thinking we do to reach decisions and solve problems is called **critical thinking**. This type of reasoning, or clear thinking, includes a number of steps.

Defining the Issue   The first step is to make sure that the issue or question is

Although computers have an important place in U.S. education, they cannot replace the human ability to think critically.

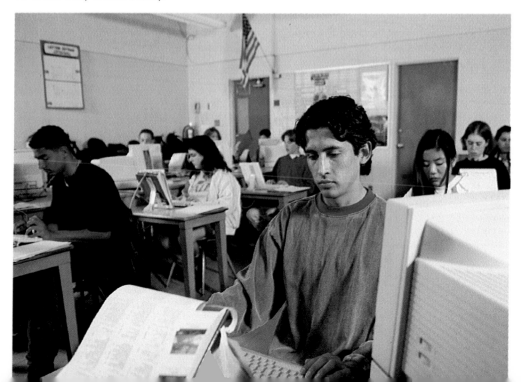

Guided Practice

Have students list the influences on their thinking and then rank those influences in order of importance. Ask students whether their ranking might change for different aspects of their lives. For example, is the most important influence on their political beliefs different from the most important influence on their musical tastes? Then discuss how much students think for themselves.

Independent Practice

Have students discuss examples in everyday life where they are faced with making a decision but allow others to influence their decisions heavily or to decide for them. Then have students write short speeches on the importance of thinking for themselves. In particular, the speeches should address the dangers of allowing others to decide things for them. Call on volunteers to give their speeches to the class.

CIVICS SIDELIGHT

Researchers studying the influences on adolescents' political views have found few clear patterns. Political views of parents do influence those of their children, but such influence is believed to be limited. The political views of young people often will diverge from the views of their parents. Many researchers agree that once political views are established in adolescence, however, those views tend to remain stable over time.

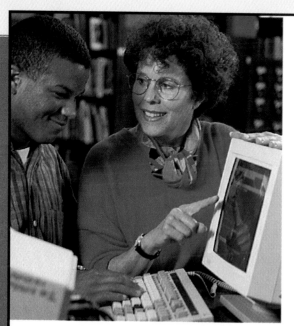
For individuals to receive a good education, they must have a great deal of help from teachers, relatives, and volunteers.

clearly defined in your mind. That is, you need to make certain that you fully understand it and any terms that might be involved. You may find it helpful to write down the issue or question. If it is a difficult one, you might outline the main ideas. Look for relationships between the ideas. Are some of the ideas causes and others effects?

Distinguishing Fact from Opinion Once the issue is clear to you, you can look for evidence that will help you understand and judge the issues involved. What are the facts? It may surprise you to discover that often there are disagreements over facts. One side may say one thing, and the other side may claim something very different. Therefore, it is important in critical thinking always to distinguish between fact and opinion.

To illustrate how difficult it can be to determine what is fact, consider the following example. A newspaper reporter may write that a person "angrily pounded on a neighbor's door until he broke it down." The fact that the door

pounding took place can be proved. Several witnesses may have seen it. But was the person angry? This is the reporter's judgment. The person may have pounded on the door not in anger, but to warn the neighbor of a fire.

A person's emotions, such as anger or happiness, are difficult to check or measure accurately. It is important, therefore, to know whether you are dealing with facts or with information colored by judgments.

Weighing the Evidence In thinking through an issue, it also is important to learn to weigh all the evidence. Are the facts used by the speaker or writer the ones you need to know? Are important facts missing? Have you studied all the tables, graphs, maps, and other available sources? In learning to think clearly, you also must learn to judge whether the given facts fit the problem. You must learn to judge which side of the argument the facts seem to support.

Reaching a Conclusion After you have weighed the evidence, you can reach your own conclusion. Try to keep an open mind. Remember that if new evidence is found, it may be necessary to change your conclusion.

Sometimes there is more than one possible answer to a question or solution to a problem. In trying to decide which solution is best, you may want to test how each solution might work. You may do this by mentally checking the facts against each possible solution. You might imagine the problem in a real-life setting. Determine which of the possible solutions would work best in such a situation. Knowing which solution is most appropriate to the circumstances is an important part of making decisions and solving problems.

Who Influences Your Thinking?

Clear thinking also demands that you realize how other people influence your thinking. How much are you influenced by what others say or do?

Closure

Briefly discuss with students how learning to think is a life skill. Then invite students to imagine what their lives might be like 10 years from now. Have them write an autobiographical sketch of themselves as if they were in their mid-twenties, incorporating examples of how they might apply the thinking skills described in this section. Ask students to consider the kinds of problems they may face in 10 years and how they can learn what will be necessary to solve those problems.

Reviewing

Have students complete the Section 3 Review.

Reteaching

Assign Section 3 of the Chapter 14 Reteaching Worksheet.

No one can do our thinking for us. Other people, however, do help determine what we think. Families, teachers, and friends have a great influence on our opinions. Sometimes we are influenced by some well-known person we admire. As you recall, we also receive ideas from the mass media. Many of these ideas are propaganda. That is, they are used to try to influence us.

Sometimes people think and behave in certain ways because they are members of particular groups in society. In a labor dispute, for example, employers may have opinions that differ from those of workers.

Because of these influences people often have opinions that favor one side or the other. Few people can be impartial, or completely objective, all the time. All of us have certain fixed feelings, or prejudices. **Prejudice** is an opinion that is not based on a careful and reasonable investigation of the facts. We must be careful not to be ruled by our prejudices or those of others.

Think for Yourself

You live in a nation that values the freedom of independent thought. Take advantage of this freedom to learn how to think for yourself. Study the way that you make decisions. Learn how to gather information and how to interpret it. Most important, believe in yourself enough to arrive at your own conclusions.

This republic can work only if citizens are willing to think for themselves and not simply accept what others tell them. Your school can help you learn to think clearly. By examining the information you learn in class and making up your own mind, you will learn the skills you need to vote wisely, understand current issues, and solve problems.

SECTION 3 REVIEW

1. Define or identify the following terms: experience, conditioning, habit, motivation, insight, creativity, critical thinking, prejudice.

2. What is the relationship between learning and experience? What role does insight play in the thinking process?

3. What steps are involved in learning to think critically?

4. What is the difference between fact and opinion? Why should you learn to think for yourself?

5. **THINKING CRITICALLY** If you were a high school teacher, how might you encourage your students to think critically about information rather than to simply memorize facts?

CHAPTER 14 SUMMARY

The U.S. educational system has changed and grown in many ways, and it continues to grow. Americans consider education to be the cornerstone of democracy.

Your school teaches many worthwhile things. It teaches you the basic skills of learning. It offers a variety of subjects. Education also prepares you to be a good citizen in your family and in the nation.

One of the most important skills you learn in school is the ability to read well and understand what you read. Schools also help people think clearly and make decisions. Everyone must learn to gather and study the facts, weigh the evidence, and consider alternative solutions before reaching conclusions.

In learning to think for yourself, you need to consider how opinions are formed. For example, you may sometimes be influenced by people you admire. You must also be aware that some people are biased because of the kind of work they do or because of the groups to which they belong. As a citizen, you must learn how to think for yourself.

Tell students that politicians campaigning for office must try to "sell" themselves to the voters. This kind of selling often includes the use of both facts and opinions. As an extending exercise, have students write 10 statements that might appear in a political campaign, some of which are fact and some of which are opinion. Have students exchange papers. Then have each student categorize as fact or opinion the statements made in the other student's list. Papers should then be returned to their originators to be "graded."

SOCIAL STUDIES SKILL
Distinguishing Fact from Opinion

One of the keys to evaluating what you read and hear is the ability to distinguish between fact and opinion. A fact is something that can be proved true. Facts can be counted, measured, or documented in some way. In contrast, opinions are personal beliefs about what is true. Because people often use facts to back up their opinions, it is important to learn how to distinguish between the two. Once you learn this skill, you will be better able to evaluate the information you read and hear on a daily basis.

How to Distinguish Fact from Opinion

1. **Determine if the information can be proved.** You can begin to identify facts by asking the same questions a reporter uses to write a good news story. If the information answers the questions *who, what, when, where,* or *how,* it probably contains facts. Next, determine if these facts can be documented, perhaps through other types of sources. Facts can be verified. Opinions cannot be checked.
2. **Note how the facts are used.** Keep in mind that a single word often can change a statement from fact to opinion. Certain phrases, such as "In our judgment . . . ," "I believe that . . . ,"or "I think that . . . ," clearly signal that the speaker or writer is about to give an opinion.
3. **Identify "loaded" words.** Loaded words are words that carry an emotional appeal, such as *beautiful, boring, exciting,* and *extremely.* These descriptive words signal an opinion because they express the speaker's or writer's personal viewpoint. Do not allow loaded words to color your judgment about the facts.

Applying the Skill

Read the campaign flyer below. Then complete the following activities.

1. Identify the loaded words in the following sentence: "Janice Green is a dedicated, hardworking educator who has served successfully on the school board for an impressive 12 years." How might these loaded words affect a person's interpretation of the facts?
2. Imagine that you are a reporter for a local newspaper. What facts from the flyer would you include in your news story?
3. Use the facts contained in the flyer to write an editorial supporting Janice Green.

JANICE GREEN
FOR CITY COUNCIL

Janice Green is determined to improve our city. If elected Green will:

★ increase the number of buses running during rush hour. Thirty percent of public buses do not run during rush hour.

★ ensure that our city taxes are reasonable. Over the past 10 years, city taxes have been increased six times.

★ add to and improve facilities for the elderly. At present, there are over 100 persons waiting to take part in this city's programs for the elderly.

Janice Green knows our city well. She is a dedicated educator who has served successfully on the school board for more than 12 years.

Elect Janice Green

She will make this a better city in which to live!

1. "dedicated," "hardworking," "successfully," "impressive;" might persuade people to look favorably on the candidate

2. Reporters would first have to verify the accuracy of the flyer's statements. If their accuracy is verified, the following statements are facts: Thirty percent of public buses do not run during rush hour; city taxes have increased six times over a 10-year period; more than 100 people are waiting to take part in the city's programs for the elderly; Green has served on the school board for more than 12 years.

3. Students should make careful use of the facts to support their opinions and to influence the opinions of others.

Vocabulary Workshop

1. critical thinking
2. ability to find new ways of thinking and doing things
3. community college
4. Examples should reflect opinions not based on careful and reasonable

investigation of facts.
5. conditioning
6. mainstreaming

Reviewing Main Ideas

1. against—said no to taxes to educate other children, would ruin business for private schools, education should be controlled by church and home; for—democratic society requires educated citizenry

2. advances in knowledge, many jobs require higher education, brings higher income; challenges— education reform, school violence
3. nursery, kindergarten, elementary, junior high and middle, high school, junior college, college, university, graduate school
4. teach basic skills, teach cooperation, help develop healthy habits, prepare for job training and opportunities, prepare for active citizenship, teach considerate behavior, teach to use leisure time wisely
5. use study helps, note headings, read carefully, take notes, do reviews, build card file; notes—helps one remember key ideas, prepare for tests

Thinking Critically

1. Answers should include opinions on the advantages and disadvantages.
2. Students should use sound reasoning in their responses.
3. Students should recognize the value of both.

CHAPTER 14

R·e·v·i·e·w

Vocabulary Workshop

1. What term describes the kind of thinking one does to reach decisions and solve problems?
2. What is creativity?
3. What is another term for a junior college?
4. Give three examples of prejudice.
5. What term is used for learning that is the result of a reward system?
6. What is the term for the practice of putting students with special needs into regular schools and classes?

Reviewing Main Ideas

1. Why were some people in the 1800s opposed to public education? What argument did supporters of public education make?
2. Why is it important to earn as much education as possible? What challenges face today's schools?
3. What are the levels of education in the U.S. educational system?
4. Identify the seven goals of U.S. education.
5. What can you do to get the most out of your textbooks? How can taking notes while you study help you learn?

Thinking Critically

1. Why do you think some families wish to educate their children at home? What might be the advantages and disadvantages of doing so?
2. As you have learned, efforts are being made to reform the U.S. educational system. What recommendations would you make to reform U.S. education?
3. Which do you think is more important to the learning process—critical thinking or creative thinking? Explain your answer.

Citizenship in Your Community

Cooperative Project

With your group, interview older members of your families, school administrators, and former students to learn about their educational experiences. What courses were required? What problems were present in the schools? What extracurricular activities were available? Based on the responses, each group member should write a paragraph answering the question, "Is it more difficult to be a student today than in earlier times?" Gather your group's paragraphs into an anthology, or collection, entitled "Working for a Diploma: Then and Now." Distribute your anthology to the rest of the class.

Building Your Portfolio

The second step of your unit portfolio project (see page 309) is to consider good citizenship in your school by observing young citizens in action there. For one week write down every act of good citizenship that you observe in school. At the end of the week, tally your results and show this information in a chart. What generalizations can you make from this information? Is good citizenship more likely to occur when people are alone or in groups? Do people receive praise for such acts? Do such acts encourage others to be good citizens? Answer these questions in a caption below your chart. Title your chart "Young Citizens Help Strengthen Their Schools." Place your chart in your individual portfolio for later use.

Citizenship in Your Community

Reports should focus on changes in education over time.

Building Your Portfolio

Assign Portfolio Assessment Worksheet 14 in the *Portfolio Assessment Worksheets* booklet.

Assessment

- **Chapter 14 Tests**, *Chapter Tests* booklet
- **Test Generator**, Chapter 14
- **Portfolio**, Portfolio Assessment Worksheet 14, *Portfolio Assessment Worksheets* booklet

CHAPTER 15

Citizenship in the Community

TEXTBOOK	TEACHING RESOURCES	OTHER AVAILABLE RESOURCES
Chapter	• Skills Worksheet 15 • Challenge/Enrichment Worksheet 15	
Section **1** Kinds of Communities Page 275	• Reteaching Worksheet 15.1	
2 Purposes of Communities Page 279	• Reteaching Worksheet 15.2	
3 Citizens Serve Communities Page 282	• Reteaching Worksheet 15.3	
Review and Assessment **Chapter 15 Review,** Page 287	• Test, Form A • Test, Form B • Portfolio Assessment Worksheet 15	• *Test Generator,* Chapter 15

ADDITIONAL RESOURCES

BOOKS FOR TEACHERS

Aronson, Elliot, *The Social Animal,* W. H. Freeman.

Etzioni, Amitai, *The Spirit of Community: Rights, Responsibilities, and the Communitarian Agenda,* Crown.

Leslie, Gerald R., and Sheila K. Korman, *The Family in Social Context,* Oxford University Press.

Wilkinson, Kenneth, *The Community in Rural America,* Greenwood.

BOOKS FOR STUDENTS

Kozol, Jonathan, *Rachel and Her Children: Homeless Families in America,* Fawcett. Examines the problem of homelessness in our nation's cities, focusing especially on homeless families.

Warren, Roland L., *The Community in America,* University Press of America. In-depth analysis of the importance of community life to the American people.

Warren, Roland L., *Studying Your Community,* Free Press. Contains numerous instructive and practical suggestions for conducting community surveys.

MULTIMEDIA RESOURCES

The Farmer in a Changing America (VHS, c, 27 min.), EBEC. Depicts how farming has come to be a huge business enterprise.

The People Places (VHS, c, 22 min.), EBEC. Examines how the automobile has significantly changed the look and form of U.S. cities.

U.S. Cities: Growth and Development (VHS, c, 19 min.), EBEC. Looks at the ori-

gins and growth patterns of our great cities.

THE INTERNET

Have students use these search words to locate more information about chapter topics on the Internet: *communities, rural communities, urban communities, metropolitan areas, urban renewal.*

 GLOBAL SKILL BUILDER

You might wish to use **Navigating the Internet** from the interactive *Global Skill Builder* CD-ROM to aid students' understanding of the Internet as a resource.

Abbreviations: b&w=black and white; c=color; f=film; fs=filmstrip; sd=sound; tr=transparency; VHS=videotape

CIVICS SKILLS

Students will learn how to work effectively in group situations. Students also will learn vocabulary terms important to understanding the role of citizenship in the community.

CITIZENSHIP VALUES

★ **Building Communities** Students will learn about the various kinds of communities found in the United States and the main purposes and functions of communities. Students also will learn about towns and cities that have solved various community problems. Students will be encouraged to appreciate the contributions that communities make to the American way of life, to do their share in improving life in their community, and to value the important work done by the nation's many volunteer groups.

MEETING INDIVIDUAL NEEDS

LIMITED ENGLISH PROFICIENCY (LEP)

Have pairs of students create word webs or other graphic organizers to describe *community*. For example, have one student draw a circle and label it *community*. Then have both students brainstorm terms that describe *community* and things that are found in many communities. *(examples—city, suburb, farm, recreational facilities, schools, places of worship, and volunteer organizations)*

LEARNERS HAVING DIFFICULTY

Provide students with a partially completed outline of Chapter 15 that includes the section titles and subheads within each section. Pair students to work together to complete the chapter outline by listing the important points found under each subhead in the sections throughout the chapter.

AUDITORY LEARNERS

Invite a member of your state, county, or local historical society to speak to the class about what your local area was like when your community was founded and also how your community has changed since its early days. Have students prepare a list of pertinent questions to ask the speaker.

VISUAL LEARNERS

Have students plan and prepare a community newspaper. The newspaper might contain articles on health, recreation, education, transportation, communication, community services, and volunteer groups in your local community. One student might write an editorial about a community problem. Another might draw a cartoon illustrating some aspect of local politics. Have volunteers type or print the material, arrange it as in a newspaper, and make enough copies for the entire class.

TACTILE/KINESTHETIC LEARNERS

Invite students to imagine that a federal official wants to tour your community. To this end, students are to plan a field trip that will best show your community's strengths. Have students work together to plan the itinerary and make all the arrangements. If feasible, take the trip that students planned, and have students write down their impressions as if they were visitors to the community. Afterward, ask students to identify the community's strengths and its weaknesses.

GIFTED LEARNERS

Have each student research and report on a volunteer organization that works for the betterment of society. Such organizations on a national or international level include VISTA, the Peace Corps, and the American Cancer Society. Most communities have local volunteer organizations that deal with specific needs. Such groups include volunteer fire departments, literacy projects, Meals on Wheels, and groups providing services for people living with AIDS or other medical problems.

Chapter 15 focuses on the development and purposes of the nation's many communities, from the rural farm to the sprawling megalopolis. It also investigates some of the ways in which citizens can take part in community life. The underlying theme of the chapter is that citizens have a responsibility to help solve community problems.

Motivator

Ask: In what communities do you live? Then write this four-part definition of a community on the chalkboard: (1) a group of people (2) having common interests (3) who live in the same area and (4) are governed by the same laws. Then ask the question again to see whether students want to change their answers. *(New answers might include family, school, neighborhood, and nation.)*

CHAPTER OBJECTIVES

After studying Chapter 15, students should be able to do the following.

1. Describe how communities develop.
2. Identify kinds of communities.
3. Describe the advantages of living in communities.
4. Explain how people can improve their communities.

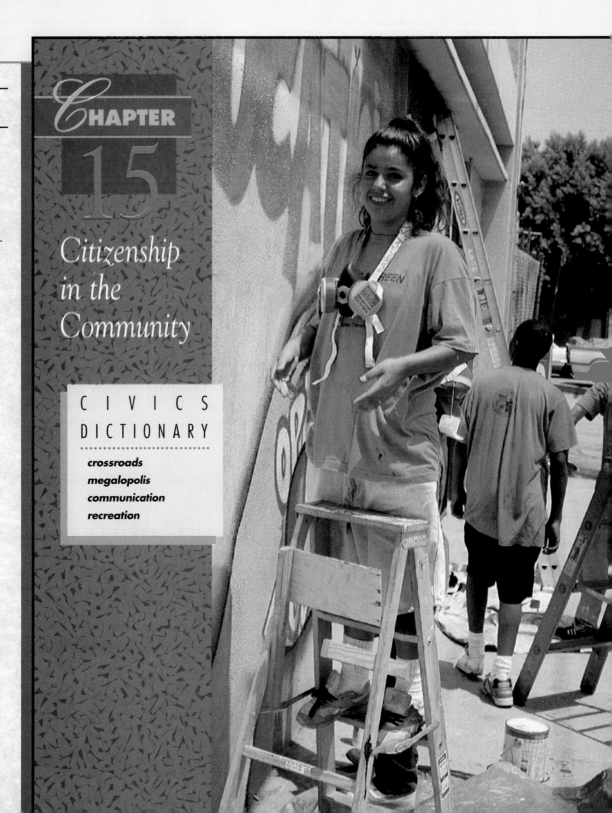

CHAPTER 15

Citizenship in the Community

CIVICS DICTIONARY

crossroads
megalopolis
communication
recreation

After studying Section 1, students should be able to do the following.

1. Identify the effects of transportation, resources, and climate on the location of communities.

2. Describe the two rural Americas, and explain what makes a community an urban area.

3. Identify how many metropolitan areas exist in the United States.

4. Define metropolitan areas and megalopolises.

Teaching Section 1
Building a Vocabulary

Have a volunteer draw a **crossroads** on the chalkboard. Ask: Why have crossroads always been important features of the land? *(People traveling in different directions could meet there and exchange goods and information.)* Have students use the word parts of **megalopolis** to deduce the meaning of this term. *(mega- or megalo-, meaning "great" or "larger," and* polis, *meaning "city")*

CHAPTER FOCUS

What do you think of when you hear the word *community*? Most probably, you think of the place where you and your friends live, go to school, have fun, and plan for the future. You think of a place that touches your life on a daily basis, a place that you, like most Americans, consider to be "home."

Communities have played a vital role in the lives of American citizens ever since the nation began. Most people find life easier when they can share it with others. Communities help people find common bonds and interests. They provide rules that guide and protect their citizens. Communities also provide goods and services that citizens cannot easily provide for themselves. In return for the benefits of community life, however, it is your responsibility to help make your community a good place to call home.

• •

STUDY GUIDE

● How do communities develop, and what kinds of communities exist?

● What special advantages do people enjoy by living in communities?

● How do people make life better in their communities?

1 Kinds of Communities

Early American settlers chose locations for their settlements that had natural advantages. Farmers were attracted to the fertile river valleys and later to the plains. Those interested in trade knew that a place with a good harbor would help build a prosperous business. A natural dam site along a river would provide power for factories. A bend in the river provided a good landing place for riverboats. Even today the natural advantages of a warm, sunny climate, beautiful sandy beaches, or snow-capped mountains can determine where a new community is located.

Crossroads Settlements

As people moved farther inland, they often settled where two main roads met. A **crossroads** was generally a good place to sell supplies to local farmers and travelers. An enterprising settler built an inn at the crossroads. A blacksmith found business there shoeing horses and repairing wagons. Farmers came to this small settlement to trade. In time the crossroads settlement grew and became a thriving town and then perhaps a city.

Transportation Centers

The American colonies depended largely on ships and boats for transportation. The country's waterways thus helped determine the location of many cities. The largest cities in the American colonies were deepwater ports on the Atlantic coast. Boston, New York, Philadelphia, and Charleston were such cities.

Most of the large inland cities grew up at lake ports or along major rivers. St. Paul and Minneapolis, for example, are located at easy-to-reach stopping points on the upper Mississippi River. New Orleans prospered because it is at the mouth of the Mississippi River where goods coming down the river were loaded onto oceangoing vessels. These cities became important transportation centers because of their location on major bodies of water.

CIVICS SIDELIGHT

Approximately 88 percent of all U.S. workers drive to work. New technology has made the trip much more productive for these computer-age commuters. Their cars have become extensions of their offices. More than 24 million Americans use cellular phones. Other electronic devices available to the modern commuter include laptop computers (for use during traffic jams), dictation machines, fax machines, and pagers.

Cars in some ways have become extensions of home, also. Some businesses are marketing portable refrigerators and portable ovens for cars. Some commuters read books, groom themselves, eat, and even exercise as they drive to work—which leads some officials to wonder why there are not more accidents involving distracted drivers.

Organize the class into small groups, and have each group use classroom and school library resources to research a large U.S. city. Individual group members should determine how transportation options, availability of resources, or climate affected development of the city. One member should investigate the development of the city's transportation system and links with other cities. Have the group present the information in a brochure of the city's history. Encourage students to include visual guides (such as maps).

Guided Practice

Help students develop a map on the board to aid a discussion about rural and urban communities. Have volunteers draw and label an urban area surrounded by rural areas on the chalkboard. Have other volunteers draw roads, suburbs, small towns, and farms. Call on volunteers to suggest what features characterize each of the areas shown in the illustration: urban, suburban, and rural. Then have students use the map to describe the two rural Americas.

GLOBAL PERSPECTIVES

Just less than half (45.2 percent) of the world's population lived in urban areas in 1995. That percentage was an increase from 35.5 percent in 1965. Africa (34.7 percent) and Asia (34.0 percent) remained the continents with the lowest percentage of urban residents, though Africa's urban population had nearly doubled from 20.6 percent in 1965. Among the continents, Australia (at 85.2 percent) and South America (at 78 percent) had the largest percentages of urban dwellers in 1995. Only 55.9 percent of South Americans had lived in urban areas in 1965. In 1995 75 percent of Europeans (excluding those in the republics of the former U.S.S.R.) and 74 percent of North and Central Americans lived in urban areas.

Among the countries with the highest percentages of their populations living in urban areas were Singapore, 100 percent; Belgium, 96.7 percent; Israel, 92.7 percent; Venezuela, 92.9 percent; Argentina, 87.5 percent; and Djibouti, 82.8 percent. In the United States, 78.2 percent of the population lived in urban areas in 1995, up from 71.9 percent in 1965.

The coming of the railroad also helped cities grow. After 1840 railroad lines began to crisscross the country, connecting its many regions. The railroads contributed to the growth of existing towns and cities and created new cities. Inland cities that were not on rivers or lakes sprang up as the railroads provided a new and speedy method of transportation. Indianapolis, Dallas, Denver, and many other cities grew prosperous because they were located along busy railroad lines.

Today Americans depend heavily on automobiles for transportation. As a result, new communities have grown up along the nation's

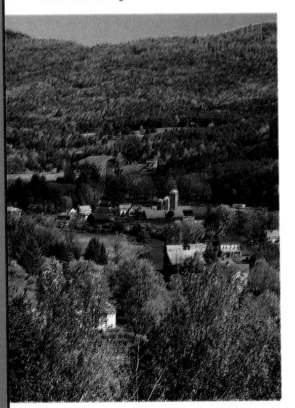

The United States still has many rural communities, like this one in Vermont. In recent years some rural communities have grown.

highways. Some of these communities provide services to travelers. Others are home to people who commute along the highways to jobs in the cities.

Resources and Climate

The United States is a nation with rich natural resources. It has a variety of climates in which vigorous activity is possible. Its broad, navigable lakes and rivers and long coastlines furnish many good ports and harbors. The nation also has vast stretches of fertile soil, adequate rainfall, good pastureland, and abundant forests. Beneath the soil are rich deposits of uranium and other metals, petroleum, and coal.

Climate and natural resources have encouraged the growth of many U.S. communities. Duluth, Minnesota, for example, is a port on Lake Superior. It owes much of its growth to the great iron-ore deposits located nearby in the Mesabi Range. In contrast, large numbers of people have flocked to central California cities because of the pleasant climate and good soil, which allow many crops to be grown.

Many New England communities were settled near waterfalls. The early textile mills needed waterpower to turn machines that spun thread and wove cloth. Many settlers in the Midwest, meanwhile, moved there because of the rich, fertile soil—one of nature's most important resources.

Rural Communities

As you know, a rural area is a region of farms and small towns. When you travel along the nation's highways, you see many different kinds of rural communities. One way to classify them is by their size. Another way is to notice the various kinds of buildings located in the community and the way in which the people make their living.

Rural Farm Communities The people who live and work on farms make up America's smallest kind of community—the rural farm community. In many parts of the

Independent Practice

Obtain from a local automobile association, airline, or travel agent information about the cities in the Boston–Washington, Chicago–Pittsburgh, or San Francisco–San Diego megalopolises. Have students write a travelogue as if they were driving through these urban areas. Students should begin at one city and work their way to the other, commenting on the urban landscape as they go. The travelogues should be written for visitors from foreign countries and should include helpful illustrations.

Closure

Invite students to write a quiz that consists of one statement describing each of the following types of communities: rural farm community, small country town, suburb, metropolitan area, and megalopolis. Each student should develop an answer key for his or her quiz. Have students exchange papers and take each other's quizzes.

United States, you will pass farm after farm as you travel through the countryside. All parts of the United States have farms. Farms differ from region to region, however, because of climate differences.

In Pennsylvania, for example, you will see farms on which a variety of crops are grown and some pigs, cows, and chickens are raised. These farms are called mixed farms. In Wisconsin you will see a large number of dairy farms. Farther west, in Wyoming, you will see large ranches that raise cattle or sheep.

In southern states you will pass tobacco, soybean, and cotton farms. West of the Mississippi River, you will see large wheat farms. In the Imperial Valley of California, there are farms that grow fruits and vegetables for city markets. In Hawaii you will see sugarcane and pineapple plantations.

Today there are about two million farms in the United States. Some farms are located near other farms, main highways, or roads. Other farms are isolated and are a long distance from their nearest neighbors.

Small Country Towns There is another kind of rural community—the small country town. It has a population of less than 2,500 and usually is located near open farmland. Most country towns have served as places where farmers could buy supplies and where rural people could shop, go to the movies, and send mail. They also have been marketing centers for farm crops.

During the 1930s many of the rural areas of the country experienced severe droughts and hard economic times. As a result, these areas lost population as farmers moved to the cities to find jobs.

Recently, however, some rural areas have begun to grow again. The newcomers are not farmers, but workers who commute to new businesses in the countryside. Land here is cheaper and operating costs are lower. As a result, there are now two rural Americas. One holds the old rural farm communities and small country towns. The other has farms but also businesses that have left the cities.

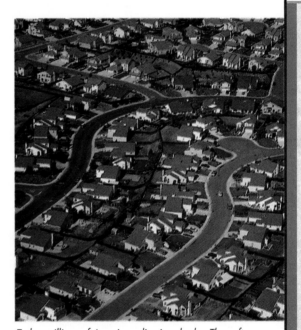

Today millions of Americans live in suburbs. They often travel to large cities to work but prefer to live in communities with more open space.

Suburbs

As you have read, a town, village, or community located on the outskirts of a city is called a suburb. People who live in the suburbs often work in the city. Each morning they travel from their homes to their city offices or other places of employment.

There are several reasons why people wish to live in the suburbs. Suburbs are smaller than cities, and some people prefer life in a smaller community. Others want their children to grow up in a community with more open spaces, trees, and places to play. They want a house with a backyard. Some families want to get away from city crowds, noise, pollution, and traffic.

Suburbs make it possible for people to live away from the city even though they earn their living in the city. Suburbs have been growing rapidly, however, and are now facing

GLOBAL PERSPECTIVES

The percentage of people living in cities with at least 750,000 inhabitants increased from 14.7 percent in 1965 to 17.4 percent in 1995. Asia, with 149 in all, had the largest number of cities with at least 750,000 inhabitants. North America had 56 such cities.

Calculating the population of urban areas is difficult for various reasons. One of those difficulties is actually defining the boundaries of an urban area. Various sources and almanacs may provide differing numbers. Some sources list the metropolis of Tokyo–Yokohama in Japan as the most populous urban area in the world (with more than 28 million inhabitants in 1995). Mexico City follows at nearly 24 million. The next eight are São Paulo, Brazil; Seoul, South Korea; New York City; Osaka–Kobe–Kyoto, Japan; Bombay, India; Calcutta, India; Rio de Janeiro, Brazil; and Buenos Aires, Argentina.

Reviewing

Have students complete the Section 1 Review.

Reteaching

Assign Section 1 of the Chapter 15 Reteaching Worksheet.

Extension

Encourage students who have visited nearby cities to describe their impressions in short paragraphs. Students might also create illustrations from photos they took or from other sources. In their paragraphs, students should compare their impressions about the cities with what they know about their own community.

MULTICULTURAL PERSPECTIVES

Metropolitan areas have always been a magnet for immigrants. Members of distinct culture groups often have settled in particular areas of a city. Living close to others from the same country or culture made adjusting to life in a new country less difficult. In this way, "cities within cities" arose. Some of these communities have names that associate them with the immigrants' native land: Little Italy, Chinatown, Little Havana. Visitors to these communities find many elements from the rich cultures of these immigrants' former countries. You might have students investigate such communities in your city or nearby cities.

New York City, like many of the nation's large cities, is a city of contrasts. It includes private homes, skyscrapers, theaters, parks, hotels, and restaurants.

many of the same challenges as cities, including crime and traffic jams.

Urban Areas

Cities, villages, towns, and boroughs of 2,500 or more people are called urban areas. Urban areas vary greatly in size. For example, Camilla, Georgia, has 5,124 people, making it an urban area. In contrast, New York City, another urban area, has a population of about seven million. Most urban areas in the United States have populations between the sizes of Camilla and New York City.

About three quarters of all Americans today live in urban communities. Those who live in the large cities are near theaters, restaurants, museums, art galleries, and other cultural advantages that cities offer. They enjoy the hustle and bustle of city living. Recent studies show, however, that the suburbs are growing faster than the cities. More than half the urban population lives outside the central

cities. A number of large cities actually have shown a loss in population in recent years.

Metropolitan Areas

Some cities, such as New York City, Dallas, Chicago, and Los Angeles, have become so large that it is difficult to tell where the city ends and the surrounding towns and suburbs begin. For this reason, as you have read, a large city and its surrounding towns and suburbs are referred to as a metropolitan area, or a metropolis. The metropolitan area of Chicago, Illinois, for example, includes several large cities in neighboring states, such as Gary, Indiana. There are 269 metropolitan areas in the United States today. Forty of these metropolitan areas have a population of at least one million each.

Some metropolitan areas have grown so large that they form a continuous urban chain. This type of giant urban area is referred to as a **megalopolis**. The metropolitan areas of

SECTION OBJECTIVES

After studying Section 2, students should be able to do the following.

1. Explain how communities influence the ways people live and the things people learn.

2. Identify ways people communicate with each other.

3. Describe how communities help people enjoy their lives, and identify various purposes of community recreational facilities.

4. Explain why communities need laws and regulations.

Teaching Section 2
Building a Vocabulary

Have students give examples of **recreation**. Ask: Can one person alone engage in recreation? *(yes)* Then ask: Can one person alone engage in **communication**? Explain to students that communication cannot take place unless there is a "sender" and a "receiver." The sender formulates and transmits a message, and the receiver interprets it.

Boston, New York, Philadelphia, Baltimore, and Washington, D.C., for example, form a megalopolis along the Atlantic coast.

SECTION 1 REVIEW

1. Define or identify the following terms: crossroads, megalopolis.

2. How did transportation help determine the location of many U.S. communities?

3. How do resources and climate help determine the kind of community a settlement will become?

4. How do the two rural Americas differ?

5. What kind of community can be called an urban area? How many metropolitan areas are there in the United States?

6. Which U.S. cities form a megalopolis along the Atlantic coast?

7. **THINKING CRITICALLY** Identify the advantages and disadvantages of city living. Then identify the advantages and disadvantages of life in the suburbs. In which type of community would you choose to live? Why?

---

2 Purposes of Communities

As you know, a community is a group of people having common interests who live in the same area and are governed by the same laws. What are some of these common interests? Also, how does a community serve its people and their interests?

Living and Learning in a Community

One of the most important things communities do is teach people how to live and work together. The first lessons in living and getting along with others are learned in the home. The family, as a small community, teaches important lessons in sharing and cooperating. As we grow up, we also learn from teachers, schoolmates, neighbors, and friends.

The people of our communities teach us to talk and behave the way we do. They teach us values by which to live happy and productive lives. The food we like, our respect for the law, the kind of person we want to be, and hundreds of other things are learned by living with the people of our community.

By building homes for people in need, these citizens are also building their community's future.

SECTION 1 REVIEW
ANSWERS

1. See the following pages: crossroads (p. 275); megalopolis (p. 278).

2. People settled in areas accessible by various means of transportation.

3. Natural resources help determine economic livelihoods. Climate helps determine economic livelihoods and lifestyles.

4. traditional rural America— made up of regions with rural farm communities and small country towns; newer rural America—has farms but also has factories and businesses built in the countryside, as well as commuting workers

5. village, town, borough, or city with a population of 2,500 or more; 269

6. Boston, New York, Philadelphia, Baltimore, Washington

7. Students who prefer cities might want access to the many activities found in cities. Those who prefer suburbs might want space, cleaner air, and safer neighborhoods.

Illustrating Ideas

Have students use newspapers and other periodicals to create collages illustrating the ways communities teach people how to live and work together. For example, some collages might include pictures of school sports teams and coaches working together toward a goal. Some students might include news articles on parenting or pictures of parents talking to their children. Each illustration should include an explanatory caption. Encourage students to be creative. Display the collages for the class to discuss.

Choose a prominent issue currently being discussed in your community. Then have small groups of students communicate the "story" in various ways: a television news story, a radio broadcast, a newspaper or magazine article, or any other method group members choose. Roles for members include producer, writer, reporter, narrator, headline writer, and technician. Have each group demonstrate for the class how each method of communication imparts the same information to its audience.

CIVICS SIDELIGHT

Americans have a wide choice of sources for getting information, and fewer are choosing newspapers as their sources. In 1994, 60 million U.S. residents subscribed to a daily newspaper. That figure was down from 62 million in 1970 and 63 million throughout much of the 1980s. Over the same time period, the U.S. population increased by more than 55 million people, from about 205 million in 1970 to nearly 261 million in 1994.

So where else are Americans getting their information? In 1994, 99 percent of U.S. households had at least one radio, 98 percent had at least one television, and 62 percent received cable television service. Also in 1994, 94 percent of U.S. households had telephone service. It seems that "word of mouth" exceeds the printed word as a preferred source of information for many Americans.

Communication

We continue to learn as long as we live. Almost every day we share information we have learned with others. This passing along of information, ideas, and beliefs from one person to another is known as **communication**.

One reason people live in communities is to be able to communicate with each other easily. The problems people face sometimes can be eased by talking them over with someone else. People also enjoy hearing about the latest happenings and learning new ideas from other people in the community.

Every community has a number of important means of communication. The most common one, as mentioned above, is conversation. Such modern inventions as telephones, computers, radios, and televisions have increased our ability to learn and share information. We

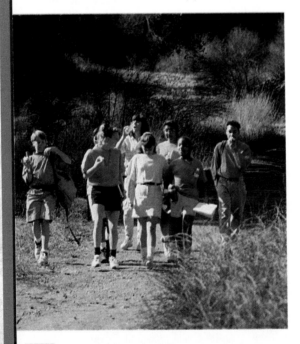

Communities often provide recreation areas, like this park. Community funds and community employees maintain these areas for all to enjoy.

also communicate in writing through letters and notes.

One of the main means of communication is the newspaper. Newspapers report events happening around the world. They also provide community news, such as what laws are passed, who is running for office, and when public meetings are held. In addition, newspapers tell us about births, marriages, and deaths in the community. Books and magazines are other important ways of communicating ideas and facts. Most U.S. communities provide free public libraries so that citizens have easy access to news, information, and ideas.

Recreation

One important reason people form communities is to enjoy the company of other people. Nearly every U.S. city and town has movie theaters, bowling alleys, skating rinks, parks, and other places of recreation that are open to the public. **Recreation** is relaxation or amusement by playing or doing something different from one's usual activities. Many larger cities have professional baseball, football, hockey, and basketball teams whose games are eagerly attended by sports fans.

Many recreational facilities are maintained at public expense. Taxes support public playgrounds, athletic fields, picnic grounds, basketball courts, and golf courses. There are also worthwhile activities sponsored by groups of citizens willing to volunteer their own time and money. The YMCA, YWCA, YMHA, Boy Scouts, Girl Scouts, Camp Fire Boys and Girls, Big Brothers/Big Sisters, and 4-H Clubs are examples of groups that help the members of the community relax and learn together.

Many communities have learned to take advantage of an unusually good climate or geographical location. They have promoted and developed these advantages not only for their own residents but also to attract tourists. Lake communities and seaside towns have developed boating, waterskiing, and swimming as special attractions. Rural communities promote hunting and fishing opportunities in

Writing to Persuade

Invite students to imagine that they live in a community with few or no recreational facilities. Have them write a letter to the editor of the local newspaper explaining the value of recreation and the purposes of recreational facilities. Letters should include proposals for the establishment of a place for the community to enjoy recreational activities.

Closure

Refer students to the chart on this page. Invite students to imagine what life would be like if one of these purposes of community life were missing. What if communities did not foster behaviors that teach citizens how to live and work with each other? What if government services such as police and fire departments did not exist? Have students write short paragraphs addressing similar questions about each of the five purposes of community shown in the chart.

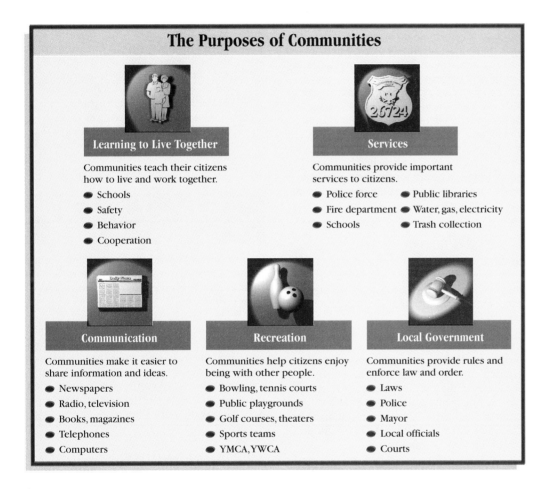

The Purposes of Communities

Learning to Live Together

Communities teach their citizens how to live and work together.

- Schools
- Safety
- Behavior
- Cooperation

Services

Communities provide important services to citizens.

- Police force
- Public libraries
- Fire department
- Water, gas, electricity
- Schools
- Trash collection

Communication

Communities make it easier to share information and ideas.

- Newspapers
- Radio, television
- Books, magazines
- Telephones
- Computers

Recreation

Communities help citizens enjoy being with other people.

- Bowling, tennis courts
- Public playgrounds
- Golf courses, theaters
- Sports teams
- YMCA, YWCA

Local Government

Communities provide rules and enforce law and order.

- Laws
- Police
- Mayor
- Local officials
- Courts

their areas. Other communities have developed skiing, horseback riding, rock climbing, and hiking facilities.

Good community recreational facilities serve a number of purposes:

- They provide worthwhile ways for Americans to use their leisure time by giving people interesting and healthful things to do.
- They help members of the community keep physically fit. Well-managed swimming pools, playgrounds, and recreation centers encourage good health habits and help members of the community build healthy bodies.

- They expand people's knowledge and may help develop new interests and hobbies. A community cooking class or reading club, for example, can teach much about geography and history.
- They help people benefit from recreation by relaxing and having fun in the company of others. Recreation helps "re-create" the individual—to feel like a new person.

Community Services

One of the reasons communities form is to provide services to their citizens. There are certain things the people of a community

SECTION OBJECTIVES

After studying Section 3, students should be able to do the following.

1. Explain how a person can live in several communities at the same time.

2. Identify challenges facing U.S. communities.

3. Describe how volunteer groups help improve the communities in which we live.

4. Explain how good citizenship is related to developing good communities.

SECTION 2 REVIEW ANSWERS

1. See the following page: communication, recreation (p. 280).

2. People learn many things (such as ways of talking, behavior, and values) by interacting with other people in the community.

3. conversation, telephones, computers, radios, television, letters, notes, newspapers, books, magazines

4. provide recreational facilities and activities, volunteer groups, services; purposes— give people interesting and healthy things to do, enable people to keep physically fit, expand the mind through new interests and hobbies, enable people to spend time in company of others

5. to maintain peace and order

6. Students might mention such things as additional recreational services, youth centers, enhanced police and fire protection, and improved transportation services.

282

working together can do more effectively than each person can separately. A good police force and fire department help ensure public safety. Public schools provide education.

People living as neighbors in a community also need pure water, an efficient sewage system, regular trash removal, and dependable gas and electric services. Sometimes the people of a community join together and vote to have these needed services furnished by their local government in return for the taxes they pay. In other cases some services are provided by private companies.

Local Government

In the United States, communities of all sizes serve their citizens by providing local government. When people live together in a community, some kinds of laws and regulations are needed to keep order.

Suppose that two neighbors argue over the location of the boundary that separates their properties. If there were no laws or local government, these neighbors might use force to settle their difficulties. Fortunately, as you have learned, communities provide local government and laws. Local courts, judges, and law enforcement officers help maintain peace and order in our communities.

SECTION 2 REVIEW

1. Define or identify the following terms: communication, recreation.

2. How do communities influence what people learn?

3. What methods do people use to communicate with each other?

4. How do communities help people enjoy their lives? What are four purposes of community recreational facilities?

5. Why do local communities need laws and regulations?

6. THINKING CRITICALLY You have just been named to head the Community Services division of your local government. Explain how the existing services in your local community might be improved. What new services might benefit the people of your community? How will these new services be funded?

3 Citizens Serve Communities

Communities depend on cooperation among people. Only by people working together for their common benefit can communities serve their citizens well.

To encourage cooperation some citizenship services are compulsory. For example, members of a community must obey its laws or suffer the penalty established. Likewise, young citizens must attend school. In most matters, however, communities rely on their members to respect the rights of others simply because it is the right thing to do.

Your Communities

Each of us lives in a number of different communities. We profit from their services, and we owe certain duties and responsibilities in return. In many ways the family is a kind of community. The obligations of cooperation and respect for members of our family—the smallest community in which we live—have already been discussed in Chapter 13. This cooperation and respect should extend to people living in our immediate neighborhood and to the larger communities of our town or city, state, and nation.

Every community faces challenges that must be met so that life in that community can be pleasant. These challenges can be met if every member of the community takes an interest in them.

Ask students how they would illustrate the idea that each of us lives in several communities at the same time. Encourage students to express their ideas freely. Here is one possibility: a chart with a small circle to represent the family, surrounded by a larger circle that encloses the community, surrounded by a representation of your state, and all encircled by an outline of the United States. Some students might choose to use pictures and captions to illustrate the communities in which they live.

COOPERATIVE LEARNING

Have small groups use newspapers and other periodicals to identify an important challenge facing your community. Each group should then develop a course of action for meeting the challenge. Plans need not be too detailed, but they should include general goals and proposals for achieving them. The group should appoint a chairperson and a recording secretary. Another member should illustrate the plan of action with a flowchart or other graphic device. One or two members should present the plan to the class.

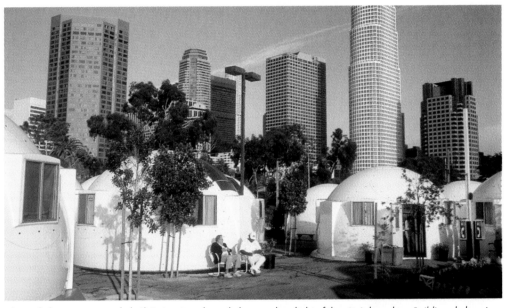

These shelters were recently built in Los Angeles to help ease the plight of the city's homeless. Building shelters is just one example of how communities work to solve problems.

Improving Communities

Groups of concerned citizens are taking action on many issues in their communities. Consider Las Vegas, New Mexico, a town of about 15,000 people. For years the streets and sidewalks of Las Vegas were in need of repair. The town also had few recreation centers. Nevertheless, the citizens of Las Vegas were proud of their community and wanted to work to improve it.

The mayor headed the community's improvement program. A new gymnasium was added to the high school. A community swimming pool was built. As streets and sidewalks were rebuilt, the town began to show new signs of life. More projects were planned to continue Las Vegas's program of improvement.

Each year other U.S. communities face similar issues and do something about them. For example, the citizens of Decatur, Illinois, undertook a program to improve their downtown areas, clear slums, and reduce traffic jams. Decatur cleared and rebuilt a large part

of its business district. In similar fashion, the city of Worcester, Massachusetts, established a successful new program consisting of better schools, playgrounds, museums, and retirement homes.

When the people of Pittsburgh, Pennsylvania, took a critical look at their city, they were not pleased with what they saw. The smoke from the steel mills and factories was so thick that Pittsburgh was known as "the Smoky City." Traffic jams choked city streets, and the central city was in poor repair.

The people of Pittsburgh voted to spend the money needed to improve their city. New skyscrapers were built. A successful campaign against air pollution reduced the smoke in the air. More roads were built, a new water system was planned, and parks and recreation centers were added.

Proud of their efforts, the citizens of Pittsburgh learned that their city must continue to plan, build, and change if it is to meet their needs in the future. Across the nation, cities such as Baltimore, Philadelphia, Houston,

CIVICS SIDELIGHT

The need for community improvement took on a new intensity after riots shattered much of south central Los Angeles in 1992. Henry G. Cisneros, the former mayor of San Antonio, Texas, and then U.S. Secretary of Housing and Urban Development, offered this advice on how to reinvigorate the city: "Bring people together in a more consistent, systematic, tireless and structured way than ever before. That means informal as well as formal leaders, not just people who head organizations or run corporations, but people who work in the neighborhoods and have churches in the area and speak for community organizations—and even some in the gang structure. At a minimum, take the temperature of the community regularly and try to understand what people are thinking and saying."

Guided Practice

Have students list on the chalkboard the various volunteer groups that contribute to the improvement of their communities. Ask students how these volunteer groups contribute. Then help students create a class volunteer project. The class should choose an important cause and debate the best way students can volunteer their efforts. You might invite a spokesperson from a volunteer organization in your community to speak to the class about particular needs his or her organization has.

Independent Practice

Have students write letters to the editor describing how volunteer work promotes good citizenship and how good citizenship is related to good communities. Students might choose particular volunteer projects to use as examples in their letters. Call on volunteers to read their letters to the class. Encourage students to send the final drafts of their letters to a local newspaper.

CIVICS SIDELIGHT

Former president Jimmy Carter has been a model of the volunteer spirit through his work with Habitat for Humanity International, a Georgia-based non-profit organization that helps people in need build homes for themselves. Carter and his wife, Rosalyn, have, on numerous occasions, rolled up their sleeves and worked side by side with other volunteers (and the future homeowners) pounding nails, sawing lumber, and otherwise making direct contributions to the well-being of less fortunate individuals.

The former president also has become something of a freelance international diplomat. Carter has served in a variety of roles around the world since he left office, including as an election observer and a negotiator in international disputes.

GLOBAL CONNECTIONS

Volunteerism in Russia

Volunteerism has a long history in the United States. George Washington, Benjamin Franklin, and Paul Revere, for example, all served in volunteer fire companies. In fact, Benjamin Franklin started the nation's first volunteer fire company. Since that time, volunteer groups and organizations have become a common feature of life in the United States.

Some nations, however, are just beginning to experiment with organized volunteerism. In Russia, for example, Big Brothers/Big Sisters of Moscow recently opened. Like its U.S. counterpart, this volunteer organization links volunteers aged 21 or older with young people aged 7 to 18 who are in need of role models. The volunteers spend several hours a week with their young friends, giving them guidance and friendship. The organization is financed by contributions from Russian businesses.

Organizers in Moscow learned about the Big Brothers/Big Sisters program by reading a U.S. newspaper account that reported increases in self-esteem and optimism among the organization's volunteers. They then asked the executive director of New York City's Big Brothers/Big Sisters to help them open a chapter of the organization in Moscow. By the time it dedicated its office in 1992, Big Brothers/Big Sisters of Moscow had screened and assigned its first 50 volunteers.

Denver, and St. Paul have rebuilt older areas of their cities. These improvement programs have turned the areas into business and entertainment centers.

Community Volunteers

Another way citizens can improve their communities is by becoming volunteers. As you recall, a volunteer is someone who offers to work without pay. Many Americans do not realize how much work is done by volunteers.

Volunteers help the sick, the needy, older citizens, and people with disabilities. They collect money for charities. In some areas volunteers put out fires and drive ambulances. Volunteers help in schools, libraries, museums, sports groups, and many other organizations.

Communities rely on the help of volunteers because no government can know all the needs of local areas. Volunteers also help provide services a community might otherwise be unable to afford. It is up to all of us to help keep communities healthy, clean, and safe.

Volunteer Groups

The United States has many different kinds of volunteer groups. Some are small local groups. Others are large national organizations that depend on local volunteers to carry out their work. A small group may be formed for a specific purpose, such as cleaning up the neighborhood. After the problem is solved, the group disbands. Some areas, however, have permanent neighborhood groups that meet regularly to discuss community needs.

Many towns, cities, and counties have permanent volunteer groups. They include hospital volunteers, volunteer firefighters, and student-parent-teacher associations. Such groups rely on the help of citizens of all ages. Some high school students, for example, take older citizens to doctor appointments. Retired people may spend a few hours each week helping in libraries, hospitals, and other community facilities.

Some groups require that volunteers take short courses to learn specific skills, such as

Closure

Have students work together to create posters encouraging young people to volunteer in their communities. The posters should show the connection between good citizenship and good communities. Invite your school principal to view the posters, and arrange to have them placed around the school as part of a campaign to promote volunteerism.

Reviewing

Have students complete the Section 3 Review.

Reteaching

Assign Section 3 of the Chapter 15 Reteaching Worksheet.

---

first aid and operating special equipment. Those people who take part in these programs have the satisfaction of performing a valuable service for their community. They also learn useful new skills.

Among the large national volunteer groups are the League of Women Voters, the American Cancer Society, the American Red Cross, and Volunteers of America. These associations are supported by money from private contributors and depend on the services of volunteers. A large group such as the American Red Cross has millions of volunteers working for it. Local branches of these organizations are usually started by concerned citizens. Community members can support these groups with time, ideas, and money.

Good Citizens Make Good Communities

Right now you are an active member of your local community. You attend its schools and enjoy its parks and recreation centers. You are protected by its police and fire departments. You depend on it to provide you with many other services. Someday you may work and raise a family in your community. It is important, therefore, that you be a good citizen in your local community.

It is also important that you be a good citizen in the other communities in which you live. These communities include your state and your nation. Remember that you are also a member of the global community—the community of all people in the world. To be a good global citizen, you must stay informed about world events.

Because you enjoy the benefits of all the communities of which you are a member, you have certain duties and responsibilities to those communities. These range from picking up litter to offering your services as a volunteer. For communities to continue to benefit citizens, citizens must make contributions to their communities. It is up to you to take pride in your communities and practice good citizenship wherever you are.

SECTION 3 REVIEW

1. How can a person live in several communities at the same time?

2. What are some of the challenges facing U.S. communities?

3. How do volunteer groups help improve communities?

4. How is good citizenship related to good communities?

5. **THINKING CRITICALLY** Identify volunteer groups in your community. Which group are you most interested in joining? Why? How much time each week could you give to this group? How might your community benefit from your involvement in this group?

CHAPTER 15 SUMMARY

The United States is a nation of many communities. These communities differ greatly in size and population. They face many common challenges, however, wherever they are located—in rural or in urban areas.

Communities serve many important purposes. They help us enjoy living among other citizens, receive a good education, and earn a living. Communities also provide needed services and maintain law and order. The prosperity of a community depends on its location, climate, natural and industrial resources, and hardworking citizens.

Many communities are carrying out planned programs of improvement. Cities such as Pittsburgh and Houston have attracted many different industries and built cleaner and more beautiful cities. Much work remains to be done in the nation's communities. Citizens can help to improve their communities by becoming volunteers and by fulfilling the responsibilities of citizenship.

SECTION 3 REVIEW ANSWERS

1. Families, neighborhoods, cities, towns, rural areas, states, the nation, and the world each constitute a community.

2. need for infrastructure repair and better and new community facilities; pollution; traffic congestion; crime; slums

3. help the sick, the needy, older citizens, and people with disabilities; collect money for charities; serve as firefighters; drive ambulances and assist emergency personnel; help in schools, libraries, sports groups, other organizations; provide other services communities otherwise could not afford

4. If citizens did not fulfill their duties and responsibilities, the quality of life in communities would suffer.

5. Students should realize that their contributions would help make their communities better places to live.

Point out that the process of government at the local, state, and national levels is largely carried out by groups. Volunteer groups organize efforts to meet community needs. Groups of employees in business work together to create and sell products and to provide services.

Have pairs of students study one group in government, business, or the community at large. Each pair should use the guidelines on this page to explain how its assigned group works effectively. Students should write short reports or outlines and provide visual guides to present to the class.

Developing Civics Skills

LIFE SKILL
Working in Groups

1. Most people work with various groups of people throughout their lives. Knowing how to work with others helps make a group more effective and time spent with the group more enjoyable.

2. Leaders keep groups focused on goals and ensure that members have the opportunity to contribute ideas. Students might say that a leader should be serious, flexible, fair, and knowledgeable.

3. Compromise must be used to achieve agreement among members, all of whom may have different ideas about how something should be done.

4. Students should realize that following the guidelines will improve the quality of group activities.

Chances are that you will work with some group of people nearly every day of your life. That group may be your family, your classmates, your friends, or your coworkers. It is important that you know how to work effectively as a member of all these groups. This knowledge will make your group more effective and make your time with the group much more enjoyable.

How to Work in Groups

1. **Identify the group's purpose.** Groups are usually formed to accomplish a particular task. For example, your teacher may organize the class into groups to complete a project. It is important that the members of each group understand the group's goal, or purpose. Otherwise, the resulting confusion among members can interfere with achieving that goal.

2. **Create an agenda.** An agenda is an itemized plan of the topics to be covered in a meeting. It is useful for keeping group members on task. The agenda for the first meeting of a group might include the election of the group's leader, a discussion of the group's goals, and the assignment of individual tasks.

3. **Choose a group leader.** Because groups are made up of many people, it is often helpful to have a leader. The leader can help keep the group's discussion focused on the group's goal. The leader also can make sure that all of the items on the group's agenda are covered. Equally important is the leader's role in making sure that all group members have the opportunity to contribute their ideas.

4. **Be a good communicator.** Communication in a group means speaking *and* listening. Organize your thoughts before you

speak so that you are sure about the ideas you want to contribute. Do not interrupt other members of the group. Speak clearly so that you will be understood by everyone. When other group members are speaking, listen closely to what they have to say. Ask questions if you are unclear on their ideas.

5. **Compromise to reach a decision.** Groups are made up of a number of people who usually have different ideas about how things should be done. How do groups agree on what action to take? Group members compromise to reach an agreement. For people to compromise, each side needs to make sure the other side receives something in return. In this way all members of a group will accept a proposal even though it might not completely satisfy everyone. As you have learned, compromise is a vital part of the democratic process.

Applying the Skill

Answer the following questions.

1. Why is it important to know how to work with a group of people?

2. Why is having a leader helpful for a group? What qualities do you think an effective group leader should have?

3. Why is compromise vital to the achievement of group goals?

4. Identify a group of people you have worked with recently. The group may have been at home, at school, or elsewhere. Did the group follow the guidelines on this page? If so, explain how this benefited the group. If your group did not follow these guidelines, explain how its work differed.

CHAPTER 15 REVIEW
A N S W E R S

Vocabulary Workshop
1. crossroads
2. megalopolis
3. communication
4. recreation

Reviewing Main Ideas
1. communicate with others easily, enjoy company of others, health and safety, to fulfill need for goods and services; Families, local areas, states, the nation, and the world all are communities.
2. People settled in areas accessible by various means of transportation. Natural factors help determine economy and industry in an area.
3. Volunteers serve varied needs; provide services community cannot afford; help the sick, the needy, older citizens, and people with disabilities; collect money for charities; serve as firefighters and other emergency personnel; help in schools, libraries, and various organizations.
4. suburbs—smaller communities, more space, cleaner, quieter; cities—variety of activities, cultural advantages, excitement, action
5. infrastructure repair; pollution; traffic congestion; crime; slums
6. traditional rural America—made up of regions with rural farm communities and small country towns; newer rural America—has farms, factories, businesses built in the countryside, commuting workers

Thinking Critically
1. Students should make reasoned arguments.
2. Community service may teach offenders responsibility and respect for others.

Citizenship in Your Community
Profiles should address factors in the community's development.

Building Your Portfolio
Assign Portfolio Assessment Worksheet 15 in the *Portfolio Assessment Worksheets* booklet.

Assessment
• **Chapter 15 Tests**, *Chapter Tests* booklet
• **Test Generator**, Chapter 15
• **Portfolio**, Portfolio Assessment Worksheet 15, *Portfolio Assessment Worksheets* booklet

CHAPTER 15
R • e • v • i • e • w

Vocabulary Workshop
1. What is the term for a place where two main roads meet?
2. When a number of cities grow together, what giant urban area forms?
3. What term is used to describe the passing along of information, ideas, and beliefs from one person to another?
4. What term refers to relaxation or amusement by doing something other than one's usual activities?

Reviewing Main Ideas
1. Why do people live and work in communities? How is it possible to live in several communities at the same time?
2. What role did transportation play in determining the location of early American communities? How do natural factors influence the development of communities?
3. In what ways are volunteer organizations essential to a community's success?
4. What are some advantages to living in the suburbs? Why do some people choose to live in cities?
5. What problems do communities in the United States face?
6. How do the "two rural Americas" differ?

Thinking Critically
1. Some U.S. communities require students to volunteer for community service activities in order to pass particular courses or to graduate from school. Do you think being required to volunteer adds to or detracts from the spirit of volunteerism?
2. People who commit minor crimes sometimes are ordered to perform community service rather than go to jail or pay a fine. What is the purpose of such a sentence? Do you think this type of sentencing for minor crimes is more beneficial to a community than jail time or fines? Why?

Citizenship in Your Community

Individual Project
Conduct library research and contact historical associations in your area to learn about the factors that influenced where your community was founded. Did your community serve as a transportation center? What kinds of transportation did your community's early settlers use? What natural resources made your community an attractive place to settle? Use your findings to create a community profile showing the community's location, natural resources, and economic activities.

Building Your Portfolio

The third step of your unit portfolio project (see page 309) is to consider good citizenship in the community by conducting a survey of young citizens in your school. Ask the citizens about their involvement in volunteer activities. What percentage belong to volunteer groups? What kinds of volunteer work do they perform? How much time do they donate? How did they become involved in volunteer work? Show in a collage the volunteer work these young citizens perform. Below the images write a caption answering the above questions. Title your collage "Young Citizens Help Strengthen Their Communities." Place your collage in your individual portfolio for later use.

PLANNING GUIDE

TEXTBOOK	TEACHING RESOURCES	OTHER AVAILABLE RESOURCES
Chapter	• Skills Worksheet 16 • Challenge/Enrichment Worksheet 16	
Section **1** Crime in the United States Page 289	• Reteaching Worksheet 16.1	
2 The Criminal Justice System Page 293	• Reteaching Worksheet 16.2	
3 Juvenile Crime Page 300	• Reteaching Worksheet 16.3	
Review and Assessment **Chapter 16 Review**, Page 307 **Unit 5 Review**, Page 308	• *Test, Form A* • *Test, Form B* • Portfolio Assessment Worksheet 16 • Unit 5 Portfolio Assessment Worksheet	• *Test Generator*, Chapter 16 • *Test Generator*, Unit 5

ADDITIONAL RESOURCES

BOOKS FOR TEACHERS

Barr, Robert D., *Values and Youth*, National Council for the Social Studies.

Bortner, M. A., *Delinquency & Justice: An Age of Crisis*, McGraw-Hill.

Currie, Elliott, *Confronting Crime: An American Challenge*, Pantheon.

Prothrow-Stith, Deborah, *Deadly Consequences*, HarperCollins.

BOOKS FOR STUDENTS

Anonymous, *Go Ask Alice*, Avon. Diary of an adolescent drug abuser.

La Vert, Marianne, *Crime in America*, Facts on File. Packed with information about the nature of crime and violence, cultural sources of violence, and the various types of crime in the United States.

Meltzer, Milton, *Crime in America*, Morrow. This comprehensive overview of crime examines street crime, abused

family members, organized crime, and law enforcement.

Wekesser, Carol, ed., *The Death Penalty: Opposing Viewpoints*, Greenhaven. Essays reflect various positions on capital punishment.

MULTIMEDIA RESOURCES

The Death Penalty: What Is Fair? (fs, sd), SRS. A balanced presentation of the history of and controversy surrounding capital punishment.

Gangs (VHS, c, 45 min.), COR/MTI. Tells the story of two brothers in East Los Angeles whose attitudes differ about involvement in gang life.

Great American Trials (fs, sd), SRA. Six filmstrips include "Peter Zenger," "The Scopes Trial," and "The Chicago Seven."

Street Law Mock Trials Series (simulations), SSSS. Offers learning experiences that

deal with issues such as divorce, guardianship, and juvenile crime.

The Vandals (VHS, c, 25 min.), GA. Examines the social causes of vandalism.

THE INTERNET

Have students use these search words to locate more information about chapter topics on the Internet: *crime statistics, organized crime, criminal justice, police officers, juvenile crime.*

GLOBAL SKILL BUILDER

You might wish to use **Navigating the Internet** from the interactive *Global Skill Builder* CD-ROM to aid students' understanding of the Internet as a resource.

Abbreviations: b&w=black and white; c=color; f=film; fs=filmstrip; sd=sound; tr=transparency; VHS=videotape

CIVICS SKILLS

Students will learn how to conduct library research. Students also will learn terms important to understanding the value of laws in society.

CITIZENSHIP VALUES

✭ **Rights and Responsibilities** Students will be encouraged to understand the criminal justice system, to appreciate the work of the police in fighting crime, and to recognize ways to practice juvenile responsibility.

AMERICAN GOVERNMENT

✭ **Structures and Functions** Students will learn about the categories and causes of crime. They will learn about the criminal justice system, the training of police and the work they perform, the process a suspect must undergo after arrest, and the various ways of punishing lawbreakers. Students also will learn about juvenile crime, its causes, and juvenile courts.

MEETING INDIVIDUAL NEEDS

LIMITED ENGLISH PROFICIENCY (LEP)

Pair an LEP student with a student who is proficient in English. Have them write each chapter vocabulary term on a card and put each definition or descriptive sketch of the term's meaning on another card. Have them shuffle and lay out the cards on a table. Students should take turns turning over a pair of cards to try to match a term with its definition. If a player makes a "match," he or she takes those two cards out of play. Unmatched cards are replaced in their original positions on the table. Pairs may or may not wish to keep score.

LEARNERS HAVING DIFFICULTY

Ask each student to prepare a quiz consisting of 10 questions about information in the chapter. On a separate sheet of paper, students should write the answers to their quizzes for later use. Then have students take each other's quizzes. When they are done, have the quiz makers grade the quizzes.

AUDITORY LEARNERS

Invite a police officer to speak to the class about how people can avoid becoming victims of crime. Have students prepare for the talk by thinking about what they can do to avoid becoming victims of certain types of crime. Students should take notes about what the officer has to say and then should summarize his or her talk by writing news articles entitled "Ten Ways to Prevent Crime."

VISUAL LEARNERS

Have students create anti-crime posters. Each student should determine whether his or her poster's audience is made up of children, teenagers, adults, or the general public. The posters should address such topics as ways to prevent crime and how to avoid being a crime victim.

TACTILE/KINESTHETIC LEARNERS

Have students list the causes of juvenile crime on the chalkboard. Encourage them to choose one cause and express their feelings about it in a drawing, a poem, a rap, or in some other creative way. Invite volunteers to present their projects to the class.

GIFTED LEARNERS

Have students research crime in other countries. Students should investigate such information as crime rates, punishments, and societal attitudes toward crime. Students should compile their information in oral reports supported by visual guides that help explain their research.

CHAPTER OVERVIEW

Chapter 16 examines the problem of crime, including its alarming increase among young people. It also considers how the U.S. criminal justice system tries to protect citizens from crime and still uphold the rights of the accused. The underlying theme of the chapter is that American society depends on responsible citizens who obey the law and support the officials who bring criminals to justice.

Motivator

Bring a week's worth of newspapers to class and have students find as many articles about crime as they can in those newspapers. Call on volunteers to list on the chalkboard the different kinds of crime written about in the newspapers. Ask: Is anyone in society not affected by crime? Why or why not? Lead a brief discussion concerning how crime affects people's everyday lives, physically, financially, and psychologically.

CHAPTER OBJECTIVES

After studying Chapter 16, students should be able to do the following.

1. Define crime and explain how crimes are categorized.
2. Identify the causes and costs of crime.
3. Explain how the U.S. criminal justice system works.
4. Explain how the juvenile justice system operates.

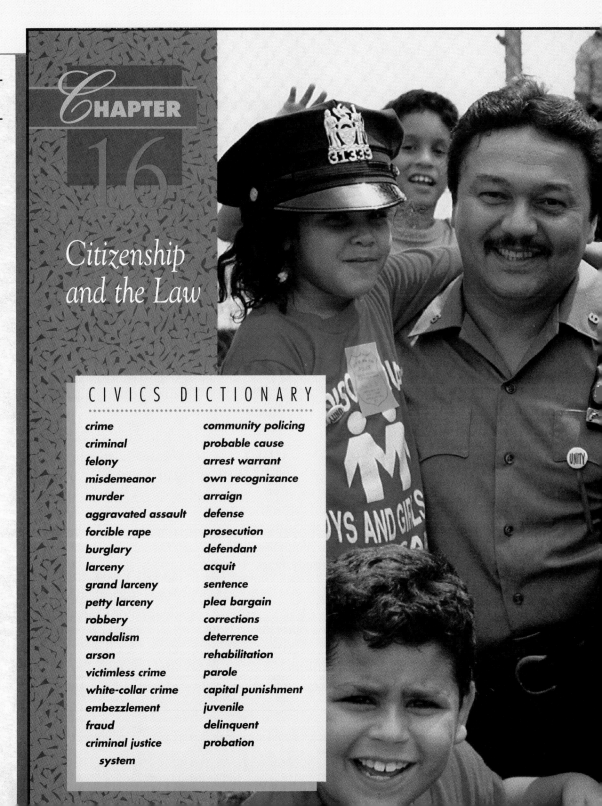

CHAPTER 16

Citizenship and the Law

CIVICS DICTIONARY

crime	community policing
criminal	probable cause
felony	arrest warrant
misdemeanor	own recognizance
murder	arraign
aggravated assault	defense
forcible rape	prosecution
burglary	defendant
larceny	acquit
grand larceny	sentence
petty larceny	plea bargain
robbery	corrections
vandalism	deterrence
arson	rehabilitation
victimless crime	parole
white-collar crime	capital punishment
embezzlement	juvenile
fraud	delinquent
criminal justice	probation
system	

SECTION OBJECTIVES

After studying Section 1, students should be able to do the following.

1. Identify the main source of information about U.S. crime.
2. Distinguish crimes against persons from crimes against property.
3. Explain why everyone pays for white-collar crimes.
4. Explain the difficulty in catching members of organized crime.
5. Identify four possible reasons for crime.

Teaching Section 1

Building a Vocabulary

Explain that state laws distinguish between the seriousness of crimes, categorizing some crimes as **felonies** and less serious crimes as **misdemeanors**. You might invite a lawyer to your class to provide examples of each kind of crime. Help students understand the concept by having them suggest school rules, categorize them according to seriousness, and explain why violations of some rules are more serious than violations of others.

CHAPTER FOCUS

Have you or anyone you know ever been the victim of crime? If so, you know what a high psychological, economic, and even physical toll crime can take on its victims. Crime also takes a serious toll on the nation's prosperity and quality of life.

Although it is the duty of all citizens to obey the law, some people choose to break the law. Thus we must rely on a system of police, courts, and prisons to protect us. But you also must do your part. You must learn and obey the laws and encourage others to do the same. Only if all Americans work toward solving the problem of crime can we feel safe in our homes, communities, and nation.

. . . .

STUDY GUIDE

● What is crime, and how are crimes categorized?

● What are the causes and costs of crime?

● How does the criminal justice system operate in the United States?

● How does the juvenile justice system operate?

CIVICS SIDELIGHT

The FBI annually publishes its *Crime Clock* statistics, which show how often certain crimes occur in the United States when averaged out over the whole year. The 1994 *Crime Clock* revealed that, on average, a violent crime took place every 17 seconds and a property crime took place every 3 seconds. It also showed that there was one murder every 23 minutes, one forcible rape every 5 minutes, one robbery every 51 seconds, one aggravated assault every 28 seconds, one burglary every 12 seconds, one larceny-theft every 4 seconds, and one motor-vehicle theft every 20 seconds.

1 Crime in the United States

The Federal Bureau of Investigation (FBI) is the main source of information on crime in the United States. According to the FBI, serious crime in the United States has risen almost 17 percent over the past decade. In recent years more than 14 million serious crimes have been reported each year. Americans have become increasingly alarmed by the extent of crime in the United States.

What is considered a crime? A **crime** is any act that breaks the law and for which a punishment has been established. A **criminal** is a person who commits any type of crime. The FBI identifies 29 types of crime. Serious crimes, such as murder and kidnapping, are called **felonies**. Less serious offenses, such as traffic violations and disorderly conduct, are called **misdemeanors**.

The 29 types of crime are categorized in other ways as well. Five main crime categories are crimes against persons, crimes against property, victimless crimes, white-collar crimes, and organized crimes.

Crimes Against Persons

Crimes against persons are violent crimes, or acts that harm or end a person's life or that threaten to do so. The most serious of such crimes is **murder,** or the willful killing of one person by another person. Nearly 25,000 murders are committed in the nation each year.

The most common type of violent crime is aggravated assault. **Aggravated assault** is any kind of physical injury that is done intentionally to another person. Such assault is often committed during the act of robbing someone. The FBI records more than one million cases of aggravated assault each year.

Another type of violent crime is **forcible rape,** or the sexual violation of a person by force and against the person's will. According to the FBI, more than 100,000 forcible rapes take place in the United States each year.

Crimes Against Property

Most crimes committed in the United States are crimes against property. This type of crime includes actions that involve stealing or destroying someone else's property. The forcible

Writing a Dialogue

Invite students to imagine they are newspaper reporters who need to find out the latest crime statistics. Ask: Who would you call? *(FBI)* Have students write the dialogue that might take place between a reporter and the FBI. Tell students that, of course, the reporter wants to be sure the FBI's figures are accurate and complete. Ask: Is that possible? *(It is impossible to know how many crimes are committed each year.)* Students should include their answers in their fictional dialogues.

Learning from Examples

Bring to class lists of police calls printed in your local newspaper or obtain such lists from local law enforcement authorities. Using the lists, describe various crimes reported to police and have students discuss what kind of crime probably has been committed (such as burglary, larceny, or robbery). You might send students' responses along with the lists to a police officer and have him or her determine whether students' answers are correct.

GLOBAL PERSPECTIVES

The history of the term *vandalism* goes back to ancient Roman times. Among the Germanic tribes who overran the Roman Empire in the fifth century was a particularly terrifying group known as the Vandals. They sacked Rome in 455, looting its treasures in a destructive rampage. Today the term *vandal* is applied to anyone who destroys property deliberately or out of ignorance.

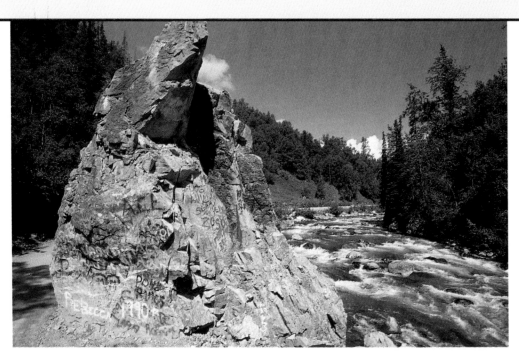

Each year thousands of people are arrested in the United States for vandalism. This photograph shows how vandalism can harm a beautiful area.

or illegal entry into someone's home or other property with the intention to steal is called **burglary**. Around three million burglaries a year were reported in recent years.

Larceny is theft of property without the use of force or violence. Examples of larceny include stealing from a cash drawer and shoplifting. If the property is worth more than a certain amount of money (which varies from state to state), the theft is called **grand larceny**. A theft of goods valued under this amount is called **petty larceny**.

The theft of automobiles, or motor vehicle theft, is a common crime against property and a serious national problem. More than 1.5 million cars are reported stolen each year. Many cars are taken by organized gangs that resell them or strip them and sell the parts. Other cases involve young people who risk arrest to steal the cars, drive them for a while, and then abandon them.

Robbery is a crime that involves both property and persons. It may be defined as taking something from a person by threatening the person with injury. The robber may demand "your money or your life" and back the threat with a weapon. More than 600,000 robberies take place in the United States each year. Many of them involve the use of firearms. A murder committed during a robbery, even if the murder is unplanned, may be punished by life imprisonment.

Another kind of crime against property is **vandalism**, or the willful destruction of property. **Arson** is the destruction of property by setting fire to it. The damaging of schools and other public property by vandalism and arson has been increasing. These forms of crime hurt all citizens in a community.

Victimless Crimes

Some crimes, such as gambling and the use of illegal drugs, are called **victimless crimes**. In such crimes there is no victim whose rights are invaded by another person. These crimes

Have students list on the chalkboard reasons people commit crimes. Help them understand these reasons by making up specific examples, or scenarios, of fictional characters who turn to crime—one example for each reason listed on the chalkboard. Then ask: Why do you think members of organized crime turn to illegal activities?

Have students write newspaper editorials on how to decrease crime rates. The editorials should include references to the causes of crime, though students are free to argue that one (or more) of these causes has less to do with crime than others do. Each editorial should include proposals for addressing the causes of crime and other methods for reducing crime. Some students might want to focus on efforts to fight organized crime. Call on volunteers to read their editorials to their class.

mainly harm the lawbreakers themselves. Nevertheless, victimless crimes are harmful to society. The sale and possession of illegal drugs increases the death rate and often leads to other types of crime, such as robbery. Gamblers who lose their money may turn to stealing and other crimes.

White-Collar Crimes

Crimes committed for illegal gain by people in the course of their work are called **white-collar crimes**. These crimes range from stealing office supplies to embezzlement and fraud. **Embezzlement** is taking for one's own use money that has been entrusted to one's care. **Fraud** is taking someone else's money or property through dishonesty. A person commits fraud when charging for services that were not performed, for example.

Although it is impossible to know exactly how much money such crimes cost U.S. businesses each year, experts estimate it is billions of dollars. Everyone pays for white-collar crime, because the financial costs of these crimes are passed on to consumers in the form of higher prices.

Many white-collar crimes involve computers. Today most businesses and government offices use computers. Some criminals break into these computer systems to commit electronic theft, fraud, and embezzlement.

Organized Crime

When most people think of criminals, they think of individuals who act on their own to commit crimes. This is not always the case. Some criminals are part of organized crime. That is, they belong to a crime syndicate, or a large organization of professional criminals.

Organized crime syndicates specialize in providing illegal goods and services, such as gambling, drug trafficking, prostitution, and loan-sharking, or lending money at extremely high interest rates. Often these crime syndicates engage in legal business pursuits that serve as a front, or cover, for illegal activities. Criminals in crime syndicates are difficult to catch. They often use terror tactics and violence to keep people from going to the police.

Rising Fear of Crime

National statistics on crime are collected from local police departments by the FBI. The U.S. Bureau of Justice Statistics, meanwhile, collects information on crime from crime victims. Even with all this information, however, it is impossible to know how many crimes are committed each year. One reason is that many crimes go undetected. Also, citizens do not always report crimes to the police. For these reasons, the crime rate undoubtedly is higher than statistics indicate.

According to a recent poll, nine out of ten adults believe that crime in the United States is on the rise. With crime comes fear, not only for adults but for young people as well. A recent poll of teenagers found that many of them have changed their daily routine in order to avoid becoming victims of crime.

Causes of Crime

Although no one really knows why people commit crimes, there are many theories. The causes usually given for crime and its increase are poverty, illegal drug use, and certain trends in society.

Poverty One cause of crime is poverty. Many poor people live in slums, where there is overcrowding, poor education, and unstable family life. Under these conditions, many people do not receive the training they need for good jobs. In such an environment, people often feel helpless and angry. Some people break the law to "get even" with society for the kind of life they have.

Illegal Drug Use In recent years the use of illegal drugs has risen in the United States. Arrests related to drug use add to the crime rate, and people who use illegal drugs often turn to other types of crime to support expensive drug habits.

GLOBAL PERSPECTIVES

The FBI is the U.S. agency responsible for investigating federal crimes. FBI officials often work together with police forces in other countries in their attempt to thwart crime that crosses national borders. The International Criminal Police Organization (Interpol) was founded in 1923 to help coordinate the fight against international crime. Interpol agents do not, as a rule, hunt down criminals in foreign countries. Interpol's main weapon is the extradition treaty, with which it can target such international criminals as drug smugglers, counterfeiters, and those who have fled from one country to another to avoid arrest. Interpol also maintains a central library of extensive information about specific international criminals. Law enforcement authorities can obtain needed information by various means, including through Interpol's telecommunications network.

Closure

Have students draw cartoons illustrating the cost of crime to everyone. Some students might illustrate crime in general terms. Other students might choose to illustrate white-collar crime or particular aspects of crime. The cartoons should emphasize the costs of crime to society financially, physically, and/or psychologically.

Reviewing

Have students complete the Section 1 Review.

Reteaching

Assign Section 1 of the Chapter 16 Reteaching Worksheet.

25 account for almost half of all the arrests in the United States. Most of those people arrested are young men.

SECTION 1 REVIEW
A N S W E R S

1. See the following pages: crime, criminal, felony, misdemeanor, murder, aggravated assault, forcible rape (p. 289); burglary, larceny, grand larceny, petty larceny, robbery, vandalism, arson, victimless crime (p. 290); white-collar crime, embezzlement, fraud (p. 291).

2. FBI

3. against persons—crimes that harm or end a person's life or that threaten to do so; against property—actions that involve stealing or destroying someone else's property

4. Financial costs are passed on to consumers through higher prices.

5. use terror tactics and violence to keep people from going to the police

6. poverty, illegal drug use, permissive society, population shifts; Many crimes go undetected or unreported.

7. Students should explain ways citizens can work to protect themselves against crime.

292

One of the costs of crime is fear. As a result of increases in crime, many people have taken precautions to protect their lives and property.

Permissive Society Some people believe a permissive society contributes to the increase in crime. They say many parents spoil their children and permit them to do anything they want. These children sometimes find it difficult to control their behavior when they are older. They have not learned to act responsibly in their own lives and toward others.

Other people believe the courts are too permissive. They say judges often are too lenient with convicted criminals.

Population Shifts Some experts point to two other reasons for the increase in crime—urbanization and the large percentage of young people now in the population.

More offenses have always been committed in cities than in rural areas. As the United States increasingly has become a nation of cities, it is not surprising that crime, too, is increasing. Crime is also on the increase due to the many kinds of crime committed by young people. In fact, today people under the age of

Fighting Crime

Whatever its causes, crime is a problem that harms every citizen. Partly in response to the growing public outcry about crime, Congress passed a new national crime bill in 1994. This bill aims to prevent crime and provide tougher penalties for people who commit crime.

Strategies for achieving these goals include life sentences for three-time violent offenders, grants to build new prisons, and grants to state and local communities to hire more police. Crime-prevention education in the schools is another tool in the fight against crime.

Putting an end to crime, however, requires citizen involvement. Citizens must report all crimes that they see, and take precautions to ensure their safety and the safety of others. Citizens also must lend their support to police officers, who work to serve and protect all the members of a community.

SECTION 1 REVIEW

1. Define or identify the following terms: crime, criminal, felony, misdemeanor, murder, aggravated assault, forcible rape, burglary, larceny, grand larceny, petty larceny, robbery, vandalism, arson, victimless crime, white-collar crime, embezzlement, fraud.

2. What is the main source of information about crime in the United States?

3. Distinguish between crimes against persons and crimes against property.

4. Why can it be said that everyone pays for white-collar crimes?

5. Why are members of organized crime difficult to catch?

Witnessing a Trial

If possible, take your class to a local courtroom to witness a trial. Try to attend a case likely to be decided in a short amount of time, such as a traffic dispute. Students should take notes about the proceedings. In particular, students should identify the dispute, the defendant, and the witnesses. Students also should summarize testimony and procedures used to ensure a fair and impartial trial.

Debating Ideas

Discuss with students the concept of plea bargaining. Then facilitate a panel debate between students who support and those who oppose plea bargaining. Students on each side of the debate must be able to cite specific reasons for their positions. Students should gather information and examples from newspapers and other periodicals in preparation for the debate. Have class members who are not participating in the debate take notes on each side's arguments.

can be used against them in a court of law. If a suspect is not given this information before questioning, any statements he or she makes cannot be used as evidence in court.

After the arrest the suspect is taken to the police station for "booking." That is, a record of the arrest is made. An officer writes down the name of the suspect, the time of the arrest, and the charges involved. The suspect is fingerprinted and photographed.

Preliminary Hearing   Usually within the next 24 hours, a preliminary hearing is held. During this procedure a judge must decide if there is enough evidence to send the case to trial. If there is not, the judge can dismiss, or drop, the charges against the suspect. If the charges are not dropped, the judge must decide whether or not to set bail. Bail, as you recall, is money a suspect posts as a guarantee that he or she will return for trial.

The bail amount is determined by the seriousness of the offense. If the offense is minor, the judge may agree to release the suspect on his or her **own recognizance**, or without bail. If the suspect lives in the community and has a good reputation, he or she usually is released without bail. It is assumed that the suspect's community ties will ensure his or her appearance in court for the trial.

Indictment   Next, a formal charge must be made. In some states a grand jury hears the evidence to decide whether to send the case to trial. If the grand jury finds probable cause, the suspect is indicted, or charged formally with the crime.

Arraignment   The accused person then appears before a judge to be **arraigned**. This means the accused enters a plea of guilty or not guilty of the charge. If the person pleads guilty, no trial is necessary.

Trial   If the accused person pleads not guilty to the charge, the case goes to trial. The **defense** represents the accused person's side of the case. The government's side of the case is presented by the **prosecution**. The defense and prosecution lawyers choose the jurors for the trial from a large group of people. Both lawyers have the right to question prospective jurors and to reject those people they believe to be prejudiced against their case.

After the jury has been selected, the prosecutor and the defense lawyer make opening statements to the jury. Each lawyer outlines the facts he or she will try to prove.

First, the prosecutor presents the case against the **defendant**, or accused person. Witnesses are sworn in, questioned by the prosecutor, and cross-examined. Next, the defense presents its case. The defendant may choose whether to testify. Under the U.S. Constitution, no defendant can be forced to testify against himself or herself.

After all the evidence is presented by each side, each lawyer makes a closing statement that summarizes his or her arguments. Before the jury leaves the courtroom to reach a verdict, the judge tells the jurors what they can and cannot consider in reaching their verdict.

The defendant is always presumed to be innocent. It is the prosecution's job to prove that the accused person is guilty beyond a

(continued on page 298)

Under the Constitution all persons accused of crimes are entitled to due process of the law. When arrested they must be informed of their rights immediately.

CIVICS SIDELIGHT

Many cable television viewers have received an education in due process by watching a cable network, known as Court TV, devoted to court cases. This 24-hour cable network was first telecast in 1991. By 1995 viewers in 25 million households could watch live coverage of high-profile trials, as well as shows on consumer law and small-claims court cases.

295

Illustrating Ideas

Have students draw flowcharts to summarize the Gideon case. They should box each item and connect items with an arrow to show time order. The first item might be "Someone broke into a pool hall and stole money and food." The last item might be "Gideon was found innocent and given his freedom."

CIVICS SIDELIGHT

In the case of *Gideon v. Wainwright*, the Supreme Court ruled that an attorney must be furnished to any defendant who cannot afford to hire one. In many places around the nation, judges assign attorneys from the local community or from legal aid societies to handle these cases. Since *Gideon v. Wainwright*, however, a growing number of state and local governments have established tax-supported public defender systems. Attorneys who work in public defender systems receive a salary for their work and handle only indigent cases. In 1970 Congress passed legislation authorizing the appointment of federal public defenders by federal courts of appeal. The public defender system is designed to ensure that the poor have the same access to legal counsel as the wealthy of society.

CLARENCE GIDEON

When the founders of the nation wrote the Constitution of the United States, they sought to secure the blessings of liberty and justice for all Americans. The Bill of Rights was added to the Constitution to protect the rights and freedoms of all citizens.

One of these rights is guaranteed by the Sixth Amendment. It is the right of a person accused of a crime to have "the assistance of counsel," or the help and advice of an attorney. Before the 1960s, however, people on trial in state courts had to pay for their own attorneys. State courts were required to provide counsel for defendants who could not afford it only in cases in which the death penalty was involved.

As a result, many poor people were tried without adequate representation. But one man's fight for justice has ensured that all Americans, rich or poor, now can have the help of counsel if they want it. That man is Clarence Gideon.

Clarence Gideon Is Arrested

In 1961 someone broke into a pool hall in Florida and stole money and food from a vending machine. Clarence Gideon, a Florida resident, was arrested for the crime. Gideon, because he was penniless, asked the state court to appoint free legal counsel for his defense at the trial.

The court refused Gideon's request, saying that in cases such as Gideon's, only federal courts were required to provide counsel. The state court's ruling left Gideon with only two choices: hire a lawyer on his own or represent himself in court. Because he had no money, Gideon was forced to serve as his own attorney at the trial.

Although he was determined to convince the jury of his innocence, Gideon did not have any legal expertise. The prosecution, a professional attorney, easily won the case. The court found Gideon guilty of the crime and sentenced him to five years in prison.

Not satisfied with the state court's decision, Gideon spent his long hours in prison

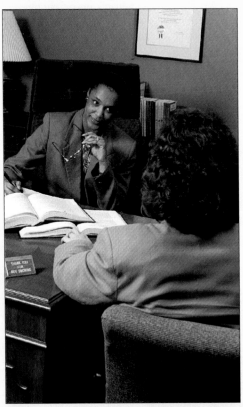

All Americans, rich or poor, are entitled to have the help of an attorney to defend themselves.

Closure

Invite five volunteers to form a discussion panel composed of the following characters: a businessperson, a police officer, a judge, a gang leader, and a concerned citizen. Panel members should be prepared to suggest ways in which they might help control crime. Encourage "cross questioning" within the panel as well as questions from other members of the class in the audience.

Reviewing

Have students complete the Section 2 Review.

Reteaching

Assign Section 2 of the Chapter 16 Reteaching Worksheet.

United States generally includes imprisonment, parole, and capital punishment.

Imprisonment While less serious crimes may be punished by fines or suspended sentences, more serious crimes are typically punished by imprisonment. People generally agree that lawbreakers should be removed from society for a period of time. Although most people believe in imprisonment as a fair punishment for crime, they disagree on the purpose imprisonment serves.

Some people see the purpose of imprisonment as retribution, or revenge. They believe that society has the right to make the criminal pay for his or her crime. Other people view imprisonment as a **deterrence** to crime. They believe that the threat of a long prison term discourages people from breaking the law.

A third view of imprisonment is that it serves as a means of **rehabilitation**. People who hold this view believe that the purpose of imprisonment is to reform criminals and return them to society as law-abiding citizens.

Still other people view imprisonment as a means of social protection. People who are imprisoned cannot commit additional crimes or pose a threat to people or property.

Parole After serving a part of their sentences, many prisoners are eligible for **parole**, or early release. People are paroled on the condition that they obey certain rules and keep out of trouble. Parole generally is granted only to those prisoners who behave well and who show signs of rehabilitation. In recent years, however, prison overcrowding has forced the early release of prisoners who would otherwise serve their full sentences.

A parole board reviews each application for parole carefully and makes a decision on it. When a prisoner is paroled, he or she must report regularly to a parole officer. Parole usually lasts until the end of the maximum part of the person's sentence.

Capital Punishment The harshest punishment for crimes that are committed in

Prison sentences punish criminals and remove them from society for a time. Some prisons offer training programs to help people find jobs after their release.

the nation is **capital punishment**, or the death penalty. People who oppose capital punishment believe it violates the Eighth Amendment's prohibition against "cruel and unusual" punishment. Other people say the death penalty is a just punishment, especially for a person who has committed murder. In 1976 the U.S. Supreme Court ruled that capital punishment as a penalty for murder is constitutional. Each state passes its own laws about capital punishment.

SECTION 2 REVIEW

1. Define or identify the following terms: criminal justice system, community policing, probable cause, arrest warrant, own recognizance, arraign, defense, prosecution, defendant, acquit,

SECTION 2 REVIEW
A N S W E R S

1. See the following pages: criminal justice system (p. 293); community policing, probable cause, arrest warrant (p. 294); own recognizance, arraign, defense, prosecution, defendant (p. 295); acquit, sentence, plea bargain, corrections (p. 298); deterrence, rehabilitation, parole, capital punishment (p. 299).

2. protect life and property, prevent crime, arrest criminals, protect rights, maintain peace, control traffic; to become officer—investigation, pass intelligence, physical, psychological exams, police academy

3. silence, attorney, must be told own words can be used against them

4. booking, hearing, indictment, arraignment, trial

5. retribution, deterrence, rehabilitation, protection of society

6. for—just punishment; against—cruel and unusual punishment

7. Students should make reasoned arguments.

After studying Section 3, students should be able to do the following.

1. Identify possible causes of juvenile delinquency.

2. Compare past and present treatment of juvenile offenders in the United States.

3. Explain why juveniles are tried in special courts.

4. Describe what happens when juveniles are charged and found guilty of breaking the law.

Teaching Section 3
Building a Vocabulary

Write the following Latin words and their meanings on the chalkboard: *juvenis* ("young person") and *delinquere* ("to offend"). Ask: Based on the Latin roots, what is a juvenile delinquent? *(a young person who offends, or breaks the law)* Then tell them that the Latin word *probare* means "to test or to prove." Have students use this information and their own knowledge to deduce a definition of **probation**. *(a time of testing or proving)*

Photo Caption Answer

Such programs help build stronger bonds between police and young people.

CIVICS SIDELIGHT

The social problem of youth gangs in major cities is not an entirely recent development. Law enforcement officials in many cities have had to deal with gang-related crime for many years. Gangs, gang-related problems, and juvenile delinquency have been themes in many movies, television shows, and theatrical productions. For example, New York City was the setting for a classic Broadway show and movie about a gang-related tragedy. *West Side Story,* first produced in 1957, is loosely based on Shakespeare's *Romeo and Juliet.* Tony and Maria, from separate ethnic groups whose neighborhoods are ruled by separate gangs, fall in love. In the climactic scene, Tony is gunned down by a member of the rival gang.

Programs like the Police Athletic League work to bring police officers and young people together. Why might police departments support such programs?

sentence, plea bargain, corrections, deterrence, rehabilitation, parole, capital punishment.

2. What are the duties of police officers? How do people become police officers?

3. What rights of due process are guaranteed to suspects?

4. What steps do suspects go through from arrest to sentencing?

5. What are the four views on the purpose of imprisonment?

6. What are the arguments for and against capital punishment?

7. THINKING CRITICALLY Consider the positive and negative consequences of plea bargaining. Then write a position statement for or against the elimination of plea bargaining from the U.S. criminal justice system. What might replace the current system?

3 Juvenile Crime

Young people are responsible for a large number of the nation's crimes. They commit many of the crimes against property, such as burglary, larceny, vandalism, arson, and automobile theft, and many of the more serious crimes. The rate of violent crime among young people has climbed steadily over the years.

Defining Juvenile Crime

Every state has special laws for dealing with young offenders. The ages to which these laws apply vary from state to state. Most states, however, define a **juvenile** as a person under the age of 18. Some set the age as low as 16. Juveniles become **delinquents** when they are found guilty of breaking a law.

Statistics show that young people commit many of the serious crimes reported to the police. Others commit minor offenses that bring them into conflict with society. Juveniles who

Conducting a Poll

Have students ask people (relatives, neighbors, friends, or other students) the following question: What do you think is the primary cause of teenage crime? Have students report their findings in class and tally the results to determine which cause was cited most often. Students should discuss these results and compare their findings with the causes listed in the section.

Practicing Interviewing Skills

Discuss with students society's treatment of juvenile crime before the late 1800s and today. (See page 304.) Ask: Why are juveniles tried in special courts? *(to make sure a juvenile's rights are protected)* Then invite a judge or a lawyer specializing in juvenile cases to your class to discuss the processes of the juvenile justice system. Have students prepare and ask questions about what juveniles accused of crimes encounter in the justice system. Then have students write newspaper articles about the "interviews."

prove to be unmanageable by their parents or who repeatedly run away from home may be termed unruly. The laws concerning unruly behavior vary from community to community. Where such behavior is unlawful, a young person who is repeatedly unruly may be turned over to the juvenile authorities.

Causes of Juvenile Crime

Why do some young people break the law or become unruly, while most live law-abiding and productive lives? According to experts who have studied the problem, there is no single answer. The following are some of the main causes of juvenile crime. Some of these are the same as for crime in general.

Poor Home Conditions Many juvenile offenders come from homes in which parents take little responsibility for their children. Often one parent has permanently left or is rarely at home. Young people whose parents are alcoholics, illegal drug users, or child abusers may spend a lot of time on the streets, where they get into trouble.

Poor Neighborhood Conditions The poorer areas of cities frequently have higher rates of crime than other areas. People who live crowded together in poverty often feel hopeless and angry. Many young people in these areas get into trouble while seeking outlets for their frustration and unhappiness. Some young people view delinquency and crime as their only way out of poverty.

Gang Membership The number of youth gangs in the United States has risen dramatically in recent years. More than 125 U.S. cities have serious gang problems, up from 10 cities only a decade ago. Increasingly, gang members are engaging in serious crimes involving firearms and illegal drugs.

School Dropouts and Unemployment When young people have nothing to do, no place to go, and no money to spend,

they may be headed for trouble. A person who drops out of high school is not necessarily headed for a life of crime. Nevertheless, studies show that unemployed youths with little training often become delinquents.

Alcohol and Drugs Laws forbid the sale of alcoholic beverages to anyone under a certain age. They also ban the sale of habit-forming drugs to anyone who does not have a prescription from a doctor. Yet many young people use these substances and other illegal drugs. Under the influence of alcohol or drugs, they may do things that they would not do otherwise. People addicted to drugs, who need money to pay for their habit, often turn to crime—sometimes violent crime.

Peer Pressure Some young people get into trouble because they are pressured by their friends to commit crimes. Everyone wants to be liked, but people who pressure others to break the law are not true friends.

(continued on page 304)

One way to stay out of trouble is to take part in sports.

The Supreme Court ruled in a case called *In re Gault* in 1967 that juveniles have the same rights to due process as do adults. The ruling revolved around a sentence that had been handed down by a lower court against 15-year-old Gerald Gault. Gault had been convicted of making an obscene telephone call to a female neighbor and sentenced to nearly six years in the Arizona State Industrial School. At the time, an adult convicted of the same crime might have served 30 days in jail and paid a $50 fine. The Supreme Court ruled that the Arizona statute violated the due process rights of juveniles under the Fourteenth Amendment.

Applying Ideas

Make up a case for students to consider in their own "Student Court." The case should involve some violation of a school rule, such as a rule concerning conduct or grades. Assign each student a role in the court, including defendant, prosecuting and defense attorneys, clerks, bailiffs, and jurors. For the purposes of this exercise, students might also be assigned the role of judge. Ask students to think about what their duties are in the teen court. Have students orally describe and act out their roles in a trial of the defendant.

CIVICS SIDELIGHT

Some Teen Courts are actively involved in making parents share the responsibility for the misbehavior of their children. In Dallas, Texas, for example, one Teen Court fines parents $25 to $100 for each time their child is truant from school. These rulings carry the weight of law and appear to be effective in curtailing truancy. One mother, for example, explained to the Teen Court jurors that it was difficult for her to make her young daughter go to school. When she found out that her seven-year-old daughter's 49 absences from first grade were going to cost her $1,800 in fines, however, the woman promised the court that she would see to it that her daughter was in school. To hold the mother to this promise, the teenage jurors sentenced her to spend three days a week with her daughter at the child's elementary school.

Citizenship IN ACTION

TEEN COURT

In the United States adults who are accused of breaking the law have the right to be judged by a jury of their peers. In general, however, juveniles have no such right. Young people who break the law usually have their cases heard by a judge without the benefit of a jury. In some places around the nation, however, a new program allows teenage offenders to have their cases heard by their peers—other teenagers. This program is called Teen Court.

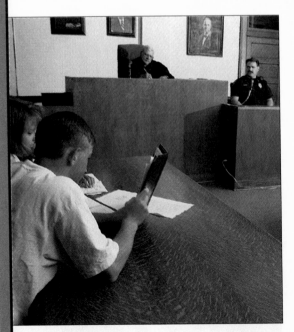

Teen prosecuting attorneys call witnesses in presenting their case before a judge and jury.

What Is Teen Court?

Teen Court is a real courtroom situation in which first-time juvenile offenders are tried and sentenced by a jury of their peers. Originally begun in Odessa, Texas, in 1983, these courts now operate in Texas, Arizona, Florida, Oregon, California, Michigan, New York, Georgia, Indiana, and Colorado. More states are expected to use Teen Court programs in the future.

Except for the judge, participants in Teen Court usually are between the ages of 14 and 17. Judges who preside over Teen Court typically are retired district judges. The young people assume all other courtroom roles, serving as prosecuting and defense attorneys, clerks, bailiffs, and jurors. Teenagers who volunteer to serve on Teen Court usually sign a contract pledging to give six months of service. They also must undergo training before they begin their service.

Teenage jurors usually hear cases involving offenses such as theft, possession of drugs

Extending Ideas

Have pairs of students work together to develop a list of proposed punishments for offenses committed by teenagers who appear in Teen Courts. In short paragraphs or statements next to each punishment they propose, students should explain how the punishment (or range of possible punishments) is appropriate to each offense. Then invite volunteers to present their lists to the class for a discussion of the purposes of punishment and whether or not each pair's punishments are fair.

or alcohol, disorderly conduct, breaking curfew, speeding, and truancy. After the prosecuting and defense attorneys have presented their cases to the court, and after all witnesses have been called, the teenage jurors consider the facts of the case and decide the sentence. Most judges who sit for Teen Court agree that the teenage jurors are tougher than adult judges on the offenders. Teenage jurors tend to give harsher sentences.

In Plano, Texas, for example, Teen Court jurors heard the case of a 16-year-old boy who had been caught by the police with an open container of beer. The teenage jurors sentenced the boy to 36 hours of community service.

In Houston, Texas, Teen Court jurors sentenced a 16-year-old girl charged with speeding in an elementary school zone to 90-days probation, 30 hours of community service, and two-weeks' duty as a crossing guard. The girl also had to write a letter of apology to the elementary school.

Other typical punishments include fines and counseling. Offenders who successfully complete their sentences have the offenses for which they were charged erased from their permanent records.

Does Teen Court Work?

Juvenile justice experts who have studied Teen Courts generally agree that it is an effective way to keep young people from committing further offenses. Teenagers who have their cases heard by other teenagers know that they are telling their stories to people with whom they can identify and who have shared the experiences of teenage life. Thus they are more likely to accept their sentences and successfully complete them.

Also, by fulfilling sentences that involve counseling and community service work, teenage offenders learn to respect other people. Perhaps most important, they learn to respect themselves. In fact, Teen Court has been so successful that many of the young people sentenced by teenage jurors later volunteer to serve on Teen Court themselves.

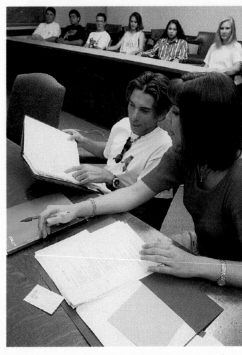

Teenage jurors hear all the evidence in a case and decide the offender's sentence.

YOU DECIDE

1 What is the purpose of Teen Court? What are the courtroom roles of teenagers serving on Teen Court?

2 Why might teenage jurors tend to give harsher sentences than adult judges?

3 Conduct research to learn if there is a Teen Court in your area. Who can serve on this court? What kinds of cases does it hear? What types of sentences does it give? How effective is it in reducing the number of teenage offenses?

Guided Practice

To help students understand the differences between juvenile and adult courts, stage a scene from each type of court. Divide the class in half. One half will provide characters for juvenile court and the other half characters for adult court. Set up both courts at the same time. Have judge, defendant, lawyers, and others take their proper positions in each "court" and identify themselves. Then lead a class discussion of any differences in the court's arrangements, involved parties, and procedures.

Independent Practice

Have students write editorials either supporting or opposing the following statement: "Juveniles who commit serious crimes should be tried as adults." Students should consider the purposes of the juvenile justice system. You might wish to have students hold a formal debate to argue this issue before (or after) writing their editorials.

CIVICS SIDELIGHT

In recent years some officials have championed military-style boot camps for juvenile offenders. Proponents believe these boot camps instill discipline in juvenile offenders and help prevent their return to crime. However, some studies have not shown that boot camps significantly reduce the number of repeat offenders.

Colorado officials are trying an approach that combines the discipline of boot camp with counseling and job training. After a 30-day boot camp filled with exercise, work, and drills, offenders are enrolled in job training programs at the detention center. They also take part in vocational programs and group discussions on violence prevention. Finally, after a period in a halfway house, offenders are returned home or to another supportive environment. They are expected to attend group meetings and to work or go to school. Proponents hope the program will prevent at least some of these juvenile offenders from running into problems with the law again.

Boot camps are an experiment in rehabilitating juvenile offenders. The camps aim to give young offenders self-discipline and positive goals.

Treating Juvenile Crime

Before the late 1800s juveniles at least 14 years old were held responsible for their crimes. They were tried in adult courts and sentenced to prison and even death. During the 1870s, however, reformers began working to change the way young offenders were treated. They believed that juveniles need special understanding rather than punishment.

As a result, many communities set up juvenile court systems. Their purpose was not to punish but to remove children from harmful environments. Reformers hoped to reeducate offenders by giving them care, treatment, discipline, and supervision.

Instead of trials, juvenile courts hold hearings, which are attended only by parents or guardians and other people directly involved in the case. The purpose of the hearings is to determine the guilt or innocence of juveniles. The meetings are informal, and the records of them are kept secret.

The purpose of a separate juvenile court system is to do what is best for the young people involved. Many believed that the parents and court officials would protect juveniles' rights. Sometimes, though, juveniles were denied equal protection under the law.

In 1967 a Supreme Court decision brought major changes to the juvenile justice system. The Court ruled that juveniles accused of breaking the law have the same rights of due process as adults. That is, juveniles have the right to be informed of the charges brought against them, to be represented by a lawyer, to question all witnesses, and to refuse to testify against themselves in court. The Supreme Court later ruled, however, that juveniles accused of crimes do not have the right to a jury trial. Nevertheless, a number of states allow young people to be tried before juries.

Punishing Juvenile Crime

After hearing all the evidence, the judge must decide the guilt or innocence of the juvenile offender. If the juvenile is found guilty, several outcomes are possible. The judge may order that the juvenile be placed in a foster home. In serious cases the judge may have the youth sent to a juvenile corrections facility.

One type of corrections facility for people under the age of 18 is a training school. Youthful offenders placed in training schools usually stay there from six to nine months. Juveniles who are confined for shorter periods of time usually are sent to juvenile detention centers. The main goal of both of these types of facilities is to rehabilitate, rather than punish, the young offenders.

Another possible outcome for the juvenile offender is probation. **Probation** is a period of time during which a person guilty of an offense is given an opportunity to show that he or she can reform. Offenders placed on probation must obey strict rules, such as being home by a certain time each night and avoiding bad influences. They also must report regularly to a probation officer.

The juvenile justice system also is experimenting with use of "boot camps" to rehabilitate young offenders. Like military boot camps, these rehabilitative boot camps provide a highly disciplined, structured environment. The goal of such facilities is to help young offenders gain positive values.

Closure

Encourage student reaction to the four items listed under the heading "Juvenile Decency" on this page. Then ask: Is this list complete? What else can teenagers do to ensure that they stay out of trouble with the law? Have students create posters on the theme of juvenile decency. Invite the principal to view the posters before displaying them in your school as part of a campaign promoting juvenile decency.

Reviewing

Have students complete the Section 3 Review.

Reteaching

Assign Section 3 of the Chapter 16 Reteaching Worksheet.

Serious Crimes by Juveniles

In recent years the number of serious crimes committed by young people has increased. As a result, many Americans want to eliminate juvenile court systems and to try juvenile offenders as adults.

Under the traditional juvenile justice system, a young person who commits murder may be on the street again after only a few years in a juvenile corrections facility. Despite the good intentions of corrections officers, that juvenile may not be reformed. He or she may commit another serious crime. In response to public demand for protection, some states now punish juveniles convicted of serious crimes as they would punish adults.

Juvenile Decency

Most of the nation's young people are good citizens who stay out of trouble and obey the law. Criminologists—scientists who study crime and the behavior of criminals—give the following suggestions to young people who want to avoid trouble with the law.

- Do not use drugs. People who use drugs often end up in criminal courts and correction facilities or jails.
- Stay in school and earn the best education possible. School opens new opportunities and increases your chances for a good job.
- Have the courage to say no when friends suggest illegal acts. Anyone can go along with the crowd—it takes courage to stand up to one.
- Try to live a full life, with plenty of physical activity and interesting hobbies. A person who is busy doing challenging things does not become bored and turn to criminal activities as an outlet.

SECTION 3 REVIEW

1. Define or identify the following terms: juvenile, delinquent, probation.

2. What are six possible causes of juvenile delinquency?

3. How has the treatment of juvenile offenders changed over the years?

4. Describe what happens when a juvenile is arrested and charged.

5. What happens when juveniles are found guilty of breaking the law?

6. **THINKING CRITICALLY** You head a committee to encourage juvenile decency in your community. Create a chart showing five goals you want your committee to achieve and suggestions for achieving each goal. How can young people work to achieve these goals?

CHAPTER 16 SUMMARY

Americans want and need to be protected from crime. Such protection is one of the services governments provide for their citizens. Crime has become an increasingly serious problem in the United States. The financial and psychological costs of crime are high.

The U.S. criminal justice system operates to protect everyone, even those people who have been accused of committing criminal actions. Police officers are trained to deal with the public, handle emergencies, control situations that may lead to crime, and deal with criminals. They must also inform suspects of their constitutional rights. From the moment of arrest, all people suspected of crimes are entitled to the due process of law.

Although most of the nation's young people are law-abiding citizens, juvenile crime has become an increasingly pressing problem in the United States. A large percentage of offenses, including serious ones, are committed by young people each year. Special courts and corrections facilities have been set up to deal with juvenile offenders.

SECTION 3 REVIEW ANSWERS

1. See the following pages: juvenile, delinquent (p. 300); probation (p. 304).

2. poor home conditions, poor neighborhood conditions, gang membership, dropping out of school and unemployment, alcohol and drugs, peer pressure

3. Before the late 1800s, juveniles at least 14 years of age were treated as adults by the justice system. During the late 1800s, reformers worked to set up juvenile court systems and sought to reeducate offenders to make them better citizens. In 1967 the U.S. Supreme Court ruled juveniles have the same rights to due process as adults have.

4. hearing attended only by parents or guardians and by others involved in case; same due process rights as adults, except for trial by jury (some states allow jury trials)

5. may be placed in foster homes, juvenile correction facilities, boot camps, or on probation

6. Goals should be backed by specific proposals.

Tell students that juvenile crime has become a common topic for writers and publishers. Have students use the *Readers' Guide to Periodical Literature* to list as many magazine articles about juvenile crime as they can find for a particular year. Randomly assign specific years to students. Then have students tally the total number of articles for each year and report their tallies to the class. Keep track of the tallies on the chalkboard. Have students discuss any trends that can be deduced from the annual tallies of articles on juvenile crime. If, for example, increasing numbers of articles are being written on juvenile crime each year, could this be a sign of increasing juvenile crime, growing fear of juvenile crime, or both?

Developing Civics Skills

SOCIAL STUDIES SKILL
Conducting Library Research

Throughout your school career you will conduct research on many different topics. Your school library and your local public library contain a wide collection of reference books especially designed to help you in your research. All reference books contain facts, but the type of facts varies with the reference. Choosing the right reference book will save you time.

How to Conduct Library Research

1. **Reacquaint yourself with encyclopedias.** Most students are familiar with encyclopedias. These reference books contain articles on a wide range of topics. Most encyclopedias consist of a number of volumes in which topics are arranged alphabetically. Some, however, have all their information in only one or two volumes.
2. **Become familiar with almanacs.** A handy source of both historical and up-to-date facts is an almanac, such as the *World Almanac and Book of Facts*. Here you will find statistics on topics ranging from crime to presidential elections. Almanacs are updated each year and present much of their information in easy-to-reference tables, graphs, and charts.
3. **Consult sources on people.** If you are looking for information on well-known people, you might go to a biographical dictionary. This reference book summarizes the key events and dates in a person's life. For important people in U.S. history, consult the *Dictionary of American Biography*. For famous people in the present, consult *Who's Who in America* or *Current Biography*.
4. **Sharpen your geography skills.** To locate maps and statistics on the United States or other parts of the world, use an atlas. An atlas is a book of maps that also provides useful facts and figures, including information on population and climate.
5. **Be aware of current events.** Whenever you want current information on a topic, refer to the *Readers' Guide to Periodical Literature*. This book records all of the articles that have appeared in many popular magazines. To find articles on a particular topic, turn to that subject heading in the *Guide*. If an article on the topic has been published, it will be listed along with the name, date, and page numbers of the magazine in which it appeared.
6. **Consult the librarian.** Your most valuable resource is the librarian. This trained professional can help you find the best reference materials for your needs. Do not hesitate to consult with the librarian before you begin your research.

Applying the Skill

Answer the following questions.

1. Where would you look to find how many cases of arson occurred in the United States in recent years?
2. Where would you look to find Billy the Kid's real name?
3. What would be the best source of information on the history of the juvenile justice system?
4. Where would you find recent articles on crimes involving handguns?
5. You are writing a report on crime in the United States. You want to show crime figures on a map of the country. Where would you find the map and crime statistics you need?

ANSWERS TO Applying the Skill

1. almanac
2. *Dictionary of American Biography* or an encyclopedia
3. encyclopedia
4. listed in *Readers' Guide to Periodical Literature*
5. atlas, almanac

306

Vocabulary Workshop

1. Examples should include crimes of embezzlement and/or fraud.

2. defense; prosecution

3. grand—theft of property over a certain amount; petty—theft of property under a certain amount

4. police, courts, corrections

5. parole—early release from prison; probation—no prison, must follow certain rules

6. aggravated assault

7. arson

Reviewing Main Ideas

1. against persons, against property, victimless, white-collar, organized

2. Many crimes go unreported.

3. foster home, juvenile correction facility, boot camp, or probation

4. poverty, drugs, permissive society, population shifts; poor home and neighborhood conditions, gangs, dropping out, unemployment, alcohol, drugs, peer pressure

5. booking, hearing, indictment, arraignment, trial; rights to silence, attorney, other due process rights

6. retribution, deterrence, rehabilitation, protection

7. Some say it results in inadequate punishment and encourages people to give up trial rights. Some say it is cruel and unusual, while others say it is just punishment.

8. juveniles 14 and over once treated as adults; late 1800s reformers created juvenile courts, sought to reeducate; 1967 Court ruled juveniles have due process rights

Thinking Critically

1. Students should suggest harmful effects of gangs.

2. Students should use sound reasoning in their responses.

Citizenship in Your Community

Students should research roles.

BUILDING YOUR PORTFOLIO

Assign Portfolio Assessment Worksheet 16 in the *Portfolio Assessment Worksheets* booklet.

Assessment

- **Chapter 16 Tests**, *Chapter Tests* booklet
- **Test Generator**, Chapter 16
- **Portfolio**, Portfolio Assessment Worksheet 16, *Portfolio Assessment Worksheets* booklet

---

CHAPTER 16

R·e·v·i·e·w

Vocabulary Workshop

1. Give two examples of white-collar crime.

2. What is the term for an accused person's side of a court case? What is the term for the government's side?

3. What is the difference between grand larceny and petty larceny?

4. What three parts make up the criminal justice system?

5. Distinguish between parole and probation.

6. Which is the most common type of violent crime?

7. What term is used to describe the destruction of property by setting fire to it?

Reviewing Main Ideas

1. Identify and describe five categories of crime.

2. Why is the crime rate undoubtedly higher than official statistics indicate?

3. What may a judge do if he or she finds a juvenile guilty of a crime?

4. What are the possible causes of crime? of juvenile delinquency?

5. What steps does a criminal suspect go through from the time of arrest to the time of sentencing? What rights do all criminal suspects have?

6. What are four points of view concerning the purpose of imprisonment?

7. Why is plea bargaining controversial? Why is capital punishment the subject of debate?

8. How has the juvenile justice system changed over the years?

Thinking Critically

1. Youth gangs have become a serious social problem in the United States. Why do you think young people join gangs? How is gang membership harmful?

2. Should juveniles who commit serious crimes such as murder be tried in adult courts? Should those convicted of these crimes face the same punishments as adult offenders? Explain your answers.

Citizenship in Your Community

Cooperative Project

With your group, locate a current local newspaper article about a teenager involved in a serious crime. Use the facts in the case to conduct a mock trial. Assign various members of your group to play the roles of judge, attorneys, defendant, and witnesses. Choose 12 members of the class (who are not in your group) to serve as a jury. Have group members research their roles so that the trial can be as realistic as possible. What was the outcome of the trial? How were the rights of the defendant protected?

Building Your Portfolio

The fourth step of your unit portfolio project (see page 309) is to consider good citizenship in dealing with the law. What can young citizens do to protect their rights and the rights of others? Answer this question by creating a plan to organize a Crime Watch program in your school. In your plan, list the precautions your school has taken to protect the health and safety of its students and teachers. What else can young citizens do to make your school a safe place? Title your plan "Young Citizens on the Watch." Place your plan for a school Crime Watch program in your individual portfolio for later use.

Reviewing Main Ideas

1. to work in factories; families had to earn money to buy what they had once produced on farms, had to share influence on children with schools and churches

2. development of individual citizens and development of the nation; ladder—nursery school, kindergarten, elementary school, junior high (middle) school, high school, junior college, college, university, graduate school

3. purposes—help people find common bonds and interests, provide rules that guide and protect citizens, provide needed goods and services; volunteers—No government can know all the needs of local areas, and volunteers help provide services communities otherwise could not afford.

4. same rights as adults; right to jury trial

5. has become less complicated and less expensive, women are less likely to stay in unhappy marriages for financial reasons, society more tolerant of divorce

6. use terror tactics and violence to keep people from going to the police; police duties—protect life and property, prevent crime, arrest lawbreakers, protect rights, maintain peace and order, control traffic

Thinking Critically

1. Answers will vary. Students should use sound reasoning in their responses.

308

2. Students might suggest that employers must seek ways to prevent theft without infringing on the rights of their employees.

Practicing Civics Skills

1. Students should describe various aspects of a news program.

2. Students should identify specific facts and opinions.

3. Students should consider all necessary aspects of such a program.

Citizenship in Your Community

Reports and diagrams should clearly compare criminal justice systems of the United States and the foreign country under study.

R·e·v·i·e·w

Reviewing Main Ideas

1. Why did families begin moving from farms to cities? How did this move affect family life in the United States?

2. What are the main purposes of education? Through what levels may one progress on the U.S. educational ladder?

3. What purposes do communities serve? Why are volunteers important to a community's success?

4. What rights of due process are given to juveniles? What right is denied to juveniles?

5. What are the reasons for the high U.S. divorce rate?

6. Why are members of crime syndicates difficult to catch? What are the duties of police officers?

Thinking Critically

1. Based on what you know about the changing American family, describe family life in the year 2020.

2. Many companies have installed security cameras and other devices to catch employees who steal. Do these devices infringe on the privacy rights of employees? Do they protect the rights of employers to guard against theft?

Practicing Civics Skills

1. Watch a television news program. What news stories and features does the program cover? How much time is devoted to sports and weather? Does the program include a commentary? If so, what is its topic?

2. Collect several product advertisements from magazines and newspapers. Identify which statements in each advertisement are facts and which are opinions.

3. Work with a group of students to develop a recycling program in your school. Organize the group, elect a leader, and follow the guidelines on page 286 to help your group make its project a success.

Citizenship in Your Community

Individual Project

Conduct research to learn about the criminal justice system in a foreign nation. What type of training do police officers receive, and what type of relationship do the police have with citizens? Are the rights of the accused protected? Do suspects have the right to a jury trial? to a lawyer? How is the court system organized? Compare your chosen nation's criminal justice system with the U.S. criminal justice system in a written report. You might create diagrams of each system to accompany your report.

Learning from Technology

College by Computer

Thanks to the computer revolution, many Americans can receive a college education in their own homes. People with a computer and a modem (a telephone link-up device) can enroll in and pay for college classes, receive and submit assignments, and "talk" to instructors and other students, all by computer. What are the advantages and disadvantages of such a system? Does this system strengthen the community by extending educational opportunities or weaken it by isolating citizens in their homes?

Have students use newspapers and other periodicals to locate articles on how the U.S. government has acted as a referee in a specific business deal. Some students might find, for example, articles about government intervention when a large communications company wants to purchase another television station or newspaper. Have students create flowcharts, diagrams, or other visual guides (such as collages) to help explain the economic issues in the story to the class.

Review with students the basic economic freedoms that are a crucial part of the nation's free-enterprise system. Then ask students to consider what life would be like in the United States if these economic freedoms were taken away. Have them write a list of things that might be different. Call on volunteers to read their lists to the class. Then have students discuss which freedoms are related to specific items on each volunteer's list.

---

placing these machines in factories in which large numbers of workers were employed, businesses were able to produce large quantities of goods at lower prices.

The owners of these large factories and businesses made huge profits. Some owners hoping to make great fortunes, however, used business practices that would be considered unfair or illegal today.

Monopolies

Unfair business practices harm a free economy. They may interfere with the free market and affect the prices people have to pay for goods and services.

One unfair practice used by big business owners in the late 1800s and early 1900s was the forming of monopolies. A company has a **monopoly** if it is the only firm selling a product or providing a service. If there is no competition for the product or service, and if it is something people really need (such as food), the monopolist controls the price. People are then forced to pay the asking price in order to acquire the product or service.

A merger may lead to the forming of a monopoly. A **merger** occurs when two or more companies combine to form one company. If all the companies in an industry merge, a monopoly forms. There is no longer real competition in the industry.

Another way to create a monopoly is to form a **trust**. That is, several companies create a board of trustees. Even though each company remains a separate business, the board of trustees makes sure the companies no longer compete with one another. If all the companies in an industry became part of the trust, a monopoly is created.

To understand how monopolies form and how they operate, consider the example of a large coffee company that wants to lessen its competition. It might buy all the small coffee companies, or it might force them out of business by lowering its prices below its costs.

If the large company lowered its prices below its costs, soon the small coffee companies would have to lower their prices to compete and stay in business. Every coffee firm would be selling coffee at a loss. Because the large company has more capital than the small companies, however, it can afford to lose money longer. The small companies most likely would be forced to sell their businesses, merge with the large company, or go out of business altogether.

The large company would then be a monopoly. It alone would produce all the coffee on the market, allowing it to raise the price of coffee. Because there would be no other companies selling coffee, people would have to buy their coffee from the big company at the price charged, or drink something else.

Importance of Big Business

Not all large companies are monopolies. Today most big businesses in the United States face competition from other big companies and from foreign producers. Also, if a company's profits are high, other companies seeking profits are encouraged to enter the industry. Competition is then quickly restored.

Today's big businesses are essential to the economy. Many of the goods and services we need cannot be produced efficiently by small companies. To produce steel, electricity, automobiles, and ships, for example, large and very expensive equipment is needed. **Economies of scale** describes the situation in which things can be produced more efficiently and cheaply by larger companies.

Because of economies of scale, a few large companies account for most of the production and sales in some industries today. If these companies should form a trust and agree on how much to produce and what to charge for their products, they might be abusing their size and power. As you will learn, however, there are laws to prevent such abuse.

Regulating Monopolies

The referee of a basketball or football game ensures that the teams observe the rules of the

Large pharmaceutical companies are good examples of big businesses that have the considerable resources sometimes needed to develop a product—in this case, medicines. These resources include the "intellectual capital" provided by teams of scientists employed by the company to work on developing new medicines. Because these scientists are employed by the company, patents for drugs discovered and developed by them typically are awarded to the company.

Some people believe that awarding these patents on drugs is problematic because no drug is actually "new." These critics argue that "new" drugs actually evolve based on the previous work of other scientists. They also argue that the patents permit drug companies to monopolize the market for newly discovered drugs and to reap huge profits as a result. Pharmaceutical companies argue that the patents and the money they make on the sales of drugs are fair and necessary, considering the sometimes enormous resources they invest in developing the drugs.

Reviewing

Have students complete the Section 1 Review.

Reteaching

Assign Section 1 of the Chapter 17 Reteaching Worksheet.

Extension

Have pairs of students research arguments for and against the Sherman Antitrust Act of 1890 and other trustbusting efforts of the late 1800s and early 1900s. Students should investigate circumstances leading up to the events and identify major participants. Have each pair prepare oral reports and visual guides to explain and illustrate their research for the class.

CIVICS SIDELIGHT

Conglomerates often produce a wide variety of brand-name products. Typical U.S. conglomerates include the Sara Lee Corporation (Sara Lee®, Ball Park®, Hanes®, L'eggs®, Ty-D-bol®, Kiwi®); Pepsico (Pepsi®, Mountain Dew®, Doritos®, Lay's®, KFC®, Pizza Hut®, Taco Bell®); and Philip Morris (Marlboro®, Cool Whip®, Cracker Barrel®, Jell-O®, Kool-Aid®, Maxwell House®, Oscar Mayer®, Miller®, Toblerone®).

game. In much the same way, the federal government enforces rules to protect the U.S. free-enterprise system.

To prevent monopolies and trusts from forming, Congress has passed antimonopoly and antitrust laws. The Sherman Antitrust Act of 1890, for example, was passed to prevent monopolies. It was strengthened by the Clayton Act of 1914, which forbade practices that would weaken competition. The Antitrust Division of the Justice Department and the Federal Trade Commission are responsible for enforcing these laws.

During the past several decades the number of large business combinations known as conglomerates has increased significantly. A **conglomerate** is formed by the merger of businesses that produce, supply, or sell a number of unrelated goods and services. For example, a single conglomerate may control communication systems, insurance companies, hotel chains, and other types of businesses.

The government watches mergers of large companies to ensure that conglomerates do not gain too much control over an industry or any part of the economy. If a conglomerate gains so much power that it threatens competition in the free economy, the government may step in as referee.

In some industries monopolies are legal. These legal monopolies are **public utilities**, companies that provide essential services to the public. Electric and natural gas companies are examples of public utilities. Their capital equipment is so expensive that it would be wasteful to have more than one company providing the same service in the same area. Therefore, one company is allowed to have a monopoly, but only under strict government regulation of services and prices.

Comparing Economic Systems

As you have learned, the freedom of buyers and sellers is essential to the U.S. economic system. The economy, however, has grown large and complex. As a result, the federal

Free enterprise and entrepreneurship are transforming China's economy into a bustling, powerful force.

After studying Section 2, students should be able to do the following.

1. Compare sole proprietorships with partnerships.

2. Describe the corporate form of organization.

3. Explain how corporations raise money and how the debts of a corporation are paid if the corporation fails.

4. Identify the purposes of nonprofit organizations.

5. Distinguish preferred stock from common stock.

6. Explain why corporations issue bonds.

Teaching Section 2
Building a Vocabulary

Help students understand the meaning of **corporation** by explaining that the Latin word *corpus* means "body" and that a corporation is a body, or organization, formed to act as a single person. Then tell students that corporations sometimes pay **dividends**. Ask students to find a word within the term *dividend*. *(divide)* Tell them that a company's profits are divided up among investors. Each share is a dividend.

---

government sometimes acts as referee and makes economic decisions. Although the government makes many more economic decisions now than it did 100 years ago, the U.S. economy remains a free economy. Most economic decisions are made by individuals.

In an economy like that of Cuba, however, the opposite is true. Most economic decisions are made by government officials who head planning agencies. Individuals are allowed only limited private enterprise. The Cuban government, for the most part, decides what goods and services to provide. Cuban workers are limited in the jobs they can hold. Young people are directed toward training for certain jobs and careers.

For these reasons, Cuba's economy is called a command economy. A **command economy** is the opposite of a free economy. In a command economy the government owns almost all of the capital, tools, and production equipment. The government tells the managers and workers in factories and on farms what and how much to produce. Most economic decisions thus are made by the government, rather than by individuals in a free market.

The U.S. economy is free, but it does have some features of a command economy. For example, the government regulates businesses to make sure that working conditions are safe. Because the United States has features of a command economy in its mostly free system, the U.S. economic system can be described as a **mixed economy**.

SECTION 1 REVIEW

1. Define or identify the following terms: standard of living, free market, free competition, profit motive, invest, copyright, patent, scarcity, law of supply, law of demand, capitalism, capital, free-enterprise system, monopoly, merger, trust, economies of scale, conglomerate, public utility, command economy, mixed economy.

2. What five freedoms are found in the U.S. economic system?

3. What does the problem of scarcity force people to do?

4. How do supply and demand affect prices?

5. What role does the government play in the U.S. economy?

6. Why are most monopolies illegal? Why are some legal?

7. **THINKING CRITICALLY** Imagine that you have a pen pal who lives in a nation that has a command economy. Write a letter to your pen pal describing how the U.S. economic system differs from the economic system under which your pen pal lives.

2 Business Organizations

More than 100 years ago, a young clerk in a small New York town used a new idea to increase his store's business. He gathered several small items from the store's shelves and placed them on a table near the entrance. He put up a sign reading "Everything on this table, 5 cents each." Customers who came into the store to buy thread or cloth stopped at the table for a bag of clothespins, an eggbeater, or some other item that caught their eye.

The young man then decided to open his own store and to sell only five-cent and ten-cent items. Unfortunately, his new store failed. He lost all the money he had saved and borrowed to start the business. Rather than give up, however, he borrowed the money he needed to buy new goods and started over. This time his business was a success.

The young man with the new idea was Frank W. Woolworth. With the profits from his successful business, he soon opened another

SECTION 1 REVIEW ANSWERS

1. See the following pages: standard of living, free market, free competition (p. 313); profit motive, invest, copyright, patent, scarcity, law of supply, law of demand (p. 314); capitalism, capital (p. 315); free-enterprise system (p. 316); monopoly, merger, trust, economies of scale (p. 317); conglomerate, public utility (p. 318); command economy, mixed economy (p. 319).

2. buy and sell, compete for customers, compete for jobs, earn profit, own property

3. choose which wants and needs can be satisfied

4. Production (supply) and prices rise and fall based on demand.

5. ensure fair competition

6. block competition; some legal because they provide essential services using expensive capital equipment

7. Letters should cite differences between free-market and command economies.

Writing a Journal Entry

Invite students to imagine each is the sole proprietor of a business. Tell them to think about what kind of business it is and how hard they have to work to make it run. Ask each student to write a journal entry at the end of a particularly long day that sums up both the advantages and disadvantages of being a sole proprietor. Invite students to read their journal entries to the class as part of a discussion of sole proprietorships.

Writing a Letter

Ask each student to write a letter to a friend as if he or she is the sole owner of a business who has decided to try to find a partner to help the business expand. In their letters students should explain why they want to enter into a partnership. They might also discuss their concerns about having to give up complete control over the business, as well as their desire for some relief from the burdens of sole ownership. Call on volunteers to share their letters with the class.

ULTICULTURAL PERSPECTIVES

Throughout U.S. history many immigrants have earned livings by running sole proprietorships. One such immigrant, a Vietnamese refugee, tells his story: "In Vietnam, I was like your U.S. Senators. I was very respected and an important man, but when I came to your country I had to start all over again. I knew that I could not be in the government here so I asked my boys to help me think of ways that we could begin our own business here in Hawaii. It was after that when we started our lawn business and now I have nine crews working for me."

Many grocery stores in the United States are sole proprietorships. This owner works long hours to keep his grocery store operating at a profit.

store, and then another and another. When he died in 1919, Woolworth had established more than 1,000 five-and-ten-cent stores in the United States and Canada. He became a wealthy man because he had a good idea and the business ability to make it succeed.

Sole Proprietorships

There are more than 20 million business firms in the United States today. Of these, more than 15 million are small businesses owned by one person. They include gas stations, grocery stores, hair salons, drugstores, and other businesses that serve people who live nearby. These small businesses, each owned by one person, are called **sole proprietorships**.

You probably know some of the advantages of going into business for yourself. Sole proprietors are their own bosses. They decide the hours the businesses will be open and how the businesses will operate. Because they are the owners, they take all the profits.

Yet there are disadvantages to being a sole proprietor. Owners must supply all the money needed to rent or buy buildings or office space and equipment. If they need to hire help, they must be able to pay their employees. They must also pay taxes. Owners are hardworking people. Although they can hire others to help them, they alone are responsible for the success or failure of their businesses.

If their businesses fail, proprietors must face the losses. While workers may lose their jobs, proprietors may have to sell everything they own to pay their business debts.

Partnerships

Each year in the United States many small businesses are started and many others fail. Some fail because the sole proprietor lacks enough capital or the business ability to earn a good profit. For such reasons, the owner of a small business sometimes seeks another person to become a part owner of the business.

Such **partnerships** give the business a greater amount of capital and a better chance of success. In a partnership there is more than one person to provide capital, share responsibility, furnish ideas, and do the work. The partners also share the risks. If the business fails, the partners share responsibility for the debts.

Any two or more persons can form a partnership. Usually they sign an agreement setting up the partnership. Unwritten partnership agreements, however, are legal and are recognized by the courts. There are a few large U.S. businesses that are organized as partnerships. Most partnerships, though, are small.

It is possible to recognize a partnership by the name of the business firm: Kim and Jackson, Contractors; Reilley, Cortés, and Clark, Attorneys. If *Inc.*, an abbreviation, or short form, of "Incorporated," appears after the names, the business is organized as a corporation, a third form of business organization.

Corporations

Establishing a big business requires large sums of money—to buy land, build factories and

Assign each small group one of the following companies: General Motors, USX Corp., International Business Machines, American Telephone and Telegraph Co., Exxon, or Du Pont. Have each group use available resources to prepare a report, using flowcharts or other visual guides, about the growth of its assigned corporation. Individual tasks include researching, writing, editing, and illustrating. Conclude by asking: Do you think a corporation starting today can grow the way older corporations have grown? Why or why not?

Tell students that they are all stockholders in the Classroom Corporation, and it is time for the annual stockholders meeting. Have students elect a board of directors. Have the board choose executive officers. Ask the board and the officers to describe their duties. Then ask the whole class: If the Classroom Corporation fails, who among you is responsible for paying its debts? *(None of the stockholders are responsible for paying the debts. The company's assets are sold to pay its debts.)*

---

offices, purchase tools and machinery, and employ workers. A big business seldom can be set up by an individual or even by a number of partners. Another form of business organization—a **corporation**—is needed.

The corporation is the most common form of business organization for most of the nation's large companies and for many smaller ones. The corporation is a permanent organization. It is unlike proprietorships and partnerships, which end when their owners die.

Corporations play a vital role in the U.S. economy. How does a corporation work? How is it organized? The following are its most important features.

Raising Money Corporations raise money by selling **stocks**, or shares of ownership. Each share of stock represents part of the ownership of the corporation. The people who buy corporate stocks are called **stockholders**.

Suppose that a new corporation needs $1 million to set up business. The corporation has the legal right to raise this money from investors. For example, it could sell 10,000 shares of its stock at $100 a share. Each purchaser of a single share of stock would then own one ten-thousandth of the company.

When profits are divided each year, each owner of a single share of stock would receive

(continued on page 324)

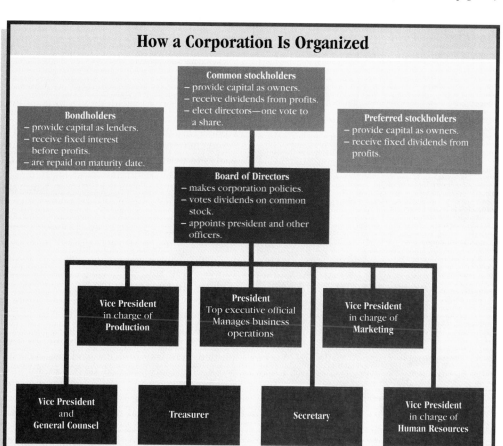

How a Corporation Is Organized

Common stockholders
- provide capital as owners.
- receive dividends from profits.
- elect directors—one vote to a share.

Bondholders
- provide capital as lenders.
- receive fixed interest before profits.
- are repaid on maturity date.

Preferred stockholders
- provide capital as owners.
- receive fixed dividends from profits.

Board of Directors
- makes corporation policies.
- votes dividends on common stock.
- appoints president and other officers.

Vice President in charge of **Production**

President Top executive official Manages business operations

Vice President in charge of **Marketing**

Vice President and **General Counsel**

Treasurer

Secretary

Vice President in charge of **Human Resources**

Summarizing

Have students write a list of the steps that Rosa and Jonathan's Junior Achievement group took to get their business started, to make it work, and to end it at the close of the school year. Students should illustrate the steps in a diagram, such as a flowchart or time line. Have students use their illustrations (with explanatory captions) to create posters to display in class.

CIVICS SIDELIGHT

In addition to teaching high school students how to organize and operate their own businesses, Junior Achievement provides programs that introduce elementary school students and middle school students to the world of economics and business. At the elementary school level, Junior Achievement programs teach students more about themselves as consumers and workers. Middle school students engage in activities designed to help them learn about the U.S. economic system, personal finance, long-term goal setting, and the importance of getting a good education.

Junior Achievement also offers a dropout prevention program. This program uses board games, charts, and role-playing exercises to teach middle school students about the economic consequences of dropping out of school. Students also learn to make budgets based on their potential incomes.

Citizenship IN ACTION

STUDENT BUSINESSES

Running a business takes thought, hard work, and patience. Rosa Furvo and Jonathan Banks should know. In their sophomore year in high school, Rosa and Jonathan learned the responsibilities of organizing and running a small business. Rosa worked as company president, factory worker, and door-to-door salesperson. Jonathan was company treasurer, package handler, and salesperson.

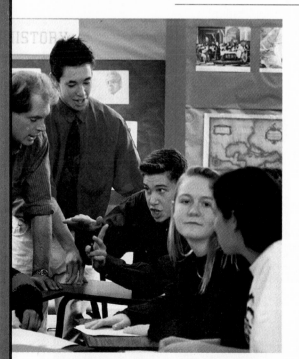

Junior Achievement advisers are community business-people who volunteer their time and expertise. Together, students and advisers run successful companies.

Junior Achievement

Rosa and Jonathan did all these jobs in a Junior Achievement *Company Program.* Each year students around the nation form hundreds of JA companies. JA is a national organization whose goal is to teach high school students about the free-enterprise system. Students learn to organize, run, and shut down a business. Some students meet once a week for two hours a week for 15 weeks. Even others run Junior Achievement companies as after-school clubs.

Rosa and Jonathan's group named the company Double-M—for Double the Money. It made and sold desk lamps and decorated T-shirts. To raise money to buy materials and run the business, the students sold stock in their company. They sold 130 shares, mostly to family and friends, at $1 a share.

After the stock was sold, the students elected company officers and assigned the work. They also settled on prices for their products. Help came from two sources. One source was national JA materials. The materials point out typical manufacturing and sales costs. They also discuss how much the students should add to the selling price to keep the price competitive yet profitable.

Tell students that nonprofit organizations often use strategies found in the business world. Have small groups of students develop campaigns for selling tickets to an event to raise funds for a new school library. The groups should identify potential ticket buyers and strategies to sell the tickets. Roles for students include creating and illustrating the ticket, illustrating and writing the sales pitch, and preparing advertising. Have each group present its project to the rest of the class.

The second source of help was an adult consultant who attended the company meetings. JA consultants are local businesspeople who volunteer their time to start JA programs. They ask local industries to donate funds for a space where student companies can meet and work. Rosa's and Jonathan's company worked in a former bakery rented by the consultants.

Meeting the Challenge

Most people who start their own businesses do not have to learn how to do several jobs in a few weeks. What was it like for students to learn all those new jobs so quickly?

As president of Double-M, Rosa had a lot of work to do. She learned that "the president really has to get out and work. She or he can't just sit back and watch."

As treasurer, Jonathan had to learn to give financial details his constant attention. "It's so easy to forget to write down a few cents here and a few cents there. But it makes a difference in the long run."

All members of the company cooperated in decorating the T-shirts and making the desk lamps. When the products were ready, all company members sold the products door-to-door. By May most of the products were sold, except for a half dozen desk lamps. The students worked extra hard and found new ways to sell the lamps quickly, so that they could close the company by the end of the school year.

Closing the Company

The students ended their business by publishing an annual report and closing their record books. Like most JA companies, Double-M declared a profit. This meant that the company not only returned the $1 that each stockholder had invested but also paid a dividend.

How did Rosa and Jonathan feel about having spent so much time on their JA company in addition to their regular schoolwork? Both agreed that the experience had more than repaid their effort. "We learned a lot and are ready to go again," they said.

Junior Achievement students play a board game about the free-enterprise system. These games help students learn about organizing and running small businesses.

YOU DECIDE

1. What are the advantages and disadvantages of doing several jobs in the same company?
2. Why is it necessary to keep track of all the money earned and spent by a company?
3. Why is running a Junior Achievement company a good way to learn about the free-enterprise system? How else might a person learn how the U.S. economic system works?

GLOBAL PERSPECTIVES

Junior Achievement programs are not limited to the United States. Around half a million students in 85 countries around the world participate in Junior Achievement activities. Junior Achievement's international affiliates include such countries as Argentina, China, Costa Rica, Ireland, New Zealand, South Africa, Uruguay, and many of the formerly communist countries of eastern Europe.

. . . .

ANSWERS TO YOU DECIDE

. . . .

1. Students probably will note that learning to do several jobs allows a person to know more thoroughly how a company operates. A possible disadvantage is the difficulty of concentrating on several jobs at once.

2. to keep track of profits and losses

3. hands-on experience; Students also may learn about the economic system by reading, watching the news, and talking with businesspeople.

Independent Practice

Have students write the "obituary" for an imaginary failed corporation. They should give some history of the corporation and the reasons for its failure (cause of death), but they should also focus on how the corporation's debts were paid off. Students should explain what has happened to the company's stockholders, including any liabilities they have regarding the company's failure. Invite volunteers to read their obituaries to the class.

Closure

Invite a business owner and the director (or spokesperson) of a nonprofit organization to talk to the class about differences and similarities between the two kinds of organizations. Have students prepare pertinent questions for the guests. Then have students write short paragraphs summarizing the guests' comments.

CIVICS SIDELIGHT

Sometimes a corporation is just too big to fail. Or more accurately, the government will not allow it to fail, for fear that the overall economy might suffer a serious downturn. Such was the case with the Chrysler Corporation. During the 1970s rising fuel prices hurt sales of large, fuel-inefficient cars, of which Chrysler had a large inventory. By 1979 the company faced bankruptcy. As the newly hired chairman of Chrysler, Lee Iacocca asked the federal government to help the company. Congress, after much debate, voted to "bail out" Chrysler with guaranteed loans totaling $1.5 billion, while Chrysler agreed to find another $2 billion from other sources. The company also slashed its workforce, cut wages, and closed plants to save money. The plan worked. By 1981 Chrysler had bounced back, and in 1984 the company enjoyed record profits (more than $2.4 billion).

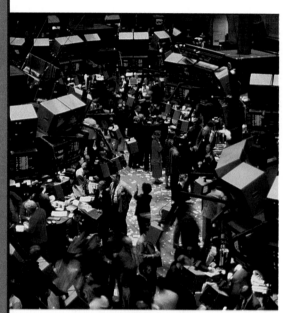

In a maze of people and computers, traders place stock orders on the floor of the New York Stock Exchange. Millions of shares of stock are bought and sold on the exchange each day.

one ten-thousandth of the profits. Corporation profits paid to stockholders are called **dividends**. Some stockholders own a few shares of stock. Other stockholders own many more shares. Each stockholder receives a share of the profits in proportion to the number of stock shares owned.

Rights to Operate Corporations receive their rights to operate from state governments. States give businesses charters, or grants, of incorporation. These charters recognize corporations' right to conduct business, sell stock to the public, and receive the protection of state laws.

In return for these benefits, corporations must obey state regulations in regard to their organization, the reports they make public, the taxes they pay, and the way in which they sell their stocks to the public.

Elected Directors The directors of corporations are elected by the stockholders. Every corporation is required by law to hold at least one meeting of its stockholders each year. All stockholders have the right to attend and address this meeting—even if they own only one share.

At this annual meeting, the stockholders elect a board of directors. They may also vote on changes in the corporation's business. Each share of stock entitles its owner to one vote. Major stockholders, therefore, cast most of the votes. The board of directors, representing the stockholders, meets during the year to make decisions about the corporation.

Choosing Executives The board of directors chooses corporation executives, or the people who will manage the affairs of the corporation. The executives include the president of the company, vice presidents, secretary, and treasurer. The president usually chooses the other major assistants. Together, these officials oversee the daily operations of the corporation.

Debt Responsibility Corporations, as you recall, are owned by the stockholders. The money received from the sale of stock becomes the corporation's capital. The purchase of shares gives the stockholders the right to receive a part of the company's profits.

But what if the business fails? Are the stockholders responsible for paying a corporation's debts? No. The most that stockholders may lose is the amount they paid for their shares of stock.

Are the corporation's executives responsible for the debts? No. Individuals are not responsible for the debts of a corporation. This is the advantage the corporation has in gathering large amounts of capital. If the corporation fails, owing many debts, neither the stockholders nor the officers of the corporation are responsible for its debts. Instead, if a corporation goes out of business, its assets (property, buildings, and other valuables) are sold. The money raised from this sale is then used to pay off the corporation's debts.

Extension

Have students find representative samples of local businesses that are sole proprietorships, partnerships, and corporations, both for-profit and nonprofit. They might use the telephone directory and the local Chamber of Commerce to find their sample businesses. Students should choose one of each type of business and prepare reports to the class about how each business is structured and raises money.

Preferred and Common Stock

A corporation may issue two kinds of stock—preferred stock and common stock. Owners of **preferred stock** take less risk when they invest their money. As long as the company makes a profit, they are guaranteed a fixed dividend every year. The corporation must pay dividends to the preferred stockholders before paying other stockholders their dividends. Because preferred stockholders take less risk, they usually do not have a vote in the company's affairs. They are owners, but they have no voice in managing the company.

Owners of **common stock** take more risk when they invest their money. They receive dividends only if the company makes good profits. Why, then, would anyone want to risk buying common stock? There are three main advantages in owning common stock:

- If the company's profits are high, owners of common stock may receive higher dividends than owners of preferred stock.
- If the company's profits are high, the market price, or selling price, of the common stock usually increases. This means stockholders can sell their shares, if they wish, for more than they paid for them.
- Common stock owners have a vote in electing the board of directors and in deciding certain company policies.

Corporate Bonds

Even with the sale of preferred and common stocks, corporations sometimes need additional large sums of money to carry on and expand operations. In such cases corporations, like governments, may issue bonds.

As you know, bonds are certificates stating how much the original purchaser paid. They also declare the percentage of interest on this amount that the corporation will pay the bondholder each year. Interest, as you also know, is the percentage paid to individuals or banks for the use of their money. The company must pay the interest on its bonds before

it pays dividends to stockholders. This interest must be paid whether or not the company earns any profits for the year.

If the company cannot repay the money by the date stated on the bonds, the bondholders may take over the business. They may close the corporation and sell its property and other assets to raise the money owed them. Or they may keep the business in operation, perhaps with new management. This is done in the hope that the corporation will be able to repay the amount owed on the bonds.

Nonprofit Organizations

Some business organizations provide goods and services without seeking to earn a profit. These **nonprofit organizations** vary in size and include charities, scientific research associations, and organizations dedicated to cultural and educational programs. Among the many nonprofit organizations in the United States are the American Red Cross, the American Heart Association, the United Way, Boy Scouts, and Girl Scouts. Nonprofit organizations are not taxed by the government.

SECTION 2 REVIEW

1. Define or identify the following terms: sole proprietorship, partnership, corporation, stock, stockholder, dividend, preferred stock, common stock, nonprofit organization.

2. What are the advantages and disadvantages of a sole proprietorship? of a partnership?

3. Why is the corporation form of organization well suited to large industries? How do corporations raise money? How are the debts of a corporation paid if the corporation fails?

4. What are the purposes of nonprofit organizations?

SECTION 2 REVIEW ANSWERS

1. See the following pages: sole proprietorship, partnership (p. 320); corporation, stock, stockholder (p. 321); dividend (p. 324); preferred stock, common stock, nonprofit organization (p. 325).

2. proprietorship—owner is own boss and does not share profits, but supplies all capital, pays salaries and taxes, is responsible for failure; partnership—more than one person responsible for expenses, workload, possible failure, but profits and decision-making shared

3. provides large sums of money needed to operate; sell stocks; assets sold

4. provide goods and services without seeking profit

5. preferred—fixed dividend but no voice in managing company; common—dividend if profits are high, gives voting rights; bonds issued to obtain money

6. Students should cite the advantages and disadvantages of their type of organization.

After studying Section 3, students should be able to do the following.

1. Explain the role of the four factors of production in starting a business.

2. Explain the relationship between good management and profits.

3. Distinguish wages from salaries and net income from gross income.

4. Describe government's role in business and concerns about government regulation.

Write the French word *entreprendre* on the chalkboard, and tell students that it means "to undertake or attempt." Have students use this information to define **entrepreneur**. Then have students distinguish **gross income** from **net income**. Tell them that the word *gross* comes from the French word *gros*, meaning "large." Students should understand that gross income is larger than net income.

GLOBAL PERSPECTIVES

Factors such as taxes and availability of space help determine how expensive office space will be. For example, office space in the prime business area of Stockholm, Sweden, cost $25 a square foot in 1994. Taxes and charges other than rent accounted for less than 10 percent of that cost. In comparison, a square foot of office space cost nearly four times as much in London, where taxes and charges other than rent accounted for about half of total cost. At $170 a square foot, Tokyo had the most expensive office space among the world's large cities in 1994, but taxes and charges other than rent accounted for only about 12 percent of those costs. Space was about a third cheaper in New York City, where taxes and charges other than rent accounted for about 34 percent of costs.

CIVICS TRANSPARENCIES

An overhead transparency of "Factors of Production" is available in *Teaching Transparencies with Teacher's Notes.*

326

5. How does preferred stock differ from common stock? Why do corporations issue bonds?

6. **THINKING CRITICALLY** Consider the advantages and disadvantages of the four types of business organizations in the United States. If you were to start a business of your own, would you organize it as a sole proprietorship, a partnership, a corporation, or a nonprofit organization? Explain your answer.

3 Making Business Decisions

You know that Americans operate businesses as individual proprietors, as members of a partnership, or as managers of a corporation. No matter how a business is organized, its success depends mainly on decisions about the use of four resources, or **factors of production**: land, capital, labor, and management.

Land

Suppose that Maria Moreno decides to start a bakery. She will need a place to conduct her business. That is, she needs land. Every business enterprise needs land.

Land refers not only to a place to locate a store, factory, or office, but also to the natural resources that come from the land. The wheat used to make flour for Maria's bakery comes from the land. The wood for her bread racks comes from trees grown on the land. All the raw materials needed to produce goods of all kinds come from the mines, fields, and forests that are a part of the land.

The nation's total supply of land is limited. In some places land is so scarce that many businesses occupy each city block. People who start businesses must decide on which piece of land they want to locate their business.

Maria, for example, must decide whether to own the property on which her business will be located. She can buy either a piece of land with a building on it or land on which she can build. Or she can pay rent for a building. **Rent** is the money a person pays to use land or other property belonging to someone else.

Rents and land prices in crowded business areas where land is scarce are higher than in

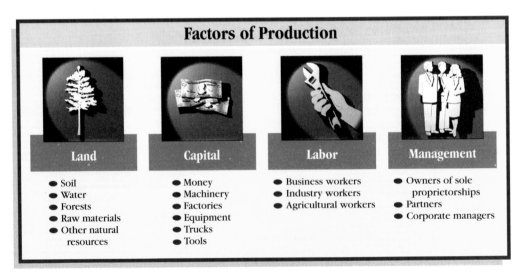

Factors of Production

Land	Capital	Labor	Management
• Soil	• Money	• Business workers	• Owners of sole
• Water	• Machinery	• Industry workers	proprietorships
• Forests	• Factories	• Agricultural workers	• Partners
• Raw materials	• Equipment		• Corporate managers
• Other natural resources	• Trucks		
	• Tools		

CIVICS THEMES

AMERICAN ECONOMIC SYSTEM
✷ **Structures and Functions** Students will learn the various components of mass production, the reasons business relies on a good system of transportation, examples of mass marketing, and the role of advertising in the U.S. economy.

✷ **Managing Finances** Students will learn the advantages and disadvantages of using charge accounts and installment plans and what consumers should do to buy quality goods at reasonable prices.

CIVICS SKILLS
Students will learn to read a product's ingredient and nutrition labels. Students also will learn terms important to understanding how goods are produced and distributed to consumers.

CITIZENSHIP VALUES
✷ **Rights and Responsibilities** Students will be encouraged to recognize the responsibilities of the consumer in the marketplace.

MEETING INDIVIDUAL NEEDS

LIMITED ENGLISH PROFICIENCY (LEP)
Pair an LEP student with a student who is proficient in English. Have them work together to make a crossword puzzle, using the terms in the Chapter 18 Civics Dictionary. They should exchange their puzzles with other pairs of students and then solve them.

LEARNERS HAVING DIFFICULTY
Ask a question that will lead students to summarize each section in the chapter. Section 1's first paragraph ends with an appropriate question. For Section 2 you might ask: What are the key elements of the distribution system for U.S. goods? For Section 3 you might ask: What does it take to be a smart consumer? Each student should then write a short summarizing paragraph to answer your focus question.

AUDITORY LEARNERS
Read aloud an article from a consumer magazine concerning the testing of a product in which students would be interested. Ask students to take notes as you read. Then have them discuss the main points of the article and come to some decisions about which of the tested brands appeals to them most and why.

VISUAL LEARNERS
Have students bring to class local department store flyers or newspaper advertising supplements. Ask

them to list 20 items from the flyer that they think are bargains and 20 items they think are not bargains. For each item students should give a reason to support their judgment. Students' reasons might fall into the categories of quality, price, usefulness, and comparisons with similar products offered at other department stores.

TACTILE/KINESTHETIC LEARNERS
Tell students that they have a 50-pound package that must go to a distant city (name a specific city), and they must find the cheapest way to send it there. To do so, students should contact airlines, parcel delivery services (post office, United Parcel Service, and others), interstate bus lines, railroads, and trucking companies. Have students organize the information in a chart showing comparative prices. Then have students discuss the importance of transportation to the economy.

GIFTED LEARNERS
Have students research how colonial powers used rail transport in their colonies for economic and military purposes. Examples include the British in India and several European nations in Africa, beginning in the 1800s. Some students might wish to research the effects of the railroad on settlement of the American West. Invite volunteers to present their findings to the class for discussion.

CHAPTER OVERVIEW

Chapter 18 examines an American innovation—mass production. It also looks at the ways in which the nation's many products are transported and sold. Of particular interest in the chapter is the discussion of one of the most important components of a free economy—the consumer. The underlying theme of the chapter is that everyone plays a role in maintaining the high standard of living created by the U.S. system of production.

Motivator

Have students look around the classroom and note all the different kinds of products, from chairs to clothing. Ask: How many products were handmade, and how many were produced in a factory? *(Most goods are factory-produced.)* Tell students that in this section they will learn how such goods are produced and then distributed from the factory to the store and ultimately to the consumer.

CHAPTER OBJECTIVES

After studying Chapter 18, students should be able to do the following.

1. Describe mass production and explain why it works well in a free economy.
2. Explain how businesses distribute goods.
3. Explain how people can become wise consumers.

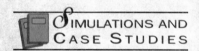

SIMULATIONS AND CASE STUDIES

Lesson 17: Group Consumerism Reports

Block Scheduling Option

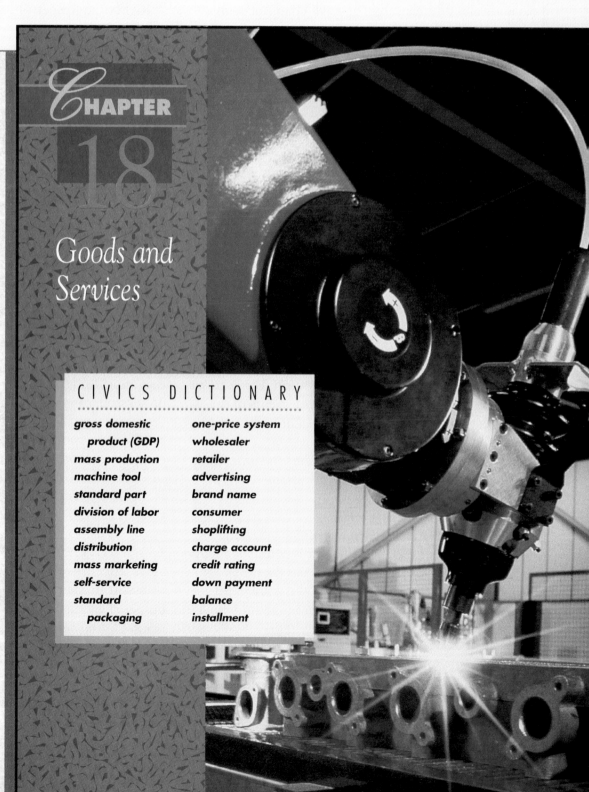

CHAPTER 18

Goods and Services

CIVICS DICTIONARY

gross domestic
   product (GDP)
mass production
machine tool
standard part
division of labor
assembly line
distribution
mass marketing
self-service
standard
   packaging

one-price system
wholesaler
retailer
advertising
brand name
consumer
shoplifting
charge account
credit rating
down payment
balance
installment

SECTION OBJECTIVES

After studying Section 1, students should be able to do the following.

1. Identify the three main features of mass production.
2. Explain how the sources of power for U.S. factories have changed over the years.
3. Explain the role of the assembly line and the feeder line in mass production.
4. Explain how the profit motive affects the economic system in the United States.

Teaching Section 1
Building a Vocabulary

Write separately on the chalkboard the three words of the term **gross domestic product**. Have students recall the meaning of *gross* from the last chapter. *(total; without deductions)* Then ask for the meaning of *domestic (from within a country)* and *product (something made).* Help students deduce the meaning of the whole term. *(value of all goods produced in the United States)* You might explain other vocabulary terms in a similar way.

CHAPTER FOCUS

From cereal to compact discs, sunglasses to basketballs, and blue jeans to popcorn, almost any type of product you might wish to buy is made somewhere in the United States. In fact, the U.S. economic system has an extraordinary ability to produce. In recent years, the United States has produced more than $6 trillion worth of goods and services annually, more than any other nation in the world.

The dollar value of all goods and services produced in the United States each year is called the **gross domestic product (GDP).** Economists use GDP as one measure of how well the U.S. economy is performing. Other measures of the economy's well-being include the number of unemployed people, the number of business failures, and the amount of tax revenue produced by citizens and businesses in the nation.

The U.S. economy has remained relatively strong for more than two centuries. Much of its strength lies in the way U.S. products are made and distributed.

•••••••••••••••••••••••••••••

STUDY GUIDE

- What is mass production, and why does it work so well in a free economy?
- How do businesses distribute goods?
- How can you become a wise consumer?

1 U.S. Production

During one recent year, the United States produced nearly 11 million automobiles, trucks, and buses. In a single year it produced almost 101 million tons (92 million metric tons) of steel and more than 280 million tons (254 million metric tons) of corn. Millions of other goods are produced each year in the nation. What makes this huge production possible?

Mass Production

There are many factors that make the United States capable of such an enormous output.

One factor is **mass production,** or the rapid production by machine of large numbers of identical objects. Mass production requires many large, complex machines and vast amounts of power. Inventors have developed machines that can make, or help make, almost any product.

One of the first inventors to make mass production possible was Eli Whitney. (You may remember him as the inventor of the cotton gin.) In 1798 Whitney signed a contract to make muskets, or guns, for the U.S. Army. He promised to manufacture and deliver 10,000 guns in two years.

Whitney's promise seemed impossible to keep because up to that time guns had been made by hand, one at a time. To prove that he could keep his promise, Whitney showed some government officials how he planned to make so many guns so quickly.

From a box Whitney took 10 gun barrels, 10 triggers, 10 stocks, and 10 locks for exploding the gunpowder. He asked the officials to choose one of each of these parts. Whitney then took the four parts and quickly put together a finished musket. To show that the parts were all alike, he continued to put together muskets until all 10 were completed.

GLOBAL PERSPECTIVES

The Industrial Revolution of the 18th and early 19th centuries dramatically transformed production methods, making power-driven machinery and factories the engines of production. The British textile industry led the revolution with the invention of various machines, such as the spinning mule for spinning yarns and the flying shuttle for weaving. Textile mills spread throughout England beginning in the 1740s. The development of power sources, such as the steam engine, and other basic resources, such as coal and iron ore, also increased manufacturing capacity.

Labor, in abundant supply as people moved from rural areas to cities in search of jobs, and the increased flow of capital helped fuel the expansion of industrialization. The population of Greater London, for example, more than doubled in the first half of the 19th century to nearly 2.7 million people by 1850. As the need for capital to sustain development increased, the number of banks in London rose from 20 in 1750 to 70 in 1800.

Applying Ideas

Ask students to choose a product (other than automobiles) that is mass-produced and consider how the three main features of mass production apply to that product. That is, students should decide what kind of machine tools are needed, what the standard parts are, and how division of labor is used to manufacture the product. Have students present their information orally, with visual guides if helpful.

Assign each small group one of the following sources of power: waterpower, steam engine, internal combustion engine, electrical power. Have each group use classroom and library resources to research and then illustrate for the class how each source of power works and was (or is) used in industry. You might have some groups research how the various sources of electrical power are used by industry. Tasks for students might include researching, writing, editing, illustrating, and presenting.

GLOBAL PERSPECTIVES

Point out that the major sources of electricity can vary significantly from country to country. Nuclear power, in particular, has become an important source of electricity for many industrialized countries. For example, around 73 percent of France's electricity was supplied by nuclear power plants in 1992. Nuclear power plants supplied just about 22 percent of U.S. electricity in 1992. (The United States, however, is the world's largest producer of energy from nuclear power plants.) Following are the percentages (for 1992) of electricity from nuclear power plants for selected countries: Canada, 15 percent; Japan, 27 percent; Germany, 30 percent; Switzerland, 40 percent; and Sweden, 43 percent.

For the world, the amount of electricity produced from nuclear power plants increased by nearly 200 percent between 1980 and 1993. Nevertheless, nuclear power accounted for only about 6 percent of the world's energy production in 1993. The largest source of energy over the 1980–1993 period was petroleum, which accounted for nearly 40 percent of the world's energy in 1993.

He had made 10 identical guns from a box containing identical, interchangeable parts. Moreover, he was able to make them rapidly.

Eli Whitney's methods have become the basis of all mass production, from radios and sewing machines to automobiles and tractors. What are these methods?

Machine Tools Whitney developed **machine tools**, or machinery built to produce parts that are exactly the same. Instead of boring each gun barrel by hand, for example, Whitney made a machine that did nothing but bore gun barrels, all in the same way.

Standard Parts Each of Whitney's machine tools made parts that were exactly alike, called **standard parts**. That is, any Whitney gun barrel would fit any gun stock made by Whitney. Other parts were also identical, or interchangeable, and would fit any of the guns. This was a great advantage. If a part wore out, it could easily be replaced by a new standard, identical part.

Division of Labor Barrels, triggers, stocks, and locks for Whitney's guns were

Inventor Eli Whitney's methods of making muskets formed the basis of mass production.

made by different groups of workers, each operating a separate machine. No one worker made a complete gun. The job was divided into several tasks among the various workers. In this **division of labor**, each worker was a specialist at part of the job. Specialization speeded the entire process.

The use of machine tools, standard parts, and division of labor helped increase production. The early machines used by Whitney and others were small and still relatively inefficient, however. These early machines needed a better source of power.

Power Sources

For many years Americans used the force of falling water, or waterpower, as the main source of power to operate their machines. Early factories therefore were located near streams. Dams were built to hold back water so that it could be released when necessary to turn waterwheels. As these big wheels turned, they generated power to run machines within the factory.

Steam power began to replace waterpower in the late 1700s. Scottish engineer James Watt's invention of a practical steam engine made steam power possible. Steam power continued to be the leading source of industrial power during the 1800s.

In the late 1800s several new sources of power were developed. The internal combustion engine used the power released by exploding gasoline. It was often used to run small machines and, of course, automobiles.

The source of power that contributed most to modern mass production was electricity. In the late 1800s the work of Thomas Edison made the widespread use of electricity practical and affordable.

At first electricity was used mainly for lighting. As time passed, it was used in many other ways. American families today use electricity to run toasters, fans, refrigerators, air conditioners, washers, dryers, vacuum cleaners, radios, televisions, and so on. Today nearly every U.S. factory uses electricity as its main

Guided Practice

Review with students the difference between the assembly line and the feeder line. Then use the chalkboard to help students diagram the assembly process at a factory, including both kinds of lines. Then have the class demonstrate the assembly process by producing something simple, such as a hand-held fan made with cardboard and ice cream sticks or a booklet of papers stapled together. Have an "assembly line" compete against individuals to see who can produce the most items in a given period of time.

Independent Practice

Have students diagram the assembly process for the mass-produced product they chose in the Applying Ideas activity on page 334. Students should decide what kinds of workers are needed and what skills the workers must have. Encourage students to be creative, such as by developing work-saving steps in the assembly process. Remind students that advances in technology often result in revisions in a company's assembly process. Call on volunteers to present their work to the class for discussion.

Foundations of Modern Mass Production

Machine Tools	**Standard Parts**	**Division of Labor**	**Source of Power**
are used to make standard parts.	are used to make identical products.	speeds production along the assembly line.	operates machinery cheaply and efficiently.

---

source of power. Scientists continue to search for even better sources of power.

Mass Production in an Automobile Factory

One of the best ways to understand modern mass production is to visit an automobile manufacturing plant. Suppose you were to go to Detroit, Michigan, to make such a visit. What would you see?

When you first enter the factory, it may take a few minutes to get used to all the activity and noise. As you look about, you can see how Eli Whitney's methods of manufacturing are still used by U.S. industry.

As an engine block moves by, a team of workers begins its tasks. First a huge machine tool bores dozens of holes into the block. As the block moves along, workers fit pistons, valves, and bolts into the holes. The block has become an internal combustion engine. Other teams of workers fasten carburetors, ignitions, and other parts to the engine. One automobile engine after another is made in this way, each exactly alike.

How does modern mass production use Whitney's methods? Think about what you have just seen in the automobile plant. You saw a machine tool produce identical parts—bored engine blocks. You saw examples of the division of labor. Each worker does a specialized job and has become highly skilled. You saw standard parts, such as valves, being used. Each valve fits exactly into a hole in the engine block. Eli Whitney's ideas have spread to all types of industry, including ones that did not exist in his lifetime.

The Assembly Line

One feature of modern mass production, however, is different from Whitney's day. That feature is the **assembly line**. How does an assembly line work?

Back in the automobile plant, you see a frame of a car moving along on a very large conveyor belt. The belt slowly moves many car frames at a time through the factory.

As a car frame moves along the assembly line, the wheels are added to the frame. Then the engine, transmission, windshield, steering wheel, and gears are added. Seats, door panels, lights, and the dashboard are put on next. The car moves to the paint shop where it is spray-painted and dried. Finally, the car is driven off

Closure

Have students write letters to fictional pen pals in some of the countries instituting free-market reforms (such as in eastern Europe and the independent republics of the former Soviet Union). Students should explain how the profit motive affects the U.S. economic system. The letters should relate how the profit motive encouraged the development of mass production techniques and technologies and how those innovations in turn help business increase profits. Call on volunteers to read their letters to the class.

Reviewing

Have students complete the Section 1 Review.

Reteaching

Assign Section 1 of the Chapter 18 Reteaching Worksheet.

GLOBAL PERSPECTIVES

Many countries that once had command economies have instituted reforms to ease or remove government control of business. The People's Republic of China, for example, has experienced phenomenal economic growth as the central government loosened its grips on the economy over the past decade. Profitable businesses owned by regional and local governments successfully compete against money-losing businesses owned and run by the central government. Growing prosperity is spreading from coastal regions into the poorer interior of the country. Chinese entrepreneurs are getting rich as an emerging Chinese middle class buys televisions, cars, and other consumer goods. Massive amounts of foreign investment also are fueling China's economic growth. Some observers believe that this foreign investment will help spread the ideas of entrepreneurialism and even political reform throughout the country.

This U.S. airplane manufacturing plant includes many features of modern mass production. Here skilled workers use standard parts to build the aircraft.

the assembly line and tested. It is now ready to be shipped to an automobile dealer's showroom and sold.

How do the various parts arrive at the assembly line just in time to become parts of the finished automobile? At the beginning of your tour, you recall, you saw an engine being made. This engine was not on the main assembly line. It was on a side line, or feeder line. The engine's movement along the feeder line was timed so that the engine was completed just as the feeder line met the main assembly line. In this way feeder lines are used to assemble many parts of the car and bring them to the main assembly line exactly when and where they are needed.

Other large industries use these same methods of production. Bread from a large bakery, for example, is made in a similar way to automobiles. Flour and other ingredients are dumped into huge mixers from overhead bins.

Conveyor belts running from the storage rooms supply the bins. After the loaf is shaped, it is carried on a conveyor belt through a long oven. By the time it reaches the other end of the oven, the bread is baked.

The finished loaf travels through another machine that slices and wraps it. Still another machine packs loaves in boxes. A conveyor belt transports the boxes to trucks for delivery to stores.

Mass Production in the World

Mass production was first developed in the United States, but it has spread to other nations around the world. Mass production is used more effectively in some nations than in others, however.

Cuba, for example, uses mass production methods, but it has not been as successful as

After studying Section 2, students should be able to do the following.

1. Explain the importance and history of transportation in the U.S. economic system.

2. Explain why a shopping mall is an efficient marketing system and why specialty shops are important to local communities.

3. Identify the roles of wholesalers and retailers in the economy of the United States.

Teaching Section 2

Building a Vocabulary

Explain that one meaning of *mass* implies a quantity, such as a large amount of something: "a great mass of people." Have students deduce the meaning of **mass marketing**. *(selling, or marketing, goods in large, or mass, quantities)*
Ask: Who is **advertising** aimed at? *(the public; consumers)*
Ask: Why is advertising important in mass marketing? *(Advertising informs the public about the mass of products and encourages consumers to purchase them.)*

---

other nations. One reason may be that in Cuba, as you recall, the government controls the economy. Property is not privately owned, and private enterprise is allowed only on a limited basis. The government generally decides what prices to charge and the amount of goods and services to produce.

A command economy like Cuba's does not have the same incentives, or motives, of a free economy. The lack of a profit motive in particular discourages people from working hard and producing more. In turn, lower productivity means that there is less money for modernizing factories.

In contrast, a free-market economy encourages businesspeople to take risks. When there is no incentive to make a profit by taking a risk, people may be less inclined to take risks. What, for example, was Eli Whitney's incentive? He invented a new method of production because he hoped to profit from it. So did all the other businesspeople who adopted and improved the system of mass production.

Businesspeople must be quick to grasp new ideas. To remain competitive they must be ready to change from old ways to new ways. They must do this even if it means building new factories, modernizing old ones, and buying costly new machinery.

SECTION 1 REVIEW

1. Define or identify the following terms: gross domestic product (GDP), mass production, machine tool, standard part, division of labor, assembly line.

2. What are the three main features of mass production?

3. How have the sources of power used by U.S. factories changed since the early years of the nation?

4. How does the assembly line enable the mass production of products? What is the purpose of a feeder line?

5. How does the profit motive affect the U.S. economic system?

6. **THINKING CRITICALLY** Imagine that you work in the U.S. automobile factory described in this section. Create a flowchart of an automobile moving through the factory on an assembly line. Be sure to label each step.

2 Distributing Goods

U.S. businesses and industries produce goods and services that supply people's needs. Production, however, is only one part of supplying those needs. The other part is **distribution**. After goods are made, they must be distributed, or spread, to the people who want them.

Distribution has two sides: transportation and marketing. Transportation is essential for bringing goods from the places where they are made to the places where people can buy or use them. Persuading people to buy goods is called marketing.

Railroads

In such a vast land as the United States, transportation always has been important. Early in the nation's history, a good system of transportation was necessary to bring together, or unify, the nation. As a result, the young nation experienced a long period of road, canal, and railroad building. This made it possible for U.S. businesses and industries to transport their goods to all parts of the nation.

U.S. industry was greatly helped by the growth of railroads. Railroads that crisscrossed the nation helped create a single, large market for products. Long freight trains rolled from coast to coast carrying raw materials and finished products. The railroads brought up-to-date products to every U.S. city, to most towns, and within reach of farms. They gave

SECTION **1** REVIEW
A N S W E R S

1. See the following pages: gross domestic product (GDP), mass production (p. 333); machine tool, standard part, division of labor (p. 334); assembly line (p. 335).

2. machine tools, standard parts, division of labor

3. In the earliest years, water was the main source of power. Steam power was developed in the late 1700s and was important throughout the 19th century. Gasoline and electrical power became important in the late 19th century. Electricity has come to be the main source of power for industry.

4. Identical items are produced rapidly. Feeder lines make parts available on the main assembly line when needed.

5. motivates people to work hard and produce more, providing capital to invest; also motivates people to be innovative and to take risks

6. Flowcharts should illustrate assembly and feeder lines.

CIVICS SIDELIGHT

The Erie Canal played a vital role in the fantastic growth of industry in the Midwest and in New York City in the 1800s. Opened on October 25, 1825, the 363-mile-long Erie Canal linked the Great Lakes with New York City by way of the Hudson River. Many settlers used the canal on their moves west. Their farm produce was sent back east on boats and barges pulled by horses along the canal. Those same boats and barges carried manufactured goods back to the Midwest at a tenth of the cost of shipping them over land. The state of New York paid more than $7 million to construct the Erie Canal. The canal more than paid for itself through the tolls charged for its use. The tolls ended in 1882, and the canal today is part of the New York State Barge Canal System. The system connects Lake Champlain and the Hudson River to Lake Erie and Lake Ontario.

businesspeople a means of rapid travel and communication.

Railroads were the nation's chief method of transportation for nearly a century. In the mid-1900s, however, railroads found it difficult to compete with other means of transportation—trucks, buses, automobiles, and airplanes. In the 1960s and 1970s many railroads went out of business. Railroads today carry a much smaller percentage of passengers and freight than before.

Although efforts are being made to modernize the U.S. railroad system, the tracks and equipment of many of the nation's railroad lines are in poor condition. Also, U.S. trains are not as fast as more modern trains in some nations. For example, today's trains travel between New York City and Washington, D.C., at speeds over 100 miles (161 km) an hour. Trains in France, meanwhile, travel at speeds of up to 186 miles (300 km) an hour. Germany,

the United Kingdom, and other European countries also operate high-speed trains.

Railroads, though, are still an important part of the nation's transportation system. They carry bulk cargo, such as coal and grain. They also carry passengers and provide jobs. In an effort to support the railroads, Congress created a national rail passenger system called Amtrak in 1970. Organized with funds from the federal government, Amtrak is working to improve the nation's railroads.

Air Transportation

Railroads today must compete with other forms of transportation. In passenger transportation, for example, the airlines have grown rapidly. In 1950 railroads carried more than 6 percent of the passengers traveling between cities. Airlines carried less than 2 percent. By 1993 the airlines had more than 17 percent of

Railroads helped make possible the tremendous growth of U.S. industry. Today railroads remain an important part of the nation's transportation system.

Visiting a Supermarket

If possible, take your class to a nearby supermarket. Have pairs of students count the number of various kinds of products available on each aisle (one aisle per pair). Have each pair also note the variety of brands available for each kind of product. Then pool each pair's numbers to produce a rough estimate of the number of items offered by the supermarket. Discuss with the class how this exercise illustrates mass marketing. Invite the store manager to talk to your class about how mass marketing works for his or her store.

Guided Practice

Have students list all the stores they can think of in a local shopping center or mall familiar to students. (You may wish to analyze more than one shopping center.) Ask them to categorize the stores as chains or independents. (A volunteer might call to settle any disagreements.) Then have students analyze the variety of goods in the shopping center. Have them draw a conclusion about the efficiency of the "one-stop shopping" offered by the shopping center or mall.

---

passenger traffic, and the railroads had less than 1 percent. Modern research, equipment, and management methods have made airlines in the United States among the best and safest in the world.

Airlines now carry all first-class mail between U.S. cities located over a certain distance apart. They are also important in transporting freight. Airlines can carry all kinds of freight—from small packages to large industrial machinery and automobiles—with great speed.

The Highway System

The automobile is the leading means of transportation in the United States. Automobiles carry about 81 percent of passengers—more than all other kinds of transportation combined. More than 146 million cars—about one vehicle for every two persons—are registered in the United States.

Rapid highway transportation depends on good roads. To speed motor traffic the nation maintains a vast highway system. The country now has more than 3.9 million miles (6.3 million km) of roads.

Some of the nation's highways are toll roads. Drivers must pay a toll, or fee, to use these roads. Other roads are freeways, which are free of charge. Together these roads form an interstate highway system that reaches every part of the nation.

Buses, cars, and trucks travel the highways at all hours. This heavy traffic on highways and roads has caused a number of problems, including traffic jams, accidents, air pollution, and heavy use of gasoline and oil.

Among the steps citizens and communities are taking to solve these problems are lower speed limits, stricter automobile emission laws, smaller cars, and improved public transportation systems.

Mass Marketing

Selling goods in large quantities is called **mass marketing**. Modern supermarkets and large

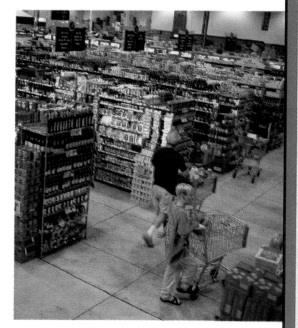

It may seem hard to believe today, but the term supermarket did not exist 50 years ago. Now supermarkets such as this one are a common sight.

department stores use this kind of large-scale selling. They also use a type of marketing called **self-service**. Self-service is an efficient and inexpensive way to sell goods because it saves time and labor.

In supermarkets, for example, customers push carts up and down the aisles, selecting items and "serving" themselves. When a customer has finished shopping, he or she rolls the cart to the checkout counter. A clerk rings up the purchases on a cash register or scans them with an electronic device.

Self-service is a modern method of marketing. Prior to the use of self-service marketing, storekeepers hired clerks to sell the goods. Each clerk helped only one customer at a time. In today's self-service stores, many customers can shop at the same time, and one clerk can help many more people.

(continued on page 342)

Proposing a New Magazine

Call on volunteers to list on the chalkboard reasons for the success of *Foxfire* magazine. Then have students brainstorm ideas for a magazine that would appeal to their communities. Have pairs of students draw up proposals for such a magazine and present them to the class. The class should discuss the chances of success for some of the magazines they propose.

Citizenship IN ACTION

FOXFIRE TURNS BIG BUSINESS

Can a group of teenagers in a rural high school start a successful magazine? They can, and they did. Students in Rabun-Gap Nacooche School in northeastern Georgia publish a magazine that is read throughout the country. Foxfire magazine began with one small group of teenagers, but generations of students have expanded the project to include books and even sound recordings.

Creating a Magazine

The idea for the magazine started with an English teacher in Rabun-Gap Nacooche School. He wanted to find a way to help his students learn language arts skills. He also wanted to help them understand their own backgrounds and the community in which they live. Only by knowing how their community works, he believed, could they become committed to its future and help plan improvements.

A magazine published by the students seemed an ideal way to fulfill these goals. Moreover, publishing a magazine would give students the opportunity to create and run a business. From the start the plan called for students to do all the work—from raising money to writing articles and preparing material for the printer.

The contents of the magazine were drawn from the students' own community in the Appalachian Mountains—an area with a rich culture and heritage. The articles included stories about the people of the community. Older citizens told students about their experiences and what they had learned from them. Relatives and neighbors also demonstrated, step by step, many traditional skills such as wood carving, weaving, and building a log cabin.

The students named their magazine *Foxfire,* after a lichen, or mosslike plant, that glows in the dark. The students went from door to door asking for contributions to help

Pages from some early editions of Foxfire.

Summarizing

Have students summarize the article by asking and answering these five questions: *Who? What? When? Where? How?* The summaries may take the form of outlines or news stories, either in periodicals or for broadcast by radio or television stations. Call on volunteers to present their summaries to the class.

them pay the printer for the first issue. They collected $440, enough for 600 copies of the magazine. When they sold those copies, they had enough money to print the next issue. In a short time the magazine paid for itself.

The Magazine Is a Success

The students published *Foxfire* four times a year, and readers kept asking for it year after year. Soon the magazine was known throughout the country. Articles from the magazine were collected in *The Foxfire Book,* which sold more than three million copies. Many other *Foxfire* books have followed.

Many years have passed since *Foxfire* was started in 1966. New groups of students have taken over, and the magazine has branched into new fields. Income from the magazine and books pays for college scholarships and enables *Foxfire* to hire students to work during the summer. Today more than half the staff members are former students who returned after graduating from college.

These staff members also work at the high school. They help students continue to publish the magazine and books. Students also produce and market a series of sound recordings and conduct environmental studies in the region. When the operation needed more space, the students were able to buy land on which they reconstructed 27 traditional log buildings.

The magazine continues to be popular. One reason for its success is that it is filled with useful information. It explains, for example, how to use common items to make quilts, toys, and baskets. Readers have learned about blacksmithing and well digging.

The students who worked on the magazine discovered that the people of their community possess a vast amount of information that is appreciated by millions of other Americans. The success of *Foxfire* encouraged students in other communities to start similar projects. Similar magazines are now published in high schools across the country.

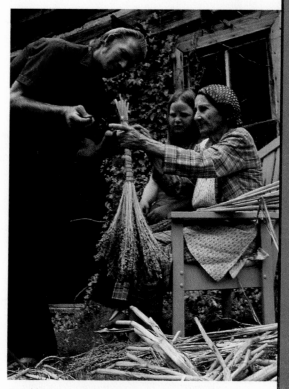

An older citizen demonstrates a traditional craft for a young person. The Appalachian Mountains region has a rich culture that is passed down through generations.

YOU DECIDE

1 How does *Foxfire* make use of the special human resources of the Appalachian region?

2 What might students learn about business by publishing magazines such as *Foxfire*?

3 What type of magazine would you like to publish? What aspects of your community's culture might you be able to explore in a local magazine?

ANSWERS TO YOU DECIDE

1. People in the small towns of the Appalachian region have preserved a wealth of American folklore and traditions. This information is communicated by them and made public through *Foxfire*.

2. Among other things, students should refer to the production and distribution aspects of business. Students also should address ideas for obtaining the necessary capital for running a business.

3. Answers will vary but should address the kinds of information students would cover in their magazines.

Independent Practice

Remind students that the convenience of shopping malls often does not provide all of the benefits that specialty stores can provide to local communities. Have students create collages illustrating these specialty stores and the benefits they provide for their communities. For example, students might use a homemade craft or a picture of a neighborhood crafts store to show the value of community businesses as sales outlets for local artists. Display the collages for the class.

Closure

Ask students to draw illustrated flowcharts that show how products move from factory to wholesaler to retailer and then to the general public. Have them insert advertising into their charts where they think it is appropriate. Students should write explanatory captions for each part of their flowcharts. Display and discuss selected charts.

CIVICS SIDELIGHT

The proliferation of shopping malls is the subject of a book whimsically titled *The Malling of America* by William Kowinski. In the book Kowinski claims that there are more shopping centers in the United States than movie theaters, hotels, or hospitals, and more enclosed malls than cities, four-year colleges, or television stations. He calls the mall a "great consumer paradise." Yet the quotation that introduces the first chapter suggests that there is more to the mall phenomenon than meets the eye. The quotation is from Charles Kuralt, who says: "Twenty-five years ago, they weren't here. Today they're everywhere. What used to be farms or woods or country crossroads have become malls. . . . If you want to find America today, this is where you have to look."

DID YOU KNOW THAT...

Advertising was used to settle the United States. In the late 1800s the Great Plains had few settlers. Railroad companies, extending their tracks into the region, had land they wanted to sell. They also hoped to profit from farmers who would ship freight on their lines. So the railroads started an advertising campaign to encourage men and women to settle in the West.

The railroads ran advertisements in newspapers and put up hundreds of posters. Sometimes they even offered immigrants free transportation to visit their native lands if they agreed to persuade others to return to the United States with them. Thousands of people responded, and many new communities grew up almost overnight.

Standard packaging also adds to the efficiency of the self-service system. Goods come from factories already wrapped. Crackers, for instance, are sealed in wrappers and sold in boxes. Sugar comes in boxes or bags of different weights. Years ago crackers were sold from a barrel. They were weighed out for each customer. Sugar also was scooped out of a barrel. It was poured into a paper bag and weighed for each customer. Today only a few items must be weighed or measured in a store.

Another feature of mass marketing is the **one-price system**, in which prices are stamped or bar-coded on products. The one-price system was first used by Wanamaker's department store in Philadelphia, Pennsylvania, more than 100 years ago. Now it is a standard practice almost everywhere.

Before the one-price system, customers often bargained with salespeople to lower the price. Imagine how much time a shopper would spend in buying the week's groceries if he or she had to bargain for every item. Instead, shoppers today pay the price marked on the product. Americans do, however, tend to bargain for large items such as houses, boats, and automobiles.

Shopping Malls

An outgrowth of the supermarket and department store is the shopping mall, or shopping center. These large complexes feature different types of stores, partly or completely surrounded by parking areas. The center of the mall is usually a supermarket or a department store. There may also be a drugstore, shoe store, hardware store, restaurants, and dozens more stores and shops.

The shopping mall is an example of highly efficient marketing. Customers can drive in, park their cars, and buy almost everything they need. Many stores can afford to sell goods at lower prices because so many goods are being sold so rapidly in the shopping center.

Chain Stores and Specialty Shops

Many of the stores in a shopping mall or center are chain stores. A chain store is owned and operated by a company that has many of the same kind of stores. The company may purchase its goods directly from a factory or farm, or it may have its own factory or farm. The chain store can offer its products at lower cost because it buys or produces those goods in large quantities.

Many other stores are independent. That is, they do not belong to a chain of stores. Some are specialty shops. They sell only certain kinds of goods or offer a particular kind of service. They may sell only women's or men's clothing, books, or toys and games.

Reviewing

Have students complete the Section 2 Review.

Reteaching

Assign Section 2 of the Chapter 18 Reteaching Worksheet.

Extension

Have pairs of students research how goods were distributed and sold in the mid-1800s. Have each pair draw an illustrated map of the United States showing how a particular product (such as wheat, minerals, or textiles, for example) moved from where it was produced or mined to various markets. Call on volunteers to explain their research and maps to the class.

These small, independent stores can offer special services not provided by larger stores. For instance, smaller stores often carry special products for which there is not a large demand. These locally owned stores play an important part in most communities. The businesspeople who own and operate them contribute to the prosperity of their communities.

Wholesalers and Retailers

Products may pass through several hands from the time they leave the factory to the time they reach the customer. A factory often sells goods in large quantities to a **wholesaler**. This businessperson owns a large warehouse where goods are stored. The wholesaler then sells the goods to retailers. **Retailers**, or retail stores, sell goods directly to the public.

Wholesalers are also called distributors. They perform a service in linking the factory and the retailer. In the end, of course, the customer must pay for this service. Chain stores, large department stores, and supermarkets often have their own warehouses and have no need for distributors. As a result, sometimes they can offer goods at lower prices.

The distribution and marketing of goods, whatever methods are used, cost a great deal of money. Sometimes it costs as much to market a product as it did to make it. Inefficient marketing can add to the price you pay for a product. Just as in mass production, efficiency in mass distribution reduces the prices of the items you buy.

Advertising

Mass marketing of goods would not be possible without advertising. **Advertising** informs people about products and tries to persuade them to buy these products. It also speeds the movement of goods from factories and farms to the public.

In the competition between producers of similar products, advertising often makes the difference between the success of one product and the failure of another. Some people believe this system is inefficient. They claim it would be better and less wasteful not to have so many products. Other people argue that competition among mass producers, marketers, and advertisers helps keep the quality of products high and prices low.

National advertising makes it possible for producers to sell their products throughout the country. Such advertising increases people's recognition of products and their brand names. A **brand name** product is a widely advertised and distributed product. When customers shop, they often choose a product with a brand name they have heard about most favorably or most often. By using national advertising, small producers may be able to grow into large national producers with brand name products. Then they can mass-produce their products for a larger market at lower costs.

Shoppers sometimes are confused by advertising, especially when several producers claim that their product is best or most effective. Advertising, however, can be a useful way for a producer to inform shoppers about a new product. In the next section you will learn how you can receive good value for your money in the American system of mass production and mass marketing.

SECTION 2 REVIEW

1. Define or identify the following terms: distribution, mass marketing, self-service, standard packaging, one-price system, wholesaler, retailer, advertising, brand name.

2. Why is transportation essential to the U.S. economic system? How did the growth of railroads affect U.S. business?

3. How has the U.S. transportation system changed over time?

4. Why is the shopping mall an efficient system of marketing? Why are specialty shops important to local communities?

SECTION 2 REVIEW
A N S W E R S

1. See the following pages: distribution (p. 337); mass marketing, self-service (p. 339); standard packaging, one-price system (p. 342); wholesaler, retailer, advertising, brand name (p. 343).

2. brings goods from producers to consumers; helped to create a single, large market for products by providing means of transportation and communication

3. Trucks, buses, automobiles, and airplanes overtook trains as main means of transportation by the mid-20th century.

4. Customers can drive in, park, and buy anything they need in one place. Specialty shops offer special services not provided by larger stores.

5. Retailers sell goods directly to the public. Wholesalers sell goods to retailers after purchasing goods from manufacturers.

6. Articles should address possible advantages and disadvantages, as well as answer the questions, *who, what, where,* and *when.*

After studying Section 3, students should be able to do the following.

1. Identify ways of saving money on purchases.
2. Explain how the Nutrition Labeling and Education Act helps consumers, and identify what meat labels must tell consumers.
3. Describe how independent organizations and the government help consumers.
4. Explain the advantages and disadvantages of charge accounts and installment plans.

Tell students to think of certain long-term assignments as being completed in **installments**. For example, each chapter includes a portfolio assignment—an installment, in a way, toward completion of the final unit portfolio project. Have students use this reasoning to deduce the meaning of *installments* when applied to buying something. *(A portion of the cost is paid at set times.)* Ask: What do you call the amount of money left when you subtract the amount paid from the total? *(the **balance**, the amount still owed)*

CIVICS SIDELIGHT

More and more Americans are passing up brand-name products in the supermarket, particularly when household budgets are tight. For years many stores have offered their own store brands at lower cost than the nationally advertised brands. Traditionally, these private label products have lacked the jazzy wrappers and catchy names that grab shoppers' attention. The sales of these nondescript products have been rising, however. According to a poll taken in 1994, one out of every three U.S. consumers reported buying store brands more often.

Such success has led some retailers to make some changes in marketing their brands. Retailers have begun to "sell" their store brands more enthusiastically by improving their packaging. They have also increased the advertising and promotion of these "no-name" brands. Shifting the marketing focus from cost savings to just another battle between brands might backfire for retailers, however. Some observers believe such a contest would be fought on the turf of makers of name-brand products that still retain significant consumer loyalty.

344

5. What are the roles of wholesalers and retailers in the U.S. economy?

6. **THINKING CRITICALLY** Imagine you are a newspaper reporter covering a debate on the role of advertising in the U.S. economy. One side argues that advertising is necessary and beneficial. The other side argues that advertising is unnecessary and costly. Write a newspaper article outlining the arguments made by each side in the debate. Be sure to answer the questions *who, what, where,* and *when.*

3 You, the Consumer

Each of us is a consumer. A **consumer** is a person who buys or uses goods and services. As consumers, we play an important part in the U.S. free-enterprise system.

Each year businesses spend billions of dollars to encourage us to buy their products. They run advertisements in newspapers and magazines, on billboards, and on radio and television. They create slogans they hope we will remember. They know that some of us will buy the product whose slogan appeals to us. Often, however, the slogan has nothing to do with the quality or usefulness of the product.

Some shoppers are impulse buyers. They make a quick decision to buy a product—they like the product's slogan or the advertising commercial on television. They buy without thinking about the price or about the usefulness of the product. Other people put more thought into their purchases. Anyone can learn to be a wise shopper.

Learning Where and When to Buy

There are a number of ways that consumers can get the most for their limited shopping dollars. For example, wise food shoppers study food advertisements in the newspaper. They find out which stores are having special sales. At certain times of the year, for example, turkey may be priced low. Using cents-off coupons also can help buyers save money.

By watching for sales and coupons you can buy clothing, books, furniture, hardware, and other items at reduced prices. Some people never pay the full price for an item. They stock up when the price is low.

A low price on an item, however, does not always mean the item is a bargain. An item is not a bargain if it is something you cannot really use or if it is poorly made. It is not a bargain if an item you already have is just as good as a new one.

Judging Price and Quality

Wise shoppers must be able to judge the quality of a product and know how they plan to use the product. They also must make sure that they choose goods and services that are best suited to their own needs.

To do this, many consumers shop only at well-known stores that guarantee the quality of every item they sell or service they provide. Others shop at various stores to compare products and look for bargains.

Many people buy items by brand name because they trust certain business firms. They believe that all products bearing the brand names of these firms must be of good quality. This may or may not be true. Large nationwide firms, as you have learned, sell their products under brand names. They spend billions of dollars making consumers aware of these names. The only way to be sure of the quality of a product, however, is to study its labeling.

Studying Labels

Labels are placed on foods, clothing, and other items to protect consumers. The government requires that certain kinds of information be included on these labels to help consumers judge the quality of products.

Expressing Ideas

Have students consider the term *consumer*. Ask: When something is consumed, what happens to it? Elicit that it disappears; for example, people consume food, a fire consumes wood. Have students make drawings to express the idea of people as consumers. Conclude by discussing whether students' illustrations depict consumers in positive or negative ways. Help students understand that consumers and wise consumption are important to the U.S. economic system.

Have small groups design and create product advertisements for print, radio, or television. Group members should try to persuade consumers of the high value of the product being advertised. Roles for students might include writers, designers, and illustrators. Groups should present their finished advertisements to the class and have the class discuss how consumers can balance personal wants and needs, and their household budgets, with the interests of advertisers.

CIVICS SIDELIGHT

Reading food product labels is important if consumers are to make wise choices. Some labels, however, are misleading. For example, the term *natural* on a label might lead a person to believe that all the ingredients are healthful. In reality, "natural" ingredients may include refined sugar, salt, fat, starches, fillers, and other additives that come from nature but have little or no nutritional value.

Wise consumers often wait for an item to go on sale. Shopping sales is a good way to buy something you need at a reduced price.

There are a number of federal laws on labeling. The Fair Packaging and Labeling Act requires businesses to supply certain information on the packages of the goods they sell. This information includes the name and address of the manufacturer, the contents of the package, and the weight or quantity of the items in the package.

The Nutrition Labeling and Education Act of 1990, which was amended in 1994, requires all food companies to place standard labels on their food products. In addition to listing standard serving sizes, these labels identify the amount of fat, cholesterol, sodium, fiber, and nutrients contained in each serving. The figures are given as a percentage of a person's daily dietary allowance.

In addition to weight and content information, meat packages now must carry labels with instructions for the safe handling and cooking of meats. The labels also must warn consumers that improper handling or cooking of the meat may lead to illness, even though the meat has passed government inspection.

Many products, such as bread, milk, and cheese, must be stamped with the date by which the product must be sold or used. Dating a product ensures that it will be fresh when purchased by consumers.

Some laws require unit pricing. That is, the price tag must show how much money is being asked per unit of the product—per ounce or gram, for example. A 10-ounce (284-g) can of peaches might be a better buy than a can at the same price with only 8 ounces (227 g). Larger sizes often are a better bargain because they have a lower price per unit. This is not always true, however. You must read labels carefully for the best bargain.

Unless people are able to read labels intelligently, the labels are of no help to them. Beware of terms like "highest quality." These words sound good, but they often have no real meaning. A label that says a piece of clothing

Practicing Interviewing Skills

Invite a representative from the local branch of the Better Business Bureau, or another organization that helps to educate consumers, to come talk to the class. Have students develop questions for the guest, covering such topics as making wise purchases and wise consumer judgments about products. Then have students write articles about the interview for submission to the school newspaper. Some students might want to use the interview to write editorials urging students to be smart consumers.

Drawing a Poster

Have students list on the chalkboard all the organizations (private and governmental) that are available to help or protect consumers. Have them choose one organization and create a poster that informs the public about its services. Students may wish to research the organization to gather more information before they begin. Display completed posters for the rest of the school.

CIVICS SIDELIGHT

In 1993 there were approximately 1.2 million incidents of shoplifting in the United States. Shoplifting accounted for 15 percent of all the larceny-thefts known to police, up from 11 percent in 1980. A 1993 study showed that shoplifting costs businesses more than $11 billion each year.

is "preshrunk" also means little. The label does not tell you how much the piece of clothing is likely to shrink when it is washed. If the label says "Sanforized," however, you know the clothing will not shrink more than 1 percent. *Sanforized* is a standard term that means the same throughout the clothing industry.

Consumer Protection Organizations

Sometimes consumers find that a product has been falsely labeled or advertised. If you believe you have been misled by an unfair business practice, you should first try to seek satisfaction from the business that sold you

The variety of products available in the United States means that consumers must compare quality and price before making a purchase.

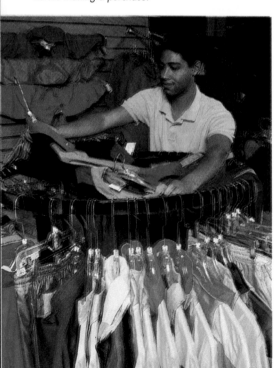

the product or service. Many businesses have consumer service departments.

If you still are not satisfied, you should contact the local Better Business Bureau. There is a bureau in or near most communities. This organization gives advice and assistance to people who believe they have been cheated or treated unfairly by a business firm.

The federal government also protects consumers. The Federal Trade Commission (FTC), for instance, has the power to bring to court any business firm that uses false or misleading advertising or false labeling. The National Institute of Standards and Technology tests and grades many products. The Department of Agriculture inspects and grades meat, poultry, and certain other foods sold in interstate commerce, or trade between states. The U.S. Postal Service makes sure that businesses and individuals do not cheat the public through the mail. The Consumer Product Safety Commission (CPSC) checks products to make sure they do not cause injuries.

Most states and many cities also have consumer protection offices. They publish advice for consumers and issue warnings to business firms that violate consumer laws. The firms are brought to court if they continue to cheat or mislead consumers.

A number of private organizations help consumers as well. Among these is Consumers Union, which tests and rates nearly every product the public buys. Consumers Union publishes the results of its tests in magazines and special reports. A visit to the library to examine these and other publications will help you compare various brands of the same product. In this way you can learn which product is best suited to your needs and which product is the best buy.

Problems Caused by Consumers

Consumers often accuse businesses of misleading advertising, poor service, and inferior products. Sometimes, however, consumers cause problems for businesses.

Have students make two charts on the chalkboard in which they list the advantages and disadvantages of charge accounts and installment purchases. Then lead the class in writing a fictional sketch of each of the following characters: (1) a person for whom a charge account or installment buying is a great help; (2) a person for whom a charge account or installment buying is problematic.

Have each student create an application for a charge account. The students may include any questions they believe are important in determining whether a person should be approved for the account. Then invite a credit counselor to the class to discuss which questions are actually permitted on such applications. Afterward, have students write short paragraphs about whether they believe they deserve an account and whether they want one. Invite volunteers to read their paragraphs to the class for discussion.

Shoplifting, or stealing items displayed in stores, costs businesses in the United States billions of dollars each year. Sometimes people break or damage a store owner's property. Sometimes they demand refunds for merchandise they have already used or abused. Items in motels, hotels, and restaurants are often stolen or damaged. Sometimes people fail to pay for purchases obtained on credit.

These people are not professional criminals. Many believe their actions are unimportant. They may argue that the business—especially if it is a big business—can afford the loss. They may be hurting other consumers, though, because these dishonest acts add to the costs of doing business. Businesses pass these costs on to consumers in the form of higher prices.

Pay Now or Later?

When you buy something, you may pay cash. You also may charge it, or you may buy it on an installment plan. What are the advantages and disadvantages of buying merchandise in these three ways?

Cash The person who pays cash is likely a careful buyer. Because the buyer must pay the full amount at the time of purchase, he or she is likely to think carefully before handing the money to the salesclerk. A person with cash is sometimes able to buy a product for a lower price than someone who has to rely on credit to make the purchase.

Charge Accounts Suppose you find a bargain on something you need, but you do not have the cash on hand to pay for it. At such times, a charge account can be of help. A **charge account** is a form of credit that stores grant to many of their customers.

People who have a steady job and a record of paying their bills on time can usually open a charge account. A charge account permits customers to buy now and pay later. That is, they can make their purchases during the month but not pay for them until they receive a bill from the store.

Shopping Tips for Consumers

Before you buy:

- Think about what you need and what product or service features are important to you.

- Compare brands. Ask for word-of-mouth recommendations, and look for formal product comparison reports. Check your local library for magazines and other publications that contain product comparisons.

- Compare stores. Look for a store with a good reputation, and plan ahead to take advantage of sales. Check with your local Better Business Bureau to find out if the company is reputable.

- Read warranties to understand what you must do and what the manufacturer must do if you have a problem. Read contract terms carefully. Make sure all blank spaces are filled in before you sign a contract. Ask the sales person to explain the store's return or exchange policy.

After you buy:

- Read and follow the instructions on how to use the product or service.

- Read and understand the warranty. Keep in mind that you may have additional warranty rights in your state. Keep all sales receipts, warranties, and instructions.

- If trouble develops, report the problem to the company as soon as possible. Keep a file of your efforts to resolve the problem. It should include the names of the individuals with whom you speak and the date, time, and outcome of the conversations. Also, keep copies of the letters you send to the company and any replies it sends to you.

Source: *U.S. Office of Consumer Affairs.*

CIVICS SIDELIGHT

Even in the early years of the U.S. republic, credit was widely used in business transactions. The young United States was a nation of farmers. Farmers earned money by selling their harvested crops, usually in the fall. If they wanted a new horse, plow, clock, or chair, they often had to buy it on credit. Farmers paid off their bills with money earned from selling their crops after harvesting.

Retail credit boomed after World War I, especially with the rising demand for expensive technological products such as automobiles, washing machines, and vacuum cleaners. So many people opened charge accounts that clerks could not recognize all the customers who had been granted credit. Some form of identification was needed, and many businesses issued charge cards with identifying information. In addition to their use for identification purposes, charge cards strengthened ties between customers and the retailers who issued the cards.

Closure

Have students reread the list of "Qualities of a Good Citizen" on pages 5–6. Then have students compile a list called "Qualities of a Good Consumer." Ask: How are the two lists similar? How are they different? Which of the points on your list do you think is most important? Why? Conclude by discussing the steps students should take when making a purchase, according to what they have studied in the section.

Reviewing

Have students complete the Section 3 Review.

Reteaching

Assign Section 3 of the Chapter 18 Reteaching Worksheet.

CIVICS SIDELIGHT

A customer's credit rating is usually determined by a credit bureau, an organization that accumulates information about individuals based on past credit history, employment history, statements from landlords, public records, newspapers, and first-hand investigation. Computerization allows credit bureaus to maintain tens of millions of files on individual consumers. Computerization, however, does not guarantee accuracy. According to critics, up to 40 percent of credit reports contain erroneous information, which could lead to problems when applying for a mortgage, a car loan, or other types of credit. Consumer advocates have urged consumers to check the accuracy of these credit reports, and these advocates have pushed for legislation, such as the Fair Credit Reporting Act of 1971, that makes it easier for consumers to do so.

"It's a red-letter day — she took her first step, and she received her first credit card application form."

Many people are eager to apply for a credit card and start making purchases on credit. Credit must be used wisely, however. What should this father tell his daughter—when she is older—about using credit?

If customers fail to pay their bills when they are due, the store may close their charge accounts. Such customers become bad credit risks. As a result, they may find it difficult to obtain a charge account elsewhere. Stores report credit information to centralized credit bureaus. Stores, banks, and other companies contact these bureaus to learn about a person's credit history.

There are advantages to using charge accounts. A charge account makes it easy for you to keep track of what you have bought and what you paid for various items. You do not have to carry large amounts of cash with you when you go shopping. If you have a charge account, it is often easier for you to return purchases you do not want. Charge account customers often receive notices of sales before the sales are advertised in the newspapers.

Most important, though, when you have charge accounts and pay your bills regularly, you establish a good credit rating for yourself. A **credit rating** is a report that shows how reliable a customer is in paying bills. A good credit rating is essential when you want to apply for a bank loan or buy a house.

There also are some disadvantages to having a charge account. Because charge accounts are so easy to use, some people use them to buy items without shopping around for the best values. These customers also may buy things on impulse that they do not need. In addition, customers who order items over the telephone using their account numbers run the risk of having these numbers used by thieves. The same is true for people whose charge cards are lost or stolen.

Stores that offer charge accounts usually charge high interest on unpaid balances. If the bill is not paid by the due date (usually 10 to 30 days after the customer receives the bill), most stores add a percentage of the unpaid balance to the bill. The interest can be as much as 19 percent or more a year. Many consumers have financial troubles because they use charge accounts unwisely.

Installment Plans Installment plans also allow consumers to buy goods without paying the full amount in cash when they make their purchases. In this system of buying, the buyer uses cash to pay part of the purchase price. This money is called a **down payment**. The rest of what the buyer owes is called the **balance**. The balance is paid in equal payments, or **installments**, over a period of

Extension

Have students research specific government laws and regulations designed to protect consumers. For example, students might research the history of U.S. Agriculture Department regulations regarding the handling of fresh meats and fish. Other possible topics include regulation of medicines by the Food and Drug Administration and regulations regarding children's car seats and flame-retardant children's pajamas. Have students prepare oral reports, with diagrams such as flowcharts, for the class.

weeks, months, or years. An installment plan allows a buyer to have the use of a product while paying for it.

Automobiles, houses, refrigerators, furniture, and other large items are often bought on an installment plan. The purchaser signs a written contract with the seller. The contract states how much the installment payments are and how often they must be paid. It also states that the item still belongs to the seller.

If the customer does not make the payments on time or complete the necessary number of payments, the seller can repossess, or take back, the item. When this happens, the purchaser loses the item. He or she also loses the amount of money that has already been paid on the item.

Buying an item on an installment plan increases its cost. In addition to the regular price, a service charge as well as interest on the unpaid balance is included in the installment payments.

If you consider buying something on an installment plan, you may find it cheaper to borrow the money from a bank. You can then pay cash for the item and pay the bank back in installments. This form of credit is called installment credit. Banks usually charge only interest, and not an additional service charge, for installment loans. The interest paid to the bank may be less than the combined service charge and interest under an installment plan.

Whether you buy an item under an installment plan or installment credit, it is wise to make as large a down payment as possible. It is also wise to pay off the balance as quickly as possible to reduce the item's total cost.

SECTION 3 REVIEW

1. Define or identify the following terms: consumer, shoplifting, charge account, credit rating, down payment, balance, installment.

2. How can wise shoppers save money?

3. How does the Nutrition Labeling and Education Act help consumers? What must meat labels tell consumers?

4. How do independent organizations and the government help consumers?

5. What are the advantages and disadvantages of charge accounts and installment plans?

6. **THINKING CRITICALLY** Imagine that a friend has asked you for advice on choosing a new computer. Write a list of steps you recommend that your friend take to find the highest quality product for the lowest possible price.

CHAPTER 18 SUMMARY

The U.S. system of mass production makes available a wide variety of goods and services. Mass production is made possible by machine tools, standard parts, and the division of labor. These elements of mass production are organized in assembly lines on which products move as they are made. Such methods of production require great sources of power.

Once products are made, a good system of distribution—transportation and marketing—is needed to bring the products to market. Railroads, trucks, ships, and airplanes transport goods from factories, farms, and warehouses to places where consumers can buy them.

The mass marketing system helps sell goods and services to customers. Advertising and many kinds of stores are part of the U.S. marketing system.

As consumers, each of us plays an important role in the economy. In knowing how to judge price and quality and in buying wisely, we help manufacturers and retailers know how they can serve us best. By using consumer organizations and by learning the best ways to pay for goods—with cash or on credit—we receive value for our money.

SECTION 3 REVIEW
A N S W E R S

1. See the following pages: consumer (p. 344); shoplifting, charge account (p. 347); credit rating, down payment, balance, installment (p. 348).

2. sales, coupons, be good judge of quality and prices

3. helps consumers judge quality; meat—weight, content information, and how to handle and cook meat properly

4. set and enforce regulations, publish product comparisons and reports, help consumers when treated unfairly, publish consumer information

5. charge: advantages—keeps track of purchases, no need to carry cash, easier to return purchases, prior notice of sales, establishes credit rating; disadvantages—unwise use, theft, interest charges; installment: advantage—can use product while paying for it, can buy expensive items over time; disadvantage—possible repossession, increased costs

6. Lists should include steps for being a wise consumer.

Have students bring to class food products in jars or cans carrying the standard labels mandated by the Nutrition Labeling and Education Act of 1994. You might also bring to class meat labels with their instructions for safe handling and cooking. Have students devise questions about the information on each label and then answer each other's questions.

Invite a nutritionist or dietician to class to clarify the terms and the percentages shown on food labels and to advise students how to find nutritious foods. Then have students create posters encouraging elementary school students to pay attention to the nutritional value of the food they eat. Posters should include references to food labels.

LIFE SKILL
Reading Labels

You go to the supermarket to buy, among other things, a can of vegetable soup. That seems simple enough. When you get to the aisle that has soup, though, you see a dozen different brands of vegetable soup. Which brand should you buy? Reading the cans' labels will help you make this decision. As you know, product labels help and protect you, the consumer.

How to Read Labels

1. **Identify the ingredients.** Federal law requires companies to list the ingredients in each package of food. The ingredients must be listed in the order of their amounts. The main ingredient appears first, and the ingredient used in the least amount appears last. If there are foods you wish to avoid, such as those that contain large amounts of sugar or salt, reading the list of ingredients will help you choose the right product.

2. **Read the nutrition facts.** The federal government requires that food labels tell consumers how many servings are in the container, the size of a serving, and the number of calories and calories from fat that are in a serving. Labels must also tell consumers what percentage of their total daily allowance (daily value) of fat, cholesterol, sodium, carbohydrates, and protein are in one serving of the food. You should strive to buy nutritious food.

3. **Study the other information.** Note that the label tells you that the percentages of daily values are based on a 2,000-calorie diet. Your own daily values may be higher or lower, depending on the number of calories in your diet.

4. **Be a comparison shopper.** Comparing labels for ingredients and nutritional

content will help you make intelligent purchases.

Applying the Skill

Study the food label below. Then answer the following questions.

1. What is the main ingredient?
2. Which ingredient is found in the smallest amount?
3. What percentage of your daily value of fat is supplied by one serving?
4. What percentage of your daily value of sodium will a serving supply?
5. How large is one serving size? How many servings are contained in this can of soup?

ANSWERS TO
Applying
the Skill

1. water
2. oleoresin paprika
3. 3 percent
4. 37 percent
5. one-half cup (120 mL); about 2.5

VEGETARIAN
VEGETABLE
—SOUP—

Nutrition Facts	Amount / serving	% DV*	Amount / serving	% DV*
Serv. Size ½ cup (120mL) condensed soup	Total Fat 2g	3%	Total Carb. 15g	5%
Servings About 2.5	Sat. Fat 0g	0%	Fiber 2g	8%
Calories 90	Cholest. 0mg	0%	Sugars 5g	
Fat Cal. 20	Sodium 880mg	37%	Protein 3g	
*Percent Daily Values (DV) are based on a 2,000 calorie diet.	Vitamin A 35% • Vitamin C 4% • Calcium 2% • Iron 4%.			

INGREDIENTS: WATER, POTATOES, TOMATO PUREE (WATER, TOMATO PASTE), CARROTS, PEAS, GREEN BEANS, HIGH FRUCTOSE CORN SYRUP, ENRICHED ALPHABET MACARONI PRODUCT (ENRICHED WITH NIACIN, FERROUS SULFATE, THIAMINE MONONITRATE AND RIBOFLAVIN), CORN, ONIONS, CELERY, POTATO STARCH, SALT, VEGETABLE OIL (CORN, COTTONSEED OR PARTIALLY HYDROGENATED SOYBEAN OIL), YEAST EXTRACT AND HYDROLYZED WHEAT GLUTEN AND SOY PROTEIN, MONOSODIUM GLUTAMATE, DEHYDRATED GARLIC, SPICE EXTRACT AND OLEORESIN PAPRIKA.

CHAPTER 18 REVIEW
A N S W E R S

Vocabulary Workshop

1. wholesalers—sell goods to retailers after purchasing them from manufacturers; retailers—sell goods directly to public
2. distribution
3. consumers

4. mass marketing
5. marketing system where customer serves himself or herself

Reviewing Main Ideas

1. machine tools, standard parts, division of labor
2. charge: advantages—keeps track of purchases, no need to carry cash, easier to return purchases, prior notice of sales, establishes credit; disadvantages—unwise use, risk of theft, interest charges; installment: advantages—can use product while paying for it, can buy expensive items over time; disadvantages—possible repossession, increased costs
3. set and enforce regulations, publish comparisons and reports, publish consumer information
4. electricity; allows large numbers of identical items to be produced rapidly
5. gets raw materials and goods from producers to people who want them
6. self-service—saves labor, inexpensive, many customers can shop at one time; standard packaging—saves labor and money for business, convenient for consumers
7. needed to get loan; to judge quality, nutritive value, proper handling

Thinking Critically

1. Students should discuss wise credit use.
2. Students should make reasoned arguments.

Citizenship in Your Community

Brochures should address the services of the organization.

Building Your Portfolio

Assign Portfolio Assessment Worksheet 18 in the *Portfolio Assessment Worksheets* booklet.

Assessment

- **Chapter 18 Tests**, *Chapter Tests* booklet
- **Test Generator**, Chapter 18
- **Portfolio**, Portfolio Assessment Worksheet 18, *Portfolio Assessment Worksheets* booklet

CHAPTER 18 R·e·v·i·e·w

Vocabulary Workshop

1. Distinguish between wholesalers and retailers.
2. What part of the economic system is made up of transportation and marketing?
3. What term describes people who buy or use goods and services?
4. What is the term for the selling of goods in large quantities?
5. Define the term *self-service*.

Reviewing Main Ideas

1. What are the three main features of mass production?
2. What are the advantages and disadvantages of charge accounts? of installment plans?
3. How do private organizations and the government help consumers?
4. What is the main source of power in today's factories? How does the assembly line help factories mass-produce goods?
5. Why is the U.S. transportation system vital to the economy?
6. How do self-service and standard packaging contribute to the efficiency of mass marketing?
7. Why is it important to have a good credit rating? Why should shoppers always study the labels on products?

Thinking Critically

1. Many Americans are in financial difficulty because they are burdened with too much credit debt. Are charge accounts too easy to open in the United States?
2. To stop shoplifting many stores have installed security cameras and other devices. Does this infringe on the privacy rights of shoppers? Do business owners have the right to protect themselves from theft? Should they be allowed to place security cameras in dressing rooms?

Citizenship in Your Community

Individual Project

Create a brochure for a consumer protection organization in your state or community. Your brochure should explain the services offered by the organization. Does it register consumer complaints, evaluate products, or publish consumer information? How do consumers contact this organization? Illustrate your brochure with sketches of the services available from the organization. If possible, make copies to share with the class.

Building Your Portfolio

The second step of your unit portfolio project (see page 421) is to sketch the design of your mousetrap. Consider where the mousetrap will be used, whether mice will be caught singly or in groups, and what you will use for bait. How will you name, package, and advertise your product? What methods of mass production will you use to make the mousetrap? How will you distribute it? Create an advertising poster that includes the sketch of your mousetrap. The poster should emphasize how efficiently your mousetrap can be made and distributed. Place your poster in your individual portfolio for later use.

CHAPTER 19

Managing Money

TEXTBOOK	TEACHING RESOURCES	OTHER AVAILABLE RESOURCES
Chapter	• Skills Worksheet 19 • Challenge/Enrichment Worksheet 19	• Simulations and Case Studies Lesson 18
Section **1 Money and Credit** Page 353	• Reteaching Worksheet 19.1	
2 Banks and Banking Page 357	• Reteaching Worksheet 19.2	
3 Saving and Investing Page 362	• Reteaching Worksheet 19.3	• Transparency 22: Saving Keeps the Nation Prosperous
4 Insurance Against Hardship Page 367	• Reteaching Worksheet 19.4	
Review and Assessment Chapter 19 Review, Page 375	• Test, Form A • Test, Form B • Portfolio Assessment Worksheet 19	• *Test Generator,* Chapter 19

ADDITIONAL RESOURCES

BOOKS FOR TEACHERS

Levi, Maurice, *Thinking Economically: How Economic Principles Can Contribute to Clear Thinking,* Basic Books.

Mayer, Thomas, *Money, Banking, and the Economy,* Norton.

Teweles, Richard J., et al., *The Stock Market,* Wiley.

Zelizer, Viviana A., *The Social Meaning of Money,* Basic Books.

BOOKS FOR STUDENTS

Bungum, Jane E., *Money and Financial Institutions,* Lerner. Provides a history of money and banking, including discussions of uncommon currencies and the Federal Reserve System.

Fisher, Clayton P., *The Stock Market Explained for Young Investors,* Business

Classics. Explains what stocks are and how to trade them.

Maestro, Betsy, *The Story of Money,* Clarion. This explanation of the invention of money includes a listing of the money of other countries.

MULTIMEDIA RESOURCES

Money and Banking (VHS, c, 19 min.), EBEC. Discusses the Federal Reserve System and banks in the United States.

Money: Summing It Up (f, VHS, c, 23 min.), NGS. Chronicles the use of barter, commodity money, gold, silver, and paper money.

Using Money Wisely (VHS, c, 17 min.), JF. Uses humor to teach the techniques of personal money management.

Your Credit Is Good (VHS, c, 14 min.), JF. Reveals the potential hazards of credit.

THE INTERNET

Have students use these search words to find more information about chapter topics on the Internet: *currency, credit cards, savings and loans, credit unions, Federal Reserve, insurance, Social Security.*

 GLOBAL SKILL BUILDER

You might wish to use **Navigating the Internet** from the interactive *Global Skill Builder* CD-ROM to aid students' understanding of the Internet as a resource.

Abbreviations: b&w=black and white; c=color; f=film; fs=filmstrip; sd=sound; tr=transparency; VHS=videotape

CIVICS SKILLS

Students will learn how to write a personal check. Students also will learn terms important to understanding the institutions and processes involved in managing money.

CITIZENSHIP VALUES

✯ **Structures and Functions** Students will be encouraged to appreciate the need for currency and credit in the smooth management of a free economy, to recognize why the federal government regulates certain banking practices, and to realize the importance of social insurance programs.

AMERICAN ECONOMIC SYSTEM

✯ **Structures and Functions** Students will learn about forms of money and the system of credit in the United States, the function of banks, and the responsibilities of the Federal Reserve System. Students also will learn how the government protects savings and investments and how to distinguish between private and social insurance.

MEETING INDIVIDUAL NEEDS

LIMITED ENGLISH PROFICIENCY (LEP)

Pair up LEP students with students who are proficient in English. Have the pairs create flash cards, one set of cards with vocabulary terms and another set of cards with vocabulary definitions or sketches of the words' meanings. Then have the students take turns quizzing each other with the flash cards.

LEARNERS HAVING DIFFICULTY

Have students write quizzes on the material in the chapter. Then have students exchange quizzes, write the answers, and return the quizzes to their originators for grading. Discuss questions and answers from the quizzes in class.

AUDITORY LEARNERS

Have students write a poem, a song, or a rap about the importance of maintaining good credit. Then invite volunteers to present their creations to the class. Have students note the points each poem, song, or rap makes about maintaining a good credit record. Have students use their notes as study guides.

VISUAL LEARNERS

Ask students to look through newspapers for bank advertisements and any other information related to those banks, such as mortgage rates. Have students evaluate all the information related to each bank to draw conclusions about how the banks are attempting to attract customers. Then have students create their own advertisements that would help to bring more customers to the bank. Use the advertisements to facilitate a discussion about the roles of banks in the economy.

TACTILE/KINESTHETIC LEARNERS

Have students design credit cards for a fictitious company. Then have students determine qualifications for owners of their credit cards and develop advertising campaigns to persuade consumers to obtain and use the cards. Call on volunteers to present their cards and advertising campaigns to the class, and lead a discussion about the advantages and disadvantages of credit cards.

GIFTED LEARNERS

Have students compare social insurance programs in the United States to those in other countries. Students should note the kinds of social insurance available in each country, eligibility requirements for the programs, and the history and cost of the programs. Call on volunteers to report their findings to the class. Students might use charts or other graphics to help explain the comparisons.

CHAPTER OVERVIEW

Chapter 19 begins with a discussion of money, examining the most common kinds of money in the United States—coins, paper money, checks, and credit. The chapter also discusses banks and how Americans use money to save, invest, and ensure their financial security. The underlying theme of the chapter is that a system of sound financial exchange serves both the individual citizen and the nation.

Motivator

Invite students to imagine that the government has removed all money from society. Have pairs of students create short stories or skits that describe what life would be like without money. Students should address such dilemmas as how people would obtain what they want or need and how businesses would operate. Call on volunteers to read their stories or present their skits to the class. Lead a discussion on the advantages of having a uniform medium of exchange (money) for conducting business.

CHAPTER OBJECTIVES

After studying Chapter 19, students should be able to do the following.

1. Explain the ways currency, checks, and credit serve the economy.
2. Describe the kinds of banks in the United States.
3. Explain why saving and insurance are important for all Americans.

SIMULATIONS AND CASE STUDIES

Lesson 18: Money Scramble

CHAPTER 19

Managing Money

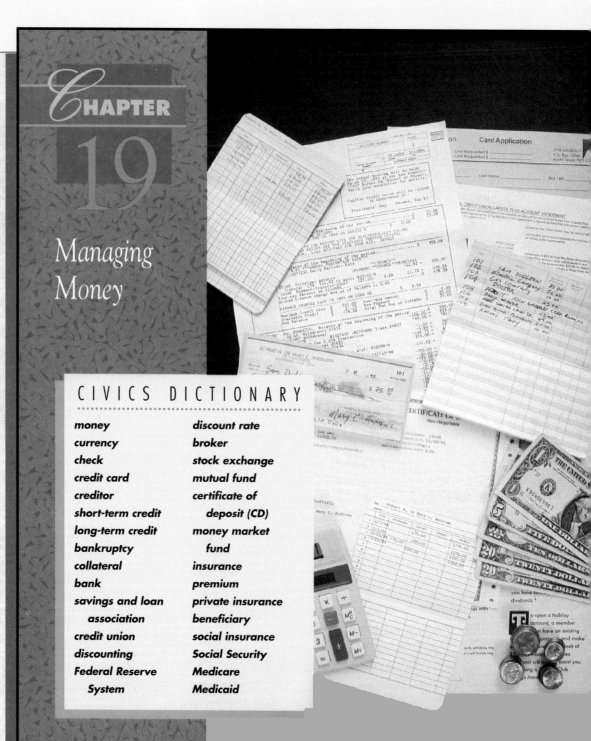

CIVICS DICTIONARY

money
currency
check
credit card
creditor
short-term credit
long-term credit
bankruptcy
collateral
bank
savings and loan
   association
credit union
discounting
Federal Reserve
   System

discount rate
broker
stock exchange
mutual fund
certificate of
   deposit (CD)
money market
   fund
insurance
premium
private insurance
beneficiary
social insurance
Social Security
Medicare
Medicaid

SECTION OBJECTIVES

After studying Section 1, students should be able to do the following.

1. Identify the common features of all currencies.

2. Identify the coins and bills issued by the federal government and explain why people accept coins not made of silver or gold.

3. Explain why sellers accept checks even though they are not legal tender.

4. Distinguish credit cards from charge cards and explain how too much debt can harm businesses and families.

Teaching Section 1
Building a Vocabulary

Ask students what a **credit card** is. Tell them that *credit* comes from the Latin word *credere,* which means "to believe or entrust." Have them use that meaning to define **creditor.** *(one who entrusts money to someone else)* Then ask students: Who would be paying on an installment plan, someone with **short-term credit** or someone with **long-term credit**? *(Installment credit and long-term credit generally mean the same thing.)*

CHAPTER FOCUS

Imagine that money did not exist today and that everyone had to barter for what they wanted. Barter is the swapping of one product for another. How would such a system work?

Suppose that in your spare time you like to make ceramic bowls. Today, however, you would like to see a movie. How will you "buy" a movie ticket? You will have to swap a bowl for it.

You take some bowls and set off for the theater. Luckily, the bus driver will give you a ride for one of your bowls. When you arrive at the theater, the owner tells you that she does not need a bowl, but she will give you a ticket in exchange for some tomatoes. You have a friend who grows tomatoes, so you head for his house.

Unfortunately, your friend has just traded his last pound of tomatoes for some new shoes. He agrees, however, to give you the pair of shoes for a bowl. You then take them to another friend who needs new shoes. Luckily, this friend's mother gives you some tomatoes for the shoes. You take the tomatoes back to the theater to trade for your movie ticket. Of course, now you are too tired to enjoy the movie and leave in the middle of it.

After giving the bus driver your last bowl, you think to yourself that there must be a better way of doing business. In this chapter you will learn about that better way.

· ·

STUDY GUIDE

● What are the roles of currency, checks, and credit in the economy?

● What kinds of banks exist in the nation?

● Why are saving and insurance important for Americans?

1 Money and Credit

At various times and in various places, people have used many different items as money. Cows, pigs, guns, playing cards, furs, salt, olive oil, stones, knives, tobacco, copper, iron, wampum beads, shells, rings, silver, and diamonds all have been used as money.

What is money? **Money** is something that sellers will take in exchange for whatever they have to sell. Buyers can exchange it for whatever they want to buy. Money is a medium, or means, of exchange.

To a banker, the term *money* may include checks, bank accounts, and other kinds of writing on pieces of paper. You will read later about some of these kinds of money. For now, think about the "jingling money" and "folding money" that people carry in their pockets or purses. Another term used for these kinds of money is **currency.**

Paper bills and coins do not have value as means of exchange just because the government prints them or stamps them out of metal. Money in these forms has value only because it will buy things.

For a nation's currency to be worth something, the nation's economy must produce something for its people to buy. One reason the United States can produce so much is that American citizens are able to buy what is produced. U.S. currency is also valuable in the world's markets because the United States produces so much.

MULTICULTURAL PERSPECTIVES

Although the use of metals (such as gold and silver) as money has been traced back as far as the 20th century B.C., throughout history various cultures have used many different mediums of exchange. Some Native Americans used *wampum*—beads made of shells. Brightly colored shells called *cowries* served as currency in India. Among the Fiji islanders of the South Pacific, whales' teeth were prized as a medium of exchange. For many cultures cattle were the currency of choice. In fact, the term *pecuniary* ("relating to money") comes from the Latin word *pecus,* meaning "cow."

◀ *Money varies in shape, size, and form.*   **CHAPTER 19** MANAGING MONEY **353**

Tell students that they are citizens of a country that has just achieved independence and needs a new currency. Have small groups devise a currency that meets the four requirements listed in the section and describe it in detail through words and drawings. Roles for group members include writer, designer, illustrator, and presenter. Have each group present its proposed currency to the class and explain how it meets each of the four requirements. The class should vote to determine the new currency.

Seeing Relationships

Let students examine as many U.S. coins and bills as you can make available. Have them list the characteristics of each item of currency. Then have the class compare and contrast the coins and bills. Ask questions such as this: Is a quarter worth more than a dime because it might have more silver in it? *(No U.S. coin issued today has silver in it.)* Then ask: Why do Americans accept coins with no precious metals in them? *(They have faith in the U.S. government.)*

◈ CIVICS SIDELIGHT

Historically, a nation's coins have carried the likeness of its monarch or ruler. In the United States, where the president is a respected citizen but not an object of worship, presidents' portraits did not appear on coins until 1909, when Congress approved the minting of the Lincoln penny. A non-president graced the most recent coin to be minted —the Susan B. Anthony dollar. Anthony (1820–1906) was a leader in the woman's suffrage movement in the United States. Ill-fated in part because of its similarity in size to a quarter, the Susan B. Anthony dollar was produced for just three years, from 1979 to 1981.

Currencies

Every nation in the world has a currency. All currencies share four common features:

- Currency must be easy to carry and must take up little space. People must be able to carry it with them for everyday use.
- Currency must be based on a system of units that are easy to multiply and divide. That is, it should not take too long to figure the number of coins and bills needed to exchange for an item.
- Currency must be durable, or last a long time. It should not wear out too quickly or fall apart. People must be able to keep currency until they are ready to spend it.
- Currency must be made in a standard form and must be guaranteed by the nation's government. In this way the nation's citizens can be certain that their coins and bills will be accepted by everyone else in exchange for goods and services.

The currency used by Americans is issued, or made, by the federal government. All U.S. paper money and coins are considered legal tender. That is, the law requires that every American accept this money as payment in exchange for all goods and services.

Coins and Paper Money

You may recall that one of the weaknesses of the nation under the Articles of Confederation was the lack of a standard currency. Each state issued its own money. The Constitution solved this weakness by granting to Congress the sole right "to coin money, [regulating] the value thereof. . . ."

In 1792 a mint, or plant where coins are made, was opened in Philadelphia. This mint and another in Denver now make most coins for general circulation. Mints in San Francisco and West Point, New York, make commemorative, or special occasion, coins.

Coins are sometimes called "hard money" because they are usually made of hard metal. In the United States, five coins are used: pennies, nickels, dimes, quarters, and half-dollars.

These coins are parts of one dollar. Dollar coins have not been made since 1981.

For many years the value of a coin was decided by the amount of metal it contained. A silver dollar, for example, yielded about a dollar's worth of silver when melted down. In the past, many Americans would accept only hard money. They thought it was more valuable and reliable than paper money.

Coins make up only a small percentage of the total U.S. money supply. They no longer contain gold or silver. All coins are alloys, or mixtures, of metals. Pennies are copper-coated zinc. Nickels, dimes, quarters, and half-dollars are alloys of copper and nickel.

Why do Americans accept coins that are not made of gold or silver? They accept them because they have faith in the U.S. government. They know that the coins will be accepted as legal tender, or money, when they are presented at stores, banks, or elsewhere. They also know that the government has a supply of gold and silver bullion, or bars. This bullion is kept in a depository at Fort Knox, Kentucky. If necessary, it could pay those U.S. debts owed to foreign nations. It also helps strengthen the nation's financial position.

Most of the money issued by the government today is paper money. It is printed in Washington, D.C., at the Bureau of Engraving and Printing of the Department of the Treasury. Bills are printed in denominations of $1, $5, $10, $20, $50, and $100. These bills are being redesigned to help guard against counterfeiting. Bills in denominations of $2, $500, $1,000, $5,000, and $10,000 are no longer issued, but some are still in circulation. As these bills reach the nation's central bank, they are removed from circulation.

Checks

Very little of what is bought and sold in the United States is paid for with either coins or paper money. Americans make greater use of another kind of money, the kind represented by checks. A **check** is a written and signed order to a bank to pay a sum of money from a

Ask: What kinds of substitutes do many people and businesses use for money? *(checks, credit cards)* Then ask: Why do sellers accept these substitutes? *(There are penalties for "bouncing" checks; credit cards are backed by major lending institutions.)* Have students role-play a store owner who accepts cash only and a customer who insists on paying by check or credit card. The scene should focus on the advantages and disadvantages to sellers of a cash-only policy.

Help students complete two flowcharts: one flowchart diagramming how store charge cards work (including how the store is paid) and another flowchart similarly diagramming how credit cards work. Call on volunteers to suggest each step in both processes. Ask: How can using a credit card increase the cost of a purchase? *(Interest charges on unpaid credit balances in effect increase the cost of a purchase.)*

checking account to the person or business named on the check.

Much of the total U.S. money supply is in the form of bank deposits. Bank deposits are the figures in bank accounts, including checking accounts. These figures represent the amount of credit held in a person's or business firm's account. Credit is what the bank owes the person or the firm. The person or business firm can spend money at any time from a checking account by writing a check.

Checks are just pieces of paper. They are not legal tender because they are not guaranteed by the federal government. Most sellers, however, will accept a check that has been written by a responsible person or business firm. The person or firm who writes the check maintains the account by depositing cash or checks—such as paychecks—from other persons or businesses.

A signature on a check is a promise that there is sufficient credit in an account to cover the amount of a check. People who knowingly write checks without having sufficient funds may be subject to criminal penalties.

Many people never see most of their money because they use checks. What they see instead is a column of figures the bank sends them on a monthly statement. The statement tells them how many checks they have written in the month, the amounts of the checks, and how much credit remains in their checking account.

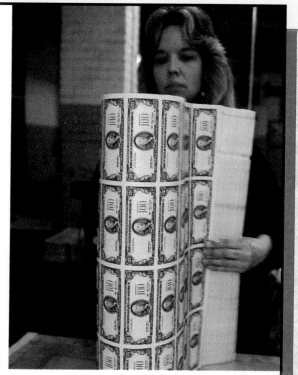

This worker is handling sheets of newly printed $100 bills. The bills have been printed in the new design that the government hopes will discourage counterfeiters.

Charge Accounts and Credit Cards

As you know, a charge account is a method by which a store extends credit to customers. Customers receive charge cards, which allow them to buy things without paying cash at the time of purchase. The amount of the purchases is added to their charge accounts. Customers then receive a monthly bill.

The customer writes a check for all or part of the bill, keeping in mind that interest is charged on the unpaid portion. The store deposits the check in its own bank, which then

sends the check to the customer's bank. The customer's bank subtracts the amount of the check from the customer's account. No currency changes hands. (Banks do not actually collect from each other check by check. They use computerized systems that handle huge numbers of checks.)

Credit cards are a substitute for money issued by banks and other major lending institutions. Examples of credit cards include American Express®, VISA®, and MasterCard®. Unlike charge cards, which only can be used at specific stores, credit cards can be used at thousands of stores and other businesses throughout the nation and the world.

The customer shows the credit card when making a purchase. The store or business then charges the credit card company. The credit card company pays the store or business and

GLOBAL PERSPECTIVES

Today credit cards such as American Express®, VISA®, and MasterCard® can be used not only in the United States but also in foreign countries. They have become an international medium of exchange. More than a hundred years ago, the writer Edward Bellamy predicted just such a situation. In 1888 Bellamy wrote *Looking Backward 2000– 1887*, in which he predicted what life would be like in the year 2000. In a prophetic passage Bellamy described a future that sounds familiar: "An American credit card," he wrote, ". . . is just as good in Europe as American gold used to be."

Independent Practice

Tell students that consumers often need an established credit history (a credit rating) before they can obtain a credit card. Have students write letters to a credit card company supporting or opposing the following statement: Consumers should be allowed to acquire their own credit cards *before* they establish a credit rating. In their letters students should address the concerns creditors have about the consequences of a consumer who cannot pay his or her debts.

Closure

Have students imagine that they are going to buy the following items: (1) house, (2) toaster, (3) furnace, (4) automobile, (5) paperback book, (6) compact disc player. For each item, have students determine which type of credit (long-term or short-term) would be most appropriate to use. Also discuss which purchases might be better made with cash rather than credit. Students should use what they have learned to defend their answers.

Are we becoming a cashless society? This woman uses a credit card to pay for a purchase. When the bill arrives, she probably will pay it by check.

charges the customer. As with charge cards, the customer pays all or part of the credit card bill with one check once a month. Interest charges, which often are quite high, are added to the unpaid portion of the monthly bill. Again, no currency changes hands.

Credit in Business

Credit is used instead of currency in most sales involving large amounts of goods. A wholesale grocer may order a truckload of canned goods, for example. He or she promises to pay for this order at the end of the month or, sometimes, within 90 days. Because the wholesaler has good credit, he or she can take the canned goods right away.

If the wholesaler sells the canned goods before the debt is due, he or she will have the money to repay the debt. Credit allows wholesalers to do a larger amount of business than if they had to pay for the goods immediately.

Credit, however, is sometimes used unwisely. Suppose businesspeople use credit more often than they should. When it is time to pay their bills, they find themselves in trouble. They cannot pay the bills they piled up by using credit. Then their **creditors**—those people to whom they owe money—may force them to sell their businesses to pay their debts.

Credit in the Family

If used wisely, credit also can help the average American family. Emergencies happen at one time or another in most families. Sometimes a product or service is needed immediately. A refrigerator, for example, may break down. If the family does not have enough money in the bank to pay for a new refrigerator, the machine usually can be bought on credit.

If the family plans to pay for an item within a few weeks or months, it needs only **short-term credit**. If, however, the family needs many months to pay, it will pay a certain amount each month until the total has been paid. This **long-term credit**, as you have learned, is also called installment credit. Most

SECTION OBJECTIVES

After studying Section 2, students should be able to do the following.

1. Identify the most numerous type of bank in the United States, and explain the functions of the FDIC.

2. Describe the savings and loan crisis of the 1980s and the purpose of the Resolution Trust Corporation (RTC).

3. Explain the origin of savings banks, and identify who owns credit unions.

4. Explain the origins and functions of the Federal Reserve System.

American families use this kind of credit to make large purchases, such as homes, automobiles, large appliances, and furniture.

Like some businesspeople, some families use credit unwisely. Suppose a family buys so much on credit that it cannot afford to make the payments. What will happen? The stores may take back their products. Or, the debts may be so high that the family has no choice but to declare bankruptcy. **Bankruptcy** is a legal declaration that a person cannot pay his or her debts. (Businesses can also declare bankruptcy.) Declaring bankruptcy can hurt a family's credit rating for years.

Credit in the Economy

Credit, as you have read, plays several important roles in the buying and selling of goods and services in a free market. It also plays an important role in the successful operation of the U.S. economy as a whole.

In a healthy economic system, the supply of money must increase or decrease in relation to the general condition of the economy. When production picks up and business is brisk, there must be plenty of money available to consumers. Otherwise, goods that are produced cannot be sold. In that case, production has to slow again. Free-flowing money in the form of credit makes it possible for consumers to buy whenever there are goods to be sold.

If too much money is available when production slows, prices may rise too high. That would happen because there would be more money to spend than there were goods to buy. Customers would try to outbid each other to buy the limited supply of goods. To slow consumer spending, banks may extend less credit to customers when production drops. Buying by consumers tends to slow when credit is less available. In this way credit helps keep the economy in balance.

The United States is made up, for the most part, of honest people. As a result, the widespread use of credit is possible as a means of exchange. If buyers and sellers could not trust each other, credit would not be possible.

SECTION 1 REVIEW

1. Define or identify the following terms: money, currency, check, credit card, creditor, short-term credit, long-term credit, bankruptcy.

2. What four common features do all currencies have?

3. What coins and denominations of bills are issued by the U.S. government? Why do people accept coins not made of silver or gold?

4. Why are checks not considered legal tender? Why do sellers accept them?

5. How do credit cards differ from charge cards? How can having too much credit debt harm businesses and families?

6. **THINKING CRITICALLY** Some people believe that the widespread use of credit has turned the United States into a "cashless society." Do you agree or disagree with this statement? What might be the advantages and disadvantages of such a society? Explain your answers.

---

2 Banks and Banking

Money presented a problem 1,000 years ago just as it does for many people today. In fact, money was even a problem for the wealthy. They had difficulty finding a safe place to keep their money. Carrying it made them the target of thieves. Hiding it in their homes did not guarantee its safety.

How Banking Began

In most communities, however, there were goldsmiths who kept their wealth heavily

SECTION 1 REVIEW
ANSWERS

1. See the following pages: money, currency (p. 353); check (p. 354); credit card (p. 355); creditor, short-term credit, long-term credit (p. 356); bankruptcy (p. 357).

2. easy to carry and take up little space, based on system of units that are easy to multiply and divide, durable, made in standard form and guaranteed by government

3. coins—penny, nickel, dime, quarter, half-dollar; bills—$1, $5, $10, $20, $50, $100; faith in government and know that coins are legal tender

4. not guaranteed by government; accept as promise that sufficient funds exist to cover them

5. credit—accepted by thousands of stores and businesses, charge—accepted only by stores that issue them; too much debt—can force businesses to close or families to go bankrupt

6. Answers will vary. Students might say that the widespread use of checks and credit has turned the nation into a virtual "cashless society."

Ask students to help you define **collateral**. Ask them what a lateral is in football. *(a pass tossed to the side)* Tell students that *lateral* comes from a Latin word meaning "side." Elicit that collateral is property "off to the side" of a deal and that a borrower offers collateral as security to a lender. Then ask students what the **Federal Reserve System** holds in reserve. *(money)*

Have students create a chart on the chalkboard that displays details about the four types of banks discussed in the section. When the chart is completed, have students compare the different types of banks. Ask: Which is the most numerous type of bank? Why? *(Commercial banks offer a full range of services to customers.)* Then have students explain how the government secures customers' deposits in each bank. *(FDIC, NCUA)* Students should copy the chart for use as a study guide.

GLOBAL PERSPECTIVES

Gold has been important throughout world history. In the 1400s and 1500s, sailors seeking gold opened new trade routes around the world. Spanish conquistadors, for example, scoured the Americas on a quest for gold, and the Portuguese extracted gold from Africa. Why was gold such an important mineral? Gold's valued properties include its beauty, softness (permitting its use in many ways and shapes), and its scarcity. In 1905 a statistician determined that all the gold taken from the earth to that time would fill just a 10-meter cube (the equivalent of a cube whose sides measure 33 feet). As of 1992 it was estimated that the cumulative amount of gold mined throughout history could fit into a cube with sides no longer than 18 meters (59 feet).

guarded. Because gold was so valuable, the goldsmiths kept it in strong, sturdy safes.

In time the townspeople began to bring their money to the goldsmiths for safekeeping. Before long, local goldsmiths had entered the money-keeping business. They began to charge a small fee for this service.

Eventually, goldsmiths took on money-lending services. Townspeople who needed money came to the goldsmiths for loans. In return for the loans, they signed a paper promising to repay the money by a certain date and to pay interest for using the money.

Borrowers guaranteed their loans by promising to give their property to the money-lender if the loans were not repaid on time. Property used to guarantee that a loan will be repaid is called **collateral**. These practices developed over centuries into the banking system we know today.

What Is a Bank?

Banks are familiar sights in every U.S. town and city. A **bank** is a business that deals in money and credit. Banks safeguard the deposits of customers and provide people with a convenient means of paying bills. Banks also make loans to customers, usually in the form of checks or credits to their checking accounts.

Most people rely on banks for their checking and savings accounts. Money deposited in a checking account is called a demand deposit. That is, the bank must give depositors their money when they request ("demand") it by writing checks. Depositors usually do not earn interest on regular checking accounts.

Money deposited in a savings account is called a time deposit. Most banks require depositors to keep the money in their accounts for a period of time. Savings accounts pay interest to depositors. The amount of interest paid depends on the type of account.

An increasingly popular type of bank account combines checking and savings—the negotiable order of withdrawal (NOW) account. With a NOW account, the customer can write checks and receive interest on the money in

the account. Most banks require depositors to maintain a certain minimum balance in their NOW accounts.

Types of Banks

A bank chartered under state laws is a state bank. One chartered under federal laws is a national bank. The type of charter determines whether the bank is supervised by state or federal officials. It also determines many of the rules that guide the bank.

There are four main types of banks in the United States: commercial banks, savings and loan associations, savings banks, and credit unions. Although the differences among these banks have blurred in recent years, some important differences remain.

Commercial Banks The most numerous banks in the United States are commercial banks, which offer a full range of services. Commercial banks offer checking, savings, and NOW accounts. They make loans to individuals and businesses. They issue credit cards and manage retirement accounts. They also have departments that help customers manage property and invest money.

Accounts in commercial banks are insured by a government agency called the Federal Deposit Insurance Corporation (FDIC). Each depositor is insured up to $100,000. This means that if for some reason a bank is unable to give its depositors their money, the FDIC will do so, but only up to $100,000 per depositor.

Like corporations, commercial banks are owned by stockholders who buy shares in the bank. Shareholders receive cash dividends from the profits made by the bank.

Savings and Loan Associations Banks known as **savings and loan associations** began in the mid-1800s to help people buy homes. They still account for a large percentage of home mortgage loans. In recent years, though, federal regulations have allowed them to expand their services to include many of those offered by commercial banks. In addition

◈ 𝒞OOPERATIVE LEARNING

Have small groups of students research and present reports on aspects of the 1980s savings and loan crisis. Areas of research might include local bank failures; deregulation as a cause of the crisis; the Resolution Trust Corporation; and prosecutions of specific individuals. Assign each student a role, such as researcher, writer, illustrator, or presenter. To form a complete picture of the crisis, have students take notes during presentations by each group. Then have the class discuss the consequences of the crisis.

Guided Practice

Draw a web diagram on the chalkboard to organize the information about the Federal Reserve System. The central circle of the web should contain the term *Federal Reserve System*. Have students add connected circles to the central circle and to each other as they develop more information about the Federal Reserve System, such as its purpose, structure, and powers. Have students copy the diagram for use as a study guide.

to obtaining loans, customers can open checking, savings, and NOW accounts and can apply for credit cards.

In the past, almost all savings and loans were owned and operated by their depositors. Today nearly half of them are owned and operated by stockholders.

Until 1989, deposits in savings and loans were insured by the Federal Savings and Loan Insurance Corporation (FSLIC). During the 1980s, however, many of these banks were involved in risky loans, bad investments, and fraud. As a result, hundreds of savings and loans throughout the nation failed.

Faced with paying the costs of these failures, the FSLIC ran out of money. The government passed the FSLIC's insurance obligations on to the FDIC. It also formed the Resolution Trust Corporation (RTC) to sort out the savings and loan crisis. During its six years of operation, the RTC disposed of some 747 failed savings and loans. The final cost of the bailout to taxpayers was $145 billion.

Savings Banks Savings banks began in the early 1800s to encourage savings by people who could make only very small deposits. Today these banks offer a variety of services, including home loans. Most savings banks are located in the northeast region of the United States. As with commercial banks, deposits in savings banks are insured by the FDIC up to a maximum of $100,000 per depositor.

Prior to the mid-1980s most savings banks were called mutual savings banks, and they passed on their profits to depositors in the form of interest. Now, however, many savings banks are owned by shareholders who receive dividends from the profits. Shareholders elect a board of directors to manage the daily operation of the bank.

Credit Unions Most **credit unions** are established by people who work for the same company or belong to the same organization. Credit unions are owned and operated by their members. When members make deposits, they buy interest-paying shares in the credit union. These deposits are pooled to make low-interest loans available to members. Depositors also may write checks, which are called share drafts.

Deposits in credit unions are insured by a government agency called the National Credit Union Administration (NCUA). Each depositor is insured up to $100,000.

George McClain Gets a Bank Loan

What happens when a person borrows money from a bank? Consider the example of George McClain, who owns and operates a small gas station. George needs $5,000 to buy some new equipment. He visits a commercial bank to speak to a loan officer. After listening to George, the loan officer tells him that he probably will receive the loan, but George must show that he is a good credit risk.

George brings in his business records, which show that his gas station makes a profit.

Many small business owners like this one depend on bank loans to help them start their businesses.

Have students analyze the board of governors of the Federal Reserve System. They should consider the board's powers, how governors are appointed, and for how long. Then have students diagram at least one way the Federal Reserve affects the growth of the economy. Students should save these diagrams for use as study guides.

Ask: In a nation that believes in free enterprise, why is government involved so deeply in banking? Have students write an editorial for a fictional banking magazine in support of or in opposition to government banking regulation. Each student should address the advantages and disadvantages of government banking regulation. Call on volunteers to read their editorials to the class for discussion.

CIVICS SIDELIGHT

Until recently, the Federal Reserve has destroyed its old, worn-out greenbacks by shredding them and then dumping them into the nearest landfill. Now the government agency wants to recycle the 7,000 tons of used bills that are retired each year (nearly $10 billion, or about 3 percent of the value of currency in circulation). The Federal Reserve has contracted with companies to use the refuse to make roofing tiles, particle board, fuel pellets, stationery, and packing material. The Federal Reserve also is continuing to look for other ways to recycle the shredded currency.

George also points out that he owns his home, and that he has no large business debts. This information convinces the bank that George will be able to repay the loan. The bank agrees to make the loan and to consider George's house as collateral.

Some commercial bank loans are short-term loans that must be repaid in 30, 60, or 90 days. George receives a short-term loan of $5,000, due in 90 days. George does not receive the full $5,000 credit, however. The bank takes out a small sum in advance as the interest it is charging for the loan. George receives the remainder as a credit in his checking account. Deducting the interest on a loan in advance is known as **discounting**.

After he receives the loan, George buys the new equipment. He begins to take in more money because his gas station can now offer better service to his customers.

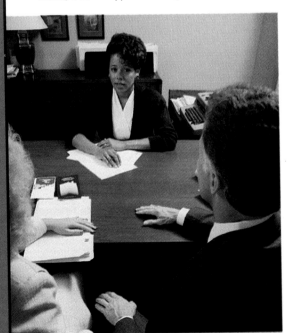

People applying for a bank loan must speak to a loan officer, who will approve or deny the loan.

The equipment company, richer now by George's borrowed credit, uses the money to expand its business. In fact, with George's check and the checks of other customers coming in, the equipment company may borrow money from a commercial bank for its own expansion. In this way, credit circulates throughout the U.S. economy.

Renewing the Loan

What happens when the loan is due at the end of the 90-day period? If George's business has done well, he can repay the loan. But suppose the new equipment was late in arriving, or business did not increase quite as fast as expected. George may have to go to the bank and ask that his loan be renewed, or continued. If the bank agrees, George will not have to repay the loan for another 90 days.

Usually a bank will renew a loan to a person like George McClain, whose credit is good. George, of course, will have to pay interest again on the loan renewal.

Suppose, however, that bank officials think George has done a poor job managing his business with the new equipment. They may decide he is no longer a good risk and may refuse to renew the loan. George must then find some way to repay the loan at once. To save his house, which is the collateral for his loan, he may have to sell his car or other possessions. He may even have to sell his business. As you can see, a loan involves a risk for the bank and for the borrower.

Government Regulation

There was a time when banks were allowed to conduct business with few rules. They sometimes loaned money without enough collateral or did not keep enough money in reserve.

Under these conditions, rumors might spread that the bank was shaky. Depositors would start "a run on the bank." That is, people would panic, go to the bank, and demand their money. Sometimes so many depositors withdrew their money at once that the bank

Reviewing

Have students complete the Section 2 Review.

Reteaching

Assign Section 2 of the Chapter 19 Reteaching Worksheet.

Extension

Have pairs of students develop proposals to organize and operate a "Students' Savings Bank" in your school. Students should decide operating rules of the bank, the tracking system for deposits and withdrawals, how the safety of the deposits can be guaranteed, rules regarding loans, and interest rates on the loans. The written proposals should include graphics, such as charts, that help explain the structure and policies of the bank. Call on volunteers to present their proposals to the class for discussion.

had no funds left. (Remember, the bank has used some of the funds to make loans.) As a result, some depositors lost their money.

Bank failures happened often enough in the nation's history that the federal government finally stepped in with a plan to regulate U.S. banking. In 1913 Congress established the **Federal Reserve System**. All national banks were required to belong to this system. State banks could join the system if they wished, and many did.

For many years the Federal Reserve had direct control only over its member banks. For example, only the member banks had to keep part of their deposits on reserve with the "Fed," as the system is called. Then in 1980 a law was passed stating that all banks must meet the Fed's reserve requirements.

The Federal Reserve System

The Federal Reserve System divides the United States into 12 Federal Reserve districts. A large Federal Reserve bank is located in each district. The Federal Reserve banks do not usually do business with individuals or business firms. Instead, they act as bankers for the federal government and for other banks.

The Federal Reserve banks serve two main purposes. First, the federal government uses the Federal Reserve banks to handle its own banking needs. The secretary of the U.S. Treasury deposits government funds in these banks. The secretary writes checks on the federal government's account, just as an individual does who has a checking account. The Federal Reserve banks also handle the sale of bonds issued by the government. Most U.S. currency is put into circulation through the Federal Reserve System.

Second, the 12 Federal Reserve banks provide services to the state and national banks and control the banking system. Even banks sometimes have to borrow money. A member bank can go to the Federal Reserve bank in its district and borrow money to increase its own reserve. The member bank then is able to

make more loans or investments. The bank must pay interest on these loans. The rate of interest charged by the Federal Reserve is called the **discount rate**.

The Federal Reserve at Work

The Federal Reserve System is managed by a seven-member board of governors in Washington, D.C. Each member is appointed by the president, with the consent of the Senate, for a single 14-year term. The board of governors makes most of the major decisions for the Federal Reserve System.

Through its influence over the banking system, the Fed tries to keep the right amount of money in circulation. When the economy is growing, more money is needed in circulation. Remember, money is simply a useful tool that helps us exchange goods and services efficiently. If more goods and services are being produced, more money is needed.

If the supply of money grows faster than the supply of goods, prices will rise. To prevent this, the Federal Reserve may try to slow the growth of the money supply or even take money out of circulation.

If the Federal Reserve wants to speed economic growth, it puts more money into circulation. It usually does this by buying U.S. government bonds from banks or individuals. These banks or people then have more money to spend or lend, and the money enters the economy. To take money out of circulation, the Federal Reserve does the opposite. It sells government bonds back to banks or people. After buying these bonds, individuals or banks have less money to spend or lend.

SECTION 2 REVIEW

1. Define or identify the following terms: collateral, bank, savings and loan association, credit union, discounting, Federal Reserve System, discount rate.

After studying Section 3, students should be able to do the following.

1. Explain why saving money is important, and identify ways to save or invest.

2. Compare the risk of buying U.S. savings bonds with the risk of investing in stocks.

3. Describe how savers help the U.S. economy.

4. Explain how the federal government helps protect bank depositors and buyers of stocks and bonds.

Teaching Section 3
Building a Vocabulary

Remind students that stocks are shares of ownership in a company. (See Chapter 17.) Stockholders trade, or exchange, stock at a **stock exchange**. The exchange of stocks is arranged by a **broker**. *Broker* comes from an Anglo-French word meaning "negotiator." Some investors try to lessen their risks in stock investing by buying into **mutual funds**. Ask students to suggest meanings of *mutual. (joint or shared)* Then have students deduce the meaning of *mutual funds. (investments in stocks from many companies)*

CIVICS SIDELIGHT

Many people who are saving to buy a house usually are concerned mostly with being able to save enough money to make the required down payment. But they might also consider how monthly house payments will affect their ability to save. For a 30-year mortgage on an $80,000 home loan at a 10 percent interest rate, the buyers will end up paying $702.06 per month (not including taxes and insurance on the home). Lenders commonly require that monthly payments be no more than 28 percent of gross income. Thus, buyers applying for an $80,000 home loan at 10 percent interest would need a total annual income of at least $30,088.

2. Which is the most numerous type of bank in the United States? How does the FDIC help depositors?

3. What caused the savings and loan crisis in the 1980s? What was the purpose of the Resolution Trust Corporation?

4. Why were savings banks first begun? Who owns and operates credit unions?

5. Why was the Federal Reserve System established? How does the Fed keep the right amount of money in circulation?

6. **THINKING CRITICALLY** Imagine that you are the bank loan officer considering George McClain's loan application. Will you approve or deny his application? Why?

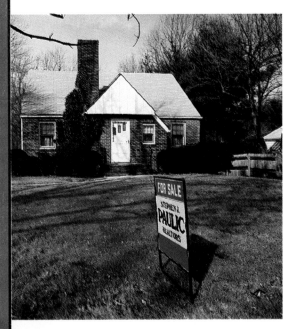

For many, owning a home is part of the American Dream. Careful attention to saving is one way to help make that dream become a reality.

3 Saving and Investing

Most of us want money to spend. We do not have to spend it right away, however. One of the features of money is that it can be stored and spent later. Most people set aside some money in case they have unexpected expenses. Keeping money by setting it aside is called saving. Saving is important for individuals and for the nation.

Why People Save

Almost everyone saves or tries to save. Families set aside money for their children's education or to buy a house. They save money to meet emergencies, such as medical and hospital bills, loss of a job, or other unexpected difficulties. People save money for their retirement years. Saving is an important part of knowing how to manage money wisely.

Why do we need to save money in a credit system? True, the credit system in the United States allows people to buy goods and services without paying cash for them at the time of purchase. Even when using credit, however, the customer often must make a fairly large down payment.

The largest purchases most people make are houses and cars. To buy a house, you must first pay a sizable part of the total cost as a down payment. Builders may advertise "Only 10 percent down." Ten percent of the cost of an $85,000 house is still a large sum though—$8,500. The average family has to save a long time to have $8,500.

Used-car dealers may advertise "No money down, drive it home today!" Without a down payment, though, the monthly payments on an automobile may be higher than the buyer can afford. The smaller the down payment, the greater the amount of interest and the larger the monthly payments. The extra interest will also make the total cost of the car higher. Thus saving money throughout life is wise for everyone.

Writing Creatively

Have students write a short poem about the virtues of saving or about the problems people might encounter in life if they do not save "for a rainy day." Encourage students to be creative. Each student should pick an audience, such as teenagers or young adults, for his or her poem. Call on volunteers to read their poems to the class. Have students identify key points from each poem for discussion.

COOPERATIVE LEARNING

Have each small group write a story in which an investor chooses one or more ways of saving money: putting it in a savings account, buying bonds, buying stocks, investing in a CD or money-market fund, or buying valuable items. Each group's story should indicate the level of risk for its assigned savings strategy and why such an investment choice is good. Have each student contribute by researching, writing, editing, or reading aloud the story to the class.

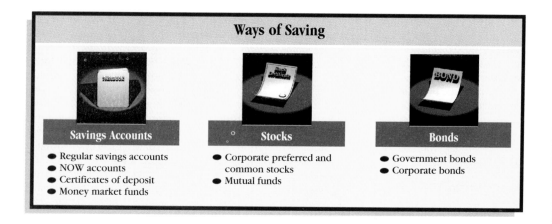

Ways of Saving

Savings Accounts	Stocks	Bonds
● Regular savings accounts ● NOW accounts ● Certificates of deposit ● Money market funds	● Corporate preferred and common stocks ● Mutual funds	● Government bonds ● Corporate bonds

GLOBAL PERSPECTIVES

If asked to name a stock exchange, many Americans would probably think of the New York Stock Exchange (NYSE). But many other nations have well-established stock exchanges. Investors pay particular attention to averages that indicate trends in the overall value of stocks in a particular stock exchange. The Dow Jones average of the value of common stocks for 30 U.S. firms serves such a function for the NYSE. Such indexes in other countries include the Nikkei in Tokyo, the DAX in Frankfurt, the CAC 40 in Paris, Australia's All Ordinaries index in Sydney, and the *Financial Times*–Stock Exchange 100 in London.

Stock exchanges do not exist just in wealthy countries. Brazil, India, Thailand, Malaysia, Turkey, and many other industrializing countries with capitalist economic systems have what are termed "emerging markets." The People's Republic of China, a communist country with a mixed economy, also has created a stock exchange.

How People Save

There are various ways to save money. You can hide your money under a mattress, put it in a cookie jar, or keep it in a piggy bank. Most Americans, however, find that there are better ways to save money.

Putting Money in the Bank Many Americans set aside a regular amount each week or each month in a savings account at a bank. The bank pays interest on money deposited in a savings account. By saving in this way, a person's money earns more money for him or her. The money is always there to be withdrawn when it is needed.

Regular savings accounts sometimes are called "passbook accounts" because some banks give depositors a small book in which to record their transactions. Regular savings accounts usually require only a small minimum balance. Some banks, though, charge a service fee if the account falls below the minimum balance or if no transactions have taken place within a certain length of time.

Buying Bonds You probably remember that when you buy a bond, you are lending money to the business or government that issues the bond. When the bond reaches maturity, you get the money back. In the meantime, your money is earning interest. The federal government, many state and local governments, and some corporations issue bonds.

U.S. government bonds, as well as the bonds of most states, localities, and corporations, are a relatively safe form of savings. In most cases bondholders receive regular interest payments.

One form of bond, the U.S. savings bond, does not pay interest until it is cashed in by the bondholder. For example, a savings bond bought for $100 earns $100 in interest after an average of 12 years. The purchaser who paid $100 for a bond receives $200 when he or she cashes it in. Meanwhile, the buyer's money is safe because the federal government will always repay its debt. The interest rate for savings bonds, however, usually is not as high as it is for many other kinds of investments because there is less risk involved.

Buying Stocks You read about common stocks and preferred stocks in Chapter 17. Business organizations known as brokerage houses buy and sell stocks for their customers. The people employed by brokerage houses are called **brokers**. Each brokerage house is a member of a **stock exchange**. Millions of shares of stock are bought and sold every working day at a stock exchange.

Anyone can buy stocks by getting in touch with a brokerage house. People need to know a

Guided Practice

Invite students to make an imaginary deposit of $100 into a savings account and "follow" it through the economic system. Have volunteers draw a class chart on the chalkboard (supplying fictional names for the bank and the business firm) to show how their $100 changes from a deposit to a bank loan to a means of producing specific goods or services. Ask: How does the federal government encourage and protect savings and investments? *(by federally insuring deposits [FDIC and NCUA] and by regulating investment markets [SEC])*

Independent Practice

Have students create advertising campaigns emphasizing the importance of saving money. Students might create posters, public service announcements, or other strategies to encourage students to save money. Invite the principal and an economics teacher to judge the campaigns. Invite the student with the best campaign to implement his or her campaign in your school.

CIVICS SIDELIGHT

Some people invest money in rare or popular collectibles. For example, a form of saving that has grown tremendously in the past 20 years is collecting baseball cards. Many of the old and rare cards are very valuable, and their worth keeps rising. A 1914 card picturing "Shoeless" Joe Jackson, for example, was worth $9,000 in 1995. A Mickey Mantle card from 1952 was worth about $2,400 in 1995; a 1952 Willie Mays card was valued at about $1,600; and a Pete Rose baseball card from 1963 was selling for $1,000. The value of a collectible baseball card is greatest if it is in mint (original) or near-mint condition.

great deal about the stock market, however, before they buy stocks. Stock prices depend heavily on expectations of how well a company will perform in the future, making stocks a relatively risky investment.

People who buy common stocks are taking a chance. They hope their investment will earn more money—perhaps much more—than it would earn in a savings account or a bond purchase. Annual stock dividends may be higher than interest earned from a savings account or a bond. Also, if the value of a stock rises in the stock exchange, the customer may sell that stock and take a profit. The stock, however, may pay small dividends or none at all. Moreover, its value on the stock market may fall.

To reduce the amount of risk in stock purchases, many people buy shares in **mutual funds**. These funds are managed by people who are familiar with stock market conditions. Because mutual fund managers buy many different stocks, the risk in any one stock is not so great. By buying a share in a mutual fund, the purchaser owns a small piece of a large number of stocks.

Before buying shares in a mutual fund, however, a consumer should research the fund—what stocks it holds, its performance over time, and its management. A mutual fund that is poorly managed can be risky.

Other Ways of Saving In recent years Americans have saved in other ways, too. They have invested in certificates of deposit and money market funds. These often pay higher rates of interest than regular savings deposits and bonds.

Certificates of deposit (CDs) are issued by banks and other financial institutions. Savers invest a certain amount of money for a specified period of time. The amount of money invested in a CD may range from $500 to $100,000. The interest to be paid when the CD matures is set at the time of purchase and usually remains constant.

CDs can have terms of three months to three years or more. Usually the longer the money is invested, the higher the interest paid

on the CD. Investors who withdraw any money before the end of the specified period of time lose a percentage of the interest.

Money market funds, like mutual funds, buy types of investments that most individuals could not purchase alone. Savers can withdraw their money at any time. Money market funds do not guarantee a specified amount of interest. The rate of interest may rise or fall. Moreover, this form of saving is not insured by the government.

People also buy gold, silver, jewels, paintings, sculptures, antiques, and other valuable items as a form of saving. They hope the value of these items will rise sharply in the future. If the value does rise, the owners may make more money than people who put their savings in stocks, bonds, or savings accounts. People receive no interest or dividends on these holdings, however. Also, the items' values can fall as sharply as they can rise.

Savings in the Economy

What happens to the money that Americans have in savings accounts, bonds, stocks, and other forms of saving? That money is used to help expand the nation's economy. In fact, saving by individual citizens is vital in a free economy. It makes the continued growth of production possible. How does saving promote such growth?

Continued growth is possible only if factories and other means of production are continually expanded. In turn, the means of production expand only when there is capital available to pay for new factories, machine tools, and other capital goods. (You read about capital in Chapter 17.) But what is the source of this capital?

It comes from savings. Suppose you have $10. You spend $5 of it and put the other $5 in a bank. The $5 you spend represents goods that you consume. That is, you spend the money for something you want. You do not consume the $5 you deposit in the bank, however. This money can be invested. The bank can use this money to make loans to businesspeople. Thus

Closure

Begin an outline of the section by writing the major section headings on the chalkboard. Then have students complete the outline by listing important points from each subsection under each outline heading. Use Roman numerals for major section headings, and capital letters, Arabic numbers, and lowercase letters for subsequent entries. Have students save the outlines for use as study guides.

Reviewing

Have students complete the Section 3 Review.

Reteaching

Assign Section 3 of the Chapter 19 Reteaching Worksheet.

---

savings provide capital for the continued growth of production.

Using Savings to Invest

Saving and investing are not the same. Money in a piggy bank is saved, but it is not invested. Money you deposit in a savings account in a bank is both saved and invested. It is saved by you. It is invested by the bank. When people buy stocks, bonds, CDs, and money market funds, they are saving and investing.

When you invest, you turn your money into capital. What your money buys is not consumed. It is used to produce goods and services. Thus investing money results in the production of goods and services. This production results in more profits.

The ability of the American people to save money, and the ability of the U.S. economic system to invest this money, help keep the nation prosperous. The ability of a free economy to raise large amounts of capital has made it possible for U.S. business firms to build large factories that turn out vast amounts of goods.

Business firms also save to raise part of their own capital. The managers of most corporations put aside a certain portion of their

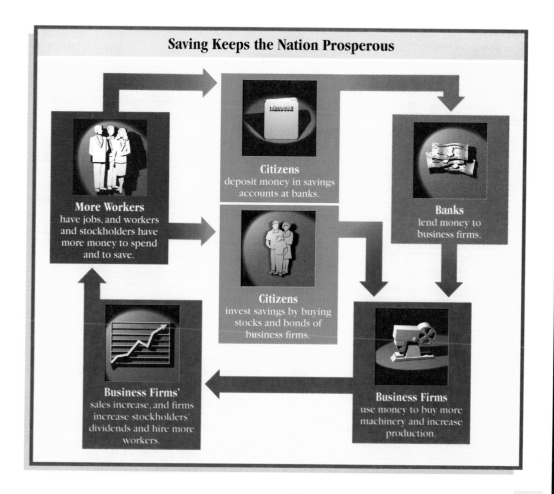

Saving Keeps the Nation Prosperous

More Workers have jobs, and workers and stockholders have more money to spend and to save.

Citizens deposit money in savings accounts at banks.

Banks lend money to business firms.

Citizens invest savings by buying stocks and bonds of business firms.

Business Firms' sales increase, and firms increase stockholders' dividends and hire more workers.

Business Firms use money to buy more machinery and increase production.

GLOBAL PERSPECTIVES

Nations tend to value a high rate of saving among its citizens because a high rate of saving usually means there is sufficient capital for investment. The savings rate may be thought of as the percentage of a nation's Gross Domestic Product (GDP) (page 333) that is not consumed (spent) by citizens and government. The United States is often referred to as a nation of consumers but rarely as a nation of savers. In 1993 the U.S. ratio of savings to disposable income was 4.1. This is low compared with many other industrialized countries, such as Italy (16.8), France (13.8), Germany (12.3), Canada (9.1), and Japan (14.6).

CIVICS TRANSPARENCIES

An overhead transparency of "Saving Keeps the Nation Prosperous" is available in *Teaching Transparencies with Teacher's Notes.*

Extension

Congress has passed legislation that allows workers to deduct a percentage of their before-tax income and defer paying taxes on the money if they put it in retirement accounts. Money in the accounts is invested, and the balance is not taxed until it is withdrawn by the retiree. Have students research the advantages of various types of such funds (such as IRAs and 401K accounts). Students should consider the value of saving for retirement when they are young. Have volunteers report their findings to the class.

Section 3 Review
A N S W E R S

1. See the following pages: broker, stock exchange (p. 363); mutual fund, certificate of deposit (CD), money market fund (p. 364).

2. because large purchases sometimes require large down payments; also helps to secure one's future against unexpected expenses

3. putting money in banks; buying bonds or stocks; also investing in CDs, money market funds, valuable items

4. The government will always repay its debt. Stock prices depend on expectations of future company earnings.

5. Depositor's savings provide capital (through bank loans) for continued growth of productivity.

6. regulates activities of savings institutions and insures deposits through FDIC and NCUA; Securities and Exchange Commission

7. Students should discuss the importance of saving and investing wisely.

366

companies' profits before they pay dividends to stockholders. This money is then put back into their business in the form of new capital.

The new capital helps businesses invest in new machines or expand factories. It also helps businesses establish new branches or add new lines of products to what they already produce. This new capital for expansion is in addition to the money set aside for new buildings and equipment when old ones need replacing.

Protecting Savings

When people put their money into a bank, they want to know their money will be safe. They want to know they will be able to get it back when they ask for it. Also, when people buy stocks or bonds, they want to be sure they are not taking unnecessary risks.

For these reasons, the federal and state governments have passed laws to regulate the activities of those institutions that handle the savings of others. All banks must receive a state or federal charter to operate. The government charters only those banks that are properly organized and have enough capital.

After a bank is chartered, it is inspected regularly by state or federal officials. The bank's directors are responsible for ensuring that their bank obeys all banking laws. Also, you may recall, all banks must keep reserve funds in Federal Reserve banks.

Despite these regulations, banks sometimes fail. The officials of the bank may make unwise investments or bad loans, and the bank may be forced to close. What happens to the savings that people have deposited in a bank if the bank fails?

Insuring Savings Most savings are now protected by the federal government. During the 1930s many banks closed their doors because businesses were in financial trouble. As a result, many people lost all or most of their savings. As a result, Congress took steps to protect depositors. As you recall, it established the Federal Deposit Insurance Corporation (FDIC). Similarly, the National

Credit Union Association (NCUA) was formed to protect deposits in all federal and most state-chartered credit unions.

You can tell if your bank or credit union is an FDIC or NCUA member. It will display signs in its windows and in its advertising. Each bank or credit union that is insured by the FDIC or the NCUA contributes to a fund held by the federal government. If any member bank or credit union fails, depositors will be paid the amount of their deposits up to $100,000 per depositor.

Regulating Stock Exchanges In the 1930s Congress also established the Securities and Exchange Commission (SEC). This organization ensures that all offerings of stocks and bonds on the nation's stock exchanges are honest.

In years past, people sometimes sold "watered-down" stock. This stock did not fully represent the value claimed for it. There were also many other types of stock fraud and deception by which dishonest people and firms cheated the American public.

The regulations of the Securities and Exchange Commission were established to stop such practices. The SEC constantly monitors the practices of the nation's stock exchanges and of the brokers who buy and sell stock. This does not mean that all stocks are safe investments or that all brokers are honest. A company can be perfectly honest, meet all the SEC's rules, and still fail.

Regulating Savings Organizations As you have learned, all of the nation's savings organizations come under state or federal government supervision. Banking practices are closely monitored. Savings and loan associations are also regulated by laws. Even company credit unions must allow government accountants to examine their records regularly to determine if they are operating properly. Because saving is so important to the prosperity of the United States and its citizens, it is in the best interest of the nation that individual savings be protected.

SECTION OBJECTIVES

After studying Section 4, students should be able to do the following.

1. Describe how insurance works.

2. Distinguish private from social insurance and Medicare from Medicaid.

3. Explain why insurance fraud hurts all citizens.

4. Explain the origin of and challenges for Social Security.

5. Describe unemployment compensation, and explain the purpose of workers' compensation.

Teaching Section 4
Building a Vocabulary

Tell students that both **Medicare** and **Medicaid** are social insurance programs that help people who need medical attention. Help students understand the difference between the terms by using the endings *-care* and *-aid*. Medicare is "care for people over 65." Medicaid is "aid to poor people." Have students use words or word parts to help identify other section vocabulary terms.

SECTION 3 REVIEW

1. Define or identify the following terms: broker, stock exchange, mutual fund, certificate of deposit (CD), money market fund.

2. Why is it important to save money even though the United States has an extensive system of credit?

3. What are three ways that Americans can save or invest money?

4. Why are U.S. savings bonds a relatively safe investment? Why are stocks a relatively risky investment?

5. How does saving by individuals help the U.S. economy?

6. How does the federal government help protect bank depositors? How does the federal government help protect people who buy stocks and bonds?

7. **THINKING CRITICALLY** Prepare a presentation on the topic "How to Save and Invest Wisely" for a class of elementary schoolchildren. What main points should you emphasize? What props and visuals will you need to make? If possible, give your presentation to an interested elementary class.

4 Insurance Against Hardship

Life is full of risks and uncertainties. There is the chance of illness or accident. There is the possibility of losing one's job. A fire or flood could damage one's house. There is the uncertainty of reaching an age when a person cannot earn a living. The U.S. economic system includes arrangements that protect people, at least in part, against such risks and uncertainties. These protections are called insurance.

What Is Insurance?

Suppose you figured that your losses could total $100,000 in the event of a fire, flood, or accident. Would you be willing to pay a much smaller sum—perhaps $750 each year—to make sure you did not run this risk? **Insurance** is a system of paying a small amount to avoid the risk of a large loss.

The small amount a person pays for this protection is called a **premium**. Premiums may be paid yearly or at regular times throughout the year. The contract that gives this kind of protection is an insurance policy.

Private Insurance

Private insurance is voluntary. That is, individuals and companies choose whether to pay for it. There are many different kinds of private

Health insurance helps this teenager's family pay for his visit to the doctor.

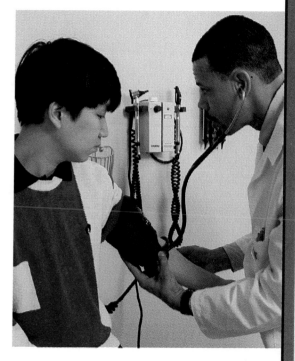

CIVICS SIDELIGHT

Insurance is not a new idea. As long ago as 3000 B.C., the merchants of Babylon (near present-day Baghdad in Iraq) insured their ships against loss at sea. Shipping at the time was quite hazardous (due to high rates of piracy, for example), and thus interest on loans to merchants was high. If the goods were lost at sea, merchants paying these higher interest rates did not have to repay the loans. Throughout history this kind of insurance helped expand international trade, encouraging merchants to take risks that they otherwise might fear to take.

Creating an Insurance Policy

Have pairs of students create insurance policies for teenagers. Each pair should consider the kinds of risks faced by a typical teenager, such as losing one's homework, failing a test, or becoming ill and missing a date. Then have each pair place some sort of value on each risk (not necessarily a financial value) and determine what premiums (not necessarily financial) would be a fair price for protection against such a risk. Have each pair draw up a sample policy and try to "sell" it to classmates.

COOPERATIVE LEARNING

Have small groups create pamphlets that distinguish between private insurance and social insurance. Each type of insurance should be defined, and students should illustrate (with explanatory captions) the different kinds of insurance one would find in private insurance and social insurance. Each group member should be responsible for illustrating and explaining at least one kind of insurance. Make copies of the pamphlets so that all group members have one for use as a study guide.

GLOBAL PERSPECTIVES

What company insured such valued property as Elizabeth Taylor's diamonds, Jimmy Durante's nose, and Liberace's fingers? Why, Lloyd's of London, of course. Lloyd's began as a coffeehouse frequented by insurance underwriters, bankers, and merchants. After a while, the establishment's proprietor formed a group of underwriters who insured marine shipping. The company grew along with British sea power in the 1700s and 1800s. Today, marine insurance remains its main area of business, but Lloyd's is still best known for insuring the property—and body parts—of the rich and famous.

insurance companies that write insurance policies covering almost every possible kind of economic and physical risk.

How can insurance companies take small amounts of money from people, yet pay them a large sum if a hardship occurs? The reason is simple—not everyone has a hardship. You may pay premiums on accident insurance all your life and never collect a cent because you never have an accident. You cannot, however, be sure you will never have an accident. Most people, therefore, consider it wise to buy insurance against such a risk.

A large insurance company has millions of policyholders who pay their premiums regularly. Part of this money goes into a reserve fund. State laws specify how much of a reserve fund a company must maintain. The amount depends on the kind of insurance the company issues and the number of policyholders.

When someone has a hardship of the type specified in the company's policies, payment of the amount of the policy is made from the reserve fund. Even with millions of policyholders, there may be only a few thousand payments out of the reserve fund each year.

Except for money held in reserve funds, insurance companies invest the premiums they collect. They buy stocks and bonds and make other forms of investment. The dividends, interest, and other income from the investments pay the expenses of these companies and earn profits for their shareholders.

Life Insurance   The main purpose of life insurance is to provide the policyholder's family with money in case the policyholder dies. In this way the family is protected from financial hardship. The person named in the policy to receive the money when the policyholder dies is called the **beneficiary**.

Two kinds of life insurance are term insurance and whole life insurance. Term insurance covers only a specified period of time. This

A home is the largest investment most people ever make. They usually buy insurance that will pay for unexpected damage, such as that caused by this tree falling.

insurance is often chosen by couples who have young children or very high bills. Because it expires at the end of the specified term, it is relatively inexpensive. It will, however, allow the surviving spouse to care for the children and pay off large debts. Whole life insurance covers the policyholder throughout his or her life, and is more expensive.

Disability Income and Health Insurance

There are many forms of insurance policies that cover policyholders if they are injured in an accident or suffer an illness. Disability income insurance, for example, provides payments to replace lost wages when a person cannot work due to total disability or partial disability.

Some policies cover all kinds of accidents, even breaking a leg by slipping on the soap in the bathtub. Other policies cover only accidents on common carriers—that is, on airplanes, trains, buses, and other means of public transportation. In case of death, the beneficiary receives the amount of the policy.

Major medical expense insurance pays a large portion of the medical costs resulting from a serious illness or injury. Major medical insurance premiums are higher than disability premiums because people are more likely to become ill than they are to become disabled.

Hospital expense insurance pays part of a policyholder's hospital expenses. Other insurance plans pay doctor and dentist bills and other medical expenses. Premiums for these kinds of insurance are often paid in part by the policyholders and in part by their employers.

Property and Liability Insurance

Some types of insurance protect the personal property of policyholders and also protect them against liability claims. Homeowners' insurance, for example, combines property and liability coverage. It protects people's homes and personal property from events such as fires, hurricanes, vandalism, and theft. The liability portion of the policy provides coverage if a visitor is accidentally injured while on or using the homeowner's property.

The most widely purchased form of property and liability insurance is automobile insurance, which protects policyholders against financial losses due to automobile accidents. It also provides coverage if a policyholder's car is stolen, vandalized, or damaged in an accident or by an act of nature such as a tornado.

Insurance Fraud

People who purchase insurance policies of any type must take care to deal only with honest, reliable insurance companies. Although insurance companies are regulated by the states, some dishonest people and companies ignore or find ways to avoid state regulations.

Sometimes it is the insurance companies themselves that are the victims of fraud. For example, dishonest doctors, dentists, pharmacists, and other health-care providers may submit claims to insurance companies for work they have not performed or may pad the claims with nonexistent expenses.

Citizens also contribute to the high cost of insurance fraud. Some people, for example, may claim severe injuries when their injuries are actually minor or nonexistent. Other people engage in insurance scams by regularly staging false slip-and-fall accidents in stores. Still others pretend to be hit by cars or buses so that they may submit false claims.

Insurance fraud hurts everyone. Estimates suggest that such fraud drains $67 billion a year from the U.S. economy. Moreover, the costs of insurance fraud usually are passed on to the consumer. Each U.S. family pays about $823 in higher insurance premiums because of insurance fraud. In an effort to crack down on insurance fraud, 13 states recently passed stronger antifraud laws. Another 12 states are in the process of strengthening their antifraud laws.

Social Insurance

The business failures of the 1930s caused much hardship and suffering among the American

CIVICS SIDELIGHT

The cost of insurance—especially automobile insurance—may vary widely from state to state. Some of the highest automobile insurance rates, for example, are in highly urbanized eastern states. Drivers in the midwestern states of the Dakotas, Iowa, and Nebraska have some of the lowest auto insurance rates. (More densely populated areas have higher frequency rates for collisions.) Other factors affecting insurance rates are traffic patterns, quality of roads and traffic law enforcement, and costs of auto repair and medical services in an area.

The Bureau of Labor Statistics has calculated that the average U.S. household spends 6.3 percent of its income on insurance of all kinds. Families used to spend the greatest amount on automobile insurance. After 1990 more of Americans' budgets went to pay health insurance expenses. The cost of homeowners' insurance ranked third on the list.

Linking the Past with the Present

Review the origins of unemployment compensation in the Great Depression. Ask students whether unemployment compensation is still necessary. Have students answer by writing a position statement in which they state their opinions and briefly defend them. Students might consider the hardship facing the worker who is suddenly out of a job, as well as the burden on the employer who must pay for the unemployment compensation.

Reading a Chart

Direct students' attention to the chart on page 371. Ask students to interpret each part of the chart by describing it in their own words. Students should be able to distinguish who pays for each program, who administers it, and who regulates it. Have the class take notes as volunteers offer their descriptions. Students should save their notes for use as study guides.

CIVICS SIDELIGHT

Not everyone agreed that there was a need for the social insurance programs and other governmental programs passed as part of Roosevelt's New Deal. Conservative critics accused Roosevelt of turning the United States toward socialism. Alf Landon, Roosevelt's Republican opponent in the 1936 presidential election, adopted the campaign slogan "Save the American Way of Life." Many others also thought the New Deal's social programs were too radical, but FDR believed they were necessary to restore Americans' faith in their democratic government.

people. Many businesses and factories closed. Millions of men and women lost their jobs. Banks failed, and thousands of people lost their life savings. Money they saved for their old age was gone.

To solve the problems of this troubled period, called the Great Depression, President Franklin D. Roosevelt recommended and Congress passed many new laws. Together these laws were called the New Deal. Some of the new laws brought immediate assistance to needy people. Other laws, looking to the future, offered protection against severe economic risks and hardships.

Government programs that are meant to protect individuals from future hardship are called **social insurance**. Social insurance is required by state and federal laws. Individuals and companies must pay for social insurance programs. In this way almost everyone can receive its benefits.

An important program of social insurance was adopted by Congress and President Roosevelt in the Social Security Act of 1935. The act set up an insurance system called **Social Security**. It has three major parts: old-age, survivors, and disability insurance; unemployment insurance; and workers' compensation.

Old-age, Survivors, and Disability Insurance The basic idea of this type of insurance is simple. People pay a percentage of their salaries each month while they work to receive cash benefits later when they most need them. During the years when workers earn money, they and their employers make contributions to a fund. When workers retire, or if they become disabled and their earnings stop, they receive payments from the fund as long as they live.

If workers die before reaching retirement age, their families receive survivors payments. A payment is made for each child under 18 and for the widow or widower. Payments for children stop when they reach the age of 18.

Paying for Social Security Monthly contributions made under the Social

Security Act are paid equally by workers and by employers. The contributions actually are a tax, because they are compulsory, or required. The program was made compulsory because Congress wanted as many U.S. citizens as possible to be spared the financial hardships experienced during the Great Depression.

Today the Social Security program extends to workers in almost every industry, business, and profession. Self-employed people must also participate. They pay the entire contribution themselves.

Receiving Social Security The benefits paid by Social Security have gradually increased since 1935. The amount of the required contribution also has increased. The amount that workers and employers pay depends on how much money the workers earn each year. The benefits received by workers when they retire is based on their average earnings over a long period of time. Retired workers, their survivors, and disabled workers receive monthly checks.

Some people worry that the Social Security program will not be able to care for future generations of retired workers. The general aging of the population, longer life expectancies, and lower birthrates mean that an ever-increasing segment of the population will be made up of people of retirement age. As a result, fewer workers will be supporting a growing number of retirees. Many fear Social Security taxes will continue to rise. Social Security, however, was never intended to provide the total income of retirees. It is simply a cushion against the worst hardship.

Unemployment Compensation When the Social Security Act was passed in 1935, unemployment was a serious problem. Millions of Americans were unemployed. Most had lost their jobs because of the Great Depression. The Social Security Act of 1935 contained a plan to help workers in the future who lost their jobs due to circumstances beyond their control. This plan is called the unemployment compensation program.

Illustrating Ideas

Review the workers' compensation program with students. Then ask: Why do employers, not employees, pay the cost of workers' compensation in most states? Then have pairs of students create posters about the responsibilities of employers and employees to maintain safe workplaces and why. Invite volunteers to explain their posters to the class.

Drawing a Political Cartoon

Tell students that some people describe social insurance and other government social welfare programs as providing a "safety net" for people who run into rough times. Have students draw political cartoons illustrating this "safety net." Students might focus on one aspect of social insurance or take a more general view. Other students might see negative aspects of this governmental "safety net" and will want to draw cartoons illustrating such drawbacks. Call on volunteers to explain their cartoons to the class.

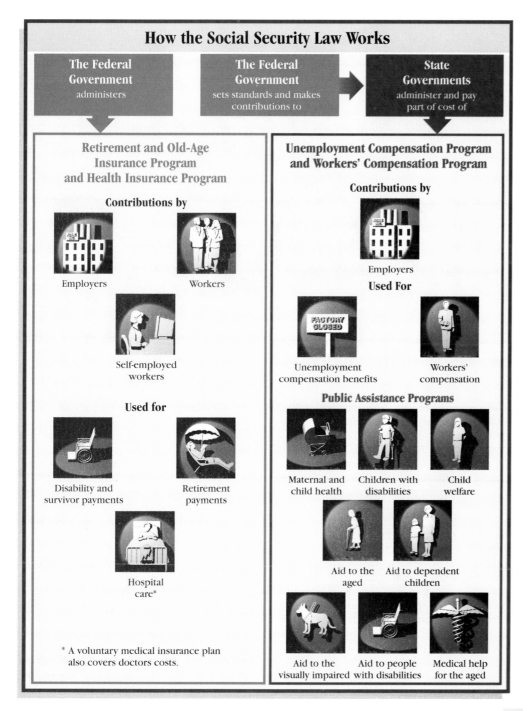

How the Social Security Law Works

The Federal Government administers → **The Federal Government** sets standards and makes contributions to → **State Governments** administer and pay part of cost of

Retirement and Old-Age Insurance Program and Health Insurance Program

Contributions by

Employers • Workers • Self-employed workers

Used for

Disability and survivor payments • Retirement payments • Hospital care*

* A voluntary medical insurance plan also covers doctors costs.

Unemployment Compensation Program and Workers' Compensation Program

Contributions by

Employers

Used For

Unemployment compensation benefits • Workers' compensation

Public Assistance Programs

Maternal and child health • Children with disabilities • Child welfare

Aid to the aged • Aid to dependent children

Aid to the visually impaired • Aid to people with disabilities • Medical help for the aged

CIVICS SIDELIGHT

Because many people have been concerned that the Social Security program will lack the funds to meet the demands of retiring baby boomers in the 21st century, Congress passed legislation in 1983 that was designed to keep the program solvent through the middle of the next century. The legislation raised Social Security taxes, required the participation of more people in the program, and made other changes, all designed to make sure enough money would be available to pay the benefits of baby-boom retirees. Some people have noted, however, that Congress has borrowed from Social Security funds to cover more of the government's general budget. Some observers fear that, without changes, such budgetary practices could prevent the Social Security program from building a sufficient surplus of funds necessary to pay for the increased numbers of retirees in the next century.

Guided Practice

Begin a simple chart on the chalkboard by writing *Medicare* and *Medicaid* as the two headings. Then call on volunteers to provide descriptions of each program. Tell students that these programs were passed as part of President Lyndon Baines Johnson's "Great Society" efforts in the 1960s. Have students discuss the importance of these two social insurance programs.

Independent Practice

Explain that some critics believe Medicare, Medicaid, and other social programs passed under the "Great Society" label are too expensive and have done more harm to society than good. Proponents say these programs meet needs otherwise not provided for. Have students write position statements supporting or opposing specifically Medicare and Medicaid. Students should develop rational arguments and back them up with facts. Have the class critique the letters of students who volunteer to read them to the class.

CIVICS SIDELIGHT

One job-related injury that has taken center stage in recent years is carpal tunnel syndrome, which affects the wrist. The wrist is also known as the carpus, and the carpal tunnel is a narrow opening in the wrist through which nerves and blood vessels pass. In carpal tunnel syndrome, caused by repetitive flexing of the wrist, the nerves become painfully compressed. Carpal tunnel syndrome affects typists, cashiers, musicians, carpenters, butchers, and others, and it is a significant source of workers' compensation claims.

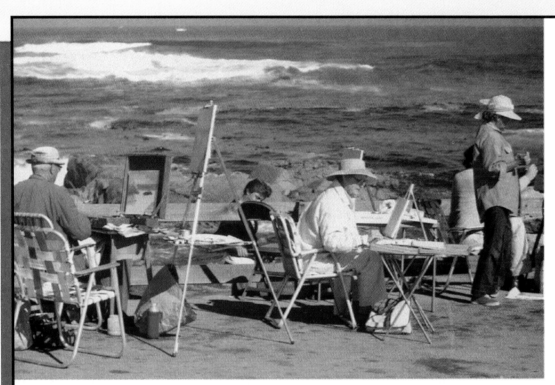

People pay Social Security taxes during the years they are working. They hope Social Security benefits will help prevent financial hardship when they retire.

To receive benefits, unemployed workers must register with a state employment office. They report periodically to the office to see if it can help them find jobs. If the job search is unsuccessful, unemployed workers receive weekly benefits based on their average earnings over a certain period of time. The amount paid varies from state to state, but most provide benefits for up to 26 weeks. The amount received is small, but it helps families support themselves while workers look for jobs.

The unemployment compensation program is financed by employers. Federal law requires all businesses that employ at least four workers to pay a special tax to the federal government. The state governments pay unemployment compensation benefits out of the money collected by the federal government.

Workers' Compensation The workers' compensation program helps people who have job-related injuries or who develop an illness as a result of working conditions at their jobs. The program pays these workers' medical expenses and helps replace any lost income. Workers' compensation also pays death benefits to the survivors of workers killed while on the job. In return for these medical and death benefits, workers give up their right to sue their employers to receive compensation for their work-related injuries.

The benefits received by workers vary by state and depend on the kind of disability the worker has and how long it lasts. The benefits also depend on the worker's weekly salary.

Workers' compensation is administered by the state or by a private insurance company. In some states administration is shared by a state agency and a private insurance company. Employers in all 50 states are required to participate in the program, and most states require employers to pay the cost.

Closure

Tell students that a family's combined monthly payments for health, life, and automobile insurance can amount to several hundred dollars. Yet if family members remain healthy and have no accidents, they receive nothing tangible in return for their premiums. Have students write a letter to the editor critical of the high cost of private insurance or praising the system that provides security for those who are insured.

Reviewing

Have students complete the Section 4 Review.

Reteaching

Assign Section 4 of the Chapter 19 Reteaching Worksheet.

Medicare and Medicaid The federal government also has programs to help older citizens and poor citizens pay their medical expenses. In 1965 Congress passed the health insurance program called **Medicare**. This program helps U.S. citizens who are 65 years of age and older pay for hospital care and for some nursing home care. In addition, Medicare includes a voluntary medical insurance plan to help older citizens pay their doctors' bills. People with disabilities who are unable to work also are eligible for Medicare benefits after two years.

Congress passed the **Medicaid** health insurance program in 1965. Under this program, the federal government provides money to help states pay medical costs of poor people.

SECTION 4 REVIEW

1. Define or identify the following terms: insurance, premium, private insurance, beneficiary, social insurance, Social Security, Medicare, Medicaid.

2. On what principle is insurance based? How can insurance companies cover large risks in return for relatively small premiums?

3. Distinguish between private insurance and social insurance.

4. Why does insurance fraud hurt everyone?

5. Why did President Roosevelt recommend Social Security as part of the New Deal legislation? Why are some people worried about the future of Social Security?

6. Who pays for the unemployment compensation program? What is the purpose of the workers' compensation program?

7. What is the difference between Medicare and Medicaid?

8. THINKING CRITICALLY Some people argue that Social Security has encouraged Americans to become too dependent on the state and federal governments for their support. Do you agree or disagree with this view? If the Social Security system were to fail before you reach the age of retirement, how might you support yourself? What will you do in the coming years to plan for your retirement?

CHAPTER 19 SUMMARY

Money is a medium of exchange. We give it in return for goods and services. Most modern money has no value in itself. We value it because the government guarantees it. We also value it because sellers will accept it in exchange for the things we want to buy.

Very little of what is bought and sold is paid for with currency. Checks are written to pay for most goods and services. Banks play a key role in the process of paying by check. They provide the checking service that transfers balances from one account to another when checks are written to pay for goods and services. Banks are safe places in which to keep money. Banks also help businesses and individuals by making loans.

The Federal Reserve System regulates banking in the nation. Federal Reserve banks are the banks in which the federal government keeps its funds. They also are the banks that service other banks. They help regulate the use of credit and maintain the proper money supply in the economy.

The federal and state governments help protect savings and investments by regulating banks, insurance companies, and the sale of stocks and bonds. Insurance companies, as well as the federal government, issue policies that seek to protect American citizens from many of life's financial hazards.

SECTION 4 REVIEW
ANSWERS

1. See the following pages: insurance, premium, private insurance (p. 367); beneficiary, (p. 368); social insurance, Social Security (p. 370); Medicare, Medicaid (p. 373).

2. protection against risk; Relatively few people need to collect on their policies.

3. private—voluntary; social—required

4. Costs of fraud are passed on through higher premiums.

5. wanted people to be protected against kinds of losses experienced during Depression; fewer workers to be supporting more retirees

6. employers; help people with job-related injuries or illness

7. Medicare—government-sponsored health insurance for the elderly and for people with disabilities who cannot work; Medicaid—government-sponsored health insurance for the poor

8. Students can prepare for retirement by saving and investing their money wisely.

Point out to students that some people pay for nearly everything, from the electric bill to groceries, by check. Checks are helpful to people who are trying to follow a budget—they provide an accurate record of expenses. Checks are also a safe way to pay bills by mail. Caution students never to send cash through the mail. There is no way to trace cash stolen from a letter. A check, on the other hand, is not cash. It must be signed and presented to a bank teller or other check-cashing agent who is on guard against stolen checks. As an extending exercise, have students bring in brochures and other literature from banks explaining various types of checking accounts.

Developing Civics Skills

LIFE SKILL
Writing Checks

As you have learned, checks are a convenient way to make purchases and pay bills. Because a signed check represents money you have in your account, it is important that you follow certain procedures when you write a check.

How to Write Checks

1. **Examine your checks.** Most checks are printed with the account owner's name and address in the upper left corner. Near the bottom left side of the check, you will see a series of numbers. The first part of these numbers is the bank's identification number. The second part is your checking account number.
2. **Date your checks.** Near the check number is a place for you to write the date.
3. **Tell the bank whom to pay.** In the middle of the left-hand side of the check are the words "Pay to the Order of" and a blank space. By filling in the blank, you tell the bank whom you want it to pay.
4. **Write the amount of the payment.** You must write the amount of the check twice—once in figures and once in words.
5. **Sign your checks.** Signing your name on the check authorizes the bank to carry out your wishes. Banks will not accept unsigned checks.

Applying the Skill

Study the sample check below. Then answer the following questions.

1. To whom is the check written? What did Paul buy? How much did he pay?
2. What is the name of Paul's bank? Where is his bank located?

Vocabulary Workshop

1. collateral

2. amount a person pays for insurance

3. easy to carry, take up little space, based on units easy to multiply and divide, durable, made in standard form, guaranteed by government

4. buy and sell stocks for customers

5. handles banking needs of U.S. government, provides services to banks, controls banking system

6. banks—mostly commercial, stockholder-owned; savings and loans—stockholder- or member-owned, begun to help people buy homes but now involved in commercial business; credit unions—member-owned

Reviewing Main Ideas

1. not guaranteed by government

2. charge—accepted only by stores that issue them, credit—accepted by thousands of stores and businesses; can be forced to close business or go bankrupt

3. FDIC—insures bank deposits; NCUA—insures credit union deposits; FSLIC—out of money because of savings and loan crisis

4. Government will always pay its debts. Market may fluctuate wildly. Buy mutuals.

5. to protect against risk

6. old-age, survivors, disability insurance; unemployment compensation; workers' compensation; Workers and businesses pay through taxes.

Thinking Critically

1. The Fed's powers greatly influence the economy.

2. Students should use sound reasoning in their responses.

3. Students might point to the drain on tax dollars.

R·e·v·i·e·w
CHAPTER 19

Vocabulary Workshop

1. What term refers to property that one uses to guarantee that a loan will be repaid?

2. What is a premium?

3. Name the common features shared by all currencies.

4. What is the job of a broker?

5. What are the purposes of the Federal Reserve System?

6. Distinguish between a bank, a savings and loan association, and a credit union.

Reviewing Main Ideas

1. Why are checks not considered legal tender?

2. How do charge cards differ from credit cards? What may happen if businesses or people are unable to pay their creditors?

3. What is the difference between the FDIC and the NCUA? Why did the FSLIC run out of money?

4. Why are government bonds a relatively safe form of investment? Why are stocks relatively risky? How can a person reduce the risk in stock buying?

5. Why do people buy insurance?

6. What are the three major parts of the Social Security system? Who pays for Social Security, and how do they pay?

Thinking Critically

1. As you know, the Federal Reserve System's board of governors is appointed by the president with the consent of the Senate. Why do Fed board members require such high-level appointment?

2. Periodically in the United States there is debate about abolishing the penny. Do you think the penny should be abolished? How might this affect the economy?

3. Some people believe the 1980s savings and loan crisis will affect Americans for years to come. In what ways do you think Americans might be affected by the crisis?

Cooperative Project

With your group, investigate the savings institutions in your community. How many banks, credit unions, and savings and loan associations are there? Where are they located? Are they local institutions or branches of larger organizations? If possible, interview loan officers in each institution. What types of loans do they make? What services do they offer? Present your findings in a community "banking map." Indicate the location of each institution, and write a short profile of each on the map.

The third step of your unit portfolio project (see page 421) is to decide how you will fund the mousetrap project. (Acme may not pay your full fee up front.) Will you need a bank loan? Is your project a good risk? Should you buy insurance for your company and your product? What type? Write a letter to your local bank requesting a loan and explaining how the money will be used. Place your letter in your individual portfolio for later use.

Citizenship in Your Community

Maps should identify community savings institutions.

BUILDING YOUR PORTFOLIO

Assign Portfolio Assessment Worksheet 19 in the *Portfolio Assessment Worksheets* booklet.

Assessment

- **Chapter 19 Tests**, *Chapter Tests* booklet
- **Test Generator**, Chapter 19
- **Portfolio**, Portfolio Assessment Worksheet 19, *Portfolio Assessment Worksheets* booklet

TEXTBOOK	TEACHING RESOURCES	OTHER AVAILABLE RESOURCES
Chapter	• Skills Worksheet 20 • Challenge/Enrichment Worksheet 20	
Section **1** The Business Cycle Page 377 **2** Coping with Economic Challenges Page 381 **3** Labor and Management Page 385	• Reteaching Worksheet 20.1 • Reteaching Worksheet 20.2 • Reteaching Worksheet 20.3	
Review and Assessment Chapter 20 Review, Page 395	• Test, Form A • Test, Form B • Portfolio Assessment Worksheet 20	• *Test Generator,* Chapter 20

ADDITIONAL RESOURCES

BOOKS FOR TEACHERS

Bradshaw, Thornton, ed., *America's New Competitors: The Challenges of the Newly Industrializing Countries,* Harper Business.

Malabre, Alfred L., Jr., *Understanding the New Economy,* Irwin.

Sherman, Howard J., *The Business Cycle: Growth and Crisis Under Capitalism,* Princeton University Press.

BOOKS FOR STUDENTS

Glassman, Bruce, *The Crash of '29 and the New Deal,* Silver Burdett. Relates and explains events of the Great Depression era.

Greene, Laura, *Child Labor: Then and Now,* Watts. A well-documented history of child labor in England and the United States.

Mitchell, Wesley, *Business Cycles and Their Causes,* Porcupine Press. Examines the causes and effects of depressions and recessions.

O'Neill, Terry, and Karin Swisher, eds., *Economics in America: Opposing Viewpoints,* Greenhaven. The pros and cons of suggested solutions to many of the problems facing the economy.

MULTIMEDIA RESOURCES

The Great Depression (VHS, c, series), PBS. Seven videos tell the powerful story of how the American people lived through the Great Depression.

The Growth of the Labor Movement (VHS, c, 37 min.), GA. Discusses the historic development and present status of the U.S. labor movement.

Pacific Horizons: Economic Change and Challenge (VHS, c, 14 min.), CU. A lively introduction to the economic relationship between the United States and the nations of the Pacific Rim.

Union Maids (VHS, c, 48 min.), NDF. Documents the story of the women who fought for workers' rights in the turbulent 1930s.

What Is a Recession? An Introduction to Economics (VHS, c, 19 min.), SRA. A student's guide to economics, narrated by three respected economists.

What Is Inflation? (f, VHS, c, 13 min.), PHX. Explains inflation and how the government tries to deal with it.

THE INTERNET

Have students use these search words to locate more information about chapter topics on the Internet: *business cycle, inflation, United States fiscal policy, labor, labor unions.*

 GLOBAL SKILL BUILDER

You might wish to use **Navigating the Internet** from the interactive *Global Skill Builder* CD-ROM to aid students' understanding of the Internet as a resource.

Abbreviations: b&w=black and white; c=color; f=film; fs=filmstrip; sd=sound; tr=transparency; VHS=videotape

AMERICAN ECONOMIC SYSTEM

★ **Structures and Functions** Students will learn the components of the business cycle and the role of the government in influencing the cycle, the various causes and effects of inflation, possible ways to control inflation, and the difference between a recession and a depression. Students also will learn about labor-management organization, unions, closed shops, open shops, union shops, and agency shops.

★ **Resolving Differences** Students will learn about major labor laws and how management and labor settle their disputes through the process of collective bargaining.

CHALLENGES IN TODAY'S WORLD

Students will be encouraged to become aware of the challenges facing the American system of free enterprise and to help improve the nation's economy.

CIVICS SKILLS

Students will learn to read a line graph and will learn terms important to understanding the challenges in a free-enterprise system.

MEETING INDIVIDUAL NEEDS

LIMITED ENGLISH PROFICIENCY (LEP)

Pair an LEP student with a student who is proficient in English. Have the students write each vocabulary term on a card and put the definition or sketch of a term's meaning on another card. Then have the students shuffle the cards and lay them face up in two vertical rows next to each other. Students should take turns matching cards labeled with terms to the appropriate definition or illustration cards.

LEARNERS HAVING DIFFICULTY

Have pairs of students outline the chapter. Students should use Roman numerals for section heads, capital letters for subsection heads, and Arabic numerals and lowercase letters for information found within each of the subsections. Make a copy of each pair's outline so that both students may use it as a study guide.

AUDITORY LEARNERS

Play some of the music that was written during the Great Depression, such as "Brother, Can You Spare a Dime?" or songs written by Woody Guthrie. Obtain lyrics to some songs from a local music store or from the school's music teacher. After each song, invite students to discuss the lyrics. Encourage them to see art as a reflection of the times. Ask: What will historians of the future learn about the 1990s from the music you listen to today?

VISUAL LEARNERS

If you have any Depression-era murals on the walls of public buildings in your community, take students on a field trip to view these works of art. (If there are no such murals in your area, have students examine books that deal with the art commissioned through the Works Progress Administration. Your school's art teacher may be able to help locate good sources.) Ask students to interpret the murals in light of what they know about the Great Depression. Ask students if they believe the artists were optimistic or pessimistic about the future. Why?

TACTILE/KINESTHETIC LEARNERS

Have students create political cartoons that portray the business cycle and its effects on business and workers. Encourage students to be creative. Invite the cartoonists to present and explain their work to the class.

GIFTED LEARNERS

Have students research and write biographical sketches of important figures in labor union history, such as the following: Samuel Gompers, John L. Lewis, Mary Harris ("Mother") Jones, Rose Schneiderman, A. Philip Randolph, and George Meany. Students should investigate the role each played in the development and history of organized labor.

CHAPTER OVERVIEW

Chapter 20 examines the business cycle and government's role in the U.S. economy. The chapter also investigates the relationship between labor and management. The underlying theme of the chapter is that the smooth operation of the free-enterprise system in the United States depends on the commitment of the American people to meet the challenges facing the economy.

Motivator

Ask students if they have noticed a rise in prices over time for various products. What products have they seen become more expensive? Have they ever noticed prices decrease for various products? Explain that in this chapter they will learn why prices rise, or inflate, and how those price changes are related to the state of the economy overall.

CHAPTER OBJECTIVES

After studying Chapter 20, students should be able to do the following.

1. Describe the business cycle and the economic challenges it poses.
2. Explain how the federal government helps the economy.
3. Explain why it is important for workers and management to compromise.

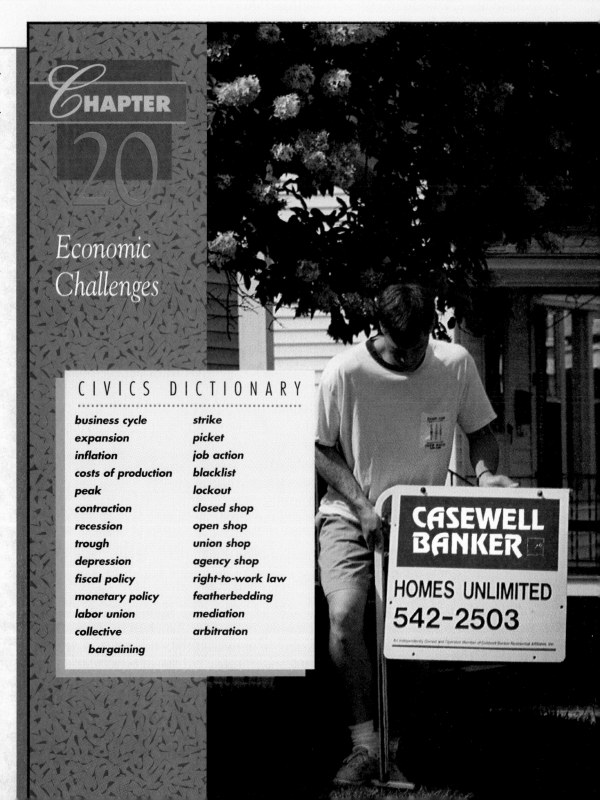

CHAPTER 20

Economic Challenges

CIVICS DICTIONARY

business cycle
expansion
inflation
costs of production
peak
contraction
recession
trough
depression
fiscal policy
monetary policy
labor union
collective
   bargaining

strike
picket
job action
blacklist
lockout
closed shop
open shop
union shop
agency shop
right-to-work law
featherbedding
mediation
arbitration

CASEWELL BANKER

HOMES UNLIMITED
542-2503

An Independently Owned and Operated Member of Coldwell Banker Residential Affiliates, Inc.

SECTION OBJECTIVES

After studying Section 1, students should be able to do the following.

1. Relate expansion of the economy to the Gross Domestic Product (GDP) and to inflation.
2. Explain why the economy sometimes contracts and what happens to the economy during a recession.
3. Relate the Great Depression to the New Deal.
4. Explain how the New Deal handled problems with unemployment and with the stock market.

Teaching Section 1
Building a Vocabulary

Ask students for the meanings of **trough**. *(a container from which cows or pigs eat; the low point between waves)* Tell students that in economics, a trough is a low point in the **business cycle**. Ask what the opposite of a trough might be. *(a crest or a **peak**)* Then write the common definitions of **contraction** *(reduction in size)* and **expansion** *(growth, increase in size)* on the chalkboard. Have students deduce the economic meanings of these terms.

CHAPTER FOCUS

You are a part of the U.S. economy. Every time you make a purchase, deposit money in the bank, or perform work, you are contributing to the economy. As part of the economy, you are affected by its ups and downs.

Throughout most of the nation's history, business has been good. During these good times of economic growth, more goods and services have been produced than ever before. But periods of slow economic growth also have occurred. Some businesses have failed, people have lost jobs, and fewer goods and services have been produced. These ups and downs in the economy cause problems that affect all Americans. You must do your part to work toward a healthy economy.

• •

STUDY GUIDE

● What is the business cycle, and what economic challenges does it bring?

● How does the federal government help the economy?

● Why is it important for workers and management to compromise?

1 | The Business Cycle

Although Americans enjoy a high standard of living, the economy does not always behave the way we want it to. Sometimes there is a period of prosperity, called a boom. During a boom, business is good. Jobs are plentiful, and profits are high. Then business activity slows. Some companies begin to lose money, and many workers lose their jobs. The nation enters a period of hard times, known as a bust. This tendency—to go from good times to bad, then back to good times again, and so on—is called the **business cycle**. The business cycle is common to free-market economies.

Steps in the Business Cycle

The chart on this page shows the various parts of the business cycle. When the economy is booming, the gross domestic product (GDP) increases. (As you recall, the GDP is the total amount of goods and services produced by the nation in one year.) This period of growth is called **expansion** because the economy is expanding, or growing.

The expansion of the economy during a boom is generally good: most people have jobs

The Business Cycle

Peak

Expansion

Peak

Contraction

Expansion

Trough

Gross Domestic Product (GDP)

Time

Writing a Speech

Invite each student to imagine he or she is the chairperson of the Federal Reserve Board at a time when the economy is expanding. Have each student write a short statement to Congress describing this expansion, including the growth of the country's Gross Domestic Product (GDP), what the expansion means for consumers and business, and possible hazards, such as inflation, down the road. Call on volunteers to read their statements to the class. Have students discuss the relationship between inflation and expansion in the economy.

COOPERATIVE LEARNING

Have small groups of students create collages illustrating the parts of the business cycle: expansion, inflation, contraction, recession, and recovery. Each group member should be responsible for illustrating one part of the business cycle. Each illustration should be accompanied by an explanatory caption. Have each group present its project to the class for a discussion on how each part of the cycle is related to the others.

GLOBAL PERSPECTIVES

We associate the Great Depression with the stock market crash and the failure of huge banks in the United States. The Great Depression was not, however, confined to the United States or even to the capitalist countries of the West. The Depression was a global phenomenon.

The Depression began in the industrialized countries but soon affected industrializing nations whose economies relied on the export of goods. Because of rising unemployment and decreasing wages, the demand for goods imported into the United States, for example, shrunk dramatically. Also, the United States enacted protectionist tariff laws, such as the Smoot-Hawley Tariff Act of 1930, that posed another barrier to U.S. imports. Many countries in return hiked tariffs on their imports, thus adding to problems for U.S. businesses, which found export markets virtually closed to them.

and businesses do well. Expansion, however, can cause problems. One problem that often accompanies a boom is inflation. **Inflation** refers to a rise in the costs of goods and services.

During periods of prosperity, people have money to spend, causing the demand for goods and services to increase. Prices rise, or inflate, as customers compete with each other to buy scarce products.

The costs of doing business also increase during a period of economic expansion. Businesses have to pay higher prices for raw materials and transportation, which are also scarce. They may also have to increase the wages of their workers to keep them, since jobs are more plentiful. Wages, payments for raw materials, transportation, rent, and interest on

During the Great Depression millions of Americans were unemployed and tried to make a living any way they could.

money borrowed are the **costs of production**. When inflation makes these costs rise, business firms may have to increase the prices of their products to pay these costs and still make a profit.

At some point, the expansion of the economy and the inflation that goes with it stops. When this happens, the business cycle has reached a **peak**, or high point.

After the economy peaks, business activity begins to slow. This economic slowdown is the opposite of an expansion and is called a **contraction**. If the contraction becomes severe enough, a **recession** may occur. During a recession, businesses fail, more people are unemployed, and profits fall.

When the economy reaches its lowest point, it is said to be in a **trough**. A trough is the opposite of a peak. When the trough is especially low, times are very hard, and economists say the economy is in a depression. During a **depression**, the number of people without jobs is high. Unemployed people cannot buy many goods and services, so businesses suffer. Many businesses close.

Usually troughs are not so low as to throw the economy into a depression. Some people lose jobs and businesses fail, but the economy bounces back and begins to grow again. Business activity increases, more people have jobs, and another period of expansion occurs as the business cycle continues.

The Great Depression

The worst depression in the nation's history took place during the 1930s. This period, as you have read, is known as the Great Depression. The first sign of trouble came in October 1929, when the prices of stocks on the New York stock exchange fell sharply. Many banks failed, and people lost their savings.

By 1932 business was producing only half as much as in 1929. Thousands of businesses closed. Farm prices were lower than ever before. By 1933 about one of every four American workers had lost his or her job. Most of these people had families to support. Unable to pay

Ask: Why were old theories of the business cycle questioned after the Great Depression? To help students answer this question, draw a two-column chart on the chalkboard. In the first column have volunteers list the old theories. Then in the second column have them explain how the events of the Great Depression went against the economic thinking of the past.

Have each student write a journal entry about the Great Depression as if he or she were an official in the Roosevelt administration. The journal entries should focus on the New Deal's role in helping unemployed workers and in attempting to end illegal practices in the stock market. Invite students to read aloud their completed entries for discussion.

Does this look like a desert? It is farmland that was turned into a "Dust Bowl" by drought. During the 1930s many farmers lost their land due to drought and dust storms.

their mortgages, many people lost their homes. People suffered these and many other severe hardships during the Great Depression.

Old Theories of the Business Cycle

Before the Great Depression of the 1930s, most economists believed the business cycle should be left alone. They maintained that it was unwise for the government to interfere in the economy to control inflation, boost production, or end unemployment.

These economists believed the problems that came with the business cycle would cure themselves. If prices rose too high, people would stop buying goods and services until prices fell again. Also, high prices and attractive profits would convince some people to go into business. The supply of goods and services would therefore increase. This increase would prevent prices from rising.

Many economists also thought that recessions could not last long. Workers who lost their jobs would soon be willing to accept lower wages. Businesses would then be able to hire people for lower pay. Other costs of production also would be low. This situation would encourage businesses to produce more.

As businesses expanded and increased their spending, they would help other businesses. Soon new businesses would be started. The economy would improve. Salaries would be raised and more people would be hired. People would buy more, and so on. Then came the Great Depression. The old theories did not seem to work.

Government Efforts

Wages were very low during the Great Depression. Rather than be without work, millions of unemployed people were willing to accept any pay, no matter how low. Businesses, however, were in great financial difficulty and could not afford to hire workers. Moreover, those businesses that did survive did not expand because there was no point in producing more goods when few people had enough money to buy them. To the surprise of the economists, the Great Depression did not end in a fairly short time. It continued year after year.

MULTICULTURAL PERSPECTIVES

During the New Deal the federal government made specific efforts to help Native Americans cope with the Great Depression. Funds from the Civilian Conservation Corps (CCC) and the Indian Emergency Conservation Work Program (IECW) provided employment and income to many impoverished Indians. At the same time, CCC projects improved the reservation environment through reforestation and erosion control. New Deal programs also helped African Americans, who were hit especially hard by unemployment. Franklin Roosevelt promised to include African Americans "absolutely and impartially" in the New Deal. Whether or not that promise was kept is a matter of debate, but as a result of Roosevelt's efforts, masses of African Americans turned toward his Democratic party and away from the Republican party, to which many had been loyal since Reconstruction.

Closure

Ask: What part of the business cycle is the economy in to-day? Have students establish the status of the economy according to the categories discussed in the section. Students might want to refer to articles in newspapers and other periodicals about the state of the U.S. economy. Then ask students what would be different if the economy today were in a different part of the business cycle. Have them list a few of the differences not only in the national economy but also in their own lives.

Reviewing

Have students complete the Section 1 Review.

Reteaching

Assign Section 1 of the Chapter 20 Reteaching Worksheet.

SECTION 1 REVIEW
A N S W E R S

1. See the following pages: business cycle, expansion (p. 377); inflation, costs of production, peak, contraction, recession, trough, depression (p. 378).

2. GDP increases; inflation—People have money to spend, which increases demand and causes prices to rise.

3. slowing of economy because consumer demand drops and money for increased production, investment, and expansion is scarce

4. recession is severe, prolonged contraction; profits fall, businesses fail, unemployment rises

5. hardships, unexpected duration of Depression convinced Roosevelt that action needed

6. government hired workers; created Securities and Exchange Commission

7. Entries should address the effects of the New Deal on life during the Great Depression.

380

In this painting called "Building a Dam," American artist William Gropper portrays government efforts to put people back to work in the 1930s.

Finally, many people were willing to have the government take steps to improve the economy. As you recall, President Franklin D. Roosevelt established a program called the New Deal. Under this program, unemployed workers were hired by the government to do useful work, such as create parks and build schools. Young people could join the Civilian Conservation Corps. They worked on projects to restore the forests and other natural resources. Homeowners and farmers could get loans to help pay their mortgages.

As you know from Chapter 19, the Federal Deposit Insurance Corporation (FDIC) was set up to insure bank deposits. Because dishonesty and fraud in the stock market had been at least partially responsible for the Great Depression, the Securities and Exchange Commission (SEC) also was established to oversee the buying and selling of stocks and bonds.

Another important part of the New Deal program was the organization of the Social Security system, which was established to give regular payments to retired citizens and help others in need. Unemployment compensation was created to provide workers with some money when they lost their jobs.

Many of the measures established during the Great Depression remain in effect today. These measures, however, have not ended the economic challenges facing the nation.

SECTION 1 REVIEW

1. Define or identify the following terms: business cycle, expansion, inflation, costs of production, peak, contraction, recession, trough, depression.

2. What happens to the gross domestic product when the economy is in a period of expansion? Why does

SECTION OBJECTIVES

After studying Section 2, students should be able to do the following.

1. Explain how inflation hurts the dollar's purchasing power and how too much money and credit fuel inflation.

2. Explain why unemployment rises during recessions.

3. Describe how too much spending stifles expansion.

4. Explain why U.S. businesses move to other countries and how such moves affect U.S. workers.

5. Describe monetary and fiscal policies.

Teaching Section 2
Building a Vocabulary

Ask students what **monetary policy** concerns. *(the money supply)* Tell them that the Latin word *moneta* once referred to "the stamp upon money" and later meant the money itself. Ask students what **fiscal policy** concerns. *(government spending and taxing)* Tell them that the Latin word for treasury is *fiscus.* Students might distinguish between these terms by remembering that monetary policy directly affects the amount of money in the economy and that fiscal policy directly affects the amount of money in the treasury.

inflation sometimes accompany expansion?

3. What causes the economy to enter a period of contraction?

4. What is the difference between a contraction and a recession? What happens to the economy and to people during a recession?

5. What is the relationship between the Great Depression and the New Deal?

6. How did the New Deal help unemployed workers? How did the New Deal attempt to end fraud and dishonesty in the stock market?

7. **THINKING CRITICALLY** Imagine that you are growing up during the Great Depression. Write a journal entry explaining how the New Deal will affect your life and that of your family members.

Coping with Economic Challenges

Since the time of the Great Depression, government has expanded its role in the economy. Maintaining a healthy economy is not easy, however. As you have learned, the business cycle is often accompanied by economic challenges such as inflation, unemployment, and recession. The government must find ways to deal with these challenges while at the same time encourage economic growth. This job is difficult because, as you will learn, many factors can affect the nation's economic health.

Causes of Economic Problems

Problems such as inflation, unemployment, and recession pose serious challenges to the economy and to individual citizens. Consider

inflation, for example. When prices increase faster than wages, people cannot buy as much with their money.

For instance, suppose that you work during the summer to buy a new bicycle that you have seen priced at $180. After earning the $180, you find that the price is now $200. You are a victim of inflation. Rising prices hurt the purchasing power of the dollar and can lower the standard of living.

Unemployment also hurts the economy. Unemployed workers cannot pay their bills. They cannot pay the taxes that help fund government. They buy fewer goods and services, which hurts U.S. businesses. Sometimes unemployed people must seek government assistance, which costs taxpayers money.

How Inflation Affects the Standard of Living

$40,000

$35,971

$30,000

$20,000

$20,000

$10,000

0

1980   Standard of Living   1994

In 1980 a family had $20,000 in income. In 1994 the same family needed an income of nearly $36,000 to have the same standard of living.

SOURCE: *1996 Information Please Almanac.*

MULTICULTURAL PERSPECTIVES

Layoffs during economic recessions typically have hit minorities and women particularly hard. The seniority system in many companies is based on the credo "last hired, first fired." Seniority refers to the preference accorded workers with more years of continuous service. Since equal opportunity laws have been enacted, many more minorities and women have won their battles to be hired for jobs that used to go largely to white males. But, say some observers, they lack the seniority to hold on to those jobs when companies lay off workers. For example, from 1987 to 1991, 11.8 percent of Hispanic workers and 8.8 percent of African American workers were "displaced" (lost their jobs). In comparison, 7.9 percent of white workers were displaced during the same period (which included the 1990–1991 recession). Since that time, the number of displaced workers has decreased.

Writing Creatively

Tell students of the old complaint, "A dollar just doesn't buy as much as it used to." Have students discuss why this saying is a comment on inflation. Then invite students to come up with their own sayings (or other forms, such as rhyming couplets) that express an opinion about the causes or effects of inflation, unemployment, and recession. Encourage students to read their sayings to the class as part of a discussion of the economic challenges of inflation, unemployment, and recession.

COOPERATIVE LEARNING

Have small groups of students illustrate the effects of various factors on inflation. Some groups might diagram an "inflation machine" or "inflation monster" that is fueled by various factors. Other groups might use formal diagrams or flowcharts to illustrate these causes of inflation. Each group member should prepare a short caption explaining how one of the factors shown contributes to inflation. Have groups present their illustrations to the class for a discussion of the causes of inflation.

CIVICS SIDELIGHT

Milton Friedman, former chairperson of the Federal Reserve Board, had his own opinion about the primary cause of inflation. In an interview in 1977 he said, "There's only one place where inflation is made: that's in Washington . . . in response to pressures from the people at large. . . . The voting public . . . ask their Congressmen to enact goodies in the form of spending, but they are unhappy about having taxes raised to pay for those goodies."

This unemployed woman looks for help from passersby. Unemployment affects not only individuals but also the U.S. economy as a whole.

Production, spending, and consumer demand decline during periods of recession. Because businesses are producing less, they need fewer workers. As a result, unemployment increases. Individuals cannot save much money, and therefore banks have less money to lend to businesses.

As you can see, inflation, unemployment, and recession pose serious challenges to the economy. What causes these economic difficulties? Not all economists agree. They point to many different reasons.

Too Much Money In Chapter 19 you learned how the Federal Reserve tries to control the amount of money and credit in the economy. Some economists believe that a major cause of inflation is the circulation of too much money. They argue that the Federal Reserve has put too much money into the economy. As people spend this additional money, they cause prices to rise.

Too Much Credit Some economists blame banks for making too many loans. This has the same effect as putting more money into the economy. People and businesses borrow from the banks and then spend what they have borrowed. This can contribute to inflation. Also, businesses that borrow and expand too rapidly may produce more than they can sell. These businesses must then slow their production to match the low level of consumer demand. Such slowdowns can contribute to economic recession.

Government Spending As you know, the government spends many billions of dollars each year. It spends for roads, dams, education, national defense, pollution control, and many other things. Members of Congress, federal judges, postal workers, and many others employed by the government must be paid. Much of the money spent by the government comes from taxes paid by individuals and business firms. The government also borrows some of the money it spends.

Many people believe the government is borrowing and spending too much. Government borrowing, like bank loans to individuals, puts more money into the economy and helps raise prices. It also adds to the national debt. The increased taxes that are needed to pay this debt take money out of the hands of individuals, who then find it difficult to pay the inflated prices of goods and services.

Consumer Spending Consumers share some of the responsibility for the nation's economic difficulties. Many people borrow money to buy things they cannot afford and do not need. Paying back this credit debt means that consumers can save only a small part of their income. Too little consumer saving reduces the amount of money available

Help students create a two-column chart on the chalkboard that shows factors that contribute to slower business expansion and contraction. Explain that some of the factors involved in creating inflation are at work here, also. Have volunteers write all of these factors in the first column of the chart. In the second column students should explain how the factors contribute to slowed growth, contraction, and/or inflation. Have students copy the chart in their notebooks for use as a review guide.

Have students make posters encouraging actions that will help ensure a healthy economy. Refer students to factors that cause inflation and slow business expansion (shown in the chart the class made in the Guided Practice activity). Display completed posters in the classroom. Have students discuss how the actions of consumers differ from the actions of government in affecting the health of the economy.

for business expansion. Too much spending may be partly responsible for inflation.

Productivity Productivity, as you recall, refers to the amount a worker produces in an hour. Rising productivity usually leads to higher wages, higher profits, and lower prices. In recent years, however, worker productivity in some other nations has increased faster than in the United States. This means that foreign products can be made and sold less expensively than American-made products. Although this allows consumers to buy less expensive products, it hurts U.S. businesses and can contribute to unemployment.

Many U.S. businesses find that the only way they can increase productivity is to spend millions of dollars modernizing their factories. Rather than do this, many American businesses have moved their operations to other countries where wages are low and govern-

ment regulations are few. Although this allows U.S. businesses to reduce their costs and increase productivity, it has resulted in the loss of thousands of American jobs.

The Government's Response

There are a number of ways that government can respond to challenges facing the U.S. economy. For example, the federal government can change its **fiscal policy**, or its policy of taxing and spending. If the economy is entering a recession, for instance, the government may reduce the amount of taxes that individuals must pay. Lower taxes give people more money to spend and to save. Increased spending encourages businesses to produce more, which leads to the creation of more jobs. Increased saving gives banks more money to lend to expanding businesses.

CIVICS SIDELIGHT

Economic events are not entirely predictable, much less controllable. For example, in the 1970s, during the presidency of Jimmy Carter, the economy was gripped by a seeming contradiction—rising inflation with stagnant output and rising unemployment. In classical economic theory, high unemployment should put a damper on inflation. In the 1970s, however, it did not. Economists dubbed this strange set of circumstances "stagflation."

Some economists have tried to explain stagflation by arguing that periods of high inflation (such as the early and mid-1970s) lead to expectations that prices will continue to increase. Such expectations then influence labor negotiations, bringing about higher wages to match expected price increases. According to this argument, the spiral of higher wages and higher prices then continues even during difficult economic times, thus producing stagflation.

Many U.S. businesses have moved part of their operations to foreign countries where labor costs are lower and government regulations are less strict. This U.S. automobile factory in Mexico may mean higher productivity for the company, but it also means fewer jobs for U.S. workers.

Closure

Review the actions that the government and the Federal Reserve might take during a recession or, conversely, during an expansion period. Have students draw diagrams to explain these actions, the reasons for the actions, and the expected results. Call on volunteers to present their diagrams to the class for discussion.

Reviewing

Have students complete the Section 2 Review.

Reteaching

Assign Section 2 of the Chapter 20 Reteaching Worksheet.

GLOBAL PERSPECTIVES

Varying circumstances make inflation a more serious problem in some countries than in others at specific times in history. For the twelve months prior to June 1994, for example, consumer prices in the United States rose an average of 2.5 percent while American officials debated various fiscal and monetary policies necessary to keep inflation under control. In Brazil, however, economic mismanagement had left consumer prices rising at a rate of nearly 50 percent a month by mid-1994. The Brazilian government made various efforts at fiscal and monetary reform, including the introduction of a new currency, in an effort to slow down the inflation rate. At the same time, officials in the People's Republic of China were trying to reign in an inflation rate of more than 20 percent in an economy experiencing rapid growth. Anti-inflation efforts included measures to slow down public spending in an effort to ease the pace of economic growth in the country.

During recessions, the government may increase its own spending. It buys more goods and hires more people to work for the government. In the past, the government has employed people to build public projects such as dams and bridges. The government also may give larger payments to the unemployed, the poor, and older citizens.

The government also may respond to economic difficulties by changing its **monetary policy**, or money policy. This policy is handled by the Federal Reserve System. As you have learned, the Federal Reserve serves as the nation's central bank. The Fed works to control the amount of money in the economy.

If the nation is entering a recession, for example, the Fed may increase the money supply

One way you can help the economy is to buy American-made products whenever possible.

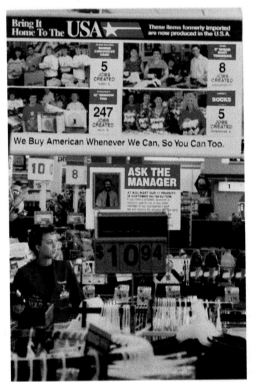

by making it easier for banks to lend money to businesses. It may do this by buying government bonds back from banks. Or it may lower the rate of interest that banks must pay the Fed for their loans. The banks then can lower their own interest rates on loans to businesses. It is hoped this will encourage businesses to expand, thus creating more jobs and income.

If the nation is in a boom period, these actions may be reversed. When inflation becomes too high, for example, the federal government may raise taxes and reduce its spending. The Federal Reserve may make it more difficult for banks to lend money to businesses by raising interest rates. This decreases the amount of money in the economy.

We have not yet learned to control the economy. Some people believe that it does not need to be controlled. They argue that the government should not interfere in the economy. They also believe that social welfare programs begun under the New Deal and later have contributed to problems such as inflation. Other people believe that the government can help the economy. These people argue that without government actions, economic difficulties would worsen. Another serious and prolonged depression might even occur.

Other Ways to Help the Economy

The government constantly struggles to maintain the proper balance between economic growth and inflation. Fiscal and monetary policies, however, do not always ensure a healthy economy. What more can be done?

Reduce Government Spending Government can reduce wasteful spending and halt unnecessary government programs. Many people believe that the government should also try to spend only the money it receives from taxes. With a balanced budget, the government would not have to borrow money and could work to reduce the national debt.

Increase Saving Consumers can help the economy by reducing their spending

Extension

Have students research specific efforts employed in the recent past to tame inflation. Some examples include wage and price controls during the Nixon administration, the "Whip Inflation Now" campaign during the Ford administration, and budget-cutting efforts during subsequent administrations. Have students investigate how successful each of these efforts was and prepare a short report with illustrations for the class.

After studying Section 3, students should be able to do the following.

1. Explain the history of U.S. labor unions, and identify ways unions and employers have dealt with each other.
2. Explain the debate over closed shops and open shops.
3. Explain the reasons for the merger of the AFL and CIO.
4. Identify labor laws and their guarantees.
5. Explain the importance of compromise in labor-management relations.

---

and saving more of their incomes. They should use credit only for buying things that they really need.

Buy American-Made Products When consumers buy products that are made in the United States, they help U.S. businesses prosper. This in turn helps preserve jobs for American workers and create more jobs.

Increase Productivity If the total amount produced each hour increases, the supply of goods increases. Business managers should try to operate their businesses more efficiently. Workers should try to do their jobs better and to make fewer mistakes. If workers' productivity increases, they can earn higher wages without contributing to inflation. Some economists suggest that, to keep inflation low, wages should not increase faster than productivity increases.

The health of the U.S. economy is of vital importance to everyone. Consumers, workers, business owners, and government must do all they can to help ensure that the United States remains a strong and prosperous nation.

SECTION 2 REVIEW

1. Define or identify the following terms: fiscal policy, monetary policy.

2. How does inflation hurt the purchasing power of the dollar? Why does unemployment increase during periods of recession?

3. How do too much money and too much credit in the economy contribute to inflation?

4. How might too much consumer spending make it difficult for businesses to expand?

5. Why should Americans buy American-made products? Why have many U.S. businesses moved their operations to other countries? How has this move affected U.S. workers?

6. Why might the government reduce taxes during a recession? How does the Federal Reserve reduce the supply of money in circulation?

7. **THINKING CRITICALLY** Write a letter to the president. In your letter, tell the president what you view as the most serious economic issue facing the nation today, and what might be done to address this issue. Be sure to discuss how this issue affects your life now and might affect your life in the future.

---

3 | Labor and Management

One day you will join the nation's working population. You may already have joined it if you have an after-school or summer job. As a full-time worker in the future, you may be part of the labor force—perhaps a worker in the computer or health-care industry. You may be part of management—one of the owners or managers of a business. In either case you will need to understand the relationship between labor and management.

Past Working Conditions

In the early days of the nation, many Americans were self-employed. They worked for themselves on small farms or in their own workshops or stores. They sold the goods they made to neighbors and friends. Most businesses were small. They employed only a few workers, or wage earners. Wage earners often worked side by side with the owner of a business. They knew the owner personally.

Usually if workers were not satisfied, they could speak to the owner and ask for better wages or improved working conditions. If the

1. See the following pages: fiscal policy (p. 383); monetary policy (p. 384).

2. When prices increase faster than wages, people cannot buy as much with their money. When businesses produce less and so need fewer workers, unemployment rises.

3. As people charge more and spend more money, the money in circulation increases, which in turn causes prices to rise.

4. Banks have less money to lend to businesses because savings rates decline.

5. Buying American helps U.S. businesses prosper and in turn helps preserve and create jobs. Lower wages and fewer government regulations attract U.S. businesses to foreign countries, resulting in loss of U.S. jobs.

6. Lower taxes give people more money to spend and save. The Fed may raise interest rates or sell bonds to decrease the money supply.

7. Letters will vary but should address specific problems and possible solutions.

Teaching Section 3
Building a Vocabulary

Ask students to suggest terms having the word part *medi-*. *(for example:* medium, *"in a middle position";* medieval, *"of the Middle Ages")* Tell students the root comes from the Latin word *mediare,* "to be in the middle." Then have them define **mediation**. *("intervention to promote compromise")* Ask students to define **arbitration**. *("objective judging,"* or, in other words, *"to find a middle ground between positions")* Tell them that the word *arbiter* means "umpire or judge" in both English and Latin.

Writing a Journal Entry

Invite students to imagine they are workers living in the 1800s before the rise of unions. Have them write journal entries that express the workers' frustration at the long hours, low wages, and poor working conditions in the factory. Each student might express a willingness on the worker's part to join with others in a united stand against the employer. Use journal entries from volunteers to lead a discussion of the origins of U.S. labor unions.

GLOBAL PERSPECTIVES

Communist governments have claimed to rule on behalf of the working people. Yet in communist countries strikes have been illegal. To settle differences, labor unions would submit petitions to a higher authority for legislative or administrative action. Nevertheless, strikes did occur in the communist countries of Poland and Hungary in 1956 and again in Poland and in Yugoslavia in the 1980s. In 1989 Poland's Solidarity union, led by Lech Walesa, became the first independent labor union in a Soviet-bloc country. After a period during which the government again repressed the activities of independent unions, Solidarity was allowed to participate in free elections in 1989, which led to the collapse of communism in Poland.

owner refused, they could quit their jobs. They could work elsewhere because industry was growing and the nation was expanding westward. There was little laborsaving machinery. Most of the time, there were more jobs than workers. Because workers were in demand, employers usually treated their employees fairly and honestly.

Between 1800 and 1850, working conditions for many wage earners changed greatly. Large factories were built, using machines to make products. Many of these factories employed hundreds of workers, including many young children.

In these new factories relations between employers and workers were different. Factory managers and owners had little or no contact with their workers. The working day was long—12 or even 16 hours. Wages were low and working conditions were often harsh, but workers could do little to improve their situation. As more and more settlers poured into western lands, it became more difficult for dissatisfied workers to leave their jobs and start on their own.

Rise of Labor Unions

As U.S. businesses continued to expand between 1850 and 1900, the number of workers also increased. U.S. workers began to organize in groups, hoping to improve wages and working conditions. These organizations of workers became known as **labor unions**.

A number of small labor unions had been established on a local basis earlier. Local unions, however, were not always successful in dealing with employers. Workers came to believe they needed national union organizations to be powerful enough to deal with employers as equals.

In the late 1800s and early 1900s the growing labor unions wanted the right to bargain with employers for better wages, shorter hours, and improved working conditions. The unions worked hard to show that the best way for employers and workers to settle their differences was through collective bargaining.

In **collective bargaining** representatives of a labor union meet with representatives of an employer to reach an agreement. The terms of the agreement are put into a written contract. This labor contract is signed by the employer and the officers of the union.

The labor contract details the agreed-on wage rates, hours, and working conditions. The agreement is for a fixed period of time—usually one, two, or three years. When the contract nears its ending date, representatives of the union and the employer meet again and bargain for a new contract.

Methods Used by Labor

In the early years of union organization, collective bargaining often broke down. Sometimes employers refused to bargain at all. To force business owners to bargain with them, labor unions used the strike. In a **strike**, union members walk off the job if employers do not agree to labor's demands. Production stops, and the company loses money.

What prevents a company from hiring other workers when there is a strike? The strikers try to prevent the hiring of replacement workers by **picketing**. Picketing strikers walk back and forth, often carrying signs, in front of company buildings. They discourage other workers from entering and taking over their jobs. Workers who cross picket lines and enter the buildings to work during the strike are called scabs. Sometimes fights have broken out between strikers and scabs. The law now limits the use of scabs by employers.

Instead of striking, workers sometimes stay on the job but work much more slowly than usual. This union action is called a slowdown. Any kind of slowdown, or action short of a strike, is called a **job action**. The union, for example, may tell its members to follow all written orders to the letter and to check and recheck their work several times. This job action slows production and costs the company money. Sometimes it gains as much for the union as a strike.

Creating a Chart

Have students create on the chalkboard a chart listing the methods used by labor and by employers in relations with each other, particularly during the early years of labor organizing. Volunteers should supply appropriate methods used by each under headings labeled "Labor Methods" and "Employer Methods." Have students copy the chart in their notebooks for use as a study guide.

COOPERATIVE LEARNING

Have students apply the information in "Creating a Chart" to specific strategies either for organizing unions or opposing their establishment in a fictional business of the 1800s. Randomly assign the roles of "labor" and "employer" to small groups. Each group should choose the kind of business involved and give the business and union fictitious names. Each group should illustrate its strategy and write a short description of specific methods to secure its interests. Have groups present their projects to the class.

Strikes, such as this one in New York City, are one way workers can make their concerns known to management.

CIVICS SIDELIGHT

A forerunner of the American Federation of Labor (AFL) was the Knights of Labor. Founded in 1869 as a secret organization devoted to merchants and farmers as well as laborers, the Knights of Labor began meeting openly in 1879 and had 700,000 members by 1886. That year in the United States there were 1,600 strikes, many of them violent, which turned many Americans against unions. As a result, the influence of the Knights of Labor declined.

Methods Used by Employers

Most early business owners viewed union workers as troublemakers. Organizations of employers were formed to oppose the growing power of labor.

Sometimes employers hired new workers who were not members of the union. They took over the jobs of workers who were on strike. Private police were sometimes hired by employers to ensure that the picketing strikers did not prevent other workers from entering the plant. A period of conflict and struggle, which sometimes turned violent, began between employers and labor.

Employers used other methods to fight the unions. They created **blacklists** containing the names of workers who were active in the labor unions. They sent these blacklists to other companies and asked them not to hire anyone whose name was listed.

Employers also found a way to fight labor slowdowns. They closed the factory and "locked out" the workers. **Lockouts** prevented workers from earning wages. With no income, workers were soon forced to agree to return to work as usual.

Closed and Open Shops

Early labor leaders quickly realized that unions needed money to succeed. To raise money, unions began to charge their members union dues, or fees. This money was used by the unions to pay their officials. During strikes or lockouts, it helped feed union members and their families.

To gather strength, the early labor unions tried to enroll every worker as a union member. It became the aim of the unions to establish a closed shop in every factory. In a **closed shop** workers cannot be hired unless they first become members of the union.

The employers opposed the closed shop. They did not want unions to have that much

(continued on page 390)

Illustrating Ideas

Have students draw flowcharts to illustrate important events in the history of the farmworkers' movement. Each event might be boxed, with an arrow leading to the next event. Students might begin with César Chávez's experiences growing up in a migrant family. Call on volunteers to present their flowcharts to the class.

Linking Civics and History

Have pairs of students research various aspects of the farmworkers' movement, such as the years before the 1960s; the cultural background of farmworkers; the nationwide lettuce boycott; the reasons why migrant labor is vital to the U.S. economy; the United Farm Workers union today; and the situation of migrant workers today. Students should prepare short oral reports, with helpful visual guides such as pictures or diagrams, to present to the class for discussion.

Throughout his many years as an activist for the rights of agricultural workers, César Chávez always pursued social change through nonviolent means. According to Chávez, he learned the principles of nonviolent social action from Martin Luther King, Jr., and India's Mohandas (Mahatma) Gandhi. Putting these principles into action, however, often took their toll on Chávez's health. In 1965, for example, Chávez underwent a 25-day fast to call worldwide attention to the plight of migrant farmworkers. He ended the fast only when Senator Robert F. Kennedy convinced him that he was more valuable alive than dead. In 1988 Chávez lived on nothing but water for 36 days to urge Americans to boycott grapes. Many people believe that these fasts and others that Chávez undertook may have contributed to his death in 1993 at the age of 66.

Case STUDY

FARMWORKERS UNITE

The life of migrant farmworkers is not an easy one. Migrant farmworkers are seasonal workers, traveling from city to city and state to state picking food crops as the crops come in season. There is no job security, wages are low, and conditions are often harsh.

During the 1960s, however, the efforts of one man helped agricultural workers in California join together to fight for better wages and working conditions and a better life. That man was César Chávez.

César Chávez dedicated himself to fighting for better working conditions for farmworkers. His efforts sparked a unionization movement among farmworkers in California in the early 1960s.

The Need for Unity

Mexican American César Chávez had first-hand experience with the rigors of life as a migrant farmworker. He grew up as the son of migrant workers, and he later toiled in the fields himself.

Through these experiences, Chávez learned that the living quarters provided by growers were crowded and of poor quality. High charges for room and board were taken out of already low wages. Hours under the hot sun were long, and few breaks were given. The farmworkers often had to sneak food into the fields because many growers did not allow them to eat while they worked. No sanitary facilities were provided in the fields, and often there was only one shared cup from which to drink water.

Although the need to move constantly kept Chávez from finishing school, he was a keen reader with a bright mind. He realized that the conditions under which the farmworkers were forced to live were unjust. Chávez therefore committed himself to fighting for better wages and better lives for the farmworkers. To do this, however, the farmworkers needed to organize a union.

A Union Forms

Chávez visited thousands of Mexican American farmworkers in the San Joaquin Valley of central California, urging them to join together to form a union. When the first meeting of the National Farm Workers Association was held on September 26, 1962, nearly 300 workers attended.

Interest in the association rose dramatically in 1965 when Filipino farmworkers went on strike, demanding higher wages from grape

Writing Creatively

Ask students to write the story of a day in the life of a migrant worker. Students might choose a setting and the type of crop being harvested. They might try to construct scenes that reflect the difficult life of farmworkers. Call on volunteers to present their stories to the class. Have the class discuss how the United Farm Workers union helps protect and support such individuals.

growers. (The Filipino workers had formed their own union.) The members of the National Farm Workers Association supported the strike. They picketed the grape growers, and they marched 300 miles (483 km) to California's state capital. Finally, the strikers won a contract with a large, important grower. A month later, the union of Mexican American farmworkers and the union of Filipino farmworkers joined together to form the United Farm Workers union.

This union dedicated itself to nonviolent forms of action, including strikes, work slowdowns, and protests. To persuade other grape growers to sign contracts, the union urged a nationwide boycott of grapes in 1965. Millions of Americans declared their solidarity with the union's cause by refusing to buy grapes. The boycott ended five years later when growers in the San Joaquin Valley agreed to a contract with the union.

Chávez strived to include all union members in working toward the goals of the United Farm Workers. He also studied management techniques and applied them to the union. His aim was to better spread the union's message of improving life for migrant farmworkers.

The Work Continues

At its peak, the United Farm Workers had more than 100,000 farmworkers in California working under collective-bargaining contracts. Although it has far fewer members today, the union continues its struggle to improve the lives of U.S. farmworkers. César Chávez died in 1993, but the union he helped create in the 1960s carries on his fight for justice.

In fact, Chávez's son-in-law, Arturo Rodriguez, has taken up the fight. Rodriguez's main goal is to increase the union's membership. Like his father-in-law, Rodriguez works long hours for little pay as the union's leader. He often stays in the homes of union members when he travels around the country on union business. In this and other ways Rodriguez remains close to the concerns of his fellow union members.

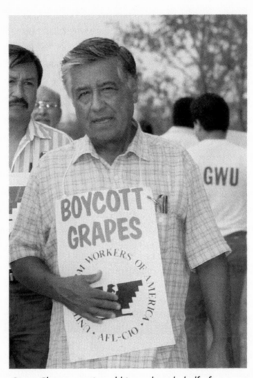

César Chávez continued his work on behalf of farmworkers for over two decades. He marched in hundreds of protests to support the causes of the United Farm Workers union.

YOU DECIDE

1 How did César Chávez know what the working conditions of migrant farmworkers were like?

2 How was the United Farm Workers union able to convince grape growers to sign a union contract?

3 Do you think unions have the right to hurt the livelihood of business owners and possibly the public's well-being by going on strike? Explain your answer.

GLOBAL PERSPECTIVES

The use of the boycott as a tool of social protest can be traced to late 19th-century Ireland. Charles Boycott, an English land agent in Ireland, refused to comply with demands by Irish tenant farmers that he lower their high rents. To retaliate, the farmers persuaded other businesspeople in the county to refuse to do business with Boycott. This plan was so successful that Boycott and his family eventually were forced to move away from the area. Afterward, refusing to do business with someone became known as "boycotting."

ANSWERS TO YOU DECIDE

1. He grew up as the son of migrant farmworkers and later worked as a migrant farmworker.

2. Farmworkers went on strike and picketed the growers.

3. Student opinions will vary, though students should consider the rights of both workers and employers.

Debating an Issue

Have half the class prepare arguments in favor of outlawing closed shops and the other half prepare arguments in favor of outlawing open shops. Then debate the issue informally, first by asking students to take turns reading their arguments aloud and then seeking counterarguments. Conclude by discussing how union shops and agency shops might be seen as compromise positions.

Writing a Newspaper Article

Invite students to imagine they are reporters for a foreign newspaper that covers events in the United States. Have them write an article to explain, in simple terms, the merging of the AFL and the CIO. Students should organize their article properly, with a headline, dateline, and summarizing opening paragraph. Call on volunteers to read their articles to the class. Have students take notes to use as review and study guides.

CIVICS SIDELIGHT

In 1981 U.S. air traffic controllers challenged the no-strike laws of the federal government and lost. President Ronald Reagan fired 11,400 members of PATCO, the Professional Air Traffic Controllers Organization, after they staged a nationwide walkout. Reagan justified his actions by pointing to regulations prohibiting government employees (such as air traffic controllers) from striking. Twelve years later, in 1993, the Clinton administration decided to lift the ban on the dismissed workers, allowing them to apply for employment again with the federal government. The move was seen by some observers as calculated to solidify organized labor's support behind the Democratic administration. The job openings for air traffic controllers, however, were few.

influence over hiring practices. They insisted on an open shop in every factory. In an **open shop** anyone can be hired. Workers do not have to be union members or join the union.

Much later a third type of shop was organized, the union shop. In a **union shop** an employer can hire any qualified worker, union or nonunion. Within a short period of time, however, new workers must join the union to keep their jobs.

Today there is also a fourth type of shop, called the agency shop. In an **agency shop** a worker cannot be forced to join the union, but he or she must pay union dues. The unions believe workers should help pay for the protection they receive from unions. If the union fights for higher pay and better conditions, nonmembers also benefit.

Many states have passed **right-to-work laws**. In these states no one may be forced to join a union. That is, only the open shop is legal. Union members as well as nonunion members may work in the same company.

The AFL Versus the CIO

Early unions were organized according to jobs or occupations. All members of the same skilled trade joined together in a craft union, or trade union. The carpenters throughout the nation, the plumbers, the bakers, and so on, each had their own union.

In 1886 some craft unions formed a large organization called the American Federation of Labor (AFL). Under the leadership of Samuel Gompers, the AFL grew into a powerful labor group. Each craft union in the AFL had its own officers and local branches around the nation. Each union worked to improve conditions for members in its own craft. These craft unions, however, joined with others in the AFL to strengthen their bargaining power.

As the nation's factories and businesses grew in size, some labor leaders argued that a new type of union should be formed. They believed unions should include unskilled workers as well as skilled craft workers. These leaders pointed out that modern mass

production methods had weakened the power of craft unions in the United States. They insisted that all workers in an industry, such as those in the steel, automobile, and coal mining industries, should be members of the same union, no matter what kind of jobs they had. This kind of union is an industrial union.

Industrial unions grew rapidly during the 1930s. Industry after industry—steel, automobile, electrical equipment, rubber—was organized by labor leaders. Led by Walter Reuther and others, the industrial unions lured members away from some of the craft unions. In 1938 the industrial unions formed one large organization called the Congress of Industrial Organizations (CIO).

Workers in many industries found it difficult to choose between the CIO and the AFL. The rivalry between the two large union organizations continued for many years. An agreement was finally reached in 1955 when the AFL and the CIO merged to form a single labor organization, the AFL-CIO.

Today the AFL-CIO is the largest U.S. labor group. It has a membership of more than 13 million workers. Not every union belongs to this large organization, however. Some large unions have decided to be independent.

Union Problems

Individual unions sometimes have problems with one another as well as with employers. For example, perhaps two unions want to organize the workers in the same company. In that case the unions compete to see which can get more workers to join. This may cause confusion on the part of the workers. They may even decide not to join either union.

Sometimes there are problems within a union. Many unions are called national unions because they have members in all parts of the nation. Even national unions, however, are divided into smaller groups called local unions. Sometimes the locals disagree with the national organization's leaders. They may think the national leaders are trying to control them or are not giving them enough support.

Recent Union Organization

During the 1960s the most successful attempts to organize workers took place among hospital workers and among migrant farm-workers. (See "Case Study: Farmworkers Unite" on pages 388–389.)

During the 1970s the labor movement also made gains among the people who work for the government. Despite laws that prohibit strikes by federal employees, many teachers, police, air traffic controllers, and other public workers have gone on strike.

In recent years unions have not grown as rapidly as in the past. Although nearly 108 million workers were in the workforce by 1994, only about 17 million belonged to unions. Thus, only about 16 percent of all workers are union members.

That the percentage of union members is small does not mean that U.S. labor unions are weak. Many major industries are unionized. Strikes in these industries can cause serious problems for the country.

Labor Laws

Over the years Congress has passed a number of laws dealing with labor-management relations. It has done so for several reasons. One reason is that Congress wants to protect the public. When workers go on strike, the whole country may suffer. For example, a strike by coal miners might cause a coal shortage in the nation. A strike by truck drivers might halt the delivery of some products.

Congress also has passed laws to prevent employers from using unfair practices in dealing with workers and to make unions act fairly in their disputes with employers. Congress has tried to stop dishonest actions by some union

GLOBAL PERSPECTIVES

Article 23 of the United Nations' *Universal Declaration of Human Rights* states: "Everyone has the right to form and to join trade unions for the protection of his interests." Many nations, such as Japan, have enacted labor laws to support this right. Japan's Trade Union Law, like the United States' National Labor Relations Act, guarantees the right of workers to organize and encourages collective bargaining. The Japanese constitution, which went into effect in 1947, includes provisions that directly protect trade-union activity. Among the provisions are those that affirm the right to strike; set standards for wages, hours, and working conditions; and bar the exploitation of children. Japan also established a Labor Relations Commission that helps settle disputes between labor and management.

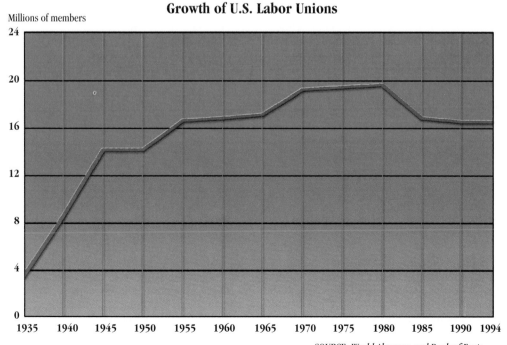

Growth of U.S. Labor Unions

Millions of members

SOURCE: *World Almanac and Book of Facts.*

Independent Practice

Have students draw political cartoons to illustrate a fictional confrontation between labor and management. Encourage students to focus on how a labor law affects the negotiations or how both sides reach a compromise. Students should write captions for their cartoons. Remind students that political cartoons rely on symbols to express information in a kind of shorthand. Invite volunteers to present and explain their cartoons to the class. Ask: How have the various labor laws affected relationships between labor and employers?

Closure

Review the information about collective bargaining today (pages 392–393). Then lead a discussion in which students identify qualities they believe an effective mediator or arbitrator should have and why. What issues must mediators and arbitrators deal with?

At one time the main issue in collective bargaining was how much of a raise union members would get. Beginning in the early 1980s, that changed. The issue often focused on how much the unions would give back to management in the form of reduced salaries and benefits in return for increased job security. In an era of cost-cutting and lay-offs, job security became the primary goal of many unions.

The largest labor organization in the United States is the National Education Association, a teachers union with more than 2 million members as of 1995. Following in size, all with more than a million members, are the International Brotherhood of Teamsters; the United Food and Commercial Workers International Union; the American Federation of State, County and Municipal Employees; and the Service Employees International Union.

leaders and to ensure that unions are run democratically. The following are some of the major labor laws passed by Congress.

National Labor Relations Act This law, usually called the Wagner Act, was passed by Congress in 1935. It guarantees the right of workers to organize and bargain collectively through representatives. The law also provides ways of settling disputes between labor unions and employers.

In addition, this act set up an independent government agency, the National Labor Relations Board (NLRB). The board judges the fairness of the activities of unions and employers toward each other. The NLRB also conducts elections within a company when a union wants to organize the workers. The workers vote to decide which union they want. They also can vote to have no union at all.

Labor-Management Relations Act This law, usually referred to as the Taft-Hartley Act, was passed in 1947. It revised the Wagner Act in several ways. The Taft-Hartley Act allows the president of the United States to order any union to delay a strike for 80 days when such a strike would threaten the national welfare. During this "cooling-off" period, a fact-finding commission may meet and recommend a settlement. At the end of the 80 days, the union may strike if no settlement is reached.

The Taft-Hartley Act also forbids the closed shop and condemns featherbedding. **Featherbedding** occurs when a union forces employers to hire more workers than are needed. In addition, the law enabled states to pass right-to-work laws.

Landrum-Griffin Act This law was passed in 1959 to prevent certain abuses by union officials. It prohibits convicted criminals from serving as union officials. It requires unions to file reports of their finances with the secretary of labor each year. The law also guarantees union members the right to a secret ballot in union elections and to freedom of speech in union meetings.

Labor Relations Today

As you have learned, employers and workers have struggled over the past 100 years, sometimes with the help of government, to work out new relationships. The attitudes of most union leaders and employers today are different from those of the past.

Modern union leaders realize that companies must make profits. If the union demands such high wages that a company goes out of business, jobs will be lost. Therefore, some modern unions help companies find new business opportunities or develop more efficient ways of operating.

Modern employers know that their workers must have good wages and working conditions. Well-paid workers are better able to buy the goods and services they produce. Some companies share a certain portion of the profits with their workers. Others allow workers to decide their work schedules or give them a voice in how the work is performed. Such actions make workers more satisfied with their jobs. They produce more goods, are absent less often, and feel more needed.

Collective Bargaining Today

Most disputes between employers and unions are settled peacefully through collective bargaining. Despite improved labor-management relations, however, strikes occur each year. In 1994, for example, the country's major league baseball players went on strike.

When a strike happens, both sides may suffer. Workers lose money during a strike because they are not receiving their wages. The company, too, loses money when it has to shut down because of a strike. Other people also are hurt by strikes. For example, during the baseball strike many small businesses located near the ballparks lost much of their business.

Often a strike will not be settled until both sides agree to compromise. That is, each side gives up some of its demands. The company may agree to give a greater wage increase than it originally offered. The union may agree to

Reviewing

Have students complete the Section 3 Review.

Reteaching

Assign Section 3 of the Chapter 20 Reteaching Worksheet.

Extension

Have students research and report to the class on organizations whose purpose it is to represent certain groups of people in nonlabor disputes. Examples include the American Association of Retired Persons (AARP) and the National Association for the Advancement of Colored People (NAACP). Have students discuss any similarities between tactics used by these associations in pursuit of their interests and those used by unions in labor disputes. Have the class discuss what role arbitration and compromise can play in areas other than labor disputes.

drop its demand for a seven-hour day and accept an eight-hour day. Thus, both sides will be able to feel that they have won.

Unions and employers prefer to settle their differences through collective bargaining. If they are unable to reach an agreement, however, they may call for help. A third party who is an expert on labor-management relations may be asked to examine both sides of the issue and recommend a solution. This method is called **mediation**. The recommendations of the mediator are not binding on either the union or the employer. Sometimes another method, called **arbitration**, is used instead. In these cases the decision of the arbitrator is binding on both sides.

When collective bargaining takes place today, both sides must consider ways to increase productivity and profits. The decisions of labor and management have a powerful influence on the nation's prosperity and on its future.

SECTION 3 REVIEW

1. Define or identify the following terms: labor union, collective bargaining, strike, picket, job action, blacklist, lockout, closed shop, open shop, union shop, agency shop, right-to-work law, featherbedding, mediation, arbitration.

2. Why did U.S. workers form labor unions during the 1800s?

3. What methods do labor unions use to persuade employers to agree to union demands? What methods did employers use in the early years of labor unions to fight the unions?

4. Why did labor unions support closed shops? Why did employers support open shops?

5. Why did the AFL and the CIO merge?

6. What law gives workers the right to organize and bargain collectively?

7. What has the federal government done to guarantee union members the right to speak freely in union meetings?

8. Why is compromise an important part of labor-management relations?

9. **THINKING CRITICALLY** Imagine that you head the nurse's union in a large urban hospital. You and the other nurses are unhappy with the level of your pay, but the hospital management refuses to increase your wages. If the nurses go on strike, there will not be enough workers to care for the patients in the hospital. Should you recommend a strike? Explain the reasoning behind your decision.

CHAPTER 20 SUMMARY

The U.S. economy is one of the most productive in the world. The free-enterprise system, however, faces several challenges.

During the business cycle the economy experiences a period of expansion, which may be accompanied by inflation. Following a peak, or high point, in economic growth, the economy slows and may enter a recession or depression. Many businesses fail and unemployment increases during a recession or a depression.

The hardships experienced during the Great Depression encouraged government to establish programs to help citizens and the economy. Since that time, government has expanded its role in the economy.

The economy also suffers when labor and management cannot settle their differences peacefully. The public can be hurt if a major strike prevents an industry from providing an important product or service. The government often tries to help settle labor-management disputes that will hurt the public. Most unions and companies, however, solve their problems on their own.

SECTION 3 REVIEW ANSWERS

1. See the following pages: labor union, collective bargaining, strike, picket, job action (p. 386); blacklist, lockout, closed shop (p. 387); open shop, union shop, agency shop, right-to-work law (p. 390); featherbedding (p. 392); mediation, arbitration (p. 393).

2. to gain strength for bargaining over wages and working conditions

3. labor—strikes, picketing, job actions; employers—hired new workers and private police, blacklisted activists, locked out strikers

4. to increase power of unions by making all workers join; employers sought to limit power of unions

5. ended years of rivalry and competition for members

6. National Labor Relations Act

7. Landrum–Griffin Act in 1959

8. allows both sides to feel that they have won something

9. Students should address the competing interests of all.

Help students distinguish between bar graphs (page 64) and line graphs by asking the following questions: Which type of graph is better for comparing quantities, or amounts? *(bar graph)* Which type is better for showing changes in data, such as prices, over time? *(line graph)*

Refer students to the Chapter 16 "Developing Civics Skills" activity (page 306) in which they tracked the total number of articles about juvenile crime listed each year in the *Readers' Guide to Periodical Literature.* Have students create line graphs that show the trend in the annual number of articles about juvenile crime over the period of time covered in that activity. Encourage students to be creative in designing their line graphs.

🌐 GLOBAL SKILL BUILDER

You might wish to use **Reading Graphs** and **Presenting Data Graphically** from the interactive *Global Skill Builder* CD-ROM to reinforce students' understanding of line graphs and other types of graphs.

. . . .

A N S W E R S   T O
Applying the Skill
. . . .

1. steep increases

2. 1978–1981, 1985–1986, 1988–1990

3. $1.20; a little more than 90¢

4. drivers, economists, policy makers; to help make decisions on purchases and financial and economic plans

5. The indicator line makes it easier to trace changes in price over time.

Developing Civics Skills

S O C I A L   S T U D I E S   S K I L L
Reading Line Graphs

Do you consider yourself a victim of inflation? Are the prices of the items you buy increasing? Many Americans answer "yes" to these questions.

Suppose you are tired of paying more for goods and services, and you want Congress to take action to curb inflation. How might you make this point to your representatives in Congress in a simple yet dramatic way? An excellent way would be to use a line graph. As you have learned, graphs help people understand data by placing large amounts of information in easy-to-read diagrams.

How to Read Line Graphs

1. **Determine the subject.** Read the title of the graph to determine its subject and purpose.
2. **Study the labels.** Line graphs usually have two labels. One label reads across the bottom of the graph. This label identifies the data on the horizontal axis. The other label appears above the line that runs up and down. This label identifies the data on the vertical axis of the graph.
3. **Examine the indicator line.** The purpose of a line graph is to show changes in amounts over time. It does so with an indicator line. By following the indicator line from left to right, you are following the amount indicated on the vertical axis through time. The period of time being studied is shown on the horizontal axis. In the line graph on this page, for example, the indicator line shows how the price of gasoline in the United States changed from 1978 to 1994.
4. **Put the data to use.** Use the graph to draw conclusions about the data. Identify any trends from the graph.

Applying the Skill

Study the line graph below. Then answer the following questions.

1. What was the trend in gasoline prices between 1978 and 1981?
2. During what years did the price of gasoline change most significantly?
3. What was the average price of a gallon of gasoline in 1985? What was the average price one year later?
4. Who might be interested in this graph's information? Why?
5. Why is a line graph better than a bar graph for showing this kind of data?

Gasoline Prices: 1978–1994

Average price per gallon

1978 1980 1982 1984 1986 1988 1990 1992 1994
Year

Have students answer the "Knowing Yourself" questionnaire created in the "Guided Practice" activity. Encourage students to be honest with themselves. Explain that interests and abilities change over time and ask students to consider what kinds of careers seem to be the best for them today. Have students create collages illustrating the kinds of careers they believe best suit them. Invite volunteers to discuss their collages with the class.

Have groups of students write four articles to submit to a fictional "Careers" magazine. Each article should focus on one of the following points: the importance of free choice, reasons for choosing certain careers, the importance of knowing oneself, and the kinds of skills and education employers want in employees. Each group member should focus on one of the topics. Have each group collect the articles and include them in its "magazine," which should include a cover and illustrations.

and your nation. A good education is certainly worth all of your efforts. As you learned in Chapter 14, your years of education pay off in hard cash. On average, the more years of schooling a person has, the higher his or her income. Education does not guarantee success, but it improves your chances for earning a higher income during your lifetime.

More important than money, though, is the satisfaction that comes from knowing you have given your best effort. Moreover, each person has the potential to make unique contributions to the world. Doing less than your best shortchanges everyone.

Some students find school difficult and drop out. Dropouts believe that when they quit school and go to work they will have a head start in earning money. Leaving school, however, is the worst thing to do if you are interested in a good income.

Although dropouts can begin to earn money sooner than students who remain in school, most dropouts earn low wages. They do not have the education, training, and skills needed for most of today's occupations and can obtain only the lowest-paying jobs.

Furthermore, dropouts often find themselves without work. With every year that passes, a person who does not finish high school will find it more difficult to earn a living. To make matters worse, many tasks that were once done by unskilled workers are now being done by machines.

The Kinds of Workers Employers Want

Employers want workers who have a good general education. If special training is needed for a position, it is sometimes given on the job. When hiring a secretary, for example, an employer wants someone who types well, has computer skills, and does neat work. The employer also seeks a person who can spell accurately, follow directions, and develop new skills. When hired, the secretary is not expected to know much about the company's products. Such things can be learned on the job.

The young man or woman who does well at a job builds on information and skills learned in school. For example, a young person hired as a clerk in a small grocery store may

These students are taking advantage of their high school's training program in electronics. The skills they are acquiring will help them find jobs after graduation.

Reviewing

Have students complete the Section 1 Review.

Reteaching

Assign Section 1 of the Chapter 21 Reteaching Worksheet.

Extension

Have students research the kinds of careers that were most common at different times in the country's history. Have students investigate the levels of education required for these jobs. Have students prepare oral reports and illustrations that help explain their findings to the class.

SECTION 1 REVIEW
A N S W E R S

1. allows people to choose careers that best suit their interests, abilities, intelligence, and desires

2. choices based on interests, personal values, talents, abilities, opportunities, rewards

3. more likely to make wise career choice if one knows own abilities, interests, skills, strengths, and weaknesses

4. A good education makes a worker more marketable, improves chances for earning higher income, and adds to personal satisfaction. Dropouts often must take low-paying jobs, have lifetime earnings that do not equal earnings of people who stay in school, and often are unemployed.

5. Students should make honest assessments of their strengths and weaknesses.

400

become the store manager if he or she has a good education and is able to solve practical problems. The employer knows that the clerk can learn how to manage the store while working. The best way, therefore, to prepare for your future job—no matter what it may be—is to learn everything you can in school.

Beginning Your Search

You may be asking yourself, "If business is changing so rapidly, how can I know what job to prepare for and what kind of education to seek?" Fortunately, you do not need to make your choice now. If you stay in school, you have several more years in which to study the possibilities before you choose.

The first thing you can do to prepare yourself is study various careers and understand the type of work each one involves. Then consider the personal qualities each career requires, such as originality or mechanical ability. Once you have done this, examine your own interests and abilities. Determine how well they fit with various careers.

Gradually, you will begin to focus on one career (or perhaps several) that may be best for you. When you have made your choice or choices, you will want to begin preparing for your career. The next four sections of this chapter will help you start thinking about the career that may be in your future.

SECTION 1 REVIEW

1. Why is freedom of career choice important?

2. What are some reasons that people choose various types of careers?

3. Why is getting to know yourself important in choosing a career?

4. Why should young people stay in school? What problems do school dropouts face?

GLOBAL CONNECTIONS

The Examination War in Japan

American students who work hard and achieve good grades usually are accepted into college. In Japan, however, colleges are open only to those students who can pass grueling entrance examinations.

These examinations are so competitive that most students spend their entire educational lives preparing for them. To win the "examination war," as it is called, Japanese students spend an average of 20 hours a week on homework. Many also take extra classes on weekends and during vacations and hire special tutors to help them study. Students who pass the examinations and are admitted into college are virtually assured future employment in Japan's largest corporations.

With such importance attached to them, the exams receive wide media attention in the country each year.

5. **THINKING CRITICALLY** Create a chart with four columns. In the first column list the rewards you hope your future career will bring. In the second and third columns, list your strengths and weaknesses. In the fourth column describe what you can do to overcome each weakness. Explain in a chart caption how using your strengths and overcoming your weaknesses will help you achieve the rewards you seek.

SECTION OBJECTIVES

After studying Section 2, students should be able to do the following.

1. Explain why professions require years of education and training.

2. Identify categories of workers.

3. Describe training needs of workers.

4. Identify future job prospects of groups of workers.

5. Explain why demand for laborers and agricultural workers has decreased over time.

Teaching Section 2
Building a Vocabulary

Help students deduce the meaning of **automation** by asking: On what word is this term based? *(from* automatic, *from the Greek* automatos, *meaning "self-acting")* Then ask students to explain another vocabulary term, *agribusiness*. *(merging of the words* agriculture *and* business) Ask: What does this merging suggest? *(farming as a big business)*

2 The World of Work

You are already familiar with many of the career opportunities in the nation. You have learned about jobs from your family and friends. Perhaps you have worked at part-time jobs. All these experiences have helped acquaint you with various fields of work. Now it is time to examine the world of work in a systematic way.

Hundreds of different occupations are available to workers in the United States. You will explore some of these occupations by examining four main categories of workers: white-collar workers, blue-collar workers, service workers, and agricultural workers.

White-Collar Workers

The largest group of workers in the nation today is made up of white-collar workers. **White-collar workers** are those people who are in the professions or who perform technical, managerial, sales, or administrative support work.

Professionals Jobs that require many years of education and training, and in which the work tends to be mental rather than physical, are referred to as professions. Examples of **professionals** include doctors, nurses, lawyers, architects, and teachers.

In the field of science, professional workers include chemists, biologists, botanists, geologists, and many other specialists. In the business world, professionals include accountants, economists, computer programmers, and engineers. Among the professionals in the arts are writers, painters, conductors, composers, and entertainers.

As the economy has changed and grown, the demand for professional workers also has increased. Among today's fastest growing career fields are those in the computer and health-care professions.

Technicians The jobs performed by **technicians** require some specialized skill in addition to a solid, basic education. Among these skilled workers are medical laboratory technicians, medical X-ray technicians, physical therapists, and dental hygienists. Other technicians are employed in radio and television, the film industry, manufacturing, and computer industries.

A high school education is the foundation on which the technician builds. Some technicians learn their skills on the job. Most take special courses in colleges or in technical or vocational schools.

Managers, Administrators, and Executives As you know, the people in charge of large businesses and corporations are managers and administrators. They also are called executives because they execute, or carry out, the operations of a business.

U.S. businesses are experiencing stiff competition from other nations of the world. If the United States is to remain competitive in the

Advances in computer technology in recent years have changed the way many offices operate.

MULTICULTURAL PERSPECTIVES

The percentage of managers, administrators, and executives who are African Americans rose from 4.7 percent to 6.8 percent between 1983 and 1994. During the same period the percentage of Hispanic Americans in those positions rose from 2.8 percent to 4.9 percent. Both figures represent progress, though they lag behind the percentage of African Americans (12.5 percent) and Hispanic Americans (10 percent) in the total U.S. population in 1994. Women also have made gains in management, occupying 43 percent of such jobs in 1994, up from 32.4 percent in 1983.

Have pairs of students construct charts that compare and contrast different categories of workers. Column headings should be "White-Collar Workers," "Blue-Collar Workers," "Service Workers," and "Agricultural Workers." Students should list examples of jobs, typical education and training requirements, and any other distinguishing features of the workers in each category. Call on volunteers to discuss their charts with the class. Students should save their charts for use as study guides.

On the chalkboard draw figures representing the different kinds of careers discussed in this section. Next to each figure, have volunteers come to the board to write past job opportunities for each of these careers. Then have other volunteers write future job prospects for each of these careers. Have the class discuss why various future job prospects are brighter than others.

CIVICS SIDELIGHT

The U.S. Bureau of Labor Statistics has predicted the number of retail sales jobs is expected to increase by almost 25 percent between 1990 and 2005. Sales work, depending on the type of selling involved, can be among the lowest paying jobs or among the most lucrative. In either case, selling is a skill that is always in demand. After all, nearly every product or service must be sold in order to move it from producer to consumer. And some products are sold more than once. Traditionally, the people who climbed the "corporate ladder" most quickly were those in the sales force. Today sales skills are still important to the nation's top executives. Even the president of the United States—the chief executive—must be able to "sell" policies and programs to the American people. Ronald Reagan, for example, honed his persuasive skills as a spokesperson for General Electric during his television career.

global economy, U.S. businesses must have experienced, well-educated, and well-trained managers and executives. Businesses build on the ideas and skills of these individuals.

The owners of U.S. businesses know that their success depends on good management. They work hard to hire, train, and develop managers. Intelligent, hardworking executives are needed as heads of departments, branch offices, research divisions, and special projects. Government, too, needs executives to keep the nation's affairs running smoothly. In every

This woman is employed as a plumber. Her work requires skills developed through observation, training, and practice.

community there are many opportunities for those people who wish to manage and run small businesses.

A person with executive ability has a good chance for success in a free economy. Special training is needed, however, if one is to become a successful executive. Today many top executives are college graduates who studied management in university or college business schools. Large businesses often have their own executive training programs.

Many managers and executives are self-employed workers. They prefer to work for themselves. They take risks and hope to profit from their own efforts. Self-employed workers are often owners of small businesses, builders, or contractors.

Managers and executives, however, are not the only people who are self-employed. Many professionals, such as doctors, dentists, and lawyers, work for themselves. This is true for many writers, painters, musicians, and other kinds of workers as well.

Administrative Support and Sales Workers Bookkeepers, secretaries, office clerks, and word processors are examples of administrative support workers. They do much of the paperwork required to keep U.S. businesses and industries operating smoothly. According to the Bureau of Labor Statistics, the United States will need many more of these workers in the years ahead.

People who sell goods and services are sales workers. Sales workers may be clerks in retail stores. They may sell from door to door. They also may sell to other businesses, to institutions, or to governments.

Sales workers are much in demand. The skills these workers need do not require long periods of training and may be learned by intelligent, hardworking individuals. Many receive their training on the job. Other sales workers, such as real estate agents, insurance agents, and specialized sales representatives, often have college educations. Some workers are required to take special courses and pass state examinations.

Have students create editorial cartoons that portray the job prospects in various careers. Some students might want to illustrate in some way the expanding opportunities in some fields and the declining opportunities in others. Other students might want to portray the popularity of some careers and the skills required for work in those fields. Call on volunteers to explain their cartoons to the class. Ask: What kinds of options do workers have if they find themselves in a career with declining job prospects?

Have students evaluate how this section's breakdown of occupations into categories has helped clarify the world of work for them. Call on volunteers to come to the board to list one advantage or one disadvantage of careers in white-collar, blue-collar, service, or agricultural fields. Have students discuss what kind of work appeals to them.

Blue-Collar Workers

Workers who perform jobs that require manual labor are known as **blue-collar workers**. They work in construction, steel, petroleum, transportation, manufacturing, mining, and many other industries. Over the past decade, the percentage of blue-collar workers in the United States has decreased.

Craft Workers People who work in trades or handicrafts are craft workers. They include carpenters, electricians, machinists, bricklayers, plumbers, printers, bakers, auto mechanics, painters, shoemakers, and construction workers.

The most important requirement for workers in crafts, or trades, is manual ability. That is, they must be able to do accurate and sometimes difficult work with their hands. They must also be good at practical mathematics. In some cases they must have great physical strength to do parts of their jobs.

To train for a craft, the new worker usually serves an **apprenticeship**, or fixed period of on-the-job training. An apprentice receives an income while learning. The length of on-the-job training varies according to the job. Some industries and unions reduce the amount of apprenticeship time by giving credit for job training courses completed in high school or trade school.

When apprentices have learned their craft to a certain level, they receive a certificate of completion of apprenticeship. After gaining some job experience, these people may become master craft workers and receive the highest wages in their trade.

Each craft has its own labor union. The number of people admitted into the crafts each year is limited by union rules, the needs of the industry, and the available supply of trained workers. Some craft workers, such as plumbers and electricians, must pass state examinations and receive licenses to practice their crafts.

The future holds many opportunities for young people who can work with their hands as well as their heads and who can become skilled in the crafts. In the past, craft jobs were held almost entirely by men. Women now work in almost all trades.

Operators People who operate machines or equipment in factories, mills, industrial plants, gas stations, mines, and laundries are called **operators**. Other factory workers, such as those who inspect, assemble, and package goods, are included in this group. Drivers of trucks and buses also are operators.

Many operators receive their training on the job. Their work usually does not require long periods of training because they often repeat the same task many times. The qualities employers look for in an operator are dependability, good health, and some manual skill. Because a job does not require long periods of training does not mean that everyone can handle it. A good truck driver gains skill only after many years. This skill comes with practice, good judgment, and good health.

Some operators face an uncertain future. The number of machine operators in U.S. industry has declined as factories have come to rely more on **automation**, or the use of machines instead of workers to provide goods and services. This trend will likely continue.

Laborers There are and probably always will be jobs calling for little or no training. Workers without special skills are often employed to mix cement, carry bricks, dig ditches, and handle freight and other heavy loads. Workers who perform this type of heavy physical work are called **laborers**.

The demand for laborers, however, will grow more slowly than the demand for other types of workers in the years ahead. Automation increasingly is replacing muscle power. More and more, machines are used to mix cement, dig ditches, load freight, and do many other jobs requiring heavy manual labor.

Service Workers

Today one of every seven employed Americans is a service worker. Service workers provide the

GLOBAL PERSPECTIVES

Economists can learn a great deal about a country by analyzing the proportion of the population working in various fields. In the United States, an industrially developed country, just one out of 28 employed Americans worked in agriculture, forestry, or fishing. This proportion is similar to other industrialized countries, such as Austria, where about one out of every 15 workers worked in these fields in 1993. In many nonindustrialized or industrializing countries, the proportion of workers working in these fields is much higher. For example, in Thailand in 1991, more than 60 percent of employed people worked in agriculture, forestry, or fishing. In Pakistan in 1994, nearly half of the workforce was engaged in this kind of work. And in Burma (Myanmar), slightly less than 70 percent of workers were employed in agriculture, forestry, or fishing.

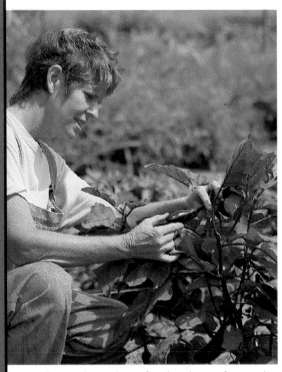

SECTION 2 REVIEW
A N S W E R S

1. See the following pages:
   white-collar worker, professional, technician (p. 401);
   blue-collar worker, apprenticeship, operator, automation, laborer (p. 403); service
   industry, agribusiness
   (p. 404).

2. mental; technicians; service
   workers

3. administrative support
   workers

4. apprenticeship, followed by
   some years of job experience

5. 60 percent

6. Automation increasingly is
   replacing muscle power.
   Agribusinesses rely heavily
   on mechanized equipment
   and can produce larger
   yields with fewer workers.

7. Students might say such a
   workforce is more productive,
   creative, and innovative.
   Also, such a workforce is
   more easily retrained as technology advances.

SECTION OBJECTIVES

After studying Section 3, students should be able to do the following.

1. Identify the nation's largest employer and explain how to get a job with this employer.
2. Identify the qualifications required for entry into officer-training school.
3. Explain the phrase "an equal opportunity employer."
4. Explain why women are being urged to train for scientific and technical jobs.

make up nearly 60 percent of the workers in service occupations.

Agricultural Workers

The need for agricultural workers has decreased greatly during this century. Agricultural workers are people who operate, manage, or work on farms. The need for such workers has declined as many small family farms have been replaced by large farms known as **agribusinesses**. Agribusinesses are owned by corporations and rely heavily on mechanized equipment. They are able to produce larger yields using fewer workers.

There is always plenty of work to do on a farm. In this vegetable field, for example, many farmworkers are needed at harvest time.

public with some type of needed assistance. For example, some service workers provide protection services. In this group are firefighters, police officers, correctional institution officers, and security guards. Other service workers provide health services. Among these workers are paramedics, dental and nursing assistants, and orderlies.

Service workers are employed by many kinds of firms. Business firms that sell services rather than products are called **service industries**. They include hospitals, security companies, hotels, restaurants, dry cleaners, laundries, barbershops, and hair salons.

Some service-industry jobs require a college education or training courses. Others teach needed skills on the job. Women today

SECTION 2 REVIEW

1. Define or identify the following terms: white-collar worker, professional, technician, blue-collar worker, apprenticeship, operator, automation, laborer, service industry, agribusiness.

2. Do professions require mainly mental or physical work? What category of workers includes physical therapists and dental hygienists? What category includes firefighters and police officers?

3. What group of workers performs much of the paperwork of business and industry?

4. What training must workers receive to become master craft workers?

5. What percentage of the workers in service occupations are women?

6. Why has the demand for laborers and agricultural workers decreased?

7. **THINKING CRITICALLY** Explain why having a well-educated, well-trained workforce is crucial to helping U.S. businesses remain competitive in the global economy.

Remind students that *civil* comes from a Latin word meaning "citizen." "Civil service," therefore, means "service of citizens." A **civil service examination** is a test to qualify for most federal jobs. Ask students for a term that describes who works in such federal jobs. *(civil servants)*

Have pairs of students identify specific needs student government could meet by creating "student service" agencies. Have each pair prepare job descriptions for necessary jobs in the "student service" and prepare a "student service examination" to give to applicants. Have students present their job descriptions and "student service examinations" to the class for discussion.

3 — Opportunities Unlimited

Whether a person is a professional, technician, craft worker, service worker, or laborer, there are opportunities for advancement. For example, young men and women who complete a high school trade or technical course might start their careers as word processors, clerks, or bookkeepers. By attending night school, they may qualify for better paying positions.

They might study accounting, for example, and learn to keep business financial records. Skilled accountants are needed by management as part of a business team. If young men and women are prepared, they will be ready when the right opportunity arises.

Government Jobs

The nation's largest employer is the U.S. government. More than three million Americans work for the federal government, not including those men and women who serve in the armed forces. Federal employees perform a wide range of jobs.

Some workers deliver the mail, care for war veterans, or protect against counterfeiting. Others run the national parks, forecast the weather, or inspect food and medicines to make sure they are pure. Many thousands of clerks, word processors, and secretaries are also needed to carry out the everyday business of the federal government.

Applicants must take a test to qualify for most federal jobs. These tests are called **civil service examinations**. The procedures for taking the tests are announced when government job openings are available. People who receive the highest test scores on the examinations usually fill the job openings.

State and local governments also employ many different kinds of workers. Like federal employees, state and local workers usually are

(continued on page 408)

CIVICS SIDELIGHT

Filling a position in the federal bureaucracy can seem quite complex to some people. For example, if more than three people are eligible for any civil service job opening, the three who have scored highest on the examination will be considered first. This principle is known as the "rule-of-three." The highest scoring applicant will not necessarily get the job, but one of those three most likely will. Of those three, a veteran of the armed services who scores higher on the test than a nonveteran must receive preference. Although rare, the hiring agency can reject, with documented justification, all three candidates and ask to interview the next three eligible people.

CIVICS TRANSPARENCIES

An overhead transparency of "Job Opportunities Today and Tomorrow" is available in *Teaching Transparencies with Teacher's Notes.*

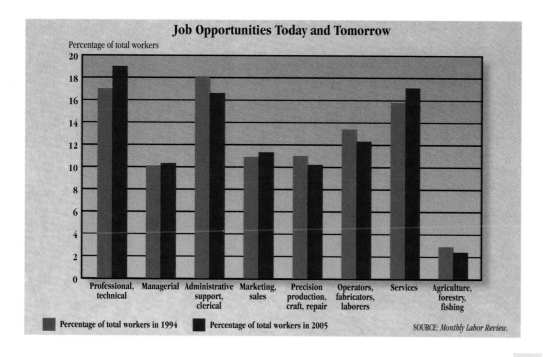

Job Opportunities Today and Tomorrow

Percentage of total workers

Categories: Professional, technical; Managerial; Administrative support, clerical; Marketing, sales; Precision production, craft, repair; Operators, fabricators, laborers; Services; Agriculture, forestry, fishing

■ Percentage of total workers in 1994   ■ Percentage of total workers in 2005

SOURCE: *Monthly Labor Review.*

Summarizing

Have students practice summarizing several paragraphs of information. For this feature, ask students to write a short summary for each of the three individuals described in the feature. Call on volunteers to read their summaries aloud. Have the class discuss which summaries most efficiently provide the necessary information. Have students discuss the value of summaries as study tools.

Citizenship IN ACTION   A JUMP ON CAREERS

Would you know how to make a monkey take its medicine, or how to interest a six-year-old in the alphabet? Could you run a television news show? Each of these tasks requires special talents—ones that could help you choose a career someday.

Janice Buhl, Cassandra Cole, and Mark Shichtman began their career search even before finishing high school. Janice worked in a zoo. Cassandra ran a school on her back porch. Mark started his own news show on cable television. Each of them learned the skilled mentioned above—and much more.

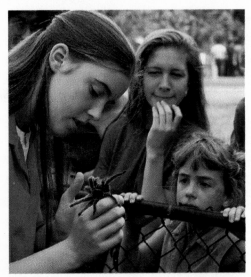

What skills would be useful in working at a zoo? What might you learn by working there?

Working at the Zoo

The high school in Hawaii that Janice Buhl attended offered a special class in zoo work. Janice, who has a strong interest in animals, signed up for the course. It required one class a week at the school and two mornings a week at the city zoo.

Janice was amazed at the variety of jobs in a zoo. One of her jobs was to escort tour groups through the zoo. Her work taught her about many kinds of animals. She had to learn enough information to tell the groups about the animals and to be able to answer any questions they might ask.

After she graduated from school, Janice took a part-time job at the zoo. She helped feed the animals and clean their cages. She also helped treat sick animals.

One of Janice's biggest problems was figuring out how to give the animals their medicine. Then she learned to use animals' eating habits. For example, many animals retain their appetites unless they are very sick. One monkey, she remembers, "always ate as if it were starving. When it became sick, I put a pill in a banana, and the monkey was in such a hurry to eat that it never noticed the medicine."

Janice learned a lot about zoos and animals. She learned, too, that she wanted to make working with animals her career.

Seeing Relationships

Tell students that without even trying, they have acquired many skills that will help them in a career. Have students think about the skills required, for example, in playing a team sport *(communication, physical endurance)* or painting a picture *(manual dexterity, organization, planning)*. Have students create newspaper want ads for various jobs, complete with descriptions of the skills and interests required for applicants. Call on volunteers to present their advertisements to the class for discussion.

Reporting the News

Appearing on television became routine for Mark Shichtman. His show—*Kids News*—appeared every Thursday afternoon. It was seen in thousands of homes in New York City.

Mark became a TV news reporter when he was in the fifth grade. He approached a cable television company with the idea for a news program by and for young people. The company agreed, and soon Mark and several friends were on television.

Kids News reported on a wide range of events. Mark and the rest of the team gathered most of their stories from newspapers or from other TV news shows. They covered local, national, and international news, as well as weather and sports. Modern camera and videotape equipment now makes it possible for students to film stories as they happen. As Mark knows, news gathering and reporting is an up-to-date job.

A School of Her Own

Cassandra Cole knew at the age of 12 that she wanted to teach, so she opened her own summer school on the porch of her home in Chicago, Illinois. She gathered materials to use in the school, signed up some students, and went to work. Her goal was to help younger children do well during the regular school year. Cassandra's teenage cousin helped her teach.

The classes were held from 12:30 to 3:00 on weekday afternoons. A typical class began with the Pledge of Allegiance. The first subject was reading, followed by spelling. After a break, the students studied mathematics. The afternoon ended with a short game. After receiving their homework assignments, the students helped clean up.

Cassandra's own teachers praised her drive and leadership skills. Her summer school was covered in newspapers and magazines, and the class appeared on a local television program. What did Cassandra think about her success? She said that someday she would like to have her own nursery school.

These students are learning firsthand what it is like to report the news.

YOU DECIDE

1 What talents might a person need to work in a zoo?

2 What tasks might be involved in producing a local weekly television news program?

3 What do you think Cassandra and her cousin learned from their teaching experience?

4 What are your special interests? What careers might be well-suited to these interests?

Organize the class into small groups. Assign each group one of the following goals: to work for the U.S. government in civil service; to join the armed forces; to enter an officer training school. Have each group design and produce a brochure that explains how to achieve its goal. Individual roles might include researcher, recording secretary, writer, and illustrator. After groups have presented their projects, store the brochures in a "Career Folder" to which students can refer as needed.

Guided Practice

Review the meaning of the phrase "an equal opportunity employer." Ask students what this phrase means about an employer. *(Such employers provide equal opportunities for jobs to all applicants.)* Obtain an equal opportunity statement from a local employer or government employment office and read it to the class. Have students identify specific groups of people protected from discrimination. Ask: What agency upholds fair employment standards? *(Equal Employment Opportunity Commission [EEOC])*

CIVICS SIDELIGHT

Not surprisingly, some people tend to remain employed in some occupations and with some employers for longer periods of time than others. For example, barbers on average stay in their occupations for 27.2 years and with one particular employer for 11 years. Other jobs with long average occupational tenures: farmers, 21.8 years; locomotive operators, 19.8 years; veterinarians, 14 years; musicians and composers, 15.2 years; airplane pilots and navigators, 12.2 years; and secondary school teachers, 14.1 years.

chosen on the basis of their civil service examination scores. Notices of job openings in federal, state, and local governments are sent to school counselors. You also may see these notices on U.S. post office bulletin boards or in local newspapers.

The Armed Forces

Although the federal government has reduced the number of military personnel in the nation over the past few years, many opportunities

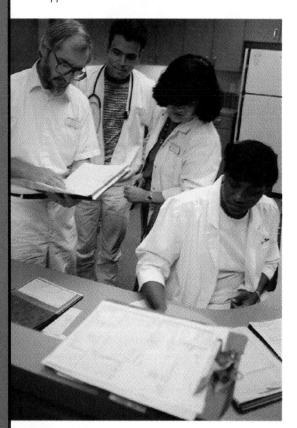

Nurses make an invaluable contribution to the quality of medical care in the United States. Nursing provides opportunities for men and women alike.

still remain in the armed forces. A high school diploma is required for most good jobs in the armed forces.

Training in the military is available for jobs such as electronics technician, radar operator and technician, medical equipment technician, motor mechanic, and surveyor. In addition, some combat aircraft and combat ship positions recently have been opened to women in the armed forces.

As you know, the United States has four officer training schools. To qualify for the Army, Navy, Air Force, or Coast Guard academies, you must be a high school graduate. Applicants must be recommended by their U.S. senator or representative. They must also pass scholastic and physical tests.

Workers in Demand

The U.S. Department of Labor constantly studies jobs and job opportunities. Each year it reports where men and women are working and what jobs they are performing. It also determines which jobs will need more workers in the coming years.

The following list includes those jobs that are expected to have the largest growth in the United States over the next decade. As you can see, the health-care and computer fields in particular will need many more workers in the years to come.

Home health aides
Human services workers
Personal and home care aides
Computer engineers and scientists
Systems analysts
Special education teachers
Medical assistants
Correction officers
Child care workers
Radiologic technologists
Legal secretaries
Preschool and kindergarten teachers
Guards
Amusement and recreation
    attendants

Some kinds of workers, too, are almost always in demand. For example, law enforcement officers and teachers are always needed. Keep in mind that the need for a particular type of worker may be greater in some parts of the nation than in others. Also remember that in all jobs there is a constant turnover because of promotions, job changes, or retirements. These events almost always create job openings. The well-prepared person will be ready to seize opportunities when they happen.

Equal Employment Opportunity

In your study of career opportunities, you may have noticed in newspaper classified advertisements the phrase "an equal opportunity employer." This phrase means that the employer does not discriminate against job applicants because of their sex, age, race, skin color, religion, or ethnic background.

Congress passed the Civil Rights Acts of 1964 and 1968 to help end discrimination in hiring and in wage rates. (See page 560.) These acts have created new job opportunities for women and members of minority groups. The Equal Employment Opportunity Commission, appointed by the president, upholds fair employment standards. Most states have similar commissions.

The struggle by women for equal rights has opened many doors. Today women are members of Congress, judges, doctors, scientists, engineers, pilots, and cab drivers. In industry, distinctions between women's and men's jobs are lessening.

U.S. businesses are urging women to study for scientific and technical jobs that once were open only to men. The Women's Bureau of the Department of Labor predicts that the nation's future needs for technical and scientific workers cannot be met unless more women enter these fields.

Likewise, fields traditionally dominated by women are now opening their doors to men. The nursing profession is a field in which

In the early days of computers, the people who worked with them were mostly men. Today women are entering computer fields in growing numbers.

men as well as women are urgently needed. Many men are lending their talents to kindergarten and elementary school teaching. Also, more men are finding job satisfaction as secretaries and word processors.

Unemployment

As you read in Chapter 20, there are times when the U.S. economy experiences a recession or depression. During such times many people are without work. Others are working but cannot find jobs in their chosen fields or are working only part-time.

The young person studying careers should remember that there have always been periods of unemployment. It is wise to have more than one interest and if possible to develop skills in more than one area of work.

After studying Section 4, students should be able to do the following.

1. Explain how to find information about careers.

2. Describe how part-time jobs and hobbies play a role in choosing a career.

3. Explain why it is important to ask yourself questions when considering possible careers.

Have students offer definitions of *salary* and then **salary range**. Tell students that the word *salary* comes from the Latin word *salarium*, which means "salt money." Ancient Roman soldiers received special salt rations as part of their wages. From this practice came the saying "not worth his salt," meaning that a soldier was not earning his pay.

SECTION 3 REVIEW
A N S W E R S

1. See the following page: civil service examination (p. 405).

2. U.S. government; take civil service examination

3. high school diploma, recommendation from U.S. senator or representative, successful completion of scholastic and physical tests

4. The employer does not discriminate against job applicants because of sex, age, race, skin color, religion, or ethnic background.

5. The nation's future needs in these fields cannot be met unless more women enter these careers.

6. Students might point to advances in technology that are quickly computerizing the world. Also, more workers will be needed in health care because of an aging population and advances in the health industry.

SECTION 3 REVIEW

1. Identify the following term: civil service examination.

2. Who is the nation's largest employer? What must people do to get jobs with this employer?

3. What are the qualifications for entry into an officer training school?

4. What does the phrase "an equal opportunity employer" mean?

5. Why are women being urged to study for scientific and technical jobs?

6. **THINKING CRITICALLY** As you know, the U.S. Bureau of Labor Statistics expects that the health-care and computer fields will need many more workers in the years to come. What do you think accounts for the fact that these two fields in particular are expected to experience large growth?

4 Learning More About Careers

You are probably discovering that you already know a great deal about careers and jobs. In your earlier studies you often have read about the careers of well-known men and women. No single book, however, not even one on careers, can give you all the information you need about various jobs. You may have to spend time looking in many places to find the facts you need to choose a career.

Reading About Careers

One of the best ways to learn about careers is to read the many available books, magazines, and pamphlets on the subject. Explore your library, newsstands, and any literature you may have at home. Your local state employment office has a number of booklets about careers in your community. Usually these booklets may be obtained free of charge. Because large business firms are always looking for good employees, many of them publish brochures that contain useful job information.

Another source of information about jobs is the U.S. Department of Labor. It publishes the *Occupational Outlook Handbook*, an important reference for job seekers. Also helpful is the *Encyclopedia of Careers and Vocational Guidance*.

Reading about career opportunities to find a career that interests you is like doing detective work. One clue leads to another. You may find a clue in a novel or biography. You may find another bit of evidence in a newspaper column or magazine article. You are acting as a detective in solving the challenge of planning your career.

As you read about jobs, of course, you must remember your own interests, needs, and abilities. You should also try to keep an open mind. You may discover a career you never thought about before.

Watching Others at Work

You will learn a great deal about careers by investigating job opportunities in your community. Through school-sponsored trips, you can find out about the jobs available in nearby factories, offices, and stores. Someone in your family may be able to arrange for you to visit his or her place of employment. You can also learn about jobs as you go about your daily affairs. Observe the work of bus drivers, police officers, teachers, salespeople, office workers, and others you meet each day.

You will gain more from watching people at work if you go about it in a carefully planned manner. Take notes on what you learn. Ask questions. Interview people who are working at jobs that interest you. Ask them what they like best and what they like least

Drawing a Flyer

Invite students to imagine each is the person in charge of next month's Career Day presentation at a local gathering place, such as a mall. The title of the presentation will be "Searching for Career Clues." Have students create flyers advertising the presentation. Flyers should briefly list sources of information about jobs and careers. They should also include the location, date, and time of the presentation. Display the flyers for the class to discuss.

Organize the class into small groups. Have each group write a fictional story about someone who turned a hobby into a successful career. Invite students to read their stories to the class. Assign each student a role, such as group leader, recording secretary, writer, and storyteller. One group member should provide illustrations, such as sketches or photographs, for the story.

Here are just four of the hundreds of careers you might choose—telemarketer, park ranger, botanist, stock trader. What kinds of work does each job involve? What kinds of skills does each require?

Photo Caption Answer

Encourage students to study the photographs for clues to the many kinds of work and skills each job requires.

GLOBAL PERSPECTIVES

Women in the United States are fortunate in that they are free to pursue any career that interests them. Although many countries around the world restrict female employment, this situation appears to be changing somewhat. In Saudi Arabia, for example, women must receive written permission from men to travel and are forbidden to drive or show their faces in public. However, the number of Saudi Arabian businesswomen registered with the Chamber of Commerce as working in the capital, Riyadh, has increased 500 percent in the past five years. In addition, Bangladesh now reserves 10 percent of all high-level civil service jobs for women, and Pakistan reserves 5 percent of government jobs for women. Even though women around the world have made some strides in the workplace, in a worldwide average women earn 30 to 40 percent less than men for the same work.

about their work. Talk about jobs with your family, friends, and counselors. Discussing your thoughts with others will help make ideas clearer in your own mind.

Learning by Working

Another good way to discover more about careers is to work at a job. For many students, responsibilities at home make having a job impossible. Some students, though, have enough time to work at part-time or summer jobs. You can learn something from any job. (See "Citizenship in Action: A Jump on Careers" on pages 406–407.)

Baby-sitting, for example, may lead you to think about a future job in child care. If not, it will at least allow you to learn more about people. Baby-sitting also can teach you why being prompt, responsible, and dependable is important in any job. Being a newspaper carrier, supermarket clerk, gasoline station attendant, or movie usher are other ways you can learn about work.

Review the job questions beginning on this page. Ask students why it is helpful to have a list of specific questions when considering a career. *(The answers to the questions give a job seeker concrete data with which to analyze the job.)* Have students suggest similar questions that might be helpful in deciding whether or not to participate in an extracurricular activity or to pursue a certain hobby. Have the class discuss similarities in the decision-making processes of choosing activities and careers.

Ask students to choose any career they wish to research. Then have them consult reference books, as well as friends and relatives, to answer a "job quiz" they develop based on the seven main job questions about that career. Encourage students to share their findings so the class can assemble a careers booklet as a classroom resource.

CIVICS SIDELIGHT

The best way to learn a job skill is to work at the job. This can present a problem, however. It is the classic complaint of a young job seeker—the "Catch-22" of employment: "How can I get a job where they want experience when I need a job to get experience?" Apprenticeship in a craft trade is one way to get around this dilemma. Another kind of on-the-job training is called internship. Medical doctors serve a period of internships as part of their residency requirement, for example. Law students often intern as law clerks. Budding politicians often gain experience by working as interns on the staffs of elected officials. You might have students research the opportunities for internships in various careers.

Do not overlook hobbies as a means of finding out what you like to do and can do well. Many people have turned their hobbies into their life's work. Hobbies may help you determine whether you have special talents. You can then begin to think about jobs that require similar abilities.

Another good way to explore your abilities is to take an active interest in school life. Try writing for the school newspaper. Manage a sports team. Serve on a class committee. Help decorate for school dances. Sell tickets for local events. These and other activities will tell you whether you enjoy writing, managing, selling, decorating, or some other skill that might be useful later in a job.

Questions to Ask Yourself

As you consider your future career, you can avoid some guesswork if you ask yourself the following questions. Your answers will help reveal if you are making a wise choice.

1. *What kind of work will I do in this job?* Will I be working alone or with other people? Will I be working mostly with my hands or with my mind? What skills will I need to develop to perform the job well? Does the job involve a great deal of study and careful planning, or does it involve repeating the same task?

2. *What personal qualities does the job require?* How important in this job are neatness, promptness, dependability, and a pleasant personality? Must I be able to follow directions? Will I be expected to give directions and to lead others? Does the job call for physical strength?

3. *How much education and training does the job require?* Must I be a college graduate? Is a graduate school degree necessary? Is any specialized training required?

Working on a school newspaper is a hobby for these students now. If they like the work, they may choose careers in the news field.

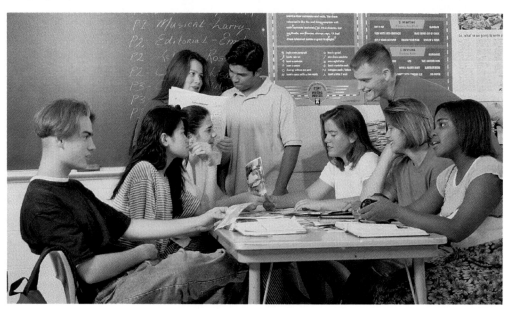

Closure

Seek students' concerns about the variety of jobs open to them and about the availability of these jobs. Discuss the advantages of the enormous number of careers open to young people today. Have small groups plan a Career Day for your school. Each group should decide what kinds of careers will be represented and what kinds of presentations will be offered. Students should develop a program of events they believe will make a successful Career Day. Possible presentations might be "Choosing a Career" and "Learning to Ask the Right Questions."

Reviewing

Have students complete the Section 4 Review.

Reteaching

Assign Section 4 of the Chapter 21 Reteaching Worksheet.

Is a period of apprenticeship needed? If so, how long does it last?

4. *What are the job opportunities in this field?* Are there many openings in this field now? Is this a growing field of work? Will there be more openings when I am ready to look for a job? Is this the kind of career in which I can develop my abilities and move ahead?

5. *What salary does the job pay?* Is the starting salary only the first step toward a higher income? What training must I have to receive salary increases? Will I be satisfied with the **salary range** (beginning salary, possible raises, and highest salary) that the work offers? What other benefits, such as insurance, sick pay, retirement benefits, and pleasant working conditions, are available?

6. *How do I feel about this job?* Do I believe this is a job worth doing? Will I be making a contribution to the community? Will I be happy with the kinds of people who may be working with me?

7. *Where will I have to live and work for this kind of job?* Will I have to move to another part of the country? Does the job require that I travel often? Will I have to live in a large city? Are most workers in this field employed in factories, on farms, in offices, or in their own homes?

A Sample Job Quiz

Answering these questions is one of the best ways to find out whether the job you are considering is right for you. For example, suppose that Kim Asato, a ninth-grade student, is interested in a job as a medical laboratory technician. Answering the above seven main job questions will help Kim decide if she wants that kind of career.

Question 1: What kind of work will I do in this job?

Answer: Medical technicians usually work with doctors in the laboratories of hospitals and clinics. Medical technicians perform tests that help doctors decide how to treat illnesses.

They take blood tests, for example, and report the results of these tests.

Question 2: What personal qualities does the job require?

Answer: Medical technicians must be dependable, accurate people who are interested in science. They must be intelligent, careful, and able to follow directions. They must also have good eyesight and skillful hands.

Question 3: How much education and training does the job require?

Answer: At least four years of college are required, including special training in a hospital to learn laboratory procedures.

Question 4: What are the job opportunities in this field?

Answer: There is a shortage of medical technicians. Well-trained workers should have no trouble getting jobs. The work can lead to a job in medical research, to ownership of an independent laboratory, or to a job as a laboratory supervisor.

Question 5: What salary does the job pay?

Answer: The starting salary of a college-trained medical technician is about $21,600. It can be more or less than this, depending on the exact nature of the job. Also, salaries vary in different parts of the country. Salaries increase with experience.

Question 6: How do I feel about this job?

Answer: Medical technicians perform interesting and important work. They help the sick get well again.

Question 7: Where will I have to live and work for this kind of job?

Answer: Medical technicians work in the hospitals, medical centers, private laboratories, clinics, and doctors' offices that are located in most communities throughout the nation. They can live anywhere within commuting distance of the job.

This job quiz should help Kim decide whether to become a medical technician. It should also give you and the rest of your class an idea of the work performed by a medical technician. You and your classmates can apply these job questions to any occupations that interest you.

CIVICS SIDELIGHT

There are a number of sources available to students who are interested in learning about the salaries paid for various types of jobs. Among these sources are the *American Almanac of Jobs and Salaries* (for median weekly salary) and the *Encyclopedia of Careers and Vocational Guidance* (for average annual salary).

The *Statistical Abstract of the United States* is another good source of information about salaries. This book provides the median weekly salaries for the major categories of occupations. The following are the 1994 median weekly salaries for selected occupational groups, broken down by sex: professional speciality, $809 (male), $623 (female); executive, administrative, managerial, $797 (male), $541 (female); sales, $575 (male), $324 (female); protective services, $538 (male), $430 (female); mechanics and repairers, $519 (male), $520 (female); machine operators, assemblers, and inspectors, $415 (male), $292 (female).

1. Explain why it is helpful to practice filling out applications for jobs.

2. Explain why employers are interested in a job seeker's school history and special interests.

3. Identify the special skills needed in various types of jobs.

Teaching Section 5
Creating a Résumé

Explain that job applicants often present their work histories and other relevant information in a résumé. Obtain a sample copy of a résumé from a counselor or from a library resource to use as an example for students. Have pairs of students create ideal résumés for a teenager. Each résumé should include name, address, work history, educational achievements, activities, and special interests. Call on volunteers to lead a class discussion on why various items were included.

SECTION 4 REVIEW
A N S W E R S

1. See the following page: salary range (p. 413).

2. information—read books and other publications one can find in libraries, newsstands, employment offices, businesses, and the U.S. Department of Labor; watch people at work; learn by working, such as at part-time and summer jobs; detective work—one clue leads to another

3. part-time jobs—give people experience in working and help teach people what skills and interests are necessary for certain jobs; hobbies—reveal special talents, interests, and abilities that may be useful in various careers

4. helps people discover if they are suited to particular types of work

5. Students should create feasible, efficient plans.

SECTION 4 REVIEW

1. Define the following term: salary range.

2. How can a person find information about careers? How is learning about careers like doing detective work?

3. How are part-time jobs helpful in choosing a career? What role do hobbies play in career choice?

4. Why is it important to ask yourself a number of questions when considering possible careers?

5. **THINKING CRITICALLY** Create an action plan that will help you in your search for a career. What types of information will you read? How will you learn about jobs in your community? What are the most important questions to ask yourself?

5 Learning More About Yourself

Some jobs may interest you because they seem exciting and glamorous. Many young people think about becoming singers, actors, or professional athletes. Many of them discover, however, that opportunities in these fields are limited. They sometimes find they are more interested in another type of job.

Of course, if you believe that you have what it takes to be a success in one of these fields, you should work as hard as you can to enter it. Likewise, if you examine your interests and abilities and discover you are more likely to succeed in another occupation, you would be wise to choose that career. Again, be honest with yourself.

Learning about yourself is not easy. It is difficult for most of us to look at ourselves honestly and to judge our own qualifications. We also must learn how we appear to other people. Often others can help us see ourselves better. What are some ways in which we can learn to know ourselves?

Preparing to Apply for a Job

When you look for your first job, you will probably have to fill out a job application. An application is a printed form on which you are asked to supply information about yourself. Your job application helps the employer decide if you are the right person for the job.

Large businesses and corporations have personnel workers whose job it is to hire or recommend new employees. Personnel workers examine job applications and interview people to determine the best-qualified applicant for the available job.

You will find it helpful to practice filling out a job application. Then when you apply for a job later, you will know what type of information you will be asked to supply.

You can practice completing job applications in several ways. Perhaps you can fill out a real application used by a local business firm. You also can prepare an outline of important facts about yourself. Many students prefer to write short autobiographies that include the chief facts about their lives.

What Employers Want to Know

In general, employers want to know the following facts about a person applying for a job.

School History Your school record tells the employer a lot about you. List the subjects you have taken in the last two years and the grades you received. Then look at the reasons for these grades. What do grades mean? Perhaps you have high marks in English because you enjoy expressing yourself through writing. This may show that you should consider an occupation in which you can use your writing talent. In contrast, you may have poor grades in mathematics. Does this mean you

◆ 𝒞OOPERATIVE LEARNING

Have small groups act as employers who wish to hire workers for entry-level jobs. Have each group choose the skills needed for the job and then design a job application to use in determining the qualifications of prospective employees. Have all students "apply" for one of the jobs offered by the class's groups. Individual group roles might include group leader, designer, and writer. Have a representative from each group explain the reasoning used to develop his or her group's job application.

Guided Practice

List on the chalkboard the following skill categories: Motor Skills, Number Skills, Perceptual Skills, Language Skills, and Interpersonal Skills. Have volunteers write job titles under each category on the chalkboard, including the ones given in the textbook as well as any others they can think of. Have students copy the lists for use in the "Independent Practice" activity on page 416.

should not consider a job that requires mathematical ability? Not necessarily.

Grades do not always tell the whole story. Some students who have received low marks in mathematics may be late in discovering their ability in this subject. After special effort, they may be catching up in their studies. They may now be on their way to mastering math and earning higher grades. Low grades in a subject are not necessarily a sign that the student cannot learn that subject. Low marks often indicate a lack of effort or support rather than a lack of ability.

Perhaps in listing your subjects and grades you should include a third column entitled "Reasons for the Grades." This column will help you judge your own abilities and interests. It also will tell you how well you have used them.

Health Record   Good health is an important qualification for any job. Some occupations even require that workers have special physical qualifications and pass physical examinations. Sometimes good eyesight is essential. A medical technician, surgeon, or jeweler, for instance, needs good eyesight. You should examine your health record and review your program for keeping fit.

Americans with disabilities also strive to keep fit. There are many job opportunities for these citizens. The history of U.S. business and industry, for example, contains countless stories of successful people with disabilities. Thomas Edison, the great inventor, was deaf. Yet his life was filled with outstanding achievements. Americans believe that everyone should have an equal chance to succeed. To this end, recent civil rights legislation has made it illegal for employers to discriminate against people with disabilities.

Outside Activities   Make a list of your hobbies, the school offices you have held, sports in which you take part, school organizations to which you belong, and your part-time and summer jobs. After you have completed this list, take another look at it. Does it show

many different activities? What part of each activity did you like best? This review can tell you and an employer a great deal about your potential job skills.

Special Interests   The things that interest you now may also point the way to the future. List all your interests that you think might help you make a career choice. Consider the subjects you like best in school. Determine whether your interests have helped you do well in these subjects. Finally, review your hobbies and your part-time jobs to find which interests they emphasize.

A future employer will know and understand you better if he or she is aware of your special interests. These interests will tell the employer whether you prefer indoor or outdoor work, whether you would rather work alone or with others, or whether you are a leader or a follower. Your interests help determine your job needs.

These young people are developing their motor skills. The skills required to repair a bicycle could lead to rewarding careers in the future.

𝒞IVICS SIDELIGHT

Many well-known public figures besides Thomas Edison had disabilities. Franklin D. Roosevelt, though he had no use of his legs as a result of a polio attack, ran for and won the U.S. presidency a record four times. Helen Keller, who became deaf and blind as an infant, became a popular writer. Ray Charles, blind from the age of seven, began playing piano professionally at age 15. He has won 10 Grammy awards for his recordings. Jim Abbott, born with just one hand, grew up to be a pitcher for the California Angels and the New York Yankees Major League Baseball teams. All of these people succeeded in spite of the odds against them.

Independent Practice

Have each student write a brief biographical sketch of a fictional character who used his or her skills to move from one kind of job to another. For example, the person might have started out as an editor but then used her or his language skills to become an advertising specialist and later a publishing or marketing executive. Call on volunteers to read their biographical sketches to the class. Ask students to identify skills that are useful in a wide variety of careers.

Closure

Have students write opinion columns for the school newspaper explaining how to apply for a job, what employers look for in applicants, and why it is important that students develop important skills to make them attractive potential employees. Have volunteers read their columns while the rest of the class takes notes.

CIVICS SIDELIGHT

A vocational interest inventory is one kind of test for measuring a person's interests and experiences. An inventory asks questions about people's preferences and things they enjoy doing. The questions may be indirect, so a person taking the test might not even realize what a particular item is intended to reveal. Nevertheless, taken together, the answers build a picture of an individual's interests and aptitudes. From the answers to the inventory, an interest profile is generated. This can be correlated to interest profiles of people already working in different fields. In this way an individual can learn what kinds of occupations might be appealing and appropriate. You might want to obtain a vocational interest inventory from a school counselor or job counselor and review it with the class.

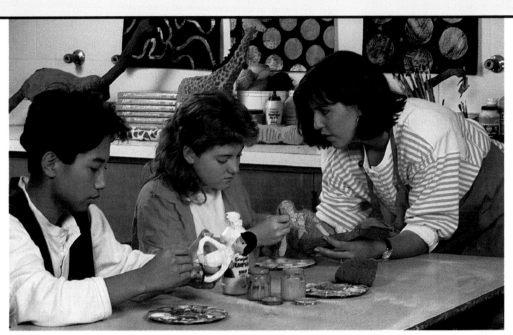

Art classes give students the chance to develop their creative talents and abilities. These students might pursue careers in art or graphic design.

Study Your Test Record

Tests are another means of helping you understand yourself and your abilities. Every test you take in school measures certain skills. You have probably taken tests that show how well you study, how accurately you remember what you read, and how well you express yourself. Review your test scores and consider the reasons for these scores. Here are some of the strengths such tests seek to measure.

Motor Skills Certain tests are used to determine how well people can use their hands—their motor skills. They measure how fast individuals can do things with their hands. They also check for accuracy. Certain other tests determine how well people can handle and arrange small objects. Such skills are useful to a watchmaker or a worker assembling small electronic equipment.

Number Skills One of the most common tests measures a person's ability to work quickly and accurately with numbers.

Such number skills are essential to bookkeepers, carpenters, and accountants. Most scientists also need to be skilled in using numbers.

Perceptual Skills How well can you picture things—that is, see them in your mind? To read a blueprint, for example, you must be able to picture in your mind the way a building will look when finished. You must be able to see depth and width in a flat drawing. The ability to think in this way is a part of perceptual skills.

Language Skills A teacher explaining an idea to students, a salesperson talking to a customer, and a parent describing to a child how to do something all are using language skills. An editor, an advertising specialist, and an executive in a business firm must be skilled in using written language. Many kinds of tests determine language skills.

Special Talents Some tests include sections that try to discover whether a person has artistic and creative talent. There also may be a section that measures the ability to organize and present facts. People can use these special talents in many kinds of jobs. Publishing companies and advertising agencies, for example, need designers and writers.

Interpersonal Skills   There are tests to check how well you handle personal relationships, or how you get along with others. These interpersonal skills are important in many jobs, such as teaching, sales, and others in which workers deal with the public.

Interests and Aptitudes   There are certain other tests given in school that can help you to know yourself better. These are called interest tests, or aptitude tests. They are easy to take and reveal interesting things about you. Your teacher or counselor can explain the results of these tests.

Such tests probably will not tell you the exact job you should seek. No test can map out the future for you. What these tests can do is help you discover your abilities and interests. It is up to you to match what you have discovered about yourself with what you have learned about various career opportunities.

By now you probably have made a good start in getting to know yourself better. As you study careers, compare your opportunities with your abilities. Your present goal should be to choose a general field of work—a type of work rather than a specific job. Leave the door open so that you can enter another field of work if necessary. Remember, a person's first job choice may not be the final one.

SECTION 5 REVIEW

1. Why is it helpful to practice filling out job applications?

2. Why is your school history important to employers? What can your special interests tell your future employer?

3. What type of special skill do accountants and bookkeepers need? What type of skill do editors, teachers, and advertisers require?

4. THINKING CRITICALLY   Create a two-column chart. In the first column list the seven types of skills discussed in the section. In the second column make an honest assessment of your level of skill. In which areas are you most skilled? How do these skills relate to your personal interests? In which areas are you least skilled? How can you improve your level of skill in these areas?

CHAPTER 21 SUMMARY

All young Americans must plan their careers. There are many career opportunities for young people, but these opportunities keep changing. You must gather up-to-date job information if you are to make a wise career choice.

In considering career possibilities, you should know about the work performed by professionals, managers, technicians, service workers, craft workers, operators, and agricultural workers. Your career choice must be made by you alone. There are, however, certain general guides that you may find helpful. You can read about jobs, explore jobs in your community, interview workers, and work at a part-time job.

An important step in deciding on a career is to learn more about yourself. Your school and health records, your special interests, your outside activities, and your work experience will be of interest to prospective employers.

You can prepare yourself now so that you will know what employers look for when hiring new workers. Learn about jobs that are available, not only in your community but throughout the country. Use your school years wisely. The skills and knowledge you acquire in school will help you for the rest of your life.

1. It helps to know the types of information employers will ask for.

2. School history indicates a person's special abilities and talents. Special interests help employers determine your job needs and desires.

3. accountants and bookkeepers—number skills; editors, teachers, advertisers—language skills

4. Students should make an honest assessment of their skills. Those who find that they are weak in certain areas might suggest that additional study and practice would strengthen their skills in those areas.

Bring to class major newspapers from around the country, and have students compare the want ads in these newspapers with the want ads in your community's newspaper. Have the class discuss the kinds of jobs advertised in other cities. Ask students to identify required skills and qualifications listed in the want ads.

Then invite students to imagine they are personnel managers for a fictitious company. Students should develop strategies for filling a position in the firm. Have each student write a classified ad for the position, including details about the job, its requirements, and other relevant information. Invite volunteers to share their job advertisements with the class.

LIFE SKILL
Reading Help Wanted Ads

Choosing an occupation is one of the most important decisions you will ever make. You want to find a job that you will enjoy doing on a year-round basis for many years.

A good source of information on jobs available in your community is the classified section of your newspaper. The classified section contains the help wanted ads listing employment opportunities in your area and sometimes in other parts of the country.

Look through as many newspapers as possible. Employers may not advertise in all local papers. The Sunday editions usually contain the largest selection of help wanted ads.

How to Read Help Wanted Ads

1. **Become familiar with the organization.** Most help wanted ads follow the same general organization. They are divided into major categories such as "Accounting/Bookkeeping," "Engineering," "Medical," "Office/Clerical," "Professional," and "Sales." Within each of these categories, jobs are listed in rough alphabetical order. The type of job usually is listed at the top of each ad to help you spot job possibilities. Be sure to scan the entire classified section because some ads may appear in unlikely or incorrect categories.

2. **Read the ads carefully.** Note what training or experience is required. Also, study any promises made in the ad. What is the salary? Are benefits such as vacations, sick leave, and medical and dental insurance discussed? The answers to these questions will help you decide if you want to apply for the job.

    Pay special attention to ads placed by employment agencies, or businesses that charge money to fill a position. The company that has the job opening usually pays the agency's fee, but sometimes the successful applicant must pay it.

3. **Keep your options open.** Look under several of the major headings in the classified section. You may find that the type of job you are looking for is listed under more than one category.

Applying the Skill

Read the help wanted ad shown below. Then answer the following questions.

1. What qualifications are needed for this job?
2. Who is advertising the position?
3. Is there a fee involved?
4. What features about the job are used to attract applicants?
5. If you wanted to apply for the job, how would you go about it?
6. What other information should you ask about the job?

RECEPTIONIST
ART GALLERY

$225/fee paid

Bright, energetic, enthusiastic H.S. grad. to handle front desk and busy phones. Typing 55 w.p.m.

Neat appearance and punctuality a must. Knowledge of modern art and word processing useful. Excellent vacation and fringe benefits. Immediate hire.

Winston Agency   **555-3791**
An Equal Opportunity Employer

Vocabulary Workshop

1. craft worker

2. white-collar—workers in the professions or in technical, managerial, sales, or administrative support work; blue-collar—workers in jobs that require manual labor

3. beginning salary, possible raises, highest salary

4. possible answers—hospitals, security companies, hotels, restaurants, dry cleaners, laundries, barbershops

5. civil service examination

Reviewing Main Ideas

1. career often chosen on basis of personal values; helps one discover own abilities, interests, skills, weaknesses

2. craft—skilled, long training period, needs manual and mathematical ability; operator—less skill and manual ability, short training period; technician—specialized skill, most training in college, technical, or vocational schools

3. more marketable worker, higher income, personal satisfaction; dropouts—low-paying jobs, often unemployed

4. health-care, computers

5. See pages 412–413.

6. school history, health record, outside activities, special interests, past work

7. U.S. government; high school diploma, recommendation from U.S. senator or representative, pass scholastic and physical tests

Thinking Critically

1. Students might mention such traits as independence and personal drive.

2. Students might note that women today work in virtually all fields.

R·e·v·i·e·w

Vocabulary Workshop

1. Who might serve an apprenticeship?

2. Distinguish between white-collar workers and blue-collar workers.

3. What is a salary range?

4. Name three types of service industries.

5. What test must people pass when applying for federal jobs?

Reviewing Main Ideas

1. What is the relationship between personal values and career choice? How can an honest study of yourself help you choose a career?

2. How does a craft worker differ from an operator? from a technician?

3. Why is it important to earn as much education as you can? How does dropping out of school harm an individual?

4. Which two career fields will experience high growth over the next decade?

5. What questions are important to ask yourself when considering careers?

6. What types of information do employers want to know about job applicants?

7. Who is the nation's largest employer? How do people qualify for military officer training school?

Thinking Critically

1. Many people in the United States are self-employed. What kinds of personal qualities do you think self-employed people must have to be successful?

2. Watch several television programs from the 1950s and 1960s. What types of jobs do women in these programs hold? How do these jobs compare to those held by women on programs today? What do you think accounts for the difference?

Citizenship in Your Community

Cooperative Project

With your group, conduct interviews of people in your community who hold various types of jobs. Assign group members to interview workers in each of the following categories (if possible): white-collar workers, blue-collar workers, service workers, and agricultural workers.

Ask the interviewees the following questions: Why did the person choose this particular job? How long has he or she held this job? What does the person like most about the job? What does he or she like least? What would the person like to change about the job? Write brief profiles of the interviewees and organize them by work category into a booklet. Are there any similarities among the categories? any differences? Answer these questions in the booklet's introduction. Present your booklet to the class.

Building Your Portfolio

The fifth step of your unit portfolio project (see page 421) is to anticipate any problems with the mousetrap project. What will you do if the project encounters technical or design difficulties? How will you fill Acme's order if your distributor goes out of business? Create a two-column chart. In the first column list the problems the project might face. In the second column list the skills, talents, and education of your company's employees that could help solve those problems quickly. Place your chart in your individual portfolio for later use.

Thinking Critically

1. Students might mention such traits as independence and personal drive.

2. Students might note that women today work in virtually all fields.

Citizenship in Your Community

Students should compare workers in the four categories.

Building Your Portfolio

Assign Portfolio Assessment Worksheet 21 in the *Portfolio Assessment Worksheets* booklet.

Assessment

- **Chapter 21 Tests**, *Chapter Tests* booklet
- **Test Generator**, Chapter 21
- **Portfolio**, Portfolio Assessment Worksheet 21, *Portfolio Assessment Worksheets* booklet

UNIT 6 · R·e·v·i·e·w

Reviewing Main Ideas

1. How do supply and demand affect product prices? How does a capitalist economy differ from a command economy?

2. What four types of business organizations exist in the United States?

3. What are the components of modern mass production? How do standard packaging and the one-price system help mass marketing work?

4. What are the advantages and disadvantages of charge accounts? How can too much money and too much credit hurt the economy?

5. What is the difference between private insurance and social insurance?

6. What are the four parts of the business cycle? What is inflation, and how can it hurt the economy?

Thinking Critically

1. Imagine that you have started your own business and have a limited budget for advertising. How will you make potential customers aware of your new business?

2. You have just won $1,000 in an essay contest on "How to Use Money Wisely." What will you do with the money?

3. Write an editorial for your school newspaper that speaks to the importance of staying in school and earning a good education.

Practicing Civics Skills

1. You have just bought a portable compact disc player for $139. Draw a picture of the check you wrote to pay for it. Then write a warranty for the product.

2. Visit a grocery store and compare labels of cereal brands. Which cereals have the highest nutritional value? the lowest?

3. Read the classified section of your Sunday newspaper and choose several jobs that interest you. What qualifications are needed for these jobs?

4. Research how the average cost of a college education has changed since 1980. Use this information to draw a line graph.

Citizenship in Your Community

Individual Project

Collect newspaper articles that focus on economic issues in your community. Next, collect articles that focus on national economic issues. How do the economic problems in your community compare to the nation's economic difficulties? Summarize your findings in a paragraph.

Learning from Technology

Telecommuting

Thanks to modern technology, more than nine million U.S. employees now can work for their companies at least part-time in their homes. These "telecommuters" typically work at home one or two days a week. They communicate with their offices through computer linkups, fax machines, and telephones. The number of telecommuters is expected to grow as even more sophisticated technology becomes available.

How does telecommuting benefit workers? What drawbacks might there be? What businesses might be best suited to telecommuting? For example, could someone telecommute to his or her job at a fast-food restaurant?

Paragraphs should compare and contrast the economic situation of your community with that of the nation.

Answers will vary. Students should use sound reasoning in their responses. Students should list jobs they believe are well-suited to telecommuting.

Students have been working on a Building Your Portfolio project throughout Unit 6. You might ask volunteers to present their work to the class. Have all of the students add their work to their individual portfolios. Assign the Unit 6 Portfolio Assessment Worksheet in the *Portfolio Assessment Worksheets* booklet.

Building Your Portfolio

Individually or in a group, complete the following project to show your understanding of the civics concepts involved.

A Better Mousetrap

An abundance of food and a lack of cats have caused the mouse population in the halls of Acme Grain Corporation to rise. Acme has asked you and several other business firms to design and build an all-terrain mousetrap. Acme will award the project to the firm with the best mousetrap. To prepare your proposal, you will need to do the following.

1. Write a background profile of your business that highlights your company's stability and experience. How are the four factors of production involved in your company? How does your company take advantage of the opportunities and freedoms in a capitalist system? Is your company organized as a sole proprietorship, a partnership, or a corporation? In your profile, include an organizational chart of your business organization. Who is responsible for what tasks?

2. Sketch the design of your mousetrap. Consider where the mousetrap will be used, whether mice will be caught singly or in groups, and what you will use for bait. How will you name, package, and advertise your product? What methods of mass production will you use to make the mousetrap? How will you distribute it? Create an advertising poster that includes the sketch of your mousetrap. The poster should emphasize how efficiently your mousetrap can be made and distributed.

3. Decide how you will fund the mousetrap project. (Acme may not pay your full fee up front.) Will you need a bank loan? Is your project a good risk? Should you buy insurance for your company and your product? What type? Write a letter to your local bank requesting a loan and explaining how the money will be used.

4. Determine if the market is right for the mousetrap project. In what part of the business cycle is the economy? Are interest rates high? Is the demand for mousetrap products high (in case Acme cannot follow through on the project)? Are your workers unionized and demanding higher wages? Write a company memo summarizing the mousetrap market and stating why you recommend pursuing the project.

5. Anticipate any problems with the mousetrap project. What will you do if the project encounters technical or design difficulties? How will you fill Acme's order if your distributor goes out of business? Create a two-column chart. In the first column list the problems the project might face. In the second column list the skills, talents, and education of your company's employees that could help solve those problems quickly.

Organize your materials, and present your proposal to Acme (the rest of the class).

THE UNITED STATES AND THE WORLD

Using the Quotation

Have students read the quotation and suggest the year or span of years in which this statement might have been made. *(Roosevelt was president from 1933 to 1945.)* Ask: Could these words have been spoken today? Discuss how the desire to achieve peace has been a goal of U.S. and world leaders for generations.

About the Author

Franklin Delano Roosevelt (1882–1945) served as president of the United States longer than any other U.S. chief executive. Swept into office by voters seeking relief from the Great Depression, Roosevelt served from 1933 to his death in April 1945. As president, Roosevelt led the United States through the world's greatest conflagration to that time, World War II. His policies led to a great expansion of the role of government in American economic life.

"The overwhelming majority of the peoples and nations of the world today want to live in peace. They seek the removal of barriers against trade. They want to exert themselves [work hard] in industry, in agriculture and in business, that they may increase their wealth through the production of wealth-producing goods rather than striving to produce military planes and bombs and machine guns and cannon for the destruction of human lives and useful property."

—*Franklin D. Roosevelt*

32ND PRESIDENT OF THE UNITED STATES

Unit 7 stresses the obligations of citizens to be aware of world problems that affect them and the nation. Throughout the unit students examine international situations and measures the United States must take to ensure peace. Students are introduced to the concept of foreign policy and learn how U.S. leaders formulate that policy. The unit also focuses on past and future foreign policy challenges for the United States.

After studying Unit 7, students should be able to accomplish the following.

1. Explain how U.S. foreign policy is established.

2. Discuss the chief goal of U.S. foreign policy and the role played by the UN in pursuit of this goal.

3. Describe the development and history of U.S. foreign policy.

4. Identify changes in U.S. relations with other nations.

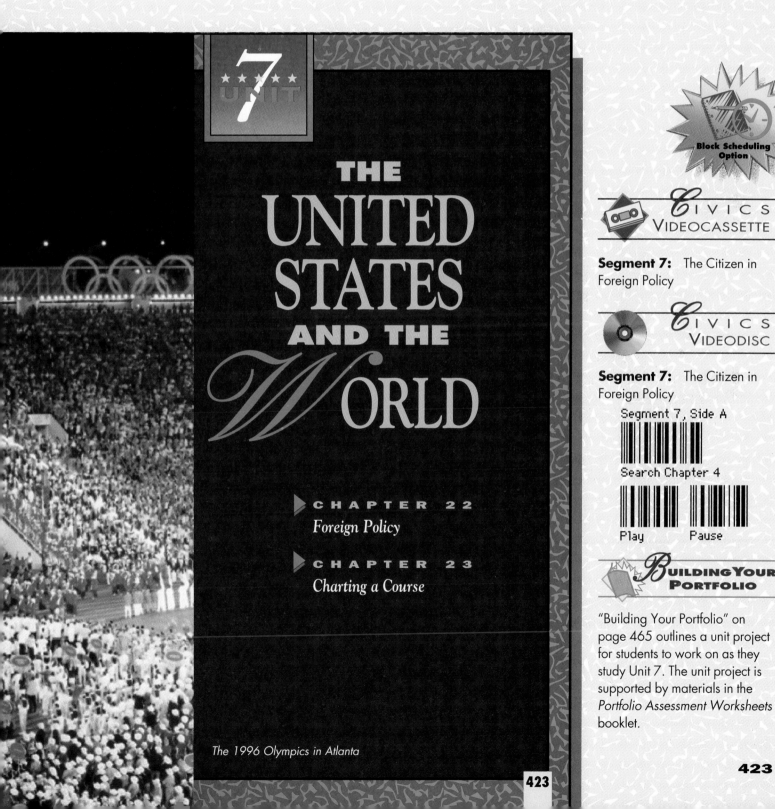

UNIT 7

THE UNITED STATES AND THE World

▶ CHAPTER 22
Foreign Policy

▶ CHAPTER 23
Charting a Course

The 1996 Olympics in Atlanta

Block Scheduling Option

CIVICS VIDEOCASSETTE

Segment 7: The Citizen in Foreign Policy

CIVICS VIDEODISC

Segment 7: The Citizen in Foreign Policy

Segment 7, Side A

Search Chapter 4

Play   Pause

BUILDING YOUR PORTFOLIO

"Building Your Portfolio" on page 465 outlines a unit project for students to work on as they study Unit 7. The unit project is supported by materials in the *Portfolio Assessment Worksheets* booklet.

CHAPTER 22

Foreign Policy

TEXTBOOK	TEACHING RESOURCES	OTHER AVAILABLE RESOURCES
Chapter	• Skills Worksheet 22 • Challenge/Enrichment Worksheet 22	• Simulations and Case Studies Lesson 19
Section **1** Conducting Foreign Relations Page 425	• Reteaching Worksheet 22.1	
2 Working for Peace Page 432	• Reteaching Worksheet 22.2	
3 The United Nations Page 436	• Reteaching Worksheet 22.3	• Transparency 24: Organization of the United Nations
Review and Assessment Chapter 22 Review, Page 443	• Test, Form A • Test, Form B • Portfolio Assessment Worksheet 22	• *Test Generator*, Chapter 22

Block Scheduling Option

ADDITIONAL RESOURCES

BOOKS FOR TEACHERS

Claude, Inis, *Swords into Ploughshares: The Problems and Progress of International Organizations*, McGraw-Hill.

Hunt, Michael, *Ideology and U.S. Foreign Policy*, Yale University Press.

Kennan, George, *American Diplomacy*, University of Chicago Press.

Matsuura, Kumiko, et al., *Chronology and Fact Book of the United Nations*, Oceana.

BOOKS FOR STUDENTS

Cooney, James, *Foreign Policy: The United States and the World*, Walker. Explores the making of U.S. foreign policy.

Schirokauer, Conrad, *Modern China and Japan*, Harcourt Brace & Company. Historical and contemporary perspectives on these two powerful nations.

MULTIMEDIA RESOURCES

International Relations (VHS, c, 77 min.), CU. Explains the underlying complexities of international relations.

Peacekeeping (VHS, c, 19 min.), CINGLD. Examines the role of UN peacekeeping forces in the trouble spots of the world.

The United Nations: It's More Than You Think (VHS, c, 31 min.), CSS. Introduction to the United Nations and its changing role after the Cold War.

U.S. Response: The Making of U.S. Foreign Policy (simulation), CU. A role-play simulation game of foreign-policy crises.

THE INTERNET

Have students use these search words to locate more information about chapter topics on the Internet: *foreign relations, Department of State, Department of Defense, international trade, United Nations.*

 GLOBAL SKILL BUILDER

You might wish to use **Navigating the Internet** from the interactive *Global Skill Builder* CD-ROM to aid students' understanding of the Internet as a resource.

Abbreviations: b&w=black and white; c=color; f=film; fs=filmstrip; sd=sound; tr=transparency; VHS=videotape

CHALLENGES IN TODAY'S WORLD

✴ **Structures and Functions** Students will learn about the constitutional powers of the president and Congress in setting U.S. foreign policy and about the role of various government departments and agencies in carrying out that foreign policy.

✴ **World Leadership** Students will learn how the United States works to promote peace and how the foreign policies of other nations can affect our balance of trade. Students also will learn about the history and structure of the United Nations, as well as the debate for and against this organization of nations.

CIVICS SKILLS

Students will learn how to comprehend data in table form. Students also will learn terms important to understanding the development of U.S. foreign policy.

CITIZENSHIP VALUES

Students will be encouraged to stay informed about foreign policy issues and to appreciate the need to work for world peace.

MEETING INDIVIDUAL NEEDS

LIMITED ENGLISH PROFICIENCY (LEP)

Have pairs of students write large, block letters of the alphabet on small squares of paper. Then have the students take turns using the letters to form acronyms for the U.S. foreign policy agencies, international security organizations, and agencies of the United Nations. After one student forms the acronym, the other student should supply the name and purpose of the agency or organization. Both students should develop lists of the organizations as a study guide.

LEARNERS HAVING DIFFICULTY

Invite each student to imagine that he or she is a U.S. ambassador to the United Nations. Tell them that they must explain the purpose of U.S. foreign policy to the UN General Assembly. Have them write out their explanations, and then have volunteers present their explanations orally.

AUDITORY LEARNERS

Organize students into pairs. Have them read aloud parts of the chapter to each other and then orally review and summarize the material they have covered. Each student should take notes on the passages read aloud by his or her partner.

VISUAL LEARNERS

Have pairs of students illustrate the foreign policy powers of the president and of Congress. The students should use newspapers, other periodicals, and their own drawings to create a collage (with descriptive captions) illustrating the powers of the president and Congress. Have students present and explain their illustrations to the class.

TACTILE/KINESTHETIC LEARNERS

Invite students to work together to create a work of art that symbolizes the quest for world peace. Students may choose to make a sculpture, a painting, a collage, a song, or a poem. Each project should somehow address the role of the president, Congress, the United Nations, U.S. citizens, or another entity in fostering world peace. Have students present their work to the rest of the class.

GIFTED LEARNERS

Have students research and create illustrated time lines about the history of the Peace Corps. Students should extend the time lines to 2025 to show what they think the future of the organization will be. Illustrations in time lines should be accompanied by explanatory captions. Call on volunteers to present their time lines to the class for discussion.

423B

Chapter 22 focuses on U.S. foreign policy—its form and its content, who establishes it, and how it is carried out. The chapter also examines the organization and role of the United Nations, including the debate over its effectiveness. The underlying theme of the chapter is that the chief goal of U.S. foreign policy is the preservation of world peace.

Motivator

Ask students to recall some of the domestic concerns facing the United States. *(crime, pollution, unemployment, economic issues)* Then ask them why the United States should spend so much of its time and money on the problems of foreign countries—why not simply concentrate on domestic concerns? *(The nations of the world are interconnected politically and economically; the United States can better avoid problems and address the future if it is involved in world affairs.)*

CHAPTER OBJECTIVES

After studying Chapter 22, students should be able to do the following.

1. Identify the roles of the executive and legislative branches in foreign policy.
2. Describe how the United States has met the challenges of global security and the global economy.
3. Describe the United Nations and how it tries to improve life for all people.

SIMULATIONS AND CASE STUDIES

Lesson 19: Foreign Aid Case Studies

Block Scheduling Option

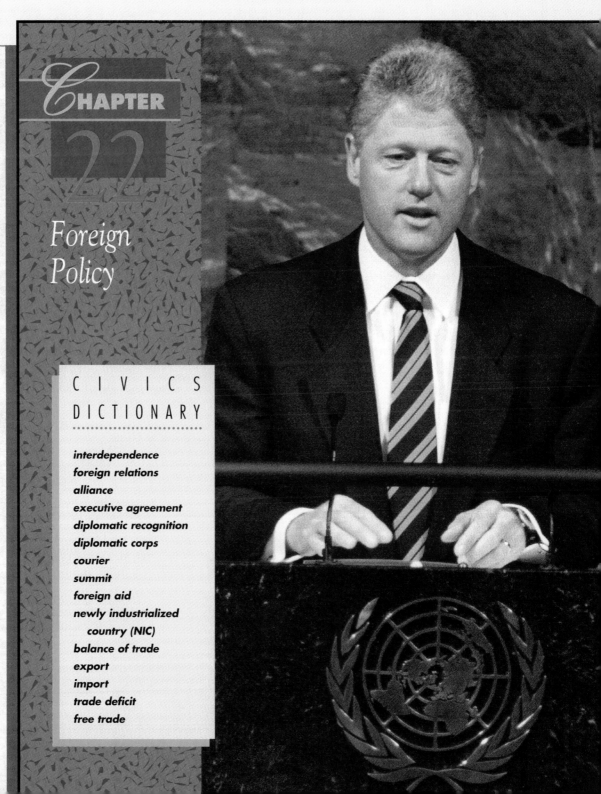

CHAPTER 22

Foreign Policy

CIVICS DICTIONARY

interdependence
foreign relations
alliance
executive agreement
diplomatic recognition
diplomatic corps
courier
summit
foreign aid
newly industrialized country (NIC)
balance of trade
export
import
trade deficit
free trade

SECTION OBJECTIVES

After studying Section 1, students should be able to do the following.

1. Identify the purposes of foreign policy.

2. Describe the effects of business and tourism on U.S. foreign relations.

3. Name the president's military and diplomatic powers, and explain how Congress can limit the president's activities in international affairs.

4. Identify the foreign policy roles of the Department of State and the Department of Defense.

Teaching Section 1
Building a Vocabulary

Review the term *diplomacy*. (See page 99.) Have students suggest the meaning of ***diplomatic recognition*** (page 426) and ***diplomatic corps*** (page 427). Tell them that *corps* comes from the Latin word meaning "body." A corps is a body of persons with a common purpose. Then have students describe what a **courier** does. Tell them that the Latin word *currere* means "to run." In ancient times messages were often delivered by runners.

CHAPTER FOCUS

Have you ever traveled to a foreign land and talked to people living there? Have you made friends with schoolmates who are visiting the United States from another nation? Do you have a pen pal who lives in another country? If you answer yes to any of these questions, you have helped conduct U.S. foreign policy.

The main goal of U.S. foreign policy is to promote peace and friendship with the other nations of the world. As you know, events happening in one nation can dramatically affect events in other nations. Advances in communication and transportation have made the world a smaller place and have encouraged the **interdependence**, or mutual reliance, of the world's nations. Such interdependence means that nations must cooperate in seeking world peace, freedom, and prosperity.

Forming U.S. foreign policy is a complex process. The government must strike a balance between cooperation and competition with other nations. The process requires the work of thousands of government officials. It also requires the support of citizens like you.

. . . .

STUDY GUIDE

● What are the roles of the executive and legislative branches in foreign policy?

● How has the United States met the challenges of global security and the global economy?

● What is the United Nations, and how does it work to improve life for all people?

1 | Conducting Foreign Relations

As you recall, the plan that a nation follows in dealing with other nations is called foreign policy. The way in which this policy is carried out and its success or failure affects a country's **foreign relations**. That means it affects the way a country deals with other nations.

In establishing its foreign policy, the United States depends on many people. Government officials meet with the leaders of other nations. Small businesses and large corporations carry on foreign trade. Even U.S. tourists traveling in other nations may influence attitudes toward the United States.

The President's Role

President Truman once said, "I make American foreign policy." By this he meant that the president is responsible for the conduct of foreign policy. Although assisted by officials of the Department of State and other advisers, the president is responsible for major decisions. Article II, Section 2, of the Constitution gives the president the following powers concerning foreign relations.

Military Powers As commander in chief of the U.S. armed forces, the president makes recommendations to Congress about the military's size and equipment. The president can order troops, planes, and warships into action. For example, in 1994 President Clinton sent U.S. troops to Haiti to help restore democracy in that country. Only Congress, however, can declare war. In addition, the War Powers Act requires U.S. troops sent abroad to be recalled within 60 days unless Congress approves the action.

Treaty-Making Powers As you know, treaties are written agreements between

CIVICS SIDELIGHT

President Woodrow Wilson used his treaty-making powers extensively. In a break with tradition, he traveled to Europe in 1918 to meet with U.S. allies to draft a peace treaty ending World War I. Many of his advisers opposed Wilson's trip, suggesting he was putting his prestige and power on the line by becoming a mere negotiator. Wilson decided, however, that the matter was too important to trust it to anyone else.

Summarizing

Have students look through newspapers and other periodicals to find articles about U.S. foreign policy. Have students summarize their articles in brief paragraphs. Call on volunteers to read their paragraphs to the class. Use the subjects of the articles to lead a class discussion about the purposes of foreign policy. *(promoting peace and friendship with other nations of the world)*

COOPERATIVE LEARNING

Ask: How can businesses and tourists affect U.S. foreign relations? Organize the class into small groups. Have each group use information from the section to create an illustrated story in which a U.S. business in a foreign market or an American tourist in a foreign country affects foreign relations. Groups might present their finished stories to the class. Assign each student a role, including discussion leader, writer, editor, illustrator, and presenter.

CIVICS SIDELIGHT

Presidents have the power to break off relations with a foreign country, but they can also restore them in full or in stages. In 1994 President Clinton decided to lift the United States' 19-year-old trade embargo against the Southeast Asian nation of Vietnam. His stated reasons for normalizing trade relations included the Vietnamese government's willingness to help account fully for U.S. soldiers missing in action (MIA) from the Vietnam War. In 1995 the United States formally established diplomatic relations with Vietnam.

In his roles of foreign policy leader and chief diplomat, the president meets often with officials from other countries. Here President Clinton meets with Chancellor Helmut Kohl of Germany.

nations. They are an important part of U.S. foreign relations. With the advice and consent of the Senate, the president has the power to make three types of treaties.

Peace treaties are agreements to end wars. They spell out the terms for ending the fighting. All sides in the conflict must consent to such treaties. Alliance treaties are agreements between nations to help each other for defense, economic, scientific, or other reasons. The United States has established such **alliances** with many nations of the world. Commercial treaties, or trade treaties, are solely economic agreements between two or more nations to trade with each other on favorable terms. All treaties must be approved by a two-thirds vote of the Senate.

Agreements between nations do not always require treaties. The president and the leader of a foreign government may meet and establish a mutual understanding, or **executive agreement**. The agreement is announced in a joint statement to the people of the two nations. The leaders also may exchange official letters or notes in which they spell out details of their agreement. Executive agreements have been used often in recent years.

Diplomatic Powers The president, again with the approval of the Senate, appoints ambassadors to represent the United States in foreign nations. The president also receives ambassadors from other nations.

The president's right to receive ambassadors from foreign nations includes the power of **diplomatic recognition**. That is, the president may decide whether to recognize the government of a foreign nation. To recognize a foreign government means to establish official relations with that government. Sending a U.S. ambassador to that country and in turn receiving that nation's ambassador means that official recognition has taken place.

The president may refuse to recognize a government whose foreign policies are considered unfriendly or dangerous to the United States or its allies. For many years, the United States refused to recognize the Communist government of China. When recognition was granted in the 1970s, the two countries exchanged ambassadors.

Sometimes it is necessary to break off relations, or end all official dealings, with a foreign nation. This action occurs rarely and only when two nations cannot settle a serious dispute. The United States, for example, broke off diplomatic relations with Iraq in late 1990 when Iraqi troops invaded the neighboring country of Kuwait.

In establishing and carrying out U.S. foreign policy, the president may call on any department of the government for assistance. The president also hires foreign policy experts. These experts are part of the Executive Office of the President.

Writing a Speech

Invite each student to imagine he or she is the president of the United States and is seeking a second term in office. Have students write short speeches describing how they have used their military, diplomatic, and treaty-making powers wisely. Students might refer to actual or fictional foreign policy dilemmas facing the United States. Call on volunteers to read their speeches aloud, and have the class discuss how each speech demonstrates the president's foreign policy powers.

Guided Practice

Have students list on the chalkboard the people who attend meetings of the National Security Council. Then lead the class in the creation of a dialogue that might take place at an NSC meeting during the following crisis: A U.S. warship has been fired upon by an unidentified ship in the South Pacific Ocean off the Antarctic coast. Have students locate the area on a map before they begin suggesting dialogue for each person at the meeting. Students should demonstrate an understanding of the role of the NSC.

Department of State

The Department of State is the principal organization for carrying out U.S. foreign policy as established by the president. It also acts as "the eyes and ears of the president" in obtaining information on which U.S. foreign relations are based.

The Department of State is headed by the secretary of state, who is appointed by the president with the approval of the Senate. The secretary of state reports directly to the president and is assisted by a deputy secretary, undersecretaries, and many others.

The secretary of state advises the president and supervises the activities of American ambassadors, ministers, and consuls. These officials and their assistants are members of the **diplomatic corps**.

As you learned in Chapter 6, members of the diplomatic corps work toward friendly relations with the nations in which they are stationed. They report to the secretary of state on any events of importance taking place there. Their reports may be carried by special messengers called **couriers**. Sometimes ambassadors or ministers will meet with the secretary of state or the president about a special concern.

Information from the diplomatic corps helps the president and advisers to decide U.S. policy toward other countries. U.S. consuls also send regular reports on business and trade conditions. These reports help U.S. businesses plan their operations in foreign countries.

Department of Defense

An important source of military information for the president is the Department of Defense. The secretary of defense advises the president on troop movements, placement of military bases, and weapons development.

The secretary of defense and the president receive advice on military matters from the Joint Chiefs of Staff. As you recall, the Joint Chiefs include a chairperson and the highest-ranking military officer of the Army, Navy, Air Force, and Marines.

AMERICAN BIOGRAPHY

Colin Powell

Colin Powell was born in 1937 in the Harlem section of New York City. Powell's parents taught their children that education is the key to opportunity. Powell realized this while he was a student at City College of New York.

On his way to class one day, Powell stopped to watch the Reserve Officers Training Corps (ROTC). Impressed by what he saw, he joined the ROTC. He graduated from college with the highest grades in his ROTC class and the highest rank in the Corps—cadet colonel.

Powell swiftly moved up the military ranks. After serving in Vietnam, where he earned numerous medals, he was selected to help plan military and defense policies.

In 1987 Powell became the first African American to head the National Security Council. Two years later, General Powell assumed the nation's top military post— chairperson of the Joint Chiefs of Staff. Powell's military expertise largely was responsible for the U.S. victory against Iraq in the 1991 Persian Gulf War. Powell retired from the Army in 1993, after 35 years of distinguished service. He has continued to play a role in foreign affairs, however, such as in his diplomatic mission to Haiti in 1994.

Other Sources of Assistance

The other executive departments assist in foreign policy in various ways. The secretary of agriculture, for example, keeps the president

(continued on page 430)

CIVICS SIDELIGHT

The Central Intelligence Agency was established by President Harry Truman in 1947 and was an indirect descendant of the Office of Strategic Services (OSS) in World War II. The CIA uses a wide variety of techniques to gather information, including using undercover agents, listening to foreign radio and television broadcasts, and using high-tech listening devices and spy satellites in orbit around the earth.

The CIA is forbidden from spying on U.S. citizens. Nevertheless, a government commission in 1975 reported that the CIA had spied on thousands of Americans who had opposed the Vietnam War. The resulting controversy led to stricter congressional oversight of the secretive agency.

Writing a Letter

Ask students to imagine they were one of the student demonstrators in Tiananmen Square in 1989. Have them write a letter to a relative or friend in which they describe one aspect of the seven-week demonstration from their personal perspective. Have students suggest reasons why they believe the Chinese government felt threatened by the student demonstrations.

GLOBAL PERSPECTIVES

Freedom of the press is a fundamental right in the United States, but journalists around the world often find themselves the victims of attack by governments that want to suppress the truth. According to the New York-based Committee to Protect Journalists, for example, the number of reporters being arrested and imprisoned is on the rise. In 1993 alone, at least 126 journalists were held in prisons in 28 countries around the world. China imprisoned 22 journalists, some for minor offenses. Moreover, 56 journalists were killed in 1993, many of them the victims of deliberate assassination.

Case STUDY

TIANANMEN SQUARE

Gunfire pierced the early morning hours of June 5, 1989, in downtown Beijing, the capital of China. With the gunfire came other noises: wailing sirens, rumbling tanks, and, worst of all, the sounds of tens of thousands of people fleeing in terror.

Chinese students built this "Goddess of Liberty," based on the Statue of Liberty, to symbolize their desire for freedom and democracy.

These people were ordinary citizens who had gathered in Beijing's Tiananmen Square to call for democratic reforms in China's communist government. Over the previous seven weeks, more than one million people had gathered to proclaim with one voice their desire for democracy.

Tensions grew in Tiananmen Square as it became clear that the government would not address the citizens' pleas for democratic reforms. The government finally ended the seven-week demonstration brutally: they ordered units of the Chinese army to clear the square. Firing on their fellow citizens, the army troops injured thousands of people and killed more than 1,000 others.

What had prompted so many people to risk their lives? This question was answered by a demonstrator a few days before the massacre. He said simply, "We want the rights Americans have."

One of the rights Americans cherish and the Chinese citizens bravely sought is guaranteed by the First Amendment to the Constitution. This right is freedom of the press.

A Call for Truth

Many people in China had grown increasingly frustrated in the months leading to the Tiananmen Square massacre. They believed that the Chinese communist government was corrupt, and that government decisions served the leaders rather than the nation and its people.

An end to government corruption, however, was not all the protesters sought. Their most deeply felt desire was for democracy, and they knew that the first step toward democracy is the creation of a free press. The protesters believed that an open and honest exchange

Drawing a Political Cartoon

Have students draw political cartoons related to the Tiananmen Square demonstrations or massacre. Some students may wish to focus on the role the press (Chinese or foreign) played in this event. The political cartoons should include descriptive captions. Encourage students to be creative. Call on volunteers to explain their cartoons to the class.

of ideas in a free press would expose government corruption and pave the way for democratic reforms.

Power of the Press

China, like most totalitarian countries, has a long history of suppressing the news. The government censors reporters and newspapers. It uses the news media as a pipeline for government propaganda. By controlling the press, leaders also stop critics of the government from expressing their views to the public. Controlling the press and other media is the key to controlling a nation's people.

The protesters in Beijing knew the power of the press. They also knew that a government that fears a free press is a government that fears the truth. Among the protesters' strongest supporters were Chinese journalists. For years, these men and women had been forced to report only what the government wanted them to say. With great courage, many of them reported on the protests in Tiananmen Square, only to have the government quickly censor them.

The Truth Is Revealed

The communist leaders of China tried to keep the news of the Tiananmen Square massacre from reaching the rest of the world. They warned foreign journalists who were in China not to report the protests. Government leaders also banned all live broadcasts from China. The tactics that censored reporters in China, however, could not stop the foreign journalists from reporting the news of the massacre to a shocked world.

Reporters from the United States, a country founded on the ideal of free expression, went to great lengths to tell the story of Tiananmen Square. The bravery of these journalists and their dedication to discovering and reporting the truth proved the power of the press. Without the American right to freedom of the press, we might never have known about the hunger of others for democracy.

Over one million Chinese citizens gathered in Tiananmen Square in 1989 to proclaim the need for changes in the Chinese communist government. Because of the First Amendment right to a free press, Americans were able to witness this historic plea for democracy.

YOU DECIDE

1 Why were Chinese citizens protesting in Tiananmen Square?

2 How did the Chinese government respond to the protesters in Tiananmen Square?

3 How do the events surrounding the protest illustrate the power of a free press?

ANSWERS TO YOU DECIDE

1. The citizens were calling for democratic reforms in the communist government. They sought a generally more democratic country, an end to government corruption, and freedom of the press.

2. It used violence to end the demonstrations by ordering the army to clear the square of protesters.

3. The free press of other countries brought the events of Tiananmen Square to the attention of the world.

Independent Practice

Ask students to review the departments and agencies (including those organizations whose directors are part of the National Security Council) described on pages 426, 430, and 431. Have them choose the agency for which they would most like to work and write a journal entry explaining a day in the life of a member of that particular organization. The entries should refer to the foreign policy role of the particular department or agency the student has chosen. Encourage students to share their entries with the class.

Closure

Begin a chart on the chalkboard with "President's Role" and "Congress's Role" as heads. Call on volunteers to supply the foreign policy powers of the president and Congress, writing the powers under the appropriate headings. Then ask: How do the foreign policy powers of Congress check those of the president? Have students copy the chart for use as a study guide.

GLOBAL PERSPECTIVES

Radio Free Europe/Radio Liberty is a government-funded radio service similar to the Voice of America. Authorized by the U.S. Congress, this independent service reaches more than 30 million people in eastern Europe and the former Soviet Union from its broadcast center in Prague, capital of the Czech Republic. Daily programming includes news broadcasts and analyses, world press reviews, reports by correspondents, and feature presentations.

Both Radio Free Europe and Radio Liberty were set up in the 1950s as alternative sources of information for people living behind the "iron curtain." The two broadcasters merged in 1976. The budgets for the radio services have been cut significantly since the end of the Cold War. The broadcasters decided in 1994 to move their operations from Munich, Germany, to Prague to reduce costs.

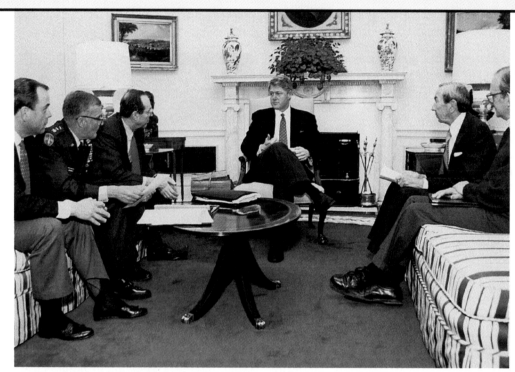

President Bill Clinton meets often with his Cabinet members and advisers to decide important foreign and domestic policy issues.

advised of available surplus foods that may be sent to needy nations. The secretary of the treasury handles the financial transactions relating to assistance to other countries. The secretary of health and human services supplies information essential to medical assistance for foreign lands.

In addition to the assistance and the advice provided by the executive departments, Congress has established a number of specialized agencies to help establish and carry out the nation's foreign policy.

The Central Intelligence Agency (CIA) is responsible for gathering information essential to national defense. The CIA also helps keep the president informed about political trends and developments in various nations.

The National Security Council (NSC) is part of the Executive Office of the President. Its members are the president, the vice president, and the secretaries of state and defense.

The chairperson of the Joint Chiefs of Staff and the director of the CIA attend all NSC meetings. The NSC was created to help coordinate U.S. military and foreign policy.

The United States Information Agency (USIA) helps keep the world informed about the American way of life and about American points of view on world issues. It does so through information centers set up in countries around the world. The USIA also publishes booklets, distributes films, and sponsors Voice of America radio programs.

The Arms Control and Disarmament Agency (ACDA) seeks to prevent dangerous weapons-building races. It does so by negotiating with other nations and seeking agreements on arms limitations.

Another agency that assists in foreign relations is the Agency for International Development (AID). It provides technical and financial assistance to developing nations. This agency

Reviewing

Have students complete the Section 1 Review.

Reteaching

Assign Section 1 of the Chapter 22 Reteaching Worksheet.

Extension

Have students research the foreign policy organizations of other countries. Students should use charts and diagrams to compare the structures and roles of foreign policy organizations in these countries with those of the United States. Students should address such issues as who establishes the country's foreign policy and whether the foreign policy power of those persons or organizations can be checked by other parts of their governments. Call on volunteers to present their findings and diagrams to the class.

has provided billions of dollars worth of raw materials, modern machinery, food, fuel, medical supplies, and loans to help the world's peoples. The agency also provides money and technical assistance during emergencies resulting from floods, outbreaks of disease, and other disasters.

Congress's Role

The president leads the nation in dealing with world affairs, but Congress also plays a major role. It is essential that the president work closely with leaders in both houses of Congress when deciding foreign policy issues. The Senate Foreign Relations Committee and the House Committee on Foreign Affairs make recommendations to Congress and the president on foreign relations issues.

Approval Powers The Senate, as you know, must approve by a two-thirds vote all treaties between the United States and other nations. What happens if the Senate refuses to approve a treaty?

After World War I, President Woodrow Wilson wanted the United States to join the League of Nations. A provision for joining this peacekeeping organization was included as a part of the Treaty of Versailles that ended World War I.

A powerful group of senators, however, opposed U.S. membership in the League of Nations. These senators wanted the United States to stay out of European affairs and to concentrate on solving its own problems. They eventually succeeded in preventing a two-thirds majority vote of the Senate in favor of the treaty. As a result, the United States did not approve the Treaty of Versailles or join the League of Nations.

The Senate also must approve by majority vote the appointment of all ambassadors. The president's nominations of ambassadors are almost always approved.

War-Making Powers Under the U.S. Constitution, as you recall, only Congress

can declare war. Over the years, however, presidents have sent troops to foreign countries without a declaration of war. In 1973 Congress passed the War Powers Act. This act limits the president's power to send troops abroad without the approval of Congress.

Financial Powers As you have read, both houses of Congress must approve all expenditures of public funds. This power, too, allows Congress to influence foreign affairs. All spending for national defense, for example, must be approved by Congress. The president may recommend that a new weapon be built or that the armed forces be expanded. Unless Congress votes for the necessary money, however, these policies cannot be carried out.

SECTION 1 REVIEW

1. Define or identify the following terms: interdependence, foreign relations, alliance, executive agreement, diplomatic recognition, diplomatic corps, courier.

2. What is the purpose of foreign policy? How do businesses and tourists affect U.S. foreign relations?

3. What military powers does the president have? diplomatic powers?

4. What three types of treaties does the president have the power to make?

5. How do the Department of State and the Department of Defense help the president carry out foreign policy?

6. How can Congress limit the president's activities in international affairs?

7. **THINKING CRITICALLY** Should citizens be kept informed of all foreign policy decisions, or should the president have the power to keep secret decisions that might affect national security?

SECTION 1 REVIEW ANSWERS

1. See the following pages: interdependence, foreign relations (p. 425); alliance, executive agreement, diplomatic recognition (p. 426); diplomatic corps, courier (p. 427).

2. have a plan for dealing with other nations; affect foreign trade and influence attitudes toward the United States

3. makes recommendations about military, can send military to trouble spots; appoints ambassadors, receives foreign ambassadors, may grant or end diplomatic recognition

4. peace, alliance, commercial

5. State—obtains information on which policy is based, advises, carries out policy, supervises diplomats; Defense—provides military information, advises on military matters, oversees military

6. must approve treaties, appointments; has power to declare war; War Powers Act, controls finances

7. Students should use sound reasoning in their responses.

SECTION OBJECTIVES

After studying Section 2, students should be able to do the following.

1. Explain the president's role as chief diplomat.
2. Explain the purposes of security alliances.
3. Describe NATO and Partnership for Peace.
4. Describe the history and purpose of U.S. foreign aid.
5. Explain the challenges posed by Pacific Rim countries and the goals of the European Union.
6. Describe the purposes of NAFTA, GATT, and APEC.

Teaching Section 2
Building a Vocabulary

Ask students for synonyms for the word **summit**. *(peak, height)* Then ask: Why is a meeting of the leaders of two nations called a summit? *(They are the nations' highest political leaders.)* Then teach the terms **import** and **export** by isolating the root *port* (from the Latin word meaning "carry") from its prefixes *im-*, meaning "in," and *ex-*, meaning "out." Finally, ask students what the word *free* in the term **free trade** means. *(no restrictions)*

CIVICS SIDELIGHT

During the Cold War, Americans got used to dramatic summit meetings between U.S. presidents and the leaders of the Soviet Union. The purposes of these meetings were to find common ground on issues of mutual concern and to reduce tensions between the superpowers. U.S. presidents and Soviet leaders met 16 times from 1961 to 1991. Five of those summits were held in the United States. U.S. presidents traveled to the Soviet Union for five summits. Six summits were held in other countries.

2 Working for Peace

That so many departments and agencies of the government devote so much time to foreign affairs indicates its importance. The chief goal of U.S. foreign policy is to maintain peace in the world. Government officials work in many ways to achieve this goal.

Diplomacy

The process of conducting relations between nations, as you recall, is called diplomacy. It is used to prevent war, negotiate an end to conflicts, solve problems, and establish communication between nations. The president is the nation's chief diplomat.

To carry out this role, presidents often use personal diplomacy. That is, they travel to other countries to meet with foreign leaders. They also consult with foreign officials in the United States. One such example of personal diplomacy is a summit. A **summit** is a meeting among the leaders of two or more nations to discuss issues that concern those nations.

Diplomacy is also carried out by other government officials. For example, State Department officials often represent the president in trying to settle conflicts between other nations. In recent years U.S. diplomats have traveled back and forth between different nations so often that this kind of peace seeking has become known as "shuttle diplomacy."

Alliances

The United States has alliances with many nations, including Japan, South Korea, and the Philippines. It has also established alliances with several large groups of nations.

In the Western Hemisphere, for example, the United States and most nations of Latin America formed the Organization of American States (OAS) in 1948. The goal of the OAS is mutual defense and the peaceful settlement of disputes among member nations. In 1951 Australia, New Zealand, and the United States

President Clinton and President Boris Yeltsin of Russia have used summits to forge effective communications between their two nations.

Conducting a Panel Discussion

Call on volunteers to list on the chalkboard the purposes of diplomacy. *(prevent war, negotiate end to conflicts, solve problems, establish communication between nations)* Then conduct a panel discussion on the personal and professional qualities a president needs to be a successful chief diplomat for the United States. Call on volunteers to use the panel discussion to list these qualities on the chalkboard to create a profile of the "ideal" chief diplomat.

Expressing a Point of View

Review the purpose of NATO, and briefly discuss the fall of communism in eastern Europe and the Soviet Union. Then ask: Should NATO continue to exist? Does the Partnership for Peace program extend or counteract NATO's purposes? Have students write newspaper opinion pieces supporting or opposing the disbanding of NATO. Call on volunteers to read aloud their opinion pieces to begin a discussion of the purposes of security alliances.

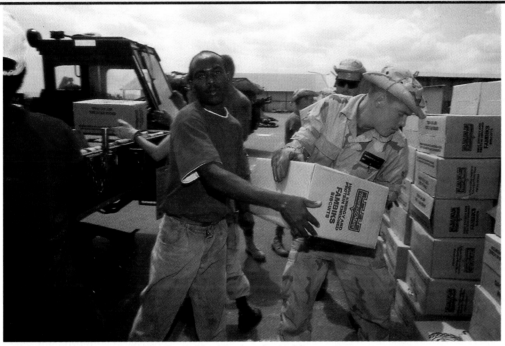

U.S. foreign aid sometimes takes the form of food for the victims of famine. Here food arrives for starving people in eastern Africa.

formed an alliance called ANZUS. The purpose of ANZUS is to provide mutual defense in case of attack.

Perhaps the most important security alliance of which the United States is a member is the North Atlantic Treaty Organization (NATO). NATO, to which most western European nations belong, was formed in 1949 to establish a united front against the threat of aggression by the Soviet Union and its communist eastern European allies. NATO members pledge that attack against one member will be considered an attack on all.

Since the breakup of the Soviet Union in the early 1990s and the move toward democracy in eastern Europe, several of the Soviet Union's former allies and other countries interested in peacekeeping have applied for NATO membership. Wary of forging new alliances too quickly, however, NATO has accepted 26 of these countries as members in its Partnership for Peace program. The program,

designed by the United States, allows countries to join NATO in military exercises, peacekeeping operations, and other activities as preparation for possible future membership. Partnership nations, however, are not included in NATO's mutual security guarantee.

Foreign Aid

Another important part of U.S. foreign policy is foreign aid. **Foreign aid** is any government program that provides economic or military assistance to other nations. The United States first gave large amounts of foreign aid during World War II. After the war's devastation, the nations of western Europe needed help. People needed food, clothing, and housing.

In 1947 U.S. Secretary of State George Marshall proposed a plan to help the war-torn nations of Europe rebuild their factories, farms, homes, and transportation systems. Under the Marshall Plan, Congress granted over

GLOBAL PERSPECTIVES

In 1992 industrialized nations provided nearly $116 billion in aid to other nations. The U.S. share was $33.5 billion, the highest total of any donor nation. Yet figured in per-capita terms, the United States, at $46 a person, ranked well behind Norway ($296), Sweden ($283), Denmark ($270), France ($144), Japan ($90), and several other countries.

Nations receiving the largest share of foreign aid from the United States in 1992 included Egypt, Israel, Peru, the Philippines, and Brazil. Israel received $4.75 billion, the most U.S. foreign assistance to any one country in 1992. Egypt received $2.5 billion that year, followed by Peru, in third place at $607 million.

Invite small groups of students to imagine that they are representing the United States at an international conference on foreign aid. Each group is to prepare a presentation on the history of U.S. foreign aid. As part of its presentation, each group should focus on a specific example of such aid, such as the Marshall Plan or aid to specific countries such as Israel, Egypt, and various Latin American, African, and Asian countries. Roles for group members include chairperson, researchers, writers, illustrators, and presenters.

Debating Ideas

Call on volunteers to come to the chalkboard to list the reasons the United States provides aid to foreign countries. Then organize the class into two groups to debate the following proposition: The United States, as one of the world's wealthiest nations, should increase the amount of money it provides in foreign aid. Make sure students on each side of the proposition make reasoned arguments for their positions. Call on a volunteer to serve as moderator during the class debate.

ℊlobal Perspectives

The value of U.S. exports in 1994 was estimated at about $513 billion, while the estimated value of imports to the United States was more than $663 billion. Canada was the largest U.S. trading partner in 1994, with exports to the United States valued at more than $128 billion and imports from the United States valued at more than $114 billion. The value of Japan's 1994 exports to the United States was estimated at about $119 billion, while that country's U.S. imports were valued at more than $53 billion. Germany, South Korea, and Taiwan were the next three largest importers of U.S. goods in 1994. China, Germany, and Taiwan were the next three top exporters of goods to the United States.

As a group, the value of exports from Pacific Rim countries to the United States was estimated at more than $261 billion in 1994. The same countries imported nearly $148 billion in U.S. goods the same year.

Peace Corps volunteers work in many countries throughout the world. This volunteer is helping with health care for children.

$13 billion in aid to these nations. By 1952 the economies of western Europe had recovered to a remarkable degree. Marshall Plan aid, having accomplished its goal, ended.

Since World War II, the United States has given or loaned nearly $440 billion in foreign aid. Almost 35 percent of the total money spent on U.S. foreign aid has been for military assistance. This money has helped nations throughout the world maintain their independence. U.S. economic assistance has helped nations in Africa, Asia, and Latin America become self-supporting.

The United States also participates in humanitarian aid efforts. In the early 1990s, for example, Somalia in Africa was torn apart by

civil war. Many Somali people had little or no food, and the fighting prevented relief workers from bringing help. As a result, thousands of Somali people died of starvation. In 1992 the United States joined other nations in sending troops to Somalia to help relief workers bring food and supplies to the starving people. In addition, the United States sent foodstuffs such as wheat, corn, and rice.

Individual Americans provide another type of foreign aid. The Peace Corps, established by President John F. Kennedy in the early 1960s, sends volunteers to countries that request assistance. Peace Corps volunteers in fields such as teaching, engineering, agriculture, and health care work in countries throughout the world.

Foreign Trade

As you have learned, the U.S. government must constantly struggle with economic challenges facing the nation. The economy at home, however, is not the government's only economic concern. The United States is linked with other nations through billions of dollars' worth of international trade. Economic events in other countries can pose serious challenges to the United States. Thus foreign trade is a central focus of U.S. foreign policy.

The United States has long held a position of strength in the global economy. In recent decades, however, foreign competition and economic alliances in other parts of the world have challenged the economic position of the United States.

The nations of the Pacific Rim, for example, compete with the United States in producing and selling goods. These nations include, among others, Australia, China, Hong Kong, Indonesia, Japan, Malaysia, Singapore, New Zealand, the Philippines, South Korea, and Taiwan. The ability of Pacific Rim nations to produce high-quality, low-priced goods such as automobiles, computers, and electronic equipment has created a high demand for these goods in the United States and many other countries around the world.

Guided Practice

Assign a dollar value to various "products" (such as books, pencils, paper, and chalk) and have three groups of students demonstrate the concepts of *balance of trade* and *trade deficit* by "exporting" and "importing" various quantities of products to and from each other. Have each group calculate its balance of trade. Ask: What economic challenge do the countries of the Pacific Rim and the EU present to the United States? *(Their growing economic strength challenges the once dominant position of the United States in world trade.)*

Independent Practice

Ask students to choose one of the following: NAFTA, APEC, or GATT. Have them write editorials describing how membership in NAFTA, association with APEC, or participation in GATT can help the United States meet the economic challenges posed by the Pacific Rim nations and the European Union. Call on volunteers to read their editorials to the class for discussion.

Although Japan is the economic leader in the Pacific Rim region, Hong Kong, Singapore, South Korea, and Taiwan also compete successfully in world markets. These countries, known as **newly industrialized countries (NICs)**, have experienced rapid industrialization and economic growth in recent years.

The success of the Pacific Rim nations in the global economy has had a significant impact on the U.S. **balance of trade**, or the difference in the value of the nation's exports and imports. **Exports** are those goods and services that the United States sells to other countries. **Imports** are those goods and services that the United States buys from other countries. In recent years the United States has suffered serious **trade deficits**. That is, the nation spends more money to buy foreign goods (imports) than it earns from sales of American-made goods (exports) to other countries.

Economic alliances among other countries also challenge the U.S. position in the global economy. For example, the European Union (EU) was formed in 1993 when 12 western European nations signed the Maastricht Treaty. EU nations were formerly and more loosely allied as the European Community (EC).

Among the goals of the now 15-member EU are the free movement of goods, workers, and capital among member nations. The European Union also seeks the expansion of its membership and a single currency. If the EU is successful in its plans, member nations will share an economic relationship similar to that found among the states of the United States. This will make the EU an extremely powerful trade group in the global economy.

Meeting Global Economic Challenges

Foreign competition has led the United States to seek ways to strengthen its position in the global economy. For example, the United States recently signed the North American Free-Trade Agreement (NAFTA), which allows free trade among the United States, Canada, and Mexico. **Free trade** is trade that is not

Container ships, such as the one shown below, carry much of the world's trade. Trade is an important part of any nation's foreign relations. The United States, for example, trades with most of the world's nations.

CIVICS SIDELIGHT

Not every American saw the North American Free-Trade Agreement as a step in the right direction. Many labor groups opposed NAFTA, claiming that U.S. jobs would go south, to Mexico. Ross Perot, the Texas billionaire who ran for president in 1992, suggested that Mexico's lack of environmental controls, low labor costs, and limited health care and retirement benefits for workers would draw U.S. industries into Mexico. Some observers say time will tell whether Perot was correct. As an extending exercise, you might have students research the results of NAFTA since it went into effect.

435

Closure

Have students draw political cartoons about the role of security alliances and international trade agreements in U.S. foreign policy. Some students might choose to focus on a specific security alliance or trade agreement. Call on volunteers to explain their cartoons to the class.

Reviewing

Have students complete the Section 2 Review.

Reteaching

Assign Section 2 of the Chapter 22 Reteaching Worksheet.

SECTION 2 REVIEW
ANSWERS

1. See the following pages: summit (p. 432); foreign aid (p. 433); newly industrialized country (NIC), balance of trade, export, import, trade deficit, free trade (p. 435).

2. personal diplomacy, summits; mutual defense, maintain peace, security

3. united front against threat of aggression from Soviet Union; does not extend mutual security guarantee

4. during and after World War II, to help war-torn Europe; purpose—humanitarian and security goals; forms—economic, military, technological

5. great demand for their products, thus threatening U.S. balance of trade; EU—free movement of goods, workers, and capital, membership expansion, single currency

6. encourages free trade, which helps jobs and growth; GATT—encourage free and fair trade around world

7. Students should make reasoned arguments.

436

restricted by tariffs and other trade barriers. As you know, tariffs are taxes on imports that make foreign goods more expensive. By eliminating such trade barriers, NAFTA members hope to open new markets, create jobs, and encourage economic growth in member nations.

The United States also hopes to improve its economic position through its membership in the Asia-Pacific Economic Cooperation Group (APEC). APEC is made up of the United States, Canada, Chile, Mexico, and 14 other nations of the Pacific Rim. Its goal is to promote cooperation among Asia-Pacific nations. In its association with APEC, the United States hopes to encourage the Pacific Rim nations, particularly Japan, to lower restrictions on U.S. exports and expand trade in the region.

Because the stability of the global economy has worldwide importance, the United States has joined with more than 100 other nations in the General Agreement on Tariffs and Trade (GATT). The GATT, which began in 1947 with 23 participants, is designed to encourage free trade among the nations of the world. It also works to establish fair and common standards in the way that each nation conducts trade with other nations.

The latest round of GATT talks, called the Uruguay Round, began in 1986 and concluded in 1994 after making groundbreaking advances in world trade agreements. To address changes in the global economy, this round also restructured the GATT by replacing it with the World Trade Organization (WTO).

Debating Free Trade

Although the WTO and the NAFTA agreement are expected to help U.S. consumers and producers in the long run, not all Americans support such measures. Opponents of free trade believe that tariffs are needed to protect U.S. industries and jobs from foreign competition. They maintain that raising the prices of foreign goods through tariffs will encourage U.S. consumers to buy American-made goods.

In contrast, supporters of free trade believe that opening the United States to foreign trade will help the nation gain greater access to foreign markets. This, they claim, will lead to increased economic growth for the United States and a strengthening of the nation's position in the global economy.

SECTION 2 REVIEW

1. Define or identify the following terms: summit, foreign aid, newly industrialized country (NIC), balance of trade, export, import, trade deficit, free trade.

2. How does the president carry out the role of chief diplomat? What are the purposes of security alliances?

3. Why did NATO form? How does membership in Partnership for Peace differ from membership in NATO?

4. When and why did the United States first give large amounts of foreign aid? What is the purpose of foreign aid, and what forms can it take?

5. Why do Pacific Rim nations present an economic challenge to the United States? What are the goals of the European Union?

6. How might membership in NAFTA and APEC help the U.S. economy? What is the purpose of the GATT?

7. **THINKING CRITICALLY** Do you think the United States should support or oppose free-trade policies? Why?

3 — The United Nations

In 1941 President Franklin D. Roosevelt met with Winston Churchill, the prime minister of Great Britain, to discuss the aims of the World War II Allies. The meeting was held on a ship in the Atlantic Ocean off the coast of Newfoundland. The agreement reached by these

SECTION OBJECTIVES

After studying Section 2, students should be able to do the following.

1. Describe Marx's ideas about communism.

2. Explain how the Soviet Union was formed.

3. Explain how the Cold War began and how Soviet influence spread.

4. Describe important events of the Cold War, including the U.S. response to the Berlin blockade, the Cuban missile crisis, the Korean War, and the Vietnam War.

as a part of the treaty ending World War I. Many Americans, however, including some powerful senators, opposed U.S. membership in the League. They feared that if the United States joined the League, the nation would be drawn into European conflicts. The spirit of U.S. isolationism remained strong. It helped keep the United States out of the League of Nations.

The beginning of World War II found the United States again in a neutral position. Congress passed a series of neutrality laws in the mid-1930s forbidding the sale of arms, or weapons, to warring nations. In 1939 the United States did agree to sell arms, but only on a cash-and-carry basis. That is, the arms sold had to be carried in foreign ships and paid for in cash, not on credit. Soon the United States, however, agreed to lend or lease (rent) billions of dollars' worth of arms to the cash-poor Allies. The United States became the "arsenal of democracy."

U.S. neutrality was shattered completely with the bombing of Pearl Harbor by the Japanese on December 7, 1941. The attack shocked the American people, who realized that isolationism in a worldwide conflict was impossible. The United States declared war on Japan and, soon afterward, on Germany and Italy.

While World War II was still being fought, plans were underway for a postwar organization of nations to maintain peace. In 1945, as you have learned, the United States joined with many other nations around the world to form the United Nations.

SECTION 1 REVIEW

1. Define or identify the following terms: isolationism, doctrine, corollary, dollar diplomacy, neutrality.

2. Why did the United States follow a policy of isolationism in its early history? Why was it difficult to maintain this policy?

3. Why was the War of 1812 a turning point in U.S. foreign policy? Describe relations between the United States and Canada today.

4. Why was the Monroe Doctrine put into effect? Why did the United States adopt the Good Neighbor Policy?

5. Why did the United States not remain neutral during World War I and World War II?

6. THINKING CRITICALLY Some people believe that the U.S. government should resume a policy of isolationism and concentrate on domestic issues. Others believe that a U.S. retreat from global issues would threaten the future of the nation and the world. What is your position on this issue, and why?

2   The Cold War

During World War II, the United States and the former Soviet Union were allied in fighting Nazi Germany. Soon after the war ended, however, the two nations came into conflict. What caused this change in relations? The roots of the conflict were in the two nations' very different economic systems and forms of government. The United States has always been a representative democracy, while the former Soviet Union was a communist nation.

Roots of Communism

The ideas behind modern communism come mainly from a German writer named Karl Marx. He believed that factory owners, or capitalists, throughout the world were getting rich by treating workers unfairly. With another writer, Friedrich Engels, Marx wrote a book called the *Communist Manifesto*.

In this book, written in 1848, Marx and Engels proposed a new economic system called

Teaching Section 2
Building a Vocabulary

Ask students to describe a satellite. *(any body, such as a moon or a spacecraft, that orbits another body)* Have students use that idea to define the term **satellite nation**. *(a nation controlled by [in orbit around] another nation)* Tell students that the term **communism** comes from the French word meaning "common," reflecting the idea that property is held in common, not privately, in such a system.

To help students review the philosophy of communism, have small groups create informative brochures or pamphlets that explain the roots of communism. The booklets should include written descriptions and illustrations explaining the economic and political views of communism. Roles for students include group leader, writers, illustrators, and production managers (to keep work flowing). Make copies of the booklets so that all group members have one for use as a study guide.

GLOBAL PERSPECTIVES

Winston Churchill, Great Britain's prime minister through much of World War II, sounded the alarm about the spread of communism in his famous speech at Westminster College in Fulton, Missouri, on March 5, 1946. To U.S. President Harry Truman and the rest of the audience that day, he said, in part: "From Stettin in the Baltic to Trieste in the Adriatic, an iron curtain has descended across the Continent."

Churchill contended that the Soviet Union had brought nearly all of eastern Europe under its control by installing communist parties in power there. Although they remained under the control of communist parties, Yugoslavia (in 1948) and Albania (in 1961) broke with Moscow and charted courses independent of the Soviet bloc. Other communist-ruled countries of eastern Europe remained behind the "iron curtain" until the end of the Cold War.

communism. They argued that in the future the workers, called the proletariat, would take over factories and businesses. Under communism, Marx said, the proletariat in all nations would own or control all the means of production—the land, capital, and labor. Private individuals (capitalists) would not be permitted to own or control the means of production to make profits. Later Marx expanded these ideas in another book called *Das Kapital* (from the German word meaning "capital").

According to Marx, the proletariat would run the government. Everything from raw materials to finished products would be owned by the government in the name of the workers. In the process, capitalism would be overthrown, by force if necessary. The workers would establish a "dictatorship of the proletariat" around the world. Communism thus would be both an economic and a political system.

Communism in the Soviet Union

In 1917 Russia became the first nation to adopt a communist system. Russia's ruler, the czar,

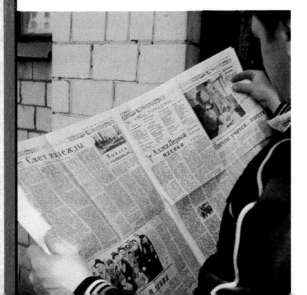

In the former Soviet Union the government strictly controlled the press for decades. The people received news from the government news agency, Tass.

was overthrown, and a communist government was established under Vladimir Ilich Lenin. Russia became the Union of Soviet Socialist Republics (USSR), or the Soviet Union. Lenin was succeeded by Joseph Stalin, and a new, harsh rule began. Stalin established a communist dictatorship that completely controlled the people of the Soviet Union.

For decades, the Communist party of the Soviet Union was all-powerful. The communist government made all economic decisions for the nation. It owned and managed all of the nation's industries and farms. It also controlled most aspects of citizens' lives.

Most people, for example, had little choice concerning the type of job they held, the education they received, or even where they could travel or live within the country. For years, no political party except the Communist party was allowed to exist. There was no free press to tell the truth to the people. Journalists reported only what the government told them to report. The Soviet people had little control over their lives and their government.

The people of the Soviet Union suffered other hardships under communism. For example, through enforced programs, the government drove its citizens to make the Soviet Union a modern industrial nation. By 1950 the country ranked second among the industrial powers of the world, surpassed only by the United States. This rapid progress was an amazing feat.

Such progress had a high price, however. The standard of living in the Soviet Union was much lower than that in the United States. Because the Soviet government concentrated its production efforts on the machinery needed for industrialization, there often were shortages of basic consumer goods, including food. These shortages caused widespread hardship. People often waited long hours just to buy a pair of shoes or a loaf of bread.

Communism Spreads

After World War II, hopes were high that the Soviet Union and the United States, allies in

Have students imagine that they are living in Russia sometime after the communist takeover of 1917. Assign students to write journal entries describing life in the country, including how political and economic decisions are made. Invite volunteers to share their entries with the class as part of a discussion about the origins of the Soviet Union.

Have pairs of students sketch maps of the world. Students might want to trace the outline of the world from the map on pages 520–521. As students study this section, they should shade the parts of their world map that came under communist control at various times. Suggest that they use different colors to denote the different time periods of communism's spread. Students should use legends to identify the colors and time periods. Call on volunteers to use their maps to explain the spread of communism and the U.S. response (the policy of containment).

---

the war, would remain friends. It was hoped that the Soviet Union would share the ideals expressed in the Atlantic Charter and the United Nations Charter. People of all nations wished that the world might now find a way to live in peace.

These hopes were soon shattered. During World War II, the Soviet Union occupied large parts of Poland and Romania. After the war, Russia used its presence in the region to interfere in the affairs of eastern Europe. In country after country leaders of political parties opposed to communism were jailed, forced to flee, or assassinated. Within a few years communist governments were set up in Poland, Romania, Bulgaria, Hungary, Czechoslovakia, Albania, and East Germany. The Soviet Union had turned the countries along its borders into **satellite nations**, or nations that are controlled by another country.

Soviet leaders maintained that these actions were necessary so that the Soviet Union would never again be attacked by Germany or any other nation of western Europe. Leaders in the United States and western Europe, however, believed the Soviets had more in mind than the defense of their country. They believed the Soviet Union, with its great new military strength, would try to impose Soviet-dominated communist governments throughout the world.

Only the fear of U.S. nuclear bombs, some believed, prevented Soviet forces from overrunning all of western Europe. At that time only the United States had nuclear weapons.

The Cold War Begins

With the satellite nations of eastern Europe under its control, the Soviet Union tried to increase its power in the eastern Mediterranean Sea and Southwest Asia, also called the Middle East. The Soviet Union sought an ice-free route for Soviet ships into the oceans of the world. It also wanted influence in the oil-rich lands of Southwest Asia.

Soviet troops had occupied part of Iran, with its rich oil fields, during World War II.

Instead of withdrawing after the war, Soviet troops remained and even increased in number. A communist party was encouraged by the Soviets in Greece. Turkey was faced with a demand for a Soviet naval base on its territory. The United States and other noncommunist nations saw these southward thrusts of Soviet power as serious threats to their national security and to world peace.

Thus soon after the end of World War II, much of the world was caught up in a competition for global power and influence, which came to be known as the Cold War. On one side of the conflict was the Soviet Union and its satellite nations. On the other side was the United States and other noncommunist nations.

Both sides in the Cold War used propaganda, spying, alliances, foreign aid, and other methods to "win" the war. Issues related to the Cold War occupied most of U.S. foreign policy in the years following World War II.

The Policy of Containment

The president of the United States in the immediate postwar period was Harry Truman. He warned the Soviet Union that it must withdraw its troops from Iran. The Soviet Union agreed to do so. President Truman then asked Congress to provide military equipment and economic aid to Greece and Turkey to help them resist Soviet influence. Partly because of this aid, Greece and Turkey did not become satellites of the Soviet Union.

The success of U.S. aid to Greece and Turkey encouraged the U.S. government to give similar aid to other European nations. This policy of helping free nations resist communist aggression became known as the Truman Doctrine.

The idea behind this policy came to be called **containment**. The purpose of containment was to prevent Soviet communism from spreading. The forces of the Soviet Union were to be "contained" within the area they had occupied up to 1948. U.S. policy makers expected, however, that the Soviet Union would test U.S. commitment to the policy.

CIVICS SIDELIGHT

In 1960 Americans were introduced to a previously secret side of the Cold War. In May of that year the Soviet Union announced that it had shot down a high-flying U.S. reconnaissance ("spy") plane known as a U-2. The pilot, Francis Gary Powers, was held prisoner in Moscow. (Powers was exchanged for a Soviet spy two years later.) The U-2 incident helped reheat the Cold War by cutting short a summit meeting in Paris attended by leaders of the United States, the Soviet Union, Great Britain, and France. The United States and the Soviet Union continued to use various methods, including orbiting satellites, to spy on each other.

Assign each small group one of the following topics: the Berlin blockade, the communist takeover in China, the Cuban missile crisis, the Korean War, or the Vietnam War. Have each group prepare a "You Are There" newscast about its assigned topic. The newscast should describe important actions and the role of U.S. policy in each event. Roles for students include narrator (or "news anchor"), reporters, scriptwriters, directors, and producers. Have each group present its newscast to the class.

Guided Practice

On the chalkboard begin a time line illustrating the history of the Soviet Union, the spread of communism, and the Cold War. Call on volunteers to come to the board to write (in the time line) and explain important events they have studied in this section. Have students copy the time line into their notebooks for use as a study guide.

The 1948 Berlin airlift brought needed food and supplies to people in West Berlin.

The Berlin Blockade

The first real test of containment came in 1948 in Berlin. At the end of World War II, Germany was divided into two separate nations. East Germany became a communist nation while West Germany became a democratic republic. The city of Berlin, although located in East Germany, was not part of that nation.

Berlin was occupied by troops of four nations—France, Great Britain, the United States, and the Soviet Union. Each nation controlled a part of the city. The Soviet Union had access to Berlin through Soviet-controlled East Germany. The noncommunist nations had free access to the city over special land routes through East Germany.

In June 1948 the Soviet Union closed these routes. That is, it started a blockade of Berlin. Soviet strategy in closing East German routes into Berlin was to force the noncommunist occupation forces to leave. The Soviets planned to make the city a communist center.

As a result of the blockade, the German people living in the British, French, and American sections of the city, called West Berlin, could not receive food and coal. They faced cold and starvation.

The United States and Great Britain took prompt action. They began a massive airlift of fuel, food, clothing, and other vital items. Airplanes loaded with supplies flew into the city. Day after day, in all kinds of weather, U.S. and British planes landed in West Berlin. More than 250,000 flights brought two million tons of needed supplies to West Berlin. Their blockade failing, the Soviets agreed in 1949 to reopen the land routes to Berlin.

Communism in China

After World War II, a full-scale civil war broke out in China. In 1949 Chinese Communists defeated the government led by Chiang Kaishek. Chiang's forces fled to the island of Taiwan, off the southeast coast of China. There they set up a government in exile, called Nationalist China, or the Republic of China.

The Communists held the mainland—known as the People's Republic of China. The first head of the People's Republic of China was Mao Zedong.

The United States refused to recognize the People's Republic of China. Instead, it provided economic and military aid to Nationalist China (Taiwan). With the support of the United States and other noncommunist nations, Nationalist China was allowed to remain a member of the United Nations. In 1971, however, Nationalist China was expelled from, or forced out of, the United Nations and replaced by the People's Republic of China.

The Cuban Missile Crisis

The Cold War between the United States and the Soviet Union took a dangerous turn when the Soviet Union developed its own nuclear weapons during the 1950s. Leaders of both countries recognized that a **balance of power**, or situation in which countries are about equal

Have students use classroom and library resources to illustrate the history of Arab-Israeli relations since 1948. Students might create collages or time lines, for example, that help explain the series of historical events leading from Israeli independence through various wars to the peace table. Illustrations and diagrams should include explanatory captions. Call on volunteers to present and explain their work to the class for discussion.

Review with students the relationship between China and the United States, particularly since the Chinese government's crackdown in Tiananmen Square in 1989. Explain that some policy makers believe the best way to encourage economic and political reform in China is to maintain positive U.S. relations through trade and other diplomatic efforts. Critics of this policy believe the United States should take a harder line against the Chinese government. Have students write newspaper editorials on the issue.

because it contains much of the world's oil. Though the United States has tried to maintain good relations with all nations in Southwest Asia, this has not always been possible.

In 1990 the nation of Kuwait was invaded by Iraqi troops. The government of Iraq, led by the dictator Saddam Hussein, wished to take control of Kuwait's rich oil fields. Many feared that Iraq might also invade Saudi Arabia.

The United States led the members of the United Nations in condemning Iraq's actions. Troops from the United States and other nations were sent to the region to protect it from Iraqi aggression. In early 1991 the United States led a ground and air assault on Iraq. The U.S.-allied victory in the Persian Gulf War freed Kuwait from Iraqi control.

Another area of Southwest Asia that has been plagued by troubles is Israel and its surrounding Arab neighbors. Because of differences in religion and culture, and because of boundary disputes, Israel has fought several wars with its neighbors since its creation as a nation in 1948. A major source of conflict has been tension between Israelis and Palestinians concerning territorial control and Palestinian self-rule.

U.S. officials have worked for years to help bring about lasting peace in the area. In September 1993 President Bill Clinton hosted the signing of an historic peace agreement between Israeli prime minister Yitzhak Rabin and Palestinian leader Yasser Arafat. This agreement and later ones allow for Palestinian self-rule in certain areas. Although many difficult issues remain to be settled, the United States is hopeful that the peace agreement will end years of bitter fighting in the region.

South Africa

The nation of South Africa is located at the southern tip of the continent of Africa. For decades, South Africa operated under a system of **apartheid**, or separation of the races. Under apartheid, all political, social, and economic power in the country was held by the white South Africans, who made up a minority of the

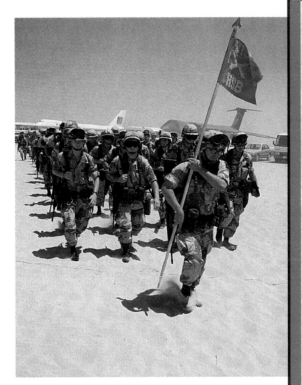

These U.S. soldiers marching in Saudi Arabia were sent to that nation in 1990 to protect it from its aggressive northern neighbor, Iraq.

population. Black South Africans and those of mixed race had limited access to housing, employment, education, and health care. In addition, their personal rights and freedoms were severely restricted.

The United States and other nations around the world condemned the system of apartheid. Responding to international pressure and growing internal unrest, the South African government announced important reforms in 1990.

Although the process was slow and often violent, apartheid officially ended in 1993. The nation's first free elections were held in 1994. Anti-apartheid leader Nelson Mandela became the new president of South Africa.

(continued on page 460)

GLOBAL PERSPECTIVES

Even before the creation of a Jewish state in Southwest Asia, many Jews from across the globe had begun to return to their biblical homeland. After the state of Israel was established in 1948, the Knesset (Israel's national legislature) passed the Law of Return, which gave every Jew in the world the right to immigrate to Israel. Jews from the United States, Russia, Egypt, and many other countries poured into Israel. Of Israel's 1995 population of more than 5.1 million, 82 percent was Jewish. Since the time Israel became a nation in 1948, it endured decades of conflict with its Arab neighbors. In the 1990s, however, much progress was being made toward ending the conflict and bringing peace to this area of the world. The peace process suffered a severe setback in 1995, when Prime Minister Yitzhak Rabin was assassinated by a Jewish student who opposed Rabin's peace agreement with Palestinian leader Yasser Arafat. Rabin, who was a recipient of the Nobel Peace prize, had served as Israel's prime minister since 1992.

Linking Civics and History

Have small groups of students research the effects of human rights issues on U.S. foreign policy in the past. Students should note not only the policy the United States adopted toward a country but also criticism of that policy. Possible areas of study include China, South Africa, El Salvador, Iran (before and after 1979), the Philippines, and Haiti. Have students report their findings to the class.

GLOBAL PERSPECTIVES

The Universal Declaration of Human Rights, drafted by a United Nations commission headed by Eleanor Roosevelt, was created largely in response to the horrors of World War II's Nazi Holocaust. During the Holocaust, millions of people, especially Jews, were killed on the basis of their religious or ethnic backgrounds. The commission wanted to produce a document that would help put an end to such crimes against humanity. In enumerating the basic human rights to which all people of the world are entitled, the commission also included basic survival rights. These rights include the right to sufficient food, shelter, health care, education, and work. Although the Universal Declaration of Human Rights set a standard for the humane treatment of people everywhere, it is not a legally enforceable document.

Citizenship IN ACTION

POWER OF THE PEN

In 1948 the United States joined with other nations to create the *Universal Declaration of Human Rights*. This document set a worldwide standard for basic human rights. Although the document has helped improve conditions for the world's people, many governments continue to abuse the rights of their citizens. Thanks to the efforts of teenagers across the United States, however, these governments are learning that they cannot hide human-rights violations from the rest of the world.

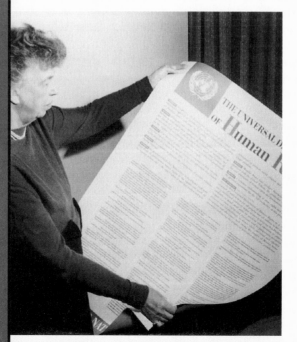

In 1948 former first lady Eleanor Roosevelt helped draft the Universal Declaration of Human Rights.

The Fight for Human Rights

The students who are fighting for human rights are members of Amnesty International. This worldwide organization works for the release of people who have been unfairly imprisoned, for fair and speedy trials for political prisoners, and for an end to government torture and abuse of citizens. Nearly 2,000 middle schools and high schools in the United States have chapters that help Amnesty International in its work.

When the organization learns of a human rights abuse occurring in some part of the world, student members in different chapters jump into action. One of their efforts is to launch massive letter-writing campaigns.

In Brockton, Massachusetts, for example, student members at Brockton High School learned that a 10-year-old boy in Guatemala had been shot and paralyzed when government soldiers attacked his father, a union activist. The Brockton High students wrote letters to raise money and were able to bring the boy to the United States for needed medical care.

Gathering Information

Have the class write to Amnesty International to learn more about letter-writing campaigns to help victims of human rights abuses. Students might request copies of typical letters that individuals have written in the past, as well as information about how students can become involved in the process. Students may write to Amnesty International/ USA at 322 Eighth Avenue, New York, NY 10001-4808.

In Maine, students helped free a man in Ethiopia who had been jailed because he belonged to an ethnic group the government disliked and because he spoke out against government oppression. The Amnesty letter writers waged a years-long campaign, asking the Ethiopian government to release the man. The government finally released the prisoner. One year later he visited Maine to thank the Amnesty members for their efforts.

Student Amnesty members also write letters to ask governments to investigate the murder or disappearance of citizens. They send petitions calling for the humane treatment of prisoners. One political prisoner in the Dominican Republic, for example, had his clothes taken away in jail. After the government received 200 letters from Amnesty International, guards returned the man's clothes to him. After the government received 3,000 letters, the man was released.

In addition to letter-writing campaigns, students across the nation work to raise money to help political prisoners worldwide. In Plattsburgh, New York, for example, Amnesty members from Plattsburgh High School held a "rock-athon" to raise money for human rights. These students rocked in rocking chairs for eight hours to earn pledges of support. In Napa County, California, students participated in an art exhibit to benefit the cause of human rights. The exhibit, titled "The Power of Hope," made the public aware of human-rights issues.

The Need for Involvement

Why have these students and thousands of others across the nation become involved in protecting human rights? They have done so because they want to put an end to human suffering. Of course, this is not an easy task. According to Amnesty International, nearly half the world's nations imprison people without trials. One of every three nations uses torture. Securing human rights for the world's people requires the commitment of everyone who values freedom, justice, and equality.

An Amnesty International poster

YOU DECIDE

1 What is Amnesty International?

2 Do you think Americans have the right to question the actions of governments other than their own? Why or why not?

3 Research the human-rights groups active in your community or state. How do these groups further the cause of human rights? What can teenagers do to help?

CIVICS SIDELIGHT

Amnesty International was founded in 1961. The organization particularly focuses its efforts on helping what it calls "prisoners of conscience"—people imprisoned primarily for their political or religious beliefs. Amnesty International has approximately 400,000 members in the United States, and branches of the organization can be found in many nations around the world.

ANSWERS TO YOU DECIDE

1. worldwide organization that works for the release of people who have been unfairly imprisoned, for fair and speedy trials for political prisoners, and for an end to government torture and abuse of citizens

2. Answers will vary. Students should use sound reasoning in their responses.

3. Students may find a variety of groups in your community or state. Students should suggest concrete actions teenagers can take to help.

Guided Practice

Create a chart with three headings, one each for Japan, Canada, and Mexico. Under each heading have students suggest actions the United States has taken to promote freer trade with each country and identify reasons why freer trade is important to each nation. *(In general, freer trade helps lower the U.S. trade deficit, strengthens U.S. and foreign economies by facilitating export sales, and lowers the costs of goods for consumers in all involved countries).*

Independent Practice

Have students illustrate the advantages of free trade by creating posters for an advertising campaign advocating free trade. Students should identify their audiences and gear their advertisements toward them. Display the posters for the class, and call on volunteers to explain their projects.

GLOBAL PERSPECTIVES

Nelson Mandela, South Africa's first black president, spent more than 27 years in prison in South Africa for his part in the struggle against apartheid. Freed in 1990 at the age of 71, Mandela immediately took up the struggle once more. He sat at the negotiating table with the leader of the South African government, F. W. de Klerk. Together they worked out a solution that would eventually give control of the government to the black majority. For their efforts, both men received the Nobel Prize for peace in 1993.

Much of U.S. foreign policy is influenced by the importance of trade. Here, representatives from the United States, Canada, and Mexico discuss the North American Free-Trade Agreement.

China

With the breakup of the Soviet Union and the fall of communism in eastern Europe, the People's Republic of China is one of the few remaining communist nations in the world. Until the 1970s, U.S. relations with China were strained. In 1971, however, the two nations entered a period of détente.

Since that time, the United States has moved forward in its relations with China. For example, the two nations have opened their doors to an exchange of journalists, students, and scholars. Trade between the two countries is also booming. China has introduced many free-market reforms, allowing its citizens to start new businesses. Although disagreements over trade practices remain, U.S. businesses are eager to expand trade with China.

U.S. attempts to improve relations with China were dealt a blow in 1989, however. In that year the Chinese government brutally ended demonstrations in Beijing by Chinese citizens who were calling for democratic reforms. (See "Case Study: Tiananmen Square" on pages 428–429.) The United States condemned this action and has since looked for ways to encourage the protection of human rights in China.

Japan and the Pacific Rim

As you know, the countries of the Pacific Rim include, among others, the United States, Australia, Indonesia, Japan, New Zealand, the Philippines, Singapore, and South Korea. Trade issues dominate much of the foreign relations between the United States and the Pacific Rim nations, particularly Japan. Trade across the Pacific has soared in recent years as televisions, cameras, stereos, automobiles, computers, clothing, timber, and agricultural products pour across the ocean.

The huge U.S. trade deficit with Japan, however, causes alarm among many U.S. economists and government officials. As you recall, a trade deficit means the United States buys many more goods and services from Japan than it sells to Japan.

Many economists and officials believe the trade deficit weakens the U.S. economy. They also believe the deficit is caused in part by the refusal of Japan's government to open its markets fully to U.S. and other foreign goods and services. The U.S. government continues to work at improving trade relations with Japan and expanding free trade across the Pacific.

Latin America

For many years the United States was concerned about the possible spread of communism to some Latin American countries. The communist government established in Cuba by Fidel Castro in 1959, for example, remains in place. Since the breakup of the Soviet Union and the end of communism in eastern Europe, however, the Cuban economy has been in shambles. Cuba relied heavily on the Soviet Union for financial aid. The United States does not trade with Cuba and does not offer foreign aid to the country.

The main goal of U.S. foreign policy in Latin America today has shifted to expanding trade and opening new markets. As you have learned, the United States recently entered into the North American Free-Trade Agreement (NAFTA) with Canada and Mexico. All three countries hope to create new jobs and markets in their countries under the agreement. The United States is interested in forming similar economic alliances with Central and South American countries.

Understanding Foreign Policy

The basic goal of U.S. foreign policy—to promote peace, trade, and friendship throughout the world—does not change. The ways in which the United States tries to achieve this goal, however, change with changing times. New situations and new problems constantly challenge U.S. policy makers. New problems require new solutions. As a U.S. citizen, it is your responsibility to stay informed about the nation's foreign policy and let your government representatives know your concerns.

SECTION 3 REVIEW

1. Define or identify the following terms: *glasnost, perestroika,* détente, nationalism, reunification, apartheid.

2. What events marked the end of the Cold War? Why is the United States concerned about the rise of nationalism in Russia?

3. How did the fall of the Berlin Wall affect East and West Germany? Why did civil war break out in former Yugoslavia?

4. Why did the United States fight in the Persian Gulf War? What recent event has brought hopes of peace in Southwest Asia?

5. How have U.S. relations with China changed over time? What issues dominate relations between the United States and Japan?

6. What is the goal of NAFTA?

7. **THINKING CRITICALLY** Imagine that you are a foreign adviser to the president. What do you think should be the position of the United States concerning trade with nations that violate human rights? Should the United States limit or stop trading with these nations? Explain your answer.

CHAPTER 23 SUMMARY

Forming U.S. foreign policy is a complex and continually changing process as new international challenges appear. Through the years, the United States has moved from a policy of isolationism to deep involvement in world affairs. In this century the nation has fought in two world wars.

After World War II, the world was dominated by two opposing groups of nations. The worldwide struggle between communist and noncommunist nations, using every means short of all-out war, became known as the Cold War. Under its policy of containment, the United States fought limited wars against communist forces in Korea and Vietnam.

In recent years the breakup of the Soviet Union, the fall of the Berlin Wall, and the collapse of communism in eastern Europe signaled the end of the Cold War. The United States has revised its foreign policy to adapt to these changes and to changes taking place in other parts of the world.

SECTION 3 REVIEW ANSWERS

1. See the following pages: *glasnost, perestroika,* détente (p. 455); nationalism, reunification (p. 456); apartheid (p. 457).

2. Soviet reforms under Gorbachev, fall of communism in eastern Europe, dismantling of Berlin Wall, collapse of Soviet Union; fear that Russia may again force its will on the former Soviet republics

3. ultimately led to reunification; Yugoslavia—ethnic conflict and end of strong central government

4. to protect Kuwait and its neighbors from Iraqi aggression; recent event—peace accord between Israel and Palestinians

5. U.S. relations with China were strained before 1970, but then improved until the Tiananmen incident. Japan—trade issues

6. create new jobs and markets by eliminating trade barriers

7. Students should consider consequences of limiting or not limiting trade.

Invite students to imagine that they are newspaper reporters in the year 2050. Each student will write an in-depth article on the history of the Cold War in the 20th century. Have students make lists of some specific primary sources they would need to review to write their articles. *(Possible primary sources include specific speeches by government officials and diplomats, UN documents and resolutions, letters and journal entries of leaders and ordinary citizens, government documents listing military and political information and strategies, and eyewitness accounts and interviews that were published or broadcast.)*

Developing Civics Skills

SOCIAL STUDIES SKILL
Using Primary Sources

Primary sources of information are written by people who witnessed or participated in historical events. Primary sources differ from secondary sources. Secondary sources are usually written after an event has taken place. They are often written by an author using primary source materials.

Both primary and secondary sources provide important facts. Only primary sources, however, allow you to see events through the eyes of the people who experienced them. They not only provide information about the event, but also give you glimpses of the attitudes, feelings, and concerns of people who lived in the past.

You will find many primary sources in your research. You need to know how to use them.

How to Use Primary Sources

1. **Identify the source's background.** To judge the accuracy and reliability of a primary source, you must understand who wrote the source and the conditions under which it was written. As you read, ask yourself if the author is biased in some way. Research what was happening in the world at the time the source was written. Answering these and similar questions will help you decide if the source is accurate and reliable.
2. **Read the source.** Read the source several times until you are confident you understand its meaning. Look up any words you do not know. As you read the source, be sure to identify all facts. Also note any statements that give you insight into the opinions of the author and the period in which the author lived.
3. **Draw conclusions.** Use your careful reading of the source to draw conclusions about the topic or event discussed.

Applying the Skill

The primary source on this page is part of a speech written by President George Washington as he was about to leave office in 1796. Read the source. Then answer the following questions.

1. Why might Washington's speech be a good source of information on early U.S. foreign policy?
2. What is the basic message of this part of the speech?
3. What arguments does the president use to support his position?
4. Based on the secondary source information in this textbook, why might Washington have taken this position?

The great rule of conduct for us is to extend our commercial relations with foreign nations, but to have as little political connection with foreign nations as possible. Let us fulfill our previous commitments. Here let us stop.

Europe's interests have little relation to ours. It is engaged in frequent controversies that are not important to us. Thus it is unwise for us to let artificial ties involve us in Europe's politics.

Our distance from Europe permits us to pursue a different course. Why give up the advantages of our special situation? Why entangle our peace and prosperity in the web of European ambition, rivalry, interest, and whim?

It is our true policy to steer clear of permanent alliances with any foreign nation.

ANSWERS TO Applying the Skill

1. Washington, as the first U.S. president, was important in developing early U.S. foreign policy.
2. The United States should avoid political entanglements with foreign nations, particularly European nations.
3. Europe's interests and controversies have little relation to those of the United States; distance from Europe insulates the United States from European problems.
4. The United States was working to develop its economy and faced other problems that needed the attention of the government.

CHAPTER 23 REVIEW
A N S W E R S

Vocabulary Workshop
1. apartheid
2. Mikhail Gorbachev
3. statement of policy
4. include Poland, Romania, Hungary, Czechoslovakia, Bulgaria, and East Germany; controlled by another country (U.S.S.R.)
5. neutrality
6. situation in which two countries are about equal in strength

Reviewing Main Ideas
1. to prevent new Latin American nations from being conquered again by any European nation; help nations resist communist aggression
2. was in debt, needed to develop economy and solve domestic problems; Isolationism became impractical because of tensions with other nations.
3. Both heightened tensions between U.S. and Soviet Union; fall of communism, fall of Berlin Wall, breakup of Soviet Union
4. to defend South Korea from communist aggression; Iraq driven from Kuwait
5. Russia might seek to regain control over former Soviet republics; NAFTA—remove trade barriers between U.S., Canada, and Mexico

Thinking Critically
1. Students should consider current and future foreign policy challenges.
2. Students might compare world affairs in the late 18th century and today.

Citizenship in Your Community
Posters should illustrate the effects of the Cold War.

Building Your Portfolio
Assign Portfolio Assessment Worksheet 23 in the *Portfolio Assessment Worksheets* booklet.

Assessment
- **Chapter 23 Tests**, *Chapter Tests* booklet
- **Test Generator**, Chapter 23
- **Portfolio**, Portfolio Assessment Worksheet 23, *Portfolio Assessment Worksheets* booklet

CHAPTER 23 R · e · v · i · e · w

Vocabulary Workshop
1. What term is used to describe South Africa's former policy of racial separation?
2. Who began the policies of *glasnost* and *perestroika* in the former Soviet Union?
3. What is a doctrine?
4. Identify three former satellite nations in eastern Europe. Why are these nations included in this category?
5. What term refers to a policy of refusing to take sides in a conflict?
6. Define the term *balance of power*.

Reviewing Main Ideas
1. Why did the United States adopt the Monroe Doctrine? What was the main purpose of the Truman Doctrine?
2. Why did the United States seek to stay out of world affairs in its early years? Why did this policy change?
3. How did the Berlin blockade and the Cuban missile crisis contribute to the Cold War? What events signaled the end of the Cold War?
4. Why did the United States participate in the Korean War? What was the outcome of the Persian Gulf War?
5. How might the rise of Russian nationalism be dangerous to world peace? What is the goal of NAFTA?

Thinking Critically
1. Because the Cold War has ended, the United States has reduced spending on the military and national defense. Do you believe this policy is wise, or should the United States maintain the troop levels of the Cold War? Why?
2. If the founders of the nation were alive today, would they promote U.S. isolationism or would they promote involvement in global affairs? Explain your answer.

Citizenship in Your Community

Cooperative Project
With your group, research the effects of the Cold War on your community or state. Were many people employed in defense-related industries? How has the end of the Cold War affected their jobs? You might search newspaper files and interview residents to learn if fears of nuclear war affected people in your community or state. Create a poster that displays the information your group has collected. Be sure to title your poster and label any images or drawings.

Building Your Portfolio

The second step of your unit portfolio project (see page 465) is to create a four-column chart of the alliances you hope to pursue with the other nations of the world. In the first column list the country or group of countries with which New Populous hopes to ally itself. You may list existing alliances or outline new alliances. In the second column indicate the type of alliance New Populous is proposing—economic, scientific, defense, and so on. In the third column list the benefits New Populous will gain from the alliances listed in the first column. Finally, in the fourth column list the resources New Populous will bring to each alliance. How will its membership in each alliance benefit the other members? Place your chart in your individual portfolio for later use.

UNIT 7 REVIEW
A N S W E R S

Reviewing Main Ideas

1. nation's plan for dealing with other nations; Conduct of foreign policy affects relations with foreign countries.
2. economic system in which means of production are owned by and economy managed by government in the name of the workers; U.S. policy of containment
3. to present united front against communist aggression; plan to prepare former communist nations for possible future NATO membership but no mutual security guarantee
4. U.S. policy to protect new Latin American nations against aggression by Spain or by any European nation; to assure Latin American nations that U.S. would stay out of their affairs
5. détente—easing of tensions; *glasnost, perestroika*, efforts at détente with U.S.
6. for—promotes negotiation over conflict, provides forum for all nations; against—U.S. pays more than its fair share for cost of operations, ineffective because no permanent UN army that can end military disputes, large countries can be outvoted by more numerous small countries
7. war fought without using nation's full military power; U.S. sought to contain communism by supporting South Vietnam
8. These nations produce goods and services that compete

with U.S. goods and services, affecting U.S. balance of trade.

Thinking Critically

1. Students should consider the advantages and disadvantages of providing aid, as well as the possible consequences of not providing aid.
2. Students might say the existence of nuclear weapons might bring about an even more devastating war.

Practicing Civics Skills

1. Students should base their generalizations on figures from the table.
2. Summaries should compare the fighting in the two conflicts.

accounts, and identify how the fighting differed in the two conflicts.

Reviewing Main Ideas

1. What is foreign policy? How does foreign policy differ from foreign relations?
2. What is communism? What was the U.S. response to the spread of communism in the years after World War II?
3. Why was NATO formed? What is the Partnership for Peace program?
4. What was the Monroe Doctrine? Why was it replaced by the Good Neighbor Policy?
5. What is détente? What were Mikhail Gorbachev's reform policies?
6. What are the arguments for and against the United Nations?
7. What is a limited war? Why did the United States send troops to Vietnam?
8. Why do the Pacific Rim nations and the European Union present economic challenges to the United States?

Thinking Critically

1. If Russia is to achieve full democracy and the goal of a free-market economy, it will need billions of dollars in foreign aid. Should the United States provide economic aid to Russia? Why or why not?
2. How might a world war fought today differ from the two world wars fought earlier in this century?

Practicing Civics Skills

1. Research the U.S. balance of trade with Japan for the past 10 years. Show this information in a table. What generalizations can you make from this information?
2. Read firsthand accounts of the fighting in two wars in which the United States was involved in this century. Summarize these

Citizenship in Your Community

Individual Project

Interview at least five members of your community about current U.S. foreign policy. About what issue or issues are local residents most concerned? Next, research foreign policy concerns of the American people as a whole. You can find the results of public opinion polls and newspaper and periodical articles on foreign policy in your school or local library. Use the information you have gathered to write a newspaper article for your school newspaper. In your article compare the concerns of your community to the concerns of the nation as a whole. You may want to include excerpts of your interviews to highlight the main points of your article.

Learning from Technology

On-line Computer Services

On-line computer companies offer a wide variety of services, including electronic mail, bulletin boards, games, clubs, and news. Some on-line services emphasize user interaction, allowing subscribers from different cities and nations to "talk" to each other via their computers. How might such international "conversations" affect foreign relations? Might they present national security problems? Should the government have the power to monitor computer conversations of people they consider national security risks? In such cases, which should take priority—individual privacy or national security?

Articles should reflect research into community and national concerns.

Student answers should focus on both the positive and negative aspects of international computer communications.

Students have been working on a Building Your Portfolio project throughout Unit 7. You might ask volunteers to present their work to the class. Have all students add their work to their individual portfolios. Assign the Unit 7 Portfolio Assessment Worksheet in the *Portfolio Assessment Worksheets* booklet.

Building Your Portfolio

Individually or in a group, complete the following project to show your understanding of the civics concepts involved.

New Populous

New Populous is the newest country on Earth. It has just peacefully established its independence. You are a foreign policy official in the New Populous government. You and your fellow officials wish to take your first foreign policy action by applying to the United Nations for membership. To submit your application you will need to do the following.

1. Create a background profile of your country. Include the following information: the country's location, land area, population, capital city, form of government, and foreign policy goals (free trade or limited trade, independence or interdependence, cooperation or competition, and so on). Your profile should also include a map of your country showing its borders, lakes, rivers, deserts, mountains, major cities, and neighboring countries. In addition, include a sketch of the New Populous flag. The flag's design should reflect your country's foreign policy goals.

2. Create a four-column chart of the alliances you hope to pursue with the other nations of the world. In the first column list the country or group of countries with which New Populous hopes to ally itself. You may list existing alliances or outline new alliances. In the second column indicate the type of alliance New Populous is proposing—economic, scientific, defense, and so on. In the third column list the benefits New Populous will gain from the alliances listed in the first column. Finally, in the fourth column list the resources New Populous will bring to each alliance. How will its membership in each alliance benefit the other members?

Organize your materials, and present your application to the members of the United Nations (the rest of the class).

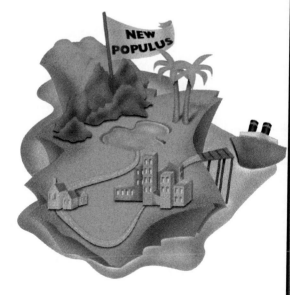

MEETING FUTURE CHALLENGES

Using the Quotation

Have students read the quotation and think about what it asks of them as citizens, now and in the future. Explain that Gaudiani is calling for more than just activism. She wants citizens "to act out of civic virtue." Discuss possible meanings for this phrase, considering her reference to the ideals of the founding documents. Ask: What are some of these ideals? *(freedom, equality, democracy, responsibility)*

About the Author

Claire L. Gaudiani (1944–   ) became president of Connecticut College in 1988. In addition to her numerous academic accomplishments, she has been a strong advocate of what she calls "global civic virtues." These civic virtues, she contends, are increasingly important at home and in the emerging democratic nations of the world. She also has been a strong advocate of volunteerism and of increased efforts to make a college education more accessible to everyone.

" I think you and I must look at contemporary [current] America, examine the communities we are a part of and activate ourselves as citizens, not just the kind of citizens that demand rights or support the demand of rights for others but citizens who call upon ourselves to act out of civic virtue. We need to rethink contemporary civic virtue all over this country, community by community, and commit ourselves to making the ideals we studied in those founding documents come closer to reality in the lives of Americans today."

— Claire L. Gaudiani
PRESIDENT OF CONNECTICUT COLLEGE

Unit 8 explores the issues facing the United States in the coming years. Americans already have taken steps to meet some of these challenges, but more must be done. In this unit students discover how they may work to improve their communities and secure the civil rights, health, and safety of all citizens. They also investigate the need to protect the scarce resources of planet Earth.

After studying Unit 8, students should be able to accomplish the following.

1. Explain the pattern of growth experienced by many U.S. communities.

2. Describe how the government helps protect people's rights, health, and safety.

3. Identify causes and effects of pollution.

4. Analyze present and future sources of energy.

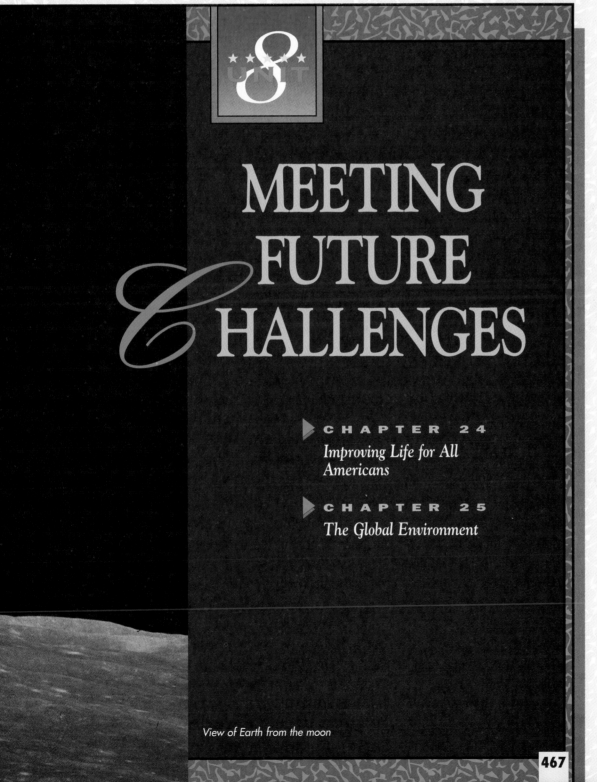

UNIT 8

MEETING FUTURE CHALLENGES

▶ **CHAPTER 24**
Improving Life for All Americans

▶ **CHAPTER 25**
The Global Environment

View of Earth from the moon

Block Scheduling Option

CIVICS VIDEOCASSETTE

Segment 8: Building the Future

CIVICS VIDEODISC

Segment 8: Building the Future

Segment 8, Side B

Search Chapter 4

Play   Pause

BUILDING YOUR PORTFOLIO

"Building Your Portfolio" on page 515 outlines a unit project for students to work on as they study Unit 8. The unit project is supported by materials in the *Portfolio Assessment Worksheets* booklet.

CHAPTER

24

Improving
Life for All
Americans

TEXTBOOK	TEACHING RESOURCES	OTHER AVAILABLE RESOURCES
Chapter	• Skills Worksheet 24 • Challenge/Enrichment Worksheet 24	• Simulations and Case Studies Lessons 21 and 22
Section **1 Improving Communities** Page 469	• Reteaching Worksheet 24.1	• Transparency 25: How Many U.S. Communities Grew
2 Ensuring Rights for All Page 475	• Reteaching Worksheet 24.2	
3 Protecting Citizens' Health and Safety Page 482	• Reteaching Worksheet 24.3	
Review and Assessment Chapter 24 Review, Page 489	• Test, Form A • Test, Form B • Portfolio Assessment Worksheet 24	• Test Generator, Chapter 24

Block Scheduling Option

ADDITIONAL RESOURCES

BOOKS FOR TEACHERS

Kennedy, Paul M., *Preparing for the Twenty-first Century*, Random House.

Stanback, Thomas, *The New Suburbanization: Challenge to the Central City*, Westview.

Torres-Gil, Fernando M., *The New Aging: Politics and Change in America*, Auburn House.

BOOKS FOR STUDENTS

Anonymous, *Go Ask Alice*, Avon Books. Diary of an adolescent drug abuser.

Hyde, Margaret O., and Elizabeth H. Forsyth, *AIDS: What Does It Mean to You?* Walker. Discusses the spread and transmission of the AIDS virus as well as prevention and treatment.

Kozol, Jonathan, *Rachel and Her Children: Homeless Families in America*, Fawcett. Looks at the growing problem of homeless families in the United States.

Levine, Ellen, *Freedom's Children: Young*

Civil Rights Activists Tell Their Own Stories, Putnam. First-person accounts of the civil rights movement by 30 African Americans who were children or teenagers at the time.

MULTIMEDIA RESOURCES

AIDS: Facts and Fears, Crisis and Controversy (VHS, c, 56 min.), GA. Provides comprehensive information about AIDS and offers a sensitive portrayal of an AIDS patient and his family.

The Fateful Decade: From Little Rock to the Civil Rights Bill (VHS, c, 27 min.), FH. Recounts the turbulent events that marked the struggle for civil rights in the United States.

Inside Life Outside (VHS, c, 57 min.), NDF. Follows a group of homeless people as they struggle for survival and dignity on the streets of New York City.

The Possible Dream? The Quest for Racial and Ethnic Harmony in American

Schools (VHS, c, 45 min.), CSS. Students discuss racial differences and look for solutions to racial issues in schools.

Urbanization: The Growth of Cities (Apple, IBM, Macintosh), SSSS. Students deal with issues of urbanization as they examine the patterns of growth of U.S. cities and towns.

THE INTERNET

Have students use these search words to locate more information about chapter topics on the Internet: *communities, urban renewal, homelessness, civil rights.*

 GLOBAL SKILL BUILDER

You might wish to use **Navigating the Internet** from the interactive *Global Skill Builder* CD-ROM to aid students' understanding of the Internet as a resource.

Abbreviations: b&w=black and white; c=color; f=film; fs=filmstrip; sd=sound; tr=transparency; VHS=videotape

CHALLENGES IN TODAY'S WORLD

★ **Building Communities** Students will learn about problems facing many of the country's communities and the purposes of regional planning.

★ **Living in a Diverse Society** Students will learn about minority groups, the civil rights movement, and the principles of civil rights established by the government.

★ **Promoting the General Welfare** Students will learn about serious health and safety problems in the United States and how federal, state, and local governments work to solve these problems. Students also will learn how citizens can help improve the health and safety of their communities.

CIVICS SKILLS

Students will learn how to compare points of view on issues. Students also will learn terms important to understanding the challenges of improving life for all Americans.

CITIZENSHIP VALUES

Students will be encouraged to appreciate the importance of equal rights in the American way of life, to recognize the importance of avoiding substance abuse, and to realize the need to practice good health and safety habits.

MEETING INDIVIDUAL NEEDS

LIMITED ENGLISH PROFICIENCY (LEP)

Have pairs of students make flash cards with a chapter vocabulary term on one side of each card and its definition or descriptive illustration on the other side. Each pair should use the cards to quiz each other until both students have mastered all of the vocabulary terms.

LEARNERS HAVING DIFFICULTY

Have pairs of students work together to outline the chapter. Section heads should be designated by Roman numerals. Subheads should be designated by capital letters. Information under each subhead should be designated by Arabic numbers. Make copies of the outlines so both students have one for use as a study guide.

AUDITORY LEARNERS

Have students prepare radio advertisements discouraging teenagers from smoking. They might gather information about smoking and its effects on health from the chapter or from other sources. Call on volunteers to read their advertisements aloud or tape-record them and play them back for the class.

VISUAL LEARNERS

Have students create posters about protecting citizens' health and safety. The posters should be aimed at elementary schoolchildren and should illustrate health and safety challenges facing everyone. Posters should also emphasize what schoolchildren can do to protect themselves and should contain a slogan and illustrations that will appeal to young people.

TACTILE/KINESTHETIC LEARNERS

Explain that more people are moving to "planned communities," where areas are set aside ahead of time for residential, commercial, and recreational purposes. Have students map a hypothetical planned community. Maps also should indicate main traffic arteries for the community.

GIFTED LEARNERS

Have each student research and prepare a report about one of the following diseases: smallpox, tuberculosis, polio, bubonic plague, typhus, yellow fever, cholera. Students should determine the causes of the disease, how people combatted it, and the status of the disease in the world today.

CHAPTER OVERVIEW

Chapter 24 studies U.S. communities today—their growth, their challenges, and the efforts to meet these challenges. The chapter points out that to achieve a high quality of life in communities, everyone must enjoy equal rights and a healthy and safe environment. The underlying theme of the chapter is that citizens must be ready to meet the challenges that arise with growth and change.

Motivator

Obtain a map of a large metropolitan area, such as Los Angeles, New York, Chicago, or Houston. Help students identify the primary city in the urban area; suburban cities; and transportation routes, such as highways and railways. Ask: Why is the transportation network so extensive? *(need to connect inner city with the outlying cities and suburbs)* Tell students that this chapter will describe the growth of communities and the challenges, such as transportation, that go with such growth.

CHAPTER OBJECTIVES

After studying Chapter 24, students should be able to do the following.

1. Identify challenges facing U.S. cities and what can be done to meet these challenges.
2. Describe how citizens have worked toward ensuring equal rights for all Americans.
3. Identify wellness and explain what Americans can do to achieve it.

SIMULATIONS AND CASE STUDIES

Lesson 21: Get to Know Your Lemon: A Multicultural Awareness Activity

Lesson 22: Case Studies on Equality Laws

Block Scheduling Option

CHAPTER 24

Improving Life for All Americans

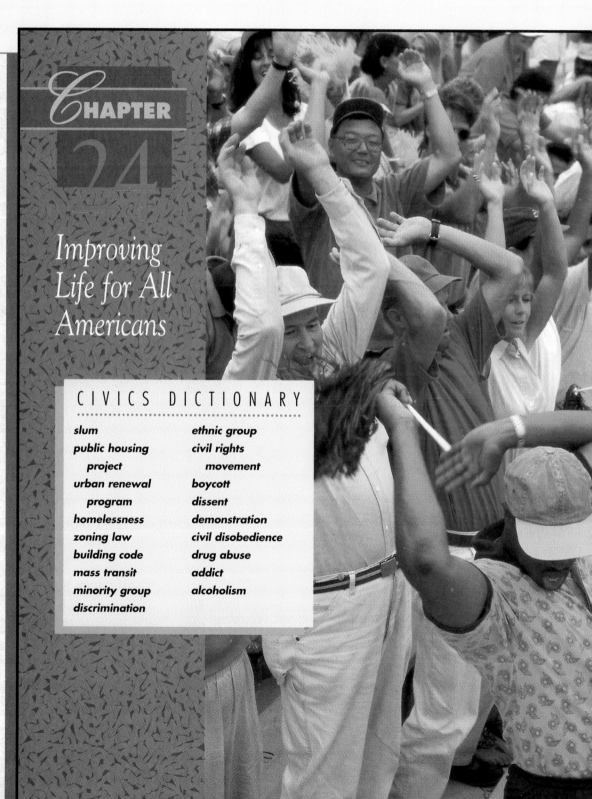

CIVICS DICTIONARY

slum
public housing
   project
urban renewal
   program
homelessness
zoning law
building code
mass transit
minority group
discrimination

ethnic group
civil rights
   movement
boycott
dissent
demonstration
civil disobedience
drug abuse
addict
alcoholism

SECTION OBJECTIVES

After studying Section 1, students should be able to do the following.

1. Identify the pattern of growth of many U.S. cities.

2. Explain the movement of people away from central cities and its effects.

3. Describe slums and the actions taken to eliminate them.

4. Describe the nature of homelessness today.

5. Discuss the challenges facing mass transit and the need for regional planning.

Teaching Section 1

Building a Vocabulary

Ask students what the word *public* in **public housing project** means. *(government funded)* Then ask them what the word *mass* in **mass transit** refers to. *(large numbers of people)* Then tell them that *transit* comes from the Latin word meaning "to go across." Have students define *mass transit*. *(transportation of large numbers of people)* Ask students to identify examples of mass transit. *(buses, subways, trains)*

CHAPTER FOCUS

Where do you live? Have you ever moved? Where have your parents lived? Chances are that your family's experiences mirror larger trends in the United States. Americans have always moved to new communities in search of a better life for themselves and their children.

Many communities today, however, face serious challenges, such as overcrowding, crime, and unemployment. People are working together to solve these problems. Our communities and our nation also face the challenges of ensuring rights for all citizens and protecting citizens' health and safety. The United States was founded on the ideal of equal rights and opportunities for all. We must strive to ensure that this ideal is fully realized.

● ●

STUDY GUIDE

● What challenges are facing U.S. cities, and what can be done to meet these challenges?

● How have citizens worked toward ensuring equal rights for all Americans?

● What is "wellness," and what can Americans do to achieve it?

1 | *Improving Communities*

As you know, the United States has many different kinds of communities—from small rural towns to huge cities. Many of these urban areas face serious challenges, including poor housing, inefficient transportation systems, and crime. Such problems exist not only in cities but also in suburbs and rural areas. They are found in communities throughout the world as well.

The problems of our communities affect all of us. Addressing these challenges and making our communities more pleasant places in which to live are important issues for all American citizens.

Growth of U.S. Cities

America began as a rural country with small, scattered settlements. Small communities that grew into cities usually spread over the surrounding countryside in a typical pattern. Most cities have spread outward, away from the original settlement. If you were to draw a diagram showing the growth of a typical city, it would look like a target. As you can see in the diagram on page 470, the older downtown area would be in the center. It would be surrounded by several circles, each becoming larger the farther it is from the center.

The older, central part of the city usually is the downtown business center. Stores, office buildings, factories, and warehouses are found here. Sometimes modern hotels and luxury apartment houses also are located in the downtown section. Areas in and around this section, however, are often run-down.

Apartment buildings, private homes, and neighborhood shops and stores occupy the next circle outward from the downtown area. These buildings are often built side by side with little or no space between them.

The next circle is sometimes called the greenbelt. Houses with yards and lawns, trees, and shrubbery are often found in this section. The greenbelt usually lies only partly within the city boundaries. It also extends beyond city lines, where it is called the suburbs. Suburbs, as you have learned, are smaller, independent communities that surround a city.

GLOBAL PERSPECTIVES

The older, central part of many foreign cities is marked by a wall built to keep out invaders in earlier times. For example, the stone fortifications of Istanbul (formerly Constantinople), Turkey, enclose palaces, churches, and mosques that are hundreds of years old. Canada's oldest city, Quebec, also has a walled section. The walled section contains buildings dating back to the 1600s, when Quebec was a French outpost in North America. Tokyo, the capital of Japan, is different. At its center lies the Imperial Palace, surrounded by stone walls and moats. But the rest of central Tokyo has a modern look. An earthquake, tidal wave, and fire in 1923, as well as Allied bombing during World War II, destroyed nearly all of the city's oldest structures.

Point out that all three cities listed here have much in common with U.S. cities. Neighborhoods surround business and cultural centers, for example. Also, various modes of transportation link the cities to outlying regions and suburbs.

Organize the class into small groups. Have each group devise a growth model of your community, based on the chart on this page. They might use paper, wood, or other materials to represent the various areas and well-known structures in your city or town. Students should label areas of growth from the oldest to the newest. Assign tasks such as researcher, designer, and model maker.

Drawing a Political Cartoon

Review with the class the reasons why people are leaving the cities. *(to seek fresh air, more space, lower levels of crime, lower rents and taxes, better schools, and a slower pace of life; to be near new jobs)* Then ask: What are the consequences of this movement? Have students draw political cartoons illustrating some aspect of the move from inner cities and the consequences of this migration. Call on volunteers to present and explain their cartoons to the class.

CIVICS SIDELIGHT

The U.S. Census Bureau groups certain cities and nearby counties into standard metropolitan statistical areas (SMSA) in order to more accurately reflect the population of an urban area. A consolidated metropolitan statistical area (CMSA) combines contiguous metropolitan statistical areas. The largest CMSA in 1992 was New York–Northern New Jersey–Long Island, which also included nearby parts of Pennsylvania and Connecticut. The population of this CMSA was 19.7 million. The Los Angeles–Riverside–Orange County CMSA had a population of 15 million in 1992. Chicago–Gary–Kenosha CMSA was the third largest area with a population of 8.4 million people.

CIVICS TRANSPARENCIES

An overhead transparency of "How Many U.S. Communities Grew" is available in *Teaching Transparencies with Teacher's Notes.*

On the edge of the greenbelt is the rural-urban fringe, or the area where the city meets the countryside. Farms and small towns occupy this area. The rural-urban fringe may stretch as far as 50 to 100 miles (80 to 161 km) from the downtown center.

In recent years many factories, businesses, and stores have moved from cities to rural areas. These industries and businesses have left cities because rural areas often offer cheaper land, lower taxes, better housing, and less crowded traffic and parking conditions.

Move of Middle-Income Families

As you have read, a large city with its surrounding area of suburbs and small towns is known as a metropolitan area. Although the number of metropolitan areas has been growing, the centers of U.S. cities have been losing population. More people have moved out of the central cities than have moved to them.

How Many U.S. Communities Grew

Nearby small towns · Suburbs · Apartment buildings · Private homes · Private homes · Original downtown center · Small stores · Small stores · Two-family dwellings · Suburbs · Nearby small towns

Between 1970 and 1990, 21 of the nation's 50 largest cities lost a combined total of nearly four million residents.

Why are people leaving the cities? There are many reasons. Some people seek fresh air, sunshine, and neighborhoods with yards. The number of crimes in some cities is so high that many people are afraid to live there.

Others have left the cities to avoid paying high rents and city taxes. Some seek better schools and an escape from urban noise, grime, and bustle. People also move to be near the new jobs that are created in suburbs as businesses move there.

This shift of people to the suburbs has seriously affected U.S. cities. For the most part, those who move are middle-income or upper-income families. Many of these people still work in the city and use its services. Those people who travel from suburban homes to city places of business are called commuters. Commuters often pay few or no taxes to city governments.

Furthermore, because much of the federal government's financial aid to cities is based on urban population figures, the cities lose federal aid when people leave. As residents move out, urban areas lose federal funds for housing, schools, transportation, public assistance, and other services. Cities also lose voters when people move to the suburbs. Fewer voters means fewer representatives in state government and in Congress.

Spread of Slums

As people moved to suburbs, the older areas of many cities became slums. A **slum** is a run-down section of a city in which buildings are neglected and people live crowded together.

Life is difficult for people living in slums. In these crowded areas the rates of disease and death are high. Compared with other sections of cities, slums have more people living in poverty, more unemployment, and more crime. Perhaps worst of all is the feeling among people who live in slums that they have little hope for a better future.

Writing a Letter

Have students each write a letter to the editor of a city newspaper describing the effects of the movement to the suburbs. Topics for letters might include commuters who use city services but pay few or no taxes to help maintain the city; the loss of federal funds, which are based on population; and the loss of representation in Congress. Students should offer solutions to the problems they discuss.

COOPERATIVE LEARNING

Invite small groups of students to imagine that each group is a city Development Commission. Each group should create a "Development Action Plan" to eliminate the city's slums and help the residents who live there. Each group should identify and describe the problems (perhaps in a list or chart) and propose actions necessary to solve the problems. Each group should use illustrations and graphics to develop a formal presentation. Roles for members include illustrators, writers, and presenters.

Slums create problems for everyone, not just for those who live in them. For instance, slums cost everyone money. The number of fires is greater in slum areas. More police officers are also needed to protect these areas because they tend to have more crime than other neighborhoods. More of the city's money must be spent on health needs, public assistance, child care, and other services in slum areas than in any other part of the city. Thus all the people in the city help pay the cost of allowing slums to exist.

Recovering Slums

U.S. cities have tried several plans to eliminate slums. Some communities have replaced slum dwellings with **public housing projects**, or apartment buildings built with public funds. Rents in public housing projects are low, and the apartments are open primarily to low-income families.

Another plan to eliminate slums calls for redeveloping, or completely rebuilding, the center of the city. Sometimes run-down buildings are torn down and replaced by new public buildings to form a civic center. Facilities are built for business conferences, concerts, sporting events, and public exhibits. Private corporations often take part in the redevelopment project. Those people whose homes are torn down for redevelopment usually are provided better housing nearby.

A third plan to eliminate slums is to restore and maintain the buildings in the area. Buildings that can be saved are repaired by their owners. Sometimes owners receive financial help from the city. Buildings that cannot be repaired are replaced with new dwellings or with parks and playgrounds.

The programs you have just read about are called **urban renewal programs**. These programs usually are planned and carried out by local agencies with financial support from the federal government.

Some urban renewal programs have achieved great successes. Many new schools, libraries, hospitals, and other community

Large cities like this one often have urban renewal programs to improve the city's quality of life. Such programs can include better parks and schools.

centers have improved the lives of local residents. These improvements also have helped revive businesses in former slum areas, providing jobs for many people. To encourage growth in these areas, many communities have established "enterprise zones" that offer lower taxes to businesses that move there.

Unfortunately, urban renewal programs are expensive. They can also disrupt people's lives. When run-down areas are redeveloped, people must move to make room for the new development. Often, as you have read, they are relocated to public housing projects. The public housing projects in some areas, meanwhile, have become run-down and dangerous.

CIVICS SIDELIGHT

In some places massive urban renewal programs directed by the federal government have given way to community development projects directed by local citizens. In a South Boston neighborhood, African American and Hispanic American residents joined forces to turn vacant lots into playgrounds, parks, a business center, and refurbished housing. A similar group in West Baltimore worked to secure new houses, job-training programs, school improvements, and food banks for their community. The Atlanta Project, meanwhile, has targeted 20 poverty clusters throughout the Georgia capital with money and programs to battle such problems as crime, teenage pregnancy, homelessness, unemployment, and drug abuse. Each cluster has a corporate sponsor that supplies funds and representatives to work with community leaders. Neighborhood groups in Chicago, Los Angeles, Houston, and other cities have also launched their own projects that encourage and help residents to improve their communities.

Writing a Journal Entry

Invite students to imagine they are homeless children. Have them write a journal entry about their first week on the streets. Students should think through their circumstances before they begin writing. Encourage students to consider where they would sleep, what they would do during the day, and how they would find food to eat. Invite volunteers to read their entries to the class. Then lead a discussion about the causes of homelessness.

Creating a Map

Have pairs of students create zoning maps for a hypothetical city. Each pair should use various colors to identify zones permitting different kinds of businesses (such as stores, restaurants, and office buildings), industry (such as factories and processing plants), single-unit and multiple-unit housing, and recreational and designated nondevelopment areas (such as parks). Each map should include a color key identifying the purposes of the zones. Invite volunteers to present their maps to the class and explain the reasoning behind their zoning decisions.

According to some studies, many of the homeless on America's streets—perhaps 25 percent of them—have severe mental illnesses. In years past these people might have spent their lives in an institution. Beginning in the 1970s, however, public policy shifted toward de-institutionalization. People with mental illnesses were moved out of hospitals and into the community. With the help of federal entitlement funds and community support programs, many benefited from and succeeded in living outside the structured environment of the institution. Others, however, did not succeed. As a result of drug abuse, failure to take medicine or follow treatment guidelines, and the inability of family and community to cope with mental illness, many of these individuals have ended up living on the streets.

Photo Caption Answer

The igloo is too tall. Student opinions on zoning laws will vary but should include reasoned arguments.

Homelessness

One of the most pressing and difficult problems facing many U.S. communities today is **homelessness**. For the first time since the Great Depression of the 1930s, many Americans do not have a place to live.

There have always been homeless people in the United States. Most of these have been single men. Another large group has been made up of people who have mental illnesses. What has brought homelessness to the attention of the American people in recent years is that a growing percentage of the homeless population is made up of families. Many children now are among the nation's homeless.

Being homeless makes life very difficult. Some homeless people spend nights in shelters set up to house the homeless, but these places

What "irregularity" has the zoning commission found? Should communities have zoning laws?

"THE ZONING COMMISSION WOULD LIKE TO POINT OUT AN IRREGULARITY!"

fill quickly. In addition, some shelters for the homeless are unhealthy and dangerous places. As a result, many homeless people sleep in bus stations, under bridges, on benches, or in their cars. Because they have no home, they are forced to carry their few possessions with them. Poverty is a constant companion, and children who are homeless find it difficult to attend school regularly.

One reason for the increase in homelessness is the lack of affordable housing. Across the country the price of housing has increased dramatically in recent years. Moreover, millions of low-cost apartments and houses have been lost in the past 15 years. These buildings are abandoned, or, more often, converted to high-cost housing. Cutbacks in federal funding of programs designed to provide low-cost housing have added to the problem.

Many Americans are working to solve the problem of homelessness. Some private groups have set up shelters and programs to help the homeless. More and more city governments recognize the problem and are working to establish shelters and more low-cost housing. Notable entertainers hold concerts and other benefits to help homeless Americans.

The federal government also is trying to ease the problem. In 1987 Congress passed the Homeless Assistance Act, which has provided more than $1 billion in aid for the homeless. Most of this money is used for shelters and other services needed by the homeless. Among these services are health care, educational programs, housing, and job training.

Zoning Laws

U.S. communities act not only to solve existing housing problems but also to prevent new problems. For example, suppose a company wants to build an oil refinery next to your house. Luckily, the company cannot build in your neighborhood because of the local **zoning laws**. Such laws regulate the kinds of buildings and businesses that may locate in a zone, or area. Only certain types of buildings or businesses are allowed in each zone.

Obtain a transit map (such as for buses and subways) from your local transit authority, a nearby city, or from the library (which might carry such maps for large cities). Review with students the various types of mass transit. Ask students to describe, in detail if possible, what they know about each type of transportation. Then help students use the transit map to understand how mass transit moves people from place to place across large distances in urban areas.

Invite pairs of students to imagine they are transit authority officials working in a large metropolitan area that has highways, commuter trains, subways, and buses. Students must create an advertisement encouraging people to use mass transit. The students can create a print or billboard advertisement, or they might want to create a radio or television advertisement. Each advertisement should explain the advantages of using mass transit. Have volunteers present their advertisements to the class.

Towns and cities also pass laws that builders must follow in making new structures safe and attractive. To keep track of these new buildings, local governments require builders to obtain permits before they start working. Other laws require owners to keep their buildings comfortable and in good repair. As a result, new buildings, as well as all apartment houses, office buildings, and other buildings open to the public, are inspected regularly to ensure that local regulations are followed. Such laws are part of an area's **building code**.

Suburban Challenges

Suburbs and other small communities also face challenges. Over time stores and homes may become run-down. Gas stations, billboards, junkyards, and convenience stores may be built without careful planning.

In addition, as suburbs and other communities have grown in size and population, they have faced problems with their water supply, trash removal, and sewage disposal, and with increasing crime and high taxes. Like large cities, these communities have established programs to redevelop their run-down areas. They, too, have tried to prevent problems through zoning laws and community action.

The Transportation Tangle

Do you use mass transit in your community? **Mass transit** includes various forms of public transportation, such as subways, buses, and commuter railroads. All of these transportation systems face challenges: fewer passengers, fewer services, higher fares. What are the causes of these problems? Is there a remedy?

The movement of large numbers of city workers to the suburbs is one cause of the decline of mass transportation. Many suburban commuters prefer to drive their cars, even though highways leading to cities are choked with traffic. The loss of riders has caused mass transit systems to lose money.

Rising wages for workers and higher maintenance costs on mass transit lines are another cause. Higher operating costs mean higher fares. Higher fares mean a further drop in the number of passengers. As service worsens, still other passengers take to the highways or, if possible, walk or bicycle to work.

These factors, plus the high cost of gasoline, have led some cities to build new mass transit systems or to modernize existing ones. For example, Bay Area Rapid Transit (BART) began running in 1972 to link San Francisco, California, with nearby communities. More than $2 billion was spent in recent years on a Metrorail system in Miami, Florida. Such systems are often paid for by local taxes and federal and state government funds.

Despite their problems, mass transit systems are essential to every large city. They are as vital as the highways and airlines that connect cities with the rest of the nation and with the world. They must be made to succeed if cities and their surrounding communities are to flourish.

Planning for the Future

So many people have moved out of the inner, or central, city to suburbs and rural areas that a number of problems have been created in the entire metropolitan area. How, for example, can essential services, such as water supply, trash removal, electric power, and mass transportation, be provided for such large numbers of people in a metropolitan area?

Many counties, cities, and towns have community planning commissions that work to improve conditions. Some large groups of cities also have regional planning groups, which study the problems of an entire region. These regional groups may be made up of private citizens.

All planning groups employ experts to help them study the land and its uses. Among the specialists they consult are traffic engineers, population experts, economists, health experts, architects, and scientists.

One area that often requires regional planning is transportation. City streets and suburban roads and highways are a part of one large

CIVICS SIDELIGHT

The transportation system of many cities still relies mainly on highways, which are becoming more and more clogged with traffic each year. The 1990 U.S. census found that nearly three-fourths of the country's 115 million workers drove to their jobs alone. Just over 5 percent of commuters used public transportation alternatives.

According to a 1993 study, the most traffic-congested city in the United States was Los Angeles, followed by Washington, D.C., San Francisco–Oakland, Miami, and Chicago. The 1994 earthquake in Los Angeles created more commuter headaches. With major freeways and streets impassable, some travelers turned to Metrolink, the little-used commuter rail system in the city. The number of daily train riders went from 900 before the earthquake to 22,000 a week after it. Still, hundreds of thousands of commuters could not kick the automobile habit. Fortunately for commuters, the Santa Monica Freeway, the country's busiest, was reopened two-and-a-half months ahead of schedule.

Closure

Invite students to imagine that they have been chosen by the government to plan the "ideal community." In developing their plans, students should consider a number of questions, such as how the city would prevent homelessness and the creation of slums. Would people be close enough to their jobs to walk to work, or would they need other means of transportation? What kind of transportation would be good for this "ideal community"? Why? Encourage students to be creative. What would they call this ideal city?

Reviewing

Have students complete the Section 1 Review.

Reteaching

Assign Section 1 of the Chapter 24 Reteaching Worksheet.

SECTION 1 REVIEW
ANSWERS

1. See the following pages: slum (p. 470); public housing project, urban renewal program (p. 471); homelessness, zoning law (p. 472); building code, mass transit (p. 473).

2. spread outward from original settlement

3. lower cost of living, less crime, better schools, slower pace; consequences—loss of tax money, federal funds, voters, governmental representatives for the city

4. run-down, crowded, neglected section of town; urban renewal programs

5. growing percentage of homeless are families; one cause— lack of affordable housing

6. low ridership, fewer services, higher fares; city and suburbs make up one large transportation system

7. Students should suggest ways to address the issue.

Have you ever been caught in a scene like this? What steps might communities take to avoid traffic jams?

transportation system. Traffic jams, air pollution, and related problems cross over city boundary lines. Therefore many cities and suburbs have formed metropolitan transit authorities. Representatives from the city and suburban communities are part of the transit authorities. These groups study regional traffic problems and work to solve them.

Similar groups are working to meet other challenges facing U.S. communities. Among these challenges are pollution, drug abuse, overcrowding, crime, poor school systems, and unemployment. Poverty also is a problem that can devastate people's lives. People who live in poverty have shorter life expectancies, are ill more often, and have fewer opportunities for education and jobs.

Solutions to the problems facing our communities are not always easy to find or carry out. Many solutions require a great deal of money. Money alone, however, is not the answer. Communities also need imaginative

planning. Above all, they need citizens who are willing to do their part and accept responsibility to make their communities better places in which to live.

SECTION 1 REVIEW

1. Define or identify the following terms: slum, public housing project, urban renewal program, homelessness, zoning law, building code, mass transit.

2. What pattern of growth have many U.S. cities followed?

3. Why have people been moving away from the central cities? How has this move affected urban areas?

4. What are slums? What actions have been taken to eliminate slums?

Have students research the issue of homeless people in foreign countries. Students should investigate the causes of homelessness, what actions have been taken to alleviate the problem in these countries, and how effective these actions have been. Have students report their results to the class. Then have the class discuss whether any of the actions taken in other countries might be effective in the United States.

After studying Section 2, students should be able to do the following.

1. Describe how civil rights activists combatted discrimination against African Americans.

2. Explain how the Twenty-fourth Amendment strengthened the rights of minority groups.

3. Describe the political advances of Hispanic Americans, Native Americans, older Americans, and women.

4. Describe the Americans with Disabilities Act.

---

5. How has the nature of homelessness changed in recent years? Why has homelessness increased?

6. What challenges face mass transit systems? Why do transportation systems often require regional planning?

7. **THINKING CRITICALLY** What is the most pressing issue facing your community today? What is the government doing to address this issue? What are citizens doing to help? What more do you think can be done?

2 Ensuring Rights for All

The quality of life in U.S. communities depends not only on beautiful buildings, well-kept parks, and efficient services. It requires, too, that all Americans have equal rights and opportunities. These rights, of course, are guaranteed to all citizens by the U.S. Constitution. Despite this guarantee, however, Americans have not always shared these rights equally. Some groups of Americans have struggled to win their rights as citizens.

A Rich Cultural Heritage

As you learned in Chapter 1, people from all over the world have settled in the United States and contributed to its heritage. As group after group came to the United States, they brought with them different languages, ideas, and customs. Almost every language in the world is spoken somewhere in the United States. The holidays, foods, clothing, and other customs of the many groups in U.S. society add a richness to the lives of all Americans.

The nation's many different groups are proud of their varied backgrounds. Sometimes, however, differences in customs and beliefs have led to misunderstandings and problems between groups. Such miscommunication and

conflict has occurred not only in this country but in every land throughout history.

Minority Groups

Some groups of people in society are referred to as **minority groups**. The word *minority* in this case does not necessarily mean that the group is outnumbered. Rather, it means that it is not the group in power. It also means that the group is set apart from other groups of people in society because of ethnic background, language, customs, or religion.

Minority groups often have met with prejudice and discrimination. As you recall, prejudice is an opinion not based on a careful and reasonable review of facts. **Discrimination** refers to unfair actions taken against people because they belong to a particular group. Prejudice and discrimination have been present throughout human history. In the United States, too, some Americans have looked at those who were different from them with fear and distrust.

Prejudice and discrimination were not uncommon in the early years of the nation. For example, Native Americans were often treated harshly by the settlers from Europe. Some English settlers did not welcome the early Scotch-Irish and Germans. In later years some Americans feared arriving Catholics from Ireland and Germany. Still later, some people opposed the arrival of immigrants from southern and eastern Europe.

Throughout the nation's history, African Americans have suffered greatly as a result of prejudice and discrimination. Also, Mexican Americans, other Hispanic Americans, and Asian Americans often have faced resentment and hostility.

The minority groups you have been reading about are ethnic groups. An **ethnic group** is a group of people of the same race, nationality, or religion who share a common and distinctive culture and heritage.

In recent years women, older Americans, and people with physical and mental disabilities also have been regarded as minority

GLOBAL PERSPECTIVES

History provides many examples of conflicts among ethnic groups living within the same borders. The Roman Empire, however, managed to establish unity throughout its vast territory by offering many conquered peoples a valuable reward for their loyalty: citizenship. People from lands as distant as Syria, Britain, and Spain could all declare, *"Civis romanus sum."* ("I am a Roman citizen.") Citizens throughout the empire received the same rights accorded those in Rome, and they received the protection of the Roman army and the highly regarded Roman legal system. They also gained economic opportunities and access to government jobs. Although these liberal citizenship laws surely did not eliminate all hostility among the empire's conquered peoples, some historians point to them as one reason the empire lasted as long as it did.

Teaching Section 2
Building a Vocabulary

Tell students that the word *ethnic* comes from the Greek word *ethnikos,* meaning "national." Have students identify **ethnic groups** in your community. Then ask students: Do members of these ethnic groups sometimes encounter **discrimination?** Explain that people who belong to **minority groups** (people set apart from others in society because of such things as ethnicity and language) often have faced discrimination. Call on volunteers to describe ways in which some people discriminate.

Writing a Speech

Invite students to imagine they are civil rights leaders in the 1950s. Have each student write a speech describing discrimination against African Americans at that time and why such discrimination threatens all citizens' civil rights and should be stopped. Call on volunteers to read their speeches to the class.

MULTICULTURAL PERSPECTIVES

The goal of the NAACP's founders was to end the legal abuses of African Americans. Ten years after its founding, and despite efforts in some states to make it illegal, the NAACP had nearly 100,000 members across the country. The NAACP counted more than 500,000 members in 1995. Among the NAACP's triumphs have been the 1954 *Brown* decision, the passage of the 1964 Civil Rights Act, and the 1944 Supreme Court decision in *Smith v. Allwright* that political parties (specifically the Texas Democratic party) could not prohibit African Americans from voting in their primary elections. The ruling against the so-called "white primary" was a major victory for African American voters.

groups. These groups have not been set apart by language, race, or religion. Many of these people believe, however, that they have not been given their full equal rights.

The Struggle for Equal Rights

As you learned in Chapter 4, the basic rights of citizenship to which all Americans are entitled are called civil rights. They include the right to vote, the right to equal treatment under the law, and the right to be considered for any job for which one is qualified. Civil rights include, too, the right to use public places and facilities.

The struggle for equal rights has a long history. For more than 200 years, African Americans were forced to live in slavery. Although slavery ended after the Civil War, most African Americans still were denied their civil rights. Laws in many states treated them as second-class citizens.

Some of the southern states passed laws to prevent African Americans from voting. These states also passed segregation laws. As you have read, these laws separated the races. There were separate schools, separate parks, separate drinking fountains, and other separate facilities for African Americans. African Americans could not buy homes in certain communities. They were not allowed to work at certain jobs.

African Americans in the North were also denied full civil rights. Although the northern states did not pass laws that took away their civil rights, African Americans in the North had trouble finding jobs. They were forced to live in areas where only African Americans lived and where schools for African American students were inferior to those attended by white students.

African Americans have worked for many years to achieve equal rights. One of the earliest groups formed to help in this struggle was the National Association for the Advancement of Colored People (NAACP), founded in 1909. The NAACP remains an active force today.

An important step toward obtaining equal rights for all Americans was made in 1954. As you learned in Chapter 7, in that year the Supreme Court made its landmark decision in the case of *Brown v. Board of Education of Topeka.* The Court ruled that segregation in public schools is unconstitutional.

The Civil Rights Movement

After the *Brown* decision, the struggle for equal rights grew even stronger under leaders such as Dr. Martin Luther King. (See page 559.) This struggle is known as the **civil rights movement**. Americans who supported the civil rights movement opposed laws that denied equal rights to African Americans.

An important test of such laws came in 1955 in Montgomery, Alabama. Under the South's segregation laws, African Americans were forced to ride in the back of public buses. They also had to give their seats to white passengers when the front section reserved for whites was filled.

In December 1955, Rosa Parks, an African American seamstress, was riding the bus home from work one night when the bus driver demanded that she give her seat to a white passenger. Parks refused, was arrested, and was later convicted of violating the city's segregation laws.

In protest, Montgomery's civil rights leaders asked African American citizens to **boycott**, or stop using, the buses. The months-long, and often violent, boycott was successful. In 1956 the Supreme Court overturned Parks's conviction and ruled that segregation on buses is unconstitutional.

Americans can express their **dissent**, or disagreement, with a law in many ways. People involved in the civil rights movement used many different methods of dissent. In addition to staging boycotts, they wrote letters, made phone calls, and sent telegrams to their elected lawmakers. They wrote books, made speeches, and organized mass demonstrations. During a **demonstration**, dissenters march in public carrying signs, singing songs, and making

Illustrating Ideas

Have students use the textbook and other classroom and library resources to create illustrated time lines showing the history of the struggle for civil rights. Each entry on the time line should be accompanied by an explanatory caption. Call on volunteers to present and explain their time lines to the class.

In 1963 more than 200,000 Americans staged a "March on Washington." They came from all over the nation to urge the passage of civil rights legislation.

MULTICULTURAL PERSPECTIVES

When civil rights demonstrators practiced civil disobedience, they were following tactics devised by the great philosopher and leader Mohandas K. Gandhi of India. Gandhi used nonviolent resistance to lead the Indian independence movement against Britain. India won its independence in 1947. African Americans had long followed the struggle of Gandhi and his people in African American newspapers. Also, a number of African American leaders learned directly about Gandhi's philosophy of nonviolence when they met with him in India before World War II. Gandhi was also a major influence on Martin Luther King, Jr., who saw a connection between Christian teachings and Gandhi's concept of nonviolence. "Christ furnished the spirit and motivation, while Gandhi furnished the method," King said.

speeches. (See "Case Study: The Birmingham March" on pages 478–479.)

The right of all Americans to express their dissent against laws in these and many other ways is protected by the Constitution. People do not have the right, however, to break the laws while expressing their dissent.

What can citizens do if they have used the above forms of dissent without results? Is there anything more they can do to change laws they believe are wrong or unjust?

During the civil rights movement, and at other times in the past, some Americans have shown their dissent by intentionally disobeying laws they believed to be wrong. This practice is called **civil disobedience**.

As you know, people who disobey a law must face the consequences. Civil rights supporters who disobeyed laws they believed to be wrong knew they could be arrested. They hoped the willingness to lose their freedom would make other people work to have the

laws changed. Such activists generally use civil disobedience only when other tactics fail.

Progress in Civil Rights

The civil rights movement has had a great impact on the nation. In response to demands for equal rights, Congress passed several civil rights laws. These civil rights laws established the following principles to guarantee the rights of American minority groups:

- The right to vote cannot be denied because of race or color.
- Discrimination in public schools must not be allowed.
- The right to work or belong to a union shall not be denied because of race or color.
- Any business open to the public, such as restaurants and theaters, shall be open equally to all people.

(continued on page 480)

Drawing a Political Cartoon

Invite students to draw political cartoons depicting the events in Birmingham in 1963. Students might wish to focus on Eugene "Bull" Connor's role in trying to prevent the demonstration or on the Supreme Court's upholding of the constitutional right to assemble peaceably. Remind students to use symbols and labels in their cartoons.

CIVICS SIDELIGHT

There are a number of organizations in the United States today that work to protect the constitutional and civil rights of American citizens. The American Civil Liberties Union (ACLU), for example, is dedicated to defending civil rights and constitutional freedoms, and supports court tests of these freedoms. The ACLU has been a strong supporter of school integration, the rights of the accused, free speech, and strict separation of church and state. Providing constitutional and civil rights for citizens means, however, that the rights of unpopular groups also must be protected. Acknowledging this fact, the ACLU in 1978 defended the right of the American Nazi party to march in Skokie, Illinois, and to display Nazi symbols during its march. The march proceeded despite a massive outcry from the Skokie community, which has a large Jewish population.

Case Study: THE BIRMINGHAM MARCH

The city of Birmingham, Alabama, was rocked in the spring of 1963 by massive demonstrations that captured the attention of people throughout the world. The demonstrators were African Americans and their supporters who gathered in Birmingham to protest decades of racial injustice. Primary among their concerns were segregation laws that denied African Americans equal access to education, jobs, and thus the opportunities for economic success.

Leading the demonstrators was the Reverend Martin Luther King, Jr., who called Birmingham "the country's chief symbol of racial intolerance." King believed that effective demonstrations in this southern city could lead to sweeping changes in the laws that denied equality to African Americans.

King was right. The events of 1963 helped pave the way for important civil rights legislation. But these events could not have taken place without a fundamental freedom guaranteed to all Americans in the Constitution of the United States. That freedom is "the right of the people peaceably to assemble," and it is guaranteed by the First Amendment.

The police in Birmingham, Alabama, used fire hoses on these protesters in an effort to keep them from demonstrating for equal rights.

A Permit to Demonstrate

In April 1963, King and his supporters sent representatives to request a demonstration permit from the city of Birmingham. They needed the permit to hold a legal demonstration.

The city's Commissioner of Public Safety, Eugene "Bull" Connor, denied the request personally. Other city officials agreed with Connor's decision. They cited an ordinance that allowed them to stop a gathering if they believed it would disturb "the public welfare, peace, safety, health, decency, good order, morals or convenience" of the city.

Two days later the demonstrators tried again. They requested a permit to demonstrate "against the injustices of segregation and discrimination." Again, Connor saw to it that the request was denied. He sent a telegram to the protest leaders, "I insist that you and your people do not start any picketing on the streets in Birmingham, Alabama."

Exploring Ideas

Have interested students work together to find out more about Martin Luther King, Jr., and his ideas about peaceful protest. They might wish to locate quotations from King's speeches or books and give a reading for the class. Other students might wish to provide a biographical sketch of King for the class to discuss.

The leaders of the protest felt certain that city officials were using the ordinance as an excuse to deny the protesters their civil rights. They knew that their cause was just, and they proceeded with the march anyway.

An Appeal for Justice

The police wasted no time in breaking up the march and arresting the protest leaders. The leaders were soon tried in court, convicted, and sentenced to prison. When the case went to the Alabama Supreme Court, the convictions were upheld.

The leaders of the protest were not satisfied with the state court's decision. One of the leaders, Fred L. Shuttlesworth, represented all of the demonstrators when he appealed his conviction to the U.S. Supreme Court. He charged that the city had violated his constitutional right to gather with others in peaceful demonstration.

In 1969 the Supreme Court heard the case. The Court agreed that the city ordinance was applied unfairly and that the demonstrators had indeed been denied their right to assemble. Arguing that "fundamental rights" were at stake, the Court maintained that the city of Birmingham had acted "to deny . . . the right of assembly and the opportunities for the communication of thought."

Protecting the Right of Assembly

Martin Luther King's vision of a nation with equality for all people was given new promise with the demonstrations of 1963. These demonstrations prompted President John F. Kennedy to seek sweeping federal civil rights legislation aimed at social, political, and economic justice for all.

The achievements of the 1960s and beyond could not have been realized without the freedom of citizens to work together for change. The continuing fight for equal justice for all people requires that we protect our First Amendment right of assembly.

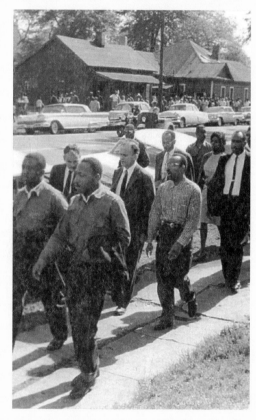

These marchers in Birmingham, Alabama, used their First Amendment right of assembly to make the entire nation aware of injustice.

YOU DECIDE

1 Why do you think the protesters were denied a permit to demonstrate?

2 What was the result of Fred Shuttlesworth's appeal to the U.S. Supreme Court?

3 How is the freedom of assembly related to the freedom of speech?

CIVICS SIDELIGHT

In attempting to stop the Birmingham demonstrators from exercising their constitutional rights, Public Safety Commissioner Eugene "Bull" Connor unwittingly added fuel to the growing civil rights movement. His use of fire hoses and dogs against the demonstrators was so outrageous that newspapers across the nation gave the story front-page coverage, adding support for federal civil rights legislation.

ANSWERS TO YOU DECIDE

1. City officials wanted to keep them from exercising their civil rights.

2. The Court decided that the city had acted to deny the protesters their constitutional rights, particularly the right of assembly.

3. When people gather together in free assembly, they exercise their freedom of speech by sharing their ideas and opinions on issues.

Drawing Conclusions

Have a volunteer read aloud the Twenty-fourth Amendment (page 548). Ask: What did this amendment do? *(prohibited poll tax)* Is there any mention of African Americans or any other minority group? *(no)* Then ask: Why was this such an important amendment for all Americans? *(removed financial status as a factor in being permitted to vote)*

Guided Practice

Begin a chart on the chalkboard with the following headings: Hispanic Americans, Native Americans, Women, Older Citizens, and Americans with Disabilities. Then call on volunteers to fill in columns under each heading with information from this section about each group's struggle for equal rights. Have students copy the chart in their notebooks for use as a study guide.

CIVICS SIDELIGHT

Civil rights laws prohibit discrimination in the sale of houses. Such discrimination does not always take the form of an owner refusing to sell to a member of a minority group. An example of indirect discrimination is redlining. This term describes a questionable banking practice that reflects some banks' unwillingness to provide mortgage financing within areas that they decide are in danger of becoming slums. In effect, the banks draw a red line around those areas and refuse to do business there. Thus the banks contribute to the decline of the area. Because of the concentration of racial minorities in many of these poverty-stricken areas, some people call redlining another form of racial discrimination.

AMERICAN BIOGRAPHY

Héctor Pérez García

Héctor Pérez García was born in Mexico in 1914 and later moved with his family to Texas. García graduated from college in 1936 and became a doctor in 1940. Two years later he joined the Army, where he served in the Medical Corps during World War II. García's service as a combat surgeon earned him a Bronze Star and six Battle Stars.

When the war ended, García opened a medical practice in Texas. While seeing patients in a local veterans hospital, he found that Mexican American veterans were treated with prejudice and discrimination. The experience spurred García to found the American G.I. Forum in 1948. Originally established to work for the civil rights of Mexican American veterans, the G.I. Forum soon set its sights on securing civil rights for all Mexican Americans.

As a civil rights activist, García also joined the League of United Latin American Citizens and helped found the Political Association of Spanish-Speaking Organizations. In 1968 he became the first Mexican American to serve on the U.S. Commission on Civil Rights. García's efforts have brought him many honors and awards, including the U.S.A. Medal of Freedom and the Outstanding Democracy Forward Award.

- Public places of amusement, such as parks and swimming pools, shall be open to all people.
- Discrimination in the rental or sale of houses must not be allowed.

The voting rights of minority groups were further strengthened by various voting rights acts and by the Twenty-fourth Amendment to the Constitution. This amendment, ratified in 1964, prohibits the use of poll taxes or other taxes as a requirement for voting.

Extending Equal Rights

In recent years the progress made by African Americans has encouraged other minority groups to work to end discrimination. These groups include Hispanic Americans, Native Americans, women, older citizens, and Americans with disabilities.

Hispanic Americans One of the fastest growing minority groups in the United States is Hispanic Americans. Hispanic Americans include people whose origins can be traced to Mexico, Puerto Rico, Cuba, and other parts of Central and South America. Like African Americans, Hispanic Americans have suffered discrimination in many areas of life.

Hispanic Americans have become increasingly united in their struggle for civil rights. They now hold more than 5,000 elected and appointed offices in the United States. In addition, two Hispanic Americans, Henry Cisneros and Federico Pena, now head executive departments in the federal government.

Native Americans Native Americans make up one of the country's smallest minority groups. For most of the nation's history, the federal government considered Native Americans to be conquered peoples with their own separate governments. As a result, they were long denied many of their civil rights. For example, Native Americans could not vote until 1924, when they were granted U.S. citizenship.

Since the 1960s, Native Americans have used protests, court cases, and lobbying efforts to secure their civil rights. Increased awareness of Native American issues led to the founding in 1989 of a museum of Native American history in Washington, D.C., as part of the Smithsonian Institution.

Invite students to imagine that they are living in the year 2076. As part of a project commemorating 300 years of U.S. independence, students should write newspaper headlines for retrospective articles about the equal rights struggles of the 20th century. Students should write a descriptive headline for such a story about the equal rights struggles of each group discussed in this section. Call on volunteers to share their headlines with the class.

Invite students to imagine they are the authors of a constitution for a newly independent country. Students should consider how the constitution will guarantee equal rights to all citizens of the country. Have each student write the section, article, or amendment that meets that goal. Students should review the U.S. Constitution (pages 529–549) and the Voting Rights Act (page 561). Invite volunteers to read their finished products to the class.

Women From the earliest period in the nation's history, women have not had the same rights as men. (See page 552.) For many years women could not own property. They could not vote until the Nineteenth Amendment to the Constitution was passed in 1920. They also did not enjoy the same educational and career opportunities as men.

In recent years women's efforts to secure equal rights have brought many changes. For example, women now outnumber men on college campuses. In addition, women now work in most of the occupations that once were closed to them, including medicine, law, and engineering. Men, however, still greatly outnumber women in the highest-paying jobs. Also, women do not always receive the same pay as men working in the same jobs. As a result, the movement for women's rights continues today.

Older Citizens As you know, the U.S. population is growing older. Today about 33 million Americans are age 65 and over. As the number of older citizens has increased, so have their demands for equal rights.

Older Americans, like other minority groups, have faced discrimination. This discrimination is based on the unfounded belief that older Americans are unproductive. This prejudice has cost the nation a great deal. Older citizens, with their wealth of experience, are particularly able to make valuable contributions to society.

In recent years older citizens have used strong lobbying efforts to make their concerns known to legislators. In addition, groups such as the American Association of Retired Persons (AARP) and the Gray Panthers work on behalf of older Americans.

Americans with Disabilities The 46 million Americans with disabilities have faced discrimination in areas such as housing, employment, and transportation. In 1990 activists won their most important victory with the passage of the Americans with Disabilities Act (ADA). The ADA, whose provisions went into effect over a period of several years, addresses four main areas. These areas are employment, public services, public accommodations, and telecommunications.

In employment, for example, the ADA makes it illegal to discriminate against people with disabilities in job applications, hiring, advancement, and salary and benefits. In the area of public services, the ADA requires that all new public buses and trains provide easy access to people with disabilities.

The ADA also requires changes in public accommodations. This means that businesses such as hotels and restaurants must install ramps, widen doors, and make other needed changes to provide access to people with disabilities. In telecommunications, the ADA requires that people with hearing and speech

Modern technology, such as this Braille computer, has allowed many Americans with disabilities to contribute their skills and talents to the workforce.

CIVICS
SIDELIGHT

The Wyoming territorial legislature gave women the right to vote in 1869, more than five decades before ratification of the Nineteenth Amendment to the U.S. Constitution. Wyoming voters also elected the first woman to be governor of a state when Nellie Tayloe Ross won the governorship in 1924.

Have students complete the Section 2 Review.

Assign Section 2 of the Chapter 24 Reteaching Worksheet.

SECTION OBJECTIVES

After studying Section 3, students should be able to do the following.

1. Explain why health-care costs have risen dramatically.

2. Describe how the government promotes citizens' health.

3. Explain why Americans should be concerned about drug abuse, alcoholism, and smoking.

4. Explain how AIDS is transmitted and why it is such a serious health problem.

5. Identify ways to ensure safety on highways and at home.

SECTION 2 REVIEW
A N S W E R S

1. See the following pages: minority group, discrimination, ethnic group (p. 475); civil rights movement, boycott, dissent, demonstration (p. 476); civil disobedience (p. 477).

2. enslaved, denied voting rights, segregated, not allowed to live in certain areas or work in certain jobs; dissent—boycotts, spoke out, demonstrated, used civil disobedience

3. prohibited use of poll taxes as requirement for voting

4. now hold many elected and appointed offices; not considered U.S. citizens.

5. more attend college and work in nontraditional jobs; want access to highest-paying jobs and equal pay

6. that they are unproductive

7. protects people with disabilities from discrimination in employment, public services and accommodations, telecommunications

8. Statements should focus on the denial of equal rights.

482

impairments have round-the-clock access to telephone services.

Protecting Citizens' Rights

Much has been accomplished in moving toward the goal of equal rights for all Americans. Many groups throughout the nation, however, continue to work toward achieving full civil rights and opportunities.

The United States was founded and made free through the efforts and contributions of the many groups that settled here. Over the years many of these groups have struggled to secure their lawful rights. It is up to all of us as responsible citizens to uphold the laws that guarantee these rights.

SECTION 2 REVIEW

1. Define or identify the following terms: minority group, discrimination, ethnic group, civil rights movement, boycott, dissent, demonstration, civil disobedience.

2. How were African Americans discriminated against prior to the civil rights movement? What forms of dissent did civil rights activists use?

3. How did the Twenty-fourth Amendment strengthen the rights of minority groups?

4. What political strides have Hispanic Americans made? Why were Native Americans denied the right to vote until 1924?

5. What gains have women made in recent years in their efforts to secure equal rights? Why does the women's movement continue today?

6. What unfounded belief forms the basis of discrimination against older Americans?

7. How does the Americans with Disabilities Act protect civil rights?

8. **THINKING CRITICALLY** Imagine that you are a lawyer living in the South during the 1950s. Prepare a statement that you will present to the Supreme Court explaining why segregation on buses is unconstitutional. You may want to read your statement to the class.

3 Protecting Citizens' Health and Safety

Being healthy means more than not being sick. The World Health Organization of the United Nations defines health as "a state of complete physical, mental, and social well-being and not merely the absence of disease or infirmity." Many people also refer to this state of well-being as "wellness."

Everyone has the responsibility to look after his or her own wellness. The lack of wellness in individuals can affect an entire community. Thus the welfare of our communities and the nation depends on the wellness of *all* citizens. For this and other reasons, the health and safety of U.S. citizens are of concern to the government. How does the government promote wellness?

The Federal Government's Role

The federal government has many divisions that promote the health of the American people. The Department of Health and Human Services, for example, spends billions of dollars each year on health programs. It advises state and local governments and distributes federal funds to local health programs.

One of the department's most important agencies is the U.S. Public Health Service. It conducts medical research in treating ailments such as cancer and heart disease. In addition, it

Help students understand the meaning of *addict* by pointing out that the word originates from the Latin *addictus*, meaning "favored." In a way, an addict favors, or likes, something too much. In fact, the body can become addicted to something (favor it) so much that taking it away can cause physical symptoms in a person. Ask students to suggest various things to which a person might become addicted. *(drugs, alcohol, tobacco)*

Review the reasons for the recent rise in health-care costs. Explain that advances in science and technology have indirect effects on costs. Have students discuss how such advances affect the aging population *(keep people alive longer)* and rising costs. *(New equipment, medicines, and therapies used to detect and combat disease can be very expensive.)* Have students use available resources to create flowcharts and other diagrams showing how technical advances contribute to rising medical costs.

works with foreign governments to prevent the spread of disease and maintains the world's largest medical library. The Public Health Service directs many other health-related agencies, including the Food and Drug Administration and the National Institutes of Health.

In recent years health care has become an issue of major concern in the nation. An aging population, rising doctor and hospital fees, and rising insurance premiums have caused health-care costs to skyrocket. By 1993 the problem prompted President Bill Clinton to call for an overhaul of the U.S. health-care system. The government continues to look for ways to ensure that all Americans have access to health insurance, including the estimated 41 million people now uninsured.

State Government's Role

Each state has a department of public health. Its function is to see that health laws are carried out in every part of the state. This department has broad powers covering every city, town, village, and rural community.

State public health departments assist local boards of health in several ways. They work with local boards during outbreaks of contagious diseases, such as measles or the flu. They provide laboratory services to diagnose diseases. State health departments regularly publish useful information for the general public. They also provide medicines and vaccines for the prevention of diseases.

State public health departments have other duties as well. They must examine all plans for public buildings. They inspect all public buildings and factories and other workplaces to determine if they are safe and have satisfactory air quality and clean conditions. Also under the supervision of these departments are state water systems and the disposal of garbage and sewage.

Local Government's Role

Nearly every U.S. city and town has a local health department to enforce proper rules of

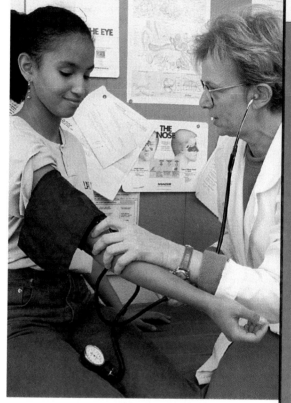

Local governments help keep community members healthy by preventing and treating health problems.

sanitation and cleanliness. These local departments also offer help in the prevention and cure of disease. They record cases of disease and act to stop the spread of disease.

Most health departments have laboratories that test foods to determine their purity. They inspect all restaurants and other places that perform services that could affect citizens' health.

Most communities have local hospitals that are supported in part by local funds. Some communities also provide public clinics that offer free or low-cost medical care.

Drugs and Drug Abuse

Widespread use of legal and illegal drugs has become a major issue for people concerned

CIVICS SIDELIGHT

The chief executive of the Public Health Service is called the surgeon general. President Clinton appointed Joycelyn Elders to this post in 1993. Like other surgeons general before her, Dr. Elders brought many years of education and experience to the position as the nation's top public health official. She attended Philander Smith College in Little Rock, Arkansas, to which she won a full scholarship at the age of 15. After a stint in the Army, she enrolled as the first female African American student at the University of Arkansas Medical School, after which she became a pediatric endocrinologist. Dr. Elders later became a professor of pediatrics at the University of Arkansas and also served as director of the Arkansas public health department. Elders left her position as surgeon general at the end of 1994.

Creating a Chart

Have pairs of students create charts that list the roles of federal, state, and local governments in protecting the public's health. Students should list information about each level of government under the appropriate headings. Have students copy the chart so that both students can add it to their notebooks for use as a study guide.

Developing Health Warnings

Ask students to read the "Surgeon General's Warnings on Cigarette Packages." Then have pairs of students develop similar warnings about drug and alcohol use as part of an overall campaign to combat drug, alcohol, and tobacco use. Call on volunteers to read their alcohol and drug warnings to the class for discussion.

CIVICS SIDELIGHT

The 1993 National Household Survey on Drug Abuse revealed that 11.7 million Americans— 5.6 percent of the population age 12 and older—had used an illegal drug in the month preceding the survey. While slightly higher than the figure for 1992 (11.4 million), the 1993 figure was far below the 24.3 million drug users reported in 1979. Since that date, there has generally been a steady decline in the use of illegal drugs, especially among so-called casual users. In discussing the report, government officials said the remaining drug users were chronic, hard-core users who were more difficult to help.

with health and safety in U.S. communities. We live in a society in which drugs are a part of everyday life for many people. The medicine chest in the average American home usually contains several kinds of drugs. Depending on their use, they may be helpful or harmful.

Drugs are prescribed by physicians in the treatment of disease. When taken as directed, they benefit people. Drugs also are used in self-medication. If used correctly, they may be helpful. Some people, however, take drugs for the wrong reasons. They take drugs to seek a new thrill or to forget or escape from problems. Using drugs in this way is called **drug abuse**.

Most of the drugs used by drug abusers are habit-forming and can cause life-threatening health problems. Drug abuse can have other side effects as well. For example, a drug abuser shows poor judgment when driving, putting his or her life and those of others in danger.

Continued use of drugs causes the users to become **addicts**, or slaves to the habit. Addicts must have the drug or they suffer headaches and pains in the stomach, muscles, and bones. As their dependence on the drug grows, they often need stronger and stronger doses of the drug to reach the effect they desire.

The quality of drugs sold illegally by drug "pushers" is not regulated. Therefore, the drugs may be too strong or mixed with something harmful. When this happens, individuals may take too strong a dose, or overdose. They may imagine terrible things are happening to them and have to be hospitalized. An overdose may also lead to death.

Much of the increase in crime in the United States is related to the sale, possession, and purchase of illegal drugs. Often needing hundreds of dollars a day to buy drugs, an addict may turn to crime. Many crimes of mugging, shoplifting, and burglary are committed by habitual drug users in search of money.

Drug addiction alone is not a crime but an illness. Both public and private hospitals have programs for treating and rehabilitating addicts. Private groups also run special centers where addicts may live while being treated. Recovering from drug addiction, however, is a difficult process. The best way to treat drug abuse and drug addiction is to prevent it. Therefore, public health officials offer many prevention programs to educate students, school officials, and parents.

Alcohol and Alcohol Abuse

Many people do not think of drinking alcohol as a problem, but too much alcohol can be harmful to your health. In fact, alcohol is a drug, and, like many drugs, it is habit-forming. Nearly 11 million Americans are problem drinkers, or alcoholics. They suffer from a disease called **alcoholism**.

The costs of alcohol abuse to the nation are tremendous. Alcohol is a factor in nearly half of all fatal automobile accidents. In addition, thousands of people die each year from physical illnesses brought on by drinking too much alcohol. People who drink too much strain family relationships and have trouble keeping jobs. Also, many crimes are committed by people who have been drinking alcohol.

It is important to remember that alcohol, like other drugs, can be dangerous to your health and well-being. The best way to avoid the dangers of alcohol is to not use it.

Surgeon General's Warnings on Cigarette Packages

● Smoking causes lung cancer, heart disease, emphysema, and may complicate pregnancy.

● Quitting smoking now greatly reduces serious risks to your health.

● Smoking by pregnant women may result in fetal injury, premature birth, and low birth weight.

● Cigarette smoke contains carbon monoxide.

Have small groups create pamphlets designed to provide high school students with information about AIDS. The pamphlets should include a brief history of the disease, projections for the future, and information about how HIV is transmitted. Roles for students include group leader, writers, and illustrators. Invite the principal to review the pamphlets to decide if any are appropriate for distribution throughout your school.

Guided Practice

If possible, bring to class newspapers for students to use to locate stories about accidents and emergency situations that have occurred. *(automobile accidents, falls, poisonings, drownings, fires, and others)* Ask: How can these accidents and emergency situations be avoided? What role does the government play in prevention?

Smoking

Since the 1950s scientists have studied the lives and health of people who smoke. These officials have reported that smokers are much more likely than nonsmokers to have lung cancer, respiratory ailments, and heart disease. So powerful was their evidence that Congress in 1970 banned cigarette advertisements from television. A federal law also requires all cigarette packages and all cigarette advertisements to carry a warning about the dangers of smoking. (See the chart on page 484.)

In 1993 a report issued by the Environmental Protection Agency concluded that environmental tobacco smoke, or secondhand smoke, poses a health risk not only to smokers but to nonsmokers as well. This report has fueled a mounting drive across the nation to ban smoking in public places, including workplaces. In 1994 the Department of Defense announced a ban on smoking in the workplace at U.S. military sites around the world. In addition, smoking now is banned on domestic airline flights in the United States.

In recent years, seven states in the nation have filed lawsuits against the tobacco industry to recover billions of Medicaid dollars spent on tobacco-related illnesses. A number of other states are now considering similar actions.

AIDS

In 1981 the Centers for Disease Control and Prevention began recording cases of a new, deadly disease in the United States. This disease is Acquired Immune Deficiency Syndrome (AIDS). In just a few years, a few hundred cases turned into an epidemic, or a disease affecting large numbers of people. By the late 1980s the U.S. Surgeon General identified AIDS as the country's most serious health problem.

AIDS is believed to be caused by the human immunodeficiency virus (HIV). HIV destroys a body's immune system, leaving it unable to fight infection and illness. As a result, people with AIDS have no protection against diseases such as cancer and pneumonia.

Reported Cases of AIDS in the United States

Year	Number of Cases
1981–1986	28,414
1987	27,795
1988	34,068
1989	39,252
1990	41,008
1991	42,472
1992	28,215
1993	103,360
1994	78,279

SOURCE: *Statistical Abstract of the United States.*

Although the federal government and other organizations have spent millions of dollars on AIDS research, there is still no cure for this deadly disease. Aids researchers believe it will be years before a vaccine or a cure for the disease is found.

People who contract AIDS may not show any signs of illness for many years. Thus it is difficult to know exactly how many people are infected with HIV. It is certain, however, that the disease is spreading rapidly.

It is estimated that one million Americans are infected with HIV and will eventually become ill. By the year 2000 an estimated 80,000 children and adolescents in the United States will lose their mothers to AIDS.

Researchers originally identified homosexual and bisexual men as the group in the U.S. population most likely to contract AIDS. Another group at high risk was users of intravenous drugs (drugs injected with a needle).

In recent years the number of new cases among homosexual and bisexual men has decreased, while the number of cases among intravenous drug users has increased. Moreover, AIDS appears to be spreading faster among

GLOBAL PERSPECTIVES

The number of world AIDS cases and HIV infections continues to increase rapidly. By mid-1995, nearly 1.2 million AIDS cases had been reported to the World Health Organization (WHO) since the disease was first reported in this country in 1981. WHO officials estimated that, because many cases are not diagnosed and because of reporting problems, the cumulative number of AIDS cases by mid-1995 actually was about 4.5 million—an 80 percent increase over the estimate of 2.5 million in 1993. WHO officials also estimated that, by mid-1995, around 1.5 million children had been infected by HIV since the late 1970s.

All parts of the world have been affected by the pandemic. WHO estimated that nearly two thirds of world AIDS cases by mid-1995 had occurred in Africa. About 9 percent had occurred in the United States and another 9 percent in the rest of North and South America. Health officials were increasingly concerned about the rapid spread of HIV in Asia, particularly in South and Southeast Asia.

Independent Practice

Have students write editorials for the school newspaper encouraging students to take steps to prevent accidents and emergencies such as fires. The editorials should include specific prevention advice. Encourage volunteers to read their editorials to the class and to submit their pieces to the school newspaper for publication.

Closure

Lead a discussion of government's role in protecting Americans and also citizens' responsibilities to protect themselves and others. Have students make a chart of the problems discussed in the section, including problems concerning health, substance abuse, and accidents. For each problem, students should suggest what preventive actions citizens and federal, state, and local government might reasonably be expected to take.

CIVICS SIDELIGHT

A poll conducted in 1992 suggested that Americans are much more safety conscious than they used to be, at least when it comes to driving. According to the poll, more than two thirds of all Americans used seat belts regularly. Less than a fifth of Americans in 1983 said they buckled up regularly. As of 1995, all states in the nation except Maine and New Hampshire had some form of seatbelt use law.

As another safety feature, more and more auto manufacturers are adding air bags to vehicles that they produce. Air bags inflate upon impact and then deflate almost immediately.

heterosexuals, including women, than among any other group. Heterosexual cases, however, still make up only a small percentage of reported AIDS cases in the United States.

AIDS is a worldwide problem. The World Health Organization estimates that at least 14 million people in the world are infected with HIV. By the year 2000 that number is expected to rise to between 30 and 40 million.

How AIDS Is Transmitted

The AIDS virus is transmitted through blood and other body fluids. Most people who contract AIDS are infected with the virus through sexual contact or by using needles that were used by people who carry the virus. Pregnant women who have the AIDS virus can pass it on to their unborn children. Before 1985 recipients of blood transfusions sometimes contracted the virus by receiving infected blood. Today the nation's blood supply is checked carefully to avoid this method of transmission.

People sometimes think that they can catch the AIDS virus by associating with people who have the disease. There is no evidence, however, that a person can catch AIDS through casual contact. Medical research has established that casual social contact—at school, in restaurants, in swimming pools—does not pose any threat of infection.

Accidents

Every American wants to live in a community in which it is safe to live, work, and play. Each year, however, about 62 million Americans are injured in accidents. About 18 million of these people are disabled for at least one day after the accident. Around 90,000 Americans die in accidents each year, and accidents cost more than $400 billion annually in medical care, wage loss, property damage, and other costs.

What kinds of accidents cause so much suffering? Automobile accidents, falls, poisonings, and drownings are among the leading categories of accidents in the United States. Many of these accidents take place at home or on the job. The rest occur on highways, in schools, in parks, and in other public places.

Safety on the Highway

Most of the nation's serious accidents take place on streets and highways. Nearly six million people are injured each year in the United States in accidents involving motor vehicles. About 42,000 people are killed in these automobile accidents.

Nearly half of these deaths involve alcohol. That is, drinking and driving contribute in some way to almost 17,000 deaths each year. In recent years local and state governments have responded to the growing public outcry over drinking and driving by passing stricter drunk driving laws. (See "Case Study: Mothers Against Drunk Driving" on pages 214–215.)

The main cause of automobile accidents is speeding. For this reason, law enforcement officials devote much time and energy to catching people who exceed the speed limit. Police issue tickets, and, in many states, a driver with a certain number of tickets loses his or her driver's license.

Government officials also promote safety on the highway by encouraging the use of seat belts. Many state governments now have laws that require everyone to wear a seat belt. Experts estimate that thousands of lives could be saved each year if everyone wore a seat belt. In addition, many state governments have passed child-restraint laws, which require that children riding in cars be placed in specially designed child seats or harnesses.

These government measures save lives. The burden of highway safety, however, still rests with individual citizens. Americans must act with care and responsibility on the nation's roadways.

Fire

Nearly two million fires occur in the United States each year. These fires cause the deaths of nearly 5,000 people annually and cost more than $8 billion in property damage.

What causes all of these fires? Most are caused either by carelessness or by defective equipment. Thus most fires that occur in the United States could be prevented. In fact, the

Reviewing

Have students complete the Section 3 Review.

Reteaching

Assign Section 3 of the Chapter 24 Reteaching Worksheet.

Extension

Have students research the history of the U.S. Public Health Service. Students should investigate how and when the service was begun, as well as the histories of the agencies the service directs. Have students compile their information in short, written reports that include graphics such as time lines. Invite volunteers to present their reports to the class.

best way to fight a fire is to prevent it from happening. Every citizen has the responsibility to follow commonsense rules of fire prevention in the home, at school, at work, in the community, and while outdoors.

One of the best ways to avoid the hazards of fire is to install smoke detectors in homes and other buildings. A smoke detector is a small device that sounds an alarm when it detects smoke. This early warning can help people in a home or other building escape safely. Most U.S. communities require that smoke detectors be installed in newly constructed homes and office buildings.

Protecting Your Safety

Safety is a life-and-death matter. Fortunately, many health problems, accidents, and fires can be prevented. The key is education. All Americans have the responsibility to learn and follow the commonsense rules of safety. As citizens protect their health and safety, the nation becomes safer for everyone.

SECTION 3 REVIEW

1. Define or identify the following terms: drug abuse, addict, alcoholism.

2. What has caused health-care costs to skyrocket in recent years?

3. How does the government promote health? Why does drug abuse and alcoholism concern all Americans?

4. Why is there a movement to ban smoking in public places?

5. Why is AIDS considered to be the nation's most serious health problem? How is the virus that causes AIDS transmitted?

6. How does the government promote highway safety? What can citizens do to protect their homes from fire?

7. **THINKING CRITICALLY** The Department of Health and Human Services has asked you to deliver a televised speech to the nation on "Wellness in the Year 2000." In your speech discuss current health issues facing the nation and what can be done to address these issues.

CHAPTER 24 SUMMARY

Americans have always sought to improve their way of life. Early in the nation's history, for example, men and women began moving to the cities to find new and better jobs. There they hoped to make a better life for themselves and their children.

As time passed and the population continued to grow, however, Americans began leaving large cities for smaller towns and suburbs. For the most part, the problems of the nation's cities are responsible for this movement of the American people.

Many city centers have deteriorated, and some areas are now slums. Mass transportation has declined. As the populations of small towns and suburbs have grown, these areas have developed similar problems. Many communities across the country are working hard to improve conditions.

The United States is home to many minority groups. These groups have contributed much to the richness of American society. Unfortunately, many groups have faced prejudice and discrimination. They continue to work to achieve their full civil rights.

The wellness of people in our communities is important, as it affects the health of our communities and of the nation as a whole. There are many things that each person can do to safeguard his or her health and safety and that of others. For example, you can learn about preventing alcoholism and drug abuse and seek safety training.

SECTION 3 REVIEW ANSWERS

1. See the following page: drug abuse, addict, alcoholism (p. 484).

2. aging population, rising doctor and hospital costs, rising insurance premiums

3. health departments and agencies, research, distribution of information and medicines, track spread of disease, inspect public facilities, fund and operate public health facilities; abuse causes health problems and is associated with crime, accidents, poor relationships

4. evidence of significant health risks of secondhand smoke

5. It is a fatal, incurable disease that is spreading rapidly. It is transmitted through blood and other body fluids, usually through sexual activity or by sharing needles.

6. drunk driving and traffic laws, encouraging or requiring use of automobile safety restraints; smoke detectors

7. Speeches should focus on specific health issues.

Suggest to students that one of the best ways to compare points of view about local issues is to read the newspaper every day. Tell them that issues evolve over time. Local leaders on both sides of a question consider the facts as they emerge and draw conclusions from them. Those conclusions often appear in newspaper articles. If students follow the issue closely, they will be able to sort out the arguments on both sides, distinguish facts from opinions, and come to their own conclusions about issues.

Have students research a local issue by reading about it in back issues of your community newspaper at the library. Then have students create charts that describe the points of view on both sides of the issue and how each side argued its point. Students should note how the issue was settled.

Developing Civics Skills

CITIZENSHIP SKILL
Comparing Points of View

ANSWERS TO
Applying the Skill

1. whether carmakers should be required to install air bags in all new cars

2. arguments—Valerie: Air bags are better than seat belts because they cannot be ignored. They would save lives. Luis: Air bags are too expensive and would violate consumers' freedom of choice. evidence—Valerie: government and insurance industry studies; Luis: auto industry studies; opinions—Valerie: Saving lives is the most important thing, and air bags are best way to do this. Also, 30 to 55 percent is a large percentage, and government action will save lives. Luis: Consumers should have a choice on whether to accept the cost and risks of air bags.

3. Answers will vary. Students should use sound reasoning in their responses.

As a citizen, you are free to make choices and take stands on issues. During your lifetime, you will face hundreds of questions such as: Whom will you vote for? and Which proposals do you support?

Different people will have different answers to these questions. Comparing the points of view on an issue will enable you to make a well-informed, fair, and reasonable decision.

How to Compare Points of View

1. Identify the issue. Before you can compare points of view, you must understand the issue. Often, it helps to put the issue in the form of a question. For example, the issue in a discussion about who should be elected governor might be phrased as "Who should be governor of the state?"

2. List each side's arguments. Listing the arguments side-by-side on a piece of paper will help you compare each side's argument on a point-by-point basis.

3. Examine the evidence. Just because someone gives a reason for a position does not mean the position is a valid one. Evaluate the evidence and facts behind each position to determine its validity.

4. Distinguish between facts and opinions. When comparing points of view, focus on the relevant facts, not the opinions expressed by the writer or speaker.

Applying the Skill

Compare the points of view below. Then answer the following questions.

1. What issue is being discussed?
2. What arguments does each person use to support his or her view? What evidence does each person offer? What are the opinions expressed?
3. State your own point of view on the issue under consideration.

Valerie's Point of View:
There is nothing more important than saving lives on American highways. The best way to do this is to require carmakers to install air bags in all new cars. Air bags are better than seat belts: people can ignore seat belts, but they cannot ignore air bags. Government studies show that deaths from auto accidents would drop as much as 30 to 55 percent if all cars were equipped with air bags. This is a large percentage. Studies done by the insurance industry also show that air bags save lives. The sooner the government acts, the sooner more American lives will be saved.

Luis's Point of View:
Air bags are expensive and will add hundreds of dollars to the price of a car. If the government requires air bags to be installed in all new cars, American consumers will lose their choice as to whether to pay extra for air bags. Moreover, according to auto industry studies, it can cost as much as $2,000 to restore an air bag after it has been used. Who can afford that? And what if the air bag inflated accidentally? That could cause an accident. The cost and risk of air bags are things American consumers should have a choice about. The government should not require that air bags be installed in new cars.

CHAPTER 24 REVIEW
A N S W E R S

Vocabulary Workshop
1. slum
2. mass transit
3. unfair actions against people because they belong to a certain group
4. intentionally disobeying a law one believes to be wrong

5. help prevent future problems by setting aside parts of cities for specific purposes; keep buildings safe, comfortable, and in good repair

Reviewing Main Ideas
1. loss of tax money, federal funds, voters, representatives for cities
2. increasing lack of affordable housing
3. equal rights; write letters, make telephone calls, send telegrams, march, demonstrate, boycott, use civil disobedience
4. forbids discrimination in employment, public services and accommodations, telecommunications
5. have a variety of departments that conduct research, distribute information, enforce health laws, check purity of food and water, set up health centers, perform other health-related activities
6. Addicts may turn to other crimes to get money for drugs. ban—eliminate exposure to secondhand smoke
7. HIV; through blood and other body fluids primarily through sexual activity or sharing needles

Thinking Critically
1. Students should use sound reasoning in their responses.
2. Students should provide workable solutions.
3. Students should understand that these U.S. ideals apply to all Americans.

Citizenship in Your Community
Reports should focus on homelessness in your community.

BUILDING YOUR PORTFOLIO
Assign Portfolio Assessment Worksheet 24 in the *Portfolio Assessment Worksheets* booklet.

Assessment
- **Chapter 24 Tests**, *Chapter Tests* booklet
- **Test Generator**, Chapter 24
- **Portfolio**, Portfolio Assessment Worksheet 24, *Portfolio Assessment Worksheets* booklet

CHAPTER 24 R·e·v·i·e·w

Vocabulary Workshop
1. What is the term for a run-down section of a city where buildings are neglected and people live crowded together?
2. What collective term is used to describe subways, buses, and commuter railroads?
3. Define the term *discrimination*.
4. What is civil disobedience?
5. How do building codes and zoning laws benefit communities?

Reviewing Main Ideas
1. What problems have resulted from the movement of middle-income families away from cities?
2. Why has homelessness been on the rise?
3. What is the goal of the civil rights movement? What are some of the methods by which Americans can show their dissent?
4. How does the Americans with Disabilities Act help citizens with disabilities?
5. How do the federal, state, and local governments promote health?
6. How does drug abuse contribute to the rising rate of crime? Why is there a movement to ban smoking in public places?
7. What causes AIDS? How is the AIDS virus transmitted?

Thinking Critically
1. The movement to ban smoking in public places is widely debated. Nonsmokers believe that they should not be forced to breathe secondhand smoke. Smokers believe that they should not be forced to give up their right to smoke. What is your position on this issue?
2. You have just been elected mayor of a large city. What actions will you take to eliminate slums in your city?
3. Explain how prejudice and discrimination are contrary to the ideals of freedom, justice, and democracy on which the United States is based.

Citizenship in Your Community

Individual Project

Research and report on homelessness in your community. Approximately how many people in your community are without homes? What organizations exist to help the homeless in your community? How is your local government helping solve the problem? How can individuals contribute to these efforts? You may wish to create charts or other visuals to illustrate the information you collect.

Building Your Portfolio

The first step of your unit portfolio (see page 515) is to research what impact the drive for equal rights has had on your school over time. What is the ethnic makeup of your school? How has it changed over time? Are certain classes now open to girls that once were closed? Do boys now take classes that once were taken only by girls? What multicultural education classes are taught in your school? What has your school done to comply with the Americans with Disabilities Act? What more can be done to ensure equal educational opportunities for all students? Show your findings in a series of graphs that compare the answers to these questions now and in the past. Place your graphs in your individual portfolio for later use.

PLANNING GUIDE

TEXTBOOK	TEACHING RESOURCES	OTHER AVAILABLE RESOURCES
Chapter	• Skills Worksheet 25 • Challenge/Enrichment Worksheet 25	
Section **1** Understanding Ecology Page 491 **2** Pollution Page 496 **3** Energy Resources Page 503 **4** Our Future on Earth Page 507	• Reteaching Worksheet 25.1 • Reteaching Worksheet 25.2 • Reteaching Worksheet 25.3 • Reteaching Worksheet 25.4	
Review and Assessment **Chapter 25 Review,** Page 513 **Unit 8 Review,** Page 514	• Test, Form A • Test, Form B • Portfolio Assessment Worksheet 25 • Unit 8 Portfolio Assessment Worksheet	• *Test Generator,* Chapter 25 • *Test Generator,* Unit 8

ADDITIONAL RESOURCES

BOOKS FOR TEACHERS

Carless, Jennifer, *Taking Out the Trash: A No-Nonsense Guide to Recycling*, Island Press.

Carson, Rachel, *Silent Spring*, Houghton Mifflin.

Lappé, Marc, *Chemical Deception: The Toxic Threat to Health and the Environment*, Sierra Club Books.

Pick, Maritza, *How to Save Your Neighborhood, City, or Town: The Sierra Club Guide to Community Organizing*, Sierra Club Books.

BOOKS FOR STUDENTS

Gay, Kathlyn, *Global Garbage: Exporting Trash and Toxic Waste*, Watts. Studies issues concerning the international disposal of hazardous wastes.

Krensky, Stephen, *Four Against the Odds: The Struggle to Save Our Environment*, Scholastic. Portrays the courageous ef-

forts of John Muir, Rachel Carson, Lois Gibbs, and Chico Mendes to preserve the environment.

Pack, Janet, *Fueling the Future*, Childrens. Discusses the impact of fossil fuels on the environment and examines alternative sources of energy.

Patent, Dorothy Hinshaw, *Habitats: Saving Wild Places*, Enslow. Discusses preserving wildlife habitats and how to influence U.S. government actions.

MULTIMEDIA RESOURCES

Earth's Natural Resources: Can They Last? (fs/cassettes, c, 35 min.), NGS. Explains how we rely on and deplete resources.

The Fragile Soil (VHS, c, 22 min.), BEA. Discusses erosion and destruction of the soil ecosystem by pollutants.

Recycling: The Endless Circle (f, VHS, c, 25 min.), NGS. Explains how recycling keeps waste out of landfills.

Spaceship Earth: Our Global Environment (VHS, c, 25 min.), CSS. Demonstrates the global interdependence of human, natural, and technological systems.

THE INTERNET

Have students use these search words to locate more information about chapter topics on the Internet: *ecology, farming, pollution, natural resources, Environmental Protection Agency.*

 GLOBAL SKILL BUILDER

You might wish to use **Navigating the Internet** from the interactive *Global Skill Builder* CD-ROM to aid students' understanding of the Internet as a resource.

Abbreviations: b&w=black and white; c=color; f=film; fs=filmstrip; sd=sound; tr=transparency; VHS=videotape

CIVICS SKILLS

Students will learn how to read maps. Students also will learn terms important to understanding environmental challenges facing the earth.

CITIZENSHIP VALUES

Students will be encouraged to recognize the need to treat the earth's resources with care, to become aware of the need to conserve scarce energy resources, to appreciate the work of conservation groups, and to cooperate in conservation measures.

CHALLENGES IN TODAY'S WORLD

★ **Protecting the Environment** Students will learn about ecosystems, threats to the "balance of nature," and the conservation movement. Students also will learn ways in which people can conserve available energy resources and how government works to protect the environment.

MEETING INDIVIDUAL NEEDS

LIMITED ENGLISH PROFICIENCY (LEP)

Have students list the kinds of alternative sources of energy discussed on pages 506–507. Then have them create illustrations that describe the name of each energy source. For example, students might draw a picture of the sun to illustrate *solar* power and water and lightning bolts to illustrate *hydro*electric power. Encourage students to be creative.

LEARNERS HAVING DIFFICULTY

Ask students to prepare 10-question quizzes about information presented in the chapter. Have them write the answers on a separate sheet of paper. Then, as a review, students should answer each other's quizzes, returning them for grading. Graded quizzes should be kept as study guides.

AUDITORY LEARNERS

Have students create radio advertisements about actions one can take to promote conservation. Then call on volunteers to present their advertisements to the class as part of a discussion of conservation.

VISUAL LEARNERS

Have students use newspapers, other periodicals, and their own drawings to create collages illustrating different ecosystems. The illustrations should include explanatory captions. Call on volunteers to present and explain their collages to the class as part of a discussion of ecosystems.

TACTILE/KINESTHETIC LEARNERS

Bring to class a flower, a piece of driftwood, a pine cone, a colorful stone, or some other piece of nature. Invite students to look closely at and touch the object. Then have them create a poem or song or work of art that describes the world without the object. Encourage students to consider possible consequences to human and animal life. For example, for a flower: Bees and other insects would lose a food source, and many human-made products that depend on plants (perfume, rosewater, cosmetics, foods, some medicines) might not be available. Students might also consider the beauty of the object as important by itself. Encourage students to be creative.

GIFTED LEARNERS

Have students research the Biosphere II project near Tucson, Arizona, from 1991 to 1993. Then have students develop plans for changing your school into a self-contained biosphere. Students should decide what kinds of skills inhabitants of the school biosphere would need and how ecosystems would be created within the school biosphere. Students might want to illustrate their ideas. Call on volunteers to present their plans to the class.

CHAPTER OVERVIEW

Chapter 25 opens by considering the need to preserve the balance of nature. It then examines the problems of pollution and scarce energy resources. The chapter concludes with a discussion of environmental history and how students can help conserve resources. The underlying theme of the chapter is that wise use of resources will ensure continued prosperity into the future.

Motivator

Invite students to imagine what they would have seen if they could have flown over the United States a thousand years ago. Then discuss what they would see today. Ask: How has the landscape changed? Is the change good or bad? Elicit that there is no clear answer. Many changes that brought prosperity also caused environmental damage. One sign of progress is that we are now able to see and, sometimes, anticipate mistakes.

CHAPTER OBJECTIVES

After studying Chapter 25, students should be able to do the following.

1. Define an ecosystem, and explain the interdependence of all living things in a particular ecosystem.
2. Identify kinds of pollution and the ways in which pollution can be reduced.
3. Identify the types of energy available and which types offer promise for the future.
4. Describe what governments, private organizations, and individuals can do to protect the planet.

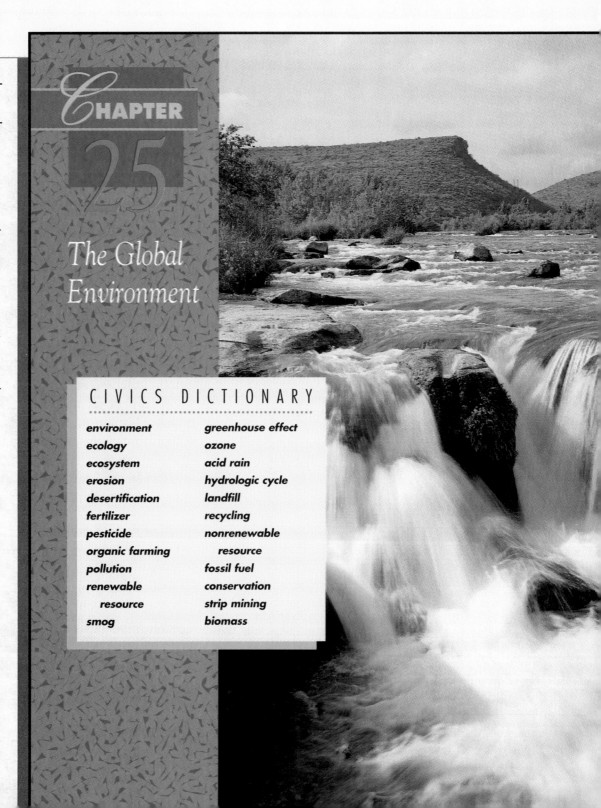

CHAPTER 25

The Global Environment

CIVICS DICTIONARY

environment
ecology
ecosystem
erosion
desertification
fertilizer
pesticide
organic farming
pollution
renewable
    resource
smog

greenhouse effect
ozone
acid rain
hydrologic cycle
landfill
recycling
nonrenewable
    resource
fossil fuel
conservation
strip mining
biomass

SECTION OBJECTIVES

After studying Section 1, students should be able to do the following.

1. Explain the interdependence of all living things in an ecosystem.
2. Explain how humans have upset the balance of nature.
3. Identify how farmers care for the soil, and explain why farmland is still being lost.
4. List the advantages and disadvantages of pesticide use.
5. Describe the problems of overpopulation.

Teaching Section 1
Building a Vocabulary

Explain that **environment**, from the French word *environ*, meaning "around," is the world around us. Tell students the Greek root *eco-* means "habitat" or "environment." Also, one meaning of the Greek root *-logy* is "doctrine" or "science." Thus, **ecology** is the study, or science, of living things in relation to each other and to their environment. Have students break **ecosystem** into parts to deduce its meaning. *(community, or system, of interdependent living things in an environment)*

CHAPTER FOCUS

December 1968: U.S. astronaut James Lovell, halfway to the moon, looked out the window of his spacecraft. There among the stars he saw a planet. One side of it was in shadow. The other side was streaked with beautiful colors—blue, brown, green, and white. To Lovell and the other astronauts, the earth, too, seemed to be a kind of spacecraft among the stars. We are all riding on it, passengers together, dependent on the earth for all the necessities of life.

The earth has been good to us. It provides us with air to breathe, water to drink, food to eat, and materials to make life easier. Over the years these resources have been taken for granted, as though they could never be used up. We now know, however, that the resources of the earth are not limitless. They need protection.

STUDY GUIDE

- What is an ecosystem, and why are all living things in an ecosystem interdependent?
- What kinds of pollution exist today, and what can be done to reduce pollution?
- What types of energy are available, and which offer promise for the future?
- What can governments, organizations, and individuals do to protect the planet?

1 Understanding Ecology

The world around us is our **environment**. It is made up of layers of air, water covering about three fourths of the surface of the globe, and land. We depend on the environment for everything we need to live.

What happens, however, when the environment changes? Each day new buildings go up. Highways are built. Jet planes streak through the skies. These changes can be helpful. They can also create serious problems.

What Is Ecology?

All living things depend on each other for survival. The study of living things in relation to each other and to their environment is called **ecology**. The entire earth can be considered one large ecological unit. Usually, however, ecologists study the earth by dividing it into a number of ecosystems. An **ecosystem** is a community of interdependent living things existing in balance with their physical environment. Typical examples of ecosystems are a desert, a forest, and a pond.

All living things within an ecosystem play a vital role in maintaining the stability of the system. Human beings and animals, for example, depend on green plants for the oxygen they breathe. Plants take carbon dioxide out of the air. They then break it down into carbon and oxygen. The plants use the carbon to make their own food.

The pure oxygen, which plants cannot use, is released back into the atmosphere. Human beings and animals breathe in this oxygen, which they need to live. They breathe out carbon dioxide, and the cycle begins again. Without green plants and the oxygen they supply, no animal or human being could live.

The living things within an ecosystem depend on each other in other ways as well. Bacteria, for example, feed on fallen leaves, causing the leaves to decay. This decaying

CIVICS SIDELIGHT

Point out that the move by people into previously undeveloped areas has consequences for both wildlife and humans. For example, humans living in some areas inhabited by deer must be on the alert for Lyme disease. Lyme disease, named after the town in Connecticut where it was first observed, is primarily a problem in parts of the northeastern and midwestern United States, in northern California, and in the Pacific Northwest. The disease is spread by ticks that feed on the blood of infected mice and deer. As the suburbs increasingly push out into forested rural areas, human populations come into greater contact with deer and the ticks they carry. Left untreated, the disease can damage the joints and the nervous system. The disease can be treated effectively with antibiotics.

Understanding Ideas

Draw a web diagram on the chalkboard with your school in the center. Ask students to add other elements, such as students, teachers, custodians, and parents, as well as education, taxes/tuition, and jobs; then have students specify how these elements are interdependent. *(For example, without teachers there would be no education, and students would not learn enough to get a good job.)* Call on volunteers to compare this interdependence with that characterizing an ecosystem.

Writing to Learn

Tell students that Native Americans of the Great Plains, such as the Sioux and Pawnee, relied on the buffalo for many of their needs, including food, clothing, and housing. As American settlers moved westward, however, Native Americans had to compete for land and buffalo. By the late 1800s, the buffalo had been nearly wiped out. Have students write an imaginary interview with a Native American from the late 1800s. The interviews should focus on how the decline of the buffalo affected life for Native Americans.

MULTICULTURAL PERSPECTIVES

European claims to Native American land were a foreign concept to Native Americans, who believed people could not "own" land. Native Americans believed they simply were part of the ecosystem that existed on the land. In 1806 Chief Tecumseh of the Shawnee protested against the notion that anyone could own the land. The land, he said, "was never divided, but belongs to all. No tribe has the right to sell, even to each other, much less to strangers. Sell a country! Why not sell the air, the great sea, as well as the earth?"

Photo Caption Answer

Economic development, growth of cities, and pollution are some of the factors affecting the balance of nature.

matter enriches the soil, so that more plants and trees can grow. The plants in turn supply food for insects, birds, other animals, and eventually, more bacteria.

Likewise, tiny marine animals called plankton live in marshes and wetlands and provide food for shrimp, oysters, and minnows. These in turn become food for larger fish and make possible the great schools of fish on which human beings, dolphins, seals, bears, and many other animals depend for food.

As these examples show, all living things in an ecosystem are like links in a chain. Take away one link and all living things depending on that link will suffer. For example, reducing the amount of forests in the world also reduces the wild bird population that lives in the forests. Without enough birds to eat them, insects will multiply quickly. Increased numbers of insects will do more damage to the food crops on which they feed. As a result, people who depend on the crops for a living (farmers) and for food (consumers) will suffer.

Similarly, reducing the amount of undeveloped areas of a country also reduces the number of eagles, hawks, coyotes, mountain lions, and other predators living there. Without these natural enemies, other animals, such as mice and deer, will increase quickly. With too many plant-eating animals, not enough plants will decay to enrich the soil and hold moisture. Later there will be fewer plants, and the plant eaters, too, will suffer.

As you can see, all living things depend on a delicate balance of nature within their environment. People sometimes do not realize they are part of this balance. They do not understand that their activities can have harmful side effects that upset the balance of nature. Because changes in the environment can have far-reaching effects, we must all learn that our actions have consequences.

America's Early Environment

The North American continent is a land of great natural wealth and beauty. This part of the world has moderate climates, with plenty of sunshine and a good supply of rain in most

Water, plants, trees, and other wildlife all have their place in the balance of nature. How have people upset nature's balance over the years?

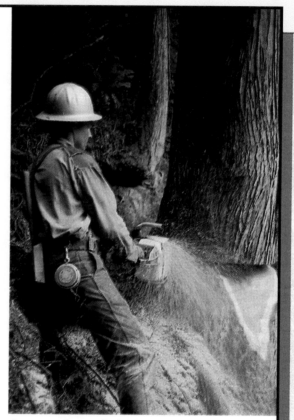

COOPERATIVE LEARNING

Have small groups use flowcharts or other diagrams to illustrate the balance of nature in an ecosystem. Diagrams should illustrate how all species in an ecosystem rely on other species for survival. Have the group use captions to explain the consequences to the ecosystem should one species in the balance of nature become extinct. Groups might want to use classroom and library resources to provide specific examples of such occurrences. Roles for students include researchers, writers, and illustrators.

Comparing Points of View

Invite students to role-play a meeting among agricultural officials from the United Nations, from an industrializing nation, and from the United States. The officials should try to find ways to protect the nations' environments while at the same time developing their economies. For example, a plan for the United States might stress industries that use recyclable materials. A plan for the industrializing nation might focus on ways to prevent widespread deforestation.

---

places. Before the continent was heavily settled, trees grew thick and tall in the forests. The plains were covered with wild grasses. The river valleys were fertile and green. Many kinds of wild animals roamed the land.

America's abundance was the result of natural forces that had been at work for thousands of years. The sun, wind, and rain had worn away huge rocks and reduced them to soil. Melting snow had formed streams that carried soil down from the mountains into the valleys. Huge rivers formed. These rivers dug out great channels and canyons and deposited more soil in their paths.

Plants grew in this soil. When they decayed, their leaves and roots further enriched the soil. Trees were able to take root and grow. Some of these trees grew in rocky places. Their roots helped break up the rocks and make more soil. Other trees took root and huge forests were born.

These great forests provided protection and food for many kinds of animals. Other animals, such as the great herds of American bison (buffalo), grazed on the open plains. Various species of birds, insects, and animals kept each other in balance. Each plant or animal took what it needed from the environment. In turn each contributed to the needs of other living things.

People also were part of the balance of nature. Native Americans hunted animals for food and used the hides for clothing and shelter. They usually killed only what they needed. Although their ways of life have changed, many Native Americans continue to have great respect for the earth and for the environment.

Upsetting America's Ecology

The early European settlers were amazed by the natural wealth of America. In Europe most of the land had been farmed for hundreds of years. There were few forests and few wild animals left. Thus the fertile land, forests, and wildlife of America seemed unlimited to the European settlers.

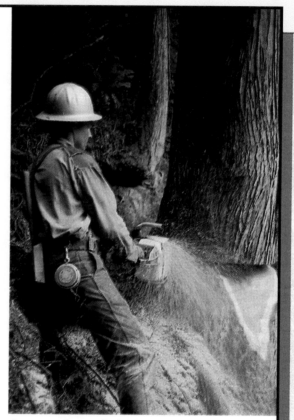

The cutting of vast timberlands in the past and today has greatly affected the ecology of the United States. In recent years more care has been taken in some areas to replant forests as trees are cut.

America's forests were so thick with growth that settlers in the East first had to clear the trees to grow crops. They used some of the wood to build their houses and furniture. They burned what they did not need or shipped it to Europe as lumber. The tallest and straightest trees were used to make the masts of great sailing ships.

As the number of settlers in America increased and the demand for wood grew, more forests were cut down. No new trees were planted in their place. If people wanted more wood, there were more forests to the west.

As settlers destroyed the forests, however, they destroyed something more. As the trees

GLOBAL PERSPECTIVES

American settlers turned forestland into cropland by cutting down and burning trees. They also sold wood for a profit. Today settlers in the tropical forests of developing countries carry on these practices as their nations' economies grow. Many scientists, however, now warn that such practices pose a danger to the forests, their ecosystems, and the world environment. Many forested regions of the world are shrinking rapidly. Deforestation can cause losses of entire species of plants and animals and lead to erosion and other harmful environmental effects. Deforestation during the 1980s was particularly severe in Brazil, Indonesia, Malaysia, Zaire, and Colombia. Governments in these countries have tried to implement plans designed to sustain development in the forests while protecting the regions from widespread deforestation.

Guided Practice

Help students develop a chart on the advantages and disadvantages of pesticide use. Begin two columns of the chart by writing "Advantages" and "Disadvantages" on the chalkboard. Then call on volunteers to supply appropriate information under each column heading. Have students copy the chart in their notebooks for use as a study guide.

Independent Practice

Explain that pesticides often are used to increase crop yields to feed the rapidly increasing populations of many industrializing countries. Have students consider other environmental consequences of overpopulation, such as the overuse and depletion of natural resources. Then have students create illustrated flowcharts or other diagrams, with explanatory captions, that show how overpopulation is connected with these environmental consequences.

MULTICULTURAL PERSPECTIVES

Some of the agricultural methods that work so well today have a long history in the Americas. For example, the Incas of South America mastered the art of terrace farming well before the arrival of Europeans in the 1400s. The Incas lived and farmed on the slopes of the Andes, where fertile soil was at a minimum. They could not afford to have soil wash away down the hillside, so they constructed elaborate terraces, with stone walls to hold the soil in place. Like farmers today, the Incas built irrigation canals and drainage channels. They also practiced crop rotation, alternating their plantings of maize, potatoes, beans, and other crops from year to year.

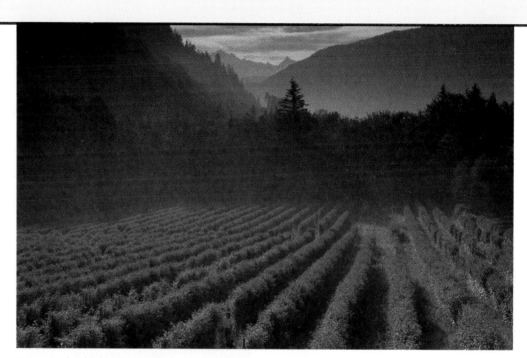

Science and technology have helped make U.S. farmland among the most productive in the world. This organic raspberry farm uses no artificial substances, such as pesticides.

disappeared, so did much of the wildlife that depended on them for food and shelter. Many other wild animals were killed by settlers, not only for food but also for their furs or for sport.

Beavers were trapped by the millions because beaver hats were popular in Europe. Whole herds of buffalo were shot for hides or for sport, and their meat was left to rot. Other animals and birds of prey, including foxes, bears, mountain lions, owls, hawks, and eagles, were shot as pests because they sometimes attacked livestock.

Destroying these animals upset the balance of nature. These creatures fed mostly on other animals, including mice and snakes. Soon mice and other small animal populations began to grow unchecked. Another result of the thoughtless killing of so many animals was that some species were destroyed or almost destroyed. These endangered species are now protected by special laws, but their future is still uncertain.

Farming the Land

The land cleared for farming was at first very fertile. This rich soil produced large crops of vegetables, wheat, oats, cotton, and tobacco. When the farmer planted a crop and harvested it, however, nothing was left to decay and rebuild the soil. As the land was farmed year after year, the supply of plant food in the soil was used up and nothing was put back.

In the West, cattle ranchers and sheepherders also took the land for granted. Their huge herds ate all the grasses and plants on the prairies. Without plants to hold water, the land dried out. Much good grassland was ruined in this way. People seemed to think that new land would always be available.

By the early 1900s the vast North American continent was filling with people. There was no longer a seemingly endless supply of land. Farmers plowed up more and more of the flat grasslands on the Great Plains. When the plains went through a long dry period in the

Have pairs of students create brochures that could be used to educate the public about the interdependence of ecosystems. The brochures should include diagrams or other visual guides that help describe ways in which ecosystems and the balance of nature are threatened, such as through irresponsible economic development, overuse of pesticides, and overpopulation. The brochures also should include ways ecosystems can be protected. Call on volunteers to present their brochures to the class for discussion.

Have students complete the Section 1 Review.

Assign Section 1 of the Chapter 25 Reteaching Worksheet.

1930s, no grass was left to hold the soil in place. Huge amounts of rich soil were blown away by the wind. A few years later, all that was left was a barren "dust bowl."

In the 1930s President Franklin D. Roosevelt urged Congress to pass a program to conserve the nation's farmlands. Under this program, called the soil bank, landowners were rewarded if they did not farm some of their land. They were paid to grow trees or grass instead. These practices were designed to preserve a supply of good land for the future.

Modern Agriculture

Today farmers in the United States and other areas of the world use modern science and technology to care for the soil. To prevent **erosion**, or the wearing away of land by water and wind, some farmers use contour farming. By plowing and planting across the slope of the land, farmers prevent the soil from being washed away. Many farmers also build drainage channels, dams, and terraces—flat spaces on the slopes—to prevent water erosion.

Other farmers plant cover crops, such as clover and soybeans, because their roots hold the soil in place better than other crops. They also practice crop rotation—planting different crops on the land each year. Crop rotation helps keep the soil from wearing out.

Despite modern agricultural techniques, however, some of the world's available farmland is lost each year. In industrialized nations such as the United States, farmland mainly is being lost to the spread of urban and suburban areas. Other nations are losing their soil to a process called **desertification**. This occurs when years of overgrazing and removal of trees and plants harm the soil to the extent that once-fertile areas become deserts.

Fertilizers and Pesticides

To help grow more food on less land, many farmers around the world use chemical fertilizers and pesticides. **Fertilizers** are plant foods that make crops grow faster and bigger. The most important fertilizers are nitrates, which contain nitrogen. Nitrates can be mixed with water and pumped into the ground, or they can be spread as powder to soak in with the next rain. Crops fertilized with nitrates grow so quickly that much more food can be harvested.

Pesticides are chemicals that kill insect pests and weeds. Many insects attack food plants, ruining entire crops. Weeds also lower crop production. The use of chemical pesticides has dramatically reduced crop losses to insects and weeds.

Although the thousands of pesticides used around the world increase production, they pose potential health and environmental hazards. In 1972, for example, the United States severely restricted the use of the pesticide DDT, first introduced in 1939. Scientists found that several species of birds were dying out because the DDT weakened the shells of the eggs they laid. (See "American Biography: Rachel Carson" on page 501.) DDT, however, still is used in many parts of the world and may be responsible for higher rates of death and disease among people in these areas.

Pesticides also kill insects that are beneficial to plants, such as ladybugs and honeybees. Moreover, many damaging insects build a tolerance to pesticides over time, requiring new and stronger chemicals to defeat them. Pesticides also leak into the surrounding soil and water, where they may stay active for many years. Many of the long-term effects of pesticides on humans, animals, and the environment are still undetermined.

Because of the problems caused by pesticide use, some people practice **organic farming**, or farming without using artificial substances. By using natural substances, beneficial insects, and special farming methods to increase crop yields and control pests, farmers can avoid using chemicals. (See "Global Connections: Pest Management in Indonesia" on page 509.)

Overpopulation

The population of the world has been increasing at an astonishing rate. It took more than a

GLOBAL PERSPECTIVES

Agricultural planning in the former Soviet Union led to an ecological disaster in the early 1990s. In order to irrigate farmland, planners had diverted water from two rivers that flowed into the Aral Sea—formerly the fourth largest inland body of water in the world. As a result of the diversion of water, the Aral Sea had shrunk to less than half of its original size by the early 1990s. As the water receded, salt and mineral content in the sea rose, killing the fish that inhabited the sea. Port cities were left high and dry. The local climate became harsher, with greater extremes of heat and cold. In addition, fertilizer residues mixed with parched soil and produced a toxic dust that the wind spread throughout the area. Incidences of anemia and infant mortality rose, and life expectancy fell. In 1994 several former Soviet republics agreed to set up a committee and a fund to try to save the Aral Sea.

Extension

Have students research actions taken by various governments and the United Nations to end overuse of pesticides (such as in Indonesia), to slow deforestation (such as in Brazil), or to save endangered species (such as with Tiger Preserves in India). Have students prepare oral reports, accompanied by appropriate visual guides, such as charts, diagrams, maps, or photographs, to present to the class.

SECTION OBJECTIVES

After studying Section 2, students should be able to do the following.

1. Explain why pollution is an international concern.

2. Describe the possible effects of global warming and the thinning of the ozone layer.

3. Describe conditions that reduce the quantity and quality of water.

4. Identify problems with landfills.

5. Identify agreements made at the Earth Summit.

SECTION 1 REVIEW ANSWERS

1. See the following pages: environment, ecology, ecosystem (p. 491); erosion, desertification, fertilizer, pesticide, organic farming (p. 495).

2. All living things within an ecosystem play a vital role in maintaining the stability of the system.

3. some factors—development, urban growth, pollution

4. crop rotation and contour farming and other techniques to prevent erosion; spread of urban and suburban areas, desertification

5. advantages—reduces crop losses to insects and weeds; disadvantages—potential health and environmental hazards, kill beneficial insects, targeted insects build up tolerance

6. strains resources such as food, minerals, water, energy, timber; more waste produced

7. Students might point out that many people might not be able to afford the higher costs of organic foods.

---

million years for the human population to reach one billion, by the year 1850. In 1930, after only 80 years, however, this figure had doubled to two billion. By 1975 the world population had doubled again. Today the population of the world is more than five and a half billion people. If the present rate of growth continues, the world's population will reach more than six billion by the year 2000 and more than eight billion by the year 2025.

Such rapid population growth strains the world's resources. Growing numbers of people, for example, need more food. In many of the world's poorer nations, food production cannot keep pace with population growth. Even with aid from wealthier nations, millions of people die from hunger-related causes each year.

Overpopulation strains other natural resources as well. Growing numbers of people use more minerals, water, energy, and timber. For example, it is estimated that 49 million acres of the earth's tropical rain forest are lost each year. The continuing destruction of tropical rain forests at this high rate may have global consequences. These forests produce 20 percent of the world's oxygen. In addition, many of the plants that have been identified as having cancer-fighting properties are found only in the rain forests.

Growing numbers of people also produce more waste that can harm the environment and upset the balance of nature. Controlling global population growth so that all the world's people can have better lives and a healthier environment is a challenge that faces all the nations of the world.

SECTION 1 REVIEW

1. Define or identify the following terms: environment, ecology, ecosystem, erosion, desertification, fertilizer, pesticide, organic farming.

2. How are all living things in an ecosystem interdependent?

---

3. How have human beings upset the balance of nature?

4. What are farmers doing to care for the soil? Why is farmland still being lost?

5. What are the advantages and disadvantages of using pesticides?

6. What problems accompany overpopulation?

7. **THINKING CRITICALLY** As you have read, some farmers do not use chemical fertilizers and pesticides. Organically grown food, however, is usually more expensive than food grown using pesticides. Are you willing to pay more for food that is free of pesticides? Why or why not?

---

2 Pollution

Our natural resources are precious. Unfortunately, however, many people have taken for granted the air, land, and water around us. They have polluted the environment.

Pollution results when we cause any part of the environment to become contaminated, or unfit for use. Pollution can destroy plants and animals and can upset the balance of nature. Among the countless living creatures that pollution harms are the ones who cause it—human beings.

A Global Concern

During the 1960s and 1970s many Americans became concerned about the possible dangers posed by pollution. They believed that pollution was causing health problems, killing vegetation and wildlife, and harming the quality of life in U.S. communities. In response to public concerns about pollution, Congress passed a series of laws to protect the environment.

Building a Vocabulary

Help students understand the term **hydrologic cycle** by telling students that *hydro-* means "water." Explain that *cycle* comes from the Greek word *kyklos*, meaning "circle" or "wheel." Use the chalkboard to help students conceptualize a wheel that illustrates water evaporating to form clouds and then falling back to earth as rain. Point out that cycles involve successive, recurring events. Then ask students where water can be found in nature. *(oceans, lakes, rivers, ponds, water vapor in the atmosphere)*

Illustrating Ideas

Tell students that we often think of political boundaries as walls, but they are usually just arbitrary lines drawn on a map. Airborne and waterborne pollutants pass right through these borders. Invite students to represent this phenomenon visually, through a drawing or a political cartoon. Display students' finished work on a bulletin board titled "Global Pollution." Then ask: How do these drawings illustrate why pollution is an international concern? *(Pollution in one country can affect other countries.)*

In the 1980s, however, new environmental problems arose. In 1986 an explosion at the Chernobyl nuclear power plant near Kiev, Ukraine, killed at least 31 plant workers. More than 135,000 people living near the plant were evacuated. Even more devastating, the explosion scattered radioactive material over wide areas of the former Soviet Union and Europe. Many people were contaminated by radiation, and much plant life died.

The Chernobyl accident made it frighteningly clear that environmental pollution is not contained by national borders. Pollution in one nation can affect neighboring nations and the world environment. It can harm the air we breathe and the water we need for life. It can devastate the land on which we live. Pollution is a problem of global concern.

Air Pollution

The air we breathe is a mixture of nitrogen, oxygen, carbon dioxide, and small amounts of other gases. It is a **renewable resource**. That is, it can be replaced. Under normal conditions, natural processes clean the air of dirt and harmful gases released by furnaces, factories, and automobiles. In recent years, however, the pollution in the air has become so great that nature cannot easily get rid of it.

As a result, the air over many of the world's cities is filled with **smog**—a combination of smoke, gases, and fog. Smog burns the eyes and lungs. High levels of smog can be harmful to human health. A 1995 study, for example, found that people who live in the U.S. cities with the highest levels of air pollution are more likely to die at younger ages than people who live in the nation's cleanest cities.

Air pollution has caused other problems as well. Over the past century the level of carbon dioxide and other gases released into the atmosphere has risen dramatically. At the same time, millions of acres of forests whose trees absorb carbon dioxide have been destroyed. Many scientists believe the resulting high level of carbon dioxide traps the sun's heat and raises the temperature of the earth's atmosphere, creating a **greenhouse effect**.

The greenhouse effect is of concern because it may lead to global warming, a general

(continued on page 500)

Factories produce many goods that we enjoy. Unfortunately, some factories also produce unwanted and harmful by-products—air pollution, ground pollution, and water pollution.

GLOBAL PERSPECTIVES

The burning of fossil fuels produces carbon dioxide, a waste product that pollutes the air. The United States and other industrialized nations have tried to limit this kind of air pollution, often through legislation aimed at cleaning up emissions of factories, power plants, and automobiles. Industrializing nations, trying to "catch up" to the developed nations, often cannot afford the expensive technology needed to keep these pollutants in check. As of 1992, according to the U.S. Energy Department, industrializing nations produced a little more than half of the world's energy-related carbon dioxide emissions. In 1970 industrializing nations produced 43 percent of the world's carbon dioxide emissions. In part, the increase reflects growth in the developing nations, especially in the areas of transportation and the generation of electricity.

497

Presenting a Newscast

Have groups of students present mock newscasts centered on a project of Kids Against Pollution. Students should first decide what the project is, perhaps using their own community as the locale. Then they should determine how the news team will cover the story. They might use reporting, interviews, and accounts of past KAP exploits.

Citizenship IN ACTION

PROTECTING THE EARTH

You may never have heard of Closter, New Jersey. What happened in this small suburb of New York City, though, has echoed throughout the United States and in many other nations around the world. As you will learn, the town of Closter is home to a group of young citizens who have made it their goal to save the planet.

Kids Against Pollution

Kids Against Pollution (KAP) was founded by a group of civics students and their teacher at Tenakill School in Closter, New Jersey, in 1988. From the original 19 members, KAP has grown to include thousands of members and hundreds of chapters in the United States and in several foreign countries as well. KAP members have testified before various local and state governments, appeared as witnesses before hearings of the Environmental Protection Agency (EPA), proposed an amendment to the U.S. Constitution, and even made presentations at the United Nations.

What has prompted so many young citizens to do so much? One eighth-grade KAP member gave this answer: "I want my generation to be known as the one that did something about the environment."

Other KAP members agree. Distressed by what they saw as the spoiling and abuse of the environment, the original KAP group in Closter decided to do something about it. They immediately formed KAP and adopted as their motto a simple yet moving phrase: "Save the Earth, Not Just For Us, But For Future Generations." They were on their way.

Making a Difference

The first action of the newly formed KAP group was to petition their school district to stop using plastic foam products. Plastic foam, or polystyrene, can be dangerous to the environment. It takes up space in landfills, does not decay, and gives off toxic fumes when

Members of Kids Against Pollution (KAP) have testified to Congress about their environmental concerns.

Gathering Information

Have students research other groups that are working to protect the environment, such as the Sierra Club and Greenpeace. Students should research the group's history, goals, and specific projects. Call on volunteers to report their findings to the class. Suggest that students might want to start their own antipollution group.

burned in trash incinerators. Impressed by KAP's logical and poised presentation, the school district agreed with the students' proposal. KAP had won its first victory.

The many victories that have followed KAP's early success have not been won as easily. The students learned that changing long-standing practices and people's minds is hard work. KAP members believe strongly, however, that the planet must be saved from pollution and that their hard work is well worth the effort.

Realizing Actions Have Consequences

KAP's balloon protest is a good example. A hospital was planning to use helium-filled balloons as part of a promotion. When KAP members learned of the plan, they were concerned. They feared that some of the balloons might eventually land in the sea and kill the sea animals that tried to eat them. Birds might also try to eat them. The kids of KAP sprang into action.

KAP members from several chapters organized a large demonstration to urge the hospital not to use balloons. They spent long hours researching the effects of balloons on the environment and organizing the demonstration. KAP's hard work and dedication paid off. Hospital administrators listened to the facts and agreed not to use the balloons.

Since its beginning, Kids Against Pollution has organized and participated in hundreds of similar projects, all aimed at helping the planet. KAP efforts have even led to change as far away as Europe and Asia. This worldwide movement of young people all started with one civics class in one small town in the United States.

You can find out more about KAP and its activities by writing to:

Kids Against Pollution (KAP)
Tenakill School
275 High St.
Closter, NJ 07624

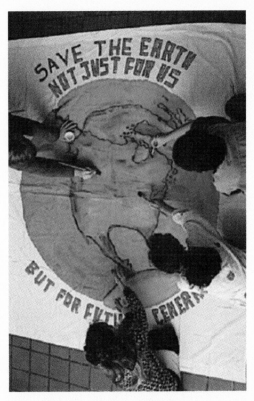

The members of KAP are doing everything they can to ensure that the world is a clean and healthy place to live, now and in the future.

YOU DECIDE

1 What is the goal of Kids Against Pollution (KAP)?

2 What are some activities KAP members have organized to help achieve this goal?

3 Do you think young people can make a difference in saving the earth? Explain your answer.

GLOBAL PERSPECTIVES

Caring for the earth is a global concern, one that calls for the co-operation of people throughout the world. Acknowledging this fact, 2,000 young people from nearly 60 nations gathered together in New York City in 1992 to participate in the Global Youth Forum, sponsored by the United Nations Environment Program. At this meeting the participants ratified the Youth Declaration to the Earth Summit, a pledge to work together to address global issues and environmental concerns.

ANSWERS TO
YOU DECIDE

1. save the planet for future generations

2. testifying before government Environmental Protection Agency and United Nations; proposing constitutional amendment; campaigning for use of recyclable materials; protesting actions dangerous to the environment

3. Answers should indicate ways young people can make a difference in saving the earth.

Writing a Speech

Have students imagine they are attending an international conference on pollution. Each student should prepare a short speech, accompanied by diagrams as visual guides, explaining either global warming or depletion of the ozone layer. Call on volunteers to present their speeches to the class for discussion.

COOPERATIVE LEARNING

Assign each small group one of the following topics: air pollution, water pollution, ground pollution, and responses to pollution. Have groups of students use drawings, newspapers, and other periodicals to create collages illustrating each of these topics. Illustrations should be accompanied by explanatory captions. Have groups explain their collages to the class. The group(s) illustrating responses to pollution should present its collage last. Individual tasks might include writing, illustrating, and presenting.

CIVICS SIDELIGHT

With the hole in the ozone layer allowing more and more ultraviolet light through the atmosphere, scientists expect cases of skin cancer to continue rising. The most serious kind of skin cancer is melanoma. Between 1973 and 1992, the number of Americans diagnosed with melanoma increased about 4 percent each year. The number of melanoma deaths increased about 34 percent for the same time period. The American Cancer Society estimated that approximately 38,000 people would be diagnosed with melanoma in 1996. Moreover, estimates suggest that 1 in 87 Americans will get the disease during their lifetime, a figure that is expected to rise to 1 in 75 by the year 2000.

There are preventive measures that people can take. No one, especially people with fair complexions, should be exposed to the sun (particularly the midday sun) for long periods of time without protection. Protection includes tightly woven clothing, hats, and the generous use of effective sunscreens.

increase in the temperature of the earth. This could have devastating effects on the environment by changing world climates and weather patterns, possibly destroying ecosystems.

Another problem posed by air pollution is a thinning of the earth's ozone layer. The **ozone** layer is a thin layer in the earth's upper atmosphere that shields the planet from the sun's ultraviolet rays. These rays can be dangerous to living things. Scientists have discovered that chemicals called chlorofluorocarbons (CFCs), used in items such as refrigerators, air conditioners, and aerosol spray cans, rise in the atmosphere and destroy the ozone layer. Many countries have banned the use of CFCs in new products.

The greatest damage to the ozone layer thus far has been over Antarctica, but scientists suspect that other areas of the ozone layer are thinning as well. As the damaged ozone layer allows more ultraviolet radiation to reach the earth, scientists anticipate increased cases of skin cancer and eye disease in humans and increased levels of damage to marine life, crops, and forests.

Air pollution also has led to acid rain. **Acid rain** occurs when pollution from burning gas, oil, and coal mixes with water vapor in the air to form acid. This acid then falls to the earth with snow and rain. Acid rain increases the levels of acid in soil, lakes, and streams, making them less able to support plant and animal life. Gradually, trees die and lakes and streams become unfit for fish and plant life.

The Water Supply

Water, like air, is essential to life on the planet. Protecting the planet and ourselves requires us to protect the water supply.

All fresh water comes from clouds—as rain, snow, or other forms of precipitation. It sinks into the earth, follows underground routes, and forms underground pools. The excess water runs into rivers, lakes, and oceans. Eventually it evaporates into the atmosphere, to fall again as precipitation. This process is called the **hydrologic cycle**.

Underground water reserves are a key part of the cycle. Underground water nourishes plants. Bubbling up in wells and springs, it helps supply water to people and animals. A good supply of underground water is assured when trees, plants, and grasses cover the earth's soil. The roots of trees and other plants help keep the soil moist by slowing the flow of water. Trees and plants release moisture into the atmosphere as part of the hydrologic cycle.

When trees and other plants are removed from large areas of land, the rain tends to rush down slopes instead of sinking slowly into the ground. This has happened in many parts of the United States. The level of water under the ground—the water table—is slowly sinking. As a result, the nation's supply of usable water is decreasing. This is occurring also in nations whose rapidly growing populations are placing great demands on the water supply.

Along with the quantity of available water, the quality of the earth's water is a matter of international concern. Increasingly the waters of the world are being polluted. This poses hazards not only for human beings, but also for the thousands of species of marine and plant life that live in and depend on the sea.

Water Pollution

Anything in the water that makes the water less useful or less healthful is a pollutant. Water pollution is classified into five types: chemical, sewage, thermal, silt, and crud.

Chemical pollutants come mainly from industrial plants. In fact, industry—factories, mills, and mines—accounts for more than half of all water pollution. Pesticides and artificial fertilizers used in agriculture are also major sources of chemical water pollution.

There are other forms of chemical pollution. For instance, many washing detergents contain substances called phosphates, which make detergents act more quickly. Phosphates also, however, pollute the waters in much the same way as fertilizers.

Sewage comes mainly from cities, towns, and other communities that dump raw waste,

Ask: Why must nations cooperate to solve environmental problems? Have students list problems on the board that call for international cooperation. For each one, have students discuss how cooperation can lead to a solution. Ask students why international cooperation can be a complex and difficult process. *(Some nations pollute more than others; some have more resources than others.)*

Invite students to imagine they are delegates to another Earth Summit. Each student should draw up a proposed international treaty on pollution that builds on the agreements made at the first Earth Summit. A preamble to the treaty should state the reasons why such a treaty is necessary. The treaty also should include goals and ways for countries to meet those goals. Call on volunteers to present their treaties to the class. Then have the class discuss ways all nations can help everyone meet those goals.

including that made by people, into lakes, rivers, and streams. Water contaminated by untreated sewage is extremely dangerous to human beings. The diseases of cholera, typhoid, amebic dysentery, and hepatitis, for example, are transmitted in human waste. In addition, this polluted water eventually makes its way to the sea, where it can contaminate and kill fish and other marine life.

Thermal pollution occurs when industries use cold water from streams or lakes to cool their products, then pump the warmer water back into the streams or lakes. Steel plants and nuclear power plants, for example, pump warmed water into streams. The temperature of the water, raised in this manner, may kill fish and other marine life.

In addition, algae, or tiny water plants, may grow in the warmer water and begin to smell. Algae draw large amounts of oxygen from the water as they die and rot, depriving oxygen from other marine life. Algae also block the sun's energy from reaching lower levels of the water. In these ways thermal pollution upsets the balance of nature that helps renew the earth's water.

Silt is soil, sand, or mud that has washed into streams. Silt comes mainly from sloping land that does not have enough trees or other plants to hold the soil in place. Silt pollution often is caused by improper mining and agricultural practices, road building, and earth moving. In some bodies of water, such as mountain streams, even small amounts of silt can interfere with the reproduction of water insects that are eaten by fish. Without the insects to eat, the fish die.

Crud, usually a slang word, can also refer to trash, such as old tires, bottles, and other used items. Such items become crud when they are discarded by people into lakes, rivers, and streams, as well as on land.

Crud poses many hazards to living things. Aquatic birds, for example, can drown when they become entangled in the plastic rings used to hold aluminum cans together. Marine animals can eat pieces of plastic and other trash that eventually injures or kills them.

Rachel Carson

Rachel Carson was born in 1907 in Springdale, Pennsylvania. After graduating from Johns Hopkins University with a Master of Arts degree, Carson went to work as a biologist with the U.S. Bureau of Fisheries. In this position she conducted research and wrote brochures promoting the nation's wildlife resources.

In 1941 Carson published her first book, *Under the Sea Wind*, which focused on the Atlantic coast sea floor. Her 1951 publication, *The Sea Around Us*, was on the U.S. nonfiction best-seller list for 39 weeks and won the National Book Award.

It was her 1962 publication of *Silent Spring*, however, for which Carson is best known. In this book Carson painted a gloomy picture of a world destroyed by the overuse of pesticides, particularly DDT. The book sparked a nationwide debate over the use of pesticides.

As a spokesperson for environmental protection, Carson in 1963 testified before a Senate committee studying pesticides. Her testimony helped to pass a law requiring warning labels on all chemical products. Although Carson died in 1964, her dedication to the care of the environment started a movement that continues strong to this day.

Ground Pollution

As the global population has grown and as more goods have been produced, many cities of the world have become overwhelmed by an

Providing clean, fresh water for the expanding world population promises to be a hot issue in years to come. About 97 percent of the earth's water is salty. Only 3 percent is fresh, and two-thirds of that is locked up as ice. That does not leave a lot of fresh water to go around. Yet, in the United States we often take water for granted. Americans use about 1,300 gallons of water a day per person, which is three times the average usage rate in Europe and many times the rate in industrializing nations.

Most fresh water is used for agriculture. Innovative irrigation methods in the United States and elsewhere have helped reduce water use. In Israel, for example, a "drip irrigation" program uses computers and sensing monitors to make sure plants receive just the right amount of water they need to thrive.

Closure

Have students write descriptive science fiction paragraphs that illustrate what life in the United States might be like by the year 2500 if pollution is not controlled today. The paragraphs should refer to conditions in the 20th century and efforts made then to solve environmental problems. Students also may wish to illustrate their paragraphs. Encourage students to share their finished work with the class.

Reviewing

Have students complete the Section 2 Review.

Reteaching

Assign Section 2 of the Chapter 25 Reteaching Worksheet.

SECTION 2 REVIEW
ANSWERS

1. See the following pages: pollution (p. 496); renewable resource, smog, greenhouse effect (p. 497); ozone, acid rain, hydrologic cycle (p. 500); landfill, recycling (p. 502).

2. Pollution is not contained within national borders. It can affect neighboring and even distant regions.

3. could change climates and weather patterns; ozone layer protects earth from sun's dangerous ultraviolet rays

4. less water sinks into ground to replenish underground reserves; chemical, sewage, thermal, silt, crud

5. long decomposition periods required, leaking of toxic materials into surrounding environment, difficulty in finding new locations to build; summit—reduce global warming, preserve forests, limit ocean pollution, protect all species

6. Students should present feasible suggestions.

---

ever-increasing amount of garbage. This ground pollution, and what to do about it, is a matter of urgent concern.

In Tokyo, Japan, for example, the city's inhabitants produce 22,000 tons of garbage each day. Some of this garbage is burned; some is turned into items that can be used. Most of it, however, ends up in dump sites. Tokyo is running out of room for these dump sites and has built artificial islands in Tokyo Bay to hold the garbage. It cannot continue to do so, though, without threatening both its fishing and shipping industries.

In the United States most garbage is deposited in landfills. **Landfills** are huge pits dug in the ground as a place to store large amounts of garbage. The garbage is supposed to decompose, much as leaves on the forest floor decay. Unfortunately, recent discoveries show that garbage does not decompose as rapidly as once thought. Some materials can take decades to decompose.

Moreover, landfills often leak toxic materials into the surrounding soil and groundwater. Another problem is that no one wants to live near a landfill. Thus as existing landfills become full, it becomes more difficult to locate places to dig new ones.

Responding to Pollution

The problems of environmental pollution have no political boundaries. Polluted air and water from one nation may drift into the air and water of other nations and affect the global environment. Thus providing solutions to the problem of pollution calls for international cooperation. Acknowledging this fact, delegates from 178 nations met in 1992 for the United Nations Conference on Environment and Development—the Earth Summit.

At the Earth Summit, held in Rio de Janeiro, Brazil, the participants signed treaties and other agreements to reduce global warming, preserve forests, limit ocean pollution, and protect the world's animal, plant, and microbe species. It will take a great deal of time, money, and effort, however, to put these agreements into effect. Some people worry that nations will not carry through the agreements. Still, the Earth Summit stands as the largest international effort to deal with the problems facing the global environment.

Individuals, too, are taking steps to help protect the environment. Many communities, for example, have started recycling programs. **Recycling** is the process of turning waste into something that can be used again. Aluminum cans, for example, can be melted and used to make new cans. Recycling reduces the amount of trash that ends up in landfills.

Individuals also help the environment by reducing the amount of disposable goods, water, and energy that they use on a daily basis. Some people, for example, bring cloth bags to the grocery store so that they do not have to use the store's paper or plastic bags. People can also recycle many of the items that they typically use and discard.

Plastic forks and spoons, for instance, can be washed and reused. Some people are walking and riding bicycles whenever possible, instead of driving. Even something as simple as turning the water off when you brush your teeth or switching off the light when you leave a room helps save the world's resources.

Everyone in the world depends on the environment for life. The future of the earth as a home for all living things depends on how well we all cooperate to prevent pollution.

SECTION 2 REVIEW

1. Define or identify the following terms: pollution, renewable resource, smog, greenhouse effect, ozone, acid rain, hydrologic cycle, landfill, recycling.

2. Why is pollution an international concern?

3. How might global warming affect the environment? Why is the thinning of the ozone layer a matter of concern?

SECTION OBJECTIVES

After studying Section 3, students should be able to do the following.

1. Identify the uses of petroleum and coal and the disadvantages of using each.
2. Explain why natural gas burns cleanly.
3. Explain why nuclear energy is controversial.
4. Identify alternative energy sources.
5. Describe opposing positions in the debate between development and conservation.

Teaching Section 3
Building a Vocabulary

Tell students that the word part *bio-* comes from the Greek word *bios*, meaning "life," and that *bio-* refers to plant and animal matter. **Biomass** is a quantity of plant or animal matter that can be used for fuel. Then have students study the term **conservation**. Tell them that the Latin root is *conservare*, from the word parts *con-* ("together") and *servare* ("keep" or "guard"). Have students deduce the meaning of *conservation* in relation to energy. *(to safeguard natural resources by using them wisely)*

4. What can happen to the water supply when vegetation is removed from areas of land? What are five types of water pollutants?

5. What problems are associated with landfills? What agreements were made at the Earth Summit?

6. **THINKING CRITICALLY** You are your community's recycling coordinator. How will you encourage residents to recycle their trash?

3 Energy Resources

The people of the world depend on energy resources to run their factories, to provide heat and light for their homes, to drive their automobiles, and to cook their food. Some of these resources are renewable. Every day, for example, the sun bathes the earth in rich supplies of energy. The resources that are sustained by the sun—trees and plants, for example—are also renewable.

Some resources, however, are nonrenewable. **Nonrenewable resources** are resources that can be used only once. Minerals, metals, and ores are examples of nonrenewable resources. Formed millions of years ago, the world's deposits of these resources cannot grow. They can only decrease.

The earth's nonrenewable resources also include **fossil fuels**—petroleum, natural gas, and coal. Fossil fuels are believed to have formed over millions of years from the fossilized remains of plants and animals.

As the world continues to industrialize and increase in population, greater demands are placed on its nonrenewable energy sources. Although improvements in technology can stretch the world's supply, these resources eventually will run out. Dealing with shortages of nonrenewable energy sources and seek-

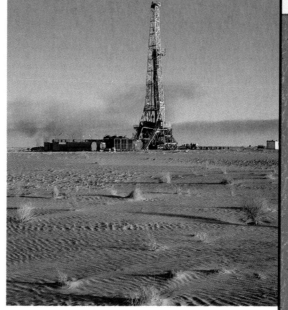

The world's largest reserves of petroleum are found in the Persian Gulf region of Southwest Asia.

ing new sources of energy are issues that concern all the world's people.

Petroleum

Petroleum, or oil as it is commonly called, lies deep within the earth in great pools. These pools are believed to have formed from microscopic plants and animals that lived millions of years ago. They were covered with mud, rocks, and water. After centuries of decay and pressure from the earth, petroleum formed.

Pumped to the surface and refined, petroleum furnishes the energy to heat homes, the gasoline to power automobiles, and the lubricating oil to grease the wheels of industry. It also is the basis of a wide variety of by-products, such as plastics, fertilizers, dyes, and many chemicals.

The world's largest reserves of petroleum today are found in Saudi Arabia and the neighboring countries of the Persian Gulf region. The largest oil reserves in the United States are found in Alaska, Texas, and Louisiana.

CIVICS SIDELIGHT

Oil spills are a major source of pollution. In 1989 the *Exxon Valdez* spilled 10.8 million gallons of oil into pristine Alaskan waters. It was a disaster for plants, birds, and other life forms along the coast. That oil spill was dwarfed by the spill resulting from the Iraqi sabotage of Kuwait's oil terminals during the Persian Gulf War in 1991. That mammoth spill dumped more than 250 million gallons of oil into the Persian Gulf.

Various techniques, including skimming and vacuuming, are used to clean up oil spills. One innovative technique has been used with increasing frequency since the *Exxon Valdez* spill. In a process called bioremediation, authorities release into the spill microbes that actually eat the oil. The digested oil becomes a fatty acid, which then is devoured by other marine life.

Creating a Poster

Have students create posters as part of a campaign promoting conservation. Each poster should emphasize the limits of nonrenewable resources, as well as ways people can conserve those resources. Display the posters as part of a contest. Invite the principal, an official from a local utility company, and other teachers to serve as judges. Encourage volunteers to explain their posters to the panel of judges.

COOPERATIVE LEARNING

Have small groups create energy pamphlets explaining the advantages and disadvantages of petroleum, coal, natural gas, and nuclear energy as energy sources. Each group member should focus on one of these energy sources. The pamphlet should include pictures and other illustrations. Have the groups present their pamphlets to the class.

CIVICS SIDELIGHT

Several different types of heating fuel are available to U.S. home owners. About half the homes in the United States are heated by natural gas, and another 6 percent use bottled gas or liquid propane. About 26 percent of homes heat with electricity, 12 percent use oil, and 4 percent burn wood. Less than one percent of homes are heated with coal, solar energy, or other energy sources.

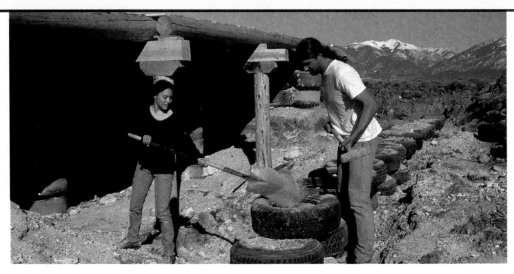

These people are working to conserve resources by using recycled materials to build a house. What steps can you take to help conserve resources?

The use of petroleum as an energy source is not without problems. For example, burning oil to heat homes and gasoline to power automobiles contributes to air pollution and possibly to global warming. The millions of tons of plastic produced from petroleum each year end up in dump sites and landfills, where they can pollute the ground, soil, and water. Plastic and other petroleum products also take a very long time to decompose.

In addition, the world's supply of oil is limited. Some experts believe that the world's existing oil reserves will run out sometime in the next century. Of course, discovery of new oil deposits could extend the supply. With the increasing worldwide dependence on oil as an energy source, however, it is difficult to estimate how long existing and new deposits might last.

One way to stretch available oil resources is through conservation. **Conservation** refers to the safeguarding of natural resources by using them wisely. Using smaller cars, for example, helps save oil because smaller cars travel more miles (kilometers) per gallon of gas than larger cars. Likewise, many industries have installed new machinery that requires less energy to run, thus conserving oil.

Home owners also can do their part to help conserve oil. Lowering home temperatures, insulating attics and walls, and installing storm windows and doors are ways to use less heating oil. People can also reduce their reliance on and recycle plastic, a petroleum-based product.

Natural Gas

Natural gas, another fossil fuel, usually is found with petroleum. At one time, natural gas was burned off as it came out of an oil well. This clean-burning fuel, however, found favor with industry and home owners. Its use around the world as an energy source is growing rapidly.

Most of the energy contained in natural gas is used to generate steam for electricity and steam engines, to heat buildings, and for cooking. The world's largest reserves of natural gas today are found in Russia and in the nations of the Persian Gulf region.

Natural gas is the cleanest-burning fossil fuel because it is refined naturally during its formation in the earth. As a result, natural gas does not release harmful pollutants or by-products when it burns. Because it is a clean-burning energy source, worldwide demand

Have students keep a record, for one day, of every time they use electric power. When students have completed their records, ask: In what ways do teenagers seem to use the most electricity? Then discuss how students might work to conserve electrical energy.

Have students create charts for listing alternative sources of energy. The first column should list the name of the energy source. Information in the second column should describe how the source works. The third column should include information about where these alternative sources are used. Students might want to consult library and classroom resources to help complete the third column. Students should share their charts and use them as study guides.

for natural gas has increased greatly in recent years. At its present rate of consumption, natural gas reserves may last only slightly longer than petroleum reserves.

In addition, natural gas usually is shipped great distances through overland pipelines. These pipelines often require large areas of land, and they can interfere with the migration patterns of wildlife.

Coal

Coal is a fossil fuel that developed over millions of years when plant debris accumulated in ancient swamps and bogs. The partially decomposing debris formed layers of peat, which became buried below marine sediments. The weight of the marine sediments compressed the peat and formed coal.

Coal is an important source of energy. Much of the heat energy in coal is used to produce electricity or operate steam engines. Coal also is used in the manufacture of steel, and it is the source of many chemical products, such as plastics, paints, and synthetic rubber. In many countries of Asia and Europe, coal is used to heat homes and other buildings. The largest reserves of coal today are found in the United States, Russia, China, and Australia.

Although coal is the most plentiful fossil fuel available, it too is a nonrenewable resource. Experts believe that available coal reserves might last another 200 years. Coal, however, is difficult to remove from the ground. Coal mines sometimes cave in and can release dangerous gases. Miners working underground to remove coal are subject to accidents and to diseases such as black lung. Coal also is costly to transport.

Some deposits of coal lie near the earth's surface and can be reached by stripping off the top layers of soil. This practice of **strip mining**, however, is harmful to the environment. It often leaves large pits and ugly scars on the land. Without trees or plants to hold it in place, the soil washes down the hills and valleys into streams. It pollutes the water with silt and sometimes clogs waterways.

In addition, burning coal can result in air pollution and acid rain. Many of the world's large coal-burning power plants have installed scrubbers and filters to control the level of pollutants emitted, but such devices are costly. Techniques also exist to turn coal into a cleaner-burning liquid or gas, but these techniques are extremely expensive as well.

Nuclear Energy

Some people believe nuclear energy is the answer to the world's growing shortages of fossil fuels. Nuclear reactors run on a small amount of fuel and produce large amounts of energy efficiently. Much controversy, however, surrounds the use of nuclear energy.

In 1979, for example, an accident occurred at the nuclear-powered electric plant at Three Mile Island in Middletown, Pennsylvania. Because of a series of human and mechanical errors, the radioactive core of the reactor started to overheat. This caused some radioactive gas to escape into the air. It was days before the danger of an explosion at the plant ended.

The Chernobyl nuclear power plant in the Ukraine was not so lucky. As you have read, a major explosion occurred at this plant in 1986. The radioactive material released by the explosion was detected as far away as Canada and Japan. Human beings, plants, and animals were contaminated by the radiation. It still is too early to know the long-term effects of this contamination.

In addition, the use of nuclear energy brings with it the problem of how to dispose of nuclear waste. The wastes from nuclear plants remain radioactive and hazardous for thousands of years. At present the best method for disposing of nuclear waste is to bury it in sealed containers underground in solid rock. Even sealed containers may leak, however. Moreover, transporting nuclear waste to storage facilities increases the risk of accidents.

Because of the problems and hazards associated with nuclear energy, many people question its use. The United States has no plans to expand its present number of nuclear power

Civics Sidelight

A colorful term used by some U.S. critics to convey the dangers of nuclear power plants is *China syndrome*. This imagined chain of events refers to the catastrophe that might result if the cooling system of a nuclear reactor failed. Theoretically, enough energy might be released to melt the reactor and create an intensely hot nuclear lava flow. Nobody really knows for sure what would happen next, but it is possible that the molten core could burn through the floor of the nuclear facility and into the earth and, some say, "all the way through to China." In truth, U.S. reactors are designed to flood the core to cool it if the regular cooling system fails.

Independent Practice

Have students consider the debate between proponents of economic development and those urging conservation. Have students write newspaper editorials on the possibilities regarding the use of alternative energy sources as one way to prevent environmental harm caused by development. Students should consider the advantages and disadvantages of such an approach, including whether such alternatives might be cost-effective and feasible. Invite volunteers to read their editorials to the class for discussion.

Closure

Tell students that each of them has mysteriously been transformed into "Conservation Person," a new superhero whose job it is to make sure people conserve precious resources. Students should create cartoon panels for a short story about "Conservation Person" in action. For example, "Conservation Person" might swoop out of the sky to educate someone about alternative energy sources or to persuade a new-car buyer to purchase a fuel-efficient vehicle. Invite volunteers to share their cartoons with the class.

GLOBAL PERSPECTIVES

The people of Iceland generate much of their energy from hydroelectric power plants. But the island, in a highly volcanic region, also has an abundance of geothermal energy. Iceland's nearly 36,000 acres of greenhouses are heated by these geothermal sources.

Cartoon Caption Answer

The cartoon implies that the government, consumers, and oil companies did not plan well for the future.

plants. Other nations, including Sweden and Germany, are phasing out their existing nuclear plants. Some nations have declared their intentions never to build nuclear power plants.

Alternative Sources of Energy

With the growing shortages of available fossil fuels and the problems involved in the use of nuclear energy, the nations of the world have turned their attention to alternative sources of energy. It is hoped that these alternative energy sources will enable the world's nations and people to lessen their reliance on nonrenewable resources.

In the 1970s Americans truly realized that gasoline supplies were limited. What does this cartoon suggest about the possible causes of the shortage?

"Who Was Navigating, Anyhow?"

One of the most promising sources of energy for the future is energy from the sun, or solar energy. The sun gives off an enormous amount of energy, which cannot be used up in the near future. Solar energy involves capturing the sun's energy and converting it into heat and electricity. Solar energy is a clean, efficient way to heat and cool specially constructed homes and offices.

Another alternative source of energy is geothermal energy, or underground heat. This energy is generated whenever water comes in contact with hot underground rocks and produces steam. The steam, released through hot springs and geysers, can be captured and used to generate electricity. Nations throughout the world, including the United States, Italy, Japan, and New Zealand, have developed geothermal power plants.

Hydroelectric energy, or energy from water, is another alternative source of power. Hydroelectric power is produced by storing water behind large dams. When the water is released under pressure, it spins special engines that produce pollution-free electricity. Hydroelectric plants now contribute to energy production in nations such as Norway, Russia, Canada, and the United States.

Some nations are using the power of the wind to generate energy. In fact, windmills are one of the world's oldest devices for producing power. Today's windmills provide a cheap, clean source of energy. Wind energy, however, usually is practical only in areas that have strong, steady winds.

Also being considered as a possible source of alternative energy is **biomass**, or wood and waste products (garbage, yard trimmings, and so on) that can be burned or used to make fuel. Biomass is a commonly used household fuel in many of the world's poorer nations. Although burning biomass produces some degree of air pollution, researchers are testing new ways to turn biomass into more efficient, convenient, and clean-burning fuel products.

These alternative energy sources rely mainly on the world's renewable resources, such as sun, water, and wind. To meet the

Reviewing

Have students complete the Section 3 Review.

Reteaching

Assign Section 3 of the Chapter 25 Reteaching Worksheet.

After studying Section 4, students should be able to do the following.

1. Describe U.S. environmental policy before the 1950s.
2. Explain provisions of the clean air and water acts.
3. Explain the purpose of an endangered species list.
4. Identify duties of the Environmental Protection Agency.
5. Explain the purpose and importance of Earth Day.

---

ever-increasing global demand for energy, these alternative sources and others must be studied, improved, and used.

Development and Conservation

Care must be taken whenever new energy sources are developed. Each time an area is developed, delicate ecosystems may be upset. Development, of course, is necessary for the growth and well-being of nations. Today, however, people in nations around the world are determined to halt the environmental harm that has been common in the past.

Some people worry about the high costs of keeping the environment clean. They argue that new safeguards and equipment make it too costly to build new plants or begin new development. To have the energy and raw materials we need, some people say we must continue to use the land and its resources as we always have. They believe it even may be necessary to relax some of the standards for a cleaner environment that have been set in recent years.

Conservationists, in contrast, argue that continuing to pollute the environment and upset the balance of nature is dangerous. They charge that whatever harms the land, sea, and air harms human beings and all other living things. They also remind us that conservation is concerned not only with the situation of the earth today. Conservation's main goal is to ensure that the earth is a healthy and livable place for future generations.

SECTION 3 REVIEW

1. Define or identify the following terms: nonrenewable resource, fossil fuel, conservation, strip mining, biomass.

2. What are the uses of petroleum? What are the disadvantages of using petroleum?

3. Why is natural gas the cleanest-burning fossil fuel?

4. How is coal used? What are the disadvantages of using coal?

5. Why is the use of nuclear energy controversial? What alternative sources of energy are being explored?

6. Describe the debate between development and conservation.

7. **THINKING CRITICALLY** You are the U.S. secretary of energy, and you must decide how to use limited research funds. To which alternative source of energy will you devote the most funds?

4 Our Future on Earth

The United States has had a long interest in conservation and the environment. In 1872, for example, the U.S. government set aside a portion of northwestern Wyoming as a national park. The land was to remain in its natural state, to be enjoyed by all. Yellowstone National Park was the first national park in the world. In recent years the United States has become a leading force in addressing environmental issues. Caring for the earth requires the ongoing efforts of government, business, and individual citizens.

Early Conservation Efforts

The National Park Service of the United States is only one of many agencies that help to preserve the natural resources of the country. Early in the 1900s President Theodore Roosevelt called a conference of the governors of the states to consider how best to conserve the land and its resources.

The National Forest Service was established to supervise vast areas of forest land and

---

SECTION 3 REVIEW ANSWERS

1. See the following pages: nonrenewable resource, fossil fuel (p. 503); conservation (p. 504); strip mining (p. 505); biomass (p. 506).

2. uses—heat, gasoline, lubricating oil, various byproducts; disadvantages—pollution, long decomposition period for byproducts, exists in limited supply

3. refined naturally

4. produce electricity, operate steam engines, manufacture steel, heat, source of various chemical products; disadvantages—difficult to mine, can be harmful to environment, costly to transport, exists in limited supply

5. accidents, nuclear waste; solar, geothermal, hydroelectric, wind, biomass

6. development—resources needed for industry, antipollution equipment and safeguards too expensive; conservation—development upsets balance of nature, harms environment

7. Students should use sound reasoning in their responses.

Drawing a Time Line

Have students make time lines that show the U.S. government's environmental efforts in a historical context. To do this, students might place dates and events related to the environment above the line and dates of other historically significant events from the same period below the line. Explanatory captions should accompany the environmental entries on the time lines. Students should save the time lines for use as study guides.

Creating a Chart

Have pairs of students create study charts describing provisions of the clean air and clean water acts. Each student should complete one column of the chart, which should have two column headings: "Clean Air" and "Clean Water." Information in each column should include the dates the legislation passed and specific provisions of the acts. Each student should copy the chart into his or her notebook to use as a study guide.

GLOBAL PERSPECTIVES

The United States established the world's first national park in 1872. Since then, most other countries have also set aside land for national parks. These parks, which number in the hundreds, showcase not only great natural scenery but also beautiful or rare animals and plants, as the following limited selection shows. Finders Chase in Australia is home to kangaroos, anteaters, koalas, and emus. Amazônia in Brazil is 3,838 square miles of plains and rain forest. Banff in Canada contains mountain goats and bighorn sheep. Fuji-Hakone-Izu in Japan is the site of Mount Fuji volcano. Serengeti in Tanzania is a vast, open grassland where lions, antelopes, and zebras roam. Victoria Falls in Zimbabwe boasts a spectacular 400-foot waterfall that is over a mile (1.6 km) wide.

to help conserve their timber. Later, laws were passed to limit the amount of oil and minerals that could be taken from the ground each year. Laws governing grazing practices helped stop the destruction of grasslands. The U.S. Department of Agriculture and state governments encouraged and helped farmers use soil conservation methods.

Under President Franklin D. Roosevelt, a program of soil banks was established. Land was set aside to be improved and renewed. Dams were built to irrigate farmlands and control floods. The dams also provide electricity and recreation areas.

These efforts, however, did not stop waste and pollution. By the 1950s large numbers of concerned citizens began to point out that the misuse of resources was placing an enormous and damaging strain on the environment. Today we know that firm conservation measures are needed.

Oil spilled from tankers or offshore wells can wash up on nearby beaches, threatening wildlife and entire ecosystems. Here, a volunteer is helping to clean an oil-soaked bird.

The Federal Government and Conservation

The U.S. Congress has passed a number of laws to reduce pollution and restore the environment. The following are the most significant of these acts.

The National Environmental Policy Act This 1969 act is sometimes called the Environmental Bill of Rights. It set up the Council on Environmental Quality to advise the president on environmental issues and oversee the nation's pollution controls. As a result of advice from this body, stricter laws were passed regulating pesticides, oil spills, and ocean dumping.

The 1969 act also provides that every federal agency must make and publish an environmental impact statement. This document must describe the expected effects on the environment of any project to be undertaken with federal assistance.

Clean Air Acts The first clean air act was passed in 1963 and has been amended and strengthened several times, most recently in 1990. The clean air acts provide funds for research and set standards to be met by all industries and buildings. They make it possible for the government to reduce certain forms of air pollution. The automobile industry, for example, must develop engines that give off reduced amounts of exhaust pollution by a certain year.

Water Pollution Control Acts As early as 1899, Congress passed a law making it a crime to dump refuse into any navigable waterway. This law, however, was not strictly enforced until recent times. It was strengthened by the Water Quality Act of 1965. This law sets standards of water quality for the interstate and coastal waters of the United States.

Again in 1966 and 1969, clean water acts were passed by Congress. Under these acts the federal government has helped local communities build sewage treatment plants. In 1972 a

Review with students the discussion of the interdependence of species in an ecosystem on pages 491–492. You might want students to review their Cooperative Learning projects (from page 493) on how the extinction of a species can upset the balance of nature in an ecosystem. Ask: How has the U.S. government addressed the danger of extinction for some species? *(Endangered Species Act)* Explain that some critics of this legislation say it threatens jobs by stifling economic development. Facilitate a panel debate on the issue.

Invite each student to imagine he or she has been hired as a spokesperson for the Environmental Protection Agency. Each spokesperson's first task is to write a press release stating the purposes and duties of the EPA. The press release should include a letterhead, a date, and a contact person for the news media. The press releases should be written in the style of a news story. Invite volunteers to share their press releases with the class.

law was passed to limit the discharge of wastes into the waters.

Other Acts of Congress Americans have become aware of the problems of using and disposing of chemicals. These substances pollute the land, water, and air in ever-increasing amounts. Some chemicals are toxic, or poisonous. To protect citizens' health, Congress passed the Resource Conservation and Recovery Act in 1976. It enables the government to regulate the transportation and storage of dangerous chemicals.

Americans have also pressed Congress to preserve the beauty of the land and protect its wildlife. The National Wild Rivers Act and the Wilderness Act set aside areas of land to be kept in their natural state. Environmentalists are also urging Congress to provide financial aid to farmers who practice conservation and reduce their reliance on chemical fertilizers and pesticides.

Hundreds of plants and animals in the United States alone are threatened with extinction. These species, such as the brown pelican and woodland caribou, are protected under the Endangered Species Acts. Such laws have helped some species partially recover. In 1994, for example, the American bald eagle was reclassified as "threatened," rather than as the more serious "endangered." Many species, however, remain near extinction.

The United States is also concerned with saving wildlife in other parts of the world. Federal laws forbid the importation of the feathers, skins, and other parts of many endangered animals from other countries.

The Environmental Protection Agency

Many federal bureaus that deal with pollution and other environmental issues have been organized under an independent government agency, called the Environmental Protection Agency (EPA). The head of the EPA reports directly to the president.

The EPA includes several offices responsible for controlling and monitoring water and

GLOBAL CONNECTIONS

Pest Management in Indonesia

While many U.S. farmers are looking for ways to reduce their reliance on chemical pesticides, farmers on Java, Indonesia, have found success with a system called Integrated Pest Management (IPM). The Food and Agriculture Organization (FAO) of the United Nations helped start the program.

For years Indonesian farmers used pesticides heavily. At first crop yields rose, but after a few years, farmers found that the pesticides were causing many problems. In addition to posing health and environment hazards, the pesticides were killing beneficial insects. Also, the harmful insects became resistant to the pesticides.

Under the IPM system, Indonesian farmers now use pesticides only when absolutely necessary and only in small amounts. They count the number of beneficial and harmful insects on their crops to determine if pesticides are needed. They also plan crops carefully to avoid providing a constant source of food to the harmful insects. In these ways the harmful pests can be controlled without endangering people and the environment. Farmers' crop yields are rising again, too.

air pollution. Other divisions oversee the management of solid wastes and radiation. In addition, the EPA deals with pesticide problems and performs studies of ecosystems.

CIVICS SIDELIGHT

The removal of the American bald eagle from the endangered species list was a victory for environmentalists. Some estimates have put the number of bald eagles at the time of European settlement in North America at between 25,000 and 75,000. Researchers identified only 417 breeding pairs of the birds in the 48 contiguous states in 1963. Researchers estimated that about 14,000 bald eagles existed in those states in 1993.

The key to this victory was the banning of the insecticide DDT in 1972 by the Environmental Protection Agency—10 years after Rachel Carson's 1962 publication of *Silent Spring*, which called attention to the plight of the national bird and other birds of the United States. Eagles are particularly susceptible to DDT poisoning, which weakens egg shells. DDT accumulates in the tissue of insects, which are then eaten by other animals that pass the DDT up the food chain. Removal of DDT from the environment eliminated the greatest danger to the eagle's survival.

Guided Practice

Review with students state and local activities designed to protect the environment. Then help the class create a "School Protection Agency." Members of the class should act as student government representatives in proposing legislation on how the agency can protect the school's environment. To keep work flowing smoothly, you should serve as leader and direct discussion and action. Call on volunteers to write the proposed legislation on the board. Then conduct a debate and final vote on the legislation.

Independent Practice

Have students review the textbook discussion of Earth Day and then plan activities for a "School Environment Day." Students should review the goals of the "School Protection Agency" to help them focus on their proposed School Environment Day activities. Students should propose goals for School Environment Day and activities to mark the event and accomplish the goals. Students also should create posters and flyers advertising the event. You might ask the principal to review the proposals and consider having such a School Environment Day.

Photo Caption Answer

Damage to the environment threatens us all. Refer students to "Your Role in Conservation" beginning on this page.

CIVICS SIDELIGHT

Recycling—a vital part of any conservation program—is not a new idea. The possibility of turning waste into wealth has fascinated scientists and inventors since the early 1900s. During World War II, Americans saw conservation as a patriotic duty. They willingly recycled paper, metal cans, and food wastes that manufacturers needed.

But the end of the war brought a return to old habits. Postwar U.S. consumers favored convenience over conservation. Industry obliged, replacing returnable bottles and cans with nonreturnables. As more and more landfills were built (as many as 400 a year by the early 1970s), Americans began to see problems in the growing mounds of trash. Today many communities have recycling programs.

Why is it important to conserve natural areas like this one? What can you do to help safeguard the nation's remaining wilderness areas?

State and Local Activities

Every state government and most local governments in the nation have laws that seek to provide quality environments for their citizens. These laws range from provisions for the preservation of the state's natural resources to local laws governing the disposal of trash.

Some states have taken giant steps forward by studying large areas and starting programs to preserve or restore their ecological balance. Oregon, for example, has made its entire Pacific shoreline public property. It also has a program to preserve the state's natural beauty. Thirty U.S. states now require that environmental education be a part of the public school curriculum.

Local communities act to preserve the environment as well. Many communities regulate the amount of pollution released by factories. More cities are starting recycling programs. These and similar actions are largely the result of growing citizen concern about the environment.

Earth Day

One example of citizen involvement is Earth Day. Earth Day on April 22 is an unofficial holiday dedicated to caring for the earth. The first Earth Day, in 1970, was the largest organized political demonstration in history. About 20 million Americans participated in Earth Day activities, ranging from neighborhood clean-ups to massive demonstrations. The government responded with a number of laws to protect the environment.

Today hundreds of millions of people around the world take part in annual Earth Day events. These people have made caring for the planet an important part of their lives.

Your Role in Conservation

Federal, state, and local laws cannot guarantee that the environment will be protected. Nor can private environmental organizations do the job alone. The future of the nation and the planet depends on the cooperation of individuals. Protecting the earth begins with you, the citizen. Only through your action to preserve the environment is there hope for the future.

Here are some steps you can take to help conserve resources:

1. Prevent waste of all kinds in your home and school. Do not waste food, water, electricity, and other resources.

Closure

Have pairs of students outline the section by using Roman numerals to identify section heads and capital letters and Arabic numbers to identify important information under each main head. Students should save the outlines for use as study guides.

Reviewing

Have students complete the Section 4 Review.

Reteaching

Assign Section 4 of the Chapter 25 Reteaching Worksheet.

---

2. With your class take part in a conservation project, such as planting trees, cleaning up streams, or picking up litter.

3. Take an interest in the natural resources in your community. Study ways in which they might be used more wisely.

4. Participate in recycling projects. Newspapers, cans, bottles, and other materials can be reused in new products. Find out about companies in your area that accept recyclable materials, and join in collection projects. Reduce your reliance on disposable goods, and reuse items as many times as possible.

5. Beware of the danger of fire when in a forest or wooded area. Put out your campfire with water. Then shovel dirt on it to make sure the fire is out.

6. Do not destroy wildlife or damage public resources. Vandalism is a serious crime against the environment.

7. Obey laws against open burning, littering, polluting, and other actions that damage the environment.

8. Stay informed on ecological issues in your area. Make your opinions known by writing to your government representatives. Attend meetings and support petitions for a better environment.

9. Make it a point to appreciate the beauty of the natural world.

10. Think about what you can do to keep the world a fit place for people, including you.

SECTION 4 REVIEW

1. Prior to the 1950s, how did the U.S. government protect the environment?

2. What are some provisions of the clean air acts? How have clean water acts helped the environment?

3. What is an endangered species list's purpose? What are some of the duties of the Environmental Protection Agency?

4. Why is Earth Day a good example of global environmental cooperation?

5. **THINKING CRITICALLY** Imagine that the president has appointed you to head the Environmental Protection Agency. Identify three environmental problems that will be the top priorities of your agency. Then explain how you will try to solve these problems.

CHAPTER 25 SUMMARY

The global environment is rich in natural resources. Many human practices, however, have upset the balance of nature. Air, water, and ground pollution are among the most serious environmental problems. Combating pollution is costly, but the cost must be met to preserve the balance of nature.

To understand the effects of pollution, we must understand ecology—the study of living things in relation to each other and to their environment. Damage to any part of an ecosystem can have devastating effects.

An ever-growing global population, the misuse of natural resources, and unchecked pollution have resulted in many environmental problems of global concern. Among the problems with which the world now must deal are the greenhouse effect and global warming, destruction of the ozone layer, and acid rain.

In addition, the world must find solutions to global shortages of energy sources, particularly fossil fuels. Many people are turning to alternative sources of power, such as solar energy, geothermal energy, hydroelectric energy, wind, and biomass.

The United States has long been a leader in addressing environmental concerns. To help protect the environment, laws have been passed to ensure the wise use of natural resources. It is up to individual citizens, however, to do their share and to work toward a cleaner environment, now and for the future.

SECTION 4 REVIEW
A N S W E R S

1. created parks; National Forest Service sought to conserve timber; laws limited grazing and extraction of oil and minerals; promoted soil conservation; built dams for irrigation and flood control

2. air—provides funds for research, sets standards to be met by all industries and buildings, allows regulation of pollution-producing activities; water—prohibited waste dumping in waters, set water quality standards, helped in construction of sewage plants

3. to target endangered species for protection; control water and air pollution, oversee management of solid wastes and radiation, deal with pesticide problems, study ecosystems

4. Hundreds of millions of people around the world participate in Earth Day activities.

5. Students should identify three priorities and three feasible strategies.

Impress upon students that they will apply map skills often in their lives. In addition to helping a person locate an important address or route, map skills are necessary to working in such fields as architecture, construction, trucking, and the armed forces.

Obtain enough local city road maps (from students, travel agencies, and the library) for pairs of students to work together, using one map per pair. Then have students use the maps to describe the most direct routes between various points that you identify. Call on volunteers to read their directions to the class to see which pairs have identified the most direct route between the points.

GLOBAL SKILL BUILDER

There are several map-related activities on the interactive *Global Skill Builder* CD-ROM. You might wish to use some of these, such as **Using Map Legends and Symbols** and **Identifying Different Types of Maps**, to reinforce students' map skills.

ANSWERS TO
Applying the Skill

1. hazardous waste sites in the United States

2. number of waste sites represented by a particular color

3. 32 states; highest—New Jersey and Pennsylvania

4. between 21 and 40; between 61 and 80

5. a little over 1,000 miles

Developing Civics Skills

SOCIAL STUDIES SKILL

Reading Maps

Maps are flat diagrams of all or part of the earth's surface. Maps can show roads, political boundaries, natural features, and many other kinds of information. Like charts and graphs, they are excellent ways to organize large amounts of data.

How to Read Maps

1. **Determine the subject.** Reading the title of the map will alert you to the kinds of information you can learn from the map. Note the area shown on the map.
2. **Study the legend.** Examine the legend, or key, to learn the meanings of the map's symbols and colors.
3. **Use the scale and the compass rose.** The scale of a map tells you how distances on the map compare with the actual distances on the surface of the earth. The compass rose on a map indicates direction and orientation.
4. **Study the labels.** The names of important geographic features and key terms often appear on the map.
5. **Put the data to use.** Taking all of the map's information into account, draw conclusions about what the map shows.

Applying the Skill

Study the map below. Then answer the following questions.

1. What is the subject of the map?
2. What does the legend tell you?
3. How many states have between 0 and 20 hazardous waste sites? Which two states have the highest number?
4. How many hazardous waste sites are in Illinois? in Michigan?
5. What is the approximate distance between the southern tip of Florida and the southern tip of Illinois?

Hazardous Waste Sites in the United States

LEGEND
- 0-20 Sites
- 21-40 Sites
- 41-60 Sites
- 61-80 Sites
- 81-100 Sites
- 101+ Sites

SCALE
0   250   500
Miles

Vocabulary Workshop

1. environment
2. possible—cans, glass, newspapers, plastic products
3. wearing away by water and wind
4. Carbon dioxide traps sun's heat; may cause global warming.
5. renewable—can be replaced; nonrenewable—used only once
6. fossil—petroleum, natural gas, coal; alternatives—solar, geothermal, hydroelectric, wind, biomass

Reviewing Main Ideas

1. Species in an ecosystem are interdependent. techniques—contour farming, drainage channels, dams, terraces, cover crops, crop rotation
2. danger to wildlife and humans; more people use more resources, produce more waste
3. lets ultraviolet rays reach the earth; acid rain—pollution from burning fossil fuels mixes with water vapor in air to form acid
4. chemical, sewage, thermal, silt, crud; summit—world pollution
5. can cause pollution
6. nuclear—accidents, waste; landfills—long decomposition periods, leaking of toxic materials
7. development—resources needed for industry, anti-pollution equipment and safeguards too expensive; conservation—pollution upsets balance of nature, harms environment

Thinking Critically

1. Students should offer specific proposals.
2. Students should make reasoned arguments.

R·e·v·i·e·w

Vocabulary Workshop

1. What term refers to the world around us?
2. Identify five items you use every day that can be recycled.
3. What is erosion?
4. What is the greenhouse effect, and why is it a matter of global concern?
5. Distinguish between renewable resources and nonrenewable resources.
6. Identify three fossil fuels and three alternative sources of energy.

Reviewing Main Ideas

1. How can upsetting the balance of nature within an ecosystem have global implications? What modern agricultural techniques help farmers care for the land?
2. Why was DDT banned in the United States? How does rapid population growth strain global resources?
3. Why is the thinning of the ozone layer a matter of concern? What is acid rain?
4. What are five kinds of water pollutants? What was the Earth Summit's purpose?
5. How can the use of petroleum and coal harm the environment?
6. What problems are associated with nuclear energy? with landfills?
7. What arguments underlie the debate between development and conservation?

Thinking Critically

1. Some businesspeople claim that environmental regulations make it too costly to operate in the United States. Thus many U.S. companies have moved to countries that do not have such strict controls. How can government persuade these companies to stay and protect the environment at the same time?

2. Some of the chemicals used on fruit and vegetables enhance their color and protect them from bruising. Many farmers argue that they must use these chemicals because consumers will not buy unattractive produce. Do you agree with this argument? Explain your answer.

Citizenship in Your Community

Cooperative Project

With your group, create a list of things that teenagers can do to help protect your community's environment. Some members of the group might interview local citizens for their suggestions. Other members might illustrate the items on your group's list with drawings, poems, or songs. Use your materials to create a pamphlet entitled "Protecting the Environment of *(your community's name)*."

Building Your Portfolio

The second step of your unit portfolio project (see page 515) is to create an environmental profile of your school. What can be done to make your school more energy efficient? What can the school do to conserve more electricity, water, and other resources? Are such items as newspapers, bottles, and cans recycled? Do students help keep the classrooms and school grounds free of litter? Has the school planted enough trees and other vegetation to hold the soil in place and reduce the need for air conditioning? Place your profile in your individual portfolio for later use.

Citizenship in Your Community

Pamphlets should include ways teenagers can help protect your community's environment.

Building Your Portfolio

Assign Portfolio Assessment Worksheet 25 in the *Portfolio Assessment Worksheets* booklet.

Assessment

- **Chapter 25 Tests**, *Chapter Tests* booklet
- **Test Generator**, Chapter 25
- **Portfolio**, Portfolio Assessment Worksheet 25, *Portfolio Assessment Worksheets* booklet

Reviewing Main Ideas

1. could change world climates and weather patterns, possibly destroying ecosystems; use of chlorofluorocarbons damages ozone layer
2. promoted equal rights by prohibiting segregation in schools; civil disobedience—draw attention to laws people believe to be wrong
3. urban renewal programs; homelessness—lack of affordable housing
4. fossil fuels—petroleum, natural gas, coal formed over millions of years from the fossilized remains of plants and animals; can be used only once and can't be replaced; hope that alternative energy sources will bring less reliance on nonrenewable resources
5. transmitted through blood and other body fluids, primarily through sexual activity or sharing needles
6. chemical, sewage, thermal, silt, crud

Thinking Critically

1. Students should make reasoned arguments and consider the national experience with Prohibition.
2. Many are highly mobile, many do not want to be found, and many do not want to communicate with public officials.

Practicing Civics Skills

1. In assessing the editorials, students should demonstrate an understanding of the difference between fact and opinion.
2. Students should note the decline in the world's tropical rain forests.

Citizenship in Your Community

Students should consider all aspects of a school recycling program.

Learning from Technology

Students might argue that the use of telemetry, while costly, has improved the quality and delivery of health care in the United States.

R·e·v·i·e·w

Reviewing Main Ideas

1. What environmental problems might global warming cause? What is responsible for the thinning of the ozone layer?
2. How did the Supreme Court decision in *Brown v. Board of Education of Topeka* affect the civil rights movement? What is the purpose of civil disobedience?
3. How have cities tried to solve the problem of slums? What is responsible for the increase in homelessness in recent years?
4. What are fossil fuels, and why are they considered nonrenewable resources? Why are we seeking alternative energy sources?
5. How is AIDS transmitted?
6. Identify five types of water pollution.

Thinking Critically

1. As you know, the health hazards associated with smoking have led to a movement to ban it in public places. Alcohol also is a substance that endangers many lives each year. Should there be a ban on drinking alcohol in public places? Consider the Eighteenth and Twenty-first Amendments to the Constitution in your answer.
2. The Bureau of the Census acknowledges that the number of homeless people in the nation is undoubtedly underestimated. Why is it difficult to count the number of homeless Americans?

Practicing Civics Skills

1. Locate two editorials on the use of pesticides: one arguing for pesticide use and one arguing against it. Compare the two editorials. Identify and list the arguments and evidence used by each author. Which is more convincing? Why?
2. Locate a current map of the world's tropical rain forests. Then locate a map that shows the parts of the world that had rain forests in the past. Write a paragraph comparing the two maps.

Citizenship in Your Community

Cooperative Project

With your group, organize a recycling program in your school. Determine what materials can be recycled and what recycling facilities exist in your community. How will you persuade students and teachers to participate? How and when will you collect the materials? Where will you take them? What financial and environmental benefits will such a program have?

Learning from Technology

Telemetry

Telemetry uses radio waves to transmit measurable information over great distances. Many ambulances, for example, now carry telemetry that sends to the hospital the pulse rate, heart rate, and respiration of ambulance patients. Telemetry also enables people who wear electronic devices such as pacemakers to have their devices monitored from home, simply by using their telephones. How do you think telemetry might affect the delivery of health care in the United States? How might it affect people's chances for surviving an accident? How might home telemetry affect the cost of health care?

Building Your Portfolio

Students have been working on a Building Your Portfolio project throughout Unit 8. You might ask volunteers to present their work to the class. Have all students add their work to their individual portfolios. Assign the Unit 8 Portfolio Assessment Worksheet in the *Portfolio Assessment Worksheets* booklet.

Building Your Portfolio

Individually or in a group, complete the following project to show your understanding of the civics concepts involved.

Operation 2010

The members of your local school board have asked you to draft a proposal that will help your school prepare itself for the challenges of the future. Specifically, the board wants to develop a long-term plan for meeting challenges through the year 2010. To plan for future challenges, however, the board also must know how challenges were dealt with in the past. To prepare your proposal for "Operation 2010," you will need to do the following.

1. Research what impact the drive for equal rights has had on your school over time. What is the ethnic makeup of your school? How has it changed over time? Are certain classes now open to girls that once were closed? Do boys now take classes that once were taken only by girls? What multicultural education classes are taught in your school? What has your school done to comply with the Americans with Disabilities Act? What more can be done to ensure equal educational opportunities for all students? Show your findings in a series of graphs that compare the answers to these questions now and in the past.

2. Create an environmental profile of your school. What can be done to make your school more energy efficient? What can the school do to conserve more electricity, water, and other resources? Are such items as newspapers, bottles, and cans recycled? Do students help keep the classrooms and school grounds free of litter? Has the school planted enough trees and other vegetation to hold the soil in place and reduce the need for air conditioning?

Organize your materials, and present your proposal to the members of the school board (the rest of the class).

*R*eference Section

517

PACIFIC TIME   MOUNTAIN TIME   CENTRAL TIME

Seattle
Olympia   WASHINGTON   River   Helena   MONTANA   NORTH DAKOTA   Farg
Portland   Columbia   Bismarck
Salem
CASCADE RANGE   OREGON   IDAHO   Billings   BLACK HILLS   SOUTH DAKOTA   Pierre
                Boise   Snake   River   WYOMING   Sioux Fa

COASTAL   Carson City   Great Salt Lake   Salt Lake City   Cheyenne   NEBRASKA
SIERRA   Sacramento   NEVADA   UTAH   Denver   Linco
San Francisco   NEVADA RANGE   COLORADO   KANSAS

CALIFORNIA   Las Vegas   Wichita

            River   Santa Fe   Oklahoma City
Los Angeles   Albuquerque   Amarillo   OKLAHOM
                Colorado   ARIZONA   Phoenix   NEW MEXICO
San Diego   Lubbock
PACIFIC OCEAN   Dall

                Tucson   El Paso   TEXAS
To understand the relative locations of Alaska and Hawaii as well
as the vast distances separating them from the rest of the United
States, see the map on page 532.

Kauai   HAWAII TIME   ARCTIC OCEAN   Austin
Nihau   Oahu   Honolulu
        Molokai
HAWAII   Lanai   Maui   Arctic Circle
PACIFIC OCEAN   ALASKA   San Antonio
                Hawaii   0   100 Miles
                        0   100 Kilometers   Rio Grande
                            Yukon   River   Fairbanks
        0   250   500 Miles   Mt. McKinley
        0   250   500 Kilometers   20,320 ft   Anchorage
Bering Sea   6,194 m

PACIFIC OCEAN   Gulf of Alaska   Juneau
        ALEUTIAN ISLANDS   ALASKA TIME

THE MAYFLOWER COMPACT

On November 21, 1620, the tiny ship *Mayflower* carrying the Pilgrims to North America reached shore. The ship was far off its course, and the Pilgrims had no charter to settle in New England or to form a government. Faced with the need to form a government, the Pilgrim leaders wrote the Mayflower Compact. This document created a government based on cooperation and the consent of the governed.

NOVEMBER 21, 1620

In the name of God, Amen. We whose names are underwritten, the loyal subjects of our dread [revered and feared] sovereign Lord King James, by the grace of God, of Great Britain, France, and Ireland, King, Defender of the Faith, etc., having undertaken for the glory of God, and advancement of the Christian faith, and honor of our king and country, a voyage to plant the first colony in the northern parts of Virginia, do by these presents [this document] solemnly and mutually in the presence of God, and one of another, covenant [promise] and combine ourselves together into a civil body politic [group organized for government] for our better ordering and preservation and furtherance of the ends aforesaid; and by virtue [authority] hereof, to enact, constitute, and frame such just and equal laws, ordinances [regulations], acts, constitutions, and offices from time to time, as shall be thought most meet [fitting] and convenient for the general good of the colony unto which we promise all due submission and obedience.

In WITNESS whereof we have hereunto subscribed our names at Cape Cod, the eleventh of November [November 21 by the modern-day calendar system], in the year of the reign of our sovereign Lord King James of England, France, and Ireland the eighteenth, and of Scotland the fifty-fourth. *Anno Domini,* 1620.

[Signed by forty-one men on the *Mayflower*]

PATRICK HENRY'S SPEECH TO THE VIRGINIA CONVENTION

Patrick Henry had attended the First Continental Congress as a delegate from Virginia. After the Congress, he returned to Virginia believing that war would soon break out with Great Britain. Soon after his return, Patrick Henry addressed the Virginia Convention, which was meeting to consider the political situation in the colony. There he delivered his most famous speech—a rousing call to fight for liberty and freedom, which continues to inspire Americans today.

MARCH 23, 1775

Mr. President: No man thinks more highly than I do of the patriotism, as well as abilities, of the very worthy gentlemen who have just addressed the House. But different men often see the same subjects in different lights; and, therefore, I hope that it will not be thought disrespectful to those gentlemen if, entertaining as I do, opinions of a character very opposite to theirs, I shall speak forth my sentiments freely and without reserve. This is no time for ceremony. The question before the House is one of awful moment [importance] to this country. . . .

It is in vain, sir, to extenuate [prolong] the matter. Gentlemen may cry peace, peace. But there is no peace. The war is actually begun! The next gale that sweeps from the north will bring to our ears the clash of resounding arms! Our brethren are already in the field! Why stand we here idle? What is it that gentlemen wish? What would they have? Is life so dear, or peace so sweet, as to be purchased at the price of chains and slavery? Forbid it, Almighty God! I know not what course others may take; but as for me, give me liberty or give me death!

THE DECLARATION OF INDEPENDENCE

▶ *In Congress, July 4, 1776*
The Unanimous Declaration of the
Thirteen United States of America

Why the Declaration Was Written

When, in the course of human events, it becomes necessary for one people to dissolve the political bands which have connected them with another, and to assume, among the powers of the earth, the separate and equal station to which the laws of nature and of nature's God entitle them, a decent respect to the opinions of mankind requires that they should declare the causes which impel them to the separation.

Statement of Basic Human Rights

We hold these truths to be self-evident: That all men are created equal; that they are endowed by their Creator with certain unalienable rights; that among these are life, liberty, and the pursuit of happiness.

Government Must Safeguard Human Rights

That to secure these rights, governments are instituted among men, deriving their just powers from the consent of the governed;

That whenever any form of government becomes destructive of these ends, it is the right of the people to alter or to abolish it, and to institute a new government, laying its foundation on such principles, and organizing its powers in such form, as to them shall seem most likely to effect their safety and happiness. Prudence, indeed, will dictate that governments long established should not be changed for light and transient causes; and accordingly all experience hath shown that mankind are more disposed to suffer while evils are sufferable, than to right themselves by abolishing the forms to which they are accustomed. But when a long train of abuses and usurpations, pursuing invariably the same object, evinces a design to reduce them under absolute despotism, it is their right, it is their duty, to throw off such government, and to provide new guards for their future security.

Abuses of Human Rights by the King

Such has been the patient sufferance of these colonies; and such is now the necessity which constrains them to alter their former systems of government. The history of the present King of Great Britain is a history of repeated injuries and usurpations, all having in direct object the establishment of an absolute tyranny over these states. To prove this, let facts be submitted to a candid world.

He has refused his assent to laws the most wholesome and necessary for the public good.

He has forbidden his governors to pass laws of immediate and pressing importance, unless suspended in their operation till his assent should be obtained; and, when so suspended, he has utterly neglected to attend to them.

He has refused to pass other laws for the accommodation of large districts of people, unless those people would relinquish the right of representation in the legislature, a right inestimable to them, and formidable to tyrants only.

He has called together legislative bodies at places unusual, uncomfortable, and distant from the depository of their public records, for the sole purpose of fatiguing them into compliance with his measures.

He has dissolved representative houses repeatedly, for opposing, with manly firmness, his invasions on the rights of the people.

He has refused, for a long time after such dissolutions, to cause others to be elected, whereby the legislative powers, incapable of annihilation, have returned to the people at large for their exercise; the state remaining, in the mean time, exposed to all the dangers of invasion from without and convulsions within.

He has endeavored to prevent the population of these states; for that purpose obstructing the laws of naturalization of foreigners, refusing to pass others to encourage their migrations hither, and raising the conditions of new appropriations of lands.

He has obstructed the administration of justice, by refusing his assent to laws for establishing judiciary powers.

He has made judges dependent on his will alone for the tenure of their offices, and the amount and payment of their salaries.

He has erected a multitude of new offices, and sent hither swarms of officers to harass our people and eat out their substance.

He has kept among us, in times of peace, standing armies, without the consent of our legislatures.

He has affected to render the military independent of, and superior to, the civil power.

He has combined with others to subject us to a jurisdiction foreign to our constitution, and unacknowledged by our laws; giving his assent to their acts of pretended legislation:

For quartering large bodies of armed troops among us;

For protecting them, by a mock trial, from punishment for any murders which they should commit on the inhabitants of these states;

For cutting off our trade with all parts of the world;

For imposing taxes on us without our consent;

For depriving us, in many cases, of the benefits of trial by jury;

For transporting us beyond seas, to be tried for pretended offenses;

For abolishing the free system of English laws in a neighboring province, establishing therein an arbitrary government, and enlarging its boundaries, so as to render it at once an example and fit instrument for introducing the same absolute rule into these colonies;

For taking away our charters, abolishing our most valuable laws, and altering, fundamentally, the forms of our governments;

For suspending our own legislatures, and declaring themselves invested with power to legislate for us in all cases whatsoever.

He has abdicated government here, by declaring us out of his protection and waging war against us.

He has plundered our seas, ravaged our coasts, burnt our towns, and destroyed the lives of our people.

He is at this time transporting large armies of foreign mercenaries to complete the works of death, desolation, and tyranny already begun with circumstances of cruelty and perfidy scarcely paralleled in the most barbarous ages, and totally unworthy of the head of a civilized nation.

He has constrained our fellow citizens, taken captive on the high seas, to bear arms against their country, to become the executioners of their friends and brethren, or to fall themselves by their hands.

He has excited domestic insurrections amongst us, and has endeavored to bring on the inhabitants of our frontiers the merciless Indian savages, whose known rule of warfare is an undistinguished destruction of all ages, sexes, and conditions.

Colonial Efforts to Avoid Separation

In every stage of these oppressions we have petitioned for redress in the most humble terms; our repeated petitions have been answered only by repeated injury.

A prince whose character is thus marked by every act which may define a tyrant is unfit to be the ruler of a free people.

Nor have we been wanting in our attentions to our British brethren. We have warned them, from time to time, of attempts by their legislature to extend an unwarrantable jurisdiction over us. We have reminded them of the circumstances of our emigration and settlement here. We have appealed to their native justice and magnanimity; and we have conjured them, by the ties of our common kindred, to disavow these usurpations, which would inevitably interrupt our connections and correspondence. They, too, have been deaf to the voice of justice and consanguinity. We must, therefore, acquiesce in the necessity which denounces our separation, and hold them, as we hold the rest of mankind, enemies in war, in peace friends.

The Colonies Declare Independence

We, therefore, the representatives of the United States of America, in General Congress assembled, appealing to the Supreme Judge of the world for the rectitude of our intentions, do, in the name and by the authority of the good people of these colonies, solemnly publish and declare, That these united colonies are, and of right ought to be, free and independent states; that they are absolved from all allegiance to the British crown, and that all political connection between them and the state of Great Britain is, and ought to be, totally dissolved; and that, as free and independent states, they have full power to levy war, conclude peace, contract alliances, establish commerce, and to do all other acts and things which independent states may of right do. And, for the support of this declaration, with a firm reliance on the protection of Divine Providence, we mutually pledge to each other our lives, our fortunes, and our sacred honor.

President

NEW HAMPSHIRE
Josiah Bartlett
William Whipple
Matthew Thornton

MASSACHUSETTS
Samuel Adams
John Adams
Robert Treat Paine
Elbridge Gerry

RHODE ISLAND
Stephen Hopkins
William Ellery

CONNECTICUT
Roger Sherman
Samuel Huntington
William Williams
Oliver Wolcott

NEW YORK
William Floyd
Philip Livingston
Francis Lewis
Lewis Morris

NEW JERSEY
Richard Stockton
John Witherspoon
Francis Hopkinson
John Hart
Abraham Clark

PENNSYLVANIA
Robert Morris
Benjamin Rush
Benjamin Franklin
John Morton
George Clymer
James Smith

George Taylor
James Wilson
George Ross

DELAWARE
Caesar Rodney
George Read
Thomas McKean

MARYLAND
Samuel Chase
William Paca
Thomas Stone
Charles Carroll of
    Carrollton

VIRGINIA
George Wythe
Richard Henry Lee
Thomas Jefferson

Benjamin Harrison
Thomas Nelson, Jr.
Francis Lightfoot Lee
Carter Braxton

NORTH CAROLINA
William Hooper
Joseph Hewes
John Penn

SOUTH CAROLINA
Edward Rutledge
Thomas Heyward, Jr.
Thomas Lynch, Jr.
Arthur Middleton

GEORGIA
Button Gwinnett
Lyman Hall
George Walton

NATHAN HALE'S SPEECH

Nathan Hale, a captain in the American Revolutionary Army, volunteered for a secret mission behind the British lines. Pretending that he was a Dutch schoolmaster, Hale slipped into British-held territory. When Hale tried to return to American lines, he was captured by the British and condemned to die by hanging. Before his death Hale made a brief speech, which has since served as an inspiration to all Americans. It states a deep devotion to the principle of freedom.

SEPTEMBER 22, 1776

The cause for which I am dying I did not take up in an idle moment. I was born in it, as are all my countrymen. If the belief in man's right to freedom is held in any other place on earth, I have not heard of it. I am proud to have lived in the country where freedom is a reality. Living, it has been my privilege to fight for it. In death I shall hold it forever. If I were to be born a thousand times, I would choose no other life but service to American freedom. I have only one sorrow. I only regret that I have but one life to lose for my country.

THE CONSTITUTION OF THE UNITED STATES

The parts of the text crossed out in blue have been changed by the passing of time or by later amendments. Explanations and comments are also in blue.

Preamble

We the people of the United States, in order to form a more perfect union, establish justice, insure domestic tranquillity, provide for the common defense, promote the general welfare, and secure the blessings of liberty to ourselves and our posterity, do ordain and establish this Constitution for the United States of America.

The **Preamble**, or introduction, to the Constitution states the purposes of the Constitution. It also makes clear that the government is established by consent of the governed. "We the people, . . . ordain and establish" the government.

By separating the functions of government among branches concerned with making laws (Article 1), executing laws (Article 2), and interpreting laws (Article 3), the framers of the Constitution were applying the principle of **separation of powers**. They were also developing a system of **checks and balances**. They hoped it would prevent any part of the federal government from becoming too powerful.

ARTICLE 1. Legislative Branch

SECTION 1. CONGRESS

All legislative powers herein granted shall be vested in a Congress of the United States, which shall consist of a Senate and House of Representatives.

The power to make laws is given to Congress. Congress is made up of two houses—the Senate and the House of Representatives.

SECTION 2. HOUSE OF REPRESENTATIVES

1. Election of Members and Term of Office. The House of Representatives shall be composed of members chosen every second year by the people of the several States, and the electors in each State shall have the qualifications requisite for electors of the most numerous branch of the State Legislature.

Members of the House of Representatives are chosen every two years. They are elected directly by the voters who are qualified to vote for members of their state legislatures.

2. Qualifications. No person shall be a Representative who shall not have attained to the age of twenty-five years, and been seven years a citizen of the United States, and who shall not, when elected, be an inhabitant of that State in which he shall be chosen.

Members of the House of Representatives must be at least 25 years old, U.S. citizens for at least seven years, and residents of the states they represent.

3. Division of Representatives and Direct Taxes Among the States. Representatives and direct taxes shall be apportioned among the several States which may be included within this Union, according to their respective

The number of representatives for each state is based on its population.

numbers, which shall be determined by adding to the whole number of free persons, including those bound to service for a term of years, and excluding Indians not taxed, three fifths of all other persons. The actual enumeration shall be made within three years after the first meeting of the Congress of the United States, and within every subsequent term of ten years, in such manner as they shall by law direct. The number of Representatives shall not exceed one for every thirty thousand, but each State shall have at least one Representative; and until such enumeration shall be made, the state of New Hampshire shall be entitled to choose three; Massachusetts, eight; Rhode Island and Providence Plantations, one; Connecticut, five; New York, six; New Jersey, four; Pennsylvania, eight; Delaware, one; Maryland, six; Virginia, ten; North Carolina, five; South Carolina, five; and Georgia, three.

A **census**, or count of the population, must be taken by the federal government every 10 years.

4. Filling Vacancies. When vacancies happen in the representation from any State, the Executive authority thereof shall issue writs of election to fill such vacancies.

Vacancies in the House of Representatives are filled by special elections called by the governor of the state.

5. Officers; Impeachment. The House of Representatives shall choose their Speaker and other officers; and shall have the sole power of impeachment.

The House of Representatives has the power to choose its **Speaker**, or presiding officer, and other officers. It also has the power to **impeach**, or accuse, an official in the executive branch or a federal judge. The trial of the impeached official takes place in the Senate. (See Section 3, Clause 6.)

SECTION 3. SENATE

1. Number of Members and Term of Office. The Senate of the United States shall be composed of two Senators from each State, chosen by the Legislature thereof, for six years; and each Senator shall have one vote.

In the Senate, each state is represented equally by two senators. (Amendment 17 provides for the direct election of senators.)

2. Classification; Filling Vacancies. Immediately after they shall be assembled in consequence of the first election, they shall be divided as equally as may be into three classes. The seats of the Senators of the first class shall be vacated at the expiration of the second year, of the second class at the expiration of the fourth year, and of the third class at the expiration of the sixth year, so that one third may be chosen every second year; and if vacancies happen by resignation, or otherwise, during the recess of the Legislature of any State, the executive thereof may make temporary appointments until the next meeting of the Legislature, which shall then fill such vacancies.

One third of the senators are elected every two years for a six-year term. As a result, the terms of senators overlap, making the Senate a "continuing" body.

Under Amendment 17, Senate vacancies are filled by new senators appointed by the governor of the state.

3. Qualifications of Members. No person shall be a Senator who shall not have attained to the age of thirty years, and been nine years a citizen of the United States, and who shall not, when elected, be an inhabitant of that State for which he shall be chosen.

Senators must be at least 30 years old, U.S. citizens for at least nine years, and residents of the states they represent.

4. President of the Senate. The Vice President of the United States shall be President of the Senate, but shall have no vote, unless they be equally divided.

The vice president is the presiding officer of the Senate but may vote only in the case of a tie.

5. Other Senate Officers. The Senate shall choose their other officers, and also a President *pro tempore*, in the absence of the Vice President, or when he shall exercise the office of President of the United States.

The Senate elects a temporary presiding officer from among its members. The **president *pro tempore*** serves when the vice president is absent or becomes president.

6. Trial of Impeachments. The Senate shall have the sole power to try all impeachments. When sitting for that purpose, they shall be on oath or affirmation. When the President of the United States is tried, the Chief Justice shall preside; and no person shall be convicted without the concurrence of two thirds of the members present.

The Senate has power to try impeachment cases. A two-thirds vote is needed to convict an impeached official.

7. Penalty for Conviction in Impeachment Cases. Judgment in cases of impeachment shall not extend further than to removal from office, and disqualification to hold and enjoy any office of honor, trust, or profit under the United States; but the party convicted shall nevertheless be liable and subject to indictment, trial, judgment, and punishment, according to law.

If the Senate convicts an impeached official, it can only punish the official so far as to remove him or her from office and disqualify him or her from holding office again. An official who has been impeached and convicted may also be tried in a court of law if he or she has broken the law.

SECTION 4. BOTH HOUSES

1. Holding Elections. The times, places, and manner of holding elections for Senators and Representatives shall be prescribed in each State by the Legislature thereof; but the Congress may at any time by law make or alter such regulations, except as to the places of choosing Senators.

Election regulations are set by the states, but Congress may pass laws overruling the state regulations.

2. Meetings. The Congress shall assemble at least once in every year, and such meeting shall be on the first Monday in December, unless they shall by law appoint a different day.

Congress must meet at least once a year. The meeting time of Congress was set by Amendment 20 at January 3.

SECTION 5. EACH HOUSE ALONE

1. Organization. Each house shall be the judge of the elections, returns, and qualifications of its own members, and a majority of each shall constitute a quorum to do business; but a smaller number may adjourn from day to day, and may be authorized to compel the attendance of absent members, in such manner, and under such penalties, as each house may provide.

Each house of Congress decides whether its members are qualified and have been elected fairly. A **quorum**, or a majority of the members, must be present to carry on the work of each house. Members of either house of Congress may be ordered to attend so that business can be handled.

2. Proceedings. Each house may determine the rules of its proceedings, punish its members for disorderly behavior, and, with the concurrence of two thirds, expel a member.

Each house may establish rules for carrying on its business and may punish members who break these rules. In either house, a two-thirds vote is required to expel a member of that house.

3. Journal. Each house shall keep a journal of its proceedings, and from time to time publish the same, excepting such parts as may in their judgment require secrecy; and the yeas and nays of the members of either house on any question shall, at the desire of one fifth of those present, be entered on the journal.

Each house of Congress must keep and publish an official record of its activities. *The Congressional Record* is published every day that Congress is in session. It provides a daily account of what the members of Congress do and say.

The two houses of Congress must remain in session for the same period of time and in the same place.

Members of Congress are paid salaries and receive additional sums of money for certain expenses.

Members of Congress cannot be sued or arrested for anything they say in Congress. They can be arrested for major crimes while Congress is in session.

Members of Congress cannot hold any other federal office while serving in Congress. Members also cannot resign and then accept federal jobs that were created during their term in Congress.

Appropriation bills, or money-raising bills, must begin in the House of Representatives. The Senate, however, can suggest changes in these bills.

A bill passed by Congress must be sent to the president. If the president approves and signs the bill, it becomes a law. If the president **vetoes**, or refuses to sign, the bill, it is returned to the house in which it started.

The president's veto may be overruled by a two-thirds vote of each house of Congress. The president can let a bill become a law without signing it by holding it for 10 days (excluding Sundays) while Congress is in session. But a bill sent to the president during the last 10 days of a session of Congress is rejected by a **pocket veto** if the president does not sign it.

4. *Adjournment.* Neither house, during the session of Congress, shall, without the consent of the other, adjourn for more than three days, nor to any other place than that in which the two houses shall be sitting.

SECTION 6. PRIVILEGES AND RESTRICTIONS

1. *Pay and Privileges.* The Senators and Representatives shall receive a compensation for their services, to be ascertained by law, and paid out of the treasury of the United States. They shall in all cases, except treason, felony, and breach of the peace, be privileged from arrest during their attendance at the session of their respective houses, and in going to and returning from the same; and for any speech or debate in either house they shall not be questioned in any other place.

2. *Members Cannot Hold Other Offices.* No Senator or Representative shall, during the time for which he was elected, be appointed to any civil office under the authority of the United States, which shall have been created, or the emoluments whereof shall have been increased, during such time; and no person holding any office under the United States shall be a member of either house during his continuance in office.

SECTION 7. METHOD OF PASSING LAWS

1. *Revenue Bills.* All bills for raising revenue shall originate in the House of Representatives; but the Senate may propose or concur with amendments as on other bills.

2. *How a Bill Becomes a Law.* Every bill which shall have passed the House of Representatives and the Senate shall, before it become a law, be presented to the President of the United States; if he approve he shall sign it, but if not he shall return it with his objections to that house in which it shall have originated, who shall enter the objections at large on their journal, and proceed to reconsider it. If after such reconsideration two thirds of that house shall agree to pass the bill, it shall be sent together with the objections, to the other house, by which it shall likewise be reconsidered, and, if approved by two thirds of that house, it shall become a law. But in all such cases the votes of both houses shall be determined by yeas and nays, and the names of the persons voting for and against the bill shall be entered on the journal of each house respectively. If any bill shall not be returned by the President within ten days (Sundays excepted) after it shall have been presented to him, the same shall be a law, in like manner as if he had signed it, unless the Congress by their adjournment prevent its return, in which case it shall not be a law.

3. *Presidential Approval or Veto.* Every order, resolution, or vote to which the concurrence of the Senate and House of Representatives may be necessary (except on a question of adjournment) shall be presented to the President of the United States; and, before the same shall take effect, shall be approved by him, or, being disapproved by him, shall be repassed by two thirds of the Senate and House of Representatives, according to the rules and limitations prescribed in the case of a bill.

The president must sign or veto every resolution, except those on adjournment, passed by both houses.

SECTION 8. POWERS GRANTED TO CONGRESS
The Congress shall have power

The specific powers delegated, or granted, to Congress are:

1. To lay and collect taxes, duties, imposts, and excises, to pay the debts and provide for the common defense and general welfare of the United States; but all duties, imposts, and excises shall be uniform throughout the United States;

to levy and collect uniform taxes to pay government debts and provide for the defense and general welfare of the nation,

2. To borrow money on the credit of the United States;

to borrow money,

3. To regulate commerce with foreign nations, and among the several states, and with the Indian tribes;

to regulate interstate and foreign commerce, or trade,

4. To establish a uniform rule of naturalization, and uniform laws on the subject of bankruptcies throughout the United States;

to set up uniform laws concerning **naturalization**, or becoming a citizen, and concerning bankruptcy,

5. To coin money, regulate the value thereof, and of foreign coin, and fix the standard of weights and measures;

to coin money and set standards of weights and measures,

6. To provide for the punishment of counterfeiting the securities and current coin of the United States;

to provide for the punishment of **counterfeiting**,

7. To establish post offices and post roads;

to establish post offices and post roads,

8. To promote the progress of science and useful arts, by securing for limited times to authors and inventors the exclusive right to their respective writings and discoveries;

to issue **patents** and **copyrights**,

9. To constitute tribunals inferior to the Supreme Court;

to set up a system of federal courts,

10. To define and punish piracies and felonies committed on the high seas, and offences against the law of nations;

to define and punish piracy,

11. To declare war, grant letters of marque and reprisal, and make rules concerning captures on land and water;

to declare war,

12. To raise and support armies, but no appropriation of money to that use shall be for a longer term than two years;

to raise and support armies,

13. To provide and maintain a navy;

to provide and maintain a navy,

14. To make rules for the government and regulation of the land and naval forces;

to make rules and regulations for the armed forces,

15. To provide for calling forth the militia to execute the laws of the Union, suppress insurrections, and repel invasions;

to provide for calling out the militia (National Guard),

16. To provide for organizing, arming, and disciplining the militia, and for governing such part of them as may be employed in the service of the

to help states maintain their militias,

United States, reserving to the States respectively, the appointment of the officers, and the authority of training the militia according to the discipline prescribed by Congress.

17. To exercise exclusive legislation, in all cases whatsoever, over such district (not exceeding ten miles square) as may, by cession of particular States, and the acceptance of Congress, become the seat of the government of the United States; and to exercise like authority over all places purchased by the consent of the Legislature of the State in which the same shall be, for the erection of forts, magazines, arsenals, dock-yards, and other needful buildings; and

18. To make all laws which shall be necessary and proper for carrying into execution the foregoing powers, and all other powers vested by this Constitution in the government of the United States, or in any department or officer thereof.

SECTION 9. POWERS FORBIDDEN TO THE FEDERAL GOVERNMENT

[Amendments 1 to 10 also directly or indirectly limit the powers of the federal government.]

1. The migration or importation of such persons as any of the States now existing shall think proper to admit, shall not be prohibited by the Congress prior to the year one thousand eight hundred and eight, but a tax or duty may be imposed on such importation, not exceeding ten dollars for each person.

2. The privilege of the writ of *habeas corpus* shall not be suspended, unless when in cases of rebellion or invasion the public safety may require it.

3. No bill of attainder or *ex post facto* law shall be passed.

4. No capitation or other direct tax shall be laid, unless in proportion to the census or enumeration herein before directed to be taken.

5. No tax or duty shall be laid on articles exported from any State.

6. No preference shall be given by any regulation of commerce or revenue to the ports of one State over those of another; nor shall vessels bound to, or from, one State, be obliged to enter, clear, or pay duties in another.

---

to establish and govern the nation's capital, the District of Columbia, and govern other federal property,

to make all "necessary and proper" laws for carrying out the powers of the federal government. This **elastic clause** allows Congress to take many actions not named in the Constitution.

The powers forbidden to Congress are:

to interfere with the foreign slave trade before 1808 (Congress outlawed the slave trade in 1808.),

to suspend the **writ of habeas corpus** except during emergencies (The guarantee of the writ of *habeas corpus* means that people may not be held in jail on little or no evidence.),

to pass **bills of attainder** or *ex post facto* laws (A bill of attainder is a law, passed by the legislature, that condemns and punishes a person without a jury trial. An *ex post facto* law is a law that punishes a person for doing something that was not illegal at the time it was done.),

to levy direct taxes except in proportion to population (see Amendment 16),

to tax exports,

to pass any laws that would favor the trade of a particular state,

7. No money shall be drawn from the treasury, but in consequence of appropriations made by law; and a regular statement and account of the receipts and expenditures of all public money shall be published from time to time.

to spend money without appropriating it by law,

8. No title of nobility shall be granted by the United States; and no person holding any office of profit or trust under them shall, without the consent of the Congress, accept of any present, emolument, office, or title, of any kind whatever, from any king, prince, or foreign state.

to grant or accept any title of nobility,

SECTION 10. POWERS FORBIDDEN TO THE STATES
[Supplemented by Amendments 14 and 15]

The powers forbidden to the states are:

1. No State shall enter into any treaty, alliance, or confederation; grant letters of marque and reprisal; coin money; emit bills of credit; make anything but gold and silver coin a tender in payment of debts; pass any bill of attainder, *ex post facto* law, or law impairing the obligation of contracts; or grant any title of nobility.

to make treaties or alliances,
to coin money,
to pass bills of attainder,
to pass ex post facto laws,
to pass laws excusing people from carrying out lawful obligations,
to grant titles of nobility.

2. No State shall, without the consent of the Congress, lay any imposts or duties on imports or exports, except what may be absolutely necessary for executing its inspection laws; and the net produce of all duties and imposts, laid by any State on imports and exports, shall be for the use of the Treasury of the United States; and all such laws shall be subject to the revision and control of the Congress.

to levy taxes or tariffs on goods sent into or out of the state without permission of Congress,

3. No State shall, without the consent of Congress, lay any duty of tonnage, keep troops or ships of war in time of peace, enter into any agreement or compact with another State, or with a foreign power, or engage in war, unless actually invaded, or in such imminent danger as will not admit of delay.

to keep troops or warships in peacetime or deal with another state or a foreign nation without consent of Congress or engage in war unless invaded.

ARTICLE 2. Executive Branch

SECTION 1. PRESIDENT; VICE PRESIDENT

1. *Term of Office.* The executive power shall be vested in a President of the United States of America. He shall hold his office during the term of four years, and, together with the Vice President, chosen for the same term, be elected as follows:

Executive power is given to the president, who holds office for a four-year term.

2. *The Electoral System.* Each State shall appoint, in such manner as the Legislature thereof may direct, a number of Electors equal to the whole number of Senators and Representatives to which the State may be entitled in the Congress; but no Senator or Representative, or person holding an office of trust or profit under the United States shall be appointed an Elector.

*The president and vice president are elected by **electors**, or members of the **Electoral College**, chosen by the voters. Each state is entitled to the number of electors equal to the number of its senators and representatives.*

3. *A Discarded Way of Using the Electoral System.* The Electors shall meet in their respective States, and vote by ballot for two persons, of whom one at least shall not be an inhabitant of the same State with themselves. And they shall make a list of all the persons voted for, and of the number of

This procedure for electing the president and vice president was changed by Amendment 12.

votes for each; which list they shall sign and certify, and transmit sealed to the seat of the government of the United States, directed to the President of the Senate. The President of the Senate shall, in the presence of the Senate and House of Representatives, open all the certificates, and the votes shall then be counted. The person having the greatest number of votes shall be the President, if such number be a majority of the whole number of Electors appointed; and if there be more than one who have such majority, and have an equal number of votes, then the House of Representatives shall immediately choose by ballot one of them for President; and if no person have a majority, then from the five highest on the list the said house shall in like manner choose the President. But in choosing the President, the votes shall be taken by States, the representation from each State having one vote; a quorum for this purpose shall consist of a member or members from two thirds of the States, and a majority of all the States shall be necessary to a choice. In every case, after the choice of the President, the person having the greatest number of votes of the Electors shall be the Vice President. But if there should remain two or more who have equal votes, the Senate shall choose from them by ballot the Vice President.

4. Time of Elections. Congress may determine the time of choosing the Electors, and the day on which they shall give their votes; which day shall be the same throughout the United States.

5. Qualifications for the President. No person except a natural-born citizen, or a citizen of the United States at the time of the adoption of this Constitution, shall be eligible to the office of President; neither shall any person be eligible to that office who shall not have attained to the age of thirty-five years, and been fourteen years a resident within the United States.

6. Filling Vacancies. In case of the removal of the President from office, or of his death, resignation, or inability to discharge the power and duties of the said office, the same shall devolve on the Vice President, and the Congress may by law provide for the case of removal, death, resignation, or inability, both of the President and Vice President, declaring what officer shall then act as President, and such officer shall act accordingly, until the disability be removed, or a President shall be elected.

7. Salary. The President shall, at stated times, receive for his services a compensation, which shall neither be increased nor diminished during the period for which he shall have been elected, and he shall not receive within that period any other emolument from the United States, or any of them.

8. Oath of Office. Before he enter on the execution of his office, he shall take the following oath or affirmation: "I do solemnly swear (or affirm) that I will faithfully execute the office of President of the United States, and will,

Today presidential elections are held on the first Tuesday after the first Monday in November. Electoral votes are cast on the first Monday after the second Wednesday in December.

The president must be a natural-born U.S. citizen, at least 35 years old, and a resident of the United States for at least 14 years.

If the president dies, or for any reason cannot carry out the duties of office, the vice president will act as president. In the event that both officials are unable to serve, Congress has declared that the order of succession is as follows: (1) Speaker of the House, (2) president *pro tempore* of the Senate, and (3) the cabinet members in the order in which their offices were created. (See also Amendment 25.)

The president receives a salary, the amount of which may not be changed during the term of office.

The president takes an oath of office before beginning the duties as chief executive.

to the best of my ability, preserve, protect, and defend the Constitution of the United States."

SECTION 2. POWERS OF THE PRESIDENT

1. Military Powers. The President shall be Commander in Chief of the army and navy of the United States, and of the militia of the several States, when called into the actual service of the United States; he may require the opinion, in writing, of the principal officer in each of the executive departments, upon any subject relating to the duties of their respective offices, and he shall have power to grant reprieves and pardons for offences against the United States, except in cases of impeachment.

The president is commander in chief of the armed forces.

The head of each executive department is, in practice, a member of the president's **cabinet**.

The president may grant pardons for offenses against the United States, except in cases of impeachment.

2. Treaty-making Power; Power of Appointment. He shall have power, by and with the advice and consent of the Senate, to make treaties, provided two thirds of the Senators present concur; and he shall nominate, and, by and with the advice and consent of the Senate, shall appoint ambassadors, other public ministers, and consuls, judges of the Supreme Court, and all other officers of the United States, whose appointments are not herein otherwise provided for, and which shall be established by law; but the Congress may by law vest the appointment of such inferior officers, as they think proper, in the President alone, in the courts of law, or in the heads of departments.

The president has the power to make treaties and to appoint such officials as ambassadors, federal judges, and presidential advisers provided that they are approved by the Senate.

3. Filling Vacancies. The President shall have power to fill up all vacancies that may happen during the recess of the Senate, by granting commissions which shall expire at the end of their next session.

The president may appoint officials to fill vacancies temporarily without the consent of the Senate if Congress is not in session.

SECTION 3. DUTIES OF THE PRESIDENT

He shall from time to time give to the Congress information of the state of the Union, and recommend to their consideration such measures as he shall judge necessary and expedient; he may, on extraordinary occasions, convene both houses, or either of them, and in case of disagreement between them, with respect to the time of adjournment, he may adjourn them to such time as he shall think proper; he shall receive ambassadors and other public ministers; he shall take care that the laws be faithfully executed, and shall commission all the officers of the United States.

The president is required to send or to read a report on the state of the Union—the condition of the nation—at the opening of each session of Congress. The president also sends special messages to Congress.

The president may call special sessions of Congress.

The president is required to receive ambassadors, to ensure that the laws of the nation are carried out, and to sign papers that give officers in the armed forces the right to hold their positions.

SECTION 4. IMPEACHMENT

The President, Vice President, and all civil officers of the United States, shall be removed from office on impeachment for, and conviction of, treason, bribery, or other high crimes and misdemeanors.

The president and all civil officers may be removed from office if impeached and convicted of treason, bribery, or other high crimes. (See also Article 1, Section 3, clauses 6 and 7.)

ARTICLE 3. Judicial Branch

SECTION 1. FEDERAL COURTS

The Supreme Court and Lower Federal Courts. The judicial power of the United States shall be vested in one Supreme Court, and in such inferior

Judicial power is given to a Supreme Court and lower

federal courts established by Congress.

Federal judges hold office for life, but they may be removed by the impeachment process.

Federal courts may try cases involving the Constitution, federal laws, treaties, and laws relating to ships on the high seas and navigable waters. They may also try cases involving the U.S. government, foreign diplomatic officials, two or more state governments, and citizens of different states.

Cases involving ambassadors or officials of foreign nations and cases involving states are tried in the Supreme Court. Other cases begin in lower courts but may be appealed to the Supreme Court.

Every person accused of a federal crime, except someone undergoing impeachment, is guaranteed a jury trial in the state where the crime took place.

Treason is carefully defined as waging war against the nation or helping its enemies. A person cannot be convicted of treason without the testimony of two witnesses to the same act, unless the person confesses in court.

Punishment for treason is determined by Congress and may not extend to the family of the convicted person.

All states are required to honor each other's laws, records, and legal decisions.

---

courts as the Congress may from time to time ordain and establish. The judges, both of the Supreme and inferior courts, shall hold their offices during good behavior, and shall, at stated times, receive for their services a compensation, which shall not be diminished during their continuance in office.

SECTION 2. JURISDICTION OF THE FEDERAL COURTS

1. General Jurisdiction. The judicial power shall extend to all cases, in law and equity, arising under this Constitution, the laws of the United States, and treaties made, or which shall be made, under their authority; to all cases affecting ambassadors, other public ministers and consuls; to all cases of admiralty and maritime jurisdiction; to controversies to which the United States shall be a party; to controversies between two or more States, between a State and citizens of another State [see Amendment 11], between citizens of different States, between citizens of the same State claiming lands under grants of different States, and between a State, or the citizens thereof, and foreign states, citizens, or subjects.

2. The Supreme Court. In all cases affecting ambassadors, other public ministers, and consuls, and those in which a State shall be party, the Supreme Court shall have original jurisdiction. In all the other cases before mentioned, the Supreme Court shall have appellate jurisdiction, both as to law and fact, with such exceptions, and under such regulations, as the Congress shall make.

3. Conduct of Trials. The trial of all crimes, except in cases of impeachment, shall be by jury; and such trial shall be held in the State where the said crimes shall have been committed, but when not committed within any State, the trial shall be at such place or places as the Congress may by law have directed. [Expanded by Amendments 5, 6, and 7.]

SECTION 3. TREASON

1. Definition. Treason against the United States shall consist only in levying war against them, or in adhering to their enemies, giving them aid and comfort. No person shall be convicted of treason unless on the testimony of two witnesses to the same overt act, or on confession in open court.

2. Punishment. The Congress shall have power to declare the punishment of treason, but no attainder of treason shall work corruption of blood, or forfeiture, except during the life of the person attainted.

ARTICLE 4. *Relation of the States to Each Other*

SECTION 1. OFFICIAL ACTS

Full faith and credit shall be given in each State to the public acts, records, and judicial proceedings of every other State. And the Congress may by general laws prescribe the manner in which such acts, records, and proceedings shall be proved, and the effect thereof.

for as President, and of all persons voted for as Vice President, and of the number of votes for each, which lists they shall sign and certify, and transmit sealed to the seat of the government of the United States, directed to the President of the Senate;—the President of the Senate shall, in the presence of the Senate and House of Representatives, open all the certificates, and the votes shall then be counted;—the person having the greatest number of votes for President shall be the President, if such number be a majority of the whole number of Electors appointed; and if no person have such majority, then from the persons having the highest numbers not exceeding three on the list of those voted for as President, the House of Representatives shall choose immediately, by ballot, the President. But in choosing the President, the votes shall be taken by States, the representation from each State having one vote; a quorum for this purpose shall consist of a member or members from two thirds of the States, and a majority of all the States shall be necessary to a choice. And if the House of Representatives shall not choose a President, whenever the right of choice shall devolve upon them, before the fourth day of March next following, then the Vice President shall act as President, as in the case of the death or other constitutional disability of the President. [See Amendment 20.] The person having the greatest number of votes as Vice President shall be the Vice President, if such number be a majority of the whole number of Electors appointed, and if no person have a majority, then from the two highest numbers on the list the Senate shall choose the Vice President; a quorum for the purpose shall consist of two thirds of the whole number of Senators, and a majority of the whole number shall be necessary to a choice. But no person constitutionally ineligible to the office of President shall be eligible to that of Vice President of the United States.

without specifying which person was to be president and which vice president.

The candidate receiving the majority of electoral votes became president; the person with the next largest number became vice president. In the election of 1800, there was a tie. Amendment 12 was established to prevent such situations. It instructs electors to cast separate ballots for the president and for the vice president.

AMENDMENT 13. *Abolishment of Slavery (1865)*

SECTION 1. SLAVERY ENDED IN THE UNITED STATES
Neither slavery nor involuntary servitude, except as a punishment for crime whereof the party shall have been duly convicted, shall exist within the United States, or any place subject to their jurisdiction.

Slavery no longer will be allowed in the United States or in any areas governed by the United States.

SECTION 2. ENFORCEMENT
Congress shall have power to enforce this article by appropriate legislation.

AMENDMENT 14. *Rights of Citizens (1868)*

SECTION 1. CITIZENSHIP DEFINED
All persons born or naturalized in the United States, and subject to the jurisdiction thereof, are citizens of the United States and of the State wherein they reside. No State shall make or enforce any law which shall abridge the privileges or immunities of citizens of the United States; nor shall any State deprive any person of life, liberty, or property, without due process of law; nor deny to any person within its jurisdiction the equal protection of the laws.

Citizenship is given to African Americans. The states are forbidden to deny equal privileges and protection by law to any citizen. In effect, the basic protections of the Bill of Rights apply to state governments as well as to the federal government.

SECTION 2. APPORTIONMENT OF REPRESENTATIVES

Representatives shall be apportioned among the several States according to their respective numbers, counting the whole number of persons in each State, excluding Indians not taxed. But when the right to vote at any election for the choice of electors for President and Vice President of the United States, Representatives in Congress, the executive and judicial officers of a State, or the members of the Legislature thereof, is denied to any of the male inhabitants of such State, being twenty-one years of age and citizens of the United States, or in any way abridged, except for participation in rebellion or other crime, the basis of representation therein shall be reduced in the proportion which the number of such male citizens shall bear to the whole number of male citizens twenty-one years of age in such State.

SECTION 3. DISABILITY FOR ENGAGING IN INSURRECTION

No person shall be a Senator or Representative in Congress, or Elector of President and Vice President, or hold any office, civil or military, under the United States, or under any State, who, having previously taken an oath, as a member of Congress, or as an officer of the United States, or as a member of any State Legislature, or as an executive or judicial officer of any State, to support the Constitution of the United States, shall have engaged in insurrection or rebellion against the same, or given aid or comfort to the enemies thereof. But Congress may, by a vote of two thirds of each house, remove such disability.

SECTION 4. PUBLIC DEBT

The validity of the public debt of the United States, authorized by law, including debts incurred for payment of pensions and bounties for services in suppressing insurrection or rebellion, shall not be questioned. But neither the United States, nor any State shall assume or pay any debt or obligation incurred in aid of insurrection or rebellion against the United States, or any claim for the loss or emancipation of any slave; but all such debts, obligations, and claims shall be held illegal and void.

SECTION 5. ENFORCEMENT

The Congress shall have power to enforce, by appropriate legislation, the provisions of this article.

AMENDMENT 15. *Right of Suffrage (1870)*

SECTION 1. EXTENSION OF VOTING RIGHTS

The right of citizens of the United States to vote shall not be denied or abridged by the United States, or by any State, on account of race, color, or previous condition of servitude.

SECTION 2. ENFORCEMENT

The Congress shall have power to enforce this article by appropriate legislation.

Side notes:

A state's representation in Congress may be reduced if the state denies the right to vote to any eligible citizen.

Certain former officials of the Confederate states were barred from holding public office.

All debts of the federal government connected with the Civil War are to be paid. All debts of the Confederate states are declared illegal and will not be paid by the federal government. No payment will be made for the loss of former slaves.

Citizens cannot be denied the right to vote because of their race or color, or because of prior enslavement.

AMENDMENT 16. *Taxes on Income (1913)*

The Congress shall have power to lay and collect taxes on incomes, from whatever source derived, without apportionment among the several States, and without regard to any census or enumeration.

Congress is given the power to pass a law taxing incomes. (This amendment changes Article 1, Section 9, Clause 4.)

AMENDMENT 17. *Election of Senators (1913)*

SECTION 1. DIRECT POPULAR VOTE
The Senate of the United States shall be composed of two Senators from each State, elected by the people thereof, for six years; and each Senator shall have one vote. The electors in each State shall have the qualifications requisite for electors of the most numerous branch of the State legislatures.

Senators are to be elected by the voters of each state. (This amendment changes Article 1, Section 3, Clause 1, under which senators were elected by state legislatures.)

SECTION 2. FILLING SENATORIAL VACANCIES
When vacancies happen in the representation of any State in the Senate, the executive authority of such State shall issue writs of election to fill such vacancies. Provided, that the Legislature of any State may empower the executive thereof to make temporary appointment until the people fill the vacancies by election as the Legislature may direct.

A vacancy in the Senate may be filled by a special election. Also, the governor of the state may be given the power by the state legislature to appoint someone temporarily to fill the vacancy.

SECTION 3. LIMITATION ON AMENDMENT
This amendment shall not be so construed as to affect the election or term of any Senator chosen before it becomes valid as part of the Constitution.

AMENDMENT 18. *National Prohibition (1919)*

SECTION 1. PROHIBITIONS ON ALCOHOL
After one year from the ratification of this article the manufacture, sale, or transportation of intoxicating liquors within, the importation thereof into, or the exportation thereof from the United States and all territory subject to the jurisdiction thereof, for beverage purposes is hereby prohibited.

The making, sale, and transportation of alcoholic beverages in the United States are prohibited. (This amendment was repealed by Amendment 21.)

SECTION 2. ENFORCEMENT
The Congress and the several States shall have concurrent power to enforce this article by appropriate legislation.

SECTION 3. LIMITATION ON AMENDMENT
This article shall be inoperative unless it shall have been ratified as an amendment to the Constitution by the Legislatures of the several States as provided in the Constitution within seven years from the date of the submission hereof to the States by the Congress.

AMENDMENT 19. *Women's Suffrage (1920)*

SECTION 1. EXTENSION OF VOTING RIGHTS
The right of citizens of the United States to vote shall not be denied or abridged by the United States or by any State on account of sex.

The right of women to vote is guaranteed nationwide.

SECTION 2. ENFORCEMENT
Congress shall have power to enforce this article by appropriate legislation.

AMENDMENT 20. *"Lame Duck" Amendment* (1933)

SECTION 1. BEGINNING OF TERMS OF OFFICE

The terms of the President and Vice President shall end at noon on the 20th day of January, and the terms of Senators and Representatives at noon on the 3rd day of January, of the years in which such terms would have ended if this article had not been ratified; and the terms of their successors shall then begin.

A defeated candidate who holds office after his or her replacement has been elected has little influence and therefore is called a lame duck. This amendment shortens the time in office of lame ducks. The president and vice president are to take office on January 20 (instead of March 4). Members of Congress are to take office January 3. (Previously, new members of Congress had to wait 13 months before taking their seats.)

Congress is to meet at least once a year.

SECTION 2. BEGINNING OF CONGRESSIONAL SESSIONS

The Congress shall assemble at least once in every year, and such meeting shall begin at noon on the 3rd day of January, unless they shall by law appoint a different day.

SECTION 3. PRESIDENTIAL SUCCESSION

If, at the time fixed for the beginning of the term of the President, the President-elect shall have died, the Vice President-elect shall become President. If a President shall not have been chosen before the time fixed for the beginning of his term, or if the President-elect shall have failed to qualify, then the Vice President-elect shall act as President until a President shall have qualified; and the Congress may by law provide for the case wherein neither a President-elect nor a Vice President-elect shall have qualified, declaring who shall then act as President, or the manner in which one who is to act shall be selected, and such person shall act accordingly until a President or Vice President shall have qualified.

If the president-elect should die before January 20 or fail to qualify, the office of president is to be filled temporarily by the vice president.

SECTION 4. FILLING PRESIDENTIAL VACANCY

The Congress may by law provide for the case of the death of any of the persons from whom the House of Representatives may choose a President whenever the right of choice shall have devolved upon them, and for the case of the death of any of the persons from whom the Senate may choose a Vice President whenever the right of choice shall have devolved upon them.

This amendment gives Congress the power to decide what to do in the event a presidential candidate dies when the election must be decided by the House. Congress may also make a determination in similar cases when a candidate dies and the Senate must elect a vice president.

SECTION 5. EFFECTIVE DATE

Sections 1 and 2 shall take effect on the 15th day of October following the ratification of this article.

SECTION 6. LIMITATION ON AMENDMENT

This article shall be inoperative unless it shall have been ratified as an amendment to the Constitution by the Legislatures of three fourths of the several States within seven years from the date of its submission.

AMENDMENT 21. *National Prohibition Repealed (1933)*

SECTION 1. REPEAL OF AMENDMENT 18
The eighteenth article of amendment to the Constitution of the United States is hereby repealed.

Amendment 18 is repealed.

SECTION 2. STATE CONTROL
The transportation or importation into any State, Territory, or possession of the United States for delivery or use therein of intoxicating liquors, in violation of the laws thereof, is hereby prohibited.

States may prohibit the transportation, sale, and possession of alcoholic beverages.

SECTION 3. LIMITATION ON AMENDMENT
This article shall be inoperative unless it shall have been ratified as an amendment to the Constitution by conventions in the several States, as provided in the Constitution, within seven years from the date of the submission hereof to the States by Congress.

AMENDMENT 22. *Two-Term Limit for Presidents (1951)*

SECTION 1. TERM LIMITS
No person shall be elected to the office of the President more than twice, and no person who has held the office of President, or acted as President, for more than two years of a term to which some other person was elected President, shall be elected to the office of the President more than once. But this article shall not apply to any person holding the office of President when this article was proposed by the Congress, and shall not prevent any person who may be holding the office of President, or acting as President, during the term within which this article becomes operative from holding the office of President, or acting as President, during the remainder of such term.

A president is limited to two full terms in office. If a vice president has already served more than two years as president, this person may be elected president only once.

This amendment did not apply to Harry Truman, who was president when the amendment was proposed.

SECTION 2. LIMITATION ON AMENDMENT
This article shall be inoperative unless it shall have been ratified as an amendment to the Constitution by the Legislatures of three fourths of the several States within seven years from the date of its submission to the States by the Congress.

AMENDMENT 23. *Presidential Electors for District of Columbia (1961)*

SECTION 1. APPOINTING ELECTORS
The District constituting the seat of Government of the United States shall appoint in such manner as Congress may direct: A number of Electors of President and Vice President equal to the whole number of Senators and Representatives in Congress to which the District would be entitled if it were a State, but in no event more than the least populous State; they shall be in addition to those appointed by the States, but they shall be considered, for the purposes of the election of President and Vice President, to be Electors appointed by a State; and they shall meet in the District and perform such duties as provided by the twelfth article of amendment.

Residents of Washington, D.C., are given the right to vote for president and vice president. In effect, this amendment gives the District of Columbia three electoral votes.

SECTION 2. ENFORCEMENT

The Congress shall have power to enforce this article by appropriate legislation.

AMENDMENT 24. *Prohibition of Poll Taxes for National Elections (1964)*

SECTION 1. EXTENSION OF VOTING RIGHTS

The right of citizens of the United States to vote in any primary or other election for President or Vice President, for Electors for President or Vice President, or for Senator or Representative in Congress, shall not be denied or abridged by the United States or any State by reason of failure to pay any poll tax or other tax.

A poll tax may not be a requirement for voting for federal officials. In 1966 the Supreme Court ruled that poll taxes were also illegal as a requirement for voting in state and local elections.

SECTION 2. ENFORCEMENT

The Congress shall have power to enforce this article by appropriate legislation.

AMENDMENT 25. *Presidential Succession (1967)*

SECTION 1. PRESIDENTIAL VACANCY

In case of the removal of the President from office or of his death or resignation, the Vice President shall become President.

If the office of the president becomes vacant due to death or resignation, the vice president becomes president.

SECTION 2. VICE PRESIDENTIAL VACANCY

Whenever there is a vacancy in the office of the Vice President, the President shall nominate a Vice President who shall take office upon confirmation by a majority vote of both houses of Congress.

If the office of vice president becomes vacant, the president may appoint someone to fill this office. The appointment must be approved by a majority vote in both houses of Congress.

SECTION 3. PRESIDENTIAL INABILITY

Whenever the President transmits to the President *pro tempore* of the Senate and the Speaker of the House of Representatives his written declaration that he is unable to discharge the powers and duties of his office, and until he transmits to them a written declaration to the contrary, such powers and duties shall be discharged by the Vice President as Acting President.

If the president believes he or she is unable to carry out the duties of office, the president is to notify Congress in a written message. The vice president takes over as acting president until the president is again able to carry out the duties of office.

SECTION 4. PRESIDENTIAL INABILITY DETERMINED BY CONGRESS

Whenever the Vice President and a majority of either the principal officers of the executive departments, or of such other body as Congress may by law provide, transmit to the President *pro tempore* of the Senate and the Speaker of the House of Representatives their written declaration that the President is unable to discharge the powers and duties of his office, the Vice President shall immediately assume the powers and duties of the office as Acting President.

If the vice president and a majority of the Cabinet members believe that the president is unable to carry out the duties of office, they are to notify Congress in a written message. The vice president then takes over as acting president.

Thereafter, when the President transmits to the President *pro tempore* of the Senate and the Speaker of the House of Representatives his written declaration that no inability exists, he shall resume the powers and duties of his office unless the Vice President and a majority of either the principal officers of the executive departments, or of such other body as Congress may by law provide, transmit within four days to the President *pro tempore* of the Senate and the Speaker of the House of Representatives their written declaration that the President is unable to discharge the powers and duties of his office. Thereupon Congress shall decide the issue, assembling within 48 hours for that purpose if not in session. If the Congress, within 21 days after receipt of the latter written declaration, or, if Congress is not in session, within 21 days after Congress is required to assemble, determines by two-thirds vote of both houses that the President is unable to discharge the powers and duties of his office, the Vice President shall continue to discharge the same as Acting President; otherwise, the President shall resume the powers and duties of his office.

When the president feels ready to carry out the duties again, the president may notify Congress. If the vice president and a majority of the Cabinet members do not agree, then Congress must decide who is president by a two-thirds vote within 21 days.

AMENDMENT 26. *Voting Age Lowered to 18* *(1971)*

SECTION 1. EXTENSION OF VOTING RIGHTS
The right of citizens of the United States, who are 18 years of age or older, to vote shall not be denied or abridged by the United States or by any state on account of age.

The minimum voting age is lowered to 18 in all federal, state, and local elections.

SECTION 2. ENFORCEMENT
The Congress shall have the power to enforce this article by appropriate legislation.

AMENDMENT 27. *Congressional Pay Raises* *(1992)*

No law, varying the compensation for the services of the Senators and Representatives, shall take effect until an election of Representatives shall have intervened.

Any increase in congressional pay does not go into effect until after the next regular election of the House of Representatives.

THOMAS JEFFERSON'S FIRST INAUGURAL ADDRESS

Thomas Jefferson, a Republican, won the presidency in the election of 1800, defeating the Federalist candidate. Jefferson's inauguration marked the first time that the power to govern passed peacefully from one political party to another.

Jefferson's Inaugural Address is one of the great speeches of all time. In it he reassures his Federalist opponents of his respect for their rights and views. He also advocates the ideals of limited government and representative democracy.

MARCH 4, 1801

Friends and Fellow Citizens: . . .

All . . . will bear in mind this sacred principle, that though the will of the majority is in all cases to prevail, that will to be rightful must be reasonable; that the minority possess their equal rights, which equal law must protect, and to violate would be oppression. Let us, then, fellow citizens, unite with one heart and one mind. . . . And let us reflect that, having banished from our land that religious intolerance under which mankind so long bled and suffered, we have yet gained little if we countenance [allow] a political intolerance as despotic, as wicked, and capable of as bitter and bloody persecutions. . . . But every difference of opinion is not a difference of principle. We have called by different names brethren of the same principle. We are all Republicans; we are all Federalists. If there be any among us who would wish to dissolve this Union or to change its republican form, let them stand undisturbed as monuments of the safety with which error of opinion may be tolerated where reason is left free to combat it. . . .

Let us, then, with courage and confidence pursue our own Federal and Republican principles, our attachment to union and representative government. . . .

Relying, then, on the patronage of your good will, I advance with obedience to the work, ready to retire from it whenever you become sensible how much better choice it is in your power to make. And may that Infinite Power which rules the destinies of the universe lead our councils to what is best, and give them a favorable issue for your peace and prosperity.

THE MONROE DOCTRINE

The Monroe Doctrine is not a law passed by Congress. It is a statement of foreign policy made by President James Monroe in a State of the Union Address to Congress. The Monroe Doctrine is one of the most important documents in the nation's history. It has influenced U.S. foreign policy to the present time. The Monroe Doctrine asserts the nation's dedication to freedom. It warns foreign nations that the Americas—North, South, and Central—are closed to colonization.

DECEMBER 2, 1823

. . . [It is] a principle in which the rights and interests of the United States are involved, that the American continents, by the free and independent condition which they have assumed and maintain, are henceforth not to be considered as subjects for future colonization by any European powers. . . .

. . . We owe it, therefore, to candor and to the amicable [friendly] relations existing between the United States and those powers to declare that we should consider any attempt on their part to extend their system to any portion of this hemisphere as dangerous to our peace and safety. With the existing colonies or dependencies of any European power, we have not interfered and shall not interfere. But with the governments who have declared their independence and maintained it, and whose independence we have, on great consideration and on just principles, acknowledged, we could not view any interposition [interference] for the purpose of oppressing them, or controlling in any other manner their destiny, by any European power in any other light than as the manifestation [evidence] of an unfriendly disposition toward the United States.

THE SENECA FALLS DECLARATION

The first women's rights convention in the United States met in 1848 in Seneca Falls, New York. At that convention, the delegates adopted a series of resolutions stating their belief in the equality of men and women. The document appeals to the principles of freedom and equality set forth in the Declaration of Independence. The Seneca Falls Declaration states the delegates' determination to strive for legal recognition in the United States of women's equality with men.

JULY 19, 1848

When, in the course of human events, it becomes necessary for one portion of the family of man to assume among the people of the earth a position different from that which they have hitherto occupied, but one to which the laws of nature and of nature's God entitle them, a decent respect to the opinions of mankind requires that they should declare the causes that impel them to such a course.

We hold these truths to be self-evident: that all men and women are created equal; that they are endowed by their Creator with certain inalienable rights; that among these are life, liberty, and the pursuit of happiness; that to secure these rights governments are instituted, deriving their just powers from the consent of the governed. . . .

RESOLUTIONS

Resolved, That all laws which prevent woman from occupying such a station in society as her conscience shall dictate, or which place her in a position inferior to that of man, are contrary to the great precept of nature, and, therefore, of no force or authority.

Resolved, That woman is man's equal—was intended to be so by the Creator, and the highest good of the race demands that she should be recognized as such. . . .

Resolved, That it is the duty of the women of this country to secure to themselves their sacred right to the elective franchise [the vote]. . . .

Resolved, That the equality of human rights results necessarily from the fact of the identity [sameness of essential character] of the race in capabilities and responsibilities.

THE EMANCIPATION PROCLAMATION

President Abraham Lincoln wrote the Emancipation Proclamation in September 1862 but did not officially issue it until January 1, 1863. Before the Proclamation, the Civil War was fought mainly to save the Union. After that time, the war also became a crusade to end slavery. Many historians believe the Proclamation greatly helped the Union cause. The Proclamation's commitment to freedom remains a source of inspiration for Americans to the present day.

JANUARY 1, 1863

Whereas on the twenty-second day of September, A.D. 1862, a proclamation was issued by the President of the United States, containing, among other things, the following, to wit:

"That on the first day of January, A.D. 1863, all persons held as slaves within any state or designated part of a state, the people whereof shall then be in rebellion against the United States, shall be then, thenceforward, and forever free; and the executive government of the United States, including the military and naval authority thereof, will recognize and maintain the freedom of such persons and will do no act or acts to repress such persons or any of them, in any efforts they may make for their actual freedom.

"That the Executive will on the first day of January aforesaid, by proclamation, designate the states and parts of states, if any, in which the people thereof, respectively, shall then be in rebellion against the United States; and the fact that any state or the people thereof shall on that day be in good faith represented in the Congress of the United States by members chosen thereto at elections wherein a majority of the qualified voters of such states shall have participated shall, in the absence of strong countervailing [opposing] testimony, be deemed conclusive evidence that such state and the people thereof are not then in rebellion against the United States."

THE GETTYSBURG ADDRESS

In November 1863 President Abraham Lincoln dedicated the national cemetery at Gettysburg, Pennsylvania. Just four months earlier, Gettysburg had been the scene of one of the bloodiest battles of the Civil War. Lincoln's brief speech, *The Gettysburg Address,* has inspired generations of Americans. It reaffirms Americans' dedication to liberty and to the equality of all, and it continues to inspire citizens today.

NOVEMBER 19, 1863

Fourscore and seven years ago our fathers brought forth on this continent a new nation, conceived in liberty, and dedicated to the proposition that all men are created equal.

Now we are engaged in a great civil war, testing whether that nation, or any nation so conceived and so dedicated, can long endure. We are met on a great battlefield of that war. We have come to dedicate a portion of that field as a final resting place for those who here gave their lives that that nation might live. It is altogether fitting and proper that we should do this.

But, in a larger sense, we cannot dedicate—we cannot consecrate—we cannot hallow—this ground. The brave men, living and dead, who struggled here, have consecrated it far above our poor power to add or detract. The world will little note nor long remember what we say here, but it can never forget what they did here. It is for us, the living, rather, to be dedicated here to the unfinished work which they who fought here have thus far so nobly advanced. It is rather for us to be here dedicated to the great task remaining before us—that from these honored dead we take increased devotion to that cause for which they gave the last full measure of devotion; that we here highly resolve that these dead shall not have died in vain; that this nation, under God, shall have a new birth of freedom; and that government of the people, by the people, for the people, shall not perish from the earth.

THE AMERICAN'S CREED

The American's Creed was written during World War I by William Tyler Page, who was the clerk of the House of Representatives. It includes phrases from the Constitution of the United States, the Declaration of Independence, and several famous speeches. The American's Creed was adopted by the House of Representatives in 1918 as the "best summary of the political faith of America." The American's Creed states principles that all American citizens cherish.

1918

I believe in the United States of America as a government of the people, by
    the people, for the people;
whose just powers are derived from the consent of the governed;
a democracy in a Republic;
a sovereign Nation of many sovereign States;
a perfect Union, one and inseparable;
established upon those principles of freedom, equality, justice, and humanity
    for which American patriots sacrificed their lives and fortunes.

I therefore believe it is my duty to my country to love it;
to support its Constitution;
to obey its laws;
to respect its flag;
and to defend it against all enemies.

FRANKLIN D. ROOSEVELT'S FOUR FREEDOMS

President Franklin D. Roosevelt gave a State of the Union Address before Congress in January 1941. In his address Roosevelt warned the nation about the war that was raging around the world (World War II). President Roosevelt also stated four freedoms to which the United States was firmly committed. These four freedoms inspired Americans during World War II, and the four freedoms remain at the heart of the nation's policies, both foreign and domestic.

JANUARY 6, 1941

I address you, the members of the Seventy-seventh Congress, at a moment unprecedented in the history of the Union. I use the word "unprecedented," because at no previous time has American security been as seriously threatened from without as it is today. . . .

Every realist knows that the democratic way of life is at this moment being directly assailed in every part of the world—assailed either by arms, or by . . . propaganda. . . .

In the future days, which we seek to make secure, we look forward to a world founded upon four essential human freedoms.

The first is freedom of speech and expression—everywhere in the world.

The second is freedom of every person to worship God in his own way—everywhere in the world.

The third is freedom from want—which, translated into world terms, means economic understandings which will secure to every nation a healthy peacetime life for its inhabitants—everywhere in the world.

The fourth is freedom from fear—which, translated into world terms, means a world-wide reduction of armaments to such a point and in such a thorough fashion that no nation will be in a position to commit an act of physical aggression against any neighbor—anywhere in the world. . . .

This nation has placed its destiny in the hands and heads and hearts of its millions of free men and women; and its faith in freedom under the guidance of God. Freedom means the supremacy of human rights everywhere. Our support goes to those who struggle to gain those rights or keep them. Our strength is in our unity of purpose.

To that high concept there can be no end save victory.

BROWN V. BOARD OF EDUCATION OF TOPEKA

Brown v. Board of Education of Topeka is a landmark decision in the struggle for equal rights. In this decision the Supreme Court struck down segregation in the public schools. In doing so, the Court overturned the "separate but equal" doctrine established in the case of *Plessy v. Ferguson.* The Court's decision in *Brown* inspired Americans to continue the struggle for equality, and it has helped make the United States a nation where all men and women are equal.

MAY 17, 1954

[In this case,] segregation was alleged to deprive the plaintiffs of the equal protection of the laws under the Fourteenth Amendment. . . .

The plaintiffs contend that segregated public schools are not "equal" and cannot be made "equal," and that hence they are deprived of the equal protection of the law. . . .

In approaching this problem, we cannot turn the clock back to 1868 when the [Fourteenth] Amendment was adopted, or even to 1896 when *Plessy v. Ferguson* was written. We must consider public education in the light of its full development and its present place in American life throughout the Nation. . . .

We come then to the question presented: Does segregation of children in public schools solely on the basis of race, even though the physical facilities and other "tangible" factors may be equal, deprive the children of the minority group of equal educational opportunities? We believe that it does. . . .

We conclude that in the field of public education the doctrine of "separate but equal" has no place. Separate educational facilities are inherently unequal. Therefore, we hold that the plaintiffs . . . are, by reason of the segregation complained of, deprived of the equal protection of the laws guaranteed by the Fourteenth Amendment.

JOHN F. KENNEDY'S INAUGURAL ADDRESS

John F. Kennedy, at age 43, was the youngest person ever elected president in the nation's history. His Inaugural Address is one of the greatest speeches ever delivered. In it President Kennedy challenges Americans to join together in a "struggle against poverty, disease, and war itself." Kennedy's address inspired "a new generation of Americans." It continues to inspire citizens today as Americans reach for the goals set forth by President Kennedy.

JANUARY 20, 1961

My Fellow Citizens:

We observe today not a victory of party but a celebration of freedom—symbolizing an end as well as a beginning—signifying renewal as well as change. For I have sworn before you and Almighty God the same solemn oath our forebears prescribed nearly a century and three-quarters ago. . . .

We dare not forget today that we are the heirs of that first revolution. Let the word go forth from this time and place, to friend and foe alike, that the torch has been passed to a new generation of Americans—born in this century, tempered by war, disciplined by a hard and bitter peace, proud of our ancient heritage—and unwilling to witness or permit the slow undoing of those human rights to which this nation has always been committed, and to which we are committed today at home and around the world.

Let every nation know, whether it wishes us well or ill, that we shall pay any price, bear any burden, meet any hardship, support any friend, oppose any foe to assure the survival and the success of liberty. This much we pledge—and more. . . .

And so, my fellow Americans: Ask not what your country can do for you—ask what you can do for your country.

My fellow citizens of the world: Ask not what America will do for you, but what together we can do for the freedom of man.

Finally, whether you are citizens of America or citizens of the world, ask of us here the same high standards of strength and sacrifice which we ask of you. With a good conscience our only sure reward, with history the final judge of our deeds, let us go forth.

I Have a Dream

Martin Luther King, Jr., symbolizes the dream of equality for all Americans. In 1963 Dr. King addressed more than 200,000 Americans at the March on Washington, the largest rally for racial equality in the nation's history. Dr. King's speech, made to the huge crowd assembled before the Lincoln Memorial, sets forth his dream of a nation where all Americans are truly equal and free.

AUGUST 28, 1963

I say to you today, my friends, that in spite of the difficulties and frustrations of the moment I still have a dream. It is a dream deeply rooted in the American Dream.

I have a dream that one day this nation will rise up and live out the true meaning of its creed: "We hold these truths to be self-evident: that all men are created equal. . . ."

I have a dream that my four little children will one day live in a nation where they will not be judged by the color of their skin but by the content of their character. . . .

I have a dream today.

This is our hope. This is the faith with which I return to the South. With this faith we will be able to cut out of the mountain of despair a stone of hope. With this faith we will be able to change the jangling discords of our nation into a beautiful symphony of brotherhood. With this faith we will be able to work together, to pray together, to struggle together, to go to jail together, to stand up for freedom together, knowing that we will be free one day.

This will be the day when all of God's children will be able to sing with new meaning "My country 'tis of thee, sweet land of liberty, of thee I sing. Land where my fathers died, land of the pilgrim's pride, from every mountainside, let freedom ring. . . ."

When we let freedom ring, when we let it ring from every village and every hamlet, from every state and every city, we will be able to speed up that day when all of God's children, black people and white people, Jews, Protestants, and Catholics, will be able to join hands and sing in the words of the old Negro spiritual, "Free at last! Free at last, thank God almighty we are free at last!"

THE CIVIL RIGHTS ACT
OF 1964

The Civil Rights Act of 1964 is landmark legislation. The act prohibits discrimination on the basis of race, color, religion, or national origin. Under the terms of this act, discrimination is outlawed in the exercise of voting rights, and in public places, public education, and employment practices. This act supported the principles set forth in the Fourteenth and Fifteenth Amendments and helped the nation toward the goal of achieving equality for all Americans.

JULY 2, 1964

VOTING RIGHTS

No person acting under color of law shall—

in determining whether any individual is qualified under State law or laws to vote in any Federal election, apply any standard, practice, or procedure different from the standards, practices, or procedures applied under such law or laws to other individuals within the same county, parish, or similar political subdivision who have been found by State officials to be qualified to vote. . . .

DISCRIMINATION IN PLACES OF PUBLIC ACCOMMODATION

All persons shall be entitled to the full and equal enjoyment of the goods, services, facilities, privileges, advantages, and accommodations of any place of public accommodation, as defined in this section, without discrimination or segregation on the ground of race, color, religion, or national origin. . . .

EQUAL EMPLOYMENT OPPORTUNITY

It shall be an unlawful employment practice for an employer—

to fail or refuse to hire or to discharge any individual, or otherwise to discriminate against any individual with respect to his compensation, terms, conditions, or privileges of employment, because of such individual's race, color, religion, sex, or national origin; or

to limit, segregate, or classify his employees in any way . . . because of such individual's race, color, religion, sex, or national origin.

THE VOTING RIGHTS ACT
OF 1965

The Voting Rights Act of 1965 strengthened the Civil Rights Act of 1964. The Voting Rights Act extends the prohibition of voting discrimination to federal, state, and local elections. It also outlaws the use of literacy tests as a way of preventing people from voting. This act increased the number of people who were eligible to vote, thus making the United States a more democratic nation. Extensions of this act ensure that its guarantees remain in effect.

MAY 26, 1965

To assure that the right of citizens of the United States to vote is not denied or abridged on account of race or color, no citizen shall be denied the right to vote in any Federal, State, or local election because of his failure to comply with any test or device in any State. . . .

The phrase "test or device" shall mean any requirement that a person as a prerequisite for voting or registration for voting (1) demonstrate the ability to read, write, understand, or interpret any matter, (2) demonstrate any educational achievement or his knowledge of any particular subject, (3) possess good moral character, or (4) prove his qualifications by the voucher of registered voters or members of any other class. . . .

Section 12. (a) Whoever shall deprive or attempt to deprive any person of any right . . . shall be fined not more than $5,000, or imprisoned not more than five years, or both.

AMERICAN PRESIDENTS

1
George Washington
1732–1799
Elected from: Virginia
In office: 1789–1797

2
John Adams
1735–1826
Elected from: Massachusetts
Federalist
In office: 1797–1801

3
Thomas Jefferson
1743–1826
Elected from: Virginia
Democratic-Republican
In office: 1800–1809

4
James Madison
1750–1836
Elected from: Virginia
Democratic-Republican
In office: 1809–1817

5
James Monroe
1758–1831
Elected from: Virginia
Democratic-Republican
In office: 1817–1825

6
John Quincy Adams
1767–1848
Elected from: Massachusetts
Democratic-Republican
In office: 1825–1829

7
Andrew Jackson
1767–1845
Elected from: Tennessee
Democrat
In office: 1829–1837

8
Martin Van Buren
1782–1862
Elected from: New York
Democrat
In office: 1837–1841

9
William Henry Harrison
1773–1841
Elected from: Ohio
Whig
In office: 1841

10
John Tyler
1790–1862
Elected from: Virginia
Whig
In office: 1840–1845

11
James K. Polk
1795–1849
Elected from: Tennessee
Democrat
In office: 1845–1849

17
Andrew Johnson
1808–1875
Elected from: Tennessee
Republican
In office: 1865–1869

12
Zachary Taylor
1784–1850
Elected from: Louisiana
Whig
In office: 1849–1850

18
Ulysses S. Grant
1822–1885
Elected from: Illinois
Republican
In office: 1869–1877

13
Millard Fillmore
1800–1874
Elected from: New York
Whig
In office: 1850–1853

19
Rutherford B. Hayes
1822–1893
Elected from: Ohio
Republican
In office: 1877–1881

14
Franklin Pierce
1804–1869
Elected from: New Hampshire
Democrat
In office: 1853–1857

20
James A. Garfield
1831–1881
Elected from: Ohio
Republican
In office: 1881

15
James Buchanan
1791–1868
Elected from: Pennsylvania
Democrat
In office: 1857–1861

21
Chester A. Arthur
1831–1886
Elected from: New York
Republican
In office: 1880–1885

16
Abraham Lincoln
1809–1865
Elected from: Illinois
Republican
In office: 1860–1865

22
Grover Cleveland
1837–1908
Elected from: New York
Democrat
In office: 1885–1889

23
Benjamin Harrison
1833–1901
Elected from: Indiana
Republican
In office: 1889–1893

29
Warren G. Harding
1865–1923
Elected from: Ohio
Republican
In office: 1920–1923

24
Grover Cleveland
1837–1908
Elected from: New York
Democrat
In office: 1893–1897

30
Calvin Coolidge
1872–1933
Elected from: Massachusetts
Republican
In office: 1923–1929

25
William McKinley
1843–1901
Elected from: Ohio
Republican
In office: 1897–1901

31
Herbert C. Hoover
1874–1964
Elected from: California
Republican
In office: 1929–1933

26
Theodore Roosevelt
1858–1919
Elected from: New York
Republican
In office: 1900–1909

32
**Franklin D.
Roosevelt**
1882–1945
Elected from: New York
Democrat
In office: 1933–1945

27
William H. Taft
1857–1930
Elected from: Ohio
Republican
In office: 1909–1913

33
Harry S. Truman
1884–1972
Elected from: Missouri
Democrat
In office: 1945–1953

28
Woodrow Wilson
1856–1924
Elected from: New Jersey
Democrat
In office: 1913–1921

34
**Dwight D.
Eisenhower**
1890–1969
Elected from: Pennsylvania
Republican
In office: 1953–1961

35
John F. Kennedy
1917–1963
Elected from:
Massachusetts
Democrat
In office: 1960–1963

36
Lyndon B. Johnson
1908–1973
Elected from: Texas
Democrat
In office: 1963–1969

37
Richard M. Nixon
1913–1994
Elected from: California
Republican
In office: 1969–1974

38
Gerald R. Ford
1913–
Elected from: Michigan
Republican
In office: 1974–1977

39
Jimmy Carter
1924–
Elected from: Georgia
Democrat
In office: 1977–1981

40
Ronald W. Reagan
1911–
Elected from: California
Republican
In office: 1980–1989

41
George Bush
1924–
Elected from: Texas
Republican
In office: 1989–1993

42
William Clinton
1946–
Elected from: Arkansas
Democrat
In office: 1993–

THE 50 STATES

The number in parentheses is the order in which each state was admitted to the Union. For the original 13 states, this is the order in which each state approved the Constitution. Population figures are taken from the U.S. Bureau of the Census. The nickname of each state is listed in *italics*.

Alabama (22)
Admitted to Union: 1819
Capital: Montgomery
Population: 4,219,000
Yellowhammer State

Colorado (38)
Admitted to Union: 1876
Capital: Denver
Population: 3,656,000
Centennial State

Alaska (49)
Admitted to Union: 1959
Capital: Juneau
Population: 606,278
The Last Frontier

Connecticut (5)
Admitted to Union: 1788
Capital: Hartford
Population: 3,275,000
Nutmeg State

Arizona (48)
Admitted to Union: 1912
Capital: Phoenix
Population: 4,071,650
Grand Canyon State

Delaware (1)
Admitted to Union: 1787
Capital: Dover
Population: 706,000
First State

Arkansas (25)
Admitted to Union: 1836
Capital: Little Rock
Population: 2,453,000
Land of Opportunity

Florida (27)
Admitted to Union: 1845
Capital: Tallahassee
Population: 13,953,000
Sunshine State

California (31)
Admitted to Union: 1850
Capital: Sacramento
Population: 31,431,000
Golden State

Georgia (4)
Admitted to Union: 1788
Capital: Atlanta
Population: 7,055,000
Peach State

Hawaii (50)
Admitted to Union: 1959
Capital: Honolulu
Population: 1,178,564
Aloha State

Idaho (43)
Admitted to Union: 1890
Capital: Boise
Population: 1,133,034
Gem State

Illinois (21)
Admitted to Union: 1818
Capital: Springfield
Population: 11,752,000
Prairie State

Indiana (19)
Admitted to Union: 1816
Capital: Indianapolis
Population: 5,752,000
Hoosier State

Iowa (29)
Admitted to Union: 1846
Capital: Des Moines
Population: 2,829,000
Hawkeye State

Kansas (34)
Admitted to Union: 1861
Capital: Topeka
Population: 2,554,000
Sunflower State

Kentucky (15)
Admitted to Union: 1792
Capital: Frankfort
Population: 3,827,000
Bluegrass State

Louisiana (18)
Admitted to Union: 1812
Capital: Baton Rouge
Population: 4,315,000
Pelican State

Maine (23)
Admitted to Union: 1820
Capital: Augusta
Population: 1,240,000
Pine Tree State

Maryland (7)
Admitted to Union: 1788
Capital: Annapolis
Population: 5,006,000
Free State

Massachusetts (6)
Admitted to Union: 1788
Capital: Boston
Population: 6,041,000
Bay State

Michigan (26)
Admitted to Union: 1837
Capital: Lansing
Population: 9,496,000
Wolverine State

Minnesota (32)
Admitted to Union: 1858
Capital: St. Paul
Population: 4,567,000
North Star State

Mississippi (20)
Admitted to Union: 1817
Capital: Jackson
Population: 2,669,000
Magnolia State

Missouri (24)
Admitted to Union: 1821
Capital: Jefferson City
Population: 5,278,000
Show-me State

New York (11)
Admitted to Union: 1788
Capital: Albany
Population: 18,169,000
Empire State

Montana (41)
Admitted to Union: 1889
Capital: Helena
Population: 856,000
Treasure State

North Carolina (12)
Admitted to Union: 1789
Capital: Raleigh
Population: 7,070,000
Tar Heel State

Nebraska (37)
Admitted to Union: 1867
Capital: Lincoln
Population: 1,623,000
Cornhusker State

North Dakota (39)
Admitted to Union: 1889
Capital: Bismarck
Population: 638,000
Peace Garden State

Nevada (36)
Admitted to Union: 1864
Capital: Carson City
Population: 1,457,000
Sagebrush State

Ohio (17)
Admitted to Union: 1803
Capital: Columbus
Population: 11,102,198
Buckeye State

New Hampshire (9)
Admitted to Union: 1788
Capital: Concord
Population: 1,137,000
Granite State

Oklahoma (46)
Admitted to Union: 1907
Capital: Oklahoma City
Population: 3,258,000
Sooner State

New Jersey (3)
Admitted to Union: 1787
Capital: Trenton
Population: 7,904,000
Garden State

Oregon (33)
Admitted to Union: 1859
Capital: Salem
Population: 3,086,000
Beaver State

New Mexico (47)
Admitted to Union: 1912
Capital: Santa Fe
Population: 1,654,000
Land of Enchantment

Pennsylvania (2)
Admitted to Union: 1787
Capital: Harrisburg
Population: 12,052,000
Keystone State

Rhode Island (13)
Admitted to Union: 1790
Capital: Providence
Population: 997,000
Ocean State

Vermont (14)
Admitted to Union: 1791
Capital: Montpelier
Population: 580,000
Green Mountain State

South Carolina (8)
Admitted to Union: 1788
Capital: Columbia
Population: 3,664,000
Palmetto State

Virginia (10)
Admitted to Union: 1788
Capital: Richmond
Population: 6,552,000
Old Dominion

South Dakota (40)
Admitted to Union: 1889
Capital: Pierre
Population: 721,000
Coyote State

Washington (42)
Admitted to Union: 1889
Capital: Olympia
Population: 5,343,000
Evergreen State

Tennessee (16)
Admitted to Union: 1796
Capital: Nashville
Population: 5,175,000
Volunteer State

West Virginia (35)
Admitted to Union: 1863
Capital: Charleston
Population: 1,822,000
Mountain State

Texas (28)
Admitted to Union: 1845
Capital: Austin
Population: 18,418,300
Lone Star State

Wisconsin (30)
Admitted to Union: 1848
Capital: Madison
Population: 5,082,000
Badger State

Utah (45)
Admitted to Union: 1896
Capital: Salt Lake City
Population: 1,908,000
Beehive State

Wyoming (44)
Admitted to Union: 1890
Capital: Cheyenne
Population: 474,970
Equality State

THE AMERICAN FLAG

The American flag is a symbol of the nation. It is recognized instantly, whether it is a big banner waving in the wind or a tiny emblem worn on a lapel. The flag is so important that it is a major theme of the national anthem, "The Star-Spangled Banner." One of the most popular names for the flag is the "Stars and Stripes." It is also known as "Old Glory."

The Meaning of the Flag

The American flag has 13 stripes—7 red and 6 white. In the upper-left corner of the flag is the Union—50 white stars against a blue background.

The 13 stripes stand for the original 13 American states, and the 50 stars represent the states of the nation today. According to the U.S. Department of State, the colors of the flag also are symbolic:

> Red stands for courage.
> White symbolizes purity.
> Blue is the color of vigilance, perseverance, and justice.

Early American Flags

Before the United States declared its independence in 1776, the colonies used many different flags. A favorite colonial design of the southern colonies was a flag with a rattlesnake and the motto, "Don't Tread on Me." Another colonial symbol was the pine tree, which symbolized the strength and courage of New England.

The first flag to represent all the colonies was called the "Continental

Colors." It has 13 alternating red and white stripes and the British flag at the upper left (showing that the colonies belonged to Great Britain).

Adopting the Stars and Stripes

After the Declaration of Independence was adopted, the Continental Congress no longer wanted the British flag to be part of the American flag. On June 14, 1777, the Congress decided that the flag of the United States should have 13 red and white stripes and 13 stars "representing a new constellation."

According to legend, a Philadelphia seamstress named Betsy Ross helped design this American flag and made the first one. The story is probably not true, although she did design and make other flags.

After Vermont and Kentucky joined the Union in the 1790s, two additional stars and stripes were added to the flag.

As you can imagine, adding a stripe for every new state would have created problems. Therefore in 1818 Congress ruled that the number of stripes should remain at 13, with a star added for each new state.

Displaying the Flag

The American flag should not be displayed in bad weather. It should be displayed outdoors only from sunrise to sunset, except on certain occasions. In a few special places, however, the flag is always allowed to be flown day and night. When flown at night, the flag must be spotlighted.

Near a speaker's platform, the flag should occupy the place of honor at the speaker's right. When carried in a parade with other flags, the American flag should be on the marching right or in front at the center. When flying with the flags of the 50 states, the national flag must be at the center and the highest point. In a group of national flags, all should be of equal size and all should be flown from staffs, or flag poles, of equal height.

The flag should never touch the ground, the floor, or water. It should not be marked with any insignia, pictures, or words. Nor should it be used in any disrespectful way—as an advertising decoration, for instance. The flag should never be dipped to honor any person or thing.

Saluting the Flag

The United States, like other countries, has a flag code, or rules for displaying and honoring the flag. For example, all those present should stand at attention facing the flag and salute it when it is being raised or lowered or when it is carried past them in a parade or other procession. A man wearing a hat should take it off and hold it with his right hand over his heart. All women and hatless men should stand with their right hands over their hearts to show their respect.

The flag over the Capitol

Special Occasions

When the flag is flown upside down, with the stars at the bottom, it is a signal of distress. Flown at half-mast, it is a symbol of mourning. For example, when a president or other important official dies, flags around the country fly at half-mast. The flag also may be draped over the casket of a person who has served in the U.S. armed forces. After the funeral, this flag is folded and given to a family member.

One of the best-known occasions for displaying the American flag was the first landing of Americans on the moon in July 1969. The astronauts placed a metal flag there because the moon has no atmosphere, and thus no wind.

The flag on the moon

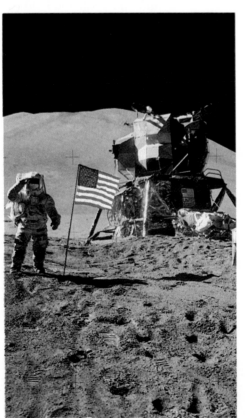

As far as we know, the American flag is still there.

The Pledge of Allegiance

The Pledge of Allegiance was written in 1892 by a Massachusetts magazine editor named Francis Bellamy. (The words "under God" were added in 1954.) These are the words:

> I pledge allegiance to the Flag of the United States of America and to the Republic for which it stands, one Nation under God, indivisible, with liberty and justice for all.

Civilians should say the Pledge of Allegiance with their right hands on their hearts. People in the armed forces give the military salute. By saying the Pledge of Allegiance, we promise loyalty ("pledge allegiance") to the United States and its ideals.

"The Star-Spangled Banner"

"The Star-Spangled Banner" is the national anthem of the United States. It was written by Francis Scott Key during the War of 1812. While being held aboard a British ship on September 13, 1814, Key watched the bombardment of the U.S. Fort McHenry at Baltimore. The attack lasted 25 hours. The smoke was so thick that Key could not tell who had won. When the air cleared, Key saw the American flag that was still flying over the fort.

To express his joy, Key wrote most of the words of the song in a few minutes on the back of an envelope. "The Star-Spangled Banner" is sung to music written by John Stafford Smith. In 1931 Congress adopted "The Star-Spangled Banner" as the national anthem.

The Star-Spangled Banner

I

Oh, say can you see by the dawn's
    early light
What so proudly we hail'd at the twi-
    light's last gleaming?
Whose broad stripes and bright stars
    through the perilous fight,
O'er the ramparts we watched were so
    gallantly streaming?
And the rockets' red glare, the bombs
    bursting in air,
Gave proof through the night that our
    flag was still there.
Oh, say does that star-spangled banner
    yet wave
O'er the land of the free and the home
    of the brave?

II

On the shore, dimly seen through the
    mists of the deep,
Where the foe's haughty host in dread
    silence reposes,
What is that which the breeze, o'er the
    towering steep,
As it fitfully blows, half conceals, half
    discloses?
Now it catches the gleam of the morn-
    ing's first beam,
In full glory reflected now shines in
    the stream:
'Tis the star-spangled banner! Oh, long
    may it wave
O'er the land of the free and the home
    of the brave!

III

And where is that band who so vaunt-
    ingly swore
That the havoc of war and the battle's
    confusion,
A home and a country should leave us
    no more!
Their blood has washed out their foul
    footstep's pollution.
No refuge could save the hireling and
    slave
From terror of flight, or the gloom of
    the grave:
And the star-spangled banner in tri-
    umph doth wave
O'er the land of the free and the home
    of the brave!

IV

Oh! thus be it ever, when freemen
    shall stand
Between their loved home and the
    war's desolation!
Blest with victory and peace, may the
    heaven rescued land
Praise the Power that hath made and
    preserved us a nation.
Then conquer we must, when our
    cause it is just,
And this be our motto: "In God is our
    trust."
And the star-spangled banner in tri-
    umph shall wave
O'er the land of the free and the home
    of the brave!

AMERICAN HOLIDAYS

Holidays are special occasions usually marked by celebrations and vacations from school and work. Religious holidays are celebrated by people of various faiths. For example, Christians celebrate Christmas (marking the birth of Jesus), and Jews celebrate Rosh Hashanah (marking the beginning of the Jewish New Year). On legal holidays, banks, schools, and most government and business offices are closed.

National holidays usually commemorate, or remind people of, a special event in a nation's past. Strictly speaking, the United States has no official national holidays. It is up to the states, not the federal government, to determine which days will be celebrated. The federal government, however, influences these by designating the days to be observed in Washington, D.C., and by all federal employees. Along with New Year's Day (January 1) and Christmas (December 25), the following eight legal holidays are observed throughout the United States.

Martin Luther King's Birthday

(third Monday in January)

An act of Congress established the newest federal holiday—the birthday of Martin Luther King, Jr. Dr. King helped begin the civil rights movement in the 1950s, working to end discrimination against African Americans. He led many peaceful protest marches and demonstrations in cities across the United States. Largely because of Dr. King's efforts, Congress passed the Civil Rights Act of 1964.

Dr. King's brilliant career was cut short when he was assassinated on April 4, 1968. After Dr. King's death, many people called for a national holiday to recognize his efforts. The holiday became official in 1986.

President's Day

(third Monday in February)

President's Day is a combined observance of George Washington's birthday and Abraham Lincoln's birthday. Although this holiday is widely recognized throughout the United States, some states observe the two presidents' birthdays as separate holidays.

February 22 is the day celebrated as George Washington's birthday. Washington was actually born, however, on February 11 according to the calendar in use in 1732, the year of his birth. In the 1970s the celebration of his birthday was changed to the third Monday in February.

Abraham Lincoln was born on February 12, 1809. Lincoln's birthday first became a federal holiday in 1892.

Memorial Day

(last Monday in May)

Originally, Memorial Day honored the soldiers who died in the Civil War. Today the holiday honors all those Americans who died in all the wars in which the United States has fought. Memorial Day, sometimes called Decoration Day, was first celebrated on May 30. Some states celebrate the holiday on the traditional day.

Independence Day

(July 4)

Fireworks, parades, and picnics mark this holiday, regarded as the birthday of the country. It commemorates the day in 1776 when the Continental Congress adopted the Declaration of Independence.

Even then, John Adams, one of the leaders in the struggle for American independence, said of the day: "I am apt to believe that it will be celebrated by succeeding generations as the great anniversary festival." Time has proved John Adams to be right about Independence Day celebrations.

Labor Day

(first Monday in September)

A union leader, Peter J. McGuire, first suggested a holiday to honor working people across the nation. Various states observed the day in the 1880s. Labor Day has been celebrated as a federal holiday since 1894.

Labor Day is marked with parades and speeches honoring workers. It also has come to mean the end of summer and often is celebrated with a last day at the beach, a picnic or cookout, or community festivities.

Columbus Day

(second Monday in October)

On October 12, 1492, Christopher Columbus first reached the Americas. Today we honor Columbus's first voyage to the Americas on the second Monday in October.

Parades and special banquets mark this holiday. The first Columbus Day was celebrated in New York City, New York, in 1792—the 300th anniversary of Columbus's voyage. Columbus Day

has been celebrated as a federal holiday in the United States since 1920.

Veterans Day

(November 11)

This holiday is unusual because it is also a special day in many European nations. Formerly called Armistice Day, it originally marked the truce, or armistice, that ended World War I on November 11, 1918.

In 1954 the United States changed the observance of this holiday to honor all the men and women who have served in the U.S. armed forces. Military parades are common on Veterans Day. Reenactments of famous battles sometimes are held. Special services are also held at the Tomb of the Unknown Soldier in Arlington National Cemetery, near the nation's capital, Washington, D.C.

Thanksgiving Day

(fourth Thursday in November)

For hundreds of years, people have held autumn festivals to give thanks for a good harvest. The American celebration of Thanksgiving began with the Pilgrims in Plymouth Colony. They observed the first Thanksgiving in 1621 to mark the end of their first difficult year in America and the gathering of the harvest. Their celebration lasted three days. During that time the Pilgrims and their Native American friends feasted on good food.

Thereafter, many communities observed a day of thanksgiving at various times in the fall. Finally, in 1863, President Abraham Lincoln declared that the day should be celebrated nationally. Thanksgiving Day is, above all, a time for family togetherness, commitment, and celebration.

AMERICAN SYMBOLS

The Statue of Liberty

At the entrance to New York Harbor, on Liberty Island, stands one of the best-known symbols of the United States—the Statue of Liberty. The official name of this colossal figure is *Liberty Enlightening the World.* Slightly over 151 feet (45 m) tall, it is the largest statue ever made.

The statue was a gift from the people of France to the United States. It was presented as a symbol of friendship and in honor of the 100th anniversary of American independence. It was designed by Frédéric Bartholdi and constructed by Alexandre Eiffel.

The Statue of Liberty was built in Paris, taken apart, and then shipped to the United States in 214 crates. It was placed on a pedestal built with money raised by the American people. President Grover Cleveland dedicated the statue in 1886.

The statue represents a woman dressed in long flowing robes and wearing a crown with seven spikes. At her feet are the broken chains of tyranny. Her right arm holds a torch high in the air. In her left hand is a law book with the date of the Declaration of Independence, July 4, 1776.

An elevator in the pedestal brings visitors to the foot of the statue. From there they may climb a long, narrow, spiral staircase to the statue's crown, which provides a beautiful view of New York Harbor.

The Statue of Liberty has long been a symbol of freedom for millions of immigrants to the United States. "The New Colossus," a poem by Emma Lazarus to welcome immigrants, was inscribed on a tablet in the pedestal in 1903. It ends with the following lines:

> Give me your tired, your poor,
> Your huddled masses yearning
>   to breathe free,
> The wretched refuse of your
>   teeming shore.
> Send these, the homeless,
>   tempest-tost to me,
> I lift my lamp beside the
>   golden door!

Over the years, rust and corrosion from weather and pollution have damaged the Statue of Liberty. By the early 1980s, the statue was badly in need of repair. In 1982 President Ronald Reagan formed a special commission of private citizens to oversee the statue's restoration. The project was funded by millions of dollars in private donations. Special rededication ceremonies took place in July 1986.

The Liberty Bell

The Liberty Bell has been a symbol of American freedom ever since it rang on July 8, 1776, to announce the adoption of the Declaration of Independence. This giant bronze bell was made in England in 1752 for the State House (now Independence Hall) in Philadelphia, Pennsylvania. The bell's inscription—"Proclaim Liberty throughout all the land unto all the inhabitants thereof"—is from the Bible.

The Liberty Bell cracked soon after its arrival in Philadelphia and had to be recast. It rang at every anniversary of the Declaration of Independence until 1835. In that year it cracked again while tolling after the death of John

Marshall, chief justice of the Supreme Court. Finally, while ringing in honor of George Washington's birthday in 1846, the bell was damaged so badly that it could not be tolled again.

The bell was on display in Independence Hall until 1976. In celebration of the nation's 200th anniversary, the bell was moved to its own building where thousands of visitors view it each year.

The Great Seal of the United States

For more than 1,000 years, officials have used seals, or engraved stamps, as guarantees that documents are authentic. At one time monarchs even wore signet, or seal, rings. The Great Seal of the United States was adopted by the new nation in 1782. Today it is kept in the Department of State and is used only on certain important kinds of documents, such as treaties. Only the face of the seal is used to seal official documents. Both sides of the seal, however, appear on the back of the $1 bill.

The face of the seal shows an American bald eagle with raised wings. On its breast is a shield with 13 alternate red and white stripes representing the original states. In the eagle's right claw is an olive branch with 13 leaves and 13 olives. In its left claw are 13 arrows. These symbols indicate the nation's wish to live in peace, but also its ability to wage war.

In the eagle's beak is a ribbon with the words *E Pluribus Unum*. This Latin phrase means "from many [states], one [nation]." Above the eagle's head are 13 stars surrounded by rays of light breaking through a cloud.

The reverse side of the Great Seal shows a pyramid made up of 13 layers of stone, representing the new nation. The base of the pyramid has a date shown in Roman numerals—MDCCLXXVI (1776)—the year of the signing of the Declaration of Independence. The pyramid is guarded by an eye surrounded by rays of light. Above are the Latin words *Annuit Coeptis*, meaning "He [God] has favored our undertaking." Below is the phrase *Novus Ordo Seclorum*, which means "a new order of the ages."

The Bald Eagle

The bald eagle, which appears on the Great Seal, is the official emblem of the United States. This bird is not actually bald, but sometimes appears to be so because its head and neck are pure white. The eagle has symbolized official power since the days of ancient Egyptian civilizations.

The bald eagle was chosen as the national bird of the United States in 1872. The choice was not unanimous, though. Benjamin Franklin preferred a native bird, the turkey, but he was overruled.

The Great Seal

Uncle Sam

The figure of Uncle Sam is an American symbol as widely recognized as the American flag. He has symbolized the United States since the War of 1812.

One legend has it that during that war, a storeyard in Troy, New York, stamped the initials "U.S." on barrels of salted meat for American soldiers. The "U.S." stood for United States. Workers, though, jokingly claimed that the initials really stood for "Uncle Sam" (Samuel) Wilson, who managed the storeyard. The idea of equating Uncle Sam with the United States spread rapidly. After all, Great Britain, the nation's opponent in the War of 1812, already had a personal symbol of its own—the figure of an English farmer, John Bull.

Uncle Sam as we know him today was first drawn in the 1860s by the American cartoonist Thomas Nast. The symbol of Uncle Sam usually has long hair and a white beard. His pants have red and white stripes, his stovepipe hat is decorated with stars and stripes, and he wears a cutaway coat.

The Donkey and the Elephant

Two well-known symbols—the donkey and the elephant—represent the major political parties in the United States. They were first drawn as symbols of the Democratic party and the Republican party by American cartoonist Thomas Nast.

The donkey was used for the first time as a political symbol by Andrew Jackson after his opponents in the 1828 presidential election called him a "jackass." Later, Nast used the donkey in his cartoons to stand for the Democratic party. The donkey soon became recognized as the symbol of the Democratic party.

The elephant as a symbol of the Republican party first appeared in a cartoon by Nast in *Harper's Weekly* in 1874. He used the elephant to represent the Republican vote. It soon came to stand for the Republican party.

GLOSSARY

A

absolute monarch a king or queen with absolute, or total, power, 21

acid rain acid formed when pollution from burning gas, oil, and coal mixes with water vapor in the air, 500

acquit to find a defendant not guilty, 298

act a law, 84

addict a slave to a habit, such as the use of drugs, 484

administrative law law made by government agencies, 116

adopt to legally establish a child as one's own, 247

advertising the use of the mass media by businesses to inform people about products and to persuade them to buy these products, 343

agency shop a business in which workers cannot be forced to join a union but must pay union dues, 390

aggravated assault a physical injury done intentionally to another person, 289

agribusiness large farms that are owned by corporations and that rely heavily on mechanized equipment, 404

alcoholism a disease in which a person is addicted to alcohol, 484

alien a person who lives in a nation but is not a citizen of that nation, 9

alliance an agreement in which two or more nations commit to helping each other for defense, economic, scientific, or other reasons, 426

ambassador the highest-ranking official representing a government in a foreign country, 102

amendment a written change to the Constitution, 46

Anti-Federalist an opponent of the Constitution who urged its rejection in 1787, 33

apartheid a system that separates the races, 457

appeal the right of a convicted person to ask a higher court to review his or her case, 118

appellate jurisdiction the authority of some courts to review decisions made by lower courts, 119

apportion to distribute, as in the seats in the House of Representatives, 72

apprenticeship a fixed period of job training, 403

appropriation bill a bill approving the spending of public money, 84

arbitration a method of settling differences between labor unions and employers in which a third party's decision must be accepted by both sides, 393

arraign to bring an accused person before a court to enter a plea of guilty or not guilty, 295

arrest warrant an authorization by a court for police to make an arrest, 294

arson the destruction of property by setting fire to it, 290

assembly line a system in which individual workers perform specialized jobs in making a product that travels on a conveyor belt, 335

attorney general the chief legal officer of the nation or of a state, 102

audit an examination by an accountant of a government's or business's income and expenditures, 235

automation the use of machines instead of workers to provide goods and services, 403

B

bail money or property an accused person gives a court to hold as a guarantee that he or she will appear for trial, 57

balance the remainder owed on a bill or a loan, 348

balanced budget a budget in which revenue equals expenditures, 233

balance of power a situation in which countries or groups of countries have equal levels of strength, 452

balance of trade the difference in value between a nation's imports and exports, 435

bank a business that deals in money and credit, 358

bankruptcy a legal declaration that a person or business cannot pay his or her or its debts, 357

beneficiary the person named in an insurance policy to receive the amount of the policy when the policyholder dies, 368

bicameral consisting of two houses, as in a lawmaking body, 29

bill a proposed law being considered by a lawmaking body, 77

bill of attainder a law sentencing a person to jail without a trial, 82

Bill of Rights the first 10 amendments to the Constitution, which set forth basic rights guaranteed to all Americans, 51

biomass wood or waste products that can be burned or used to make fuel, 506

birthrate the annual number of live births per 1,000 members of a population, 11

blacklist a method once used by employers in which companies create and share lists of workers active in labor unions and refuse to hire those workers, 387

blended family a family in which one or both partners brings children from a previous marriage into the new marriage, 246

block grant federal funds given to state and local governments for broad purposes, 176

blue-collar worker a person who performs a job requiring manual labor, 403

bond a certificate of debt issued by governments and corporations to persons from whom they have borrowed money, 226

borough a term used in Alaska for a county; also, a unit of local government similar to a town, 160

boycott to stop buying or using a good or service, 476

brand name a widely advertised product usually distributed over a large area, 343

brief a written statement explaining the main points of one side's argument in a court case, 127

broker a brokerage house employee who buys and sells stock, 363

budget a plan of income and spending, 101

building code a set of local laws that regulate the construction and repair of buildings in a community, 473

bureaucracy the many departments and agencies at all levels of government, 111

burglary the forcible or illegal entry into a home or other property with the intent to steal, 290

business cycle the tendency of a free-market economy to go back and forth between good times and bad times, 377

C

Cabinet the leaders of the executive departments who also act as advisers to the president, 47

candidate a person who runs for election to public office, 186

capital money invested in business; also, property and equipment used to produce goods or services, 315

capitalism an economic system based on private ownership of the means of production, 315

capital punishment the death penalty, 299

caucus a meeting of party leaders to determine party policy or to choose the party's candidates for public office, 76

censure the formal disapproval of the actions of a member of Congress by the other members, 75

census an official count of the number of people in a country, 11

certificate of deposit (CD) an investment in which an amount of money invested for a specified period of time earns a guaranteed rate of interest, 364

charge account a form of credit that stores grant to customers to buy goods now and pay for them later, 347

charter a basic plan of government granted by a state legislature to a local government, 159

check a written and signed order to a bank to pay a sum of money from a checking account to the person or business named on the check, 354

checks and balances a system in which the powers of government are balanced among different branches so that each branch can check, or limit, the power of the other branches, 42

child abuse the mental, physical, or sexual mistreatment of a child, 247

circuit the judicial district covered by a court of appeals, 121

citizen a member of a nation, 3

city the largest type of municipality, 166

city council the lawmaking body of a city, 167

civics the study of what it means to be a U.S. citizen, 3

civil case a court case involving disputes over money or property between individuals or businesses, 151

civil disobedience the intentional breaking of a law to show dissent, 477

civilian a nonmilitary person, 103

civil rights the rights guaranteed to all U.S. citizens, 58

civil rights movement the struggle for equal rights for all Americans, 476

civil service examination a test given to applicants for government jobs, 405

closed primary a primary election in which only voters who are members of the party can vote for the party's candidates, 196

closed shop a business in which only union members can be hired, 387

cloture a limit on the debate of a bill in the Senate, 88

coalition an agreement between two or more political parties to work together to run a government, 188

collateral property used to guarantee that a loan will be repaid, 358

collective bargaining a process in which representatives of a labor union and an employer work to reach an agreement about wages and working conditions, 386

college a four-year institution of higher learning, 260

command economy an economic system in which the government controls a nation's economy, 319

commission a local government body that has both legislative and executive powers, 169

committee a small group in Congress formed to consider bills, 77

common law customary law that develops from judges' decisions and is followed in situations not covered by statutory law, 116

common stock shares in a corporation that do not earn a fixed dividend but give shareholders a voice in managing the company, 325

communication the passing along of ideas, information, and beliefs from one person to another, 280

communism an economic system based on the theories of Marx and Engels in which the means of production are owned by the government and the government decides what will be produced, 450

community policing a system in which police officers and citizens are encouraged to work together to prevent crime in a community, 294

commutation making a convicted person's sentence less severe, 99

complaint a lawsuit, 151

compromise an agreement in which each side gives up part of its demands, 30

concealed propaganda propaganda presented as fact and whose source is kept secret, 208

concurrent power a power shared by the federal government and the states, 39

concurring opinion a statement written by a Supreme Court justice who agrees with the majority's decision but for different reasons, 128

conditioning learning that is the result of a reward system or of experience involving the motor nerves, 268

confederation a loose association of states, 25

conference committee a temporary congressional committee made up of senators and representatives who try to reach an agreement on different versions of a bill, 78

conglomerate a large company formed by the merger of businesses that produce, supply, or sell a number of unrelated goods and services, 318

conservation safeguarding of natural resources through wise use, 504

constable an officer who enforces township laws, 164

constituent a person represented by members of a lawmaking body, 83

constitution a written plan of government, 23

constitutional law law based on the Constitution and Supreme Court decisions, 116

consul an official who works to promote U.S. trade in a foreign country, 102

consulate the office of a consul, 103

consumer a person who buys or uses products and services, 344

containment the U.S. foreign policy of preventing the spread of communism, 451

contraction a period in a business cycle during which the economy is slowing, 378

copyright an exclusive right, granted by law, to publish or sell a written, musical, or art work for a certain number of years, 314

corollary a statement that follows as a natural or logical result, 447

corporation a business organization chartered by a state government and given power to conduct business, sell stock, and receive protection of state laws, 321

corrections methods used to punish lawbreakers, 298

costs of production business costs, such as wages, payments for raw materials, transportation, rent, and interest on borrowed money, 378

council member-at-large a member of a local council who is elected by all the voters of a community, 167

counterfeiting the making or distributing of fake money, 103

county a subdivision of state government formed to carry out state laws, collect taxes, and supervise elections, 160

county clerk the official who keeps county records, 162

county seat the town or city in which a county government is located, 161

courier a special government messenger, 427

court-martial a trial of a person in the armed services accused of breaking military law, 122

court of appeals a federal court that reviews decisions appealed from district courts, 121

creativity the ability to find new ways of thinking and doing things, 269

credit card a form of credit issued by banks and other major lending institutions and accepted by most businesses worldwide, 355

creditor a person who is owed money, 356

credit rating a report that shows how reliable a customer is in paying his or her bills, 348

credit union a bank established by people with common interests to create a pool of money for low-interest loans, 359

crime any act that breaks the law and for which a punishment has been established, 289

criminal a person who commits any type of crime, 289

criminal case a court case in which a person is accused of breaking a criminal law, 150

criminal justice system the system of police, courts, and corrections used to bring criminals to justice, 293

critical thinking a type of thinking one does to reach decisions and solve problems, 269

cross-examine to question an opponent's witness in court, 118

crossroads a location where two roads meet, 275

currency coins and paper money, 353

D

death rate the annual number of deaths per 1,000 members of a population, 11

deduction an expense taxpayers are allowed to subtract in figuring their taxable income, 227

defendant a person accused of a crime in a court case, 295

defense an accused person's side in a court case, 295

deficit the amount by which expenditures exceed income, 233

delayed marriage the tendency to marry at older ages, 245

delegate a representative, 28

delegated power a power given to the federal government by the Constitution, 39

delinquent a juvenile who breaks the law, 300

democracy a form of government in which the people of a nation either rule directly or through elected representatives, 21

demonstration a gathering in which people express dissent by marching, carrying signs, singing songs, and making speeches, 476

deport to force a person to leave a nation, such as an illegal alien, 9

depression a sharp decline in a nation's business activity, during which many workers lose their jobs and many businesses close down, 378

desertification the loss of soil, due to overgrazing and removal of trees and plants, that results in once-fertile areas becoming deserts, 495

détente a lessening of tensions, 455

deterrence discouraging people from certain behavior by the threat of punishment, 299

dictatorship a form of government in which all power is in the hands of one person or a small group of people, 21

diplomacy the art of dealing with foreign governments, 99

diplomatic corps the ambassadors and other representatives of a nation serving in foreign countries, 427

diplomatic note a written communication between leaders of different governments, 99

diplomatic recognition the power of the president to decide whether to establish official relations with a foreign government, 426

direct democracy a form of government in which all the people meet together at one place to make laws and decide what actions to take, 21

discounting the practice of deducting interest on a loan before money is given to the borrower, 360

discount rate the rate of interest charged by Federal Reserve banks on loans to member banks, 361

discrimination unfair actions taken against people because they belong to a particular group, 475

dissent disagreement, as with a law, 476

dissenting opinion a statement written by a Supreme Court justice who disagrees with the majority's decision, 128

distribution a process of spreading goods from manufacturers to the people who want them, 337

district attorney the official who represents the state government in county trials, 162

district court a lower federal court that has original jurisdiction in most cases involving federal laws, 119

dividend a profit paid to corporate stockholders, 324

division of labor a system in which each worker performs a specialized portion of a total job, 334

divorce a legal ending of a marriage, 250

docket a calendar of cases to be heard by a court, 126

doctrine a statement that sets forth a new government policy with respect to other nations, 447

dollar diplomacy the practice of sending U.S. troops to other countries to protect U.S. investments, 447

double jeopardy being tried a second time for the same crime, 56

down payment an initial cash payment on an installment loan or on an item bought under an installment plan, 348

draft a policy requiring men to serve in the military, 61

drug abuse the use of drugs for escape or excitement, 484

due process of law the right to a fair trial, 56

E

ecology the study of living things in relation to each other and to their environment, 491

economies of scale a situation in which goods can be produced more efficiently and cheaply by larger companies, 317

ecosystem a community of interdependent living things existing in balance with their physical environment, 491

elastic clause Article 1, Section 8, of the Constitution; known also as the "necessary and proper" clause that allows Congress to extend its delegated powers, 80

elector a person elected by the voters in a presidential election as a member of the Electoral College, 202

Electoral College the group of electors who cast the official votes that elect the president and vice president, 202

electoral vote the vote cast by the Electoral College for president and vice president, 202

embassy the official residence of an ambassador in a foreign country, 102

embezzlement taking for one's own use money that has been entrusted to one's care, 291

eminent domain the power of the government to take private property for public use, 57

entrepreneur a business owner, 328

environment the air, water, and soil that make up the world around us, 491

erosion the wearing away of land by water and wind, 495

estate tax a tax on all the wealth left by a person who has died, 231

ethnic group a group of people of the same race, nationality, or religion who share a common and distinctive culture and heritage, 475

excise tax a federal tax collected on certain luxury items produced and sold in the United States, 230

executive agreement a mutual understanding between the president of the United States and the leader of a foreign government, 426

executive branch the branch of government that carries out the laws, 41

executive department a department in the executive branch of the federal government, 101

executive order an order issued by the head of the executive branch to set up methods of enforcing laws, 147

exemption an amount of money a taxpayer is allowed

to subtract from taxable income for themselves and for dependents, 227

expansion a period in a business cycle during which the economy is growing, 377

experience direct observation or participation in events, 268

export a good or service sold to another country, 435

ex post facto **law** a law that applies to an action that took place before the law was passed, 82

expulsion the removal of a member of Congress for serious misconduct, 74

extradition a legal process for returning criminals to the state from which they fled, 142

F

factors of production the four resources, or means, of production—land, capital, labor, and management, 326

family law the legal regulation of marriage, divorce, and the duties of parents and children, 247

favorite son or daughter a man or woman, popular in his or her home state, who is nominated for president by the state's delegates on the first ballot at the national nominating convention, 200

featherbedding a practice once used by unions to force employers to hire more workers than are needed, 392

federalism a system of government in which the powers of government are divided between the national government, which governs the whole nation, and the state governments, which govern the people of each state, 30

Federalist a supporter of the Constitution who urged its adoption in 1787, 32

federal magistrate a district court official who hears evidence in a case and decides if the case should be brought before a grand jury, 121

Federal Reserve System the U.S. banking system that handles the banking needs of the federal government and regulates the money supply, 361

fee a small government charge for a service or license, 225

felony a serious crime, such as burglary, kidnapping, and murder, 289

fertilizer a plant food that makes crops grow faster and bigger, 495

filibuster a method of delaying action on a bill in the Senate by making long speeches, 88

fine money paid as a penalty for breaking certain laws, 225

fiscal policy a government's policy of taxation and spending, 383

fixed expense an expense that occurs regularly, 252

floor leader a political party leader in Congress who works for the passage of bills the party favors, 76

forcible rape the sexual violation of a person by force and against the person's will, 289

foreign aid a government program that provides economic and military assistance to other nations, 433

foreign policy a nation's plan for dealing with other nations of the world, 97

foreign relations the way in which a nation deals with the governments of other nations, 425

fossil fuel a nonrenewable resource (petroleum, natural gas, or coal) that is believed to have formed over millions of years from the fossilized remains of plants and animals, 503

foster home a home of people who are unrelated to a child but who agree to act as the child's parents, 247

franking privilege the right of members of Congress to mail official letters free of charge, 74

fraud taking someone else's money or property through dishonesty, 291

free competition a system in which business owners compete among themselves for customers, 313

free-enterprise system an economic system in which people are free to operate their businesses as they see fit, 316

free market an exchange between buyers and sellers who are free to choose, 313

free trade trade that is unrestricted by tariffs and other trade barriers, 435

full faith and credit clause the provision in the Constitution ensuring that each state will accept the decisions of courts in other states, 142

G

general election an election in which the voters elect their leaders, 196

general trial court a court that handles major criminal and civil cases, 154

gerrymandering the process of drawing congressional district lines to favor a political party, 72

gift tax a tax on items received as gifts that are worth more than $10,000, 231

glasnost a policy of openness begun by Mikhail Gorbachev that aimed to give more freedom to the people of the Soviet Union, 455

government an authority that acts on behalf of a group of people, 3

governor the chief executive of a state government, 147

graduate school an institution of higher learning that offers advanced degrees, 260

grand jury a group that hears the evidence in a criminal case and decides whether there is enough evidence to bring the accused person to trial, 56

grand larceny the theft of goods worth more than a certain amount, 290

grant-in-aid federal funds given to state and local governments for specific projects, 176

grassroots originating, as in political support, from many individuals rather than from national parties and large organizations, 196

greenhouse effect the trapping of the sun's heat by high levels of carbon dioxide in the atmosphere, resulting in the possible long-term raising of temperatures on Earth, 497

gross domestic product (GDP) the value of all goods and services produced in a nation each year, 333

gross income the total amount of money a company receives from the sale of its goods and services, 328

guardian a person appointed by a state court to look after an individual who is not an adult or who is unable to care for himself or herself, 247

H

habit an action performed automatically, 268

homelessness the situation of being without a place to live, 472

home rule the power of a city to write its own municipal charter and to manage its own affairs, 167

human rights the basic rights to which all people are entitled as human beings, 25

hung jury a jury that cannot reach a verdict, 118

hydrologic cycle the process in which water circulates through the earth's environment, 500

I

ideal a belief or standard of conduct that people try to live up to, 4

immigrant a person who comes to a nation to settle as a permanent resident, 7

immunity legal protection, 74

impeachment a formal charge brought against a government official, 81

implied power a power not specifically granted to Congress by the Constitution but which is suggested to be necessary to carry out its delegated powers, 81

import a good or service bought from another country, 435

income tax a tax on the income that individuals and companies earn, 227

independent agency an agency in the executive branch of the federal government formed by Congress to help enforce laws and regulations not covered by the executive departments, 109

independent voter a voter who is not a member of a political party, 196

indict to formally accuse a person of a crime, 56

inflation a rise in the costs of goods and services, 378

inheritance tax a tax on money and property received from an estate, 231

initiative a process by which citizens of a state may propose a law by collecting signatures on a petition, 146

insight a process by which people unconsciously take what they know about a subject and apply it to a problem or question in order to find an answer, 269

installment a payment made on a balance owed, 348

insurance a system of protection in which people pay small sums periodically to avoid the risk of a large loss, 367

interdependence mutual reliance, 425

interest payment for the use of loaned money, 223

interest group an organization of people with common interests who try to influence government policies and decisions, 212

invest to put money into businesses or valuable articles in hopes of making a profit, 314

isolationism a policy of avoiding involvement in foreign affairs, 445

item veto the power of the head of the executive branch to reject one part of a bill but approve the rest of it, 146

J

job action any kind of slowdown or action short of a strike, 386

Joint Chiefs of Staff the group made up of the highest-ranking officers from the Army, Navy, and Air Force that advises the president on military affairs, 106

joint committee a committee made up of members of both houses of Congress to deal with matters of mutual concern, 78

judicial branch the branch of government that interprets the laws and punishes lawbreakers, 42

judicial review the power of the U.S. Supreme Court to determine if a law passed by Congress or a presidential action is in accord with the Constitution, 126

junior college a two-year community college, 260

jurisdiction the authority to interpret and administer the law; also, the range of that authority, 119

juror a member of a trial jury who judges evidence and determines the verdict in a court case, 117

jury duty serving on a jury, 117

justice a member of the Supreme Court, 123

justice of the peace a judge who presides over a state justice court, usually in rural areas and small towns, and who tries misdemeanors and civil cases involving small sums, 151

juvenile in most states, a person under the age of 18, 300

L

labor human effort used to make goods and services, 327

laborer a person who performs unskilled or heavy physical labor, 403

labor union an organization of workers formed to bargain for higher wages and improved working conditions and to protect workers' rights, 386

landfill a huge pit dug to store garbage, 502

larceny the theft of property without the use of force or violence, 290

law a rule of conduct enforced by government, 22

law of demand an economic rule that states that buyers will demand more products when they can buy them at lower prices and fewer products when they must buy them at higher prices, 314

law of supply an economic rule that states that businesses will provide more products when they can sell them at higher prices and fewer products when they must sell them at lower prices, 314

legislative branch the lawmaking branch of government, 41

legislature a lawmaking body of government, 30

libel written falsehoods that damage another person's reputation, 52

lieutenant governor the official who succeeds the governor if the governor dies, resigns, or is removed from office, 149

limited government a system in which government powers are carefully spelled out to prevent government from becoming too powerful, 40

limited war a war fought without using a nation's full power, particularly nuclear weapons, 453

lobby an interest group, 212

lobbyist a person paid to represent an interest group's viewpoint, 212

lockout a method once used by employers to fight labor slowdowns by locking workers out, thus preventing them from earning wages, 387

long-term credit an advance of money to be repaid over a long period of time in installments, 356

M

machine tool machinery built to produce identical parts, 334

mainstreaming the practice of placing students with special needs in regular schools and classes, 261

majority party the political party that has more members in Congress or in a state legislature, 76

majority rule a system in which the decision of more than half the people is accepted by all, 38

marshal an official in each federal district court who makes arrests, delivers subpoenas, keeps order in courtrooms, and carries out court orders, 120

mass marketing the process of selling goods in large quantities, 339

mass media forms of communication that transmit information to large numbers of people, 208

mass production the rapid production by machine of large numbers of identical objects, 333

mass transit public transportation, including buses, subways, and commuter railroads, 473

mayor the chief executive of a city government, 167

mediation a method of settling disputes between labor unions and employers through the use of a third party who offers a nonbinding solution, 393

Medicaid a federal program that helps the states pay the medical costs of poor people, 373

Medicare a federal program of health insurance for people aged 65 and over, 373

megalopolis a continuous, giant urban area that includes many cities, 278

merger a combination of two or more companies into one company, 317

metropolitan area a large city and its suburbs, 15

migration the movement of people from region to region, 15

minister an official sent to a small country to represent the U.S. government, 102

minority group a group not in power and set apart from other groups of people in society because of ethnic background, language, customs, or religion, 475

minority party the political party that has fewer members in Congress or in a state legislature, 76

misdemeanor a less serious crime, such as a traffic violation, 289

mixed economy an economic system that combines elements of free and command economies, 319

monetary policy a government's policy of regulating the amount of money in the economy, 384

money a means of exchange, 353

money market fund an investment similar to a mutual fund, 364

monopoly a situation in which one company controls all production of a good or service, 317

motivation an internal drive that stirs people and directs their behavior, 268

multiparty system a political system in which many political parties play a role in government, 188

municipal court a court in a large city that handles minor civil and criminal cases, 151

municipality a local governmental unit that is incorporated by the state and has a large degree of self-government, 159

murder the willful killing of one person by another person, 289

mutual fund an investment that reduces risk to shareholders by investing in many different stocks, 364

N

national debt the total amount of money owed by the U.S. government plus the interest that must be paid on this borrowed money, 234

nationalism a drive to put the interests of one's own country above all others, 456

native-born citizen an American born as a citizen of the United States, 8

naturalization a legal process by which aliens become citizens, 10

net income the money a company has left over after all its costs have been paid, 328

neutrality a policy of not favoring one side or the other in a conflict, 448

newly industrialized country (NIC) a nation experiencing rapid industrialization and economic growth, 435

no-fault divorce a divorce in which a couple states the marriage has problems that cannot be resolved, 250

nominate to select candidates to run for public office, 186

nonprofit organization a business organization that provides goods and services without seeking to earn a profit, 325

nonrenewable resource a natural wealth that can be used only once, 503

one-parent family a family with only one parent, 246

one-party system a political system in which a single political party controls the government and all other parties are banned, 189

one-price system a system in which the price is stamped or bar-coded on a product, 342

open primary a primary election in which voters may vote for the candidates of any party, 196

open shop a business that employs both union and nonunion workers, 390

operator a person who operates machinery, who inspects, assembles, and packs goods in a factory, or who drives a truck, bus, or automobile, 403

opinion a written statement by the U.S. Supreme Court explaining its reasoning behind a decision, 127

ordinance a regulation that governs a local governmental unit, 160

organic farming farming without the use of artificial substances, 495

original jurisdiction the authority of a court to be the first court to hold trials in certain kinds of cases, 119

own recognizance the legal responsibility for one's own behavior, as in an arrested suspect being released without bail, 295

ozone a thin layer in the earth's upper atmosphere that shields the planet from the sun's ultraviolet rays, 500

pardon an official act by the president or by a governor forgiving a person convicted of a crime and freeing that person from serving out his or her sentence, 99

parish a term used in Louisiana for a county, 160

Parliament the lawmaking body of British government, 29

parole an early release from prison on certain conditions, 299

partnership a business organization in which two or more persons share responsibilities, costs, profits, and losses, 320

party platform a written statement outlining a political party's views on issues and describing the programs it proposes, 199

party whip the assistant to the floor leader in each house of Congress who tries to persuade party members to vote for bills the party supports, 76

passport a document that allows a U.S. citizen to travel abroad, 103

patent an exclusive right given to a person to make and sell an invention for a certain number of years, 314

patronage a system in which government jobs are given to people recommended by political party leaders and officeholders, 150

peak a high point in a business cycle, 378

penal code a set of criminal laws, 150

perestroika a policy by which Mikhail Gorbachev sought to restructure and improve the economy of the Soviet Union, 455

personal property possessions such as money, stocks, jewelry, and cars, 230

pesticide a chemical that kills insect pests and weeds, 495

petition a formal request, 53

petit jury a trial jury of 6 to 12 persons, 117

petty larceny the theft of goods worth less than a certain amount, 290

picket to march in front of one's workplace, often with signs urging others not to work for the company or buy its goods and services, 386

plaintiff the person or company filing the complaint in a civil lawsuit, 151

plea bargain an agreement between the prosecutor and the defense in which an accused person pleads guilty to a reduced charge, 298

pocket veto a way in which the president can reject a bill, when Congress is not in session, by not signing it, 89

political action committee (PAC) the political arm of an interest group that collects voluntary contributions from members to fund political candidates and parties the interest group favors, 218

political party an organization of citizens who have similar views on issues and who work to put their ideas into effect through government action, 185

poll a survey taken to measure public opinion, 210

polling place a place where citizens go to vote, 191

poll tax a special tax that had to be paid in order to vote, 60

pollution contaminants of the earth, air, or water, 496

popular sovereignty government by consent of the governed, 37

popular vote the votes cast by citizens in a presidential election, 202

Preamble the beginning of the U.S. Constitution, which describes its purposes, 37

precedent an earlier court decision that guides judges' decisions in later cases, 116

precinct a local voting district in a county, city, or ward, 191

preferred stock shares in a corporation that earn a fixed dividend but do not give shareholders a voice in managing the company, 325

prejudice an opinion not based on careful and reasonable investigation of the facts, 271

premium a payment made for insurance protection, 367

presidential primary a primary election in which voters in a state select the presidential candidate they wish their delegates to support at the party's national nominating convention, 199

presidential succession the order in which the office of president is to be filled if it becomes vacant, 95

president *pro tempore* the official who presides over the Senate in the vice president's absence, 76

primary election an election in which the voters of various parties choose candidates to run for office in a general election, 196

private insurance insurance individuals and companies voluntarily pay to cover unexpected losses, 367

probable cause the reason for an arrest, based on the knowledge of a crime and the available evidence, 294

probation a period of time during which a person guilty of an offense does not go to prison but instead must follow certain rules and report to a probation officer, 304

productivity the amount of work produced by a worker in an hour, 327

professional a person whose job requires many years of education and training and who performs mostly mental, rather than physical, work, 401

profit the income a business has left after paying its expenses, 229

profit motive the desire to make money from a business or investment, 314

progressive tax a tax that takes a larger percentage of income from high-income groups than from low-income groups, 228

propaganda ideas used to influence people's thinking or behavior, 208

property tax a local or state tax collected on real property or personal property, 230

proposition a proposed law resulting from a petition, 146

prosecution the government's side in a criminal case, 295

public housing project a complex of apartment houses for low-income families that are built with public funds and that charge low rents, 471

public interest group a group seeking to promote the interests of the general public rather than just one part of it, 213

public opinion the total of the opinions held concerning a particular issue, 207

public utility a legal monopoly that provides essential services to the public, 318

quorum the minimum number of members who must be present before a legislative body can conduct business, 88

quota a limit on the number of immigrants who may enter a country each year, 8

ratification approval by a formal vote, 32

real property land and buildings, 230

recall a process by which voters may remove an elected official from office, 146

recession a severe contraction in a business cycle, 378

recreation relaxation or amusement, 280

recycling the process of turning waste into something that can be used again, 502

referendum a method of referring a bill to the voters for approval before the bill can become law, 146

refugee a person who flees persecution in his or her homeland to seek safety in another nation, 8

regressive tax a tax that takes a larger percentage of income from low-income groups than from high-income groups, 229

regulatory commission an independent agency created by Congress that can make rules concerning certain activities and bring violators to court, 110

rehabilitation reforming criminals and returning them to society as law-abiding citizens, 299

remand to return an appealed case to a lower court for a new trial, 127

remarriage a marriage in which one or both of the partners has been married before, 246

renewable resource any natural wealth that can be replaced, 497

rent a payment for the use of land or other property belonging to another person, 326

repeal to cancel or revoke, 46

representative democracy a form of government in which the people elect representatives to carry on the work of government for them, 22

reprieve a postponement in the carrying out of a prison sentence, 99

republic a form of government in which the people elect representatives to carry on the work of government for them, 22

reserved power   a power set aside by the Constitution for the states or for the people, 39

retailer   a businessperson who sells goods directly to the public, 343

reunification   a joining together, 456

revealed propaganda   propaganda that openly attempts to influence people, 209

revenue   income, 224

right-to-work law   a law passed by certain states that forbids closed shops and makes union membership voluntary, 390

robbery   a theft accompanied by the threat of force, 290

roll-call vote   a vote in Congress in which a record is made of how each member votes, 88

runoff primary   an election in which voters choose between the two leading candidates in a primary to determine the party's candidate in the general election, 196

rural area   a region of farms and small towns, 14

salary range   the lowest to highest earnings for a particular job, 413

sales tax   a state or city tax on items or services sold to the public, 229

satellite nation   a country that is controlled by another country, 451

savings and loan association   a type of bank originally established to help people buy homes, 358

scarcity   the problem of limited resources, 314

search warrant   a legal document granted by a judge that permits police to enter and search a place where there is reason to believe evidence of a crime will be found, 53

secretary   an official who heads an executive department in the federal government, 102

secret ballot   a method of voting in which the voter marks a ballot in secret, 197

segregate   to separate on the basis of race, 128

select committee   a temporary House or Senate committee appointed to deal with an issue not handled by a standing committee, 78

self-incrimination   testifying against oneself, 56

self-service   a type of marketing in which customers serve themselves, 339

seniority system   the custom of giving leadership of committees to members of Congress with the most years of service, 79

sentence   a punishment given to a person convicted of a crime, 298

separation of church and state   the division between religion and government, 51

separation of powers   the three-way division of power among the branches of the federal government, 41

service industry   a business that sells services rather than products, 404

session   a meeting of Congress, 75

sheriff   the chief law-enforcement official in some county governments, 162

shoplifting   stealing items displayed in a store, 347

short-term credit   an advance of money to be repaid within a short period of time, 356

slander   spoken false statements that damage another person's reputation, 52

slum   a run-down section of a city in which buildings are neglected and families live crowded together, 470

small claims court   a state court that hears civil cases involving small amounts of money, 151

smog   a combination of smoke, gases, and fog in the air, 497

social insurance   government programs that are meant to protect individuals from future hardship and that individuals and businesses are required to pay for by state and federal laws, 370

Social Security   a system of government insurance that provides benefits for retired people, people with disabilities, unemployed people, and people with job-related injuries or illnesses, 370

Social Security tax   a kind of income tax that is used mainly to provide income to retired people and people with disabilities, 229

sole proprietorship   a business organization owned by one person, 320

Speaker   the presiding officer of the House of Representatives, 76

special district   a unit of local government set up to provide a specific service, 165

split ticket   a ballot on which a person votes for the candidates of more than one political party, 198

standard of living   the well-being of a nation's population, based on the amount of goods and services the population can afford, 313

standard packaging   the practice of wrapping and weighing goods before they reach customers, 342

standard part   an identical, interchangeable part of a manufactured product, 334

standing committee   a permanent House or Senate committee that considers bills in a certain area, 77

State of the Union Address   a yearly report by the president to Congress describing the nation's condition and recommending programs and policies, 97

statutory law   law passed by Congress and by lawmaking bodies of state or local governments, 115

stock   a share of ownership in a corporation, 321

stock exchange   a market where stocks are bought and sold, 363

stockholder   a person who owns corporate stock, 321

straight ticket   a ballot on which a person votes for all the candidates of one political party, 198

strike a situation in which workers walk off the job and refuse to work until labor issues are settled, 386

strip mining the practice of stripping away the top layer of soil to remove the minerals underneath, 505

subcommittee a division of a standing congressional committee that deals with specific issues in the area handled by the committee as a whole, 77

subpoena an official court order requiring a person to appear in court, 120

suburb a residential community near a large city, 15

suffrage the right to vote, 59

summit a meeting among the leaders of two or more nations, 432

Sunbelt a U.S. region made up of states in the South and West, 15

surplus an amount by which income exceeds expenditures, 233

tariff a tax on products imported from other countries, 231

tax a payment of money that citizens and businesses must make to help pay the costs of government, 224

taxable income the amount of income, less deductions, on which individuals and businesses must pay taxes, 228

technician a skilled worker who handles complex instruments or machinery, 401

term limits laws that limit the number of terms elected officials can serve, 73

territorial court a federal court that administers justice to people living in U.S. territories, 122

territory an area that is eligible to become a state, 141

testimony evidence given in court by a witness, 118

third party a minor political party in a two-party system, 188

totalitarian government a government that has total control over the lives of the people, 21

town a unit of local government, usually larger than a village and smaller than a city, 162

town meeting a form of government in which all citizens meet regularly to discuss town issues, 163

township a unit of local government that maintains local roads and rural schools within counties, 164

trade deficit a situation in which a nation spends more money to buy foreign goods than it earns through the sale of its goods to other countries, 435

treason an act that betrays and endangers one's country, 81

treaty a written agreement between nations, 98

trough a low point in a business cycle, 378

trust a form of business organization in which several companies create a board of trustees that ensures the companies no longer compete with one another, 317

two-earner family a family in which both partners work, 245

two-party system a political system with two strong political parties, 187

unconstitutional in conflict with the Constitution of the United States, 126

unicameral consisting of one house, as in a lawmaking body, 143

union *See* **labor union**

union shop a business in which a nonunion worker may be hired but must join a union within a certain period of time, 390

university an institution of higher learning that includes one or more colleges as well as graduate programs, 260

urban area a city or large town, 14

urban renewal program a program to recover a run-down area of a city, 471

vandalism the willful destruction of property, 290

verdict a decision of a jury, 118

veto a refusal of the president or of a governor to sign a bill, 42

victimless crime a crime in which there is no victim whose rights are invaded by another person, 290

village a unit of local government, usually smaller than a town, 163

visa a document that allows people from one country to visit another country, 103

volunteer a person who works without pay to help others, 218

ward an election district within a city or county, 167

warrant an order to pay out government funds, 149

white-collar crime a crime committed for illegal gain by people in the course of their work, 291

white-collar worker a person in a profession or who performs technical, managerial, sales, or administrative support work, 401

wholesaler a businessperson who buys goods from manufacturers and sells to retailers, 343

writ of *habeas corpus* a court order requiring that an accused person be brought to court to determine if there is enough evidence to hold the person for trial, 82

Z

zoning law a local law that regulates the kinds of buildings that may be constructed in a certain area, 472

INDEX

hydroelectric power, 506
hydrologic cycle, (def.) 500

I

Idaho, m 72, m 202, m 229, m 518, 567
ideals: (def.) 4; in Constitution, 37–40; in Declaration of Independence, 25, 257
"I Have a Dream" speech, 559
illegal aliens, 9
Illinois, m 72, 105, 174, m 202, m 229, 283, m 519, 567
immigration: (def.) 7, 8, p 8, 80, 475; naturalization, 10–11; and population growth, 11, 14
Immigration and Naturalization Service (INS), U.S., 9, 106
Immigration Reform and Control Act, 9
immunity, (def.) 74
impeachment, (def.) 81; recommendation for Nixon, 45
implied powers, (def.) 81
imports: (def.) 435; balance of trade and, 435, g 442; taxes on, 83, 225, 231
imprisonment, 299
Inauguration Day, 93
income: of businesses, 328; business cycles and, g 377, 378, 379, 381–82, 384–85; education and, 260, g 260, 398–99. See also wages
income taxes, (def.) 227–29, m 229
Independence Day, 575
Independence Hall, p 20, 28, 576
independent agencies, (def.) 109
independent candidates, 188–189, p 188, 196–97
independent voters, (def.) 196
Indiana, m 72, m 202, m 229, 278; m 519, 567
Indian Affairs, Bureau of, 106
Indians, American. See Native Americans
indictments, (def.) 56, 117, 295
Indonesia, 434, m 521
industrial unions, 390
industry: mass production, 333–37, g 335, p 336; monopolies and, 317–18; and pollution, 497, p 497, 500–502, 508, 509; regulation of, 80, 317–18; service,

403–404. See also business; corporations
inflation: (def.) 378, 379, 381–82, g 381; monetary policy and, 384; during recessions, 383–84, wages and, 378, 385
inheritance taxes, (def.) 231
initiatives, (def.) 146
Inouye, Daniel, 77, p 77
insight, (def.) 269
installment credit, 349, 356
installment plans, 348–49
installments, (def.), 348
insurance: (def.) 367, 368–73, p 368; for bank accounts, 358–59; and fraud, 369; private, 367–69; social, 369–73, g 371
interest: (def.) 223; on charge accounts, 348; charged by Federal Reserve banks, 361; on corporate bonds, 325; discounting, 360; on government bonds, 226, 363; on installment plans, 349; on savings, 358, 359, 363, 364
interest groups, (def.) 212–13, p 213, 216, 218
Interior, Department of the, 106, g 107
Internal Revenue Service (IRS), 103, 122, 232
International Atomic Energy Agency, 438
International Bank for Reconstruction and Development (IBRD), 440
International Court of Justice, g 438, 438–39
International Development Association (IDA), 440
International Finance Corporation (IFC), 440
international law, 438
International Telecommunication Union (ITU), 440
Interstate Commerce Commission (ICC), 110
interstate highway system, 175
investments: (def.) 314, 315; by insurance companies; 368; in Latin America, 447; of savings, 363–64. See also stocks; bonds
Iowa, 15, m 72, 124, 125, m 202, m 229, m 519, 567
Iran, 451, 456, m 521
Iraq, 426, 427, 456, 457, m 521
isolationism, (def.) 445, 448–49

Israel, p 97, 456, 457, m 521
Italy, 189, 449, m 521
item vetoes, (def.) 146

J

Jackson, Andrew, 187–88, p 562
Jackson, Jesse, 94, p 199
Japan: m 521; and education, 400; and pollution, 502; and trade, 434, 435, 436, 460; in World War II, 449
Jefferson, Thomas: 25, p 562; Declaration of Independence written by, 25, p 24; Democratic-Republican party and, 187, p 187; First Inaugural Address of, 550
job actions, (def.) 386
job applications, 414–15
jobs: g 405, 410–13; as agricultural workers, 404, p 404; applications, 414–15; blue-collar, p 402, 403; choice of, 397–98; discrimination in, 409, 476; early starts in, 406–407; education for, 398–99; equal employment opportunity in, 409; in government, 405, 408; help wanted ads for, 418, p 418; opportunities in, 405, g 405, 408–409; as service workers, 403–404; training for, 263, p 263; white-collar, 401–402
Johnson, Andrew, 81, p 563
Johnson, Lyndon B., 454, p 565
Joint Chiefs of Staff, (def.) 106, 427
joint committees, (def.) 78
joint sessions, 75, p 76
Jordan, 456, m 521
Jordan, Barbara, 182
judges, p 121, 123, 151, 302–303, p 302
judicial branch: g 40, g 41, (def.) 42; federal courts, of, 119–23, g 120, 126–31; presidential appointments to, 99; of state governments, 150–51, 154–55; Supreme Court in, 123, 126–31, p 127. See also Supreme Court of the United States
judicial review, (def.) 126
Judiciary Act, 119, 126
Junior Achievement, 322–23, p 322, p 323
junior colleges, (def.) 260

599

For permission to reprint copyrighted material, grateful acknowledgment is made to the following sources:

The American Red Cross National Headquarters: From "Volunteering in 2001" by Charlotte J. Lunsford delivered before The 1988 National Volunteer Conference, San Francisco, CA, June 21, 1988. Copyright © 1988 by The American Red Cross. **The Denver Post Corporation:** From "Kids Helping Kids: Tutoring's payoffs yield toys as well as better grades at Teller" by Carol Kreck from *The Denver Post,* January 4, 1994. Copyright © 1994 by The Denver Post Corporation. **Claire L. Gaudiani:** From "Developing Global Civic Virtues" by Claire L. Gaudiani delivered to Phi Beta Kappa, University of Connecticut, Storrs, CT, May 1, 1993. Copyright © 1993 by Claire L. Gaudiani. **Barbara Jordan:** From a statement of the Honorable Barbara Jordan, a United States Representative from The State of Texas, at the 1976 Democratic Convention. Copyright © 1976 by Barbara Jordan. **Little, Brown and Company:** From *Epic of America* by James Truslow Adams. Copyright 1931, 1933 by James Truslow Adams; copyright renewed © 1959 by James Truslow Adams. **Writers House, Inc. as agent for the proprietor of The Heirs to the Estate of Martin Luther King, Jr.:** From the speech "I Have a Dream" by Martin Luther King, Jr., August 28, 1963. Copyright © 1963 by Martin Luther King, Jr.; copyright renewed © 1991 by Coretta Scott King.

The following excerpt also appears in *American Civics*:
From "Bush Honors Miami Teenage Volunteer" by Linda Brockman from *Miami Jewish Tribune*, April 14–20, 1989, p. 8A. Copyright © 1989 by Miami Jewish Tribune.

Photo Credits

Abbreviations used: (t) top, (c) center, (b) bottom, (l) left, (r) right, (bckgd) background, (bdr) border.

Front Cover and Title Page, Long Photo/Sports Light, 1994;
Page: v(t), Richard Bloom/SABA; v(bl), Mary Kate Denny/PhotoEdit; v(br), vi(t), Paul Conklin; vi(b), HRW photo by Peter Van Steen; vii(tl), Laurence Parent; vii(tr), © The National Geographic Society, courtesy of The Supreme Court Historical Society; vii(bl), Sepp Seitz/Woodfin Camp & Associates; viii(tl), Tomas Muscionico/Contact Press Images; viii(b), David Woo/Sygma; ix(tl), Tony Freeman/PhotoEdit; ix(tr), Charles Gupton/Tony Stone Images; ix(bl), Michael Newman/PhotoEdit; x(tl), Henry Friedman; x(r), Richard B. Levine; x(b), HRW photo by Eric Beggs; xi(tl), Joel Stettenheim/SABA; xi(c), Larry Kolvoord; xi(b), Reuters/Bettmann; xii(t), Poster illustrated by Seymour Chwast for Amnesty International USA; xii(bl), AP/Wide World Photos; xii(br), Laurence Parent; xiii(t), Erich Hartmann/Magnum; xiii(b), Najlah Feanny/SABA; xiv(l), Sheila Stieglitz; xiv(r), David Burnett/Contact Press Images; xviii(c), Richard Bloom/SABA; 2, Paul Gero/Nawrocki Stock Photo; 4, Jeffry W. Myers/Uniphoto; 5, Steven E. Sutton/Duomo; 6, Ronnie Kaufman/The Stock Market; 8(tl), Phil Schofield/Tony Stone Images; 8(tr), 8(bl), 8(bc), 8(br), HRW photos by Sam Dudgeon; 9, Alon Reininger/Contact Press Images; 12, 13, Sheila Stieglitz; 15, Matt Bradley/Tom Stack & Associates; 16, David R. Frazier; 20, Henry Groskinsky; 23(l), Rad Sinyak; 23(r), Tom Myers/Photo Researchers; 24, The Bettmann Archive; 26, Culver Pictures; 27, William S. Nawrocki/Nawrocki Stock Photography; 28(l), The Bettmann Archive; 28(r), National Archives; 29, The Print and Picture Collection, The Free Library of Philadelphia; 31, Library of Congress; 32, 34, The Bettmann Archive; 36, National Archives; 39, David Young-Wolff/PhotoEdit; 44, UPI/Bettmann Newsphoto; 45, Dennis Brack/Black Star; 50, Mary Kate Denny/PhotoEdit; 52, Elizabeth Zuckerman/PhotoEdit; 53, Nubar Alexanian/Woodfin Camp & Associates; 54, Paul Conklin; 55, Brad Markel/Gamma-Liaison; 58, The Bettmann Archive; 60, HRW photo by Sam Dudgeon; 61, Patrick Dunn; 68(l), Masa Uemura/Tony Stone Images; 68-69(r), Chuck Pefley/Tony Stone Images; 70, Michael J. Howell/Superstock, Inc.; 76, Paul Conklin; 77, courtesy of Senator Daniel Inouye; 82, Ted Soqui/Sygma; 86, Jay Mallin; 90, 1975 by Herblock in The Washington Post; 92, M Win/Washington Stock Photo; 94, Reuters/Bettmann; 95, AP/Wide World Photo; 97, 99, Reuters/Bettmann; 102(l), Library of Congress; 102(r), Dennis Brack/Black Star; 104, Sullivan/TexaStock; 105, Dennis Brack/Black Star; 109, Mark Richards/PhotoEdit; 114, Stock Montage; 117, John Neubauer/FPG International; 117, John Neubauer; 121, HRW photo by Peter Van Steen; 122, Mary Gow; 124, UPI/Bettmann Newsphotos; 126, The Bettmann Archive; 127, © National Geographic Society, courtesy, The Supreme Court Historical Society; 129, AP/Wide World Photos; 129 (inset), UPI/Bettmann; 130, © The National Geographic Society, courtesy of The Supreme Court Historical Society; 136-137, Mary Gow; 138, Laurence Parent; 141, HRW photo by Sam Dudgeon; 146, Photograph by The Texas House of Representatives Photography Department; 151, James L. Shaffer/PhotoEdit; 152, Paul Conklin; 153, James L. Shaffer/PhotoEdit; 154, Drawing by Tom Little, from the Nashville Tennessean; 158, Sepp Seitz/Woodfin Camp & Associates; 163, George A. Robinson/Tony Stone Images; 165, HRW photo by Eric Beggs; 167, Gwendolen Cates/Sygma; 169, Oscar Palmquist/Lightwave; 172, Larry Armbrust; 173(t), Paul Vandevelder/Gamma-Liaison; 173(b), courtesy of Larry Armbrust; 174, Jeffry W. Myers/Corbis; 175, Michael Newman/PhotoEdit; 176, Courtesy of Austin Fire Department; 182–183, Larry Kolvoord; 184, Smithsonian Institution; 187(l), National Portrait Gallery, Smithsonian Institution, Gift of the Regents of the Smithsonian Institution, the Thomas Jefferson Memorial Foundation, and the Enid and Crosby Kemper Foundation/Art Resource; 187(r), National Portrait Gallery, Smithsonian Institution/Art Resource; 188, Matthew McVay/Tony Stone Images; 192, Tom Myers; 193(l), Tomas Muscionico/Contact Press Images; 194, I. Wyman/Sygma; 196, Paul Conklin/PhotoEdit; 198, Charles Gupton/The Stock Market; 200(l), UPI/Bettmann; 200(r), Donna Binder/Impact Visuals; 201, HRW photo by Sam Dudgeon; 204, 206, Paul Conklin/PhotoEdit; 208, North American Syndicate; 212, David Burnett/Contact Press Images; 213, Paul Gero/Sygma; 214, Joseph A.

DiChello, Jr.; 215, Larry Lawfer/The Picture Cube; 217, Jack Bender, Waterloo Courier, Iowa/Rothco; 218, HRW photo by Peter Van Steen; 222, HRW photo by Sam Dudgeon; 225, David Woo/Sygma; 226, P.R. Dunn; 228, 233, HRW photo by Sam Dudgeon; 240–241, Kristin Finnegan/Tony Stone Images; 242, Charles Gupton/Tony Stone Images; 244, The Bettmann Archive; 248, Library of Congress; 250, Phil Schermeister/Corbis; 252, Freeman - Grishaber/PhotoEdit; 253, Kennedy/TexaStock; 256, HRW photo by Peter Van Steen; 258, The Saint Louis Art Museum; 263, Dana White; 264, Tony Freeman/PhotoEdit; 264(r), Ewing Galloway; 265, Elena Roorald/PhotoEdit; 266, Tony Freeman/PhotoEdit; 269, 270, Dana White; 274, Michael Newman/PhotoEdit; 276, Craig Aurness/Woodfin Camp & Associates; 277, Dave Lawrence/The Stock Market; 278, Tom Zimberoff/Sygma; 279, Mark Richards/PhotoEdit; 280, David Young-Wolff/PhotoEdit; 283, Robert Yager/Tony Stone Images; 288, Richard B. Levine; 290, Nancy Simmerman/Tony Stone Images; 292, Peter Steiner/The Stock Market; 294, Michael Newman/PhotoEdit; 295, P.R. Dunn; 296, Larry Kolvoord; 297, Flip Schullke, Life Magazine/© Time, Inc.; 298, Terry Thompson/Sygma; 299, HRW photo by Sam Dudgeon; 300, 301, Steven Shames/Matrix; 302, 303, Larry Kolvoord; 304, Alon Reininger/Contact Press Images; 310–311, C. Bruce Forster/Tony Stone Images; 312, Barbara Leslie/FPG International; 316(l), Tony Freeman/PhotoEdit; 316(r), John P. Endress/The Stock Market; 318, Dennis Cox/ChinaStock; 320, Henry Friedman; 322, Junior Achievement; 323, © 1990 Victor Powell, Chicago/Junior Achievement; 324, Robert McElroy/Woodfin Camp & Associates; 327, Brownie Harris/The Stock Market; 332, Tony Price/Ace/Nawrocki; 334, Yale University Art Gallery, Gift of George Hoadley, B.A. 1801; 336, Chris Sorensen; 338, Charlie Westerman/Gamma-Liaison; 339, Larry Kolvoord; 340, The Foxfire Fund, Inc.; 341, Michal Heron/Woodfin Camp & Associates; 345, HRW photo by Sam Dudgeon; 346, HRW photo by Eric Beggs; 348, Etta Hulme cartoon reprinted by permission of NEA, Inc.; 352, HRW photo by Sam Dudgeon; 355, Frank Fournier/Contact Press Images; 356, HRW photo by Sam Dudgeon; 359, John Henley/The Stock Market; 360, Jim Pickerell/Comstock; 362, George Goodwin/The Picture Cube; 367, Ira Wyman/Sygma; 368, Fredrik D. Bodin/Stock Boston; 372, Richard Weiss/Peter Arnold; 376, Joel Stettenheim/SABA; 378, UPI/Corbis-Bettmann; 379, The Bettmann Archive; 380, U.S. Department of the Interior; 382, Steven Baratz/The Picture Cube; 383, Abbas/Magnum; 384, Larry Kolvoord; 387, Kim Keitt/Globe Photos; 388, Kennedy/TexaStock; 389, Najlah Feanny/SABA; 396, HRW photo by Sam Dudgeon; 398, Charles Gupton/Tony Stone Images; 399, Dennis MacDonald/PhotoEdit; 401, Kaluzny/Thatcher/Tony Stone Images; 402, Michael Newman/PhotoEdit; 404, P.R. Dunn; 406, Paul Conklin; 407, Bachmann/PhotoEdit; 408, Larry Kolvoord; 409, C. Bruce Forster/Tony Stone Images; 411(tl), Pictor Uniphoto; 411(tr), N. Tully/Sygma; 411(bl), Joe McNally/Sygma; 411(br), HRW photo by Dennis Carlyle Darling; 412, 415, HRW photo by Sam Dudgeon; 416, Bill Bachman/f/Stop Pictures; 422–423, William R. Sallaz/Duomo; 424, Reuters/Bettmann; 426, Reuters/Bettmann; 427, Office of the Assistant to the Secretary of Defense; 428, AP/Wide World Photos; 429, Joe Japho/Picture Group; 430, AP/Wide World Photos; 432, Reuters/Bettmann; 433, Liz Gilbert/Sygma; 434, Olivier Rebbot/Woodfin Camp & Associates; 435, Robert Essel/The Stock Market; 437, Jon Riley/Tony Stone Images; 440, Wernher Krutein/Photovault; 444, Kainulain/Lehtikuva Oy/SABA; 446, The Bettmann Archive; 447, The Plain Dealer; 448, Culver Pictures; 450, Fred Hibon/Sygma; 452, Walter Sanders, Life Magazine/© Time Warner, Inc.; 453, UPI/Bettmann Newsphotos; 455, Alain Nogues/Sygma; 457, Jacques Langevin/Sygma; 458, Franklin D. Roosevelt Library; 459, Poster illustrated by Seymour Chwast for Amnesty International USA.; 460, Reuters/Corbis-Bettmann; 466, NASA; 468, Chuck Savage/The Stock Market; 471, Tim Thompson/Corbis; 472, Reprinted by permission: Tribune Media Services; 474, Philip Gould/Corbis; 477, Fred Ward/Black Star; 478, AP/Wide World Photos; 479, AP/Wide World Photos; 480, Dr. Hector P. Garcia Papers, Special Collections and Archives, Texas A&M University-Corpus Christi Library; 481, James D. Wilson/Woodfin Camp & Associates; 483, Michael Newman/PhotoEdit; 490, 492, Laurence Parent; 493, David Barnes/The Stock Market; 494, Kevin Morris/Corbis; 497, Laurence Parent; 498, 499, Charlie Archambault/U.S. News and World Report; 501, Erich Hartmann/Magnum; 503, George Hunter/Tony Stone Images; 504, Roger Ressmeyer/Corbis; 506, From ""Herblock On All Fronts" (New American Library, 1980); 508, Michael Baytoff/Black Star; 510, Laurence Parent; 562, all Library of Congress except: (1), Metropolitan Museum of Art, Gift of H.O. Havemeyer, 1888; (5) Metropolitan Museum of Art, Bequest of Seth Low, 1929; 563, all Library of Congress except: (12), Charles Phelps Cushing; (16) The Bettmann Archive; 564, all Library of Congress except: (29), (30), Ewing Galloway; (31), photo by Bachrach; (32), Franklin D. Roosevelt Library, Hyde Park, NY; (33), Charles Phelps Cushing; (34), Chase News Photo; 565 (35), Henry Grossman; (36), Photo by Bachrach; (37), The White House; (38) Courtesy of President Gerald Ford; (39), The White House; (40), UPI/Bettmann Newsphotos; (41), David Valdez/The White House; (42), The White House; 571, Evan H. Sheppard/Folio; 572, NASA; 577, U.S. Department of State.

Illustrations

Durke, Stephen: 30.

Morgan Cain & Associates: XIV, 7, 10, 25, 38, 40, 41, 42, 46, 48, 56, 59, 62, 74, 78, 80, 81, 85, 87, 98, 101, 103, 107, 112, 118, 120, 128, 135, 140, 144, 148, 160, 161, 168, 171, 181, 186, 191, 197, 209, 224, 227, 230, 234, 239, 245, 249, 259, 281, 284, 293, 309, 315, 321, 326, 328, 335, 342, 363, 365, 371, 400, 438, 465, 484, 485, 488, 509, 515.

Morrow, Michael: XV, 215, 236, 260, 261, 377, 381, 391, 394, 405, 442, 470.